Sourcebook on EU
Competition Law
2012-2013
Volume 1

www.larcier.com   www.stradalex.com

© Groupe De Boeck s.a., 2012 – Minimenstraat 39 – 1000 Brussel

Authors and editors have attempted to ensure utmost correctness of the Larcier Thematic Code – Sourcebook on EU Competition Law 2012-2013, but they cannot be held responsible for any remaining errors or omissions.

All rights reserved. No part of this publication may be reproduced, stored in a retrieval system, or transmitted in any form or by any means, mechanical, photocopying, recording, or otherwise, without prior written permission of the publishers. Permission to use this content must be obtained from the copyright owner.

D2012/0031/262   ISBN 978-2-8044-5401-2

LARCIER THEMATIC CODE

Sourcebook on EU
Competition Law
2012-2013
Volume 1

Wouter Devroe
Paul Nihoul
Anne-Marie Van den Bossche
Christophe Verdure

This book reflects the state of the law on 1 July 2012

Preface

One risks to drown in the flood of ever more regulatory texts and judgments on European competition law. This third English language edition of the Sourcebook on Competition Law aims to bring some order to this subject.

The body of European competition law has grown so rapidly over the past decades that each effort to map this vast area of law necessarily entails choices. Several concise selections of regulatory texts are already on the market, as are casebooks, collections of references and complete multi-volume text collections. However, we believe that there is need for a guide which combines as much as possible the advantages of a practical overview of the law as it stands with the depth of more thorough collections. This combination should enable practitioners and academics quickly to find answers to a wide range of competition law issues, as well as to be put on the right track towards a more in-depth search.

With this purpose in mind this Sourcebook on Competition Law offers:

(a) an extensive full-text collection of European Union documents on competition law comprising core Articles of the Treaty on the Functioning of the European Union, relevant Protocols, European Union secondary legislation, Commission notices and communications and the like;

(b) excerpts of relevant judgments of the General Court and the Court of Justice of the European Union;

(c) an extensive bibliography focusing on the years 2005-2012 with books, articles and overviews of case law in English, French, German, and Dutch; and

(d) notification forms brought together in a separate section of the book.

The book follows a structure which the reader may recognize from Commission documents, web sites and textbooks. It should allow the reader to distinguish easily between essential provisions and documents which rank lower in the hierarchy of norms. Competition law provisions which are primarily addressed to undertakings (restrictive practices, abuse of dominant position, merger control) are followed by provisions which primarily concern Member State behaviour (state aid, public undertakings and services of general economic interest). Within each of the five branches of competition law, the reader is first directed towards the most essential documents, and subsequently to implementing documents, first of a substantive and then of a procedural nature.

As we have aimed to combine thoroughness with practicability, the book cannot possibly be exhaustive. As editors we have had to select texts, and we fully realize that this implies a degree of subjectivity. This becomes particularly apparent in the overview of the Union courts' case law, much too voluminous to reproduce in full text, and in the bibliography. Similarly, only the most important sectoral rules have been included, and texts of a purely institutional or programmatory nature, less vital in practice, have been left out.

We thank researchers Lieve Hoornaert and Evi Mattioli, publishers Lien Van Hecke and Shanna Maertens, as well as our students, readers and colleagues who provided feedback and comments on this code and related research.

We welcome all suggestions for improvement:
Wouter.Devroe@law.kuleuven.be;
Paul.Nihoul@uclouvain.be;
Anne-Marie.VandenBossche@ua.ac.be;
Verdure@fusl.ac.be.

Wouter Devroe   Paul Nihoul   Anne-Marie Van den Bossche   Christophe Verdure

HOW TO USE THIS BOOK

We would like to inform the reader about certain choices that were made regarding the structure, content and presentation of this book.

a. Provisions concerning public undertakings and services of general economic interest (Art. 106 TFEU) are dealt with under the heading "Rules primarily addressed to Member States". We realize that these provisions (like state aid provisions for that matter) are also in part addressed to undertakings, but we could obviously not include them twice. The fact that many of the documents concerning services of general economic interest are closely related to state aid comforts us in our choice.

b. As indicated in the Preface, the following categories of regulatory documents have as a rule not been included: (i) texts of a merely institutional nature (e.g. the appointment of the Hearing Officer), (ii) White and Green Papers, resolutions and other documents of a mainly programmatic nature, (iii) proposals for regulatory texts and (iv) sectoral regulation, with the exception of block exemption regulations in the insurance and motor vehicle sector. As "sectoral" we consider not only regulation applied by national regulatory authorities (NRA's) and/or their supranational counterparts, but also sector-specific competition law rules (e.g. a Council regulation "applying certain rules of competition to the production of and trade in certain agricultural products"). As for block exemptions, the enabling Council regulations which authorize the Commission to adopt regulations are not included, while the Commission regulations adopted on the basis thereof are included.

c. The following has not been considered for insertion in the bibliographical section: sector-specific texts, texts emphasizing economic rather than legal aspects of competition, and individual contributions in collective works (generally, only the collective work is mentioned).

d. Most judgments in the case law section of this book are excerpted. For most judgments, it was possible to do this in such a way that the facts of the case became clear from the excerpted text. Where this was not possible, a separate brief description of the facts has been added to the excerpt.

e. The old Treaty numbering has been respected throughout the excerpts of the judgments, but the first time that the Court refers to an Article using the old numbering, the current numbering is mentioned between brackets.

Most commonly consulted documents

1. Treaty on the functioning of the European Union (TFEU)
   Restrictive practices.................................... 1
   State aid 425
   Services of general interest 664
2. Regulation 1/2003 (implementation of Articles 101-102 TFEU, modernisation)... 3
3. Notice on agreements of minor importance (*de minimis*) 21
4. Regulation 330/2010 (block exemption - Vertical restraints) 63
5. Regulations 1217 - 1218/2010 (block exemptions - Horizontal restraints)... 112
6. Guidelines on the method of setting fines 269
7. Notice on Immunity from fines and reduction of fines in cartel cases (Leniency) 272
8. Regulation 139/2004 (Merger Regulation) 288
9. Consolidated Jurisdictional Notice on the control of concentrations.. 357
10. Regulation 800/2008 (State aid - General block exemption regulation).. 433

Selected Case law.. 724
Bibliography 791
Forms 812

Table of contents

LEGISLATION

1. Treaty on the Functioning of the European Union

Consolidated version of the Treaty on the functioning of the European Union *(O.J. C 115, 9 May 2008, p. 47, corrig., O.J. C 290, 30 November 2009, p. 1)* 1

2. Rules adressed to undertakings

2.1. Cartels and abuse of dominant position

2.1.1. Core legislation

Protocol N° 27 on the internal market and competition *(OJ C 115, 9 May 2008, p. 309)*........................ 5

Council Regulation (EC) N° 1/2003, 16 December 2002 on the implementation of the rules on competition laid down in Articles 81 and 82 of the Treaty (Text with EEA relevance) *(OJ L 1, 4 January 2003, p. 1)* 5

2.1.2. Substantive rules

2.1.2.1. General rules

Commission Notice on the definition of relevant market for the purposes of Community competition law *(OJ C 372, 9 December 1997, p. 5)* 19

Commission Notice on agreements of minor importance which do not appreciably restrict competition under Article 81(1) of the Treaty establishing the European Community (de minimis) *(OJ C 368, 22 December 2001, p. 13)* 25

Guidelines on the effect on trade concept contained in Articles 81 and 82 of the Treaty *(OJ C 101, 27 April 2004, p. 81)*.. 27

Guidelines on the application of Article 81(3) of the Treaty *(OJ C 101, 27 April 2004, p. 97)* 39

Guidance on the Commission's enforcement priorities in applying Article 102 to abusive exclusionary conduct by dominant undertakings *(OJ C 45, 24 February 2009, p. 7)* 54

2.1.2.2. Vertical agreements

Commission Regulation (EU) N° 330/2010, 20 April 2010 on the application of Article 101(3) of the Treaty on the functioning of the European Union to categories of vertical agreements and concerted practices *(OJ L 102, 23 April 2010, p. 1)* 66

Guidelines on Vertical Restraints *(OJ C 130, 19 May 2010, p. 1)*... 70

Commission Regulation (EU) N° 461/2010, 27 May 2010 on the application of Article 101(3) of the Treaty on the functioning of the European Union to categories of vertical agreements and concerted practices in the motor vehicle sector *(OJ L 129, 28 May 2010, p. 52)* 103

Supplementary guidelines on vertical restraints in agreements for the sale and repair of motor vehicles and for the distribution of spare parts for motor vehicles *(OJ C 138, 28 May 2010, p. 16)*....................... 106

2.1.2.3. Horizontal agreements

Commission Regulation (EU) N° 1217/2010, 14 December 2010 on the application of Article 101(3) of the Treaty on the Functioning of the European Union to certain categories of research and development agreements *(OJ L 335, 18 December 2010, p. 36)*............ 116

Commission Regulation (EU) N° 1218/2010, 14 December 2010 on the application of Article 101(3) of the Treaty on the Functioning of the European Union to certain categories of specialisation agreements *(OJ L 335, 18 December 2010, p. 43)*.................. 121

Guidelines on the applicability of Article 101 of the Treaty on the Functioning of the European Union to horizontal co-operation agreements *(OJ C 11, 14 January 2011, p. 1, corrig., OJ C 33, 2 February 2011, p. 20)* ... 124

2.1.2.4. Transfer of technology

Commission Regulation (EC) N° 772/2004, 27 April 2004 on the application of Article 81(3) of the Treaty to categories of technology transfer agreements *(OJ L 123, 27 April 2004, p. 11, rect., OJ L 127, 29 April 2004, p. 158)* 168

Guidelines on the application of Article 81 of the EC Treaty to technology transfer agreements *(OJ C 101, 27 April 2004, p. 2)*...................................... 172

Index of the guidelines............................... 203

2.1.2.5. Insurance sector

Commission Regulation (EU) N° 267/2010, 24 March 2010 on the application of Article 101(3) of the Treaty on the functioning of the European Union to certain categories of agreements, decisions and concerted practices in the insurance sector *(OJ L 83, 30 March 2010, p. 1)* ... 205

Communication from the Commission on the application of Article 101(3) of the Treaty on the functioning of the European Union to certain categories of agreements, decisions and concerted practices in the insurance sector *(OJ C 82, 30 March 2010, p. 20)*............ 209

2.1.3. Procedural rules

Communication 6 January 2010 – Guidance on procedures of the Hearing Officers in proceedings relating to Articles 101 and 102 TFEU 213

Commission Regulation (EC) N° 773/2004, 7 April 2004 relating to the conduct of proceedings by the Commission pursuant to Articles 81 and 82 of the EC Treaty *(OJ L 123, 27 April 2004, p. 18)*.................. 220

Best Practices for the submission of economic evidence and data collection in cases concerning the application of Articles 101 and 102 TFEU and in Merger cases, not published in the Official Journal 224

Commission Notice on co-operation within the Network of Competition Authorities *(OJ C 101, 27 April 2004, p. 43)* 232

Commission Notice on the co-operation between the Commission and the courts of the EU Member States in the application of Articles 81 and 82 EC *(OJ C 101, 27 April 2004, p. 54)* 239

Commission Notice on the handling of complaints by the Commission under Articles 81 and 82 of the EC Treaty *(OJ C 101, 27 April 2004, p. 65)* 245

Commission Notice on informal guidance relating to novel questions concerning Articles 81 and 82 of the EC Treaty that arise in individual cases *(OJ C 101, 27 April 2004, p. 78)* 253

Commission Notice on the rules for access to the Commission file in cases pursuant to Articles 81 and 82 of the EC Treaty, Articles 53, 54 and 57 of the EEA Agreement and Council Regulation (EC) N° 139/2004 *(OJ C 325, 22 December 2005, p. 7)* 255

Guidelines on the method of setting fines imposed pursuant to Article 23(2)(a) of Regulation N° 1/2003 *(OJ C 210, 1 September 2006, p. 2)*. 261

Commission Notice on Immunity from fines and reduction of fines in cartel cases *(OJ C 298, 8 December 2006, p. 17)* 263

Inspections – Explanatory note to an authorization to conduct an inspection in execution of a Commission Decision under Article 20(4) of Council Regulation N° 1/2003, March 2008 268

Commission Notice on the conduct of settlement procedures in view of the adoption of Decisions pursuant to Article 7 and Article 23 of Council Regulation (EC) n° 1/2003 in cartel cases *(OJ C 167, 2 July 2008, p. 1)*. 269

White Paper 2 April 2008 on Damages Actions for Breach of the EC antitrust rules, COM(2008) 165 274

Commission staff working paper 2 April 2008 accompanying the White paper on damages actions for breach of the EC antitrust rules 278

Commission Staff Working Paper 2 April 2008 – document accompanying document to the White paper on damages actions for breach of the EC antitrust rules – Impact assessment.. 278

DG Competition, Draft Guidance paper: Quantifying harm in actions for damages on breaches of Article 101 or 102 of the Treaty on the Functioning of the European Union, June 2011, not published in the Official Journal 278

Decision of the President of the European Commission 13 October 2011 on the function and terms of reference of the hearing officer in certain competition proceedings (Text with EEA relevance) *(PB. L 275, 20 October 2011, p. 29)* 309

Commission notice Best practices for the conduct of proceedings concerning Articles 101 and 102 TFEU *(O.J. C 308, 20 October 2011, p. 6)* 315

Brochure DG Competition – Compliance matters, November 2011, – What companies can do better to respect EU competition rules, not published in the Official Journal 332

2.2. Concentration control

2.2.1. Core legislation

Council Regulation (EC) N° 139/2004, 20 January 2004 on the control of concentrations between undertakings (the EC Merger Regulation) *(OJ L 24, 29 January 2004, p. 1)* 338

Communication 18 June 2009 from the Commission to the Council – Report on the functioning of Regulation N° 139/2004, COM (2009) 281 final 354

Commission Regulation (EC) N° 802/2004, 21 April 2004 implementing Council Regulation N° 139/2004 on the control of concentrations between undertakings *(OJ L 133, 30 April 2004, p. 1)* 356

2.2.2. Substantive rules

Commission Notice on the definition of relevant market for the purposes of Community competition law *(OJ C 372, 9 December 1997, p. 5)* 363

Commission Notice on remedies acceptable under Council Regulation (EC) N° 139/2004 and under Commission Regulation (EC) N° 802/2004 *(OJ C 267, 22 October 2008, p. 1)*................................... 363

Merger Remedies Study, October 2005 381

Guidelines on the assessment of horizontal mergers under the Council Regulation on the control of concentrations between undertakings *(OJ C 31, 5 February 2004, p. 5)*... 381

Guidelines on the assessment of non-horizontal mergers under the Council Regulation on the control of concentrations between undertakings *(OJ C 265, 18 October 2008, p. 6)*....................................... 392

Commission Notice on restrictions directly related and necessary to concentrations *(OJ C 56, 5 March 2005, p. 24)* 404

Commission Consolidated Jurisdictional Notice under Council Regulation (EC) N° 139/2004 on the control of concentrations between undertakings *(OJ C 95, 16 April 2008, p. 1)* 408

Simplified method to obtain the average rate used to calculate the turnover.............................. 435

2.2.3. Procedural rules

Best Practice Guidelines – The Commission's Model Texts for Divestiture Commitments and the Trustee Mandate under the EC Merger Regulation, not published in the Official Journal 436

Model texts for divestiture commitments – Commitments to the European Commission, 2 May 2003, not published in the Official Journal 440

Model texts for trustee mandates, 2 May 2003, not published in the Official Journal 440

Best Practices on the conduct of EC merger control proceedings, 20 January 2004, not published in the Official Journal 440

DG Competition Information note on Art. 6, (1), c), 2nd sentence, of Regulation 139/2004 (abandonment of concentrations), 20 January 2004, not published in the Official Journal 445

Communication from the Commission pursuant to Article 23(1) of Commission Regulation (EC) N° 802/2004 implementing Council Regulation (EC) N° 139/2004 on the control of concentrations between undertakings *(OJ C 139, 19 May 2004, p. 2)* 446

Commission Notice on case referral in respect of concentrations *(OJ C 56, 5 March 2005, p. 2)* 446

Commission Notice on a simplified procedure for treatment of certain concentrations under Council Regulation (EC) N° 139/2004 *(OJ C 56, 5 March 2005, p. 32)*.. 461

Communication pursuant to Article 3(2) of Commission Regulation (EC) N° 802/2004 implementing Council Regulation (EC) N° 139/2004 on the control of concentrations between undertakings *(OJ C 251, 17 October 2006, p. 2)*... 463

Commission Notice on the rules for access to the Commission file in cases pursuant to Articles 81 and 82 of the EC Treaty, Articles 53, 54 and 57 of the EEA Agreement and Council Regulation (EC) N° 139/2004 *(OJ C 325, 22 December 2005, p. 7)* 464

Merger notification and procedures template, March 2008, not published in the Official Journal 464

Market share ranges in non confidential versions of merger decisions (11 December 2008) 474

Best practices for the submission of economic evidence and data collection in cases concerning the application of Articles 101 and 102 TFEU and in Merger cases, not published in the Official Journal..................... 475

Decision of the President of the European Commission 13 October 2011 on the function and terms of reference of the hearing officer in certain competition proceedings (Text with EEA relevance) *(PB. L 275, 20 October 2011, p. 29)*... 475

EU Merger Working Group 8 November 2011 Best Practices on Cooperation between EU National Competition Authorities in Merger Review, not published in the Official Journal... 475

3. Rules addressed to Member States

3.1. State aid

3.1.1. Substantive law

3.1.2.1. General rules

Council Regulation (EC) N° 994/98, 7 May 1998 on the application of Articles 92 and 93 of the Treaty establishing the European Community to certain categories of horizontal State aid *(OJ L 142, 14 May 1998, p. 1)*...... 478

Commission Regulation (EC) N° 1998/2006, 15 December 2006 on the application of Articles 87 and 88 of the Treaty to de minimis aid *(OJ L 379, 28 December 2006, p. 5)*.. 481

Commission Regulation (EC) N° 800/2008, 6 August 2008 declaring certain categories of aid compatible with the common market in application of Articles 87 and 88 of the Treaty (General block exemption Regulation) *(OJ L 214, 9 August 2008, p. 3)* 485

3.1.2.2. Regional aid

Commission Regulation (EC) N° 800/2008, 6 August 2008 declaring certain categories of aid compatible with the common market in application of Articles 87 and 88 of the Treaty (General block exemption Regulation) *(OJ L 214, 9 August 2008, p. 3)* 510

Communication from the Commission – Multisectoral framework on regional aid for large investment projects *(OJ C 70, 19 March 2002, p. 8)*....................... 510

Communication from the Commission – Guidelines on national regional aid for 2007-2013 *(OJ C 54, 4 March 2006, p. 13)*.. 517

Communication from the Commission concerning the criteria for an in-depth assessment of regional aid to large investment projects *(OJ C 223, 16 September 2009, p. 3)*. 533

Communication of the Commission on the review of the State aid status and the aid ceiling of the statistical effect regions in the following National regional State aid maps for the period 1.1.2011- 31.12.2013 – Guidelines on National Regional aid for 2007-2013 *(OJ C 222, 17 August, 2010, p. 2)*..................... 538

3.1.2.3. SME aid

Commission Regulation (EC) N° 800/2008, 6 August 2008 declaring certain categories of aid compatible with the common market in application of Articles 87 and 88 of the Treaty (General block exemption Regulation) *(OJ L 214, 9 August 2008, p. 3)* 540

Community guidelines on state aid to promote risk capital investments in small and medium-sized enterprises *(OJ C 194, 18 August 2006, p. 2)*................ 540

Communication from the Commission amending the Community guidelines on State aid to promote risk capital investments in small and medium-sized enterprises *(OJ C 329, 7 December, 2010, p. 4)* 551

3.1.2.4. Environmental aid

Commission Regulation (EC) N° 800/2008, 6 August 2008 declaring certain categories of aid compatible with the common market in application of Articles 87 and 88 of the Treaty (General block exemption Regulation) *(OJ L 214, 9 August 2008, p. 3)* 552

Community guidelines on State aid for environmental protection *(OJ C 82, 1 April 2008, p. 1)* 552

3.1.2.5. Aid for Research, Development and Innovation

Commission Regulation (EC) N° 800/2008, 6 August 2008 declaring certain categories of aid compatible with the common market in application of Articles 87 and 88 of the Treaty (General block exemption Regulation) *(OJ L 214, 9 August 2008, p. 3)* 576

Communication of the Commission – Community framework for state aid for research and development and innovation *(OJ C 323, 30 December 2006, p. 1)* 576

3.1.2.6. Training aid

Commission Regulation (EC) N° 800/2008, 6 August 2008 declaring certain categories of aid compatible with the common market in application of Articles 87 and 88 of the Treaty (General block exemption Regulation) *(OJ L 214, 9 August 2008, p. 3)* 594

Communication from the Commission – Criteria for the analysis of the compatibility of State aid for training subject to individual notification *(OJ C 188, 11 August 2009, p. 1)*... 594

3.1.2.7. Aid to disadvantaged and disabled workers

Commission Regulation (EC) N° 800/2008, 6 August 2008 declaring certain categories of aid compatible with the common market in application of Articles 87 and 88 of the Treaty (General block exemption Regulation) *(OJ L 214, 9 August 2008, p. 3)* 597

Communication from the Commission – Criteria for the analysis of the compatibility of State aid for the employment of disadvantaged and disabled workers subject to individual notification *(OJ C 188, 11 August 2009, p. 6)* ... 597

3.1.2.8. Aid related to the current financial and economic crisis

Communication from the Commission – The application of State aid rules to measures taken in relation to financial institutions in the context of the current global financial crisis *(OJ C 270, 25 October 2008, p. 8)* ... 600

Communication from the Commission — The recapitalisation of financial institutions in the current financial crisis: limitation of aid to the minimum necessary and safeguards against undue distortions of competition *(OJ C 10, 15 January 2009, p. 2)* ... 605

Communication from the Commission on the treatment of impaired assets in the Community banking sector *(OJ C 72, 26 March 2009, p. 1)* ... 611

Commission communication on the return to viability and the assessment of restructuring measures in the financial sector in the current crisis under the State aid rules *(OJ C 195, 19 August 2009, p. 9)* ... 624

Communication of the Commission – Temporary Union framework for State aid measures to support access to finance in the current financial and economic crisis *(OJ C 6, 11 January, 2011, p. 5)* ... 632

Communication from the Commission 6 December 2011 on the application, from 1 January 2012, of State aid rules to support measures in favour of banks in the context of the financial crisis (Text with EEA relevance) *(PB. C 356, 6 December 2011, p. 7)* ... 637

Communication from the Commission 21 April 2012 amending the Communication of the Commission to the Member States pursuant to Article 93(1) of the EC Treaty applying Articles 92 and 93 of the Treaty to short-term export-credit insurance *(PB. C 117, 21 April 2012, p. 1)* .. 640

3.1.2.9. Other aid

Commission Communication on State aid elements in sales of land and buildings by public authorities *(OJ C 209, 10 July 1997, p. 3)* ... 641

Communication of the Commission to the Member States pursuant to Article 93 (1) of the EC Treaty applying Articles 92 and 93 of the Treaty to short-term export-credit insurance *(OJ C 281, 17 September 1997, p. 4)* ... 643

Communication of the Commission – Commission Notice on the application of the State aid rules to measures relating to direct business taxation *(OJ C 384, 10 December 1998, p. 3)* ... 647

Communication from the Commission – Community guidelines on State aid for rescuing and restructuring firms in difficulty *(OJ C 244, 1 October 2004, p. 2)* ... 651

Communication from the Commission concerning the prolongation of the Community Guidelines on State aid for Rescuing and Restructuring Firms in Difficulty *(OJ C 156, 9 July 2009, p. 3)* ... 662

Communication of the Commission – Commission Notice on the application of Articles 87 and 88 of the EC Treaty to State aid in the form of guarantees *(OJ C 155, 20 June 2008, p. 10)* ... 662

Communication of the Commission amending the period of application of Communication of the Commission to the Member States pursuant to Article 93(1) of the EC Treaty applying Articles 92 and 93 of the Treaty to short-term export-credit insurance *(OJ C 329, 7 December, 2010, p. 6)* ... 670

Communication from the Commission 21 April 2012 amending the Communication of the Commission to the Member States pursuant to Article 93(1) of the EC Treaty applying Articles 92 and 93 of the Treaty to short-term export-credit insurance *(PB. C 117, 21 April 2012, p. 1)* .. 670

3.1.2. Procedural rules

Council Regulation (EC) N° 659/1999, 22 March 1999 laying down detailed rules for the application of Article 93 of the EC Treaty *(OJ L 83, 27 March 1999, p. 1)* ... 671

Commission Regulation (EC) N° 794/2004, 21 April 2004 implementing Council Regulation (EC) N° 659/1999 laying down detailed rules for the application of Article 93 of the EC Treaty (consolidated version) *(OJ L 140, 30 April 2004, p. 1)* ... 677

State aid complaint form – Form for the submission of complaints concerning alleged unlawful State aid 683

Commission communication 1 December 2003 on professional secrecy in State aid decisions *(OJ C 297, 9 December 2003, p. 3)* ... 683

Communication – Details of arrangement for the electronic transmission of State aid notifications including addresses together with the arrangements for the protection of confidential information – Article 3(6) of Commission Regulation (EC) N° 794/2004 of 21 April 2004 implementing Council Regulation (EC) N° 659/1999 laying down detailed rules for the application of Article 93 of the EC Treaty *(OJ C 237, 27 September 2005, p. 3)* 686

Commission notice on the enforcement of State Aid Law by National Courts *(OJ C 85, 9 April 2009, p. 1)* ... 687

Commission Notice – Towards an effective implementation of Commission decisions ordering Member States to recover unlawful and incompatible State aid *(OJ C 272, 15 November 2007, p. 4)* ... 699

Communication from the Commission on the revision of the method for setting the reference and discount rates *(OJ C 14, 19 January, 2008, p. 6)* ... 707

Notice from the Commission on a simplified procedure for treatment of certain types of State Aid *(OJ C 136, 16 June 2009, p. 3)* ... 709

Communication from the Commission – Code of Best Practice for the conduct of State aid control procedures *(OJ C 136, 16 June 2009, p. 13)* ... 715

3.2. Public undertakings and services of general interest

3.2.1. Core legislation

Charter of Fundamental Rights of the European Union *(OJ C 303, 14 December 2007, p. 1)* ... 720

Protocol N° 26 on services of general interest *(OJ C 115, 9 May 2008, p. 308)* ... 720

3.2.2. Other documents

Commission communication to the Member States – Application of Articles 92 and 93 of the EEC Treaty and of Article 5 of Commission Directive 80/723/EEC to public undertakings in the manufacturing sector *(OJ C 307, 13 November 1993, p. 3)* 721

Communication from the Commission 12 May 2004 to the European Parliament, the Council, the European Economic and Social Committee and the Committee of the Regions – White Paper on services of general interest, COM (2004) 374 final........................... 730

Commission decision 2005/842/CE, 28 November 2005 on the application of Article 86(2) of the EC Treaty to State aid in the form of public service compensation granted to certain undertakings entrusted with the operation of services of general economic interest *(OJ L 312, 29 November 2005, p. 67)* 740

Communication from the Commission on a Community framework for State aid in the form of public service compensation (Altmark-communication) *(OJ C 297, 29 November 2005, p. 4)*................................ 741

Commission Directive 2006/111/EC 16 November 2006 on the transparency of financial relations between Member States and public undertakings as well as on financial transparency within certain undertakings *(OJ L 318, 17 November 2006, p. 17)*.............. 745

Communication from the Commission on services of general interest, including social services of general interest: a new European commitment, COM (2007) 725 748

Commission staff working document 20 November 2007 – Progress since the 2004 White paper on services of general interest – Accompanying document to the Communication on «Services of general interest, including social services of general interest: a new European commitment».................................... 754

Commission staff working paper 23 March 2011 – The Application of EU State Aid rules on Services of General Economic Interest since 2005 and the Outcome of the Public Consultation 754

Communication from the Commission 23 March 2011 to the European Parliament, the Council, the European Economic and Social Committee and the Committee of the Regions – Reform of the EU State Aid Rules on Services of General Economic Interest.................... 772

Communication from the Commission on the application of the European Union State aid rules to compensation granted for the provision of services of general economic interest (Text with EEA relevance) *(O.J. C 8, 11 January 2012, p. 4)*............................... 777

Communication from the Commission – European Union framework for State aid in the form of public service compensation (2011) (Text with EEA relevance) *(O.J. C 8, 11 January 2012, p. 15)*..................... 786

Commission Decision 20 December 2011 on the application of Article 106(2) of the Treaty on the Functioning of the European Union to State aid in the form of public service compensation granted to certain undertakings entrusted with the operation of services of general economic interest (notified under document C(2011) 9380) (Text with EEA relevance) *(O.J. L 7, 11 January 2012, p. 3)* 791

Commission Regulation (EU) No 360/2012, 25 April 2012 on the application of Articles 107 and 108 of the Treaty on the Functioning of the European Union to de minimis aid granted to undertakings providing services of general economic interest (Text with EEA relevance) *(O.J. L 114, 26 April 2012, p. 8)*....................... 797

SELECTED CASE LAW

I. Competition law predominantly applicable to undertakings (Articles 101-102 TFEU and Concentration control................................... 725

ECJ judgment of 13 February 1969, Case 14/68, Walt Wilhelm a.o. v. Bundeskartellamt [1969] ECR 1........ 725

ECJ judgment of 21 February 1973, Case 6/72, Europemballage Corporation and Continental Can Company Inc. v Commission [1973] ECR 215............. 726

ECJ judgment of 25 October 1977, Case 26/76, Metro SaBa-Großmärkte & Co. v Commission [1977] ECR 1875 727

ECJ judgment of 21 September 1988, Case 267/86, Van Eycke v. ASPA [1988] ECR 4769..................... 728

ECJ judgment of 27 September 1988, Joined Cases 89, 104, 114, 116, 117 and 125 to 129/85, A. Ahlstrom Osakeyhtio a.o. v. Commission (Wood pulp I) [1988] ECR 5193... 729

ECJ judgment of 31 March 1993, Joined Cases 89, 104, 114, 116, 117 and 125 to 129/85, A. Ahlstrom Osakeyhtio a.o. v. Commission (Wood pulp II) [1993] ECR I-1307..... 729

ECJ judgment of 17 November 1993, Case C-2/91, Criminal proceedings against Wolf W. Meng [1993] ECR I-5751 730

ECJ judgment of 9 June 1994, Case C-153/93, Germany v. Delta Schiffahrt und Speditionsgesellschaft [1994] ECR I-2517 731

ECJ judgment of 16 November 1995, Case C-244/94, Fédération Française des Sociétés d'Assurance (FFSA) a.o. v. Ministère de l'Agriculture et de la Pêche [1995] ECR I-4013 732

ECJ judgment of 24 October 1996, Case C-73/95 P, Viho Europe v. Commission [1996] ECR I-5457........ 733

ECJ judgment of 18 March 1997, Case C-343/95, Diego Calí & Figli v. Servizi Ecologici Porto di Genova [1997] ECR I-1547 734

ECJ judgment of 18 June 1998, Case C-35/96, Commission v. Italy (CNSD) [1998] ECR I-3851 735

ECJ judgment of 1 October 1998, Case C-38/97, Autotrasporti Librandi Snc di Librandi F. & C. v. Cuttica Spedizioni e Servizi Internazionali [1998] ECR I-5955 .. 735

ECJ judgment of 26 November 1998, Case C-7/97, Oscar Bronner v. Mediaprint [1998] ECR I-7791 737

ECJ judgment of 21 September 1999, Case C-219/97, Maatschappij Drijvende Bokken v. Stichting Pensioenfonds voor de Vervoer- en Havenbedrijven [1999] ECR I-6125.... 738

CFI judgment of 18 September 2001, Case T-112/99, Métropole Télévision (M6), Suez-Lyonnaise des Eaux, France Télécom, and Télévision Française 1 SA (TF1) v. Commission [2001] ECR II-2459 739

ECJ judgment of 20 September 2001, Case C-453/99, Courage v. Bernard Crehan [2001] ECR I-6297 743

ECJ judgment of 19 February 2002, Case C-35/99, Arduino a.o. [2002] ECR I-1529. 745

ECJ judgment of 19 February 2002, Case C-309/99, Wouters a.o. v. Algemene Raad van de Nederlandse Orde van Advocaten [2002] ECR I-1577 746

ECJ judgment of 13 July 2006, Joined Cases C-295/04, C-296/04, C-297/04 and C-298/04, Manfredi [2006] ECR I-6619. 749

CJ judgment of 18 July 2006, Case C-519/04 P, Meca-Medina and Macjen v Commission [2006] ECR I-6991. 754

CFI judgment of 8 July 2008, T-99/04, AC-Treuhand v Commission [2008] ECR II-1501. 757

ECJ judgment of 29 June 2010, Case C-441/07P, Commission v Alrosa Company Ltd, not yet reported 759

ECJ judgment of 7 December 2010, Case C-439/08, VEBIC, not yet reported 765

ECJ judgment of 14 September 2010, Case C-550/07 P, Akzo Nobel Chemicals and Akcros Chemicals v Commission, not yet reported 768

ECJ judgment of 17 February 2011, Case C-52/09, TeliaSonera Sverige, not yet reported 773

ECJ judgment of 14 June 2011, Case C-360/09, Pfleiderer AG v Bundeskartellamt, not yet reported 773

ECJ judgment of 29 September 2011, Case C-520/09P, Arkema v. Commission, not yet reported 857

GC judgment of 12 October 2011, Case T-224/10, Test-Aankoop/Test-achats v. Commission, not yet reported 858

ECJ judgment of 14 February 2012, Case C-17/10, Toshiba et al. v. Commission, not yet reported. 863

ECJ Judgment of 27 March 2012, Case C-209/10, Post Danmark, not yet reported 869

II. Competition law predominantly applicable to Member States, public undertakings, and undertakings entrusted with special rights or performing services of general economic interest (Articles 107-108 TFEU). 776

ECJ judgment of 24 January 1978, Case 82/77, Openbaar Ministerie of the Kingdom of the Netherlands v. Van Tiggele [1978] ECR 25 776

ECJ judgment of 30 January 1985, Case 290/83, Commission v. France («Aid to farmers») [1985] ECR 445 . . 776

ECJ judgment of 17 March 1993, Joined Cases C-72/91 and C-73/91, Sloman Neptun Schiffahrts AG v. Seebetriebsrat Bodo Ziesemer der Sloman Neptun Schiffahrts AG [1993] ECR I-887 777

ECJ judgment of 15 June 1993, Case C 225/91, Matra v. Commission [1993] ECR I 3203 778

ECJ judgment of 30 November 1993, Case C-189/91, Petra Kirsammer-Hack v. Nurhan Sidal [1993] ECR I-6185 780

ECJ judgment of 7 May 1998, Joined Cases C-52/97, C-53/97 and C-54/97, Epifanio Viscido a.o. v. Ente Poste Italiane [1998] ECR I-3949. 780

ECJ judgment of 16 September 1999, Case C-22/98, Criminal proceedings against Becu a.o. [1999] ECR I-5682 780

ECJ judgment of 25 October 2001, Case C-475/99, Firma Ambulanz Glöckner v Landkreis Südwestpfalz [2001] ECR I-8089 781

ECJ judgment of 16 May 2002, Case C-482/99, France v. Commission («Stardust Marine») [2002] ECR I-4397. 784

ECJ judgment of 24 July 2003, Case C-280/00, Altmark Trans GmbH, Regierungspräsidium Magdeburg v Nahverkehrsgesellschaft Altmark GmbH [2003] ECR I-7747 . 785

ECJ judgment of 15 July 2004, Case C-345/02, Pearle BV, Hans Prijs Optiek Franchise BV and Rinck Opticiëns BV v Hoofdbedrijfschap Ambachten [2004] ECR I-7139. 786

ECJ judgment of 6 September 2006, Case C-88/03, Portugal v Commission («regional taxation Azores») [2006] ECR I-7115. 787

ECJ judgment of 10 June 2010, Case C-140/09, Fallimento Traghetti del Mediterraneo SpA v Presidenza del Consiglio dei Ministri, not yet reported. 788

BIBLIOGRAPHY

List of Periodicals and Abbreviations consulted for the Bibliography 886

Selected Bibliography European Competition Law (2005-2012) 888

FORMS

Complaint form Articles 101 and 102 TFEU

Commission Regulation (EC) N° 773/2004, 7 April 2004 relating to the conduct of proceedings by the Commission pursuant to Articles 81 and 82 of the EC Treaty (OJ L 123, 27 April 2004, p. 18) 909

Inspection authorisation

Authorisation to conduct an inspection under Article 20(4) of Council Regulation (EC) N° 1/2003, March 2008 910

Notification forms Concentration control

Commission Regulation (EC) N° 802/2004, 21 April 2004 implementing Council Regulation N° 139/2004 on the control of concentrations between undertakings: FORM CO (OJ L 133, 30 April 2004, p. 1). 911

Commission Regulation (EC) N° 802/2004, 21 April 2004 implementing Council Regulation N° 139/2004 on the control of concentrations between undertakings: SHORT FORM (OJ L 133, 30 April 2004, p. 1). 919

Commission Regulation (EC) N° 802/2004, 21 April 2004 implementing Council Regulation N° 139/2004 on the control of concentrations between undertakings: FORM RS (OJ L 133, 30 April 2004, p. 1) 924

Commission Regulation (EC) N° 802/2004, 21 April 2004 implementing Council Regulation N° 139/2004 on the control of concentrations between undertakings: FORM RM (OJ L 133, 30 April 2004, p. 1) 929

Model texts Concentration control

Model texts for divestiture commitments – Commitments to the European Commission, 2 May 2003, not published in the Official Journal 930

Model texts for trustee mandates, 2 May 2003, not published in the Official Journal 935

Notification forms State aid

Notification form regional aid

Communication from the Commission – Multisectoral framework on regional aid for large investment projects: NOTIFICATION FORM *(OJ C 70, 19 March 2002, p. 8)* 941

Forms for the provisions of summary information under the reporting obligations of Regulation (EC) N° 800/2008

Commission Regulation (EC) N° 800/2008, 6 August 2008 declaring certain categories of aid compatible with the common market in application of Articles 87 and 88 of the Treaty (General block exemption Regulation): Summary information R&D aid *(OJ L 214, 9 August 2008, p. 3)* 943

Commission Regulation (EC) N° 800/2008, 6 August 2008 declaring certain categories of aid compatible with the common market in application of Articles 87 and 88 of the Treaty (General block exemption Regulation): Summary information article 9(1) *(OJ L 214, 9 August 2008, p. 3)* 944

Complaint form State aid

State aid complaint form – Form for the submission of complaints concerning alleged unlawful State aid 946

Public holidays 2012 and 2013

List of public holidays for 2012 for the institutions of the European Union *(OJ C 320, 25 November 2010, p. 3)* ... 948

Commission Decision 19 August 2011 on public holidays for 2013 for the institutions of the European Union *(OJ C 243, 20 August 2011)* 948

LEGISLATION

TABLE OF CONTENTS

1. Treaty on the Functioning of the European Union 1
2. Rules adressed to undertakings 5
3. Rules addressed to Member States 478

1. Treaty on the Functioning of the European Union

Consolidated version of the Treaty on the functioning of the European Union

(O.J. C 115, 9 May 2008, p. 47, corrig., O.J. C 290, 30 November 2009, p. 1)

(Extract)
(art. 3, 7–17, 42, 50, 93, 101–109)

PART ONE
PRINCIPLES

Art. 3. 1. The Union shall have exclusive competence in the following areas:

(b) the establishing of the competition rules necessary for the functioning of the internal market;

TITLE II
PROVISIONS HAVING GENERAL APPLICATION

Art. 7. The Union shall ensure consistency between its policies and activities, taking all of its objectives into account and in accordance with the principle of conferral of powers.

Art. 8 (ex Article 3(2) TEC) (2)

In all its activities, the Union shall aim to eliminate inequalities, and to promote equality, between men and women.

(2) These references are merely indicative. For more ample information, please refer to the tables of equivalences between the old and the new numbering of the Treaties.

Art. 9. In defining and implementing its policies and activities, the Union shall take into account requirements linked to the promotion of a high level of employment, the guarantee of adequate social protection, the fight against social exclusion, and a high level of education, training and protection of human health.

Art. 10. In defining and implementing its policies and activities, the Union shall aim to combat discrimination based on sex, racial or ethnic origin, religion or belief, disability, age or sexual orientation.

Art. 11 (ex Article 6 TEC)

Environmental protection requirements must be integrated into the definition and implementation of the Union policies and activities, in particular with a view to promoting sustainable development.

Art. 12 (ex Article 153(2) TEC)

Consumer protection requirements shall be taken into account in defining and implementing other Union policies and activities.

Art. 13. In formulating and implementing the Union's agriculture, fisheries, transport, internal market, research and technological development and space policies, the Union and the Member States shall, since animals are sentient beings, pay full regard to the welfare requirements of animals, while respecting the legislative or administrative provisions and customs of the Member States relating in particular to religious rites, cultural traditions and regional heritage.

Art. 14 (ex Article 16 TEC)

Without prejudice to Article 4 of the Treaty on European Union or to Articles 93, 106 and 107 of this Treaty, and given the place occupied by services of general economic interest in the shared values of the Union as well as their role in promoting social and territorial cohesion, the Union and the Member States, each within their respective powers and within the scope of application of the Treaties, shall take care that such services operate on the basis of principles and conditions, particularly economic and financial conditions, which enable them to fulfil their missions. The European Parliament and the Council, acting by means of regulations in accordance with the ordinary legislative procedure, shall establish these principles and set these conditions without prejudice to the competence of Member States, in compliance with the Treaties, to provide, to commission and to fund such services.

Art. 15 (ex Article 255 TEC)

1. In order to promote good governance and ensure the participation of civil society, the Union institutions, bodies, offices and agencies shall conduct their work as openly as possible.

2. The European Parliament shall meet in public, as shall the Council when considering and voting on a draft legislative act.

3. Any citizen of the Union, and any natural or legal person residing or having its registered office in a Member State, shall have a right of access to documents of the Union institutions, bodies, offices and agencies, whatever their medium, subject to the principles and the conditions to be defined in accordance with this paragraph.

General principles and limits on grounds of public or private interest governing this right of access to documents shall be determined by the European Parliament and the Council, by means of regulations, acting in accordance with the ordinary legislative procedure.

Each institution, body, office or agency shall ensure that its proceedings are transparent and shall elaborate in its own Rules of Procedure specific provisions regarding access to its documents, in accordance with the regulations referred to in the second subparagraph.

The Court of Justice of the European Union, the European Central Bank and the European Investment Bank shall be subject to this paragraph only when exercising their administrative tasks.

The European Parliament and the Council shall ensure publication of the documents relating to the legislative procedures under the terms laid down by the regulations referred to in the second subparagraph.

Art. 16 (ex Article 286 TEC)

1. Everyone has the right to the protection of personal data concerning them.

2. The European Parliament and the Council, acting in accordance with the ordinary legislative procedure, shall lay down the rules relating to the protection of individuals with regard to the processing of personal data by Union institutions, bodies, offices and agencies, and by the Member States when carrying out activities which fall within the scope of Union law, and the rules relating to the free movement of such data. Compliance with these rules shall be subject to the control of independent authorities.

The rules adopted on the basis of this Article shall be without prejudice to the specific rules laid down in Article 39 of the Treaty on European Union.

Art. 17. 1. The Union respects and does not prejudice the status under national law of churches and religious associations or communities in the Member States.

2. The Union equally respects the status under national law of philosophical and non-confessional organisations.

3. Recognising their identity and their specific contribution, the Union shall maintain an open, transparent and regular dialogue with these churches and organisations.

PART THREE

UNION POLICIES AND INTERNAL ACTIONS

TITLE III

AGRICULTURE AND FISHERIES

Art. 42. (ex Article 36 TEC)

The provisions of the Chapter relating to rules on competition shall apply to production of and trade in agricultural products only to the extent determined by the European Parliament and the Council within the framework of Article 43(2) and in accordance with the procedure laid down therein, account being taken of the objectives set out in Article 39.

The Council, on a proposal from the Commission, may authorise the granting of aid:

(a) for the protection of enterprises handicapped by structural or natural conditions;

(b) within the framework of economic development programmes.

TITLE IV

FREE MOVEMENT OF PERSONS, SERVICES AND CAPITAL

CHAPTER 2

RIGHT OF ESTABLISHMENT

Art. 50. (ex Article 44 TEC)

1. In order to attain freedom of establishment as regards a particular activity, the European Parliament and the Council, acting in accordance with the ordinary legislative procedure and after consulting the Economic and Social Committee, shall act by means of directives.

2. The European Parliament, the Council and the Commission shall carry out the duties devolving upon them under the preceding provisions, in particular:

(a) by according, as a general rule, priority treatment to activities where freedom of establishment makes a particularly valuable contribution to the development of production and trade;

(b) by ensuring close cooperation between the competent authorities in the Member States in order to ascertain the particular situation within the Union of the various activities concerned;

(c) by abolishing those administrative procedures and practices, whether resulting from national legislation or from agreements previously concluded between Member States, the maintenance of which would form an obstacle to freedom of establishment;

(d) by ensuring that workers of one Member State employed in the territory of another Member State may remain in that territory for the purpose of taking up activities therein as self-employed persons, where they satisfy the conditions which they would be required to satisfy if they were entering that State at the time when they intended to take up such activities;

(e) by enabling a national of one Member State to acquire and use land and buildings situated in the territory of another Member State, in so far as this does not conflict with the principles laid down in Article 39(2);

(f) by effecting the progressive abolition of restrictions on freedom of establishment in every branch of activity under consideration, both as regards the conditions for setting up agencies, branches or subsidiaries in the territory of a Member State and as regards the subsidiaries in the territory of a Member State and as regards the conditions governing the entry of personnel belonging to the main establishment into managerial or supervisory posts in such agencies, branches or subsidiaries;

(g) by coordinating to the necessary extent the safeguards which, for the protection of the interests of members and others, are required by Member States of companies or firms within the meaning of the second paragraph of Article 54 with a view to making such safeguards equivalent throughout the Union;

(h) by satisfying themselves that the conditions of establishment are not distorted by aids granted by Member States.

TITLE VI

TRANSPORT

Art. 93. (ex Article 73 TEC)

Aids shall be compatible with the Treaties if they meet the needs of coordination of transport or if they represent reimbursement for the discharge of certain obligations inherent in the concept of a public service.

TITLE VII
COMMON RULES ON COMPETITION, TAXATION AND APPROXIMATION OF LAWS

CHAPTER 1
RULES ON COMPETITION

Section 1
Rules applying to undertakings

Art. 101 (ex Article 81 TEC)

1. The following shall be prohibited as incompatible with the internal market: all agreements between undertakings, decisions by associations of undertakings and concerted practices which may affect trade between Member States and which have as their object or effect the prevention, restriction or distortion of competition within the internal market, and in particular those which:

(a) directly or indirectly fix purchase or selling prices or any other trading conditions;

(b) limit or control production, markets, technical development, or investment;

(c) share markets or sources of supply;

(d) apply dissimilar conditions to equivalent transactions with other trading parties, thereby placing them at a competitive disadvantage;

(e) make the conclusion of contracts subject to acceptance by the other parties of supplementary obligations which, by their nature or according to commercial usage, have no connection with the subject of such contracts.

2. Any agreements or decisions prohibited pursuant to this Article shall be automatically void.

3. The provisions of paragraph 1 may, however, be declared inapplicable in the case of:

– any agreement or category of agreements between undertakings;

– any decision or category of decisions by associations of undertakings;

– any concerted practice or category of concerted practices,

which contributes to improving the production or distribution of goods or to promoting technical or economic progress, while allowing consumers a fair share of the resulting benefit, and which does not:

(a) impose on the undertakings concerned restrictions which are not indispensable to the attainment of these objectives;

(b) afford such undertakings the possibility of eliminating competition in respect of a substantial part of the products in question.

Art. 102 (ex Article 82 TEC)

Any abuse by one or more undertakings of a dominant position within the internal market or in a substantial part of it shall be prohibited as incompatible with the internal market in so far as it may affect trade between Member States.

Such abuse may, in particular, consist in:

(a) directly or indirectly imposing unfair purchase or selling prices or other unfair trading conditions;

(b) limiting production, markets or technical development to the prejudice of consumers;

(c) applying dissimilar conditions to equivalent transactions with other trading parties, thereby placing them at a competitive disadvantage;

(d) making the conclusion of contracts subject to acceptance by the other parties of supplementary obligations which, by their nature or according to commercial usage, have no connection with the subject of such contracts.

Art. 103 (ex Article 83 TEC)

1. The appropriate regulations or directives to give effect to the principles set out in Articles 101 and 102 shall be laid down by the Council, on a proposal from the Commission and after consulting the European Parliament.

2. The regulations or directives referred to in paragraph 1 shall be designed in particular:

(a) to ensure compliance with the prohibitions laid down in Article 101(1) and in Article 102 by making provision for fines and periodic penalty payments;

(b) to lay down detailed rules for the application of Article 101(3), taking into account the need to ensure effective supervision on the one hand, and to simplify administration to the greatest possible extent on the other;

(c) to define, if need be, in the various branches of the economy, the scope of the provisions of Articles 101 and 102;

(d) to define the respective functions of the Commission and of the Court of Justice of the European Union in applying the provisions laid down in this paragraph;

(e) to determine the relationship between national laws and the provisions contained in this Section or adopted pursuant to this Article.

Art. 104 (ex Article 84 TEC)

Until the entry into force of the provisions adopted in pursuance of Article 103, the authorities in Member States shall rule on the admissibility of agreements, decisions and concerted practices and on abuse of a dominant position in the internal market in accordance with the law of their country and with the provisions of Article 101, in particular paragraph 3, and of Article 102.

Art. 105 (ex Article 85 TEC)

1. Without prejudice to Article 104, the Commission shall ensure the application of the principles laid down in Articles 101 and 102. On application by a Member State or on its own initiative, and in cooperation with the competent authorities in the Member States, which shall give it their assistance, the Commission shall investigate cases of suspected infringement of these principles. If it finds that there has been an infringement, it shall propose appropriate measures to bring it to an end.

2. If the infringement is not brought to an end, the Commission shall record such infringement of the principles in a reasoned decision. The Commission may publish its decision and authorise Member States to take the measures, the conditions and details of which it shall determine, needed to remedy the situation.

3. The Commission may adopt regulations relating to the categories of agreement in respect of which the Council has adopted a regulation or a directive pursuant to Article 103(2)(b).

Art. 106 (ex Article 86 TEC)

1. In the case of public undertakings and undertakings to which Member States grant special or exclusive rights, Member States shall neither enact nor maintain in force any measure contrary to the rules contained in the Treaties, in particular to those rules provided for in Article 18 and Articles 101 to 109.

2. Undertakings entrusted with the operation of services of general economic interest or having the character of a revenue-producing monopoly shall be subject to the rules contained in the Treaties, in particular to the rules on competition, in so far as the application of such rules does not obstruct the performance, in law or in fact, of the particular tasks assigned to them. The development of trade must not be affected to such an extent as would be contrary to the interests of the Union.

3. The Commission shall ensure the application of the provisions of this Article and shall, where necessary, address appropriate directives or decisions to Member States.

Section 2

Aids granted by states

Art. 107 (ex Article 87 TEC)

1. Save as otherwise provided in the Treaties, any aid granted by a Member State or through State resources in any form whatsoever which distorts or threatens to distort competition by favouring certain undertakings or the production of certain goods shall, in so far as it affects trade between Member States, be incompatible with the internal market.

2. The following shall be compatible with the internal market:

(a) aid having a social character, granted to individual consumers, provided that such aid is granted without discrimination related to the origin of the products concerned;

(b) aid to make good the damage caused by natural disasters or exceptional occurrences;

(c) aid granted to the economy of certain areas of the Federal Republic of Germany affected by the division of Germany, in so far as such aid is required in order to compensate for the economic disadvantages caused by that division. Five years after the entry into force of the Treaty of Lisbon, the Council, acting on a proposal from the Commission, may adopt a decision repealing this point.

3. The following may be considered to be compatible with the internal market:

(a) aid to promote the economic development of areas where the standard of living is abnormally low or where there is serious underemployment, and of the regions referred to in Article 349, in view of their structural, economic and social situation;

(b) aid to promote the execution of an important project of common European interest or to remedy a serious disturbance in the economy of a Member State;

(c) aid to facilitate the development of certain economic activities or of certain economic areas, where such aid does not adversely affect trading conditions to an extent contrary to the common interest;

(d) aid to promote culture and heritage conservation where such aid does not affect trading conditions and competition in the Union to an extent that is contrary to the common interest;

(e) such other categories of aid as may be specified by decision of the Council on a proposal from the Commission.

Art. 108 (ex Article 88 TEC)

1. The Commission shall, in cooperation with Member States, keep under constant review all systems of aid existing in those States. It shall propose to the latter any appropriate measures required by the progressive development or by the functioning of the internal market.

2. If, after giving notice to the parties concerned to submit their comments, the Commission finds that aid granted by a State or through State resources is not compatible with the internal market having regard to Article 107, or that such aid is being misused, it shall decide that the State concerned shall abolish or alter such aid within a period of time to be determined by the Commission.

If the State concerned does not comply with this decision within the prescribed time, the Commission or any other interested State may, in derogation from the provisions of Articles 258 and 259, refer the matter to the Court of Justice of the European Union direct.

On application by a Member State, the Council may, acting unanimously, decide that aid which that State is granting or intends to grant shall be considered to be compatible with the internal market, in derogation from the provisions of Article 107 or from the regulations provided for in Article 109, if such a decision is justified by exceptional circumstances. If, as regards the aid in question, the Commission has already initiated the procedure provided for in the first subparagraph of this paragraph, the fact that the State concerned has made its application to the Council shall have the effect of suspending that procedure until the Council has made its attitude known.

If, however, the Council has not made its attitude known within three months of the said application being made, the Commission shall give its decision on the case.

3. The Commission shall be informed, in sufficient time to enable it to submit its comments, of any plans to grant or alter aid. If it considers that any such plan is not compatible with the internal market having regard to Article 107, it shall without delay initiate the procedure provided for in paragraph 2. The Member State concerned shall not put its proposed measures into effect until this procedure has resulted in a final decision.

4. The Commission may adopt regulations relating to the categories of State aid that the Council has, pursuant to Article 109, determined may be exempted from the procedure provided for by paragraph 3 of this Article.

Art. 109 (ex Article 89 TEC)

The Council, on a proposal from the Commission and after consulting the European Parliament, may make any appropriate regulations for the application of Articles 107 and 108 and may in particular determine the conditions in which Article 108(3) shall apply and the categories of aid exempted from this procedure.

2. Rules adressed to undertakings

TABLE OF CONTENTS

2.1. Cartels and abuse of dominant position 5
2.2. Concentration control 338

2.1. Cartels and abuse of dominant position

TABLE OF CONTENTS

2.1.1. Core legislation 5
2.1.2. Substantive rules 19
2.1.3. Procedural rules 213

2.1.1. Core legislation

Protocol N° 27 – Internal market and competition 5
Council Regulation (EC) N° 1/2003, 16 December 2002 – Rules on competition Art. 101 and 102 Treaty, implementation. 5

Protocol N° 27 on the internal market and competition

(OJ C 115, 9 May 2008, p. 309)

THE HIGH CONTRACTING PARTIES,

CONSIDERING that the internal market as set out in Article 3 of the Treaty on European Union includes a system ensuring that competition is not distorted,

HAVE AGREED that:

To this end, the Union shall, if necessary, take action under the provisions of the Treaties, including under Article 352 of the Treaty on the Functioning of the European Union.

This protocol shall be annexed to the Treaty on European Union and to the Treaty on the Functioning of the European Union.

Council Regulation (EC) N° 1/2003, 16 December 2002 on the implementation of the rules on competition laid down in Articles 81 and 82 of the Treaty (Text with EEA relevance)

(OJ L 1, 4 January 2003, p. 1)

Amended by:
Council Regulation (EC) N° 411/2004 of 26 February 2004. *Official Journal* L 68, p. 1, 6.3.2004.
Council Regulation (EC) N° 1419/2006 of 25 september 2006. *Official Journal* L 269, p 1, 28.9.2006

1. Article 81 EC is now Article 101 TFEU and Article 82 EC is now Article 102 TFEU.

THE COUNCIL OF THE EUROPEAN UNION,
Having regard to the Treaty establishing the European Community, and in particular Article 83 thereof,
Having regard to the proposal from the Commission (1),
Having regard to the opinion of the European Parliament (2),
Having regard to the opinion of the European Economic and Social Committee (3),
Whereas:
(1) In order to establish a system which ensures that competition in the common market is not distorted, Articles 81 and 82 of the Treaty must be applied effectively and uniformly in the Community. Council Regulation N° 17 of 6 February 1962, First Regulation implementing Articles 81 and 82 (*) of the Treaty (4), has allowed a Community competition policy to develop that has helped to disseminate a competition culture within the Community. In the light of experience, however, that Regulation should now be replaced by legislation designed to meet the challenges of an integrated market and a future enlargement of the Community.

(2) In particular, there is a need to rethink the arrangements for applying the exception from the prohibition on agreements, which restrict competition, laid down in Article 81(3) of the Treaty. Under Article 83(2)(b) of the Treaty, account must be taken in this regard of the need to ensure effective supervision, on the one hand, and to simplify administration to the greatest possible extent, on the other.

(3) The centralised scheme set up by Regulation N° 17 no longer secures a balance between those two objectives. It hampers application of the Community competition rules by the courts and competition authorities of the Member States, and the system of notification it involves prevents the Commission from concentrating its resources on curbing the most serious infringements. It also imposes considerable costs on undertakings.

(4) The present system should therefore be replaced by a directly applicable exception system in which the competition authorities and courts of the Member States have the power to apply not only Article 81(1) and Article 82 of the Treaty, which have direct applicability by virtue of the case-law of the Court of Justice of the European Communities, but also Article 81(3) of the Treaty.

(5) In order to ensure an effective enforcement of the Community competition rules and at the same time the respect of fundamental rights of defence, this Regulation should regulate the burden of proof under Articles 81 and 82 of the Treaty. It should be for the party or the authority alleging an infringement of Article 81(1) and Article 82 of the Treaty to prove the existence thereof to the required legal standard. It should be for the undertaking or association of undertakings invoking the benefit of a defence against a finding of an infringement to demonstrate to the required legal standard that the conditions for applying such defence are satisfied. This Regulation affects neither national rules on the standard of proof nor obligations of competition authorities and courts of the Member States to ascertain the relevant facts of a case, provided that such rules and obligations are compatible with general principles of Community law.

(6) In order to ensure that the Community competition rules are applied effectively, the competition authorities of the Member States should be associated more closely with their application. To this end, they should be empowered to apply Community law.

(7) National courts have an essential part to play in applying the Community competition rules. When deciding disputes between private individuals, they protect the subjective rights under Community law, for example by awarding damages to the victims of infringements. The role of the national courts here complements that of the competition authorities of the Member States. They should therefore be allowed to apply Articles 81 and 82 of the Treaty in full.

(8) In order to ensure the effective enforcement of the Community competition rules and the proper functioning of the cooperation mechanisms contained in this Regulation, it is necessary to oblige the competition authorities and courts of the Member States to also apply Articles 81 and 82 of the Treaty where they apply national competition law to agreements and practices which may affect trade between Member States. In order to create a level playing field for agreements, decisions by associations of undertakings and concerted practices within the internal market, it is also necessary to determine pursuant to Article 83(2)*(e)* of the Treaty the relationship between national laws and Community competition law. To that effect it is necessary to provide that the application of national competition laws to agreements, decisions or concerted practices within the meaning of Article 81(1) of the Treaty may not lead to the prohibition of such agreements, decisions and concerted practices if they are not also prohibited under Community competition law. The notions of agreements, decisions and concerted practices are autonomous concepts of Community competition law covering the coordination of behaviour of undertakings on the market as interpreted by the Community Courts. Member States should not under this Regulation be precluded from adopting and applying on their territory stricter national competition laws which prohibit or impose sanctions on unilateral conduct engaged in by undertakings. These stricter national laws may include provisions which prohibit or impose sanctions on abusive behaviour toward economically dependent undertakings. Furthermore, this Regulation does not apply to national laws which impose criminal sanctions on natural persons except to the extent that such sanctions are the means whereby competition rules applying to undertakings are enforced.

(9) Articles 81 and 82 of the Treaty have as their objective the protection of competition on the market. This Regulation, which is adopted for the implementation of these Treaty provisions, does not preclude Member States from implementing on their territory national legislation, which protects other legitimate interests provided that such legislation is compatible with general principles and other provisions of Community law. In so far as such national legislation pursues predominantly an objective different from that of protecting competition on the market, the competition authorities and courts of the Member States may apply such legislation on their territory. Accordingly, Member States may under this Regulation implement on their territory national legislation that prohibits or imposes sanctions on acts of unfair trading practice, be they unilateral or contractual. Such legislation pursues a specific objective, irrespective of the actual or presumed effects of such acts on competition on the market. This is particularly the case of legislation which prohibits undertakings from imposing on their trading partners, obtaining or attempting to obtain from them terms and conditions that are unjustified, disproportionate or without consideration.

(10) Regulations such as 19/65/EEC (5), (EEC) N° 2821/71 (6), (EEC) N° 3976/87 (7), (EEC) N° 1534/91 (8), or (EEC) N° 479/92 (9) empower the Commission to apply Article 81(3) of the Treaty by Regulation to certain categories of agreements, decisions by associations of undertakings and concerted practices. In the areas defined by such Regulations, the Commission has adopted and may continue to adopt so called «block» exemption Regulations by which it declares Article 81(1) of the Treaty inapplicable to categories of agreements, decisions and concerted practices. Where agreements, decisions and concerted practices to which such Regulations apply nonetheless have effects that are incompatible with Article 81(3) of the Treaty, the Commission and the competition authorities of the Member States should have the power to withdraw in a particular case the benefit of the block exemption Regulation.

(11) For it to ensure that the provisions of the Treaty are applied, the Commission should be able to address decisions to undertakings or associations of undertakings for the purpose of bringing to an end infringements of Articles 81 and 82 of the Treaty. Provided there is a legitimate interest in

doing so, the Commission should also be able to adopt decisions which find that an infringement has been committed in the past even if it does not impose a fine. This Regulation should also make explicit provision for the Commission's power to adopt decisions ordering interim measures, which has been acknowledged by the Court of Justice.

(12) This Regulation should make explicit provision for the Commis-sion's power to impose any remedy, whether behavioural or structural, which is necessary to bring the infringement effectively to an end, having regard to the principle of proportionality. Structural remedies should only be imposed either where there is no equally effective behavioural remedy or where any equally effective behavioural remedy would be more burdensome for the undertaking concerned than the structural remedy. Changes to the structure of an undertaking as it existed before the infringement was committed would only be proportionate where there is a substantial risk of a lasting or repeated infringement that derives from the very structure of the undertaking.

(13) Where, in the course of proceedings which might lead to an agreement or practice being prohibited, undertakings offer the Commission commitments such as to meet its concerns, the Commission should be able to adopt decisions which make those commitments binding on the undertakings concerned. Commitment decisions should find that there are no longer grounds for action by the Commission without concluding whether or not there has been or still is an infringement. Commitment decisions are without prejudice to the powers of competition authorities and courts of the Member States to make such a finding and decide upon the case. Commitment decisions are not appropriate in cases where the Commission intends to impose a fine.

(14) In exceptional cases where the public interest of the Community so requires, it may also be expedient for the Commission to adopt a decision of a declaratory nature finding that the prohibition in Article 81 or Article 82 of the Treaty does not apply, with a view to clarifying the law and ensuring its consistent application throughout the Community, in particular with regard to new types of agreements or practices that have not been settled in the existing case-law and administrative practice.

(15) The Commission and the competition authorities of the Member States should form together a network of public authorities applying the Community competition rules in close cooperation. For that purpose it is necessary to set up arrangements for information and consultation. Further modalities for the cooperation within the network will be laid down and revised by the Commission, in close cooperation with the Member States.

(16) Notwithstanding any national provision to the contrary, the exchange of information and the use of such information in evidence should be allowed between the members of the network even where the information is confidential. This information may be used for the application of Articles 81 and 82 of the Treaty as well as for the parallel application of national competition law, provided that the latter application relates to the same case and does not lead to a different outcome. When the information exchanged is used by the receiving authority to impose sanctions on undertakings, there should be no other limit to the use of the information than the obligation to use it for the purpose for which it was collected given the fact that the sanctions imposed on undertakings are of the same type in all systems. The rights of defence enjoyed by undertakings in the various systems can be considered as sufficiently equivalent. However, as regards natural persons, they may be subject to substantially different types of sanctions across the various systems. Where that is the case, it is necessary to ensure that information can only be used if it has been collected in a way which respects the same level of protection of the rights of defence of natural persons as provided for under the national rules of the receiving authority.

(17) If the competition rules are to be applied consistently and, at the same time, the network is to be managed in the best possible way, it is essential to retain the rule that the competition authorities of the Member States are automatically relieved of their competence if the Commission initiates its own proceedings. Where a competition authority of a Member State is already acting on a case and the Commission intends to initiate proceedings, it should endeavour to do so as soon as possible. Before initiating proceedings, the Commission should consult the national authority concerned.

(18) To ensure that cases are dealt with by the most appropriate authorities within the network, a general provision should be laid down allowing a competition authority to suspend or close a case on the ground that another authority is dealing with it or has already dealt with it, the objective being that each case should be handled by a single authority. This provision should not prevent the Commission from rejecting a complaint for lack of Community interest, as the case-law of the Court of Justice has acknowledged it may do, even if no other competition authority has indicated its intention of dealing with the case.

(19) The Advisory Committee on Restrictive Practices and Dominant Positions set up by Regulation N° 17 has functioned in a very satisfactory manner. It will fit well into the new system of decentralised application. It is necessary, therefore, to build upon the rules laid down by Regulation N° 17, while improving the effectiveness of the organisational arrangements. To this end, it would be expedient to allow opinions to be delivered by written procedure. The Advisory Committee should also be able to act as a forum for discussing cases that are being handled by the competition authorities of the Member States, so as to help safeguard the consistent application of the Community competition rules.

(20) The Advisory Committee should be composed of representatives of the competition authorities of the Member States. For meetings in which general issues are being discussed, Member States should be able to appoint an additional representative. This is without prejudice to members of the Committee being assisted by other experts from the Member States.

(21) Consistency in the application of the competition rules also requires that arrangements be established for cooperation between the courts of the Member States and the Commission. This is relevant for all courts of the Member States that apply Articles 81 and 82 of the Treaty, whether apply-

ing these rules in lawsuits between private parties, acting as public enforcers or as review courts. In particular, national courts should be able to ask the Commission for information or for its opinion on points concerning the application of Community competition law. The Commission and the competition authorities of the Member States should also be able to submit written or oral observations to courts called upon to apply Article 81 or Article 82 of the Treaty. These observations should be submitted within the framework of national procedural rules and practices including those safeguarding the rights of the parties. Steps should therefore be taken to ensure that the Commission and the competition authorities of the Member States are kept sufficiently well informed of proceedings before national courts.

(22) In order to ensure compliance with the principles of legal certainty and the uniform application of the Community competition rules in a system of parallel powers, conflicting decisions must be avoided. It is therefore necessary to clarify, in accordance with the case-law of the Court of Justice, the effects of Commission decisions and proceedings on courts and competition authorities of the Member States. Commitment decisions adopted by the Commission do not affect the power of the courts and the competition authorities of the Member States to apply Articles 81 and 82 of the Treaty.

(23) The Commission should be empowered throughout the Community to require such information to be supplied as is necessary to detect any agreement, decision or concerted practice prohibited by Article 81 of the Treaty or any abuse of a dominant position prohibited by Article 82 of the Treaty. When complying with a decision of the Commission, undertakings cannot be forced to admit that they have committed an infringement, but they are in any event obliged to answer factual questions and to provide documents, even if this information may be used to establish against them or against another undertaking the existence of an infringement.

(24) The Commission should also be empowered to undertake such inspections as are necessary to detect any agreement, decision or concerted practice prohibited by Article 81 of the Treaty or any abuse of a dominant position prohibited by Article 82 of the Treaty. The competition authorities of the Member States should cooperate actively in the exercise of these powers.

(25) The detection of infringements of the competition rules is growing ever more difficult, and, in order to protect competition effectively, the Commission's powers of investigation need to be supplemented. The Commission should in particular be empowered to interview any persons who may be in possession of useful information and to record the statements made. In the course of an inspection, officials authorised by the Commission should be empowered to affix seals for the period of time necessary for the inspection. Seals should normally not be affixed for more than 72 hours. Officials authorised by the Commission should also be empowered to ask for any information relevant to the subject matter and purpose of the inspection.

(26) Experience has shown that there are cases where business records are kept in the homes of directors or other people working for an undertaking. In order to safeguard the effectiveness of inspections, therefore, officials and other persons authorised by the Commission should be empowered to enter any premises where business records may be kept, including private homes. However, the exercise of this latter power should be subject to the authorisation of the judicial authority.

(27) Without prejudice to the case-law of the Court of Justice, it is useful to set out the scope of the control that the national judicial authority may carry out when it authorises, as foreseen by national law including as a precautionary measure, assistance from law enforcement authorities in order to overcome possible opposition on the part of the undertaking or the execution of the decision to carry out inspections in non-business premises. It results from the case-law that the national judicial authority may in particular ask the Commission for further information which it needs to carry out its control and in the absence of which it could refuse the authorisation. The case-law also confirms the competence of the national courts to control the application of national rules governing the implementation of coercive measures.

(28) In order to help the competition authorities of the Member States to apply Articles 81 and 82 of the Treaty effectively, it is expedient to enable them to assist one another by carrying out inspections and other fact-finding measures.

(29) Compliance with Articles 81 and 82 of the Treaty and the fulfilment of the obligations imposed on undertakings and associations of undertakings under this Regulation should be enforceable by means of fines and periodic penalty payments. To that end, appropriate levels of fine should also be laid down for infringements of the procedural rules.

(30) In order to ensure effective recovery of fines imposed on associations of undertakings for infringements that they have committed, it is necessary to lay down the conditions on which the Commission may require payment of the fine from the members of the association where the association is not solvent. In doing so, the Commission should have regard to the relative size of the undertakings belonging to the association and in particular to the situation of small and medium-sized enterprises. Payment of the fine by one or several members of an association is without prejudice to rules of national law that provide for recovery of the amount paid from other members of the association.

(31) The rules on periods of limitation for the imposition of fines and periodic penalty payments were laid down in Council Regulation (EEC) N° 2988/74 (10), which also concerns penalties in the field of transport. In a system of parallel powers, the acts, which may interrupt a limitation period, should include procedural steps taken independently by the competition authority of a Member State. To clarify the legal framework, Regulation (EEC) N° 2988/74 should therefore be amended to prevent it applying to matters covered by this Regulation, and this Regulation should include provisions on periods of limitation.

(32) The undertakings concerned should be accorded the right to be heard by the Commission, third parties whose interests may be affected by a decision should be given the opportunity of submitting their observations beforehand, and the decisions taken should be widely publicised. While

ensuring the rights of defence of the undertakings concerned, in particular, the right of access to the file, it is essential that business secrets be protected. The confidentiality of information exchanged in the network should likewise be safeguarded.

(33) Since all decisions taken by the Commission under this Regulation are subject to review by the Court of Justice in accordance with the Treaty, the Court of Justice should, in accordance with Article 229 thereof be given unlimited jurisdiction in respect of decisions by which the Commission imposes fines or periodic penalty payments.

(34) The principles laid down in Articles 81 and 82 of the Treaty, as they have been applied by Regulation N° 17, have given a central role to the Community bodies. This central role should be retained, whilst associating the Member States more closely with the application of the Community competition rules. In accordance with the principles of subsidiarity and proportionality as set out in Article 5 of the Treaty, this Regulation does not go beyond what is necessary in order to achieve its objective, which is to allow the Community competition rules to be applied effectively.

(35) In order to attain a proper enforcement of Community competition law, Member States should designate and empower authorities to apply Articles 81 and 82 of the Treaty as public enforcers. They should be able to designate administrative as well as judicial authorities to carry out the various functions conferred upon competition authorities in this Regulation. This Regulation recognises the wide variation which exists in the public enforcement systems of Member States. The effects of Article 11(6) of this Regulation should apply to all competition authorities. As an exception to this general rule, where a prosecuting authority brings a case before a separate judicial authority, Article 11(6) should apply to the prosecuting authority subject to the conditions in Article 35(4) of this Regulation. Where these conditions are not fulfilled, the general rule should apply. In any case, Article 11(6) should not apply to courts insofar as they are acting as review courts.

(36) As the case-law has made it clear that the competition rules apply to transport, that sector should be made subject to the procedural provisions of this Regulation. Council Regulation N° 141 of 26 november 1962 exempting transport from the application of Regulation N° 17 (11) should therefore be repealed and Regulations (EEC) N° 1017/68 (12), (EEC) N° 4056/86 (13) and (EEC) N° 3975/87 (14) should be amended in order to delete the specific procedural provisions they contain.

(37) This Regulation respects the fundamental rights and observes the principles recognised in particular by the Charter of Fundamental Rights of the European Union. Accordingly, this Regulation should be interpreted and applied with respect to those rights and principles.

(38) Legal certainty for undertakings operating under the Community competition rules contributes to the promotion of innovation and investment. Where cases give rise to genuine uncertainty because they present novel or unresolved questions for the application of these rules, individual undertakings may wish to seek informal guidance from the Commission. This Regulation is without prejudice to the ability of the Commission to issue such informal guidance,

HAS ADOPTED THIS REGULATION:

(1) O.J. C 365 E, 19.12.2000, p. 284.

(2) O.J. C 72 E, 21.3.2002, p. 305.

(3) O.J. C 155, 29.5.2001, p. 73.

(*) The title of Regulation N° 17 has been adjusted to take account of the renumbering of the Articles of the EC Treaty, in accordance with Article 12 of the Treaty of Amsterdam; the original reference was to Articles 85 and 86 of the Treaty.

(4) O.J. 13, 21.2.1962, p. 204/62. Regulation as last amended by Regulation (EC) N° 1216/1999 (O.J. L 148, 15.6.1999, p. 5).

(5) Council Regulation N° 19/65/EEC of 2 March 1965 on the application of Article 81(3) (The titles of the Regulations have been adjusted to take account of the renumbering of the Articles of the EC Treaty, in accordance with Article 12 of the Treaty of Amsterdam; the original reference was to Article 85(3) of the Treaty) of the Treaty to certain categories of agreements and concerted practices (O.J. 36, 6.3.1965, p. 533). Regulation as last amended by Regulation (EC) N° 1215/1999 (O.J. L 148, 15.6.1999, p. 1).

(6) Council Regulation (EEC) N° 2821/71 of 20 december 1971 on the application of Article 81(3) (The titles of the Regulations have been adjusted to take account of the renumbering of the Articles of the EC Treaty, in accordance with Article 12 of the Treaty of Amsterdam; the original reference was to Article 85(3) of the Treaty) of the Treaty to categories of agreements, decisions and concerted practices (O.J. L 285, 29.12.1971, p. 46). Regulation as last amended by the Act of Accession of 1994.

(7) Council Regulation (EEC) N° 3976/87 of 14 december 1987 on the application of Article 81(3) (The titles of the Regulations have been adjusted to take account of the renumbering of the Articles of the EC Treaty, in accordance with Article 12 of the Treaty of Amsterdam; the original reference was to Article 85(3) of the Treaty) of the Treaty to certain categories of agreements and concerted practices in the air transport sector (O.J. L 374, 31.12.1987, p. 9). Regulation as last amended by the Act of Accession of 1994.

(8) Council Regulation (EEC) N° 1534/91 of 31 May 1991 on the application of Article 81(3) (The titles of the Regulations have been adjusted to take account of the renumbering of the Articles of the EC Treaty, in accordance with Article 12 of the Treaty of Amsterdam; the original reference was to Article 85(3) of the Treaty) of the Treaty to certain categories of agreements, decisions and concerted practices in the insurance sector (O.J. L 143, 7.6.1991, p. 1).

(9) Council Regulation (EEC) N° 479/92 of 25 February 1992 on the application of Article 81(3) (The titles of the Regulations have been adjusted to take account of the renumbering of the Articles of the EC Treaty, in accordance with Article 12 of the Treaty of Amsterdam; the original reference was to Article 85(3) of the Treaty) of the Treaty to certain categories of agreements, decisions and concerted practices between liner shipping companies (Consortia) (O.J. L 55, 29.2.1992, p. 3). Regulation amended by the Act of Accession of 1994.

(10) Council Regulation (EEC) N° 2988/74 of 26 november 1974 concerning limitation periods in proceedings and the enforcement of sanctions under the rules of the European Economic Community relating to transport and competition (O.J. L 319, 29.11.1974, p. 1).

(11) O.J. 124, 28.11.1962, p. 2751/62; Regulation as last amended by Regulation N° 1002/67/EEC (O.J. 306, 16.12.1967, p. 1).

(12) Council Regulation (EEC) N° 1017/68 of 19 July 1968 applying rules of competition to transport by rail, road and inland waterway (O.J. L 175, 23.7.1968, p. 1). Regulation as last amended by the Act of Accession of 1994.

(13) Council Regulation (EEC) N° 4056/86 of 22 december 1986 laying down detailed rules for the application of Articles 81 and 82 (The title of the Regulation has been adjusted to take account of the renumbering of the Articles of the EC Treaty, in accordance with Article 12 of the Treaty of Amsterdam; the original reference was to Articles 85 and 86 of the Treaty) of the Treaty to maritime transport (O.J. L 378, 31.12.1986, p. 4). Regulation as last amended by the Act of Accession of 1994.

(14) Council Regulation (EEC) N° 3975/87 of 14 december 1987 laying down the procedure for the application of the rules on competition to undertakings in the air transport sector (O.J. L 374, 31.12.1987, p. 1). Regulation as last amended by Regulation (EEC) N° 2410/92 (O.J. L 240, 24.8.1992, p. 18)

CHAPTER I
PRINCIPLES

Art. 1. *Application of Articles 81 and 82 of the Treaty*

1. Agreements, decisions and concerted practices caught by Article 81(1) of the Treaty which do not satisfy the conditions of Article 81(3) of the Treaty shall be prohibited, no prior decision to that effect being required.

2. Agreements, decisions and concerted practices caught by Article 81(1) of the Treaty which satisfy the conditions of Article 81(3) of the Treaty shall not be prohibited, no prior decision to that effect being required.

3. The abuse of a dominant position referred to in Article 82 of the Treaty shall be prohibited, no prior decision to that effect being required.

Art. 2. *Burden of proof*

In any national or Community proceedings for the application of Articles 81 and 82 of the Treaty, the burden of proving an infringement of Article 81(1) or of Article 82 of the Treaty shall rest on the party or the authority alleging the infringement. The undertaking or association of undertakings claiming the benefit of Article 81(3) of the Treaty shall bear the burden of proving that the conditions of that paragraph are fulfilled.

Art. 3. *Relationship between Articles 81 and 82 of the Treaty and national competition laws*

1. Where the competition authorities of the Member States or national courts apply national competition law to agreements, decisions by associations of undertakings or concerted practices within the meaning of Article 81(1) of the Treaty which may affect trade between Member States within the meaning of that provision, they shall also apply Article 81 of the Treaty to such agreements, decisions or concerted practices. Where the competition authorities of the Member States or national courts apply national competition law to any abuse prohibited by Article 82 of the Treaty, they shall also apply Article 82 of the Treaty.

2. The application of national competition law may not lead to the prohibition of agreements, decisions by associations of undertakings or concerted practices which may affect trade between Member States but which do not restrict competition within the meaning of Article 81(1) of the Treaty, or which fulfil the conditions of Article 81(3) of the Treaty or which are covered by a Regulation for the application of Article 81 (3) of the Treaty. Member States shall not under this Regulation be precluded from adopting and applying on their territory stricter national laws which prohibit or sanction unilateral conduct engaged in by undertakings.

3. Without prejudice to general principles and other provisions of Community law, paragraphs 1 and 2 do not apply when the competition authorities and the courts of the Member States apply national merger control laws nor do they preclude the application of provisions of national law that predominantly pursue an objective different from that pursued by Articles 81 and 82 of the Treaty.

CHAPTER II
POWERS

Art. 4. *Powers of the Commission*

For the purpose of applying Articles 81 and 82 of the Treaty, the Commission shall have the powers provided for by this Regulation.

Art. 5. *Powers of the competition authorities of the Member States*

The competition authorities of the Member States shall have the power to apply Articles 81 and 82 of the Treaty in individual cases. For this purpose, acting on their own initiative or on a complaint, they may take the following decisions:
– requiring that an infringement be brought to an end;
– ordering interim measures;
– accepting commitments;
– imposing fines, periodic penalty payments or any other penalty provided for in their national law.

Where on the basis of the information in their possession the conditions for prohibition are not met they may likewise decide that there are no grounds for action on their part.

Art. 6. *Powers of the national courts*

National courts shall have the power to apply Articles 81 and 82 of the Treaty.

CHAPTER III
COMMISSION DECISIONS

Art. 7. *Finding and termination of infringement*

1. Where the Commission, acting on a complaint or on its own initiative, finds that there is an infringement of Article 81 or of Article 82 of the Treaty, it may by decision require the undertakings and associations of undertakings concerned to bring such infringement to an end. For this purpose, it may impose on them any behavioural or structural remedies which are proportionate to the infringement committed and necessary to bring the infringement effectively to an end. Structural remedies can only be imposed either where there is no equally effective behavioural remedy or where any equally effective behavioural remedy would be more burdensome for the undertaking concerned than the structural remedy. If the Commission has a legitimate interest in doing so, it may also find that an infringement has been committed in the past.

2. Those entitled to lodge a complaint for the purposes of paragraph 1 are natural or legal persons who can show a legitimate interest and Member States.

Art. 8. *Interim measures*

1. In cases of urgency due to the risk of serious and irreparable damage to competition, the Commission, acting on its own initiative may by decision, on the basis of a prima facie finding of infringement, order interim measures.

2. A decision under paragraph 1 shall apply for a specified period of time and may be renewed in so far this is necessary and appropriate.

Art. 9. *Commitments*

1. Where the Commission intends to adopt a decision requiring that an infringement be brought to an end and the undertakings concerned offer commitments to meet the concerns expressed to them by the Commission in its preliminary assessment, the Commission may by decision make those commitments binding on the undertakings. Such a decision may be adopted for a specified period and shall conclude that there are no longer grounds for action by the Commission.

2. The Commission may, upon request or on its own initiative, reopen the proceedings:

(a) where there has been a material change in any of the facts on which the decision was based;

(b) where the undertakings concerned act contrary to their commitments; or

(c) where the decision was based on incomplete, incorrect or misleading information provided by the parties.

Art. 10. *Finding of inapplicability*

Where the Community public interest relating to the application of Articles 81 and 82 of the Treaty so requires, the Commission, acting on its own initiative, may by decision find that Article 81 of the Treaty is not applicable to an agreement, a decision by an association of undertakings or a concerted practice, either because the conditions of Article 81(1) of the Treaty are not fulfilled, or because the conditions of Article 81(3) of the Treaty are satisfied.

The Commission may likewise make such a finding with reference to Article 82 of the Treaty.

CHAPTER IV
COOPERATION

Art. 11. *Cooperation between the Commission and the competition authorities of the Member States*

1. The Commission and the competition authorities of the Member States shall apply the Community competition rules in close cooperation.

2. The Commission shall transmit to the competition authorities of the Member States copies of the most important documents it has collected with a view to applying Articles 7, 8, 9, 10 and Article 29 (1). At the request of the competition authority of a Member State, the Commission shall provide it with a copy of other existing documents necessary for the assessment of the case.

3. The competition authorities of the Member States shall, when acting under Article 81 or Article 82 of the Treaty, inform the Commission in writing before or without delay after commencing the first formal investigative measure. This information may also be made available to the competition authorities of the other Member States.

4. No later than 30 days before the adoption of a decision requiring that an infringement be brought to an end, accepting commitments or withdrawing the benefit of a block exemption Regulation, the competition authorities of the Member States shall inform the Commission. To that effect, they shall provide the Commission with a summary of the case, the envisaged decision or, in the absence thereof, any other document indicating the proposed course of action. This information may also be made available to the competition authorities of the other Member States. At the request of the Commission, the acting competition authority shall make available to the Commission other documents it holds which are necessary for the assessment of the case. The information supplied to the Commission may be made available to the competition authorities of the other Member States. National competition authorities may also exchange between themselves information necessary for the assessment of a case that they are dealing with under Article 81 or Article 82 of the Treaty.

5. The competition authorities of the Member States may consult the Commission on any case involving the application of Community law.

6. The initiation by the Commission of proceedings for the adoption of a decision under Chapter III shall relieve the competition authorities of the Member States of their competence to apply Articles 81 and 82 of the Treaty. If a competition authority of a Member State is already acting on a case, the Commission shall only initiate proceedings after consulting with that national competition authority.

Art. 12. *Exchange of information*

1. For the purpose of applying Articles 81 and 82 of the Treaty the Commission and the competition authorities of the Member States shall have the power to provide one another with and use in evidence any matter of fact or of law, including confidential information.

2. Information exchanged shall only be used in evidence for the purpose of applying Article 81 or Article 82 of the Treaty and in respect of the subject-matter for which it was collected by the transmitting authority. However, where national competition law is applied in the same case and in parallel to Community competition law and does not lead to a different outcome, information exchanged under this Article may also be used for the application of national competition law.

3. Information exchanged pursuant to paragraph 1 can only be used in evidence to impose sanctions on natural persons where:

– the law of the transmitting authority foresees sanctions of a similar kind in relation to an infringement of Article 81 or Article 82 of the Treaty or, in the absence thereof;

– the information has been collected in a way which respects the same level of protection of the rights of defence of natural persons as provided for under the national rules of the receiving authority. However, in this case, the information exchanged cannot be used by the receiving authority to impose custodial sanctions.

Art. 13. *Suspension or termination of proceedings*

1. Where competition authorities of two or more Member States have received a complaint or are acting on their own initiative under Article 81 or Article 82 of the Treaty against the same agreement, decision of an association or practice, the fact that one authority is dealing with the case shall be sufficient grounds for the others to suspend the proceedings before them or to reject the complaint. The Commission may likewise reject a complaint on the ground that a competition authority of a Member State is dealing with the case.

2. Where a competition authority of a Member State or the Commission has received a complaint against an agreement, decision of an association or practice which has already been dealt with by another competition authority, it may reject it.

Art. 14. *Advisory Committee*

1. The Commission shall consult an Advisory Committee on Restrictive Practices and Dominant Positions prior to the taking of any decision under Articles 7, 8, 9, 10, 23, Article 24(2) and Article 29(1).

2. For the discussion of individual cases, the Advisory Committee shall be composed of representatives of the competition authorities of the Member States. For meetings in which issues other than individual cases are being discussed, an additional Member State representative competent in competition matters may be appointed. Representatives may, if unable to attend, be replaced by other representatives.

3. The consultation may take place at a meeting convened and chaired by the Commission, held not earlier than 14 days after dispatch of the notice convening it, together with a summary of the case, an indication of the most important documents and a preliminary draft decision. In respect

of decisions pursuant to Article 8, the meeting may be held seven days after the dispatch of the operative part of a draft decision. Where the Commission dispatches a notice convening the meeting which gives a shorter period of notice than those specified above, the meeting may take place on the proposed date in the absence of an objection by any Member State. The Advisory Committee shall deliver a written opinion on the Commission's preliminary draft decision. It may deliver an opinion even if some members are absent and are not represented. At the request of one or several members, the positions stated in the opinion shall be reasoned.

4. Consultation may also take place by written procedure. However, if any Member State so requests, the Commission shall convene a meeting. In case of written procedure, the Commission shall determine a time-limit of not less than 14 days within which the Member States are to put forward their observations for circulation to all other Member States. In case of decisions to be taken pursuant to Article 8, the time-limit of 14 days is replaced by seven days. Where the Commission determines a time-limit for the written procedure which is shorter than those specified above, the proposed time-limit shall be applicable in the absence of an objection by any Member State.

5. The Commission shall take the utmost account of the opinion delivered by the Advisory Committee. It shall inform the Committee of the manner in which its opinion has been taken into account.

6. Where the Advisory Committee delivers a written opinion, this opinion shall be appended to the draft decision. If the Advisory Committee recommends publication of the opinion, the Commission shall carry out such publication taking into account the legitimate interest of undertakings in the protection of their business secrets.

7. At the request of a competition authority of a Member State, the Commission shall include on the agenda of the Advisory Committee cases that are being dealt with by a competition authority of a Member State under Article 81 or Article 82 of the Treaty. The Commission may also do so on its own initiative. In either case, the Commission shall inform the competition authority concerned.

A request may in particular be made by a competition authority of a Member State in respect of a case where the Commission intends to initiate proceedings with the effect of Article 11(6).

The Advisory Committee shall not issue opinions on cases dealt with by competition authorities of the Member States. The Advisory Committee may also discuss general issues of Community competition law.

Art. 15. *Cooperation with national courts*

1. In proceedings for the application of Article 81 or Article 82 of the Treaty, courts of the Member States may ask the Commission to transmit to them information in its possession or its opinion on questions concerning the application of the Community competition rules.

2. Member States shall forward to the Commission a copy of any written judgment of national courts deciding on the application of Article 81 or Article 82 of the Treaty. Such copy shall be forwarded without delay after the full written judgment is notified to the parties.

3. Competition authorities of the Member States, acting on their own initiative, may submit written observations to the national courts of their Member State on issues relating to the application of Article 81 or Article 82 of the Treaty. With the permission of the court in question, they may also submit oral observations to the national courts of their Member State. Where the coherent application of Article 81 or Article 82 of the Treaty so requires, the Commission, acting on its own initiative, may submit written observations to courts of the Member States. With the permission of the court in question, it may also make oral observations.

For the purpose of the preparation of their observations only, the competition authorities of the Member States and the Commission may request the relevant court of the Member State to transmit or ensure the transmission to them of any documents necessary for the assessment of the case.

4. This Article is without prejudice to wider powers to make observations before courts conferred on competition authorities of the Member States under the law of their Member State.

Art. 16. *Uniform application of Community competition law*

1. When national courts rule on agreements, decisions or practices under Article 81 or Article 82 of the Treaty which are already the subject of a Commission decision, they cannot take decisions running counter to the decision adopted by the Commission. They must also avoid giving decisions which would conflict with a decision contemplated by the Commission in proceedings it has initiated. To that effect, the national court may assess whether it is necessary to stay its proceedings. This obligation is without prejudice to the rights and obligations under Article 234 of the Treaty.

2. When competition authorities of the Member States rule on agreements, decisions or practices under Article 81 or Article 82 of the Treaty which are already the subject of a Commission decision, they cannot take decisions which would run counter to the decision adopted by the Commission.

CHAPTER V
POWERS OF INVESTIGATION

Art. 17. *Investigations into sectors of the economy and into types of agreements*

1. Where the trend of trade between Member States, the rigidity of prices or other circumstances suggest that competition may be restricted or distorted within the common market, the Commission may conduct its inquiry into a particular sector of the economy or into a particular type of agreements across various sectors. In the course of that inquiry, the Commission may request the undertakings or associations of undertakings concerned to supply the information necessary for giving effect to Articles 81 and 82 of the Treaty and may carry out any inspections necessary for that purpose.

The Commission may in particular request the undertakings or associations of undertakings concerned to communicate to it all agreements, decisions and concerted practices.

The Commission may publish a report on the results of its inquiry into particular sectors of the economy or particular types of agreements across various sectors and invite comments from interested parties.

2. Articles 14, 18, 19, 20, 22, 23 and 24 shall apply *mutatis mutandis*.

Art. 18. *Requests for information*

1. In order to carry out the duties assigned to it by this Regulation, the Commission may, by simple request or by

decision, require undertakings and associations of undertakings to provide all necessary information.

2. When sending a simple request for information to an undertaking or association of undertakings, the Commission shall state the legal basis and the purpose of the request, specify what information is required and fix the time-limit within which the information is to be provided, and the penalties provided for in Article 23 for supplying incorrect or misleading information.

3. Where the Commission requires undertakings and associations of undertakings to supply information by decision, it shall state the legal basis and the purpose of the request, specify what information is required and fix the time-limit within which it is to be provided. It shall also indicate the penalties provided for in Article 23 and indicate or impose the penalties provided for in Article 24. It shall further indicate the right to have the decision reviewed by the Court of Justice.

4. The owners of the undertakings or their representatives and, in the case of legal persons, companies or firms, or associations having no legal personality, the persons authorised to represent them by law or by their constitution shall supply the information requested on behalf of the undertaking or the association of undertakings concerned. Lawyers duly authorised to act may supply the information on behalf of their clients. The latter shall remain fully responsible if the information supplied is incomplete, incorrect or misleading.

5. The Commission shall without delay forward a copy of the simple request or of the decision to the competition authority of the Member State in whose territory the seat of the undertaking or association of undertakings is situated and the competition authority of the Member State whose territory is affected.

6. At the request of the Commission the governments and competition authorities of the Member States shall provide the Commission with all necessary information to carry out the duties assigned to it by this Regulation.

Art. 19. *Power to take statements*

1. In order to carry out the duties assigned to it by this Regulation, the Commission may interview any natural or legal person who consents to be interviewed for the purpose of collecting information relating to the subject-matter of an investigation.

2. Where an interview pursuant to paragraph 1 is conducted in the premises of an undertaking, the Commission shall inform the competition authority of the Member State in whose territory the interview takes place. If so requested by the competition authority of that Member State, its officials may assist the officials and other accompanying persons authorised by the Commission to conduct the interview.

Art. 20. *The Commission's powers of inspection*

1. In order to carry out the duties assigned to it by this Regulation, the Commission may conduct all necessary inspections of undertakings and associations of undertakings.

2. The officials and other accompanying persons authorised by the Commission to conduct an inspection are empowered:

(a) to enter any premises, land and means of transport of undertakings and associations of undertakings;

(b) to examine the books and other records related to the business, irrespective of the medium on which they are stored;

(c) to take or obtain in any form copies of or extracts from such books or records;

(d) to seal any business premises and books or records for the period and to the extent necessary for the inspection;

(e) to ask any representative or member of staff of the undertaking or association of undertakings for explanations on facts or documents relating to the subject-matter and purpose of the inspection and to record the answers.

3. The officials and other accompanying persons authorised by the Commission to conduct an inspection shall exercise their powers upon production of a written authorisation specifying the subject matter and purpose of the inspection and the penalties provided for in Article 23 in case the production of the required books or other records related to the business is incomplete or where the answers to questions asked under paragraph 2 of the present Article are incorrect or misleading. In good time before the inspection, the Commission shall give notice of the inspection to the competition authority of the Member State in whose territory it is to be conducted.

4. Undertakings and associations of undertakings are required to submit to inspections ordered by decision of the Commission. The decision shall specify the subject matter and purpose of the inspection, appoint the date on which it is to begin and indicate the penalties provided for in Articles 23 and 24 and the right to have the decision reviewed by the Court of Justice. The Commission shall take such decisions after consulting the competition authority of the Member State in whose territory the inspection is to be conducted.

5. Officials of as well as those authorised or appointed by the competition authority of the Member State in whose territory the inspection is to be conducted shall, at the request of that authority or of the Commission, actively assist the officials and other accompanying persons authorised by the Commission. To this end, they shall enjoy the powers specified in paragraph 2.

6. Where the officials and other accompanying persons authorised by the Commission find that an undertaking opposes an inspection ordered pursuant to this Article, the Member State concerned shall afford them the necessary assistance, requesting where appropriate the assistance of the police or of an equivalent enforcement authority, so as to enable them to conduct their inspection.

7. If the assistance provided for in paragraph 6 requires authorisation from a judicial authority according to national rules, such authorisation shall be applied for. Such authorisation may also be applied for as a precautionary measure.

8. Where authorisation as referred to in paragraph 7 is applied for, the national judicial authority shall control that the Commission decision is authentic and that the coercive measures envisaged are neither arbitrary nor excessive having regard to the subject matter of the inspection. In its control of the proportionality of the coercive measures, the national judicial authority may ask the Commission, directly or through the Member State competition authority, for detailed explanations in particular on the grounds the Commission has for suspecting infringement of Articles 81 and 82 of the Treaty, as well as on the seriousness of the suspected infringement and on the nature of the involvement of the undertaking concerned. However, the national judicial authority may not call into question the necessity for the inspection nor demand that it be provided with the information in the Commission's file. The lawfulness of the Commission decision shall be subject to review only by the Court of Justice.

Art. 21. *Inspection of other premises*

1. If a reasonable suspicion exists that books or other records related to the business and to the subject-matter of the inspection, which may be relevant to prove a serious violation of Article 81 or Article 82 of the Treaty, are being kept in any other premises, land and means of transport, including the homes of directors, managers and other members of staff of the undertakings and associations of undertakings concerned, the Commission can by decision order an inspection to be conducted in such other premises, land and means of transport.

2. The decision shall specify the subject matter and purpose of the inspection, appoint the date on which it is to begin and indicate the right to have the decision reviewed by the Court of Justice. It shall in particular state the reasons that have led the Commission to conclude that a suspicion in the sense of paragraph 1 exists. The Commission shall take such decisions after consulting the competition authority of the Member State in whose territory the inspection is to be conducted.

3. A decision adopted pursuant to paragraph 1 cannot be executed without prior authorisation from the national judicial authority of the Member State concerned. The national judicial authority shall control that the Commission decision is authentic and that the coercive measures envisaged are neither arbitrary nor excessive having regard in particular to the seriousness of the suspected infringement, to the importance of the evidence sought, to the involvement of the undertaking concerned and to the reasonable likelihood that business books and records relating to the subject matter of the inspection are kept in the premises for which the authorisation is requested. The national judicial authority may ask the Commission, directly or through the Member State competition authority, for detailed explanations on those elements which are necessary to allow its control of the proportionality of the coercive measures envisaged.

However, the national judicial authority may not call into question the necessity for the inspection nor demand that it be provided with information in the Commission's file. The lawfulness of the Commission decision shall be subject to review only by the Court of Justice.

4. The officials and other accompanying persons authorised by the Commission to conduct an inspection ordered in accordance with paragraph 1 of this Article shall have the powers set out in Article 20 (2)*(a)*, *(b)* and *(c)*. Article 20(5) and (6) shall apply *mutatis mutandis*.

Art. 22. *Investigations by competition authorities of Member States*

1. The competition authority of a Member State may in its own territory carry out any inspection or other fact-finding measure under its national law on behalf and for the account of the competition authority of another Member State in order to establish whether there has been an infringement of Article 81 or Article 82 of the Treaty. Any exchange and use of the information collected shall be carried out in accordance with Article 12.

2. At the request of the Commission, the competition authorities of the Member States shall undertake the inspections which the Commission considers to be necessary under Article 20(1) or which it has ordered by decision pursuant to Article 20(4). The officials of the competition authorities of the Member States who are responsible for conducting these inspections as well as those authorised or appointed by them shall exercise their powers in accordance with their national law.

If so requested by the Commission or by the competition authority of the Member State in whose territory the inspection is to be conducted, officials and other accompanying persons authorised by the Commission may assist the officials of the authority concerned.

CHAPTER VI
PENALTIES

Art. 23. *Fines*

1. The Commission may by decision impose on undertakings and associations of undertakings fines not exceeding 1 % of the total turnover in the preceding business year where, intentionally or negligently:

(a) they supply incorrect or misleading information in response to a request made pursuant to Article 17 or Article 18(2);

(b) in response to a request made by decision adopted pursuant to Article 17 or Article 18(3), they supply incorrect, incomplete or misleading information or do not supply information within the required time-limit;

(c) they produce the required books or other records related to the business in incomplete form during inspections under Article 20 or refuse to submit to inspections ordered by a decision adopted pursuant to Article 20(4);

(d) in response to a question asked in accordance with Article 20(2)*(e)*,

– they give an incorrect or misleading answer;

– they fail to rectify within a time-limit set by the Commission an incorrect, incomplete or misleading answer given by a member of staff; or

– they fail or refuse to provide a complete answer on facts relating to the subject-matter and purpose of an inspection ordered by a decision adopted pursuant to Article 20(4);

(e) seals affixed in accordance with Article 20(2)*(d)* by officials or other accompanying persons authorised by the Commission have been broken.

2. The Commission may by decision impose fines on undertakings and associations of undertakings where, either intentionally or negligently:

(a) they infringe Article 81 or Article 82 of the Treaty; or

(b) they contravene a decision ordering interim measures under Article 8; or

(c) they fail to comply with a commitment made binding by a decision pursuant to Article 9.

For each undertaking and association of undertakings participating in the infringement, the fine shall not exceed 10 % of its total turnover in the preceding business year.

Where the infringement of an association relates to the activities of its members, the fine shall not exceed 10 % of the sum of the total turnover of each member active on the market affected by the infringement of the association.

3. In fixing the amount of the fine, regard shall be had both to the gravity and to the duration of the infringement.

4. When a fine is imposed on an association of undertakings taking account of the turnover of its members and the association is not solvent, the association is obliged to call for contributions from its members to cover the amount of the fine.

Where such contributions have not been made to the association within a time-limit fixed by the Commission, the

Commission may require payment of the fine directly by any of the undertakings whose representatives were members of the decision-making bodies concerned of the association.

After the Commission has required payment under the second subparagraph, where necessary to ensure full payment of the fine, the Commission may require payment of the balance by any of the members of the association which were active on the market on which the infringement occurred.

However, the Commission shall not require payment under the second or the third subparagraph from undertakings which show that they have not implemented the infringing decision of the association and either were not aware of its existence or have actively distanced themselves from it before the Commission started investigating the case.

The financial liability of each undertaking in respect of the payment of the fine shall not exceed 10 % of its total turnover in the preceding business year.

5. Decisions taken pursuant to paragraphs 1 and 2 shall not be of a criminal law nature.

Art. 24. *Periodic penalty payments*

1. The Commission may, by decision, impose on undertakings or associations of undertakings periodic penalty payments not exceeding 5 % of the average daily turnover in the preceding business year per day and calculated from the date appointed by the decision, in order to compel them:

(a) to put an end to an infringement of Article 81 or Article 82 of the Treaty, in accordance with a decision taken pursuant to Article 7;

(b) to comply with a decision ordering interim measures taken pursuant to Article 8;

(c) to comply with a commitment made binding by a decision pursuant to Article 9;

(d) to supply complete and correct information which it has requested by decision taken pursuant to Article 17 or Article 18(3);

(e) to submit to an inspection which it has ordered by decision taken pursuant to Article 20(4).

2. Where the undertakings or associations of undertakings have satisfied the obligation which the periodic penalty payment was intended to enforce, the Commission may fix the definitive amount of the periodic penalty payment at a figure lower than that which would arise under the original decision. Article 23(4) shall apply correspondingly.

CHAPTER VII
LIMITATION PERIODS

Art. 25. *Limitation periods for the imposition of penalties*

1. The powers conferred on the Commission by Articles 23 and 24 shall be subject to the following limitation periods:

(a) three years in the case of infringements of provisions concerning requests for information or the conduct of inspections;

(b) five years in the case of all other infringements.

2. Time shall begin to run on the day on which the infringement is committed. However, in the case of continuing or repeated infringements, time shall begin to run on the day on which the infringement ceases.

3. Any action taken by the Commission or by the competition authority of a Member State for the purpose of the investigation or proceedings in respect of an infringement shall interrupt the limitation period for the imposition of fines or periodic penalty payments. The limitation period shall be interrupted with effect from the date on which the action is notified to at least one undertaking or association of undertakings which has participated in the infringement. Actions which interrupt the running of the period shall include in particular the following:

(a) written requests for information by the Commission or by the competition authority of a Member State;

(b) written authorisations to conduct inspections issued to its officials by the Commission or by the competition authority of a Member State;

(c) the initiation of proceedings by the Commission or by the competition authority of a Member State;

(d) notification of the statement of objections of the Commission or of the competition authority of a Member State.

4. The interruption of the limitation period shall apply for all the undertakings or associations of undertakings which have participated in the infringement.

5. Each interruption shall start time running afresh. However, the limitation period shall expire at the latest on the day on which a period equal to twice the limitation period has elapsed without the Commission having imposed a fine or a periodic penalty payment. That period shall be extended by the time during which limitation is suspended pursuant to paragraph 6.

6. The limitation period for the imposition of fines or periodic penalty payments shall be suspended for as long as the decision of the Commission is the subject of proceedings pending before the Court of Justice.

Art. 26. *Limitation period for the enforcement of penalties*

1. The power of the Commission to enforce decisions taken pursuant to Articles 23 and 24 shall be subject to a limitation period of five years.

2. Time shall begin to run on the day on which the decision becomes final.

3. The limitation period for the enforcement of penalties shall be interrupted:

(a) by notification of a decision varying the original amount of the fine or periodic penalty payment or refusing an application for variation;

(b) by any action of the Commission or of a Member State, acting at the request of the Commission, designed to enforce payment of the fine or periodic penalty payment.

4. Each interruption shall start time running afresh.

5. The limitation period for the enforcement of penalties shall be suspended for so long as:

(a) time to pay is allowed;

(b) enforcement of payment is suspended pursuant to a decision of the Court of Justice.

CHAPTER VIII
HEARINGS AND PROFESSIONAL SECRECY

Art. 27. *Hearing of the parties, complainants and others*

1. Before taking decisions as provided for in Articles 7, 8, 23 and Article 24(2), the Commission shall give the undertakings or associations of undertakings which are the subject of the proceedings conducted by the Commission the opportunity of being heard on the matters to which the Commission has taken objection. The Commission shall base its decisions only on objections on which the parties concerned have been able to comment. Complainants shall be associated closely with the proceedings.

2. The rights of defence of the parties concerned shall be fully respected in the proceedings. They shall be entitled to have access to the Commission's file, subject to the legitimate interest of undertakings in the protection of their business secrets. The right of access to the file shall not extend to confidential information and internal documents of the Commission or the competition authorities of the Member States. In particular, the right of access shall not extend to correspondence between the Commission and the competition authorities of the Member States, or between the latter, including documents drawn up pursuant to Articles 11 and 14. Nothing in this paragraph shall prevent the Commission from disclosing and using information necessary to prove an infringement.

3. If the Commission considers it necessary, it may also hear other natural or legal persons. Applications to be heard on the part of such persons shall, where they show a sufficient interest, be granted. The competition authorities of the Member States may also ask the Commission to hear other natural or legal persons.

4. Where the Commission intends to adopt a decision pursuant to Article 9 or Article 10, it shall publish a concise summary of the case and the main content of the commitments or of the proposed course of action. Interested third parties may submit their observations within a time limit which is fixed by the Commission in its publication and which may not be less than one month. Publication shall have regard to the legitimate interest of undertakings in the protection of their business secrets.

Art. 28. *Professional secrecy*

1. Without prejudice to Articles 12 and 15, information collected pursuant to Articles 17 to 22 shall be used only for the purpose for which it was acquired.

2. Without prejudice to the exchange and to the use of information foreseen in Articles 11, 12, 14, 15 and 27, the Commission and the competition authorities of the Member States, their officials, servants and other persons working under the supervision of these authorities as well as officials and civil servants of other authorities of the Member States shall not disclose information acquired or exchanged by them pursuant to this Regulation and of the kind covered by the obligation of professional secrecy. This obligation also applies to all representatives and experts of Member States attending meetings of the Advisory Committee pursuant to Article 14.

CHAPTER IX
EXEMPTION REGULATIONS

Art. 29. *Withdrawal in individual cases*

1. Where the Commission, empowered by a Council Regulation, such as Regulations 19/65/EEC, (EEC) N° 2821/71, (EEC) N° 3976/87, (EEC) N° 1534/91 or (EEC) N° 479/92, to apply Article 81(3) of the Treaty by regulation, has declared Article 81(1) of the Treaty inapplicable to certain categories of agreements, decisions by associations of undertakings or concerted practices, it may, acting on its own initiative or on a complaint, withdraw the benefit of such an exemption Regulation when it finds that in any particular case an agreement, decision or concerted practice to which the exemption Regulation applies has certain effects which are incompatible with Article 81(3) of the Treaty.

2. Where, in any particular case, agreements, decisions by associations of undertakings or concerted practices to which a Commission Regulation referred to in paragraph 1 applies have effects which are incompatible with Article 81(3) of the Treaty in the territory of a Member State, or in a part thereof, which has all the characteristics of a distinct geographic market, the competition authority of that Member State may withdraw the benefit of the Regulation in question in respect of that territory.

CHAPTER X
GENERAL PROVISIONS

Art. 30. *Publication of decisions*

1. The Commission shall publish the decisions, which it takes pursuant to Articles 7 to 10, 23 and 24.

2. The publication shall state the names of the parties and the main content of the decision, including any penalties imposed. It shall have regard to the legitimate interest of undertakings in the protection of their business secrets.

Art. 31. *Review by the Court of Justice*

The Court of Justice shall have unlimited jurisdiction to review decisions whereby the Commission has fixed a fine or periodic penalty payment. It may cancel, reduce or increase the fine or periodic penalty payment imposed.

Art. 33. *Implementing provisions*

1. The Commission shall be authorised to take such measures as may be appropriate in order to apply this Regulation. The measures may concern, inter alia:

(a) the form, content and other details of complaints lodged pursuant to Article 7 and the procedure for rejecting complaints;

(b) the practical arrangements for the exchange of information and consultations provided for in Article 11;

(c) the practical arrangements for the hearings provided for in Article 27.

2. Before the adoption of any measures pursuant to paragraph 1, the Commission shall publish a draft thereof and invite all interested parties to submit their comments within the time-limit it lays down, which may not be less than one month. Before publishing a draft measure and before adopting it, the Commission shall consult the Advisory Committee on Restrictive Practices and Dominant Positions.

CHAPTER XI
TRANSITIONAL, AMENDING AND FINAL PROVISIONS

Art. 34. *Transitional provisions*

1. Applications made to the Commission under Article 2 of Regulation N° 17, notifications made under Articles 4 and 5 of that Regulation and the corresponding applications and notifications made under Regulations (EEC) N° 1017/68, (EEC) N° 4056/86 and (EEC) N° 3975/87 shall lapse as from the date of application of this Regulation.

2. Procedural steps taken under Regulation N° 17 and Regulations (EEC) N° 1017/68, (EEC) N° 4056/86 and (EEC) N° 3975/87 shall continue to have effect for the purposes of applying this Regulation.

Art. 35. *Designation of competition authorities of Member States*

1. The Member States shall designate the competition authority or authorities responsible for the application of Articles 81 and 82 of the Treaty in such a way that the provisions of this regulation are effectively complied with. The measures necessary to empower those authorities to apply those Articles shall be taken before 1 May 2004. The authorities designated may include courts.

2. When enforcement of Community competition law is entrusted to national administrative and judicial authorities, the Member States may allocate different powers and functions to those different national authorities, whether administrative or judicial.

3. The effects of Article 11(6) apply to the authorities designated by the Member States including courts that exercise functions regarding the preparation and the adoption of the types of decisions foreseen in Article 5. The effects of Article 11(6) do not extend to courts insofar as they act as review courts in respect of the types of decisions foreseen in Article 5.

4. Notwithstanding paragraph 3, in the Member States where, for the adoption of certain types of decisions foreseen in Article 5, an authority brings an action before a judicial authority that is separate and different from the prosecuting authority and provided that the terms of this paragraph are complied with, the effects of Article 11(6) shall be limited to the authority prosecuting the case which shall withdraw its claim before the judicial authority when the Commission opens proceedings and this withdrawal shall bring the national proceedings effectively to an end.

Art. 36. *Amendment of Regulation (EEC) N° 1017/68*

Regulation (EEC) N° 1017/68 is amended as follows:

1. Article 2 is repealed;

2. in Article 3(1), the words «The prohibition laid down in Article 2» are replaced by the words

The prohibition in Article 81(1) of the Treaty

3. Article 4 is amended as follows:

(a) In paragraph 1, the words «The agreements, decisions and concerted practices referred to in Article 2» are replaced by the words

Agreements, decisions and concerted practices pursuant to Article 81(1) of the Treaty

(b) Paragraph 2 is replaced by the following:

2. If the implementation of any agreement, decision or concerted practice covered by paragraph 1 has, in a given case, effects which are incompatible with the requirements of Article 81(3) of the Treaty, undertakings or associations of undertakings may be required to make such effects cease.

4. Articles 5 to 29 are repealed with the exception of Article 13(3) which continues to apply to decisions adopted pursuant to Article 5 of Regulation (EEC) N° 1017/68 prior to the date of application of this Regulation until the date of expiration of those decisions;

5. in Article 30, paragraphs 2, 3 and 4 are deleted.

Art. 37. *Amendment of Regulation (EEC) N° 2988/74*

In Regulation (EEC) N° 2988/74, the following Article is inserted:

Art. 7a. Exclusion

This Regulation shall not apply to measures taken under Council Regulation (EC) N° 1/2003 of 16 december 2002 on the implementation of the rules on competition laid down in Articles 81 and 82 of the Treaty (*).

(*) O.J. L 1, 4.1.2003, p. 1.

Art. 38. *Amendment of Regulation (EEC) N° 4056/86.*

Regulation (EEC) N° 4056/86 is amended as follows:

1. Article 7 is amended as follows:

(a) Paragraph 1 is replaced by the following:

1. Breach of an obligation

Where the persons concerned are in breach of an obligation which, pursuant to Article 5, attaches to the exemption provided for in Article 3, the Commission may, in order to put an end to such breach and under the conditions laid down in Council Regulation (EC) N° 1/2003 of 16 december 2002 on the implementation of the rules on competition laid down in Articles 81 and 82 of the Treaty (*) adopt a decision that either prohibits them from carrying out or requires them to perform certain specific acts, or withdraws the benefit of the block exemption which they enjoyed.

(*) O.J. L 1, 4.1.2003, p. 1.

(b) Paragraph 2 is amended as follows:

(i) In point *(a)*, the words «under the conditions laid down in Section II» are replaced by the words

under the conditions laid down in Regulation (EC) N° 1/2003

(ii) The second sentence of the second subparagraph of point *(c)* (i) is replaced by the following:

At the same time it shall decide, in accordance with Article 9 of Regulation (EC) N° 1/2003, whether to accept commitments offered by the undertakings concerned with a view, inter alia, to obtaining access to the market for non-conference lines.

2. Article 8 is amended as follows:

(a) Paragraph 1 is deleted.

(b) In paragraph 2 the words «pursuant to Article 10» are replaced by the words

pursuant to Regulation (EC) N° 1/2003

(c) Paragraph 3 is deleted;

3. Article 9 is amended as follows:

(a) In paragraph 1, the words «Advisory Committee referred to in Article 15» are replaced by the words

Advisory Committee referred to in Article 14 of Regulation (EC) N° 1/2003

(b) In paragraph 2, the words «Advisory Committee as referred to in Article 15» are replaced by the words

Advisory Committee referred to in Article 14 of Regulation (EC) N° 1/2003

4. Articles 10 to 25 are repealed with the exception of Article 13(3) which continues to apply to decisions adopted pursuant to Article 81(3) of the Treaty prior to the date of application of this Regulation until the date of expiration of those decisions;

5. in Article 26, the words «the form, content and other details of complaints pursuant to Article 10, applications pursuant to Article 12 and the hearings provided for in Article 23(1) and (2)» are deleted.

Art. 39. *Amendment of Regulation (EEC) N° 3975/87*

Articles 3 to 19 of Regulation (EEC) N° 3975/87 are repealed with the exception of Article 6(3) which continues to apply to decisions adopted pursuant to Article 81(3) of the Treaty prior to the date of application of this Regulation until the date of expiration of those decisions.

Art. 40. *Amendment of Regulations N° 19/65/EEC, (EEC) N° 2821/71 and (EEC) N° 1534/91*

Article 7 of Regulation N° 19/65/EEC, Article 7 of Regulation (EEC) N° 2821/71 and Article 7 of Regulation (EEC) N° 1534/91 are repealed.

Art. 41. *Amendment of Regulation (EEC) N° 3976/87*

Regulation (EEC) N° 3976/87 is amended as follows:

1. Article 6 is replaced by the following:

Art. 6. The Commission shall consult the Advisory Committee referred to in Article 14 of Council Regulation (EC) N° 1/2003 of 16 december 2002 on the implementation of the rules on competition laid down in Articles 81 and 82 of the Treaty (*) before publishing a draft Regulation and before adopting a Regulation.

(*) O.J. L 1, 4.1.2003, p. 1.

2. Article 7 is repealed.

Art. 42. *Amendment of Regulation (EEC) N° 479/92*

Regulation (EEC) N° 479/92 is amended as follows:

1. Article 5 is replaced by the following:

Art. 5. Before publishing the draft Regulation and before adopting the Regulation, the Commission shall consult the Advisory Committee referred to in Article 14 of Council Regulation (EC) N° 1/2003 of 16 december 2002 on the implementation of the rules on competition laid down in Articles 81 and 82 of the Treaty (*)

(*) O.J. L 1, 4.1.2003, p. 1.

2. Article 6 is repealed.

Art. 43. *Repeal of Regulations N° 17 and N° 141*

1. Regulation N° 17 is repealed with the exception of Article 8(3) which continues to apply to decisions adopted pursuant to Article 81(3) of the Treaty prior to the date of application of this Regulation until the date of expiration of those decisions.

2. Regulation N° 141 is repealed.

3. References to the repealed Regulations shall be construed as references to this Regulation.

Art. 44. *Report on the application of the present Regulation*

Five years from the date of application of this Regulation, the Commission shall report to the European Parliament and the Council on the functioning of this Regulation, in particular on the application of Article 11(6) and Article 17.

On the basis of this report, the Commission shall assess whether it is appropriate to propose to the Council a revision of this Regulation.

Art. 45. *Entry into force*

This Regulation shall enter into force on the 20th day following that of its publication in the Official Journal of the European Communities.

It shall apply from 1 May 2004.

This Regulation shall be binding in its entirety and directly applicable in all Member States.

2.1.2. Substantive rules

TABLE OF CONTENTS

2.1.2.1. General rules..................................	19
2.1.2.2. Vertical agreements	66
2.1.2.3. Horizontal agreements......................	116
2.1.2.4. Transfer of technology	168
2.1.2.5. Insurance sector..............................	205

2.1.2.1. General rules

Commission Notice – Relevant market...	19
Commission Notice – Agreements of minor importance	25
Guidelines on the effect on trade concept.......................................	27
Guidelines on the application of Art. 101(3)	39
Guidance on the Commission's enforcement priorities in applying Article 102 to abusive exclusionary conduct by dominant undertakings.................................	54

Commission Notice on the definition of relevant market for the purposes of Community competition law

(OJ C 372, 9 December 1997, p. 5)

1. See above, section 2.1.2.1. General rules
2. In 1999, Articles 85 and 86 became Articles 81 and 82 EC, and are now Articles 101 and 102 TFEU.

I. INTRODUCTION

1. The purpose of this notice is to provide guidance as to how the Commission applies the concept of relevant product and geographic market in its ongoing enforcement of Community competition law, in particular the application of Council Regulation N° 17 and (EEC) N° 4064/89, their equivalents in other sectoral applications such as transport, coal and steel, and agriculture, and the relevant provisions of the EEA Agreement (1). Throughout this notice, references to Articles 85 and 86 of the Treaty and to merger control are to be understood as referring to the equivalent provisions in the EEA Agreement and the ECSC Treaty.

(1) The focus of assessment in State aid cases is the aid recipient and the industry/sector concerned rather than identification of competitive constraints faced by the aid recipient. When consideration of market power and therefore of the relevant market are raised in any particular case, elements of the approach outlined here might serve as a basis for the assessment of State aid cases.

2. Market definition is a tool to identify and define the boundaries of competition between firms. It serves to establish the framework within which competition policy is applied by the Commission. The main purpose of market definition is to identify in a systematic way the competitive constraints that the undertakings involved (2) face. The objective of defining a market in both its product and geographic dimension is to identify those actual competitors of the undertakings involved that are capable of constraining those undertakings' behaviour and of preventing them from behaving independently of effective competitive pressure. It is from this perspective that the market definition makes it possible inter alia to calculate market shares that would convey meaningful information regarding market power for the purposes of assessing dominance or for the purposes of applying Article 85.

(2) For the purposes of this notice, the undertakings involved will be, in the case of a concentration, the parties to the concentration; in investigations within the meaning of Article 86 of the Treaty, the undertaking being investigated or the complainants; for investigations within the meaning of Article 85, the parties to the Agreement.

3. It follows from point 2 that the concept of «relevant market» is different from other definitions of market often used in other contexts. For instance, companies often use the term 'market` to refer to the area where it sells its products or to refer broadly to the industry or sector where it belongs.

4. The definition of the relevant market in both its product and its geographic dimensions often has a decisive influence on the assessment of a competition case. By rendering public the procedures which the Commission follows when considering market definition and by indicating the criteria and evidence on which it relies to reach a decision, the Commission expects to increase the transparency of its policy and decision-making in the area of competition policy.

5. Increased transparency will also result in companies and their advisers being able to better anticipate the possibility that the Commission may raise competition concerns in an individual case. Companies could, therefore, take such a possibility into account in their own internal decision-making when contemplating, for instance, acquisitions, the creation of joint ventures, or the establishment of certain agreements. It is also intended that companies should be in a better position to understand what sort of information the Commission considers relevant for the purposes of market definition.

6. The Commission's interpretation of «relevant market» is without prejudice to the interpretation which may be given by the Court of Justice or the Court of First Instance of the European Communities.

II. DEFINITION OF RELEVANT MARKET

Definition of relevant product market and relevant geographic market

7. The Regulations based on Article 85 and 86 of the Treaty, in particular in section 6 of Form A/B with respect to Regulation N° 17, as well as in section 6 of Form CO with respect to Regulation (EEC) N° 4064/89 on the control of concentrations having a Community dimension have laid down the following definitions. «Relevant product markets» are defined as follows:

«A relevant product market comprises all those products and/or services which are regarded as interchangeable or substitutable by the consumer, by reason of the products' characteristics, their prices and their intended use».

8. «Relevant geographic markets» are defined as follows:

«The relevant geographic market comprises the area in which the undertakings concerned are involved in the supply and demand of products or services, in which the conditions of competition are sufficiently homogeneous and which can be distinguished from neighbouring areas because the conditions of competition are appreciably different in those area».

9. The relevant market within which to assess a given competition issue is therefore established by the combination of the product and geographic markets. The Commission interprets the definitions in paragraphs 7 an 8 (which reflect the case-law of the Court of Justice and the Court of First Instance as well as its own decisionmaking practice) according to the orientations defined in this notice.

Concept of relevant market and objectives of Community competition policy

10. The concept of relevant market is closely related to the objectives pursued under Community competition policy. For example, under the Community's merger control, the objective in controlling structural changes in the supply of a product/service is to prevent the creation or reinforcement of a dominant position as a result of which effective competition would be significantly impeded in a substantial part of the common market. Under the Community's competition rules, a dominant position is such that a firm or group of firms would be in a position to behave to an appreciable extent independently of its competitors, customers and ultimately of its consumers (3). Such a position would usually arise when a firm or group of firms accounted for a large share of the supply in any given market, provided that other factors analysed in the assessment (such as entry barriers, customers' capacity to react, etc.) point in the same direction.

(3) Definition given by the Court of Justice in its judgment of 13 February 1979 in Case 85/76, Hoffmann-La Roche [1979] ECR 461, and confirmed in subsequent judgments.

11. The same approach is followed by the Commission in its application of Article 86 of the Treaty to firms that enjoy a single or collective dominant position. Within the meaning of Regulation N° 17, the Commission has the power to investigate and bring to an end abuses of such a dominant position, which must also be defined by reference to the relevant market. Markets may also need to be defined in the application of Article 85 of the Treaty, in particular, in determining whether an appreciable restriction of competition exists or in establishing if the condition pursuant to Article 85 (3) *(b)* for an exemption from the application of Article 85 (1) is met.

12. The criteria for defining the relevant market are applied generally for the analysis of certain types of behaviour in the market and for the analysis of structural changes in the supply of products. This methodology, though, might lead to different results depending on the nature of the competition issue being examined. For instance, the scope of the geographic market might be different when analysing a concentration, where the analysis is essentially prospective, from an analysis of past behaviour. The different time horizon considered in each case might lead to the result that different geographic markets are defined for the same products depending on whether the Commission is examining a change in the structure of supply, such as a concentration or a cooperative joint venture, or examining issues relating to certain past behaviour.

Basic principles for market definition

Competitive constraints

13. Firms are subject to three main sources or competitive constraints: demand substitutability, supply substitutability and potential competition. From an economic point of view, for the definition of the relevant market, demand substitution constitutes the most immediate and effective disciplinary force on the suppliers of a given product, in particular in relation to their pricing decisions. A firm or a group of firms cannot have a significant impact on the prevailing conditions of sale, such as prices, if its customers are in a position to switch easily to available substitute products or to suppliers located elsewhere. Basically, the exercise of market definition consists in identifying the effective alternative sources of supply for the customers of the undertakings involved, in terms both of products/services and of geographic location of suppliers.

14. The competitive constraints arising from supply side substitutability other then those described in paragraphs 20 to 23 and from potential competition are in general less immediate and in any case require an analysis of additional factors. As a result such constraints are taken into account at the assessment stage of competition analysis.

Demand substitution

15. The assessment of demand substitution entails a determination of the range of products which are viewed as substitutes by the consumer. One way of making this determination can be viewed as a speculative experiment, postulating a hypothetical small, lasting change in relative prices and evaluating the likely reactions of customers to that increase. The exercise of market definition focuses on prices for operational and practical purposes, and more precisely on demand substitution arising from small, permanent changes in relative prices. This concept can provide clear indications as to the evidence that is relevant in defining markets.

16. Conceptually, this approach means that, starting from the type of products that the undertakings involved sell and the area in which they sell them, additional products and areas will be included in, or excluded from, the market definition depending on whether competition from these other products and areas affect or restrain sufficiently the pricing of the parties' products in the short term.

17. The question to be answered is whether the parties' customers would switch to readily available substitutes or to suppliers located elsewhere in response to a hypothetical small (in the range 5% to 10%) but permanent relative price increase in the products and areas being considered. If substitution were enough to make the price increase unprofitable because of the resulting loss of sales, additional substitutes and areas are included in the relevant market. This would be done until the set of products and geographical areas is such that small, permanent increases in relative prices would be profitable. The equivalent analysis is applicable in cases concerning the concentraiton of buying power, where the starting point would then be the supplier and the price test serves to identify the alternative distribution channels or outlets for the supplier's products. In the application of these principles, careful account should be taken of certain particular situations as described within paragraphs 56 and 58.

18. A practical example of this test can be provided by its application to a merger of, for instance, soft-drink bottlers. An issue to examine in such a case would be to decide whether different flavours of soft drinks belong to the same market. In practice, the question to address would be whether consumers of flavour A would switch to other flavours when confronted with a permanent price increase of 5% to 10% for flavour A. If a sufficient number of consumers would switch to, say, flavour B, to such an extent that the price increase for flavour A would not be profitable owing to the resulting loss of sales, then the market would comprise at least flavours A and B. The process would have to be extended in addition to other available flavours until a set of products is identified for which a price rise would not induce a sufficient substitution in demand.

19. Generally, and in particular for the analysis of merger cases, the price to take into account will be the prevailing market price. This may not be the case where the prevailing price has been determined in the absence of sufficient competition. In particular for the investigation of abuses of dominant positions, the fact that the prevailing price might already have been substantially increased will be taken into account.

Supply substitution

20. Supply-side substitutability may also be taken into account when defining markets in those situations in which its effects are equivalent to those of demand substitution in terms of effectiveness and immediacy. This means that suppliers are able to switch production to the relevant products and market them in the short term (4) without incurring significant additional costs or risks in response to small and permanent changes in relative prices. When these conditions are met, the additional production that is put on the market will have a disciplinary effect on the competitive behaviour of the companies involved. Such an impact in terms of effectiveness and immediacy is equivalent to the demand substitution effect.

(4) That is such a period that does not entail a significant adjustment of existing tangible and intangible assets (see paragraph 23).

21. These situations typically arise when companies market a wide range of qualities or grades of one product; even if, for a given final customer or group of consumers, the different qualities are not substitutable, the different qualities will be grouped into one product market, provided that most of the suppliers are able to offer and sell the various qualities immediately and without the significant increases in costs described above. In such cases, the relevant product market will encompass all products that are substitutable in demand and supply, and the current sales of those products will be aggregated so as to give the total value or volume of the market. The same reasoning may lead to group different geographic areas.

22. A practical example of the approach to supply-side substitutability when defining product markets is to be found in the case of paper. Paer is usually supplied in a range of different qualities, from standard writing paper to high quality papers to be used, for instance, to publish art books. From a demand point of view, different qualities of paper cannot be used for any given use, i.e. an art book or a high quality publication cannot be based on lower quality papers. However, paper plants are prepared to manufacture the different qualities, and production can be adjusted with negligible costs and in a short time-frame. In the absence of particular difficulties in distribution, paper manufacturers are able therefore, to compete for orders of the various qualities, in particular if orders are placed with sufficient lead time to allow for modification of production plans. Under such circumstances, the Commission would not define a separate market for each quality of paper and its respective use. The various qualities of paper are included in the relevant market, and their sales added up to estimate total market galue and volume.

23. When supply-side substitutability would entail the need to adjust significantly existing tangible and intangible assets, additional investments, strategic decisions or time delays, it will not be considered at the stage of market definition. Examples where supply-side substitution did not induce the Commission to enlarge the market are offered in the area of consumer products, in particular for branded beverages. Although bottling plants may in principle bottle different beverages, there are costs and lead times involved (in terms of advertising, product testing and distribution) before the products can actually be sold. In these cases, the effects of supply-side substitutability and other forms of potential competition would then be examined at a later stage.

Potential competition

24. The third source of competitive constraint, potential competition, is not taken into account when defining markets, since the conditions under which potential competition will actually represent an effective competitive constraint depend on the analysis of specific factors and circumstances related to the conditions of entry. If required, this analysis is only carried out at a subsequent stage, in general once the position of the companies involved in the relevant market has already been ascertained, and when such position gives rise to concerns from a competition point of view.

III. EVIDENCE RELIED ON TO DEFINE RELEVANT MARKETS

The process of defining the relevant market in practice

Product dimension

25. There is a range of evidence permitting an assessment of the extent to which substitution would take place. In individual cases, certain types of evidence will be determinant, depending very much on the characteristics and specificity of the industry and products or services that are being examined. The same type of evidence may be of no importance in other cases. In most cases, a decision will have to be based on the consideration of a number of criteria and different items of evidence. The Commission follows an open approach to empirical evidence, aimed at making an effective use of all available information which may be relevant in individual cases. The Commission does not follow a rigid hierarchy of different sources of information or types of evidence.

26. The process of defining relevant markets may be summarized as follows: on the basis of the preliminary information available or information submitted by the undertakings involved, the Commission will usually be in a position to broadly establish the possible relevant markets within which, for instance, a concentration or a restriction of competition has to be assessed. In general, and for all practical purposes when handling individual cases, the question will usually be to decide on a few alternative possible relevant markets. For instance, with respect to the product market, the issue will often be to establish whether product A and product B belong or do not belong to the same product market. it is often the case that the inclusion of product B would be enough to remove any competition concerns.

27. In such situations it is not necessary to consider whether the market includes additional products, or to reach a definitive conclusion on the precise product market. If under the conceivable alternative market definitions the operation in question does not raise competition concerns, the question of market definition will be left open, reducing thereby the burden on companies to supply information.

Geographic dimension

28. The Commission's approach to geographic market definition might be summarized as follows: it will take a preliminary view of the scope of the geographic market on the basis of broad indications as to the distribution of market shares between the parties and their competitors, as well as a preliminary analysis of pricing and price differences at national and Community or EEA level. This initial view is used basically as a working hypothesis to focus the Commission's enquiries for the purposes of arriving at a precise geographic market definition.

29. The reasons behind any particular configuration of prices and market shares need to be explored. Companies might enjoy high market shares in their domestic markets just because of the weight of the past, and conversely, a homogeneous presence of companies throughout the EEA might be consistent with national or regional geographic markets. The initial working hypothesis will therefore be checked against an analysis of demand characteristics (importance of national or local preferences, current patterns of purchases of customers, product differentiation/brands, other) in order to establish whether companies in different areas do indeed constitute a real alternative source of supply for consumers. The theoretical experiment is again based on substitution arising from changes in relative prices, and the question to answer is again whether the customers of the parties would switch their orders to companies located elsewhere in the short term and at a negligible cost.

30. If necessary, a further check on supply factors will be carried out to ensure that those companies located in differing areas do not face impediments in developing their sales on competitive terms throughout the whole geographic market. This analysis will include an examination of requirements for a local presence in order to sell in that area the conditions of access to distribution channels, costs associated with setting up a distribution network, and the presence or absence of regulatory barriers arising from public procurement, price regulations, quotas and tariffs limiting trade or production, technical standards, monopolies, freedom of establishment, requirements for administrative authorizations, packaging regulations, etc. In short, the Commission will identify possible obstacles and barriers isolating companies located in a given area from the competitive pressure of companies located outside that area, so as to determine the precise degree of market interpenetration at national, European or global level.

31. The actual pattern and evolution of trade flows offers useful supplementary indications as to the economic importance of each demand or supply factor mentioned above, and the extent to which they may or may not constitute actual barriers creating different geographic markets. The analysis of trade flows will generally address the question of transport costs and the extent to which these may hinder trade between different areas, having regard to plant location, costs of production and relative price levels.

Market integration in the Community

32. Finally, the Commission also takes into account the continuing process of market integration, in particular in the Community, when defining geographic markets, especially in the area of concentrations and structural joint ventures. The measures adopted and implemented in the internal market programme to remove barriers to trade and further integrate the Community markets cannot be ignored when assessing the effects on competition of a concentration or a structural joint venture. A situation where national markets have been artificially isolated from each other because of the existence of legislative barriers that have now been removed will generally lead to a cautious assessment of past evidence regarding prices, market shares or trade patterns. A process of market integration that would, in the short term, lead to wider geographic markets may therefore be taken into consideration when defining the geographic market for the purposes of assessing concentrations and joint ventures.

The process of gathering evidence

33. When a precise market definition is deemed necessary, the Commission will often contact the main customers and the main companies in the industry to enquire into their views about the boudaries of product and geographic markets and to obtain the necessary factual evidence to reach a conclusion. The Commission might also contact the relevant professional associations, and companies active in upstream markets, so as to be able to define, in so far as necessary, separate product and geographic markets, for different levels of production or distribution of the products/services in question. It might also request additional information to the undertakings involved.

34. Where appropriate, the Commission will address written requests for information to the market players mentioned above. These requests will usually include questions relating to the perceptions of companies about reactions to hypothetical price increases and their views of the boundaries of the relevant market. They will also ask for provision of the factual information the Commission deems necessary to reach a conclusion on the extent of the relevant market. The Commission might also discuss with marketing directors or other officers of those companies to gain a better understanding on how negotiations between suppliers and customers take place and better understand issues relating to the definition of the relevant market. Where appropriate, they might also carry out visits or inspections to the premises of the parties, their customers and/or their competitors, in order to better understand how products are manufactured and sold.

35. The type of evidence relevant to reach a conclusion as to the product market can be categorized as follows:

Evidence to define markets – product dimension

36. An analysis of the product characteristics and its intended use allows the Commission, as a first step, to limit the field of investigation of possible substitutes. However, product characteristics and intended use are insufficient to show whether two products are demand substitutes. Functional interchangeability or similarity in characteristics may not, in themselves, provide sufficient criteria, because the responsiveness of customers to relative price changes may be determined by other considerations as well. For example, there may be different competitive contraints in the original equipment market for car components and in spare parts, thereby leading to a separate delineation of two relevant markets. Conversely, differences in product characteristics are not in themselves sufficient to exclude demand substitutability, since this will depend to a large extent on how customers value different characteristics.

37. The type of evidence the Commission considers relevant to assess whether two products are demand substitutes can be categorized as follows:

38. *Evidence of substitution in the recent past.* In certain cases, it is possible to analyse evidence relating to recent past events or shocks in the market that offer actual examples of substituion between two products. When available, this sort of information will normally be fundamental for market definition. If there have been changes in relative prices in the past (all else being equal), the reactions in terms of quantities demanded will be determinant in establishing substitutability. Launches of new products in the past can also offer useful information, when it is possible to precisely analyse which products have lost sales to the new product.

39. There are a number of *quantitative tests* that have specifically been designed for the purpose of delineating markets. These tests consist of various econometric and statistical approaches estimates of elasticities and cross-price elasticities (5) for the demand of a product, tests based on similarity of price movements over time, the analysis of causality between price series and similarity of price levels and/or their convergence. The Commission takes into account the available quantitative evidence capable of withstanding rigorous scrutiny for the purposes of establishing patterns of substitution in the past.

(5) Own-price elasticity of demand for product X is a measure of the responsiveness of demand for X to percentage change in its own price. Cross-prise elasticity between products X and Y is the responsiveness of demand for product X to percentage change in the price of product Y.

40. *Views of customers and competitors.* The Commission often contacts the main customers and competitors of the companies involved in its enquiries, to gather their views on the boundaries of the product market as well as most of the factual information it requires to reach a conclusion on the scope of the market. Reasoned answers of customers and competitors as to what would happen if relative prices for the candidate products were to increase in the candidate geographic area by a small amount (for instance of 5% to 10%) are taken into account when they are sufficiently backed by factual evidence.

41. *Consumer preferences.* In the case of consumer goods, it may be difficult for the Commission to gather the direct views of end consumers about substitute products. Marketing studies that companies have commissioned in the past and that are used by companies in their own decision-making as to pricing of their products and/or marketing actions may provide useful information for the Commission's delineation of the relevant market. Consumer surveys on usage patterns and attitudes, data from consumer's purchasing patterns, the views expressed by retailers and more generally, market research studies submitted by the parties and their competitors are taken into account to establish whether an economically significant proportion of consumers consider two products as substitutable, also taking into account the importance of brands for the products in question. The methodology followed in consumer surveys carried out ad hoc by the undertakings involved or their competitors for the purposes of a merger procedure or a procedure pursuant to Regulation N° 17 will usually be scrutinized with utmost care. Unlike preexisting studies, they have not been prepared in the normal course of business for the adoption of business decisions.

42. *Barriers and costs associated with switching demand to potential substitutes.* There are a number of barriers and costs that might prevent the Commission from considering two prima facie demand substitutes as belonging to one single product market. It is not possible to provide an exhaustive list of all the possible barriers to substitution and of switching costs. These barriers or obstacles might have a wide range of origins, and in its decisions, the Commission has been confronted with regulatory barriers or other forms of State intervention, constraints arising in downstream markets, need to incur specific capital investment or loss in current output in order to switch to alternative inputs, the location of customers, specific investment in production process, learning and human capital investment, retooling costs or other investments, uncertainty about quality and reputation of unknown suppliers, and others.

43. *Different categories of customers and price discrimination.* The extent of the product market might be narrowed in the presence of distinct groups of customers. A distinct group of customers for the relevant product may constitute a narrower, distinct market when such ha group could be subject to price discrimination. This will usually be the case when two conditions are met: (a) it is possible to identify clearly which group an individual customer belongs to at the moment of selling the relevant products to him, and (b) trade among customers or arbitrage by third parties should not be feasible.

Evidence for defining markets – geographic dimension

44. The type of evidence the Commission considers relevant to reach a conclusion as to the geographic market can be categorized as follows:

45. Past evidence of diversion of orders to other areas. In certain cases, evidence on changes in prices between different areas and consequent reactions by customers might be available. Generally, the same quantitative tests used for product market definition might as well be used in geographic market definition, bearing in mind that international comparisons of prices might be more complex due to a number of factors such as exchange rate movements, taxation and product differentiation.

46. *Basic demand characteristics.* The nature of demand for the relevant product may in itself determine the scope of the geographical market. Factors such as national preferences or preferences for national brands, language, culture and life style, and the need for a local presence have a strong potential to limit the geographic scope of competition.

47. *Views of customers and competitors.* Where appropriate, the Commission will contact the main customers and competitors of the parties in its enquiries, to gather their views on the boundaries of the geographic market as well as most of the factual information it requires to reach a conclusion on the scope of the market when they are sufficiently backed by factual evidence.

48. *Current geographic pattern of purchases.* An examination of the customers' current geographic pattern of purchases provides useful evidence as to the possible scope of the geographic market. When customers purchase from companies located anywhere in the Community or the EEA on similar terms, or they procure their supplies through effective tendering procedures in which companies from anywhere in the Community or the EEA submit bids, usually the geographic market will be considered to be Community-wide.

49. *Trade flows/pattern of shipments.* When the number of customers is so large that it is not possible to obtain through them a clear picture of geographic purchasing patterns, information on trade flows might be used alternatively, provided that the trade statistics are available with a sufficient degree of detail for the relevant products. Trade flows, and above all, the rationale behind trade flows provide useful insights and information for the purpose of establishing the scope of the geographic market but are not in themselves conclusive.

50. *Barriers and switching costs associated to divert orders to companies located in other areas.* The absence of transborder purchases or trade flows, for instance, does not necessarily mean that the market is at most national in scope. Still, barriers isolating the national market have to identified before it is concluded that the relevant geographic market in such a case is national. Perhaps the clearest obstacle for a customer to divert its orders to other areas is the impact of transport costs and transport restrictions arising from legislation or from the nature of the relevant products. The impact of transport costs will usually limit the scope of the geographic market for bulky, low-value products, bearing in mind that a transport disadvantage might also be compensated by a comparative advantage in other costs (labour costs or raw materials). Access to distribution in a given area, regulatory barriers still existing in certain sectors, quotas and custom tariffs might also constitute barriers isolating a geographic area from the competitive pressure of companies located outside that area. Significant switching costs in procuring supplies from companies located in other countries constitute additional sources of such barriers.

51. On the basis of the evidence gathered, the Commission will then define a geographic market that could range from a local dimension to a global one, and there are examples of both local and global markets in past decisions of the Commission.

52. The paragraphs above describe the different factors which might be relevant to define markets. This does not imply that in each individual case it will be necessary to obtain evidence and assess each of these factors. Often in practice the evidence provided by a susbset of these factors will be sufficient to reach a conclusion, as shown in the past decisional practice of the Commission.

IV. CALCULATION OF MARKET SHARE

53. The definition of the relevant market in both its product and geograhic dimensions allows the identification the suppliers and the customers/consumers active on that market. On that basis, a total market size and market shares for each supplier can be calculated on the basis of their sales of the relevant products in the relevant area. In practice, the total market size and market shares are often available from market sources, i.e. companies' estimates, studies commissioned from industry consultants and/or trade associations. When this is not the case, or when available estimates are not reliable, the Commission will usually ask each supplier in the relevant market to provide its own sales in order to calculate total market size and market shares.

54. If sales are usually the reference to calculate market shares, there are nevertheless other indications that, depending on the specific products or industry in question, can offer useful information such as, in particular, capacity, the number of players in bidding markets, units of fleet as in aerospace, or the reserves held in the case of sectors such as mining.

55. As a rule of thumb, both volume sales and value sales provide useful information. In cases of differentiated products, sales in value and their associated market share will usually be considered to better reflect the relative position and strength of each supplier.

V. ADDITIONAL CONSIDERATIONS

56. There are certain areas where the application of the principles above has to be undertaken with care. This is the case when considering primary and secondary markets, in particular, when the behaviour of undertakings at a point in time has to be analysed pursuant to Article 86. The method of defining markets in these cases is the same, i.e. assessing the responses of customers based on their purchasing decisions to relative price changes, but taking into account as well, constraints on substitution imposed by conditions in the connected markets. A narrow definition of market for secondary products, for instance, spare parts, may result when compatibility with the primary product is important. Problems of finding compatible secondary products together with the existence of high prices and a long lifetime of the primary products may render relative price increases of secondary products profitable. A different market definition may result if significant substitution between secondary products is possible or if the characteristics of the primary products make quick and direct consumer responses to relative price increases of the secondary products feasible.

57. In certain cases, the existence of chains of substitution might lead to the definition of a relevant market where products or areas at the extreme of the market are not directly substitutable. An example might be provided by the geographic dimension of a product with significant transport costs. In such cases, deliveries from a given plant are limited to a certain area around each plant by the impact of transport costs. In principle, such an area could constitute the relevant geographic market. However, if the distribution of plants is such that there are considerable overlaps between the areas around different plants, it is possible that the pricing of those products will be constrained by a chain substitution effect, and lead to the definition of a broader geographic market. The same reasoning may apply if product B is a demand substitute for products A and C. Even if products A and C are not direct demand substitutes, they might be found to be in the same relevant product market since their respective pricing might be constrained by substitution to B.

58. From a practical perspective, the concept of chains of substitution has to be corroborated by actual evidence, for instance related to price interdependence at the extremes of the chains of substitution, in order to lead to an extension of the relevant market in an individual case. Price levels at the extremes of the chains would have to be of the same magnitude as well.

Commission Notice on agreements of minor importance which do not appreciably restrict competition under Article 81(1) of the Treaty establishing the European Community (de minimis)

(OJ C 368, 22 December 2001, p. 13)

1. Article 81 EC is now Article 101 TFEU.

I

1. Article 81(1) prohibits agreements between undertakings which may affect trade between Member States and which have as their object or effect the prevention, restriction or distortion of competition within the common market. The Court of Justice of the European Communities has clarified that this provision is not applicable where the impact of the agreement on intra- Community trade or on competition is not appreciable.

2. In this notice the Commission quantifies, with the help of market share thresholds, what is not an appreciable restriction of competition under Article 81 of the EC Treaty. This negative definition of appreciability does not imply that agreements between undertakings which exceed the thresholds set out in this notice appreciably restrict competition. Such agreements may still have only a negligible effect on competition and may therefore not be prohibited by Article 81(1) (1).

(1) See, for instance, the judgment of the Court of Justice in Joined Cases C-215/96 and C-216/96 *Bagnasco (Carlos) v Banca Popolare di Novara and Casa di Risparmio di Genova e Imperia* (1999) ECR I-135, points 34-35. This notice is also without prejudice to the principles for assessment under Article 81(1) as expressed in the Commission notice «Guidelines on the applicability of Article 81 of the EC Treaty to horizontal cooperation agreements», O.J. C 3, 6.1.2001, in particular points 17-31 inclusive, and in the Commission notice «Guidelines on vertical restraints», O.J. C 291, 13.10.2000, in particular points 5-20 inclusive.

3. Agreements may in addition not fall under Article 81(1) because they are not capable of appreciably affecting trade between Member States. This notice does not deal with this issue. It does not quantify what does not constitute an appreciable effect on trade. It is however acknowledged that agreements between small and medium-sized undertakings, as defined in the Annex to Commission Recommendation 96/280/EC (2), are rarely capable of appreciably affecting trade between Member States. Small and medium-sized undertakings are currently defined in that recommendation as undertakings which have fewer than 250 employees and have either an annual turnover not exceeding EUR 40 million or an annual balance-sheet total not exceeding EUR 27 million.

(2) O.J. L 107, 30.4.1996, p. 4. This recommendation will be revised. It is envisaged to increase the annual turnover threshold from EUR 40 million to EUR 50 million and the annual balance-sheet total threshold from EUR 27 million to EUR 43 million.

4. In cases covered by this notice the Commission will not institute proceedings either upon application or on its own initiative. Where undertakings assume in good faith that an agreement is covered by this notice, the Commission will not impose fines. Although not binding on them, this notice also intends to give guidance to the courts and authorities of the Member States in their application of Article 81.

5. This notice also applies to decisions by associations of undertakings and to concerted practices.

6. This notice is without prejudice to any interpretation of Article 81 which may be given by the Court of Justice or the Court of First Instance of the European Communities.

II

7. The Commission holds the view that agreements between undertakings which affect trade between Member States do not appreciably restrict competition within the meaning of Article 81(1):

(a) if the aggregate market share held by the parties to the agreement does not exceed 10 % on any of the relevant markets affected by the agreement, where the agreement

is made between undertakings which are actual or potential competitors on any of these markets (agreements between competitors) (3); or

(b) if the market share held by each of the parties to the agreement does not exceed 15 % on any of the relevant markets affected by the agreement, where the agreement is made between undertakings which are not actual or potential competitors on any of these markets (agreements between non-competitors). In cases where it is difficult to classify the agreement as either an agreement between competitors or an agreement between non-competitors the 10 % threshold is applicable.

(3) On what are actual or potential competitors, see the Commission notice «Guidelines on the applicability of Article 81 of the EC Treaty to horizontal cooperation agreements», O.J. C 3, 6.1.2001, paragraph 9. A firm is treated as an actual competitor if it is either active on the same relevant market or if, in the absence of the agreement, it is able to switch production to the relevant products and market them in the short term without incurring significant additional costs or risks in response to a small and permanent increase in relative prices (immediate supply-side substitutability). A firm is treated as a potential competitor if there is evidence that, absent the agreement, this firm could and would be likely to undertake the necessary additional investments or other necessary switching costs so that it could enter the relevant market in response to a small and permanent increase in relative prices.

8. Where in a relevant market competition is restricted by the cumulative effect of agreements for the sale of goods or services entered into by different suppliers or distributors (cumulative foreclosure effect of parallel networks of agreements having similar effects on the market), the market share thresholds under point 7 are reduced to 5 , both for agreements between competitors and for agreements between non-competitors. Individual suppliers or distributors with a market share not exceeding 5 % are in general not considered to contribute significantly to a cumulative foreclosure effect (4). A cumulative foreclosure effect is unlikely to exist if less than 30 % of the relevant market is covered by parallel (networks of) agreements having similar effects.

(4) See also the Commission notice «Guidelines on vertical restraints», O.J. C 291, 13.10.2000, in particular paragraphs 73, 142, 143 and 189. While in the guidelines on vertical restraints in relation to certain restrictions reference is made not only to the total but also to the tied market share of a particular supplier or buyer, in this notice all market share thresholds refer to total market shares.

9. The Commission also holds the view that agreements are not restrictive of competition if the market shares do not exceed the thresholds of respectively 10 %, 15 % and 5 % set out in point 7 and 8 during two successive calendar years by more than 2 percentage points.

10. In order to calculate the market share, it is necessary to determine the relevant market. This consists of the relevant product market and the relevant geographic market. When defining the relevant market, reference should be had to the notice on the definition of the relevant market for the purposes of Community competition law (5). The market shares are to be calculated on the basis of sales value data or, where appropriate, purchase value data. If value data are not available, estimates based on other reliable market information, including volume data, may be used.

(5) O.J. C 372, 9.12.1997, p. 5.

11. Points 7, 8 and 9 do not apply to agreements containing any of the following hardcore restrictions:

(1) as regards agreements between competitors as defined in point 7, restrictions which, directly or indirectly, in isolation or in combination with other factors under the control of the parties, have as their object (6):

(a) the fixing of prices when selling the products to third parties;

(b) the limitation of output or sales;

(c) the allocation of markets or customers;

(2) as regards agreements between non-competitors as defined in point 7, restrictions which, directly or indirectly, in isolation or in combination with other factors under the control of the parties, have as their object:

(a) the restriction of the buyer's ability to determine its sale price, without prejudice to the possibility of the supplier imposing a maximum sale price or recommending a sale price, provided that they do not amount to a fixed or minimum sale price as a result of pressure from, or incentives offered by, any of the parties;

(b) the restriction of the territory into which, or of the customers to whom, the buyer may sell the contract goods or services, except the following restrictions which are not hardcore:

– the restriction of active sales into the exclusive territory or to an exclusive customer group reserved to the supplier or allocated by the supplier to another buyer, where such a restriction does not limit sales by the customers of the buyer,

– the restriction of sales to end users by a buyer operating at the wholesale level of trade,

– the restriction of sales to unauthorised distributors by the members of a selective distribution system, and

– the restriction of the buyer's ability to sell components, supplied for the purposes of incorporation, to customers who would use them to manufacture the same type of goods as those produced by the supplier;

(c) the restriction of active or passive sales to end users by members of a selective distribution system operating at the retail level of trade, without prejudice to the possibility of prohibiting a member of the system from operating out of an unauthorised place of establishment;

(d) the restriction of cross-supplies between distributors within a selective distribution system, including between distributors operating at different levels of trade;

(e) the restriction agreed between a supplier of components and a buyer who incorporates those components, which limits the supplier's ability to sell the components as spare parts to end users or to repairers or other service providers not entrusted by the buyer with the repair or servicing of its goods;

(3) as regards agreements between competitors as defined in point 7, where the competitors operate, for the purposes of the agreement, at a different level of the production or distribution chain, any of the hardcore restrictions listed in paragraph (1) and (2) above.

(6) Without prejudice to situations of joint production with or without joint distribution as defined in Article 5, paragraph 2, of Commission Regulation (EC) N° 2658/2000 and Article 5, paragraph 2, of Commission Regulation (EC) N° 2659/2000, O.J. L 304, 5.12.2000, pp. 3 and 7 respectively.

12. (1) For the purposes of this notice, the terms «undertaking», «party to the agreement», «distributor», «supplier» and «buyer» shall include their respective connected undertakings.

(2) «Connected undertakings» are:

(a) undertakings in which a party to the agreement, directly or indirectly:

– has the power to exercise more than half the voting rights, or

– has the power to appoint more than half the members of the supervisory board, board of management or bodies legally representing the undertaking, or

– has the right to manage the undertaking's affairs;

(b) undertakings which directly or indirectly have, over a party to the agreement, the rights or powers listed in *(a)*;

(c) undertakings in which an undertaking referred to in *(b)* has, directly or indirectly, the rights or powers listed in *(a)*;

(d) undertakings in which a party to the agreement together with one or more of the undertakings referred to in *(a)*, *(b)* or *(c)*, or in which two or more of the latter undertakings, jointly have the rights or powers listed in *(a)*;

(e) undertakings in which the rights or the powers listed in *(a)* are jointly held by:

– parties to the agreement or their respective connected undertakings referred to in *(a)* to *(d)*, or

– one or more of the parties to the agreement or one or more of their connected undertakings referred to in *(a)* to *(d)* and one or more third parties.

(3) For the purposes of paragraph 2*(e)*, the market share held by these jointly held undertakings shall be apportioned equally to each undertaking having the rights or the powers listed in paragraph 2*(a)*.

Guidelines on the effect on trade concept contained in Articles 81 and 82 of the Treaty

(OJ C 101, 27 April 2004, p. 81)

1. Article 81 EC is now Article 101 TFEU and Article 82 EC is now Article 102 TFEU.

1. INTRODUCTION

1. Articles 81 and 82 of the Treaty are applicable to horizontal and vertical agreements and practices on the part of undertakings which «may affect trade between Member States».

2. In their interpretation of Articles 81 and 82, the Community Courts have already substantially clarified the content and scope of the concept of effect on trade between Member States.

3. The present guidelines set out the principles developed by the Community Courts in relation to the interpretation of the effect on trade concept of Articles 81 and 82. They further spell out a rule indicating when agreements are in general unlikely to be capable of appreciably affecting trade between Member States (the non-appreciable affectation of trade rule or NAAT-rule). The guidelines are not intended to be exhaustive. The aim is to set out the methodology for the application of the effect on trade concept and to provide guidance on its application in frequently occurring situations. Although not binding on them, these guidelines also intend to give guidance to the courts and authorities of the Member States in their application of the effect on trade concept contained in Articles 81 and 82.

4. The present guidelines do not address the issue of what constitutes an appreciable restriction of competition under Article 81(1). This issue, which is distinct from the ability of agreements to appreciably affect trade between Member States, is dealt with in the Commission Notice on agreements of minor importance which do not appreciably restrict competition under Article 81(1) of the Treaty (1) (the de minimis rule). The guidelines are also not intended to provide guidance on the effect on trade concept contained in Article 87(1) of the Treaty on State aid.

(1) *O.J.* C 368, 22.12.2001, p. 13.

5. These guidelines, including the NAAT-rule, are without prejudice to the interpretation of Articles 81 and 82 which may be given by the Court of Justice and the Court of First Instance.

2. THE EFFECT ON TRADE CRITERION

2.1. General principes

6. Article 81(1) provides that «the following shall be prohibited as incompatible with the common market: all agreements between undertakings, decisions of associations of undertakings and concerted practices which may affect trade between Member States and which have as their object or effect the prevention, restriction or distortion of competition within the common market». For the sake of simplicity the terms «agreements, decisions of associations of undertakings and concerted practices» are collectively referred to as «agreements».

7. Article 82 on its part stipulates that «any abuse by one or more undertakings of a dominant position within the common market or in a substantial part thereof shall be prohibited as incompatible with the common market insofar as it may affect trade between Member States». In what follows the term «practices» refers to the conduct of dominant undertakings.

8. The effect on trade criterion also determines the scope of application of Article 3 of Regulation 1/2003 on the implementation of the rules on competition laid down in Articles 81 and 82 of the Treaty (2).

(2) *O.J.* L 1, 4.1.2003, p. 1.

9. According to Article 3(1) of that Regulation the competition authorities and courts of the Member States must apply Article 81 to agreements, decisions by associations of undertakings or concerted practices within the meaning of Article 81(1) of the Treaty which may affect trade between Member States within the meaning of that provision, when they apply national competition law to such agreements, decisions or concerted practices. Similarly, when the competition authorities and courts of the Member States apply national competition law to any abuse prohibited by Article 82 of the Treaty, they must also apply Article 82 of the Treaty. Article 3(1) thus obliges the competition authorities and courts of the Member States to also apply Articles 81 and 82 when they apply national competition law to agreements and abusive practices which may affect trade between Member States. On the other hand, Article 3(1) does not oblige national competition authorities and courts to apply national competition law when they apply Articles 81 and 82 to agreements, decisions and concerted practices and to abuses which may affect trade between Member States. They may in such cases apply the Community competition rules on a stand alone basis.

10. It follows from Article 3(2) that the application of national competition law may not lead to the prohibition of agreements, decisions by associations of undertakings or concerted practices which may affect trade between Member States but which do not restrict competition within the meaning of Article 81(1) of the Treaty, or which fulfil the conditions of Article 81(3) of the Treaty or which are covered by a Regulation for the application of Article 81(3) of the Treaty. Member States, however, are not under Regulation 1/2003 precluded from adopting and applying on their territory stricter national laws which prohibit or sanction unilateral conduct engaged in by undertakings.

11. Finally it should be mentioned that Article 3(3) stipulates that without prejudice to general principles and other provisions of Community law, Article 3(1) and (2) do not apply when the competition authorities and the courts of the Member States apply national merger control laws, nor do they preclude the application of provisions of national law that predominantly pursue an objective different from that pursued by Articles 81 and 82 of the Treaty.

12. The effect on trade criterion is an autonomous Community law criterion, which must be assessed separately in each case. It is a jurisdictional criterion, which defines the scope of application of Community competition law (3). Community competition law is not applicable to agreements and practices that are not capable of appreciably affecting trade between Member States.

(3) See e.g. Joined Cases 56/64 and 58/64, Consten and Grundig, [1966] ECR p. 429, and Joined Cases 6/73 and 7/73, Commercial Solvents, [1974] ECR p. 223.

13. The effect on trade criterion confines the scope of application of Articles 81 and 82 to agreements and practices that are capable of having a minimum level of cross-border effects within the Community. In the words of the Court of Justice, the ability of the agreement or practice to affect trade between Member States must be «appreciable» (4).

(4) See in this respect Case 22/71, Béguelin, [1971] ECR p. 949, paragraph 16.

14. In the case of Article 81 of the Treaty, it is the agreement that must be capable of affecting trade between Member States. It is not required that each individual part of the agreement, including any restriction of competition which may flow from the agreement, is capable of doing so (5). If the agreement as a whole is capable of affecting trade between Member States, there is Community law jurisdiction in respect of the entire agreement, including any parts of the agreement that individually do not affect trade between Member States. In cases where the contractual relations between the same parties cover several activities, these activities must, in order to form part of the same agreement, be directly linked and form an integral part of the same overall business arrangement (6). If not, each activity constitutes a separate agreement.

(5) See Case 193/83, Windsurfing, [1986] ECR p. 611, paragraph 96, and Case T-77/94, Vereniging van Groothandelaren in Bloemkwekerijprodukten, [1997] ECR II-759, paragraph 126.

(6) See paragraphs 142 to 144 of the judgment in Vereniging van Groothandelaren in Bloemkwekerijprodukteten cited in the previous footnote.

15. It is also immaterial whether or not the participation of a particular undertaking in the agreement has an appreciable effect on trade between Member States (7). An undertaking cannot escape Community law jurisdiction merely because of the fact that its own contribution to an agreement, which itself is capable of affecting trade between Member States, is insignificant.

(7) See e.g. Case T-2/89, Petrofina, [1991] ECR II-1087, paragraph 226.

16. It is not necessary, for the purposes of establishing Community law jurisdiction, to establish a link between the alleged restriction of competition and the capacity of the agreement to affect trade between Member States. Non-restrictive agreements may also affect trade between Member States. For example, selective distribution agreements based on purely qualitative selection criteria justified by the nature of the products, which are not restrictive of competition within the meaning of Article 81(1), may nevertheless affect trade between Member States. However, the alleged restrictions arising from an agreement may provide a clear indication as to the capacity of the agreement to affect trade between Member States. For instance, a distribution agreement prohibiting exports is by its very nature capable of affecting trade between Member States, although not necessarily to an appreciable extent (8).

(8) The concept of appreciability is dealt with in section 2.4 below.

17. In the case of Article 82 it is the abuse that must affect trade between Member States. This does not imply, however, that each element of the behaviour must be assessed in isolation. Conduct that forms part of an overall strategy pursued by the dominant undertaking must be assessed in terms of its overall impact. Where a dominant undertaking adopts various practices in pursuit of the same aim, for instance practices that aim at eliminating or foreclosing competitors, in order for Article 82 to be applicable to all the practices forming part of this overall strategy, it is sufficient that at least one of these practices is capable of affecting trade between Member States (9).

(9) See in this respect Case 85/76, Hoffmann-La Roche, [1979] ECR p. 461, paragraph 126.

18. It follows from the wording of Articles 81 and 82 and the case law of the Community Courts that in the application of the effect on trade criterion three elements in particular must be addressed:

(a) The concept of «trade between Member States»,

(b) The notion of «may affect», and

(c) The concept of «appreciability».

2.2. The concept of «trade between Member States»

19. The concept of «trade» is not limited to traditional exchanges of goods and services across borders (10). It is a wider concept, covering all cross-border economic activity including establishment (11). This interpretation is consistent with the fundamental objective of the Treaty to promote free movement of goods, services, persons and capital.

(10) Throughout these guidelines the term «products» covers both goods and services.

(11) See Case 172/80, Züchner, [1981] ECR p. 2021, paragraph 18. See also Case C-309/99, Wouters, [2002] ECR I-1577, paragraph 95, Case C-475/99, Ambulanz Glöckner, [2001] ECR I-8089, paragraph 49, Joined Cases C-215/96 and 216/96, Bagnasco, [1999] ECR I-135, paragraph 51, Case C-55/96, Job Centre, [1997] ECR I-7119, paragraph 37, and Case C-41/90, Höfner and Elser, [1991] ECR I-1979, paragraph 33.

20. According to settled case law the concept of «trade» also encompasses cases where agreements or practices affect the competitive structure of the market. Agreements and practices that affect the competitive structure inside the Community by eliminating or threatening to eliminate a competitor operating within the Community may be subject to the Community competition rules (12). When an undertaking is or risks being eliminated the competitive structure within the Community is affected and so are the economic activities in which the undertaking is engaged.

(12) See e.g. Joined Cases T-24/93 and others, Compagnie maritime belge, [1996] ECR II-1201, paragraph 203, and paragraph 23 of the judgment in Commercial Solvents cited in footnote.

21. The requirement that there must be an effect on trade «between Member States» implies that there must be an impact on cross-border economic activity involving at least two Member States. It is not required that the agreement or practice affect trade between the whole of one Member State and the whole of another Member State. Articles 81 and 82 may be applicable also in cases involving part of a Member State, provided that the effect on trade is appreciable (13).

(13) See e.g. Joined Cases T-213/95 and T-18/96, SCK and FNK, [1997] ECR II-1739, and sections 3.2.4 and 3.2.6 below.

22. The application of the effect on trade criterion is independent of the definition of relevant geographic markets. Trade between Member States may be affected also in cases where the relevant market is national or sub-national (14).

(14) See section 3.2 below.

2.3. The notion «may affect»

23. The function of the notion «may affect» is to define the nature of the required impact on trade between Member States. According to the standard test developed by the Court of Justice, the notion «may affect» implies that it must be possible to foresee with a sufficient degree of probability on the basis of a set of objective factors of law or fact that the agreement or practice may have an influence, direct or indirect, actual or potential, on the pattern of trade between Member States (15) (16). As mentioned in paragraph 20 above the Court of Justice has in addition developed a test based on whether or not the agreement or practice affects the competitive structure. In cases where the agreement or practice is liable to affect the competitive structure inside the Community, Community law jurisdiction is established.

(15) See e.g. the judgment in Züchner cited in footnote 11 and Case 319/82, Kerpen & Kerpen, [1983] ECR 4173, Joined Cases 240/82 and others, Stichting Sigarettenindustrie, [1985] ECR 3831, paragraph 48, and Joined Cases T-25/95 and others, Cimenteries CBR, [2000] ECR II-491, paragraph 3930.

(16) In some judgments mainly relating to vertical agreements the Court of Justice has added wording to the effect that the agreement was capable of hindering the attainment of the objectives of a single market between Member States, see e.g. Case T-62/98, Volkswagen, [2000] ECR II-2707, paragraph 179, and paragraph 47 of the Bagnasco judgment cited in footnote 11, and Case 56/65, Société Technique Minière, [1966] ECR 337. The impact of an agreement on the single market objective is thus a factor which can be taken into account.

24. The «pattern of trade»-test developed by the Court of Justice contains the following main elements, which are dealt with in the following sections:

(a) «A sufficient degree of probability on the basis of a set of objective factors of law or fact»,

(b) An influence on the «pattern of trade between Member States»,

(c) «A direct or indirect, actual or potential influence» on the pattern of trade.

2.3.1. A sufficient degree of probability on the basis of a set of objective factors of law or fact

25. The assessment of effect on trade is based on objective factors. Subjective intent on the part of the undertakings concerned is not required. If, however, there is evidence that undertakings have intended to affect trade between Member States, for example because they have sought to hinder exports to or imports from other Member States, this is a relevant factor to be taken into account.

26. The words «may affect» and the reference by the Court of Justice to «a sufficient degree of probability» imply that, in order for Community law jurisdiction to be established, it is not required that the agreement or practice will actually have or has had an effect on trade between Member States. It is sufficient that the agreement or practice is «capable» of having such an effect (17).

(17) See e.g. Case T-228/97, Irish Sugar, [1999] ECR II-2969, paragraph 170, and Case 19/77, Miller, [1978] ECR 131, paragraph 15.

27. There is no obligation or need to calculate the actual volume of trade between Member States affected by the agreement or practice. For example, in the case of agreements prohibiting exports to other Member States there is no need to estimate what would have been the level of parallel trade between the Member States concerned, in the absence of the agreement. This interpretation is consistent with the jurisdictional nature of the effect on trade criterion. Community law jurisdiction extends to categories of agreements and practices that are capable of having cross-border effects, irrespective of whether a particular agreement or practice actually has such effects.

28. The assessment under the effect on trade criterion depends on a number of factors that individually may not be decisive (18). The relevant factors include the nature of the agreement and practice, the nature of the products covered by the agreement or practice and the position and importance of the undertakings concerned (19).

(18) See e.g. Case C-250/92, Gøttrup-Klim [1994] ECR II-5641, paragraph 54.

(19) See e.g. Case C-306/96, Javico, [1998] ECR I-1983, paragraph 17, and paragraph 18 of the judgment in Béguelin cited in footnote 4.

29. The nature of the agreement and practice provides an indication from a qualitative point of view of the ability of the agreement or practice to affect trade between Member States. Some agreements and practices are by their very nature capable of affecting trade between Member States, whereas others require more detailed analysis in this respect. Cross-border cartels are an example of the former, whereas joint ventures confined to the territory of a single Member State are an example of the latter. This aspect is further examined in section 3 below, which deals with various categories of agreements and practices.

30. The nature of the products covered by the agreements or practices also provides an indication of whether trade between Member States is capable of being affected. When by their nature products are easily traded across borders or are important for undertakings that want to enter or expand their activities in other Member States, Community jurisdiction is more readily established than in cases where due to their nature there is limited demand for products offered by suppliers from other Member States or where the products are of limited interest from the point of view of cross-border establishment or the expansion of the economic activity carried out from such place of establishment (20). Establishment includes the setting-up by undertakings in one Member State of agencies, branches or subsidiaries in another Member State.

(20) Compare in this respect the judgments in Bagnasco and Wouters cited in footnote 11.

31. The market position of the undertakings concerned and their sales volumes are indicative from a quantitative point of view of the ability of the agreement or practice concerned to affect trade between Member States. This aspect, which forms an integral part of the assessment of appreciability, is addressed in section 2.4 below.

32. In addition to the factors already mentioned, it is necessary to take account of the legal and factual environment in which the agreement or practice operates. The relevant economic and legal context provides insight into the potential for an effect on trade between Member States. If there are absolute barriers to cross-border trade between Member States, which are external to the agreement or practice, trade is only capable of being affected if those barriers are likely to disappear in the foreseeable future. In cases where the barriers are not absolute but merely render cross-border activities more difficult, it is of the utmost importance to ensure that agreements and practices do not further hinder such activities. Agreements and practices that do so are capable of affecting trade between Member States.

2.3.2. An influence on the «pattern of trade between Member States»

33. For Articles 81 and 82 to be applicable there must be an influence on the «pattern of trade between Member States».

34. The term «pattern of trade» is neutral. It is not a condition that trade be restricted or reduced (21). Patterns of trade can also be affected when an agreement or practice causes an increase in trade. Indeed, Community law jurisdiction is established if trade between Member States is likely to develop differently with the agreement or practice compared to the way in which it would probably have developed in the absence of the agreement or practice (22).

(21) See e.g. Case T-141/89, Tréfileurope, [1995] ECR II-791, Case T-29/92, Vereniging van Samenwerkende Prijsregelende Organisaties in de Bouwnijverheid (SPO), [1995] ECR II-289, as far as exports were concerned, and Commission Decision in Volkswagen (II) (O.J. L 264, 2.10.2001, p. 14).

(22) See in this respect Case 71/74, Frubo, [1975] ECR 563, paragraph 38, Joined Cases 209/78 and others, Van Landewyck, [1980] ECR 3125, paragraph 172, Case T-61/89, Dansk Pelsdyravler Forening, [1992] ECR II-1931, paragraph 143, and Case T-65/89, BPB Industries and British Gypsum, [1993] ECR II-389, paragraph 135.

35. This interpretation reflects the fact that the effect on trade criterion is a jurisdictional one, which serves to distinguish those agreements and practices which are capable of having cross-border effects, so as to warrant an examination under the Community competition rules, from those agreements and practices which do not.

2.3.3. A «direct or indirect, actual or potential influence» on the pattern of trade

36. The influence of agreements and practices on patterns of trade between Member States can be «direct or indirect, actual or potential».

37. Direct effects on trade between Member States normally occur in relation to the products covered by an agreement or practice. When, for example, producers of a particular product in different Member States agree to share markets, direct effects are produced on trade between Member States on the market for the products in question. Another example of direct effects being produced is when a supplier limits distributor rebates to products sold within the Member State in which the distributors are established. Such practices increase the relative price of products destined for exports, rendering export sales less attractive and less competitive.

38. Indirect effects often occur in relation to products that are related to those covered by an agreement or practice. Indirect effects may, for example, occur where an agreement or practice has an impact on cross-border economic activities of undertakings that use or otherwise rely on the products covered by the agreement or practice (23). Such effects can, for instance, arise where the agreement or practice relates to an intermediate product, which is not traded, but which is used in the supply of a final product, which is traded. The Court of Justice has held that trade between Member States was capable of being affected in the case of an agreement involving the fixing of prices of spirits used in the production of cognac (24). Whereas the raw material was not exported, the final product - cognac - was exported. In such cases Community competition law is thus applicable, if trade in the final product is capable of being appreciably affected.

(23) See in this respect Case T-86/95, Compagnie Générale Maritime and others, [2002] ECR II-1011, paragraph 148, and paragraph 202 of the judgment in Compagnie maritime belge cited in footnote 12.

(24) See Case 123/83, BNIC v Clair, [1985] ECR 391, paragraph 29.

39. Indirect effects on trade between Member States may also occur in relation to the products covered by the agreement or practice. For instance, agreements whereby a manufacturer limits warranties to products sold by distributors within their Member State of establishment create disincentives for consumers from other Member States to buy the products because they would not be able to invoke the warranty (25). Export by official distributors and parallel traders is made more difficult because in the eyes of consumers the products are less attractive without the manufacturer's warranty (26).

(25) See Commission Decision in Zanussi, O.J. L 322, 16.11.1978, p. 36, paragraph 11.

(26) See in this respect Case 31/85, ETA Fabrique d'Ébauches, [1985] ECR 3933, paragraphs 12 and 13.

40. Actual effects on trade between Member States are those that are produced by the agreement or practice once it is implemented. An agreement between a supplier and a distributor within the same Member State, for instance one that prohibits exports to other Member States, is likely to produce actual effects on trade between Member States. Without the agreement the distributor would have been free to engage in export sales. It should be recalled, however, that it is not required that actual effects are demonstrated. It is sufficient that the agreement or practice be capable of having such effects.

41. Potential effects are those that may occur in the future with a sufficient degree of probability. In other words, foreseeable market developments must be taken into account (27). Even if trade is not capable of being affected at the time the agreement is concluded or the practice is implemented, Articles 81 and 82 remain applicable if the factors which led to that conclusion are likely to change in the foreseeable future. In this respect it is relevant to consider the impact of liberalisation measures adopted by the Community or by the Member State in question and other foreseeable measures aiming at eliminating legal barriers to trade.

(27) See Joined Cases C-241/91 P and C-242/91 P, RTE (Magill), [1995] ECR I-743, paragraph 70, and Case 107/82, AEG, [1983] ECR 3151, paragraph 60.

42. Moreover, even if at a given point in time market conditions are unfavourable to cross-border trade, for example because prices are similar in the Member States in question, trade may still be capable of being affected if the situation may change as a result of changing market conditions (28). What matters is the ability of the agreement or practice to affect trade between Member States and not whether at any given point in time it actually does so.

(28) See paragraph 60 of the AEG judgment cited in the previous footnote.

43. The inclusion of indirect or potential effects in the analysis of effects on trade between Member States does not mean that the analysis can be based on remote or hypothetical effects. The likelihood of a particular agreement to produce indirect or potential effects must be explained by the authority or party claiming that trade between Member States is capable of being appreciably affected. Hypothetical or speculative effects are not sufficient for establishing Community law jurisdiction. For instance, an agreement that raises the price of a product which is not tradable reduces the disposable income of consumers. As consumers have less money to spend they may purchase fewer products imported from other Member States. However, the link between such income effects and trade between Member States is generally in itself too remote to establish Community law jurisdiction.

2.4. The concept of appreciability

2.4.1. General principle

44. The effect on trade criterion incorporates a quantitative element, limiting Community law jurisdiction to agreements and practices that are capable of having effects of a certain magnitude. Agreements and practices fall outside the scope of application of Articles 81 and 82 when they affect the market only insignificantly having regard to the weak position of the undertakings concerned on the market for the products in question (29). Appreciability can be appraised in particular by reference to the position and the importance of the relevant undertakings on the market for the products concerned (30).

(29) See Case 5/69, Völk, [1969] ECR 295, paragraph 7.

(30) See e.g. paragraph 17 of the judgment in Javico cited in footnote 19, and paragraph 138 of the judgment in BPB Industries and British Gypsum cited in footnote 22.

45. The assessment of appreciability depends on the circumstances of each individual case, in particular the nature of the agreement and practice, the nature of the products covered and the market position of the undertakings concerned. When by its very nature the agreement or practice is capable of affecting trade between Member States, the appreciability threshold is lower than in the case of agreements and practices that are not by their very nature capable of affecting trade between Member States. The stronger the market position of the undertakings concerned, the more likely it is that an agreement or practice capable of affecting trade between Member States can be held to do so appreciably (31).

(31) See paragraph 138 of the judgment in BPB Industries and British Gypsum cited in footnote 22.

46. In a number of cases concerning imports and exports the Court of Justice has considered that the appreciability requirement was fulfilled when the sales of the undertakings concerned accounted for about 5% of the market (32). Market share alone, however, has not always been considered the decisive factor. In particular, it is necessary also to take account of the turnover of the undertakings in the products concerned (33).

(32) See e.g. paragraphs 9 and 10 of the Miller judgment cited in footnote 17, and paragraph 58 of the AEG judgment cited in footnote 27.

(33) See Joined Cases 100/80 and others, Musique Diffusion Française, [1983] ECR 1825, paragraph 86. In that case the products in question accounted for just above 3 % of sales on the national markets concerned. The Court held that the agreements, which hindered parallel trade, were capable of appreciably affecting trade between Member States due to the high turnover of the parties and the relative market position of the products, compared to those of products produced by competing suppliers.

47. Appreciability can thus be measured both in absolute terms (turnover) and in relative terms, comparing the position of the undertaking(s) concerned to that of other players on the market (market share). This focus on the position and importance of the undertakings concerned is consistent with the concept «may affect», which implies that the assessment is based on the ability of the agreement or practice to affect trade between Member States rather than on the impact on actual flows of goods and services across borders. The market position of the undertakings concerned and their turnover in the products concerned are indicative of the ability of an agreement or practice to affect trade between Member States. These two elements are reflected in the presumptions set out in paragraphs and 53 below.

48. The application of the appreciability test does not necessarily require that relevant markets be defined and market shares calculated (34). The sales of an undertaking in absolute terms may be sufficient to support a finding that the impact on trade is appreciable. This is particularly so in the case of agreements and practices that by their very nature are liable to affect trade between Member States, for example because they concern imports or exports or because they cover several Member States. The fact that in such circumstances turnover in the products covered by the agreement may be sufficient for a finding of an appreciable effect on trade between Member States is reflected in the positive presumption set out in paragraph below.

(34) See in this respect paragraphs 179 and 231 of the Volkswagen judgment cited in footnote 16, and Case T-213/00, CMA CGM and others, [2003] ECR I-, paragraphs 219 and 220.

49. Agreements and practices must always be considered in the economic and legal context in which they occur. In the case of vertical agreements it may be necessary to have regard to any cumulative effects of parallel networks of similar agreements (35). Even if a single agreement or network of agreements is not capable of appreciably affecting trade between Member States, the effect of parallel networks of agreements, taken as a whole, may be capable of doing so. For that to be the case, however, it is necessary that the individual agreement or network of agreements makes a significant contribution to the overall effect on trade (36).

(35) See e.g. Case T-7/93, Langnese-Iglo, [1995] ECR II-1533, paragraph 120.

(36) See paragraphs 140 and 141 of the judgment in Vereniging van Groothandelaren in Bloemkwekerijprodukten cited in footnote 5.

2.4.2. Quantification of appreciability

50. It is not possible to establish general quantitative rules covering all categories of agreements indicating when trade between Member States is capable of being appreciably affected. It is possible, however, to indicate when trade is normally not capable of being appreciably affected. Firstly, in its notice on agreements of minor importance which do not appreciably restrict competition in the meaning of Article 81(1) of the Treaty (the de minimis rule) (37) the Commission has stated that agreements between small and medium-sized undertakings (SMEs) as defined in the Annex to Commission Recommendation 96/280/EC (38) are normally not capable of affecting trade between Member States. The reason for this presumption is the fact that the activities of SMEs are normally local or at most regional in nature. However, SMEs may be subject to Community law jurisdiction in particular where they engage in cross-border economic activity. Secondly, the Commission considers it appropriate to set out general principles indicating when trade is normally not capable of being appreciably affected, i.e. a standard defining the absence of an appreciable effect on trade between Member States (the NAAT-rule). When applying Article 81, the Commission will consider this standard as a negative rebuttable presumption applying to all agreements within the meaning of Article 81(1) irrespective of the nature of the restrictions contained in the agreement, including restrictions that have been identified as hardcore restrictions in Commission block exemption regulations and guidelines. In cases where this presumption applies the Commission will normally not institute proceedings either upon application or on its own initiative. Where the undertakings assume in good faith that an agreement is covered by this negative presumption, the Commission will not impose fines.

(37) See Commission Notice on agreements of minor importance which do not appreciably restrict competition under Article 81(1) of the Treaty (O.J. C 368, 22.12.2001, p. 13, paragraph 3).

(38) O.J. L 107, 30.4.1996, p. 4. With effect from 1.1.2005 this recommendation will be replaced by Commission Recommendation 2003/361/EC concerning the definition of micro, small and medium-sized enterprises (O.J. L 124, 20.5.2003, p. 36).

51. Without prejudice to paragraph below, this negative definition of appreciability does not imply that agreements, which do not fall within the criteria set out below, are automatically capable of appreciably affecting trade between Member States. A case by case analysis is necessary.

52. The Commission holds the view that in principle agreements are not capable of appreciably affecting trade between Member States when the following cumulative conditions are met:

(a) The aggregate market share of the parties on any relevant market within the Community affected by the agreement does not exceed 5%, and

(b) In the case of horizontal agreements, the aggregate annual Community turnover of the undertakings concerned (39) in the products covered by the agreement does not exceed 40 million euro. In the case of agreements concerning the joint buying of products the relevant turnover shall be the parties' combined purchases of the products covered by the agreement.

In the case of vertical agreements, the aggregate annual Community turnover of the supplier in the products covered by the agreement does not exceed 40 million euro. In the case of licence agreements the relevant turnover shall be the aggregate turnover of the licensees in the products incorporating the licensed technology and the licensor's own turnover in such products. In cases involving agreements concluded between a buyer and several suppliers the relevant turnover shall be the buyer's combined purchases of the products covered by the agreements.

The Commission will apply the same presumption where during two successive calendar years the above turnover threshold is not exceeded by more than 10% and the above market threshold is not exceeded by more than 2 percentage points. In cases where the agreement concerns an emerging not yet existing market and where as a consequence the parties neither generate relevant turnover nor accumulate any relevant market share, the Commission will not apply this presumption. In such cases appreciability may have to be assessed on the basis of the position of the parties on related product markets or their strength in technologies relating to the agreement.

(39) The term «undertakings concerned» shall include connected undertakings as defined in paragraph 12.2 of the Commission's Notice on agreements of minor importance which do not appreciably restrict competition under Article 81(1) of the Treaty establishing the European Community (O.J. C 368, 22.12.2001, p. 13).

53. The Commission will also hold the view that where an agreement by its very nature is capable of affecting trade between Member States, for example, because it concerns imports and exports or covers several Member States, there is a rebuttable positive presumption that such effects on trade are appreciable when the turnover of the parties in the products covered by the agreement calculated as indicated in paragraphs 52 and 54 exceeds 40 million euro. In the case of agreements that by their very nature are capable of affecting trade between Member States it can also often be presumed that such effects are appreciable when the market share of the parties exceeds the 5% threshold set out in the previous paragraph. However, this presumption does not apply where the agreement covers only part of a Member State (see paragraph 90 below).

54. With regard to the threshold of 40 million euro (cf. paragraph 52 above), the turnover is calculated on the basis of total Community sales excluding tax during the previous financial year by the undertakings concerned, of the products covered by the agreement (the contract products). Sales between entities that form part of the same undertaking are excluded (40).

(40) See the previous footnote.

55. In order to apply the market share threshold, it is necessary to determine the relevant market (41). This consists of the relevant product market and the relevant geographic market. The market shares are to be calculated on the basis of sales value data or, where appropriate, purchase value data. If value data are not available, estimates based on other reliable market information, including volume data, may be used.

(41) When defining the relevant market, reference should be made to the notice on the definition of the relevant market for the purposes of Community competition law (O.J. C 372, 9.12.1997, p. 5).

56. In the case of networks of agreements entered into by the same supplier with different distributors, sales made through the entire network are taken into account.

57. Contracts that form part of the same overall business arrangement constitute a single agreement for the purposes of the NAAT-rule (42). Undertakings cannot bring themselves inside these thresholds by dividing up an agreement that forms a whole from an economic perspective.

(42) See also paragraph 14 above.

3. THE APPLICATION OF THE ABOVE PRINCIPLES TO COMMON TYPES OF AGREEMENTS AND ABUSES

58. The Commission will apply the negative presumption set out in the preceding section to all agreements, including agreements that by their very nature are capable of affecting trade between Member States as well as agreements that involve trade with undertakings located in third countries (*cf.* section 3.3 below).

59. Outside the scope of negative presumption, the Commission will take account of qualitative elements relating to the nature of the agreement or practice and the nature of the products that they concern (see paragraphs and above). The relevance of the nature of the agreement is also reflected in the positive presumption set out in paragraph 53 above relating to appreciability in the case of agreements that by their very nature are capable of affecting trade between Member States. With a view to providing additional guidance on the application of the effect on trade concept it is therefore useful to consider various common types of agreements and practices.

60. In the following sections a primary distinction is drawn between agreements and practices that cover several Member States and agreements and practices that are confined to a single Member State or to part of a single Member State. These two main categories are broken down into further subcategories based on the nature of the agreement or practice involved. Agreements and practices involving third countries are also dealt with.

3.1. Agreements and abuse covering or implemented in several Member States

61. Agreements and practices covering or implemented in several Member States are in almost all cases by their very nature capable of affecting trade between Member States. When the relevant turnover exceeds the threshold set out in paragraph above it will therefore in most cases not be necessary to conduct a detailed analysis of whether trade between Member States is capable of being affected. However, in order to provide guidance also in these cases and to illustrate the principles developed in section 2 above, it is useful to explain what are the factors that are normally used to support a finding of Community law jurisdiction.

3.1.1. Agreements concerning imports and exports

62. Agreements between undertakings in two or more Member States that concern imports and exports are by their very nature capable of affecting trade between Member States. Such agreements, irrespective of whether they are restrictive of competition or not, have a direct impact on patterns of trade between Member States. In Kerpen & Kerpen, for example, which concerned an agreement between a French producer and a German distributor covering more than 10% of exports of cement from France to Germany, amounting in total to 350000 tonnes per year, the Court of Justice held that it was impossible to take the view that such an agreement was not capable of (appreciably) affecting trade between Member States (43).

(43) See paragraph 8 of the judgment in Kerpen & Kerpen cited in footnote 15. It should be noted that the Court does not refer to market share but to the share of French exports and to the product volumes involved.

63. This category includes agreements that impose restrictions on imports and exports, including restrictions on active and passive sales and resale by buyers to customers in other Member States (44). In these cases there is an inherent link between the alleged restriction of competition and the effect on trade, since the very purpose of the restriction is to prevent flows of goods and services between Member States, which would otherwise be possible. It is immaterial whether the parties to the agreement are located in the same Member State or in different Member States.

(44) See e.g. the judgment in Volkswagen cited in footnote 16 and Case T-175/95, BASF Coatings, [1999] ECR II-1581. For a horizontal agreement to prevent parallel trade see Joined Cases 96/82 and others, IAZ International, [1983] ECR 3369, paragraph 27.

3.1.2. Cartels covering several Member States

64. Cartel agreements such as those involving price fixing and market sharing covering several Member States are by their very nature capable of affecting trade between Member States. Cross-border cartels harmonise the conditions of competition and affect the interpenetration of trade by cementing traditional patterns of trade (45). When undertakings agree to allocate geographic territories, sales from other areas into the allocated territories are capable of being eliminated or reduced. When undertakings agree to fix prices, they eliminate competition and any resulting price differentials that would entice both competitors and customers to engage in cross-border trade. When undertakings agree on sales quotas traditional patterns of trade are preserved. The undertakings concerned abstain from expanding output and thereby from serving potential customers in other Member States.

(45) See e.g. Case T-142/89, Usines Gustave Boël, [1995] ECR II-867, paragraph 102.

65. The effect on trade produced by cross-border cartels is generally also by its very nature appreciable due to the market position of the parties to the cartel. Cartels are normally only formed when the participating undertakings together hold a large share of the market, as this allows them to raise price or reduce output.

3.1.3. Horizontal cooperation agreements covering several Member States

66. This section covers various types of horizontal cooperation agreements. Horizontal cooperation agreements may for instance take the form of agreements whereby two or more undertakings cooperate in the performance of a particular economic activity such as production and distribution (46). Often such agreements are referred to as joint ventures. However, joint ventures that perform on a lasting basis all the functions of an autonomous economic entity are covered by the Merger Regulation (47). At the level of the Community such full function joint ventures are not dealt with under Articles 81 and 82 except in cases where Article 2(4) of the Merger Regulation is applicable (48). This section therefore does not deal with full-function joint ventures. In the case of non-full function joint ventures the joint entity does not operate as an autonomous supplier (or buyer) on any market. It merely serves the parents, who themselves operate on the market (49).

(46) Horizontal cooperation agreements are dealt with in the Commission Guidelines on the applicability of Article 81 of the EC Treaty to horizontal cooperation agreements (O.J. C 3, 6.1.2001, p. 2). Those guidelines deal

with the substantive competition assessment of various types of agreements but do not deal with the effect on trade issue.

(47) See Council Regulation (EC) N° 139/2004 on the control of concentrations between undertakings (*O.J.* L 24, 29.1.2004, p. 1).

(48) The Commission Notice on the concept of full-function joint ventures under the Merger Regulation (*O.J.* C 66, 2.3.1998, p. 1) gives guidance on the scope of this concept.

(49) See e.g. the Commission Decision in Ford/Volkswagen (*O.J.* L 20, 28.1.1993, p. 14).

67. Joint ventures which engage in activities in two or more Member States or which produce an output that is sold by the parents in two or more Member States affect the commercial activities of the parties in those areas of the Community. Such agreements are therefore normally by their very nature capable of affecting trade between Member States compared to the situation without the agreement (50). Patterns of trade are affected when undertakings switch their activities to the joint venture or use it for the purpose of establishing a new source of supply in the Community.

(50) See in this respect paragraph 146 of the Compagnie Générale Maritime judgment cited in footnote 23 above.

68. Trade may also be capable of being affected where a joint venture produces an input for the parent companies, which is subsequently further processed or incorporated into a product by the parent undertakings. This is likely to be the case where the input in question was previously sourced from suppliers in other Member States, where the parents previously produced the input in other Member States or where the final product is traded in more than one Member State.

69. In the assessment of appreciability it is important to take account of the parents' sales of products related to the agreement and not only those of the joint entity created by the agreement, given that the joint venture does not operate as an autonomous entity on any market.

3.1.4. Vertical agreements implemented in several Member States

70. Vertical agreements and networks of similar vertical agreements implemented in several Member States are normally capable of affecting trade between Member States if they cause trade to be channelled in a particular way. Networks of selective distribution agreements implemented in two or more Member States for example, channel trade in a particular way because they limit trade to members of the network, thereby affecting patterns of trade compared to the situation without the agreement (51).

(51) See in this respect Joined Cases 43/82 and 63/82, VBVB and VBBB, [1984] ECR 19, paragraph 9.

71. Trade between Member States is also capable of being affected by vertical agreements that have foreclosure effects. This may for instance be the case of agreements whereby distributors in several Member States agree to buy only from a particular supplier or to sell only its products. Such agreements may limit trade between the Member States in which the agreements are implemented, or trade from Member States not covered by the agreements. Foreclosure may result from individual agreements or from networks of agreements. When an agreement or networks of agreements that cover several Member States have foreclosure effects, the ability of the agreement or agreements to affect trade between Member States is normally by its very nature appreciable.

72. Agreements between suppliers and distributors which provide for resale price maintenance (RPM) and which cover two or more Member States are normally also by their very nature capable of affecting trade between Member States (52). Such agreements alter the price levels that would have been likely to exist in the absence of the agreements and thereby affect patterns of trade.

(52) See in this respect Case T-66/89, Publishers Association, [1992] ECR II-1995.

3.1.5. Abuses of dominant positions covering several Member States

73. In the case of abuse of a dominant position it is useful to distinguish between abuses that raise barriers to entry or eliminate competitors (exclusionary abuses) and abuses whereby the dominant undertaking exploits its economic power for instance by charging excessive or discriminatory prices (exploitative abuses). Both kinds of abuse may be carried out either through agreements, which are equally subject to Article 81(1), or through unilateral conduct, which as far as Community competition law is concerned is subject only to Article 82.

74. In the case of exploitative abuses such as discriminatory rebates, the impact is on downstream trading partners, which either benefit or suffer, altering their competitive position and affecting patterns of trade between Member States.

75. When a dominant undertaking engages in exclusionary conduct in more than one Member State, such abuse is normally by its very nature capable of affecting trade between Member States. Such conduct has a negative impact on competition in an area extending beyond a single Member State, being likely to divert trade from the course it would have followed in the absence of the abuse. For example, patterns of trade are capable of being affected where the dominant undertaking grants loyalty rebates. Customers covered by the exclusionary rebate system are likely to purchase less from competitors of the dominant firm than they would otherwise have done. Exclusionary conduct that aims directly at eliminating a competitor such as predatory pricing is also capable of affecting trade between Member States because of its impact on the competitive market structure inside the Community (53). When a dominant firm engages in behaviour with a view to eliminating a competitor operating in more than one Member State, trade is capable of being affected in several ways. First, there is a risk that the affected competitor will cease to be a source of supply inside the Community. Even if the targeted undertaking is not eliminated, its future competitive conduct is likely to be affected, which may also have an impact on trade between Member States. Secondly, the abuse may have an impact on other competitors. Through its abusive behaviour the dominant undertaking can signal to its competitors that it will discipline attempts to engage in real competition. Thirdly, the very fact of eliminating a competitor may be sufficient for trade between Member States to be capable of being affected. This may be the case even where the undertaking that risks being eliminated mainly engages in exports to third countries (54). Once the effective competitive market structure inside the Community risks being further impaired, there is Community law jurisdiction.

(53) See in this respect the judgment in Commercial Solvents cited in footnote 3, in the judgment in Hoffmann-La Roche, cited in footnote, paragraph 125, and in RTE and ITP cited in footnote, as well as Case 6/72, Con-

tinental Can, [1973] ECR 215, paragraph 16, and Case 27/76, United Brands, [1978] ECR 207, paragraphs 197 to 203.

(54) See paragraphs 32 and 33 of the judgment in Commercial Solvents cited in footnote 3.

76. Where a dominant undertaking engages in exploitative or exclusionary abuse in more than one Member State, the capacity of the abuse to affect trade between Member States will normally also by its very nature be appreciable. Given the market position of the dominant undertaking concerned, and the fact that the abuse is implemented in several Member States, the scale of the abuse and its likely impact on patterns of trade is normally such that trade between Member States is capable of being appreciably affected. In the case of an exploitative abuse such as price discrimination, the abuse alters the competitive position of trading partners in several Member States. In the case of exclusionary abuses, including abuses that aim at eliminating a competitor, the economic activity engaged in by competitors in several Member States is affected. The very existence of a dominant position in several Member States implies that competition in a substantial part of the common market is already weakened (55). When a dominant undertaking further weakens competition through recourse to abusive conduct, for example by eliminating a competitor, the ability of the abuse to affect trade between Member States is normally appreciable.

(55) According to settled case law dominance is a position of economic strength enjoyed by an undertaking which enables it to prevent effective competition being maintained on the relevant market by affording it the power to act to an appreciable extent independently of its competitors, its customers and ultimately of the consumers, see e.g. paragraph 38 of the judgment in Hoffmann-La Roche cited in footnote 9.

3.2. Agreements and abuses covering a single, or only part of a, Member State

77. When agreements or abusive practices cover the territory of a single Member State, it may be necessary to proceed with a more detailed inquiry into the ability of the agreements or abusive practices to affect trade between Member States. It should be recalled that for there to be an effect on trade between Member States it is not required that trade is reduced. It is sufficient that an appreciable change is capable of being caused in the pattern of trade between Member States. Nevertheless, in many cases involving a single Member State the nature of the alleged infringement, and in particular, its propensity to foreclose the national market, provides a good indication of the capacity of the agreement or practice to affect trade between Member States. The examples mentioned hereafter are not exhaustive. They merely provide examples of cases where agreements confined to the territory of a single Member State can be considered capable of affecting trade between Member States.

3.2.1. Cartels covering a single Member State

78. Horizontal cartels covering the whole of a Member State are normally capable of affecting trade between Member States. The Community Courts have held in a number of cases that agreements extending over the whole territory of a Member State by their very nature have the effect of reinforcing the partitioning of markets on a national basis by hindering the economic penetration which the Treaty is designed to bring about (56).

(56) See for a recent example paragraph 95 of the Wouters judgment cited in footnote 11.

79. The capacity of such agreements to partition the internal market follows from the fact that undertakings participating in cartels in only one Member State, normally need to take action to exclude competitors from other Member States (57). If they do not, and the product covered by the agreement is tradable (58), the cartel risks being undermined by competition from undertakings from other Member States. Such agreements are normally also by their very nature capable of having an appreciable effect on trade between Member States, given the market coverage required for such cartels to be effective.

(57) See e.g. Case 246/86, Belasco, [1989] ECR 2117, paragraph 32-38.

(58) See paragraph 34 of the Belasco judgment cited in the previous footnote and more recently Joined Cases T-202/98 a.o., British Sugar, [2001] ECR II-2035, paragraph 79. On the other hand this is not so when the market is not susceptible to imports, see paragraph 51 of the Bagnasco judgment cited in footnote 11.

80. Given the fact that the effect on trade concept encompasses potential effects, it is not decisive whether such action against competitors from other Member States is in fact adopted at any given point in time. If the cartel price is similar to the price prevailing in other Member States, there may be no immediate need for the members of the cartel to take action against competitors from other Member States. What matters is whether or not they are likely to do so, if market conditions change. The likelihood of that depends on the existence or otherwise of natural barriers to trade in the market, including in particular whether or not the product in question is tradable. In a case involving certain retail banking services (59) the Court of Justice has, for example, held that trade was not capable of being appreciably affected because the potential for trade in the specific products concerned was very limited and because they were not an important factor in the choice made by undertakings from other Member States regarding whether or not to establish themselves in the Member State in question (60).

(59) Guarantees for current account credit facilities.

(60) See paragraph 51 of the Bagnasco judgment cited in footnote 11.

81. The extent to which the members of a cartel monitor prices and competitors from other Member States can provide an indication of the extent to which the products covered by the cartel are tradable. Monitoring suggests that competition and competitors from other Member States are perceived as a potential threat to the cartel. Moreover, if there is evidence that the members of the cartel have deliberately fixed the price level in the light of the price level prevailing in other Member States (limit pricing), it is an indication that the products in question are tradable and that trade between Member States is capable of being affected.

82. Trade is normally also capable of being affected when the members of a national cartel temper the competitive constraint imposed by competitors from other Member States by inducing them to join the restrictive agreement, or if their exclusion from the agreement places the competitors at a competitive disadvantage (61). In such cases the agreement either prevents these competitors from exploiting any competitive advantage that they have, or raises their costs, thereby having a negative impact on their competitiveness and their sales. In both cases the agreement hampers the operations of competitors from other Member States on the national market in question. The same is true when a cartel agreement confined to a single Member

State is concluded between undertakings that resell products imported from other Member States (62).

(61) See in this respect Case 45/85, Verband der Sachversicherer, [1987] ECR 405, paragraph 50, and Case C-7/95 P, John Deere, [1998] ECR I-3111. See also paragraph 172 of the judgment in Van Landewyck cited in footnote 22, where the Court stressed that the agreement in question reduced appreciably the incentive to sell imported products.

(62) See e.g. the judgment in Stichting Sigarettenindustrie, cited in footnote 15, paragraphs 49 and 50.

3.2.2. Horizontal cooperation agreements covering a single Member State

83. Horizontal cooperation agreements and in particular non-full function joint ventures (cf. paragraph 66 above), which are confined to a single Member State and which do not directly relate to imports and exports, do not belong to the category of agreements that by their very nature are capable of affecting trade between Member States. A careful examination of the capacity of the individual agreement to affect trade between Member States may therefore be required.

84. Horizontal cooperation agreements may, in particular, be capable of affecting trade between Member States where they have foreclosure effects. This may be the case with agreements that establish sector-wide standardisation and certification regimes, which either exclude undertakings from other Member States or which are more easily fulfilled by undertakings from the Member State in question due to the fact that they are based on national rules and traditions. In such circumstances the agreements make it more difficult for undertakings from other Member States to penetrate the national market.

85. Trade may also be affected where a joint venture results in undertakings from other Member States being cut off from an important channel of distribution or source of demand. If, for example, two or more distributors established within the same Member State, and which account for a substantial share of imports of the products in question, establish a purchasing joint venture combining their purchases of that product, the resulting reduction in the number of distribution channels limits the possibility for suppliers from other Member States of gaining access to the national market in question. Trade is therefore capable of being affected (63). Trade may also be affected where undertakings which previously imported a particular product form a joint venture which is entrusted with the production of that same product. In this case the agreement causes a change in the patterns of trade between Member States compared to the situation before the agreement.

(63) See in this respect Case T-22/97, Kesko, [1999] ECR II-3775, paragraph 109.

3.2.3. Vertical agreements covering a single Member State

86. Vertical agreements covering the whole of a Member State may, in particular, be capable of affecting patterns of trade between Member States when they make it more difficult for undertakings from other Member States to penetrate the national market in question, either by means of exports or by means of establishment (foreclosure effect). When vertical agreements give rise to such foreclosure effects, they contribute to the partitioning of markets on a national basis, thereby hindering the economic interpenetration which the Treaty is designed to bring about (64).

(64) See e.g. Case T-65/98, Van den Bergh Foods, [2003] ECR II-..., and the judgment in Langnese-Iglo, cited in footnote 35 paragraph 120.

87. Foreclosure may, for example, occur when suppliers impose exclusive purchasing obligations on buyers (65). In Delimitis (66), which concerned agreements between a brewer and owners of premises where beer was consumed whereby the latter undertook to buy beer exclusively from the brewer, the Court of Justice defined foreclosure as the absence, due to the agreements, of real and concrete possibilities of gaining access to the market. Agreements normally only create significant barriers to entry when they cover a significant proportion of the market. Market share and market coverage can be used as an indicator in this respect. In making the assessment account must be taken not only of the particular agreement or network of agreements in question, but also of other parallel networks of agreements having similar effects (67).

(65) See e.g. judgment of 7.12.2000, Case C-214/99, Neste, ECR I-11121.

(66) See judgment of 28.2.1991, Case C-234/89, Delimitis, ECR I-935.

(67) See paragraph 120 of the Langnese-Iglo judgment cited in footnote 35.

88. Vertical agreements which cover the whole of a Member State and which relate to tradable products may also be capable of affecting trade between Member States, even if they do not create direct obstacles to trade. Agreements whereby undertakings engage in resale price maintenance (RPM) may have direct effects on trade between Member States by increasing imports from other Member States and by decreasing exports from the Member State in question (68). Agreements involving RPM may also affect patterns of trade in much the same way as horizontal cartels. To the extent that the price resulting from RPM is higher than that prevailing in other Member States this price level is only sustainable if imports from other Member States can be controlled.

(68) See e.g. Commission Decision in Volkswagen (II), cited in footnote 21, paragraphs 81 et seq.

3.2.4. Agreements covering only part of a Member State

89. In qualitative terms the assessment of agreements covering only part of a Member State is approached in the same way as in the case of agreements covering the whole of a Member State. This means that the analysis in section 2 applies. In the assessment of appreciability, however, the two categories must be distinguished, as it must be taken into account that only part of a Member State is covered by the agreement. It must also be taken into account what proportion of the national territory is susceptible to trade. If, for example, transport costs or the operating radius of equipment render it economically unviable for undertakings from other Member States to serve the entire territory of another Member State, trade is capable of being affected if the agreement forecloses access to the part of the territory of a Member State that is susceptible to trade, provided that this part is not insignificant (69).

(69) See in this respect paragraphs 177 to 181 of the judgment in SCK and FNK cited in footnote 13.

90. Where an agreement forecloses access to a regional market, then for trade to be appreciably affected, the volume of sales affected must be significant in proportion to the overall volume of sales of the products concerned inside the Member State in question. This assessment cannot be based merely on geographic coverage. The market share of the parties to the agreement must also be given fairly limited weight. Even if the parties have a high market share in a properly defined regional market, the size of that market in terms of volume may still be insignificant when compared to total sales of the products concerned within the Member State in question. In general, the best indicator of the capacity of the agreement to (appreciably) affect trade between Member States is therefore considered to be the share of the national market in terms of volume that is being foreclosed. Agreements covering areas with a high concentration of demand will thus weigh more heavily than those covering areas where demand is less concentrated. For Community jurisdiction to be established the share of the national market that is being foreclosed must be significant.

91. Agreements that are local in nature are in themselves not capable of appreciably affecting trade between Member States. This is the case even if the local market is located in a border region. Conversely, if the foreclosed share of the national market is significant, trade is capable of being affected even where the market in question is not located in a border region.

92. In cases in this category some guidance may be derived from the case law concerning the concept in Article 82 of a substantial part of the common market (70). Agreements that, for example, have the effect of hindering competitors from other Member States from gaining access to part of a Member State, which constitutes a substantial part of the common market, should be considered to have an appreciable effect on trade between Member States.

(70) See as to this notion the judgment in Ambulanz Glöckner, cited in footnote 11, paragraph 38, and Case C-179/90, Merci convenzionali porto di Genova, [1991] ECR I-5889, and Case C-242/95, GT-Link, [1997] ECR I-4449.

3.2.5. Abuses of dominant positions covering a single Member State

93. Where an undertaking, which holds a dominant position covering the whole of a Member State, engages in exclusionary abuses, trade between Member States is normally capable of being affected. Such abusive conduct will generally make it more difficult for competitors from other Member States to penetrate the market, in which case patterns of trade are capable of being affected (71). In Michelin (72), for example, the Court of Justice held that a system of loyalty rebates foreclosed competitors from other Member States and therefore affected trade within the meaning of Article 82. In Rennet (73) the Court similarly held that an abuse in the form of an exclusive purchasing obligation on customers foreclosed products from other Member States.

(71) See e.g. paragraph 135 of the judgment in BPB Industries and British Gypsum cited in footnote.

(72) See Case 322/81, Nederlandse Banden Industrie Michelin, [1983] ECR 3461

(73) See Case 61/80, Coöperative Stremsel- en Kleurselfabriek, [1981] ECR 851, paragraph 15.

94. Exclusionary abuses that affect the competitive market structure inside a Member State, for instance by eliminating or threatening to eliminate a competitor, may also be capable of affecting trade between Member States. Where the undertaking that risks being eliminated only operates in a single Member State, the abuse will normally not affect trade between Member States. However, trade between Member States is capable of being affected where the targeted undertaking exports to or imports from other Member States (74) and where it also operates in other Member States (75). An effect on trade may arise from the dissuasive impact of the abuse on other competitors. If through repeated conduct the dominant undertaking has acquired a reputation for adopting exclusionary practices towards competitors that attempt to engage in direct competition, competitors from other Member States are likely to compete less aggressively, in which case trade may be affected, even if the victim in the case at hand is not from another Member State.

(74) See in this respect judgment in Irish Sugar, cited in footnote 17 paragraph 169.

(75) See paragraph 70 of the judgment in RTE (Magill) cited in footnote 27.

95. In the case of exploitative abuses such as price discrimination and excessive pricing, the situation may be more complex. Price discrimination between domestic customers will normally not affect trade between Member States. However, it may do so if the buyers are engaged in export activities and are disadvantaged by the discriminatory pricing or if this practice is used to prevent imports (76). Practices consisting of offering lower prices to customers that are the most likely to import products from other Member States may make it more difficult for competitors from other Member States to enter the market. In such cases trade between Member States is capable of being affected.

(76) See the judgment in Irish Sugar cited in footnote 17.

96. As long as an undertaking has a dominant position which covers the whole of a Member State it is normally immaterial whether the specific abuse engaged in by the dominant undertaking only covers part of its territory or affects certain buyers within the national territory. A dominant firm can significantly impede trade by engaging in abusive conduct in the areas or vis-à-vis the customers that are the most likely to be targeted by competitors from other Member States. For example, it may be the case that a particular channel of distribution constitutes a particularly important means of gaining access to broad categories of consumers. Hindering access to such channels can have a substantial impact on trade between Member States. In the assessment of appreciability it must also be taken into account that the very presence of the dominant undertaking covering the whole of a Member State is likely to make market penetration more difficult. Any abuse which makes it more difficult to enter the national market should therefore be considered to appreciably affect trade. The combination of the market position of the dominant undertaking and the anti-competitive nature of its conduct implies that such abuses have normally by their very nature an appreciable effect on trade. However, if the abuse is purely local in nature or involves only an insignificant share of the sales of the dominant undertaking within the Member State in question, trade may not be capable of being appreciably affected.

3.2.6. Abuse of a dominant position covering only part of a Member State

97. Where a dominant position covers only part of a Member State some guidance may, as in the case of agreements, be derived from the condition in Article 82 that the dominant position must cover a substantial part of the common market. If the dominant position covers part of a Member State that constitutes a substantial part of the common market and the abuse makes it more difficult for competitors from other Member States to gain access to the market where the undertaking is dominant, trade between Member States must normally be considered capable of being appreciably affected.

98. In the application of this criterion regard must be had in particular to the size of the market in question in terms of volume. Regions and even a port or an airport situated in a Member State may, depending on their importance, constitute a substantial part of the common market (77). In the latter cases it must be taken into account whether the infrastructure in question is used to provide cross-border services and, if so, to what extent. When infrastructures such as airports and ports are important in providing cross-border services, trade between Member States is capable of being affected.

(77) See e.g. the case law cited in footnote 70.

99. As in the case of dominant positions covering the whole of a Member State (cf. paragraph 95 above), trade may not be capable of being appreciably affected if the abuse is purely local in nature or involves only an insignificant share of the sales of the dominant undertaking.

3.3. Agreements and abuses involving imports and exports with undertakings located in third countries, and agreements and practices involving undertakings located in third countries

3.3.1. General remarks

100. Articles 81 and 82 apply to agreements and practices that are capable of affecting trade between Member States even if one or more of the parties are located outside the Community (78). Articles 81 and 82 apply irrespective of where the undertakings are located or where the agreement has been concluded, provided that the agreement or practice is either implemented inside the Community (79), or produce effects inside the Community (80). Articles 81 and 82 may also apply to agreements and practices that cover third countries, provided that they are capable of affecting trade between Member States. The general principle set out in section 2 above according to which the agreement or practice must be capable of having an appreciable influence, direct or indirect, actual or potential, on the pattern of trade between Member States, also applies in the case of agreements and abuses which involve undertakings located in third countries or which relate to imports or exports with third countries.

(78) See in this respect Case 28/77, Tepea, [1978] ECR 1391, paragraph 48, and paragraph 16 of the judgment in Continental Can cited in footnote 53.

(79) See Joined Cases C-89/85 and others, Ahlström Osakeyhtiö (Woodpulp), [1988] ECR 651, paragraph 16.

(80) See in this respect Case T-102/96, Gencor, [1999] ECR II-753, which applies the effects test in the field of mergers.

101. For the purposes of establishing Community law jurisdiction it is sufficient that an agreement or practice involving third countries or undertakings located in third countries is capable of affecting cross-border economic activity inside the Community. Import into one Member State may be sufficient to trigger effects of this nature. Imports can affect the conditions of competition in the importing Member State, which in turn can have an impact on exports and imports of competing products to and from other Member States. In other words, imports from third countries resulting from the agreement or practice may cause a diversion of trade between Member States, thus affecting patterns of trade.

102. In the application of the effect on trade criterion to the above mentioned agreements and practices it is relevant to examine, inter alia, what is the object of the agreement or practice as indicated by its content or the underlying intent of the undertakings involved (81).

(81) See to that effect paragraph 19 of the judgment in Javico cited in footnote 19.

103. Where the object of the agreement is to restrict competition inside the Community the requisite effect on trade between Member States is more readily established than where the object is predominantly to regulate competition outside the Community. Indeed in the former case the agreement or practice has a direct impact on competition inside the Community and trade between Member States. Such agreements and practices, which may concern both imports and exports, are normally by their very nature capable of affecting trade between Member States.

3.3.2. Arrangements that have as their object the restriction of competition inside the Community

104. In the case of imports, this category includes agreements that bring about an isolation of the internal market (82). This is, for instance, the case of agreements whereby competitors in the Community and in third countries share markets, e.g. by agreeing not to sell in each other's home markets or by concluding reciprocal (exclusive) distribution agreements (83).

(82) See in this respect Case 51/75, EMI v CBS, [1976] ECR 811, paragraphs 28 and 29.

(83) See Commission Decision in Siemens/Fanuc (O.J. L 376, 31.12.1985, p. 29).

105. In the case of exports, this category includes cases where undertakings that compete in two or more Member States agree to export certain (surplus) quantities to third countries with a view to co-ordinating their market conduct inside the Community. Such export agreements serve to reduce price competition by limiting output inside the Community, thereby affecting trade between Member States. Without the export agreement these quantities might have been sold inside the Community (84).

(84) See in this respect Joined Cases 29/83 and 30/83, CRAM and Rheinzinc, [1984] ECR 1679, and Joined Cases 40/73 and others, Suiker Unie, [1975] ECR 1663, paragraphs 564 and 580.

3.3.3. Other arrangements

106. In the case of agreements and practices whose object is not to restrict competition inside the Community, it is normally necessary to proceed with a more detailed analysis of whether or not cross-border economic activity inside the Community, and thus patterns of trade between Member States, are capable of being affected.

107. In this regard it is relevant to examine the effects of the agreement or practice on customers and other operators inside the Community that rely on the products of the undertakings that are parties to the agreement or practice (85). In Compagnie maritime belge (86), which concerned agreements between shipping companies operating between Community ports and West African ports, the agreements were held to be capable of indirectly affecting trade between Member States because they altered the catchment areas of the Community ports covered by the agreements and because they affected the activities of other undertakings inside those areas. More specifically, the agreements affected the activities of undertakings that relied on the parties for transportation services, either as a means of transporting goods purchased in third countries or sold there, or as an important input into the services that the ports themselves offered.

(85) See paragraph 22 of the judgment in Javico cited in footnote 19.

(86) See paragraph 203 of the judgment in Compagnie maritime belge cited in footnote 12.

108. Trade may also be capable of being affected when the agreement prevents re-imports into the Community. This may, for example, be the case with vertical agreements between Community suppliers and third country distributors, imposing restrictions on resale outside an allocated territory, including the Community. If in the absence of the agreement resale to the Community would be possible and likely, such imports may be capable of affecting patterns of trade inside the Community (87).

(87) See in this respect the judgment in Javico cited in footnote 19.

109. However, for such effects to be likely, there must be an appreciable difference between the prices of the products charged in the Community and those charged outside the Community, and this price difference must not be eroded by customs duties and transport costs. In addition, the product volumes exported compared to the total market for those products in the territory of the common market must not be insignificant (88). If these product volumes are insignificant compared to those sold inside the Community, the impact of any re-importation on trade between Member States is considered not to be appreciable. In making this assessment, regard must be had not only to the individual agreement concluded between the parties, but also to any cumulative effect of similar agreements concluded by the same and competing suppliers. It may be, for example, that the product volumes covered by a single agreement are quite small, but that the product volumes covered by several such agreements are significant. In that case the agreements taken as a whole may be capable of appreciably affecting trade between Member States. It should be recalled, however (cf. paragraph 49 above), that the individual agreement or network of agreements must make a significant contribution to the overall effect on trade.

(88) See in this respect paragraphs 24 to 26 of the Javico judgment cited in footnote 19.

Guidelines on the application of Article 81(3) of the Treaty

(OJ C 101, 27 April 2004, p. 97)

1. Article 81 EC is now Article 101 TFEU.

1. INTRODUCTION

1. Article 81(3) of the Treaty sets out an exception rule, which provides a defence to undertakings against a finding of an infringement of Article 81(1) of the Treaty. Agreements, decisions of associations of undertakings and concerted practices (1) caught by Article 81(1) which satisfy the conditions of Article 81(3) are valid and enforceable, no prior decision to that effect being required.

(1) In the following the term «agreement» includes concerted practices and decisions of associations of undertakings.

2. Article 81(3) can be applied in individual cases or to categories of agreements and concerted practices by way of block exemption regulation. Regulation 1/2003 on the implementation of the competition rules laid down in Articles 81 and 82 (2) does not affect the validity and legal nature of block exemption regulations. All existing block exemption regulations remain in force and agreements covered by block exemption regulations are legally valid and enforceable even if they are restrictive of competition within the meaning of Article 81(1) (3). Such agreements can only be prohibited for the future and only upon formal withdrawal of the block exemption by the Commission or a national competition authority (4). Block exempted agreements cannot be held invalid by national courts in the context of private litigation.

(2) O.J. L 1, 4.1.2003, p. 1.

(3) All existing block exemption regulations and Commission notices are available on the DG Competition web-site: http://www.europa.eu.int/comm/dgs/competition.

(4) See paragraph 36 below.

3. The existing guidelines on vertical restraints, horizontal cooperation agreements and technology transfer agreements (5) deal with the application of Article 81 to various types of agreements and concerted practices. The purpose of those guidelines is to set out the Commission's view of the substantive assessment criteria applied to the various types of agreements and practices.

(5) See Commission Notice on Guidelines on vertical restraints (O.J. C 291, 13.10.2000, p. 1), Commission Notice on Guidelines on the application of Article 81 of the Treaty to horizontal cooperation agreements (O.J. C 3, 6.1.2001, p. 2), and Commission Notice on Guidelines on the application of Article 81 of the Treaty to technology transfer agreements, not yet published.

4. The present guidelines set out the Commission's interpretation of the conditions for exception contained in Article 81(3). It thereby provides guidance on how it will apply Article 81 in individual cases. Although not binding on them, these guidelines also intend to give guidance to the courts and authorities of the Member States in their application of Article 81(1) and (3) of the Treaty.

5. The guidelines establish an analytical framework for the application of Article 81(3). The purpose is to develop a methodology for the application of this Treaty provision. This methodology is based on the economic approach already introduced and developed in the guidelines on vertical restraints, horizontal co-operation agreements and technology transfer agreements. The Commission will follow the present guidelines, which provide more detailed guidance on the application of the four conditions of Article 81(3) than the guidelines on vertical restraints, horizontal co-operation agreements and technology transfer agreements, also with regard to agreements covered by those guidelines.

6. The standards set forth in the present guidelines must be applied in light of the circumstances specific to each case. This excludes a mechanical application. Each case must be assessed on its own facts and the guidelines must be applied reasonably and flexibly.

7. With regard to a number of issues, the present guidelines outline the current state of the case law of the Court of Justice. However, the Commission also intends to explain its policy with regard to issues that have not been dealt with in the case law, or that are subject to interpretation. The Commission's position, however, is without prejudice to the case law of the Court of Justice and the Court of First Instance concerning the interpretation of Article 81(1) and (3), and to the interpretation that the Community Courts may give to those provisions in the future.

2. THE GENERAL FRAMEWORK OF ARTICLE 81 EC

2.1. The Treaty provisions

8. Article 81(1) prohibits all agreements between undertakings, decisions by associations of undertakings and concerted practices which may affect trade between Member States (6) and which have as their object or effect the prevention, restriction or distortion of competition (7).

(6) The concept of effect on trade between Member States is dealt with in separate guidelines.

(7) In the following the term «restriction» includes the prevention and distortion of competition.

9. As an exception to this rule Article 81(3) provides that the prohibition contained in Article 81(1) may be declared inapplicable in case of agreements which contribute to improving the production or distribution of goods or to promoting technical or economic progress, while allowing consumers a fair share of the resulting benefits, and which do not impose restrictions which are not indispensable to the attainment of these objectives, and do not afford such undertakings the possibility of eliminating competition in respect of a substantial part of the products concerned.

10. According to Article 1(1) of Regulation 1/2003 agreements which are caught by Article 81(1) and which do not satisfy the conditions of Article 81(3) are prohibited, no prior decision to that effect being required (8). According to Article 1(2) of the same Regulation agreements which are caught by Article 81(1) but which satisfy the conditions of Article 81(3) are not prohibited, no prior decision to that effect being required. Such agreements are valid and enforceable from the moment that the conditions of Article 81(3) are satisfied and for as long as that remains the case.

(8) According to Article 81(2) such agreements are automatically void.

11. The assessment under Article 81 thus consists of two parts. The first step is to assess whether an agreement between undertakings, which is capable of affecting trade between Member States, has an anti-competitive object or actual or potential (9) anti-competitive effects. The second step, which only becomes relevant when an agreement is found to be restrictive of competition, is to determine the pro-competitive benefits produced by that agreement and to assess whether these pro-competitive effects outweigh the anti-competitive effects. The balancing of anticompetitive and pro-competitive effects is conducted exclusively within the framework laid down by Article 81(3) (10).

(9) Article 81(1) prohibits both actual and potential anti-competitive effects, see e.g. Case C-7/95 P, John Deere, [1998] ECR I-3111, paragraph 77.

(10) See Case T-65/98, Van den Bergh Foods, [2003] ECR II ..., paragraph 107 and Case T-112/99, Métropole télévision (M6) and others, [2001] ECR II-2459, paragraph 74, where the Court of First Instance held that it is only in the precise framework of Article 81(3) that the pro- and anti-competitive aspects of a restriction may be weighed.

12. The assessment of any countervailing benefits under Article 81(3) necessarily requires prior determination of the restrictive nature and impact of the agreement. To place Article 81(3) in its proper context it is appropriate to briefly outline the objective and principal content of the prohibition rule of Article 81(1). The Commission guidelines on vertical restraints, horizontal co-operation agreements and technology transfer agreements (11) contain substantial guidance on the application of Article 81(1) to various types of agreements. The present guidelines are therefore limited to recalling the basic analytical framework for applying Article 81(1).

(11) See note above.

2.2. The prohibition rule of Article 81(1)

2.2.1. General remarks

13. The objective of Article 81 is to protect competition on the market as a means of enhancing consumer welfare and of ensuring an efficient allocation of resources. Competition and market integration serve these ends since the creation and preservation of an open single market promotes an efficient allocation of resources throughout the Community for the benefit of consumers.

14. The prohibition rule of Article 81(1) applies to restrictive agreements and concerted practices between undertakings and decisions by associations of undertakings in so far as they are capable of affecting trade between Member States. A general principle underlying Article 81(1) which is expressed in the case law of the Community Courts is that each economic operator must determine independently the policy, which he intends to adopt on the market (12). In view of this the Community Courts have defined «agreements», «decisions» and «concerted practices» as Community law concepts which allow a distinction to be made between the unilateral conduct of an undertaking and co-ordination of behaviour or collusion between undertakings (13). Unilateral conduct is subject only to Article 82 of the Treaty as far as Community competition law is concerned. Moreover, the convergence rule set out in Article 3(2) of Regulation 1/2003 does not apply to unilateral conduct. This provision applies only to agreements, decisions and concerted practices, which are capable of affecting trade between Member States. Article 3(2) provides that when such agreements, decisions and concerted practices are not prohibited by Article 81, they cannot be prohibited by national competition law. Article 3 is without prejudice to the fundamental principle of primacy of Community law, which entails in particular that agreements and abusive practices that are prohibited by Articles 81 and 82 cannot be upheld by national law (14).

(12) See e.g. Case C-49/92 P, Anic Partecipazioni, [1999] ECR I-4125, paragraph 116; and Joined Cases 40/73 to 48/73 and others, Suiker Unie, [1975] ECR page 1663, paragraph 173.

(13) See in this respect paragraph 108 of the judgment in Anic Partecipazioni cited in the previous note and Case C-277/87, Sandoz Prodotti, [1990] ECR I-45.

(14) See in this respect e.g. Case 14/68, Walt Wilhelm, [1969] ECR 1, and more recently Case T-203/01, Michelin (II), [2003] ECR II ..., paragraph 112.

15. The type of co-ordination of behaviour or collusion between undertakings falling within the scope of Article 81(1) is that where at least one undertaking vis-à-vis another undertaking undertakes to adopt a certain conduct on the market or that as a result of contacts between them uncertainty as to their conduct on the market is eliminated or at least substantially reduced (15). It follows that co-ordination can take the form of obligations that regulate the market conduct of at least one of the parties as well as of arrangements that influence the market conduct of at least one of the parties by causing a change in its incentives. It is not required that co-ordination is in the interest of all the undertakings concerned (16). Co-ordination must also not necessarily be express. It can also be tacit. For an agreement to be capable of being regarded as having been concluded by tacit acceptance there must be an invitation from an undertaking to another undertaking, whether express or implied, to fulfil a goal jointly (17). In certain circumstances an agreement may be inferred from and imputed to an ongoing commercial relationship between the parties (18). However, the mere fact that a measure adopted by an undertaking falls within the context of on-going business relations is not sufficient (19).

(15) See Joined Cases T-25/95 and others, Cimenteries CBR, [2000] ECR II-491, paragraphs 1849 and 1852; and Joined Cases T-202/98 and others, British Sugar, [2001] ECR II-2035, paragraphs 58 to 60.

(16) See to that effect Case C-453/99, Courage v Crehan, [2001] ECR I-6297, and paragraph 3444 of the judgment in Cimenteries CBR cited in the previous note.

(17) See in this respect Joined Cases C-2/01 P and C-3/01 P, Bundesverband der Arzneimittel-Importeure, [2004] ECR I ..., paragraph 102.

(18) See e.g. Joined Cases 25/84 and 26/84, Ford, [1985] ECR 2725.

(19) See in this respect paragraph 141 of the judgment in Bundesverband der Arzneimittel-Importeure cited in note.

16. Agreements between undertakings are caught by the prohibition rule of Article 81(1) when they are likely to have an appreciable adverse impact on the parameters of competition on the market, such as price, output, product quality, product variety and innovation. Agreements can have this effect by appreciably reducing rivalry between the parties to the agreement or between them and third parties.

2.2.2. The basic principles for assessing agreements under Article 81(1)

17. The assessment of whether an agreement is restrictive of competition must be made within the actual context in which competition would occur in the absence of the agreement with its alleged restrictions (20). In making this assessment it is necessary to take account of the likely impact of the agreement on inter-brand competition (i.e. competition between suppliers of competing brands) and on intra-brand competition (i.e. competition between distributors of the same brand). Article 81(1) prohibits restrictions of both inter-brand competition and intra-brand competition (21).

(20) See Case 56/65, Société Technique Minière, [1966] ECR 337, and paragraph 76 of the judgment in John Deere, cited in note 9.

(21) See in this respect e.g. Joined Cases 56/64 and 58/66, Consten and Grundig, [1966] ECR 429.

18. For the purpose of assessing whether an agreement or its individual parts may restrict inter-brand competition and/or intra-brand competition it needs to be considered how and to what extent the agreement affects or is likely to affect competition on the market. The following two questions provide a useful framework for making this assessment. The first question relates to the impact of the agreement on inter-brand competition while the second question relates to the impact of the agreement on intra-brand competition. As restraints may be capable of affecting both inter-brand competition and intra-brand competition at the same time, it may be necessary to analyse a restraint in light of both questions before it can be concluded whether or not competition is restricted within the meaning of Article 81(1):

(1) Does the agreement restrict actual or potential competition that would have existed without the agreement? If so, the agreement may be caught by Article 81(1). In making this assessment it is necessary to take into account competition between the parties and competition from third parties. For instance, where two undertakings established in different Member States undertake not to sell products in each other's home markets, (potential) competition that existed prior to the agreement is restricted. Similarly, where a supplier imposes obligations on his distributors not to sell competing products and these obligations foreclose third party access to the market, actual or potential competition that would have existed in the absence of the agreement is restricted. In assessing whether the parties to an agreement are actual or potential competitors the economic and legal context must be taken into account. For instance, if due to the financial risks involved and the technical capabilities of the parties it is unlikely on the basis of objective factors that each party would be able to carry out on its own the activities covered by the agreement the parties are deemed to be non-competitors in respect of that activity (22). It is for the parties to bring forward evidence to that effect.

(22) See in this respect e.g. Commission Decision in Elopak/Metal Box – Odin (O.J. 1990 L 209, p. 15) and in TPS (O.J. 1999 L 90, p. 6).

(2) Does the agreement restrict actual or potential competition that would have existed in the absence of the contractual restraint(s)? If so, the agreement may be caught by Article 81(1). For instance, where a supplier restricts its distributors from competing with each other, (potential) competition that could have existed between the distributors absent the restraints is restricted. Such restrictions include resale price maintenance and territorial or customer sales restrictions between distributors. However, certain restraints may in certain cases not be caught by Article 81(1) when the restraint is objectively necessary for the existence of an agreement of that type or that nature (23). Such exclusion of the application of Article 81(1) can only be made on the basis of objective factors external to the parties themselves and not the subjective views and characteristics of the parties. The question is not whether the parties in their particular situation would not have accepted to conclude a less restrictive agreement, but whether given the nature of the agreement and the characteristics of the market a less restrictive agreement would not have been concluded by undertakings in a similar setting. For instance, territorial restraints in an agreement between a supplier and a distributor may for a certain period of time fall outside Article 81(1), if the restraints are objectively necessary in order for the distributor to penetrate a new market (24). Similarly, a prohibition imposed on all distributors not to sell to certain categories of end users may not be restrictive of competition if such restraint is objectively necessary for reasons of safety or health related to the dangerous nature of the product in question. Claims that in the absence of a restraint the supplier would have resorted to vertical integration are not sufficient. Decisions on whether or not to vertically integrate depend on a broad range of complex economic factors, a number of which are internal to the undertaking concerned.

(23) See in this respect the judgment in Société Technique Minière cited in note 20 and Case 258/78, Nungesser, [1982] ECR 2015.

(24) See rule 10 in paragraph 119 of the Guidelines on vertical restraints cited in note above, according to which inter alia passive sales restrictions – a hardcore restraint – are held to fall outside Article 81(1) for a period of 2 years when the restraint is linked to opening up new product or geographic markets.

19. In the application of the analytical framework set out in the previous paragraph it must be taken into account that Article 81(1) distinguishes between those agreements that have a restriction of competition as their object and those agreements that have a restriction of competition as their effect. An agreement or contractual restraint is only prohibited by Article 81(1) if its object or effect is to restrict inter-brand competition and/or intra-brand competition.

20. The distinction between restrictions by object and restrictions by effect is important. Once it has been established that an agreement has as its object the restriction of competition, there is no need to take account of its concrete effects (25). In other words, for the purpose of applying Article 81(1) no actual anti-competitive effects need to be demonstrated where the agreement has a restriction of competition as its object. Article 81(3), on the other hand, does not distinguish between agreements that restrict competition by object and agreements that restrict competition by effect. Article 81(3) applies to all agreements that fulfil the four conditions contained therein (26).

(25) See e.g. paragraph 99 of the judgment in Anic Partecipazioni cited in note 12.

(26) See paragraph 46 below.

21. Restrictions of competition by object are those that by their very nature have the potential of restricting competition. These are restrictions which in light of the objectives pursued by the Community competition rules have such a high potential of negative effects on competition that it is unnecessary for the purposes of applying Article 81(1) to demonstrate any actual effects on the market. This presumption is based on the serious nature of the restriction and on experience showing that restrictions of competition by object are likely to produce negative effects on the market and to jeopardise the objectives pursued by the Community competition rules. Restrictions by object such as price fixing and market sharing reduce output and raise prices, leading to a misallocation of resources, because goods and services demanded by customers are not produced. They also lead to a reduction in consumer welfare, because consumers have to pay higher prices for the goods and services in question.

22. The assessment of whether or not an agreement has as its object the restriction of competition is based on a number of factors. These factors include, in particular, the content of the agreement and the objective aims pursued by it. It may also be necessary to consider the context in which it is (to be) applied and the actual conduct and behaviour of the parties on the market (27). In other words, an examination of the facts underlying the agreement and the specific circumstances in which it operates may be required before it can be concluded whether a particular restriction constitutes a restriction of competition by object. The way in which an agreement is actually implemented may reveal a restriction by object even where the formal agreement does not contain an express provision to that effect. Evidence of subjective intent on the part of the parties to restrict competition is a relevant factor but not a necessary condition.

(27) See Joined Cases 29/83 and 30/83, CRAM and Rheinzink, [1984] ECR 1679, paragraph 26, and Joined Cases 96/82 and others, ANSEAU-NAVEWA, [1983] ECR 3369, paragraphs 23-25.

23. Non-exhaustive guidance on what constitutes restrictions by object can be found in Commission block exemption regulations, guidelines and notices. Restrictions that are black-listed in block exemptions or identified as hardcore restrictions in guidelines and notices are generally considered by the Commission to constitute restrictions by object. In the case of horizontal agreements restrictions of competition by object include price fixing, output limitation and sharing of markets and customers (28). As regards vertical agreements the category of restrictions by object includes, in particular, fixed and minimum resale price maintenance and restrictions providing absolute territorial protection, including restrictions on passive sales (29).

(28) See the Guidelines on horizontal cooperation agreements, cited in note, paragraph 25, and Article 5 of Commission Regulation 2658/2000 on the application of Article 81(3) of the Treaty to categories of specialisation agreements (O.J. L 304, 5.12.2000, p. 3).

(29) See Article 4 Commission Regulation 2790/1999 on the application of Article 81(3) of the Treaty to categories of vertical agreements and concerted practices (O.J. L 336, 29.12.1999, p. 21) and the Guidelines on Vertical Restraints, cited in note, paragraph 46 et seq. See also Case 279/87, Tipp-Ex, [1990] ECR I-261, and Case T-62/98, Volkswagen v Commission, [2000] ECR II-2707, paragraph 178.

24. If an agreement is not restrictive of competition by object it must be examined whether it has restrictive effects on competition. Account must be taken of both actual and potential effects (30). In other words the agreement must have likely anti-competitive effects. In the case of restrictions of competition by effect there is no presumption of anti-competitive effects. For an agreement to be restrictive by effect it must affect actual or potential competition to such an extent that on the relevant market negative effects on prices, output, innovation or the variety or quality of goods and services can be expected with a reasonable degree of probability (31). Such negative effects must be appreciable.

The prohibition rule of Article 81(1) does not apply when the identified anti-competitive effects are insignificant (32). This test reflects the economic approach which the Commission is applying. The prohibition of Article 81(1) only applies where on the basis of proper market analysis it can be concluded that the agreement has likely anti-competitive effects on the market (33). It is insufficient for such a finding that the market shares of the parties exceed the thresholds set out in the Commission's de minimis notice (34). Agreements falling within safe harbours of block exemption regulations may be caught by Article 81(1) but this is not necessarily so. Moreover, the fact that due to the market shares of the parties, an agreement falls outside the safe harbour of a block exemption is in itself an insufficient basis for finding that the agreement is caught by Article 81(1) or that it does not fulfil the conditions of Article 81(3). Individual assessment of the likely effects produced by the agreement is required.

(30) See paragraph 77 of the judgment in John Deere cited in note 9.

(31) It is not sufficient in itself that the agreement restricts the freedom of action of one or more of the parties, see paragraphs 76 and 77 of the judgment in Métropole television (M6) cited in note 10. This is in line with the fact that the object of Article 81 is to protect competition on the market for the benefit of consumers.

(32) See e.g. Case 5/69, Völk, [1969] ECR 295, paragraph 7. Guidance on the issue of appreciability can be found in the Commission Notice on agreements of minor importance which do not appreciably restrict competition under Article 81(1) of the Treaty (O.J. C 368, 22.12.2001, p. 13) The notice defines appreciability in a negative way. Agreements, which fall outside the scope of the de minimis notice, do not necessarily have appreciable restrictive effects. An individual assessment is required.

(33) See in this respect Joined Cases T-374/94 and others, European Night Services, [1998] ECR II-3141.

(34) See note 32.

25. Negative effects on competition within the relevant market are likely to occur when the parties individually or jointly have or obtain some degree of market power and the agreement contributes to the creation, maintenance or strengthening of that market power or allows the parties to exploit such market power. Market power is the ability to maintain prices above competitive levels for a significant period of time or to maintain output in terms of product quantities, product quality and variety or innovation below competitive levels for a significant period of time. In markets with high fixed costs undertakings must price significantly above their marginal costs of production in order to ensure a competitive return on their investment. The fact that undertakings price above their marginal costs is therefore not in itself a sign that competition in the market is not functioning well and that undertakings have market power that allows them to price above the competitive level. It is when competitive constraints are insufficient to maintain prices and output at competitive levels that undertakings have market power within the meaning of Article 81(1).

26. The creation, maintenance or strengthening of market power can result from a restriction of competition between the parties to the agreement. It can also result from a restriction of competition between any one of the parties and third parties, e.g. because the agreement leads to foreclosure of competitors or because it raises competitors' costs, limiting their capacity to compete effectively with the contracting parties. Market power is a question of degree. The degree of market power normally required for the finding of an infringement under Article 81(1) in the case of agreements that are restrictive of competition by effect is less than the degree of market power required for a finding of dominance under Article 82.

27. For the purposes of analysing the restrictive effects of an agreement it is normally necessary to define the relevant market (35). It is normally also necessary to examine and assess, inter alia, the nature of the products, the market position of the parties, the market position of competitors, the market position of buyers, the existence of potential competitors and the level of entry barriers. In some cases, however, it may be possible to show anti-competitive effects directly by analysing the conduct of the parties to the agreement on the market. It may for example be possible to ascertain that an agreement has led to price increases. The guidelines on horizontal cooperation agreements and on vertical restraints set out a detailed framework for analysing the competitive impact of various types of horizontal and vertical agreements under Article 81(1) (36).

(35) See in this respect Commission notice on the definition of the relevant market for the purposes of Community competition law (O.J. C 372, 9.12.1997, p. 1).

(36) For the reference in the O.J. see note 5.

2.2.3. Ancillary restraints

28. Paragraph 18 above sets out a framework for analysing the impact of an agreement and its individual restrictions on inter-brand competition and intra-brand competition. If on the basis of those principles it is concluded that the main transaction covered by the agreement is not restrictive of competition, it becomes relevant to examine whether individual restraints contained in the agreement are also compatible with Article 81(1) because they are ancillary to the main non-restrictive transaction.

29. In Community competition law the concept of ancillary restraints covers any alleged restriction of competition which is directly related and necessary to the implementation of a main non-restrictive transaction and proportionate to it (37). If an agreement in its main parts, for instance a distribution agreement or a joint venture, does not have as its object or effect the restriction of competition, then restrictions, which are directly related to and necessary for the implementation of that transaction, also fall outside Article 81(1) (38). These related restrictions are called ancillary restraints. A restriction is directly related to the main transaction if it is subordinate to the implementation of that transaction and is inseparably linked to it. The test of necessity implies that the restriction must be objectively necessary for the implementation of the main transaction and be proportionate to it. It follows that the ancillary restraints test is similar to the test set out in paragraph 18(2) above. However, the ancillary restraints test applies in all cases where the main transaction is not restrictive of competition (39). It is not limited to determining the impact of the agreement on intra-brand competition.

(37) See paragraph 104 of the judgment in Métropole télévision (M6) and others, cited in note 10.

(38) See e.g. Case C-399/93, Luttikhuis, [1995] ECR I-4515, paragraphs 12 to 14.

(39) See in this respect paragraphs 118 et seq. of the Métropole television judgment cited in note 10.

30. The application of the ancillary restraint concept must be distinguished from the application of the defence under Article 81(3) which relates to certain economic benefits produced by restrictive agreements and which are balanced against the restrictive effects of the agreements. The application of the ancillary restraint concept does not involve any weighing of pro-competitive and anticompetitive effects. Such balancing is reserved for Article 81(3) (40).

(40) See paragraph 107 of the judgment in Métropole télévision judgement cited in note 10.

31. The assessment of ancillary restraints is limited to determining whether, in the specific context of the main non-restrictive transaction or activity, a particular restriction is necessary for the implementation of that transaction or activity and proportionate to it. If on the basis of objective factors it can be concluded that without the restriction the main non-restrictive transaction would be difficult or impossible to implement, the restriction may be regarded as objectively necessary for its implementation and proportionate to it (41). If, for example, the main object of a franchise agreement does not restrict competition, then restrictions, which are necessary for the proper functioning of the agreement, such as obligations aimed at protecting the uniformity and reputation of the franchise system, also fall outside Article 81(1) (42). Similarly, if a joint venture is not in itself restrictive of competition, then restrictions, which are necessary for the functioning of the agreement are deemed to be ancillary to the main transaction and are therefore not caught by Article 81(1). For instance in TPS (43) the Commission concluded that an obligation on the parties not to be involved in companies engaged in distribution and marketing of television programmes by satellite was ancillary to the creation of the joint venture during the initial phase. The restriction was therefore deemed to fall outside Article 81(1) for a period of three years. In arriving at this conclusion the Commission took account of the heavy investments and commercial risks involved in entering the market for pay-television.

(41) See e.g. Commission Decision in Elopak/Metal Box – Odin cited in note 22.

(42) See Case 161/84, Pronuptia, [1986] ECR 353.

(43) See note 22. The decision was upheld by the Court of First Instance in the judgment in Métropole télévision (M6) cited in note 10.

2.3. The exception rule of Article 81(3)

32. The assessment of restrictions by object and effect under Article 81(1) is only one side of the analysis. The other side, which is reflected in Article 81(3), is the assessment of the positive economic effects of restrictive agreements.

33. The aim of the Community competition rules is to protect competition on the market as a means of enhancing consumer welfare and of ensuring an efficient allocation of resources. Agreements that restrict competition may at the same time have pro-competitive effects by way of efficiency gains (44). Efficiencies may create additional value by lowering the cost of producing an output, improving the quality of the product or creating a new product. When the pro-competitive effects of an agreement outweigh its anti-competitive effects the agreement is on balance pro-competitive and compatible with the objectives of the Community competition rules. The net effect of such agreements is to promote the very essence of the competitive process, namely to win customers by offering better products or better prices than those offered by rivals. This analytical framework is reflected in Article 81(1) and Article 81(3). The latter provision expressly acknowledges that restrictive agreements may generate objective economic benefits so as to outweigh the negative effects of the restriction of competition (45).

(44) Cost savings and other gains to the parties that arise from the mere exercise of market power do not give rise to objective benefits and cannot be taken into account, cf. paragraph 49 below.

(45) See the judgment in Consten and Grundig, cited in note 21.

34. The application of the exception rule of Article 81(3) is subject to four cumulative conditions, two positive and two negative:

(a) The agreement must contribute to improving the production or distribution of goods or contribute to promoting technical or economic progress,

(b) Consumers must receive a fair share of the resulting benefits,

(c) The restrictions must be indispensable to the attainment of these objectives, and finally

(d) The agreement must not afford the parties the possibility of eliminating competition in respect of a substantial part of the products in question.

When these four conditions are fulfilled the agreement enhances competition within the relevant market, because it leads the undertakings concerned to offer cheaper or better products to consumers, compensating the latter for the adverse effects of the restrictions of competition.

35. Article 81(3) can be applied either to individual agreements or to categories of agreements by way of a block exemption regulation. When an agreement is covered by a block exemption the parties to the restrictive agreement are relieved of their burden under Article 2 of Regulation 1/2003 of showing that their individual agreement satisfies each of the conditions of Article 81(3). They only have to prove that the restrictive agreement benefits from a block exemption. The application of Article 81(3) to categories of agreements by way of block exemption regulation is based on the presumption that restrictive agreements that fall within their scope (46) fulfil each of the four conditions laid down in Article 81(3).

(46) The fact that an agreement is block exempted does not in itself indicate that the individual agreement is caught by Article 81(1).

36. If in an individual case the agreement is caught by Article 81(1) and the conditions of Article 81(3) are not fulfilled the block exemption may be withdrawn. According to Article 29(1) of Regulation 1/2003 the Commission is empowered to withdraw the benefit of a block exemption when it finds that in a particular case an agreement covered by a block exemption regulation has certain effects which are incompatible with Article 81(3) of the Treaty. Pursuant to Article 29(2) of Regulation 1/2003 a competition authority of a Member State may also withdraw the benefit of a Commission block exemption regulation in respect of its territory (or part of its territory), if this territory has all the characteristics of a distinct geographic market. In the case of withdrawal it is for the competition authorities concerned to demonstrate that the agreement infringes Article 81(1) and that it does not fulfil the conditions of Article 81(3).

37. The courts of the Member States have no power to withdraw the benefit of block exemption regulations. Moreover, in their application of block exemption regulations Member State courts may not modify their scope by extending their sphere of application to agreements not covered by the block exemption regulation in question (47). Outside the scope of block exemption regulations Member State courts have the power to apply Article 81 in full (cf. Article 6 of Regulation 1/2003).

(47) See e.g. Case C-234/89, Delimitis, [1991] ECR I-935, paragraph 46.

3. THE APPLICATION OF THE FOUR CONDITIONS OF ARTICLE 81(3)

38. The remainder of these guidelines will consider each of the four conditions of Article 81(3) (48). Given that these four conditions are cumulative (49) it is unnecessary to examine any remaining conditions once it is found that one of the conditions of Article 81(3) is not fulfilled. In individual cases it may therefore be appropriate to consider the four conditions in a different order.

(48) Article 36(4) of Regulation 1/2003 has, inter alia, repealed Article 5 of Regulation 1017/68 applying rules of competition to transport by rail, road and inland waterway. However, the Commission's case practice adopted under Regulation 1017/68 remains relevant for the purposes of applying Article 81(3) in the inland transport sector.

(49) See paragraph 42 below.

39. For the purposes of these guidelines it is considered appropriate to invert the order of the second and the third condition and thus deal with the issue of indispensability before the issue of pass-on to consumers. The analysis of pass-on requires a balancing of the negative and positive effects of an agreement on consumers. This analysis should not include the effects of any restrictions, which already fail the indispensability test and which for that reason are prohibited by Article 81.

3.1. General principles

40. Article 81(3) of the Treaty only becomes relevant when an agreement between undertakings restricts competition within the meaning of Article 81(1). In the case of non-restrictive agreements there is no need to examine any benefits generated by the agreement.

41. Where in an individual case a restriction of competition within the meaning of Article 81(1) has been proven, Article 81(3) can be invoked as a defence. According to Article 2 of Regulation 1/2003 the burden of proof under Article 81(3) rests on the undertaking(s) invoking the benefit of the exception rule. Where the conditions of Article 81(3) are not satisfied the agreement is null and void, cf. Article 81(2). However, such automatic nullity only applies to those parts of the agreement that are incompatible with Article 81, provided that such parts are severable from the agreement as a whole (50). If only part of the agreement is null and void, it is for the applicable national law to determine the consequences thereof for the remaining part of the agreement (51).

(50) See the judgment in Société Technique Minière cited in note 20.

(51) See in this respect Case 319/82, Kerpen & Kerpen, [1983] ECR 4 173, paragraphs 11 and 12.

42. According to settled case law the four conditions of Article 81(3) are cumulative (52), i.e. they must all be fulfilled for the exception rule to be applicable. If they are not, the application of the exception rule of Article 81(3) must be refused (53). The four conditions of Article 81(3) are also exhaustive. When they are met the exception is applicable and may not be made dependant on any other condition. Goals pursued by other Treaty provisions can be taken into account to the extent that they can be subsumed under the four conditions of Article 81(3) (54).

(52) See e.g. Case T-185/00 and others, Métropole télévision SA (M6), [2002] ECR II-3805, paragraph 86, Case T-17/93, Matra, ECR [1994] II-595, paragraph 85; and Joined Cases 43/82 and 63/82, VBVB and VBBB, [1984] ECR 19, paragraph 61.

(53) See Case T-213/00, CMA CGM and others, [2003] ECR II ..., paragraph 226.

(54) See to that effect implicitly paragraph 139 of the Matra judgment cited in note 52 and Case 26/76, Metro (I), [1977] ECR 1875, paragraph 43.

43. The assessment under Article 81(3) of benefits flowing from restrictive agreements is in principle made within the confines of each relevant market to which the agreement relates. The Community competition rules have as their objective the protection of competition on the market and cannot be detached from this objective. Moreover, the condition that consumers (55) must receive a fair share of the benefits implies in general that efficiencies generated by the restrictive agreement within a relevant market must be sufficient to outweigh the anti-competitive effects produced by the agreement within that same relevant market (56). Negative effects on consumers in one geographic market or product market cannot normally be balanced against and compensated by positive effects for consumers in another unrelated geographic market or product market. However, where two markets are related, efficiencies achieved on separate markets can be taken into account provided that the group of consumers affected by the restriction and benefiting from the efficiency gains are substantially the same (57). Indeed, in some cases only consumers in a downstream market are affected by the agreement in which case the impact of the agreement on such consumers must be assessed. This is for instance so in the case of purchasing agreements (58).

(55) As to the concept of consumers see paragraph 84 below where it is stated that consumers are the customers of the parties and subsequent buyers. The parties themselves are not «consumers» for the purposes of Article 81(3).

(56) The test is market specific, see to that effect Case T-131/99, Shaw, [2002] ECR II-2023, paragraph 163, where the Court of First Instance held that the assessment under Article 81(3) had to be made within the same analytical framework as that used for assessing the restrictive effects, and Case C-360/92 P, Publishers Association, [1995] ECR I-23, paragraph 29, where in a case where the relevant market was wider than national the Court of Justice held that in the application of Article 81(3) it was not correct only to consider the effects on the national territory.

(57) In Case T-86/95, Compagnie Générale Maritime and others, [2002] ECR II-1011, paragraphs 343 to 345, the Court of First Instance held that Article 81(3) does not require that the benefits are linked to a specific market and that in appropriate cases regard must be had to benefits «for every other market on which the agreement in question might have beneficial effects, and even, in a more general sense, for any service the quality or efficiency of which might be improved by the existence of that agreement». Importantly, however, in this case the affected group of consumers was the same. The case concerned intermodal transport services encompassing a bundle of, inter alia, inland and maritime transportation provided to shipping companies across the Community. The restrictions related to inland transport services, which were held to constitute a separate market, whereas the benefits were claimed to occur in relation to maritime transport services. Both services were demanded by shippers requiring intermodal transport services between northern Europe and South-East and East Asia. The judgment in CMA CGM, cited in note 53 above, also concerned a situation where the agreement, while covering several distinct services, affected the same group of consumers, namely shippers of containerised cargo between northern Europe and the Far East. Under the agreement the parties fixed charges and surcharges relating to inland transport services, port services and maritime transport services. The Court of First Instance held (cf. paragraphs 226 to 228) that in the circumstances of the case there was no need to define relevant markets for the purpose of applying Article 81(3). The agreement was restrictive of competition by its very object and there were no benefits for consumers.

(58) See paragraphs 126 and 132 of the Guidelines on horizontal co-operation agreements cited in note 5 above.

44. The assessment of restrictive agreements under Article 81(3) is made within the actual context in which they occur (59) and on the basis of the facts existing at any given point in time. The assessment is sensitive to material changes in the facts. The exception rule of Article 81(3) applies as long as the four conditions are fulfilled and ceases to apply when that is no longer the case (60). When applying Article 81(3) in accordance with these principles it is necessary to take into account the initial sunk investments made by any of the parties and the time needed and the restraints required to commit and recoup an efficiency enhancing investment. Article 81 cannot be applied without taking due account of such *ex ante* investment. The risk facing the parties and the sunk investment that must be committed to implement the agreement can thus lead to the agreement falling outside Article 81(1) or fulfilling the conditions of Article 81(3), as the case may be, for the period of time required to recoup the investment.

(59) See the Ford judgment cited in note 18.

(60) See in this respect for example Commission Decision in TPS (O.J. L 90, 2.4.1999, p. 6). Similarly, the prohibition of Article 81(1) also only applies as long as the agreement has a restrictive object or restrictive effects.

45. In some cases the restrictive agreement is an irreversible event. Once the restrictive agreement has been implemented the *ex ante* situation cannot be re-established. In such cases the assessment must be made exclusively on the basis of the facts pertaining at the time of implementation. For instance, in the case of a research and development agreement whereby each party agrees to abandon its respective research project and pool its capabilities with those of another party, it may from an objective point of view be technically and economically impossible to revive a project once it has been abandoned. The assessment of the anti-competitive and pro-competitive effects of the agreement to abandon the individual research projects must therefore be made as of the time of the completion of its implementation. If at that point in time the agreement is compatible with Article 81, for instance because a sufficient number of third parties have competing research and development projects, the parties' agreement to abandon their individual projects remains compatible with Article 81, even if at a later point in time the third party projects fail. However, the prohibition of Article 81 may apply to other parts of the agreement in respect of which the issue of irreversibility does not arise. If for example in addition to joint research and development, the agreement provides for joint exploitation, Article 81 may apply to this part of the agreement if due to subsequent market developments the agreement becomes restrictive of competition and does not (any longer) satisfy the conditions of Article 81(3) taking due account of *ex ante* sunk investments, cf. the previous paragraph.

46. Article 81(3) does not exclude a priori certain types of agreements from its scope. As a matter of principle all restrictive agreements that fulfil the four conditions of Article 81(3) are covered by the exception rule (61). However, severe restrictions of competition are unlikely to fulfil the conditions of Article 81(3). Such restrictions are usually black-listed in block exemption regulations or identified as hardcore restrictions in Commission guidelines and notices. Agreements of this nature generally fail (at least) the two first conditions of Article 81(3). They neither create objective economic benefits (62) nor do they benefit consumers (63). For example, a horizontal agreement to fix prices limits output leading to misallocation of resources. It also transfers value from consumers to producers, since it leads to higher prices without producing any countervailing value to consumers within the relevant market. Moreover, these types of agreements generally also fail the indispensability test under the third condition (64).

(61) See paragraph 85 of the Matra judgment cited in note 52.

(62) As to this requirement see paragraph 49 below.

(63) See e.g. Case T-29/92, Vereniging van Samenwerkende Prijsregelende Organisaties in de Bouwnijverheid (SPO), [1995] ECR II-289.

(64) See e.g. Case 258/78, Nungesser, [1982] ECR 2015, paragraph 77, concerning absolute territorial protection.

47. Any claim that restrictive agreements are justified because they aim at ensuring fair conditions of competition on the market is by nature unfounded and must be discarded (65). The purpose of Article 81 is to protect effective competition by ensuring that markets remain open and competitive. The protection of fair conditions of competition is a task for the legislator in compliance with Community law obligations (66) and not for undertakings to regulate themselves.

(65) See in this respect e.g. the judgment in SPO cited in note 63.

(66) National measures must, inter alia, comply with the Treaty rules on free movement of goods, services, persons and capital.

3.2. First condition of Article 81(3): Efficiency gains

3.2.1. General remarks

48. According to the first condition of Article 81(3) the restrictive agreement must contribute to improving the production or distribution of goods or to promoting technical or economic progress. The provision refers expressly only to goods, but applies by analogy to services.

49. It follows from the case law of the Court of Justice that only objective benefits can be taken into account (67). This means that efficiencies are not assessed from the subjective point of view of the parties (68). Cost savings that arise from the mere exercise of market power by the parties cannot be taken into account. For instance, when companies agree to fix prices or share markets they reduce output and thereby production costs. Reduced competition may also lead to lower sales and marketing expenditures. Such cost reductions are a direct consequence of a reduction in output and value. The cost reductions in question do not produce any pro-competitive effects on the market. In particular, they do not lead to the creation of value through an integration of assets and activities. They merely allow the undertakings concerned to increase their profits and are therefore irrelevant from the point of view of Article 81(3).

(67) See e.g. the judgment in Consten and Grundig cited in note 21.

(68) See in this respect Commission Decision in Van den Bergh Foods (O.J. 1998 L 246, p. 1).

50. The purpose of the first condition of Article 81(3) is to define the types of efficiency gains that can be taken into account and be subject to the further tests of the second and third conditions of Article 81(3). The aim of the analysis is to ascertain what are the objective benefits created by the agreement and what is the economic importance of such efficiencies. Given that for Article 81(3) to apply the pro-competitive effects flowing from the agreement must outweigh its anti-competitive effects, it is necessary to verify what is the link between the agreement and the claimed efficiencies and what is the value of these efficiencies.

51. All efficiency claims must therefore be substantiated so that the following can be verified:

(a) The nature of the claimed efficiencies;

(b) The link between the agreement and the efficiencies;

(c) The likelihood and magnitude of each claimed efficiency; and

(d) How and when each claimed efficiency would be achieved.

52. Letter (a) allows the decision-maker to verify whether the claimed efficiencies are objective in nature, cf. paragraph 49 above.

53. Letter (b) allows the decision-maker to verify whether there is a sufficient causal link between the restrictive agreement and the claimed efficiencies. This condition normally requires that the efficiencies result from the economic activity that forms the object of the agreement. Such activities may, for example, take the form of distribution, licensing of technology, joint production or joint research and development. To the extent, however, that an agreement has wider efficiency enhancing effects within the relevant market, for example because it leads to a reduction in industry wide costs, these additional benefits are also taken into account.

54. The causal link between the agreement and the claimed efficiencies must normally also be direct (69). Claims based on indirect effects are as a general rule too uncertain and too remote to be taken into account. A direct causal link exists for instance where a technology transfer agreement allows the licensees to produce new or improved products or a distribution agreement allows products to be distributed at lower cost or valuable services to be produced. An example of indirect effect would be a case where it is claimed that a restrictive agreement allows the undertakings concerned to increase their profits, enabling them to invest more in research and development to the ultimate benefit of consumers. While there may be a link between profitability and research and development, this link is generally not sufficiently direct to be taken into account in the context of Article 81(3).

(69) See in this respect Commission Decision in Glaxo Wellcome (*O.J.* 2001 L 302, p. 1).

55. Letters *(c)* and *(d)* allow the decision-maker to verify the value of the claimed efficiencies, which in the context of the third condition of Article 81(3) must be balanced against the anti-competitive effects of the agreement, see paragraph 101 below. Given that Article 81(1) only applies in cases where the agreement has likely negative effects on competition and consumers (in the case of hardcore restrictions such effects are presumed) efficiency claims must be substantiated so that they can be verified. Unsubstantiated claims are rejected.

56. In the case of claimed cost efficiencies the undertakings invoking the benefit of Article 81(3) must as accurately as reasonably possible calculate or estimate the value of the efficiencies and describe in detail how the amount has been computed. They must also describe the method(s) by which the efficiencies have been or will be achieved. The data submitted must be verifiable so that there can be a sufficient degree of certainty that the efficiencies have materialised or are likely to materialise.

57. In the case of claimed efficiencies in the form of new or improved products and other non-cost based efficiencies, the undertakings claiming the benefit of Article 81(3) must describe and explain in detail what is the nature of the efficiencies and how and why they constitute an objective economic benefit.

58. In cases where the agreement has yet to be fully implemented the parties must substantiate any projections as to the date from which the efficiencies will become operational so as to have a significant positive impact in the market.

3.2.2. The different categories of efficiencies

59. The types of efficiencies listed in Article 81(3) are broad categories which are intended to cover all objective economic efficiencies. There is considerable overlap between the various categories mentioned in Article 81(3) and the same agreement may give rise to several kinds of efficiencies. It is therefore not appropriate to draw clear and firm distinctions between the various categories. For the purpose of these guidelines, a distinction is made between cost efficiencies and efficiencies of a qualitative nature whereby value is created in the form of new or improved products, greater product variety etc.

60. In general, efficiencies stem from an integration of economic activities whereby undertakings combine their assets to achieve what they could not achieve as efficiently on their own or whereby they entrust another undertaking with tasks that can be performed more efficiently by that other undertaking.

61. The research and development, production and distribution process may be viewed as a value chain that can be divided into a number of stages. At each stage of this chain an undertaking must make a choice between performing the activity itself, performing it together with (an)other undertaking(s) or outsourcing the activity entirely to (an)other undertaking(s).

62. In each case where the choice made involves cooperation on the market with another undertaking, an agreement within the meaning of Article 81(1) normally needs to be concluded. These agreements can be vertical, as is the case where the parties operate at different levels of the value chain or horizontal, as is the case where the firms operate at the same level of the value chain. Both categories of agreements may create efficiencies by allowing the undertakings in question to perform a particular task at lower cost or with higher added value for consumers. Such agreements may also contain or lead to restrictions of competition in which case the prohibition rule of Article 81(1) and the exception rule of Article 81(3) may become relevant.

63. The types of efficiencies mentioned in the following are only examples and are not intended to be exhaustive.

3.2.2.1. Cost efficiencies

64. Cost efficiencies flowing from agreements between undertakings can originate from a number of different sources. One very important source of cost savings is the development of new production technologies and methods. In general, it is when technological leaps are made that the greatest potential for cost savings is achieved. For instance, the introduction of the assembly line led to a very substantial reduction in the cost of producing motor vehicles.

65. Another very important source of efficiency is synergies resulting from an integration of existing assets. When the parties to an agreement combine their respective assets they may be able to attain a cost/output configuration that would not otherwise be possible. The combination of two existing technologies that have complementary strengths may reduce production costs or lead to the production of a higher quality product. For instance, it may be that the production assets of firm A generate a high output per hour but require a relatively high input of raw materials per unit of output, whereas the production assets of firm B generate lower output per hour but require a relatively lower input of raw materials per unit of output. Synergies are created if by establishing a production joint venture combining the production assets of A and B the parties can attain a high(er) level of output per hour with a low(er) input of raw materials per unit of output. Similarly, if one undertaking has optimised one part of the value chain and another undertaking has optimised another part of the value chain, the combination of their operations may lead to lower costs. Firm A may for instance have a highly automated production facility resulting in low production costs per unit whereas B has developed an efficient order processing system. The system allows production to be tailored to customer demand, ensuring timely delivery and reducing warehousing and obsolescence costs. By combining their assets A and B may be able to obtain cost reductions.

66. Cost efficiencies may also result from economies of scale, i.e. declining cost per unit of output as output increases. To give an example: investment in equipment and other assets often has to be made in indivisible blocks. If an undertaking cannot fully utilise a block, its average costs will be higher than if it could do so. For instance, the cost of operating a truck is virtually the same regardless of whether it is almost empty, half-full or full. Agreements whereby undertakings combine their logistics operations may allow them to increase the load factors and reduce the number of vehicles employed. Larger scale may also allow for better division of labour leading to lower unit costs. Firms may achieve economies of scale in respect of all parts of the value chain, including research and development, production, distribution and marketing. Learning economies constitute a related type of efficiency. As experience is gained in using a particular production process or in performing particular tasks, productivity may increase because the process is made to run more efficiently or because the task is performed more quickly.

67. Economies of scope are another source of cost efficiency, which occur when firms achieve cost savings by producing different products on the basis of the same input. Such efficiencies may arise from the fact that it is possible to use the same components and the same facilities and personnel to produce a variety of products. Similarly, economies of scope may arise in distribution when several types of goods are distributed in the same vehicles. For instance, a producer of frozen pizzas and a producer of frozen vegetables may obtain economies of scope by jointly distributing their products. Both groups of products must be distributed in refrigerated vehicles and it is likely that there are significant overlaps in terms of customers. By combining their operations the two producers may obtain lower distribution costs per distributed unit.

68. Efficiencies in the form of cost reductions can also follow from agreements that allow for better planning of production, reducing the need to hold expensive inventory and allowing for better capacity utilisation. Efficiencies of this nature may for example stem from the use of 'just in time' purchasing, i.e. an obligation on a supplier of components to continuously supply the buyer according to its needs thereby avoiding the need for the buyer to maintain a significant stock of components which risks becoming obsolete. Cost savings may also result from agreements that allow the parties to rationalise production across their facilities.

3.2.2.2. Qualitative efficiencies

69. Agreements between undertakings may generate various efficiencies of a qualitative nature which are relevant to the application of Article 81(3). In a number of cases the main efficiency enhancing potential of the agreement is not cost reduction; it is quality improvements and other efficiencies of a qualitative nature. Depending on the individual case such efficiencies may therefore be of equal or greater importance than cost efficiencies.

70. Technical and technological advances form an essential and dynamic part of the economy, generating significant benefits in the form of new or improved goods and services. By cooperating undertakings may be able to create efficiencies that would not have been possible without the restrictive agreement or would have been possible only with substantial delay or at higher cost. Such efficiencies constitute an important source of economic benefits covered by the first condition of Article 81(3). Agreements capable of producing efficiencies of this nature include, in particular, research and development agreements. An example would be A and B creating a joint venture for the development and, if successful, joint production of a cell-based tyre. The puncture of one cell does not affect other cells, which means that there is no risk of collapse of the tyre in the event of a puncture. The tyre is thus safer than traditional tyres. It also means that there is no immediate need to change the tyre and thus to carry a spare. Both types of efficiencies constitute objective benefits within the meaning of the first condition of Article 81(3).

71. In the same way that the combination of complementary assets can give rise to cost savings, combinations of assets may also create synergies that create efficiencies of a qualitative nature. The combination of production assets may for instance lead to the production of higher quality products or products with novel features. This may for instance be the case for licence agreements, and agreements providing for joint production of new or improved goods or services. Licence agreements may, in particular, ensure more rapid dissemination of new technology in the Community and enable the licensee(s) to make available new products or to employ new production techniques that lead to quality improvements. Joint production agreements may, in particular, allow new or improved products or services to be introduced on the market more quickly or at lower cost (70). In the telecommunications sector, for example, cooperation agreements have been held to create efficiencies by making available more quickly new global services (71). In the banking sector cooperation agreements that made available improved facilities for making crossborder payments have also been held to create efficiencies falling within the scope of the first condition of Article 81(3) (72).

(70) See e.g. Commission Decision in GEAE/P&W (O.J. 2000 L 58, p. 16); in British Interactive Broadcasting/Open (O.J. 1999 L 312, p. 1) and in Asahi/Saint Gobain (O.J. 1994 L 354, page 87).

(71) See e.g. Commission Decision in Atlas (O.J. 1996 L 239, p. 23), and in Phoenix/Global One (O.J. 1996 L 239, p. 57).

(72) See e.g. Commission Decision in Uniform Eurocheques (O.J. 1985 L 35, p. 43).

72. Distribution agreements may also give rise to qualitative efficiencies. Specialised distributors, for example, may be able to provide services that are better tailored to customer needs or to provide quicker delivery or better quality assurance throughout the distribution chain (73).

(73) See e.g. Commission Decision in Cégétel + 4 (O.J. 1999 L 88, p. 26).

3.3. Third condition of Article 81(3): Indispensability of the restrictions

73. According to the third condition of Article 81(3) the restrictive agreement must not impose restrictions, which are not indispensable to the attainment of the efficiencies created by the agreement in question. This condition implies a two-fold test. First, the restrictive agreement as such must be reasonably necessary in order to achieve the efficiencies. Secondly, the individual restrictions of competition that flow from the agreement must also be reasonably necessary for the attainment of the efficiencies.

74. In the context of the third condition of Article 81(3) the decisive factor is whether or not the restrictive agreement and individual restrictions make it possible to perform the activity in question more efficiently than would likely have been the case in the absence of the agreement or the restriction concerned. The question is not whether in the absence of the restriction the agreement would not have been concluded, but whether more efficiencies are produced with the agreement or restriction than in the absence of the agreement or restriction (74).

(74) As to the former question, which may be relevant in the context of Article 81(1), see paragraph 18 above.

75. The first test contained in the third condition of Article 81(3) requires that the efficiencies be specific to the agreement in question in the sense that there are no other economically practicable and less restrictive means of achieving the efficiencies. In making this latter assessment the market conditions and business realities facing the parties to the agreement must be taken into account. Undertakings invoking the benefit of Article 81(3) are not required to consider hypothetical or theoretical alternatives. The Commission will not second guess the business judgment of the parties. It will only intervene where it is reasonably clear that there are realistic and attainable alternatives. The parties must only explain and demonstrate why such seemingly realistic and significantly less restrictive alternatives to the agreement would be significantly less efficient.

76. It is particularly relevant to examine whether, having due regard to the circumstances of the individual case, the parties could have achieved the efficiencies by means of another less restrictive type of agreement and, if so, when they would likely be able to obtain the efficiencies. It may also be necessary to examine whether the parties could have achieved the efficiencies on their own. For instance, where the claimed efficiencies take the form of cost reductions resulting from economies of scale or scope the undertakings concerned must explain and substantiate why the same efficiencies would not be likely to be attained through internal growth and price competition. In making this assessment it is relevant to consider, inter alia, what is the minimum efficient scale on the market concerned. The minimum efficient scale is the level of output required to minimise average cost and exhaust economies of scale (75). The larger the minimum efficient scale compared to the current size of either of the parties to the agreement, the more likely it is that the efficiencies will be deemed to be specific to the agreement. In the case of agreements that produce substantial synergies through the combination of complementary assets and capabilities the very nature of the efficiencies give rise to a presumption that the agreement is necessary to attain them.

(75) Scale economies are normally exhausted at a certain point. Thereafter average costs will stabilise and eventually rise due to, for example, capacity constraints and bottlenecks.

77. These principles can be illustrated by the following hypothetical example:

A and B combine within a joint venture their respective production technologies to achieve higher output and lower raw material consumption. The joint venture is granted an exclusive licence to their respective production technologies. The parties transfer their existing production facilities to the joint venture. They also transfer key staff in order to ensure that existing learning economies can be exploited and further developed. It is estimated that these economies will reduce production costs by a further 5%. The output of the joint venture is sold independently by A and B. In this case the indispensability condition necessitates an assessment of whether or not the benefits could be substantially achieved by means of a licence agreement, which would be likely to be less restrictive because A and B would continue to produce independently. In the circumstances described this is unlikely to be the case since under a licence agreement the parties would not be able to benefit in the same seamless and continued way from their respective experience in operating the two technologies, resulting in significant learning economies.

78. Once it is found that the agreement in question is necessary in order to produce the efficiencies, the indispensability of each restriction of competition flowing from the agreement must be assessed. In this context it must be assessed whether individual restrictions are reasonably necessary in order to produce the efficiencies. The parties to the agreement must substantiate their claim with regard to both the nature of the restriction and its intensity.

79. A restriction is indispensable if its absence would eliminate or significantly reduce the efficiencies that follow from the agreement or make it significantly less likely that they will materialise. The assessment of alternative solutions must take into account the actual and potential improvement in the field of competition by the elimination of a particular restriction or the application of a less restrictive alternative. The more restrictive the restraint the stricter the test under the third condition (76). Restrictions that are black listed in block exemption regulations or identified as hardcore restrictions in Commission guidelines and notices are unlikely to be considered indispensable.

(76) See in this respect paragraphs 392 to 395 of the judgment in Compagnie Générale Maritime cited in note 57.

80. The assessment of indispensability is made within the actual context in which the agreement operates and must in particular take account of the structure of the market, the economic risks related to the agreement, and the incentives facing the parties. The more uncertain the success of the product covered by the agreement, the more a restriction may be required to ensure that the efficiencies will materialise. Restrictions may also be indispensable in order to align the incentives of the parties and ensure that they concentrate their efforts on the implementation of the agreement. A restriction may for instance be necessary in order to avoid hold-up problems once a substantial sunk investment has been made by one of the parties. Once for instance a supplier has made a substantial relationship-specific investment with a view to supplying a customer with an input, the supplier is locked into the customer. In order to avoid that ex post the customer exploits this dependence to obtain more favourable terms, it may be necessary to impose an obligation not to purchase the component from third parties or to purchase minimum quantities of the component from the supplier (77).

(77) See for more detail paragraph 116 of the Guidelines on Vertical Restraints cited in note 5.

81. In some cases a restriction may be indispensable only for a certain period of time, in which case the exception of Article 81(3) only applies during that period. In making this assessment it is necessary to take due account of the period of time required for the parties to achieve the efficiencies justifying the application of the exception rule (78). In cases where the benefits cannot be achieved without considerable investment, account must, in particular, be taken of the period of time required to ensure an adequate return on such investment, see also paragraph 44 above.

(78) See Joined Cases T-374/94 and others, European Night Services, [1998] ECR II-3141, paragraph 230.

82. These principles can be illustrated by the following hypothetical examples:

P produces and distributes frozen pizzas, holding 15% of the market in Member State X. Deliveries are made directly to retailers. Since most retailers have limited storage capacity, relatively frequent deliveries are required, leading to low capacity utilisation and use of relatively small vehicles.

T is a wholesaler of frozen pizzas and other frozen products, delivering to most of the same customers as P. The pizza products distributed by T hold 30% of the market. T has a fleet of larger vehicles and has excess capacity. P concludes an exclusive distribution agreement with T for Member State X and undertakes to ensure that distributors in other Member States will not sell into T's territory either actively or passively. T undertakes to advertise the products, survey consumer tastes and satisfaction rates and ensure delivery to retailers of all products within 24 hours. The agreement leads to a reduction in total distribution costs of 30% as capacity is better utilised and duplication of routes is eliminated. The agreement also leads to the provision of additional services to consumers. Restrictions on passive sales are hardcore restrictions under the block exemption regulation on vertical restraints (79) and can only be considered indispensable in exceptional circumstances. The established market position of T and the nature of the obligations imposed on it indicate this is not an exceptional case. The ban on active selling, on the other hand, is likely to be indispensable. T is likely to have less incentive to sell and advertise the P brand, if distributors in other Member States could sell actively in Member State X and thus get a free ride on the efforts of T. This is particularly so, as T also distributes competing brands and thus has the possibility of pushing more of the brands that are the least exposed to free riding.

S is a producer of carbonated soft drinks, holding 40% of the market. The nearest competitor holds 20%. S concludes supply agreements with customers accounting for 25% of demand, whereby they undertake to purchase exclusively from S for 5 years. S concludes agreements with other customers accounting for 15% of demand whereby they are granted quarterly target rebates, if their purchases exceed certain individually fixed targets. S claims that the agreements allow it to predict demand more accurately and thus to better plan production, reducing raw material storage and warehousing costs and avoiding supply shortages. Given the market position of S and the combined coverage of the restrictions, the restrictions are very unlikely to be considered indispensable. The exclusive purchasing obligation exceeds what is required to plan production and the same is true of the target rebate scheme. Predictability of demand can be achieved by less restrictive means. S could, for example, provide incentives for customers to order large quantities at a time by offering quantity rebates or by offering a rebate to customers that place firm orders in advance for delivery on specified dates.

(79) See Commission Regulation No 2790/1999 on the application of Article 81(3) of the Treaty on categories of vertical agreements and concerted practices (O.J. 1999 L 336, page 21).

3.4. Second condition of Article 81(3): Fair share for consumers

3.4.1. General remarks

83. According to the second condition of Article 81(3) consumers must receive a fair share of the efficiencies generated by the restrictive agreement.

84. The concept of «consumers» encompasses all direct or indirect users of the products covered by the agreement, including producers that use the products as an input, wholesalers, retailers and final consumers, i.e. natural persons who are acting for purposes which can be regarded as outside their trade or profession. In other words, consumers within the meaning of Article 81(3) are the customers of the parties to the agreement and subsequent purchasers. These customers can be undertakings as in the case of buyers of industrial machinery or an input for further processing or final consumers as for instance in the case of buyers of impulse ice-cream or bicycles.

85. The concept of «fair share» implies that the pass-on of benefits must at least compensate consumers for any actual or likely negative impact caused to them by the restriction of competition found under Article 81(1). In line with the overall objective of Article 81 to prevent anti-competitive agreements, the net effect of the agreement must at least be neutral from the point of view of those consumers directly or likely affected by the agreement (80). If such consumers are worse off following the agreement, the second condition of Article 81(3) is not fulfilled. The positive effects of an agreement must be balanced against and compensate for its negative effects on consumers (81). When that is the case consumers are not harmed by the agreement. Moreover, society as a whole benefits where the efficiencies lead either to fewer resources being used to produce the output consumed or to the production of more valuable products and thus to a more efficient allocation of resources.

(80) See in this respect the judgment in Consten and Grundig cited in note 21, where the Court of Justice held that the improvements within the meaning of the first condition of Article 81(3) must show appreciable objective advantages of such a character as to compensate for the disadvantages which they cause in the field of competition.

(81) It is recalled that positive and negative effects on consumers are in principle balanced within each relevant market (cf. paragraph 43 above).

86. It is not required that consumers receive a share of each and every efficiency gain identified under the first condition. It suffices that sufficient benefits are passed on to compensate for the negative effects of the restrictive agreement. In that case consumers obtain a fair share of the overall benefits (82). If a restrictive agreement is likely to lead to higher prices, consumers must be fully compensated through increased quality or other benefits. If not, the second condition of Article 81(3) is not fulfilled.

(82) See in this respect paragraph 48 of the Metro (I) judgment cited in note 54.

87. The decisive factor is the overall impact on consumers of the products within the relevant market and not the impact on individual members of this group of consumers (83). In some cases a certain period of time may be required before the efficiencies materialise. Until such time the agreement may have only negative effects. The fact that pass-on to the consumer occurs with a certain time lag does not in itself exclude the application of Article 81(3). However, the greater the time lag, the greater must be the efficiencies to compensate also for the loss to consumers during the period preceding the pass-on.

(83) See paragraph 163 of the judgment in Shaw cited in note 56.

88. In making this assessment it must be taken into account that the value of a gain for consumers in the future is not the same as a present gain for consumers. The value of saving 100 euro today is greater than the value of saving the same amount a year later. A gain for consumers in the future therefore does not fully compensate for a present loss to consumers of equal nominal size. In order to allow for an appropriate comparison of a present loss to consumers with a future gain to consumers, the value of future gains must be discounted. The discount rate applied must reflect the rate of inflation, if any, and lost interest as an indication of the lower value of future gains.

89. In other cases the agreement may enable the parties to obtain the efficiencies earlier than would otherwise be possible. In such circumstances it is necessary to take account of the likely negative impact on consumers within the relevant market once this lead-time has lapsed. If through the restrictive agreement the parties obtain a strong position on the market, they may be able to charge a significantly higher price than would otherwise have been the case. For the second condition of Article 81(3) to be satisfied the benefit to consumers of having earlier access to the products must be equally significant. This may for instance be the case where an agreement allows two tyre manufacturers to bring to market three years earlier a new substantially safer tyre but at the same time, by increasing their market power, allows them to raise prices by 5%. In such a case it is likely that having early access to a substantially improved product outweighs the price increase.

90. The second condition of Article 81(3) incorporates a sliding scale. The greater the restriction of competition found under Article 81(1) the greater must be the efficiencies and the pass-on to consumers. This sliding scale approach implies that if the restrictive effects of an agreement are relatively limited and the efficiencies are substantial it is likely that a fair share of the cost savings will be passed on to consumers. In such cases it is therefore normally not necessary to engage in a detailed analysis of the second condition of Article 81(3), provided that the three other conditions for the application of this provision are fulfilled.

91. If, on the other hand, the restrictive effects of the agreement are substantial and the cost savings are relatively insignificant, it is very unlikely that the second condition of Article 81(3) will be fulfilled. The impact of the restriction of competition depends on the intensity of the restriction and the degree of competition that remains following the agreement.

92. If the agreement has both substantial anti-competitive effects and substantial pro-competitive effects a careful analysis is required. In the application of the balancing test in such cases it must be taken into account that competition is an important long-term driver of efficiency and innovation. Undertakings that are not subject to effective competitive constraints – such as for instance dominant firms – have less incentive to maintain or build on the efficiencies. The more substantial the impact of the agreement on competition, the more likely it is that consumers will suffer in the long run.

93. The following two sections describe in more detail the analytical framework for assessing consumer pass-on of efficiency gains. The first section deals with cost efficiencies, whereas the section that follows covers other types of efficiencies such as new or improved products (qualitative efficiencies). The framework, which is developed in these two sections, is particularly important in cases where it is not immediately obvious that the competitive harms exceed the benefits to consumers or vice versa (84).

(84) In the following sections, for convenience the competitive harm is referred to in terms of higher prices; competitive harm could also mean lower quality, less variety or lower innovation than would otherwise have occurred.

94. In the application of the principles set out below the Commission will have regard to the fact that in many cases it is difficult to accurately calculate the consumer pass-on rate and other types of consumer pass-on. Undertakings are only required to substantiate their claims by providing estimates and other data to the extent reasonably possible, taking account of the circumstances of the individual case.

3.4.2. Pass-on and balancing of cost efficiencies

95. When markets, as is normally the case, are not perfectly competitive, undertakings are able to influence the market price to a greater or lesser extent by altering their output (85). They may also be able to price discriminate amongst customers.

(85) In perfectly competitive markets individual undertakings are price-takers. They sell their products at the market price, which is determined by overall supply and demand. The output of the individual undertaking is so small that any individual undertaking's change in output does not affect the market price.

96. Cost efficiencies may in some circumstances lead to increased output and lower prices for the affected consumers. If due to cost efficiencies the undertakings in question can increase profits by expanding output, consumer pass-on may occur. In assessing the extent to which cost efficiencies are likely to be passed on to consumers and the outcome of the balancing test contained in Article 81(3) the following factors are in particular taken into account:

(a) The characteristics and structure of the market,
(b) The nature and magnitude of the efficiency gains,
(c) The elasticity of demand, and
(d) The magnitude of the restriction of competition.

All factors must normally be considered. Since Article 81(3) only applies in cases where competition on the market is being appreciably restricted, see paragraph 24 above, there can be no presumption that residual competition will ensure that consumers receive a fair share of the benefits. However, the degree of competition remaining on the market and the nature of this competition influences the likelihood of pass-on.

97. The greater the degree of residual competition the more likely it is that individual undertakings will try to increase their sales by passing on cost efficiencies. If undertakings compete mainly on price and are not subject to significant capacity constraints, pass-on may occur relatively quickly. If competition is mainly on capacity and capacity adaptations occur with a certain time lag, pass-on will be slower. Pass-on is also likely to be slower when the market structure is conducive to tacit collusion (86). If competitors are likely to retaliate against an increase in output by one or more parties to the agreement, the incentive to increase output may be tempered, unless the competitive advantage conferred by the efficiencies is such that the undertakings concerned have an incentive to break away from the common policy adopted on the market by the members of the oligopoly. In other words, the efficiencies generated by the agreement may turn the undertakings concerned into so-called «mavericks» (87).

(86) Undertakings collude tacitly when in an oligopolistic market they are able to coordinate their action on the market without resorting to an explicit cartel agreement.

(87) This term refers to undertakings that constrain the pricing behaviour of other undertakings in the market who might otherwise have tacitly colluded.

98. The nature of the efficiency gains also plays an important role. According to economic theory undertakings maximise their profits by selling units of output until marginal revenue equals marginal cost. Marginal revenue is the change in total revenue resulting from selling an additional unit of output and marginal cost is the change in total cost resulting from producing that additional unit of output. It follows from this principle that as a general rule output and pricing decisions of a profit maximising undertaking are not determined by its fixed costs (i.e. costs that do not vary with the rate of production) but by its variable costs (i.e. costs that vary with the rate of production). After fixed costs are incurred and capacity is set, pricing and output decisions are determined by variable cost and demand conditions. Take for instance a situation in which two companies each produce two products on two production lines operating only at half their capacities. A specialisation agreement may allow the two undertakings to specialise in producing one of the two products and scrap their second production line for the other product. At the same time the specialisation may allow the companies to reduce variable input and stocking costs. Only the latter savings will have a direct effect on the pricing and output decisions of the undertakings, as they will influence the marginal costs of production. The scrapping by each undertaking of one of their production lines will not reduce their variable costs and will not have an impact on their production costs. It follows that undertakings may have a direct incentive to pass on to consumers in the form of higher output and lower prices efficiencies that reduce marginal costs, whereas they have no such direct incentive with regard to efficiencies that reduce fixed costs. Consumers are therefore more likely to receive a fair share of the cost efficiencies in the case of reductions in variable costs than they are in the case of reductions in fixed costs.

99. The fact that undertakings may have an incentive to pass on certain types of cost efficiencies does not imply that the pass-on rate will necessarily be 100%. The actual pass-on rate depends on the extent to which consumers respond to changes in price, i.e. the elasticity of demand. The greater the increase in demand caused by a decrease in price, the greater the pass-on rate. This follows from the fact that the greater the additional sales caused by a price reduction due to an increase in output the more likely it is that these sales will offset the loss of revenue caused by the lower price resulting from the increase in output. In the absence of price discrimination the lowering of prices affects all units sold by the undertaking, in which case marginal revenue is less than the price obtained for the marginal product. If the undertakings concerned are able to charge different prices to different customers, i.e. price discriminate, pass-on will normally only benefit price-sensitive consumers (88).

(88) The restrictive agreement may even allow the undertakings in question to charge a higher price to customers with a low elasticity of demand.

100. It must also be taken into account that efficiency gains often do not affect the whole cost structure of the undertakings concerned. In such event the impact on the price to consumers is reduced. If for example an agreement allows the parties to reduce production costs by 6%, but production costs only make up one third of the costs on the basis of which prices are determined, the impact on the product price is 2%, assuming that the full amount is passed-on.

101. Finally, and very importantly, it is necessary to balance the two opposing forces resulting from the restriction of competition and the cost efficiencies. On the one hand, any increase in market power caused by the restrictive agreement gives the undertakings concerned the ability and incentive to raise price. On the other hand, the types of cost efficiencies that are taken into account may give the undertakings concerned an incentive to reduce price, see paragraph 98 above. The effects of these two opposing forces must be balanced against each other. It is recalled in this regard that the consumer pass-on condition incorporates a sliding scale. When the agreement causes a substantial reduction in the competitive constraint facing the parties, extraordinarily large cost efficiencies are normally required for sufficient pass-on to occur.

3.4.3. Pass-on and balancing of other types of efficiencies

102. Consumer pass-on can also take the form of qualitative efficiencies such as new and improved products, creating sufficient value for consumers to compensate for the anticompetitive effects of the agreement, including a price increase.

103. Any such assessment necessarily requires value judgment. It is difficult to assign precise values to dynamic efficiencies of this nature. However, the fundamental objective of the assessment remains the same, namely to ascertain the overall impact of the agreement on the consumers within the relevant market. Undertakings claiming the benefit of Article 81(3) must substantiate that consumers obtain countervailing benefits (see in this respect paragraphs 57 and 86 above).

104. The availability of new and improved products constitutes an important source of consumer welfare. As long as the increase in value stemming from such improvements exceeds any harm from a maintenance or an increase in price caused by the restrictive agreement, consumers are better off than without the agreement and the consumer pass-on requirement of Article 81(3) is normally fulfilled. In cases where the likely effect of the agreement is to increase prices for consumers within the relevant market it must be carefully assessed whether the claimed efficiencies create real value for consumers in that market so as to compensate for the adverse effects of the restriction of competition.

3.5. Fourth condition of Article 81(3): No elimination of competition

105. According to the fourth condition of Article 81(3) the agreement must not afford the undertakings concerned the possibility of eliminating competition in respect of a substantial part of the products concerned. Ultimately the protection of rivalry and the competitive process is given priority over potentially pro-competitive efficiency gains which could result from restrictive agreements. The last condition of Article 81(3) recognises the fact that rivalry between undertakings is an essential driver of economic efficiency, including dynamic efficiencies in the shape of innovation. In other words, the ultimate aim of Article 81 is to protect the competitive process. When competition is eliminated the competitive process is brought to an end and short-term efficiency gains are outweighed by longer-term losses stemming inter alia from expenditures incurred by the incumbent to maintain its position (rent seeking), misallocation of resources, reduced innovation and higher prices.

106. The concept in Article 81(3) of elimination of competition in respect of a substantial part of the products concerned is an autonomous Community law concept specific to Article 81(3) (89). However, in the application of this concept it is necessary to take account of the relationship between Article 81 and Article 82. According to settled case law the application of Article 81(3) cannot prevent the application of Article 82 of the Treaty (90). Moreover, since Articles 81 and 82 both pursue the aim of maintaining effective competition on the market, consistency requires that Article 81(3) be interpreted as precluding any application of this provision to restrictive agreements that constitute an abuse of a dominant position (91) (92). However, not all restrictive agreements concluded by a dominant undertaking constitute an abuse of a dominant position. This is for instance the case where a dominant undertaking is party to a non-full function joint venture (93), which is found to be restrictive of competition but at the same time involves a substantial integration of assets.

(89) See Joined Cases T-191/98, T-212/98 and T-214/98, Atlantic Container Line (TACA), [2003] ECR II-..., paragraph 939, and Case T-395/94, Atlantic Container Line, [2002] ECR II-875, paragraph 330.

(90) See Joined Cases C-395/96 P and C-396/96 P, Compagnie maritime belge, [2000] ECR I-1365, paragraph 130. Similarly, the application of Article 81(3) does not prevent the application of the Treaty rules on the free movement of goods, services, persons and capital. These provisions are in certain circumstances applicable to agreements, decisions and concerted practices within the meaning of Article 81(1), see to that effect Case C-309/99, Wouters, [2002] ECR I-1577, paragraph 120.

(91) See in this respect Case T-51/89, Tetra Pak (I), [1990] ECR II-309, and Joined Cases T-191/98, T-212/98 and T-214/98, Atlantic Container Line (TACA), [2003] ECR II-..., paragraph 1456.

(92) This is how paragraph 135 of the Guidelines on vertical restraints and paragraphs 36, 71, 105, 134 and 155 of the Guidelines on horizontal cooperation agreements, cited in note 5, should be understood when they state that in principle restrictive agreements concluded by dominant undertakings cannot be exempted.

(93) Full function joint ventures, i.e. joint ventures that perform on a lasting basis all the functions of an autonomous economic entity, are covered by Council Regulation (EEC) N° 4064/89 on the control of concentrations between undertakings (O.J. 1990 L 257, p. 13).

107. Whether competition is being eliminated within the meaning of the last condition of Article 81(3) depends on the degree of competition existing prior to the agreement and on the impact of the restrictive agreement on competition, i.e. the reduction in competition that the agreement brings about. The more competition is already weakened in the market concerned, the slighter the further reduction required for competition to be eliminated within the meaning of Article 81(3). Moreover, the greater the reduction of competition caused by the agreement, the greater the likelihood that competition in respect of a substantial part of the products concerned risks being eliminated.

108. The application of the last condition of Article 81(3) requires a realistic analysis of the various sources of competition in the market, the level of competitive constraint that they impose on the parties to the agreement and the impact of the agreement on this competitive constraint. Both actual and potential competition must be considered.

109. While market shares are relevant, the magnitude of remaining sources of actual competition cannot be assessed exclusively on the basis of market share. More extensive qualitative and quantitative analysis is normally called for. The capacity of actual competitors to compete and their incentive to do so must be examined. If, for example, competitors face capacity constraints or have relatively higher costs of production their competitive response will necessarily be limited.

110. In the assessment of the impact of the agreement on competition it is also relevant to examine its influence on the various parameters of competition. The last condition for exception under Article 81(3) is not fulfilled, if the agreement eliminates competition in one of its most important expressions. This is particularly the case when an agreement eliminates price competition (94) or competition in respect of innovation and development of new products.

(94) See paragraph 21 of the judgment in Metro (I) cited in note 54.

111. The actual market conduct of the parties can provide insight into the impact of the agreement. If following the conclusion of the agreement the parties have implemented and maintained substantial price increases or engaged in other conduct indicative of the existence of a considerable degree of market power, it is an indication that the parties are not subject to any real competitive pressure and that competition has been eliminated with regard to a substantial part of the products concerned.

112. Past competitive interaction may also provide an indication of the impact of the agreement on future competitive interaction. An undertaking may be able to eliminate competition within the meaning of Article 81(3) by concluding an agreement with a competitor that in the past has been a «maverick» (95). Such an agreement may change the competitive incentives and capabilities of the competitor and thereby remove an important source of competition in the market.

(95) See paragraph 97 above.

113. In cases involving differentiated products, i.e. products that differ in the eyes of consumers, the impact of the agreement may depend on the competitive relationship between the products sold by the parties to the agreement. When undertakings offer differentiated products the competitive constraint that individual products impose on each other differs according to the degree of substitutability between them. It must therefore be considered what is the degree of substitutability between the products offered by the parties, i.e. what is the competitive constraint that they impose on each other. The more the products of the parties to the agreement are close substitutes the greater the likely restrictive effect of the agreement. In other words, the more substitutable the products the greater the likely change brought about by the agreement in terms of restriction of competition on the market and the more likely it is that competition in respect of a substantial part of the products concerned risks being eliminated.

114. While sources of actual competition are usually the most important, as they are most easily verified, sources of potential competition must also be taken into account. The assessment of potential competition requires an analysis of barriers to entry facing undertakings that are not already competing within the relevant market. Any assertions by the parties that there are low barriers to market entry must be supported by information identifying the sources of potential competition and the parties must also substantiate why these sources constitute a real competitive pressure on the parties.

115. In the assessment of entry barriers and the real possibility for new entry on a significant scale, it is relevant to examine, inter alia, the following:

(i) The regulatory framework with a view to determining its impact on new entry.

(ii) The cost of entry including sunk costs. Sunk costs are those that cannot be recovered if the entrant subsequently exits the market. The higher the sunk costs the higher the commercial risk for potential entrants.

(iii) The minimum efficient scale within the industry, i.e. the rate of output where average costs are minimised. If the

minimum efficient scale is large compared to the size of the market, efficient entry is likely to be more costly and risky.

(iv) The competitive strengths of potential entrants. Effective entry is particularly likely where potential entrants have access to at least as cost efficient technologies as the incumbents or other competitive advantages that allow them to compete effectively. When potential entrants are on the same or an inferior technological trajectory compared to the incumbents and possess no other significant competitive advantage entry is more risky and less effective.

(v) The position of buyers and their ability to bring onto the market new sources of competition. It is irrelevant that certain strong buyers may be able to extract more favourable conditions from the parties to the agreement than their weaker competitors (96). The presence of strong buyers can only serve to counter a prima facie finding of elimination of competition if it is likely that the buyers in question will pave the way for effective new entry.

(vi) The likely response of incumbents to attempted new entry. Incumbents may for example through past conduct have acquired a reputation of aggressive behaviour, having an impact on future entry.

(vii) The economic outlook for the industry may be an indicator of its longer-term attractiveness. Industries that are stagnating or in decline are less attractive candidates for entry than industries characterised by growth.

(viii) Past entry on a significant scale or the absence thereof.

(96) See in this respect Case T-228/97, Irish Sugar, [1999] ECR II-2969, paragraph 101.

116. The above principles can be illustrated by the following hypothetical examples, which are not intended to establish thresholds:

Firm A is brewer, holding 70% of the relevant market, comprising the sale of beer through cafés and other on-trade premises. Over the past 5 years A has increased its market share from 60%. There are four other competitors in the market, B, C, D and E with market shares of 10%, 10%, 5% and 5%. No new entry has occurred in the recent past and price changes implemented by A have generally been followed by competitors. A concludes agreements with 20% of the on-trade premises representing 40% of sales volumes whereby the contracting parties undertake to purchase beer only from A for a period of 5 years. The agreements raise the costs and reduce the revenues of rivals, which are foreclosed from the most attractive outlets. Given the market position of A, which has been strengthened in recent years, the absence of new entry and the already weak position of competitors it is likely that competition in the market is eliminated within the meaning of Article 81(3).

Shipping firms A, B, C, and D, holding collectively more than 70% of the relevant market, conclude an agreement whereby they agree to coordinate their schedules and their tariffs. Following the implementation of the agreement prices rise between 30% and 100%. There are four other suppliers, the largest holding about 14% of the relevant market. There has been no new entry in recent years and the parties to the agreement did not lose significant market share following the price increases. The existing competitors brought no significant new capacity to the market and no new entry occurred. In light of the market position of the parties and the absence of competitive response to their joint conduct it can reasonably be concluded that the parties to the agreement are not subject to real competitive pressures and that the agreement affords them the possibility of eliminating competition within the meaning of Article 81(3).

A is a producer of electric appliances for professional users with a market share of 65% of a relevant national market. B is a competing manufacturer with 5% market share which has developed a new type of motor that is more powerful while consuming less electricity. A and B conclude an agreement whereby they establish a production joint venture for the production of the new motor. B undertakes to grant an exclusive licence to the joint venture. The joint venture combines the new technology of B with the efficient manufacturing and quality control process of A. There is one other main competitor with 15% of the market. Another competitor with 5% market share has recently been acquired by C, a major international producer of competing electric appliances, which itself owns efficient technologies. C has thus far not been active on the market mainly due to the fact that local presence and servicing is desired by customers. Through the acquisition C gains access to the service organisation required to penetrate the market. The entry of C is likely to ensure that competition is not being eliminated.

Guidance on the Commission's enforcement priorities in applying Article 102 to abusive exclusionary conduct by dominant undertakings

(OJ C 45, 24 February 2009, p. 7)

1. Article 82 EC is now Article 102 TFEU.

I. INTRODUCTION

1. Article 82 of the Treaty establishing the European Community («Article 82») prohibits abuses of a dominant position. In accordance with the case-law, it is not in itself illegal for an undertaking to be in a dominant position and such a dominant undertaking is entitled to compete on the merits. However, the undertaking concerned has a special responsibility not to allow its conduct to impair genuine undistorted competition on the common market. Article 82 is the legal basis for a crucial component of competition policy and its effective enforcement helps markets to work better for the benefit of businesses and consumers. This is particularly important in the context of the wider objective of achieving an integrated internal market.

II. PURPOSE OF THIS DOCUMENT

2. This document sets out the enforcement priorities that will guide the Commission's action in applying Article 82 to exclusionary conduct by dominant undertakings. Alongside the Commission's specific enforcement decisions, it is intended to provide greater clarity and predictability as regards the general framework of analysis which the Commission employs in determining whether it should pursue cases concerning various forms of exclusionary conduct and to help undertakings better assess whether certain behaviour is likely to result in intervention by the Commission under Article 82.

3. This document is not intended to constitute a statement of the law and is without prejudice to the interpretation of Article 82 by the Court of justice or the Court of First Instance of the European Communities. In addition, the general framework set out in this document applies without prejudice to the possibility for the Commission to reject a complaint when it considers that a case lacks priority on grounds of lack of Community interest.

4. Article 82 applies to undertakings which hold a dominant position on one or more relevant markets. Such a position may be held by one undertaking (single dominance) or by two or more undertakings (collective dominance). This document only relates to abuses committed by an undertaking holding a single dominant position.

5. In applying Article 82 to exclusionary conduct by dominant undertakings, the Commission will focus on those types of conduct that are most harmful to consumers. Consumers benefit from competition through lower prices, better quality and a wider choice of new or improved goods and services. The Commission, therefore, will direct its enforcement to ensuring that markets function properly and that consumers benefit from the efficiency and productivity which result from effective competition between undertakings.

6. The emphasis of the Commission's enforcement activity in relation to exclusionary conduct is on safeguarding the competitive process in the internal market and ensuring that undertakings which hold a dominant position do not exclude their competitors by other means than competing on the merits of the products or services they provide. In doing so the Commission is mindful that what really matters is protecting an effective competitive process and not simply protecting competitors. This may well mean that competitors who deliver less to consumers in terms of price, choice, quality and innovation will leave the market.

7. Conduct which is directly exploitative of consumers, for example charging excessively high prices or certain behaviour that undermines the efforts to achieve an integrated internal market, is also liable to infringe Article 82. The Commission may decide to intervene in relation to such conduct, in particular where the protection of consumers and the proper functioning of the internal market cannot otherwise be adequately ensured. For the purpose of providing guidance on its enforcement priorities the Commission at this stage limits itself to exclusionary conduct and in, particular, certain specific types of exclusionary conduct which, based on its experience, appear to be the most common.

8. In applying the general enforcement principles set out in this Communication, the Commission will take into account the specific facts and circumstances of each case. For example, in cases involving regulated markets, the Commission will take into account the specific regulatory environment in conducting its assessment (1). The Commission may therefore adapt the approach set out in this Communication to the extent that this would appear to be reasonable and appropriate in a given case.

(1) See for instance paragraph 82.

III. GENERAL APPROACH TO EXCLUSIONARY CONDUCT

A. Market power

9. The assessment of whether an undertaking is in a dominant position and of the degree of market power it holds is a first step in the application of Article 82. According to the case-law, holding a dominant position confers a special responsibility on the undertaking concerned, the scope of which must be considered in the light of the specific circumstances of each case (2).

(2) Case 322/81 *Nederlandsche Banden Industrie Michelin (Michelin I) v Commission* (1983) ECR 3461, paragraph 57; Case T-83/91 *Tetra Pak v Commission (Tetra Pak II)* (1993) ECR II-755, paragraph 114; Case T-111/96 *ITT Promedia v Commission* (1998) ECR II-2937, paragraph 139; Case T-228/97 *Irish Sugar v Commission* (1999) ECR II-2969, paragraph 112; and Case T-203/01 *Michelin v Commission (Michelin II)* (2003) ECR II-4071, paragraph 97.

10. Dominance has been defined under Community law as a position of economic strength enjoyed by an undertaking, which enables it to prevent effective competition being maintained on a relevant market, by affording it the power to behave to an appreciable extent independently of its competitors, its customers and ultimately of consumers (3). This notion of independence is related to the degree of competitive constraint exerted on the undertaking in question. Dominance entails that these competitive constraints are not sufficiently effective and hence that the undertaking in question enjoys substantial market power over a period of time. This means that the undertaking's decisions are largely insensitive to the actions and reactions of competitors, customers and, ultimately, consumers. The Commission may consider that effective competitive constraints are absent even if some actual or potential competition remains (4). In general, a dominant position derives from a combination of several factors which, taken separately, are not necessarily determinative (5).

(3) See Case 27/76 *United Brands Company and United Brands Continentaal v Commission* (1978) ECR 207, paragraph 65; Case 85/76 *Hoffmann-La Roche & Co. v Commission* (1979) ECR 461, paragraph 38.

(4) See Case 27/76 *United Brands Company and United Brands Continentaal v Commission* (1978) ECR 207, paragraphs 113 to 121; Case T-395/94 *Atlantic Container Line and Others v Commission* (2002) ECR II-875, paragraph 330.

(5) Case 27/76 *United Brands and United Brands Continentaal v Commission* (1978) ECR 207, paragraphs 65 and 66; Case C-250/92 *Gøttrup-Klim e.a. Grovvareforeninger v Dansk Landbrugs Grovvareselskab* (1994) ECR I-5641, paragraph 47; Case T-30/89 *Hilti v Commission* (1991) ECR II-1439, paragraph 90.

11. The Commission considers that an undertaking which is capable of profitably increasing prices above the competitive level for a significant period of time does not face sufficiently effective competitive constraints and can thus generally be regarded as dominant (6). In this Communication, the expression «increase prices» includes the power to maintain prices above the competitive level and is used as shorthand for the various ways in which the parameters of competition – such as prices, output, innovation, the variety or quality of goods or services – can be influenced to the advantage of the dominant undertaking and to the detriment of consumers (7).

(6) What is a significant period of time will depend on the product and on the circumstances of the market in question, but normally a period of two years will be sufficient.

(7) Accounting profitability may be a poor proxy for the exercise of market power. See to that effect Case 27/76 *United Brands Company and United Brands Continentaal v Commission* (1978) ECR 207, paragraph 126.

12. The assessment of dominance will take into account the competitive structure of the market, and in particular the following factors:
– constraints imposed by the existing supplies from, and the position on the market of, actual competitors (the market position of the dominant undertaking and its competitors),
– constraints imposed by the credible threat of future expansion by actual competitors or entry by potential competitors (expansion and entry),
– constraints imposed by the bargaining strength of the undertaking's customers (countervailing buyer power).

(a) Market position of the dominant undertaking and its competitors

13. Market shares provide a useful first indication for the Commission of the market structure and of the relative importance of the various undertakings active on the market (8). However, the Commission will interpret market shares in the light of the relevant market conditions, and in particular of the dynamics of the market and of the extent to which products are differentiated. The trend or development of market shares over time may also be taken into account in volatile or bidding markets.

(8) Case 85/76 *Hoffmann-La Roche & Co. v Commission* (1979) ECR 461, paragraph 39-41; Case C-62/86 *AKZO v Commission* (1991) ECR I-3359, paragraph 60; Case T-30/89 *Hilti v Commission* (1991) ECR II-1439, paragraphs 90, 91 and 92; Case T-340/03 *France Télécom v Commission* (2007) ECR II-107, paragraph 100.

14. The Commission considers that low market shares are generally a good proxy for the absence of substantial market power. The Commission's experience suggests that dominance is not likely if the undertaking's market share is below 40% in the relevant market. However, there may be specific cases below that threshold where competitors are not in a position to constrain effectively the conduct of a dominant undertaking, for example where they face serious capacity limitations. Such cases may also deserve attention on the part of the Commission.

15. Experience suggests that the higher the market share and the longer the period of time over which it is held, the more likely it is that it constitutes an important preliminary indication of the existence of a dominant position and, in certain circumstances, of possible serious effects of abusive conduct, justifying an intervention by the Commission under Article 82 (9). However, as a general rule, the Commission will not come to a final conclusion as to whether or not a case should be pursued without examining all the factors which may be sufficient to constrain the behaviour of the undertaking.

(9) As to the relationship between the degree of dominance and the finding of abuse, see Joined Cases C-395/96 P and C-396/96 P *Compagnie Maritime Belge transports, Compagnie Maritime Belge and Dafra-Lines v Commission* (2000) ECR I-1365, paragraph 119; Case T-228/97 *Irish Sugar v Commission* (1999) ECR II-2969, paragraph 186.

(b) Expansion or entry

16. Competition is a dynamic process and an assessment of the competitive constraints on an undertaking cannot be based solely on the existing market situation. The potential impact of expansion by actual competitors or entry by potential competitors, including the threat of such expansion or entry, is also relevant. An undertaking can be deterred from increasing prices if expansion or entry is likely, timely and sufficient. For the Commission to consider expansion or entry likely it must be sufficiently profitable for the competitor or entrant, taking into account factors such as the barriers to expansion or entry, the likely reactions of the allegedly dominant undertaking and other competitors, and the risks and costs of failure. For expansion or entry to be considered timely, it must be sufficiently swift to deter or defeat the exercise of substantial market power. For expansion or entry to be considered sufficient, it cannot be simply small-scale entry, for example into some market niche, but must be of such a magnitude as to be able to deter any attempt to increase prices by the putatively dominant undertaking in the relevant market.

17. Barriers to expansion or entry can take various forms. They may be legal barriers, such as tariffs or quotas, or they may take the form of advantages specifically enjoyed by the dominant undertaking, such as economies of scale and scope, privileged access to essential inputs or natural resources, important technologies (10) or an established distribution and sales network (11). They may also include costs and other impediments, for instance resulting from network effects, faced by customers in switching to a new supplier. The dominant undertaking's own conduct may also create barriers to entry, for example where it has made significant investments which entrants or competitors would have to match (12), or where it has concluded long-term contracts with its customers that have appreciable foreclosing effects. Persistently high market shares may be indicative of the existence of barriers to entry and expansion.

(10) Case T-30/89 *Hilti v Commission* (1991) ECR II-1439, paragraph 19.

(11) Case 85/76 *Hoffmann-La Roche v Commission* (1979) ECR 461, paragraph 48.

(12) Case 27/76 *United Brands v Commission* (1978) ECR 207, paragraph 91.

(c) Countervailing buyer power

18. Competitive constraints may be exerted not only by actual or potential competitors but also by customers. Even an undertaking with a high market share may not be able to act to an appreciable extent independently of customers with sufficient bargaining strength (13). Such countervailing buying power may result from the customers' size or their commercial significance for the dominant undertaking, and their ability to switch quickly to competing suppliers, to promote new entry or to vertically integrate, and to credibly threaten to do so. If countervailing power is of a sufficient magnitude, it may deter or defeat an attempt by the undertaking to profitably increase prices. Buyer power may not, however, be considered a sufficiently effective constraint if it only ensures that a particular or limited segment of customers is shielded from the market power of the dominant undertaking.

(13) See Case T-228/97 *Irish Sugar v Commission* (1999) ECR II-2969, paragraphs 97 to 104, in which the Court of First Instance considered whether the alleged lack of independence of the undertaking vis-à-vis its customers should be seen as an exceptional circumstance preventing the finding of a dominant position in spite of the fact that the undertaking was responsible for a very large part of the sales recorded on the industrial sugar market in Ireland.

B. Foreclosure leading to consumer harm («anti-competitive foreclosure»)

19. The aim of the Commission's enforcement activity in relation to exclusionary conduct is to ensure that dominant undertakings do not impair effective competition by foreclosing their competitors in an anti-competitive way, thus having an adverse impact on consumer welfare, whether in the form of higher price levels than would have otherwise prevailed or in some other form such as limiting quality or reducing consumer choice. In this document the term "anti-competitive foreclosure" is used to describe a situation where effective access of actual or potential competitors to supplies or markets is hampered or eliminated as a result of the conduct of the dominant undertaking whereby the dominant undertaking is likely to be in a position to profitably increase prices (14) to the detriment of consumers. The identification of likely consumer harm can rely on qualitative and, where possible and appropriate, quantitative evidence. The Commission will address such anti-competitive foreclosure either at the intermediate level or at the level of final consumers, or at both levels (15).

(14) For the meaning of the expression «increase price» see paragraph 11.

(15) The concept of «consumers» encompasses all direct or indirect users of the products affected by the conduct, including intermediate producers that use the products as an input, as well as distributors and final consumers both of the immediate product and of products provided by intermediate producers. Where intermediate users are actual or potential competitors of the dominant undertaking, the assessment focuses on the effects of the conduct on users further downstream.

20. The Commission will normally intervene under Article 82 where, on the basis of cogent and convincing evidence, the allegedly abusive conduct is likely to lead to anti-competitive foreclosure. The Commission considers the following factors to be generally relevant to such an assessment:

– the position of the dominant undertaking: in general, the stronger the dominant position, the higher the likelihood that conduct protecting that position leads to anti-competitive foreclosure,

– the conditions on the relevant market: this includes the conditions of entry and expansion, such as the existence of economies of scale and/or scope and network effects. Economies of scale mean that competitors are less likely to enter or stay in the market if the dominant undertaking forecloses a significant part of the relevant market. Similarly, the conduct may allow the dominant undertaking to «tip» a market characterised by network effects in its favour or to further entrench its position on such a market. Likewise, if entry barriers in the upstream and/or downstream market are significant, this means that it may be costly for competitors to overcome possible foreclosure through vertical integration,

– the position of the dominant undertaking's competitors: this includes the importance of competitors for the maintenance of effective competition. A specific competitor may play a significant competitive role even if it only holds a small market share compared to other competitors. It may, for example, be the closest competitor to the dominant undertaking, be a particularly innovative competitor, or have the reputation of systematically cutting prices. In its assessment, the Commission may also consider in appropriate cases, on the basis of information available, whether there are realistic, effective and timely counter-strategies that competitors would be likely to deploy,

– the position of the customers or input suppliers: this may include consideration of the possible selectivity of the conduct in question. The dominant undertaking may apply the practice only to selected customers or input suppliers who may be of particular importance for the entry or expansion of competitors, thereby enhancing the likelihood of anti-competitive foreclosure (16). In the case of customers, they may, for example, be the ones most likely to respond to offers from alternative suppliers, they may represent a particular means of distributing the product that would be suitable for a new entrant, they may be situated in a geographic area well suited to new entry or they may be likely to influence the behaviour of other customers. In the case of input suppliers, those with whom the dominant undertaking has concluded exclusive supply arrangements may be the ones most likely to respond to requests by customers who are competitors of the dominant undertaking in a downstream market, or may produce a grade of the product – or produce at a location – particularly suitable for a new entrant. Any strategies at the disposal of the customers or input suppliers which could help to counter the conduct of the dominant undertaking will also be considered,

– the extent of the allegedly abusive conduct: in general, the higher the percentage of total sales in the relevant market affected by the conduct, the longer its duration, and the more regularly it has been applied, the greater is the likely foreclosure effect,

– possible evidence of actual foreclosure: if the conduct has been in place for a sufficient period of time, the market performance of the dominant undertaking and its competitors may provide direct evidence of anti-competitive foreclosure. For reasons attributable to the allegedly abusive conduct, the market share of the dominant undertaking may have risen or a decline in market share may have been slowed. For similar reasons, actual competitors may have been marginalised or may have exited, or potential competitors may have tried to enter and failed,

– direct evidence of any exclusionary strategy: this includes internal documents which contain direct evidence of a strategy to exclude competitors, such as a detailed plan to engage in certain conduct in order to exclude a competitor, to prevent entry or to pre-empt the emergence of a market, or evidence of concrete threats of exclusionary action. Such direct evidence may be helpful in interpreting the dominant undertaking's conduct.

(16) Case T-228/97 *Irish Sugar v Commission* (1999) ECR II-2969, paragraph 188.

21. When pursuing a case the Commission will develop the analysis of the general factors mentioned in paragraph 20, together with the more specific factors described in the sections dealing with certain types of exclusionary conduct, and any other factors which it may consider to be appropriate. This assessment will usually be made by comparing the actual or likely future situation in the relevant market (with the dominant undertaking's conduct in place) with an appropriate counterfactual, such as the simple absence of the conduct in question or with another realistic alternative scenario, having regard to established business practices.

22. There may be circumstances where it is not necessary for the Commission to carry out a detailed assessment before concluding that the conduct in question is likely to result in consumer harm. If it appears that the conduct can only raise obstacles to competition and that it creates no efficiencies, its anti-competitive effect may be inferred. This could be the case, for instance, if the dominant undertaking prevents its customers from testing the products of competitors or provides financial incentives to its customers on condition that they do not test such products, or pays a distributor or a customer to delay the introduction of a competitor's product.

C. Price-based exclusionary conduct

23. The considerations in paragraphs 23 to 27 apply to price-based exclusionary conduct. Vigorous price competition is generally beneficial to consumers. With a view to preventing anti-competitive foreclosure, the Commission will normally only intervene where the conduct concerned has already been or is capable of hampering competition from competitors which are considered to be as efficient as the dominant undertaking (17).

(17) Case 62/86 *AKZO Chemie v Commission* (1991) ECR I-3359, paragraph 72: in relation to pricing below average total cost (ATC) the Court of Justice stated: «Such prices can drive from the market undertakings which are perhaps as efficient as the dominant undertaking but which, because of their smaller financial resources, are incapable of withstanding the competition waged against them». See also Judgment of 10 April 2008 in Case T-271/03 *Deutsche Telekom v Commission* not yet reported, paragraph 194.

24. However, the Commission recognises that in certain circumstances a less efficient competitor may also exert a constraint which should be taken into account when considering whether particular price-based conduct leads to anti-competitive foreclosure. The Commission will take a dynamic view of that constraint, given that in the absence of an abusive practice such a competitor may benefit from demand-related advantages, such as network and learning effects, which will tend to enhance its efficiency.

25. In order to determine whether even a hypothetical competitor as efficient as the dominant undertaking would be likely to be foreclosed by the conduct in question, the Commission will examine economic data relating to cost and sales prices, and in particular whether the dominant undertaking is engaging in below-cost pricing. This will require that sufficiently reliable data be available. Where available, the Commission will use information on the costs of the dominant undertaking itself. If reliable information on those costs is not available, the Commission may decide to use the cost data of competitors or other comparable reliable data.

26. The cost benchmarks that the Commission is likely to use are average avoidable cost (A.A.C.) and long-run average incremental cost (L.R.A.I.C.) (18). Failure to cover A.A.C. indicates that the dominant undertaking is sacrificing profits in the short term and that an equally efficient competitor cannot serve the targeted customers without incurring a loss. L.R.A.I.C. is usually above A.A.C. because, in contrast to A.A.C. (which only includes fixed costs if incurred during the period under examination), L.R.A.I.C. includes product specific fixed costs made before the period in which allegedly abusive conduct took place. Failure to cover L.R.A.I.C. indicates that the dominant undertaking is not recovering all the (attributable) fixed costs of producing the good or service in question and that an equally efficient competitor could be foreclosed from the market (19).

(18) Average avoidable cost is the average of the costs that could have been avoided if the company had not produced a discrete amount of (extra) output, in this case the amount allegedly the subject of abusive conduct. In most cases, A.A.C. and the average variable cost (A.V.C.) will be the same, as it is often only variable costs that can be avoided. Long-run average incremental cost is the average of all the (variable and fixed) costs that a company incurs to produce a particular product. L.R.A.I.C. and average total cost (A.T.C.) are good proxies for each other, and are the same in the case of single product undertakings. If multi-product undertakings have economies of scope, L.R.A.I.C. would be below A.T.C. for each individual product, as true common costs are not taken into account in L.R.A.I.C. In the case of multiple products, any costs that could have been avoided by not producing a particular product or range are not considered to be common costs. In situations where common costs are significant, they may have to be taken into account when assessing the ability to foreclose equally efficient competitors.

(19) In order to apply these cost benchmarks it may also be necessary to look at revenues and costs of the dominant company and its competitors in a wider context. It may not be sufficient to only assess whether the price or revenue covers the costs for the product in question, but it may be necessary to look at incremental revenues in case the dominant company's conduct in question negatively affects its revenues in other markets or of other products. Similarly, in the case of two sided markets it may be necessary to look at revenues and costs of both sides at the same time.

27. If the data clearly suggest that an equally efficient competitor can compete effectively with the pricing conduct of the dominant undertaking, the Commission will, in principle, infer that the dominant undertaking's pricing conduct is not likely to have an adverse impact on effective competition, and thus on consumers, and will therefore be unlikely to intervene. If, on the contrary, the data suggest that the price charged by the dominant undertaking has the potential to foreclose equally efficient competitors, then the Commission will integrate this in the general assessment of anti-competitive foreclosure (see section B above), taking into account other relevant quantitative and/or qualitative evidence.

D. Objective necessity and efficiencies

28. In the enforcement of Article 82, the Commission will also examine claims put forward by a dominant undertaking that its conduct is justified (20). A dominant undertaking may do so either by demonstrating that its conduct is objectively necessary or by demonstrating that its conduct produces substantial efficiencies which outweigh any anti-competitive effects on consumers. In this context, the Commission will assess whether the conduct in question is indispensable and proportionate to the goal allegedly pursued by the dominant undertaking.

(20) See Case 27/76 *United Brands v Commission* (1978) ECR 207, paragraph 184; Case 311/84 *Centre belge d'études de marché – Télémarketing (C.B.E.M.) v Compagnie luxembourgeoise de télédiffusion (C.L.T.) and information publicité Benelux (I.P.B.)* (1985) ECR 3261, paragraph 27; Case T-30/89 *Hilti v Commission* (1991) ECR II-1439, paragraphs 102 to 119; Case T-83/91 *Tetra Pak International v Commission (Tetra Pak II)* (1994) ECR II-755, paragraphs 136 and 207; Case C-95/04 P *British Airways v Commission* (2007) ECR I-2331, paragraphs 69 and 86.

29. The question of whether conduct is objectively necessary and proportionate must be determined on the basis of factors external to the dominant undertaking. Exclusionary conduct may, for example, be considered objectively necessary for health or safety reasons related to the nature of the product in question. However, proof of whether conduct of this kind is objectively necessary must take into account that it is normally the task of public authorities to set and enforce public health and safety standards. It is not the task of a dominant undertaking to take steps on its own initiative to exclude products which it regards, rightly or wrongly, as dangerous or inferior to its own product (21).

(21) See, for instance, Case T-30/89 *Hilti v Commission* (1991) ECR II-1439, paragraph 118-119; Case T-83/91 *Tetra Pak International v Commission (Tetra Pak II)* (1994) ECR II-755, paragraphs 83 and 84 and 138.

30. The Commission considers that a dominant undertaking may also justify conduct leading to foreclosure of competitors on the ground of efficiencies that are sufficient to guarantee that no net harm to consumers is likely to arise.

In this context, the dominant undertaking will generally be expected to demonstrate, with a sufficient degree of probability, and on the basis of verifiable evidence, that the following cumulative conditions are fulfilled (22):
– the efficiencies have been, or are likely to be, realised as a result of the conduct. They may, for example, include technical improvements in the quality of goods, or a reduction in the cost of production or distribution,
– the conduct is indispensable to the realisation of those efficiencies: there must be no less anti-competitive alternatives to the conduct that are capable of producing the same efficiencies,
– the likely efficiencies brought about by the conduct outweigh any likely negative effects on competition and consumer welfare in the affected markets,
– the conduct does not eliminate effective competition, by removing all or most existing sources of actual or potential competition. Rivalry between undertakings is an essential driver of economic efficiency, including dynamic efficiencies in the form of innovation. In its absence the dominant undertaking will lack adequate incentives to continue to create and pass on efficiency gains. Where there is no residual competition and no foreseeable threat of entry, the protection of rivalry and the competitive process outweighs possible efficiency gains. In the Commission's view, exclusionary conduct which maintains, creates or strengthens a market position approaching that of a monopoly can normally not be justified on the grounds that it also creates efficiency gains.

(22) See, in the different context of Article 81, the Communication from the Commission – Notice – Guidelines on the application of Article 81(3) of the Treaty (O.J. C 101, 27.4.2004, p. 97).

31. It is incumbent upon the dominant undertaking to provide all the evidence necessary to demonstrate that the conduct concerned is objectively justified. It then falls to the Commission to make the ultimate assessment of whether the conduct concerned is not objectively necessary and, based on a weighing-up of any apparent anti-competitive effects against any advanced and substantiated efficiencies, is likely to result in consumer harm.

IV. SPECIFIC FORMS OF ABUSE

A. Exclusive dealing

32. A dominant undertaking may try to foreclose its competitors by hindering them from selling to customers through use of exclusive purchasing obligations or rebates, together referred to as exclusive dealing (23). This section sets out the circumstances which are most likely to prompt an intervention by the Commission in respect of exclusive dealing arrangements entered into by dominant undertakings.

(23) The notion of exclusive dealing also includes exclusive supply obligations or incentives with the same effect, whereby the dominant undertaking tries to foreclose its competitors by hindering them from purchasing from suppliers. The Commission considers that such input foreclosure is in principle liable to result in anti-competitive foreclosure if the exclusive supply obligation or incentive ties most of the efficient input suppliers and customers competing with the dominant undertaking are unable to find alternative efficient sources of input supply.

(a) Exclusive purchasing

33. An exclusive purchasing obligation requires a customer on a particular market to purchase exclusively or to a large extent only from the dominant undertaking. Certain other obligations, such as stocking requirements, which appear to fall short of requiring exclusive purchasing, may in practice lead to the same effect (24).

(24) Case T-65/98 Van den Bergh Foods v Commission (2003) ECR II-4653. In this case the obligation to use coolers exclusively for the products of the dominant undertaking was considered to lead to outlet exclusivity.

34. In order to convince customers to accept exclusive purchasing, the dominant undertaking may have to compensate them, in whole or in part, for the loss in competition resulting from the exclusivity. Where such compensation is given, it may be in the individual interest of a customer to enter into an exclusive purchasing obligation with the dominant undertaking. But it would be wrong to conclude automatically from this that all exclusive purchasing obligations, taken together, are beneficial for customers overall, including those currently not purchasing from the dominant undertaking, and the final consumers. The Commission will focus its attention on those cases where it is likely that consumers as a whole will not benefit. This will, in particular, be the case if there are many customers and the exclusive purchasing obligations of the dominant undertaking, taken together, have the effect of preventing the entry or expansion of competing undertakings.

35. In addition to the factors mentioned in paragraph 20, the following factors will generally be of particular relevance in determining whether the Commission will intervene in respect of exclusive purchasing arrangements.

36. The capacity for exclusive purchasing obligations to result in anti-competitive foreclosure arises in particular where, without the obligations, an important competitive constraint is exercised by competitors who either are not yet present in the market at the time the obligations are concluded, or who are not in a position to compete for the full supply of the customers. Competitors may not be able to compete for an individual customer's entire demand because the dominant undertaking is an unavoidable trading partner at least for part of the demand on the market, for instance because its brand is a «must stock item» preferred by many final consumers or because the capacity constraints on the other suppliers are such that a part of demand can only be provided for by the dominant supplier (25). If competitors can compete on equal terms for each individual customer's entire demand, exclusive purchasing obligations are generally unlikely to hamper effective competition unless the switching of supplier by customers is rendered difficult due to the duration of the exclusive purchasing obligation. In general, the longer the duration of the obligation, the greater the likely foreclosure effect. However, if the dominant undertaking is an unavoidable trading partner for all or most customers, even an exclusive purchasing obligation of short duration can lead to anti-competitive foreclosure.

(25) Case T-65/98 Van den Bergh Foods v Commission (2003) ECR II-4653, paragraphs 104 and 156.

(b) Conditional rebates

37. Conditional rebates are rebates granted to customers to reward them for a particular form of purchasing behaviour. The usual nature of a conditional rebate is that the customer is given a rebate if its purchases over a defined reference period exceed a certain threshold, the rebate being granted either on all purchases (retroactive rebates) or only on those made in excess of those required to achieve the threshold (incremental rebates). Conditional rebates are not an uncommon practice. Undertakings may offer such rebates in order to attract more demand, and as such they may stimulate demand and benefit consumers. However, such rebates – when granted by a dominant undertaking – can also have actual or potential foreclosure effects similar to exclusive purchasing obligations. Conditional rebates can have such effects without necessarily entailing a sacrifice for the dominant undertaking (26).

(26) In this regard, the assessment of conditional rebates differs from that of predation, which always entails a sacrifice.

38. In addition to the factors already mentioned in paragraph 20, the following factors are of particular importance to the Commission in determining whether a given system of conditional rebates is liable to result in anti-competitive foreclosure and, consequently, will be part of the Commission's enforcement priorities.

39. As with exclusive purchasing obligations, the likelihood of anti-competitive foreclosure is higher where competitors are not able to compete on equal terms for the entire demand of each individual customer. A conditional rebate granted by a dominant undertaking may enable it to use the «non contestable» portion of the demand of each customer (that is to say, the amount that would be purchased by the customer from the dominant undertaking in any event) as leverage to decrease the price to be paid for the «contestable» portion of demand (that is to say, the amount for which the customer may prefer and be able to find substitutes) (27).

(27) See Case T-203/01 *Michelin v Commission (Michelin II)* (2003) ECR II-4071, paragraphs 162 and 163. See also Case T-219/99 *British Airways v Commission* (2003) ECR II-5917, paragraphs 277 and 278.

40. In general terms, retroactive rebates may foreclose the market significantly, as they may make it less attractive for customers to switch small amounts of demand to an alternative supplier, if this would lead to loss of the retroactive rebates (28). The potential foreclosing effect of retroactive rebates is in principle strongest on the last purchased unit of the product before the threshold is exceeded. However, what is in the Commission's view relevant for an assessment of the loyalty enhancing effect of a rebate is not simply the effect on competition to provide the last individual unit, but the foreclosing effect of the rebate system on (actual or potential) competitors of the dominant supplier. The higher the rebate as a percentage of the total price and the higher the threshold, the greater the inducement below the threshold and, therefore, the stronger the likely foreclosure of actual or potential competitors.

(28) Case 322/81 *Nederlandsche Banden Industrie Michelin v Commission (Michelin I)* (1983) ECR 3461, paragraphs 70 to 73.

41. When applying the methodology explained in paragraphs 23 to 27, the Commission intends to investigate, to the extent that the data are available and reliable, whether the rebate system is capable of hindering expansion or entry even by competitors that are equally efficient by making it more difficult for them to supply part of the requirements of individual customers. In this context the Commission will estimate what price a competitor would have to offer in order to compensate the customer for the loss of the conditional rebate if the latter would switch part of its demand («the relevant range») away from the dominant undertaking. The effective price that the competitor will have to match is not the average price of the dominant undertaking, but the normal (list) price less the rebate the customer loses by switching, calculated over the relevant range of sales and in the relevant period of time. The Commission will take into account the margin of error that may be caused by the uncertainties inherent in this kind of analysis.

42. The relevant range over which to calculate the effective price in a particular case depends on the specific facts of each case and on whether the rebate is incremental or retroactive. For incremental rebates, the relevant range is normally the incremental purchases that are being considered. For retroactive rebates, it will generally be relevant to assess in the specific market context how much of a customer's purchase requirements can realistically be switched to a competitor (the «contestable share» or «contestable portion"). If it is likely that customers would be willing and able to switch large amounts of demand to a (potential) competitor relatively quickly, the relevant range is likely to be relatively large. If, on the other hand, it is likely that customers would only be willing or able to switch small amounts incrementally, then the relevant range will be relatively small. For existing competitors their capacity to expand sales to customers and the fluctuations in those sales over time may also provide an indication of the relevant range. For potential competitors, an assessment of the scale at which a new entrant would realistically be able to enter may be undertaken, where possible. It may be possible to take the historical growth pattern of new entrants in the same or in similar markets as an indication of a realistic market share of a new entrant (29).

(29) The relevant range will be estimated on the basis of data which may have varying degrees of precision. The Commission will take this into account in drawing any conclusions regarding the dominant undertaking's ability to foreclose equally efficient competitors. It may also be useful to calculate how big a share of customers' requirements on average the entrant should capture as a minimum so that the effective price is at least as high as the L.R.A.I.C. of the dominant company. In a number of cases the size of this share, when compared with the actual market shares of competitors and their shares of the customers' requirements, may make it clear whether the rebate scheme is capable to have an anti-competitive foreclosure effect.

43. The lower the estimated effective price over the relevant range is compared to the average price of the dominant supplier, the stronger the loyalty-enhancing effect. However, as long as the effective price remains consistently above the L.R.A.I.C. of the dominant undertaking, this would normally allow an equally efficient competitor to compete profitably notwithstanding the rebate. In those circumstances the rebate is normally not capable of foreclosing in an anti-competitive way.

44. Where the effective price is below A.A.C., as a general rule the rebate scheme is capable of foreclosing even equally efficient competitors. Where the effective price is between A.A.C. and L.R.A.I.C., the Commission will investigate whether other factors point to the conclusion that entry or expansion even by equally efficient competitors is likely to be affected. In this context, the Commission will investigate whether and to what extent competitors have realistic and effective counterstrategies at their disposal, for instance their capacity to also use a «non contestable» portion of their buyers' demand as leverage to decrease the price for the relevant range. Where competitors do not have such counterstrategies at their disposal, the Commission will consider that the rebate scheme is capable of foreclosing equally efficient competitors.

45. As indicated in paragraph 27, this analysis will be integrated in the general assessment, taking into account other relevant quantitative or qualitative evidence. It is normally important to consider whether the rebate system is applied with an individualised or a standardised threshold. An individualised threshold – one based on a percentage of the total requirements of the customer or an individualised volume target – allows the dominant supplier to set the threshold at such a level as to make it difficult for customers to switch suppliers, thereby creating a maximum loyalty enhancing effect (30). By contrast, a standardised volume threshold – where the threshold is the same for all or a group of customers – may be too high for some smaller customers and/or too low for larger customers to have a loyalty enhancing effect. If, however, it can be established that a standardised volume threshold approximates the requirements of an appreciable proportion of customers, the Commission is likely to consider that such a standardised system of rebates may produce anti-competitive foreclosure effects.

(30) See Case 85/76 *Hoffmann-La Roche & Co. v Commission* (1979) ECR 461, paragraphs 89 and 90; Case T-288/97 *Irish Sugar v Commission* (1999) ECR II-2969, paragraph 213; Case T-219/99 *British Airways v Commission* (2003) ECR II-5917, paragraphs 7 to 11 and 270 to 273.

(c) Efficiencies

46. Provided that the conditions set out in section III D are fulfilled, the Commission will consider claims by dominant undertakings that rebate systems achieve cost or other advantages which are passed on to customers (31). Transaction-related cost advantages are often more likely to be achieved with standardised volume targets than with individualised volume targets. Similarly, incremental rebate schemes are in general more likely to give resellers an incentive to produce and resell a higher volume than retroactive rebate schemes (32). Under the same conditions, the Commission will consider evidence demonstrating that exclusive dealing arrangements result in advantages to particular customers if those arrangements are necessary for the dominant undertaking to make certain relationship-specific investments in order to be able to supply those customers.

(31) For instance, for rebates see Case C-95/04 P *British Airways v Commission* (2007) ECR I-2331, paragraph 86.

(32) See, to that effect, Case T-203/01 *Michelin v Commission (Michelin II)* (2003) ECR II-4071, paragraphs 56 to 60, 74 and 75.

B. Tying and bundling

47. A dominant undertaking may try to foreclose its competitors by tying or bundling. This section sets out the circumstances which are most likely to prompt an intervention by the Commission when assessing tying and bundling by dominant undertakings.

48. «Tying» usually refers to situations where customers that purchase one product (the tying product) are required also to purchase another product from the dominant undertaking (the tied product). Tying can take place on a technical or contractual basis (33). «Bundling» usually refers to the way products are offered and priced by the dominant undertaking. In the case of pure bundling the products are only sold jointly in fixed proportions. In the case of mixed bundling, often referred to as a multi-product rebate, the products are also made available separately, but the sum of the prices when sold separately is higher than the bundled price.

(33) Technical tying occurs when the tying product is designed in such a way that it only works properly with the tied product (and not with the alternatives offered by competitors). Contractual tying occurs when the customer who purchases the tying product undertakes also to purchase the tied product (and not the alternatives offered by competitors).

49. Tying and bundling are common practices intended to provide customers with better products or offerings in more cost effective ways. However, an undertaking which is dominant in one product market (or more) of a tie or bundle (referred to as the tying market) can harm consumers through tying or bundling by foreclosing the market for the other products that are part of the tie or bundle (referred to as the tied market) and, indirectly, the tying market.

50. The Commission will normally take action under Article 82 where an undertaking is dominant in the tying market (34) and where, in addition, the following conditions are fulfilled: *(i)* the tying and tied products are distinct products, and *(ii)* the tying practice is likely to lead to anti-competitive foreclosure (35).

(34) The undertaking should be dominant in the tying market, though not necessarily in the tied market. In bundling cases, the undertaking needs to be dominant in one of the bundled markets. In the special case of tying in after-markets, the condition is that the undertaking is dominant in the tying market and/or the tied after-market.

(35) Case T-201/04 *Microsoft v Commission* (2007) ECR II-3601, in particular paragraphs 842, 859 to 862, 867 and 869.

(a) Distinct products

51. Whether the products will be considered by the Commission to be distinct depends on customer demand. Two products are distinct if, in the absence of tying or bundling, a substantial number of customers would purchase or would have purchased the tying product without also buying the tied product from the same supplier, thereby allowing stand-alone production for both the tying and the tied product (36). Evidence that two products are distinct could include direct evidence that, when given a choice, customers purchase the tying and the tied products separately from different sources of supply, or indirect evidence, such as the presence on the market of undertakings specialised in the manufacture or sale of the tied product without the tying product (37) or of each of the products bundled by the dominant undertaking, or evidence indicating that undertakings with little market power, particularly in competitive markets, tend not to tie or not to bundle such products.

(36) Case T-201/04 *Microsoft v Commission* (2007) ECR II-3601, paragraphs 917, 921 and 922.

(37) Case T-30/89 *Hilti v Commission* (1991) ECR II-1439, paragraph 67.

(b) Anti-competitive foreclosure in the tied and/or tying market

52. Tying or bundling may lead to anti-competitive effects in the tied market, the tying market, or both at the same time. However, even when the aim of the tying or bundling is to protect the dominant undertaking's position in the tying market, this is done indirectly through foreclosing the tied market. In addition to the factors already mentioned in paragraph 20, the Commission considers that the following factors are generally of particular importance for identifying cases of likely or actual anti-competitive foreclosure.

53. The risk of anti-competitive foreclosure is expected to be greater where the dominant undertaking makes its tying or bundling strategy a lasting one, for example through technical tying which is costly to reverse. Technical tying also reduces the opportunities for resale of individual components.

54. In the case of bundling, the undertaking may have a dominant position for more than one of the products in the bundle. The greater the number of such products in the bundle, the stronger the likely anti-competitive foreclosure. This is particularly true if the bundle is difficult for a competitor to replicate, either on its own or in combination with others.

55. The tying may lead to less competition for customers interested in buying the tied product, but not the tying product. If there is not a sufficient number of customers who will buy the tied product alone to sustain competitors of the dominant undertaking in the tied market, the tying can lead to those customers facing higher prices.

56. If the tying and the tied product can be used in variable proportions as inputs to a production process, customers may react to an increase in price for the tying product by increasing their demand for the tied product while decreasing their demand for the tying product. By tying the two products the dominant undertaking may seek to avoid this substitution and as a result be able to raise its prices.

57. If the prices the dominant undertaking can charge in the tying market are regulated, tying may allow the dominant undertaking to raise prices in the tied market in order to compensate for the loss of revenue caused by the regulation in the tying market.

58. If the tied product is an important complementary product for customers of the tying product, a reduction of alternative suppliers of the tied product and hence a reduced availability of that product can make entry to the tying market alone more difficult.

(c) Multi-product rebates

59. A multi-product rebate may be anti-competitive on the tied or the tying market if it is so large that equally efficient competitors offering only some of the components cannot compete against the discounted bundle.

60. In theory, it would be ideal if the effect of the rebate could be assessed by examining whether the incremental revenue covers the incremental costs for each product in the dominant undertaking's bundle. However, in practice assessing the incremental revenue is complex. Therefore, in its enforcement practice the Commission will in most situations use the incremental price as a good proxy. If the incremental price that customers pay for each of the dominant undertaking's products in the bundle remains above the L.R.A.I.C. of the dominant undertaking from including that product in the bundle, the Commission will normally not intervene since an equally efficient competitor with only one product should in principle be able to compete profitably against the bundle. Enforcement action may, however, be warranted if the incremental price is below the LRAIC, because in such a case even an equally efficient competitor may be prevented from expanding or entering (38).

(38) In principle, the L.R.A.I.C. cost benchmark is relevant here as long as competitors are not able to also sell bundles (see paragraphs 23 to 27 and paragraph 61).

61. If the evidence suggests that competitors of the dominant undertaking are selling identical bundles, or could do so in a timely way without being deterred by possible additional costs, the Commission will generally regard this as a bundle competing against a bundle, in which case the relevant question is not whether the incremental revenue covers the incremental costs for each product in the bundle, but rather whether the price of the bundle as a whole is predatory.

(d) Efficiencies

62. Provided that the conditions set out in section III D are fulfilled, the Commission will look into claims by dominant undertakings that their tying and bundling practices may lead to savings in production or distribution that would benefit customers. The Commission may also consider whether such practices reduce transaction costs for customers, who would otherwise be forced to buy the components separately, and enable substantial savings on packaging and distribution costs for suppliers. It may also examine whether combining two independent products into a new, single product might enhance the ability to bring such a product to the market to the benefit of consumers. The Commission may also consider whether tying and bundling practices allow the supplier to pass on efficiencies arising from its production or purchase of large quantities of the tied product.

C. Predation

63. In line with its enforcement priorities, the Commission will generally intervene where there is evidence showing that a dominant undertaking engages in predatory conduct by deliberately incurring losses or foregoing profits in the short term (referred to hereafter as «sacrifice»), so as to foreclose or be likely to foreclose one or more of its actual or potential competitors with a view to strengthening or maintaining its market power, thereby causing consumer harm (39).

(39) The Commission may also pursue predatory practices by dominant undertakings on secondary markets on which they are not yet dominant. In particular, the Commission will be more likely to find such an abuse in sectors where activities are protected by a legal monopoly. While the dominant undertaking does not need to engage in predatory conduct to protect its dominant position in the market protected by legal monopoly, it may use the profits gained in the monopoly market to cross-subsidize its activities in another market and thereby threaten to eliminate effective competition in that other market.

(a) Sacrifice

64. Conduct will be viewed by the Commission as entailing a sacrifice if, by charging a lower price for all or a particular part of its output over the relevant time period, or by expanding its output over the relevant time period, the dominant undertaking incurred or is incurring losses that could have been avoided. The Commission will take A.A.C. as the appropriate starting point for assessing whether the dominant undertaking incurred or is incurring avoidable losses. If a dominant undertaking charges a price below A.A.C. for all or part of its output, it is not recovering the costs that could have been avoided by not producing that output: it is incurring a loss that could have been avoided (40). Pricing below A.A.C. will thus in most cases be viewed by the Commission as a clear indication of sacrifice (41).

(40) In most cases the average variable cost (A.V.C.) and A.A.C. will be the same, as often only variable costs can be avoided. However, in circumstances where A.V.C. and A.A.C. differ, the latter better reflects possible sacrifice: for example, if the dominant undertaking had to expand capacity in order to be able to predate, then the sunk costs of that extra capacity should be taken into account in looking at the dominant undertaking's losses. Those costs would be reflected in the A.A.C. but not the A.V.C.

(41) In Case 62/86 *AKZO Chemie v Commission* (1991) ECR I-3359, paragraph 71, the Court held, in relation to pricing below average variable cost (A.V.C.), that: «A dominant undertaking has no interest in applying such prices except that of eliminating competitors so as to enable it subsequently to raise its price by taking advantage of its monopolistic position, since each sale generates a loss ...».

65. However, the concept of sacrifice does not only include pricing below A.A.C. (42). In order to show a predatory strategy, the Commission may also investigate whether the allegedly predatory conduct led in the short term to net revenues lower than could have been expected from a reasonable alternative conduct, that is to say, whether the dominant undertaking incurred a loss that it could have avoided (43). The Commission will not compare the actual conduct with hypothetical or theoretical alternatives that might have been more profitable. Only economically rational and practicable alternatives will be considered which, taking into account the market conditions and business realities facing the dominant undertaking, can realistically be expected to be more profitable.

(42) If the estimate of cost is based on the direct cost of production (as registered in the undertaking's accounts), it may not adequately capture whether or not there has been a sacrifice.

(43) However, undertakings should not be penalised for incurring *ex post* losses where the *ex ante* decision to engage in the conduct was taken in good faith, that is to say, if they can provide conclusive evidence that they could reasonably expect that the activity would be profitable.

66. In some cases it will be possible to rely upon direct evidence consisting of documents from the dominant undertaking which clearly show a predatory strategy (44), such as a detailed plan to sacrifice in order to exclude a competitor, to prevent entry or to pre-empt the emergence of a market, or evidence of concrete threats of predatory action (45).

(44) See Case T-83/91 *Tetra Pak International v Commission (Tetra Pak II)* (1994) ECR II-755, paragraphs 151 and 171, and Case T-340/03 *France Télécom v Commission* (2007) ECR II-107, paragraphs 198 to 215.

(45) In Case 62/86 *AKZO Chemie v Commission* (1991) ECR I-3359, the Court accepted that there was clear evidence of AKZO threatening E.C.S. in two meetings with below cost pricing if it did not withdraw from the organic peroxides market. In addition there was a detailed plan, with figures, describing the measures that AKZO would put into effect if E.C.S. would not withdraw from the market (see paragraphs 76 to 82, 115, and 131 to 140).

(b) Anti-competitive foreclosure

67. If sufficient reliable data are available, the Commission will apply the equally efficient competitor analysis, described in paragraphs 25 to 27, to determine whether the conduct is capable of harming consumers. Normally only pricing below L.R.A.I.C. is capable of foreclosing as efficient competitors from the market.

68. In addition to the factors already mentioned in paragraph 20, the Commission will generally investigate whether and how the suspected conduct reduces the likelihood that competitors will compete. For instance, if the dominant undertaking is better informed about cost or other market conditions, or can distort market signals about profitability, it may engage in predatory conduct so as to influence the expectations of potential entrants and thereby deter entry. If the conduct and its likely effects are felt on multiple markets and/or in successive periods of possible entry, the dominant undertaking may be shown to be seeking a reputation for predatory conduct. If the targeted competitor is dependent on external financing, substantial price decreases or other predatory conduct by the dominant undertaking could adversely affect the competitor's performance so that its access to further financing may be seriously undermined.

69. The Commission does not consider that it is necessary to show that competitors have exited the market in order to show that there has been anti-competitive foreclosure. The possibility cannot be excluded that the dominant undertaking may prefer to prevent the competitor from competing vigorously and have it follow the dominant undertaking's pricing, rather than eliminate it from the market altogether. Such disciplining avoids the risk inherent in eliminating competitors, in particular the risk that the assets of the competitor are sold at a low price and stay in the market, creating a new low cost entrant.

70. Generally speaking, consumers are likely to be harmed if the dominant undertaking can reasonably expect its market power after the predatory conduct comes to an end to be greater than it would have been had the undertaking not engaged in that conduct in the first place, that is to say, if the undertaking is likely to be in a position to benefit from the sacrifice.

71. This does not mean that the Commission will only intervene if the dominant undertaking would be likely to be able to increase its prices above the level persisting in the market before the conduct. It is sufficient, for instance, that the conduct would be likely to prevent or delay a decline in prices that would otherwise have occurred. Identifying consumer harm is not a mechanical calculation of profits and losses, and proof of overall profits is not required. Likely consumer harm may be demonstrated by assessing the likely foreclosure effect of the conduct, combined with consideration of other factors, such as entry barriers (46). In this context, the Commission will also consider possibilities of re-entry.

(46) This was confirmed in Case T-83/91 *Tetra Pak International v Commission (Tetra Pak II)* (1994) ECR II-755, upheld on appeal in Case C-333/94 P *Tetra Pak International v Commission* (1996) ECR I-5951, where the Court of First Instance stated that proof of actual recoupment was not required (paragraph 150 *in fine*). More in general, as predation may turn out to be more difficult than expected at the start of the conduct, the total costs to the dominant undertaking of predating could outweigh its later profits and thus make actual recoupment impossible while it may still be rational to decide to continue with the predatory strategy that it started some time ago. See also COMP/38.233 Wanadoo Interactive, Commission Decision of 16 July 2003, paragraphs 332 to 367.

72. It may be easier for the dominant undertaking to engage in predatory conduct if it selectively targets specific customers with low prices, as this will limit the losses incurred by the dominant undertaking.

73. It is less likely that the dominant undertaking engages in predatory conduct if the conduct concerns a low price applied generally for a long period of time.

(c) Efficiencies

74. In general it is considered unlikely that predatory conduct will create efficiencies. However, provided that the conditions set out in section III D are fulfilled, the Commission will consider claims by a dominant undertaking that the low pricing enables it to achieve economies of scale or efficiencies related to expanding the market.

D. Refusal to supply and margin squeeze

75. When setting its enforcement priorities, the Commission starts from the position that, generally speaking, any undertaking, whether dominant or not, should have the right to choose its trading partners and to dispose freely of its property. The Commission therefore considers that intervention on competition law grounds requires careful consideration where the application of Article 82 would lead to the imposition of an obligation to supply on the dominant undertaking (47). The existence of such an obligation – even for a fair remuneration – may undermine undertakings' incentives to invest and innovate and, thereby, possibly harm consumers. The knowledge that they may have a duty to supply against their will may lead dominant undertakings – or undertakings who anticipate that they may become dominant – not to invest, or to invest less, in the activity in question. Also, competitors may be tempted to free ride on investments made by the dominant undertaking instead of investing themselves. Neither of these consequences would, in the long run, be in the interest of consumers.

(47) Joined Cases C-241/91 P and C-242/91 *Radio Telefis Eireann (R.T.E.) and Independent Television publications (I.T.P.) v Commission (Magill)* (1995) ECR I-743, paragraph 50; Case C-418/01 *IMS Health v NDC Health* (2004) ECR I-5039, paragraph 35; Case T-201/04 *Microsoft v Commission* (2007) ECR II-3601, paragraphs 319, 330, 331, 332 and 336.

76. Typically competition problems arise when the dominant undertaking competes on the «downstream» market with the buyer whom it refuses to supply. The term «downstream market» is used to refer to the market for which the refused input is needed in order to manufacture a product or provide a service. This section deals only with this type of refusal.

77. Other types of possibly unlawful refusal to supply, in which the supply is made conditional upon the purchaser accepting limitations on its conduct, are not dealt with in this section. For instance, halting supplies in order to punish customers for dealing with competitors or refusing to supply customers that do not agree to tying arrangements, will be examined by the Commission in line with the principles set out in the sections on exclusive dealing and tying and bundling. Similarly, refusals to supply aimed at preventing the purchaser from engaging in parallel trade (48) or from lowering its resale price are also not dealt with in this section.

(48) See Judgment of 16 September 2008 in Joined Cases C-468/06 to C-478/06 *Sot. Lélos kai Sia and Others v GlaxoSmithKline*, not yet reported.

78. The concept of refusal to supply covers a broad range of practices, such as a refusal to supply products to existing or new customers (49), refusal to license intellectual property rights (50), including when the licence is necessary to provide interface information (51), or refusal to grant access to an essential facility or a network (52).

(49) Joined Cases 6/73 and 7/73 *Istituto Chemioterapico Italiano and Commercial Solvents v Commission* (1974) ECR 223.

(50) Joined Cases C-241/91 P and C-242/91 P *Radio Telefis Eireann (R.T.E.) and Independent Television publications Ltd (I.T.P.) v Commission (Magill)* (1995) ECR 743; Case C-418/01 *IMS Health v NDC Health* (2004) ECR I-5039. Those judgments show that in exceptional circumstances a refusal to license intellectual property rights is abusive.

(51) See Case T-201/04 *Microsoft v Commission* (2007) ECR II-3601.

(52) See Commission Decision 94/19/EC of 21 December 1993 in Case IV/34.689 Sea *Containers v Stena Sealink – Interim Measures* (O.J. L 15, 18.1.1994, p. 8) and Commission Decision 92/213/EEC of 26 February 1992 in Case IV/33.544 *British Midland v Aer Lingus* (O.J. L 96, 10.4.1992, p. 34).

79. The Commission does not regard it as necessary for the refused product to have been already traded: it is sufficient that there is demand from potential purchasers and that a potential market for the input at stake can be identified (53). Likewise, it is not necessary for there to be actual refusal on the part of a dominant undertaking; «constructive refusal» is sufficient. Constructive refusal could, for example, take the form of unduly delaying or otherwise degrading the supply of the product or involve the imposition of unreasonable conditions in return for the supply.

(53) Case C-418/01 *IMS Health v NDC Health* (2004) ECR I-5039, paragraph 44.

80. Finally, instead of refusing to supply, a dominant undertaking may charge a price for the product on the upstream market which, compared to the price it charges on the downstream market (54), does not allow even an equally efficient competitor to trade profitably in the downstream market on a lasting basis (a so-called «margin squeeze»). In margin squeeze cases the benchmark which the Commission will generally rely on to determine the costs of an equally efficient competitor are the L.R.A.I.C. of the downstream division of the integrated dominant undertaking (55).

(54) Including a situation in which an integrated undertaking that sells a «system» of complementary products refuses to sell one of the complementary products on an unbundled basis to a competitor that produces the other complementary product.

(55) In some cases, however, the L.R.A.I.C. of a non-integrated competitor downstream might be used as the benchmark, for example when it is not possible to clearly allocate the dominant undertaking's costs to downstream and upstream operations.

81. The Commission will consider these practices as an enforcement priority if all the following circumstances are present:
 – the refusal relates to a product or service that is objectively necessary to be able to compete effectively on a downstream market,
 – the refusal is likely to lead to the elimination of effective competition on the downstream market, and
 – the refusal is likely to lead to consumer harm.

82. In certain specific cases, it may be clear that imposing an obligation to supply is manifestly not capable of having negative effects on the input owner's and/or other operators' incentives to invest and innovate upstream, whether *ex ante* or *ex post*. The Commission considers that this is particularly likely to be the case where regulation compatible with Community law already imposes an obligation to supply on the dominant undertaking and it is clear, from the considerations underlying such regulation, that the necessary balancing of incentives has already been made by the public authority when imposing such an obligation to supply. This could also be the case where the upstream market position of the dominant undertaking has been developed under the protection of special or exclusive rights or has been financed by state resources. In such specific cases there is no reason for the Commission to deviate from its general enforcement standard of showing likely anti-competitive foreclosure, without considering whether the three circumstances referred to in paragraph 81 are present.

(a) Objective necessity of the input

83. In examining whether a refusal to supply deserves its priority attention, the Commission will consider whether the supply of the refused input is objectively necessary for operators to be able to compete effectively on the market. This does not mean that, without the refused input, no competitor could ever enter or survive on the downstream market (56). Rather, an input is indispensable where there is no actual or potential substitute on which competitors in the downstream market could rely so as to counter – at least in the long-term – the negative consequences of the refusal (57). In this regard, the Commission will normally make an assessment of whether competitors could effectively duplicate the input produced by the dominant undertaking in the foreseeable future (58). The notion of duplication means the creation of an alternative source of efficient supply that is capable of allowing competitors to exert a competitive constraint on the dominant undertaking in the downstream market (59).

(56) Case T-201/04 *Microsoft v Commission* (2007) ECR II-3601, paragraphs 428 and 560 to 563.

(57) Joined Cases C-241/91 P and C-242/91 *Radio Telefis Eireann (R.T.E.) and Independent Television publications LTD (I.T.P.) v Commission (Magill)* (1995) ECR 743, paragraphs 52 and 53; Case 7/97 *Oscar Bronner v Mediaprint Zeitungs- und Zeitschriftenverlag, Mediaprint Zeitungsvertriebsgesellschaft and Mediaprint Anzeigengesellschaft* (1998) ECR I-7791, paragraphs 44 and 45; Case T-201/04 *Microsoft v Commission* (2007) ECR II-3601, paragraph 421.

(58) In general, an input is likely to be impossible to replicate when it involves a natural monopoly due to scale or scope economies, where there are strong network effects or when it concerns so-called «single source» information. However, in all cases account should be taken of the dynamic nature of the industry and, in particular whether or not market power can rapidly dissipate.

(59) Case 7/97 *Oscar Bronner v Mediaprint Zeitungs- und Zeitschriftenverlag, Mediaprint Zeitungsvertriebsgesellschaft and Mediaprint Anzeigengesellschaft* (1998) ECR I-7791, paragraph 46, Case C-418/01 *IMS Health v NDC Health* (2004) ECR I-5039, paragraph 29.

84. The criteria set out in paragraph 81 apply both to cases of disruption of previous supply, and to refusals to supply a good or service which the dominant company has not previously supplied to others (de novo refusals to supply). However, the termination of an existing supply arrangement is more likely to be found to be abusive than a de novo refusal to supply. For example, if the dominant undertaking had previously been supplying the requesting undertaking, and the latter had made relationship-specific investments in order to use the subsequently refused input, the Commission may be more likely to regard the input in question as indispensable. Similarly, the fact that the owner of the essential input in the past has found it in its interest to supply is an indication that supplying the input does not imply any risk that the owner receives inadequate compensation for the original investment. It would therefore be up to the dominant company to demonstrate why circumstances have actually changed in such a way that the continuation of its existing supply relationship would put in danger its adequate compensation.

(b) Elimination of effective competition

85. If the requirements set out in paragraphs 83 and 84 are fulfilled, the Commission considers that a dominant undertaking's refusal to supply is generally liable to eliminate, immediately or over time, effective competition in the downstream market. The likelihood of effective competition being eliminated is generally greater the higher the market share of the dominant undertaking in the downstream market. The less capacity-constrained the dominant undertaking is relative to competitors in the downstream market, the closer the substitutability between the dominant undertaking's output and that of its competitors in the downstream market, the greater the proportion of competitors in the downstream market that are affected, and the more likely it is that the demand that could be served by the foreclosed competitors would be diverted away from them to the advantage of the dominant undertaking.

(c) Consumer harm

86. In examining the likely impact of a refusal to supply on consumer welfare, the Commission will examine whether, for consumers, the likely negative consequences of the refusal to supply in the relevant market outweigh over time the negative consequences of imposing an obligation to supply. If they do, the Commission will normally pursue the case.

87. The Commission considers that consumer harm may, for instance, arise where the competitors that the dominant undertaking forecloses are, as a result of the refusal, prevented from bringing innovative goods or services to market and/or where follow-on innovation is likely to be stifled (60). This may be particularly the case if the undertaking which requests supply does not intend to limit itself essentially to duplicating the goods or services already offered by the dominant undertaking on the downstream market, but intends to produce new or improved goods or services for which there is a potential consumer demand or is likely to contribute to technical development (61).

(60) Case T-201/04 *Microsoft v Commission* (2007) ECR II-3601, paragraphs 643, 647, 648, 649, 652, 653 and 656.

(61) Case C-418/01 *IMS Health v NDC Health* (2004) ECR I-5039, paragraph 49; Case T-201/04 *Microsoft v Commission* (2007) ECR II-3601, paragraph 658.

88. The Commission also considers that a refusal to supply may lead to consumer harm where the price in the upstream input market is regulated, the price in the downstream market is not regulated and the dominant undertaking, by excluding competitors on the downstream market through a refusal to supply, is able to extract more profits in the unregulated downstream market than it would otherwise do.

(d) Efficiencies

89. The Commission will consider claims by the dominant undertaking that a refusal to supply is necessary to allow the dominant undertaking to realise an adequate return on the investments required to develop its input business, thus generating incentives to continue to invest in the future, taking the risk of failed projects into account. The Commission will also consider claims by the dominant undertaking that its own innovation will be negatively affected by the obligation to supply, or by the structural changes in the market conditions that imposing such an obligation will bring about, including the development of follow-on innovation by competitors.

90. However, when considering such claims, the Commission will ensure that the conditions set out in section III D are fulfilled. In particular, it falls on the dominant undertaking to demonstrate any negative impact which an obligation to supply is likely to have on its own level of innovation (62). If a dominant undertaking has previously supplied the input in question, this can be relevant for the assessment of any claim that the refusal to supply is justified on efficiency grounds.

(62) Case T-201/04 *Microsoft v Commission* (2007) ECR II-3601, paragraph 659.

2.1.2.2. Vertical agreements

Commission Regulation (EC) N° 330/2010, 20 April 2010 – Vertical agreements and
concerted practices, application Art. 101(3) Treaty 66
Guidelines on Vertical Restraints 70
Commission Regulation (EC) N° 461/2010, 27 May 2010 – Vertical agreements and
concerted practices in the motor vehicle sector................................. 103
Supplementary guidelines – Vertical agreements and concerted practices in the motor
vehicle sector.. 106

Commission Regulation (EU) N° 330/2010, 20 April 2010 on the application of Article 101(3) of the Treaty on the functioning of the European Union to categories of vertical agreements and concerted practices

(OJ L 102, 23 April 2010, p. 1)

THE EUROPEAN COMMISSION,
Having regard to the Treaty on the Functioning of the European Union,
Having regard to Regulation N° 19/65/EEC of the Council of 2 March 1965 on the application of Article 85(3) of the Treaty to certain categories of agreements and concerted practices, and in particular Article 1 thereof,
Having published a draft of this Regulation,
After consulting the Advisory Committee on Restrictive Practices and Dominant Positions,
Whereas:

(1) Regulation N° 19/65/EEC empowers the Commission to apply Article 101(3) of the Treaty on the Functioning of the European Union by regulation to certain categories of vertical agreements and corresponding concerted practices falling within Article 101(1) of the Treaty.

(2) Commission Regulation (EC) N° 2790/1999 of 22 December 1999 on the application of Article 81(3) of the Treaty to categories of vertical agreements and concerted practices defines a category of vertical agreements which the Commission regarded as normally satisfying the conditions laid down in Article 101(3) of the Treaty. In view of the overall positive experience with the application of that Regulation, which expires on 31 May 2010, and taking into account further experience acquired since its adoption, it is appropriate to adopt a new block exemption regulation.

(3) The category of agreements which can be regarded as normally satisfying the conditions laid down in Article 101(3) of the Treaty includes vertical agreements for the purchase or sale of goods or services where those agreements are concluded between non-competing undertakings, between certain competitors or by certain associations of retailers of goods. It also includes vertical agreements containing ancillary provisions on the assignment or use of intellectual property rights. The term «vertical agreements» should include the corresponding concerted practices.

(4) For the application of Article 101(3) of the Treaty by regulation, it is not necessary to define those vertical agreements which are capable of falling within Article 101(1) of the Treaty. In the individual assessment of agreements under Article 101(1) of the Treaty, account has to be taken of several factors, and in particular the market structure on the supply and purchase side.

(5) The benefit of the block exemption established by this Regulation should be limited to vertical agreements for which it can be assumed with sufficient certainty that they satisfy the conditions of Article 101(3) of the Treaty.

(6) Certain types of vertical agreements can improve economic efficiency within a chain of production or distribution by facilitating better coordination between the participating undertakings. In particular, they can lead to a reduction in the transaction and distribution costs of the parties and to an optimisation of their sales and investment levels.

(7) The likelihood that such efficiency-enhancing effects will outweigh any anti-competitive effects due to restrictions contained in vertical agreements depends on the degree of market power of the parties to the agreement and, therefore, on the extent to which those undertakings face competition from other suppliers of goods or services regarded by their customers as interchangeable or substitutable for one another, by reason of the products' characteristics, their prices and their intended use.

(8) It can be presumed that, where the market share held by each of the undertakings party to the agreement on the relevant market does not exceed 30 %, vertical agreements which do not contain certain types of severe restrictions of competition generally lead to an improvement in production or distribution and allow consumers a fair share of the resulting benefits.

(9) Above the market share threshold of 30 %, there can be no presumption that vertical agreements falling within the scope of Article 101(1) of the Treaty will usually give rise to objective advantages of such a character and size as to compensate for the disadvantages which they create for competition. At the same time, there is no presumption that those vertical agreements are either caught by Article 101(1) of the Treaty or that they fail to satisfy the conditions of Article 101(3) of the Treaty.

(10) This Regulation should not exempt vertical agreements containing restrictions which are likely to restrict competition and harm consumers or which are not indispensable to the attainment of the efficiency-enhancing effects. In particular, vertical agreements containing certain types of severe restrictions of competition such as minimum and fixed resale-prices, as well as certain types of territorial protection, should be excluded from the benefit of the block exemption established by this Regulation irrespective of the market share of the undertakings concerned.

(11) In order to ensure access to or to prevent collusion on the relevant market, certain conditions should be attached to the block exemption. To this end, the exemption of non-compete obligations should be limited to obligations which do not exceed a defined duration. For the same reasons, any direct or indirect obligation causing the mem-

bers of a selective distribution system not to sell the brands of particular competing suppliers should be excluded from the benefit of this Regulation.

(12) The market-share limitation, the non-exemption of certain vertical agreements and the conditions provided for in this Regulation normally ensure that the agreements to which the block exemption applies do not enable the participating undertakings to eliminate competition in respect of a substantial part of the products in question.

(13) The Commission may withdraw the benefit of this Regulation, pursuant to Article 29(1) of Council Regulation (EC) N° 1/2003 of 16 December 2002 on the implementation of the rules on competition laid down in Articles 81 and 82 of the Treaty, where it finds in a particular case that an agreement to which the exemption provided for in this Regulation applies nevertheless has effects which are incompatible with Article 101(3) of the Treaty.

(14) The competition authority of a Member State may withdraw the benefit of this Regulation pursuant to Article 29(2) of Regulation (EC) N° 1/2003 in respect of the territory of that Member State, or a part thereof where, in a particular case, an agreement to which the exemption provided for in this Regulation applies nevertheless has effects which are incompatible with Article 101(3) of the Treaty in the territory of that Member State, or in a part thereof, and where such territory has all the characteristics of a distinct geographic market.

(15) In determining whether the benefit of this Regulation should be withdrawn pursuant to Article 29 of Regulation (EC) N° 1/2003, the anti-competitive effects that may derive from the existence of parallel networks of vertical agreements that have similar effects which significantly restrict access to a relevant market or competition therein are of particular importance. Such cumulative effects may for example arise in the case of selective distribution or non compete obligations.

(16) In order to strengthen supervision of parallel networks of vertical agreements which have similar anti-competitive effects and which cover more than 50 % of a given market, the Commission may by regulation declare this Regulation inapplicable to vertical agreements containing specific restraints relating to the market concerned, thereby restoring the full application of Article 101 of the Treaty to such agreements,

HAS ADOPTED THIS REGULATION:

Art. 1. *Definitions*

1. For the purposes of this Regulation, the following definitions shall apply:

(a) «vertical agreement» means an agreement or concerted practice entered into between two or more undertakings each of which operates, for the purposes of the agreement or the concerted practice, at a different level of the production or distribution chain, and relating to the conditions under which the parties may purchase, sell or resell certain goods or services;

(b) «vertical restraint» means a restriction of competition in a vertical agreement falling within the scope of Article 101(1) of the Treaty;

(c) «competing undertaking» means an actual or potential competitor; «actual competitor» means an undertaking that is active on the same relevant market; «potential competitor» means an undertaking that, in the absence of the vertical agreement, would, on realistic grounds and not just as a mere theoretical possibility, in case of a small but permanent increase in relative prices be likely to undertake, within a short period of time, the necessary additional investments or other necessary switching costs to enter the relevant market;

(d) «non-compete obligation» means any direct or indirect obligation causing the buyer not to manufacture, purchase, sell or resell goods or services which compete with the contract goods or services, or any direct or indirect obligation on the buyer to purchase from the supplier or from another undertaking designated by the supplier more than 80 % of the buyer's total purchases of the contract goods or services and their substitutes on the relevant market, calculated on the basis of the value or, where such is standard industry practice, the volume of its purchases in the preceding calendar year;

(e) «selective distribution system» means a distribution system where the supplier undertakes to sell the contract goods or services, either directly or indirectly, only to distributors selected on the basis of specified criteria and where these distributors undertake not to sell such goods or services to unauthorised distributors within the territory reserved by the supplier to operate that system;

(f) «intellectual property rights» includes industrial property rights, know how, copyright and neighbouring rights;

(g) «know-how» means a package of non-patented practical information, resulting from experience and testing by the supplier, which is secret, substantial and identified: in this context, «secret» means that the know-how is not generally known or easily accessible; «substantial» means that the know-how is significant and useful to the buyer for the use, sale or resale of the contract goods or services; «identified» means that the know-how is described in a sufficiently comprehensive manner so as to make it possible to verify that it fulfils the criteria of secrecy and substantiality;

(h) «buyer» includes an undertaking which, under an agreement falling within Article 101(1) of the Treaty, sells goods or services on behalf of another undertaking;

(i) «customer of the buyer» means an undertaking not party to the agreement which purchases the contract goods or services from a buyer which is party to the agreement.

2. For the purposes of this Regulation, the terms «undertaking», «supplier» and «buyer» shall include their respective connected undertakings.

«Connected undertakings» means:

(a) undertakings in which a party to the agreement, directly or indirectly:

(i) has the power to exercise more than half the voting rights; or

(ii) has the power to appoint more than half the members of the supervisory board, board of management or bodies legally representing the undertaking; or

(iii) has the right to manage the undertaking's affairs;

(b) undertakings which directly or indirectly have, over a party to the agreement, the rights or powers listed in point *(a)*;

(c) undertakings in which an undertaking referred to in point *(b)* has, directly or indirectly, the rights or powers listed in point *(a)*;

(d) undertakings in which a party to the agreement together with one or more of the undertakings referred to in points *(a)*, *(b)* or *(c)*, or in which two or more of the latter

undertakings, jointly have the rights or powers listed in point *(a)*;

(e) undertakings in which the rights or the powers listed in point *(a)* are jointly held by:

(i) parties to the agreement or their respective connected undertakings referred to in points *(a)* to *(d)*; or

(ii) one or more of the parties to the agreement or one or more of their connected undertakings referred to in points *(a)* to *(d)* and one or more third parties.

Art. 2. *Exemption*

1. Pursuant to Article 101(3) of the Treaty and subject to the provisions of this Regulation, it is hereby declared that Article 101(1) of the Treaty shall not apply to vertical agreements.

This exemption shall apply to the extent that such agreements contain vertical restraints.

2. The exemption provided for in paragraph 1 shall apply to vertical agreements entered into between an association of undertakings and its members, or between such an association and its suppliers, only if all its members are retailers of goods and if no individual member of the association, together with its connected undertakings, has a total annual turnover exceeding EUR 50 million. Vertical agreements entered into by such associations shall be covered by this Regulation without prejudice to the application of Article 101 of the Treaty to horizontal agreements concluded between the members of the association or decisions adopted by the association.

3. The exemption provided for in paragraph 1 shall apply to vertical agreements containing provisions which relate to the assignment to the buyer or use by the buyer of intellectual property rights, provided that those provisions do not constitute the primary object of such agreements and are directly related to the use, sale or resale of goods or services by the buyer or its customers. The exemption applies on condition that, in relation to the contract goods or services, those provisions do not contain restrictions of competition having the same object as vertical restraints which are not exempted under this Regulation.

4. The exemption provided for in paragraph 1 shall not apply to vertical agreements entered into between competing undertakings. However, it shall apply where competing undertakings enter into a non-reciprocal vertical agreement and:

(a) the supplier is a manufacturer and a distributor of goods, while the buyer is a distributor and not a competing undertaking at the manufacturing level; or

(b) the supplier is a provider of services at several levels of trade, while the buyer provides its goods or services at the retail level and is not a competing undertaking at the level of trade where it purchases the contract services.

5. This Regulation shall not apply to vertical agreements the subject matter of which falls within the scope of any other block exemption regulation, unless otherwise provided for in such a regulation.

Art. 3. *Market share threshold*

1. The exemption provided for in Article 2 shall apply on condition that the market share held by the supplier does not exceed 30 % of the relevant market on which it sells the contract goods or services and the market share held by the buyer does not exceed 30 % of the relevant market on which it purchases the contract goods or services.

2. For the purposes of paragraph 1, where in a multi party agreement an undertaking buys the contract goods or services from one undertaking party to the agreement and sells the contract goods or services to another undertaking party to the agreement, the market share of the first undertaking must respect the market share threshold provided for in that paragraph both as a buyer and a supplier in order for the exemption provided for in Article 2 to apply.

Art. 4. *Restrictions that remove the benefit of the block exemption – hardcore restrictions*

The exemption provided for in Article 2 shall not apply to vertical agreements which, directly or indirectly, in isolation or in combination with other factors under the control of the parties, have as their object:

(a) the restriction of the buyer's ability to determine its sale price, without prejudice to the possibility of the supplier to impose a maximum sale price or recommend a sale price, provided that they do not amount to a fixed or minimum sale price as a result of pressure from, or incentives offered by, any of the parties;

(b) the restriction of the territory into which, or of the customers to whom, a buyer party to the agreement, without prejudice to a restriction on its place of establishment, may sell the contract goods or services, except:

(i) the restriction of active sales into the exclusive territory or to an exclusive customer group reserved to the supplier or allocated by the supplier to another buyer, where such a restriction does not limit sales by the customers of the buyer;

(ii) the restriction of sales to end users by a buyer operating at the wholesale level of trade;

(iii) the restriction of sales by the members of a selective distribution system to unauthorised distributors within the territory reserved by the supplier to operate that system; and

(iv) the restriction of the buyer's ability to sell components, supplied for the purposes of incorporation, to customers who would use them to manufacture the same type of goods as those produced by the supplier;

(c) the restriction of active or passive sales to end users by members of a selective distribution system operating at the retail level of trade, without prejudice to the possibility of prohibiting a member of the system from operating out of an unauthorised place of establishment;

(d) the restriction of cross-supplies between distributors within a selective distribution system, including between distributors operating at different level of trade;

(e) the restriction, agreed between a supplier of components and a buyer who incorporates those components, of the supplier's ability to sell the components as spare parts to end-users or to repairers or other service providers not entrusted by the buyer with the repair or servicing of its goods.

Art. 5. *Excluded restrictions*

1. The exemption provided for in Article 2 shall not apply to the following obligations contained in vertical agreements:

(a) any direct or indirect non-compete obligation, the duration of which is indefinite or exceeds five years;

(b) any direct or indirect obligation causing the buyer, after termination of the agreement, not to manufacture, purchase, sell or resell goods or services;

(c) any direct or indirect obligation causing the members of a selective distribution system not to sell the brands of particular competing suppliers.

For the purposes of point (a) of the first subparagraph, a non-compete obligation which is tacitly renewable beyond a period of five years shall be deemed to have been concluded for an indefinite duration.

2. By way of derogation from paragraph 1(a), the time limitation of five years shall not apply where the contract goods or services are sold by the buyer from premises and land owned by the supplier or leased by the supplier from third parties not connected with the buyer, provided that the duration of the non-compete obligation does not exceed the period of occupancy of the premises and land by the buyer.

3. By way of derogation from paragraph 1(b), the exemption provided for in Article 2 shall apply to any direct or indirect obligation causing the buyer, after termination of the agreement, not to manufacture, purchase, sell or resell goods or services where the following conditions are fulfilled:

(a) the obligation relates to goods or services which compete with the contract goods or services;

(b) the obligation is limited to the premises and land from which the buyer has operated during the contract period;

(c) the obligation is indispensable to protect know-how transferred by the supplier to the buyer;

(d) the duration of the obligation is limited to a period of one year after termination of the agreement.

Paragraph 1(b) is without prejudice to the possibility of imposing a restriction which is unlimited in time on the use and disclosure of know-how which has not entered the public domain.

Art. 6. *Non-application of this Regulation*

Pursuant to Article 1a of Regulation N° 19/65/EEC, the Commission may by regulation declare that, where parallel networks of similar vertical restraints cover more than 50 % of a relevant market, this Regulation shall not apply to vertical agreements containing specific restraints relating to that market.

Art. 7. *Application of the market share threshold*

For the purposes of applying the market share thresholds provided for in Article 3 the following rules shall apply:

(a) the market share of the supplier shall be calculated on the basis of market sales value data and the market share of the buyer shall be calculated on the basis of market purchase value data. If market sales value or market purchase value data are not available, estimates based on other reliable market information, including market sales and purchase volumes, may be used to establish the market share of the undertaking concerned;

(b) the market shares shall be calculated on the basis of data relating to the preceding calendar year;

(c) the market share of the supplier shall include any goods or services supplied to vertically integrated distributors for the purposes of sale;

(d) if a market share is initially not more than 30 % but subsequently rises above that level without exceeding 35 %, the exemption provided for in Article 2 shall continue to apply for a period of two consecutive calendar years following the year in which the 30 % market share threshold was first exceeded;

(e) if a market share is initially not more than 30 % but subsequently rises above 35 %, the exemption provided for in Article 2 shall continue to apply for one calendar year following the year in which the level of 35 % was first exceeded;

(f) the benefit of points (d) and (e) may not be combined so as to exceed a period of two calendar years;

(g) the market share held by the undertakings referred to in point (e) of the second subparagraph of Article 1(2) shall be apportioned equally to each undertaking having the rights or the powers listed in point (a) of the second subparagraph of Article 1(2).

Art. 8. *Application of the turnover threshold*

1. For the purpose of calculating total annual turnover within the meaning of Article 2(2), the turnover achieved during the previous financial year by the relevant party to the vertical agreement and the turnover achieved by its connected undertakings in respect of all goods and services, excluding all taxes and other duties, shall be added together. For this purpose, no account shall be taken of dealings between the party to the vertical agreement and its connected undertakings or between its connected undertakings.

2. The exemption provided for in Article 2 shall remain applicable where, for any period of two consecutive financial years, the total annual turnover threshold is exceeded by no more than 10 %.

Art. 9. *Transitional period*

The prohibition laid down in Article 101(1) of the Treaty shall not apply during the period from 1 June 2010 to 31 May 2011 in respect of agreements already in force on 31 May 2010 which do not satisfy the conditions for exemption provided for in this Regulation but which, on 31 May 2010, satisfied the conditions for exemption provided for in Regulation (EC) N° 2790/1999.

Art. 10. *Period of validity*

This Regulation shall enter into force on 1 June 2010.

It shall expire on 31 May 2022.

This Regulation shall be binding in its entirety and directly applicable in all Member States.

Guidelines on Vertical Restraints

(OJ C 130, 19 May 2010, p. 1)

Table of contents

	Pages
I. INTRODUCTION	
1. Purpose of the Guidelines (1)	70
2. Applicability of Article 101 to vertical agreements (5)	71
II. VERTICAL AGREEMENTS WHICH GENERALLY FALL OUTSIDE THE SCOPE OF ARTICLE 101(1)	
1. Agreements of minor importance and SMEs (8)	71
2. Agency agreements	
2.1. Definition of agency agreements (12)	72
2.2. The application of Article 101(1) to agency agreements (18)	72
3. Subcontracting agreements (22)	73
III. APPLICATION OF THE BLOCK EXEMPTION REGULATION	
1. Safe harbour created by the Block Exemption Regulation (23)	73
2. Scope of the Block Exemption Regulation	
2.1. Definition of vertical agreements (24)	73
2.2. Vertical agreements between competitors (27)	74
2.3. Associations of retailers (29)	75
2.4. Vertical agreements containing provisions on intellectual property rights (IPRs) (31)	75
Trade mark (39)	76
Copyright (40)	76
Know-how (43)	76
2.5. Relationship to other block exemption regulations (46)	77
3. Hardcore restrictions under the Block Exemption Regulation (47)	77
4. Individual cases of hardcore sales restrictions that may fall outside the scope of Article 101(1) or may fulfil the conditions of Article 101(3) (60)	80
5. Excluded restrictions under the Block Exemption Regulation (65)	81
6. Severability (70)	81
7. Portfolio of products distributed through the same distribution system (72)	81
IV. WITHDRAWAL OF THE BLOCK EXEMPTION AND DISAPPLICATION OF THE BLOCK EXEMPTION REGULATION	
1. Withdrawal procedure (74)	82
2. Disapplication of the Block Exemption Regulation (79)	82
V. MARKET DEFINITION AND MARKET SHARE CALCULATION	
1. Commission Notice on definition of the relevant market (86)	83
2. The relevant market for calculating the 30 % market share threshold under the Block Exemption Regulation (87)	83
3. Calculation of market shares under the Block Exemption Regulation (93)	84
VI. ENFORCEMENT POLICY IN INDIVIDUAL CASES	
1. The framework of analysis (96)	84
1.1. Negative effects of vertical restraints (100)	85
1.2. Positive effects of vertical restraints. – (106)	86
1.3. Methodology of analysis. – (110)	87
1.3.1. Relevant factors for the assessment under Article 101(1) (111)	87
1.3.2. Relevant factors for the assessment under Article 101(3) (122)	88
2. Analysis of specific vertical restraints (128)	89
2.1. Single branding (129)	89
Example of quantity forcing (150)	91
2.2. Exclusive distribution (151)	92
Example of exclusive distribution at the wholesale level (165)	93
Example of multiple exclusive dealerships in an oligopolistic market (166)	93
Example of exclusive distribution combined with exclusive sourcing (167)	94
2.3. Exclusive customer allocation (168)	94
Example of exclusive customer allocation (173)	95
2.4. Selective distribution (174)	95
Example of quantitative selective distribution (187)	97
Example of selective distribution with cumulative effects (188)	97
2.5. Franchising (189)	98
Example of franchising (191)	98
2.6. Exclusive supply (192)	98
Example of exclusive supply (202)	99
2.7. Upfront access payments (203)	99
2.8. Category Management Agreements (209)	100
2.9. Tying (214)	101
2.10. Resale price restrictions (223)	102

I. INTRODUCTION

1. Purpose of the Guidelines

1. These Guidelines set out the principles for the assessment of vertical agreements under Article 101 of the Treaty on the Functioning of the European Union (1) (hereinafter «Article 101») (2). Article 1(1)*(a)* of Commission Regulation (EU) N° 330/2010 of 20 April 2010 on the application of Article 101(3) of the Treaty on the Functioning of the European Union to categories of vertical agreements and concerted practices (3) (hereinafter referred to as the «Block Exemption Regulation») (see paragraphs (24) to (46)) defines the term «vertical agreement». These Guidelines are without prejudice to the possible parallel application of Article 102 of the Treaty on the Functioning of the European Union (hereinafter «Article 102») to vertical agreements. These Guidelines are structured in the following way:

– Section II (paragraphs (8) to (22)) describes vertical agreements which generally fall outside Article 101(1);

– Section III (paragraphs (23) to (73)) clarifies the conditions for the application of the Block Exemption Regulation;

– Section IV (paragraphs (74) to (85)) describes the principles concerning the withdrawal of the block exemption and the disapplication of the Block Exemption Regulation;

– Section V (paragraphs (86) to (95)) provides guidance on how to define the relevant market and calculate market shares;

– Section VI (paragraphs (96) to (229)) describes the general framework of analysis and the enforcement policy of the Commission in individual cases concerning vertical agreements.

(1) With effect from 1 December 2009, Articles 81 and 82 of the EC Treaty have become Articles 101 and, 102, respectively, of the Treaty on the Functioning of the European Union («TFEU»). The two sets of provisions are, in substance, identical. For the purposes of these Guidelines, references to Articles 101 and 102 of the TFEU should be understood as references to Articles 81 and 82, respectively, of the EC Treaty where appropriate. The TFEU also introduced certain changes in terminology, such as the replacement of «Community» by «Union» and «common market» by «internal market». The terminology of the TFEU will be used throughout these Guidelines.

(2) These Guidelines replace the Commission Notice – Guidelines on Vertical Restraints, *OJ* C 291, 13.10.2000, p. 1.

(3) *OJ* L 102, 23.4.2010, p. 1.

2. Throughout these Guidelines, the analysis applies to both goods and services, although certain vertical restraints are mainly used in the distribution of goods. Similarly, vertical agreements can be concluded for intermediate and final goods and services. Unless otherwise stated, the analysis and arguments in these Guidelines apply to all types of goods and services and to all levels of trade. Thus, the term «products» includes both goods and services. The terms «supplier» and «buyer» are used for all levels of trade. The Block Exemption Regulation and these Guidelines do not apply to agreements with final consumers where the latter are not undertakings, since Article 101 only applies to agreements between undertakings.

3. By issuing these Guidelines, the Commission aims to help companies conduct their own assessment of vertical agreements under EU competition rules. The standards set forth in these Guidelines cannot be applied mechanically, but must be applied with due consideration for the specific circumstances of each case. Each case must be evaluated in the light of its own facts.

4. These Guidelines are without prejudice to the case-law of the General Court and the Court of Justice of the European Union concerning the application of Article 101 to vertical agreements. The Commission will continue to monitor the operation of the Block Exemption Regulation and Guidelines based on market information from stakeholders and national competition authorities and may revise this notice in the light of future developments and of evolving insight.

2. Applicability of Article 101 to vertical agreements

5. Article 101 applies to vertical agreements that may affect trade between Member States and that prevent, restrict or distort competition («vertical restraints») (4). Article 101 provides a legal framework for the assessment of vertical restraints, which takes into consideration the distinction between anti-competitive and pro-competitive effects. Article 101(1) prohibits those agreements which appreciably restrict or distort competition, while Article 101(3) exempts those agreements which confer sufficient benefits to outweigh the anti-competitive effects (5).

(4) See inter alia judgments of the Court of Justice in Joined Cases 56/64 and 58/64 Grundig-Consten v Commission (1966) ECR 299; Case 56/65 Technique Minière v Maschinenbau Ulm (1966) ECR 235; and judgment of the Court of First Instance in Case T-77/92 Parker Pen v Commission (1994) ECR II-549.

(5) See Communication from the Commission Notice – Guidelines on the application of Article 81(3) of the Treaty, OJ C 101, 27.4.2004, p. 97 for the Commission's general methodology and interpretation of the conditions for applying Article 101(1) and in particular Article 101(3).

6. For most vertical restraints, competition concerns can only arise if there is insufficient competition at one or more levels of trade, that is, if there is some degree of market power at the level of the supplier or the buyer or at both levels. Vertical restraints are generally less harmful than horizontal restraints and may provide substantial scope for efficiencies.

7. The objective of Article 101 is to ensure that undertakings do not use agreements – in this context, vertical agreements – to restrict competition on the market to the detriment of consumers. Assessing vertical restraints is also important in the context of the wider objective of achieving an integrated internal market. Market integration enhances competition in the European Union. Companies should not be allowed to re-establish private barriers between Member States where State barriers have been successfully abolished.

II. VERTICAL AGREEMENTS WHICH GENERALLY FALL OUTSIDE THE SCOPE OF ARTICLE 101(1)

1. Agreements of minor importance and SMEs

8. Agreements that are not capable of appreciably affecting trade between Member States or of appreciably restricting competition by object or effect do not fall within the scope of Article 101(1). The Block Exemption Regulation applies only to agreements falling within the scope of application of Article 101(1). These Guidelines are without prejudice to the application of Commission Notice on agreements of minor importance which do not appreciably restrict competition under Article 81(1) of the Treaty establishing the European Community (*de minimis*) (6) or any future *de minimis* notice.

(6) OJ C 368, 22.12.2001, p. 13.

9. Subject to the conditions set out in the *de minimis* notice concerning hardcore restrictions and cumulative effect issues, vertical agreements entered into by non-competing undertakings whose individual market share on the relevant market does not exceed 15 % are generally considered to fall outside the scope of Article 101(1) (7). There is no presumption that vertical agreements concluded by undertakings having more than 15 % market share automatically infringe Article 101(1). Agreements between undertakings whose market share exceeds the 15 % threshold may still not have an appreciable effect on trade between Member States or may not constitute an appreciable restriction of competition (8). Such agreements need to be assessed in their legal and economic context. The criteria for the assessment of individual agreements are set out in paragraphs (96) to (229).

(7) For agreements between competing undertakings the *de minimis* market share threshold is 10 % for their collective market share on each affected relevant market.

(8) See judgment of the Court of First Instance in Case T-7/93 Langnese-Iglo v. Commission (1995) ECR II-1533, paragraph 98.

10. As regards hardcore restrictions referred to in the *de minimis* notice, Article 101(1) may apply below the 15 % threshold, provided that there is an appreciable effect on trade between Member States and on competition. The applicable case-law of the Court of Justice and the General Court is relevant in this respect (9). Reference is also made to the possible need to assess positive and negative effects of hardcore restrictions as described in particular in paragraph (47) of these Guidelines.

(9) See judgments of the Court of Justice in Case 5/69 Völk v. Vervaecke (1969) ECR 295; Case 1/71 Cadillon v. Höss (1971) ECR 351 and Case C-306/96 Javico v. Yves Saint Laurent (1998) ECR I-1983, paragraphs 16 and 17.

11. In addition, the Commission considers that, subject to cumulative effect and hardcore restrictions, vertical agreements between small and medium-sized undertakings as defined in the Annex to Commission Recommendation of 6 May 2003 concerning the definition of micro, small and medium-sized enterprises (10) are rarely capable of appreciably affecting trade between Member States or of appreciably restricting competition within the meaning of Article 101(1), and therefore generally fall outside the scope of Article 101(1). In cases where such agreements nonetheless meet the conditions for the application of Article 101(1), the

Commission will normally refrain from opening proceedings for lack of sufficient interest for the European Union unless those undertakings collectively or individually hold a dominant position in a substantial part of the internal market.

(10) *OJ* L 124, 20.5.2003, p. 36.

2. Agency agreements

2.1. Definition of agency agreements

12. An agent is a legal or physical person vested with the power to negotiate and/or conclude contracts on behalf of another person (the principal), either in the agent's own name or in the name of the principal, for the:
– purchase of goods or services by the principal, or
– sale of goods or services supplied by the principal.

13. The determining factor in defining an agency agreement for the application of Article 101(1) is the financial or commercial risk borne by the agent in relation to the activities for which it has been appointed as an agent by the principal (11). In this respect it is not material for the assessment whether the agent acts for one or several principals. Neither is material for this assessment the qualification given to their agreement by the parties or national legislation.

(11) See judgment of the Court of First Instance in Case T-325/01 Daimler Chrysler v. Commission (2005) ECR II-3319; judgments of the Court of Justice in Case C-217/05 Confederación Espanola de Empresarios de Estaciones de Servicio v. CEPSA (2006) ECR I-11987; and Case C-279/06 CEPSA Estaciones de Servicio SA v. LV Tobar e Hijos SL (2008) ECR I-6681.

14. There are three types of financial or commercial risk that are material to the definition of an agency agreement for the application of Article 101(1). First, there are the contract-specific risks which are directly related to the contracts concluded and/or negotiated by the agent on behalf of the principal, such as financing of stocks. Secondly, there are the risks related to market-specific investments. These are investments specifically required for the type of activity for which the agent has been appointed by the principal, that is, which are required to enable the agent to conclude and/or negotiate this type of contract. Such investments are usually sunk, which means that upon leaving that particular field of activity the investment cannot be used for other activities or sold other than at a significant loss. Thirdly, there are the risks related to other activities undertaken on the same product market, to the extent that the principal requires the agent to undertake such activities, but not as an agent on behalf of the principal but for its own risk.

15. For the purposes of applying Article 101(1), the agreement will be qualified as an agency agreement if the agent does not bear any, or bears only insignificant, risks in relation to the contracts concluded and/or negotiated on behalf of the principal, in relation to market-specific investments for that field of activity, and in relation to other activities required by the principal to be undertaken on the same product market. However, risks that are related to the activity of providing agency services in general, such as the risk of the agent's income being dependent upon its success as an agent or general investments in for instance premises or personnel, are not material to this assessment.

16. For the purpose of applying Article 101(1), an agreement will thus generally be considered an agency agreement where property in the contract goods bought or sold does not vest in the agent, or the agent does not himself supply the contract services and where the agent:

(a) does not contribute to the costs relating to the supply/purchase of the contract goods or services, including the costs of transporting the goods. This does not preclude the agent from carrying out the transport service, provided that the costs are covered by the principal;

(b) does not maintain at its own cost or risk stocks of the contract goods, including the costs of financing the stocks and the costs of loss of stocks and can return unsold goods to the principal without charge, unless the agent is liable for fault (for example, by failing to comply with reasonable security measures to avoid loss of stocks);

(c) does not undertake responsibility towards third parties for damage caused by the product sold (product liability), unless, as agent, it is liable for fault in this respect;

(d) does not take responsibility for customers' non-performance of the contract, with the exception of the loss of the agent's commission, unless the agent is liable for fault (for example, by failing to comply with reasonable security or anti-theft measures or failing to comply with reasonable measures to report theft to the principal or police or to communicate to the principal all necessary information available to him on the customer's financial reliability);

(e) is not, directly or indirectly, obliged to invest in sales promotion, such as contributions to the advertising budgets of the principal;

(f) does not make market-specific investments in equipment, premises or training of personnel, such as for example the petrol storage tank in the case of petrol retailing or specific software to sell insurance policies in case of insurance agents, unless these costs are fully reimbursed by the principal;

(g) does not undertake other activities within the same product market required by the principal, unless these activities are fully reimbursed by the principal.

17. This list is not exhaustive. However, where the agent incurs one or more of the risks or costs mentioned in paragraphs (14), (15) and (16), the agreement between agent and principal will not be qualified as an agency agreement. The question of risk must be assessed on a case-by-case basis, and with regard to the economic reality of the situation rather than the legal form. For practical reasons, the risk analysis may start with the assessment of the contract-specific risks. If contract-specific risks are incurred by the agent, it will be enough to conclude that the agent is an independent distributor. On the contrary, if the agent does not incur contract-specific risks, then it will be necessary to continue further the analysis by assessing the risks related to market-specific investments. Finally, if the agent does not incur any contract-specific risks and risks related to market-specific investments, the risks related to other required activities within the same product market may have to be considered.

2.2. The application of Article 101(1) to agency agreements

18. In the case of agency agreements as defined in section 2.1., the selling or purchasing function of the agent forms part of the principal's activities. Since the principal bears the commercial and financial risks related to the selling and purchasing of the contract goods and services all obligations imposed on the agent in relation to the contracts concluded and/or negotiated on behalf of the principal fall outside Article 101(1). The following obligations on the agent's part will be considered to form an inherent part of an agency agreement, as each of them relates to the ability of the principal to fix the scope of activity of the agent in relation to the contract goods or services, which is essential if the principal is to take the risks and therefore to be in a position to determine the commercial strategy:

(a) limitations on the territory in which the agent may sell these goods or services;

(b) limitations on the customers to whom the agent may sell these goods or services;

(c) the prices and conditions at which the agent must sell or purchase these goods or services.

19. In addition to governing the conditions of sale or purchase of the contract goods or services by the agent on behalf of the principal, agency agreements often contain provisions which concern the relationship between the agent and the principal. In particular, they may contain a provision preventing the principal from appointing other agents in respect of a given type of transaction, customer or territory (exclusive agency provisions) and/or a provision preventing the agent from acting as an agent or distributor of undertakings which compete with the principal (single branding provisions). Since the agent is a separate undertaking from the principal, the provisions which concern the relationship between the agent and the principal may infringe Article 101(1). Exclusive agency provisions will in general not lead to anti-competitive effects. However, single branding provisions and post-term non-compete provisions, which concern inter-brand competition, may infringe Article 101(1) if they lead to or contribute to a (cumulative) foreclosure effect on the relevant market where the contract goods or services are sold or purchased (see in particular Section VI.2.1.). Such provisions may benefit from the Block Exemption Regulation, in particular when the conditions provided in Article 5 of that Regulation are fulfilled. They can also be individually justified by efficiencies under Article 101(3) as for instance described in paragraphs (144) to (148).

20. An agency agreement may also fall within the scope of Article 101(1), even if the principal bears all the relevant financial and commercial risks, where it facilitates collusion. That could, for instance, be the case when a number of principals use the same agents while collectively excluding others from using these agents, or when they use the agents to collude on marketing strategy or to exchange sensitive market information between the principals.

21. Where the agent bears one or more of the relevant risks as described in paragraph (16), the agreement between agent and principal does not constitute an agency agreement for the purpose of applying Article 101(1). In that situation, the agent will be treated as an independent undertaking and the agreement between agent and principal will be subject to Article 101(1) as any other vertical agreement.

3. Subcontracting agreements

22. Subcontracting concerns a contractor providing technology or equipment to a subcontractor that undertakes to produce certain products on the basis thereof (exclusively) for the contractor. Subcontracting is covered by Commission notice of 18 December 1978 concerning the assessment of certain subcontracting agreements in relation to Article 85(1) of the EEC Treaty (12) (hereinafter «subcontracting notice»). According to that notice, which remains applicable, subcontracting agreements whereby the subcontractor undertakes to produce certain products exclusively for the contractor generally fall outside the scope of Article 101(1) provided that the technology or equipment is necessary to enable the subcontractor to produce the products. However, other restrictions imposed on the subcontractor such as the obligation not to conduct or exploit its own research and development or not to produce for third parties in general may fall within the scope of Article 101 (13).

(12) *OJ* C 1, 3.1.1979, p. 2.

(13) See paragraph 3 of the subcontracting notice.

III. APPLICATION OF THE BLOCK EXEMPTION REGULATION

1. Safe harbour created by the Block Exemption Regulation

23. For most vertical restraints, competition concerns can only arise if there is insufficient competition at one or more levels of trade, that is, if there is some degree of market power at the level of the supplier or the buyer or at both levels. Provided that they do not contain hardcore restrictions of competition, which are restrictions of competition by object, the Block Exemption Regulation creates a presumption of legality for vertical agreements depending on the market share of the supplier and the buyer. Pursuant to Article 3 of the Block Exemption Regulation, it is the supplier's market share on the market where it sells the contract goods or services and the buyer's market share on the market where it purchases the contract goods or services which determine the applicability of the block exemption. In order for the block exemption to apply, the supplier's and the buyer's market share must each be 30 % or less. Section V of these Guidelines provides guidance on how to define the relevant market and calculate the market shares. Above the market share threshold of 30 %, there is no presumption that vertical agreements fall within the scope of Article 101(1) or fail to satisfy the conditions of Article 101(3) but there is also no presumption that vertical agreements falling within the scope of Article 101(1) will usually satisfy the conditions of Article 101(3).

2. Scope of the Block Exemption Regulation

2.1. Definition of vertical agreements

24. Article 1(1)*(a)* of the Block Exemption Regulation defines a «vertical agreement» as «an agreement or concerted practice entered into between two or more undertakings each of which operates, for the purposes of the agreement or the concerted practice, at a different level of the production or distribution chain, and relating to the conditions under which the parties may purchase, sell or resell certain goods or services».

25. The definition of «vertical agreement» referred to in paragraph (24) has four main elements:

(a) The Block Exemption Regulation applies to agreements and concerted practices. The Block Exemption Regulation does not apply to unilateral conduct of the undertakings concerned. Such unilateral conduct can fall within the scope of Article 102 which prohibits abuses of a dominant position. For there to be an agreement within the meaning of Article 101 it is sufficient that the parties have expressed

their joint intention to conduct themselves on the market in a specific way. The form in which that intention is expressed is irrelevant as long as it constitutes a faithful expression of the parties' intention. In case there is no explicit agreement expressing the concurrence of wills, the Commission will have to prove that the unilateral policy of one party receives the acquiescence of the other party. For vertical agreements, there are two ways in which acquiescence with a particular unilateral policy can be established. First, the acquiescence can be deduced from the powers conferred upon the parties in a general agreement drawn up in advance. If the clauses of the agreement drawn up in advance provide for or authorise a party to adopt subsequently a specific unilateral policy which will be binding on the other party, the acquiescence of that policy by the other party can be established on the basis thereof (14). Secondly, in the absence of such an explicit acquiescence, the Commission can show the existence of tacit acquiescence. For that it is necessary to show first that one party requires explicitly or implicitly the cooperation of the other party for the implementation of its unilateral policy and second that the other party complied with that requirement by implementing that unilateral policy in practice (15). For instance, if after a supplier's announcement of a unilateral reduction of supplies in order to prevent parallel trade, distributors reduce immediately their orders and stop engaging in parallel trade, then those distributors tacitly acquiesce to the supplier's unilateral policy. This can however not be concluded if the distributors continue to engage in parallel trade or try to find new ways to engage in parallel trade. Similarly, for vertical agreements, tacit acquiescence may be deduced from the level of coercion exerted by a party to impose its unilateral policy on the other party or parties to the agreement in combination with the number of distributors that are actually implementing in practice the unilateral policy of the supplier. For instance, a system of monitoring and penalties, set up by a supplier to penalise those distributors that do not comply with its unilateral policy, points to tacit acquiescence with the supplier's unilateral policy if this system allows the supplier to implement in practice its policy. The two ways of establishing acquiescence described in this paragraph can be used jointly;

(b) The agreement or concerted practice is between two or more undertakings. Vertical agreements with final consumers not operating as an undertaking are not covered by the Block Exemption Regulation. More generally, agreements with final consumers do not fall under Article 101(1), as that article applies only to agreements between undertakings, decisions by associations of undertakings and concerted practices of undertakings. This is without prejudice to the possible application of Article 102;

(c) The agreement or concerted practice is between undertakings each operating, for the purposes of the agreement, at a different level of the production or distribution chain. This means for instance that one undertaking produces a raw material which the other undertaking uses as an input, or that the first is a manufacturer, the second a wholesaler and the third a retailer. This does not preclude an undertaking from being active at more than one level of the production or distribution chain;

(d) The agreements or concerted practices relate to the conditions under which the parties to the agreement, the supplier and the buyer, «may purchase, sell or resell certain goods or services». This reflects the purpose of the Block Exemption Regulation to cover purchase and distribution agreements. These are agreements which concern the conditions for the purchase, sale or resale of the goods or services supplied by the supplier and/or which concern the conditions for the sale by the buyer of the goods or services which incorporate these goods or services. Both the goods or services supplied by the supplier and the resulting goods or services are considered to be contract goods or services under the Block Exemption Regulation. Vertical agreements relating to all final and intermediate goods and services are covered. The only exception is the automobile sector, as long as this sector remains covered by a specific block exemption such as that granted by Commission Regulation (EC) N° 1400/2002 of 31 July 2002 on the application of Article 81(3) of the Treaty to categories of vertical agreements and concerted practices in the motor vehicle sector (16) or its successor. The goods or services provided by the supplier may be resold by the buyer or may be used as an input by the buyer to produce its own goods or services.

(14) Judgment of the Court of Justice in Case C-74/04 P Commission v. Volkswagen AG (2006) ECR I-6585.

(15) Judgment of the Court of First Instance in Case T-41/96 Bayer AG v. Commission (2000) ECR II-3383.

(16) OJ L 203, 1.8.2002, p. 30.

26. The Block Exemption Regulation also applies to goods sold and purchased for renting to third parties. However, rent and lease agreements as such are not covered, as no good or service is sold by the supplier to the buyer. More generally, the Block Exemption Regulation does not cover restrictions or obligations that do not relate to the conditions of purchase, sale and resale, such as an obligation preventing parties from carrying out independent research and development which the parties may have included in an otherwise vertical agreement. In addition, Article 2(2) to (5) of the Block Exemption Regulation directly or indirectly excludes certain vertical agreements from the application of that Regulation.

2.2. Vertical agreements between competitors

27. Article 2(4) of the Block Exemption Regulation explicitly excludes «vertical agreements entered into between competing undertakings» from its application. Vertical agreements between competitors are dealt with, as regards possible collusion effects, in the Commission Guidelines on the applicability of Article 81 of the EC Treaty to horizontal cooperation agreements (17). However, the vertical aspects of such agreements need to be assessed under these Guidelines. Article 1(1)(c) of the Block Exemption Regulation defines a competing undertaking as «an actual or potential competitor». Two companies are treated as actual competitors if they are active on the same relevant market. A company is treated as a potential competitor of another company if, absent the agreement, in case of a small but permanent increase in relative prices it is likely that this first company, within a short period of time normally not longer than one year, would undertake the necessary additional investments or other necessary switching costs to enter the relevant market on which the other company is active. That assessment must be based on realistic grounds; the mere theoretical possibility of entering a market is not sufficient (18). A distributor that provides specifications to a manufacturer to produce particular goods under the distributor's brand name is not to be considered a manufacturer of such own-brand goods.

(17) OJ C 3, 6.1.2001, p. 2. A revision of those Guidelines is forthcoming.

(18) See Commission Notice on the definition of the relevant market for the purposes of Community competition law, OJ C 372, 9.12.1997, p. 5, paragraphs 20 to 24, the Commission's Thirteenth Report on Competition Policy, point 55, and Commission Decision 90/410/EEC in Case N° IV/32.009 – Elopak/Metal Box-Odin, OJ L 209, 8.8.1990, p. 15.

28. Article 2(4) of the Block Exemption Regulation contains two exceptions to the general exclusion of vertical agreements between competitors. These exceptions concern non-reciprocal agreements. Non-reciprocal agreements between competitors are covered by the Block Exemption Regulation where *(a)* the supplier is a manufacturer and distributor of goods, while the buyer is only a distributor and not also a competing undertaking at the manufacturing level, or *(b)* the supplier is a provider of services operating at several levels of trade, while the buyer operates at the retail level and is not a competing undertaking at the level of trade where it purchases the contract services. The first exception covers situations of dual distribution, that is, the manufacturer of particular goods also acts as a distributor of the goods in competition with independent distributors of its goods. In case of dual distribution it is considered that in general any potential impact on the competitive relationship between the manufacturer and retailer at the retail level is of lesser importance than the potential impact of the vertical supply agreement on competition in general at the manufacturing or retail level. The second exception covers similar situations of dual distribution, but in this case for services, when the supplier is also a provider of products at the retail level where the buyer operates.

2.3. Associations of retailers

29. Article 2(2) of the Block Exemption Regulation includes in its application vertical agreements entered into by an association of undertakings which fulfils certain conditions and thereby excludes from the Block Exemption Regulation vertical agreements entered into by all other associations. Vertical agreements entered into between an association and its members, or between an association and its suppliers, are covered by the Block Exemption Regulation only if all the members are retailers of goods (not services) and if each individual member of the association has a turnover not exceeding EUR 50 million. Retailers are distributors reselling goods to final consumers. Where only a limited number of the members of the association have a turnover exceeding the EUR 50 million threshold and where these members together represent less than 15 % of the collective turnover of all the members combined, the assessment under Article 101 will normally not be affected.

30. An association of undertakings may involve both horizontal and vertical agreements. The horizontal agreements must be assessed according to the principles set out in the Guidelines on the applicability of Article 81 of the EC Treaty to horizontal cooperation agreements (19). If that assessment leads to the conclusion that a cooperation between undertakings in the area of purchasing or selling is acceptable, a further assessment will be necessary to examine the vertical agreements concluded by the association with its suppliers or its individual members. The latter assessment will follow the rules of the Block Exemption Regulation and these Guidelines. For instance, horizontal agreements concluded between the members of the association or decisions adopted by the association, such as the decision to require the members to purchase from the association or the decision to allocate exclusive territories to the members must first be assessed as a horizontal agreement. Once that assessment leads to the conclusion that the horizontal agreement is not anticompetitive, an assessment of the vertical agreements between the association and individual members or between the association and suppliers is necessary.

(19) See paragraph (27).

2.4. Vertical agreements containing provisions on intellectual property rights (IPRs)

31. Article 2(3) of the Block Exemption Regulation includes vertical agreements containing certain provisions relating to the assignment of IPRs to or use of IPRs by the buyer in its application and thereby excludes all other vertical agreements containing IPR provisions from the Block Exemption Regulation. The Block Exemption Regulation applies to vertical agreements containing IPR provisions where five conditions are fulfilled:

(a) The IPR provisions must be part of a vertical agreement, that is, an agreement with conditions under which the parties may purchase, sell or resell certain goods or services;

(b) The IPRs must be assigned to, or licensed for use by, the buyer;

(c) The IPR provisions must not constitute the primary object of the agreement;

(d) The IPR provisions must be directly related to the use, sale or resale of goods or services by the buyer or its customers. In the case of franchising where marketing forms the object of the exploitation of the IPRs, the goods or services are distributed by the master franchisee or the franchisees;

(e) The IPR provisions, in relation to the contract goods or services, must not contain restrictions of competition having the same object as vertical restraints which are not exempted under the Block Exemption Regulation.

32. Such conditions ensure that the Block Exemption Regulation applies to vertical agreements where the use, sale or resale of goods or services can be performed more effectively because IPRs are assigned to or licensed for use by the buyer. In other words, restrictions concerning the assignment or use of IPRs can be covered when the main object of the agreement is the purchase or distribution of goods or services.

33. The first condition makes clear that the context in which the IPRs are provided is an agreement to purchase or distribute goods or an agreement to purchase or provide services and not an agreement concerning the assignment or licensing of IPRs for the manufacture of goods, nor a pure licensing agreement. The Block Exemption Regulation does not cover for instance:

(a) agreements where a party provides another party with a recipe and licenses the other party to produce a drink with this recipe;

(b) agreements under which one party provides another party with a mould or master copy and licenses the other party to produce and distribute copies;

(c) the pure licence of a trade mark or sign for the purposes of merchandising;

(d) sponsorship contracts concerning the right to advertise oneself as being an official sponsor of an event;

(e) copyright licensing such as broadcasting contracts concerning the right to record and/or broadcast an event.

34. The second condition makes clear that the Block Exemption Regulation does not apply when the IPRs are provided by the buyer to the supplier, no matter whether the IPRs concern the manner of manufacture or of distribution. An agreement relating to the transfer of IPRs to the supplier and containing possible restrictions on the sales made by the supplier is not covered by the Block Exemption Regulation. That means, in particular, that subcontracting involving the transfer of know-how to a subcontractor (20) does not fall within the scope of application of the Block Exemption Regulation (see also paragraph (22)). However, vertical agreements under which the buyer provides only specifications to the supplier which describe the goods or services to be supplied fall within the scope of application of the Block Exemption Regulation.

(20) See the subcontracting notice (referred to in paragraph (22)).

35. The third condition makes clear that in order to be covered by the Block Exemption Regulation, the primary object of the agreement must not be the assignment or licensing of IPRs. The primary object must be the purchase, sale or resale of goods or services and the IPR provisions must serve the implementation of the vertical agreement.

36. The fourth condition requires that the IPR provisions facilitate the use, sale or resale of goods or services by the buyer or its customers. The goods or services for use or resale are usually supplied by the licensor but may also be purchased by the licensee from a third supplier. The IPR provisions will normally concern the marketing of goods or services. An example would be a franchise agreement where the franchisor sells goods for resale to the franchisee and licenses the franchisee to use its trade mark and know-how to market the goods or where the supplier of a concentrated extract licenses the buyer to dilute and bottle the extract before selling it as a drink.

37. The fifth condition highlights the fact that the IPR provisions should not have the same object as any of the hard-core restrictions listed in Article 4 of the Block Exemption Regulation or any of the restrictions excluded from the coverage of the Block Exemption Regulation by Article 5 of that Regulation (see paragraphs (47) to (69) of these Guidelines).

38. Intellectual property rights relevant to the implementation of vertical agreements within the meaning of Article 2(3) of the Block Exemption Regulation generally concern three main areas: trade marks, copyright and know-how.

Trade mark

39. A trade mark licence to a distributor may be related to the distribution of the licensor's products in a particular territory. If it is an exclusive licence, the agreement amounts to exclusive distribution.

Copyright

40. Resellers of goods covered by copyright (books, software, etc.) may be obliged by the copyright holder only to resell under the condition that the buyer, whether another reseller or the end user, shall not infringe the copyright. Such obligations on the reseller, to the extent that they fall under Article 101(1) at all, are covered by the Block Exemption Regulation.

41. Agreements, under which hard copies of software are supplied for resale and where the reseller does not acquire a licence to any rights over the software but only has the right to resell the hard copies, are to be regarded as agreements for the supply of goods for resale for the purpose of the Block Exemption Regulation. Under that form of distribution, licensing the software only occurs between the copyright owner and the user of the software. It may take the form of a «shrink wrap» licence, that is, a set of conditions included in the package of the hard copy which the end user is deemed to accept by opening the package.

42. Buyers of hardware incorporating software protected by copyright may be obliged by the copyright holder not to infringe the copyright, and must therefore not make copies and resell the software or make copies and use the software in combination with other hardware. Such use-restrictions, to the extent that they fall within Article 101(1) at all, are covered by the Block Exemption Regulation.

Know-how

43. Franchise agreements, with the exception of industrial franchise agreements, are the most obvious example of where know-how for marketing purposes is communicated to the buyer (21). Franchise agreements contain licences of intellectual property rights relating to trade marks or signs and know-how for the use and distribution of goods or the provision of services. In addition to the licence of IPR, the franchisor usually provides the franchisee during the life of the agreement with commercial or technical assistance, such as procurement services, training, advice on real estate, financial planning etc. The licence and the assistance are integral components of the business method being franchised.

(21) Paragraphs 43-45 apply by analogy to other types of distribution agreements which involve the transfer of substantial know-how from supplier to buyer.

44. Licensing contained in franchise agreements is covered by the Block Exemption Regulation where all five conditions listed in paragraph (31) are fulfilled. Those conditions are usually fulfilled as under most franchise agreements, including master franchise agreements, the franchisor provides goods and/or services, in particular commercial or technical assistance services, to the franchisee. The IPRs help the franchisee to resell the products supplied by the franchisor or by a supplier designated by the franchisor or to use those products and sell the resulting goods or services. Where the franchise agreement only or primarily concerns licensing of IPRs, it is not covered by the Block Exemption Regulation, but the Commission will, as a general rule, apply the principles set out in the Block Exemption Regulation and these Guidelines to such an agreement.

45. The following IPR-related obligations are generally considered necessary to protect the franchisor's intellectual property rights and are, where these obligations fall under Article 101(1), also covered by the Block Exemption Regulation:

(a) an obligation on the franchisee not to engage, directly or indirectly, in any similar business;

(b) an obligation on the franchisee not to acquire financial interests in the capital of a competing undertaking such as would give the franchisee the power to influence the economic conduct of such undertaking;

(c) an obligation on the franchisee not to disclose to third parties the know-how provided by the franchisor as long as this know-how is not in the public domain;

(d) an obligation on the franchisee to communicate to the franchisor any experience gained in exploiting the franchise and to grant the franchisor, and other franchisees, a non-exclusive licence for the know-how resulting from that experience;

(e) an obligation on the franchisee to inform the franchisor of infringements of licensed intellectual property rights, to take legal action against infringers or to assist the franchisor in any legal actions against infringers;

(f) an obligation on the franchisee not to use know-how licensed by the franchisor for purposes other than the exploitation of the franchise;

(g) an obligation on the franchisee not to assign the rights and obligations under the franchise agreement without the franchisor's consent.

2.5. Relationship to other block exemption regulations

46. Article 2(5) states that the Block Exemption Regulation does «not apply to vertical agreements the subject matter of which falls within the scope of any other block exemption regulation, unless otherwise provided for in such a regulation». The Block Exemption Regulation does not therefore apply to vertical agreements covered by Commission Regulation (EC) N° 772/2004 of 27 April 2004 on the application of Article 81(3) of the Treaty to categories of technology transfer agreements (22), Regulation 1400/2002 on the application of Article 81(3) of the Treaty to categories of vertical agreements and concerted practices in the motor vehicle sector (23) or Commission Regulation (EC) N° 2658/2000 of 29 November 2000 on the application of Article 81(3) of the Treaty to categories of specialisation agreements (24) and Commission Regulation (EC) N° 2659/2000 of 29 November 2000 on the application of Article 81(3) of the Treaty to categories of research and development agreements (25) exempting vertical agreements concluded in connection with horizontal agreements, or any future regulations of that kind, unless otherwise provided for in such a regulation.

(22) *OJ* L 123, 27.4.2004, p. 11.

(23) See paragraph (25).

(24) *OJ* L 304, 5.12.2000, p. 3.

(25) *OJ* L 304, 5.12.2000, p. 7.

3. Hardcore restrictions under the Block Exemption Regulation

47. Article 4 of the Block Exemption Regulation contains a list of hardcore restrictions which lead to the exclusion of the whole vertical agreement from the scope of application of the Block Exemption Regulation (26). Where such a hardcore restriction is included in an agreement, that agreement is presumed to fall within Article 101(1). It is also presumed that the agreement is unlikely to fulfil the conditions of Article 101(3), for which reason the block exemption does not apply. However, undertakings may demonstrate pro-competitive effects under Article 101(3) in an individual case (27). Where the undertakings substantiate that likely efficiencies result from including the hardcore restriction in the agreement and demonstrate that in general all the conditions of Article 101(3) are fulfilled, the Commission will be required to effectively assess the likely negative impact on competition before making an ultimate assessment of whether the conditions of Article 101(3) are fulfilled (28).

(26) This list of hardcore restrictions applies to vertical agreements concerning trade within the Union. In so far as vertical agreements concern exports outside the Union or imports/re-imports from outside the Union see judgment of the Court of Justice in Case C-306/96 Javico v. Yves Saint Laurent (1998) ECR I-1983. In that judgment the ECJ held in paragraph 20 that «an agreement in which the reseller gives to the producer an undertaking that it will sell the contractual products on a market outside the Community cannot be regarded as having the object of appreciably restricting competition within the common market or as being capable of affecting, as such, trade between Member States».

(27) See in particular paragraphs 106 to 109 describing in general possible efficiencies related to vertical restraints and Section VI.2.10. on resale price restrictions. See for general guidance on this the Communication from the Commission Notice – Guidelines on the application of Article 81(3) of the Treaty, *OJ* C 101, 27.4.2004, p. 97.

(28) Although, in legal terms, these are two distinct steps, they may in practice be an iterative process where the parties and Commission in several steps enhance and improve their respective arguments.

48. The hardcore restriction set out in Article 4*(a)* of the Block Exemption Regulation concerns resale price maintenance (RPM), that is, agreements or concerted practices having as their direct or indirect object the establishment of a fixed or minimum resale price or a fixed or minimum price level to be observed by the buyer. In the case of contractual provisions or concerted practices that directly establish the resale price, the restriction is clear cut. However, RPM can also be achieved through indirect means. Examples of the latter are an agreement fixing the distribution margin, fixing the maximum level of discount the distributor can grant from a prescribed price level, making the grant of rebates or reimbursement of promotional costs by the supplier subject to the observance of a given price level, linking the prescribed resale price to the resale prices of competitors, threats, intimidation, warnings, penalties, delay or suspension of deliveries or contract terminations in relation to observance of a given price level. Direct or indirect means of achieving price fixing can be made more effective when combined with measures to identify price-cutting distributors, such as the implementation of a price monitoring system, or the obligation on retailers to report other members of the distribution network that deviate from the standard price level. Similarly, direct or indirect price fixing can be made more effective when combined with measures which may reduce the buyer's incentive to lower the resale price, such as the supplier printing a recommended resale price on the product or the supplier obliging the buyer to apply a most-favoured-customer clause. The same indirect means and the same «supportive» measures can be used to make maximum or recommended prices work as RPM. However, the use of a particular supportive measure or the provision of a list of recommended prices or maximum prices by the supplier to the buyer is not considered in itself as leading to RPM.

49. In the case of agency agreements, the principal normally establishes the sales price, as the agent does not become the owner of the goods. However, where such an agreement cannot be qualified as an agency agreement for the purposes of applying Article 101(1) (see paragraphs (12) to (21)) an obligation preventing or restricting the agent from sharing its commission, fixed or variable, with the customer would be a hardcore restriction under Article 4*(a)* of the Block Exemption Regulation. In order to avoid including such a hardcore restriction in the agreement, the agent should thus be left free to lower the effective price paid by the customer without reducing the income for the principal (29).

(29) See, for instance, Commission Decision 91/562/EEC in Case N° IV/32.737 – Eirpage, OJ L 306, 7.11.1991, p. 22, in particular recital (6).

50. The hardcore restriction set out in Article 4(b) of the Block Exemption Regulation concerns agreements or concerted practices that have as their direct or indirect object the restriction of sales by a buyer party to the agreement or its customers, in as far as those restrictions relate to the territory into which or the customers to whom the buyer or its customers may sell the contract goods or services. This hardcore restriction relates to market partitioning by territory or by customer group. That may be the result of direct obligations, such as the obligation not to sell to certain customers or to customers in certain territories or the obligation to refer orders from these customers to other distributors. It may also result from indirect measures aimed at inducing the distributor not to sell to such customers, such as refusal or reduction of bonuses or discounts, termination of supply, reduction of supplied volumes or limitation of supplied volumes to the demand within the allocated territory or customer group, threat of contract termination, requiring a higher price for products to be exported, limiting the proportion of sales that can be exported or profit pass-over obligations. It may further result from the supplier not providing a Union-wide guarantee service under which normally all distributors are obliged to provide the guarantee service and are reimbursed for this service by the supplier, even in relation to products sold by other distributors into their territory (30). Such practices are even more likely to be viewed as a restriction of the buyer's sales when used in conjunction with the implementation by the supplier of a monitoring system aimed at verifying the effective destination of the supplied goods, such as the use of differentiated labels or serial numbers. However, obligations on the reseller relating to the display of the supplier's brand name are not classified as hardcore. As Article 4(b) only concerns restrictions of sales by the buyer or its customers, this implies that restrictions of the supplier's sales are also not a hardcore restriction, subject to what is stated in paragraph (59) regarding sales of spare parts in the context of Article 4(e) of the Block Exemption Regulation. Article 4(b) applies without prejudice to a restriction on the buyer's place of establishment. Thus, the benefit of the Block Exemption Regulation is not lost if it is agreed that the buyer will restrict its distribution outlet(s) and warehouse(s) to a particular address, place or territory.

(30) If the supplier decides not to reimburse its distributors for services rendered under the Union-wide guarantee, it may be agreed with these distributors that a distributor which makes a sale outside its allocated territory, will have to pay the distributor appointed in the territory of destination a fee based on the cost of the services (to be) carried out including a reasonable profit margin. This type of scheme may not be seen as a restriction of the distributors' sales outside their territory (see judgment of the Court of First Instance in Case T-67/01 JCB Service v. Commission (2004) ECR II-49, paragraphs 136 to 145).

51. There are four exceptions to the hardcore restriction in Article 4(b) of the Block Exemption Regulation. The first exception in Article 4(b)(i) allows a supplier to restrict active sales by a buyer party to the agreement to a territory or a customer group which has been allocated exclusively to another buyer or which the supplier has reserved to itself. A territory or customer group is exclusively allocated when the supplier agrees to sell its product only to one distributor for distribution in a particular territory or to a particular customer group and the exclusive distributor is protected against active selling into its territory or to its customer group by all the other buyers of the supplier within the Union, irrespective of sales by the supplier. The supplier is allowed to combine the allocation of an exclusive territory and an exclusive customer group by for instance appointing an exclusive distributor for a particular customer group in a certain territory. Such protection of exclusively allocated territories or customer groups must, however, permit passive sales to such territories or customer groups. For the application of Article 4(b) of the Block Exemption Regulation, the Commission interprets «active» and «passive» sales as follows:

– «Active» sales mean actively approaching individual customers by for instance direct mail, including the sending of unsolicited e-mails, or visits; or actively approaching a specific customer group or customers in a specific territory through advertisement in media, on the internet or other promotions specifically targeted at that customer group or targeted at customers in that territory. Advertisement or promotion that is only attractive for the buyer if it (also) reaches a specific group of customers or customers in a specific territory, is considered active selling to that customer group or customers in that territory.

– «Passive» sales mean responding to unsolicited requests from individual customers including delivery of goods or services to such customers. General advertising or promotion that reaches customers in other distributors' (exclusive) territories or customer groups but which is a reasonable way to reach customers outside those territories or customer groups, for instance to reach customers in one's own territory, are considered passive selling. General advertising or promotion is considered a reasonable way to reach such customers if it would be attractive for the buyer to undertake these investments also if they would not reach customers in other distributors' (exclusive) territories or customer groups.

52. The internet is a powerful tool to reach a greater number and variety of customers than by more traditional sales methods, which explains why certain restrictions on the use of the internet are dealt with as (re)sales restrictions. In principle, every distributor must be allowed to use the internet to sell products. In general, where a distributor uses a website to sell products that is considered a form of passive selling, since it is a reasonable way to allow customers to reach the distributor. The use of a website may have effects that extend beyond the distributor's own territory and customer group; however, such effects result from the technology allowing easy access from everywhere. If a customer visits the web site of a distributor and contacts the distributor and if such contact leads to a sale, including delivery, then that is considered passive selling. The same is true if a customer opts to be kept (automatically) informed by the distributor and it leads to a sale. Offering different language options on the website does not, of itself, change the passive character of such selling. The Commission thus regards the following as examples of hardcore restrictions of passive selling given the capability of these restrictions to limit the distributor's access to a greater number and variety of customers:

(a) an agreement that the (exclusive) distributor shall prevent customers located in another (exclusive) territory from viewing its website or shall automatically re-rout its customers to the manufacturer's or other (exclusive) distributors' websites. This does not exclude an agreement that the distributor's website shall also offer a number of links to websites of other distributors and/or the supplier;

(b) an agreement that the (exclusive) distributor shall terminate consumers' transactions over the internet once their credit card data reveal an address that is not within the distributor's (exclusive) territory;

(c) an agreement that the distributor shall limit its proportion of overall sales made over the internet. This does not exclude the supplier requiring, without limiting the online sales of the distributor, that the buyer sells at least a certain absolute amount (in value or volume) of the products offline to ensure an efficient operation of its brick and mortar shop (physical point of sales), nor does it preclude the supplier from making sure that the online activity of the distributor remains consistent with the supplier's distribution model (see paragraphs (54) and (56)). This absolute amount of required offline sales can be the same for all buyers, or determined individually for each buyer on the basis of objective criteria, such as the buyer's size in the network or its geographic location;

(d) an agreement that the distributor shall pay a higher price for products intended to be resold by the distributor online than for products intended to be resold offline. This does not exclude the supplier agreeing with the buyer a fixed fee (that is, not a variable fee where the sum increases with the realised offline turnover as this would amount indirectly to dual pricing) to support the latter's offline or online sales efforts.

53. A restriction on the use of the internet by distributors that are party to the agreement is compatible with the Block Exemption Regulation to the extent that promotion on the internet or use of the internet would lead to active selling into, for instance, other distributors' exclusive territories or customer groups. The Commission considers online advertisement specifically addressed to certain customers as a form of active selling to those customers. For instance, territory-based banners on third party websites are a form of active sales into the territory where these banners are shown. In general, efforts to be found specifically in a certain territory or by a certain customer group is active selling into that territory or to that customer group. For instance, paying a search engine or online advertisement provider to have advertisements displayed specifically to users in a particular territory is active selling into that territory.

54. However, under the Block Exemption the supplier may require quality standards for the use of the internet site to resell its goods, just as the supplier may require quality standards for a shop or for selling by catalogue or for advertising and promotion in general. This may be relevant in particular for selective distribution. Under the Block Exemption, the supplier may, for example, require that its distributors have one or more brick and mortar shops or showrooms as a condition for becoming a member of its distribution system. Subsequent changes to such a condition are also possible under the Block Exemption, except where those changes have as their object to directly or indirectly limit the online sales by the distributors. Similarly, a supplier may require that its distributors use third party platforms to distribute the contract products only in accordance with the standards and conditions agreed between the supplier and its distributors for the distributors' use of the internet. For instance, where the distributor's website is hosted by a third party platform, the supplier may require that customers do not visit the distributor's website through a site carrying the name or logo of the third party platform.

55. There are three further exceptions to the hardcore restriction set out in Article 4*(b)* of the Block Exemption Regulation. All three exceptions allow for the restriction of both active and passive sales. Under the first exception, it is permissible to restrict a wholesaler from selling to end users, which allows a supplier to keep the wholesale and retail level of trade separate. However, that exception does not exclude the possibility that the wholesaler can sell to certain end users, such as bigger end users, while not allowing sales to (all) other end users. The second exception allows a supplier to restrict an appointed distributor in a selective distribution system from selling, at any level of trade, to unauthorised distributors located in any territory where the system is currently operated or where the supplier does not yet sell the contract products (referred to as «the territory reserved by the supplier to operate that system» in Article 4*(b)*(iii)). The third exception allows a supplier to restrict a buyer of components, to whom the components are supplied for incorporation, from reselling them to competitors of the supplier. The term «component» includes any intermediate goods and the term «incorporation» refers to the use of any input to produce goods.

56. The hardcore restriction set out in Article 4*(c)* of the Block Exemption Regulation excludes the restriction of active or passive sales to end users, whether professional end users or final consumers, by members of a selective distribution network, without prejudice to the possibility of prohibiting a member of the network from operating out of an unauthorised place of establishment. Accordingly, dealers in a selective distribution system, as defined in Article 1(1)*(e)* of the Block Exemption Regulation, cannot be restricted in the choice of users to whom they may sell, or purchasing agents acting on behalf of those users except to protect an exclusive distribution system operated elsewhere (see paragraph (51)). Within a selective distribution system the dealers should be free to sell, both actively and passively, to all end users, also with the help of the internet. Therefore, the Commission considers any obligations which dissuade appointed dealers from using the internet to reach a greater number and variety of customers by imposing criteria for online sales which are not overall equivalent to the criteria imposed for the sales from the brick and mortar shop as a hardcore restriction. This does not mean that the criteria imposed for online sales must be identical to those imposed for offline sales, but rather that they should pursue the same objectives and achieve comparable results and that the difference between the criteria must be justified by the different nature of these two distribution modes. For example, in order to prevent sales to unauthorised dealers, a supplier can restrict its selected dealers from selling more than a given quantity of contract products to an individual end user. Such a requirement may have to be stricter for online sales if it is easier for an unauthorised dealer to obtain those products by using the internet. Similarly, it may have to be stricter for offline sales if it is easier to obtain them from a brick and mortar shop. In order to ensure timely delivery of contract products, a supplier may impose that the products be delivered instantly in the case of offline sales. Whereas an identical requirement cannot be imposed for online sales, the supplier may specify certain practicable delivery times for such sales. Specific requirements may have to be formulated for an online aftersales help desk, so as to cover the costs of customers returning the product and for applying secure payment systems.

57. Within the territory where the supplier operates selective distribution, this system may not be combined with exclusive distribution as that would lead to a hardcore restriction of active or passive selling by the dealers under Article 4*(c)* of the Block Exemption Regulation, with the exception that restrictions can be imposed on the dealer's ability to determine the location of its business premises. Selected dealers may be prevented from operating their business from different premises or from opening a new outlet in a different location. In that context, the use by a distributor of its own website cannot be considered to be the same thing as the opening of a new outlet in a different location. If the dealer's outlet is mobile, an area may be defined outside which the mobile outlet cannot be operated. In addition, the supplier may commit itself to supplying only one dealer or a limited number of dealers in a particular part of the territory where the selective distribution system is applied.

58. The hardcore restriction set out in Article 4*(d)* of the Block Exemption Regulation concerns the restriction of cross-supplies between appointed distributors within a selective distribution system. Accordingly, an agreement or concerted practice may not have as its direct or indirect object to prevent or restrict the active or passive selling of the contract products between the selected distributors. Selected distributors must remain free to purchase the contract products from other appointed distributors within the network, operating either at the same or at a different level of trade. Consequently, selective distribution cannot be combined with vertical restraints aimed at forcing distributors to purchase the contract products exclusively from a given source. It also means that within a selective distribution network, no restrictions can be imposed on appointed wholesalers as regards their sales of the product to appointed retailers.

59. The hardcore restriction set out in Article 4*(e)* of the Block Exemption Regulation concerns agreements that prevent or restrict end-users, independent repairers and service providers from obtaining spare parts directly from the manufacturer of those spare parts. An agreement between a manufacturer of spare parts and a buyer that incorporates those parts into its own products (original equipment manufacturer (OEM)), may not, either directly or indirectly, prevent or restrict sales by the manufacturer of those spare parts to end users, independent repairers or service providers. Indirect restrictions may arise particularly when the supplier of the spare parts is restricted in supplying technical information and special equipment which are necessary for the use of spare parts by users, independent repairers or service providers. However, the agreement may place restrictions on the supply of the spare parts to the repairers or service providers entrusted by the original equipment manufacturer with the repair or servicing of its own goods. In other words, the original equipment manufacturer may require its own repair and service network to buy spare parts from it.

4. Individual cases of hardcore sales restrictions that may fall outside the scope of Article 101(1) or may fulfil the conditions of Article 101(3)

60. Hardcore restrictions may be objectively necessary in exceptional cases for an agreement of a particular type or nature (31) and therefore fall outside Article 101(1). For example, a hardcore restriction may be objectively necessary to ensure that a public ban on selling dangerous substances to certain customers for reasons of safety or health is respected. In addition, undertakings may plead an efficiency defence under Article 101(3) in an individual case. This section provides some examples for (re)sales restrictions, whereas for RPM this is dealt with in section VI.2.10.

(31) See paragraph 18 of Communication from the Commission Notice – Guidelines on the application of Article 81(3) of the Treaty, *OJ* C 101, 27.4.2004, p. 97.

61. A distributor which will be the first to sell a new brand or the first to sell an existing brand on a new market, thereby ensuring a genuine entry on the relevant market, may have to commit substantial investments where there was previously no demand for that type of product in general or for that type of product from that producer. Such expenses may often be sunk and in such circumstances the distributor may not enter into the distribution agreement without protection for a certain period of time against (active and) passive sales into its territory or to its customer group by other distributors. For example such a situation may occur where a manufacturer established in a particular national market enters another national market and introduces its products with the help of an exclusive distributor and where this distributor needs to invest in launching and establishing the brand on this new market. Where substantial investments by the distributor to start up and/or develop the new market are necessary, restrictions of passive sales by other distributors into such a territory or to such a customer group which are necessary for the distributor to recoup those investments generally fall outside the scope of Article 101(1) during the first two years that the distributor is selling the contract goods or services in that territory or to that customer group, even though such hardcore restrictions are in general presumed to fall within the scope of Article 101(1).

62. In the case of genuine testing of a new product in a limited territory or with a limited customer group and in the case of a staggered introduction of a new product, the distributors appointed to sell the new product on the test market or to participate in the first round(s) of the staggered introduction may be restricted in their active selling outside the test market or the market(s) where the product is first introduced without falling within the scope of Article 101(1) for the period necessary for the testing or introduction of the product.

63. In the case of a selective distribution system, cross supplies between appointed distributors must normally remain free (see paragraph (58)). However, if appointed wholesalers located in different territories are obliged to invest in promotional activities in «their» territories to support the sales by appointed retailers and it is not practical to specify in a contract the required promotional activities, restrictions on active sales by the wholesalers to appointed retailers in other wholesalers' territories to overcome possible free riding may, in an individual case, fulfil the conditions of Article 101(3).

64. In general, an agreement that a distributor shall pay a higher price for products intended to be resold by the distributor online than for products intended to be resold offline («dual pricing») is a hardcore restriction (see paragraph (52)). However, in some specific circumstances, such an agreement may fulfil the conditions of Article 101(3). Such circumstances may be present where a manufacturer agrees such dual pricing with its distributors, because selling online leads to substantially higher costs for the manufacturer than offline sales. For example, where offline sales include home installation by the distributor but

online sales do not, the latter may lead to more customer complaints and warranty claims for the manufacturer. In that context, the Commission will also consider to what extent the restriction is likely to limit internet sales and hinder the distributor to reach more and different customers.

5. Excluded restrictions under the Block Exemption Regulation

65. Article 5 of the Block Exemption Regulation excludes certain obligations from the coverage of the Block Exemption Regulation even though the market share threshold is not exceeded. However, the Block Exemption Regulation continues to apply to the remaining part of the vertical agreement if that part is severable from the non-exempted obligations.

66. The first exclusion is provided for in Article 5(1)(a) of the Block Exemption Regulation and concerns non-compete obligations. Non-compete obligations are arrangements that result in the buyer purchasing from the supplier or from another undertaking designated by the supplier more than 80 % of the buyer's total purchases of the contract goods and services and their substitutes during the preceding calendar year (as defined by Article 1(1)(d) of the Block Exemption Regulation), thereby preventing the buyer from purchasing competing goods or services or limiting such purchases to less than 20 % of total purchases. Where, in the first year after entering in the agreement, for the year preceding the conclusion of the contract no relevant purchasing data for the buyer are available, the buyer's best estimate of its annual total requirements may be used. Such non-compete obligations are not covered by the Block Exemption Regulation where the duration is indefinite or exceeds five years. Non-compete obligations that are tacitly renewable beyond a period of five years are also not covered by the Block Exemption Regulation (see the second subparagraph of Article 5(1)). In general, non-compete obligations are exempted under that Regulation where their duration is limited to five years or less and no obstacles exist that hinder the buyer from effectively terminating the non-compete obligation at the end of the five year period. If, for instance, the agreement provides for a five-year non-compete obligation and the supplier provides a loan to the buyer, the repayment of that loan should not hinder the buyer from effectively terminating the non-compete obligation at the end of the five-year period. Similarly, when the supplier provides the buyer with equipment which is not relationship-specific, the buyer should have the possibility to take over the equipment at its market asset value once the non-compete obligation expires.

67. The five-year duration limit does not apply when the goods or services are resold by the buyer «from premises and land owned by the supplier or leased by the supplier from third parties not connected with the buyer». In such cases the non-compete obligation may be of the same duration as the period of occupancy of the point of sale by the buyer (Article 5(2) of the Block Exemption Regulation). The reason for this exception is that it is normally unreasonable to expect a supplier to allow competing products to be sold from premises and land owned by the supplier without its permission. By analogy, the same principles apply where the buyer operates from a mobile outlet owned by the supplier or leased by the supplier from third parties not connected with the buyer. Artificial ownership constructions, such as a transfer by the distributor of its proprietary rights over the land and premises to the supplier for only a limited period, intended to avoid the five-year limit cannot benefit from this exception.

68. The second exclusion from the block exemption is provided for in Article 5(1)(b) of the Block Exemption Regulation and concerns post term non-compete obligations on the buyer. Such obligations are normally not covered by the Block Exemption Regulation, unless the obligation is indispensable to protect know-how transferred by the supplier to the buyer, is limited to the point of sale from which the buyer has operated during the contract period, and is limited to a maximum period of one year (see Article 5(3) of the Block Exemption Regulation). According to the definition in Article 1(1)(g) of the Block Exemption Regulation the know-how needs to be «substantial», meaning that the know-how includes information which is significant and useful to the buyer for the use, sale or resale of the contract goods or services.

69. The third exclusion from the block exemption is provided for in Article 5(1)(c) of the Block Exemption Regulation and concerns the sale of competing goods in a selective distribution system. The Block Exemption Regulation covers the combination of selective distribution with a non-compete obligation, obliging the dealers not to resell competing brands in general. However, if the supplier prevents its appointed dealers, either directly or indirectly, from buying products for resale from specific competing suppliers, such an obligation cannot enjoy the benefit of the Block Exemption Regulation. The objective of the exclusion of such an obligation is to avoid a situation whereby a number of suppliers using the same selective distribution outlets prevent one specific competitor or certain specific competitors from using these outlets to distribute their products (foreclosure of a competing supplier which would be a form of collective boycott) (32).

(32) An example of indirect measures having such exclusionary effects can be found in Commission Decision 92/428/EEC in Case N° IV/33.542 – Parfum Givenchy, OJ L 236, 19.8.1992, p. 11.

6. Severability

70. The Block Exemption Regulation exempts vertical agreements on condition that no hardcore restriction, as set out in Article 4 of that Regulation, is contained in or practised with the vertical agreement. If there are one or more hardcore restrictions, the benefit of the Block Exemption Regulation is lost for the entire vertical agreement. There is no severability for hardcore restrictions.

71. The rule of severability does apply, however, to the excluded restrictions set out in Article 5 of the Block Exemption Regulation. Therefore, the benefit of the block exemption is only lost in relation to that part of the vertical agreement which does not comply with the conditions set out in Article 5.

7. Portfolio of products distributed through the same distribution system

72. Where a supplier uses the same distribution agreement to distribute several goods/services some of these may, in view of the market share threshold, be covered by the Block Exemption Regulation while others may not. In that case, the Block Exemption Regulation applies to those goods and services for which the conditions of application are fulfilled.

73. In respect of the goods or services which are not covered by the Block Exemption Regulation, the ordinary rules of competition apply, which means:

(a) there is no block exemption but also no presumption of illegality;

(b) if there is an infringement of Article 101(1) which is not exemptible, consideration may be given to whether there are appropriate remedies to solve the competition problem within the existing distribution system;

(c) if there are no such appropriate remedies, the supplier concerned will have to make other distribution arrangements.

Such a situation can also arise where Article 102 applies in respect of some products but not in respect of others.

IV. WITHDRAWAL OF THE BLOCK EXEMPTION AND DISAPPLICATION OF THE BLOCK EXEMPTION REGULATION

1. Withdrawal procedure

74. The presumption of legality conferred by the Block Exemption Regulation may be withdrawn where a vertical agreement, considered either in isolation or in conjunction with similar agreements enforced by competing suppliers or buyers, comes within the scope of Article 101(1) and does not fulfil all the conditions of Article 101(3).

75. The conditions of Article 101(3) may in particular not be fulfilled when access to the relevant market or competition therein is significantly restricted by the cumulative effect of parallel networks of similar vertical agreements practised by competing suppliers or buyers. Parallel networks of vertical agreements are to be regarded as similar if they contain restraints producing similar effects on the market. Such a situation may arise for example when, on a given market, certain suppliers practise purely qualitative selective distribution while other suppliers practise quantitative selective distribution. Such a situation may also arise when, on a given market, the cumulative use of qualitative criteria forecloses more efficient distributors. In such circumstances, the assessment must take account of the anti-competitive effects attributable to each individual network of agreements. Where appropriate, withdrawal may concern only a particular qualitative criterion or only the quantitative limitations imposed on the number of authorised distributors.

76. Responsibility for an anti-competitive cumulative effect can only be attributed to those undertakings which make an appreciable contribution to it. Agreements entered into by undertakings whose contribution to the cumulative effect is insignificant do not fall under the prohibition provided for in Article 101(1) (33) and are therefore not subject to the withdrawal mechanism. The assessment of such a contribution will be made in accordance with the criteria set out in paragraphs (128) to (229).

(33) Judgment of the Court of Justice of 28 February 1991 in Case C-234/89, Stergios Delimitis v. Henninger Bräu AG (1991) ECR I-935.

77. Where the withdrawal procedure is applied, the Commission bears the burden of proof that the agreement falls within the scope of Article 101(1) and that the agreement does not fulfil one or several of the conditions of Article 101(3). A withdrawal decision can only have *ex nunc* effect, which means that the exempted status of the agreements concerned will not be affected until the date at which the withdrawal becomes effective.

78. As referred to in recital 14 of the Block Exemption Regulation, the competition authority of a Member State may withdraw the benefit of the Block Exemption Regulation in respect of vertical agreements whose anti-competitive effects are felt in the territory of the Member State concerned or a part thereof, which has all the characteristics of a distinct geographic market. The Commission has the exclusive power to withdraw the benefit of the Block Exemption Regulation in respect of vertical agreements restricting competition on a relevant geographic market which is wider than the territory of a single Member State. When the territory of a single Member State, or a part thereof, constitutes the relevant geographic market, the Commission and the Member State concerned have concurrent competence for withdrawal.

2. Disapplication of the Block Exemption Regulation

79. Article 6 of the Block Exemption Regulation enables the Commission to exclude from the scope of the Block Exemption Regulation, by means of regulation, parallel networks of similar vertical restraints where these cover more than 50 % of a relevant market. Such a measure is not addressed to individual undertakings but concerns all undertakings whose agreements are defined in the regulation disapplying the Block Exemption Regulation.

80. Whereas the withdrawal of the benefit of the Block Exemption Regulation implies the adoption of a decision establishing an infringement of Article 101 by an individual company, the effect of a regulation under Article 6 is merely to remove, in respect of the restraints and the markets concerned, the benefit of the application of the Block Exemption Regulation and to restore the full application of Article 101(1) and (3). Following the adoption of a regulation declaring the Block Exemption Regulation inapplicable in respect of certain vertical restraints on a particular market, the criteria developed by the relevant case-law of the Court of Justice and the General Court and by notices and previous decisions adopted by the Commission will guide the application of Article 101 to individual agreements. Where appropriate, the Commission will take a decision in an individual case, which can provide guidance to all the undertakings operating on the market concerned.

81. For the purpose of calculating the 50 % market coverage ratio, account must be taken of each individual network of vertical agreements containing restraints, or combinations of restraints, producing similar effects on the market. Article 6 of the Block Exemption Regulation does not entail an obligation on the part of the Commission to act where the 50 % market-coverage ratio is exceeded. In general, disapplication is appropriate when it is likely that access to the relevant market or competition therein is appreciably restricted. This may occur in particular when parallel networks of selective distribution covering more than 50 % of a market are liable to foreclose the market by using selection criteria which are not required by the nature of the relevant goods or which discriminate against certain forms of distribution capable of selling such goods.

82. In assessing the need to apply Article 6 of the Block Exemption Regulation, the Commission will consider whether individual withdrawal would be a more appropriate remedy. This may depend, in particular, on the number of competing undertakings contributing to a cumulative effect on a market or the number of affected geographic markets within the Union.

83. Any regulation referred to in Article 6 of the Block Exemption Regulation must clearly set out its scope. Therefore, the Commission must first define the relevant product and geographic market(s) and, secondly, must identify the type of vertical restraint in respect of which the Block Exemption Regulation will no longer apply. As regards the latter aspect, the Commission may modulate the scope of its regulation according to the competition concern which it intends to address. For instance, while all parallel networks of single-branding type arrangements shall be taken into account in view of establishing the 50 % market coverage ratio, the Commission may nevertheless restrict the scope of the disapplication regulation only to non-compete obligations exceeding a certain duration. Thus, agreements of a shorter duration or of a less restrictive nature might be left unaffected, in consideration of the lesser degree of foreclosure attributable to such restraints. Similarly, when on a particular market selective distribution is practised in combination with additional restraints such as non-compete or quantity-forcing on the buyer, the disapplication regulation may concern only such additional restraints. Where appropriate, the Commission may also provide guidance by specifying the market share level which, in the specific market context, may be regarded as insufficient to bring about a significant contribution by an individual undertaking to the cumulative effect.

84. Pursuant to Regulation N° 19/65/EEC of 2 March 1965 of the Council on the application of Article 85(3) of the Treaty to certain categories of agreements and concerted practices (34), the Commission will have to set a transitional period of not less than six months before a regulation disapplying the Block Exemption Regulation becomes applicable. This should allow the undertakings concerned to adapt their agreements to take account of the regulation disapplying the Block Exemption Regulation.

(34) *OJ* 36, 6.3.1965, p. 533/65, English special edition: *OJ Series I* Chapter 1965-1966, p. 35.

85. A regulation disapplying the Block Exemption Regulation will not affect the exempted status of the agreements concerned for the period preceding its date of application.

V. MARKET DEFINITION AND MARKET SHARE CALCULATION

1. Commission Notice on definition of the relevant market

86. The Commission Notice on definition of the relevant market for the purposes of Community competition law (35) provides guidance on the rules, criteria and evidence which the Commission uses when considering market definition issues. That Notice will not be further explained in these Guidelines and should serve as the basis for market definition issues. These Guidelines will only deal with specific issues that arise in the context of vertical restraints and that are not dealt with in that notice.

(35) *OJ* C 372, 9.12.1997, p. 5.

2. The relevant market for calculating the 30 % market share threshold under the Block Exemption Regulation

87. Under Article 3 of the Block Exemption Regulation, the market share of both the supplier and the buyer are decisive to determine if the block exemption applies. In order for the block exemption to apply, the market share of the supplier on the market where it sells the contract products to the buyer, and the market share of the buyer on the market where it purchases the contract products, must each be 30 % or less. For agreements between small and medium-sized undertakings it is in general not necessary to calculate market shares (see paragraph (11)).

88. In order to calculate an undertaking's market share, it is necessary to determine the relevant market where that undertaking sells and purchases, respectively, the contract products. Accordingly, the relevant product market and the relevant geographic market must be defined. The relevant product market comprises any goods or services which are regarded by the buyers as interchangeable, by reason of their characteristics, prices and intended use. The relevant geographic market comprises the area in which the undertakings concerned are involved in the supply and demand of relevant goods or services, in which the conditions of competition are sufficiently homogeneous, and which can be distinguished from neighbouring geographic areas because, in particular, conditions of competition are appreciably different in those areas.

89. The product market definition primarily depends on substitutability from the buyers' perspective. When the supplied product is used as an input to produce other products and is generally not recognisable in the final product, the product market is normally defined by the direct buyers' preferences. The customers of the buyers will normally not have a strong preference concerning the inputs used by the buyers. Usually, the vertical restraints agreed between the supplier and buyer of the input only relate to the sale and purchase of the intermediate product and not to the sale of the resulting product. In the case of distribution of final goods, substitutes for the direct buyers will normally be influenced or determined by the preferences of the final consumers. A distributor, as reseller, cannot ignore the preferences of final consumers when it purchases final goods. In addition, at the distribution level the vertical restraints usually concern not only the sale of products between supplier and buyer, but also their resale. As different distribution formats usually compete, markets are in general not defined by the form of distribution that is applied. Where suppliers generally sell a portfolio of products, the entire portfolio may determine the product market when the portfolios and not the individual products are regarded as substitutes by the buyers. As distributors are professional buyers, the geographic wholesale market is usually wider than the retail market, where the product is resold to final consumers. Often, this will lead to the definition of national or wider wholesale markets. But retail markets may also be wider than the final consumers' search area where homogeneous market conditions and overlapping local or regional catchment areas exist.

90. Where a vertical agreement involves three parties, each operating at a different level of trade, each party's market share must be 30 % or less in order for the block exemption to apply. As specified in Article 3(2) of the Block Exemption Regulation, where in a multi party agreement an undertaking buys the contract goods or services from one undertaking party to the agreement and sells the contract goods or services to another undertaking party to the agreement, the block exemption applies only if its market share does not exceed the 30 % threshold both as a buyer and a supplier. If, for instance, in an agreement between a manufacturer, a wholesaler (or association of retailers) and a retailer, a non-compete obligation is agreed, then the market shares of the manufacturer and the wholesaler (or association of retailers) on their respective downstream markets must not exceed 30 % and the market share of the wholesaler (or association of retailers) and the retailer must not exceed 30 % on their respective purchase markets in order to benefit from the block exemption.

91. Where a supplier produces both original equipment and the repair or replacement parts for that equipment, the supplier will often be the only or the major supplier on the aftermarket for the repair and replacement parts. This may also arise where the supplier (OEM supplier) subcontracts the manufacturing of the repair or replacement parts. The relevant market for application of the Block Exemption Regulation may be the original equipment market including the spare parts or a separate original equipment market and after-market depending on the circumstances of the case, such as the effects of the restrictions involved, the lifetime of the equipment and importance of the repair or replacement costs (36). In practice, the issue is whether a significant proportion of buyers make their choice taking into account the lifetime costs of the product. If so, it indicates there is one market for the original equipment and spare parts combined.

(36) See for example Commission Decision in Pelikan/Kyocera (1995), COM(96) 126 (not published), point 87, and Commission Decision 91/595/EEC in Case N° IV/M.12 – Varta/Bosch, OJ L 320, 22.11.1991, p. 26, Commission Decision in Case N° IV/M.1094 – Caterpillar/Perkins Engines, OJ C 94, 28.3.1998, p. 23, and Commission Decision in Case N° IV/M.768 – Lucas/Varity, OJ C 266, 13.9.1996, p. 6. See also point 56 of the Notice on the definition of the relevant market for the purposes of Community competition law (see paragraph 86).

92. Where the vertical agreement, in addition to the supply of the contract goods, also contains IPR provisions – such as a provision concerning the use of the supplier's trademark – which help the buyer to market the contract goods, the supplier's market share on the market where it sells the contract goods is relevant for the application of the Block Exemption Regulation. Where a franchisor does not supply goods to be resold but provides a bundle of services and goods combined with IPR provisions which together form the business method being franchised, the franchisor needs to take account of its market share as a provider of a business method. For that purpose, the franchisor needs to calculate its market share on the market where the business method is exploited, which is the market where the franchisees exploit the business method to provide goods or services to end users. The franchisor must base its market share on the value of the goods or services supplied by its franchisees on this market. On such a market, the competitors may be providers of other franchised business methods but also suppliers of substitutable goods or services not applying franchising. For instance, without prejudice to the definition of such market, if there was a market for fast-food services, a franchisor operating on such a market would need to calculate its market share on the basis of the relevant sales figures of its franchisees on this market.

3. Calculation of market shares under the Block Exemption Regulation

93. The calculation of market shares needs to be based in principle on value figures. Where value figures are not available substantiated estimates can be made. Such estimates may be based on other reliable market information such as volume figures (see Article 7(a) of the Block Exemption Regulation).

94. In-house production, that is, production of an intermediate product for own use, may be very important in a competition analysis as one of the competitive constraints or to accentuate the market position of a company. However, for the purpose of market definition and the calculation of market share for intermediate goods and services, in-house production will not be taken into account.

95. However, in the case of dual distribution of final goods, that is, where a producer of final goods also acts as a distributor on the market, the market definition and market share calculation need to include sales of their own goods made by the producers through their vertically integrated distributors and agents (see Article 7(c) of the Block Exemption Regulation). «Integrated distributors» are connected undertakings within the meaning of Article 1(2) of the Block Exemption Regulation (37).

(37) For these market definition and market share calculation purposes, it is not relevant whether the integrated distributor sells in addition products of competitors.

VI. ENFORCEMENT POLICY IN INDIVIDUAL CASES

1. The framework of analysis

96. Outside the scope of the block exemption, it is relevant to examine whether in the individual case the agreement falls within the scope of Article 101(1) and if so whether the conditions of Article 101(3) are satisfied. Provided that they do not contain restrictions of competition by object and in particular hardcore restrictions of competition, there is no presumption that vertical agreements falling outside the block exemption because the market share threshold is exceeded fall within the scope of Article 101(1) or fail to satisfy the conditions of Article 101(3). Individual assessment of the likely effects of the agreement is required. Companies are encouraged to do their own assessment. Agreements that either do not restrict competition within the meaning of Article 101(1) or which fulfil the conditions of Article 101(3) are valid and enforceable. Pursuant to Article 1(2) of Council Regulation (EC) N° 1/2003 of 16 December 2002 on the implementation of the rules on competition laid down in Articles 81 and 82 of the Treaty (38) no notification needs to be made to benefit from an individual exemption under Article 101(3). In the case of an individual examination by the Commission, the latter will bear the burden of proof that the agreement in question infringes Article 101(1). The undertakings claiming the benefit of Article 101(3) bear the burden of proving that the conditions of that paragraph are fulfilled. When likely anti-competitive effects are demonstrated, undertakings may substantiate efficiency claims and explain why a certain distribution system is indispensable to bring likely benefits to consumers without eliminating competition, before the Commission decides whether the agreement satisfies the conditions of Article 101(3).

(38) OJ L 1, 4.1.2003, p. 1.

97. The assessment of whether a vertical agreement has the effect of restricting competition will be made by comparing the actual or likely future situation on the relevant market with the vertical restraints in place with the situation that would prevail in the absence of the vertical re-

straints in the agreement. In the assessment of individual cases, the Commission will take, as appropriate, both actual and likely effects into account. For vertical agreements to be restrictive of competition by effect they must affect actual or potential competition to such an extent that on the relevant market negative effects on prices, output, innovation, or the variety or quality of goods and services can be expected with a reasonable degree of probability. The likely negative effects on competition must be appreciable (39). Appreciable anticompetitive effects are likely to occur when at least one of the parties has or obtains some degree of market power and the agreement contributes to the creation, maintenance or strengthening of that market power or allows the parties to exploit such market power. Market power is the ability to maintain prices above competitive levels or to maintain output in terms of product quantities, product quality and variety or innovation below competitive levels for a not insignificant period of time. The degree of market power normally required for a finding of an infringement under Article 101(1) is less than the degree of market power required for a finding of dominance under Article 102.

(39) See Section II.1.

98. Vertical restraints are generally less harmful than horizontal restraints. The main reason for the greater focus on horizontal restraints is that such restraints may concern an agreement between competitors producing identical or substitutable goods or services. In such horizontal relationships, the exercise of market power by one company (higher price of its product) may benefit its competitors. This may provide an incentive to competitors to induce each other to behave anti-competitively. In vertical relationships, the product of the one is the input for the other-, in other words, the activities of the parties to the agreement are complementary to each other. The exercise of market power by either the upstream or downstream company would therefore normally hurt the demand for the product of the other. The companies involved in the agreement therefore usually have an incentive to prevent the exercise of market power by the other.

99. Such self-restraining character should not, however, be over-estimated. When a company has no market power, it can only try to increase its profits by optimising its manufacturing and distribution processes, with or without the help of vertical restraints. More generally, because of the complementary role of the parties to a vertical agreement in getting a product on the market, vertical restraints may provide substantial scope for efficiencies. However, when an undertaking does have market power it can also try to increase its profits at the expense of its direct competitors by raising their costs and at the expense of its buyers and ultimately consumers by trying to appropriate some of their surplus. This can happen when the upstream and downstream company share the extra profits or when one of the two uses vertical restraints to appropriate all the extra profits.

1.1. Negative effects of vertical restraints

100. The negative effects on the market that may result from vertical restraints which EU competition law aims at preventing are the following:

(a) anticompetitive foreclosure of other suppliers or other buyers by raising barriers to entry or expansion;

(b) softening of competition between the supplier and its competitors and/or facilitation of collusion amongst

these suppliers, often referred to as reduction of inter-brand competition (40);

(c) softening of competition between the buyer and its competitors and/or facilitation of collusion amongst these competitors, often referred to as reduction of intra-brand competition if it concerns distributors' competition on the basis of the brand or product of the same supplier;

(d) the creation of obstacles to market integration, including, above all, limitations on the possibilities for consumers to purchase goods or services in any Member State they may choose.

(40) By collusion is meant both explicit collusion and tacit collusion (conscious parallel behaviour).

101. Foreclosure, softening of competition and collusion at the manufacturers' level may harm consumers in particular by increasing the wholesale prices of the products, limiting the choice of products, lowering their quality or reducing the level of product innovation. Foreclosure, softening of competition and collusion at the distributors' level may harm consumers in particular by increasing the retail prices of the products, limiting the choice of price-service combinations and distribution formats, lowering the availability and quality of retail services and reducing the level of innovation of distribution.

102. On a market where individual distributors distribute the brand(s) of only one supplier, a reduction of competition between the distributors of the same brand will lead to a reduction of intra-brand competition between these distributors, but may not have a negative effect on competition between distributors in general. In such a case, if inter-brand competition is fierce, it is unlikely that a reduction of intra-brand competition will have negative effects for consumers.

103. Exclusive arrangements are generally more anti-competitive than non-exclusive arrangements. Exclusive arrangements, whether by means of express contractual language or their practical effects, result in one party sourcing all or practically all of its demand from another party. For instance, under a non-compete obligation the buyer purchases only one brand. Quantity forcing, on the other hand, leaves the buyer some scope to purchase competing goods. The degree of foreclosure may therefore be less with quantity forcing.

104. Vertical restraints agreed for non-branded goods and services are in general less harmful than restraints affecting the distribution of branded goods and services. Branding tends to increase product differentiation and reduce substitutability of the product, leading to a reduced elasticity of demand and an increased possibility to raise price. The distinction between branded and non-branded goods or services will often coincide with the distinction between intermediate goods and services and final goods and services.

105. In general, a combination of vertical restraints aggravates their individual negative effects. However, certain combinations of vertical restraints are less anti-competitive than their use in isolation. For instance, in an exclusive distribution system, the distributor may be tempted to increase the price of the products as intra-brand competition has been reduced. The use of quantity forcing or the setting of a maximum resale price may limit such price increases. Possible negative effects of vertical restraints are reinforced when several suppliers and their buyers organise their trade in a similar way, leading to so-called cumulative effects.

1.2. Positive effects of vertical restraints

106. It is important to recognise that vertical restraints may have positive effects by, in particular, promoting non-price competition and improved quality of services. When a company has no market power, it can only try to increase its profits by optimising its manufacturing or distribution processes. In a number of situations vertical restraints may be helpful in this respect since the usual arm's length dealings between supplier and buyer, determining only price and quantity of a certain transaction, can lead to a sub-optimal level of investments and sales.

107. While trying to give a fair overview of the various justifications for vertical restraints, these Guidelines do not claim to be complete or exhaustive. The following reasons may justify the application of certain vertical restraints:

(a) To solve a «free-rider» problem. One distributor may free-ride on the promotion efforts of another distributor. That type of problem is most common at the wholesale and retail level. Exclusive distribution or similar restrictions may be helpful in avoiding such free-riding. Free-riding can also occur between suppliers, for instance where one invests in promotion at the buyer's premises, in general at the retail level, that may also attract customers for its competitors. Non-compete type restraints can help to overcome free-riding (41).

For there to be a problem, there needs to be a real free-rider issue. Free-riding between buyers can only occur on pre-sales services and other promotional activities, but not on after-sales services for which the distributor can charge its customers individually. The product will usually need to be relatively new or technically complex or the reputation of the product must be a major determinant of its demand, as the customer may otherwise very well know what it wants, based on past purchases. And the product must be of a reasonably high value as it is otherwise not attractive for a customer to go to one shop for information and to another to buy. Lastly, it must not be practical for the supplier to impose on all buyers, by contract, effective promotion or service requirements.

Free-riding between suppliers is also restricted to specific situations, namely to cases where the promotion takes place at the buyer's premises and is generic, not brand specific.

(b) To «open up or enter new markets». Where a manufacturer wants to enter a new geographic market, for instance by exporting to another country for the first time, this may involve special «first time investments» by the distributor to establish the brand on the market. In order to persuade a local distributor to make these investments, it may be necessary to provide territorial protection to the distributor so that it can recoup these investments by temporarily charging a higher price. Distributors based in other markets should then be restrained for a limited period from selling on the new market (see also paragraph (61) in Section III.4.). This is a special case of the free-rider problem described under point *(a)*.

(c) The «certification free-rider issue». In some sectors, certain retailers have a reputation for stocking only «quality» products. In such a case, selling through those retailers may be vital for the introduction of a new product. If the manufacturer cannot initially limit its sales to the premium stores, it runs the risk of being de-listed and the product introduction may fail. There may, therefore, be a reason for allowing for a limited duration a restriction such as exclusive distribution or selective distribution. It must be enough to guarantee introduction of the new product but not so long as to hinder large-scale dissemination. Such benefits are more likely with «experience» goods or complex goods that represent a relatively large purchase for the final consumer.

(d) The so-called «hold-up problem». Sometimes there are client-specific investments to be made by either the supplier or the buyer, such as in special equipment or training. For instance, a component manufacturer that has to build new machines and tools in order to satisfy a particular requirement of one of its customers. The investor may not commit the necessary investments before particular supply arrangements are fixed.

However, as in the other free-riding examples, there are a number of conditions that have to be met before the risk of under-investment is real or significant. Firstly, the investment must be relationship-specific. An investment made by the supplier is considered to be relationship-specific when, after termination of the contract, it cannot be used by the supplier to supply other customers and can only be sold at a significant loss. An investment made by the buyer is considered to be relationship-specific when, after termination of the contract, it cannot be used by the buyer to purchase and/or use products supplied by other suppliers and can only be sold at a significant loss. An investment is thus relationship-specific because it can only, for instance, be used to produce a brand-specific component or to store a particular brand and thus cannot be used profitably to produce or resell alternatives. Secondly, it must be a long-term investment that is not recouped in the short run. And thirdly, the investment must be asymmetric, that is, one party to the contract invests more than the other party. Where these conditions are met, there is usually a good reason to have a vertical restraint for the duration it takes to depreciate the investment. The appropriate vertical restraint will be of the non-compete type or quantity-forcing type when the investment is made by the supplier and of the exclusive distribution, exclusive customer allocation or exclusive supply type when the investment is made by the buyer.

(e) The «specific hold-up problem that may arise in the case of transfer of substantial know-how». The know-how, once provided, cannot be taken back and the provider of the know-how may not want it to be used for or by its competitors. In as far as the know-how was not readily available to the buyer, is substantial and indispensable for the operation of the agreement, such a transfer may justify a non-compete type of restriction, which would normally fall outside Article 101(1).

(f) The «vertical externality issue». A retailer may not gain all the benefits of its action taken to improve sales; some may go to the manufacturer. For every extra unit a retailer sells by lowering its resale price or by increasing its sales effort, the manufacturer benefits if its wholesale price exceeds its marginal production costs. Thus, there may be a positive externality bestowed on the manufacturer by such retailer's actions and from the manufacturer's perspective the retailer may be pricing too high and/or making too little sales efforts. The negative externality of too high pricing by the retailer is sometimes called the «double marginalisation problem» and it can be avoided by imposing a maximum resale price on the retailer. To increase the retailer's sales efforts selective distribution, exclusive distribution or similar restrictions may be helpful (42).

(g) «Économies of scale in distribution». In order to have scale economies exploited and thereby see a lower retail price for its product, the manufacturer may want to con-

centrate the resale of its products on a limited number of distributors. To do so, it could use exclusive distribution, quantity forcing in the form of a minimum purchasing requirement, selective distribution containing such a requirement or exclusive sourcing.

(h) «Capital market imperfections». The usual providers of capital (banks, equity markets) may provide capital suboptimally when they have imperfect information on the quality of the borrower or there is an inadequate basis to secure the loan. The buyer or supplier may have better information and be able, through an exclusive relationship, to obtain extra security for its investment. Where the supplier provides the loan to the buyer, this may lead to non-compete or quantity forcing on the buyer. Where the buyer provides the loan to the supplier, this may be the reason for having exclusive supply or quantity forcing on the supplier.

(i) «Uniformity and quality standardisation». A vertical restraint may help to create a brand image by imposing a certain measure of uniformity and quality standardisation on the distributors, thereby increasing the attractiveness of the product to the final consumer and increasing its sales. This can for instance be found in selective distribution and franchising.

(41) Whether consumers actually benefit overall from extra promotional efforts depends on whether the extra promotion informs and convinces and thus benefits many new customers or mainly reaches customers who already know what they want to buy and for whom the extra promotion only or mainly implies a price increase.

(42) See however the previous footnote.

108. The nine situations listed in paragraph (107) make clear that under certain conditions, vertical agreements are likely to help realise efficiencies and the development of new markets and that this may offset possible negative effects. The case is in general strongest for vertical restraints of a limited duration which help the introduction of new complex products or protect relationship-specific investments. A vertical restraint is sometimes necessary for as long as the supplier sells its product to the buyer (see in particular the situations described in paragraph (107)*(a)*, *(e)*, *(f)*, *(g)* and *(i)*).

109. A large measure of substitutability exists between the different vertical restraints. As a result, the same inefficiency problem can be solved by different vertical restraints. For instance, economies of scale in distribution may possibly be achieved by using exclusive distribution, selective distribution, quantity forcing or exclusive sourcing. However, the negative effects on competition may differ between the various vertical restraints, which plays a role when indispensability is discussed under Article 101(3).

1.3. Methodology of analysis

110. The assessment of a vertical restraint generally involves the following four steps (43):

(a) First, the undertakings involved need to establish the market shares of the supplier and the buyer on the market where they respectively sell and purchase the contract products.

(b) If the relevant market share of the supplier and the buyer each do not exceed the 30 % threshold, the vertical agreement is covered by the Block Exemption Regulation, subject to the hardcore restrictions and excluded restrictions set out in that Regulation.

(c) If the relevant market share is above the 30 % threshold for supplier and/or buyer, it is necessary to assess whether the vertical agreement falls within Article 101(1).

(d) If the vertical agreement falls within Article 101(1), it is necessary to examine whether it fulfils the conditions for exemption under Article 101(3).

(43) These steps are not intended to present a legal reasoning that the Commission should follow in this order to take a decision.

1.3.1. Relevant factors for the assessment under Article 101(1)

111. In assessing cases above the market share threshold of 30 %, the Commission will undertake a full competition analysis. The following factors are particularly relevant to establish whether a vertical agreement brings about an appreciable restriction of competition under Article 101(1):

(a) nature of the agreement;

(b) market position of the parties;

(c) market position of competitors;

(d) market position of buyers of the contract products;

(e) entry barriers;

(f) maturity of the market;

(g) level of trade;

(h) nature of the product;

(i) other factors.

112. The importance of individual factors may vary from case to case and depends on all other factors. For instance, a high market share of the parties is usually a good indicator of market power, but in the case of low entry barriers it may not be indicative of market power. It is therefore not possible to provide firm rules on the importance of the individual factors.

113. Vertical agreements can take many shapes and forms. It is therefore important to analyse the nature of the agreement in terms of the restraints that it contains, the duration of those restraints and the percentage of total sales on the market affected by those restraints. It may be necessary to go beyond the express terms of the agreement. The existence of implicit restraints may be derived from the way in which the agreement is implemented by the parties and the incentives that they face.

114. The market position of the parties provides an indication of the degree of market power, if any, possessed by the supplier, the buyer or both. The higher their market share, the greater their market power is likely to be. This is particularly so where the market share reflects cost advantages or other competitive advantages vis-à-vis competitors. Such competitive advantages may, for instance, result from being a first mover on the market (having the best site, etc.), from holding essential patents or having superior technology, from being the brand leader or having a superior portfolio.

115. Such indicators, namely market share and possible competitive advantages, are used to assess the market position of competitors. The stronger the competitors are and the greater their number, the less risk there is that the parties will be able to individually exercise market power and foreclose the market or soften competition. It is also relevant to consider whether there are effective and timely counterstrategies that competitors would be likely to deploy. However, if the number of competitors becomes rather small and their market position (size, costs, R&D potential, etc.) is rather similar, such a market structure may increase the risk of collusion. Fluctuating or rapidly changing market shares are in general an indication of intense competition.

116. The market position of the parties' customers provides an indication of whether or not one or more of those customers possess buyer power. The first indicator of buyer power is the market share of the customer on the purchase market. That share reflects the importance of its demand for possible suppliers. Other indicators focus on the position of the customer on its resale market, including characteristics such as a wide geographic spread of its outlets, own brands including private labels and its brand image amongst final consumers. In some circumstances, buyer power may prevent the parties from exercising market power and thereby solve a competition problem that would otherwise have existed. This is particularly so when strong customers have the capacity and incentive to bring new sources of supply on to the market in the case of a small but permanent increase in relative prices. Where strong customers merely extract favourable terms for themselves or simply pass on any price increase to their customers, their position does not prevent the parties from exercising market power.

117. Entry barriers are measured by the extent to which incumbent companies can increase their price above the competitive level without attracting new entry. In the absence of entry barriers, easy and quick entry would render price increases unprofitable. When effective entry, preventing or eroding the exercise of market power, is likely to occur within one or two years, entry barriers can, as a general rule, be said to be low. Entry barriers may result from a wide variety of factors such as economies of scale and scope, government regulations, especially where they establish exclusive rights, state aid, import tariffs, intellectual property rights, ownership of resources where the supply is limited due to for instance natural limitations (44), essential facilities, a first mover advantage and brand loyalty of consumers created by strong advertising over a period of time. Vertical restraints and vertical integration may also work as an entry barrier by making access more difficult and foreclosing (potential) competitors. Entry barriers may be present at only the supplier or buyer level or at both levels. The question whether certain of those factors should be described as entry barriers depends particularly on whether they entail sunk costs. Sunk costs are those costs that have to be incurred to enter or be active on a market but that are lost when the market is exited. Advertising costs to build consumer loyalty are normally sunk costs, unless an exiting firm could either sell its brand name or use it somewhere else without a loss. The more costs are sunk, the more potential entrants have to weigh the risks of entering the market and the more credibly incumbents can threaten that they will match new competition, as sunk costs make it costly for incumbents to leave the market. If, for instance, distributors are tied to a manufacturer via a non-compete obligation, the foreclosing effect will be more significant if setting up its own distributors will impose sunk costs on the potential entrant. In general, entry requires sunk costs, sometimes minor and sometimes major. Therefore, actual competition is in general more effective and will weigh more heavily in the assessment of a case than potential competition.

(44) See Commission Decision 97/26/EC (Case N° IV/M.619 – Gencor/Lonrho), *OJ* L 11, 14.1.1997, p. 30.

118. A mature market is a market that has existed for some time, where the technology used is well known and widespread and not changing very much, where there are no major brand innovations and in which demand is relatively stable or declining. In such a market, negative effects are more likely than in more dynamic markets.

119. The level of trade is linked to the distinction between intermediate and final goods and services. Intermediate goods and services are sold to undertakings for use as an input to produce other goods or services and are generally not recognisable in the final goods or services. The buyers of intermediate products are usually well-informed customers, able to assess quality and therefore less reliant on brand and image. Final goods are, directly or indirectly, sold to final consumers that often rely more on brand and image. As distributors have to respond to the demand of final consumers, competition may suffer more when distributors are foreclosed from selling one or a number of brands than when buyers of intermediate products are prevented from buying competing products from certain sources of supply.

120. The nature of the product plays a role in particular for final products in assessing both the likely negative and the likely positive effects. When assessing the likely negative effects, it is important whether the products on the market are more homogeneous or heterogeneous, whether the product is expensive, taking up a large part of the consumer's budget, or is inexpensive and whether the product is a one-off purchase or repeatedly purchased. In general, when the product is more heterogeneous, less expensive and resembles more a one-off purchase, vertical restraints are more likely to have negative effects.

121. In the assessment of particular restraints other factors may have to be taken into account. Among these factors can be the cumulative effect, that is, the coverage of the market by similar agreements of others, whether the agreement is «imposed» (mainly one party is subject to the restrictions or obligations) or «agreed» (both parties accept restrictions or obligations), the regulatory environment and behaviour that may indicate or facilitate collusion like price leadership, pre-announced price changes and discussions on the «right» price, price rigidity in response to excess capacity, price discrimination and past collusive behaviour.

1.3.2. Relevant factors for the assessment under Article 101(3)

122. Restrictive vertical agreements may also produce pro-competitive effects in the form of efficiencies, which may outweigh their anti-competitive effects. Such an assessment takes place within the framework of Article 101(3), which contains an exception from the prohibition rule of Article 101(1). For that exception to be applicable, the vertical agreement must produce objective economic benefits, the restrictions on competition must be indispensable to attain the efficiencies, consumers must receive a fair share of the efficiency gains, and the agreement must not afford the parties the possibility of eliminating competition in respect of a substantial part of the products concerned (45).

(45) See Communication from the Commission Notice – Guidelines on the application of Article 81(3) of the Treaty, *OJ* C 101, 27.4.2004, p. 97.

123. The assessment of restrictive agreements under Article 101(3) is made within the actual context in which they occur (46) and on the basis of the facts existing at any given point in time. The assessment is sensitive to material changes in the facts. The exception rule of Article 101(3) applies as long as the four conditions are fulfilled and ceases to apply when that is no longer the case (47). When applying Article 101(3) in accordance with these principles it is necessary to take into account the investments made by any of the parties and the time needed and the restraints required to commit and recoup an efficiency enhancing investment.

(46) See Judgment of the Court of Justice in Joined Cases 25/84 and 26/84 Ford (1985) ECR 2725.

(47) See in this respect for example Commission Decision 1999/242/EC (Case N° IV/36.237 – TPS), OJ L 90, 2.4.1999, p. 6. Similarly, the prohibition of Article 101(1) also only applies as long as the agreement has a restrictive object or restrictive effects.

124. The first condition of Article 101(3) requires an assessment of what are the objective benefits in terms of efficiencies produced by the agreement. In this respect, vertical agreements often have the potential to help realise efficiencies, as explained in section 1.2., by improving the way in which the parties conduct their complementary activities.

125. In the application of the indispensability test contained in Article 101(3), the Commission will in particular examine whether individual restrictions make it possible to perform the production, purchase and/or (re)sale of the contract products more efficiently than would have been the case in the absence of the restriction concerned. In making such an assessment, the market conditions and the realities facing the parties must be taken into account. Undertakings invoking the benefit of Article 101(3) are not required to consider hypothetical and theoretical alternatives. They must, however, explain and demonstrate why seemingly realistic and significantly less restrictive alternatives would be significantly less efficient. If the application of what appears to be a commercially realistic and less restrictive alternative would lead to a significant loss of efficiencies, the restriction in question is treated as indispensable.

126. The condition that consumers must receive a fair share of the benefits implies that consumers of the products purchased and/or (re)sold under the vertical agreement must at least be compensated for the negative effects of the agreement (48). In other words, the efficiency gains must fully off-set the likely negative impact on prices, output and other relevant factors caused by the agreement.

(48) See paragraph 85 of Communication from the Commission Notice – Guidelines on the application of Article 81(3) of the Treaty, OJ C 101, 27.4.2004, p. 97.

127. The last condition of Article 101(3), according to which the agreement must not afford the parties the possibility of eliminating competition in respect of a substantial part of the products concerned, presupposes an analysis of remaining competitive pressures on the market and the impact of the agreement on such sources of competition. In the application of the last condition of Article 101(3), the relationship between Article 101(3) and Article 102 must be taken into account. According to settled case law, the application of Article 101(3) cannot prevent the application of Article 102 (49). Moreover, since Articles 101 and 102 both pursue the aim of maintaining effective competition on the market, consistency requires that Article 101(3) be interpreted as precluding any application of the exception rule to restrictive agreements that constitute an abuse of a dominant position (50). The vertical agreement may not eliminate effective competition, by removing all or most existing sources of actual or potential competition. Rivalry between undertakings is an essential driver of economic efficiency, including dynamic efficiencies in the form of innovation. In its absence, the dominant undertaking will lack adequate incentives to continue to create and pass on efficiency gains. Where there is no residual competition and no foreseeable threat of entry, the protection of rivalry and the competitive process outweighs possible efficiency gains. A restrictive agreement which maintains, creates or strengthens a market position approaching that of a monopoly can normally not be justified on the grounds that it also creates efficiency gains.

(49) See Judgment of the Court of Justice in Joined Cases C-395/96 P and C-396/96 P Compagnie Maritime Belge (2000) ECR I-1365, paragraph 130. Similarly, the application of Article 101(3) does not prevent the application of the Treaty rules on the free movement of goods, services, persons and capital. These provisions are in certain circumstances applicable to agreements, decisions and concerted practices within the meaning of Article 101(1), see to that effect Judgment of the Court of Justice in Case C-309/99 Wouters (2002) ECR I-1577, paragraph 120.

(50) See in this respect Judgment of the Court of First Instance in Case T-51/89 Tetra Pak (I) (1990) ECR II-309. See also paragraph 106 of Communication from the Commission Notice – Guidelines on the application of Article 81(3) of the Treaty, OJ C 101, 27.4.2004, p. 97.

2. Analysis of specific vertical restraints

128. The most common vertical restraints and combinations of vertical restraints are analysed in the remainder of these Guidelines following the framework of analysis developed in paragraphs (96) to (127). Other restraints and combinations exist for which no direct guidance is provided in these Guidelines. They will, however, be treated according to the same principles and with the same emphasis on the effect on the market.

2.1. Single branding

129. Under the heading of «single branding» fall those agreements which have as their main element the fact that the buyer is obliged or induced to concentrate its orders for a particular type of product with one supplier. That component can be found amongst others in non-compete and quantity-forcing on the buyer. A non-compete arrangement is based on an obligation or incentive scheme which makes the buyer purchase more than 80 % of its requirements on a particular market from only one supplier. It does not mean that the buyer can only buy directly from the supplier, but that the buyer will not buy and resell or incorporate competing goods or services. Quantity-forcing on the buyer is a weaker form of non-compete, where incentives or obligations agreed between the supplier and the buyer make the latter concentrate its purchases to a large extent with one supplier. Quantity-forcing may for example take the form of minimum purchase requirements, stocking requirements or non-linear pricing, such as conditional rebate schemes or a two-part tariff (fixed fee plus a price per unit). A so-called «English clause», requiring the buyer to report any better offer and allowing him only to accept such an offer when the supplier does not match it, can be expected to have the same effect as a single branding obligation, especially when the buyer has to reveal who makes the better offer.

130. The possible competition risks of single branding are foreclosure of the market to competing suppliers and potential suppliers, softening of competition and facilitation of collusion between suppliers in case of cumulative use and, where the buyer is a retailer selling to final consumers, a loss of in-store inter-brand competition. Such restrictive effects have a direct impact on inter-brand competition.

131. Single branding is exempted by the Block Exemption Regulation where the supplier's and buyer's market share each do not exceed 30 % and are subject to a limitation in time of five years for the non-compete obligation. The remainder of this section provides guidance for the assessment of individual cases above the market share threshold or beyond the time limit of five years.

132. The capacity for single branding obligations of one specific supplier to result in anticompetitive foreclosure arises in particular where, without the obligations, an important competitive constraint is exercised by competitors that either are not yet present on the market at the time the obligations are concluded, or that are not in a position to compete for the full supply of the customers. Competitors may not be able to compete for an individual customer's entire demand because the supplier in question is an unavoidable trading partner at least for part of the demand on the market, for instance because its brand is a «must stock item» preferred by many final consumers or because the capacity constraints on the other suppliers are such that a part of demand can only be provided for by the supplier in question (51). The market position of the supplier is thus of main importance to assess possible anti-competitive effects of single branding obligations.

(51) Judgment of the Court of First Instance in Case T-65/98 Van den Bergh Foods v. Commission (2003) ECR II-4653, paragraphs 104 and 156.

133. If competitors can compete on equal terms for each individual customer's entire demand, single branding obligations of one specific supplier are generally unlikely to hamper effective competition unless the switching of supplier by customers is rendered difficult due to the duration and market coverage of the single branding obligations. The higher its tied market share, that is, the part of its market share sold under a single branding obligation, the more significant foreclosure is likely to be. Similarly, the longer the duration of the single branding obligations, the more significant foreclosure is likely to be. Single branding obligations shorter than one year entered into by non-dominant companies are generally not considered to give rise to appreciable anti-competitive effects or net negative effects. Single branding obligations between one and five years entered into by non-dominant companies usually require a proper balancing of pro- and anti-competitive effects, while single branding obligations exceeding five years are for most types of investments not considered necessary to achieve the claimed efficiencies or the efficiencies are not sufficient to outweigh their foreclosure effect. Single branding obligations are more likely to result in anti-competitive foreclosure when entered into by dominant companies.

134. When assessing the supplier's market power, the market position of its competitors is important. As long as the competitors are sufficiently numerous and strong, no appreciable anti-competitive effects can be expected. Foreclosure of competitors is not very likely where they have similar market positions and can offer similarly attractive products. In such a case, foreclosure may, however, occur for potential entrants when a number of major suppliers enter into single branding contracts with a significant number of buyers on the relevant market (cumulative effect situation). This is also a situation where single branding agreements may facilitate collusion between competing suppliers. If, individually, those suppliers are covered by the Block Exemption Regulation, a withdrawal of the block exemption may be necessary to deal with such a negative cumulative effect. A tied market share of less than 5 % is not considered in general to contribute significantly to a cumulative foreclosure effect.

135. In cases where the market share of the largest supplier is below 30 % and the market share of the five largest suppliers is below 50 %, there is unlikely to be a single or a cumulative anti-competitive effect situation. Where a potential entrant cannot penetrate the market profitably, it is likely to be due to factors other than single branding obligations, such as consumer preferences.

136. Entry barriers are important to establish whether there is anticompetitive foreclosure. Wherever it is relatively easy for competing suppliers to create new buyers or find alternative buyers for their product, foreclosure is unlikely to be a real problem. However, there are often entry barriers, both at the manufacturing and at the distribution level.

137. Countervailing power is relevant, as powerful buyers will not easily allow themselves to be cut off from the supply of competing goods or services. More generally, in order to convince customers to accept single branding, the supplier may have to compensate them, in whole or in part, for the loss in competition resulting from the exclusivity. Where such compensation is given, it may be in the individual interest of a customer to enter into a single branding obligation with the supplier. But it would be wrong to conclude automatically from this that all single branding obligations, taken together, are overall beneficial for customers on that market and for the final consumers. It is in particular unlikely that consumers as a whole will benefit if there are many customers and the single branding obligations, taken together, have the effect of preventing the entry or expansion of competing undertakings.

138. Lastly, «the level of trade» is relevant. Anticompetitive foreclosure is less likely in case of an intermediate product. When the supplier of an intermediate product is not dominant, the competing suppliers still have a substantial part of demand that is free. Below the level of dominance an anti-competitive foreclosure effect may however arise in a cumulative effect situation. A cumulative anticompetitive effect is unlikely to arise as long as less than 50 % of the market is tied.

139. Where the agreement concerns the supply of a final product at the wholesale level, the question whether a competition problem is likely to arise depends in large part on the type of wholesaling and the entry barriers at the wholesale level. There is no real risk of anticompetitive foreclosure if competing manufacturers can easily establish their own wholesaling operation. Whether entry barriers are low depends in part on the type of wholesaling, that is, whether or not wholesalers can operate efficiently with only the product concerned by the agreement (for example ice cream) or whether it is more efficient to trade in a whole range of products (for example frozen foodstuffs). In the latter case, it is not efficient for a manufacturer selling only one product to set up its own wholesaling operation. In that case, anti-competitive effects may arise. In addition, cumulative effect problems may arise if several suppliers tie most of the available wholesalers.

140. For final products, foreclosure is in general more likely to occur at the retail level, given the significant entry barriers for most manufacturers to start retail outlets just for their own products. In addition, it is at the retail level that single branding agreements may lead to reduced in-store inter-brand competition. It is for these reasons that for final products at the retail level, significant anti-competitive effects may start to arise, taking into account all other relevant factors, if a non-dominant supplier ties 30 % or more of the relevant market. For a dominant company, even a modest tied market share may already lead to significant anti-competitive effects.

141. At the retail level, a cumulative foreclosure effect may also arise. Where all suppliers have market shares below 30 %, a cumulative anticompetitive foreclosure effect is unlikely if the total tied market share is less than 40 % and withdrawal of the block exemption is therefore unlikely. That figure may be higher when other factors like the number of competitors, entry barriers etc. are taken into account. Where not all companies have market shares below the threshold of the Block Exemption Regulation but none is dominant, a cumulative anticompetitive foreclosure effect is unlikely if the total tied market share is below 30 %.

142. Where the buyer operates from premises and land owned by the supplier or leased by the supplier from a third party not connected with the buyer, the possibility of imposing effective remedies for a possible foreclosure effect will be limited. In that case, intervention by the Commission below the level of dominance is unlikely.

143. In certain sectors, the selling of more than one brand from a single site may be difficult, in which case a foreclosure problem can better be remedied by limiting the effective duration of contracts.

144. Where appreciable anti-competitive effects are established, the question of a possible exemption under Article 101(3) arises. For non-compete obligations, the efficiencies described in points *(a)* (free riding between suppliers), *(d)*, *(e)* (hold-up problems) and *(h)* (capital market imperfections) of paragraph (107), may be particularly relevant.

145. In the case of an efficiency as described in paragraph (107)*(a)*, (107)*(d)* and (107)*(h)*, quantity forcing on the buyer could possibly be a less restrictive alternative. A non-compete obligation may be the only viable way to achieve an efficiency as described in paragraph (107)*(e)*, (hold-up problem related to the transfer of know-how).

146. In the case of a relationship-specific investment made by the supplier (see paragraph (107)*(d)*), a non-compete or quantity forcing agreement for the period of depreciation of the investment will in general fulfil the conditions of Article 101(3). In the case of high relationship-specific investments, a non-compete obligation exceeding five years may be justified. A relationship-specific investment could, for instance, be the installation or adaptation of equipment by the supplier when this equipment can be used afterwards only to produce components for a particular buyer. General or market-specific investments in (extra) capacity are normally not relationship-specific investments. However, where a supplier creates new capacity specifically linked to the operations of a particular buyer, for instance a company producing metal cans which creates new capacity to produce cans on the premises of or next to the canning facility of a food producer, this new capacity may only be economically viable when producing for this particular customer, in which case the investment would be considered to be relationship-specific.

147. Where the supplier provides the buyer with a loan or provides the buyer with equipment which is not relationship-specific, this in itself is normally not sufficient to justify the exemption of an anticompetitive foreclosure effect on the market. In case of capital market imperfection, it may be more efficient for the supplier of a product than for a bank to provide a loan (see paragraph (107)*(h)*). However, in such a case the loan should be provided in the least restrictive way and the buyer should thus in general not be prevented from terminating the obligation and repaying the outstanding part of the loan at any point in time and without payment of any penalty.

148. The transfer of substantial know-how (paragraph (107)*(e)*) usually justifies a non-compete obligation for the whole duration of the supply agreement, as for example in the context of franchising.

149. Example of non-compete obligation

The market leader in a national market for an impulse consumer product, with a market share of 40 %, sells most of its products (90 %). through tied retailers (tied market share 36 %). The agreements oblige the retailers to purchase only from the market leader for at least four years. The market leader is especially strongly represented in the more densely populated areas like the capital. Its competitors, 10 in number, of which some are only locally available, all have much smaller market shares, the biggest having 12 %. Those 10 competitors together supply another 10 % of the market via tied outlets. There is strong brand and product differentiation in the market. The market leader has the strongest brands. It is the only one with regular national advertising campaigns. It provides its tied retailers with special stocking cabinets for its product.

The result on the market is that in total 46 % (36 % + 10 %). of the market is foreclosed to potential entrants and to incumbents not having tied outlets. Potential entrants find entry even more difficult in the densely populated areas where foreclosure is even higher, although it is there that they would prefer to enter the market. In addition, owing to the strong brand and product differentiation and the high search costs relative to the price of the product, the absence of in-store inter-brand competition leads to an extra welfare loss for consumers. The possible efficiencies of the outlet exclusivity, which the market leader claims result from reduced transport costs and a possible hold-up problem concerning the stocking cabinets, are limited and do not outweigh the negative effects on competition. The efficiencies are limited, as the transport costs are linked to quantity and not exclusivity and the stocking cabinets do not contain special know-how and are not brand specific. Accordingly, it is unlikely that the conditions of Article 101(3) are fulfilled.

Example of quantity forcing

150. A producer X with a 40 % market share sells 80 % of its products through contracts which specify that the reseller is required to purchase at least 75 % of its requirements for that type of product from X. In return X is offering financing and equipment at favourable rates. The contracts have a duration of five years in which repayment of the loan is foreseen in equal instalments. However, after the first two years buyers have the possibility to terminate the contract with a six-month notice period if they repay the outstanding loan and take over the equipment at its market asset value. At the end of the five-year period the equipment becomes the property of the buyer. Most of the competing producers are small, twelve in total with the biggest having a market share of 20 %, and engage in similar contracts with different durations. The producers with market shares below 10 %

often have contracts with longer durations and with less generous termination clauses. The contracts of producer X leave 25 % of requirements free to be supplied by competitors. In the last three years, two new producers have entered the market and gained a combined market share of around 8 %, partly by taking over the loans of a number of resellers in return for contracts with these resellers.

Producer X's tied market share is 24 % (0,75 × 0,80 × 40 %). The other producers' tied market share is around 25 %. Therefore, in total around 49 % of the market is foreclosed to potential entrants and to incumbents not having tied outlets for at least the first two years of the supply contracts. The market shows that the resellers often have difficulty in obtaining loans from banks and are too small in general to obtain capital through other means like the issuing of shares. In addition, producer X is able to demonstrate that concentrating its sales on a limited number of resellers allows him to plan its sales better and to save transport costs. In the light of the efficiencies on the one hand and the 25 % non-tied part in the contracts of producer X, the real possibility for early termination of the contract, the recent entry of new producers and the fact that around half the resellers are not tied on the other hand, the quantity forcing of 75 % applied by producer X is likely to fulfil the conditions of Article 101(3).

2.2. Exclusive distribution

151. In an exclusive distribution agreement, the supplier agrees to sell its products to only one distributor for resale in a particular territory. At the same time, the distributor is usually limited in its active selling into other (exclusively allocated) territories. The possible competition risks are mainly reduced intra-brand competition and market partitioning, which may facilitate price discrimination in particular. When most or all of the suppliers apply exclusive distribution, it may soften competition and facilitate collusion, both at the suppliers' and distributors' level. Lastly, exclusive distribution may lead to foreclosure of other distributors and therewith reduce competition at that level.

152. Exclusive distribution is exempted by the Block Exemption Regulation where both the supplier's and buyer's market share each do not exceed 30 %, even if combined with other non-hardcore vertical restraints, such as a non-compete obligation limited to five years, quantity forcing or exclusive purchasing. A combination of exclusive distribution and selective distribution is only exempted by the Block Exemption Regulation if active selling in other territories is not restricted. The remainder of this section provides guidance for the assessment of exclusive distribution in individual cases above the 30 % market share threshold.

153. The market position of the supplier and its competitors is of major importance, as the loss of intra-brand competition can only be problematic if inter-brand competition is limited. The stronger the position of the supplier, the more serious is the loss of intra-brand competition. Above the 30 % market share threshold, there may be a risk of a significant reduction of intra-brand competition. In order to fulfil the conditions of Article 101(3), the loss of intra-brand competition may need to be balanced with real efficiencies.

154. The position of the competitors can have a dual significance. Strong competitors will generally mean that the reduction in intra-brand competition is outweighed by sufficient inter-brand competition. However, if the number of competitors becomes rather small and their market position is rather similar in terms of market share, capacity and distribution network, there is a risk of collusion and/or softening of competition. The loss of intra-brand competition can increase that risk, especially when several suppliers operate similar distribution systems. Multiple exclusive dealerships, that is, when different suppliers appoint the same exclusive distributor in a given territory, may further increase the risk of collusion and/or softening of competition. If a dealer is granted the exclusive right to distribute two or more important competing products in the same territory, inter-brand competition may be substantially restricted for those brands. The higher the cumulative market share of the brands distributed by the exclusive multiple brand dealers, the higher the risk of collusion and/or softening of competition and the more inter-brand competition will be reduced. If a retailer is the exclusive distributor for a number of brands this may have as result that if one producer cuts the wholesale price for its brand, the exclusive retailer will not be eager to transmit this price cut to the final consumer as it would reduce its sales and profits made with the other brands. Hence, compared to the situation without multiple exclusive dealerships, producers have a reduced interest in entering into price competition with one another. Such cumulative effect situations may be a reason to withdraw the benefit of the Block Exemption Regulation where the market shares of the suppliers and buyers are below the threshold of the Block Exemption Regulation.

155. Entry barriers that may hinder suppliers from creating new distributors or finding alternative distributors are less important in assessing the possible anti-competitive effects of exclusive distribution. Foreclosure of other suppliers does not arise as long as exclusive distribution is not combined with single branding.

156. Foreclosure of other distributors is not an issue where the supplier which operates the exclusive distribution system appoints a high number of exclusive distributors on the same market and those exclusive distributors are not restricted in selling to other non-appointed distributors. Foreclosure of other distributors may however become an issue where there is buying power and market power downstream, in particular in the case of very large territories where the exclusive distributor becomes the exclusive buyer for a whole market. An example would be a supermarket chain which becomes the only distributor of a leading brand on a national food retail market. The foreclosure of other distributors may be aggravated in the case of multiple exclusive dealership.

157. Buying power may also increase the risk of collusion on the buyers' side when the exclusive distribution arrangements are imposed by important buyers, possibly located in different territories, on one or several suppliers.

158. Maturity of the market is important, as loss of intra-brand competition and price discrimination may be a serious problem in a mature market but may be less relevant on a market with growing demand, changing technologies and changing market positions.

159. The level of trade is important as the possible negative effects may differ between the wholesale and retail level. Exclusive distribution is mainly applied in the distribution of final goods and services. A loss of intra-brand competition is especially likely at the retail level if coupled with large territories, since final consumers may be confronted with little possibility of choosing between a high price/high service and a low price/low service distributor for an important brand.

160. A manufacturer that chooses a wholesaler to be its exclusive distributor will normally do so for a larger territory, such as a whole Member State. As long as the wholesaler can sell the products without limitation to downstream retailers there are not likely to be appreciable anti-competitive effects. A possible loss of intra-brand competition at the wholesale level may be easily outweighed by efficiencies obtained in logistics, promotion etc., especially when the manufacturer is based in a different country. The possible risks for inter-brand competition of multiple exclusive dealerships are however higher at the wholesale than at the retail level. Where one wholesaler becomes the exclusive distributor for a significant number of suppliers, not only is there a risk that competition between these brands is reduced, but also that there is foreclosure at the wholesale level of trade.

161. As stated in paragraph (155), foreclosure of other suppliers does not arise as long as exclusive distribution is not combined with single branding. But even when exclusive distribution is combined with single branding anticompetitive foreclosure of other suppliers is unlikely, except possibly when the single branding is applied to a dense network of exclusive distributors with small territories or in case of a cumulative effect. In such a case it may be necessary to apply the principles on single branding set out in section 2.1. However, when the combination does not lead to significant foreclosure, the combination of exclusive distribution and single branding may be pro-competitive by increasing the incentive for the exclusive distributor to focus its efforts on the particular brand. Therefore, in the absence of such a foreclosure effect, the combination of exclusive distribution with non-compete may very well fulfil the conditions of Article 101(3) for the whole duration of the agreement, particularly at the wholesale level.

162. The combination of exclusive distribution with exclusive sourcing increases the possible competition risks of reduced intra-brand competition and market partitioning which may facilitate price discrimination in particular. Exclusive distribution already limits arbitrage by customers, as it limits the number of distributors and usually also restricts the distributors in their freedom of active selling. Exclusive sourcing, requiring the exclusive distributors to buy their supplies for the particular brand directly from the manufacturer, eliminates in addition possible arbitrage by the exclusive distributors, which are prevented from buying from other distributors in the system. As a result, the supplier's possibilities to limit intra-brand competition by applying dissimilar conditions of sale to the detriment of consumers are enhanced, unless the combination allows the creation of efficiencies leading to lower prices to all final consumers.

163. The nature of the product is not particularly relevant to the assessment of possible anti-competitive effects of exclusive distribution. It is, however, relevant to an assessment of possible efficiencies, that is, after an appreciable anti-competitive effect is established.

164. Exclusive distribution may lead to efficiencies, especially where investments by the distributors are required to protect or build up the brand image. In general, the case for efficiencies is strongest for new products, complex products, and products whose qualities are difficult to judge before consumption (so-called experience products) or whose qualities are difficult to judge even after consumption (so-called credence products). In addition, exclusive distribution may lead to savings in logistic costs due to economies of scale in transport and distribution.

Example of exclusive distribution at the wholesale level

165. On the market for a consumer durable, A is the market leader. A sells its product through exclusive wholesalers. Territories for the wholesalers correspond to the entire Member State for small Member States, and to a region for larger Member States. Those exclusive distributors deal with sales to all the retailers in their territories. They do not sell to final consumers. The wholesalers are in charge of promotion in their markets, including sponsoring of local events, but also explaining and promoting the new products to the retailers in their territories. Technology and product innovation are evolving fairly quickly on this market, and pre-sale service to retailers and to final consumers plays an important role. The wholesalers are not required to purchase all their requirements of the brand of supplier A from the producer himself, and arbitrage by wholesalers or retailers is practicable because the transport costs are relatively low compared to the value of the product. The wholesalers are not under a non-compete obligation. Retailers also sell a number of brands of competing suppliers, and there are no exclusive or selective distribution agreements at the retail level. On the EU market of sales to wholesalers A has around 50 % market share. Its market share on the various national retail markets varies between 40 % and 60 %. A has between 6 and 10 competitors on every national market. B, C and D are its biggest competitors and are also present on each national market, with market shares varying between 20 % and 5 %. The remaining producers are national producers, with smaller market shares. B, C and D have similar distribution networks, whereas the local producers tend to sell their products directly to retailers.

On the wholesale market described in this example, the risk of reduced intra-brand competition and price discrimination is low. Arbitrage is not hindered, and the absence of intra-brand competition is not very relevant at the wholesale level. At the retail level, neither intra- nor inter-brand competition are hindered. Moreover, inter-brand competition is largely unaffected by the exclusive arrangements at the wholesale level. Therefore it is likely, even if anti-competitive effects exist, that also the conditions of Article 101(3) are fulfilled.

Example of multiple exclusive dealerships in an oligopolistic market

166. On a national market for a final product, there are four market leaders, which each have a market share of around 20 %. Those four market leaders sell their product through exclusive distributors at the retail level. Retailers are given an exclusive territory which corresponds to the town in which they are located or a district of the town for large towns. In most territories, the four market leaders happen to appoint the same exclusive retailer («multiple dealership»), often centrally located and rather specialised in the product. The remaining 20 % of the national market is composed of small local producers, the largest of these producers having a market share of 5 % on the national market. Those local producers sell their products in general through other retailers, in particular because the exclusive distributors of the four largest suppliers show in general little interest in selling less well-known and cheaper brands. There is strong brand and product differentiation on the market. The four market leaders have large national advertising campaigns and strong brand images, whereas the fringe producers do not advertise their products at the national level. The market is rather mature, with stable demand and no major product and technological innovation. The product is relatively simple.

In such an oligopolistic market, there is a risk of collusion between the four market leaders. That risk is increased through multiple dealerships. Intra-brand competition is limited by the territorial exclusivity. Competition between the four leading brands is reduced at the retail level, since one retailer fixes the price of all four brands in each territory. The multiple dealership implies that, if one producer cuts the price for its brand, the retailer will not be eager to transmit this price cut to the final consumer as it would reduce its sales and profits made with the other brands. Hence, producers have a reduced interest in entering into price competition with one another. Inter-brand price competition exists mainly with the low brand image goods of the fringe producers. The possible efficiency arguments for (joint) exclusive distributors are limited, as the product is relatively simple, the resale does not require any specific investments or training and advertising is mainly carried out at the level of the producers.

Even though each of the market leaders has a market share below the threshold, the conditions of Article 101(3) may not be fulfilled and withdrawal of the block exemption may be necessary for the agreements concluded with distributors whose market share is below 30 % of the procurement market.

Example of exclusive distribution combined with exclusive sourcing

167. Manufacturer A is the European market leader for a bulky consumer durable, with a market share of between 40 % and 60 % in most national retail markets. In Member States where it has a high market share, it has less competitors with much smaller market shares. The competitors are present on only one or two national markets. A's long time policy is to sell its product through its national subsidiaries to exclusive distributors at the retail level, which are not allowed to sell actively into each other's territories. Those distributors are thereby incentivised to promote the product and provide pre-sales services. Recently the retailers are in addition obliged to purchase manufacturer A's products exclusively from the national subsidiary of manufacturer A in their own country. The retailers selling the brand of manufacturer A are the main resellers of that type of product in their territory. They handle competing brands, but with varying degrees of success and enthusiasm. Since the introduction of exclusive sourcing, A applies price differences of 10 % to 15 % between markets with higher prices in the markets where it has less competition. The markets are relatively stable on the demand and the supply side, and there are no significant technological changes.

In the high price markets, the loss of intra-brand competition results not only from the territorial exclusivity at the retail level but is aggravated by the exclusive sourcing obligation imposed on the retailers. The exclusive sourcing obligation helps to keep markets and territories separate by making arbitrage between the exclusive retailers, the main resellers of that type of product, impossible. The exclusive retailers also cannot sell actively into each other's territory and in practice tend to avoid delivering outside their own territory. As a result, price discrimination is possible, without it leading to a significant increase in total sales. Arbitrage by consumers or independent traders is limited due to the bulkiness of the product.

While the possible efficiency arguments for appointing exclusive distributors may be convincing, in particular because of the incentivising of retailers, the possible efficiency arguments for the combination of exclusive distribution and exclusive sourcing, and in particular the possible efficiency arguments for exclusive sourcing, linked mainly to economies of scale in transport, are unlikely to outweigh the negative effect of price discrimination and reduced intra-brand competition. Consequently, it is unlikely that the conditions of Article 101(3) are fulfilled.

2.3. Exclusive customer allocation

168. In an exclusive customer allocation agreement, the supplier agrees to sell its products to only one distributor for resale to a particular group of customers. At the same time, the distributor is usually limited in its active selling to other (exclusively allocated) groups of customers. The Block Exemption Regulation does not limit the way an exclusive customer group can be defined; it could for instance be a particular type of customers defined by their occupation but also a list of specific customers selected on the basis of one or more objective criteria. The possible competition risks are mainly reduced intra-brand competition and market partitioning, which may in particular facilitate price discrimination. Where most or all of the suppliers apply exclusive customer allocation, competition may be softened and collusion, both at the suppliers' and the distributors' level, may be facilitated. Lastly, exclusive customer allocation may lead to foreclosure of other distributors and therewith reduce competition at that level.

169. Exclusive customer allocation is exempted by the Block Exemption Regulation when both the supplier's and buyer's market share does not exceed the 30 % market share threshold, even if combined with other non-hardcore vertical restraints such as non-compete, quantity-forcing or exclusive sourcing. A combination of exclusive customer allocation and selective distribution is normally a hardcore restriction, as active selling to end-users by the appointed distributors is usually not left free. Above the 30 % market share threshold, the guidance provided in paragraphs (151) to (167) applies also to the assessment of exclusive customer allocation, subject to the specific remarks in the remainder of this section.

170. The allocation of customers normally makes arbitrage by the customers more difficult. In addition, as each appointed distributor has its own class of customers, non-appointed distributors not falling within such a class may find it difficult to obtain the product. Consequently, possible arbitrage by non-appointed distributors will be reduced.

171. Exclusive customer allocation is mainly applied to intermediate products and at the wholesale level when it concerns final products, where customer groups with different specific requirements concerning the product can be distinguished.

172. Exclusive customer allocation may lead to efficiencies, especially when the distributors are required to make investments in for instance specific equipment, skills or know-how to adapt to the requirements of their group of customers. The depreciation period of these investments indicates the justified duration of an exclusive customer allocation system. In general the case is strongest for new or complex products and for products requiring adaptation to the needs of the individual customer. Identifiable differentiated needs are more likely for intermediate products, that is, products sold to different types of professional buyers. Allocation of final consumers is unlikely to lead to efficiencies.

Example of exclusive customer allocation

173. A company has developed a sophisticated sprinkler installation. The company has currently a market share of 40 % on the market for sprinkler installations. When it started selling the sophisticated sprinkler it had a market share of 20 % with an older product. The installation of the new type of sprinkler depends on the type of building that it is installed in and on the use of the building (office, chemical plant, hospital etc.). The company has appointed a number of distributors to sell and install the sprinkler installation. Each distributor needed to train its employees for the general and specific requirements of installing the sprinkler installation for a particular class of customers. To ensure that distributors would specialise, the company assigned to each distributor an exclusive class of customers and prohibited active sales to each others' exclusive customer classes. After five years, all the exclusive distributors will be allowed to sell actively to all classes of customers, thereby ending the system of exclusive customer allocation. The supplier may then also start selling to new distributors. The market is quite dynamic, with two recent entries and a number of technological developments. Competitors, with market shares between 25 % and 5 %, are also upgrading their products.

As the exclusivity is of limited duration and helps to ensure that the distributors may recoup their investments and concentrate their sales efforts first on a certain class of customers in order to learn the trade, and as the possible anti-competitive effects seem limited in a dynamic market, the conditions of Article 101(3) are likely to be fulfilled.

2.4. Selective distribution

174. Selective distribution agreements, like exclusive distribution agreements, restrict the number of authorised distributors on the one hand and the possibilities of resale on the other. The difference with exclusive distribution is that the restriction of the number of dealers does not depend on the number of territories but on selection criteria linked in the first place to the nature of the product. Another difference with exclusive distribution is that the restriction on resale is not a restriction on active selling to a territory but a restriction on any sales to non-authorised distributors, leaving only appointed dealers and final customers as possible buyers. Selective distribution is almost always used to distribute branded final products.

175. The possible competition risks are a reduction in intra-brand competition and, especially in case of cumulative effect, foreclosure of certain type(s) of distributors and softening of competition and facilitation of collusion between suppliers or buyers. To assess the possible anti-competitive effects of selective distribution under Article 101(1), a distinction needs to be made between purely qualitative selective distribution and quantitative selective distribution. Purely qualitative selective distribution selects dealers only on the basis of objective criteria required by the nature of the product such as training of sales personnel, the service provided at the point of sale, a certain range of the products being sold etc. (52). The application of such criteria does not put a direct limit on the number of dealers. Purely qualitative selective distribution is in general considered to fall outside Article 101(1) for lack of anti-competitive effects, provided that three conditions are satisfied. First, the nature of the product in question must necessitate a selective distribution system, in the sense that such a system must constitute a legitimate requirement, having regard to the nature of the product concerned, to preserve its quality and ensure its proper use. Secondly, resellers must be chosen on the basis of objective criteria of a qualitative nature which are laid down uniformly for all and made available to all potential resellers and are not applied in a discriminatory manner. Thirdly, the criteria laid down must not go beyond what is necessary (53). Quantitative selective distribution adds further criteria for selection that more directly limit the potential number of dealers by, for instance, requiring minimum or maximum sales, by fixing the number of dealers, etc.

(52) See for example judgment of the Court of First Instance in Case T-88/92 Groupement d'achat Édouard Leclerc v. Commission (1996) ECR II-1961.

(53) See judgments of the Court of Justice in Case 31/80 L'Oréal v. PVBA (1980) ECR 3775, paragraphs 15 and 16; Case 26/76 Metro I (1977) ECR 1875, paragraphs 20 and 21; Case 107/82 AEG (1983) ECR 3151, paragraph 35; and judgment of the Court of First Instance in Case T-19/91 Vichy v. Commission (1992) ECR II-415, paragraph 65.

176. Qualitative and quantitative selective distribution is exempted by the Block Exemption Regulation as long as the market share of both supplier and buyer each do not exceed 30 %, even if combined with other non-hardcore vertical restraints, such as non-compete or exclusive distribution, provided active selling by the authorised distributors to each other and to end users is not restricted. The Block Exemption Regulation exempts selective distribution regardless of the nature of the product concerned and regardless of the nature of the selection criteria. However, where the characteristics of the product (54) do not require selective distribution or do not require the applied criteria, such as for instance the requirement for distributors to have one or more brick and mortar shops or to provide specific services, such a distribution system does not generally bring about sufficient efficiency enhancing effects to counterbalance a significant reduction in intra-brand competition. Where appreciable anti-competitive effects occur, the benefit of the Block Exemption Regulation is likely to be withdrawn. In addition, the remainder of this section provides guidance for the assessment of selective distribution in individual cases which are not covered by the Block Exemption Regulation or in the case of cumulative effects resulting from parallel networks of selective distribution.

(54) See for example judgments of the Court of First Instance in Case T-19/92, Groupement d'achat Edouard Leclerc v. Commission (1996) ECR II-1851, paragraphs 112 to 123; Case T-88/92 Groupement d'achat Edouard Leclerc v. Commission (1996) ECR II-1961, paragraphs 106 to 117, and the case law referred to in the preceding footnote.

177. The market position of the supplier and its competitors is of central importance in assessing possible anti-competitive effects, as the loss of intra-brand competition can only be problematic if inter-brand competition is limited. The stronger the position of the supplier, the more problematic is the loss of intra-brand competition. Another important factor is the number of selective distribution networks present in the same market. Where selective distribution is applied by only one supplier on the market, quantitative selective distribution does not normally create net negative effects provided that the contract goods, having regard to their nature, require the use of a selective distribution system and on condition that the selection criteria applied are necessary to ensure efficient distribution of the goods in question. The reality, however, seems to be that selective distribution is often applied by a number of the suppliers on a given market.

178. The position of competitors can have a dual significance and plays in particular a role in case of a cumulative effect. Strong competitors will mean in general that the reduction in intra-brand competition is easily outweighed by sufficient inter-brand competition. However, when a majority of the main suppliers apply selective distribution, there will be a significant loss of intra-brand competition and possible foreclosure of certain types of distributors as well as an increased risk of collusion between those major suppliers. The risk of foreclosure of more efficient distributors has always been greater with selective distribution than with exclusive distribution, given the restriction on sales to non-authorised dealers in selective distribution. That restriction is designed to give selective distribution systems a closed character, making it impossible for non-authorised dealers to obtain supplies. Accordingly, selective distribution is particularly well suited to avoid pressure by price discounters (whether offline or online-only distributors) on the margins of the manufacturer, as well as on the margins of the authorised dealers. Foreclosure of such distribution formats, whether resulting from the cumulative application of selective distribution or from the application by a single supplier with a market share exceeding 30 %, reduces the possibilities for consumers to take advantage of the specific benefits offered by these formats such as lower prices, more transparency and wider access.

179. Where the Block Exemption Regulation applies to individual networks of selective distribution, withdrawal of the block exemption or disapplication of the Block Exemption Regulation may be considered in case of cumulative effects. However, a cumulative effect problem is unlikely to arise when the share of the market covered by selective distribution is below 50 %. Also, no problem is likely to arise where the market coverage ratio exceeds 50 %, but the aggregate market share of the five largest suppliers (CR5) is below 50 %. Where both the CR5 and the share of the market covered by selective distribution exceed 50 %, the assessment may vary depending on whether or not all five largest suppliers apply selective distribution. The stronger the position of the competitors which do not apply selective distribution, the less likely other distributors will be foreclosed. If all five largest suppliers apply selective distribution, competition concerns may arise with respect to those agreements in particular that apply quantitative selection criteria by directly limiting the number of authorised dealers or that apply qualitative criteria, such as a requirement to have one or more brick and mortar shops or to provide specific services, which forecloses certain distribution formats. The conditions of Article 101(3) are in general unlikely to be fulfilled if the selective distribution systems at issue prevent access to the market by new distributors capable of adequately selling the products in question, especially price discounters or online-only distributors offering lower prices to consumers, thereby limiting distribution to the advantage of certain existing channels and to the detriment of final consumers. More indirect forms of quantitative selective distribution, resulting for instance from the combination of purely qualitative selection criteria with the requirement imposed on the dealers to achieve a minimum amount of annual purchases, are less likely to produce net negative effects, if such an amount does not represent a significant proportion of the dealer's total turnover achieved with the type of products in question and it does not go beyond what is necessary for the supplier to recoup its relationship-specific investment and/or realise economies of scale in distribution. As regards individual contributions, a supplier with a market share of less than 5 % is in general not considered to contribute significantly to a cumulative effect.

180. Entry barriers are mainly of interest in the case of foreclosure of the market to non-authorised dealers. In general, entry barriers will be considerable as selective distribution is usually applied by manufacturers of branded products. It will in general take time and considerable investment for excluded retailers to launch their own brands or obtain competitive supplies elsewhere.

181. Buying power may increase the risk of collusion between dealers and thus appreciably change the analysis of possible anti-competitive effects of selective distribution. Foreclosure of the market to more efficient retailers may especially result where a strong dealer organisation imposes selection criteria on the supplier aimed at limiting distribution to the advantage of its members.

182. Article 5(1)(c) of the Block Exemption Regulation provides that the supplier may not impose an obligation causing the authorised dealers, either directly or indirectly, not to sell the brands of particular competing suppliers. Such a condition aims specifically at avoiding horizontal collusion to exclude particular brands through the creation of a selective club of brands by the leading suppliers. That kind of obligation is unlikely to be exemptible when the CR5 is equal to or above 50 %, unless none of the suppliers imposing such an obligation belongs to the five largest suppliers on the market.

183. Foreclosure of other suppliers is normally not a problem as long as other suppliers can use the same distributors, that is, as long as the selective distribution system is not combined with single branding. In the case of a dense network of authorised distributors or in the case of a cumulative effect, the combination of selective distribution and a non-compete obligation may pose a risk of foreclosure to other suppliers. In that case, the principles set out in section 2.1. on single branding apply. Where selective distribution is not combined with a non-compete obligation, foreclosure of the market to competing suppliers may still be a problem where the leading suppliers apply not only purely qualitative selection criteria, but impose on their dealers certain additional obligations such as the obligation to reserve a minimum shelf-space for their products or to ensure that the sales of their products by the dealer achieve a minimum percentage of the dealer's total turnover. Such a problem is unlikely to arise if the share of the market covered by selective distribution is below 50 % or, where this coverage ratio is exceeded, if the market share of the five largest suppliers is below 50 %.

184. Maturity of the market is important, as loss of intra-brand competition and possible foreclosure of suppliers or dealers may be a serious problem on a mature market but is less relevant on a market with growing demand, changing technologies and changing market positions.

185. Selective distribution may be efficient when it leads to savings in logistical costs due to economies of scale in transport and that may occur irrespective of the nature of the product (paragraph (107)*(g)*). However, such an efficiency is usually only marginal in selective distribution systems. To help solve a free-rider problem between the distributors (paragraph (107)*(a)*) or to help create a brand image (paragraph (107)*(i)*), the nature of the product is very relevant. In general, the case is strongest for new products, complex products, products whose qualities are difficult to judge before consumption (so-called experience products) or whose qualities are difficult to judge even after consumption (so-called credence products). The combination of selective distribution with a location clause, protecting an appointed dealer against other appointed dealers opening up a shop in its vicinity, may in particular fulfil the conditions of Article 101(3) if the combination is indispensable to protect substantial and relationship-specific investments made by the authorised dealer (paragraph (107)*(d)*).

186. To ensure that the least anti-competitive restraint is chosen, it is relevant to see whether the same efficiencies can be obtained at a comparable cost by for instance service requirements alone.

Example of quantitative selective distribution

187. On a market for consumer durables, the market leader (brand A) with a market share of 35 %, sells its product to final consumers through a selective distribution network. There are several criteria for admission to the network: the shop must employ trained staff and provide pre-sales services, there must be a specialised area in the shop devoted to the sales of the product and similar hi-tech products, and the shop is required to sell a wide range of models of the supplier and to display them in an attractive manner. Moreover, the number of admissible retailers in the network is directly limited through the establishment of a maximum number of retailers per number of inhabitants in each province or urban area. Manufacturer A has 6 competitors in that market. Its largest competitors, B, C and D, have market shares of respectively 25, 15 and 10 %, whilst the other producers have smaller market shares. A is the only manufacturer to use selective distribution. The selective distributors of brand A always handle a few competing brands. However, competing brands are also widely sold in shops which are not member of A's selective distribution network. Channels of distribution are various: for instance, brands B and C are sold in most of A's selected shops, but also in other shops providing a high quality service and in hypermarkets. Brand D is mainly sold in high service shops. Technology is evolving quite rapidly in this market, and the main suppliers maintain a strong quality image for their products through advertising.

On that market, the coverage ratio of selective distribution is 35 %. Inter-brand competition is not directly affected by the selective distribution system of A. Intra-brand competition for brand A may be reduced, but consumers have access to low service/low price retailers for brands B and C, which have a comparable quality image to brand A. Moreover, access to high service retailers for other brands is not foreclosed, since there is no limitation on the capacity of selected distributors to sell competing brands, and the quantitative limitation on the number of retailers for brand A leaves other high service retailers free to distribute competing brands. In this case, in view of the service requirements and the efficiencies these are likely to provide and the limited effect on intra-brand competition the conditions of Article 101(3) are likely to be fulfilled.

Example of selective distribution with cumulative effects

188. On a market for a particular sports article, there are seven manufacturers, whose respective market shares are: 25 %, 20 %, 15 %, 15 %, 10 %, 8 % and 7 %. The five largest manufacturers distribute their products through quantitative selective distribution, whilst the two smallest use different types of distribution systems, which results in a coverage ratio of selective distribution of 85 %. The criteria for access to the selective distribution networks are remarkably uniform amongst manufacturers: the distributors are required to have one or more brick and mortar shops, those shops are required to have trained personnel and to provide pre-sale services, there must be a specialised area in the shop devoted to the sales of the article and a minimum size for this area is specified. The shop is required to sell a wide range of the brand in question and to display the article in an attractive manner, the shop must be located in a commercial street, and that type of article must represent at least 30 % of the total turnover of the shop. In general, the same dealer is appointed selective distributor for all five brands. The two brands which do not use selective distribution usually sell through less specialised retailers with lower service levels. The market is stable, both on the supply and on the demand side, and there is strong brand image and product differentiation. The five market leaders have strong brand images, acquired through advertising and sponsoring, whereas the two smaller manufacturers have a strategy of cheaper products, with no strong brand image.

On that market, access by general price discounters and online-only distributors to the five leading brands is denied. Indeed, the requirement that this type of article represents at least 30 % of the activity of the dealers and the criteria on presentation and pre-sales services rule out most price discounters from the network of authorised dealers. The requirement to have one or more brick and mortar shops excludes online-only distributors from the network. As a consequence, consumers have no choice but to buy the five leading brands in high service/high price shops. This leads to reduced inter-brand competition between the five leading brands. The fact that the two smallest brands can be bought in low service/low price shops does not compensate for this, because the brand image of the five market leaders is much better. Inter-brand competition is also limited through multiple dealership. Even though there exists some degree of intra-brand competition and the number of retailers is not directly limited, the criteria for admission are strict enough to lead to a small number of retailers for the five leading brands in each territory.

The efficiencies associated with these quantitative selective distribution systems are low: the product is not very complex and does not justify a particularly high service. Unless the manufacturers can prove that there are clear efficiencies linked to their network of selective distribution, it is probable that the block exemption will have to be withdrawn because of its cumulative effects resulting in less choice and higher prices for consumers.

2.5. Franchising

189. Franchise agreements contain licences of intellectual property rights relating in particular to trade marks or signs and know-how for the use and distribution of goods or services. In addition to the licence of IPRs, the franchisor usually provides the franchisee during the life of the agreement with commercial or technical assistance. The licence and the assistance are integral components of the business method being franchised. The franchisor is in general paid a franchise fee by the franchisee for the use of the particular business method. Franchising may enable the franchisor to establish, with limited investments, a uniform network for the distribution of its products. In addition to the provision of the business method, franchise agreements usually contain a combination of different vertical restraints concerning the products being distributed, in particular selective distribution and/or non-compete and/or exclusive distribution or weaker forms thereof.

190. The coverage by the Block Exemption Regulation of the licensing of IPRs contained in franchise agreements is dealt with in paragraphs (24) to (46). As for the vertical restraints on the purchase, sale and resale of goods and services within a franchising arrangement, such as selective distribution, non-compete obligations or exclusive distribution, the Block Exemption Regulation applies up to the 30 % market share threshold (55). The guidance provided in respect of those types of restraints applies also to franchising, subject to the following two specific remarks:

(a) The more important the transfer of know-how, the more likely it is that the restraints create efficiencies and/or are indispensable to protect the know-how and that the vertical restraints fulfil the conditions of Article 101(3);

(b) A non-compete obligation on the goods or services purchased by the franchisee falls outside the scope of Article 101(1) where the obligation is necessary to maintain the common identity and reputation of the franchised network. In such cases, the duration of the non-compete obligation is also irrelevant under Article 101(1), as long as it does not exceed the duration of the franchise agreement itself.

(55) See also paragraphs (86) to (95), in particular paragraph (92).

Example of franchising

191. A manufacturer has developed a new format for selling sweets in so-called fun shops where the sweets can be coloured specially on demand from the consumer. The manufacturer of the sweets has also developed the machines to colour the sweets. The manufacturer also produces the colouring liquids. The quality and freshness of the liquid is of vital importance to producing good sweets. The manufacturer made a success of its sweets through a number of own retail outlets all operating under the same trade name and with the uniform fun image (style of lay-out of the shops, common advertising etc.). In order to expand sales the manufacturer started a franchising system. The franchisees are obliged to buy the sweets, liquid and colouring machine from the manufacturer, to have the same image and operate under the trade name, pay a franchise fee, contribute to common advertising and ensure the confidentiality of the operating manual prepared by the franchisor. In addition, the franchisees are only allowed to sell from the agreed premises, to sell to end users or other franchisees and are not allowed to sell other sweets. The franchisor is obliged not to appoint another franchisee nor operate a retail outlet himself in a given contract territory. The franchisor is also under the obligation to update and further develop its products, the business outlook and the operating manual and make these improvements available to all retail franchisees. The franchise agreements are concluded for a duration of 10 years.

Sweet retailers buy their sweets on a national market from either national producers that cater for national tastes or from wholesalers which import sweets from foreign producers in addition to selling products from national producers. On that market the franchisor's products compete with other brands of sweets. The franchisor has a market share of 30 % on the market for sweets sold to retailers. Competition comes from a number of national and international brands, sometimes produced by large diversified food companies. There are many potential points of sale of sweets in the form of tobacconists, general food retailers, cafeterias and specialised sweet shops. The franchisor's market share of the market for machines for colouring food is below 10 %.

Most of the obligations contained in the franchise agreements can be deemed necessary to protect the intellectual property rights or maintain the common identity and reputation of the franchised network and fall outside Article 101(1). The restrictions on selling (contract territory and selective distribution) provide an incentive to the franchisees to invest in the colouring machine and the franchise concept and, if not necessary to, at least help maintain the common identity, thereby offsetting the loss of intra-brand competition. The non-compete clause excluding other brands of sweets from the shops for the full duration of the agreements does allow the franchisor to keep the outlets uniform and prevent competitors from benefiting from its trade name. It does not lead to any serious foreclosure in view of the great number of potential outlets available to other sweet producers. The franchise agreements of this franchisor are likely to fulfil the conditions for exemption under Article 101(3) in as far as the obligations contained therein fall under Article 101(1).

2.6. Exclusive supply

192. Under the heading of exclusive supply fall those restrictions that have as their main element that the supplier is obliged or induced to sell the contract products only or mainly to one buyer, in general or for a particular use. Such restrictions may take the form of an exclusive supply obligation, restricting the supplier to sell to only one buyer for the purposes of resale or a particular use, but may for instance also take the form of quantity forcing on the supplier, where incentives are agreed between the supplier and buyer which make the former concentrate its sales mainly with one buyer. For intermediate goods or services, exclusive supply is often referred to as industrial supply.

193. Exclusive supply is exempted by the Block Exemption Regulation where both the supplier's and buyer's market share does not exceed 30 %, even if combined with other non-hardcore vertical restraints such as non-compete. The remainder of this section provides guidance for the assessment of exclusive supply in individual cases above the market share threshold.

194. The main competition risk of exclusive supply is anti-competitive foreclosure of other buyers. There is a similarity with the possible effects of exclusive distribution, in particular when the exclusive distributor becomes the exclusive buyer for a whole market (see section 2.2., in particular paragraph (156)). The market share of the buyer on the upstream purchase market is obviously important for assessing the ability of the buyer to impose exclusive supply which forecloses other buyers from access to supplies. The importance of the buyer on the downstream market is however the factor which determines whether a competition problem may arise. If the buyer has no market power downstream, then no appreciable negative effects for consumers can be expected. Negative effects may arise when the market share of the buyer on the downstream supply market as well as the upstream purchase market exceeds 30 %. Where the market share of the buyer on the upstream market does not exceed 30 %, significant foreclosure effects may still result, especially when the market share of the buyer on its downstream market exceeds 30 % and the exclusive supply relates to a particular use of the contract products. Where a company is dominant on the downstream market, any obligation to supply the products only or mainly to the dominant buyer may easily have significant anti-competitive effects.

195. It is not only the market position of the buyer on the upstream and downstream market that is important but also the extent to and the duration for which it applies an exclusive supply obligation. The higher the tied supply share, and the longer the duration of the exclusive supply, the more significant the foreclosure is likely to be. Exclusive supply agreements shorter than five years entered into by non-dominant companies usually require a balancing of pro- and anti-competitive effects, while agreements lasting longer than five years are for most types of investments not considered necessary to achieve the claimed efficiencies or the efficiencies are not sufficient to outweigh the foreclosure effect of such long-term exclusive supply agreements.

196. The market position of the competing buyers on the upstream market is important as it is likely that competing buyers will be foreclosed for anti-competitive reasons, that is, to increase their costs, if they are significantly smaller than the foreclosing buyer. Foreclosure of competing buyers is not very likely where those competitors have similar buying power and can offer the suppliers similar sales possibilities. In such a case, foreclosure could only occur for potential entrants, which may not be able to secure supplies when a number of major buyers all enter into exclusive supply contracts with the majority of suppliers on the market. Such a cumulative effect may lead to withdrawal of the benefit of the Block Exemption Regulation.

197. Entry barriers at the supplier level are relevant to establishing whether there is real foreclosure. In as far as it is efficient for competing buyers to provide the goods or services themselves via upstream vertical integration, foreclosure is unlikely to be a real problem. However, there are often significant entry barriers.

198. Countervailing power of suppliers is relevant, as important suppliers will not easily allow themselves to be cut off from alternative buyers. Foreclosure is therefore mainly a risk in the case of weak suppliers and strong buyers. In the case of strong suppliers, the exclusive supply may be found in combination with non-compete obligations. The combination with non-compete obligations brings in the rules developed for single branding. Where there are relationship-specific investments involved on both sides (hold-up problem) the combination of exclusive supply and non-compete obligations that is, reciprocal exclusivity in industrial supply agreements may often be justified, in particular below the level of dominance.

199. Lastly, the level of trade and the nature of the product are relevant for foreclosure. Anticompetitive foreclosure is less likely in the case of an intermediate product or where the product is homogeneous. Firstly, a foreclosed manufacturer that uses a certain input usually has more flexibility to respond to the demand of its customers than the wholesaler or retailer has in responding to the demand of the final consumer for whom brands may play an important role. Secondly, the loss of a possible source of supply matters less for the foreclosed buyers in the case of homogeneous products than in the case of a heterogeneous product with different grades and qualities. For final branded products or differentiated intermediate products where there are entry barriers, exclusive supply may have appreciable anti-competitive effects where the competing buyers are relatively small compared to the foreclosing buyer, even if the latter is not dominant on the downstream market.

200. Efficiencies can be expected in the case of a hold-up problem (paragraph (107)(d) and (107)(e)), and such efficiencies are more likely for intermediate products than for final products. Other efficiencies are less likely. Possible economies of scale in distribution (paragraph (107)(g)) do not seem likely to justify exclusive supply.

201. In the case of a hold-up problem and even more so in the case of economies of scale in distribution, quantity forcing on the supplier, such as minimum supply requirements, could well be a less restrictive alternative.

Example of exclusive supply

202. On a market for a certain type of components (intermediate product market) supplier A agrees with buyer B to develop, with its own know-how and considerable investment in new machines and with the help of specifications supplied by buyer B, a different version of the component. B will have to make considerable investments to incorporate the new component. It is agreed that A will supply the new product only to buyer B for a period of five years from the date of first entry on the market. B is obliged to buy the new product only from A for the same period of five years. Both A and B can continue to sell and buy respectively other versions of the component elsewhere. The market share of buyer B on the upstream component market and on the downstream final goods market is 40 %. The market share of the component supplier is 35 %. There are two other component suppliers with around 20-25 % market share and a number of small suppliers.

Given the considerable investments, the agreement is likely to fulfil the conditions of Article 101(3) in view of the efficiencies and the limited foreclosure effect. Other buyers are foreclosed from a particular version of a product of a supplier with 35 % market share and there are other component suppliers that could develop similar new products. The foreclosure of part of buyer B's demand to other suppliers is limited to maximum 40 % of the market.

2.7. Upfront access payments

203. Upfront access payments are fixed fees that suppliers pay to distributors in the framework of a vertical relationship at the beginning of a relevant period, in order to get access to their distribution network and remunerate services provided to the suppliers by the retailers. This category includes various practices such as slotting allowances (56), the so called pay-to-stay fees (57), payments to have access to a distributor's promotion campaigns etc. Upfront access payments are exempted under the Block Exemption Regulation when both the supplier's and buyer's market share does not exceed 30 %. The remainder of this section provides guidance for the assessment of upfront access payments in individual cases above the market share threshold.

(56) Fixed fees that manufacturers pay to retailers in order to get access to their shelf space.

(57) Lump sum payments made to ensure the continued presence of an existing product on the shelf for some further period.

204. Upfront access payments may sometimes result in anticompetitive foreclosure of other distributors if such payments induce the supplier to channel its products through only one or a limited number of distributors. A high fee may make that a supplier wants to channel a substantial volume of its sales through this distributor in order to cover the costs of the fee. In such a case, upfront access payments may have the same downstream foreclosure effect as an exclusive supply type of obligation. The assessment of that negative effect is made by analogy to the assessment of exclusive supply obligations (in particular paragraphs (194) to (199)).

205. Exceptionally, upfront access payments may also result in anticompetitive foreclosure of other suppliers, where the widespread use of upfront access payments increases barriers to entry for small entrants. The assessment of that possible negative effect is made by analogy to the assessment of single branding obligations (in particular paragraphs (132) to (141)).

206. In addition to possible foreclosure effects, upfront access payments may soften competition and facilitate collusion between distributors. Upfront access payments are likely to increase the price charged by the supplier for the contract products since the supplier must cover the expense of those payments. Higher supply prices may reduce the incentive of the retailers to compete on price on the downstream market, while the profits of distributors are increased as a result of the access payments. Such reduction of competition between distributors through the cumulative use of upfront access payments normally requires the distribution market to be highly concentrated.

207. However, the use of upfront access payments may in many cases contribute to an efficient allocation of shelf space for new products. Distributors often have less information than suppliers on the potential for success of new products to be introduced on the market and, as a result, the amount of products to be stocked may be sub-optimal. Upfront access payments may be used to reduce this asymmetry in information between suppliers and distributors by explicitly allowing suppliers to compete for shelf space. The distributor may thus receive a signal of which products are most likely to be successful since a supplier would normally agree to pay an upfront access fee if it estimates a low probability of failure of the product introduction.

208. Furthermore, due to the asymmetry in information mentioned in paragraph (207), suppliers may have incentives to free-ride on distributors' promotional efforts in order to introduce sub-optimal products. If a product is not successful, the distributors will pay part of the costs of the product failure. The use of upfront access fees may prevent such free riding by shifting the risk of product failure back to the suppliers, thereby contributing to an optimal rate of product introductions.

2.8. Category Management Agreements

209. Category management agreements are agreements by which, within a distribution agreement, the distributor entrusts the supplier (the «category captain») with the marketing of a category of products including in general not only the supplier's products, but also the products of its competitors. The category captain may thus have an influence on for instance the product placement and product promotion in the shop and product selection for the shop. Category management agreements are exempted under the Block Exemption Regulation when both the supplier's and buyer's market share does not exceed 30 %. The remainder of this section provides guidance for the assessment of category management agreements in individual cases above the market share threshold.

210. While in most cases category management agreements will not be problematic, they may sometimes distort competition between suppliers, and finally result in anticompetitive foreclosure of other suppliers, where the category captain is able, due to its influence over the marketing decisions of the distributor, to limit or disadvantage the distribution of products of competing suppliers. While in most cases the distributor may not have an interest in limiting its choice of products, when the distributor also sells competing products under its own brand (private labels), the distributor may also have incentives to exclude certain suppliers, in particular intermediate range products. The assessment of such upstream foreclosure effect is made by analogy to the assessment of single branding obligations (in particular paragraphs (132) to (141)) by addressing issues like the market coverage of these agreements, the market position of competing suppliers and the possible cumulative use of such agreements.

211. In addition, category management agreements may facilitate collusion between distributors when the same supplier serves as a category captain for all or most of the competing distributors on a market and provides these distributors with a common point of reference for their marketing decisions.

212. Category management may also facilitate collusion between suppliers through increased opportunities to exchange via retailers sensitive market information, such as for instance information related to future pricing, promotional plans or advertising campaigns (58).

(58) Direct information exchange between competitors is not covered by the Block Exemption Regulation, see Article 2(4) of that Regulation and paragraphs 27-28 of these Guidelines.

213. However, the use of category management agreements may also lead to efficiencies. Category management agreements may allow distributors to have access to the supplier's marketing expertise for a certain group of products and to achieve economies of scale as they ensure that the optimal quantity of products is presented timely and directly on the shelves. As category management is based on customers' habits, category management agreements may lead to higher customer satisfaction as they help to better meet demand expectations. In general, the higher the inter-brand competition and the lower consumers' switching costs, the greater the economic benefits achieved through category management.

2.9. Tying

214. Tying refers to situations where customers that purchase one product (the tying product) are required also to purchase another distinct product (the tied product) from the same supplier or someone designated by the latter. Tying may constitute an abuse within the meaning of Article 102 (59). Tying may also constitute a vertical restraint falling under Article 101 where it results in a single branding type of obligation (see paragraphs (129) to (150)) for the tied product. Only the latter situation is dealt with in these Guidelines.

(59) Judgment of the Court of Justice in Case C-333/94 P Tetrapak v. Commission (1996) ECR I-5951, paragraph 37. See also Communication from the Commission – Guidance on the Commission's enforcement priorities in applying Article 82 of the EC Treaty to abusive conduct by dominant undertakings, OJ C 45, 24.2.2009, p. 7.

215. Whether products will be considered as distinct depends on customer demand. Two products are distinct where, in the absence of the tying, a substantial number of customers would purchase or would have purchased the tying product without also buying the tied product from the same supplier, thereby allowing stand-alone production for both the tying and the tied product (60). Evidence that two products are distinct could include direct evidence that, when given a choice, customers purchase the tying and the tied products separately from different sources of supply, or indirect evidence, such as the presence on the market of undertakings specialised in the manufacture or sale of the tied product without the tying product (61), or evidence indicating that undertakings with little market power, particularly on competitive markets, tend not to tie or not to bundle such products. For instance, since customers want to buy shoes with laces and it is not practicable for distributors to lace new shoes with the laces of their choice, it has become commercial usage for shoe manufacturers to supply shoes with laces. Therefore, the sale of shoes with laces is not a tying practice.

(60) Judgment of the Court of First Instance in Case T-201/04 Microsoft v. Commission (2007) ECR II-3601, paragraphs 917, 921 and 922.

(61) Judgment of the Court of First Instance in Case T-30/89 Hilti v. Commission (1991) ECR II-1439, paragraph 67.

216. Tying may lead to anticompetitive foreclosure effects on the tied market, the tying market, or both at the same time. The foreclosure effect depends on the tied percentage of total sales on the market of the tied product. On the question of what can be considered appreciable foreclosure under Article 101(1), the analysis for single branding can be applied. Tying means that there is at least a form of quantity-forcing on the buyer in respect of the tied product. Where in addition a non-compete obligation is agreed in respect of the tied product, this increases the possible foreclosure effect on the market of the tied product. The tying may lead to less competition for customers interested in buying the tied product, but not the tying product. If there is not a sufficient number of customers that will buy the tied product alone to sustain competitors of the supplier on the tied market, the tying can lead to those customers facing higher prices. If the tied product is an important complementary product for customers of the tying product, a reduction of alternative suppliers of the tied product and hence a reduced availability of that product can make entry onto the tying market alone more difficult.

217. Tying may also directly lead to prices that are above the competitive level, especially in three situations. Firstly, if the tying and the tied product can be used in variable proportions as inputs to a production process, customers may react to an increase in price for the tying product by increasing their demand for the tied product while decreasing their demand for the tying product. By tying the two products the supplier may seek to avoid this substitution and as a result be able to raise its prices. Secondly, when the tying allows price discrimination according to the use the customer makes of the tying product, for example the tying of ink cartridges to the sale of photocopying machines (metering). Thirdly, when in the case of long-term contracts or in the case of after-markets with original equipment with a long replacement time, it becomes difficult for the customers to calculate the consequences of the tying.

218. Tying is exempted under the Block Exemption Regulation when the market share of the supplier, on both the market of the tied product and the market of the tying product, and the market share of the buyer, on the relevant upstream markets, do not exceed 30 %. It may be combined with other vertical restraints, which are not hardcore restrictions under that Regulation, such as non-compete obligations or quantity forcing in respect of the tying product, or exclusive sourcing. The remainder of this section provides guidance for the assessment of tying in individual cases above the market share threshold.

219. The market position of the supplier on the market of the tying product is obviously of central importance to assess possible anti-competitive effects. In general, this type of agreement is imposed by the supplier. The importance of the supplier on the market of the tying product is the main reason why a buyer may find it difficult to refuse a tying obligation.

220. The market position of the supplier's competitors on the market of the tying product is important in assessing the supplier's market power. As long as its competitors are sufficiently numerous and strong, no anti-competitive effects can be expected, as buyers have sufficient alternatives to purchase the tying product without the tied product, unless other suppliers are applying similar tying. In addition, entry barriers on the market of the tying product are relevant to establish the market position of the supplier. When tying is combined with a non-compete obligation in respect of the tying product, this considerably strengthens the position of the supplier.

221. Buying power is relevant, as important buyers will not easily be forced to accept tying without obtaining at least part of the possible efficiencies. Tying not based on efficiency is therefore mainly a risk where buyers do not have significant buying power.

222. Where appreciable anti-competitive effects are established, the question whether the conditions of Article 101(3) are fulfilled arises. Tying obligations may help to produce efficiencies arising from joint production or joint distribution. Where the tied product is not produced by the supplier, an efficiency may also arise from the supplier buying large quantities of the tied product. For tying to fulfil the conditions of Article 101(3), it must, however, be shown that at least part of these cost reductions are passed on to the consumer, which is normally not the case when the retailer is able to obtain, on a regular basis, supplies of the same or equivalent products on the same or better conditions than those offered by the supplier which applies the tying practice. Another efficiency may exist where tying helps to ensure a certain uniformity and quality standardisation (see paragraph (107)*(i)*). However, it needs to be demonstrated that the positive effects cannot be realised equally efficiently by requiring the buyer to use or resell products satisfying minimum quality standards, without requiring the buyer to purchase these from the supplier or someone designated by the latter. The requirements concerning minimum quality standards would not normally fall within the scope of Article 101(1). Where the supplier of the tying product imposes on the buyer the suppliers from which the buyer must purchase the tied product, for instance because the formulation of minimum quality standards is not possible, this may also fall outside the scope of Article 101(1), especially where the supplier of the tying product does not derive a direct (financial) benefit from designating the suppliers of the tied product.

2.10. Resale price restrictions

223. As explained in section III.3., resale price maintenance (RPM), that is, agreements or concerted practices having as their direct or indirect object the establishment of a fixed or minimum resale price or a fixed or minimum price level to be observed by the buyer, are treated as a hardcore restriction. Where an agreement includes RPM, that agreement is presumed to restrict competition and thus to fall within Article 101(1). It also gives rise to the presumption that the agreement is unlikely to fulfil the conditions of Article 101(3), for which reason the block exemption does not apply. However, undertakings have the possibility to plead an efficiency defence under Article 101(3) in an individual case. It is incumbent on the parties to substantiate that likely efficiencies result from including RPM in their agreement and demonstrate that all the conditions of Article 101(3) are fulfilled. It then falls to the Commission to effectively assess the likely negative effects on competition and consumers before deciding whether the conditions of Article 101(3) are fulfilled.

224. RPM may restrict competition in a number of ways. Firstly, RPM may facilitate collusion between suppliers by enhancing price transparency on the market, thereby making it easier to detect whether a supplier deviates from the collusive equilibrium by cutting its price. RPM also undermines the incentive for the supplier to cut its price to its distributors, as the fixed resale price will prevent it from benefiting from expanded sales. Such a negative effect is particularly plausible where the market is prone to collusive outcomes, for instance if the manufacturers form a tight oligopoly, and a significant part of the market is covered by RPM agreements. Second, by eliminating intra-brand price competition, RPM may also facilitate collusion between the buyers, that is, at the distribution level. Strong or well organised distributors may be able to force or convince one or more suppliers to fix their resale price above the competitive level and thereby help them to reach or stabilise a collusive equilibrium. The resulting loss of price competition seems especially problematic when the RPM is inspired by the buyers, whose collective horizontal interests can be expected to work out negatively for consumers. Third, RPM may more generally soften competition between manufacturers and/or between retailers, in particular when manufacturers use the same distributors to distribute their products and RPM is applied by all or many of them. Fourth, the immediate effect of RPM will be that all or certain distributors are prevented from lowering their sales price for that particular brand. In other words, the direct effect of RPM is a price increase. Fifth, RPM may lower the pressure on the margin of the manufacturer, in particular where the manufacturer has a commitment problem, that is, where it has an interest in lowering the price charged to subsequent distributors. In such a situation, the manufacturer may prefer to agree to RPM, so as to help it to commit not to lower the price for subsequent distributors and to reduce the pressure on its own margin. Sixth, RPM may be implemented by a manufacturer with market power to foreclose smaller rivals. The increased margin that RPM may offer distributors, may entice the latter to favour the particular brand over rival brands when advising customers, even where such advice is not in the interest of these customers, or not to sell these rival brands at all. Lastly, RPM may reduce dynamism and innovation at the distribution level. By preventing price competition between different distributors, RPM may prevent more efficient retailers from entering the market or acquiring sufficient scale with low prices. It also may prevent or hinder the entry and expansion of distribution formats based on low prices, such as price discounters.

225. However, RPM may not only restrict competition but may also, in particular where it is supplier driven, lead to efficiencies, which will be assessed under Article 101(3). Most notably, where a manufacturer introduces a new product, RPM may be helpful during the introductory period of expanding demand to induce distributors to better take into account the manufacturer's interest to promote the product. RPM may provide the distributors with the means to increase sales efforts and if the distributors on this market are under competitive pressure this may induce them to expand overall demand for the product and make the launch of the product a success, also for the benefit of consumers (62). Similarly, fixed resale prices, and not just maximum resale prices, may be necessary to organise in a franchise system or similar distribution system applying a uniform distribution format a coordinated short term low price campaign (2 to 6 weeks in most cases) which will also benefit the consumers. In some situations, the extra margin provided by RPM may allow retailers to provide (additional) pre-sales services, in particular in case of experience or complex products. If enough customers take advantage from such services to make their choice but then purchase at a lower price with retailers that do not provide such services (and hence do not incur these costs), high-service retailers may reduce or eliminate these services that enhance the demand for the supplier's product. RPM may help to prevent such free-riding at the distribution level. The parties will have to convincingly demonstrate that the RPM agreement can be expected to not only provide the means but also the incentive to overcome possible free riding between retailers on these services and that the pre-sales services overall benefit consumers as part of the demonstration that all the conditions of Article 101(3) are fulfilled.

(62) This assumes that it is not practical for the supplier to impose on all buyers by contract effective promotion requirements, see also paragraph 107 point *(a)*.

226. The practice of recommending a resale price to a reseller or requiring the reseller to respect a maximum resale price is covered by the Block Exemption Regulation when the market share of each of the parties to the agreement does not exceed the 30% threshold, provided it does not amount to a minimum or fixed sale price as a result of pressure from, or incentives offered by, any of the parties. The remainder of this section provides guidance for the assessment of maximum or recommended prices above the market share threshold and for cases of withdrawal of the block exemption.

227. The possible competition risk of maximum and recommended prices is that they will work as a focal point for the resellers and might be followed by most or all of them and/or that maximum or recommended prices may soften competition or facilitate collusion between suppliers.

228. An important factor for assessing possible anti-competitive effects of maximum or recommended resale prices is the market position of the supplier. The stronger the market position of the supplier, the higher the risk that a maximum resale price or a recommended resale price leads to a more or less uniform application of that price level by the resellers, because they may use it as a focal point. They may find it difficult to deviate from what they perceive to be the preferred resale price proposed by such an important supplier on the market.

229. Where appreciable anti-competitive effects are established for maximum or recommended resale prices, the question of a possible exemption under Article 101(3) arises. For maximum resale prices, the efficiency described in paragraph (107)*(f)* (avoiding double marginalisation), may be particularly relevant. A maximum resale price may also help to ensure that the brand in question competes more forcefully with other brands, including own label products, distributed by the same distributor.

Commission Regulation (EU) N° 461/2010, 27 May 2010 on the application of Article 101(3) of the Treaty on the functioning of the European Union to categories of vertical agreements and concerted practices in the motor vehicle sector

(OJ L 129, 28 May 2010, p. 52)

THE EUROPEAN COMMISSION,
Having regard to the Treaty on the Functioning of the European Union,
Having regard to Regulation N° 19/65/EEC of the Council of 2 March 1965 on the application of Article 85(3) of the Treaty to certain categories of agreements and concerted practices, and in particular Article 1 thereof,
Having published a draft of this Regulation,
After consulting the Advisory Committee on Restrictive Practices and Dominant Positions,
Whereas:

(1) Regulation N° 19/65/EEC empowers the Commission to apply Article 101(3) of the Treaty on the Functioning of the European Union by regulation to certain categories of vertical agreements and corresponding concerted practices falling within Article 101(1) of the Treaty. Block exemption regulations apply to vertical agreements which fulfil certain conditions and may be general or sector-specific.

(2) The Commission has defined a category of vertical agreements which it regards as normally satisfying the conditions laid down in Article 101(3) of the Treaty and to this end has adopted Commission Regulation (EU) N° 330/2010 of 20 April 2010 on the application of Article 101(3) of the Treaty on the Functioning of the European Union to categories of vertical agreements and concerted practices, which replaces Commission Regulation (EC) N° 2790/1999.

(3) The motor vehicle sector, which includes both passenger cars and commercial vehicles, has been subject to specific block exemption regulations since 1985, the most recent being Commission Regulation (EC) N° 1400/2002 of 31 July 2002 on the application of Article 81(3) of the Treaty to categories of vertical agreements and concerted practices in the motor vehicle sector. Regulation (EC) N° 2790/1999 expressly stated that it did not apply to vertical agreements the subject matter of which fell within the scope of any other block exemption regulation. The motor vehicle sector therefore fell outside the scope of that Regulation.

(4) Regulation (EC) N° 1400/2002 expires on 31 May 2010. However, the motor vehicle sector should continue to benefit from a block exemption in order to simplify administration and reduce compliance costs for the undertakings concerned, while ensuring effective supervision of markets in accordance with Article 103(2)*(b)* of the Treaty.

(5) Experience acquired since 2002 regarding the distribution of new motor vehicles, the distribution of spare parts and the provision of repair and maintenance services for motor vehicles, makes it possible to define a category of vertical agreements in the motor vehicle sector which can be regarded as normally satisfying the conditions laid down in Article 101(3) of the Treaty.

(6) This category includes vertical agreements for the purchase, sale or resale of new motor vehicles, vertical agreements for the purchase, sale or resale of spare parts for motor vehicles and vertical agreements for the provision of repair and maintenance services for such vehicles, where those agreements are concluded between non-competing undertakings, between certain competitors, or by certain associations of retailers or repairers. It also includes vertical agreements containing ancillary provisions on the assignment or use of intellectual property rights. The term «vertical agreements» should be defined accordingly to include both such agreements and the corresponding concerted practices.

(7) Certain types of vertical agreements can improve economic efficiency within a chain of production or distribution by facilitating better coordination between the participating undertakings. In particular, they can lead to a reduction in the transaction and distribution costs of the parties and to an optimisation of their sales and investment levels.

(8) The likelihood that such efficiency-enhancing effects will outweigh any anticompetitive effects due to restrictions contained in vertical agreements depends on the degree of market power of the parties to the agreement and, therefore, on the extent to which those undertakings face competition from other suppliers of goods or services regarded by their customers as interchangeable or substitutable for one another, by reason of the products' characteristics, their prices and their intended use. Vertical agreements containing restrictions which are likely to restrict competition and

harm consumers, or which are not indispensable to the attainment of the efficiency-enhancing effects, should be excluded from the benefit of the block exemption.

(9) In order to define the appropriate scope of a block exemption regulation, the Commission must take into account the competitive conditions in the relevant sector. In this respect, the conclusions of the in-depth monitoring of the motor vehicle sector set out in the Evaluation Report on the operation of Commission Regulation (EC) N° 1400/2002 of 28 May 2008 and in the Commission Communication on The Future Competition Law Framework applicable to the Motor Vehicle sector of 22 July 2009 have shown that a distinction should be drawn between agreements for the distribution of new motor vehicles and agreements for the provision of repair and maintenance services and distribution of spare parts.

(10) As regards the distribution of new motor vehicles, there do not appear to be any significant competition shortcomings which would distinguish this sector from other economic sectors and which could require the application of rules different from and stricter than those set out in Regulation (EU) N° 330/2010. The market-share threshold, the non-exemption of certain vertical agreements and the other conditions laid down in that Regulation normally ensure that vertical agreements for the distribution of new motor vehicles comply with the requirements of Article 101(3) of the Treaty. Therefore, such agreements should benefit from the exemption granted by Regulation (EU) N° 330/2010, subject to all the conditions laid down therein.

(11) As regards agreements for the distribution of spare parts and for the provision of repair and maintenance services, certain specific characteristics of the motor vehicle aftermarket should be taken into account. In particular, the experience acquired by the Commission in applying Regulation (EC) N° 1400/2002 shows that price increases for individual repair jobs are only partially reflected in increased reliability of modern cars and lengthening of service intervals. These latter trends are linked to technological evolution and to the increasing complexity and reliability of automotive components that the vehicle manufacturers purchase from original equipment suppliers. Such suppliers sell their products as spare parts in the aftermarket both through the vehicle manufacturers' authorised repair networks and through independent channels, thereby representing an important competitive force in the motor vehicle aftermarket. The costs borne on average by consumers in the Union for motor vehicle repair and maintenance services represent a very high proportion of total consumer expenditure on motor vehicles.

(12) Competitive conditions in the motor vehicle aftermarket also have a direct bearing on public safety, in that vehicles may be driven in an unsafe manner if they have been repaired incorrectly, as well as on public health and the environment, as emissions of carbon dioxide and other air pollutants may be higher from vehicles which have not undergone regular maintenance work.

(13) In so far as a separate aftermarket can be defined, effective competition on the markets for the purchase and sale of spare parts, as well as for the provision of repair and maintenance services for motor vehicles, depends on the degree of competitive interaction between authorised repairers, that is to say those operating within repair networks established directly or indirectly by vehicle manufacturers, as well as between authorised and independent operators, including independent spare parts suppliers and repairers. The latters'
ability to compete depends on unrestricted access to essential inputs such as spare parts and technical information.

(14) Having regard to those specificities, the rules in Regulation (EU) N° 330/2010, including the uniform market share threshold of 30 %, are necessary but are not sufficient to ensure that the benefit of the block exemption is reserved only to those vertical agreements for the distribution of spare parts and for the provision of repair and maintenance services for which it can be assumed with sufficient certainty that the conditions of Article 101(3) of the Treaty are satisfied.

(15) Therefore, vertical agreements for the distribution of spare parts and for the provision of repair and maintenance services should benefit from the block exemption only if, in addition to the conditions for exemption set out in Regulation (EU) N° 330/2010, they comply with stricter requirements concerning certain types of severe restrictions of competition that may limit the supply and use of spare parts in the motor vehicle aftermarket.

(16) In particular, the benefit of the block exemption should not be granted to agreements that restrict the sale of spare parts by members of the selective distribution system of a vehicle manufacturer to independent repairers, which use them for the provision of repair or maintenance services. Without access to such spare parts, independent repairers would not be able to compete effectively with authorised repairers, since they could not provide consumers with good quality services which contribute to the safe and reliable functioning of motor vehicles.

(17) Moreover, in order to ensure effective competition on the repair and maintenance markets and to allow repairers to offer end users competing spare parts, the block exemption should not cover vertical agreements which, although they comply with Regulation (EU) N° 330/2010, nonetheless restrict the ability of a producer of spare parts to sell such parts to authorised repairers within the distribution system of a vehicle manufacturer, independent distributors of spare parts, independent repairers or end users. This does not affect the liability of producers of spare parts under civil law, or the ability of vehicle manufacturers to require the authorised repairers within their distribution system to only use spare parts that match the quality of the components used for the assembly of a certain motor vehicle. Moreover, in view of the vehicle manufacturers' direct contractual involvement in repairs under warranty, free servicing, and recall operations, agreements containing obligations on authorised repairers to use only spare parts supplied by the vehicle manufacturer for those repairs should be covered by the exemption.

(18) Finally, in order to allow authorised and independent repairers and end users to identify the manufacturer of motor vehicle components or of spare parts and to choose between alternative parts, the block exemption should not cover agreements by which a manufacturer of motor vehicles limits the ability of a manufacturer of components or original spare parts to place its trade mark or logo on those parts effectively and in a visible manner.

(19) In order to allow all operators time to adapt to this Regulation, it is appropriate to extend the period of application of the provisions of Regulation (EC) N° 1400/2002 relating to vertical agreements for the purchase, sale and resale of new motor vehicles until 31 May 2013. As regards vertical agreements for the distribution of spare parts and for the provision of repair and maintenance services, this Regulation should apply from 1 June 2010 so as to continue to ensure adequate protection of competition on the motor vehicle aftermarkets.

(20) The Commission will, on a continuous basis, monitor developments in the motor vehicle sector and will take appropriate remedial action if competition shortcomings arise which may lead to consumer harm on the market for the distribution of new motor vehicles or the supply of spare parts or after-sales services for motor vehicles.

(21) The Commission may withdraw the benefit of this Regulation, pursuant to Article 29(1) of Council Regulation (EC) N° 1/2003 of 16 December 2002 on the implementation of the rules on competition laid down in Articles 81 and 82 of the Treaty, where it finds in a particular case that an agreement to which the exemption provided for in this Regulation applies nevertheless has effects which are incompatible with Article 101(3) of the Treaty.

(22) The competition authority of a Member State may withdraw the benefit of this Regulation pursuant to Article 29(2) of Regulation (EC) N° 1/2003 in respect of the territory of that Member State, or a part thereof where, in a particular case, an agreement to which the exemption provided for in this Regulation applies nevertheless has effects which are incompatible with Article 101(3) of the Treaty in the territory of that Member State, or in a part thereof, and where such territory has all the characteristics of a distinct geographic market.

(23) In determining whether the benefit of this Regulation should be withdrawn pursuant to Article 29 of Regulation (EC) N° 1/2003, the anti-competitive effects that may derive from the existence of parallel networks of vertical agreements that have similar effects which significantly restrict access to a relevant market or competition therein are of particular importance. Such cumulative effects may, for example, arise in the case of selective distribution or non-compete obligations.

(24) In order to strengthen supervision of parallel networks of vertical agreements which have similar anti-competitive effects and which cover more than 50 % of a given market, the Commission may by regulation declare this Regulation inapplicable to vertical agreements containing specific restraints relating to the market concerned, thereby restoring the full application of Article 101 of the Treaty to such agreements.

(25) In order to assess the effects of this Regulation on competition in motor vehicle retailing, in the supply of spare parts and in after sales servicing for motor vehicles in the internal market, it is appropriate to draw up an evaluation report on the operation of this Regulation,

HAS ADOPTED THIS REGULATION:

CHAPTER I
COMMON PROVISIONS

Art. 1. *Definitions*

1. For the purposes of this Regulation, the following definitions shall apply:

(a) «vertical agreement» means an agreement or concerted practice entered into between two or more undertakings each of which operates, for the purposes of the agreement or the concerted practice, at a different level of the production or distribution chain, and relating to the conditions under which the parties may purchase, sell or resell certain goods or services;

(b) «vertical restraint» means a restriction of competition in a vertical agreement falling within the scope of Article 101(1) of the Treaty;

(c) «authorised repairer» means a provider of repair and maintenance services for motor vehicles operating within the distribution system set up by a supplier of motor vehicles;

(d) «authorised distributor» means a distributor of spare parts for motor vehicles operating within the distribution system set up by a supplier of motor vehicles;

(e) «independent repairer» means:

(i) a provider of repair and maintenance services for motor vehicles not operating within the distribution system set up by the supplier of the motor vehicles for which it provides repair or maintenance;

(ii) an authorised repairer within the distribution system of a given supplier, to the extent that it provides repair or maintenance services for motor vehicles in respect of which it is not a member of the respective supplier's distribution system;

(f) «independent distributor» means:

(i) a distributor of spare parts for motor vehicles not operating within the distribution system set up by the supplier of the motor vehicles for which it distributes spare parts;

(ii) an authorised distributor within the distribution system of a given supplier, to the extent that it distributes spare parts for motor vehicles in respect of which it is not a member of the respective supplier's distribution system;

(g) «motor vehicle» means a self-propelled vehicle intended for use on public roads and having three or more road wheels;

(h) «spare parts» means goods which are to be installed in or upon a motor vehicle so as to replace components of that vehicle, including goods such as lubricants which are necessary for the use of a motor vehicle, with the exception of fuel;

(i) «selective distribution system» means a distribution system where the supplier undertakes to sell the contract goods or services, either directly or indirectly, only to distributors selected on the basis of specified criteria and where these distributors undertake not to sell such goods or services to unauthorised distributors within the territory reserved by the supplier to operate that system.

2. For the purposes of this Regulation, the terms «undertaking», «supplier», «manufacturer» and «buyer» shall include their respective connected undertakings.

«Connected undertakings» means:

(a) undertakings in which a party to the agreement, directly or indirectly:

(i) has the power to exercise more than half the voting rights; or

(ii) has the power to appoint more than half the members of the supervisory board, board of management or bodies legally representing the undertaking; or

(iii) has the right to manage the undertaking's affairs;

(b) undertakings which directly or indirectly have, over a party to the agreement, the rights or powers listed in point *(a)*;

(c) undertakings in which an undertaking referred to in point *(b)* has, directly or indirectly, the rights or powers listed in point *(a)*;

(d) undertakings in which a party to the agreement together with one or more of the undertakings referred to in points *(a)*, *(b)* or *(c)*, or in which two or more of the latter

undertakings, jointly have the rights or powers listed in point *(a)*;

(e) undertakings in which the rights or the powers listed in point *(a)* are jointly held by:

(i) parties to the agreement or their respective connected undertakings referred to in points *(a)* to *(d)*; or

(ii) one or more of the parties to the agreement or one or more of their connected undertakings referred to in points *(a)* to *(d)* and one or more third parties.

CHAPTER II

VERTICAL AGREEMENTS RELATING TO THE PURCHASE, SALE OR RESALE OF NEW MOTOR VEHICLES

Art. 2. *Application of Regulation (EC) N° 1400/2002*

Pursuant to Article 101(3) of the Treaty, from 1 June 2010 until 31 May 2013, Article 101(1) of the Treaty shall not apply to vertical agreements relating to the conditions under which the parties may purchase, sell or resell new motor vehicles, which fulfil the requirements for an exemption under Regulation (EC) N° 1400/2002 that relate specifically to vertical agreements for the purchase, sale or resale of new motor vehicles.

Art. 3. *Application of Regulation (EU) N° 330/2010*

With effect from 1 June 2013, Regulation (EU) N° 330/2010 shall apply to vertical agreements relating to the purchase, sale or resale of new motor vehicles.

CHAPTER III

VERTICAL AGREEMENTS RELATING TO THE MOTOR VEHICLE AFTERMARKET

Art. 4. *Exemption*

Pursuant to Article 101(3) of the Treaty and subject to the provisions of this Regulation Article 101(1) of the Treaty shall not apply to vertical agreements relating to the conditions under which the parties may purchase, sell or resell spare parts for motor vehicles or provide repair and maintenance services for motor vehicles, which fulfil the requirements for an exemption under Regulation (EU) N° 330/2010 and do not contain any of the hardcore clauses listed in Article 5 of this Regulation.

This exemption shall apply to the extent that such agreements contain vertical restraints.

Art. 5. *Restrictions that remove the benefit of the block exemption – hardcore restrictions*

The exemption provided for in Article 4 shall not apply to vertical agreements which, directly or indirectly, in isolation or in combination with other factors under the control of the parties, have as their object:

(a) the restriction of the sales of spare parts for motor vehicles by members of a selective distribution system to independent repairers which use those parts for the repair and maintenance of a motor vehicle;

(b) the restriction, agreed between a supplier of spare parts, repair tools or diagnostic or other equipment and a manufacturer of motor vehicles, of the supplier's ability to sell those goods to authorised or independent distributors or to authorised or independent repairers or end users;

(c) the restriction, agreed between a manufacturer of motor vehicles which uses components for the initial assembly of motor vehicles and the supplier of such components, of the supplier's ability to place its trade mark or logo effectively and in an easily visible manner on the components supplied or on spare parts.

CHAPTER IV

FINAL PROVISIONS

Art. 6. *Non-application of this Regulation*

Pursuant to Article 1a of Regulation N° 19/65/EEC, the Commission may by regulation declare that, where parallel networks of similar vertical restraints cover more than 50 % of a relevant market, this Regulation shall not apply to vertical agreements containing specific restraints relating to that market.

Art. 7. *Monitoring and evaluation report*

The Commission will monitor the operation of this Regulation and draw up a report on its operation by 31 May 2021 at the latest, having regard in particular to the conditions set out in Article 101(3) of the Treaty.

Art. 8. *Period of validity*

This Regulation shall enter into force on 1 June 2010. It shall expire on 31 May 2023.

This Regulation shall be binding in its entirety and directly applicable in all Member States.

Supplementary guidelines on vertical restraints in agreements for the sale and repair of motor vehicles and for the distribution of spare parts for motor vehicles

(OJ C 138, 28 May 2010, p. 16)

I. INTRODUCTION

1. Purpose of the Guidelines

1. These Guidelines set out principles for assessing under Article 101 of the Treaty on the Functioning of the European Union (1) particular issues arising in the context of vertical restraints in agreements for the sale and repair of motor vehicles and for the distribution of spare parts. They accompany Commission Regulation (EU) N° 461/2010 on the application of Article 101(3) of the Treaty on the Functioning of the European Union to categories of vertical agreements and concerted practices in the motor vehicle sector (2) (hereinafter «the Motor Vehicle Block Exemption Regulation») and are aimed at helping companies to make their own assessment of such agreements.

(1) With effect from 1 December 2009, Articles 81 and 82 of the EC Treaty have become Articles 101 and 102, respectively, of the Treaty on the Func-

tioning of the European Union («TFEU»). The two sets of provisions are in substance identical. For the purposes of these Guidelines, references to Articles 101 and 102 of the TFEU should be understood as references to Articles 81 and 82, respectively, of the EC Treaty where appropriate. The TFEU also introduced certain changes in terminology, such as the replacement of «Community» by «Union» and «common market» by «internal market». The terminology of the TFEU will be used throughout these Guidelines.

(2) OJ L 129, 28.5.2010, p. 52.

2. These Guidelines provide clarification on issues that are particularly relevant for the motor vehicle sector, including the interpretation of certain provisions of Commission Regulation (EU) N° 330/2010 of 20 April 2010 on the application of Article 101(3) of the Treaty on the Functioning of the European Union to categories of vertical agreements and concerted practices (3) (hereinafter «the General Vertical Block Exemption Regulation»). They are without prejudice to the applicability of the Guidelines on Vertical Restraints (4) (hereinafter «the General Vertical Guidelines») and are therefore to be read in conjunction with and as a supplement to the General Vertical Guidelines.

(3) OJ L 102, 23.4.2010, p. 1.

(4) OJ C 130, 19.5.2010, p. 1.

3. These Guidelines apply to both vertical agreements and concerted practices relating to the conditions under which the parties may purchase, sell or resell spare parts and/or provide repair and maintenance services for motor vehicles, and to vertical agreements and concerted practices relating to the conditions under which the parties may purchase, sell or resell new motor vehicles. As explained in Section II of these Guidelines, the latter category of agreements and concerted practices will remain subject to the relevant provisions of Commission Regulation (EC) N° 1400/2002 of 31 July 2002 on the application of Article 81(3) of the Treaty to categories of vertical agreements and concerted practices in the motor vehicle sector (5) until 31 May 2013. Therefore, as regards vertical agreements and concerted practices for the purchase, sale or resale of new motor vehicles, these Guidelines will only apply as from 1 June 2013. These Guidelines do not apply to vertical agreements in sectors other than motor vehicles, and the principles set out herein may not necessarily be used to assess agreements in other sectors.

(5) OJ L 203, 1.8.2002, p. 30.

4. These Guidelines are without prejudice to the possible parallel application of Article 102 of the Treaty to vertical agreements in the motor vehicle sector, or to the interpretation that the Court of Justice of the European Union may give in relation to the application of Article 101 of the Treaty to such vertical agreements.

5. Unless otherwise stated, the analysis and arguments set out in these Guidelines apply to all levels of trade. The terms «supplier» and «distributor» (6) are used for all levels of trade. The General Vertical Block Exemption Regulation and the Motor Vehicle Block Exemption Regulation are collectively referred to as «the Block Exemption Regulations».

(6) Retail level distributors are commonly referred to in the sector as «dealers».

6. The standards set forth in these Guidelines must be applied to each case having regard to the individual factual and legal circumstances. The Commission will apply (7) these Guidelines reasonably and flexibly, and having regard to the experience that it has acquired in the course of its enforcement and market monitoring activities.

(7) Since the modernisation of the Union competition rules, the primary responsibility for such analysis lies with the parties to agreements. The Commission may however investigate the compatibility of agreements with Article 101 of the Treaty, on its own initiative or following a complaint.

7. The history of competition enforcement in this sector shows that certain restraints can be arrived at either as a result of explicit direct contractual obligations or through indirect obligations or indirect means which nonetheless achieve the same anti-competitive result. Suppliers wishing to influence a distributor's competitive behaviour may, for instance, resort to threats or intimidation, warnings or penalties. They may also delay or suspend deliveries or threaten to terminate the contracts of distributors that sell to foreign consumers or fail to observe a given price level. Transparent relationships between contracting parties would normally reduce the risk of manufacturers being held responsible for using such indirect forms of pressure aimed at achieving anticompetitive outcomes. Adhering to a Code of Conduct is one means of achieving greater transparency in commercial relationships between parties. Such codes may inter alia provide for notice periods for contract termination, which may be determined in function of the contract duration, for compensation to be given for outstanding relationship-specific investments made by the dealer in case of early termination without just cause, as well as for arbitration as an alternative mechanism for dispute resolution. If a supplier incorporates such a Code of Conduct into its agreements with distributors and repairers, makes it publicly available, and complies with its provisions, this will be regarded as a relevant factor for assessing the supplier's conduct in individual cases.

2. Structure of the Guidelines

8. These Guidelines are structured as follows:

(a) Scope of the Motor Vehicle Block Exemption Regulation and relationship with the General Vertical Block Exemption Regulation (Section II);

(b) The application of the additional provisions in the Motor Vehicle Block Exemption Regulation (Section III).

(c) The assessment of specific restraints: single branding and selective distribution (Section IV).

II. SCOPE OF THE MOTOR VEHICLE BLOCK EXEMPTION REGULATION AND RELATIONSHIP WITH THE GENERAL VERTICAL BLOCK EXEMPTION REGULATION

9. Pursuant to Article 4 thereof, the Motor Vehicle Block Exemption Regulation covers vertical agreements relating to the purchase, sale or resale of spare parts for motor vehicles and to the provision of repair and maintenance services for motor vehicles.

10. Article 2 of the Motor Vehicle Block Exemption Regulation extends the application of the relevant provisions of Regulation (EC) N° 1400/2002 until 31 May 2013 as far as they relate to vertical agreements for the purchase, sale or resale of new motor vehicles. Pursuant to Article 3 of the Motor Vehicle Block Exemption Regulation vertical agreements for the purchase, sale and resale of new motor vehicles will be covered by the General Vertical Block Exemption Regulation, from 1 June 2013 (8).

(8) The expiry of Regulation (EC) N° 1400/2002 and its replacement with the new legal framework explained in these Guidelines does not of itself require that existing contracts be terminated. See for example Case C-125/05 Vulcan Silkeborg A/S v. Skandinavisk Motor Co. A/S. (2006) ECR I-7637.

11. The distinction that the new framework makes between the markets for the sale of new motor vehicles and the motor vehicle aftermarkets reflects the differing competitive conditions on these markets.

12. On the basis of an in-depth market analysis set out in the Evaluation Report on the operation of Commission Regulation (EC) N° 1400/2002 of 28 May 2008 (9) and in the Commission Communication on The Future Competition Law Framework applicable to the Motor Vehicle Sector of 22 July 2009 (10), it appears that there are no significant competition shortcomings distinguishing the new motor vehicle distribution sector from other economic sectors and which could require the application of rules different from and stricter than those in the General Vertical Block Exemption Regulation. Consequently, the application of a market share threshold of 30 % (11), the non-exemption of certain vertical restraints and the conditions provided for in the General Vertical Block Exemption Regulation will normally ensure that vertical agreements for the distribution of new motor vehicles satisfy the conditions laid down in Article 101(3) of the Treaty without the need for any additional requirements over and above those applicable to other sectors.

(9) SEC(2008) 1946.

(10) COM(2009) 388.

(11) Pursuant to Article 7 of the General Vertical Block Exemption Regulation, the calculation of this market share threshold is normally based on market sales value data or, if such data are not available, on other reliable market information, including market sales volumes. In this respect, the Commission takes note of the fact that, for the distribution of new motor vehicles, market shares are currently calculated by the industry on the basis of the volume of motor vehicles sold by the supplier on the relevant market, which includes all motor vehicles that are regarded by the buyer as interchangeable or substitutable, by reason of the products' characteristics, prices and intended use.

13. However, in order to allow all operators time to adapt to the general regime, in particular in view of relationship-specific investments which have been made in the long term, the period of application of Regulation (EC) N° 1400/2002 is extended by three years until 31 May 2013 with regard to those requirements that relate specifically to vertical agreements for the purchase, sale or resale of new motor vehicles. From 1 June 2010 until 31 May 2013, those provisions of Regulation (EC) N° 1400/2002 which relate to both agreements for the distribution of new motor vehicles and agreements for the purchase, sale and resale of spare parts for motor vehicles and/or the provision of repair and maintenance services, will apply only in respect of the former. During that period these Guidelines will not be used for interpreting the provisions of Regulation (EC) N° 1400/2002. Instead, reference should be made to the Explanatory Brochure on that Regulation (12).

(12) Explanatory brochure for Commission Regulation (EC) N° 1400/2002 of 31 July 2002 – Distribution and Servicing of Motor Vehicles in the European Union.

14. As regards vertical agreements relating to the conditions under which the parties may purchase, sell or resell spare parts for motor vehicles and/or provide repair and maintenance services for motor vehicles, the Motor Vehicle Block Exemption Regulation applies from 1 June 2010. This means that, in order to be exempted pursuant to Article 4 of that Regulation, those agreements not only need to fulfil the conditions for an exemption under the General Vertical Block Exemption Regulation, but must also not contain any serious restrictions of competition, commonly referred to as hardcore restrictions as listed in Article 5 of the Motor Vehicle Block Exemption Regulation.

15. Because of the generally brand-specific nature of the markets for repair and maintenance services and for the distribution of spare parts, competition on those markets is inherently less intense compared to that on the market for the sale of new motor vehicles. While reliability has improved and service intervals have lengthened thanks to technological improvement, this evolution is outpaced by an upward price trend for individual repair and maintenance jobs. On the spare parts markets, parts bearing the motor vehicle manufacturer's brand face competition from those supplied by the original equipment suppliers (OES) and by other parties. This maintains price pressure on those markets, which in turn maintains pressure on prices on the repair and maintenance markets, since spare parts make up a large percentage of the cost of the average repair. Moreover, repair and maintenance as a whole represent a very high proportion of total consumer expenditure on motor vehicles, which itself accounts for a significant slice of the average consumer's budget.

16. In order to address particular competition issues arising on the motor vehicle aftermarkets, the General Vertical Block Exemption Regulation is supplemented with three additional hardcore restrictions in the Motor Vehicle Block Exemption Regulation applying to agreements for the repair and maintenance of motor vehicles and for the supply of spare parts. Further guidance on those additional hardcore restrictions is given in Section III of these Guidelines.

III. THE APPLICATION OF THE ADDITIONAL PROVISIONS IN THE MOTOR VEHICLE BLOCK EXEMPTION REGULATION

17. Agreements will not benefit from the block exemption if they contain hardcore restrictions. These restrictions are listed in Article 4 of the General Vertical Block Exemption Regulation and Article 5 of the Motor Vehicle Block Exemption Regulation. Including any such restrictions in an agreement gives rise to the presumption that the agreement falls within Article 101(1) of the Treaty. It also gives rise to the presumption that the agreement is unlikely to satisfy the conditions laid down in Article 101(3) of the Treaty, for which reason the block exemption does not apply. However, this is a rebuttable presumption which leaves open the possibility for undertakings to plead an efficiency defence under Article 101(3) of the Treaty in an individual case.

18. One of the Commission's objectives as regards competition policy for the motor vehicle sector is to protect access by spare parts manufacturers to the motor vehicle aftermarkets, thereby ensuring that competing brands of spare parts continue to be available to both independent and authorised repairers, as well as to parts wholesalers. The availability of such parts brings considerable benefits to consumers, especially since there are often large differences in price between parts sold or resold by a car manufacturer and alternative parts. Alternatives for parts bearing the trademark of the motor vehicle manufacturer (OEM parts) include original parts manufactured and distributed by original equipment suppliers (OES parts), while other parts matching the quality of the original components are supplied by «matching quality» parts manufacturers.

19. «Original parts or equipment» means parts or equipment which are manufactured according to the specifications and production standards provided by the motor vehicle manufacturer for the production of parts or equipment for the assembly of the motor vehicle in question. This includes parts or equipment which are manufactured on the same production line as those parts or equipment. It is presumed unless the contrary is proven, that parts constitute original parts if the part manufacturer certifies that the parts match the quality of the components used for the assembly of the motor vehicle in question and have been manufactured according to the specifications and production standards of the motor vehicle (see Article 3(26) of Directive 2007/46/EC of the European Parliament and of the Council of 5 September 2007 establishing a framework for the approval of motor vehicles and their trailers, and of systems, components and separate technical units intended for such motor vehicles (Framework Directive) (13)).

(13) *OJ* L 263, 9.10.2007, p. 1.

20. In order to be considered as «matching quality», parts must be of a sufficiently high quality that their use does not endanger the reputation of the authorised network in question. As with any other selection standard, the motor vehicle manufacturer may bring evidence that a given spare part does not meet this requirement.

21. Article 4*(e)* of the General Vertical Block Exemption Regulation describes it as a hardcore restriction for an agreement between a supplier of components and a buyer who incorporates those components, to prevent or restrict the supplier's ability to sell its components to end-users, independent repairers or other service providers not entrusted by the buyer with the repair or servicing of its goods. Article 5*(a)*, *(b)* and *(c)* of the Motor Vehicle Block Exemption Regulation lay down three additional hardcore restrictions relating to agreements for the supply of spare parts.

22. Article 5*(a)* of the Motor Vehicle Block Exemption Regulation concerns the restriction of the sale of spare parts for motor vehicles by members of a selective distribution system to independent repairers. This provision is most relevant for a particular category of parts, sometimes referred to as captive parts, which may only be obtained from the motor vehicle manufacturer or from members of its authorised networks. If a supplier and a distributor agree that such parts may not be supplied to independent repairers, this agreement would be likely to foreclose such repairers from the market for repair and maintenance services and fall foul of Article 101 of the Treaty.

23. Article 5*(b)* of the Motor Vehicle Block Exemption Regulation concerns any direct or indirect restriction agreed between a supplier of spare parts, repair tools or diagnostic or other equipment and a manufacturer of motor vehicles, which limits the supplier's ability to sell these goods to authorised and/or independent distributors and repairers. So-called «tooling arrangements» between component suppliers and motor vehicle manufacturers are one example of possible indirect restrictions of this type. Reference should be made in this respect to the Commission notice of 18 December 1978 concerning its assessment of certain subcontracting agreements in relation to Article 85(1) of the EEC Treaty (14) (the Sub-contracting Notice). Normally, Article 101(1) of the Treaty does not apply to an arrangement whereby a motor vehicle manufacturer provides a tool to a component manufacturer which is necessary for the production of certain components, shares in the product development costs, or contributes necessary (15) intellectual property rights, or know-how, and does not allow this contribution to be used for the production of parts to be sold directly in the aftermarket. On the other hand, if a motor vehicle manufacturer obliges a component supplier to transfer its ownership of such a tool, intellectual property rights, or know-how, bears only an insignificant part of the product development costs, or does not contribute any necessary tools, intellectual property rights, or know-how, the agreement at issue will not be considered to be a genuine sub-contracting arrangement. Therefore, it may be caught by Article 101(1) of the Treaty and be examined pursuant to the provisions of the Block Exemption Regulations.

(14) *OJ* C 1, 3.1.1979, p. 2.

(15) Where the motor vehicle manufacturer provides a tool, intellectual property rights (IPR) and/or know-how to a component supplier, this arrangement will not benefit from the Sub-contracting Notice if the component supplier already has this tool, IPR or know-how at its disposal, or could, under reasonable conditions obtain them, since under these circumstances the contribution would not be necessary.

24. Article 5*(c)* of the Motor Vehicle Block Exemption Regulation relates to the restriction agreed between a manufacturer of motor vehicles which uses components for the initial assembly of motor vehicles and the supplier of such components, which limits the supplier's ability to place its trade mark or logo effectively and in an easily visible manner on the components supplied or on spare parts. In order to improve consumer choice, repairers and consumers should be able to identify which spare parts from alternative suppliers match a given motor vehicle, other than those bearing the car manufacturer's brand. Putting the trade mark or logo on the components and on spare parts facilitates the identification of compatible replacement parts which can be obtained from OES. By not allowing this, motor vehicle manufacturers can restrict the marketing of OES parts and limit consumers' choice in a manner that runs counter to the provisions of Article 101 of the Treaty.

IV. THE ASSESSMENT OF SPECIFIC RESTRAINTS

25. Parties to vertical agreements in the motor vehicle sector should use these Guidelines as a supplement to and in conjunction with the General Vertical Guidelines in order to assess the compatibility of specific restraints with Article 101 of the Treaty. This section gives particular guidance as to single branding and selective distribution, which are two areas which may have particular relevance for assessing the category of agreements referred to in Section II of these Guidelines.

Section 1
Single branding obligations

(i) Assessment of single-branding obligations under the Block Exemption Regulations

26. Pursuant to Article 3 of the Motor Vehicle Block Exemption Regulation read in conjunction with Article 5(1)*(a)* of the General Vertical Block Exemption Regulation, a motor vehicle supplier and a distributor having a share of the relevant market that does not exceed 30 % may agree on a single-branding obligation that obliges the distributor to purchase motor vehicles only from the supplier or from other firms designated by the supplier, on condition that the duration of such non-compete obligations is limited to five years or less. The same principles apply to agreements between suppliers and their authorised repairers and/or spare parts distributors. A renewal beyond five years requires explicit consent of both parties, and there should be no obstacles that hinder the distributor from effectively terminating the non-compete obligation at the end of the five-year period. Non-compete obligations are not covered by the Block Exemption Regulations when their duration is indefinite or exceeds five years, although in those circumstances the Block Exemption Regulations would continue to apply to the remaining part of the vertical agreement. The same applies to non-compete obligations that are tacitly renewable beyond a period of five years. Obstacles, threats of termination, or intimations that single-branding will be re-imposed before a sufficient period has elapsed to allow either the distributor or the new supplier to amortise their sunk investments would amount to a tacit renewal of the single-branding obligation in question.

27. Pursuant to Article 5(1)(c) of the General Vertical Block Exemption Regulation, any direct or indirect obligation causing the members of a selective distribution system not to sell the brands of particular competing suppliers, are not covered by the exemption. Particular attention should be paid to the manner in which single branding obligations are applied to existing multi-brand distributors, in order to ensure that the obligations in question do not form part of an overall strategy aimed at eliminating competition from one or more specific suppliers, and in particular from newcomers or weaker competitors. This type of concern could arise in particular if the market share thresholds indicated in paragraph 34 of these Guidelines are exceeded and if the supplier applying this type of restraint has a position on the relevant market that enables it to contribute significantly to the overall foreclosure effect (16).

(16) Commission notice on agreements of minor importance which do not appreciably restrict competition under Article 81(1) of the Treaty establishing the European Community (de minimis), OJ C 368, 22.12.2001, p. 13.

28. Non-compete obligations in vertical agreements do not constitute hardcore restrictions, but depending on the market circumstances, can nonetheless have negative effects which may cause the agreements to fall under Article 101(1) of the Treaty (17). One such harmful effect may arise if barriers to entry or expansion are raised that foreclose competing suppliers, and harm consumers in particular by increasing the prices or limiting the choice of products, lowering their quality or reducing the level of product innovation.

(17) As regards the relevant factors to be taken into account to carry out the assessment of non-compete obligations under Article 101(1) of the Treaty, see the relevant section in the General Vertical Guidelines, in particular paragraphs 129 to 150.

29. However, non-compete obligations may also have positive effects which may justify the application of Article 101(3) of the Treaty. They may in particular help to overcome a «free-rider» problem, by which one supplier benefits from investments made by another. A supplier may, for instance, invest in a distributor's premises, but in doing so attract customers for a competing brand that is also sold from the same premises. The same applies to other types of investment made by the supplier which may be used by the distributor to sell motor vehicles of competing manufacturers, such as investments in training.

30. Another positive effect of non-compete obligations in the motor vehicle sector relates to the enhancement of the brand image and reputation of the distribution network. Such restraints may help to create and maintain a brand image by imposing a certain measure of uniformity and quality standardisation on distributors, thereby increasing the attractiveness of that brand to the final consumer and increasing its sales.

31. Article 1(d) of the General Vertical Block Exemption Regulation defines a non-compete obligation as:

«(a) any direct or indirect obligation causing the buyer not to manufacture, purchase, sell or resell goods or services which compete with the contract goods or services; or

(b) any direct or indirect obligation on the buyer to purchase from the supplier or from another undertaking designated by the supplier more than 80 % of the buyer's total purchases of the contract goods or services and their substitutes on the relevant market.»

32. Apart from direct means to tie the distributor to its own brand(s), a supplier may also have recourse to indirect means having the same effect. In the motor vehicle sector, such indirect means may include qualitative standards specifically designed to discourage the distributors from selling products of competing brands (18), bonuses made conditional on the distributor agreeing to sell exclusively one brand, target rebates or certain other requirements such as the requirement to set up a separate legal entity for the competing brand or the obligation to display the additional competing brand in a separate showroom in a geographic location where the fulfilment of such a requirement would not be economically viable (for example sparsely populated areas).

(18) See cases BMW, IP/06/302 – 13.3.2006 and Opel 2006, IP/06/303 – 13.3.2006.

33. The block exemption provided for in the General Vertical Block Exemption Regulation covers all forms of direct or indirect non-compete obligations provided that the market shares of both the supplier and the distributor do not exceed 30 % and the duration of the non-compete obligation does not exceed five years. However, even in cases where individual agreements satisfy those conditions, the use of non-compete obligations may result in anti-competitive effects not outweighed by their positive effects. In the motor vehicle industry, such net anti-competitive effects could in particular result from cumulative effects leading to the foreclosure of competing brands.

34. For the distribution of motor vehicles at the retail level, foreclosure of this type is unlikely to occur in markets where all suppliers have market shares below 30 % and where the total percentage of all motor vehicle sales that are subject to single-branding obligations on the market in question (that is to say the total tied market share) is below 40 % (19). In a situation where there is one non-dominant supplier with a market share of more than 30 % of the relevant market whereas all other suppliers' market shares are below 30 %, cumulative anticompetitive effects are unlikely as long as the total tied market share does not exceed 30 %.

(19) See General Vertical Guidelines at paragraph 141.

35. If access to the relevant market for the sale of new motor vehicles and competition therein is significantly restricted by the cumulative effect of parallel networks of similar vertical agreements containing single branding obligations, the benefit of the block exemption may be withdrawn by the Commission, pursuant to Article 29 of Council Regulation (EC) N° 1/2003 of 16 December 2002 on the implementation of the rules on competition laid down in Articles 81 and 82 of the Treaty (20). A withdrawal decision may be addressed in particular to those suppliers that contribute in a significant manner to a cumulative foreclosure effect on the relevant market. Where that effect occurs on a national market, the National Competition Authorities of that Member State may also withdraw the benefit of the block exemption in respect of that territory.

(20) OJ L 1, 4.1.2003, p. 1.

36. In addition, if parallel networks of agreements containing similar vertical restraints cover more than 50 % of a given market, the Commission may adopt a Regulation declaring the block exemption inapplicable to the market in question in respect of such restraints. In particular, such a situation may arise if cumulative effects resulting from the widespread use of single-branding obligations lead to consumer harm on that market.

37. With regard to the assessment of minimum purchasing obligations calculated on the basis of the distributor's total annual requirements, it may be justified to withdraw the benefit of the block exemption if cumulative anticompetitive effects arise even if the supplier imposes a minimum purchasing obligation that is below the 80 % limit established in Article 1(d) of the General Vertical Block Exemption Regulation. The parties need to consider whether, in the light of the relevant factual circumstances, an obligation on the distributor to ensure that a given percentage of its total purchases of motor vehicles bear the supplier's brand will prevent the distributor from taking on one or more additional competing brands. From that perspective, even a minimum purchasing requirement set at a level lower than 80 % of total annual purchases will amount to a single-branding obligation if it obliges a distributor wishing to take up a new brand of its choice from a competing manufacturer to purchase so many motor vehicles of the brand that it currently sells that the distributor's business is made economically unsustainable (21). Such a minimum purchasing obligation will also amount to a single branding obligation if it forces a competing supplier to split its envisaged sales volume in a given territory over several distributors, leading to duplication of investments and a fragmented sales presence.

(21) For instance, if a dealer purchases 100 cars of brand A in a year to meet demand, and wishes to buy 100 cars of brand B, an 80 % minimum purchasing obligation as regards brand A would imply that the following year, the dealer would have to buy 160 brand A cars. Given that penetration rates are likely to be relatively stable, this would likely leave the dealer with a large unsold stock of brand A. It would therefore be forced to dramatically reduce its purchases of brand B in order to avoid such a situation. Depending on the specific circumstances of the case, such a practice can be viewed as a single-branding obligation.

(ii) Assessment of single-branding obligations outside the scope of the Block Exemption Regulations

38. Parties may also be called upon to assess the compatibility with the competition rules of single-branding obligations in respect of agreements that do not qualify for block exemption because the parties' market shares exceed 30 % or the duration of the agreement exceeds five years. Such agreements will therefore be subject to individual scrutiny in order to ascertain whether they are caught by Article 101(1) of the Treaty and if so, whether efficiencies offsetting any possible anti-competitive effect can be demonstrated. If that is the case, they may be able to benefit from the exception laid down in Article 101(3) of the Treaty. For assessment in an individual case the general principles set out in Section VI.2.1 of the General Vertical Guidelines will apply.

39. In particular, agreements entered into between a motor vehicle manufacturer or its importer, on the one hand, and spare parts distributors and/or authorised repairers, on the other, will fall outside the Block Exemption Regulations when the market shares held by the parties exceed the 30 % threshold, which is likely to be the case for most such agreements. Single-branding obligations that will need to be assessed in such circumstances include all types of restriction that directly or indirectly limit authorised distributors' or repairers' ability to obtain original or matching quality spare parts from third parties. However, an obligation on an authorised repairer to use original spare parts supplied by the motor vehicle manufacturer for repairs carried out under warranty, free servicing and motor vehicle recall work would not be considered to be a single-branding obligation, but rather an objectively justified requirement.

40. Single-branding obligations in agreements for the distribution of new motor vehicles will also need to be individually assessed where their duration exceeds five years or/and where the market share of the supplier exceeds 30 %, which may be the case for certain suppliers in some Member States. In such circumstances, the parties should have regard not only to the supplier's and buyer's market share, but also to the total tied market share taking into account the thresholds indicated in paragraph 34. Above those thresholds, individual cases will be assessed in accordance with the general principles set out in Section VI.2.1 of the General Vertical Guidelines.

41. Outside the scope of the Block Exemption Regulations, the assessment of minimum purchasing obligations calculated on the basis of the distributor's total annual requirements will take into account all the relevant factual circumstances. In particular, a minimum purchasing requirement set at a level lower than 80 % of total annual purchases will amount to a single-branding obligation if it has the effect of preventing distributors from dealing in one or more additional competing brands.

2. Selective distribution

42. Selective distribution is currently the predominant form of distribution in the motor vehicle sector. Its use is widespread in motor vehicle distribution, as well as for repair and maintenance and the distribution of spare parts.

43. In purely qualitative selective distribution, distributors and repairers are only selected on the basis of objective criteria required by the nature of the product or service, such as the technical skills of sales personnel, the layout of sales facilities, sales techniques and the type of sales service to be provided by the distributor (22). The application of such criteria does not put a direct limit on the number of distributors or repairers admitted to the supplier's network. Purely qualitative selective distribution is in general considered to fall outside Article 101(1) of the Treaty for lack of anti-competitive effects, provided that three conditions are satisfied. First, the nature of the product in question must necessitate the use of selective distribution, in the sense that such a system must constitute a legitimate requirement, having regard to the nature of the product concerned, to preserve its quality and ensure its proper use. Second, distributors or repairers must be chosen on the basis of objective criteria of a qualitative nature which are laid down uniformly for all potential resellers and are not applied in a discriminatory manner. Third, the criteria laid down must not go beyond what is necessary.

(22) It should be recalled however that, in accordance with the established case law of the European Courts, purely qualitative selective distribution systems may nevertheless restrict competition where the existence of a certain number of such systems does not leave any room for other forms of distribution based on a different way of competing. This situation will generally not arise on the markets for the sale of new motor vehicles, on which leasing and other similar arrangements are a valid alternative to outright purchase of a motor vehicle, nor in the markets for repair and maintenance, as long as independent repairers provide consumers with an alternative channel for the upkeep of their motor vehicles. See for example Case T-88/92 Groupement d'achat Édouard Leclerc v. Commission (1996) ECR II-1961.

44. Whereas qualitative selective distribution involves the selection of distributors or repairers only on the basis of objective criteria required by the nature of the product or service, quantitative selection adds further criteria for selection that more directly limit the potential number of distributors or repairers either by directly fixing their number, or for instance, requiring a minimum level of sales. Networks based on quantitative criteria are generally held to be more restrictive than those that rely on qualitative selection alone, and are accordingly more likely to be caught by Article 101(1) of the Treaty.

45. If selective distribution agreements are caught by Article 101(1) of the Treaty, the parties will need to assess whether their agreements can benefit from the Block Exemption Regulations, or individually, from the exception in Article 101(3) of the Treaty.

(i) The assessment of selective distribution under the Block Exemption Regulations

46. The Block Exemption Regulations exempt selective distribution agreements, irrespective of whether quantitative or purely qualitative selection criteria are used, so long as the parties' market shares do not exceed 30 %. However, that exemption is conditional on the agreements not containing any of the hardcore restrictions set out in Article 4 of the General Vertical Block Exemption Regulation and Article 5 of the Motor Vehicle Block Exemption Regulation, or any of the excluded restrictions described in Article 5 of the General Vertical Block Exemption Regulation.

47. Three of the hardcore restrictions in the General Vertical Block Exemption Regulation relate specifically to selective distribution. Article 4(b) describes as hardcore the restriction of the territory into which, or of the customers to whom, a buyer party to the agreement may sell the contract goods or services, except the restriction of sales by the members of a selective distribution system to unauthorised distributors in markets where such a system is operated. Article 4(c) describes as hardcore agreements restricting active or passive sales to end users by members of a selective distribution system operating at the retail level of trade, without prejudice to the possibility of prohibiting a member of the system from operating out of an unauthorised place of establishment, while Article 4(d) relates to the restriction of cross-supplies between distributors within a selective distribution system, including between distributors operating at different levels of trade. Those three hardcore restrictions have special relevance for motor vehicle distribution.

48. The internal market has enabled consumers to purchase motor vehicles in other Member States and take advantage of price differentials between them, and the Commission views the protection of parallel trade in this sector as an important competition objective. The consumer's ability to buy goods in other Member States is especially important as far as motor vehicles are concerned, given the high value of the goods and the direct benefits in the form of lower prices accruing to consumers buying motor vehicles elsewhere in the Union. The Commission is therefore concerned that distribution agreements should not restrict parallel trade, since this cannot be expected to satisfy the conditions laid down in Article 101(3) of the Treaty (23).

(23) The notion that cross-border trade restrictions may harm consumers has been confirmed by the Court in Case C-551/03 P, General Motors, (2006) ECR I-3173, paragraphs 67 and 68; Case C-338/00 P, Volkswagen/Commission, (2003) ECR I-9189, paragraphs 44 and 49, and Case T-450/05, Peugeot/Commission, judgment of 9 July 2009, not yet reported, paragraphs 46-49.

49. The Commission has brought several cases against motor vehicle manufacturers for impeding such trade, and its decisions have been largely confirmed by the European Courts (24). This experience shows that restrictions on parallel trade may take a number of forms. A supplier may, for instance, put pressure on distributors, threaten them with contract termination, fail to pay bonuses, refuse to honour warranties on motor vehicles imported by a consumer or cross-supplied between distributors established in different Member States, or make a distributor wait significantly longer for delivery of an identical motor vehicle when the consumer in question is resident in another Member State.

(24) Commission Decision 98/273/EC of 28 January 1998 in Case IV/35.733 – VW, Commission Decision 2001/146/EC of 20 September 2000 in Case COMP/36.653 – Opel, OJ L 59, 28.2.2001, p. 1, Commission Decision 2002/758/EC of 10 October 2001 in Case COMP/36.264 – Mercedes-Benz, OJ L 257, 25.9.2002, p. 1, Commission Decision 2006/431/EC of 5 October 2005 in Cases F-2/36.623/36.820/37.275 – SEP et autres/Peugeot SA.

50. One particular example of indirect restrictions on parallel trade arises when a distributor is unable to obtain new motor vehicles with the appropriate specifications needed for cross-border sales. In those specific circumstances, the benefit of the block exemption may depend on whether a supplier provides its distributors with motor vehicles with specifications identical to those sold in other Member States for sale to consumers from those countries (the so-called «availability clause») (25).

(25) Joined Cases 25 and 26/84 Ford-Werke AG and Ford of Europe Inc. v. Commission of the European Communities, (1985) ECR 2725.

51. For the purposes of the application of the Block Exemption Regulations, and in particular as regards the application of Article 4(c) of the General Vertical Block Exemption Regulation, the notion of «end users» includes leasing companies. This means in particular that distributors in selective distribution systems may not be prevented from selling new motor vehicles to leasing companies of their choice. However, a supplier using selective distribution may prevent its distributors from selling new motor vehicles to leasing companies when there is a verifiable risk that those companies will resell them while still new. A supplier can therefore require a dealer to check, before selling to a particular company, the general leasing conditions applied so as to verify that the company in question is indeed a leasing company rather than an unauthorised reseller. However, an obligation on a dealer to provide its supplier with copies of each leasing agreement before the dealer sells a motor vehicle to a leasing company could amount to an indirect restriction on sales.

52. The notion of «end users» also encompasses consumers who purchase through an intermediary. An intermediary is a person or an undertaking which purchases a new motor vehicle on behalf of a named consumer without being a member of the distribution network. Those operators perform an important role in the motor vehicle sector, in particular by facilitating consumers' purchases of motor vehicles in other Member States. Evidence of intermediary status should as a rule be established by a valid mandate including the name and address of the consumer obtained prior to the transaction. The use of the Internet as a means to attract customers in relation to a given range of motor vehicles and collect electronic mandates from them does not affect intermediary status. Intermediaries are to be distinguished from independent resellers, which purchase motor vehicles for resale and do not operate on behalf of named consumers. Independent resellers are not to be considered as end users for the purposes of the Block Exemption Regulations.

(ii) The assessment of selective distribution outside the scope of the Block Exemption Regulations

53. As paragraph 175 of the General Vertical Guidelines explains, the possible competition risks brought about by selective distribution are a reduction in intra-brand competition and, especially in case of cumulative effect, foreclosure of certain type(s) of distributors and facilitation of collusion between suppliers or buyers.

54. To assess the possible anti-competitive effects of selective distribution under Article 101(1) of the Treaty, a distinction needs to be made between purely qualitative selective distribution and quantitative selective distribution. As pointed out in paragraph 43, qualitative selective distribution is normally not caught by Article 101(1) of the Treaty.

55. The fact that a network of agreements does not benefit from the block exemption because the market share of one or more of the parties is above the 30 % threshold for exemption does not imply that such agreements are illegal. Instead, the parties to such agreements need to subject them to an individual analysis to check whether they fall under Article 101(1) of the Treaty and, if so, whether they may nonetheless benefit from the exception in Article 101(3) of the Treaty.

56. As regards the specificities of new motor vehicle distribution, quantitative selective distribution will generally satisfy the conditions laid down in Article 101(3) of the Treaty if the parties' market shares do not exceed 40 %. However, the parties to such agreements should bear in mind that the presence of particular selection standards could have an effect on whether their agreements satisfy the conditions laid down in Article 101(3) of the Treaty. For instance, although the use of location clauses in selective distribution agreements for new motor vehicles, that is to say agreements containing a prohibition on a member of a selective distribution system from operating out of an unauthorised place of establishment, will usually bring efficiency benefits in the form of more efficient logistics and predictable network coverage, those benefits may be outweighed by disadvantages if the market share of the supplier is very high, and in those circumstances such clauses might not be able to benefit from the exception in Article 101(3) of the Treaty.

57. Individual assessment of selective distribution for authorised repairers also raises specific issues. Insofar as a market exists (26) for repair and maintenance services that is separate from that for the sale of new motor vehicles, this is considered to be brand-specific. On that market, the main source of competition results from the competitive interaction between independent repairers and authorised repairers of the brand in question.

(26) In some circumstances, a system market which includes motor vehicles and spare parts together may be defined, taking into account, inter alia, the life-time of the motor vehicle as well as the preferences and buying behaviour of the users. See Commission notice on the definition of the relevant market for the purposes of Community competition law, OJ C 372, 9.12.1997, p. 5, paragraph 56. One important factor is whether a significant proportion of buyers make their choice taking into account the lifetime costs of the motor vehicle or not. For instance, buying behaviour may significantly differ between buyers of trucks who purchase and operate a fleet, and who take into account maintenance costs at the moment of purchasing the motor vehicle and buyers of individual motor vehicles. Another relevant factor is the existence and relative position of part suppliers, repairers and/or parts distributors operating in the aftermarket independently from motor vehicle manufacturers. In most cases, there is likely to be a brand-specific aftermarket, in particular because the majority of buyers are private individuals or small and medium-size enterprises that purchase motor vehicles and aftermarket services separately and do not have systematic access to data permitting them to assess the overall costs of motor vehicle ownership in advance.

58. Independent repairers in particular provide vital competitive pressure, as their business models and their related operating costs are different from those in the authorised networks. Moreover, unlike authorised repairers, which to a large extent use car manufacturer-branded parts, independent garages generally have greater recourse to other brands, thereby allowing a motor vehicle owner to choose between competing parts. In addition, given that a large majority of repairs for newer motor vehicles are currently carried out in authorised repair shops, it is important that competition between authorised repairers remains effective, which may only be the case if access to the networks remains open for new entrants.

59. The new legal framework makes it easier for the Commission and National Competition Authorities to protect competition between independent garages and authorised repairers, as well as between the members of each authorised repairer network. In particular, the reduction in the market share threshold for exemption of qualitative selective distribution from 100 % to 30 % broadens the scope for competition authorities to act.

60. When assessing the competitive impact of vertical agreements on the motor vehicle aftermarkets, the parties should therefore be aware of the Commission's determination to preserve competition both between the members of authorised repair networks and between those members and independent repairers. To this end, particular attention should be paid to three specific types of conduct which may restrict such competition, namely preventing access of independent repairers to technical information, misusing the legal and/or extended warranties to exclude independent repairers, or making access to authorised repairer networks conditional upon non-qualitative criteria.

61. Although the following three subsections refer specifically to selective distribution, the same anti-competitive foreclosure effects could stem from other types of vertical agreements that limit, directly or indirectly, the number of service partners contractually linked to a motor vehicle manufacturer.

Access to technical information by independent operators

62. Although purely qualitative selective distribution is in general considered to fall outside Article 101(1) of the Treaty for lack of anti-competitive effects (27), qualitative selective distribution agreements concluded with authorised repairers and/or parts distributors may be caught by Article 101(1) of the Treaty if, within the context of those agreements, one of the parties acts in a way that forecloses independent operators from the market, for instance by failing to release technical repair and maintenance information to them. In that context, the notion of independent operators includes independent repairers, spare parts manufacturers and distributors, manufacturers of repair equipment or tools, publishers of technical information, automobile clubs, roadside assistance operators, operators offering inspection and testing services and operators offering training for repairers.

(27) As pointed out in paragraph 54 above, this will generally be the case on the markets for repair and maintenance as long as independent repairers provide consumers with an alternative channel for the upkeep of their motor vehicles.

63. Suppliers provide their authorised repairers with the full scope of technical information needed to perform repair and maintenance work on motor vehicles of their brands and are often the only companies able to provide repairers with all of the technical information that they need on the brands in question. In such circumstances, if the supplier fails to provide independent operators with appropriate access to its brand-specific technical repair and maintenance information, possible negative effects stemming from its agreements with authorised repairers and/or parts distributors could be strengthened, and cause the agreements to fall within Article 101(1) of the Treaty.

64. Moreover, a lack of access to necessary technical information could cause the market position of independent operators to decline, leading to consumer harm, in terms of a significant reduction in choice of spare parts, higher prices for repair and maintenance services, a reduction in choice of repair outlets and potential safety problems. In those circumstances, the efficiencies that might normally be expected to result from the authorised repair and parts distribution agreements would not be such as to offset these anti-competitive effects, and the agreements in question would consequently fail to satisfy the conditions laid down in Article 101(3) of the Treaty.

65. Regulation (EC) N° 715/2007 of the European Parliament and of the Council of 20 June 2007 on type approval of motor vehicles with respect to emissions from light passenger and commercial vehicles (Euro 5 and Euro 6) and on access to vehicle repair and maintenance information (28) as well as Commission Regulation (EC) N° 692/2008 of 18 July 2008 implementing and amending Regulation (EC) N° 715/2007 of the European Parliament and of the Council on type-approval of motor vehicles with respect to emissions from light passenger and commercial vehicles (Euro 5 and Euro 6) and on access to vehicle repair and maintenance information (29) provide for a system for disseminating repair and maintenance information in respect of passenger cars put on the market from 1 September 2009. Regulation (EC) N° 595/2009 of the European Parliament and of the Council of 18 June 2009 on type approval of motor vehicles and engines with respect to emissions from heavy duty vehicles (Euro 6) and on access to vehicle repair an maintenance information (30) and the ensuing implementing measures provide for such a system in respect of commercial vehicles put on the market from 1 January 2013. The Commission will take those Regulations into account when assessing cases of suspected withholding of technical repair and maintenance information concerning motor vehicles marketed before those dates. When considering whether withholding a particular item of information may lead the agreements at issue to be caught by Article 101(1) of the Treaty, a number of factors should be considered, including:

(a) whether the item in question is technical information, or information of another type, such as commercial information (31), which may legitimately be withheld;

(b) whether withholding the technical information in question will have an appreciable impact on the ability of independent operators to carry out their tasks and exercise a competitive constraint on the market;

(c) whether the technical information in question is made available to members of the relevant authorised repair network; if it is made available to the authorised network in whatever form, it should also be made available to independent operators on a non-discriminatory basis;

(d) whether the technical information in question will ultimately (32) be used for the repair and maintenance of motor vehicles, or rather for another purpose (33), such as for the manufacturing of spare parts or tools.

(28) OJ L 171, 29.6.2007, p. 1.

(29) OJ L 199, 28.7.2008, p. 1.

(30) OJ L 188, 18.7.2009, p. 1.

(31) Commercial information can be thought of as information that is used for carrying on a repair and maintenance business but is not needed to repair or maintain motor vehicles. Examples include billing software, or information on the hourly tariffs practiced within the authorised network.

(32) Such as information supplied to publishers for resupply to motor vehicle repairers.

(33) Information used for fitting a spare part to or using a tool on a motor vehicle should be considered as being used for repair and maintenance, while information on the design, production process or the materials used for manufacturing a spare part should not be considered to fall within this category, and may therefore be withheld.

66. Technological progress implies that the notion of technical information is fluid. Currently, particular examples of technical information include software, fault codes and other parameters, together with updates, which are required to work on electronic control units with a view to introducing or restoring settings recommended by the supplier, motor vehicle identification numbers or any other motor vehicle identification methods, parts catalogues, repair and maintenance procedures, working solutions resulting from practical experience and relating to problems typically affecting a given model or batch, and recall notices as well as other notices identifying repairs that may be carried out without charge within the authorised repair network. The part code and any other information necessary to identify the correct car manufacturer-branded spare part to fit a given individual motor vehicle (that is to say the part that the car manufacturer would generally supply to the members of its authorised repair networks to repair the motor vehicle in question) also constitute technical information (34). The lists of items set out in Article 6(2) of Regulation (EC) N° 715/2007 and Regulation (EC) N° 595/2009 should also be used as a guide to what the Commission views as technical information for the purposes of applying Article 101 of the Treaty.

(34) The independent operator should not have to purchase the spare part in question to be able to obtain this information.

67. The way in which technical information is supplied is also important for assessing the compatibility of authorised repair agreements with Article 101 of the Treaty. Access should be given upon request and without undue delay, the information should be provided in a usable form, and the price charged should not discourage access to it by failing to take into account the extent to which the independent operator uses the information. A supplier of motor vehicles should be required to give independent operators access to technical information on new motor vehicles at the same time as such access is given to its authorised repairers and should not oblige independent operators to purchase more than the information necessary to carry out the work in question. Article 101 of the Treaty does not, however, oblige a supplier to provide technical information in a standardised format or through a defined technical system, such as the CEN/ISO standard and the OASIS format as provided for by Regulation (EC) N° 715/2007 and Commission Regulation (EC) N° 295/2009 of 18 March 2009 concerning the classification of certain goods in the Combined Nomenclature (35).

(35) OJ L 95, 9.4.2009, p. 7.

68. The above considerations also apply to the availability of tools and training to independent operators. «Tools» in this context includes electronic diagnostic and other repair tools, together with related software, including periodic updates thereof, and after-sales services for such tools.

Misuse of warranties

69. Qualitative selective distribution agreements may also be caught by Article 101(1) of the Treaty if the supplier and the members of its authorised network explicitly or implicitly reserve repairs on certain categories of motor vehicles to the members of the authorised network. This might happen, for instance, if the manufacturer's warranty vis-à-vis the buyer, whether legal or extended, is made conditional on the end user having repair and maintenance work that is not covered by warranty carried out only within the authorised repair networks. The same applies to warranty conditions which require the use of the manufacturer's brand of spare parts in respect of replacements not covered by the warranty terms. It also seems doubtful that selective distribution agreements containing such practices could bring benefits to consumers in such a way as to allow the agreements in question to benefit from the exception in Article 101(3) of the Treaty. However, if a supplier legitimately refuses to honour a warranty claim on the grounds that the situation leading to the claim in question is causally linked to a failure on the part of a repairer to carry out a particular repair or maintenance operation in the correct manner or to the use of poor quality spare parts, this will have no bearing on the compatibility of the supplier's repair agreements with the competition rules.

Access to authorised repairer networks

70. Competition between authorised and independent repairers is not the only form of competition that needs to be taken into account when analysing the compatibility of authorised repair agreements with Article 101 of the Treaty. Parties should also assess the degree to which authorised repairers within the relevant network are able to compete with one another. One of the main factors driving this competition relates to the conditions of access to the network established under the standard authorised repairer agreements. In view of the generally strong market position of networks of authorised repairers, their particular importance for owners of newer motor vehicles, and the fact that consumers are not prepared to travel long distances to have their cars repaired, the Commission considers it important that access to the authorised repair networks should generally remain open to all firms that meet defined quality criteria. Submitting applicants to quantitative selection is likely to cause the agreement to fall within Article 101(1) of the Treaty.

71. A particular case arises when agreements oblige authorised repairers to also sell new motor vehicles. Such agreements are likely to be caught by Article 101(1) of the Treaty, since the obligation in question is not required by the nature of the contract services. Moreover, for an established brand, agreements containing such an obligation would not normally be able to benefit from the exception in Article 101(3) of the Treaty, since the impact would be to severely restrict access to the authorised repair network, thereby reducing competition without bringing corresponding benefits to consumers. However, in certain cases, a supplier wishing to launch a brand on a particular geographic market might initially find it difficult to attract distributors willing to make the necessary investment unless they could be sure that they would not face competition from «stand-alone» authorised repairers that sought to free-ride on these initial investments. In those circumstances, contractually linking the two activities for a limited period of time would have a pro-competitive effect on the motor vehicle sales market by allowing a new brand to launch, and would have no effect on the potential brand-specific repair market, which would in any event not exist if the motor vehicles could not be sold. The agreements in question would therefore be unlikely to be caught by Article 101(1) of the Treaty.

2.1.2.3. Horizontal agreements

Commission Regulation (EU) N° 1217/2010, 14 December 2010 – R&D Block Exemption Regulation. 116
Commission Regulation (EU) N° 1218/2010, 14 December 2010 – Specialisation Block Exemption Regulation. 121
Guidelines horizontal co-operation agreements 124

Commission Regulation (EU) N° 1217/2010, 14 December 2010 on the application of Article 101(3) of the Treaty on the Functioning of the European Union to certain categories of research and development agreements

(OJ L 335, 18 December 2010, p. 36)

THE EUROPEAN COMMISSION,

Having regard to the Treaty on the Functioning of the European Union,

Having regard to Regulation (EEC) N° 2821/71 of the Council of 20 December 1971 on application of Article 85(3) of the Treaty to categories of agreements, decisions and concerted practices [1],

Having published a draft of this Regulation,

After consulting the Advisory Committee on Restrictive Practices and Dominant Positions,

Whereas:

(1) Regulation (EEC) N° 2821/71 empowers the Commission to apply Article 101(3) of the Treaty on the Functioning of the European Union [2] by regulation to certain categories of agreements, decisions and concerted practices falling within the scope of Article 101(1) of the Treaty which have as their object the research and development of products, technologies or processes up to the stage of industrial application, and exploitation of the results, including provisions regarding intellectual property rights.

(2) Article 179(2) of the Treaty calls upon the Union to encourage undertakings, including small and medium-sized undertakings, in their research and technological development activities of high quality, and to support their efforts to cooperate with one another. This Regulation is intended to facilitate research and development while at the same time effectively protecting competition.

(3) Commission Regulation (EC) N° 2659/2000 of 29 November 2000 on the application of Article 81(3) of the Treaty to categories of research and development agreements [3] defines categories of research and development agreements which the Commission regarded as normally satisfying the conditions laid down in Article 101(3) of the Treaty. In view of the overall positive experience with the application of that Regulation, which expires on 31 December 2010, and taking into account further experience acquired since its adoption, it is appropriate to adopt a new block exemption regulation.

(4) This Regulation should meet the two requirements of ensuring effective protection of competition and providing adequate legal security for undertakings. The pursuit of those objectives should take account of the need to simplify administrative supervision and the legislative framework to as great an extent as possible. Below a certain level of market power it can in general be presumed, for the application of Article 101(3) of the Treaty, that the positive effects of research and development agreements will outweigh any negative effects on competition.

(5) For the application of Article 101(3) of the Treaty by regulation, it is not necessary to define those agreements which are capable of falling within Article 101(1) of the Treaty. In the individual assessment of agreements under Article 101(1) of the Treaty, account has to be taken of several factors, and in particular the market structure on the relevant market.

(6) Agreements on the joint execution of research work or the joint development of the results of the research, up to but not including the stage of industrial application, generally do not fall within the scope of Article 101(1) of the Treaty. In certain circumstances, however, such as where the parties agree not to carry out other research and development in the same field, thereby forgoing the opportunity of gaining competitive advantages over the other parties, such agreements may fall within Article 101(1) of the Treaty and should therefore be included within the scope of this Regulation.

(7) The benefit of the exemption established by this Regulation should be limited to those agreements for which it can be assumed with sufficient certainty that they satisfy the conditions of Article 101(3) of the Treaty.

(8) Cooperation in research and development and in the exploitation of the results is most likely to promote technical and economic progress if the parties contribute complementary skills, assets or activities to the cooperation. This also includes scenarios where one party merely finances the research and development activities of another party.

(9) The joint exploitation of results can be considered as the natural consequence of joint research and development. It can take different forms such as manufacture, the exploitation of intellectual property rights that substantially contribute to technical or economic progress, or the marketing of new products.

(10) Consumers can generally be expected to benefit from the increased volume and effectiveness of research and development through the introduction of new or improved products or services, a quicker launch of those products or services, or the reduction of prices brought about by new or improved technologies or processes.

(11) In order to justify the exemption, the joint exploitation should relate to products, technologies or processes for which the use of the results of the research and development is decisive. Moreover, all the parties should agree in the research and development agreement that they will all have full access to the final results of the joint research and development, including any arising intellectual property rights and know-how, for the purposes of further research and development and exploitation, as soon as the final results become available. Access to the results should generally not be

limited as regards the use of the results for the purposes of further research and development. However, where the parties, in accordance with this Regulation, limit their rights of exploitation, in particular where they specialise in the context of exploitation, access to the results for the purposes of exploitation may be limited accordingly. Moreover, where academic bodies, research institutes or undertakings which supply research and development as a commercial service without normally being active in the exploitation of results participate in research and development, they may agree to use the results of research and development solely for the purpose of further research. Depending on their capabilities and commercial needs, the parties may make unequal contributions to their research and development cooperation. Therefore, in order to reflect, and to make up for, the differences in the value or the nature of the parties' contributions, a research and development agreement benefiting from this Regulation may provide that one party is to compensate another for obtaining access to the results for the purposes of further research or exploitation. However, the compensation should not be so high as to effectively impede such access.

(12) Similarly, where the research and development agreement does not provide for any joint exploitation of the results, the parties should agree in the research and development agreement to grant each other access to their respective pre-existing know-how, as long as this know-how is indispensable for the purposes of the exploitation of the results by the other parties. The rates of any licence fee charged should not be so high as to effectively impede access to the know-how by the other parties.

(13) The exemption established by this Regulation should be limited to research and development agreements which do not afford the undertakings the possibility of eliminating competition in respect of a substantial part of the products, services or technologies in question. It is necessary to exclude from the block exemption agreements between competitors whose combined share of the market for products, services or technologies capable of being improved or replaced by the results of the research and development exceeds a certain level at the time the agreement is entered into. However, there is no presumption that research and development agreements are either caught by Article 101(1) of the Treaty or that they fail to satisfy the conditions of Article 101(3) of the Treaty once the market share threshold set out in this Regulation is exceeded or other conditions of this Regulation are not met. In such cases, an individual assessment of the research and development agreement needs to be conducted under Article 101 of the Treaty.

(14) In order to ensure the maintenance of effective competition during joint exploitation of the results, provision should be made for the block exemption to cease to apply if the parties' combined share of the market for the products, services or technologies arising out of the joint research and development becomes too great. The exemption should continue to apply, irrespective of the parties' market shares, for a certain period after the commencement of joint exploitation, so as to await stabilisation of their market shares, particularly after the introduction of an entirely new product, and to guarantee a minimum period of return on the investments involved.

(15) This Regulation should not exempt agreements containing restrictions which are not indispensable to the attainment of the positive effects generated by a research and development agreement. In principle, agreements containing certain types of severe restrictions of competition such as limitations on the freedom of parties to carry out research and development in a field unconnected to the agreement, the fixing of prices charged to third parties, limitations on output or sales, and limitations on effecting passive sales for the contract products or contract technologies in territories or to customers reserved for other parties should be excluded from the benefit of the exemption established by this Regulation irrespective of the market share of the parties. In this context, field of use restrictions do not constitute limitations of output or sales, and also do not constitute territorial or customer restrictions.

(16) The market share limitation, the non-exemption of certain agreements and the conditions provided for in this Regulation normally ensure that the agreements to which the block exemption applies do not enable the parties to eliminate competition in respect of a substantial part of the products or services in question.

(17) The possibility cannot be ruled out that anti-competitive foreclosure effects may arise where one party finances several research and development projects carried out by competitors with regard to the same contract products or contract technologies, in particular where it obtains the exclusive right to exploit the results vis-à-vis third parties. Therefore the benefit of this Regulation should be conferred on such paid-for research and development agreements only if the combined market share of all the parties involved in the connected agreements, that is to say, the financing party and all the parties carrying out the research and development, does not exceed 25 %.

(18) Agreements between undertakings which are not competing manufacturers of products, technologies or processes capable of being improved, substituted or replaced by the results of the research and development will only eliminate effective competition in research and development in exceptional circumstances. It is therefore appropriate to enable such agreements to benefit from the exemption established by this Regulation irrespective of market share and to address any exceptional cases by way of withdrawal of its benefit.

(19) The Commission may withdraw the benefit of this Regulation, pursuant to Article 29(1) of Council Regulation (EC) N° 1/2003 of 16 December 2002 on the implementation of the rules on competition laid down in Articles 81 and 82 of the Treaty [4], where it finds in a particular case that an agreement to which the exemption provided for in this Regulation applies nevertheless has effects which are incompatible with Article 101(3) of the Treaty.

(20) The competition authority of a Member State may withdraw the benefit of this Regulation pursuant to Article 29(2) of Regulation (EC) N° 1/2003 in respect of the territory of that Member State, or a part thereof where, in a particular case, an agreement to which the exemption established by this Regulation applies nevertheless has effects which are incompatible with Article 101(3) of the Treaty in the territory of that Member State, or in a part thereof, and where such territory has all the characteristics of a distinct geographic market.

(21) The benefit of this Regulation could be withdrawn pursuant to Article 29 of Regulation (EC) N° 1/2003, for example, where the existence of a research and development agreement substantially restricts the scope for third parties to carry out research and development in the relevant field because of the limited research capacity available elsewhere, where because of the particular structure of supply, the existence of the research and development agreement substan-

tially restricts the access of third parties to the market for the contract products or contract technologies, where without any objectively valid reason, the parties do not exploit the results of the joint research and development vis-à-vis third parties, where the contract products or contract technologies are not subject in the whole or a substantial part of the internal market to effective competition from products, technologies or processes considered by users as equivalent in view of their characteristics, price and intended use, or where the existence of the research and development agreement would restrict competition in innovation or eliminate effective competition in research and development on a particular market.

(22) As research and development agreements are often of a long-term nature, especially where the cooperation extends to the exploitation of the results, the period of validity of this Regulation should be fixed at 12 years,

HAS ADOPTED THIS REGULATION:

[1] *OJ* L 285, 29.12.1971, p. 46.

[2] With effect from 1 December 2009, Article 81 of the EC Treaty has become Article 101 of the Treaty on the Functioning of the European Union (TFEU). The two articles are, in substance, identical. For the purposes of this Regulation, references to Article 101 of the TFEU should be understood as references to Article 81 of the EC Treaty where appropriate. The TFEU also introduced certain changes in terminology, such as the replacement of «Community» by «Union» and «common market» by «internal market». The terminology of the TFEU will be used throughout this Regulation.

[3] *OJ* L 304, 5.12.2000, p. 7.

[4] *OJ* L 1, 4.1.2003, p. 1.

Art. 1. *Definitions*

1. For the purposes of this Regulation, the following definitions shall apply:

(a) «research and development agreement» means an agreement entered into between two or more parties which relate to the conditions under which those parties pursue:

(i) joint research and development of contract products or contract technologies and joint exploitation of the results of that research and development;

(ii) joint exploitation of the results of research and development of contract products or contract technologies jointly carried out pursuant to a prior agreement between the same parties;

(iii) joint research and development of contract products or contract technologies excluding joint exploitation of the results;

(iv) paid-for research and development of contract products or contract technologies and joint exploitation of the results of that research and development;

(v) joint exploitation of the results of paid-for research and development of contract products or contract technologies pursuant to a prior agreement between the same parties; or

(vi) paid-for research and development of contract products or contract technologies excluding joint exploitation of the results;

(b) «agreement» means an agreement, a decision by an association of undertakings or a concerted practice;

(c) «research and development» means the acquisition of know-how relating to products, technologies or processes and the carrying out of theoretical analysis, systematic study or experimentation, including experimental production, technical testing of products or processes, the establishment of the necessary facilities and the obtaining of intellectual property rights for the results;

(d) «product» means a good or a service, including both intermediary goods or services and final goods or services;

(e) «contract technology» means a technology or process arising out of the joint research and development;

(f) «contract product» means a product arising out of the joint research and development or manufactured or provided applying the contract technologies;

(g) «exploitation of the results» means the production or distribution of the contract products or the application of the contract technologies or the assignment or licensing of intellectual property rights or the communication of know-how required for such manufacture or application;

(h) «intellectual property rights» means intellectual property rights, including industrial property rights, copyright and neighbouring rights;

(i) «know-how» means a package of non-patented practical information, resulting from experience and testing, which is secret, substantial and identified;

(j) «secret», in the context of know-how, means that the know-how is not generally known or easily accessible;

(k) «substantial», in the context of know-how, means that the know-how is significant and useful for the manufacture of the contract products or the application of the contract technologies;

(l) «identified», in the context of know-how, means that the know-how is described in a sufficiently comprehensive manner so as to make it possible to verify that it fulfils the criteria of secrecy and substantiality;

(m) «joint», in the context of activities carried out under a research and development agreement, means activities where the work involved is:

(i) carried out by a joint team, organisation or undertaking;

(ii) jointly entrusted to a third party; or

(iii) allocated between the parties by way of specialisation in the context of research and development or exploitation;

(n) «specialisation in the context of research and development» means that each of the parties is involved in the research and development activities covered by the research and development agreement and they divide the research and development work between them in any way that they consider most appropriate; this does not include paid-for research and development;

(o) «specialisation in the context of exploitation» means that the parties allocate between them individual tasks such as production or distribution, or impose restrictions upon each other regarding the exploitation of the results such as restrictions in relation to certain territories, customers or fields of use; this includes a scenario where only one party produces and distributes the contract products on the basis of an exclusive licence granted by the other parties;

(p) «paid-for research and development» means research and development that is carried out by one party and financed by a financing party;

(q) «financing party» means a party financing paid-for research and development while not carrying out any of the research and development activities itself;

(r) «competing undertaking» means an actual or potential competitor;

(s) «actual competitor» means an undertaking that is supplying a product, technology or process capable of being improved, substituted or replaced by the contract product or the contract technology on the relevant geographic market;

(t) «potential competitor» means an undertaking that, in the absence of the research and development agreement, would, on realistic grounds and not just as a mere theoretical possibility, in case of a small but permanent increase in relative prices be likely to undertake, within not more than 3 years, the necessary additional investments or other necessary switching costs to supply a product, technology or process capable of being improved, substituted or replaced by the contract product or contract technology on the relevant geographic market;

(u) «relevant product market» means the relevant market for the products capable of being improved, substituted or replaced by the contract products;

(v) «relevant technology market» means the relevant market for the technologies or processes capable of being improved, substituted or replaced by the contract technologies.

2. For the purposes of this Regulation, the terms «undertaking» and «party» shall include their respective connected undertakings.

«Connected undertakings» means:

(a) undertakings in which a party to the research and development agreement, directly or indirectly:

(i) has the power to exercise more than half the voting rights;

(ii) has the power to appoint more than half the members of the supervisory board, board of management or bodies legally representing the undertaking; or

(iii) has the right to manage the undertaking's affairs;

(b) undertakings which directly or indirectly have, over a party to the research and development agreement, the rights or powers listed in point *(a)*;

(c) undertakings in which an undertaking referred to in point *(b)* has, directly or indirectly, the rights or powers listed in point *(a)*;

(d) undertakings in which a party to the research and development agreement together with one or more of the undertakings referred to in points *(a)*, *(b)* or *(c)*, or in which two or more of the latter undertakings, jointly have the rights or powers listed in point *(a)*;

(e) undertakings in which the rights or the powers listed in point *(a)* are jointly held by:

(i) parties to the research and development agreement or their respective connected undertakings referred to in points *(a)* to *(d)*; or

(ii) one or more of the parties to the research and development agreement or one or more of their connected undertakings referred to in points *(a)* to *(d)* and one or more third parties.

Art. 2. *Exemption*

1. Pursuant to Article 101(3) of the Treaty and subject to the provisions of this Regulation, it is hereby declared that Article 101(1) of the Treaty shall not apply to research and development agreements.

This exemption shall apply to the extent that such agreements contain restrictions of competition falling within the scope of Article 101(1) of the Treaty.

2. The exemption provided for in paragraph 1 shall apply to research and development agreements containing provisions which relate to the assignment or licensing of intellectual property rights to one or more of the parties or to an entity the parties establish to carry out the joint research and development, paid-for research and development or joint exploitation, provided that those provisions do not constitute the primary object of such agreements, but are directly related to and necessary for their implementation.

Art. 3. *Conditions for exemption*

1. The exemption provided for in Article 2 shall apply subject to the conditions set out in paragraphs 2 to 5.

2. The research and development agreement must stipulate that all the parties have full access to the final results of the joint research and development or paid-for research and development, including any resulting intellectual property rights and know-how, for the purposes of further research and development and exploitation, as soon as they become available. Where the parties limit their rights of exploitation in accordance with this Regulation, in particular where they specialise in the context of exploitation, access to the results for the purposes of exploitation may be limited accordingly. Moreover, research institutes, academic bodies, or undertakings which supply research and development as a commercial service without normally being active in the exploitation of results may agree to confine their use of the results for the purposes of further research. The research and development agreement may foresee that the parties compensate each other for giving access to the results for the purposes of further research or exploitation, but the compensation must not be so high as to effectively impede such access.

3. Without prejudice to paragraph 2, where the research and development agreement provides only for joint research and development or paid-for research and development, the research and development agreement must stipulate that each party must be granted access to any pre-existing know-how of the other parties, if this know-how is indispensable for the purposes of its exploitation of the results. The research and development agreement may foresee that the parties compensate each other for giving access to their pre-existing know-how, but the compensation must not be so high as to effectively impede such access.

4. Any joint exploitation may only pertain to results which are protected by intellectual property rights or constitute know-how and which are indispensable for the manufacture of the contract products or the application of the contract technologies.

5. Parties charged with the manufacture of the contract products by way of specialisation in the context of exploitation must be required to fulfil orders for supplies of the contract products from the other parties, except where the research and development agreement also provides for joint distribution within the meaning of point *(m)*, (i) or (ii), of Article 1(1) or where the parties have agreed that only the party manufacturing the contract products may distribute them.

Art. 4. *Market share threshold and duration of exemption*

1. Where the parties are not competing undertakings, the exemption provided for in Article 2 shall apply for the duration of the research and development. Where the results are jointly exploited, the exemption shall continue to apply for 7 years from the time the contract products or contract technologies are first put on the market within the internal market.

2. Where two or more of the parties are competing undertakings, the exemption provided for in Article 2 shall apply for the period referred to in paragraph 1 of this Article only if, at the time the research and development agreement is entered into:

(a) in the case of research and development agreements referred to in point *(a)*, (i), (ii) or (iii), of Article 1(1), the combined market share of the parties to a research and de-

velopment agreement does not exceed 25 % on the relevant product and technology markets; or

(b) in the case of research and agreements referred to in point (a), (iv), (v) or (vi), of Article 1(1), the combined market share of the financing party and all the parties with which the financing party has entered into research and development agreements with regard to the same contract products or contract technologies, does not exceed 25 % on the relevant product and technology markets.

3. After the end of the period referred to in paragraph 1, the exemption shall continue to apply as long as the combined market share of the parties does not exceed 25 % on the relevant product and technology markets.

Art. 5. *Hardcore restrictions*

The exemption provided for in Article 2 shall not apply to research and development agreements which, directly or indirectly, in isolation or in combination with other factors under the control of the parties, have as their object any of the following:

(a) the restriction of the freedom of the parties to carry out research and development independently or in cooperation with third parties in a field unconnected with that to which the research and development agreement relates or, after the completion of the joint research and development or the paid-for research and development, in the field to which it relates or in a connected field;

(b) the limitation of output or sales, with the exception of:

(i) the setting of production targets where the joint exploitation of the results includes the joint production of the contract products;

(ii) the setting of sales targets where the joint exploitation of the results includes the joint distribution of the contract products or the joint licensing of the contract technologies within the meaning of point (m), (i) or (ii), of Article 1(1);

(iii) practices constituting specialisation in the context of exploitation; and

(iv) the restriction of the freedom of the parties to manufacture, sell, assign or license products, technologies or processes which compete with the contract products or contract technologies during the period for which the parties have agreed to jointly exploit the results;

(c) the fixing of prices when selling the contract product or licensing the contract technologies to third parties, with the exception of the fixing of prices charged to immediate customers or the fixing of licence fees charged to immediate licensees where the joint exploitation of the results includes the joint distribution of the contract products or the joint licensing of the contract technologies within the meaning of point (m), (i) or (ii), of Article 1(1);

(d) the restriction of the territory in which, or of the customers to whom, the parties may passively sell the contract products or license the contract technologies, with the exception of the requirement to exclusively license the results to another party;

(e) the requirement not to make any, or to limit, active sales of the contract products or contract technologies in territories or to customers which have not been exclusively allocated to one of the parties by way of specialisation in the context of exploitation;

(f) the requirement to refuse to meet demand from customers in the parties' respective territories, or from customers otherwise allocated between the parties by way of specialisation in the context of exploitation, who would market the contract products in other territories within the internal market;

(g) the requirement to make it difficult for users or resellers to obtain the contract products from other resellers within the internal market.

Art. 6. *Excluded restrictions*

The exemption provided for in Article 2 shall not apply to the following obligations contained in research and development agreements:

(a) the obligation not to challenge after completion of the research and development the validity of intellectual property rights which the parties hold in the internal market and which are relevant to the research and development or, after the expiry of the research and development agreement, the validity of intellectual property rights which the parties hold in the internal market and which protect the results of the research and development, without prejudice to the possibility to provide for termination of the research and development agreement in the event of one of the parties challenging the validity of such intellectual property rights;

(b) the obligation not to grant licences to third parties to manufacture the contract products or to apply the contract technologies unless the agreement provides for the exploitation of the results of the joint research and development or paid-for research and development by at least one of the parties and such exploitation takes place in the internal market vis-à-vis third parties.

Art. 7. *Application of the market share threshold*

For the purposes of applying the market share threshold provided for in Article 4 the following rules shall apply:

(a) the market share shall be calculated on the basis of the market sales value; if market sales value data are not available, estimates based on other reliable market information, including market sales volumes, may be used to establish the market share of the parties;

(b) the market share shall be calculated on the basis of data relating to the preceding calendar year;

(c) the market share held by the undertakings referred to in point (e) of the second subparagraph of Article 1(2) shall be apportioned equally to each undertaking having the rights or the powers listed in point (a) of that subparagraph;

(d) if the market share referred to in Article 4(3) is initially not more than 25 % but subsequently rises above that level without exceeding 30 %, the exemption provided for in Article 2 shall continue to apply for a period of two consecutive calendar years following the year in which the 25 % threshold was first exceeded;

(e) if the market share referred to in Article 4(3) is initially not more than 25 % but subsequently rises above 30 %, the exemption provided for in Article 2 shall continue to apply for a period of one calendar year following the year in which the level of 30 % was first exceeded;

(f) the benefit of points (d) and (e) may not be combined so as to exceed a period of two calendar years.

Art. 8. *Transitional period*

The prohibition laid down in Article 101(1) of the Treaty shall not apply during the period from 1 January 2011 to 31 December 2012 in respect of agreements already in force on 31 December 2010 which do not satisfy the conditions for exemption provided for in this Regulation but which satisfy the conditions for exemption provided for in Regulation (EC) N° 2659/2000.

Art. 9. *Period of validity*

This Regulation shall enter into force on 1 January 2011. It shall expire on 31 December 2022.

Commission Regulation (EU) N° 1218/2010, 14 December 2010 on the application of Article 101(3) of the Treaty on the Functioning of the European Union to certain categories of specialisation agreements

(OJ L 335, 18 December 2010, p. 43)

THE EUROPEAN COMMISSION,

Having regard to the Treaty on the Functioning of the European Union,

Having regard to Regulation (EEC) N° 2821/71 of the Council of 20 December 1971 on application of Article 85(3) of the Treaty to categories of agreements, decisions and concerted practices [1],

Having published a draft of this Regulation,

After consulting the Advisory Committee on Restrictive Practices and Dominant Positions,

Whereas:

(1) Regulation (EEC) N° 2821/71 empowers the Commission to apply Article 101(3) of the Treaty on the Functioning of the European Union [2] by regulation to certain categories of agreements, decisions and concerted practices falling within the scope of Article 101(1) of the Treaty which have as their object specialisation, including agreements necessary for achieving it.

(2) Commission Regulation (EC) N° 2658/2000 of 29 November 2000 on the application of Article 81(3) of the Treaty to categories of specialisation agreements [3] defines categories of specialisation agreements which the Commission regarded as normally satisfying the conditions laid down in Article 101(3) of the Treaty. In view of the overall positive experience with the application of that Regulation, which expires on 31 December 2010, and taking into account further experience acquired since its adoption, it is appropriate to adopt a new block exemption regulation.

(3) This Regulation should meet the two requirements of ensuring effective protection of competition and providing adequate legal security for undertakings. The pursuit of those objectives should take account of the need to simplify administrative supervision and the legislative framework to as great an extent as possible. Below a certain level of market power it can in general be presumed, for the application of Article 101(3) of the Treaty, that the positive effects of specialisation agreements will outweigh any negative effects on competition.

(4) For the application of Article 101(3) of the Treaty by regulation, it is not necessary to define those agreements which are capable of falling within Article 101(1) of the Treaty. In the individual assessment of agreements under Article 101(1) of the Treaty, account has to be taken of several factors, and in particular the market structure on the relevant market.

(5) The benefit of the exemption established by this Regulation should be limited to those agreements for which it can be assumed with sufficient certainty that they satisfy the conditions of Article 101(3) of the Treaty.

(6) Agreements on specialisation in production are most likely to contribute to improving the production or distribution of goods if the parties have complementary skills, assets or activities, because they can concentrate on the manufacture of certain products and thus operate more efficiently and supply the products more cheaply. The same can generally be said about agreements on specialisation in the preparation of services. Given effective competition, it is likely that consumers will receive a fair share of the resulting benefits.

(7) Such advantages can arise from agreements whereby one party fully or partly gives up the manufacture of certain products or preparation of certain services in favour of another party (unilateral specialisation), from agreements whereby each party fully or partly gives up the manufacture of certain products or preparation of certain services in favour of another party (reciprocal specialisation) and from agreements whereby the parties undertake to jointly manufacture certain products or prepare certain services (joint production). In the context of this Regulation, the concepts of unilateral and reciprocal specialisation do not require a party to reduce capacity, as it is sufficient if they reduce their production volumes. The concept of joint production, however, does not require the parties to reduce their individual production activities outside the scope of their envisaged joint production arrangement.

(8) The nature of unilateral and reciprocal specialisation agreements presupposes that the parties are active on the same product market. It is not necessary for the parties to be active on the same geographic market. Consequently, the application of this Regulation to unilateral and reciprocal specialisation agreements should be limited to scenarios where the parties are active on the same product market. Joint production agreements can be entered into by parties who are already active on the same product market but also by parties who wish to enter a product market by way of the agreement. Therefore, joint production agreements should fall within the scope of this Regulation irrespective of whether the parties are already active in the same product market.

(9) To ensure that the benefits of specialisation will materialise without one party leaving the market downstream of production entirely, unilateral and reciprocal specialisation agreements should only be covered by this Regulation where they provide for supply and purchase obligations or joint distribution. Supply and purchase obligations may, but do not have to, be of an exclusive nature.

(10) It can be presumed that, where the parties' share of the relevant market for the products which are the subject matter of a specialisation agreement does not exceed a certain level, the agreements will, as a general rule, give rise to economic benefits in the form of economies of scale or scope or better production technologies, while allowing consumers a fair share of the resulting benefits. However, where the products manufactured under a specialisation agreement are intermediary products which one or more of the parties fully or partly use as an input for their own production of certain downstream products which they subsequently sell on the market, the exemption conferred by this Regulation should also be conditional on the parties' share on the relevant market for these downstream products not exceeding a certain level. In such a case, merely looking at the parties' market share at the level of the intermediary product would ignore the potential risk of foreclosing or increasing the price of inputs for competitors at the level of the downstream products. However, there is no presumption that specialisation agreements are either caught by Article 101(1) of the Treaty or that they fail to satisfy the conditions of Article 101(3) of the Treaty once the market share threshold set out in this Regulation is exceeded or other conditions of this Regulation are not met. In such

cases, an individual assessment of the specialisation agreement needs to be conducted under Article 101 of the Treaty.

(11) This Regulation should not exempt agreements containing restrictions which are not indispensable to the attainment of the positive effects generated by a specialisation agreement. In principle, agreements containing certain types of severe restrictions of competition relating to the fixing of prices charged to third parties, limitation of output or sales, and allocation of markets or customers should be excluded from the benefit of the exemption established by this Regulation irrespective of the market share of the parties.

(12) The market share limitation, the non-exemption of certain agreements and the conditions provided for in this Regulation normally ensure that the agreements to which the block exemption applies do not enable the parties to eliminate competition in respect of a substantial part of the products or services in question.

(13) The Commission may withdraw the benefit of this Regulation, pursuant to Article 29(1) of Council Regulation (EC) N° 1/2003 of 16 December 2002 on the implementation of the rules on competition laid down in Articles 81 and 82 of the Treaty [4], where it finds in a particular case that an agreement to which the exemption provided for in this Regulation applies nevertheless has effects which are incompatible with Article 101(3) of the Treaty.

(14) The competition authority of a Member State may withdraw the benefit of this Regulation pursuant to Article 29(2) of Regulation (EC) N° 1/2003 in respect of the territory of that Member State, or a part thereof where, in a particular case, an agreement to which the exemption established by this Regulation applies nevertheless has effects which are incompatible with Article 101(3) of the Treaty in the territory of that Member State, or in a part thereof, and where such territory has all the characteristics of a distinct geographic market.

(15) The benefit of this Regulation could be withdrawn pursuant to Article 29 of Regulation (EC) N° 1/2003 where, for example, the relevant market is very concentrated and competition is already weak, in particular because of the individual market positions of other market participants or links between other market participants created by parallel specialisation agreements.

(16) In order to facilitate the conclusion of specialisation agreements, which can have a bearing on the structure of the parties, the period of validity of this Regulation should be fixed at 12 years,

HAS ADOPTED THIS REGULATION:

[1] OJ L 285, 29.12.1971, p. 46.

[2] With effect from 1 December 2009, Article 81 of the EC Treaty has become Article 101 of the Treaty on the Functioning of the European Union (TFEU). The two Articles are, in substance, identical. For the purposes of this Regulation, references to Article 101 of the TFEU should be understood as references to Article 81 of the EC Treaty where appropriate. The TFEU also introduced certain changes in terminology, such as the replacement of «Community» by «Union» and «common market» by «internal market». The terminology of the TFEU will be used throughout this Regulation.

[3] OJ L 304, 5.12.2000, p. 3.

[4] OJ L 1, 4.1.2003, p. 1.

Art. 1. *Definitions*

1. For the purposes of this Regulation, the following definitions shall apply:

(a) «specialisation agreement» means a unilateral specialisation agreement, a reciprocal specialisation agreement or a joint production agreement;

(b) «unilateral specialisation agreement» means an agreement between two parties which are active on the same product market by virtue of which one party agrees to fully or partly cease production of certain products or to refrain from producing those products and to purchase them from the other party, who agrees to produce and supply those products;

(c) «reciprocal specialisation agreement» means an agreement between two or more parties which are active on the same product market, by virtue of which two or more parties on a reciprocal basis agree to fully or partly cease or refrain from producing certain but different products and to purchase these products from the other parties, who agree to produce and supply them;

(d) «joint production agreement» means an agreement by virtue of which two or more parties agree to produce certain products jointly;

(e) «agreement» means an agreement, a decision by an association of undertakings or a concerted practice;

(f) «product» means a good or a service, including both intermediary goods or services and final goods or services, with the exception of distribution and rental services;

(g) «production» means the manufacture of goods or the preparation of services and includes production by way of subcontracting;

(h) «preparation of services» means activities upstream of the provision of services to customers;

(i) «relevant market» means the relevant product and geographic market to which the specialisation products belong, and, in addition, where the specialisation products are intermediary products which one or more of the parties fully or partly use captively for the production of downstream products, the relevant product and geographic market to which the downstream products belong;

(j) «specialisation product» means a product which is produced under a specialisation agreement;

(k) «downstream product» means a product for which a specialisation product is used by one or more of the parties as an input and which is sold by those parties on the market;

(l) «competing undertaking» means an actual or potential competitor;

(m) «actual competitor» means an undertaking that is active on the same relevant market;

(n) «potential competitor» means an undertaking that, in the absence of the specialisation agreement, would, on realistic grounds and not just as a mere theoretical possibility, in case of a small but permanent increase in relative prices be likely to undertake, within not more than 3 years, the necessary additional investments or other necessary switching costs to enter the relevant market;

(o) «exclusive supply obligation» means an obligation not to supply a competing undertaking other than a party to the agreement with the specialisation product;

(p) «exclusive purchase obligation» means an obligation to purchase the specialisation product only from a party to the agreement;

(q) «joint», in the context of distribution, means that the parties:

(i) carry out the distribution of the products by way of a joint team, organisation or undertaking; or

(ii) appoint a third party distributor on an exclusive or non-exclusive basis, provided that the third party is not a competing undertaking;

(r) «distribution» means distribution, including the sale of goods and the provision of services.

2. For the purposes of this Regulation, the terms «undertaking» and «party» shall include their respective connected undertakings.

«Connected undertakings» means:

(a) undertakings in which a party to the specialisation agreement, directly or indirectly:

(i) has the power to exercise more than half the voting rights;

(ii) has the power to appoint more than half the members of the supervisory board, board of management or bodies legally representing the undertaking; or

(iii) has the right to manage the undertaking's affairs;

(b) undertakings which directly or indirectly have, over a party to the specialisation agreement, the rights or powers listed in point *(a)*;

(c) undertakings in which an undertaking referred to in point *(b)* has, directly or indirectly, the rights or powers listed in point *(a)*;

(d) undertakings in which a party to the specialisation agreement together with one or more of the undertakings referred to in points *(a)*, *(b)* or *(c)*, or in which two or more of the latter undertakings, jointly have the rights or powers listed in point *(a)*;

(e) undertakings in which the rights or the powers listed in point *(a)* are jointly held by:

(i) parties to the specialisation agreement or their respective connected undertakings referred to in points *(a)* to *(d)*; or

(ii) one or more of the parties to the specialisation agreement or one or more of their connected undertakings referred to in points *(a)* to *(d)* and one or more third parties.

Art. 2. *Exemption*

1. Pursuant to Article 101(3) of the Treaty and subject to the provisions of this Regulation, it is hereby declared that Article 101(1) of the Treaty shall not apply to specialisation agreements.

This exemption shall apply to the extent that such agreements contain restrictions of competition falling within the scope of Article 101(1) of the Treaty.

2. The exemption provided for in paragraph 1 shall apply to specialisation agreements containing provisions which relate to the assignment or licensing of intellectual property rights to one or more of the parties, provided that those provisions do not constitute the primary object of such agreements, but are directly related to and necessary for their implementation.

3. The exemption provided for in paragraph 1 shall apply to specialisation agreements whereby:

(a) the parties accept an exclusive purchase or exclusive supply obligation; or

(b) the parties do not independently sell the specialisation products but jointly distribute those products.

Art. 3. *Market share threshold*

The exemption provided for in Article 2 shall apply on condition that the combined market share of the parties does not exceed 20 % on any relevant market.

Art. 4. *Hardcore restrictions*

The exemption provided for in Article 2 shall not apply to specialisation agreements which, directly or indirectly, in isolation or in combination with other factors under the control of the parties, have as their object any of the following:

(a) the fixing of prices when selling the products to third parties with the exception of the fixing of prices charged to immediate customers in the context of joint distribution;

(b) the limitation of output or sales with the exception of:

(i) provisions on the agreed amount of products in the context of unilateral or reciprocal specialisation agreements or the setting of the capacity and production volume in the context of a joint production agreement; and

(ii) the setting of sales targets in the context of joint distribution;

(c) the allocation of markets or customers.

Art. 5. *Application of the market share threshold*

For the purposes of applying the market share threshold provided for in Article 3 the following rules shall apply:

(a) the market share shall be calculated on the basis of the market sales value; if market sales value data are not available, estimates based on other reliable market information, including market sales volumes, may be used to establish the market share of the parties;

(b) the market share shall be calculated on the basis of data relating to the preceding calendar year;

(c) the market share held by the undertakings referred to in point *(e)* of the second subparagraph of Article 1(2) shall be apportioned equally to each undertaking having the rights or the powers listed in point *(a)* of that subparagraph;

(d) if the market share referred to in Article 3 is initially not more than 20 % but subsequently rises above that level without exceeding 25 %, the exemption provided for in Article 2 shall continue to apply for a period of 2 consecutive calendar years following the year in which the 20 % threshold was first exceeded;

(e) if the market share referred to in Article 3 is initially not more than 20 % but subsequently rises above 25 %, the exemption provided for in Article 2 shall continue to apply for a period of 1 calendar year following the year in which the level of 25 % was first exceeded;

(f) the benefit of points *(d)* and *(e)* may not be combined so as to exceed a period of 2 calendar years.

Art. 6. *Transitional period*

The prohibition laid down in Article 101(1) of the Treaty shall not apply during the period from 1 January 2011 to 31 December 2012 in respect of agreements already in force on 31 December 2010 which do not satisfy the conditions for exemption provided for in this Regulation but which satisfy the conditions for exemption provided for in Regulation (EC) N° 2658/2000.

Art. 7. *Period of validity*

This Regulation shall enter into force on 1 January 2011. It shall expire on 31 December 2022.

Guidelines on the applicability of Article 101 of the Treaty on the Functioning of the European Union to horizontal co-operation agreements

(OJ C 11, 14 January 2011, p. 1, corrig., OJ C 33, 2 February 2011, p. 20)

Table of contents

	Pages
1. Introduction	
1.1. Purpose and scope (1)	125
1.2. Basic principles for the assessment under Article 101 (20)	127
1.2.1. Article 101(1) (23)	127
(i) Restrictions of competition by object (24)	127
(ii) Restrictive effects on competition (26)	128
Nature and content of the agreement (32)	128
Market power and other market characteristics (39)	129
1.2.2. Article 101(3) (48)	129
1.3. Structure of these guidelines (54)	130
2. General principles on the competitive assessment of information exchange	
2.1. Definition and scope (55)	130
Concerted practice (60)	131
2.2. Assessment under Article 101(1)	
2.2.1. Main competition concerns (53) (64)	132
Collusive outcome (65)	132
Anti-competitive foreclosure (69)	132
2.2.2. Restriction of competition by object (72)	132
2.2.3. Restrictive effects on competition (75)	133
(i) Market characteristics (77)	133
(ii) Characteristics of the information exchange	
Strategic information (86)	134
Market coverage (87)	134
Aggregated/individualised data (89)	135
Age of data (90)	135
Frequency of the information exchange (91)	135
Public/non-public information (92)	135
Public/non-public exchange of information (94)	136
2.3. Assessment under Article 101(3)	
2.3.1. Efficiency gains (76) (95)	136
2.3.2. Indispensability (101)	136
2.3.3. Pass-on to consumers (103)	137
2.3.4. No elimination of competition (104)	137
2.4. Examples (105)	137
3. Research and development agreements	
3.1. Definition (111)	139
3.2. Relevant markets (112)	139
Existing product markets (113)	139
Existing technology markets (116)	139
Competition in innovation (R&D efforts) (119)	139
Calculation of market shares (123)	140
3.3. Assessment under Article 101(1)	
3.3.1. Main competition concerns (127)	140
3.3.2. Restrictions of competition by object (128)	140
3.3.3. Restrictive effects on competition (129)	141
3.4. Assessment under Article 101(3)	
3.4.1. Efficiency gains (141)	142
3.4.2. Indispensability (142)	142
3.4.3. Pass-on to consumers (143)	142
3.4.4. No elimination of competition (144)	142
3.4.5. Time of the assessment (145)	142
3.5. Examples (147)	143
4. Production agreements	
4.1. Definition and scope (150)	144
4.2. Relevant markets (155)	145
4.3. Assessment under Article 101(1)	
4.3.1. Main competition concerns (157)	145
4.3.2. Restrictions of competition by object (160)	145
4.3.3. Restrictive effects on competition (162)	145
Market power (168)	146
Direct limitation of competition between the parties (174)	146
Collusive outcome (175)	147
4.4. Assessment under Article 101(3)	
4.4.1. Efficiency gains (183)	147
4.4.2. Indispensability (184)	147
4.4.3. Pass-on to consumers (185)	147
4.4.4. No elimination of competition (186)	148
4.5. Examples (187)	148
5. Purchasing agreements	
5.1. Definition (194)	150
5.2. Relevant markets (197)	150
5.3. Assessment under Article 101(1)	
5.3.1. Main competition concerns (200)	150
5.3.2. Restrictions of competition by object (205)	151
5.3.3. Restrictive effects on competition (207)	151
Market power (208)	151
Collusive outcome (213)	151
5.4. Assessment under Article 101(3)	
5.4.1. Efficiency gains (217)	152
5.4.2. Indispensability (218)	152
5.4.3. Pass-on to consumers (219)	152
5.4.4. No elimination of competition (220)	152
5.5. Examples (221)	152
6. Agreements on commercialisation	
6.1. Definition (225)	153
6.2. Relevant markets (229)	153
6.3. Assessment under Article 101(1)	
6.3.1. Main competition concerns (230)	153
6.3.2. Restrictions of competition by object (234)	154
6.3.3. Restrictive effects on competition (237)	154
Market power (240)	154
Collusive outcome (242)	154
6.4. Assessment under Article 101(3)	
6.4.1. Efficiency gains (246)	155
6.4.2. Indispensability (249)	155
6.4.3. Pass-on to consumers (250)	155
6.4.4. No elimination of competition (251)	155
6.5. Examples (252)	155
7. Standardisation agreements	
7.1. Definition	
Standardisation agreements (257)	157
Standard terms (259)	157
7.2. Relevant markets (261)	157
7.3. Assessment under Article 101(1)	
7.3.1. Main competition concerns	
Standardisation agreements (263)	158
Standard terms (270)	159
7.3.2. Restrictions of competition by object	
Standardisation agreements (273)	159
Standard terms (275)	159
7.3.3. Restrictive effects on competition	
Standardisation agreements Agreements normally not restrictive of competition (277)	159
FRAND Commitments (287)	160
Effects based assessment for standardisation agreements (292)	160
Standard terms (300)	161
7.4. Assessment under Article 101(3)	
7.4.1. Efficiency gains	
Standardisation agreements (308)	162
Standard terms (312)	163
7.4.2. Indispensability (314)	163
Standardisation agreements (315)	163
Standard terms (320)	163
7.4.3. Pass-on to consumers	
Standardisation agreements (321)	163
Standard terms (322)	163
7.4.4. No elimination of competition (324)	164
7.5. Examples (325)	164

1. INTRODUCTION

1.1. Purpose and scope

1. These guidelines set out the principles for the assessment under Article 101 of the Treaty on the Functioning of the European Union (1) («Article 101») of agreements between undertakings, decisions by associations of undertakings and concerted practices (collectively referred to as «agreements») pertaining to horizontal co-operation. Co-operation is of a «horizontal nature» if an agreement is entered into between actual or potential competitors. In addition, these guidelines also cover horizontal co-operation agreements between non-competitors, for example, between two companies active in the same product markets but in different geographic markets without being potential competitors.

(1) With effect from 1 december 2009, Article 81 of the EC Treaty has become Article 101 of the Treaty on the Functioning of the European Union («TFEU»). The two Articles are, in substance, identical. For the purposes of these guidelines, references to Article 101 of the TFEU should be understood as references to Article 81 of the EC Treaty where appropriate. The TFEU also introduced certain changes in terminology, such as the replacement of «Community» by «Union» and «common market» by «internal market». The terminology of the TFEU will be used throughout these guidelines.

2. Horizontal co-operation agreements can lead to substantial economic benefits, in particular if they combine complementary activities, skills or assets. Horizontal co-operation can be a means to share risk, save costs, increase investments, pool know-how, enhance product quality and variety, and launch innovation faster.

3. On the other hand, horizontal co-operation agreements may lead to competition problems. This is, for example, the case if the parties agree to fix prices or output or to share markets, or if the co-operation enables the parties to maintain, gain or increase market power and thereby is likely to give rise to negative market effects with respect to prices, output, product quality, product variety or innovation.

4. The Commission, while recognising the benefits that can be generated by horizontal co-operation agreements, has to ensure that effective competition is maintained. Article 101 provides the legal framework for a balanced assessment taking into account both adverse effects on competition and pro-competitive effects.

5. The purpose of these guidelines is to provide an analytical framework for the most common types of horizontal co-operation agreements; they deal with research and development agreements, production agreements including subcontracting and specialisation agreements, purchasing agreements, commercialisation agreements, standardisation agreements including standard contracts, and information exchange. This framework is primarily based on legal and economic criteria that help to analyse a horizontal co-operation agreement and the context in which it occurs. Economic criteria such as the market power of the parties and other factors relating to the market structure form a key element of the assessment of the market impact likely to be caused by a horizontal co-operation agreement and, therefore, for the assessment under Article 101.

6. These guidelines apply to the most common types of horizontal co-operation agreements irrespective of the level of integration they entail with the exception of operations constituting a concentration within the meaning of Article 3 of Council Regulation (EC) N° 139/2004 of 20 January 2004 on the control of concentrations between undertakings (2) («the Merger Regulation») as would be the case, for example, with joint ventures performing on a lasting basis all the functions of an autonomous economic entity («full-function joint ventures») (3).

(2) OJ L 24, 29.1.2004, p. 1.

(3) See Article 3(4) of the Merger Regulation. However, in assessing whether there is a full-function joint venture, the Commission examines whether the joint venture is autonomous in an operational sense. This does not mean that it enjoys autonomy from its parent companies as regards the adoption of its strategic decisions (see Commission Consolidated Jurisdictional Notice under Council Regulation (EC) N° 139/2004 on the control of concentrations between undertakings, OJ C 95, 16.4.2008, p. 1, paragraphs 91-109 («Consolidated Jurisdictional Notice»)). It also needs to be recalled that if the creation of a joint venture constituting a concentration under Article 3 of the Merger Regulation has as its object or effect the coordination of the competitive behaviour of undertakings that remain independent, then that coordination will be appraised under Article 101 of the Treaty (see Article 2(4) of the Merger Regulation).

7. Given the potentially large number of types and combinations of horizontal co-operation and market circumstances in which they operate, it is difficult to provide specific answers for every possible scenario. These guidelines will nevertheless assist businesses in assessing the compatibility of an individual co-operation agreement with Article 101. Those criteria do not, however, constitute a «checklist» which can be applied mechanically. Each case must be assessed on the basis of its own facts, which may require a flexible application of these guidelines.

8. These guidelines complement Commission Regulation (EU) N° 1217/2010 of 14 december 2010 on the application of Article 101(3) of the Treaty on the Functioning of the European Union to certain categories of research and development agreements (4) («the R&D Block Exemption Regulation») and Commission Regulation (EU) N° 1218/2010 of 14 december 2010 on the application of Article 101(3) of the Treaty on the Functioning of the European Union to certain categories of specialisation agreements (4) («the Specialisation Block Exemption Regulation»).;

(4) OJ L 335, 18.12.2010, p. 36;

(5) OJ L 335, 18.12.2010, p. 43.

9. Although these guidelines contain certain references to cartels, they are not intended to give any guidance as to what does and does not constitute a cartel as defined by the decisional practice of the Commission and the case-law of the Court of Justice of the European Union.

10. The term «competitors» as used in these guidelines includes both actual and potential competitors. Two companies are treated as actual competitors if they are active on the same relevant market. A company is treated as a potential competitor of another company if, in the absence of the agreement, in case of a small but permanent increase in relative prices it is likely that the former, within a short period of time (6), would undertake the necessary additional investments or other necessary switching costs to enter the relevant market on which the latter is active. This assessment has to be based on realistic grounds, the mere theoretical possibility to enter a market is not sufficient (see Commission Notice on the definition of the relevant market for the purposes of Community competition law) (7) («the Market Definition Notice»).

(6) What constitutes a «short period of time» depends on the facts of the case at hand, its legal and economic context, and, in particular, on whether the company in question is a party to the agreement or a third party. In the first case, that is to say, where it is analysed whether a party to an agreement

should be considered a potential competitor of the other party, the Commission would normally consider a longer period to be a «short period of time» than in the second case, that is to say, where the capacity of a third party to act as a competitive constraint on the parties to an agreement is analysed. For a third party to be considered a potential competitor, market entry would need to take place sufficiently fast so that the threat of potential entry is a constraint on the parties' and other market participants' behaviour. For these reasons, both the R&D and the Specialisation Block Exemption Regulations consider a period of not more than three years a «short period of time».

(7) OJ C 372, 9.12.1997, p. 5, paragraph 24; see also the Commission's Thirteenth Report on Competition Policy, point 55 and Commission Decision in Case IV/32.009, *Elopak/Metal Box-Odin*, OJ L 209, 8.8.1990, p. 15.

11. Companies that form part of the same «undertaking» within the meaning of Article 101(1) are not considered to be competitors for the purposes of these guidelines. Article 101 only applies to agreements between independent undertakings. When a company exercises decisive influence over another company they form a single economic entity and, hence, are part of the same undertaking. (8) The same is true for sister companies, that is to say, companies over which decisive influence is exercised by the same parent company. They are consequently not considered to be competitors even if they are both active on the same relevant product and geographic markets.

(8) See, for example, Case C-73/95, *Viho*, (1996) ECR I-5457, paragraph 51. The exercise of decisive influence by the parent company over the conduct of a subsidiary can be presumed in case of wholly-owned subsidiaries; see, for example, Case 107/82, *AEG*, (1983) ECR-3151, paragraph 50; Case C-286/98 P, *Stora*, (2000) ECR-I 9925, paragraph 29; or Case C-97/08 P, *Akzo*, (2009) ECR I-8237, paragraphs 60 *et seq*.

12. Agreements that are entered into between undertakings operating at a different level of the production or distribution chain, that is to say, vertical agreements, are in principle dealt with in Commission Regulation (EU) N° 330/2010 of 20 april 2010 on the application of Article 101(3) of the Treaty on the Functioning of the European Union to categories of vertical agreements and concerted practices (9) («the Block Exemption Regulation on Vertical Restraints») and the Guidelines on Vertical Restraints (10). However, to the extent that vertical agreements, for example, distribution agreements, are concluded between competitors, the effects of the agreement on the market and the possible competition problems can be similar to horizontal agreements. Therefore, vertical agreements between competitors fall under these guidelines (11). Should there be a need to also assess such agreements under the Block Exemption Regulation on Vertical Restraints and the Guidelines on Vertical Restraints, this will be specifically stated in the relevant chapter of these guidelines. In the absence of such a reference, only these guidelines will be applicable to vertical agreements between competitors.

(9) OJ L 102, 23.4.2010, p. 1.

(10) OJ C 130, 19.5.2010, p. 1.

(11) This does not apply where competitors enter into a non-reciprocal vertical agreement and (i) the supplier is a manufacturer and a distributor of goods, while the buyer is a distributor and not a competing undertaking at the manufacturing level; or (ii) the supplier is a provider of services at several levels of trade, while the buyer provides its goods or services at the retail level and is not a competing undertaking at the level of trade where it purchases the contract services. Such agreements are exclusively assessed under the Block Exemption Regulation and the Guidelines on Vertical Restraints (see Article 2(4) of the Block Exemption Regulation on Vertical Restraints).

13. Horizontal co-operation agreements may combine different stages of co-operation, for example research and development («R&D») and the production and/or commercialisation of its results. Such agreements are generally also covered by these guidelines. When using these guidelines for the analysis of such integrated co-operation, as a general rule, all the chapters pertaining to the different parts of the co-operation will be relevant. However, where the relevant chapters of these guidelines contain graduated messages, for example with regard to safe harbours or whether certain conduct will normally be considered a restriction of competition by object or by effect, what is set out in the chapter pertaining to that part of an integrated co-operation which can be considered its «centre of gravity» prevails for the entire co-operation (12).

(12) It should be noted that this test only applies to the relationship between the different chapters of these guidelines, not to the relationship between different block exemption regulations. The scope of a block exemption regulation is defined by its own provisions.

14. Two factors are in particular relevant for the determination of the centre of gravity of integrated co-operation: firstly, the starting point of the co-operation, and, secondly, the degree of integration of the different functions which are combined. For example, the centre of gravity of a horizontal co-operation agreement involving both joint R&D and joint production of the results would thus normally be the joint R&D, as the joint production will only take place if the joint R&D is successful. This implies that the results of the joint R&D are decisive for the subsequent joint production. The assessment of the centre of gravity would change if the parties would have engaged in the joint production in any event, that is to say, irrespective of the joint R&D, or if the agreement provided for a full integration in the area of production and only a partial integration of some R&D activities. In this case, the centre of gravity of the co-operation would be the joint production.

15. Article 101 only applies to those horizontal co-operation agreements which may affect trade between Member States. The principles on the applicability of Article 101 set out in these guidelines are therefore based on the assumption that a horizontal co-operation agreement is capable of affecting trade between Member States to an appreciable extent.

16. The assessment under Article 101 as described in these guidelines is without prejudice to the possible parallel application of Article 102 of the Treaty to horizontal co-operation agreements (13).

(13) See Case T-51/89, *Tetra Pak I*, (1990) ECR-II 309, paragraphs 25 *et seq*. and Guidance on the Commission's enforcement priorities in applying Article 82 of the EC Treaty to abusive exclusionary conduct by dominant undertakings, OJ C 45, 24.2.2009, p. 7 («Article 102 Guidance Paper»).

17. These guidelines are without prejudice to the interpretation the Court of Justice of the European Union may give to the application of Article 101 to horizontal co-operation agreements.

18. These guidelines replace the Commission guidelines on the applicability of Article 81 of the EC Treaty to horizontal co-operation agreements (14) which were published by the Commission in 2001 and do not apply to the extent that sector specific rules apply as is the case for certain agreements with regard to agriculture (15), transport (16) or insurance (17). The Commission will continue to monitor the operation of the R&D and Specialisation Block Exemption Regulations and these guidelines based on market information from stakeholders and national competition authorities and may revise these guidelines in the light of future developments and of evolving insight.

(14) OJ C 3, 6.1.2001, p. 2. These guidelines do not contain a separate chapter on «environmental agreements» as was the case in the previous guidelines.

Standard-setting in the environment sector, which was the main focus of the former chapter on environmental agreements, is more appropriately dealt with in the standardisation chapter of these guidelines. In general, depending on the competition issues «environmental agreements» give rise to, they are to be assessed under the relevant chapter of these guidelines, be it the chapter on R&D, production, commercialisation or standardisation agreements.

(15) Council Regulation (EC) N° 1184/2006 of 24 July 2006 applying certain rules of competition to the production of, and trade in, agricultural products, *OJ* L 214, 4.8.2006, p. 7.

(16) Council Regulation (EC) N° 169/2009 of 26 February 2009 applying rules of competition to transport by rail, road and inland waterway, *OJ* L 61, 5.3.2009, p. 1; Council Regulation (EC) N° 246/2009 of 26 February 2009 on the application of Article 81(3) of the Treaty to certain categories of agreements and concerted practices between liner shipping companies (consortia), *OJ* L 79, 25.3.2009, p. 1; Commission Regulation (EC) N° 823/2000 of 19 april 2000 on the application of Article 81(3) of the Treaty to certain categories of agreements, decisions and concerted practices between liner shipping companies (consortia), *OJ* L 100, 20.4.2000, p. 24; Guidelines on the application of Article 81 of the EC Treaty to maritime transport services, *OJ* C 245, 26.9.2008, p. 1.

(17) Commission Regulation (EU) N° 267/2010 of 24 March 2010 on the application of Article 101(3) of the Treaty on the Functioning of the European Union to certain categories of agreements, decisions and concerted practices in the insurance sector, *OJ* L 83, 31.3.2010, p. 1.

19. The Commission guidelines on the application of Article 81(3) of the Treaty (18) («the General Guidelines») contain general guidance on the interpretation of Article 101. Consequently, these guidelines have to be read in conjunction with the General Guidelines.

(18) *OJ* C 101, 27.4.2004, p. 97.

1.2. Basic principles for the assessment under Article 101

20. The assessment under Article 101 consists of two steps. The first step, under Article 101(1), is to assess whether an agreement between undertakings, which is capable of affecting trade between Member States, has an anti-competitive object or actual or potential (19) restrictive effects on competition. The second step, under Article 101(3), which only becomes relevant when an agreement is found to be restrictive of competition within the meaning of Article 101(1), is to determine the pro-competitive benefits produced by that agreement and to assess whether those pro-competitive effects outweigh the restrictive effects on competition (20). The balancing of restrictive and pro-competitive effects is conducted exclusively within the framework laid down by Article 101(3) (21). If the pro-competitive effects do not outweigh a restriction of competition, Article 101(2) stipulates that the agreement shall be automatically void.

(19) Article 101(1) prohibits both actual and potential anti-competitive effects; see for example Case C-7/95 P, *John Deere*, (1998) ECR I-3111, paragraph 77; Case C-238/05, *Asnef-Equifax*, (2006) ECR I-11125, paragraph 50.

(20) See Joined Cases C-501/06 P and others, GlaxoSmithKline, (2009) ECR I-9291, paragraph 95.

(21) See Case T-65/98, *Van den Bergh Foods*, (2003) ECR II-4653, paragraph 107; Case T-112/99, *Métropole télévision* (M6) and others, (2001) ECR II-2459, paragraph 74; Case T-328/03, *O2*, (2006) ECR II-1231, paragraphs 69 *et seq.*, where the General Court held that it is only in the precise framework of Article 101(3) that the pro- and anti-competitive aspects of a restriction may be weighed.

21. The analysis of horizontal co-operation agreements has certain common elements with the analysis of horizontal mergers pertaining to the potential restrictive effects, in particular as regards joint ventures. There is often only a fine line between full-function joint ventures that fall under the Merger Regulation and non-full-function joint ventures that are assessed under Article 101. Hence, their effects can be quite similar.

22. In certain cases, companies are encouraged by public authorities to enter into horizontal co-operation agreements in order to attain a public policy objective by way of self-regulation. However, companies remain subject to Article 101 if a national law merely encourages or makes it easier for them to engage in autonomous anti-competitive conduct (22). In other words, the fact that public authorities encourage a horizontal co-operation agreement does not mean that it is permissible under Article 101 (23). It is only if anti-competitive conduct is required of companies by national legislation, or if the latter creates a legal framework which precludes all scope for competitive activity on their part, that Article 101 does not apply (24). In such a situation, the restriction of competition is not attributable, as Article 101 implicitly requires, to the autonomous conduct of the companies and they are shielded from all the consequences of an infringement of that article (25). Each case must be assessed on its own facts according to the general principles set out in these guidelines.

(22) See judgment of 14 October 2010 in Case C-280/08 P, *Deutsche Telekom*, ECR I not yet reported, paragraph 82 and the case-law cited therein.

(23) See Case C-198/01, *CIF*, (2003) ECR I-8055, paragraphs 56-58; Joined Cases T-217/03 and T-245/03, *French Beef*, (2006) ECR II-4987, paragraph 92; Case T-7/92, *Asia Motor France II*, (1993) ECR II-669, paragraph 71; and Case T-148/89, *Tréfilunion*, (1995) ECR II-1063, paragraph 118.

(24) See Case C-280/08 P, *Deutsche Telekom*, paragraph 80-81. This possibility has been narrowly interpreted; see, for example, Joined Cases 209/78 and others, *Van Landewyck*, (1980) ECR 3125, paragraphs 130-134; Joined Cases 240/82 and others, *Stichting Sigarettenindustrie*, (1985) ECR 3831, paragraphs 27-29; and Joined Cases C-359/95 P and C-379/95 P, *Ladbroke Racing*, (1997) ECR I-6265, paragraphs 33 *et seq*.

(25) At least until a decision to disapply the national legislation has been adopted and that decision has become definitive; see Case C-198/01, *CIF*, paragraphs 54 *et seq*.

1.2.1. Article 101(1)

23. Article 101(1) prohibits agreements the object or effect of which is to restrict (26) competition.

(26) For the purpose of these guidelines, the term «restriction of competition» includes the prevention and distortion of competition.

(i) Restrictions of competition by object

24. Restrictions of competition by object are those that by their very nature have the potential to restrict competition within the meaning of Article 101(1) (27). It is not necessary to examine the actual or potential effects of an agreement on the market once its anti-competitive object has been established (28).

(27) See, for example, Case C-209/07, *BIDS*, (2008) ECR I-8637, paragraph 17.

(28) See, for example, Joined Cases C-501/06 P and others, *GlaxoSmithKline*, paragraph 55; Case C-209/07, *BIDS*, paragraph 16; Case C-8/08, *T-Mobile Netherlands*, ECR (2009) I-4529, paragraph 29 *et seq.*; Case C-7/95 P, *John Deere*, paragraph 77.

25. According to the settled case-law of the Court of Justice of the European Union, in order to assess whether an agreement has an anti-competitive object, regard must be had to the content of the agreement, the objectives it seeks to attain, and the economic and legal context of which it forms part. In addition, although the parties' intention is not a necessary factor in determining whether an agreement has an anti-competitive object, the Commission may nevertheless take this aspect into account in its analysis (29). Further guidance with regard to the notion of restrictions of competition by object can be obtained in the General Guidelines.

(29) See, for example, Joined Cases C-501/06 P and others, *GlaxoSmithKline*, paragraph 58; Case C-209/07, *BIDS*, paragraphs 15 *et seq*.

(ii) Restrictive effects on competition

26. If a horizontal co-operation agreement does not restrict competition by object, it must be examined whether it has appreciable restrictive effects on competition. Account must be taken of both actual and potential effects. In other words, the agreement must at least be likely to have anti-competitive effects.

27. For an agreement to have restrictive effects on competition within the meaning of Article 101(1) it must have, or be likely to have, an appreciable adverse impact on at least one of the parameters of competition on the market, such as price, output, product quality, product variety or innovation. Agreements can have such effects by appreciably reducing competition between the parties to the agreement or between any one of them and third parties. This means that the agreement must reduce the parties' decision-making independence (30), either due to obligations contained in the agreement which regulate the market conduct of at least one of the parties or by influencing the market conduct of at least one of the parties by causing a change in its incentives.

(30) See Case C-7/95 P, *John Deere*, paragraph 88; Case C-238/05, *Asnef-Equifax*, paragraph 51.

28. Restrictive effects on competition within the relevant market are likely to occur where it can be expected with a reasonable degree of probability that, due to the agreement, the parties would be able to profitably raise prices or reduce output, product quality, product variety or innovation. This will depend on several factors such as the nature and content of the agreement, the extent to which the parties individually or jointly have or obtain some degree of market power, and the extent to which the agreement contributes to the creation, maintenance or strengthening of that market power or allows the parties to exploit such market power.

29. The assessment of whether a horizontal co-operation agreement has restrictive effects on competition within the meaning of Article 101(1) must be made in comparison to the actual legal and economic context in which competition would occur in the absence of the agreement with all of its alleged restrictions (that is to say, in the absence of the agreement as it stands (if already implemented) or as envisaged (if not yet implemented) at the time of assessment). Hence, in order to prove actual or potential restrictive effects on competition, it is necessary to take into account competition between the parties and competition from third parties, in particular actual or potential competition that would have existed in the absence of the agreement. This comparison does not take into account any potential efficiency gains generated by the agreement as these will only be assessed under Article 101(3).

30. Consequently, horizontal co-operation agreements between competitors that, on the basis of objective factors, would not be able to independently carry out the project or activity covered by the co-operation, for instance, due to the limited technical capabilities of the parties, will normally not give rise to restrictive effects on competition within the meaning of Article 101(1) unless the parties could have carried out the project with less stringent restrictions (31).

(31) See also paragraph 18 of the General Guidelines.

31. General guidance with regard to the notion of restrictions of competition by effect can be obtained in the General Guidelines. These guidelines provide additional guidance specific to the competition assessment of horizontal co-operation agreements.

Nature and content of the agreement

32. The nature and content of an agreement relates to factors such as the area and objective of the co-operation, the competitive relationship between the parties and the extent to which they combine their activities. Those factors determine which kinds of possible competition concerns can arise from a horizontal co-operation agreement.

33. Horizontal co-operation agreements may limit competition in several ways. The agreement may:

– be exclusive in the sense that it limits the possibility of the parties to compete against each other or third parties as independent economic operators or as parties to other, competing agreements;

– require the parties to contribute such assets that their decision-making independence is appreciably reduced; or

– affect the parties' financial interests in such a way that their decision-making independence is appreciably reduced. Both financial interests in the agreement and also financial interests in other parties to the agreement are relevant for the assessment.

34. The potential effect of such agreements may be the loss of competition between the parties to the agreement. Competitors can also benefit from the reduction of competitive pressure that results from the agreement and may therefore find it profitable to increase their prices. The reduction in those competitive constraints may lead to price increases in the relevant market. Factors such as whether the parties to the agreement have high market shares, whether they are close competitors, whether the customers have limited possibilities of switching suppliers, whether competitors are unlikely to increase supply if prices increase, and whether one of the parties to the agreement is an important competitive force, are all relevant for the competitive assessment of the agreement.

35. A horizontal co-operation agreement may also:

– lead to the disclosure of strategic information thereby increasing the likelihood of coordination among the parties within or outside the field of the co-operation;

– achieve significant commonality of costs (that is to say, the proportion of variable costs which the parties have in common), so the parties may more easily coordinate market prices and output.

36. Significant commonality of costs achieved by a horizontal co-operation agreement can only allow the parties to more easily coordinate market prices and output where the parties have market power, the market characteristics are conducive to such coordination, the area of co-operation accounts for a high proportion of the parties' variable costs in a given market, and the parties combine their activities in the area of co-operation to a significant extent. This could, for instance, be the case, where they jointly manufacture or purchase an important intermediate product or jointly manufacture or distribute a high proportion of their total output of a final product.

37. A horizontal agreement may therefore decrease the parties' decision-making independence and as a result increase the likelihood that they will coordinate their behaviour in order to reach a collusive outcome but it may also make coordination easier, more stable or more effective for parties that were already coordinating before, either by making the coordination more robust or by permitting them to achieve even higher prices.

38. Some horizontal co-operation agreements, for example production and standardisation agreements, may also give rise to anti-competitive foreclosure concerns.

Market power and other market characteristics

39. Market power is the ability to profitably maintain prices above competitive levels for a period of time or to profitably maintain output in terms of product quantities, product quality and variety or innovation below competitive levels for a period of time.

40. In markets with fixed costs undertakings must price above their variable costs of production in order to ensure a competitive return on their investment. The fact that undertakings price above their variable costs is therefore not in itself a sign that competition in the market is not functioning well and that undertakings have market power that allows them to price above the competitive level. It is when competitive constraints are insufficient to maintain prices, output, product quality, product variety and innovation at competitive levels that undertakings have market power in the context of Article 101(1).

41. The creation, maintenance or strengthening of market power can result from superior skill, foresight or innovation. It can also result from reduced competition between the parties to the agreement or between any one of the parties and third parties, for example, because the agreement leads to anti-competitive foreclosure of competitors by raising competitors' costs and limiting their capacity to compete effectively with the contracting parties.

42. Market power is a question of degree. The degree of market power required for the finding of an infringement under Article 101(1) in the case of agreements that are restrictive of competition by effect is less than the degree of market power required for a finding of dominance under Article 102, where a substantial degree of market power is required.

43. The starting point for the analysis of market power is the position of the parties on the markets affected by the co-operation. To carry out this analysis the relevant market(s) have to be defined by using the methodology of the Commission's Market Definition Notice. Where specific types of markets, such as purchasing or technology markets, are concerned these guidelines will provide additional guidance.

44. If the parties have a low combined market share, the horizontal co-operation agreement is unlikely to give rise to restrictive effects on competition within the meaning of Article 101(1) and, normally, no further analysis will be required. What is considered to be a «low combined market share» depends on the type of agreement in question and can be inferred from the «safe harbour» thresholds set out in various chapters of these guidelines and, more generally, from the Commission Notice on agreements of minor importance which do not appreciably restrict competition under Article 81(1) of the Treaty establishing the European Community (*de minimis*) (32) («the *de minimis* Notice»). If one of just two parties has only an insignificant market share and if it does not possess important resources, even a high combined market share normally cannot be seen as indicating a likely restrictive effect on competition in the market (33). Given the variety of horizontal co-operation agreements and the different effects they may cause in different market situations, it is not possible to give a general market share threshold above which sufficient market power for causing restrictive effects on competition can be assumed.

(32) *OJ* C 368, 22.12.2001, p. 13.

(33) If there are more than two parties, then the collective share of all co-operating competitors has to be significantly greater than the share of the largest single participating competitor.

45. Depending on the market position of the parties and the concentration in the market, other factors such as the stability of market shares over time, entry barriers and the likelihood of market entry, and the countervailing power of buyers/suppliers also have to be considered.

46. Normally, the Commission uses current market shares in its competitive analysis (34). However, reasonably certain future developments may also be taken into account, for instance in the light of exit, entry or expansion in the relevant market. Historic data may be used if market shares have been volatile, for instance when the market is characterised by large, lumpy orders. Changes in historic market shares may provide useful information about the competitive process and the likely future importance of the various competitors, for instance, by indicating whether undertakings have been gaining or losing market shares. In any event, the Commission interprets market shares in the light of likely market conditions, for instance, if the market is highly dynamic in character and if the market structure is unstable due to innovation or growth.

(34) As to the calculation of market shares, see also Market Definition Notice, paragraphs 54-55.

47. When entering a market is sufficiently easy, a horizontal co-operation agreement will normally not be expected to give rise to restrictive effects on competition. For entry to be considered a sufficient competitive constraint on the parties to a horizontal co-operation agreement, it must be shown to be likely, timely and sufficient to deter or defeat any potential restrictive effects of the agreement. The analysis of entry may be affected by the presence of horizontal co-operation agreements. The likely or possible termination of a horizontal co-operation agreement may influence the likelihood of entry.

1.2.2. Article 101(3)

48. The assessment of restrictions of competition by object or effect under Article 101(1) is only one side of the analysis. The other side, which is reflected in Article 101(3), is the assessment of the pro-competitive effects of restrictive agreements. The general approach when applying Article 101(3) is presented in the General Guidelines. Where in an individual case a restriction of competition within the meaning of Article 101(1) has been proven, Article 101(3) can be invoked as a defence. According to Article 2 of Council Regulation (EC) N° 1/2003 of 16 december 2002 on the implementation of the rules on competition laid down in Articles

81 and 82 of the Treaty (35), the burden of proof under Article 101(3) rests on the undertaking(s) invoking the benefit of this provision. Therefore, the factual arguments and the evidence provided by the undertaking(s) must enable the Commission to arrive at the conviction that the agreement in question is sufficiently likely to give rise to pro-competitive effects or that it is not (36).

(35) *OJ* L 1, 4.1.2003, p. 1.

(36) See, for example, Joined Cases C-501/06 P and others, *GlaxoSmithKline*, paragraphs 93-95.

49. The application of the exception rule of Article 101(3) is subject to four cumulative conditions, two positive and two negative:
– the agreement must contribute to improving the production or distribution of products or contribute to promoting technical or economic progress, that is to say, lead to efficiency gains;
– the restrictions must be indispensable to the attainment of those objectives, that is to say, the efficiency gains;
– consumers must receive a fair share of the resulting benefits, that is to say, the efficiency gains, including qualitative efficiency gains, attained by the indispensable restrictions must be sufficiently passed on to consumers so that they are at least compensated for the restrictive effects of the agreement; hence, efficiencies only accruing to the parties to the agreement will not suffice; for the purposes of these guidelines, the concept of «consumers» encompasses the customers, potential and/or actual, of the parties to the agreement (37); and
– the agreement must not afford the parties the possibility of eliminating competition in respect of a substantial part of the products in question.

(37) More detail on the concept of consumer is provided in paragraph 84 of the General Guidelines.

50. In the area of horizontal co-operation agreements there are block exemption regulations based on Article 101(3) for research and development (38) and specialisation (including joint production) (39) agreements. Those Block Exemption Regulations are based on the premise that the combination of complementary skills or assets can be the source of substantial efficiencies in research and development and specialisation agreements. This may also be the case for other types of horizontal co-operation agreements. The analysis of the efficiencies of an individual agreement under Article 101(3) is therefore to a large extent a question of identifying the complementary skills and assets that each of the parties brings to the agreement and evaluating whether the resulting efficiencies are such that the conditions of Article 101(3) are fulfilled.

(38) R&D Block Exemption Regulation.

(39) Specialisation Block Exemption Regulation.

51. Complementarities may arise from horizontal co-operation agreements in various ways. A research and development agreement may bring together different research capabilities that allow the parties to produce better products more cheaply and shorten the time for those products to reach the market. A production agreement may allow the parties to achieve economies of scale or scope that they could not achieve individually.

52. Horizontal co-operation agreements that do not involve the combination of complementary skills or assets are less likely to lead to efficiency gains that benefit consumers. Such agreements may reduce duplication of certain costs, for instance because certain fixed costs can be eliminated. However, fixed cost savings are, in general, less likely to result in benefits to consumers than savings in, for instance, variable or marginal costs.

53. Further guidance regarding the Commission's application of the criteria of Article 101(3) can be obtained in the General Guidelines.

1.3. Structure of these guidelines

54. Chapter 2 will first set out some general principles for the assessment of the exchange of information, which are applicable to all types of horizontal co-operation agreements entailing the exchange of information. The subsequent chapters of these guidelines will each address one specific type of horizontal co-operation agreement. Each chapter will apply the analytical framework described in section 1.2 as well as the general principles on the exchange of information to the specific type of co-operation in question.

2. GENERAL PRINCIPLES ON THE COMPETITIVE ASSESSMENT OF INFORMATION EXCHANGE

2.1. Definition and scope

55. The purpose of this chapter is to guide the competitive assessment of information exchange. Information exchange can take various forms. Firstly, data can be directly shared between competitors. Secondly, data can be shared indirectly through a common agency (for example, a trade association) or a third party such as a market research organisation or through the companies' suppliers or retailers.

56. Information exchange takes place in different contexts. There are agreements, decisions by associations of undertakings, or concerted practices under which information is exchanged, where the main economic function lies in the exchange of information itself. Moreover, information exchange can be part of another type of horizontal co-operation agreement (for example, the parties to a production agreement share certain information on costs). The assessment of the latter type of information exchanges should be carried out in the context of the assessment of the horizontal co-operation agreement itself.

57. Information exchange is a common feature of many competitive markets and may generate various types of efficiency gains. It may solve problems of information asymmetries (40), thereby making markets more efficient. Moreover, companies may improve their internal efficiency through benchmarking against each other's best practices. Sharing of information may also help companies to save costs by reducing their inventories, enabling quicker delivery of perishable products to consumers, or dealing with unstable demand etc. Furthermore, information exchanges may directly benefit consumers by reducing their search costs and improving choice.

(40) Economic theory on information asymmetries deals with the study of decisions in transactions where one party has more information than the other.

58. However, the exchange of market information may also lead to restrictions of competition in particular in situations where it is liable to enable undertakings to be aware of market strategies of their competitors (41). The competitive outcome of information exchange depends on the characteristics of the market in which it takes place (such as concentration, transparency, stability, symmetry, complexity etc.) as well as on the type of information that is exchanged, which may modify the relevant market environment towards one liable to coordination.

(41) See Case C-7/95 P, *John Deere*, paragraph 88.

59. Moreover, communication of information among competitors may constitute an agreement, a concerted practice, or a decision by an association of undertakings with the object of fixing, in particular, prices or quantities. Those types of information exchanges will normally be considered and fined as cartels. Information exchange may also facilitate the implementation of a cartel by enabling companies to monitor whether the participants comply with the agreed terms. Those types of exchanges of information will be assessed as part of the cartel.

Concerted practice

60. Information exchange can only be addressed under Article 101 if it establishes or is part of an agreement, a concerted practice or a decision by an association of undertakings. The existence of an agreement, a concerted practice or decision by an association of undertakings does not prejudge whether the agreement, concerted practice or decision by an association of undertakings gives rise to a restriction of competition within the meaning of Article 101(1). In line with the case-law of the Court of Justice of the European Union, the concept of a concerted practice refers to a form of coordination between undertakings by which, without it having reached the stage where an agreement properly so-called has been concluded, practical cooperation between them is knowingly substituted for the risks of competition (42). The criteria of coordination and cooperation necessary for determining the existence of a concerted practice, far from requiring an actual plan to have been worked out, are to be understood in the light of the concept inherent in the provisions of the Treaty on competition, according to which each company must determine independently the policy which it intends to adopt on the internal market and the conditions which it intends to offer to its customers (43).

(42) See for example Case C-8/08, *T-Mobile Netherlands*, paragraph 26; Joined Cases C-89/85 and others, *Wood Pulp*, (1993) ECR 1307, paragraph 63.

(43) See Case C-7/95 P, *John Deere*, paragraph 86.

61. This does not deprive companies of the right to adapt themselves intelligently to the existing or anticipated conduct of their competitors. It does, however, preclude any direct or indirect contact between competitors, the object or effect of which is to create conditions of competition which do not correspond to the normal competitive conditions of the market in question, regard being had to the nature of the products or services offered, the size and number of the undertakings, and the volume of the said market (44). This precludes any direct or indirect contact between competitors, the object or effect of which is to influence conduct on the market of an actual or potential competitor, or to disclose to such competitor the course of conduct which they themselves have decided to adopt or contemplate adopting on the market, thereby facilitating a collusive outcome on the market (45). Hence, information exchange can constitute a concerted practice if it reduces strategic uncertainty (46) in the market thereby facilitating collusion, that is to say, if the data exchanged is strategic. Consequently, sharing of strategic data between competitors amounts to concertation, because it reduces the independence of competitors' conduct on the market and diminishes their incentives to compete.

(44) Case C-7/95 P, *John Deere*, paragraph 87.

(45) See Cases 40/73 and others, *Suiker Unie*, (1975) ECR 1663, paragraph 173 *et seq*.

(46) Strategic uncertainty in the market arises as there is a variety of possible collusive outcomes available and because companies cannot perfectly observe past and current actions of their competitors and entrants.

62. A situation where only one undertaking discloses strategic information to its competitor(s) who accept(s) it can also constitute a concerted practice (47). Such disclosure could occur, for example, through contacts via mail, emails, phone calls, meetings etc. It is then irrelevant whether only one undertaking unilaterally informs its competitors of its intended market behaviour, or whether all participating undertakings inform each other of the respective deliberations and intentions. When one undertaking alone reveals to its competitors strategic information concerning its future commercial policy, that reduces strategic uncertainty as to the future operation of the market for all the competitors involved and increases the risk of limiting competition and of collusive behaviour (48). For example, mere attendance at a meeting (49) where a company discloses its pricing plans to its competitors is likely to be caught by Article 101, even in the absence of an explicit agreement to raise prices (50). When a company receives strategic data from a competitor (be it in a meeting, by mail or electronically), it will be presumed to have accepted the information and adapted its market conduct accordingly unless it responds with a clear statement that it does not wish to receive such data (51).

(47) See for example Joined Cases T-25/95 and others, *Cimenteries*, (2000) ECR II-491, paragraph 1849: «(...) the concept of concerted practice does in fact imply the existence of reciprocal contacts (...). That condition is met where one competitor discloses its future intentions or conduct on the market to another when the latter requests it or, at the very least, accepts it».

(48) See Opinion of Advocate General Kokott, Case C-8/08, *T-Mobile Netherlands*, (2009) ECR I-4529, paragraph 54.

(49) See Case C-8/08, *T-Mobile Netherlands*, paragraph 59: «Depending on the structure of the market, the possibility cannot be ruled out that a meeting on a single occasion between competitors, such as that in question in the main proceedings, may, in principle, constitute a sufficient basis for the participating undertakings to concert their market conduct and thus successfully substitute practical cooperation between them for competition and the risks that that entails.»

(50) See Joined Cases T-202/98 and others, *Tate & Lyle v Commission*, (2001) ECR II-2035, paragraph 54.

(51) See Case C-199/92 P, *Hüls*, (1999) ECR I-4287, paragraph 162; Case C-49/92 P, *Anic Partezipazioni*, (1999) ECR I-4125, paragraph 121.

63. Where a company makes a unilateral announcement that is also genuinely public, for example through a newspaper, this generally does not constitute a concerted practice within the meaning of Article 101(1) (52). However, depending on the facts underlying the case at hand, the possibility of finding a concerted practice cannot be excluded, for example in a situation where such an announcement was followed by public announcements by other competitors, not least because strategic responses of competitors to each other's public announcements (which, to take one instance, might involve readjustments of their own earlier announcements to announcements made by competitors) could prove to be a strategy for reaching a common understanding about the terms of coordination.

(52) This would not cover situations where such announcements involve invitations to collude.

2.2. Assessment under Article 101(1)

2.2.1. Main competition concerns (53)

(53) The use of the term «main competition concerns» means that the ensuing description of competition concerns is neither exclusive nor exhaustive.

64. Once it has been established that there is an agreement, concerted practice or decision by an association of undertakings, it is necessary to consider the main competition concerns pertaining to information exchanges.

Collusive outcome

65. By artificially increasing transparency in the market, the exchange of strategic information can facilitate coordination (that is to say, alignment) of companies' competitive behaviour and result in restrictive effects on competition. This can occur through different channels.

66. One way is that through information exchange companies may reach a common understanding on the terms of coordination, which can lead to a collusive outcome on the market. Information exchange can create mutually consistent expectations regarding the uncertainties present in the market. On that basis companies can then reach a common understanding on the terms of coordination of their competitive behaviour, even without an explicit agreement on coordination. Exchange of information about intentions concerning future conduct is the most likely means to enable companies to reach such a common understanding.

67. Another channel through which information exchange can lead to restrictive effects on competition is by increasing the internal stability of a collusive outcome on the market. In particular, it can do so by enabling the companies involved to monitor deviations. Namely, information exchange can make the market sufficiently transparent to allow the colluding companies to monitor to a sufficient degree whether other companies are deviating from the collusive outcome, and thus to know when to retaliate. Both exchanges of present and past data can constitute such a monitoring mechanism. This can either enable companies to achieve a collusive outcome on markets where they would otherwise not have been able to do so, or it can increase the stability of a collusive outcome already present on the market (see Example 3, paragraph 107).

68. A third channel through which information exchange can lead to restrictive effects on competition is by increasing the external stability of a collusive outcome on the market. Information exchanges that make the market sufficiently transparent can allow colluding companies to monitor where and when other companies are attempting to enter the market, thus allowing the colluding companies to target the new entrant. This may also tie into the anti-competitive foreclosure concerns discussed in paragraphs 69 to 71. Both exchanges of present and past data can constitute such a monitoring mechanism.

Anti-competitive foreclosure

69. Apart from facilitating collusion, an exchange of information can also lead to anti-competitive foreclosure (54).

(54) With regard to foreclosure concerns that vertical agreements can give rise to, see paragraphs 100 et seq. of the Guidelines on Vertical Restraints.

70. An exclusive exchange of information can lead to anti-competitive foreclosure on the same market where the exchange takes place. This can occur when the exchange of commercially sensitive information places unaffiliated competitors at a significant competitive disadvantage as compared to the companies affiliated within the exchange system. This type of foreclosure is only possible if the information concerned is very strategic for competition and covers a significant part of the relevant market.

71. It cannot be excluded that information exchange may also lead to anti-competitive foreclosure of third parties in a related market. For instance, by gaining enough market power through an information exchange, parties exchanging information in an upstream market, for instance vertically integrated companies, may be able to raise the price of a key component for a market downstream. Thereby, they could raise the costs of their rivals downstream, which could result in anti-competitive foreclosure in the downstream market.

2.2.2. Restriction of competition by object

72. Any information exchange with the objective of restricting competition on the market will be considered as a restriction of competition by object. In assessing whether an information exchange constitutes a restriction of competition by object, the Commission will pay particular attention to the legal and economic context in which the information exchange takes place (55). To this end, the Commission will take into account whether the information exchange, by its very nature, may possibly lead to a restriction of competition (56).

(55) See, for example, Joined Cases C-501/06 P and others, *GlaxoSmithKline*, paragraph 58; Case C-209/07, *BIDS*, paragraphs 15 et seq.

(56) See also General Guidelines, paragraph 22.

73. Exchanging information on companies' individualised intentions concerning future conduct regarding prices or quantities (57) is particularly likely to lead to a collusive outcome. Informing each other about such intentions may allow competitors to arrive at a common higher price level without incurring the risk of losing market share or triggering a price war during the period of adjustment to new prices (see Example 1, paragraph 105). Moreover, it is less likely that information exchanges concerning future intentions are made for pro-competitive reasons than exchanges of actual data.

(57) Information regarding intended future quantities could for instance include intended future sales, market shares, territories, and sales to particular groups of consumers.

74. Information exchanges between competitors of individualised data regarding intended future prices or quantities should therefore be considered a restriction of competition by object (58) (59). In addition, private exchanges between competitors of their individualised intentions regarding future prices or quantities would normally be considered and fined as cartels because they generally have the object of fixing prices or quantities. Information exchanges that constitute cartels not only infringe Article 101(1), but, in addition, are very unlikely to fulfil the conditions of Article 101(3).

(58) The notion of «intended future prices» is illustrated in Example 1. In specific situations where companies are fully committed to sell in the future at the prices that they have previously announced to the public (that is to say, they can not revise them), such public announcements of future individualised prices or quantities would not be considered as intentions, and hence would normally not be found to restrict competition by object. This could occur, for example, because of the repeated interactions and the specific type of relationship companies may have with their customers, for instance since it is essential that the customers know future prices in advance or because they can already take advanced orders at these prices. This is because in these situations the information exchange would be a more costly means for reaching

a collusive outcome in the market than exchanging information on future intentions, and would be more likely to be done for pro-competitive reasons. However, this does not imply that in general price commitment towards customers is necessarily pro-competitive. On the contrary, it could limit the possibility of deviating from a collusive outcome and hence render it more stable.

(59) This is without prejudice to the fact that public announcements of intended individualised prices may give rise to efficiencies and that the parties to such exchange would have a possibility to rely on Article 101(3).

2.2.3. Restrictive effects on competition

75. The likely effects of an information exchange on competition must be analysed on a case-by-case basis as the results of the assessment depend on a combination of various case specific factors. The assessment of restrictive effects on competition compares the likely effects of the information exchange with the competitive situation that would prevail in the absence of that specific information exchange (60). For an information exchange to have restrictive effects on competition within the meaning of Article 101(1), it must be likely to have an appreciable adverse impact on one (or several) of the parameters of competition such as price, output, product quality, product variety or innovation. Whether or not an exchange of information will have restrictive effects on competition depends on both the economic conditions on the relevant markets and the characteristics of information exchanged.

(60) Case C-7/95 P, *John Deere v Commission*, paragraph 76.

76. Certain market conditions may make coordination easier to achieve, sustain internally, or sustain externally (61). Exchanges of information in such markets may have more restrictive effects compared to markets with different conditions. However, even where market conditions are such that coordination may be difficult to sustain before the exchange, the exchange of information may change the market conditions in such a way that coordination becomes possible after the exchange – for example by increasing transparency in the market, reducing market complexity, buffering instability or compensating for asymmetry. For this reason it is important to assess the restrictive effects of the information exchange in the context of both the initial market conditions, and how the information exchange changes those conditions. This will include an assessment of the specific characteristics of the system concerned, including its purpose, conditions of access to the system and conditions of participation in the system. It will also be necessary to examine the frequency of the information exchanges, the type of information exchanged (for example, whether it is public or confidential, aggregated or detailed, and historical or current), and the importance of the information for the fixing of prices, volumes or conditions of service (62). The following factors are relevant for this assessment.

(61) Information exchange may restrict competition in a similar way to a merger if it leads to more effective, more stable or more likely coordination in the market; see Case C-413/06 P, *Sony*, (2008) ECR I-4951, paragraph 123, where the Court of Justice endorsed the criteria established by the General Court in Case T-342/99, *Airtours*, (2002) ECR II-2585, paragraph 62.

(62) Case C-238/05, *Asnef-Equifax*, paragraph 54.

(i) Market characteristics

77. Companies are more likely to achieve a collusive outcome in markets which are sufficiently transparent, concentrated, non-complex, stable and symmetric. In those types of markets companies can reach a common understanding on the terms of coordination and successfully monitor and punish deviations. However, information exchange can also enable companies to achieve a collusive outcome in other market situations where they would not be able to do so in the absence of the information exchange. Information exchange can thereby facilitate a collusive outcome by increasing transparency in the market, reducing market complexity, buffering instability or compensating for asymmetry. In this context, the competitive outcome of an information exchange depends not only on the initial characteristics of the market in which it takes place (such as concentration, transparency, stability, complexity etc.), but also on how the type of the information exchanged may change those characteristics (63).

(63) It should be noted that the discussion in paragraphs 78 to 85 is not a complete list of relevant market characteristics. There may be other characteristics of the market which are important in the setting of certain information exchanges.

78. Collusive outcomes are more likely in transparent markets. Transparency can facilitate collusion by enabling companies to reach a common understanding on the terms of coordination, or/and by increasing internal and external stability of collusion. Information exchange can increase transparency and hence limit uncertainties about the strategic variables of competition (for example, prices, output, demand, costs etc.). The lower the pre-existing level of transparency in the market, the more value an information exchange may have in achieving a collusive outcome. An information exchange that contributes little to the transparency in a market is less likely to have restrictive effects on competition than an information exchange that significantly increases transparency. Therefore it is the combination of both the pre-existing level of transparency and how the information exchange changes that level that will determine how likely it is that the information exchange will have restrictive effects on competition. The pre-existing degree of transparency, inter alia, depends on the number of market participants and the nature of transactions, which can range from public transactions to confidential bilateral negotiations between buyers and sellers. When evaluating the change in the level of transparency in the market, the key element is to identify to what extent the available information can be used by companies to determine the actions of their competitors.

79. Tight oligopolies can facilitate a collusive outcome on the market as it is easier for fewer companies to reach a common understanding on the terms of coordination and to monitor deviations. A collusive outcome is also more likely to be sustainable with fewer companies. With more companies coordinating, the gains from deviating are greater because a larger market share can be gained through undercutting. At the same time, gains from the collusive outcome are smaller because, when there are more companies, the share of the rents from the collusive outcome declines. Exchanges of information in tight oligopolies are more likely to cause restrictive effects on competition than in less tight oligopolies, and are not likely to cause such restrictive effects on competition in very fragmented markets. However, by increasing transparency, or modifying the market environment in another way towards one more liable to coordination, information exchanges may facilitate coordination and monitoring among more companies than would be possible in its absence.

80. Companies may find it difficult to achieve a collusive outcome in a complex market environment. However, to some extent, the use of information exchange may simplify such environments. In a complex market environment more information exchange is normally needed to reach a common understanding on the terms of coordination and to monitor deviations. For example, it is easier to achieve a collusive outcome on a price for a single, homogeneous product, than on numerous prices in a market with many differentiated products. It is nonetheless possible that to circumvent the difficulties involved in achieving a collusive outcome on a large number of prices, companies may exchange information to establish simple pricing rules (for example, pricing points).

81. Collusive outcomes are more likely where the demand and supply conditions are relatively stable (64). In an unstable environment it may be difficult for a company to know whether its lost sales are due to an overall low level of demand or due to a competitor offering particularly low prices, and therefore it is difficult to sustain a collusive outcome. In this context, volatile demand, substantial internal growth by some companies in the market, or frequent entry by new companies, may indicate that the current situation is not sufficiently stable for coordination to be likely (65). Information exchange in certain situations can serve the purpose of increasing stability in the market, and thereby may enable a collusive outcome in the market. Moreover, in markets where innovation is important, coordination may be more difficult since particularly significant innovations may allow one company to gain a major advantage over its rivals. For a collusive outcome to be sustainable, the reactions of outsiders, such as current and future competitors not participating in the coordination, as well as customers, should not be capable of jeopardising the results expected from the collusive outcome. In this context, the existence of barriers to entry makes it more likely that a collusive outcome on the market is feasible and sustainable.

(64) See Case T-35/92, *John Deere v Commission*, (1994) ECR II-957, paragraph 78.

(65) See Commission Decision in Cases IV/31.370 and 31.446, *UK Agricultural Tractor Registration Exchange*, OJ L 68, 13.3.1992, p. 19, paragraph 51 and Case T-35/92, *John Deere v Commission*, paragraph 78. It is not necessary that absolute stability be established or fierce competition excluded.

82. A collusive outcome is more likely in symmetric market structures. When companies are homogenous in terms of their costs, demand, market shares, product range, capacities etc., they are more likely to reach a common understanding on the terms of coordination because their incentives are more aligned. However, information exchange may in some situations also allow a collusive outcome to occur in more heterogeneous market structures. Information exchange could make companies aware of their differences and help them to design means to accommodate for their heterogeneity in the context of coordination.

83. The stability of a collusive outcome also depends on the companies' discounting of future profits. The more companies value the current profits that they could gain from undercutting versus all the future ones that they could gain by the collusive outcome, the less likely it is that they will be able to achieve a collusive outcome.

84. By the same token, a collusive outcome is more likely among companies that will continue to operate in the same market for a long time, as in such a scenario they will be more committed to coordinate. If a company knows that it will interact with the others for a long time, it will have a greater incentive to achieve the collusive outcome because the stream of future profits from the collusive outcome will be worth more than the short term profit it could have if it deviated, that is to say, before the other companies detect the deviation and retaliate.

85. Overall, for a collusive outcome to be sustainable, the threat of a sufficiently credible and prompt retaliation must be likely. Collusive outcomes are not sustainable in markets in which the consequences of deviation are not sufficiently severe to convince coordinating companies that it is in their best interest to adhere to the terms of the collusive outcome. For example, in markets characterised by infrequent, lumpy orders, it may be difficult to establish a sufficiently severe deterrence mechanism, since the gain from deviating at the right time may be large, certain and immediate, whereas the losses from being punished small and uncertain, and only materialise after some time. The credibility of the deterrence mechanism also depends on whether the other coordinating companies have an incentive to retaliate, determined by their short-term losses from triggering a price war versus their potential long-term gain in case they induce a return to a collusive outcome. For example, companies' ability to retaliate may be reinforced if they are also interrelated by vertical commercial relationships which they can use as a threat of punishment for deviations.

(ii) Characteristics of the information exchange

Strategic information

86. The exchange between competitors of strategic data, that is to say, data that reduces strategic uncertainty in the market, is more likely to be caught by Article 101 than exchanges of other types of information. Sharing of strategic data can give rise to restrictive effects on competition because it reduces the parties' decision-making independence by decreasing their incentives to compete. Strategic information can be related to prices (for example, actual prices, discounts, increases, reductions or rebates), customer lists, production costs, quantities, turnovers, sales, capacities, qualities, marketing plans, risks, investments, technologies and R&D programmes and their results. Generally, information related to prices and quantities is the most strategic, followed by information about costs and demand. However, if companies compete with regard to R&D it is the technology data that may be the most strategic for competition. The strategic usefulness of data also depends on its aggregation and age, as well as the market context and frequency of the exchange.

Market coverage

87. For an information exchange to be likely to have restrictive effects on competition, the companies involved in the exchange have to cover a sufficiently large part of the relevant market. Otherwise, the competitors that are not participating in the information exchange could constrain any anti-competitive behaviour of the companies involved. For example, by pricing below the coordinated price level companies unaffiliated within the information exchange system could threaten the external stability of a collusive outcome.

88. What constitutes «a sufficiently large part of the market» cannot be defined in the abstract and will depend on the specific facts of each case and the type of information exchange in question. Where, however, an information exchange takes place in the context of another type of horizontal co-operation agreement and does not go beyond what is necessary for its implementation, market coverage below the market share thresholds set out in the relevant chapter of these guidelines, the relevant block exemption regulation (66) or the *De Minimis* Notice pertaining to the type of agreement in question will usually not be large enough for the information exchange to give rise to restrictive effects on competition.

(66) Exchanges of information in the context of an R&D agreement, if they do not exceed what is necessary for implementation of the agreement, can benefit from the safe harbour of 25 % set out in the R&D Block Exemption Regulation. For the Specialisation Block Exemption Regulation, the relevant safe harbour is 20 %.

Aggregated/individualised data

89. Exchanges of genuinely aggregated data, that is to say, where the recognition of individualised company level information is sufficiently difficult, are much less likely to lead to restrictive effects on competition than exchanges of company level data. Collection and publication of aggregated market data (such as sales data, data on capacities or data on costs of inputs and components) by a trade organisation or market intelligence firm may benefit suppliers and customers alike by allowing them to get a clearer picture of the economic situation of a sector. Such data collection and publication may allow market participants to make better-informed individual choices in order to adapt efficiently their strategy to the market conditions. More generally, unless it takes place in a tight oligopoly, the exchange of aggregated data is unlikely to give rise to restrictive effects on competition. Conversely, the exchange of individualised data facilitates a common understanding on the market and punishment strategies by allowing the co-ordinating companies to single out a deviator or entrant. Nevertheless, the possibility cannot be excluded that even the exchange of aggregated data may facilitate a collusive outcome in markets with specific characteristics. Namely, members of a very tight and stable oligopoly exchanging aggregated data who detect a market price below a certain level could automatically assume that someone has deviated from the collusive outcome and take market-wide retaliatory steps. In other words, in order to keep collusion stable, companies may not always need to know who deviated, it may be enough to learn that «someone» deviated.

Age of data

90. The exchange of historic data is unlikely to lead to a collusive outcome as it is unlikely to be indicative of the competitors' future conduct or to provide a common understanding on the market (67). Moreover, exchanging historic data is unlikely to facilitate monitoring of deviations because the older the data, the less useful it would be for timely detection of deviations and thus as a credible threat of prompt retaliation (68). There is no predetermined threshold when data becomes historic, that is to say, old enough not to pose risks to competition. Whether data is genuinely historic depends on the specific characteristics of the relevant market and in particular the frequency of price re-negotiations in the industry. For example, data can be considered as historic if it is several times older than the average length of contracts in the industry if the latter are indicative of price re-negotiations. Moreover, the threshold when data becomes historic also depends on the data's nature, aggregation, frequency of the exchange, and the characteristics of the relevant market (for example, its stability and transparency).

(67) The collection of historic data can also be used to convey a sector association's input to or analysis of a review of public policy.

(68) For example, in past cases the Commission has considered the exchange of individual data which was more than one year old as historic and as not restrictive of competition within the meaning of Article 101(1), whereas information less than one year old has been considered as recent; Commission Decision in Case IV/31.370, *UK Agricultural Tractor Registration Exchange*, paragraph 50; Commission Decision in Case IV/36.069, *Wirtschaftsvereinigung Stahl*, OJ L 1, 3.1.1998, p. 10, paragraph 17.

Frequency of the information exchange

91. Frequent exchanges of information that facilitate both a better common understanding of the market and monitoring of deviations increase the risks of a collusive outcome. In more unstable markets, more frequent exchanges of information may be necessary to facilitate a collusive outcome than in stable markets. In markets with long-term contracts (which are indicative of infrequent price re-negotiations) a less frequent exchange of information would normally be sufficient to achieve a collusive outcome. By contrast, infrequent exchanges would not tend to be sufficient to achieve a collusive outcome in markets with short-term contracts indicative of frequent price re-negotiations (69). However, the frequency at which data needs to be exchanged to facilitate a collusive outcome also depends on the nature, age and aggregation of data (70).

(69) However, infrequent contracts could decrease the likelihood of a sufficiently prompt retaliation.

(70) However, depending on the structure of the market and the overall context of the exchange, the possibility cannot be excluded that an isolated exchange may constitute a sufficient basis for the participating undertakings to concert their market conduct and thus successfully substitute practical co-operation between them for competition and the risks that that entails; see Case C-8/08, *T-Mobile Netherlands*, paragraph 59.

Public/non-public information

92. In general, exchanges of genuinely public information are unlikely to constitute an infringement of Article 101 (71). *Genuinely public information* is information that is generally equally accessible (in terms of costs of access) to all competitors and customers. For information to be genuinely public, obtaining it should not be more costly for customers and companies unaffiliated to the exchange system than for the companies exchanging the information. For this reason, competitors would normally not choose to exchange data that they can collect from the market at equal ease, and hence in practice exchanges of genuinely public data are unlikely. In contrast, even if the data exchanged between competitors is what is often referred to as being «in the public domain», it is not genuinely public if the costs involved in collecting the data deter other companies and customers from doing so (72). A possibility to gather the information in the market, for example to collect it from customers, does not necessarily mean that such information constitutes market data readily accessible to competitors (73).

(71) Joined Cases T-191/98 and others, *Atlantic Container Line (TACA)*, (2003) ECR II-3275, paragraph 1154. This may not be the case if the exchange underpins a cartel.

(72) Moreover, the fact that the parties to the exchange have previously communicated the data to the public (for example through a daily newspaper or on their websites) does not imply that a subsequent non-public exchange would not infringe Article 101.

(73) See Joined Cases T-202/98 and others, *Tate & Lyle v Commission*, paragraph 60.

93. Even if there is public availability of data (for example, information published by regulators), the existence of an additional information exchange by competitors may give rise to restrictive effects on competition if it further reduces strategic uncertainty in the market. In that case, it is the incremental information that could be critical to tip the market balance towards a collusive outcome.

Public/non-public exchange of information

94. An information exchange is genuinely public if it makes the exchanged data equally accessible (in terms of costs of access) to all competitors and customers (74). The fact that information is exchanged in public may decrease the likelihood of a collusive outcome on the market to the extent that non-coordinating companies, potential competitors, as well as costumers may be able to constrain potential restrictive effect on competition (75). However, the possibility cannot be entirely excluded that even genuinely public exchanges of information may facilitate a collusive outcome in the market.

(74) This does not preclude that a database be offered at a lower price to customers which themselves have contributed data to it, as by doing so they normally would have also incurred costs.

(75) Assessing barriers to entry and countervailing «buyer power» in the market would be relevant for determining whether outsiders to the information exchange system would be able to jeopardise the outcomes expected from coordination. However, increased transparency to consumers may either decrease or increase scope for a collusive outcome because with increased transparency to consumers, as price elasticity of demand is higher, pay-offs from deviation are higher but retaliation is also harsher.

2.3. Assessment under Article 101(3)

2.3.1. Efficiency gains (76)

(76) The discussion of potential efficiency gains from information exchange is neither exclusive nor exhaustive.

95. Information exchange may lead to efficiency gains. Information about competitors' costs can enable companies to become more efficient if they benchmark their performance against the best practices in the industry and design internal incentive schemes accordingly.

96. Moreover, in certain situations information exchange can help companies allocate production towards high-demand markets (for example, demand information) or low cost companies (for example, cost information). The likelihood of those types of efficiencies depends on market characteristics such as whether companies compete on prices or quantities and the nature of uncertainties on the market. Some forms of information exchanges in this context may allow substantial cost savings where, for example, they reduce unnecessary inventories or enable quicker delivery of perishable products to areas with high demand and their reduction in areas with low demand (see Example 6, paragraph 110).

97. Exchange of consumer data between companies in markets with asymmetric information about consumers can also give rise to efficiencies. For instance, keeping track of the past behaviour of customers in terms of accidents or credit default provides an incentive for consumers to limit their risk exposure. It also makes it possible to detect which consumers carry a lower risk and should benefit from lower prices. In this context, information exchange can also reduce consumer lock-in, thereby inducing stronger competition. This is because information is generally specific to a relationship and consumers would otherwise lose the benefit from that information when switching to another company. Examples of such efficiencies are found in the banking and insurance sectors, which are characterised by frequent exchanges of information about consumer defaults and risk characteristics.

98. Exchanging past and present data related to market shares may in some situations provide benefits to both companies and consumers by allowing companies to announce it as a signal of quality of their products to consumers. In situations of imperfect information about product quality, consumers often use indirect means to gain information on the relative qualities of products such as price and market shares (for example, consumers use best-selling lists in order to choose their next book).

99. Information exchange that is genuinely public can also benefit consumers by helping them to make a more informed choice (and reducing their search costs). Consumers are most likely to benefit in this way from public exchanges of current data, which are the most relevant for their purchasing decisions. Similarly, public information exchange about current input prices can lower search costs for companies, which would normally benefit consumers through lower final prices. Those types of direct consumer benefits are less likely to be generated by exchanges of future pricing intentions because companies which announce their pricing intentions are likely to revise them before consumers actually purchase based on that information. Consumers generally cannot rely on companies' future intentions when making their consumption plans. However, to some extent, companies may be disciplined not to change the announced future prices before implementation when, for example, they have repeated interactions with consumers and consumers rely on knowing the prices in advance or, for example, when consumers can make advance orders. In those situations, exchanging information related to the future may improve customers' planning of expenditure.

100. Exchanging present and past data is more likely to generate efficiency gains than exchanging information about future intentions. However, in specific circumstances announcing future intentions could also give rise to efficiency gains. For example, companies knowing early the winner of an R&D race could avoid duplicating costly efforts and wasting resources that cannot be recovered (77).

(77) Such efficiencies need to be weighed against the potential negative effects of, for example, limiting competition for the market which stimulates innovation.

2.3.2. Indispensability

101. Restrictions that go beyond what is necessary to achieve the efficiency gains generated by an information exchange do not fulfil the conditions of Article 101(3). For fulfilling the condition of indispensability, the parties will need to prove that the data's subject matter, aggregation, age, confidentiality and frequency, as well as coverage, of the exchange are of the kind that carries the lowest risks indispensable for creating the claimed efficiency gains. Moreover, the exchange should not involve information beyond the variables that are relevant for the attainment of the efficiency gains. For instance, for the purpose of benchmarking, an exchange of individualised data would generally not be indispensable because information aggregated in for example some form of industry ranking could also generate the claimed efficiency gains while carrying a lower risk of leading to a collusive outcome (see Example 4, paragraph 108). Finally, it is generally unlikely that the sharing of individualised data on future intentions is indispensable, especially if it is related to prices and quantities.

102. Similarly, information exchanges that form part of horizontal co-operation agreements are also more likely to fulfil the conditions of Article 101(3) if they do not go beyond what is indispensable for the implementation of the economic purpose of the agreement (for example, sharing technology necessary for an R&D agreement or cost data in the context of a production agreement).

2.3.3. Pass-on to consumers

103. Efficiency gains attained by indispensable restrictions must be passed on to consumers to an extent that outweighs the restrictive effects on competition caused by an information exchange. The lower is the market power of the parties involved in the information exchange, the more likely it is that the efficiency gains would be passed on to consumers to an extent that outweighs the restrictive effects on competition.

2.3.4. No elimination of competition

104. The criteria of Article 101(3) cannot be met if the companies involved in the information exchange are afforded the possibility of eliminating competition in respect of a substantial part of the products concerned.

2.4. Examples

105. *Exchange of intended future prices as a restriction of competition by object*
Example 1
Situation: A trade association of coach companies in country X disseminates individualised information on intended future prices only to the member coach companies. The information contains several elements, such as the intended fare and the route to which the fare applies, the possible restrictions to this fare, such as which consumers can buy it, if advanced payment or minimum stay is required, the period during which tickets can be sold for the given fare (first and last ticket date), and the time during which the ticket with the given fare can be used for travel (first and last travel dates).
Analysis: This information exchange, which is triggered by a decision by an association of undertakings, concerns pricing intentions of competitors. This information exchange is a very efficient tool for reaching a collusive outcome and therefore restricts competition by object. This is because the companies are free to change their own intended prices as announced within the association at any time if they learn that their competitors intend to charge higher prices. This allows the companies to reach a common higher price level without incurring the cost of losing market share. For example, coach Company A can announce today a price increase on the route from city 1 to city 2 for travel as of the following month. Since this information is accessible to all other coach companies, Company A can then wait and see the reaction of its competitors to this price announcement. If a competitor on the same route, say, Company B, matched the price increase, then

Company A's announcement would be left unchanged and later would likely become effective. However, if Company B did not match the price increase, then Company A could still revise its fare. The adjustment would continue until the companies converged to an increased anti-competitive price level. This information exchange is unlikely to fulfil the conditions of Article 101(3). The information exchange is only confined to competitors, that is to say, customers of the coach companies do not directly benefit from it.

106. *Exchange of current prices with sufficient efficiency gains for consumers*
Example 2
Situation: A national tourist office together with the coach companies in small country X agree to disseminate information on current prices of coach tickets through a freely accessible website (in contrast to Example 1, paragraph 105, consumers can already purchase tickets at the prices and conditions which are exchanged, thus they are not intended future prices but present prices of current and future services). The information contains several elements, such as the fare and the route to which the fare is applied, the possible restrictions to this fare, such as which consumers can buy it, if advanced payment or minimum stay is required, and the time during which the ticket with the given fare can be used for travel (first and last travel dates). Coach travel in country X is not in the same relevant market as train and air travel. It is presumed that the relevant market is concentrated, stable and relatively non-complex, and pricing becomes transparent with the information exchange.
Analysis: This information exchange does not constitute a restriction of competition by object. The companies are exchanging current prices rather than intended future prices because they are effectively already selling tickets at these prices (unlike in Example 1, paragraph 105). Therefore, this exchange of information is less likely to constitute an efficient mechanism for reaching a focal point for coordination. Nevertheless, given the market structure and strategic nature of the data, this information exchange is likely to constitute an efficient mechanism for monitoring deviations from a collusive outcome, which would be likely to occur in this type of market setting. Therefore, this information exchange could give rise to restrictive effects on competition within the meaning of Article 101(1). However, to the extent that some restrictive effects on competition could result from the possibility to monitor deviations, it is likely that the efficiency gains stemming from the information exchange would be passed on to consumers to an extent that outweighs the restrictive effects on competition in both their likelihood and magnitude. Unlike in Example 1, paragraph 105, the information exchange is public and consumers can actually purchase tickets at the prices and conditions that are exchanged. Therefore this information exchange is likely to directly benefit consumers by reducing their search costs and improving choice, and thereby also stimulating price competition. Hence, the conditions of Article 101(3) are likely to be met.

107. *Current prices deduced from the information exchanged*
Example 3
Situation: The luxury hotels in the capital of country A operate in a tight, non-complex and stable oligopoly, with largely homogenous cost structures, which constitute a separate relevant market from other hotels. They directly

exchange individual information about current occupancy rates and revenues. In this case, from the information exchanged the parties can directly deduce their actual current prices.

Analysis: Unless it is a disguised means of exchanging information on future intentions, this exchange of information would not constitute a restriction of competition by object because the hotels exchange present data and not information on intended future prices or quantities. However, the information exchange would give rise to restrictive effects on competition within the meaning of Article 101(1) because knowing the competitors' actual current prices would be likely to facilitate coordination (that is to say, alignment) of companies' competitive behaviour. It would be most likely used to monitor deviations from the collusive outcome. The information exchange increases transparency in the market as even though the hotels normally publish their list prices, they also offer various discounts to the list price resulting from negotiations or for early or group bookings, etc. Therefore, the incremental information that is non-publicly exchanged between the hotels is commercially sensitive, that is to say, strategically useful. This exchange is likely to facilitate a collusive outcome on the market because the parties involved constitute a tight, non-complex and stable oligopoly involved in a long-term competitive relationship (repeated interactions). Moreover, the cost structures of the hotels are largely homogeneous. Finally, neither consumers nor market entry can constrain the incumbents' anti-competitive behaviour as consumers have little buyer power and barriers to entry are high. It is unlikely that in this case the parties would be able to demonstrate any efficiency gains stemming from the information exchange that would be passed on to consumers to an extent that would outweigh the restrictive effects on competition. Therefore it is unlikely that the conditions of Article 101(3) can be met.

108. *Benchmarking benefits – criteria of Article 101(3) not fulfilled*

Example 4

Situation: Three large companies with a combined market share of 80 % in a stable, non-complex, concentrated market with high barriers to entry, non-publicly and frequently exchange information directly between themselves about a substantial fraction of their individual costs. The companies claim that they do this to benchmark their performance against their competitors and thereby intend to become more efficient.

Analysis: This information exchange does not in principle constitute a restriction of competition by object. Consequently, its effects on the market need to be assessed. Because of the market structure, the fact that the information exchanged relates to a large proportion of the companies' variable costs, the individualised form of presentation of the data, and its large coverage of the relevant market, the information exchange is likely to facilitate a collusive outcome and thereby gives rise to restrictive effects on competition within the meaning of Article 101(1). It is unlikely that the criteria of Article 101(3) are fulfilled because there are less restrictive means to achieve the claimed efficiency gains, for example by way of a third party collecting, anonymising and aggregating the data in some form of industry ranking. Finally, in this case, since the parties form a very tight, non-complex and stable oligopoly, even the exchange of aggregated data could facilitate a collusive outcome in the market. However, this would be very unlikely if this exchange of information happened in a non-transparent, fragmented, unstable, and complex market.

109. *Genuinely public information*

Example 5

Situation: The four companies owning all the petrol stations in a large country A exchange current gasoline prices over the telephone. They claim that this information exchange cannot have restrictive effects on competition because the information is public as it is displayed on large display panels at every petrol station.

Analysis: The pricing data exchanged over the telephone is not genuinely public, as in order to obtain the same information in a different way it would be necessary to incur substantial time and transport costs. One would have to travel frequently large distances to collect the prices displayed on the boards of petrol stations spread all over the country. The costs for this are potentially high, so that the information could in practice not be obtained but for the information exchange. Moreover, the exchange is systematic and covers the entire relevant market, which is a tight, non-complex, stable oligopoly. Therefore it is likely to create a climate of mutual certainty as to the competitors' pricing policy and thereby it is likely to facilitate a collusive outcome. Consequently, this information exchange is likely to give rise to restrictive effects on competition within the meaning of Article 101(1).

110. *Improved meeting of demand as an efficiency gain*

Example 6

Situation: There are five producers of fresh bottled carrot juice in the relevant market. Demand for this product is very unstable and vary from location to location in different points in time. The juice has to be sold and consumed within one day from the date of production. The producers agree to establish an independent market research company that on a daily basis collects current information about unsold juice in each point of sale, which it publishes on its website the following week in a form that is aggregated per point of sale. The published statistics allow producers and retailers to forecast demand and to better position the product. Before the information exchange was put in place, the retailers had reported large quantities of wasted juice and therefore had reduced the quantity of juice purchased from the producers; that is to say, the market was not working efficiently. Consequently, in some periods and areas there were frequent instances of unmet demand. The information exchange system, which allows better forecasting of oversupply and undersupply, has significantly reduced the instances of unmet consumer demand and increased the quantity sold in the market.

Analysis: Even though the market is quite concentrated and the data exchanged is recent and strategic, it is not very likely that this exchange would facilitate a collusive outcome because a collusive outcome would be unlikely to occur in such an unstable market. Even if the exchange creates some risk of giving rise to restrictive effects on competition, the efficiency gains stemming from increasing supply to places with high demand and decreasing supply in places with low demand is likely to offset potential restrictive effects. The information is exchanged in a public and aggregated form, which carries lower anti-competitive risks than if it were non-public and individualised. The information exchange therefore does not go beyond what is necessary to correct the market failure. Therefore, it is likely that this information exchange meets the criteria of Article 101(3).

3. RESEARCH AND DEVELOPMENT AGREEMENTS

3.1. Definition

111. R&D agreements vary in form and scope. They range from outsourcing certain R&D activities to the joint improvement of existing technologies and co-operation concerning the research, development and marketing of completely new products. They may take the form of a co-operation agreement or of a jointly controlled company. This chapter applies to all forms of R&D agreements, including related agreements concerning the production or commercialisation of the R&D results.

3.2. Relevant markets

112. The key to defining the relevant market when assessing the effects of an R&D agreement is to identify those products, technologies or R&D efforts that will act as the main competitive constraints on the parties. At one end of the spectrum of possible situations, innovation may result in a product (or technology) which competes in an existing product (or technology) market. This is, for example, the case with R&D directed towards slight improvements or variations, such as new models of certain products. Here possible effects concern the market for existing products. At the other end of the spectrum, innovation may result in an entirely new product which creates its own new product market (for example, a new vaccine for a previously incurable disease). However, many cases concern situations in between those two extremes, that is to say, situations in which innovation efforts may create products (or technology) which, over time, replace existing ones (for example, CDs which have replaced records). A careful analysis of those situations may have to cover both existing markets and the impact of the agreement on innovation.

Existing product markets

113. Where the co-operation concerns R&D for the improvement of existing products, those existing products and their close substitutes form the relevant market concerned by the co-operation (78).

(78) For market definition, see the Market Definition Notice.

114. If the R&D efforts aim at a significant change of existing products or even at a new product to replace existing ones, substitution with the existing products may be imperfect or long-term. It may be concluded that the old and the potentially emerging new products do not belong to the same relevant market (79). The market for existing products may nevertheless be concerned, if the pooling of R&D efforts is likely to result in the coordination of the parties' behaviour as suppliers of existing products, for instance because of the exchange of competitively sensitive information relating to the market for existing products.

(79) See also Commission Guidelines on the application of Article 81 of the EC Treaty to technology transfer agreements, OJ C 101, 27.4.2004, p. 2 («Technology Transfer Guidelines»), paragraph 33.

115. If the R&D concerns an important component of a final product, not only the market for that component may be relevant for the assessment, but also the existing market for the final product. For instance, if car manufacturers co-operate in R&D related to a new type of engine, the car market may be affected by that R&D co-operation. The market for final products, however, is only relevant for the assessment if the component at which the R&D is aimed is technically or economically a key element of those final products and if the parties to the R&D agreement have market power with respect to the final products.

Existing technology markets

116. R&D co-operation may not only concern products but also technology. When intellectual property rights are marketed separately from the products to which they relate, the relevant technology market has to be defined as well. Technology markets consist of the intellectual property that is licensed and its close substitutes, that is to say, other technologies which customers could use as a substitute.

117. The methodology for defining technology markets follows the same principles as product market definition (80). Starting from the technology which is marketed by the parties, those other technologies to which customers could switch in response to a small but non-transitory increase in relative prices need to be identified. Once those technologies are identified, market shares can be calculated by dividing the licensing income generated by the parties by the total licensing income of all licensors.

(80) See Market Definition Notice; see also Technology Transfer Guidelines, paragraphs 19 *et seq.*

118. The parties' position in the market for existing technology is a relevant assessment criterion where the R&D co-operation concerns a significant improvement to an existing technology or a new technology that is likely to replace the existing technology. The parties' market shares can, however, only be taken as a starting point for this analysis. In technology markets, particular emphasis must be placed on potential competition. If companies which do not currently license their technology are potential entrants on the technology market they could constrain the ability of the parties to profitably raise the price for their technology. This aspect of the analysis may also be taken into account directly in the calculation of market shares by basing those on the sales of the products incorporating the licensed technology on downstream product markets (see paragraphs 123 to 126).

Competition in innovation (R&D efforts)

119. R&D co-operation may not only affect competition in existing markets, but also competition in innovation and new product markets. This is the case where R&D co-operation concerns the development of new products or technology which either may – if emerging – one day replace existing ones or which are being developed for a new intended use and will therefore not replace existing products but create a completely new demand. The effects on competition in innovation are important in these situations, but can in some cases not be sufficiently assessed by analysing actual or potential competition in existing product/technology markets. In this respect, two scenarios can be distinguished, depending on the nature of the innovative process in a given industry.

120. In the first scenario, which is, for instance, present in the pharmaceutical industry, the process of innovation is structured in such a way that it is possible at an early stage to identify competing R&D poles. Competing R&D poles are R&D efforts directed towards a certain new product or technology, and the substitutes for that R&D, that is to say,

R&D aimed at developing substitutable products or technology for those developed by the co-operation and having similar timing. In this case, it can be analysed whether after the agreement there will be a sufficient number of remaining R&D poles. The starting point of the analysis is the R&D of the parties. Then credible competing R&D poles have to be identified. In order to assess the credibility of competing poles, the following aspects have to be taken into account: the nature, scope and size of any other R&D efforts, their access to financial and human resources, know-how/patents, or other specialised assets as well as their timing and their capability to exploit possible results. An R&D pole is not a credible competitor if it cannot be regarded as a close substitute for the parties' R&D effort from the viewpoint of, for instance, access to resources or timing.

121. Besides the direct effect on the innovation itself, the co-operation may also affect a new product market. It will often be difficult to analyse the effects on such a market directly as by its very nature it does not yet exist. The analysis of such markets will therefore often be implicitly incorporated in the analysis of competition in innovation. However, it may be necessary to consider directly the effects on such a market of aspects of the agreement that go beyond the R&D stage. An R&D agreement that includes joint production and commercialisation on the new product market may, for instance, be assessed differently than a pure R&D agreement.

122. In the second scenario, the innovative efforts in an industry are not clearly structured so as to allow the identification of R&D poles. In this situation, in the absence of exceptional circumstances, the Commission would not try to assess the impact of a given R&D co-operation on innovation, but would limit its assessment to existing product and/or technology markets which are related to the R&D co-operation in question.

Calculation of market shares

123. The calculation of market shares, both for the purposes of the R&D Block Exemption Regulation and of these guidelines, has to reflect the distinction between existing markets and competition in innovation. At the beginning of an R&D co-operation the reference point is the existing market for products capable of being improved, substituted or replaced by the products under development. If the R&D agreement only aims at improving or refining existing products, that market includes the products directly concerned by the R&D. Market shares can thus be calculated on the basis of the sales value of the existing products.

124. If the R&D aims at replacing an existing product, the new product will, if successful, become a substitute for the existing products. To assess the competitive position of the parties, it is again possible to calculate market shares on the basis of the sales value of the existing products. Consequently, the R&D Block Exemption Regulation bases its exemption of those situations on the market share in the relevant market for the products capable of being improved, substituted or replaced by the contract products (81). To fall under the R&D Block Exemption Regulation, that market share may not exceed 25 % (82).

(81) Point (u) of Article 1(1) of the R&D Block Exemption Regulation.

(82) Article 4(2) of the R&D Block Exemption Regulation.

125. For technology markets one way to proceed is to calculate market shares on the basis of each technology's share of total licensing income from royalties, representing a technology's share of the market where competing technologies are licensed. However, this may often be a mere theoretical and not very practical way to proceed because of lack of clear information on royalties, the use of royalty free cross-licensing, etc. An alternative approach is to calculate market shares on the technology market on the basis of sales of products or services incorporating the licensed technology on downstream product markets. Under that approach all sales on the relevant product market are taken into account, irrespective of whether the product incorporates a technology that is being licensed (83). Also for that market the share may not exceed 25 % (irrespective of the calculation method used) for the benefits of the R&D Block Exemption Regulation to apply.

(83) See also Technology Transfer Guidelines, paragraph 23.

126. If the R&D aims at developing a product which will create a completely new demand, market shares based on sales cannot be calculated. Only an analysis of the effects of the agreement on competition in innovation is possible. Consequently, the R&D Block Exemption Regulation treats those agreements as agreements between non-competitors and exempts them irrespective of market share for the duration of the joint R&D and an additional period of seven years after the product is first put on the market (84). However, the benefit of the block exemption may be withdrawn if the agreement eliminated effective competition in innovation (85). After the seven year period, market shares based on sales value can be calculated, and the market share threshold of 25 % applies (86).

(84) Article 4(1) of the R&D Block Exemption Regulation.

(85) See recitals 19, 20 and 21 in the preamble to the R&D Block Exemption Regulation.

(86) Article 4(3) of the R&D Block Exemption Regulation.

3.3. Assessment under Article 101(1)

3.3.1. Main competition concerns

127. R&D co-operation can restrict competition in various ways. First, it may reduce or slow down innovation, leading to fewer or worse products coming to the market later than they otherwise would. Secondly, on product or technology markets the R&D co-operation may reduce significantly competition between the parties outside the scope of the agreement or it may make anti-competitive coordination on those markets likely, thereby leading to higher prices. A foreclosure problem may only arise in the context of co-operation involving at least one player with a significant degree of market power (which does not necessarily amount to dominance) for a key technology and the exclusive exploitation of the results.

3.3.2. Restrictions of competition by object

128. R&D agreements restrict competition by object if they do not truly concern joint R&D, but serve as a tool to engage in a disguised cartel, that is to say, otherwise prohibited price fixing, output limitation or market allocation. However, an R&D agreement which includes the joint exploitation of possible future results is not necessarily restrictive of competition.

3.3.3. Restrictive effects on competition

129. Most R&D agreements do not fall under Article 101(1). First, this can be said for many agreements relating to co-operation in R&D at a rather early stage, far removed from the exploitation of possible results.

130. Moreover, R&D co-operation between non-competitors does generally not give rise to restrictive effects on competition (87). The competitive relationship between the parties has to be analysed in the context of affected existing markets and/or innovation. If, on the basis of objective factors, the parties are not able to carry out the necessary R&D independently, for instance, due to the limited technical capabilities of the parties, the R&D agreement will normally not have any restrictive effects on competition. This can apply, for example, to companies bringing together complementary skills, technologies and other resources. The issue of potential competition has to be assessed on a realistic basis. For instance, parties cannot be defined as potential competitors simply because the co-operation enables them to carry out the R&D activities. The decisive question is whether each party independently has the necessary means as regards assets, know-how and other resources.

(87) R&D co-operation between non-competitors can, however, produce foreclosure effects under Article 101(1) if it relates to an exclusive exploitation of results and if it is concluded between companies, one of which has a significant degree of market power (which does not necessarily amount to dominance) with respect to a key technology.

131. Outsourcing of previously captive R&D is a specific form of R&D co-operation. In such a scenario, the R&D is often carried out by specialised companies, research institutes or academic bodies, which are not active in the exploitation of the results. Normally, such agreements are combined with a transfer of know-how and/or an exclusive supply clause concerning the possible results, which, due to the complementary nature of the co-operating parties in such a scenario, do not give rise to restrictive effects on competition within the meaning of Article 101(1).

132. R&D co-operation which does not include the joint exploitation of possible results by means of licensing, production and/or marketing rarely gives rise to restrictive effects on competition within the meaning of Article 101(1). Those pure R&D agreements can only cause a competition problem if competition with respect to innovation is appreciably reduced, leaving only a limited number of credible competing R&D poles.

133. R&D agreements are only likely to give rise to restrictive effects on competition where the parties to the co-operation have market power on the existing markets and/or competition with respect to innovation is appreciably reduced.

134. There is no absolute threshold above which it can be presumed that an R&D agreement creates or maintains market power and thus is likely to give rise to restrictive effects on competition within the meaning of Article 101(1). However, R&D agreements between competitors are covered by the R&D Block Exemption Regulation provided that their combined market share does not exceed 25 % and that the other conditions for the application of the R&D Block Exemption Regulation are fulfilled.

135. Agreements falling outside the R&D Block Exemption Regulation because the combined market share of the parties exceeds 25 % do not necessarily give rise to restrictive effects on competition. However, the stronger the combined position of the parties on existing markets and/or the more competition in innovation is restricted, the more likely it is that the R&D agreement can cause restrictive effects on competition (88).

(88) This is without prejudice to the analysis of potential efficiency gains, including those that regularly exist in publicly co-funded R&D.

136. If the R&D is directed at the improvement or refinement of existing products or technologies, possible effects concern the relevant market(s) for those existing products or technologies. Effects on prices, output, product quality, product variety or innovation in existing markets are, however, only likely if the parties together have a strong position, entry is difficult and few other innovation activities are identifiable. Furthermore, if the R&D only concerns a relatively minor input of a final product, effects on competition in those final products are, if any, very limited.

137. In general, a distinction has to be made between pure R&D agreements and agreements providing for more comprehensive co-operation involving different stages of the exploitation of results (that is to say, licensing, production or marketing). As set out in paragraph 132, pure R&D agreements will only rarely give rise to restrictive effects on competition within the meaning of Article 101(1). This is in particular true for R&D directed towards a limited improvement of existing products or technologies. If, in such a scenario, the R&D co-operation includes joint exploitation only by means of licensing to third parties, restrictive effects such as foreclosure problems are unlikely. If, however, joint production and/or marketing of the slightly improved products or technologies are included, the effects on competition of the co-operation have to be examined more closely. Restrictive effects on competition in the form of increased prices or reduced output in existing markets are more likely if strong competitors are involved in such a situation.

138. If the R&D is directed at an entirely new product (or technology) which creates its own new market, price and output effects on existing markets are rather unlikely. The analysis has to focus on possible restrictions of innovation concerning, for instance, the quality and variety of possible future products or technologies or the speed of innovation. Those restrictive effects can arise where two or more of the few companies engaged in the development of such a new product start to co-operate at a stage where they are each independently rather near to the launch of the product. Such effects are typically the direct result of the agreement between the parties. Innovation may be restricted even by a pure R&D agreement. In general, however, R&D co-operation concerning entirely new products is unlikely to give rise to restrictive effects on competition unless only a limited number of credible alternative R&D poles exist. This principle does not change significantly if the joint exploitation of the results, even joint marketing, is involved. In those situations the issue of joint exploitation may only give rise to restrictive effects on competition where foreclosure from key technologies plays a role. Those problems would, however, not arise where the parties grant licences that allow third parties to compete effectively.

139. Many R&D agreements will lie somewhere in between the two situations described in paragraphs 137 and 138. They may therefore have effects on innovation as well as repercussions on existing markets. Consequently, both the existing market and the effect on innovation may be of relevance for the assessment with respect to the parties' combined positions, concentration ratios, number of players or innovators and entry conditions. In some cases there can be restrictive effects on competition in the form of increased prices or reduced output, product quality, product variety or innovation in existing markets and in the form of a negative impact on innovation by means of slowing down the development. For instance, if significant competitors on an existing technology market co-operate to develop a new technology which may one day replace existing products that co-operation may slow down the development of the new technology if the parties have market power on the existing market and also a strong position with respect to R&D. A similar effect can occur if the major player in an existing market co-operates with a much smaller or even potential competitor who is just about to emerge with a new product or technology which may endanger the incumbent's position.

140. Agreements may also fall outside the R&D Block Exemption Regulation irrespective of the parties' market power. This applies for instance to agreements which unduly restrict access of a party to the results of the R&D co-operation (89). The R&D Block Exemption Regulation provides for a specific exception to this general rule in the case of academic bodies, research institutes or specialised companies which provide R&D as a service and which are not active in the industrial exploitation of the results of R&D (90). Nevertheless, agreements falling outside the R&D Block Exemption Regulation and containing exclusive access rights for the purposes of exploitation may, where they fall under Article 101(1), fulfil the criteria of Article 101(3), particularly where exclusive access rights are economically indispensable in view of the market, risks and scale of the investment required to exploit the results of the research and development.

(89) See Article 3(2) of the R&D Block Exemption Regulation.
(90) See Article 3(2) of the R&D Block Exemption Regulation.

3.4. Assessment under Article 101(3)

3.4.1. Efficiency gains

141. Many R&D agreements – with or without joint exploitation of possible results – bring about efficiency gains by combining complementary skills and assets, thus resulting in improved or new products and technologies being developed and marketed more rapidly than would otherwise be the case. R&D agreements may also lead to a wider dissemination of knowledge, which may trigger further innovation. R&D agreements may also give rise to cost reductions.

3.4.2. Indispensability

142. Restrictions that go beyond what is necessary to achieve the efficiency gains generated by an R&D agreement do not fulfil the criteria of Article 101(3). In particular, the restrictions listed in Article 5 of the R&D Block Exemption Regulation may mean it is less likely that the criteria of Article 101(3) will be found to be met, following an individual assessment. It will therefore generally be necessary for the parties to an R&D agreement to show that such restrictions are indispensable to the co-operation.

3.4.3. Pass-on to consumers

143. Efficiency gains attained by indispensable restrictions must be passed on to consumers to an extent that outweighs the restrictive effects on competition caused by the R&D agreement. For example, the introduction of new or improved products on the market must outweigh any price increases or other restrictive effects on competition. In general, it is more likely that an R&D agreement will bring about efficiency gains that benefit consumers if the R&D agreement results in the combination of complementary skills and assets. The parties to an agreement may, for instance, have different research capabilities. If, on the other hand, the parties' skills and assets are very similar, the most important effect of the R&D agreement may be the elimination of part or all of the R&D of one or more of the parties. This would eliminate (fixed) costs for the parties to the agreement but would be unlikely to lead to benefits which would be passed on to consumers. Moreover, the higher the market power of the parties the less likely they are to pass on the efficiency gains to consumers to an extent that would outweigh the restrictive effects on competition.

3.4.4. No elimination of competition

144. The criteria of Article 101(3) cannot be met if the parties are afforded the possibility of eliminating competition in respect of a substantial part of the products (or technologies) in question.

3.4.5. Time of the assessment

145. The assessment of restrictive agreements under Article 101(3) is made within the actual context in which they occur and on the basis of the facts existing at any given point in time. The assessment is sensitive to material changes in the facts. The exception rule of Article 101(3) applies as long as the four conditions of Article 101(3) are fulfilled and ceases to apply when that is no longer the case. When applying Article 101(3) in accordance with those principles it is necessary to take into account the initial sunk investments made by any of the parties and the time needed and the restraints required to making and recouping an efficiency enhancing investment. Article 101 cannot be applied without taking due account of such *ex ante* investment. The risk facing the parties and the sunk investment that must be made to implement the agreement can thus lead to the agreement falling outside Article 101(1) or fulfilling the conditions of Article 101(3), as the case may be, for the period of time needed to recoup the investment. Should the invention resulting from the investment benefit from any form of exclusivity granted to the parties under rules specific to the protection of intellectual property rights, the recoupment period for such an investment will generally be unlikely to exceed the exclusivity period established under those rules.

146. In some cases the restrictive agreement is an irreversible event. Once the restrictive agreement has been implemented the *ex ante* situation cannot be re-established. In such cases the assessment must be made exclusively on the basis of the facts pertaining at the time of implementation. For instance, in the case of an R&D agreement whereby each party agrees to abandon its respective research project and pool its capabilities with those of another party, it may from an objective point of view be technically and economically impossible to revive a project once it has been abandoned. The assessment of the anti-competitive and pro-competitive effects of the agreement to abandon the individual research projects must therefore be made as of the time of the completion of its implementation. If at that point in time the agreement is compatible with Article 101, for instance because a sufficient number of third parties have competing R&D projects, the parties' agreement to abandon their individual projects remains compatible with Article 101, even if at a later point in time the third party projects fail. However, the prohibition of Article 101 may apply to other parts of the agreement in respect of which the issue of irreversibility does not arise. If, for example, in addition to joint R&D, the agreement provides for joint exploitation, Article 101 may apply to that part of the agreement if, due to subsequent market developments, the agreement gives rise to restrictive effects on competition and does not (any longer) satisfy the conditions of Article 101(3) taking due account of *ex ante* sunk investments.

3.5. Examples

147. *Impact of joint R&D on innovation markets/new product market*

Example 1

Situation: A and B are the two major companies on the Union-wide market for the manufacture of existing electronic components. Both have a market share of 30 %. They have each made significant investments in the R&D necessary to develop miniaturised electronic components and have developed early prototypes. They now agree to pool those R&D efforts by setting up a joint venture to complete the R&D and produce the components, which will be sold back to the parents, who will commercialise them separately. The remainder of the market consists of small companies without sufficient resources to undertake the necessary investments.

Analysis: Miniaturised electronic components, while likely to compete with the existing components in some areas, are essentially a new technology and an analysis must be made of the poles of research destined towards that future market. If the joint venture goes ahead then only one route to the necessary manufacturing technology will exist, whereas it would appear likely that A and B could reach the market individually with separate products. The agreement therefore reduces product variety. The joint production is also likely to directly limit competition between the parties to the agreement and lead them to agree on output levels, quality or other competitively important parameters. This would limit competition even though the parties will commercialise the products independently. The parties could, for instance, limit the output of the joint venture compared to what the parties would have brought to the market if they had decided their output on their own. The joint venture could also charge a high transfer price to the parties, thereby increasing the input costs for the parties which could lead to higher downstream prices. The parties have a large combined market share on the existing downstream market and the remainder of that market is fragmented. This situation is likely to become even more pronounced on the new downstream product market since the smaller competitors cannot invest in the new components. It is therefore quite likely that the joint production will restrict competition. Furthermore, the market for miniaturised electronic components is in the future likely to develop into a duopoly with a high degree of commonality of costs and possible exchange of commercially sensitive information between the parties. There may therefore also be a serious risk of anti-competitive coordination leading to a collusive outcome in the market. The R&D agreement is therefore likely to give rise to restrictive effects on competition within the meaning of Article 101(1). While the agreement could give rise to efficiency gains in the form of bringing a new technology forward quicker, the parties would face no competition at the R&D level, so their incentives to pursue the new technology at a high pace could be severely reduced. Although some of those concerns could be remedied if the parties committed to license key know-how for manufacturing miniature components to third parties on reasonable terms, it seems unlikely that this could remedy all concerns and fulfil the conditions of Article 101(3).

Example 2

Situation: A small research company (Company *a*) which does not have its own marketing organisation has discovered and patented a pharmaceutical substance based on new technology that will revolutionise the treatment of a certain disease. Company A enters into an R&D agreement with a large pharmaceutical producer Company B of products that have so far been used for treating the disease. Company B lacks any similar expertise and R&D programme and would not be able to build such expertise within a relevant timeframe. For the existing products Company B has a market share of around 75 % in all Member States, but the patents will expire over the next five years. There exist two other poles of research with other companies at approximately the same stage of development using the same basic new technology. Company B will provide considerable funding and know-how for product development, as well as future access to the market. Company B is granted a licence for the exclusive production and distribution of the resulting product for the duration of the patent. It is expected that the product could be brought to market in five to seven years.

Analysis: The product is likely to belong to a new relevant market. The parties bring complementary resources and skills to the co-operation, and the probability of the product coming to market increases substantially. Although Company B is likely to have considerable market power on the existing market, that market power will be decreasing shortly. The agreement will not lead to a loss in R&D on the part of Company B, as it has no expertise in this area of research, and the existence of other poles of research are likely to eliminate any incentive to reduce R&D efforts. The exploitation rights during the remaining patent period are likely to be necessary for Company B to make the considerable investments needed and Company A has no marketing resources of its own. The agreement is therefore unlikely to give rise to restrictive effects on competition within the meaning of Article 101(1). Even if there were such effects, it is likely that the conditions of Article 101(3) would be fulfilled.

148. *Risk of foreclosure*

Example 3

Situation: A small research company (Company A) which does not have its own marketing organisation has discovered and patented a new technology that will revolutionise the market for a certain product for which there is a monopoly producer (Company B) worldwide as no competitors can compete with Company B's current technology. There exist two other poles of research with other companies at approximately the same stage of development using the same basic new technology. Company B will provide considerable funding and know-how for product development, as well as future access to the market. Company B is granted an exclusive licence for the use of the technology for the duration of the patent and commits to funding only the development of Company A's technology.

Analysis: The product is likely to belong to a new relevant market. The parties bring complementary resources and skills to the co-operation, and the probability of the product coming to market increases substantially. However, the fact that Company B commits to Company A's new technology may be likely to lead the two competing poles of research to abandon their projects as it could be difficult to receive continued funding once they have lost the most likely potential customer for their technology. In such a situation no potential competitors would be able to challenge Company B's monopoly position in the future. The foreclosure effect of the agreement would then be likely to be considered to give rise to restrictive effects on competition within the meaning of Article 101(1). In order to benefit from Article 101(3) the parties would have to show that the exclusivity granted would be indispensable to bring the new technology to the market.

Example 4

Situation: Company A has market power on the market of which its blockbuster medicine forms part. A small company (Company b) which is engaged in pharmaceutical R&D and active pharmaceutical ingredient («API») production has discovered and filed a patent application for a new process that makes it possible to produce the API of Company A's blockbuster in a more economic fashion and continues to develop the process for industrial production. The compound (API) patent of the blockbuster expires in a little less than three years; thereafter there will remain a number of process patents relating to the medicine. Company B considers that the new process developed by it would not infringe the existing process patents of Company A and would allow the production of a generic version of the blockbuster once the API patent has expired. Company B could either produce the product itself or license the process to interested third parties, for example, generic producers or Company A. Before concluding its research and development in this area, Company B enters into an agreement with Company A, in which Company A makes a financial contribution to the R&D project being carried out by Company B on condition that it acquires an exclusive licence for any of Company B's patents related to the R&D project. There exist two other independent poles of research to develop a non-infringing process for the production of the blockbuster medicine, but it is not yet clear that they will reach industrial production.

Analysis: The process covered by Company B's patent application does not allow for the production of a new product. It merely improves an existing production process. Company A has market power on the existing market of which the blockbuster medicine forms part. Whilst that market power would decrease significantly with the actual market entry of generic competitors, the exclusive licence makes the process developed by Company B unavailable to third parties and is thus liable to delay generic entry (not least as the product is still protected by a number of process patents) and, consequently, restricts competition within the meaning of Article 101(1). As Company A and Company B are potential competitors, the R&D Block Exemption Regulation does not apply because Company A's market share on the market of which the blockbuster medicine forms part is above 25 %. The cost savings based on the new production process for Company A are not sufficient to outweigh the restriction of competition. In any event, an exclusive licence is not indispensable to obtain the savings in the production process. Therefore, the agreement is unlikely to fulfil the conditions of Article 101(3).

149. *Impact of R&D co-operation on dynamic product and technology markets and the environment*

Example 5

Situation: Two engineering companies that produce vehicle components agree to set up a joint venture to combine their R&D efforts to improve the production and performance of an existing component. The production of that component would also have a positive effect on the environment. Vehicles would consume less fuel and therefore emit less CO_2. The companies pool their existing technology licensing businesses in the area, but will continue to manufacture and sell the components separately. The two companies have market shares in the Union of 15 % and 20 % on the Original Equipment Manufacturer («OEM») product market. There are two other major competitors together with several in-house research programmes by large vehicle manufacturers. On the world-wide market for the licensing of technology for those products the parties have shares of 20 % and 25 %, measured in terms of revenue generated, and there are two other major technologies. The product life cycle for the component is typically two to three years. In each of the last five years one of the major companies has introduced a new version or upgrade.

Analysis: Since neither company's R&D effort is aimed at a completely new product, the markets to consider are those for the existing components and for the licensing of relevant technology. The parties' combined market share on both the OEM market (35 %) and, in particular, on the technology market (45 %) are quite high. However, the parties will continue to manufacture and sell the components separately. In addition, there are several competing technologies, which are regularly improved. Moreover, the vehicle manufacturers who do not currently license their technology are also potential entrants on the technology market and thus constrain the ability of the parties to profitably raise prices. To the extent that the joint venture has restrictive effects on competition within the meaning of Article 101(1), it is likely that it would fulfil the criteria of Article 101(3). For the assessment under Article 101(3) it would be necessary to take into account that consumers will benefit from a lower consumption of fuel.

4. PRODUCTION AGREEMENTS

4.1. Definition and scope

150. Production agreements vary in form and scope. They can provide that production is carried out by only one party or by two or more parties. Companies can produce jointly by way of a joint venture, that is to say, a jointly controlled company operating one or several production facilities or by looser forms of co-operation in production such as subcontracting agreements where one party (the «contractor») entrusts to another party (the «subcontractor») the production of a good.

151. There are different types of subcontracting agreements. Horizontal subcontracting agreements are concluded between companies operating in the same product market irrespective of whether they are actual or potential competitors. Vertical subcontracting agreements are concluded between companies operating at different levels of the market.

152. Horizontal subcontracting agreements comprise unilateral and reciprocal specialisation agreements as well as subcontracting agreements with a view to expanding production. Unilateral specialisation agreements are agreements between two parties which are active on the same product market or markets, by virtue of which one party agrees to fully or partly cease production of certain products or to refrain from producing those products and to purchase them from the other party, which agrees to produce and supply the products. Reciprocal specialisation agreements are agreements between two or more parties which are active on the same products market or markets, by virtue of which two or more parties agree, on a reciprocal basis, to fully or partly cease or refrain from producing certain but different products and to purchase those products from the other parties, which agree to produce and supply them. In the case of subcontracting agreements with a view to expanding production the contractor entrusts the subcontractor with the production of a good, while the contractor does not at the same time cease or limit its own production of the good.

153. These guidelines apply to all forms of joint production agreements and horizontal subcontracting agreements. Subject to certain conditions, joint production agreements as well as unilateral and reciprocal specialisation agreements may benefit from the Specialisation Block Exemption Regulation.

154. Vertical subcontracting agreements are not covered by these guidelines. They fall within the scope of the Guidelines on Vertical Restraints and, subject to certain conditions, may benefit from the Block Exemption Regulation on Vertical Restraints. In addition, they may be covered by the Commission notice of 18 december 1978 concerning its assessment of certain subcontracting agreements in relation to Article 85(1) of the EEC Treaty (91) («the Subcontracting Notice»).

(91) *OJ* C 1, 3.1.1979, p. 2.

4.2. Relevant markets

155. In order to assess the competitive relationship between the co-operating parties, it is necessary first to define the relevant market or markets directly concerned by the co-operation in production, that is to say, the markets to which the products manufactured under the production agreement belong.

156. A production agreement can also have spill-over effects in markets neighbouring the market directly concerned by the co-operation, for instance upstream or downstream to the agreement (the so-called «spill-over markets») (92). The spill-over markets are likely to be relevant if the markets are interdependent and the parties are in a strong position on the spill-over market.

(92) As also referred to in Article 2(4) of the Merger Regulation.

4.3. Assessment under Article 101(1)

4.3.1. Main competition concerns

157. Production agreements can lead to a direct limitation of competition between the parties. Production agreements, and in particular production joint ventures, may lead the parties to directly align output levels and quality, the price at which the joint venture sells on its products, or other competitively important parameters. This may restrict competition even if the parties market the products independently.

158. Production agreements may also result in the coordination of the parties' competitive behaviour as suppliers leading to higher prices or reduced output, product quality, product variety or innovation, that is to say, a collusive outcome. This can happen, subject to the parties having market power and the existence of market characteristics conducive to such coordination, in particular when the production agreement increases the parties' commonality of costs (that is to say, the proportion of variable costs which the parties have in common) to a degree which enables them to achieve a collusive outcome, or if the agreement involves an exchange of commercially sensitive information that can lead to a collusive outcome.

159. Production agreements may furthermore lead to anti-competitive foreclosure of third parties in a related market (for example, the downstream market relying on inputs from the market in which the production agreement takes place). For instance, by gaining enough market power, parties engaging in joint production in an upstream market may be able to raise the price of a key component for a market downstream. Thereby, they could use the joint production to raise the costs of their rivals downstream and, ultimately, force them off the market. This would, in turn, increase the parties' market power downstream, which could enable them to sustain prices above the competitive level or otherwise harm consumers. Such competition concerns could materialise irrespective of whether the parties to the agreement are competitors on the market in which the co-operation takes place. However, for this kind of foreclosure to have anti-competitive effects, at least one of the parties must have a strong market position in the market where the risks of foreclosure are assessed.

4.3.2. Restrictions of competition by object

160. Generally, agreements which involve price-fixing, limiting output or sharing markets or customers restrict competition by object. However, in the context of production agreements, this does not apply where:
  – the parties agree on the output directly concerned by the production agreement (for example, the capacity and production volume of a joint venture or the agreed amount of outsourced products), provided that the other parameters of competition are not eliminated; or
  – a production agreement that also provides for the joint distribution of the jointly manufactured products envisages the joint setting of the sales prices for those products, and only those products, provided that that restriction is necessary for producing jointly, meaning that the parties would not otherwise have an incentive to enter into the production agreement in the first place.

161. In these two cases an assessment is required as to whether the agreement gives rise to likely restrictive effects on competition within the meaning of Article 101(1). In both scenarios the agreement on output or prices will not be assessed separately, but in the light of the overall effects of the entire production agreement on the market.

4.3.3. Restrictive effects on competition

162. Whether the possible competition concerns that production agreements can give rise to are likely to materialise in a given case depends on the characteristics of the market in which the agreement takes place, as well as on the nature and market coverage of the co-operation and the product it concerns. These variables determine the likely effects of a production agreement on competition and thereby the applicability of Article 101(1).

163. Whether a production agreement is likely to give rise to restrictive effects on competition depends on the situation that would prevail in the absence of the agreement with all its alleged restrictions. Consequently, production agreements between companies which compete on markets on which the co-operation occurs are not likely to have restrictive effects on competition if the co-operation gives rise to a new market, that is to say, if the agreement enables the parties to launch a new product or service, which, on the basis of objective factors, the parties would otherwise not have been able to do, for instance, due to the technical capabilities of the parties.

164. In some industries where production is the main economic activity, even a pure production agreement can in itself eliminate key dimensions of competition, thereby directly limiting competition between the parties to the agreements.

165. Alternatively, a production agreement can lead to a collusive outcome or anti-competitive foreclosure by increasing the companies' market power or their commonality of costs or if it involves the exchange of commercially sensitive information. On the other hand, a direct limitation of competition between the parties, a collusive outcome or anti-competitive foreclosure is not likely to occur if the parties to the agreement do not have market power in the market in which the competition concerns are assessed. It is only market power that can enable them to profitably maintain prices above the competitive level, or profitably maintain output, product quality or variety below what would be dictated by competition.

166. In cases where a company with market power in one market co-operates with a potential entrant, for example, with a supplier of the same product in a neighbouring geographic or product market, the agreement can potentially increase the market power of the incumbent. This can lead to restrictive effects on competition if actual competition in the incumbent's market is already weak and the threat of entry is a major source of competitive constraint.

167. Production agreements which also involve commercialisation functions, such as joint distribution or marketing, carry a higher risk of restrictive effects on competition than pure joint production agreements. Joint commercialisation brings the co-operation closer to the consumer and usually involves the joint setting of prices and sales, that is to say, practices that carry the highest risks for competition. However, joint distribution agreements for products which have been jointly produced are generally less likely to restrict competition than stand-alone joint distribution agreements. Also, a joint distribution agreement that is necessary for the joint production agreement to take place in the first place is less likely to restrict competition than if it were not necessary for the joint production.

Market power

168. A production agreement is unlikely to lead to restrictive effects on competition if the parties to the agreement do not have market power in the market on which a restriction of competition is assessed. The starting point for the analysis of market power is the market share of the parties. This will normally be followed by the concentration ratio and the number of players in the market as well as by other dynamic factors such as potential entry, and changing market shares.

169. Companies are unlikely to have market power below a certain level of market share. Therefore, unilateral or reciprocal specialisation agreements as well as joint production agreements including certain integrated commercialisation functions such as joint distribution are covered by the Specialisation Block Exemption Regulation if they are concluded between parties with a combined market share not exceeding 20 % in the relevant market or markets, provided that the other conditions for the application of the Specialisation Block Exemption Regulation are fulfilled. Moreover, as regards horizontal subcontracting agreements with a view to expanding production, in most cases it is unlikely that market power exists if the parties to the agreement have a combined market share not exceeding 20 %. In any event, if the parties' combined market share does not exceed 20 % it is likely that the conditions of Article 101(3) are fulfilled.

170. However, if the parties' combined market share exceeds 20 %, the restrictive effects have to be analysed as the agreement does not fall within the scope of the Specialisation Block Exemption Regulation or the safe harbour for horizontal subcontracting agreements with a view to expanding production referred to in sentences 3 and 4 of paragraph 169. A moderately higher market share than allowed for in the Specialisation Block Exemption Regulation or the safe harbour referred to in sentences 3 and 4 of paragraph 169 does not necessarily imply a highly concentrated market, which is an important factor in the assessment. A combined market share of the parties of slightly more than 20 % may occur in a market with a moderate concentration. Generally, a production agreement is more likely to lead to restrictive effects on competition in a concentrated market than in a market which is not concentrated. Similarly, a production agreement in a concentrated market may increase the risk of a collusive outcome even if the parties only have a moderate combined market share.

171. Even if the market shares of the parties to the agreement and the market concentration are high, the risks of restrictive effects on competition may still be low if the market is dynamic, that is to say, a market in which entry occurs and market positions change frequently.

172. In the analysis of whether the parties to a production agreement have market power, the number and intensity of links (for example, other co-operation agreements) between the competitors in the market are relevant to the assessment.

173. Factors such as whether the parties to the agreement have high market shares, whether they are close competitors, whether the customers have limited possibilities of switching suppliers, whether competitors are unlikely to increase supply if prices increase, and whether one of the parties to the agreement is an important competitive force, are all relevant for the competitive assessment of the agreement.

Direct limitation of competition between the parties

174. Competition between the parties to a production agreement can be directly limited in various ways. The parties to a production joint venture could, for instance, limit the output of the joint venture compared to what the parties would have brought to the market if each of them had decided their output on their own. If the main product characteristics are determined by the production agreement this could also eliminate the key dimensions of competition between the parties and, ultimately, lead to restrictive effects on competition. Another example would be a joint venture charging a high transfer price to the parties, thereby increasing the input costs for the parties which could lead to higher downstream prices. Competitors may find it profitable to increase their prices as a response, thereby contributing to price increases in the relevant market.

Collusive outcome

175. The likelihood of a collusive outcome depends on the parties' market power as well as the characteristics of the relevant market. A collusive outcome can result in particular (but not only) from commonality of costs or an exchange of information brought about by the production agreement.

176. A production agreement between parties with market power can have restrictive effects on competition if it increases their commonality of costs (that is to say, the proportion of variable costs which the parties have in common) to a level which enables them to collude. The relevant costs are the variable costs of the product with respect to which the parties to the production agreement compete.

177. A production agreement is more likely to lead to a collusive outcome if prior to the agreement the parties already have a high proportion of variable costs in common, as the additional increment (that is to say, the production costs of the product subject to the agreement) can tip the balance towards a collusive outcome. Conversely, if the increment is large, the risk of a collusive outcome may be high even if the initial level of commonality of costs is low.

178. Commonality of costs increases the risk of a collusive outcome only if production costs constitute a large proportion of the variable costs concerned. This is, for instance, not the case where the co-operation concerns products which require costly commercialisation. An example would be new or heterogeneous products requiring expensive marketing or high transport costs.

179. Another scenario where commonality of costs can lead to a collusive outcome could be where the parties agree on the joint production of an intermediate product which accounts for a large proportion of the variable costs of the final product with respect to which the parties compete downstream. The parties could use the production agreement to increase the price of that common important input for their products in the downstream market. This would weaken competition downstream and would be likely to lead to higher final prices. The profit would be shifted from downstream to upstream to be then shared between the parties through the joint venture.

180. Similarly, commonality of costs increases the anti-competitive risks of a horizontal subcontracting agreement where the input which the contractor purchases from the subcontractor accounts for a large proportion of the variable costs of the final product with which the parties compete.

181. Any negative effects arising from the exchange of information will not be assessed separately but in the light of the overall effects of the agreement. A production agreement can give rise to restrictive effects on competition if it involves an exchange of commercially strategic information that can lead to a collusive outcome or anti-competitive foreclosure. Whether the exchange of information in the context of a production agreement is likely to lead to restrictive effects on competition should be assessed according to the guidance given in Chapter 2.

182. If the information exchange does not exceed the sharing of data necessary for the joint production of the goods subject to the production agreement, then even if the information exchange had restrictive effects on competition within the meaning of Article 101(1), the agreement would be more likely to meet the criteria of Article 101(3) than if the exchange went beyond what was necessary for the joint production. In this case the efficiency gains stemming from producing jointly are likely to outweigh the restrictive effects of the coordination of the parties' conduct. Conversely, in the context of a production agreement the sharing of data which is not necessary for producing jointly, for example the exchange of information related to prices and sales, is less likely to fulfil the conditions of Article 101(3).

4.4. Assessment under Article 101(3)

4.4.1. Efficiency gains

183. Production agreements can be pro-competitive if they provide efficiency gains in the form of cost savings or better production technologies. By producing together companies can save costs that otherwise they would duplicate. They can also produce at lower costs if the co-operation enables them to increase production where marginal costs decline with output, that is to say, by economies of scale. Producing jointly can also help companies to improve product quality if they put together their complementary skills and know-how. Co-operation can also enable companies to increase product variety, which they could not have afforded, or would not have been able to achieve, otherwise. If joint production allows the parties to increase the number of different types of products, it can also provide cost savings by means of economies of scope.

4.4.2. Indispensability

184. Restrictions that go beyond what is necessary to achieve the efficiency gains generated by a production agreement do not fulfil the criteria of Article 101(3). For instance, restrictions imposed in a production agreement on the parties' competitive conduct with regard to output outside the co-operation will normally not be considered to be indispensable. Similarly, setting prices jointly will not be considered indispensable if the production agreement does not also involve joint commercialisation.

4.4.3. Pass-on to consumers

185. Efficiency gains attained by indispensable restrictions need to be passed on to consumers in the form of lower prices or better product quality or variety to an extent that outweighs the restrictive effects on competition. Efficiency gains that only benefit the parties or cost savings that are caused by output reduction or market allocation are not sufficient to meet the criteria of Article 101(3). If the parties to the production agreement achieve savings in their variable costs they are more likely to pass them on to consumers than if they reduce their fixed costs. Moreover, the higher the market power of the parties, the less likely they will pass on the efficiency gains to consumers to an extent that would outweigh the restrictive effects on competition.

4.4.4. No elimination of competition

186. The criteria of Article 101(3) cannot be met if the parties are afforded the possibility of eliminating competition in respect of a substantial part of the products in question. This has to be analysed in the relevant market to which the products subject to the co-operation belong and in any possible spill-over markets.

4.5. Examples

187. *Commonality of costs and collusive outcomes*
Example 1
Situation: Companies A and B, two suppliers of a product X decide to close their current old production plants and build a larger, modern and more efficient production plant run by a joint venture, which will have a higher capacity than the total capacity of the old plants of Companies A and B. No other such investments are planned by competitors, which are using their facilities at full capacity. Companies A and B have market shares of 20 % and 25 % respectively. Their products are the closest substitutes in a specific segment of the market, which is concentrated. The market is transparent and rather stagnant, there is no entry and the market shares have been stable over time. Production costs constitute a major part of Company A and Company B's variable costs for product X. Commercialisation is a minor economic activity in terms of costs and strategic importance compared to production: marketing costs are low as product X is homogenous and established and transport is not a key driver of competition.

Analysis: If Companies A and B share all or most of their variable costs, this production agreement could lead to a direct limitation of competition between them. It may lead the parties to limit the output of the joint venture compared to what they would have brought to the market if each of them had decided their output on their own. In the light of the capacity constraints of the competitors this reduction output could lead to higher prices.

Even if Companies A and B were not sharing most of their variable costs, but only a significant part thereof, this production agreement could lead to a collusive outcome between Companies A and B, thereby indirectly eliminating competition between the two parties. The likelihood of this depends not only on the issue of commonality of costs (which are high in this case) but also on the characteristics of the relevant market such as, for example, transparency, stability and level of concentration.

In either of the two situations mentioned above, it is likely, in the market configuration of this example, that the production joint venture of Companies A and B would give rise to restrictive effects on competition within the meaning of Article 101(1) on the market of X.

The replacement of two smaller old production plants by the larger, modern and more efficient one may lead the joint venture to increase output at lower prices to the benefits of consumers. However, the production agreement could only meet the criteria of Article 101(3) if the parties provided substantiated evidence that the efficiency gains would be passed on to consumers to such an extent that they would outweigh the restrictive effects on competition.

188. *Links between competitors and collusive outcomes*
Example 2
Situation: Two suppliers, Companies A and B, form a production joint venture with respect to product Y. Companies A and B each have a 15 % market share on the market for Y. There are 3 other players on the market: Company C with a market share of 30 %, Company D with 25 % and Company E with 15 %. Company B already has a joint production plant with Company D.

Analysis: The market is characterised by very few players and rather symmetric structures. Co-operation between Companies A and B would add an additional link in the market, de facto increasing the concentration in the market, as it would also link Company D to Companies A and B. This co-operation is likely to increase the risk of a collusive outcome and thereby likely to give rise to restrictive effects on competition within the meaning of Article 101(1). The criteria of Article 101(3) could only be fulfilled in the presence of significant efficiency gains which are passed on to consumers to such an extent that they would outweigh the restrictive effects on competition.

189. *Anti-competitive foreclosure on a downstream market*
Example 3
Situation: Companies A and B set up a production joint venture for the intermediate product X which covers their entire production of X. The production costs of X account for 70 % of the variable costs of the final product Y with respect to which Companies A and B compete downstream. Companies A and B each have a share of 20 % on the market for Y, there is limited entry and the market shares have been stable over time. In addition to covering their own demand for X, both Companies A and B each have a market share of 40 % on the market for X. There are high barriers to entry on the market for X and existing producers are operating near full capacity. On the market for Y, there are two other significant suppliers, each with a 15 % market share, and several smaller competitors. This agreement generates economies of scale.

Analysis: By virtue of the production joint venture, Companies A and B would be able to largely control supplies of the essential input X to their competitors in the market for Y. This would give Companies A and B the ability to raise their rivals' costs by artificially increasing the price of X, or by reducing the output. This could foreclose the competitors of Companies A and B in market for Y. Because of the likely anti-competitive foreclosure downstream, this agreement is likely to give rise to restrictive effects on competition within the meaning of Article 101(1). The economies of scale generated by the production joint venture are unlikely to outweigh the restrictive effects on competition and therefore this agreement would most likely not meet the criteria of Article 101(3).

190. *Specialisation agreement as market allocation*
Example 4
Situation: Companies A and B each manufacture both products X and Y. Company A's market share of X is 30 % and of Y 10 %. B's market share of X is 10 % and of Y 30 %. To obtain economies of scale they conclude a reciprocal specialisation agreement under which Company A will only produce X and Company B only Y. They do not cross-supply the products to each other so that Company A only sells X and Company B sells only Y. The parties claim that by specialising

in this way they save costs due to the economies of scale and by focusing on only one product will improve their production technologies, which will lead to better quality products.

Analysis: With regard to its effects on competition in the market, this specialisation agreement is close to a hardcore cartel where parties allocate the market among themselves. Therefore, this agreement restricts competition by object. Because the claimed efficiencies in the form of economies of scale and improving production technology are only linked to the market allocation, they are unlikely to outweigh the restrictive effects, and therefore the agreement would not meet the criteria of Article 101(3). In any event, if Company A or B believes that it would be more efficient to focus on only one product, it can simply take the unilateral decision to only produce X or Y without at the same time agreeing that the other company will focus on producing the respective other product.

The analysis would be different if Companies A and B supplied each other with the product they focus on so that they both continue to sell X and Y. In such a case Companies A and B could still compete on price on both markets, especially if production costs (which become common through the production agreement) did not constitute a major share of the variable costs of their products. The relevant costs in this context are the commercialisation costs. Hence, the specialisation agreement would be unlikely to restrict competition if X and Y were largely heterogeneous products with a very high proportion of marketing and distribution costs (for example, 65-70 % or more of total costs). In such a scenario the risks of a collusive outcome would not be high and the criteria of Article 101(3) may be fulfilled, provided that the efficiency gains would be passed on to consumers to such an extent that they would outweigh the restrictive effects on competition of the agreement.

191. *Potential competitors*
Example 5
Situation: Company A produces final product X and Company B produces final product Y. X and Y constitute two separate product markets, in which Companies A and B respectively have strong market power. Both companies use Z as an input for their production of X and Y and they both produce Z for captive use only. X is a low added value product for which Z is an essential input (X is quite a simple transformation of Z). Y is a high value added product, for which Z is one of many inputs (Z constitutes a small part of variable costs of Y). Companies A and B agree to jointly produce Z, which generates modest economies of scale.

Analysis: Companies A and B are not actual competitors with regard to X, Y or Z. However, since X is a simple transformation of input Z, it is likely that Company B could easily enter the market for X and thus challenge Company A's position on that market. The joint production agreement with regard to Z might reduce Company B's incentives to do so as the joint production might be used for side payments and limit the probability of Company B selling product X (as Company A is likely to have control over the quantity of Z purchased by Company B from the joint venture). However, the probability of Company B entering the market for X in the absence of the agreement depends on the expected profitability of the entry. As X is a low added value product, entry might not be profitable and thus entry by Company B could be unlikely in the absence of the agreement. Given that Companies A and B already have market power, the agreement is likely to give rise to restrictive effects on competition within the meaning of Article 101(1) if the agreement does indeed decrease the likelihood of entry of Company B into Company A's market, that is to say, the market for X. The efficiency gains in the form of economies of scale generated by the agreement are modest and therefore unlikely to outweigh the restrictive effects on competition.

192. *Information exchange in a production agreement*
Example 6
Situation: Companies A and B with high market power decide to produce together to become more efficient. In the context of this agreement they secretly exchange information about their future prices. The agreement does not cover joint distribution.

Analysis: This information exchange makes a collusive outcome likely and is therefore likely have as its object the restriction of competition within the meaning of Article 101(1). It would be unlikely to meet the criteria of Article 101(3) because the sharing of information about the parties' future prices is not indispensable for producing jointly and attaining the corresponding cost savings.

193. *Swaps and information exchange*
Example 7
Situation: Companies A and B both produce Z, a commodity chemical. Z is a homogenous product which is manufactured according to a European standard which does not allow for any product variations. Production costs are a significant cost factor regarding Z. Company A has a market share of 20 % and Company B of 25 % on the Union-wide market for Z. There are four other manufacturers on the market for Z, with respective market shares of 20 %, 15 %, 10 % and 10 %. The production plant of Company A is located in Member State X in northern Europe whereas the production plant of Company B is located in Member State Y in southern Europe. Even though the majority of Company A's customers are located in northern Europe, Company A also has a number of customers in southern Europe. The majority of Company B's customers are in southern Europe, although it also has a number of customers located in northern Europe. Currently, Company A provides its southern European customers with Z manufactured in its production plant in Member State X and transports it to southern Europe by truck. Similarly, Company B provides its northern European customers with Z manufactured in Member State Y and transports it to northern Europe by truck. Transport costs are quite high, but not so high as to make the deliveries by Company A to southern Europe and Company B to northern Europe unprofitable. Transport costs from Member State X to southern Europe are lower than from Member State Y to northern Europe.

Companies A and B decide that it would be more efficient if Company A stopped transporting Z from Member State X to southern Europe and if Company B stopped transporting the Z from Member State Y to northern Europe although, at the same time, they are keen on retaining their customers. To do so, Companies A and B intend to enter into a swap agreement which allows them to purchase an agreed annual quantity of Z from the other party's plant with a view to selling the purchased Z to those of their customers which are located closer to the other party's plant. In order to calculate a purchase price which does not favour one party over the other and which takes due account of the parties' different production costs and different savings on transport costs, and in order to ensure that both parties can achieve an appropriate margin, they agree to disclose to each other their main costs with regard to Z (that is to say, production costs and transport costs).

Analysis: The fact that Companies A and B – who are competitors – swap parts of their production does not in itself give rise to competition concerns. However, the envisaged swap agreement between Companies A and B provides for the exchange of both parties' production and transport costs with regard to Z. Moreover, Companies A and B have a strong combined market position in a fairly concentrated market for a homogenous commodity product. Therefore, due to the extensive information exchange on a key parameter of competition with regard to Z, it is likely that the swap agreement between Companies A and B will give rise to restrictive effects on competition within the meaning of Article 101(1) as it can lead to a collusive outcome. Even though the agreement will give rise to significant efficiency gains in the form of cost savings for the parties, the restrictions on competition generated by the agreement are not indispensable for their attainment. The parties could achieve similar cost savings by agreeing on a price formula which does not entail the disclosure of their production and transport costs. Consequently, in its current form the swap agreement does not fulfil the criteria of Article 101(3).

5. PURCHASING AGREEMENTS

5.1. Definition

194. This chapter focuses on agreements concerning the joint purchase of products. Joint purchasing can be carried out by a jointly controlled company, by a company in which many other companies hold non-controlling stakes, by a contractual arrangement or by even looser forms of co-operation (collectively referred to as «joint purchasing arrangements»). Joint purchasing arrangements usually aim at the creation of buying power which can lead to lower prices or better quality products or services for consumers. However, buying power may, under certain circumstances, also give rise to competition concerns.

195. Joint purchasing arrangements may involve both horizontal and vertical agreements. In these cases a two-step analysis is necessary. First, the horizontal agreements between the companies engaging in joint purchasing have to be assessed according to the principles described in these guidelines. If that assessment leads to the conclusion that the joint purchasing arrangement does not give rise to competition concerns, a further assessment will be necessary to examine the relevant vertical agreements. The latter assessment will follow the rules of the Block Exemption Regulation on Vertical Restraints and the Guidelines on Vertical Restraints.

196. A common form of joint purchasing arrangement is an «alliance», that is to say an association of undertakings formed by a group of retailers for the joint purchasing of products. Horizontal agreements concluded between the members of the alliance or decisions adopted by the alliance first have to be assessed as a horizontal co-operation agreement according to these guidelines. Only if that assessment does not reveal any competition concerns does it become relevant to assess the relevant vertical agreements between the alliance and an individual member thereof and between the alliance and suppliers. Those agreements are covered – subject to certain conditions – by the Block Exemption Regulation on Vertical Restraints. Vertical agreements not covered by that Block Exemption Regulation are not presumed to be illegal but require individual examination.

5.2. Relevant markets

197. There are two markets which may be affected by joint purchasing arrangements. First, the market or markets with which the joint purchasing arrangement is directly concerned, that is to say, the relevant purchasing market or markets. Secondly, the selling market or markets, that is to say, the market or markets downstream where the parties to the joint purchasing arrangement are active as sellers.

198. The definition of relevant purchasing markets follows the principles described in the Market Definition Notice and is based on the concept of substitutability to identify competitive constraints. The only difference from the definition of «selling markets» is that substitutability has to be defined from the viewpoint of supply and not from the viewpoint of demand. In other words, the suppliers' alternatives are decisive in identifying the competitive constraints on purchasers. Those alternatives could be analysed, for instance, by examining the suppliers' reaction to a small but non-transitory price decrease. Once the market is defined, the market share can be calculated as the percentage of the purchases by the parties out of the total sales of the purchased product or products in the relevant market.

199. If the parties are, in addition, competitors on one or more selling markets, those markets are also relevant for the assessment. The selling markets have to be defined by applying the methodology described in the Market Definition Notice.

5.3. Assessment under Article 101(1)

5.3.1. Main competition concerns

200. Joint purchasing arrangements may lead to restrictive effects on competition on the purchasing and/or downstream selling market or markets, such as increased prices, reduced output, product quality or variety, or innovation, market allocation, or anti-competitive foreclosure of other possible purchasers.

201. If downstream competitors purchase a significant part of their products together, their incentives for price competition on the selling market or markets may be considerably reduced. If the parties have a significant degree of market power (which does not necessarily amount to dominance) on the selling market or markets, the lower purchase prices achieved by the joint purchasing arrangement are likely not to be passed on to consumers.

202. If the parties have a significant degree of market power on the purchasing market (buying power) there is a risk that they may force suppliers to reduce the range or quality of products they produce, which may bring about restrictive effects on competition such as quality reductions, lessening of innovation efforts, or ultimately sub-optimal supply.

203. Buying power of the parties to the joint purchasing arrangement could be used to foreclose competing purchasers by limiting their access to efficient suppliers. This is most likely if there are a limited number of suppliers and there are barriers to entry on the supply side of the upstream market.

204. In general, however, joint purchasing arrangements are less likely to give rise to competition concerns when the parties do not have market power on the selling market or markets.

5.3.2. Restrictions of competition by object

205. Joint purchasing arrangements restrict competition by object if they do not truly concern joint purchasing, but serve as a tool to engage in a disguised cartel, that is to say, otherwise prohibited price fixing, output limitation or market allocation.

206. Agreements which involve the fixing of purchase prices can have the object of restricting competition within the meaning of Article 101(1) (93). However, this does not apply where the parties to a joint purchasing arrangement agree on the purchasing prices the joint purchasing arrangement may pay to its suppliers for the products subject to the supply contract. In that case an assessment is required as to whether the agreement is likely to give rise to restrictive effects on competition within the meaning of Article 101(1). In both scenarios the agreement on purchase prices will not be assessed separately, but in the light of the overall effects of the purchasing agreement on the market.

(93) See Article 101(1)(a); Joined Cases T-217/03 and T-245/03, *French Beef*, paragraphs 83 *et seq.*; Case C-8/08, *T-Mobile Netherlands*, paragraph 37.

5.3.3. Restrictive effects on competition

207. Joint purchasing arrangements which do not have as their object the restriction of competition must be analysed in their legal and economic context with regard to their actual and likely effects on competition. The analysis of the restrictive effects on competition generated by a joint purchasing arrangement must cover the negative effects on both the purchasing and the selling markets.

Market power

208. There is no absolute threshold above which it can be presumed that the parties to a joint purchasing arrangement have market power so that the joint purchasing arrangement is likely to give rise to restrictive effects on competition within the meaning of Article 101(1). However, in most cases it is unlikely that market power exists if the parties to the joint purchasing arrangement have a combined market share not exceeding 15 % on the purchasing market or markets as well as a combined market share not exceeding 15 % on the selling market or markets. In any event, if the parties' combined market shares do not exceed 15 % on both the purchasing and the selling market or markets, it is likely that the conditions of Article 101(3) are fulfilled.

209. A market share above that threshold in one or both markets does not automatically indicate that the joint purchasing arrangement is likely to give rise to restrictive effects on competition. A joint purchasing arrangement which does not fall within that safe harbour requires a detailed assessment of its effects on the market involving, but not limited to, factors such as market concentration and possible countervailing power of strong suppliers.

210. Buying power may, under certain circumstances, cause restrictive effects on competition. Anti-competitive buying power is likely to arise if a joint purchasing arrangement accounts for a sufficiently large proportion of the total volume of a purchasing market so that access to the market may be foreclosed to competing purchasers. A high degree of buying power may indirectly affect the output, quality and variety of products on the selling market.

211. In the analysis of whether the parties to a joint purchasing arrangement have buying power, the number and intensity of links (for example, other purchasing agreements) between the competitors in the market are relevant.

212. If, however, competing purchasers co-operate who are not active on the same relevant selling market (for example, retailers which are active in different geographic markets and cannot be regarded as potential competitors), the joint purchasing arrangement is unlikely to have restrictive effects on competition unless the parties have a position in the purchasing markets that is likely to be used to harm the competitive position of other players in their respective selling markets.

Collusive outcome

213. Joint purchasing arrangements may lead to a collusive outcome if they facilitate the coordination of the parties' behaviour on the selling market. This can be the case if the parties achieve a high degree of commonality of costs through joint purchasing, provided the parties have market power and the market characteristics are conducive to coordination.

214. Restrictive effects on competition are more likely if the parties to the joint purchasing arrangement have a significant proportion of their variable costs in the relevant downstream market in common. This is, for instance, the case if retailers, which are active in the same relevant retail market or markets, jointly purchase a significant amount of the products they offer for resale. It may also be the case if competing manufacturers and sellers of a final product jointly purchase a high proportion of their input together.

215. The implementation of a joint purchasing arrangement may require the exchange of commercially sensitive information such as purchase prices and volumes. The exchange of such information may facilitate coordination with regard to sales prices and output and thus lead to a collusive outcome on the selling markets. Spill-over effects from the exchange of commercially sensitive information can, for example, be minimised where data is collated by a joint purchasing arrangement which does not pass on the information to the parties thereto.

216. Any negative effects arising from the exchange of information will not be assessed separately but in the light of the overall effects of the agreement. Whether the exchange of information in the context of a joint purchasing arrangement is likely to lead to restrictive effects on competition should be assessed according to the guidance given in Chapter 2. If the information exchange does not exceed the sharing of data necessary for the joint purchasing of the products by the parties to the joint purchasing arrangement, then even if the information exchange has restrictive effects on competition within the meaning of Article 101(1), the agreement is more likely to meet the criteria of Article 101(3) than if the exchange goes beyond what was necessary for the joint purchasing.

5.4. Assessment under Article 101(3)

5.4.1. Efficiency gains

217. Joint purchasing arrangements can give rise to significant efficiency gains. In particular, they can lead to cost savings such as lower purchase prices or reduced transaction, transportation and storage costs, thereby facilitating economies of scale. Moreover, joint purchasing arrangements may give rise to qualitative efficiency gains by leading suppliers to innovate and introduce new or improved products on the markets.

5.4.2. Indispensability

218. Restrictions that go beyond what is necessary to achieve the efficiency gains generated by a purchasing agreement do not meet the criteria of Article 101(3). An obligation to purchase exclusively through the co-operation may, in certain cases, be indispensable to achieve the necessary volume for the realisation of economies of scale. However, such an obligation has to be assessed in the context of the individual case.

5.4.3. Pass-on to consumers

219. Efficiency gains, such as cost efficiencies or qualitative efficiencies in the form of the introduction of new or improved products on the market, attained by indispensable restrictions must be passed on to consumers to an extent that outweighs the restrictive effects of competition caused by the joint purchasing arrangement. Hence, cost savings or other efficiencies that only benefit the parties to the joint purchasing arrangement will not suffice. Cost savings need to be passed on to consumers, that is to say, the parties' customers. To take a notable example, this pass-on may occur through lower prices on the selling markets. Lower purchasing prices resulting from the mere exercise of buying power are not likely to be passed on to consumers if the purchasers together have market power on the selling markets, and thus do not meet the criteria of Article 101(3). Moreover, the higher the market power of the parties on the selling market or markets the less likely they will pass on the efficiency gains to consumers to an extent that would outweigh the restrictive effects on competition.

5.4.4. No elimination of competition

220. The criteria of Article 101(3) cannot be fulfilled if the parties are afforded the possibility of eliminating competition in respect of a substantial part of the products in question. That assessment has to cover both purchasing and selling markets.

5.5. Examples

221. *Joint purchasing by small companies with moderate combined market shares*
Example 1
Situation: 150 small retailers conclude an agreement to form a joint purchasing organisation. They are obliged to purchase a minimum volume through the organisation, which accounts for roughly 50 % of each retailer's total costs. The retailers can purchase more than the minimum volume through the organisation, and they may also purchase outside the co-operation. They have a combined market share of 23 % on both the purchasing and the selling markets. Company A and Company B are their two large competitors. Company A has a 25 % share on both the purchasing and selling markets, Company B 35 %. There are no barriers which would prevent the remaining smaller competitors from also forming a purchasing group. The 150 retailers achieve substantial cost savings by virtue of purchasing jointly through the purchasing organisation.

Analysis: The retailers have a moderate market position on the purchasing and the selling markets. Furthermore, the co-operation brings about some economies of scale. Even though the retailers achieve a high degree of commonality of costs, they are unlikely to have market power on the selling market due to the market presence of Companies A and B, which are both individually larger than the joint purchasing organisation. Consequently, the retailers are unlikely to coordinate their behaviour and reach a collusive outcome. The formation of the joint purchasing organisation is therefore unlikely to give rise to restrictive effects on competition within the meaning of Article 101(1).

222. *Commonality of costs and market power on the selling market*
Example 2
Situation: Two supermarket chains conclude an agreement to jointly purchase products which account for roughly 80 % of their variable costs. On the relevant purchasing markets for the different categories of products the parties have combined market shares between 25 % and 40 %. On the relevant selling market they have a combined market share of 60 %. There are four other significant retailers each with a 10 % market share. Market entry is not likely.

Analysis: It is likely that this purchasing agreement would give the parties the ability to coordinate their behaviour on the selling market, thereby leading to a collusive outcome. The parties have market power on the selling market and the purchasing agreement gives rise to a significant commonality of costs. Moreover, market entry is unlikely. The incentive for the parties to coordinate their behaviour would be reinforced if their cost structures were already similar prior to concluding the agreement. Moreover, similar margins of the parties would further increase the risk of a collusive outcome. This agreement also creates the risk that by the parties' withholding demand and, consequently, as a result of reduced quantity, downstream selling prices would increase. Hence, the purchasing agreement is likely to give rise to restrictive effects on competition within the meaning of Article 101(1). Even though the agreement is very likely to give rise to efficiency gains in the form of cost savings, due to the parties' significant market power on the selling market, these are unlikely to be passed on to consumers to an extent that would outweigh the restrictive effects on competition. Therefore, the purchasing agreement is unlikely to fulfil the criteria of Article 101(3).

223. *Parties active in different geographic markets*
Example 3
Situation: Six large retailers, which are each based in a different Member State, form a purchasing group to buy several branded durum wheat flour-based products jointly. The parties are allowed to purchase other similar branded products outside the co-operation. Moreover, five of them also offer similar private label products. The members of the purchasing group have a combined market

share of approximately 22 % on the relevant purchasing market, which is Union-wide. In the purchasing market there are three other large players of similar size. Each of the parties to the purchasing group has a market share between 20 % and 30 % on the national selling markets on which they are active. None of them is active in a Member State where another member of the group is active. The parties are not potential entrants to each other's markets.

Analysis: The purchasing group will be able to compete with the other existing major players on the purchasing market. The selling markets are much smaller (in turnover and geographic scope) than the Union-wide purchasing market and in those markets some of the members of the group may have market power. Even if the members of the purchasing group have a combined market share of more than 15 % on the purchasing market, the parties are unlikely to coordinate their conduct and collude on the selling markets since they are neither actual nor potential competitors on the downstream markets. Consequently, the purchasing group is not likely to give rise to restrictive effects on competition within the meaning of Article 101(1).

224. Information exchange
Example 4
Situation: Three competing manufacturers A, B and C entrust an independent joint purchasing organisation with the purchase of product Z, which is an intermediary product used by the three parties for their production of the final product X. The costs of Z are not a significant cost factor for the production of X. The joint purchasing organisation does not compete with the parties on the selling market for X. All information necessary for the purchases (for example quality specifications, quantities, delivery dates, maximum purchase prices) is only disclosed to the joint purchasing organisation, not to the other parties. The joint purchasing organisation agrees the purchasing prices with the suppliers. A, B and C have a combined market share of 30 % on each of the purchasing and selling markets. They have six competitors in the purchasing and selling markets, two of which have a market share of 20 %.

Analysis: Since there is no direct information exchange between the parties, the transfer of the information necessary for the purchases to the joint purchasing organisation is unlikely to lead to a collusive outcome. Consequently, the exchange of information is unlikely to give rise to restrictive effects on competition within the meaning of Article 101(1).

6. AGREEMENTS ON COMMERCIALISATION

6.1. Definition

225. Commercialisation agreements involve co-operation between competitors in the selling, distribution or promotion of their substitute products. This type of agreement can have widely varying scope, depending on the commercialisation functions which are covered by the co-operation. At one end of the spectrum, joint selling agreements may lead to a joint determination of all commercial aspects related to the sale of the product, including price. At the other end, there are more limited agreements that only address one specific commercialisation function, such as distribution, after-sales service, or advertising.

226. An important category of those more limited agreements is distribution agreements. The Block Exemption Regulation on Vertical Restraints and Guidelines on Vertical Restraints generally cover distribution agreements unless the parties to the agreement are actual or potential competitors. If the parties are competitors, the Block Exemption Regulation on Vertical Restraints only covers non-reciprocal vertical agreements between competitors, if *(a)* the supplier is a manufacturer and a distributor of goods, while the buyer is a distributor and not a competing undertaking at the manufacturing level or; *(b)* the supplier is a provider of services at several levels of trade, while the buyer provides its goods or services at the retail level and does not provide competing services at the level of trade where it purchases the contract services (94).

(94) Article 2(4) of the Block Exemption Regulation on Vertical Restraints.

227. If competitors agree to distribute their substitute products on a reciprocal basis (in particular if they do so on different geographic markets) there is a possibility in certain cases that the agreements have as their object or effect the partitioning of markets between the parties or that they lead to a collusive outcome. The same can be true for non-reciprocal agreements between competitors. Reciprocal agreements and non-reciprocal agreements between competitors thus have first to be assessed according to the principles set out in this Chapter. If that assessment leads to the conclusion that co-operation between competitors in the area of distribution would in principle be acceptable, a further assessment will be necessary to examine the vertical restraints included in such agreements. That second step of the assessment should be based on the principles set out in the Guidelines on Vertical Restraints.

228. A further distinction should be drawn between agreements where the parties agree only on joint commercialisation and agreements where the commercialisation is related to another type of co-operation upstream, such as joint production or joint purchasing. When analysing commercialisation agreements combining different stages of co-operation it is necessary to determine the centre of gravity of the co-operation in accordance with paragraphs 13 and 14.

6.2. Relevant markets

229. To assess the competitive relationship between the parties, the relevant product and geographic market or markets directly concerned by the co-operation (that is to say, the market or markets to which the products subject to the agreement belong) have to be defined. As a commercialisation agreement in one market may also affect the competitive behaviour of the parties in a neighbouring market which is closely related to the market directly concerned by the co-operation, any such neighbouring market also needs to be defined. The neighbouring market may be horizontally or vertically related to the market where the co-operation takes place.

6.3. Assessment under Article 101(1)

6.3.1. Main competition concerns

230. Commercialisation agreements can lead to restrictions of competition in several ways. First, and most obviously, commercialisation agreements may lead to price fixing.

231. Secondly, commercialisation agreements may also facilitate output limitation, because the parties may decide on the volume of products to be put on the market, therefore restricting supply.

232. Thirdly, commercialisation agreements may become a means for the parties to divide the markets or to allocate orders or customers, for example in cases where the parties' production plants are located in different geographic markets or when the agreements are reciprocal.

233. Finally, commercialisation agreements may also lead to an exchange of strategic information relating to aspects within or outside the scope of the co-operation or to commonality of costs – in particular with regard to agreements not encompassing price fixing – which may result in a collusive outcome.

6.3.2. Restrictions of competition by object

234. Price fixing is one of the major competition concerns arising from commercialisation agreements between competitors. Agreements limited to joint selling generally have the object of coordinating the pricing policy of competing manufacturers or service providers. Such agreements may not only eliminate price competition between the parties on substitute products but may also restrict the total volume of products to be delivered by the parties within the framework of a system for allocating orders. Such agreements are therefore likely to restrict competition by object.

235. That assessment does not change if the agreement is non-exclusive (that is to say, where the parties are free to sell individually outside the agreement), as long as it can be concluded that the agreement will lead to an overall coordination of the prices charged by the parties.

236. Another specific competition concern related to distribution arrangements between parties which are active in different geographic markets is that they can be an instrument of market partitioning. If the parties use a reciprocal distribution agreement to distribute each other's products in order to eliminate actual or potential competition between them by deliberately allocating markets or customers, the agreement is likely to have as its object a restriction of competition. If the agreement is not reciprocal, the risk of market partitioning is less pronounced. It is necessary, however, to assess whether the non-reciprocal agreement constitutes the basis for a mutual understanding to avoid entering each other's markets.

6.3.3. Restrictive effects on competition

237. A commercialisation agreement is normally not likely to give rise to competition concerns if it is objectively necessary to allow one party to enter a market it could not have entered individually or with a more limited number of parties than are effectively taking part in the co-operation, for example, because of the costs involved. A specific application of this principle would be consortia arrangements that allow the companies involved to participate in projects that they would not be able to undertake individually. As the parties to the consortia arrangement are therefore not potential competitors for implementing the project, there is no restriction of competition within the meaning of Article 101(1).

238. Similarly, not all reciprocal distribution agreements have as their object a restriction of competition. Depending on the facts of the case at hand, some reciprocal distribution agreements may, nevertheless, have restrictive effects on competition. The key issue in assessing an agreement of this type is whether the agreement in question is objectively necessary for the parties to enter each other's markets. If it is, the agreement does not create competition problems of a horizontal nature. However, if the agreement reduces the decision-making independence of one of the parties with regard to entering the other parties' market or markets by limiting its incentives to do so, it is likely to give rise to restrictive effects on competition. The same reasoning applies to non-reciprocal agreements, where the risk of restrictive effects on competition is, however, less pronounced.

239. Moreover, a distribution agreement can have restrictive effects on competition if it contains vertical restraints, such as restrictions on passive sales, resale price maintenance, etc.

Market power

240. Commercialisation agreements between competitors can only have restrictive effects on competition if the parties have some degree of market power. In most cases, it is unlikely that market power exists if the parties to the agreement have a combined market share not exceeding 15 %. In any event, if the parties' combined market share does not exceed 15 % it is likely that the conditions of Article 101(3) are fulfilled.

241. If the parties' combined market share is greater than 15 %, their agreement will fall outside the safe harbour of paragraph 240 and thus the likely impact of the joint commercialisation agreement on the market must be assessed.

Collusive outcome

242. A joint commercialisation agreement that does not involve price fixing is also likely to give rise to restrictive effects on competition if it increases the parties' commonality of variable costs to a level which is likely to lead to a collusive outcome. This is likely to be the case for a joint commercialisation agreement if prior to the agreement the parties already have a high proportion of their variable costs in common as the additional increment (that is to say, the commercialisation costs of the product subject to the agreement) can tip the balance towards a collusive outcome. Conversely, if the increment is large, the risk of a collusive outcome may be high even if the initial level of commonality of costs is low.

243. The likelihood of a collusive outcome depends on the parties' market power and the characteristics of the relevant market. Commonality of costs can only increase the risk of a collusive outcome if the parties have market power and if the commercialisation costs constitute a large proportion of the variable costs related to the products concerned. This is, for example, not the case for homogeneous products for which the highest cost factor is production. However, commonality of commercialisation costs increases the risk of a collusive outcome if the commercialisation agreement concerns products which entail costly commercialisation, for example, high distribution or marketing costs. Consequently, joint advertising or joint promotion agreements can also give rise to restrictive effects on competition if those costs constitute a significant cost factor.

244. Joint commercialisation generally involves the exchange of sensitive commercial information, particularly on marketing strategy and pricing. In most commercialisation agreements, some degree of information exchange is required in order to implement the agreement. It is therefore necessary to verify whether the information exchange can give rise to a collusive outcome with regard to the parties' activities within and outside the co-operation. Any negative effects arising from the exchange of information will not be assessed separately but in the light of the overall effects of the agreement.

245. For example, where the parties to a joint advertising agreement exchange pricing information, this may lead to a collusive outcome with regard to the sale of the jointly advertised products. In any event, the exchange of such information in the context of a joint advertising agreement goes beyond what would be necessary to implement that agreement. The likely restrictive effects on competition of information exchange in the context of commercialisation agreements will depend on the characteristics of the market and the data shared, and should be assessed in the light of the guidance given in Chapter 2.

6.4. Assessment under Article 101(3)

6.4.1. Efficiency gains

246. Commercialisation agreements can give rise to significant efficiency gains. The efficiencies to be taken into account when assessing whether a commercialisation agreement fulfils the criteria of Article 101(3) will depend on the nature of the activity and the parties to the co-operation. Price fixing can generally not be justified, unless it is indispensable for the integration of other marketing functions, and this integration will generate substantial efficiencies. Joint distribution can generate significant efficiencies, stemming from economies of scale or scope, especially for smaller producers.

247. In addition, the efficiency gains must not be savings which result only from the elimination of costs that are inherently part of competition, but must result from the integration of economic activities. A reduction of transport cost which is only a result of customer allocation without any integration of the logistical system can therefore not be regarded as an efficiency gain within the meaning of Article 101(3).

248. Efficiency gains must be demonstrated by the parties to the agreement. An important element in this respect would be the contribution by the parties of significant capital, technology, or other assets. Cost savings through reduced duplication of resources and facilities can also be accepted. However, if the joint commercialisation represents no more than a sales agency without any investment, it is likely to be a disguised cartel and as such unlikely to fulfil the conditions of Article 101(3).

6.4.2. Indispensability

249. Restrictions that go beyond what is necessary to achieve the efficiency gains generated by a commercialisation agreement do not fulfil the criteria of Article 101(3). The question of indispensability is especially important for those agreements involving price fixing or market allocation, which can only under exceptional circumstances be considered indispensable.

6.4.3. Pass-on to consumers

250. Efficiency gains attained by indispensable restrictions must be passed on to consumers to an extent that outweighs the restrictive effects on competition caused by the commercialisation agreement. This can happen in the form of lower prices or better product quality or variety. The higher the market power of the parties, however, the less likely it is that efficiency gains will be passed on to consumers to an extent that outweighs the restrictive effects on competition. Where the parties have a combined market share of below 15 %, it is likely that any demonstrated efficiency gains generated by the agreement will be sufficiently passed on to consumers.

6.4.4. No elimination of competition

251. The criteria of Article 101(3) cannot be fulfilled if the parties are afforded the possibility of eliminating competition in respect of a substantial part of the products in question. This has to be analysed in the relevant market to which the products subject to the co-operation belong and in possible spill-over markets.

6.5. Examples

252. *Joint commercialisation necessary to enter a market*
Example 1
Situation: Four companies providing laundry services in a large city close to the border of another Member State, each with a 3 % market share of the overall laundry market in that city, agree to create a joint marketing arm for the selling of laundry services to institutional customers (that is to say, hotels, hospitals and offices), whilst keeping their independence and freedom to compete for local, individual clients. In view of the new segment of demand (the institutional customers) they develop a common brand name, a common price and common standard terms including, inter alia, a maximum period of 24 hours before deliveries and schedules for delivery. They set up a common call centre where institutional clients can request their collection and/or delivery service. They hire a receptionist (for the call centre) and several drivers. They further invest in vans for dispatching, and in brand promotion, to increase their visibility. The agreement does not fully reduce their individual infrastructure costs (since they are keeping their own premises and still compete with each other for the individual local clients), but it increases their economies of scale and allows them to offer a more comprehensive service to other types of clients, which includes longer opening hours and dispatching to a wider geographic coverage. In order to ensure the viability of the project, it is indispensable that all four of them enter into the agreement. The market is very fragmented, with no individual competitor having more than 15 % market share.

Analysis: Although the joint market share of the parties is below 15 %, the fact that the agreement involves price fixing means that Article 101(1) could apply. However, the parties would not have been in a position to enter the market for providing laundry services to institutional customers, either individually or in co-operation with a fewer number of parties than the four currently taking part in the agreement. As such, the agreement would not create competition concerns, irrespective of the price-fixing restriction, which in this case can be considered as indispensable to the promotion of the common brand and the success of the project.

253. *Commercialisation agreement by more parties than necessary to enter a market*
Example 2
Situation: The same facts as in Example 1, paragraph 252, apply with one main difference: in order to

ensure the viability of the project, the agreement could have been implemented by only three of the parties (instead of the four actually taking part in the co-operation).

Analysis: Although the joint market share of the parties is below 15 %, the fact that the agreement involves price fixing and could have been carried out by fewer than the four parties means that Article 101(1) applies. The agreement thus needs to be assessed under Article 101(3). The agreement gives rise to efficiency gains as the parties are now able to offer improved services for a new category of customers on a larger scale (which they would not otherwise have been able to service individually). In the light of the parties' combined market share of below 15 %, it is likely that they will sufficiently pass-on any efficiency gains to consumers. It is further necessary to consider whether the restrictions imposed by the agreement are indispensable to achieve the efficiencies and whether the agreement eliminates competition. Given that the aim of the agreement is to provide a more comprehensive service (including dispatch, which was not offered before) to an additional category of customers, under a single brand with common standard terms, the price fixing can be considered as indispensable to the promotion of the common brand and, consequently, the success of the project and the resulting efficiencies. Additionally, taking into account the market fragmentation, the agreement will not eliminate competition. The fact that there are four parties to the agreement (instead of the three that would have been strictly necessary) allows for increased capacity and contributes to simultaneously fulfilling the demand of several institutional customers in compliance with the standard terms (that is to say, meeting maximum delivery time terms). As such, the efficiency gains are likely to outweigh the restrictive effects arising from the reduction of competition between the parties and the agreement is likely to fulfil the conditions of Article 101(3).

254. *Joint internet platform*

Example 3

Situation: A number of small specialty shops throughout a Member State join an electronic web-based platform for the promotion, sale and delivery of gift fruit baskets. There are a number of competing web-based platforms. By means of a monthly fee, they share the running costs of the platform and jointly invest in brand promotion. Through the webpage, where a wide range of different types of gift baskets are offered, customers order (and pay for) the type of gift basket they want to be delivered. The order is then allocated to the specialty shop closest to the address of delivery. The shop individually bears the costs of composing the gift basket and delivering it to the client. It reaps 90 % of the final price, which is set by the web-based platform and uniformly applies to all participating specialty shops, whilst the remaining 10 % is used for the common promotion and the running costs of the web-based platform. Apart from the payment of the monthly fee, there are no further restrictions for specialty shops to join the platform, throughout the national territory. Moreover, specialty shops having their own company website are also able to (and in some cases do) sell gift fruit baskets on the internet under their own name and thus can still compete among themselves outside the co-operation. Customers purchasing over the web-based platform are guaranteed same day delivery of the fruit baskets and they can also choose a delivery time convenient to them.

Analysis: Although the agreement is of a limited nature, since it only covers the joint selling of a particular type of product through a specific marketing channel (the web-based platform), since it involves price-fixing, it is likely to restrict competition by object. The agreement therefore needs to be assessed under Article 101(3). The agreement gives rise to efficiency gains such as greater choice and higher quality service and the reduction of search costs, which benefit consumers and are likely to outweigh the restrictive effects on competition the agreement brings about. Given that the specialty stores taking part in the co-operation are still able to operate individually and to compete one with another, both through their shops and the internet, the price-fixing restriction could be considered as indispensable for the promotion of the product (since when buying through the web-based platform consumers do not know where they are buying the gift basket from and do not want to deal with a multitude of different prices) and the ensuing efficiency gains. In the absence of other restrictions, the agreement fulfils the criteria of Article 101(3). Moreover, as other competing web-based platforms exist and the parties continue to compete with each other, through their shops or over the internet, competition will not be eliminated.

255. *Sales joint venture*

Example 4

Situation: Companies A and B, located in two different Member States, produce bicycle tyres. They have a combined market share of 14 % on the Union-wide market for bicycle tyres. They decide to set up a (non full-function) sales joint venture for marketing the tyres to bicycle producers and agree to sell all their production through the joint venture. The production and transport infrastructure remains separate within each party. The parties claim considerable efficiency gains stem from the agreement. Such gains mainly relate to increased economies of scale, being able to fulfil the demands of their existing and potential new customers and better competing with imported tyres produced in third countries. The joint venture negotiates the prices and allocates orders to the closest production plant, as a way to rationalise transport costs when further delivering to the customer.

Analysis: Even though the combined market share of the parties is below 15 %, the agreement falls under Article 101(1). It restricts competition by object since it involves customer allocation and the setting of prices by the joint venture. The claimed efficiencies deriving from the agreement do not result from the integration of economic activities or from common investment. The joint venture would have a very limited scope and would only serve as an interface for allocating orders to the production plants. It is therefore unlikely that any efficiency gains would be passed on to consumers to such an extent that they would outweigh the restrictive effects on competition brought about by the agreement. Thus, the conditions of Article 101(3) would not be fulfilled.

256. *Non-poaching clause in agreement on outsourcing of services*

Example 5

Situation: Companies A and B are competing providers of cleaning services for commercial premises. Both have a market share of 15 %. There are several other competitors with market shares between 10 and 15 %. A has taken the (unilateral) decision to only focus on large customers in the future as servicing large and small customers has proved to require a somewhat different organisation of the work. Consequently, Company A has decided to no longer enter into contracts with new small customers. In addition, Companies A and B enter into an outsourcing agreement whereby Company B would directly provide cleaning services to Company A's existing small customers (which represent 1/3 of its customer base). At the same time, Company A is keen not to lose the customer relationship with those small customers. Hence, Company A will continue to keep its contractual relationships with the small customers but the direct provision of the cleaning services will be done by Company B. In order to implement the outsourcing agreement, Company A will necessarily need to provide Company B with the identities of Company A's small customers which are subject to the agreement. As Company A is afraid that Company B may try to poach those customers by offering cheaper direct services (thereby bypassing Company a), Company A insists that the outsourcing agreement contain a «non-poaching clause». According to that clause, Company B may not contact the small customers falling under the outsourcing agreements with a view to providing direct services to them. In addition, Companies A and B agree that Company B may not even provide direct services to those customers if Company B is approached by them. Without the «non-poaching clause» Company A would not enter into an outsourcing agreement with Company B or any other company.

Analysis: The outsourcing agreement removes Company B as an independent supplier of cleaning services for Company A's small customers as they will no longer be able to enter into a direct contractual relationship with Company B. However, those customers only represent 1/3 of Company A's customer base, that is to say, 5 % of the market. They will still be able to turn to Company A and Company B's competitors, which represent 70 % of the market. Hence, the outsourcing agreement will not enable Company A to profitably raise the prices charged to the customers subject to the outsourcing agreement. In addition, the outsourcing agreement is not likely to give rise to a collusive outcome as Companies A and B only have a combined market share of 30 % and they are faced with several competitors that have market shares similar to Company A's and Company B's individual market shares. Moreover, the fact that servicing large and small customers is somewhat different minimises the risk of spill-over effects from the outsourcing agreement to Company A's and Company B's behaviour when competing for large customers. Consequently, the outsourcing agreement is not likely to give rise to restrictive effects on competition within the meaning of Article 101(1).

7. STANDARDISATION AGREEMENTS

7.1. Definition

Standardisation agreements

257. Standardisation agreements have as their primary objective the definition of technical or quality requirements with which current or future products, production processes, services or methods may comply (95). Standardisation agreements can cover various issues, such as standardisation of different grades or sizes of a particular product or technical specifications in product or services markets where compatibility and interoperability with other products or systems is essential. The terms of access to a particular quality mark or for approval by a regulatory body can also be regarded as a standard. Agreements setting out standards on the environmental performance of products or production processes are also covered by this chapter.

(95) Standardisation can take different forms, ranging from the adoption of consensus based standards by the recognised European or national standards bodies, through consortia and fora, to agreements between independent companies.

258. The preparation and production of technical standards as part of the execution of public powers are not covered by these guidelines (96). The European standardisation bodies recognised under Directive 98/34/EC of the European Parliament and of the Council of 22 June 1998 laying down a procedure for the provision of information in the field of technical standards and regulations and on rules on Information Society services (97) are subject to competition law to the extent that they can be considered to be an undertaking or an association of undertakings within the meaning of Articles 101 and 102 (98). Standards related to the provision of professional services, such as rules of admission to a liberal profession, are not covered by these guidelines.

(96) See Case C-113/07, SELEX, (2009) ECR I-2207, paragraph 92.

(97) OJ L 204, 21.7.1998, p. 37.

(98) See judgment of 12 May 2010 in Case T-432/05, *EMC Development AB v. Commission*, not yet reported.

Standard terms

259. In certain industries companies use standard terms and conditions of sale or purchase elaborated by a trade association or directly by the competing companies («standard terms») (99). Such standard terms are covered by these guidelines to the extent that they establish standard conditions of sale or purchase of goods or services between competitors and consumers (and not the conditions of sale or purchase between competitors) for substitute products. When such standard terms are widely used within an industry, the conditions of purchase or sale used in the industry may become de facto aligned (100). Examples of industries in which standard terms play an important role are the banking (for example, bank account terms) and insurance sectors.

(99) Such standard terms might cover only a very small part of the clauses contained in the final contract or a large part thereof.

(100) This refers to a situation where (legally non-binding) standard terms in practice are used by most of the industry and/or for most aspects of the product/service thus leading to a limitation or even lack of consumer choice.

260. Standard terms elaborated individually by a company solely for its own use when contracting with its suppliers or customers are not horizontal agreements and are therefore not covered by these guidelines.

7.2. Relevant markets

261. Standardisation agreements may produce their effects on four possible markets, which will be defined according to the Market Definition Notice. First, standard-setting may have an impact on the product or service market or markets to which the standard or standards relates. Second, where the standard-setting involves the selection of technology and where the rights to intellectual property are marketed separately from the products to which they relate, the standard can have effects on the relevant technology market (101). Third, the market for standard-setting may be affected if different standard-setting bodies or agreements exist. Fourth, where relevant, a distinct market for testing and certification may be affected by standard-setting.

(101) See Chapter 3 on R&D agreements.

262. As regards standard terms, the effects are, in general, felt on the downstream market where the companies using the standard terms compete by selling their product to their customers.

7.3. Assessment under Article 101(1)

7.3.1. Main competition concerns

Standardisation agreements

263. Standardisation agreements usually produce significant positive economic effects (102), for example by promoting economic interpenetration on the internal market and encouraging the development of new and improved products or markets and improved supply conditions. Standards thus normally increase competition and lower output and sales costs, benefiting economies as a whole. Standards may maintain and enhance quality, provide information and ensure interoperability and compatibility (thus increasing value for consumers).

(102) See also paragraph 308.

264. Standard-setting can, however, in specific circumstances, also give rise to restrictive effects on competition by potentially restricting price competition and limiting or controlling production, markets, innovation or technical development. This can occur through three main channels, namely reduction in price competition, foreclosure of innovative technologies and exclusion of, or discrimination against, certain companies by prevention of effective access to the standard.

265. First, if companies were to engage in anti-competitive discussions in the context of standard-setting, this could reduce or eliminate price competition in the markets concerned, thereby facilitating a collusive outcome on the market (103).

(103) Depending on the circle of participants in the standard-setting process, restrictions can occur either on the supplier or on the purchaser side of the market for the standardised product.

266. Second, standards that set detailed technical specifications for a product or service may limit technical development and innovation. While a standard is being developed, alternative technologies can compete for inclusion in the standard. Once one technology has been chosen and the standard has been set, competing technologies and companies may face a barrier to entry and may potentially be excluded from the market. In addition, standards requiring that a particular technology is used exclusively for a standard or preventing the development of other technologies by obliging the members of the standard-setting organisation to exclusively use a particular standard, may lead to the same effect. The risk of limitation of innovation is increased if one or more companies are unjustifiably excluded from the standard-setting process.

267. In the context of standards involving intellectual property rights («IPR») (104), three main groups of companies with different interests in standard-setting can be distinguished in the abstract (105). First, there are upstream-only companies that solely develop and market technologies. Their only source of income is licensing revenue and their incentive is to maximise their royalties. Secondly, there are downstream-only companies that solely manufacture products or offer services based on technologies developed by others and do not hold relevant IPR. Royalties represent a cost for them, and not a source of revenue, and their incentive is to reduce or avoid royalties. Finally, there are vertically integrated companies that both develop technology and sell products. They have mixed incentives. On the one hand, they can draw licensing revenue from their IPR. On the other hand, they may have to pay royalties to other companies holding IPR essential to the standard. They might therefore cross-license their own essential IPR in exchange for essential IPR held by other companies.

(104) In the context of this chapter IPR in particular refers to patent(s) (excluding non-published patent applications). However, in case any other type of IPR in practice gives the IPR holder control over the use of the standard the same principles should be applied.

(105) In practice, many companies use a mix of these business models.

268. Third, standardisation may lead to anti-competitive results by preventing certain companies from obtaining effective access to the results of the standard-setting process (that is to say, the specification and/or the essential IPR for implementing the standard). If a company is either completely prevented from obtaining access to the result of the standard, or is only granted access on prohibitive or discriminatory terms, there is a risk of an anti-competitive effect. A system where potentially relevant IPR is disclosed up-front may increase the likelihood of effective access being granted to the standard since it allows the participants to identify which technologies are covered by IPR and which are not. This enables the participants to both factor in the potential effect on the final price of the result of the standard (for example choosing a technology without IPR is likely to have a positive effect on the final price) and to verify with the IPR holder whether they would be willing to license if their technology is included in the standard.

269. Intellectual property laws and competition laws share the same objectives (106) of promoting innovation and enhancing consumer welfare. IPR promote dynamic competition by encouraging undertakings to invest in developing new or improved products and processes. IPR are therefore in general pro-competitive. However, by virtue of its IPR, a participant holding IPR essential for implementing the standard, could, in the specific context of standard-setting, also acquire control over the use of a standard. When the standard constitutes a barrier to entry, the company could thereby control the product or service market to which the standard relates. This in turn could allow companies to behave in anti-competitive ways, for example by «holding-up» users after the adoption of the standard either by refusing to license the necessary IPR or by extracting excess rents by way of excessive (107) royalty fees thereby preventing effective access to the standard. However, even if the establishment of a standard can create or increase the market power of IPR holders possessing IPR essential to the standard, there is no presumption that holding or exercising IPR essential to a standard equates to the possession or exercise of market power. The question of market power can only be assessed on a case by case basis.

(106) See Technology Transfer Guidelines, paragraph 7.

(107) High royalty fees can only be qualified as excessive if the conditions for an abuse of a dominant position as set out in Article 102 of the Treaty and the case-law of the Court of Justice of the European Union are fulfilled. See for example Case 27/76, *United Brands*, (1978) ECR 207.

Standard terms

270. Standard terms can give rise to restrictive effects on competition by limiting product choice and innovation. If a large part of an industry adopts the standard terms and chooses not to deviate from them in individual cases (or only deviates from them in exceptional cases of strong buyer-power), customers might have no option other than to accept the conditions in the standard terms. However, the risk of limiting choice and innovation is only likely in cases where the standard terms define the scope of the end-product. As regards classical consumer goods, standard terms of sale generally do not limit innovation of the actual product or product quality and variety.

271. In addition, depending on their content, standard terms might risk affecting the commercial conditions of the final product. In particular, there is a serious risk that standard terms relating to price would restrict price competition.

272. Moreover, if the standard terms become industry practice, access to them might be vital for entry into the market. In such cases, refusing access to the standard terms could risk causing anti-competitive foreclosure. As long as the standard terms remain effectively open for use for anyone that wishes to have access to them, they are unlikely to give rise to anti-competitive foreclosure.

7.3.2. Restrictions of competition by object

Standardisation agreements

273. Agreements that use a standard as part of a broader restrictive agreement aimed at excluding actual or potential competitors restrict competition by object. For instance, an agreement whereby a national association of manufacturers sets a standard and puts pressure on third parties not to market products that do not comply with the standard or where the producers of the incumbent product collude to exclude new technology from an already existing standard (108) would fall into this category.

(108) See for example Commission Decision in Case IV/35.691, *Pre-insulated pipes*, OJ L 24, 30.1.1999, p. 1, where part of the infringement of Article 101 consisted in «using norms and standards in order to prevent or delay the introduction of new technology which would result in price reductions» (paragraph 147).

274. Any agreements to reduce competition by using the disclosure of most restrictive licensing terms prior to the adoption of a standard as a cover to jointly fix prices either of downstream products or of substitute IPR or technology will constitute restrictions of competition by object (109).

(109) This paragraph should not prevent unilateral *ex ante* disclosures of most restrictive licensing terms as described in paragraph 299. It also does not prevent patent pools created in accordance with the principles set out in the Technology Transfer Guidelines or the decision to license IPR essential to a standard on royalty-free terms as set out in this Chapter.

Standard terms

275. Agreements that use standard terms as part of a broader restrictive agreement aimed at excluding actual or potential competitors also restrict competition by object. An example would be where a trade association does not allow a new entrant access to its standards terms, the use of which is vital to ensure entry to the market.

276. Any standard terms containing provisions which directly influence the prices charged to customers (that is to say, recommended prices, rebates, etc.) would constitute a restriction of competition by object.

7.3.3. Restrictive effects on competition

Standardisation agreements
Agreements normally not restrictive of competition

277. Standardisation agreements which do not restrict competition by object must be analysed in their legal and economic context with regard to their actual and likely effect on competition. In the absence of market power (110), a standardisation agreement is not capable of producing restrictive effects on competition. Therefore, restrictive effects are most unlikely in a situation where there is effective competition between a number of voluntary standards.

(110) See by analogy paragraph 39 *et seq.* As regards market shares see also paragraph 296.

278. For those standard-setting agreements which risk creating market power, paragraphs 280 to 286 set out the conditions under which such agreements would normally fall outside the scope of Article 101(1).

279. The non-fulfilment of any or all of the principles set out in this section will not lead to any presumption of a restriction of competition within Article 101(1). However, it will necessitate a self-assessment to establish whether the agreement falls under Article 101(1) and, if so, if the conditions of Article 101(3) are fulfilled. In this context, it is recognised that there exist different models for standard-setting and that competition within and between those models is a positive aspect of a market economy. Therefore, standard-setting organisations remain entirely free to put in place rules and procedures that do not violate competition rules whilst being different to those described in paragraphs 280 to 286.

280. Where participation in standard-setting is unrestricted and the procedure for adopting the standard in question is transparent, standardisation agreements which contain no obligation to comply (111) with the standard and provide access to the standard on fair, reasonable and non-discriminatory terms will normally not restrict competition within the meaning of Article 101(1).

(111) See also paragraph 293 in this regard.

281. In particular, to ensure unrestricted participation the rules of the standard-setting organisation would need to guarantee that all competitors in the market or markets affected by the standard can participate in the process leading to the selection of the standard. The standard-setting organisations would also need to have objective and non-discriminatory procedures for allocating voting rights as well as, if relevant, objective criteria for selecting the technology to be included in the standard.

282. With respect to transparency, the relevant standard-setting organisation would need to have procedures which allow stakeholders to effectively inform themselves of upcoming, on-going and finalised standardisation work in good time at each stage of the development of the standard.

283. Furthermore, the standard-setting organisation's rules would need to ensure effective access to the standard on fair, reasonable and non discriminatory terms (112).

(112) For example effective access should be granted to the specification of the standard.

284. In the case of a standard involving IPR, a clear and balanced IPR policy (113), adapted to the particular industry and the needs of the standard-setting organisation in question, increases the likelihood that the implementers of the standard will be granted effective access to the standards elaborated by that standard-setting organisation.

(113) As specified in paragraphs 285 and 286.

285. In order to ensure effective access to the standard, the IPR policy would need to require participants wishing to have their IPR included in the standard to provide an irrevocable commitment in writing to offer to license their essential IPR to all third parties on fair, reasonable and non-discriminatory terms («FRAND commitment») (114). That commitment should be given prior to the adoption of the standard. At the same time, the IPR policy should allow IPR holders to exclude specified technology from the standard-setting process and thereby from the commitment to offer to license, providing that exclusion takes place at an early stage in the development of the standard. To ensure the effectiveness of the FRAND commitment, there would also need to be a requirement on all participating IPR holders who provide such a commitment to ensure that any company to which the IPR owner transfers its IPR (including the right to license that IPR) is bound by that commitment, for example through a contractual clause between buyer and seller.

(114) It should be noted that FRAND can also cover royalty-free licensing.

286. Moreover, the IPR policy would need to require good faith disclosure, by participants, of their IPR that might be essential for the implementation of the standard under development. This would enable the industry to make an informed choice of technology and thereby assist in achieving the goal of effective access to the standard. Such a disclosure obligation could be based on ongoing disclosure as the standard develops and on reasonable endeavours to identify IPR reading on the potential standard (115). It is also sufficient if the participant declares that it is likely to have IPR claims over a particular technology (without identifying specific IPR claims or applications for IPR). Since the risks with regard to effective access are not the same in the case of a standard-setting organisation with a royalty-free standards policy, IPR disclosure would not be relevant in that context.

(115) To obtain the sought after result a good faith disclosure does not need to go as far as to require participants to compare their IPR against the potential standard and issue a statement positively concluding that they have no IPR reading on the potential standard.

FRAND Commitments

287. FRAND commitments are designed to ensure that essential IPR protected technology incorporated in a standard is accessible to the users of that standard on fair, reasonable and non-discriminatory terms and conditions. In particular, FRAND commitments can prevent IPR holders from making the implementation of a standard difficult by refusing to license or by requesting unfair or unreasonable fees (in other words excessive fees) after the industry has been locked-in to the standard or by charging discriminatory royalty fees.

288. Compliance with Article 101 by the standard-setting organisation does not require the standard-setting organisation to verify whether licensing terms of participants fulfil the FRAND commitment. Participants will have to assess for themselves whether the licensing terms and in particular the fees they charge fulfil the FRAND commitment. Therefore, when deciding whether to commit to FRAND for a particular IPR, participants will need to anticipate the implications of the FRAND commitment, notably on their ability to freely set the level of their fees.

289. In case of a dispute, the assessment of whether fees charged for access to IPR in the standard-setting context are unfair or unreasonable should be based on whether the fees bear a reasonable relationship to the economic value of the IPR (116). In general, there are various methods available to make this assessment. In principle, cost-based methods are not well adapted to this context because of the difficulty in assessing the costs attributable to the development of a particular patent or groups of patents. Instead, it may be possible to compare the licensing fees charged by the company in question for the relevant patents in a competitive environment before the industry has been locked into the standard (*ex ante*) with those charged after the industry has been locked in (*ex post*). This assumes that the comparison can be made in a consistent and reliable manner (117).

(116) See Case 27/76, United Brands, paragraph 250; see also Case C-385/07 P, *Der Grüne Punkt – Duales System Deutschland GmbH*, (2009) ECR I-6155, paragraph 142.

(117) See Case 395/87, *Ministère public v Jean-Louis Tournier*, (1989) ECR 2521, paragraph 38; Joined Cases 110/88, 241/88 and 242/88, *Francois Lucazeau v SACEM*, (1989) ECR 2811, paragraph 33.

290. Another method could be to obtain an independent expert assessment of the objective centrality and essentiality to the standard at issue of the relevant IPR portfolio. In an appropriate case, it may also be possible to refer to *ex ante* disclosures of licensing terms in the context of a specific standard-setting process. This also assumes that the comparison can be made in a consistent and reliable manner. The royalty rates charged for the same IPR in other comparable standards may also provide an indication for FRAND royalty rates. These guidelines do not seek to provide an exhaustive list of appropriate methods to assess whether the royalty fees are excessive.

291. However, it should be emphasised that nothing in these Guidelines prejudices the possibility for parties to resolve their disputes about the level of FRAND royalty rates by having recourse to the competent civil or commercial courts.

Effects based assessment for standardisation agreements

292. The assessment of each standardisation agreement must take into account the likely effects of the standard on the markets concerned. The following considerations apply to all standardisation agreements that depart from the principles as set out in paragraphs 280 to 286.

293. Whether standardisation agreements may give rise to restrictive effects on competition may depend on whether the members of a standard-setting organisation remain free to develop alternative standards or products that do not comply with the agreed standard (118). For example, if the standard-setting agreement binds the members to only produce products in compliance with the standard, the risk of a likely negative effect on competition is significantly increased and could in certain circumstances give rise to a restriction of competition by object (119). In the same vein, standards only covering minor aspects or parts of the end-product are less likely to lead to competition concerns than more comprehensive standards.

(118) See Commission Decision in Case IV/29/151, *Philips/VCR*, OJ L 47, 18.2.1978, p. 42, paragraph 23: «As these standards were for the manufacture of VCR equipment, the parties were obliged to manufacture and distribute only cassettes and recorders conforming to the VCR system licensed by Philips. They were prohibited from changing to manufacturing and distributing other video cassette systems ...This constituted a restriction of competition under Article 85(1)(*b*)».

(119) See Commission Decision in Case IV/29/151, *Philips/VCR*, paragraph 23.

294. The assessment whether the agreement restricts competition will also focus on access to the standard. Where the result of a standard (that is to say, the specification of how to comply with the standard and, if relevant, the essential IPR for implementing the standard) is not at all accessible, or only accessible on discriminatory terms, for members or third parties (that is to say, non-members of the relevant standard-setting organisation) this may discriminate or foreclose or segment markets according to their geographic scope of application and thereby is likely to restrict competition. However, in the case of several competing standards or in the case of effective competition between the standardised solution and non-standardised solution, a limitation of access may not produce restrictive effects on competition.

295. If participation in the standard-setting process is open in the sense that it allows all competitors (and/or stakeholders) in the market affected by the standard to take part in choosing and elaborating the standard, this will lower the risks of a likely restrictive effect on competition by not excluding certain companies from the ability to influence the choice and elaboration of the standard (120). The greater the likely market impact of the standard and the wider its potential fields of application, the more important it is to allow equal access to the standard-setting process. However, if the facts at hand show that there is competition between several such standards and standard-setting organisations (and it is not necessary that the whole industry applies the same standards) there may be no restrictive effects on competition. Also, if in the absence of a limitation on the number of participants it would not have been possible to adopt the standard, the agreement would not be likely to lead to any restrictive effect on competition under Article 101(1) (121). In certain situations the potential negative effects of restricted participation may be removed or at least lessened by ensuring that stakeholders are kept informed and consulted on the work in progress (122). The more transparent the procedure for adopting the standard, the more likely it is that the adopted standard will take into account the interests of all stakeholders.

(120) In Commission Decision in Case IV/31.458, *X/Open Group*, OJ L 35, 6.2.1987, p. 36, the Commission considered that even if the standards adopted were made public, the restricted membership policy had the effect of preventing non-members from influencing the results of the work of the group and from getting the know-how and technical understanding relating to the standards which the members were likely to acquire. In addition, non-members could not, in contrast to the members, implement the standard before it was adopted (see paragraph 32). The agreement was therefore in these circumstances seen to constitute a restriction under Article 101(1).

(121) Or if the adoption of the standard would have been heavily delayed by an inefficient process, any initial restriction could be outweighed by efficiencies to be considered under Article 101(3).

(122) See Commission Decision of 14 October 2009 in Case 39.416, *Ship Classification*. The Decision can be found at: http://ec.europa.eu/competition/antitrust/cases/index/by_nr_78.html#i39_416

296. To assess the effects of a standard-setting agreement, the market shares of the goods or services based on the standard should be taken into account. It might not always be possible to assess with any certainty at an early stage whether the standard will in practice be adopted by a large part of the industry or whether it will only be a standard used by a marginal part of the relevant industry. In many cases the relevant market shares of the companies having participated in developing the standard could be used as a proxy for estimating the likely market share of the standard (since the companies participating in setting the standard would in most cases have an interest in implementing the standard) (123). However, as the effectiveness of standardisation agreements is often proportional to the share of the industry involved in setting and/or applying the standard, high market shares held by the parties in the market or markets affected by the standard will not necessarily lead to the conclusion that the standard is likely to give rise to restrictive effects on competition.

(123) See paragraph 261.

297. Any standard-setting agreement which clearly discriminates against any of the participating or potential members could lead to a restriction of competition. For example, if a standard-setting organisation explicitly excludes upstream only companies (that is to say, companies not active on the downstream production market), this could lead to an exclusion of potentially better technologies.

298. As regards standard-setting agreements with different types of IPR disclosure models from the ones described in paragraph 286, it would have to be assessed on a case by case basis whether the disclosure model in question (for example a disclosure model not requiring but only encouraging IPR disclosure) guarantees effective access to the standard. In other words, it needs to be assessed whether, in the specific context, an informed choice between technologies and associated IPR is in practice not prevented by the IPR disclosure model.

299. Finally, standard-setting agreements providing for *ex ante* disclosures of most restrictive licensing terms, will not, in principle, restrict competition within the meaning of Article 101(1). In that regard, it is important that parties involved in the selection of a standard be fully informed not only as to the available technical options and the associated IPR, but also as to the likely cost of that IPR. Therefore, should a standard-setting organisation's IPR policy choose to provide for IPR holders to individually disclose their most restrictive licensing terms, including the maximum royalty rates they would charge, prior to the adoption of the standard, this will normally not lead to a restriction of competition within the meaning of Article 101(1) (124). Such unilateral *ex ante* disclosures of most restrictive licensing terms would be one way to enable the standard-setting organisation to take an informed decision based on the disadvantages and advantages of different alternative technologies, not only from a technical perspective but also from a pricing perspective.

(124) Any unilateral *ex ante* disclosures of most restrictive licensing terms should not serve as a cover to jointly fix prices either of downstream products or of substitute IPR/technologies which is, as outlined in paragraph 274, a restriction of competition by object.

Standard terms

300. The establishment and use of standard terms must be assessed in the appropriate economic context and in the light of the situation on the relevant market in order to determine whether the standard terms at issue are likely to give rise to restrictive effects on competition.

301. As long as participation in the actual establishment of standard terms is unrestricted for the competitors in the relevant market (either by participation in the trade association or directly), and the established standard terms are non-binding and effectively accessible for anyone, such agreements are not likely to give rise to restrictive effects on competition (subject to the caveats set out in paragraphs 303, 304, 305 and 307).

302. Effectively accessible and non-binding standard terms for the sale of consumer goods or services (on the presumption that they have no effect on price) thus generally do not have any restrictive effect on competition since they are unlikely to lead to any negative effect on product quality, product variety or innovation. There are, however, two general exceptions where a more in-depth assessment would be required.

303. Firstly, standard terms for the sale of consumer goods or services where the standard terms define the scope of the product sold to the customer, and where therefore the risk of limiting product choice is more significant, could give rise to restrictive effects on competition within the meaning of Article 101(1) where their common application is likely to result in a de facto alignment. This could be the case when the widespread use of the standard terms de facto leads to a limitation of innovation and product variety. For instance, this may arise where standard terms in insurance contracts limit the customer's practical choice of key elements of the contract, such as the standard risks covered. Even if the use of the standard terms is not compulsory, they might undermine the incentives of the competitors to compete on product diversification.

304. When assessing whether there is a risk that the standard terms are likely to have restrictive effects by way of a limitation of product choice, factors such as existing competition on the market should be taken into account. For example if there is a large number of smaller competitors, the risk of a limitation of product choice would seem to be less than if there are only a few bigger competitors (125). The market shares of the companies participating in the establishment of the standard terms might also give a certain indication of the likelihood of uptake of the standard terms or of the likelihood that the standard terms will be used by a large part of the market. However, in this respect, it is not only relevant to analyse whether the standard terms elaborated are likely to be used by a large part of the market, but also whether the standard terms only cover part of the product or the whole product (the less extensive the standard terms, the less likely that they will lead, overall, to a limitation of product choice). Moreover, in cases where in the absence of the establishment of the standard terms it would not have been possible to offer a certain product, there would not be likely to be any restrictive effect on competition within the meaning of Article 101(1). In that scenario, product choice is increased rather than decreased by the establishment of the standard terms.

(125) If previous experience with standard terms on the relevant market shows that the standard terms did not lead to lessened competition on product differentiation, this might also be an indication that the same type of standard terms elaborated for a neighbouring product will not lead to a restrictive effect on competition.

305. Secondly, even if the standard terms do not define the actual scope of the end-product they might be a decisive part of the transaction with the customer for other reasons. An example would be online shopping where customer confidence is essential (for example, in the use of safe payment systems, a proper description of the products, clear and transparent pricing rules, flexibility of the return policy, etc). As it is difficult for customers to make a clear assessment of all those elements, they tend to favour widespread practices and standard terms regarding those elements could therefore become a de facto standard with which companies would need to comply to sell in the market. Even though non-binding, those standard terms would become a de facto standard, the effects of which are very close to a binding standard and need to be analysed accordingly.

306. If the use of standard terms is binding, there is a need to assess their impact on product quality, product variety and innovation (in particular if the standard terms are binding on the entire market).

307. Moreover, should the standard terms (binding or non-binding) contain any terms which are likely to have a negative effect on competition relating to prices (for example terms defining the type of rebates to be given), they would be likely to give rise to restrictive effects on competition within the meaning of Article 101(1).

7.4. Assessment under Article 101(3)

7.4.1. Efficiency gains

Standardisation agreements

308. Standardisation agreements frequently give rise to significant efficiency gains. For example, Union wide standards may facilitate market integration and allow companies to market their goods and services in all Member States, leading to increased consumer choice and decreasing prices. Standards which establish technical interoperability and compatibility often encourage competition on the merits between technologies from different companies and help prevent lock-in to one particular supplier. Furthermore, standards may reduce transaction costs for sellers and buyers. Standards on, for instance, quality, safety and environmental aspects of a product may also facilitate consumer choice and can lead to increased product quality. Standards also play an important role for innovation. They can reduce the time it takes to bring a new technology to the market and facilitate innovation by allowing companies to build on top of agreed solutions.

309. To achieve those efficiency gains in the case of standardisation agreements, the information necessary to apply the standard must be effectively available to those wishing to enter the market (126).

(126) See Commission Decision in Case IV/31.458, *X/Open Group*, paragraph 42: «The Commission considers that the willingness of the Group to make available the results as quickly as possible is an essential element in its decision to grant an exemption».

310. Dissemination of a standard can be enhanced by marks or logos certifying compliance thereby providing certainty to customers. Agreements for testing and certification go beyond the primary objective of defining the standard and would normally constitute a distinct agreement and market.

311. While the effects on innovation must be analysed on a case-by-case basis, standards creating compatibility on a horizontal level between different technology platforms are considered to be likely to give rise to efficiency gains.

Standard terms

312. The use of standard terms can entail economic benefits such as making it easier for customers to compare the conditions offered and thus facilitate switching between companies. Standard terms might also lead to efficiency gains in the form of savings in transaction costs and, in certain sectors (in particular where the contracts are of a complex legal structure), facilitate entry. Standard terms may also increase legal certainty for the contract parties.

313. The higher the number of competitors on the market, the greater the efficiency gain of facilitating the comparison of conditions offered.

7.4.2. Indispensability

314. Restrictions that go beyond what is necessary to achieve the efficiency gains that can be generated by a standardisation agreement or standard terms do not fulfil the criteria of Article 101(3).

Standardisation agreements

315. The assessment of each standardisation agreement must take into account its likely effect on the markets concerned, on the one hand, and the scope of restrictions that possibly go beyond the objective of achieving efficiencies, on the other (127).

(127) In Case IV/29/151, *Philips/VCR*, compliance with the VCR standards led to the exclusion of other, perhaps better systems. Such exclusion was particularly serious in view of the pre-eminent market position enjoyed by Philips «... (R)restrictions were imposed upon the parties which were not indispensable to the attainment of these improvements. The compatibility of VCR video cassettes with the machines made by other manufacturers would have been ensured even if the latter had to accept no more than an obligation to observe the VCR standards when manufacturing VCR equipment» (paragraph 31).

316. Participation in standard-setting should normally be open to all competitors in the market or markets affected by the standard unless the parties demonstrate significant inefficiencies of such participation or recognised procedures are foreseen for the collective representation of interests (128).

(128) See Commission Decision in Case IV/31.458, *X/Open Group*, paragraph 45: «(T)he aims of the Group could not be achieved if any company willing to commit itself to the Group objectives had a right to become a member. This would create practical and logistical difficulties for the management of the work and possibly prevent appropriate proposals being passed.» See also Commission Decision of 14 October 2009 in Case 39.416, *Ship Classification*, paragraph 36: «the Commitments strike an appropriate balance between maintaining demanding criteria for membership of IACS on the one hand, and removing unnecessary barriers to membership of IACS on the other hand. The new criteria will ensure that only technically competent CSs are eligible to become member of IACS, thus preventing that the efficiency and quality of IACS' work is unduly impaired by too lenient requirements for participation in IACS. At the same time, the new criteria will not hinder CSs, who are technically competent and willing to do so from joining IACS».

317. As a general rule standardisation agreements should cover no more than what is necessary to ensure their aims, whether this is technical interoperability and compatibility or a certain level of quality. In cases where having only one technological solution would benefit consumers or the economy at large that standard should, be set on a non-discriminatory basis. Technology neutral standards can, in certain circumstances, lead to larger efficiency gains. Including substitute IPR (129) as essential parts of a standard while at the same time forcing the users of the standard to pay for more IPR than technically necessary would go beyond what is necessary to achieve any identified efficiency gains. In the same vein, including substitute IPR as essential parts of a standard and limiting the use of that technology to that particular standard (that is to say, exclusive use) could limit inter-technology competition and would not be necessary to achieve the efficiencies identified.

(129) Technology which is regarded by users or licensees as interchangeable with or substitutable for another technology, by reason of the characteristics and intended use of the technologies.

318. Restrictions in a standardisation agreement making a standard binding and obligatory for the industry are in principle not indispensable.

319. In a similar vein, standardisation agreements that entrust certain bodies with the exclusive right to test compliance with the standard go beyond the primary objective of defining the standard and may also restrict competition. The exclusivity can, however, be justified for a certain period of time, for example by the need to recoup significant start-up costs (130). The standardisation agreement should in that case include adequate safeguards to mitigate possible risks to competition resulting from exclusivity. This concerns, inter alia, the certification fee which needs to be reasonable and proportionate to the cost of the compliance testing.

(130) In this context see Commission Decision in Cases IV/34.179, 34.202, 216, *Dutch Cranes (SCK and FNK)*, OJ L 312, 23.12.1995, p. 79, paragraph 23: «The ban on calling on firms not certified by SCK as subcontractors restricts the freedom of action of certified firms. Whether a ban can be regarded as preventing, restricting or distorting competition within the meaning of Article 85(1) must be judged in the legal and economic context. If such a ban is associated with a certification system which is completely open, independent and transparent and provides for the acceptance of equivalent guarantees from other systems, it may be argued that it has no restrictive effects on competition but is simply aimed at fully guaranteeing the quality of the certified goods or services».

Standard terms

320. It is generally not justified to make standard terms binding and obligatory for the industry or the members of the trade association that established them. The possibility cannot, however, be ruled out that making standard terms binding may, in a specific case, be indispensable to the attainment of the efficiency gains generated by them.

7.4.3. Pass-on to consumers

Standardisation agreements

321. Efficiency gains attained by indispensable restrictions must be passed on to consumers to an extent that outweighs the restrictive effects on competition caused by a standardisation agreement or by standard terms. A relevant part of the analysis of likely pass-on to consumers is which procedures are used to guarantee that the interests of the users of standards and end consumers are protected. Where standards facilitate technical interoperability and compatibility or competition between new and already existing products, services and processes, it can be presumed that the standard will benefit consumers.

Standard terms

322. Both the risk of restrictive effects on competition and the likelihood of efficiency gains increase with the companies' market shares and the extent to which the standard terms are used. Hence, it is not possible to provide any general «safe harbour» within which there is no risk of restrictive effects on competition or which would allow the presumption that efficiency gains will be passed on to consumers to an extent that outweighs the restrictive effects on competition.

323. However, certain efficiency gains generated by standard terms, such as increased comparability of the offers on the market, facilitated switching between providers, and legal certainty of the clauses set out in the standard terms, are necessarily beneficial for the consumers. As regards other possible efficiency gains, such as lower transaction costs, it is necessary to make an assessment on a case-by-case basis and in the relevant economic context whether these are likely to be passed on to consumers.

7.4.4. No elimination of competition

324. Whether a standardisation agreement affords the parties the possibility of eliminating competition depends on the various sources of competition in the market, the level of competitive constraint that they impose on the parties and the impact of the agreement on that competitive constraint. While market shares are relevant for that analysis, the magnitude of remaining sources of actual competition cannot be assessed exclusively on the basis of market share except in cases where a standard becomes a de facto industry standard (131). In the latter case competition may be eliminated if third parties are foreclosed from effective access to the standard. Standard terms used by a majority of the industry might create a de facto industry standard and thus raise the same concerns. However, if the standard or the standard terms only concern a limited part of the product or service, competition is not likely to be eliminated.

(131) *De facto* standardisation refers to a situation where a (legally non-binding) standard, is, in practice, used by most of the industry.

7.5. Examples

325. *Setting standards competitors cannot satisfy*
Example 1
Situation: A standard-setting organisation sets and publishes safety standards that are widely used by the relevant industry. Most competitors of the industry take part in the setting of the standard. Prior to the adoption of the standard, a new entrant has developed a product which is technically equivalent in terms of the performance and functional requirements and which is recognised by the technical committee of the standard-setting organisation. However, the technical specifications of the safety standard are, without any objective justification, drawn up in such a way as to not allow for this or other new products to comply with the standard.
Analysis: This standardisation agreement is likely to give rise to restrictive effects on competition within the meaning of Article 101(1) and is unlikely to meet the criteria of Article 101(3). The members of the standards development organisation have, without any objective justification, set the standard in such a way that products of their competitors which are based on other technological solutions cannot satisfy it, even though they have equivalent performance. Hence, this standard, which has not been set on a non-discriminatory basis, will reduce or prevent innovation and product variety. It is unlikely that the way the standard is drafted will lead to greater efficiency gains than a neutral one.

326. *Non-binding and transparent standard covering a large part of the market*
Example 2
Situation: A number of consumer electronics manufacturers with substantial market shares agree to develop a new standard for a product to follow up the DVD.
Analysis: Provided that: *(a)* the manufacturers remain free to produce other new products which do not conform to the new standard; *(b)* participation in the standard-setting is unrestricted and transparent, and *(c)* the standardisation agreement does not otherwise restrict competition, Article 101(1) is not likely to be infringed. If the parties agreed to only manufacture products which conform to the new standard, the agreement would limit technical development, reduce innovation and prevent the parties from selling different products, thereby creating restrictive effects on competition within the meaning of Article 101(1).

327. *Standardisation agreement without IPR disclosure*
Example 3
Situation: A private standard-setting organisation active in standardisation in the ICT (information and communication technology) sector has an IPR policy which neither requires nor encourages disclosures of IPR which could be essential for the future standard. The standard-setting organisation took the conscious decision not to include such an obligation in particular considering that in general all technologies potentially relevant for the future standard are covered by many IPR. Therefore the standard-setting organisation considered that an IPR disclosure obligation would, on the one hand, not lead to the benefit of enabling the participants to choose a solution with no or little IPR and, on the other, would lead to additional costs in analysing whether the IPR would be potentially essential for the future standard. However, the IPR policy of the standard-setting organisation requires all participants to make a commitment to license any IPR that might read on the future standard on FRAND terms. The IPR policy allows for opt-outs if there is specific IPR that an IPR holder wishes to put outside the blanket licensing commitment. In this particular industry there are several competing private standard-setting organisations. Participation in the standard-setting organisation is open to anyone active in the industry.
Analysis: In many cases an IPR disclosure obligation would be pro-competitive by increasing competition between technologies *ex ante*. In general, such an obligation allows the members of a standard-setting organisation to factor in the amount of IPR reading on a particular technology when deciding between competing technologies (or even to, if possible, choose a technology which is not covered by IPR). The amount of IPR reading on a technology will often have a direct impact on the cost of access to the standard. However, in this particular context, all available technologies seem to be covered by IPR, and even many IPR. Therefore, any IPR disclosure would not have the positive effect of enabling the members to factor in the amount of IPR when choosing technology since regardless of what technology is chosen, it can be presumed that there is IPR reading on that technology. IPR disclosure would be unlikely to contribute to guaranteeing effective access to the standard which in this scenario is sufficiently guaranteed by the blanket commitment to license any IPR that might read on the future standard on FRAND terms. On the contrary, an IPR disclosure obligation might in this context lead to additional

costs for the participants. The absence of IPR disclosure might also, in those circumstances, lead to a quicker adoption of the standard which might be important if there are several competing standard-setting organisations. It follows that the agreement is unlikely to give rise to any negative effects on competition within the meaning of Article 101(1).

328. *Standards in the insurance sector*

Example 4

Situation: A group of insurance companies comes together to agree non-binding standards for the installation of certain security devices (that is to say, components and equipment designed for loss prevention and reduction and systems formed from such elements). The non-binding standards set by the insurance companies: *(a)* are agreed in order to address a specific need and to assist insurers to manage risk and offer risk-appropriate premiums; *(b)* are discussed with the installers (or their representatives) and their views are taken on board prior to finalisation of the standards; *(c)* are published by the relevant insurance association on a dedicated section of its website so that any installer or other interested party can access them easily.

Analysis: The process for setting these standards is transparent and allows for the participation of interested parties. In addition, the result is easily accessible on a reasonable and non-discriminatory basis for anyone that wishes to have access to it. Provided that the standard does not have negative effects on the downstream market (for example by excluding certain installers through very specific and unjustified requirements for installations) it is not likely to lead to restrictive effects on competition. However, even if the standards led to restrictive effects on competition, the conditions set out in Article 101(3) would seem to be fulfilled. The standards would assist insurers in analysing to what extent such installation systems reduce relevant risk and prevent losses so that they can manage risks and offer risk-appropriate premiums. Subject to the caveat regarding the downstream market, they would also be more efficient for installers, allowing them to comply with one set of standards for all insurance companies rather than be tested by every insurance company separately. They could also make it easier for consumers to switch between insurers. In addition, they could be beneficial for smaller insurers who may not have the capacity to test separately. As regards the other conditions of Article 101(3), it seems that the non-binding standards do not go beyond what is necessary to achieve the efficiencies in question, that benefits would be passed on to the consumers (some would even be directly beneficial for the consumers) and that the restrictions would not lead to an elimination of competition.

329. *Environmental standards*

Example 5

Situation: Almost all producers of washing machines agree, with the encouragement of a public body, to no longer manufacture products which do not comply with certain environmental criteria (for example, energy efficiency). Together, the parties hold 90 % of the market. The products which will be thus phased out of the market account for a significant proportion of total sales. They will be replaced by more environmentally friendly, but also more expensive products. Furthermore, the agreement indirectly reduces the output of third parties (for example, electric utilities and suppliers of components incorporated in the products phased out). Without the agreement, the parties would not have shifted their production and marketing efforts to the more environmentally friendly products.

Analysis: The agreement grants the parties control of individual production and concerns an appreciable proportion of their sales and total output, whilst also reducing third parties' output. Product variety, which is partly focused on the environmental characteristics of the product, is reduced and prices will probably rise. Therefore, the agreement is likely to give rise to restrictive effects on competition within the meaning of Article 101(1). The involvement of the public authority is irrelevant for that assessment. However, newer, more environmentally friendly products are more technically advanced, offering qualitative efficiencies in the form of more washing machine programmes which can be used by consumers. Furthermore, there are cost efficiencies for the purchasers of the washing machines resulting from lower running costs in the form of reduced consumption of water, electricity and soap. Those cost efficiencies are realised on markets which are different from the relevant market of the agreement. Nevertheless, those efficiencies may be taken into account as the markets on which the restrictive effects on competition and the efficiency gains arise are related and the group of consumers affected by the restriction and the efficiency gains is substantially the same. The efficiency gains outweigh the restrictive effects on competition in the form of increased costs. Other alternatives to the agreement are shown to be less certain and less cost-effective in delivering the same net benefits. Various technical means are economically available to the parties in order to manufacture washing machines which do comply with the environmental characteristics agreed upon and competition will still take place for other product characteristics. Therefore, the criteria of Article 101(3) would appear to be fulfilled.

330. *Government encouraged standardisation*

Example 6

Situation: In response to the findings of research into the recommended levels of fat in certain processed food conducted by a government-funded think tank in one Member State, several major manufacturers of the processed foods in the same Member State agree, through formal discussions at an industry trade association, to set recommended fat levels for the products. Together, the parties represent 70 % of sales of the products within the Member State. The parties' initiative will be supported by a national advertising campaign funded by the think tank highlighting the dangers of a high fat content in processed foods.

Analysis: Although the fat levels are recommendations and therefore voluntary, as a result of the wide publicity resulting from the national advertising campaign, the recommended fat levels are likely to be implemented by all manufacturers of the processed foods in the Member State. It is therefore likely to become a de facto maximum fat level in the processed foods. Consumer choice across the product markets could therefore be reduced. However, the parties will be able to continue to compete with regard to a number of other characteristics of the products, such as price, product size, quality, taste, other nutritional and salt content, balance of ingredients, and branding. Moreover, competition regarding the fat levels in the product offering may increase where parties seek to offer products with the lowest levels. The agreement is therefore unlikely to give rise to restrictive effects on competition within the meaning of Article 101(1).

331. *Open standardisation of product packaging*

Example 7

Situation: The major manufacturers of a fast-moving consumer product in a competitive market in a Member State – as well as manufacturers and distributors in other Member States who sell the product into the Member State («importers») – agree with the major packaging suppliers to develop and implement a voluntary initiative to standardise the size and shape of the packaging of the product sold in that Member State. There is currently a wide variation in packaging sizes and materials within and across the Member States. This reflects the fact that the packaging does not represent a high proportion of total production costs and that switching costs for packaging producers are not significant. There is no actual or pending European standard for the packaging. The agreement has been entered into by the parties voluntarily in response to pressure from the Member State's government to meet environmental targets. Together, the manufacturers and importers represent 85 % of sales of the product within the Member State. The voluntary initiative will give rise to a uniform-sized product for sale within the Member State that uses less packaging material, occupies less shelf space, has lower transport and packaging costs, and is more environmentally friendly through reduced packaging waste. It also reduces the recycling costs of producers. The standard does not specify that particular types of packaging materials must be used. The specifications of the standard have been agreed between manufacturers and importers in an open and transparent manner, with the draft specifications having been published for open consultation on an industry website in a timely manner prior to adoption. The final specifications adopted are also published on an industry trade association website that is freely accessible to any potential entrants, even if they are not members of the trade association.

Analysis: Although the agreement is voluntary, the standard is likely to become a de facto industry practice because the parties together represent a high proportion of the market for the product in the Member State and retailers are also being encouraged by the government to reduce packaging waste. As such, the agreement could in theory create barriers to entry and give rise to potential anti-competitive foreclosure effects in the Member State market. This would in particular be a risk for importers of the product in question who may need to repackage the product to meet the de facto standard in order to sell in the Member State if the pack size used in other Member States does not meet the standard. However, significant barriers to entry and foreclosure are unlikely to occur in practice because: *(a)* the agreement is voluntary; *(b)* the standard has been agreed with major importers in an open and transparent manner; *(c)* switching costs are low; and *(d)* the technical details of the standard are accessible to new entrants, importers and all packaging suppliers. In particular, importers will have been aware of potential changes to packaging at an early stage of development and will have had the opportunity through the open consultation on the draft standards to put forward their views before the standard was eventually adopted. The agreement therefore may not give rise to restrictive effects on competition within the meaning of Article 101(1).

In any event, it is likely that the conditions of Article 101(3) will be fulfilled in this case: (i) the agreement will give rise to quantitative efficiencies through lower transport and packaging costs; (ii) the prevailing conditions of competition on the market are such that these costs reductions are likely to be passed on to consumers; (iii) the agreement includes only the minimum restrictions necessary to achieve the packaging standard and is unlikely to result in significant foreclosure effects; and (iv) competition will not be eliminated in a substantial part of the products in question.

332. *Closed standardisation of product packaging*

Example 8

Situation: The situation is the same as in Example 7, paragraph 331, except the standard is agreed only between manufacturers of the fast-moving consumer product located within the Member State (who represent 65 % of the sales of the product in the Member State), there was no open consultation on the specifications adopted (which include detailed standards on the type of packaging material that must be used) and the specifications of the voluntary standard are not published. This resulted in higher switching costs for producers in other Member States than for domestic producers.

Analysis: Similar to Example 7, paragraph 331, although the agreement is voluntary, it is very likely to become de facto standard industry practice since retailers are also being encouraged by the government to reduce packaging waste and the domestic manufacturers account for 65 % of sales of the product within the Member State. The fact that relevant producers in other Member States were not consulted resulted in the adoption of a standard which imposes higher switching costs on them compared to domestic producers. The agreement may therefore create barriers to entry and give rise to potential anti-competitive foreclosure effects on packaging suppliers, new entrants and importers – all of whom were not involved in the standard-setting process – as they may need to repackage the product to meet the de facto standard in order to sell in the Member State if the pack size used in other Member States does not meet the standard.

Unlike in Example 7, paragraph 331, the standardisation process has not been carried out in an open and transparent manner. In particular, new entrants, importers and packaging suppliers have not been given the opportunity to comment on the proposed standard and may not even be aware of it until a late stage, creating the possibility that they may not be able to change their production methods or switch suppliers quickly and effectively. Moreover, new entrants, importers and packaging suppliers may not be able to compete if the standard is unknown or difficult to comply with. Of particular relevance here is the fact that the standard includes detailed specifications on the packaging materials to be used which, because of the closed nature of the consultation and the standard, importers and new entrants will struggle to comply with. The agreement may therefore restrict competition within the meaning of Article 101(1). This conclusion is not affected by the fact the agreement has been entered into in order to meet underlying environmental targets agreed with the Member State's government.

It is unlikely that the conditions of Article 101(3) will be fulfilled in this case. Although the agreement will give rise to similar quantitative efficiencies as arise under Example 7, paragraph 331, the closed and private nature of the standardisation agreement and the non-published detailed standard on the type of packaging material that must be used are unlikely to be indispensable to achieving the efficiencies under the agreement.

333. *Non-binding and open standard terms used for contracts with end-users*

Example 9

Situation: A trade association for electricity distributors establishes non-binding standard terms for the supply of electricity to end-users. The establishment of the standard terms is made in a transparent and non-discriminatory manner. The standard terms cover issues such as the specification of the point of consumption, the location of the connection point and the connection voltage, provisions on service reliability as well as the procedure for settling the accounts between the parties to the contract (for example, what happens if the customer does not provide the supplier with the readings of the measurement devices). The standard terms do not cover any issues relating to prices, that is to say, they contain no recommended prices or other clauses related to price. Any company active within the sector is free to use the standard terms as it sees fit. About 80 % of the contracts concluded with end-users in the relevant market are based on these standard terms.

Analysis: These standard terms are not likely to give rise to restrictive effects on competition within the meaning of Article 101(1). Even if they have become industry practice, they do not seem to have any appreciable negative impact on prices, product quality or variety.

334. *Standard terms used for contracts between companies*

Example 10

Situation: Construction companies in a certain Member State come together to establish non-binding and open standard terms and conditions for use by a contractor when submitting a quotation for construction work to a client. A form of quotation is included together with terms and conditions suitable for building or construction. Together, the documents create the construction contract. Clauses cover such matters as contract formation, general obligations of the contractor and the client and non-price related payment conditions (for example, a provision specifying the contractor's right to give notice to suspend the work for non-payment), insurance, duration, handover and defects, limitation of liability, termination, etc. In contrast to Example 9, paragraph 333, these standard terms would often be used between companies, one active upstream and one active downstream.

Analysis: These standard terms are not likely to have restrictive effects on competition within the meaning of Article 101(1). There would normally not be any significant limitation in the customer's choice of the end-product, namely the construction work. Other restrictive effects on competition do not seem likely. Indeed, several of the clauses above (handover and defects, termination, etc.) would often be regulated by law.

335. *Standard terms facilitating the comparison of different companies' products*

Example 11

Situation: A national association for the insurance sector distributes non-binding standard policy conditions for house insurance contracts. The conditions give no indication of the level of insurance premiums, the amount of the cover or the excesses payable by the insured. They do not impose comprehensive cover including risks to which a significant number of policyholders are not simultaneously exposed and do not require the policyholders to obtain cover from the same insurer for different risks. While the majority of insurance companies use standard policy conditions, not all their contracts contain the same conditions as they are adapted to each client's individual needs and therefore there is no de facto standardisation of insurance products offered to consumers. The standard policy conditions enable consumers and consumer organisations to compare the policies offered by the different insurers. A consumer association is involved in the process of laying down the standard policy conditions. They are also available for use by new entrants, on a non-discriminatory basis.

Analysis: These standard policy conditions relate to the composition of the final insurance product. If the market conditions and other factors would show that there might be a risk of limitation in product variety as a result of insurance companies using such standard policy conditions, it is likely that such possible limitation would be outweighed by efficiencies such as facilitation of comparison by consumers of conditions offered by insurance companies. Those comparisons in turn facilitate switching between insurance companies and thus enhance competition. Furthermore the switching of providers, as well as market entry by competitors, constitutes an advantage for consumers. The fact that the consumer association has participated in the process could, in certain instances, increase the likelihood of those efficiencies which do not automatically benefit the consumers being passed on. The standard policy conditions are also likely to reduce transaction costs and facilitate entry for insurers on a different geographic and/or product markets. Moreover, the restrictions do not seem to go beyond what is necessary to achieve the identified efficiencies and competition would not be eliminated. Consequently, the criteria of Article 101(3) are likely to be fulfilled.

2.1.2.4. Transfer of technology

Commission Regulation (EC) N° 772/2004, 27 April 2004 – Technology transfer
    agreements. 168
Guidelines technology transfer agreements 172
Index of the guidelines 203

Commission Regulation (EC) N° 772/2004, 27 April 2004 on the application of Article 81(3) of the Treaty to categories of technology transfer agreements

(OJ L 123, 27 April 2004, p. 11, rect., OJ L 127, 29 April 2004, p. 158)

1. Article 81 EC is now Article 101 TFEU.

THE COMMISSION OF THE EUROPEAN COMMUNITIES,
Having regard to the Treaty establishing the European Community,
Having regard to Council Regulation N° 19/65/EEC of 2 March 1965 on application of Article 85(3) of the Treaty to certain categories of agreements and concerted practices (1), and in particular Article 1 thereof,
Having published a draft of this Regulation (2),
After consulting the Advisory Committee on Restrictive Practices and Dominant Positions,
Whereas:

(1) Regulation N° 19/65/EEC empowers the Commission to apply Article 81(3) of the Treaty by Regulation to certain categories of technology transfer agreements and corresponding concerted practices to which only two undertakings are party which fall within Article 81(1).

(2) Pursuant to Regulation N° 19/65/EEC, the Commission has, in particular, adopted Regulation (EC) N° 240/96 of 31 January 1996 on the application of Article 85(3) of the Treaty to certain categories of technology transfer agreements (3).

(3) On 20 December 2001 the Commission published an evaluation report on the transfer of technology block exemption Regulation (EC) N° 240/96 (4). This generated a public debate on the application of Regulation (EC) N° 240/96 and on the application in general of Article 81(1) and (3) of the Treaty to technology transfer agreements. The response to the evaluation report from Member States and third parties has been generally in favour of reform of Community competition policy on technology transfer agreements. It is therefore appropriate to repeal Regulation (EC) N° 240/96.

(4) This Regulation should meet the two requirements of ensuring effective competition and providing adequate legal security for undertakings. The pursuit of these objectives should take account of the need to simplify the regulatory framework and its application. It is appropriate to move away from the approach of listing exempted clauses and to place greater emphasis on defining the categories of agreements which are exempted up to a certain level of market power and on specifying the restrictions or clauses which are not to be contained in such agreements. This is consistent with an economics-based approach which assesses the impact of agreements on the relevant market. It is also consistent with such an approach to make a distinction between agreements between competitors and agreements between non-competitors.

(5) Technology transfer agreements concern the licensing of technology. Such agreements will usually improve economic efficiency and be pro-competitive as they can reduce duplication of research and development, strengthen the incentive for the initial research and development, spur incremental innovation, facilitate diffusion and generate product market competition.

(6) The likelihood that such efficiency-enhancing and pro-competitive effects will outweigh any anti-competitive effects due to restrictions contained in technology transfer agreements depends on the degree of market power of the undertakings concerned and, therefore, on the extent to which those undertakings face competition from undertakings owning substitute technologies or undertakings producing substitute products.

(7) This Regulation should only deal with agreements where the licensor permits the licensee to exploit the licensed technology, possibly after further research and development by the licensee, for the production of goods or services. It should not deal with licensing agreements for the purpose of subcontracting research and development. It should also not deal with licensing agreements to set up technology pools, that is to say, agreements for the pooling of technologies with the purpose of licensing the created package of intellectual property rights to third parties.

(8) For the application of Article 81(3) by regulation, it is not necessary to define those technology transfer agreements that are capable of falling within Article 81(1). In the individual assessment of agreements pursuant to Article 81(1), account has to be taken of several factors, and in particular the structure and the dynamics of the relevant technology and product markets.

(9) The benefit of the block exemption established by this Regulation should be limited to those agreements which can be assumed with sufficient certainty to satisfy the conditions of Article 81(3). In order to attain the benefits and objectives of technology transfer, the benefit of this Regulation should also apply to provisions contained in technology transfer agreements that do not constitute the primary object of such agreements, but are directly related to the application of the licensed technology.

(10) For technology transfer agreements between competitors it can be presumed that, where the combined share of the relevant markets accounted for by the parties does not exceed 20% and the agreements do not contain certain severely anti-competitive restraints, they generally lead to an improvement in production or distribution and allow consumers a fair share of the resulting benefits.

(11) For technology transfer agreements between non-competitors it can be presumed that, where the individual share of the relevant markets accounted for by each of the parties does not exceed 30% and the agreements do not contain certain severely anti-competitive restraints, they generally

lead to an improvement in production or distribution and allow consumers a fair share of the resulting benefits.

(12) There can be no presumption that above these marketshare thresholds technology transfer agreements do fall within the scope of Article 81(1). For instance, an exclusive licensing agreement between non-competing undertakings does often not fall within the scope of Article 81(1). There can also be no presumption that, above these market-share thresholds, technology transfer agreements falling within the scope of Article 81(1) will not satisfy the conditions for exemption. However, it can also not be presumed that they will usually give rise to objective advantages of such a character and size as to compensate for the disadvantages which they create for competition.

(13) This Regulation should not exempt technology transfer agreements containing restrictions which are not indispensable to the improvement of production or distribution. In particular, technology transfer agreements containing certain severely anti-competitive restraints such as the fixing of prices charged to third parties should be excluded from the benefit of the block exemption established by this Regulation irrespective of the market shares of the undertakings concerned. In the case of such hardcore restrictions the whole agreement should be excluded from the benefit of the block exemption.

(14) In order to protect incentives to innovate and the appropriate application of intellectual property rights, certain restrictions should be excluded from the block exemption. In particular exclusive grant back obligations for severable improvements should be excluded. Where such a restriction is included in a licence agreement only the restriction in question should be excluded from the benefit of the block exemption.

(15) The market-share thresholds, the non-exemption of technology transfer agreements containing severely anti-competitive restraints and the excluded restrictions provided for in this Regulation will normally ensure that the agreements to which the block exemption applies do not enable the participating undertakings to eliminate competition in respect of a substantial part of the products in question.

(16) In particular cases in which the agreements falling under this Regulation nevertheless have effects incompatible with Article 81(3), the Commission should be able to withdraw the benefit of the block exemption. This may occur in particular where the incentives to innovate are reduced or where access to markets is hindered.

(17) Council Regulation (EC) N° 1/2003 of 16 December 2002 on the implementation of the rules on competition laid down in Articles 81 and 82 of the Treaty (5) empowers the competent authorities of Member States to withdraw the benefit of the block exemption in respect of technology transfer agreements having effects incompatible with Article 81(3), where such effects are felt in their respective territory, or in a part thereof, and where such territory has the characteristics of a distinct geographic market. Member States must ensure that the exercise of this power of withdrawal does not prejudice the uniform application throughout the common market of the Community competition rules or the full effect of the measures adopted in implementation of those rules.

(18) In order to strengthen supervision of parallel networks of technology transfer agreements which have similar restrictive effects and which cover more than 50% of a given market, the Commission should be able to declare this Regulation inapplicable to technology transfer agreements containing specific restraints relating to the market concerned, thereby restoring the full application of Article 81 to such agreements.

(19) This Regulation should cover only technology transfer agreements between a licensor and a licensee. It should cover such agreements even if conditions are stipulated for more than one level of trade, by, for instance, requiring the licensee to set up a particular distribution system and specifying the obligations the licensee must or may impose on resellers of the products produced under the licence. However, such conditions and obligations should comply with the competition rules applicable to supply and distribution agreements. Supply and distribution agreements concluded between a licensee and its buyers should not be exempted by this Regulation.

(20) This Regulation is without prejudice to the application of Article 82 of the Treaty,

HAS ADOPTED THIS REGULATION:

(1) O.J. 36, 6.3.1965, p. 533/65. Regulation as last amended by Regulation (EC) N° 1/2003 (O.J. L 4.1.2003, p. 1).

(2) O.J. C 235, 1.10.2003, p. 10.

(3) O.J. L 31, 9.2.1996, p. 2. Regulation as amended by the 2003 Act of Accession.

(4) COM(2001) 786 final.

(5) O.J. L 1, 4.1.2003, p. 1. Regulation as amended by Regulation (EC) N° 411/2004 (O.J. L 68, 6.3.2004, p. 1).

Art. 1. *Definitions*

1. For the purposes of this Regulation, the following definitions shall apply:

(a) «agreement» means an agreement, a decision of an association of undertakings or a concerted practice;

(b) «technology transfer agreement» means a patent licensing agreement, a know-how licensing agreement, a softwarecopyright licensing agreement or a mixed patent, knowhow or software copyright licensing agreement, including any such agreement containing provisions which relate to the sale and purchase of products or which relate to the licensing of other intellectual property rights or the assignment of intellectual property rights, provided that those provisions do not constitute the primary object of the agreement and are directly related to the production of the contract products; assignments of patents, know-how, software copyright or a combination thereof where part of the risk associated with the exploitation of the technology remains with the assignor, in particular where the sum payable in consideration of the assignment is dependent on the turnover obtained by the assignee in respect of products produced with the assigned technology, the quantity of such products produced or the number of operations carried out employing the technology, shall also be deemed to be technology transfer agreements;

(c) «reciprocal agreement» means a technology transfer agreement where two undertakings grant each other, in the same or separate contracts, a patent licence, a know-how licence, a software copyright licence or a mixed patent, know-how or software copyright licence and where these licences concern competing technologies or can be used for the production of competing products;

(d) «non-reciprocal agreement» means a technology transfer agreement where one undertaking grants another undertaking a patent licence, a know-how licence, a soft-

ware copyright licence or a mixed patent, know-how or software copyright licence, or where two undertakings grant each other such a licence but where these licences do not concern competing technologies and cannot be used for the production of competing products;

(e) «product» means a good or a service, including both intermediary goods and services and final goods and services;

(f) «contract products» means products produced with the licensed technology;

(g) «intellectual property rights» includes industrial property rights, know-how, copyright and neighbouring rights;

(h) «patents» means patents, patent applications, utility models, applications for registration of utility models, designs, topographies of semiconductor products, supplementary protection certificates for medicinal products or other products for which such supplementary protection certificates may be obtained and plant breeder's certificates;

(i) «know-how» means a package of non-patented practical information, resulting from experience and testing, which is:

(i) secret, that is to say, not generally known or easily accessible,

(ii) substantial, that is to say, significant and useful for the production of the contract products, and

(iii) identified, that is to say, described in a sufficiently comprehensive manner so as to make it possible to verify that it fulfils the criteria of secrecy and substantiality;

(j) «competing undertakings» means undertakings which compete on the relevant technology market and/or the relevant product market, that is to say:

(i) competing undertakings on the relevant technology market, being undertakings which license out competing technologies without infringing each others' intellectual property rights (actual competitors on the technology market); the relevant technology market includes technologies which are regarded by the licensees as interchangeable with or substitutable for the licensed technology, by reason of the technologies' characteristics, their royalties and their intended use,

(ii) competing undertakings on the relevant product market, being undertakings which, in the absence of the technology transfer agreement, are both active on the relevant product and geographic market(s) on which the contract products are sold without infringing each others' intellectual property rights (actual competitors on the product market) or would, on realistic grounds, undertake the necessary additional investments or other necessary switching costs so that they could timely enter, without infringing each others' intellectual property rights, the(se) relevant product and geographic market(s) in response to a small and permanent increase in relative prices (potential competitors on the product market); the relevant product market comprises products which are regarded by the buyers as interchangeable with or substitutable for the contract products, by reason of the products' characteristics, their prices and their intended use;

(k) «selective distribution system» means a distribution system where the licensor undertakes to license the production of the contract products only to licensees selected on the basis of specified criteria and where these licensees undertake not to sell the contract products to unauthorised distributors;

(l) «exclusive territory» means a territory in which only one undertaking is allowed to produce the contract products with the licensed technology, without prejudice to the possibility of allowing within that territory another licensee to produce the contract products only for a particular customer where this second licence was granted in order to create an alternative source of supply for that customer;

(m) «exclusive customer group» means a group of customers to which only one undertaking is allowed actively to sell the contract products produced with the licensed technology;

(n) «severable improvement» means an improvement that can be exploited without infringing the licensed technology.

2. The terms «undertaking», «licensor» and «licensee» shall include their respective connected undertakings.

«Connected undertakings» means:

(a) undertakings in which a party to the agreement, directly or indirectly:

(i) has the power to exercise more than half the voting rights, or

(ii) has the power to appoint more than half the members of the supervisory board, board of management or bodies legally representing the undertaking, or

(iii) has the right to manage the undertaking's affairs;

(b) undertakings which directly or indirectly have, over a party to the agreement, the rights or powers listed in *(a)*;

(c) undertakings in which an undertaking referred to in *(b)* has, directly or indirectly, the rights or powers listed in *(a)*;

(d) undertakings in which a party to the agreement together with one or more of the undertakings referred to in *(a)*, *(b)* or *(c)*, or in which two or more of the latter undertakings, jointly have the rights or powers listed in *(a)*;

(e) undertakings in which the rights or the powers listed in *(a)* are jointly held by:

(i) parties to the agreement or their respective connected undertakings referred to in *(a)* to *(d)*, or

(ii) one or more of the parties to the agreement or one or more of their connected undertakings referred to in *(a)* to *(d)* and one or more third parties.

Art. 2. *Exemption*

Pursuant to Article 81(3) of the Treaty and subject to the provisions of this Regulation, it is hereby declared that Article 81(1) of the Treaty shall not apply to technology transfer agreements entered into between two undertakings permitting the production of contract products.

This exemption shall apply to the extent that such agreements contain restrictions of competition falling within the scope of Article 81(1). The exemption shall apply for as long as the intellectual property right in the licensed technology has not expired, lapsed or been declared invalid or, in the case of know-how, for as long as the know-how remains secret, except in the event where the know-how becomes publicly known as a result of action by the licensee, in which case the exemption shall apply for the duration of the agreement.

Art. 3. *Market-share thresholds*

1. Where the undertakings party to the agreement are competing undertakings, the exemption provided for in Article 2 shall apply on condition that the combined market share of the parties does not exceed 20% on the affected relevant technology and product market.

2. Where the undertakings party to the agreement are not competing undertakings, the exemption provided for in Article 2 shall apply on condition that the market share

of each of the parties does not exceed 30% on the affected relevant technology and product market.

3. For the purposes of paragraphs 1 and 2, the market share of a party on the relevant technology market(s) is defined in terms of the presence of the licensed technology on the relevant product market(s). A licensor's market share on the relevant technology market shall be the combined market share on the relevant product market of the contract products produced by the licensor and its licensees.

Art. 4. *Hardcore restrictions*

1. Where the undertakings party to the agreement are competing undertakings, the exemption provided for in Article 2 shall not apply to agreements which, directly or indirectly, in isolation or in combination with other factors under the control of the parties, have as their object:

(a) the restriction of a party's ability to determine its prices when selling products to third parties;

(b) the limitation of output, except limitations on the output of contract products imposed on the licensee in a non-reciprocal agreement or imposed on only one of the licensees in a reciprocal agreement;

(c) the allocation of markets or customers except:

(i) the obligation on the licensee(s) to produce with the licensed technology only within one or more technical fields of use or one or more product markets,

(ii) the obligation on the licensor and/or the licensee, in a non-reciprocal agreement, not to produce with the licensed technology within one or more technical fields of use or one or more product markets or one or more exclusive territories reserved for the other party,

(iii) the obligation on the licensor not to license the technology to another licensee in a particular territory,

(iv) the restriction, in a non-reciprocal agreement, of active and/or passive sales by the licensee and/or the licensor into the exclusive territory or to the exclusive customer group reserved for the other party,

(v) the restriction, in a non-reciprocal agreement, of active sales by the licensee into the exclusive territory or to the exclusive customer group allocated by the licensor to another licensee provided the latter was not a competing undertaking of the licensor at the time of the conclusion of its own licence,

(vi) the obligation on the licensee to produce the contract products only for its own use provided that the licensee is not restricted in selling the contract products actively and passively as spare parts for its own products,

(vii) the obligation on the licensee, in a non-reciprocal agreement, to produce the contract products only for a particular customer, where the licence was granted in order to create an alternative source of supply for that customer;

(d) the restriction of the licensee's ability to exploit its own technology or the restriction of the ability of any of the parties to the agreement to carry out research and development, unless such latter restriction is indispensable to prevent the disclosure of the licensed know-how to third parties.

2. Where the undertakings party to the agreement are not competing undertakings, the exemption provided for in Article 2 shall not apply to agreements which, directly or indirectly, in isolation or in combination with other factors under the control of the parties, have as their object:

(a) the restriction of a party's ability to determine its prices when selling products to third parties, without prejudice to the possibility of imposing a maximum sale price or recommending a sale price, provided that it does not amount to a fixed or minimum sale price as a result of pressure from, or incentives offered by, any of the parties;

(b) the restriction of the territory into which, or of the customers to whom, the licensee may passively sell the contract products, except:

(i) the restriction of passive sales into an exclusive territory or to an exclusive customer group reserved for the licensor,

(ii) the restriction of passive sales into an exclusive territory or to an exclusive customer group allocated by the licensor to another licensee during the first two years that this other licensee is selling the contract products in that territory or to that customer group,

(iii) the obligation to produce the contract products only for its own use provided that the licensee is not restricted in selling the contract products actively and passively as spare parts for its own products,

(iv) the obligation to produce the contract products only for a particular customer, where the licence was granted in order to create an alternative source of supply for that customer,

(v) the restriction of sales to end-users by a licensee operating at the wholesale level of trade,

(vi) the restriction of sales to unauthorised distributors by the members of a selective distribution system;

(c) the restriction of active or passive sales to end-users by a licensee which is a member of a selective distribution system and which operates at the retail level, without prejudice to the possibility of prohibiting a member of the system from operating out of an unauthorised place of establishment.

3. Where the undertakings party to the agreement are not competing undertakings at the time of the conclusion of the agreement but become competing undertakings afterwards, paragraph 2 and not paragraph 1 shall apply for the full life of the agreement unless the agreement is subsequently amended in any material respect.

Art. 5. *Excluded restrictions*

1. The exemption provided for in Article 2 shall not apply to any of the following obligations contained in technology transfer agreements:

(a) any direct or indirect obligation on the licensee to grant an exclusive licence to the licensor or to a third party designated by the licensor in respect of its own severable improvements to or its own new applications of the licensed technology;

(b) any direct or indirect obligation on the licensee to assign, in whole or in part, to the licensor or to a third party designated by the licensor, rights to its own severable improvements to or its own new applications of the licensed technology;

(c) any direct or indirect obligation on the licensee not to challenge the validity of intellectual property rights which the licensor holds in the common market, without prejudice to the possibility of providing for termination of the technology transfer agreement in the event that the licensee challenges the validity of one or more of the licensed intellectual property rights.

2. Where the undertakings party to the agreement are not competing undertakings, the exemption provided for in Article 2 shall not apply to any direct or indirect obligation limiting the licensee's ability to exploit its own technology or limiting the ability of any of the parties to the agreement to carry out research and development, unless such latter restriction is indispensable to prevent the disclosure of the licensed know-how to third parties.

Art. 6. *Withdrawal in individual cases*

1. The Commission may withdraw the benefit of this Regulation, pursuant to Article 29(1) of Regulation (EC) N° 1/2003, where it finds in any particular case that a technology transfer agreement to which the exemption provided for in Article 2 applies nevertheless has effects which are incompatible with Article 81(3) of the Treaty, and in particular where:

(a) access of third parties' technologies to the market is restricted, for instance by the cumulative effect of parallel networks of similar restrictive agreements prohibiting licensees from using third parties' technologies;

(b) access of potential licensees to the market is restricted, for instance by the cumulative effect of parallel networks of similar restrictive agreements prohibiting licensors from licensing to other licensees;

(c) without any objectively valid reason, the parties do not exploit the licensed technology.

2. Where, in any particular case, a technology transfer agreement to which the exemption provided for in Article 2 applies has effects which are incompatible with Article 81(3) of the Treaty in the territory of a Member State, or in a part thereof, which has all the characteristics of a distinct geographic market, the competition authority of that Member State may withdraw the benefit of this Regulation, pursuant to Article 29(2) of Regulation (EC) N° 1/2003, in respect of that territory, under the same circumstances as those set out in paragraph 1 of this Article.

Art. 7. *Non-application of this Regulation*

1. Pursuant to Article 1a of Regulation N° 19/65/EEC, the Commission may by regulation declare that, where parallel networks of similar technology transfer agreements cover more than 50% of a relevant market, this Regulation is not to apply to technology transfer agreements containing specific restraints relating to that market.

2. A regulation pursuant to paragraph 1 shall not become applicable earlier than six months following its adoption.

Art. 8. *Application of the market-share thresholds*

1. For the purposes of applying the market-share thresholds provided for in Article 3 the rules set out in this paragraph shall apply.

The market share shall be calculated on the basis of market sales value data. If market sales value data are not available, estimates based on other reliable market information, including market sales volumes, may be used to establish the market share of the undertaking concerned.

The market share shall be calculated on the basis of data relating to the preceding calendar year.

The market share held by the undertakings referred to in point *(e)* of the second subparagraph of Article 1(2) shall be apportioned equally to each undertaking having the rights or the powers listed in point *(a)* of the second subparagraph of Article 1(2).

2. If the market share referred to in Article 3(1) or (2) is initially not more than 20% respectively 30% but subsequently rises above those levels, the exemption provided for in Article 2 shall continue to apply for a period of two consecutive calendar years following the year in which the 20% threshold or 30% threshold was first exceeded.

Art. 9. *Repeal*

Regulation (EC) N° 240/96 is repealed.

References to the repealed Regulation shall be construed as references to this Regulation.

Art. 10. *Transitional period*

The prohibition laid down in Article 81(1) of the Treaty shall not apply during the period from 1 May 2004 to 31 March 2006 in respect of agreements already in force on 30 April 2004 which do not satisfy the conditions for exemption provided for in this Regulation but which, on 30 April 2004, satisfied the conditions for exemption provided for in Regulation (EC) N° 240/96.

Art. 11. *Period of validity*

This Regulation shall enter into force on 1 May 2004. It shall expire on 30 April 2014.

Guidelines on the application of Article 81 of the EC Treaty to technology transfer agreements
(OJ C 101, 27 April 2004, p. 2)

1. Article 81 EC is now Article 101 TFEU.

I. INTRODUCTION

1. These guidelines set out the principles for the assessment of technology transfer agreements under Article 81 of the Treaty. Technology transfer agreements concern the licensing of technology where the licensor permits the licensee to exploit the licensed technology for the production of goods or services, as defined in Article 1(1)*(b)* of Commission Regulation (EC) N° 773/2004 on the application of Article 81(3) of the Treaty to categories of technology transfer agreements (the TTBER) (1).

(1) *O.J.* L 123, 27.4.2004. The TTBER replaces Commission Regulation (EC) N° 240/96 of 31 January 1996 on the application of Article 85(3) of the Treaty to certain categories of technology transfer agreements (*O.J.* L 31, 9.2.1996, p. 2).

2. The purpose of the guidelines is to provide guidance on the application of the TTBER as well as on the application of Article 81 to technology transfer agreements that fall outside the scope of the TTBER. The TTBER and the guidelines are without prejudice to the possible parallel application of Article 82 of the Treaty to licensing agreements (2).

(2) See Joined Cases C-395/96 P and C-396/96 P, Compagnie Maritime Belge, [2000] ECR I-1365, paragraph 130, and paragraph 106 of the Commission Guidelines on the application of Article 81(3) of the Treaty, not yet published.

3. The standards set forth in these guidelines must be applied in light of the circumstances specific to each case. This excludes a mechanical application. Each case must be assessed on its own facts and the guidelines must be applied reasonably and flexibly. Examples given serve as illustrations only and are not intended to be exhaustive. The

Commission will keep under review the functioning of the TTBER and the guidelines in the new enforcement system created by Regulation 1/2003 (3) to consider whether changes need to be made.

(3) Council Regulation (EC) N° 1/2003 on the implementation of the rules on competition laid down in Articles 81 and 82 of the Treaty (O.J. L 1, 4.1.2003, p. 1).

4. The present guidelines are without prejudice to the interpretation of Article 81 and the TTBER that may be given by the Court of Justice and the Court of First Instance.

II. GENERAL PRINCIPLES

1. Article 81 and intellectual property rights

5. The aim of Article 81 as a whole is to protect competition on the market with a view to promoting consumer welfare and an efficient allocation of resources. Article 81(1) prohibits all agreements and concerted practices between undertakings and decisions by associations of undertakings (4) which may affect trade between Member States (5) and which have as their object or effect the prevention, restriction or distortion of competition (6). As an exception to this rule Article 81(3) provides that the prohibition contained in Article 81(1) may be declared inapplicable in the case of agreements between undertakings which contribute to improving the production or distribution of products or to promoting technical or economic progress, while allowing consumers a fair share of the resulting benefits and which do not impose restrictions which are not indispensable to the attainment of these objectives and do not afford such undertakings the possibility of eliminating competition in respect of a substantial part of the products concerned.

(4) In the following the term «agreement» includes concerted practices and decisions of associations of undertakings.

(5) See Commission Notice on the concept of effect on trade between Member States contained in Articles 81 and 82 of the Treaty, not yet published.

(6) In the following the term «restriction» includes the prevention and distortion of competition.

6. Intellectual property laws confer exclusive rights on holders of patents, copyright, design rights, trademarks and other legally protected rights. The owner of intellectual property is entitled under intellectual property laws to prevent unauthorised use of his intellectual property and to exploit it, inter alia, by licensing it to third parties. Once a product incorporating an intellectual property right has been put on the market inside the EEA by the holder or with his consent, the intellectual property right is exhausted in the sense that the holder can no longer use it to control the sale of the product (7) (principle of Community exhaustion). The right holder has no right under intellectual property laws to prevent sales by licensees or buyers of such products incorporating the licensed technology (8). The principle of Community exhaustion is in line with the essential function of intellectual property rights, which is to grant the holder the right to exclude others from exploiting his intellectual property without his consent.

(7) This principle of Community exhaustion is for example enshrined in Article 7(1) of Directive 104/89/EEC to approximate the laws of the Member States relating to trade marks (O.J. L 40, 11.2.1989, p. 1), which provides that the trade mark shall not entitle the proprietor to prohibit its use in relation to goods which have been put on the market in the Community under that trade mark by the proprietor or with his consent.

(8) On the other hand, the sale of copies of a protected work does not lead to the exhaustion of performance rights, including rental rights, in the work, see in this respect Case 158/86, Warner Brothers and Metronome Video, [1988] ECR 2605, and Case C-61/97, Foreningen af danske videogramdistributører, [1998] ECR I-5171.

7. The fact that intellectual property laws grant exclusive rights of exploitation does not imply that intellectual property rights are immune from competition law intervention. Articles 81 and 82 are in particular applicable to agreements whereby the holder licenses another undertaking to exploit his intellectual property rights (9). Nor does it imply that there is an inherent conflict between intellectual property rights and the Community competition rules. Indeed, both bodies of law share the same basic objective of promoting consumer welfare and an efficient allocation of resources. Innovation constitutes an essential and dynamic component of an open and competitive market economy. Intellectual property rights promote dynamic competition by encouraging undertakings to invest in developing new or improved products and processes. So does competition by putting pressure on undertakings to innovate. Therefore, both intellectual property rights and competition are necessary to promote innovation and ensure a competitive exploitation thereof.

(9) See e.g. Joined Cases 56/64 and 58/64, Consten and Grundig, [1966] ECR 429.

8. In the assessment of licence agreements under Article 81 it must be kept in mind that the creation of intellectual property rights often entails substantial investment and that it is often a risky endeavour. In order not to reduce dynamic competition and to maintain the incentive to innovate, the innovator must not be unduly restricted in the exploitation of intellectual property rights that turn out to be valuable. For these reasons the innovator should normally be free to seek compensation for successful projects that is sufficient to maintain investment incentives, taking failed projects into account. Technology licensing may also require the licensee to make significant sunk investments in the licensed technology and production assets necessary to exploit it. Article 81 cannot be applied without considering such *ex ante* investments made by the parties and the risks relating thereto. The risk facing the parties and the sunk investment that must be committed may thus lead to the agreement falling outside Article 81(1) or fulfilling the conditions of Article 81(3), as the case may be, for the period of time required to recoup the investment.

9. In assessing licensing agreements under Article 81, the existing analytical framework is sufficiently flexible to take due account of the dynamic aspects of technology licensing. There is no presumption that intellectual property rights and licence agreements as such give rise to competition concerns. Most licence agreements do not restrict competition and create pro-competitive efficiencies. Indeed, licensing as such is pro-competitive as it leads to dissemination of technology and promotes innovation. In addition, even licence agreements that do restrict competition may often give rise to pro-competitive efficiencies, which must be considered under Article 81(3) and balanced against the negative effects on competition (10). The great majority of licence agreements are therefore compatible with Article 81.

(10) The methodology for the application of Article 81(3) is set out in the Commission Guidelines on the application of Article 81(3) of the Treaty cited in note 2.

2. The general framework for applying Article 81

10. Article 81(1) prohibits agreements which have as their object or effect the restriction of competition. Article 81(1) applies both to restrictions of competition between the parties to an agreement and to restrictions of competition between any of the parties and third parties.

11. The assessment of whether a licence agreement restricts competition must be made within the actual context in which competition would occur in the absence of the agreement with its alleged restrictions (11). In making this assessment it is necessary to take account of the likely impact of the agreement on inter-technology competition (i.e. competition between undertakings using competing technologies) and on intra-technology competition (i.e. competition between undertakings using the same technology) (12). Article 81(1) prohibits restrictions of both inter-technology competition and intra-technology competition. It is therefore necessary to assess to what extent the agreement affects or is likely to affect these two aspects of competition on the market.

(11) See Case 56/65, Société Technique Minière, [1966] ECR 337, and Case C-7/95 P, John Deere, [1998] ECR I-3111, paragraph 76.

(12) See in this respect e.g. judgment in Consten and Grundig cited in note 9.

12. The following two questions provide a useful framework for making this assessment. The first question relates to the impact of the agreement on inter-technology competition while the second question relates to the impact of the agreement on intra-technology competition. As restraints may be capable of affecting both inter-technology competition and intra-technology competition at the same time, it may be necessary to analyse a restraint in the light of both questions before it can be concluded whether or not competition within the meaning of Article 81(1) is restricted:

(a) Does the licence agreement restrict actual or potential competition that would have existed without the contemplated agreement? If so, the agreement may be caught by Article 81(1). In making this assessment it is necessary to take into account competition between the parties and competition from third parties. For instance, where two undertakings established in different Member States cross licence competing technologies and undertake not to sell products in each other's home markets, (potential) competition that existed prior to the agreement is restricted. Similarly, where a licensor imposes obligations on his licensees not to use competing technologies and these obligations foreclose third party technologies, actual or potential competition that would have existed in the absence of the agreement is restricted.

(b) Does the agreement restrict actual or potential competition that would have existed in the absence of the contractual restraint(s)? If so, the agreement may be caught by Article 81(1). For instance, where a licensor restricts its licensees from competing with each other, (potential) competition that could have existed between the licensees absent the restraints is restricted. Such restrictions include vertical price fixing and territorial or customer sales restrictions between licensees. However, certain restraints may in certain cases not be caught by Article 81(1) when the restraint is objectively necessary for the existence of an agreement of that type or that nature (13). Such exclusion of the application of Article 81(1) can only be made on the basis of objective factors external to the parties themselves and not the subjective views and characteristics of the parties. The question is not whether the parties in their particular situation would not have accepted to conclude a less restrictive agreement, but whether, given the nature of the agreement and the characteristics of the market, a less restrictive agreement would not have been concluded by undertakings in a similar setting. For instance, territorial restraints in an agreement between non-competitors may fall outside Article 81(1) for a certain duration if the restraints are objectively necessary for a licensee to penetrate a new market. Similarly, a prohibition imposed on all licensees not to sell to certain categories of end users may not be restrictive of competition if such a restraint is objectively necessary for reasons of safety or health related to the dangerous nature of the product in question. Claims that in the absence of a restraint the supplier would have resorted to vertical integration are not sufficient. Decisions on whether or not to vertically integrate depend on a broad range of complex economic factors, a number of which are internal to the undertaking concerned.

(13) See in this respect the judgment in Société Technique Minière cited in note 11 and Case 258/78, Nungesser, [1982] ECR 2015.

13. In the application of the analytical framework set out in the previous paragraph it must be taken into account that Article 81(1) distinguishes between those agreements that have a restriction of competition as their object and those agreements that have a restriction of competition as their effect. An agreement or contractual restraint is only prohibited by Article 81(1) if its object or effect is to restrict inter-technology competition and/or intra-technology competition.

14. Restrictions of competition by object are those that by their very nature restrict competition. These are restrictions which in light of the objectives pursued by the Community competition rules have such a high potential for negative effects on competition that it is not necessary for the purposes of applying Article 81(1) to demonstrate any actual effects on the market (14). Moreover, the conditions of Article 81(3) are unlikely to be fulfilled in the case of restrictions by object. The assessment of whether or not an agreement has as its object a restriction of competition is based on a number of factors. These factors include, in particular, the content of the agreement and the objective aims pursued by it. It may also be necessary to consider the context in which it is (to be) applied or the actual conduct and behaviour of the parties on the market (15). In other words, an examination of the facts underlying the agreement and the specific circumstances in which it operates may be required before it can be concluded whether a particular restriction constitutes a hardcore restriction of competition. The way in which an agreement is actually implemented may reveal a restriction by object even where the formal agreement does not contain an express provision to that effect. Evidence of subjective intent on the part of the parties to restrict competition is a relevant factor but not a necessary condition. For licence agreements, the Commission considers that the restrictions covered by the list of hardcore restrictions of competition contained in Article 4 of the TTBER are restrictive by their very object.

(14) See in this respect e.g. Case C-49/92 P, Anic Partecipazioni, [1999] ECR I-4125, paragraph 99.

(15) See Joined Cases 29/83 and 30/83, CRAM and Rheinzink, [1984] ECR 1679, paragraph 26, and Joined Cases 96/82 and others, ANSEAU-NAVEWA, [1983] ECR 3369, paragraphs 23-25.

15. If an agreement is not restrictive of competition by object it is necessary to examine whether it has restrictive effects on competition. Account must be taken of both actual and potential effects (16). In other words the agreement must have likely anti-competitive effects. For licence agreements to be restrictive of competition by effect they must affect actual or potential competition to such an extent that on the relevant market negative effects on prices, output, innovation or the variety or quality of goods and services can be expected with a reasonable degree of probability. The likely negative effects on competition must be appreciable (17). Appreciable anticompetitive effects are likely to occur when at least one of the parties has or obtains some degree of market power and the agreement contributes to the creation, maintenance or strengthening of that market power or allows the parties to exploit such market power. Market power is the ability to maintain prices above competitive levels or to maintain output in terms of product quantities, product quality and variety or innovation below competitive levels for a not insignificant period of time. The degree of market power normally required for a finding of an infringement under Article 81(1) is less than the degree of market power required for a finding of dominance under Article 82.

(16) See the judgment in John Deere, [1998] cited in note 11.

(17) Guidance on the issue of appreciability can be found in Commission notice on agreements of minor importance which do not appreciably restrict competition under Article 81(1) of the Treaty (O.J. C 368, 22.12.2001, p. 13). The notice defines appreciability in a negative way. Agreements, which fall outside the scope of the de minimis notice, do not necessarily have appreciable restrictive effects. An individual assessment is required.

16. For the purposes of analysing restrictions of competition by effect it is normally necessary to define the relevant market and to examine and assess, inter alia, the nature of the products and technologies concerned, the market position of the parties, the market position of competitors, the market position of buyers, the existence of potential competitors and the level of entry barriers. In some cases, however, it may be possible to show anti-competitive effects directly by analysing the conduct of the parties to the agreement on the market. It may for example be possible to ascertain that an agreement has led to price increases.

17. Licence agreements, however, also have substantial pro-competitive potential. Indeed, the vast majority of licence agreements are pro-competitive. Licence agreements may promote innovation by allowing innovators to earn returns to cover at least part of their research and development costs. Licence agreements also lead to a dissemination of technologies, which may create value by reducing the production costs of the licensee or by enabling him to produce new or improved products. Efficiencies at the level of the licensee often stem from a combination of the licensor's technology with the assets and technologies of the licensee. Such integration of complementary assets and technologies may lead to a cost/output configuration that would not otherwise be possible. For instance, the combination of an improved technology of the licensor with more efficient production or distribution assets of the licensee may reduce production costs or lead to the production of a higher quality product. Licensing may also serve the pro-competitive purpose of removing obstacles to the development and exploitation of the licensee's own technology. In particular in sectors where large numbers of patents are prevalent licensing often occurs in order to create design freedom by removing the risk of infringement claims by the licensor. When the licensor agrees not to invoke his intellectual property rights to prevent the sale of the licensee's products, the agreement removes an obstacle to the sale of the licensee's product and thus generally promotes competition.

18. In cases where a licence agreement is caught by Article 81(1) the pro-competitive effects of the agreement must be balanced against its restrictive effects in the context of Article 81(3). When all four conditions of Article 81(3) are satisfied, the restrictive licence agreement in question is valid and enforceable, no prior decision to that effect being required (18). Hardcore restrictions of competition only fulfil the conditions of Article 81(3) in exceptional circumstances. Such agreements generally fail (at least) one of the first two conditions of Article 81(3). They generally do not create objective economic benefits or benefits for consumers. Moreover, these types of agreements generally also fail the indispensability test under the third condition. For example, if the parties fix the price at which the products produced under the licence must be sold, this will generally lead to a lower output and a misallocation of resources and higher prices for consumers. The price restriction is also not indispensable to achieve the possible efficiencies resulting from the availability to both competitors of the two technologies.

(18) See Article 1(2) of Council Regulation N° 1/2003 cited in note 3.

3. Market definition

19. The Commission's approach to defining the relevant market is laid down in its market definition guidelines (19). The present guidelines only address aspects of market definition that are of particular importance in the field of technology licensing.

(19) Commission notice on the definition of the relevant market for the purposes of Community competition law (O.J. C 372, 9.12.1997, p. 5).

20. Technology is an input, which is integrated either into a product or a production process. Technology licensing can therefore affect competition both in input markets and in output markets. For instance, an agreement between two parties which sell competing products and which cross license technologies relating to the production of these products may restrict competition on the product market concerned. It may also restrict competition on the market for technology and possibly also on other input markets. For the purposes of assessing the competitive effects of licence agreements it may therefore be necessary to define relevant goods and service markets (product markets) as well as technology markets (20). The term «product market» used in Article 3 of the TTBER refers to relevant goods and service markets in both their geographic and product dimension. As is clear from Article 1(1)(j) of the TTBER, the term is used merely to distinguish relevant goods and service markets from relevant technology markets.

(20) As to these distinctions see also Commission Guidelines on the applicability of Article 81 of the EC Treaty to horizontal cooperation agreements (O.J. C 3, 6.1.2001, p. 2, paragraphs 44 to 52).

21. The TTBER and these guidelines are concerned with effects both on product markets for final products and on product markets for intermediate products. The relevant product market includes products which are regarded by the buyers as interchangeable with or substitutable for the contract products incorporating the licensed technology, by reason of the products' characteristics, their prices and their intended use.

22. Technology markets consist of the licensed technology and its substitutes, i.e. other technologies which are regarded by the licensees as interchangeable with or substitutable for the licensed technology, by reason of the technologies' characteristics, their royalties and their intended use. The methodology for defining technology markets follows the same principles as the definition of product markets. Starting from the technology which is marketed by the licensor, one needs to identify those other technologies to which licensees could switch in response to a small but permanent increase in relative prices, i.e. the royalties. An alternative approach is to look at the market for products incorporating the licensed technology (cf. paragraph below).

23. Once relevant markets have been defined, market shares can be assigned to the various sources of competition in the market and used as an indication of the relative strength of market players. In the case of technology markets one way to proceed is to calculate market shares on the basis of each technology's share of total licensing income from royalties, representing a technology's share of the market where competing technologies are licensed. However, this may often be a mere theoretical and not a practical way to proceed because of lack of clear information on royalties etc. An alternative approach, which is the one used in Article 3(3) of the TTBER, is to calculate market shares on the technology market on the basis of sales of products incorporating the licensed technology on downstream product markets (see paragraph 70 below). Under this approach all sales on the relevant product market are taken into account, irrespective of whether the product incorporates a technology that is being licensed. In the case of technology markets the approach of Article 3(3) to take into account technologies that are (only) being used in-house, is justified. Indeed, this approach is in general a good indicator of the strength of the technology. First, it captures any potential competition from undertakings that are producing with their own technology and that are likely to start licensing in the event of a small but permanent increase in the price for licenses. Secondly, even where it is unlikely that other technology owners would start licensing, the licensor does not necessarily have market power on the technology market even if he has a high share of licensing income. If the downstream product market is competitive, competition at this level may effectively constrain the licensor. An increase in royalties upstream affects the costs of the licensee, making him less competitive, causing him to lose sales. A technology's market share on the product market also captures this element and is thus normally a good indicator of licensor market power. In individual cases outside the safe harbour of the TTBER it may be necessary, where practically possible, to apply both of the described approaches in order to assess more accurately the market strength of the licensor.

24. Moreover, outside the safe harbour of the TTBER it must also be taken into account that market share may not always be a good indication of the relative strength of available technologies. The Commission will therefore, inter alia, also have regard to the number of independently controlled technologies available in addition to the technologies controlled by the parties to the agreement that may be substitutable for the licensed technology at a comparable cost to the user (see paragraph 131 below).

25. Some licence agreements may affect innovation markets. In analysing such effects, however, the Commission will normally confine itself to examining the impact of the agreement on competition within existing product and technology markets (21). Competition on such markets may be affected by agreements that delay the introduction of improved products or new products that over time will replace existing products. In such cases innovation is a source of potential competition which must be taken into account when assessing the impact of the agreement on product markets and technology markets. In a limited number of cases, however, it may be useful and necessary to also define innovation markets. This is particularly the case where the agreement affects innovation aiming at creating new products and where it is possible at an early stage to identify research and development poles (22). In such cases it can be analysed whether after the agreement there will be a sufficient number of competing research and development poles left for effective competition in innovation to be maintained.

(21) See to that effect paragraphs 50 to 52 of the Guidelines on horizontal cooperation agreements, cited in the previous note.

(22) *Idem*, paragraph 51.

4. The distinction between competitors and noncompetitors

26. In general, agreements between competitors pose a greater risk to competition than agreements between non-competitors. However, competition between undertakings that use the same technology (intra-technology competition between licensees) constitutes an important complement to competition between undertakings that use competing technologies (inter-technology competition). For instance, intra-technology competition may lead to lower prices for the products incorporating the technology in question, which may not only produce direct and immediate benefits for consumers of these products, but also spur further competition between undertakings that use competing technologies. In the context of licensing it must also be taken into account that licensees are selling their own product. They are not re-selling a product supplied by another undertaking. There may thus be greater scope for product differentiation and quality-based competition between licensees than in the case of vertical agreements for the resale of products.

27. In order to determine the competitive relationship between the parties it is necessary to examine whether the parties would have been actual or potential competitors in the absence of the agreement. If without the agreement the parties would not have been actual or potential competitors in any relevant market affected by the agreement they are deemed to be non-competitors.

28. Where the licensor and the licensee are both active on the same product market or the same technology market without one or both parties infringing the intellectual property rights of the other party, they are actual competitors on the market concerned. The parties are deemed to be actual competitors on the technology market if the licensee is already licensing out his technology and the licensor enters the technology market by granting a license for a competing technology to the licensee.

29. The parties are considered to be potential competitors on the product market if in the absence of the agreement and without infringing the intellectual property rights of the other party it is likely that they would have undertaken the necessary additional investment to enter the relevant market in response to a small but permanent increase in product prices. In order to constitute a realistic competitive constraint entry has to be likely to occur within a short period. Normally a period of one to two years is appropriate. However, in individual cases longer periods can be taken into account. The period of time needed for undertakings already on the market to adjust their capacities can be used as a yardstick to determine this period. For instance, the parties are likely to be considered potential competitors on the product market where the licensee produces on the basis of its own technology in one geographic market and starts producing in another geographic market on the basis of a licensed competing technology. In such circumstances, it is likely that the licensee would have been able to enter the second geographic market on the basis of its own technology, unless such entry is precluded by objective factors, including the existence of blocking patents (see paragraph 32 below).

30. The parties are considered to be potential competitors on the technology market where they own substitutable technologies if in the specific case the licensee is not licensing his own technology, provided that he would be likely to do so in the event of a small but permanent increase in technology prices. However, for the application of the TTBER potential competition on the technology market is not taken into account (see paragraph 66 below).

31. In some cases the parties may become competitors subsequent to the conclusion of the agreement because the licensee develops and starts exploiting a competing technology. In such cases it must be taken into account that the parties were non-competitors at the time of conclusion of the agreement and that the agreement was concluded in that context. The Commission will therefore mainly focus on the impact of the agreement on the licensee's ability to exploit his own (competing) technology. In particular, the list of hardcore restrictions applying to agreements between competitors will not be applied to such agreements unless the agreement is subsequently amended in any material respect after the parties have become competitors (cf. Article 4(3) of the TTBER). The undertakings party to an agreement may also become competitors subsequent to the conclusion of the agreement where the licensee was already active on the product market prior to the licence and where the licensor subsequently enters the product market either on the basis of the licensed technology or a new technology. Also in this case the hardcore list relevant for agreements between non-competitors will continue to apply to the agreement unless the agreement is subsequently amended in any material respect (cf. article 4(3) of the TTBER.

32. If the parties own technologies that are in a one-way or two-way blocking position, the parties are considered to be non-competitors on the technology market. A one-way blocking position exists when a technology cannot be exploited without infringing upon another technology. This is for instance the case where one patent covers an improvement of a technology covered by another patent. In that case the exploitation of the improvement patent pre-supposes that the holder obtains a licence to the basic patent. A two-way blocking position exists where neither technology can be exploited without infringing upon the other technology and where the holders thus need to obtain a licence or a waiver from each other. In assessing whether a blocking position exists the Commission will rely on objective factors as opposed to the subjective views of the parties. Particularly convincing evidence of the existence of a blocking position is required where the parties may have a common interest in claiming the existence of a blocking position in order to be qualified as non-competitors, for instance where the claimed two-way blocking position concerns technologies that are technological substitutes. Relevant evidence includes court decisions including injunctions and opinions of independent experts. In the latter case the Commission will, in particular, closely examine how the expert has been selected. However, also other convincing evidence, including expert evidence from the parties that they have or had good and valid reasons to believe that a blocking position exists or existed, can be relevant to substantiate the existence of a blocking position.

33. In some cases it may also be possible to conclude that while the licensor and the licensee produce competing products, they are non-competitors on the relevant product market and the relevant technology market because the licensed technology represents such a drastic innovation that the technology of the licensee has become obsolete or uncompetitive. In such cases the licensor's technology either creates a new market or excludes the licensee's technology from the market. Often, however, it is not possible to come to this conclusion at the time the agreement is concluded. It is usually only when the technology or the products incorporating it have been available to consumers for some time that it becomes apparent that the older technology has become obsolete or uncompetitive. For instance, when CD technology was developed and players and discs were put on the market, it was not obvious that this new technology would replace LP technology. This only became apparent some years later. The parties will therefore be considered to be competitors if at the time of the conclusion of the agreement it is not obvious that the licensee's technology is obsolete or uncompetitive. However, given that both Articles 81(1) and Article 81(3) must be applied in light of the actual context in which the agreement occurs, the assessment is sensitive to material changes in the facts. The classification of the relationship between the parties will therefore change into a relationship of non-competitors, if at a later point in time the licensee's technology becomes obsolete or uncompetitive on the market.

III. APPLICATION OF THE BLOCK EXEMPTION REGULATION

1. The effects of the Block Exemption Regulation

34. Technology transfer agreements that fulfil the conditions set out in the TTBER are block exempted from the prohibition rule contained in Article 81(1). Block exempted agreements are legally valid and enforceable. Such agreements can only be prohibited for the future and only upon withdrawal of the block exemption by the Commission or a Member State competition authority. Block exempted agreements cannot be prohibited under Article 81 by national courts in the context of private litigation.

35. Block exemption of categories of technology transfer agreements is based on the presumption that such agreements – to the extent that they are caught by Article 81(1) – fulfil the four conditions laid down in Article 81(3). It is thus presumed that the agreements give rise to economic efficiencies, that the restrictions contained in the agreements are indispensable to the attainment of these efficiencies, that consumers within the affected markets receive a fair share of the efficiency gains and that the agreements do not afford the undertakings concerned the possibility of eliminating competition in respect of a substantial part of the products in question. The market share thresholds (Article 3), the hardcore list (Article 4) and the excluded restrictions (Article 5) set out in the TTBER aim at ensuring that only restrictive agreements that can reasonably be presumed to fulfil the four conditions of Article 81(3) are block exempted.

36. As set out in section IV below, many licence agreements fall outside Article 81(1), either because they do not restrict competition at all or because the restriction of competition is not appreciable (23). To the extent that such agreements would anyhow fall within the scope of the TTBER, there is no need to determine whether they are caught by Article 81(1) (24).

(23) See in this respect the Notice on agreements of minor importance cited in note 17.

(24) According to Article 3(2) of Regulation 1/2003, agreements which may affect trade between Member States but which are not prohibited by Article 81 cannot be prohibited by national competition law.

37. Outside the scope of the block exemption it is relevant to examine whether in the individual case the agreement is caught by Article 81(1) and if so whether the conditions of Article 81(3) are satisfied. There is no presumption that technology transfer agreements falling outside the block exemption are caught by Article 81(1) or fail to satisfy the conditions of Article 81(3). In particular, the mere fact that the market shares of the parties exceed the market share thresholds set out in Article 3 of the TTBER is not a sufficient basis for finding that the agreement is caught by Article 81(1). Individual assessment of the likely effects of the agreement is required. It is only when agreements contain hardcore restrictions of competition that it can normally be presumed that they are prohibited by Article 81.

2. Scope and duration of the Block Exemption Regulation

2.1. Agreements between two parties

38. According to Article 2(1) of the TTBER, the Regulation covers technology transfer agreements «between two undertakings». Technology transfer agreements between more than two undertakings are not covered by the TTBER (25). The decisive factor in terms of distinguishing between agreements between two undertakings and multiparty agreements is whether the agreement in question is concluded between more than two undertakings.

(25) Under Council Regulation 19/65, O.J. Special Edition Series I 1965-1966, p. 35, the Commission is not empowered to block exempt technology transfer agreements concluded between more than two undertakings.

39. Agreements concluded by two undertakings fall within the scope of the TTBER even if the agreement stipulates conditions for more than one level of trade. For instance, the TTBER applies to a licence agreement concerning not only the production stage but also the distribution stage, stipulating the obligations that the licensee must or may impose on resellers of the products produced under the licence (26).

(26) See recital 19 of the TTBER and further section 2.5 below.

40. Licence agreements concluded between more than two undertakings often give rise to the same issues as licence agreements of the same nature concluded between two undertakings. In its individual assessment of licence agreements which are of the same nature as those covered by the block exemption but which are concluded between more than two undertakings, the Commission will apply by analogy the principles set out in the TTBER.

2.2. Agreements for the production of contract products

41. It follows from Article 2 that for licence agreements to be covered by the TTBER they must concern «the production of contract products», i.e. products incorporating or produced with the licensed technology. In other words, to be covered by the TTBER the licence must permit the licensee to exploit the licensed technology for production of goods or services (see recital 7 of the TTBER). The TTBER does not cover technology pools. The notion of technology pools covers agreements whereby two or more parties agree to pool their respective technologies and license them as a package. The notion of technology pools also covers arrangements whereby two or more undertakings agree to license a third party and authorise him to license on the package of technologies. Technology pools are dealt with in section IV.4 below.

42. The TTBER applies to licence agreements for the production of contract products whereby the licensee is also permitted to sublicense the licensed technology to third parties provided, however, that the production of contract products constitutes the primary object of the agreement. Conversely, the TTBER does not apply to agreements that have sublicensing as their primary object. However, the Commission will apply by analogy the principles set out in the TTBER and these guidelines to such «master licensing» agreements between licensor and licensee. Agreements between the licensee and sub-licensees are covered by the TTBER.

43. The term «contract products» encompasses goods and services produced with the licensed technology. This is the case both where the licensed technology is used in the production process and where it is incorporated into the product itself. In these guidelines the term «products incorporating the licensed technology» covers both situations. The TTBER applies in all cases where technology is licensed for the purposes of producing goods and services. It is sufficient in this respect that the licensor undertakes not to exercise his intellectual property rights against the licensee. Indeed, the essence of a pure patent licence is the right to operate inside the scope of the exclusive right of the patent. It follows that the TTBER also covers so-called non-assertion agreements and settlement agreements whereby the licensor permits the licensee to produce within the scope of the patent.

44. The TTBER covers «subcontracting» whereby the licensor licenses technology to the licensee who undertakes to produce certain products on the basis thereof exclusively for the licensor. Subcontracting may also involve the supply of equipment by the licensor to be used in the production of the goods and services covered by the agreement. For the latter type of subcontracting to be covered by the TTBER, the licensed technology and not the supplied equipment must constitute the primary object of the agreement. Subcontracting is also covered by the Commission's Notice concerning the assessment of certain subcontracting agreements in relation to Article 81(1) of the Treaty (27). According to this notice, which remains applicable, subcontracting agreements whereby the subcontractor undertakes to produce certain products exclusively for the contractor generally fall outside Article 81(1). However, other restrictions imposed on the subcontractor such as the obligation not to conduct or exploit his own research and development may be caught by Article 81 (28).

(27) O.J. C 1, 3.1.1979, p. 2.

(28) See paragraph 3 of the subcontracting notice.

45. The TTBER also applies to agreements whereby the licensee must carry out development work before obtaining a product or a process that is ready for commercial exploitation, provided that a contract product has been identified. Even if such further work and investment is required, the object of the agreement is the production of an identified contract product. On the other hand, the TTBER and the guidelines do not cover agreements whereby a technology is licensed for the purpose of enabling the licensee to carry out further research and development in various fields. For instance, the TTBER and the guidelines do not cover the licensing of a technological research tool used in the process of further research activity. The framework of the TTBER and the guidelines is based on the premise that there is a direct link between the licensed technology and an identified contract product. In cases where no such link exists the main object of the agreement is research and development as opposed to bringing a particular product to the market; in that case the analytical framework of the TTBER and the guidelines may not be appropriate. For the same reasons the TTBER and the guidelines do not cover research and development sub-contracting whereby the licensee undertakes to carry out research and development in the field of the licensed technology and to hand back the improved technology package to the licensor. The main object of such agreements is the provision of research and development services aimed at improving the technology as opposed to the production of goods and services on the basis of the licensed technology.

2.3. The concept of technology transfer agreements

46. The TTBER and these guidelines cover agreements for the transfer of technology. According to Article 1(1)(b) and (h) of the TTBER the concept of «technology» covers patents and patent applications, utility models and applications for utility models, design rights, plant breeders rights, topographies of semiconductor products, supplementary protection certificates for medicinal products or other products for which such supplementary protection certificates may be obtained, software copyright, and know-how. The licensed technology should allow the licensee with or without other inputs to produce the contract products.

47. Know-how is defined in Article 1(1)(i) as a package of non-patented practical information, resulting from experience and testing, which is secret, substantial and identified. «Secret» means that the know-how is not generally known or easily accessible. «Substantial» means that the know-how includes information which is significant and useful for the production of the products covered by the licence agreement or the application of the process covered by the licence agreement. In other words, the information must significantly contribute to or facilitate the production of the contract products. In cases where the licensed know-how relates to a product as opposed to a process, this condition implies that the know-how is useful for the production the contract product. This condition is not satisfied where the contract product can be produced on the basis of freely available technology. However, the condition does not require that the contract product is of higher value than products produced with freely available technology. In the case of process technologies, this condition implies that the know-how is useful in the sense that it can reasonably be expected at the date of conclusion of the agreement to be capable of significantly improving the competitive position of the licensee, for instance by reducing his production costs. «Identified» means that it is possible to verify that the licensed know-how fulfils the criteria of secrecy and substantiality. This condition is satisfied where the licensed know-how is described in manuals or other written form. However, in some cases this may not be reasonably possible. The licensed know-how may consist of practical knowledge possessed by the licensor's employees. For instance, the licensor's employees may possess secret and substantial knowledge about a certain production process which is passed on to the licensee in the form of training of the licensee's employees. In such cases it is sufficient to describe in the agreement the general nature of the know-how and to list the employees that will be or have been involved in passing it on to the licensee.

48. The concept of «transfer» implies that technology must flow from one undertaking to another. Such transfers normally take the form of licensing whereby the licensor grants the licensee the right to use his technology against payment of royalties. It can also take the form of sub-licensing, whereby a licensee, having been authorised to do so by the licensor, grants licenses to third parties (sub-licensees) for the exploitation of the technology

49. The TTBER only applies to agreements that have as their primary object the transfer of technology as defined in that Regulation as opposed to the purchase of goods and services or the licensing of other types of intellectual property. Agreements containing provisions relating to the purchase and sale of products are only covered by the TTBER to the extent that those provisions do not constitute the primary object of the agreement and are directly related to the application of the licensed technology. This is likely to be the case where the tied products take the form of equipment or process input which is specifically tailored to efficiently exploit the licensed technology. If, on the other hand, the product is simply another input into the final product, it must be carefully examined whether the licensed technology constitutes the primary object of the agreement. For instance, in cases where the licensee is already manufacturing a final product on the basis of another technology, the licence must lead to a significant improvement of the licensee's production process, exceeding the value of the product purchased from the licensor. The requirement that the tied products must be related to the licensing of technology implies that the TTBER does not cover the purchase of products that have no relation with the products incorporating the licensed technology. This is for example the case where the tied product is not intended to be used with the licensed product, but relates to an activity on a separate product market.

50. The TTBER only covers the licensing of other types of intellectual property such as trademarks and copyright, other than software copyright, to the extent that they are directly related to the exploitation of the licensed technology and do not constitute the primary object of the agreement. This condition ensures that agreements covering other types of intellectual property rights are only block exempted to the extent that these other intellectual property rights serve to enable the licensee to better exploit the licensed technology. The licensor may for instance authorise the licensee to use his trademark on the products incorporating the licensed technology. The trademark licence may allow the licensee to better exploit the licensed technology by allowing consumers to make an immediate link between the product and the characteristics imputed to it by the licensed technology. An obligation on the licensee to use the licensor's trademark may also promote the dissemination of technology by allowing the licensor to identify himself as the source of the underlying technology. However, where the value of the licensed technology to the licensee is limited because he already employs an identical or very similar technology and the main object of the agreement is the trademark, the TTBER does not apply (29).

(29) ee in this respect Commission Decision in Mooseheah/Whitbread (O.J. L 100, 20.4.1990, p. 32).

51. The licensing of copyright for the purpose of reproduction and distribution of the protected work, i.e. the production of copies for resale, is considered to be similar to technology licensing. Since such licence agreements relate to the production and sale of products on the basis of an intellectual property right, they are considered to be of a similar nature as technology transfer agreements and normally raise comparable issues. Although the TTBER does not cover copyright other than software copyright, the Commission will as a general rule apply the principles set out in the TTBER and these guidelines when assessing such licensing of copyright under Article 81.

52. On the other hand, the licensing of rights in performances and other rights related to copyright is considered to raise particular issues and it may not be warranted to assess such licensing on the basis of the principles developed in these guidelines. In the case of the various rights related to performances value is created not by the reproduction and sale of copies of a product but by each individual performance of the protected work. Such exploitation can take various forms including the performance, showing or the renting of protected material such as films, music or sporting events. In the application of Article 81 the specificities of the work and the way in which it is exploited must be taken into account (30). For instance, resale restrictions may give rise to less competition concerns whereas particular concerns may arise where licensors impose on their licensees to extend to each of the licensors more favourable conditions obtained by one of them. The Commission will therefore not apply the TTBER and the present guidelines by way of analogy to the licensing of these other rights.

(30) See in this respect Case 262/81, Coditel (II), [1982] ECR 3381.

53. The Commission will also not extend the principles developed in the TTBER and these guidelines to trademark licensing. Trademark licensing often occurs in the context of distribution and resale of goods and services and is generally more akin to distribution agreements than technology licensing. Where a trademark licence is directly related to the use, sale or resale of goods and services and does not constitute the primary object of the agreement, the licence agreement is covered by Commission Regulation (EC) N° 2790/1999 on the application of Article 81(3) of the Treaty to categories of vertical agreements and concerted practices (31).

(31) O.J. L 336, 29.12.1999, p. 21.

2.4. Duration

54. Subject to the duration of the TTBER, the block exemption applies for as long as the licensed property right has not lapsed, expired or been declared invalid. In the case of know-how the block exemption applies as long as the licensed know-how remains secret, except where the know-how becomes publicly known as a result of action by the licensee, in which case the exemption shall apply for the duration of the agreement (cf. Article 2 of the TTBER).

55. The block exemption applies to each licensed property right covered by the agreement and ceases to apply on the date of expiry, invalidity or the coming into the public domain of the last intellectual property right which constitutes «technology» within the meaning of the TTBER (cf. paragraph above).

2.5. Relationship with other block exemption regulations

56. The TTBER covers agreements between two undertakings concerning the licensing of technology for the purpose of the production of contract products. However, technology can also be an element of other types of agreements. In addition, the products incorporating the licensed technology are subsequently sold on the market. It is therefore necessary to address the interface between the TTBER and Commission Regulation (EC) N° 2658/2000 on the application of Article 81(3) of the Treaty to categories of specialisation agreements (32), Commission Regulation 2659/2000 on the application of Article 81(3) to categories of research and development agreements (33) and Commission Regulation (EC) N° 2790/1999 on the application of Article 81(3) of the Treaty to categories of vertical agreements and concerted practices (34).

(32) O.J. L 304, 5.12.2000, p. 3.

(33) O.J. L 304, 5.12.2000, p. 7.

(34) See note 31.

1. Please note that all Block Exemption Regulations referred to in this section 2.5 have been replaced in 2010: Regulation 2658/2000 by Regulation 1218/2010; Regulation 2659/2000 by regulation 1217/2010; and Regulation 2790/1999 by Regulation 330/2010.
The interfaces described in paragraphs 57 to 64 are therefore to be read *mutatis mutandis*.

2.5.1. The Block Exemption Regulations on specialisation and R&D agreements

57. According to Article 1(1)(c) of Regulation 2658/2000 on specialisation agreements, that Regulation covers, inter alia, joint production agreements by virtue of which two or more undertakings agree to produce certain products jointly. The Regulation extends to provisions concerning the assignment or use of intellectual property rights, provided that they do not constitute the primary object of the agreement, but are directly related to and necessary for its implementation.

58. Where undertakings establish a production joint venture and license the joint venture to exploit technology, which is used in the production of the products produced by the joint venture, such licensing is subject to Regulation 2658/2000 and not the TTBER. Accordingly, licensing in the context of a production joint venture normally falls to be considered under Regulation 2658/2000. However, where the joint venture engages in licensing of the technology to third parties, the activity is not linked to production by the joint venture and therefore not covered by that Regulation. Such licensing arrangements, which bring together the technologies of the parties, constitute technology pools, which are dealt with in section IV.4 below.

59. Regulation 2659/2000 on research and development agreements covers agreements whereby two or more undertakings agree to jointly carry out research and development and to jointly exploit the results thereof. According to Article 2(11), research and development and the exploitation of the results are carried out jointly where the work involved is carried out by a joint team, organisation or undertakings, jointly entrusted to a third party or allocated between the parties by way of specialisation in research, development, production and distribution, including licensing.

60. It follows that Regulation 2659/2000 covers licensing between the parties and by the parties to a joint entity in the context of a research and development agreement. In the context of such agreements the parties can also determine the conditions for licensing the fruits of the research and development agreement to third parties. However, since third party licensees are not party to the research and development agreement, the individual licence agreement concluded with third parties is not covered by Regulation 2659/2000. Such licence agreements are block exempted by the TTBER where they fulfil the conditions of that Regulation.

2.5.2. The Block Exemption Regulation on vertical agreements

61. Commission Regulation (EC) N° 2790/1999 on vertical agreements covers agreements entered into between two or more undertakings each operating, for the purposes of the agreement, at different levels of the production or distribution chain, and relating to the conditions under which the parties may purchase, sell or resell certain goods or services. It thus covers supply and distribution agreements (35).

(35) See the guide «Competition policy in Europe – The competition rules for supply and distribution agreements», 2002.

62. Given that the TTBER only covers agreements between two parties and that a licensee, selling products incorporating the licensed technology, is a supplier for the purposes of Regulation 2790/1999, these two block exemption regulations are closely related. The agreement between licensor and licensee is subject to the TTBER whereas agreements concluded between a licensee and buyers are subject to Regulation 2790/1999 and the Guidelines on Vertical Restraints (36).

(36) O.J. C 291, 13.10.2000, p. 1, and note 31.

63. The TTBER also block exempts agreements between the licensor and the licensee where the agreement imposes obligations on the licensee as to the way in which he must sell the products incorporating the licensed technology. In particular, the licensee can be obliged to establish a certain type of distribution system such as exclusive distribution or selective distribution. However, the distribution agreements concluded for the purposes of implementing such obligations must, in order to be block exempted, comply with Regulation 2790/1999. For instance, the licensor can oblige the licensee to establish a system based on exclusive distribution in accordance with specified rules. However, it follows from Article 4(b) of Regulation 2790/1999 that distributors must be free to make passive sales into the territories of other exclusive distributors.

64. Furthermore, distributors must in principle be free to sell both actively and passively into territories covered by the distribution systems of other licensees producing their own products on the basis of the licensed technology. This is because for the purposes of Regulation 2790/1999 each licensee is a separate supplier. However, the reasons underlying the block exemption contained in that Regulation may also apply where the products incorporating the licensed technology are sold by the licensees under a common brand belonging to the licensor. When the products incorporating the licensed technology are sold under a common brand identity there may be the same efficiency reasons for applying the same types of restraints between licensees' distribution systems as within a single vertical distribution system. In such cases the Commission would be unlikely to challenge restraints where by analogy the requirements of Regulation 2790/1999 are fulfilled. For a common brand identity to exist the products must be sold and marketed under a common brand, which is predominant in terms of conveying quality and other relevant information to the consumer. It does not suffice that in addition to the licensees' brands the product carries the licensor's brand, which identifies him as the source of the licensed technology.

3. The safe harbour established by the Block Exemption Regulation

65. According to Article 3 of the TTBER the block exemption of restrictive agreements is subject to market share thresholds, confining the scope of the block exemption to agreements that although they may be restrictive of competition can generally be presumed to fulfil the conditions of Article 81(3). Outside the safe harbour created by the market share thresholds individual assessment is required. The fact that market shares exceed the thresholds does not give rise to any presumption either that the agreement is caught by Article 81(1) or that the agreement does not fulfil the conditions of Article 81(3). In the absence of hardcore restrictions, market analysis is required.

66. The market share threshold to be applied for the purpose of the safe harbour of the TTBER depends on whether the agreement is concluded between competitors or non-competitors. For the purposes of the TTBER undertakings are competitors on the relevant technology market when they license competing technologies. Potential competition on the technology market is not taken into account for the application of the market share threshold or the hardcore list. Outside the safe harbour of the TTBER potential competition on the technology market is taken into account but does not lead to the application of the hardcore list relating to agreements between competitors (see also paragraph 31 above).

67. Undertakings are competitors on the relevant product market where both undertakings are active on the same product and geographic market(s) on which the products incorporating the licensed technology are sold (actual competitors). They are also considered competitors where they would be likely, on realistic grounds, to undertake the necessary additional investments or other necessary switching costs to enter the relevant product and geographic market(s) within a reasonably short period of time (37) in response to a small and permanent increase in relative prices (potential competitors).

(37) See paragraph 29 above.

68. It follows from paragraphs 66 and 67 that two undertakings are not competitors for the purposes of the TTBER where the licensor is neither an actual nor a potential supplier of products on the relevant market and the licensee, already present on the product market, is not licensing out a competing technology even if he owns a competing technology and produces on the basis of that technology. However, the parties become competitors if at a later point in time the licensee starts licensing out his technology or the licensor becomes an actual or potential supplier of prod-

ucts on the relevant market. In that case the hardcore list relevant for agreements between non-competitors will continue to apply to the agreement unless the agreement is subsequently amended in any material respect, see Article 4(3) of the TTBER and paragraph 31 above.

69. In the case of agreements between competitors the market share threshold is 20% and in the case of agreements between non-competitors it is 30% (cf. Article 3(1) and (2) of the TTBER). Where the undertakings party to the licensing agreement are not competitors the agreement is covered if the market share of neither party exceeds 30% on the affected relevant technology and product markets. Where the undertakings party to the licensing agreement are competitors the agreement is covered if the combined market shares of the parties do not exceed 20% on the relevant technology and product markets. The market share thresholds apply both to technology markets and markets for products incorporating the licensed technology. If the applicable market share threshold is exceeded on an affected relevant market, the block exemption does not apply to the agreement for that relevant market. For instance, if the licence agreement concerns two separate product markets or two separate geographic markets, the block exemption may apply to one of the markets and not to the other.

70. In the case of technology markets, it follows from Article 3(3) of the TTBER that the licensor's market share is to be calculated on the basis of the sales of the licensor and all his licensees of products incorporating the licensed technology and this for each relevant market separately (38). Where the parties are competitors on the technology market, sales of products incorporating the licensee's own technology must be combined with the sales of the products incorporating the licensed technology. In the case of new technologies that have not yet generated any sales, a zero market share is assigned. When sales commence the technology will start accumulating market share.

(38) The reasons for this calculation rule are explained in paragraph 23 above.

71. In the case of product markets, the licensee's market share is to be calculated on the basis of the licensee's sales of products incorporating the licensor's technology and competing products, i.e. the total sales of the licensee on the product market in question. Where the licensor is also a supplier of products on the relevant market, the licensor's sales on the product market in question must also be taken into account. In the calculation of market shares for product markets, however, sales made by other licensees are not taken into account when calculating the licensee's and/or licensor's market share.

72. Market shares should be calculated on the basis of sales value data where such data are available. Such data normally provide a more accurate indication of the strength of a technology than volume data. However, where value based data are not available, estimates based on other reliable market information may be used, including market sales volume data.

73. The principles set out above can be illustrated by the following examples:
Licensing between non-competitors
Example 1
Company A is specialised in developing bio-technological products and techniques and has developed a new product Xeran. It is not active as a producer of Xeran, for which it has neither the production nor the distribution facilities. Company B is one of the producers of competing products, produced with freely available non-proprietary technologies. In year 1, B was selling EUR 25 million worth of products produced with the freely available technologies. In year 2, A gives a licence to B to produce Xeran. In that year B sells EUR 15 million produced with the help of the freely available technologies and EUR 15 million of Xeran. In year 3 and the following years B produces and sells only Xeran worth EUR 40 million annually. In addition in year 2, A is also licensing to C. C was not active on that product market before. C produces and sells only Xeran, EUR 10 million in year 2 and EUR 15 million in year 3 and thereafter. It is established that the total market of Xeran and its substitutes where B and C are active is worth EUR 200 million in each year.

In year 2, the year the licence agreement is concluded, A's market share on the technology market is 0% as its market share has to be calculated on the basis of the total sales of Xeran in the preceding year. In year 3 A's market share on the technology market is 12,5%, reflecting the value of Xeran produced by B and C in the preceding year 2. In year 4 and thereafter A's market share on the technology market is 27,5%, reflecting the value of Xeran produced by B and C in the preceding year.

In year 2 B's market share on the product market is 12,5%, reflecting B's EUR 25 million sales in year 1. In year 3 B's market share is 15% because its sales have increased to EUR 30 million in year 2. In year 4 and thereafter B's market share is 20% as its sales are EUR 40 million annually. C's market share on the product market is 0% in year 1 and 2, 5% in year 3 and 7, 5% thereafter.

As the licence agreements are between non-competitors and the individual market shares of A, B and C are below 30% each year, the agreements fall within the safe harbour of the TTBER.

Example 2
The situation is the same as in example 1, however now B and C are operating in different geographic markets. It is established that the total market of Xeran and its substitutes is worth EUR 100 million annually in each geographic market.

In this case, A's market share on the technology market has to be calculated for each of the two geographic markets. In the market where B is active A's market share depends on the sale of Xeran by B. As in this example the total market is assumed to be EUR 100 million, i.e. half the size of the market in example 1, the market share of A is 0% in year 2, 15% in year 3 and 40% thereafter. B's market share is 25% in year 2, 30% in year 3 and 40% thereafter. In year 2 and 3 both A's and B's market share does not exceed the 30% threshold. The threshold is however exceeded from year 4 and this means that, in line with Article 8(2) of the TTBER, after year 6 the licence agreement between A and B can no longer benefit from the safe harbour but has to be assessed on an individual basis.

In the market where C is active A's market share depends on the sale of Xeran by C. A's market share on the technology market, based on C's sales in the previous year, is therefore 0% in year 2, 10% in year 3 and 15% thereafter. The market share of C on the product market is the same: 0% in year 2, 10% in year 3 and 15% thereafter. The licence agreement between A and C therefore falls within the safe harbour for the whole period.

Licensing between competitors

Example 3

Companies A and B are active on the same relevant product and geographic market for a certain chemical product. They also each own a patent on different technologies used to produce this product. In year 1 A and B sign a cross licence agreement licensing each other to use their respective technologies. In year 1 A and B produce only with their own technology and A sells EUR 15 million of the product and B sells EUR 20 million of the product. From year 2 they both use their own and the other's technology. From that year onward A sells EUR 10 million of the product produced with its own technology and EUR 10 million of the product produced with B's technology. B sells from year 2 EUR 15 million of the product produced with its own technology and EUR 10 million of the product produced with A's technology. It is established that the total market of the product and its substitutes is worth EUR 100 million in each year.

To assess the licence agreement under the TTBER, the market shares of A and B have to be calculated both on the technology market and the product market. The market share of A on the technology market depends on the amount of the product sold in the preceding year that was produced, by both A and B, with A's technology. In year 2 the market share of A on the technology market is therefore 15%, reflecting its own production and sales of EUR 15 million in year 1. From year 3 A's market share on the technology market is 20%, reflecting the EUR 20 million sale of the product produced with A's technology and produced and sold by A and B (EUR 10 million each). Similarly, in year 2 B's market share on the technology market is 20% and thereafter 25%.

The market shares of A and B on the product market depend on their respective sales of the product in the previous year, irrespective of the technology used. The market share of A on the product market is 15% in year 2 and 20% thereafter. The market share of B on the product market is 20% in year 2 and 25% thereafter.

As the agreement is between competitors, their combined market share, both on the technology and on the product market, has to be below the 20% market share threshold in order to benefit from the safe harbour. It is clear that this is not the case here. The combined market share on the technology market and on the product market is 35% in year 2 and 45% thereafter. This agreement between competitors will therefore have to be assessed on an individual basis.

4. Hardcore restrictions of competition under the Block Exemption Regulation

4.1. General principles

74. Article 4 of the TTBER contains a list of hardcore restrictions of competition. The classification of a restraint as a hardcore restriction of competition is based on the nature of the restriction and experience showing that such restrictions are almost always anticompetitive. In line with the case law of the Community Courts (39) such a restriction may result from the clear objective of the agreement or from the circumstances of the individual case (cf. paragraph 14 above).

(39) See e.g. the case law cited in note 15.

75. When a technology transfer agreement contains a hardcore restriction of competition, it follows from Article 4(1) and 4(2) of the TTBER that the agreement as a whole falls outside the scope of the block exemption. For the purposes of the TTBER hardcore restrictions cannot be severed from the rest of the agreement. Moreover, the Commission considers that in the context of individual assessment hardcore restrictions of competition will only in exceptional circumstances fulfil the four conditions of Article 81(3) (cf. paragraph 18 above).

76. Article 4 of the TTBER distinguishes between agreements between competitors and agreements between non-competitors.

4.2. Agreements between competitors

77. Article 4(1) lists the hardcore restrictions for licensing between competitors. According to Article 4(1), the TTBER does not cover agreements which, directly or indirectly, in isolation or in combination with other factors under the control of the parties, have as their object:

(a) The restriction of a party's ability to determine its prices when selling products to third parties;

(b) The limitation of output, except limitations on the output of contract products imposed on the licensee in a non-reciprocal agreement or imposed on only one of the licensees in a reciprocal agreement;

(c) The allocation of markets or customers except

(i) the obligation on the licensee(s) to produce with the licensed technology only within one or more technical fields of use or one or more product markets;

(ii) the obligation on the licensor and/or the licensee, in a non-reciprocal agreement, not to produce with the licensed technology within one or more technical fields of use or one or more product markets or one or more exclusive territories reserved for the other party;

(iii) the obligation on the licensor not to license the technology to another licensee in a particular territory;

(iv) the restriction, in a non-reciprocal agreement, of active and/or passive sales by the licensee and/or the licensor into the exclusive territory or to the exclusive customer group reserved for the other party;

(v) the restriction, in a non-reciprocal agreement, of active sales by the licensee into the exclusive territory or to the exclusive customer group allocated by the licensor to another licensee provided that the latter was not a competing undertaking of the licensor at the time of the conclusion of its own licence;

(vi) the obligation on the licensee to produce the contract products only for its own use provided that the licensee is not restricted in selling the contract products actively and passively as spare parts for its own products;

(vii) the obligation on the licensee in a non-reciprocal agreement to produce the contract products only for a particular customer, where the licence was granted in order to create an alternative source of supply for that customer;

(d) The restriction of the licensee's ability to exploit its own technology or the restriction of the ability of any of the parties to the agreement to carry out research and development, unless such latter restriction is indispensable to prevent the disclosure of the licensed know-how to third parties.

78. For a number of hardcore restrictions the TTBER makes a distinction between reciprocal and non-reciprocal agreements. The hardcore list is stricter for reciprocal agreements than for non-reciprocal agreements between competitors. Reciprocal agreements are cross-licensing agreements where the licensed technologies are competing technologies or can be used for the production of competing products. A non-reciprocal agreement is an agreement where only one of the parties is licensing its technology to the other party or where in case of cross-licensing the licensed technologies are not competing technologies and cannot be used for the production of competing products. An agreement is not reciprocal merely because the agreement contains a grant back obligation or because the licensee licenses back own improvements of the licensed technology. In case at a later point in time a non-reciprocal agreement becomes a reciprocal agreement due to the conclusion of a second licence between the same parties, they may have to revise the first licence in order to avoid that the agreement contains a hardcore restriction. In the assessment of the individual case the Commission will take into account the time lapsed between the conclusion of the first and the second licence.

79. The hardcore restriction of competition contained in Article 4(1)(a) concerns agreements between competitors that have as their object the fixing of prices for products sold to third parties, including the products incorporating the licensed technology. Price fixing between competitors constitutes a restriction of competition by its very object. Price fixing can for instance take the form of a direct agreement on the exact price to be charged or on a price list with certain allowed maximum rebates. It is immaterial whether the agreement concerns fixed, minimum, maximum or recommended prices. Price fixing can also be implemented indirectly by applying disincentives to deviate from an agreed price level, for example, by providing that the royalty rate will increase if product prices are reduced below a certain level. However, an obligation on the licensee to pay a certain minimum royalty does not in itself amount to price fixing.

80. When royalties are calculated on the basis of individual product sales, the amount of the royalty has a direct impact on the marginal cost of the product and thus a direct impact on product prices (40). Competitors can therefore use cross licensing with reciprocal running royalties as a means of co-ordinating prices on downstream product markets (41). However, the Commission will only treat cross licences with reciprocal running royalties as price fixing where the agreement is devoid of any pro-competitive purpose and therefore does not constitute a bona fide licensing arrangement. In such cases where the agreement does not create any value and therefore has no valid business justification, the arrangement is a sham and amounts to a cartel.

(40) See in this respect paragraph 98 of the Guidelines on the application of Article 81(3) of the Treaty cited in note 2.

(41) This is also the case where one party grants a licence to the other party and accepts to buy a physical input from the licensee. The purchase price can serve the same function as the royalty.

81. The hardcore restriction contained in Article 4(1)(a) also covers agreements whereby royalties are calculated on the basis of all product sales irrespective of whether the licensed technology is being used. Such agreements are also caught by Article 4(1)(d) according to which the licensee must not be restricted in his ability to use his own technology (see paragraph 95 below). In general such agreements restrict competition since the agreement raises the cost of using the licensee's own competing technology and restricts competition that existed in the absence of the agreement (42). This is so both in the case of reciprocal and non-reciprocal arrangements. Exceptionally, however, an agreement whereby royalties are calculated on the basis of all product sales may fulfil the conditions of Article 81(3) in an individual case where on the basis of objective factors it can be concluded that the restriction is indispensable for pro-competitive licensing to occur. This may be the case where in the absence of the restraint it would be impossible or unduly difficult to calculate and monitor the royalty payable by the licensee, for instance because the licensor's technology leaves no visible trace on the final product and practicable alternative monitoring methods are unavailable.

(42) See in this respect Case 193/83, Windsurfing International, [1986] ECR 611, paragraph 67.

82. The hardcore restriction of competition set out in Article 4(1)(b) concerns reciprocal output restrictions on the parties. An output restriction is a limitation on how much a party may produce and sell. Article 4(1)(b) does not cover output limitations on the licensee in a non-reciprocal agreement or output limitations on one of the licensees in a reciprocal agreement provided that the output limitation only concerns products produced with the licensed technology. Article 4(1)(b) thus identifies as hardcore restrictions reciprocal output restrictions on the parties and output restrictions on the licensor in respect of his own technology. When competitors agree to impose reciprocal output limitations, the object and likely effect of the agreement is to reduce output in the market. The same is true of agreements that reduce the incentive of the parties to expand output, for example by obliging each other to make payments if a certain level of output is exceeded.

83. The more favourable treatment of non-reciprocal quantity limitations is based on the consideration that a one-way restriction does not necessarily lead to a lower output on the market while also the risk that the agreement is not a bona fide licensing arrangement is less when the restriction is non-reciprocal. When a licensee is willing to accept a one-way restriction, it is likely that the agreement leads to a real integration of complementary technologies or an efficiency enhancing integration of the licensor's superior technology with the licensee's productive assets. In a reciprocal agreement an output restriction on one of the licensees is likely to reflect the higher value of the technology licensed by one of the parties and may serve to promote pro-competitive licensing.

84. The hardcore restriction of competition set out in Article 4(1)(c) concerns the allocation of markets and customers. Agreements whereby competitors share markets and customers have as their object the restriction of competition. It is a hardcore restriction where competitors in a reciprocal agreement agree not to produce in certain territories or not to sell actively and/or passively into certain territories or to certain customers reserved for the other party.

85. Article 4(1)(c) applies irrespective of whether the licensee remains free to use his own technology. Once the licensee has tooled up to use the licensor's technology to produce a given product, it may be costly to maintain a separate production line using another technology in order to serve customers covered by the restrictions. Moreover, given the anti-competitive potential of the restraint the licensee may have little incentive to produce under his own technology. Such restrictions are also highly unlikely to be indispensable for pro-competitive licensing to occur.

86. Under Article 4(1)(c)(ii) it is not a hardcore restriction for the licensor in a non-reciprocal agreement to grant the licensee an exclusive licence to produce on the basis of the licensed technology in a particular territory and thus agree not to produce himself the contract products in or provide the contract products from that territory. Such exclusive licences are block exempted irrespective of the scope of the territory. If the licence is world-wide, the exclusivity implies that the licensor abstains from entering or remaining on the market. The block exemption also applies where the licence is limited to one or more technical fields of use or one or more product markets. The purpose of agreements covered by Article 4(1)(c)(ii) may be to give the licensee an incentive to invest in and develop the licensed technology. The object of the agreement is therefore not necessarily to share markets.

87. According to Article 4(1)(c)(iv) and for the same reason, the block exemption also applies to non-reciprocal agreements whereby the parties agree not to sell actively or passively (43) into an exclusive territory or to an exclusive customer group reserved for the other party.

(43) For a general definition of active and passive sales, reference is made to paragraph 50 of the Guidelines on vertical restraints cited in note 36.

88. According to Article 4(1)(c)(iii) it is also not a hardcore restriction if the licensor appoints the licensee as his sole licensee in a particular territory, implying that third parties will not be licensed to produce on the basis of the licensor's technology in the territory in question. In the case of such sole licences the block exemption applies irrespective of whether the agreement is reciprocal or not given that the agreement does not affect the ability of the parties to fully exploit their own technology in the respective territories.

89. Article 4(1)(c)(v) excludes from the hardcore list and thus block exempts up to the market share threshold restrictions in a non-reciprocal agreement on active sales by a licensee into the territory or to the customer group allocated by the licensor to another licensee. It is a condition, however, that the protected licensee was not a competitor of the licensor when the agreement was concluded. It is not warranted to hardcore such restrictions. By allowing the licensor to grant a licensee, who was not already on the market, protection against active sales by licensees which are competitors of the licensor and which for that reason are already established on the market, such restrictions are likely to induce the licensee to exploit the licensed technology more efficiently. On the other hand, if the licensees agree between themselves not to sell actively or passively into certain territories or to certain customer groups, the agreement amounts to a cartel amongst the licensees. Given that such agreements do not involve any transfer of technology they fall outside the scope of the TTBER.

90. According to Article 4(1)(c)(i) restrictions in agreements between competitors that limit the licence to one or more product markets or technical fields of use (44) are not hardcore restrictions. Such restrictions are block exempted up to the market share threshold of 20% irrespective of whether the agreement is reciprocal or not. It is a condition for the application of the block exemption, however, that the field of use restrictions do not go beyond the scope of the licensed technologies. It is also a condition that licensees are not limited in the use of their own technology (see Article 4(1)(d)). Where licensees are limited in the use of their own technology the agreement amounts to market sharing.

(44) Field of use restrictions are further dealt with in section IV.2.4 below.

91. The block exemption applies irrespective of whether the field of use restriction is symmetrical or asymmetrical. An asymmetrical field of use restriction in a reciprocal licence agreement implies that both parties are allowed to use the respective technologies that they license in only within different fields of use. As long as the parties are unrestricted in the use of their own technologies, it is not assumed that the agreement leads the parties to abandon or refrain from entering the field(s) covered by the licence to the other party. Even if the licensees tool up to use the licensed technology within the licensed field of use, there may be no impact on assets used to produce outside the scope of the licence. It is important in this regard that the restriction relates to distinct product markets or fields of use and not to customers, allocated by territory or by group, who purchase products falling within the same product market or technical field of use. The risk of market sharing is considered substantially greater in the latter case (see paragraph 85 above). In addition, field of use restrictions may be necessary to promote pro-competitive licensing (see paragraph 182 below).

92. Article 4(1)(c)(vi) contains a further exception, namely captive use restrictions, i.e. a requirement whereby the licensee may produce the products incorporating the licensed technology only for his own use. Where the contract product is a component the licensee can thus be obliged to produce that component only for incorporation into his own products and can be obliged not to sell the components to other producers. The licensee must be able, however, to sell the components as spare parts for his own products and must thus be able to supply third parties that perform after sale services on these products. Captive use restrictions as defined may be necessary to encourage the dissemination of technology, particularly between competitors, and are covered by the block exemption. Such restrictions are also dealt with in section IV.2.5 below.

93. Finally, Article 4(1)(c)(vii) excludes from the hardcore list an obligation on the licensee in a non-reciprocal agreement to produce the contract products only for a particular customer with a view to creating an alternative source of supply for that customer. It is thus a condition for the application of Article 4(1)(c)(vii) that the licence is limited to creating an alternative source of supply for that particular customer. It is not a condition, however, that only one such licence is granted. Article 4(1)(c)(vii) also covers situations where more than one undertaking is licensed to supply the same specified customer. The potential of such agreements to share markets is limited where the licence is granted only for the purpose of supplying a particular customer. In particular, in such circumstances it cannot be assumed that the agreement will cause the licensee to cease exploiting his own technology.

94. The hardcore restriction of competition set out in Article 4(1)(d) covers firstly restrictions on any of the parties' ability to carry out research and development. Both parties must be free to carry out independent research and development. This rule applies irrespective of whether the restriction applies to a field covered by the licence or to other fields. However, the mere fact that the parties agree to provide each other with future improvements of their respective technologies does not amount to a restriction on independent research and development. The effect on competition of such agreements must be assessed in light of the circumstances of the individual case. Article 4(1)(d) also does not extend to restrictions on a party to carry out research and development with third parties, where such restriction is necessary to protect the licensor's know-how against disclosure. In order to be covered by the exception, the restrictions imposed to protect the licensor's know-how against disclosure must be necessary and proportionate to ensure such protection. For instance, where the agreement designates particular employees of the licensee to be trained in and responsible for the use of the licensed know-how, it may be sufficient to oblige the licensee not to allow those employees to be involved in research and development with third parties. Other safeguards may be equally appropriate.

95. According to Article 4(1)(d) the licensee must also be unrestricted in the use of his own competing technology provided that in so doing he does not make use of the technology licensed from the licensor. In relation to his own technology the licensee must not be subject to limitations in terms of where he produces or sells, how much he produces or sells and at what price he sells. He must also not be obliged to pay royalties on products produced on the basis of his own technology (cf. paragraph 81 above). Moreover, the licensee must not be restricted in licensing his own technology to third parties. When restrictions are imposed on the licensee's use of his own technology or to carry out research and development, the competitiveness of the licensee's technology is reduced. The effect of this is to reduce competition on existing product and technology markets and to reduce the licensee's incentive to invest in the development and improvement of his technology.

4.3. Agreements between non-competitors

96. Article 4(2) lists the hardcore restrictions for licensing between non-competitors. According to this provision, the TTBER does not cover agreements which, directly or indirectly, in isolation or in combination with other factors under the control of the parties, have as their object:

(a) the restriction of a party's ability to determine its prices when selling products to third parties, without prejudice to the possibility to impose a maximum sale price or recommend a sale price, provided that it does not amount to a fixed or minimum sale price as a result of pressure from, or incentives offered by, any of the parties;

(b) the restriction of the territory into which, or of the customers to whom, the licensee may passively sell the contract products, except:

(i) the restriction of passive sales into an exclusive territory or to an exclusive customer group reserved for the licensor;

(ii) the restriction of passive sales into an exclusive territory or to an exclusive customer group allocated by the licensor to another licensee during the first two years that this other licensee is selling the contract products in that territory or to that customer group;

(iii) the obligation to produce the contract products only for its own use provided that the licensee is not restricted in selling the contract products actively and passively as spare parts for its own products;

(iv) the obligation to produce the contract products only for a particular customer, where the licence was granted in order to create an alternative source of supply for that customer;

(v) the restriction of sales to end users by a licensee operating at the wholesale level of trade;

(vi) the restriction of sales to unauthorised distributors by the members of a selective distribution system;

(c) the restriction of active or passive sales to end users by a licensee which is a member of a selective distribution system and which operates at the retail level, without prejudice to the possibility of prohibiting a member of the system from operating out of an unauthorised place of establishment.

97. The hardcore restriction of competition set out in Article 4(2)(a) concerns the fixing of prices charged when selling products to third parties. More specifically, this provision covers restrictions which have as their direct or indirect object the establishment of a fixed or a minimum selling price or a fixed or minimum price level to be observed by the licensor or the licensee when selling products to third parties. In the case of agreements that directly establish the selling price, the restriction is clear-cut. However, the fixing of selling prices can also be achieved through indirect means. Examples of the latter are agreements fixing the margin, fixing the maximum level of discounts, linking the sales price to the sales prices of competitors, threats, intimidation, warnings, penalties, or contract terminations in relation to observance of a given price level. Direct or indirect means of achieving price fixing can be made more effective when combined with measures to identify pricecutting, such as the implementation of a price monitoring system, or the obligation on licensees to report price deviations. Similarly, direct or indirect price fixing can be made more effective when combined with measures that reduce the licensee's incentive to lower his selling price, such as the licensor obliging the licensee to apply a most-favoured-customer clause, i.e. an obligation to grant to a customer any more favourable terms granted to any other customer. The same means can be used to make maximum or recommended prices work as fixed or minimum selling prices. However, the provision of a list of recommended prices to or the imposition of a maximum price on the licensee by the licensor is not considered in itself as leading to fixed or minimum selling prices.

98. Article 4(2)(b) identifies as hardcore restrictions of competition agreements or concerted practices that have as their direct or indirect object the restriction of passive sales by licensees of products incorporating the licensed technology (45). Passive sales restrictions on the licensee may be the result of direct obligations, such as the obligation not to sell to certain customers or to customers in certain territories or the obligation to refer orders from these customers to other licensees. It may also result from indirect measures aimed at inducing the licensee to refrain from making such sales, such as financial incentives and the implementation of a monitoring system aimed at verifying the effective destination of the licensed products. Quantity limitations may be an indirect means to restrict passive sales. The Commission will not assume that quantity limitations as such serve this purpose. However, it will be otherwise where quantity limitations are used to implement an underlying market partitioning agreement. Indications thereof include the adjustment of quantities over time to cover only local demand, the combination of quantity limitations and an obligation to sell minimum quantities in the territory, minimum royalty obligations linked to sales in the territory, differentiated royalty rates depending on the destination of the products and the monitoring of the destination of products sold by individual licensees. The general hardcore restriction covering passive sales by licensees is subject to a number of exceptions, which are dealt with below.

(45) This hardcore restriction applies to licence agreements concerning trade within the Community. As regards agreements concerning exports outside the Community or imports/re-imports from outside the Community see Case C-306/96, Javico, [1998] ECR I-1983.

99. Article 4(2)(b) does not cover sales restrictions on the licensor. All sales restrictions on the licensor are block exempted up to the market share threshold of 30%. The same applies to all restrictions on active sales by the licensee, with the exception of what is said on active selling in paragraphs 105 and 106 below. The block exemption of restrictions on active selling is based on the assumption that such restrictions promote investments, non-price competition and improvements in the quality of services provided by the licensees by solving free rider problems and hold-up problems. In the case of restrictions of active sales between licensees' territories or customer groups, it is not a condition that the protected licensee has been granted an exclusive territory or an exclusive customer group. The block exemption also applies to active sales restrictions where more than one licensee has been appointed for a particular territory or customer group. Efficiency enhancing investment is likely to be promoted where a licensee can be ensured that he will only face active sales competition from a limited number of licensees inside the territory and not also from licensees outside the territory.

100. Restrictions on active and passive sales by licensees into an exclusive territory or to an exclusive customer group reserved for the licensor do not constitute hardcore restrictions of competition (cf. Article 4(2)(b)(i)). Indeed, they are block exempted. It is presumed that up to the market share threshold such restraints, where restrictive of competition, promote pro-competitive dissemination of technology and integration of such technology into the production assets of the licensee. For a territory or customer group to be reserved for the licensor, it is not required that the licensor is actually producing with the licensed technology in the territory or for the customer group in question. A territory or customer group can also be reserved by the licensor for later exploitation.

101. Restrictions on passive sales by licensees into an exclusive territory or customer group allocated to another licensee are block exempted for two years calculated from the date on which the protected licensee first markets the products incorporating the licensed technology inside his exclusive territory or to his exclusive customer group (cf. Article 4(2)(b)(ii)). Licensees often have to commit substantial investments in production assets and promotional activities in order to start up and develop a new territory. The risks facing the new licensee are therefore likely to be substantial, in particular since promotional expenses and investment in assets required to produce on the basis of a particular technology are often sunk, i.e. they cannot be recovered if the licensee exits the market. In such circumstances, it is often the case that licensees would not enter into the licence agreement without protection for a certain period of time against (active and) passive sales into their territory by other licensees. Restrictions on passive sales into the exclusive territory of a licensee by other licensees therefore often fall outside Article 81(1) for a period of up to two years from the date on which the product incorporating the licensed technology was first put on the market in the exclusive territory by the licensee in question. However, to the extent that in individual cases such restrictions are caught by Article 81(1) they are block exempted. After the expiry of this two-year period restrictions on passive sales between licensees constitute hardcore restrictions. Such restrictions are generally caught by Article 81(1) and are unlikely to fulfil the conditions of Article 81(3). In particular, passive sales restrictions are unlikely to be indispensable for the attainment of efficiencies (46).

(46) See in this respect paragraph 77 of the judgment in Nungesser cited in note 13.

102. Article 4(2)(b)(iii) brings under the block exemption a restriction whereby the licensee is obliged to produce products incorporating the licensed technology only for his own (captive) use. Where the contract product is a component the licensee can thus be obliged to use that product only for incorporation into his own products and can be obliged not to sell the product to other producers. The licensee must however be able to actively and passively sell the products as spare parts for his own products and must thus be able to supply third parties that perform after sale services on these products. Captive use restrictions are also dealt with in section IV.2.5 below.

103. As in the case of agreements between competitors (cf. paragraph 93 above) the block exemption also applies to agreements whereby the licensee is obliged to produce the contract products only for a particular customer in order to provide that customer with an alternative source of supply (cf. Article 4(2)(b)(iv)). In the case of agreements between non-competitors, such restrictions are unlikely to be caught by Article 81(1).

104. Article 4(2)(b)(v) brings under the block exemption an obligation on the licensee not to sell to end users and thus only to sell to retailers. Such an obligation allows the licensor to assign the wholesale distribution function to the licensee and normally falls outside Article 81(1)(47).

(47) See in this respect Case 26/76, Metro (I), [1977] ECR 1875.

105. Finally Article 4(2)(b)(vi) brings under the block exemption a restriction on the licensee not to sell to unauthorised distributors. This exception allows the licensor to impose on the licensees an obligation to form part of a selective distribution system. In that case, however, the licensees must according to Article 4(2)(c) be permitted to sell both actively and passively to end users, without prejudice to the possibility to restrict the licensee to a wholesale function as foreseen in Article 4(2)(b)(v) (cf. the previous paragraph).

106. It is recalled (cf. paragraph 39 above) that the block exemption covers licence agreements whereby the licensor imposes obligations which the licensee must or may impose on his buyers, including distributors. However, these obligations must comply with the competition rules applicable to supply and distribution agreements. Since the TTBER is limited to agreements between two parties the agreements concluded between the licensee and his buyers implementing such obligations are not covered by the TTBER. Such agreements are only block exempted when they comply with Regulation 2790/1999 (cf. section 2.5.2 above).

5. Excluded restrictions

107. Article 5 of the TTBER lists four types of restrictions that are not block exempted and which thus require individual assessment of their anti-competitive and pro-competitive effects. It follows from Article 5 that the inclusion in a licence agreement of any of the restrictions contained in these provisions does not prevent the application of the block exemption to the rest of the agreement. It is only the individual restriction in question that is not block exempted, implying that individual assessment is required. Accordingly, the rule of severability applies to the restrictions set out in Article 5.

108. Article 5(1) provides that the block exemption shall not apply to the following three obligations:

(a) Any direct or indirect obligation on the licensee to grant an exclusive licence to the licensor or to a third party designated by the licensor in respect of its own severable improvements to or its new applications of the licensed technology.

(b) Any direct or indirect obligation on the licensee to assign to the licensor or to a third party designated by the licensor rights to severable improvements to or new applications of the licensed technology.

(c) Any direct or indirect obligation on the licensee not to challenge the validity of intellectual property rights held by the licensor in the common market. However, the TTBER does cover the possibility for the licensor to terminate the licence agreement in the event that the licensee challenges the validity of the licensed technology.

The purpose of Article 5(1)*(a)*, *(b)* and *(c)* is to avoid block exemption of agreements that may reduce the incentive of licensees to innovate.

109. Article 5(1)*(a)* and 5(1)*(b)* concerns exclusive grant backs or assignments to the licensor of severable improvements of the licensed technology. An improvement is severable if it can be exploited without infringing upon the licensed technology. An obligation to grant the licensor an exclusive licence to severable improvements of the licensed technology or to assign such improvements to the licensor is likely to reduce the licensee's incentive to innovate since it hinders the licensee in exploiting his improvements, including by way of licensing to third parties. This is the case both where the severable improvement concerns the same application as the licensed technology and where the licensee develops new applications of the licensed technology. According to Article 5(1)*(a)* and *(b)* such obligations are not block exempted. However, the block exemption does cover non-exclusive grant back obligations in respect of severable improvements. This is so even where the grant back obligation is non-reciprocal, i.e. only imposed on the licensee, and where under the agreement the licensor is entitled to feed-on the severable improvements to other licensees. A non-reciprocal grant back obligation may promote innovation and the dissemination of new technology by permitting the licensor to freely determine whether and to what extent to pass on his own improvements to his licensees. A feed-on clause may also promote the dissemination of technology because each licensee knows at the time of contracting that he will be on an equal footing with other licensees in terms of the technology on the basis of which he is producing. Exclusive grant backs and obligations to assign non-severable improvements are not restrictive of competition within the meaning of Article 81(1) since non-severable improvements cannot be exploited by the licensee without the licensor's permission.

110. The application of Article 5(1)*(a)* and *(b)* does not depend on whether or not the licensor pays consideration in return for acquiring the improvement or for obtaining an exclusive licence. However, the existence and level of such consideration may be a relevant factor in the context of an individual assessment under Article 81. When grant backs are made against consideration it is less likely that the obligation creates a disincentive for the licensee to innovate. In the assessment of exclusive grant backs outside the scope of the block exemption the market position of the licensor on the technology market is also a relevant factor. The stronger the position of the licensor, the more likely it is that exclusive grant back obligations will have restrictive effects on competition in innovation. The stronger the position of the licensor's technology the more likely it is that the licensee will be an important source of innovation and future competition. The negative impact of grant back obligations can also be increased in case of parallel networks of licence agreements containing such obligations. When available technologies are controlled by a limited number of licensors that impose exclusive grant back obligations on licensees, the risk of anticompetitive effects is greater than where there are a number of technologies only some of which are licensed on exclusive grant back terms.

111. The risk of negative effects on innovation is higher in the case of cross licensing between competitors where a grant back obligation on both parties is combined with an obligation on both parties to share with the other party improvements of his own technology. The sharing of all improvements between competitors may prevent each competitor from gaining a competitive lead over the other (see also paragraph 208 below). However, the parties are unlikely to be prevented from gaining a competitive lead over each other where the purpose of the licence is to permit them to develop their respective technologies and where the licence does not lead them to use the same technological base in the design of their products. This is the case where the purpose of the licence is to create design freedom rather than to improve the technological base of the licensee.

112. The excluded restriction set out in Article 5(1)*(c)* concerns non-challenge clauses, i.e. obligations not to challenge the validity of the licensor's intellectual property. The reason for excluding non-challenge clauses from the scope of the block exemption is the fact that licensees are normally in the best position to determine whether or not an intellectual property right is invalid. In the interest of undistorted competition and in conformity with the principles underlying the protection of intellectual property, invalid intellectual property rights should be eliminated. Invalid intellectual property stifles innovation rather than promoting it. Article 81(1) is likely to apply to non-challenge clauses where the licensed technology is valuable and therefore creates a competitive disadvantage for undertakings that are prevented from using it or are only able to use it against payment of royalties (48). In such cases the conditions of Article 81(3) are unlikely to be fulfilled (49). However, the Commission takes a favourable view of non-challenge clauses relating to know-how where once disclosed it is likely to be impossible or very difficult to recover the licensed know-how. In such cases, an obligation on the licensee not to challenge the licensed know-how promotes dissemination of new technology, in particular by allowing weaker licensors to license stronger licensees without fear of a challenge once the know-how has been absorbed by the licensee.

(48) If the licensed technology is outdated no restriction of competition arises, see in this respect Case 65/86, Bayer v Süllhofer, [1988] ECR 5249.

(49) As to non-challenge clauses in the context of settlement agreements see point 209 below.

113. The TTBER covers the possibility for the licensor to terminate the licence agreement in the event of a challenge of the licensed technology. Accordingly, the licensor is not forced to continue dealing with a licensee that challenges the very subject matter of the licence agreement, implying that upon termination any further use by the licensee of the challenged technology is at the challenger's own risk. Article 5(1)(c) ensures, however, that the TTBER does not cover contractual obligations obliging the licensee not to challenge the licensed technology, which would permit the licensor to sue the licensee for breach of contract and thereby create a further disincentive for the licensee to challenge the validity of the licensor's technology. The provision thereby ensures that the licensee is in the same position as third parties.

114. Article 5(2) excludes from the scope of the block exemption, in the case of agreements between non-competitors, any direct or indirect obligation limiting the licensee's ability to exploit his own technology or limiting the ability of the parties to the agreement to carry out research and development, unless such latter restriction is indispensable to prevent the disclosure of licensed know-how to third parties. The content of this condition is the same as that of Article 4(1)(d) of the hardcore list concerning agreements between competitors, which is dealt with in paragraphs 94 and 95 above. However, in the case of agreements between non-competitors it cannot be considered that such restrictions generally have negative effects on competition or that the conditions of Article 81(3) are generally not satisfied (50). Individual assessment is required.

(50) See paragraph 14 above.

115. In the case of agreements between non-competitors, the licensee normally does not own a competing technology. However, there may be cases where for the purposes of the block exemption the parties are considered non-competitors in spite of the fact that the licensee does own a competing technology. This is the case where the licensee owns a technology but does not license it and the licensor is not an actual or potential supplier on the product market. For the purposes of the block exemption the parties are in such circumstances neither competitors on the technology market nor competitors on the product market (51). In such cases it is important to ensure that the licensee is not restricted in his ability to exploit his own technology and further develop it. This technology constitutes a competitive constraint in the market, which should be preserved. In such a situation restrictions on the licensee's use of his own technology or on research and development are normally considered to be restrictive of competition and not to satisfy the conditions of Article 81(3). For instance, an obligation on the licensee to pay royalties not only on the basis of products it produces with the licensed technology but also on the basis of products it produces with its own technology will generally limit the ability of the licensee to exploit its own technology and thus be excluded from the scope of the block exemption.

(51) See paragraphs 66 and 67 above.

116. In cases where the licensee does not own a competing technology or is not already developing such a technology, a restriction on the ability of the parties to carry out independent research and development may be restrictive of competition where only a few technologies are available. In that case the parties may be an important (potential) source of innovation in the market. This is particularly so where the parties possess the necessary assets and skills to carry out further research and development. In that case the conditions of Article 81(3) are unlikely to be fulfilled. In other cases where several technologies are available and where the parties do not possess special assets or skills, the restriction on research and development is likely to either fall outside Article 81(1) for lack of an appreciable restrictive effect or satisfy the conditions of Article 81(3). The restraint may promote the dissemination of new technology by assuring the licensor that the licence does not create a new competitor and by inducing the licensee to focus on the exploitation and development of the licensed technology. Moreover, Article 81(1) only applies where the agreement reduces the licensee's incentive to improve and exploit his own technology. This is for instance not likely to be the case where the licensor is entitled to terminate the licence agreement once the licensee commences to produce on the basis of his own competing technology. Such a right does not reduce the licensee's incentive to innovate, since the agreement can only be terminated when a commercially viable technology has been developed and products produced on the basis thereof are ready to be put on the market.

6. Withdrawal and disapplication of the Block Exemption Regulation

6.1. Withdrawal procedure

117. According to Article 6 of the TTBER, the Commission and the competition authorities of the Member States may withdraw the benefit of the block exemption in respect of individual agreements that do not fulfil the conditions of Article 81(3). The power of the competition authorities of the Member States to withdraw the benefit of the block exemption is limited to cases where the relevant geographic market is no wider than the territory of the Member State in question.

118. The four conditions of Article 81(3) are cumulative and must all be fulfilled for the exception rule to be applicable (52). The block exemption can therefore be withdrawn where a particular agreement fails one or more of the four conditions.

(52) See in this respect paragraph 42 of the Guidelines on the application of Article 81(3) of the Treaty, cited in note 2.

119. Where the withdrawal procedure is applied, the withdrawing authority bears the burden of proving that the agreement falls within the scope of Article 81(1) and that the agreement does not satisfy all four conditions of Article 81(3). Given that withdrawal implies that the agreement in question restricts competition within the meaning of Article 81(1) and does not fulfil the conditions of Article 81(3), withdrawal is necessarily accompanied by a negative decision based on Articles 5, 7 or 9 of Regulation 1/2003.

120. According to Article 6, withdrawal may in particular be warranted in the following circumstances:

1. access of third parties' technologies to the market is restricted, for instance by the cumulative effect of parallel networks of similar restrictive agreements prohibiting licensees from using third party technology;

2. access of potential licensees to the market is restricted, for instance by the cumulative effect of parallel networks of similar restrictive agreements preventing licensors from licensing to other licensees;

3. without any objectively valid reason the parties refrain from exploiting the licensed technology.

121. Articles 4 and 5 of the TTBER, containing the list of hardcore restrictions of competition and excluded restrictions, aim at ensuring that block exempted agreements do not reduce the incentive to innovate, do not delay the dissemination of technology, and do not unduly restrict competition between the licensor and licensee or between licensees. However, the list of hardcore restrictions and the list of excluded restrictions do not take into account all the possible impacts of licence agreements. In particular, the block exemption does not take account of any cumulative effect of similar restrictions contained in networks of licence agreements. Licence agreements may lead to foreclosure of third parties both at the level of the licensor and at the level of the licensee. Foreclosure of other licensors may stem from the cumulative effect of networks of licence agreements prohibiting the licensees from exploiting competing technologies, leading to the exclusion of other (potential) licensors. Foreclosure of licensors is likely to arise in cases where most of the undertakings on the market that could (efficiently) take a competing licence are prevented from doing so as a consequence of restrictive agreements and where potential licensees face relatively high barriers to entry. Foreclosure of other licensees may stem from the cumulative effect of licence agreements prohibiting licensors from licensing other licensees and thereby preventing potential licensees from gaining access to the necessary technology. The issue of foreclosure is examined in more detail in section IV.2.7 below. In addition, the Commission is likely to withdraw the benefit of the block exemption where a significant number of licensors of competing technologies in individual agreements impose on their licensees to extend to them more favourable conditions agreed with other licensors.

122. The Commission is also likely to withdraw the benefit of the block exemption where the parties refrain from exploiting the licensed technology, unless they have an objective justification for doing so. Indeed, when the parties do not exploit the licensed technology, no efficiency enhancing activity takes place, in which case the very rationale of the block exemption disappears. However, exploitation does not need to take the form of an integration of assets. Exploitation also occurs where the licence creates design freedom for the licensee by allowing him to exploit his own technology without facing the risk of infringement claims by the licensor. In the case of licensing between competitors, the fact that the parties do not exploit the licensed technology may be an indication that the arrangement is a disguised cartel. For these reasons the Commission will examine very closely cases of non-exploitation.

6.2. Disapplication of the Block Exemption Regulation

123. Article 7 of the TTBER enables the Commission to exclude from the scope of the TTBER, by means of regulation, parallel networks of similar agreements where these cover more than 50% of a relevant market. Such a measure is not addressed to individual undertakings but concerns all undertakings whose agreements are defined in the regulation disapplying the TTBER.

124. Whereas withdrawal of the benefit of the TTBER by the Commission under Article 6 implies the adoption of a decision under Articles 7 or 9 of Regulation 1/2003, the effect of a Commission disapplication regulation under Article 7 of the TTBER is merely to remove, in respect of the restraints and the markets concerned, the benefit of the TTBER and to restore the full application of Article 81(1) and (3). Following the adoption of a regulation declaring the TTBER inapplicable for a particular market in respect of agreements containing certain restraints, the criteria developed by the relevant case law of the Community Courts and by notices and previous decisions adopted by the Commission will give guidance on the application of Article 81 to individual agreements. Where appropriate, the Commission will take a decision in an individual case, which can provide guidance to all the undertakings operating on the market concerned.

125. For the purpose of calculating the 50% market coverage ratio, account must be taken of each individual network of licence agreements containing restraints, or combinations of restraints, producing similar effects on the market.

126. Article 7 does not entail an obligation on the part of the Commission to act where the 50% market-coverage ratio is exceeded. In general, disapplication is appropriate when it is likely that access to the relevant market or competition therein is appreciably restricted. In assessing the need to apply Article 7, the Commission will consider whether individual withdrawal would be a more appropriate remedy. This may depend, in particular, on the number of competing undertakings contributing to a cumulative effect on a market or the number of affected geographic markets within the Community.

127. Any regulation adopted under Article 7 must clearly set out its scope. This means, first, that the Commission must define the relevant product and geographic market(s) and, secondly, that it must identify the type of licensing restraint in respect of which the TTBER will no longer apply. As regards the latter aspect, the Commission may modulate the scope of its regulation according to the competition concern which it intends to address. For instance, while all parallel networks of non-compete arrangements will be taken into account for the purpose of establishing the 50% market coverage ratio, the Commission may nevertheless restrict the scope of the disapplication regulation only to non-compete obligations exceeding a certain duration. Thus, agreements of a shorter duration or of a less restrictive nature might be left unaffected, due to the lesser degree of foreclosure attributable to such restraints. Where appropriate, the Commission may also provide guidance by specifying the market share level which, in the specific market context, may be regarded as insufficient to bring about a significant contribution by an individual undertaking to the cumulative effect. In general, when the market share of the products incorporating a technology licensed by an individual licensor does not exceed 5%, the agreement or network of agreements covering that technology is not considered to contribute significantly to a cumulative foreclosure effect (53).

(53) See in this respect paragraph 8 of the Commission Notice on agreements of minor importance, cited in note 17.

128. The transitional period of not less than six months that the Commission will have to set under Article 7(2) should allow the undertakings concerned to adapt their agreements to take account of the regulation disapplying the TTBER.

129. A regulation disapplying the TTBER will not affect the block exempted status of the agreements concerned for the period preceding its entry into force.

IV. APPLICATION OF ARTICLE 81(1) OUTSIDE THE SCOPE OF THE BLOK EXEMPTION REGULATION

1. The general framework for analysis

130. Agreements that fall outside the block exemption, for example because the market share thresholds are exceeded or the agreement involves more than two parties, are subject to individual assessment. Agreements that either do not restrict competition within the meaning of Article 81(1) or which fulfil the conditions of Article 81(3) are valid and enforceable. It is recalled that there is no presumption of illegality of agreements that fall outside the scope of the block exemption provided that they do not contain hardcore restrictions of competition. In particular, there is no presumption that Article 81(1) applies merely because the market share thresholds are exceeded. Individual assessment based on the principles described in these guidelines is required.

131. In order to promote predictability beyond the application of the TTBER and to confine detailed analysis to cases that are likely to present real competition concerns, the Commission takes the view that outside the area of hardcore restrictions Article 81 is unlikely to be infringed where there are four or more independently controlled technologies in addition to the technologies controlled by the parties to the agreement that may be substitutable for the licensed technology at a comparable cost to the user. In assessing whether the technologies are sufficiently substitutable the relative commercial strength of the technologies in question must be taken into account. The competitive constraint imposed by a technology is limited if it does not constitute a commercially viable alternative to the licensed technology. For instance, if due to network effects in the market consumers have a strong preference for products incorporating the licensed technology, other technologies already on the market or likely to come to market within a reasonable period of time may not constitute a real alternative and may therefore impose only a limited competitive constraint. The fact that an agreement falls outside the safe harbour described in this paragraph does not imply that the agreement is caught by Article 81(1) and, if so, that the conditions of Article 81(3) are not satisfied. As for the market share safe harbour of the TTBER, this additional safe harbour merely creates a negative presumption that the agreement is not prohibited by Article 81. Outside the safe harbour individual assessment of the agreement based on the principles developed in these guidelines is required.

1.1. The relevant factors

132. In the application of Article 81 to individual cases it is necessary to take due account of the way in which competition operates on the market in question. The following factors are particularly relevant in this respect:
(a) the nature of the agreement;
(b) the market position of the parties;
(c) the market position of competitors;
(d) the market position of buyers of the licensed products;
(e) entry barriers;
(f) maturity of the market; and
(g) other factors.
The importance of individual factors may vary from case to case and depends on all other factors. For instance, a high market share of the parties is usually a good indicator of market power, but in the case of low entry barriers it may not be indicative of market power. It is therefore not possible to provide firm rules on the importance of the individual factors.

133. Technology transfer agreements can take many shapes and forms. It is therefore important to analyse the nature of the agreement in terms of the competitive relationship between the parties and the restraints that it contains. In the latter regard it is necessary to go beyond the express terms of the agreement. The existence of implicit restraints may be derived from the way in which the agreement has been implemented by the parties and the incentives that they face.

134. The market position of the parties provides an indication of the degree of market power, if any, possessed by the licensor, the licensee or both. The higher their market share the greater their market power is likely to be. This is particularly so where the market share reflects cost advantages or other competitive advantages vis-à-vis competitors. These competitive advantages may for instance result from being a first mover in the market, from holding essential patents or from having superior technology.

135. In analysing the competitive relationship between the parties it is sometimes necessary to go beyond the analysis set out in the above sections II.3 on market definition and II.4 on the distinction between competitors and non-competitors. Even where the licensor is not an actual or potential supplier on the product market and the licensee is not an actual or potential competitor on the technology market, it is relevant to the analysis whether the licensee owns a competing technology, which is not being licensed. If the licensee has a strong position on the product market, an agreement granting him an exclusive licence to a competing technology can restrict competition significantly compared to the situation where the licensor does not grant an exclusive licence or licences other undertakings.

136. Market shares and possible competitive advantages and disadvantages are also used to assess the market position of competitors. The stronger the actual competitors and the greater their number the less risk there is that the parties will be able to individually exercise market power. However, if the number of competitors is rather small and their market position (size, costs, R&D potential, etc.) is rather similar, this market structure may increase the risk of collusion.

137. The market position of buyers provides an indication of whether or not one or more buyers possess buyer power. The first indicator of buying power is the market share of the buyer on the purchase market. This share reflects the importance of his demand for possible suppliers. Other indicators focus on the position of the buyer on his resale market, including characteristics such as a wide geographic spread of his outlets, and his brand image amongst final consumers. In some circumstances buyer power may prevent the licensor and/or the licensee from exercising market power on the market and thereby solve a competition problem that would otherwise have existed. This is particularly so when strong buyers have the capacity and the incentive to bring new sources of supply on to the market in the case of a small but permanent increase in relative prices. Where the strong buyers merely extract favourable terms from the supplier or simply pass on any price increase to their customers, the position of the buyers is not such as to prevent the exercise of market power by the licensee on the product market and therefore not such as to solve the competition problem on that market (54).

(54) See in this respect Case T-228/97, Irish Sugar, [1999] ECR II-2969, paragraph 101.

138. Entry barriers are measured by the extent to which incumbent companies can increase their price above the competitive level without attracting new entry. In the absence of entry barriers, easy and quick entry would render price increases unprofitable. When effective entry, preventing or eroding the exercise of market power, is likely to occur within one or two years, entry barriers can, as a general rule, be said to be low. Entry barriers may result from a wide variety of factors such as economies of scale and scope, government regulations, especially where they establish exclusive rights, state aid, import tariffs, intellectual property rights, ownership of resources where the supply is limited due to for instance natural limitations, essential facilities, a first mover advantage or brand loyalty of consumers created by strong advertising over a period of time. Restrictive agreements entered into by undertakings may also work as an entry barrier by making access more difficult and foreclosing (potential) competitors. Entry barriers may be present at all stages of the research and development, production and distribution process. The question whether certain of these factors should be described as entry barriers depends particularly on whether they entail sunk costs. Sunk costs are those costs which have to be incurred to enter or be active on a market but which are lost when the market is exited. The more costs are sunk, the more potential entrants have to weigh the risks of entering the market and the more credibly incumbents can threaten that they will match new competition, as sunk costs make it costly for incumbents to leave the market. In general, entry requires sunk costs, sometimes minor and sometimes major. Therefore, actual competition is in general more effective and will weigh more heavily in the assessment of a case than potential competition.

139. A mature market is a market that has existed for some time, where the technology used is well known and widespread and not changing very much and in which demand is relatively stable or declining. In such a market restrictions of competition are more likely to have negative effects than in more dynamic markets.

140. In the assessment of particular restraints other factors may have to be taken into account. Such factors include cumulative effects, i.e. the coverage of the market by similar agreements, the duration of the agreements, the regulatory environment and behaviour that may indicate or facilitate collusion like price leadership, pre-announced price changes and discussions on the 'right' price, price rigidity in response to excess capacity, price discrimination and past collusive behaviour.

1.2. Negative effects of restrictive licence agreements

141. The negative effects on competition on the market that may result from restrictive technology transfer agreements include the following:

1. reduction of inter-technology competition between the companies operating on a technology market or on a market for products incorporating the technologies in question, including facilitation of collusion, both explicit and tacit;

2. foreclosure of competitors by raising their costs, restricting their access to essential inputs or otherwise raising barriers to entry; and

3. reduction of intra-technology competition between undertakings that produce products on the basis of the same technology.

142. Technology transfer agreements may reduce inter-technology competition, i.e. competition between undertakings that license or produce on the basis of substitutable technologies. This is particularly so where reciprocal obligations are imposed. For instance, where competitors transfer competing technologies to each other and impose a reciprocal obligation to provide each other with future improvements of their respective technologies and where this agreement prevents either competitor from gaining a technological lead over the other, competition in innovation between the parties is restricted (see also paragraph 208 below).

143. Licensing between competitors may also facilitate collusion. The risk of collusion is particularly high in concentrated markets. Collusion requires that the undertakings concerned have similar views on what is in their common interest and on how the co-ordination mechanisms function. For collusion to work the undertakings must also be able to monitor each other's market behaviour and there must be adequate deterrents to ensure that there is an incentive not to depart from the common policy on the market, while entry barriers must be high enough to limit entry or expansion by outsiders. Agreements can facilitate collusion by increasing transparency in the market, by controlling certain behaviour and by raising barriers to entry. Collusion can also exceptionally be facilitated by licensing agreements that lead to a high degree of commonality of costs, because undertakings that have similar costs are more likely to have similar views on the terms of coordination (55).

(55) See in this respect paragraph 23 of the Guidelines on horizontal cooperation agreements, cited in note 20.

144. Licence agreements may also affect inter-technology competition by creating barriers to entry for and expansion by competitors. Such foreclosure effects may stem from restraints that prevent licensees from licensing from third parties or create disincentives for them to do so. For instance, third parties may be foreclosed where incumbent licensors impose non-compete obligations on licensees to such an extent that an insufficient number of licensees are available to third parties and where entry at the level of licensees is difficult. Suppliers of substitutable technologies may also be foreclosed where a licensor with a sufficient degree of market power ties together various parts of a technology and licenses them together as a package while only part of the package is essential to produce a certain product.

145. Licence agreements may also reduce intra-technology competition, i.e. competition between undertakings that produce on the basis of the same technology. An agreement imposing territorial restraints on licensees, preventing them from selling into each other's territory reduces competition between them. Licence agreements may also reduce intra-technology competition by facilitating collusion between licensees. Moreover, licence agreements that reduce intra-technology competition may facilitate collusion between owners of competing technologies or reduce inter-technology competition by raising barriers to entry.

1.3. Positive effects of restrictive licence agreements and the framework for analysing such effects

146. Even restrictive licence agreements mostly also produce pro-competitive effects in the form of efficiencies, which may outweigh their anti-competitive effects. This assessment takes place within the framework of Article 81(3), which contains an exception from the prohibition rule of Article 81(1). For this exception to be applicable the licence agreement must produce objective economic benefits, the restrictions on competition must be indispensable to attain the efficiencies, consumers must receive a fair share of the efficiency gains, and the agreement must not afford the parties the possibility of eliminating competition in respect of a substantial part of the products concerned.

147. The assessment of restrictive agreements under Article 81(3) is made within the actual context in which they occur (56) and on the basis of the facts existing at any given point in time. The assessment is sensitive to material changes in the facts. The exception rule of Article 81(3) applies as long as the four conditions are fulfilled and ceases to apply when that is no longer the case (57). However, when applying Article 81(3) in accordance with these principles it is necessary to take into account the initial sunk investments made by any of the parties and the time needed and the restraints required to commit and recoup an efficiency enhancing investment. Article 81 cannot be applied without considering the *ex ante* investment and the risks relating thereto. The risk facing the parties and the sunk investment that must be committed to implement the agreement can thus lead to the agreement falling outside Article 81(1) or fulfilling the conditions of Article 81(3), as the case may be, for the period of time required to recoup the investment.

(56) See Joined Cases 25/84 and 26/84, Ford, [1985] ECR 2725.

(57) See in this respect for example Commission Decision in TPS (O.J. L 90, 2.4.1999, p. 6). Similarly, the prohibition of Article 81(1) also only applies as long as the agreement has a restrictive object or restrictive effects.

148. The first condition of Article 81(3) requires an assessment of what are the objective benefits in terms of efficiencies produced by the agreement. In this respect, licence agreements have the potential of bringing together complementary technologies and other assets allowing new or improved products to be put on the market or existing products to be produced at lower cost. Outside the context of hardcore cartels, licensing often occurs because it is more efficient for the licensor to licence the technology than to exploit it himself. This may particularly be the case where the licensee already has access to the necessary production assets. The agreement allows the licensee to gain access to a technology that can be combined with these assets, allowing him to exploit new or improved technologies. Another example of potentially efficiency enhancing licensing is where the licensee already has a technology and where the combination of this technology and the licensor's technology gives rise to synergies. When the two technologies are combined the licensee may be able to attain a cost/output configuration that would not otherwise be possible. Licence agreements may also give rise to efficiencies at the distribution stage in the same way as vertical distribution agreements. Such efficiencies can take the form of cost savings or the provision of valuable services to consumers. The positive effects of vertical agreements are described in the Guidelines on Vertical Restraints (58). A further example of possible efficiency gains is agreements whereby technology owners assemble a technology package for licensing to third parties. Such pooling arrangements may in particular reduce transaction costs, as licensees do not have to conclude separate licence agreements with each licensor. Pro-competitive licensing may also occur to ensure design freedom. In sectors where large numbers of intellectual property rights exist and where individual products may infringe upon a number of existing and future property rights, licence agreements whereby the parties agree not to assert their property rights against each other are often pro-competitive because they allow the parties to develop their respective technologies without the risk of subsequent infringement claims.

(58) Cited in note 36. See in particular paragraphs 115 et seq.

149. In the application of the indispensability test contained in Article 81(3) the Commission will in particular examine whether individual restrictions make it possible to perform the activity in question more efficiently than would have been the case in the absence of the restriction concerned. In making this assessment the market conditions and the realities facing the parties must be taken into account. Undertakings invoking the benefit of Article 81(3) are not required to consider hypothetical and theoretical alternatives. They must, however, explain and demonstrate why seemingly realistic and significantly less restrictive alternatives would be significantly less efficient. If the application of what appears to be a commercially realistic and less restrictive alternative would lead to a significant loss of efficiencies, the restriction in question is treated as indispensable. In some cases, it may also be necessary to examine whether the agreement as such is indispensable to achieve the efficiencies. This may for example be so in the case of technology pools that include complementary but non-essential technologies (59), in which case it must be examined to what extent such inclusion gives rise to particular efficiencies or whether, without a significant loss of efficiencies, the pool could be limited to technologies for which there are no substitutes. In the case of simple licensing between two parties it is generally not necessary to go beyond an examination of the indispensability of individual restraints. Normally there is no less restrictive alternative to the licence agreement as such.

(59) As to these concepts see section IV.4.1 below.

150. The condition that consumers must receive a fair share of the benefits implies that consumers of the products produced under the licence must at least be compensated for the negative effects of the agreement (60). This means that the efficiency gains must fully off-set the likely negative impact on prices, output and other relevant factors caused by the agreement. They may do so by changing the cost structure of the undertakings concerned, giving them an incentive to reduce price, or by allowing consumers to gain access to new or improved products, compensating for any likely price increase (61).

(60) See paragraph 85 of the Guidelines on the application of Article 81(3) of the Treaty, cited in note 2.

(61) *Idem*, paragraphs 98 and 102.

151. The last condition of Article 81(3), according to which the agreement must not afford the parties the possibility of eliminating competition in respect of a substantial part of the products concerned, presupposes an analysis of remaining competitive pressures on the market and the impact of the agreement on such sources of competition. In the application of the last condition of Article 81(3) the relationship between Article 81(3) and Article 82 must be taken into account. According to settled case law, the application of Article 81(3) cannot prevent the application of Article 82 of the Treaty (62). Moreover, since Articles 81 and 82 both pursue the aim of maintaining effective competition on the market, consistency requires that Article 81(3) be interpreted as precluding any application of the exception rule to restrictive agreements that constitute an abuse of a dominant position (63).

(62) See paragraph 130 of the judgment cited in note 2. Similarly, the application of Article 81(3) does not prevent the application of the Treaty rules on the free movement of goods, service, persons and capital. These provisions are in certain circumstances applicable to agreements, decisions and concerted practices within the meaning of Article 81(1), see to that effect Case C-309/99, Wouters, [2002] ECR I-1577, paragraph 120.

(63) See in this respect Case T-51/89, Tetra Pak (I), [1990] ECR II-309. See also paragraph 106 of the Guidelines on the application of Article 81(3) of the Treaty cited in note 2 above.

152. The fact that the agreement substantially reduces one dimension of competition does not necessarily mean that competition is eliminated within the meaning of Article 81(3). A technology pool, for instance, can result in an industry standard, leading to a situation in which there is little competition in terms of the technological format. Once the main players in the market adopt a certain format, network effects may make it very difficult for alternative formats to survive. This does not imply, however, that the creation of a de facto industry standard always eliminates competition within the meaning of the last condition of Article 81(3). Within the standard, suppliers may compete on price, quality and product features. However, in order for the agreement to comply with Article 81(3), it must be ensured that the agreement does not unduly restrict competition and does not unduly restrict future innovation.

2. The application of Article 81 to various types of licensing restraints

153. This section deals with various types of restraints that are commonly included in licence agreements. Given their prevalence it is useful to provide guidance as to how they are assessed outside the safe harbour of the TTBER. Restraints that have already been dealt with in the preceding parts of these guidelines, in particular sections III.4 and III.5, are only dealt with briefly in the present section.

154. This section covers both agreements between non-competitors and agreements between competitors.

In respect of the latter a distinction is made – where appropriate – between reciprocal and non-reciprocal agreements. No such distinction is required in the case of agreements between non-competitors. When undertakings are neither actual nor potential competitors on a relevant technology market or on a market for products incorporating the licensed technology, a reciprocal licence is for all practical purposes no different from two separate licences. Arrangements whereby the parties assemble a technology package, which is then licensed to third parties, are technology pools, which are dealt with in section 4 below.

155. This section does not deal with obligations in licence agreements that are generally not restrictive of competition within the meaning of Article 81(1). These obligations include but are not limited to:

(a) confidentiality obligations;

(b) obligations on licensees not to sub-license;

(c) obligations not to use the licensed technology after the expiry of the agreement, provided that the licensed technology remains valid and in force;

(d) obligations to assist the licensor in enforcing the licensed intellectual property rights;

(e) obligations to pay minimum royalties or to produce a minimum quantity of products incorporating the licensed technology; and

(f) obligations to use the licensor's trade mark or indicate the name of the licensor on the product.

2.1. Royalty obligations

156. The parties to a licence agreement are normally free to determine the royalty payable by the licensee and its mode of payment without being caught by Article 81(1). This principle applies both to agreements between competitors and agreements between non-competitors. Royalty obligations may for instance take the form of lump sum payments, a percentage of the selling price or a fixed amount for each product incorporating the licensed technology. In cases where the licensed technology relates to an input which is incorporated into a final product it is as a general rule not restrictive of competition that royalties are calculated on the basis of the price of the final product, provided that it incorporates the licensed technology. In the case of software licensing royalties based on the number of users and royalties calculated on a per machine basis are generally compatible with Article 81(1).

157. In the case of licence agreements between competitors it is recalled, see paragraphs and above, that in a limited number of circumstances royalty obligations may amount to price fixing, which is a hardcore restriction (cf. Article 4(1)*(a)*). It is a hardcore restriction under Article 4(1)(a) if competitors provide for reciprocal running royalties in circumstances where the licence is a sham, in that its purpose is not to allow an integration of complementary technologies or to achieve another pro-competitive aim. It is also a hardcore restriction under Article 4(1)*(a)* and 4(1)*(d)* if royalties extend to products produced solely with the licensee's own technology.

158. Other types of royalty arrangements between competitors are block exempted up to the market share threshold of 20% even if they restrict competition. Outside the safe harbour of the block exemption Article 81(1) may be applicable where competitors cross license and impose running royalties that are clearly disproportionate compared to the market value of the licence and where such royalties have a significant impact on market prices. In assessing whether the royalties are disproportionate it is relevant to have regard to the royalties paid by other licensees on the product market for the same or substitute technologies. In such cases it is unlikely that the conditions of Article 81(3) are satisfied. Article 81(1) may also apply where reciprocal running royalties per unit increase as output increases. If the parties have a significant degree of market power, such royalties may have the effect of limiting output.

159. Notwithstanding the fact that the block exemption only applies as long as the technology is valid and in force, the parties can normally agree to extend royalty obligations beyond the period of validity of the licensed intellectual property rights without falling foul of Article 81(1). Once these rights expire, third parties can legally exploit the technology in question and compete with the parties to the agreement. Such actual and potential competition will normally suffice to ensure that the obligation in question does not have appreciable anti-competitive effects.

160. In the case of agreements between non-competitors the block exemption covers agreements whereby royalties are calculated on the basis of both products produced with the licensed technology and products produced with technologies licensed from third parties. Such arrangements may facilitate the metering of royalties. However, they may also lead to foreclosure by increasing the cost of using third party inputs and may thus have similar effects as a non-compete obligation. If royalties are paid not just on products produced with the licensed technology but also on products produced with third party technology, then the royalties will increase the cost of the latter products and reduce demand for third party technology. Outside the scope of the block exemption it must therefore be examined whether the restriction has foreclosure effects. For that purpose it is appropriate to use the analytical framework set out in section 2.7 below. In the case of appreciable foreclosure effects such agreements are caught by Article 81(1) and unlikely to fulfil the conditions of Article 81(3), unless there is no other practical way of calculating and monitoring royalty payments.

2.2. Exclusive licensing and sales restrictions

161. For the present purposes it is useful to distinguish between restrictions as to production within a given territory (exclusive or sole licences) and restrictions on the sale of products incorporating the licensed technology into a given territory and to a given customer group (sales restrictions).

2.2.1. Exclusive and sole licences

162. A licence is deemed to be exclusive if the licensee is the only one who is permitted to produce on the basis of the licensed technology within a given territory. The licensor thus undertakes not to produce itself or license others to produce within a given territory. This territory may cover the whole world. Where the licensor undertakes only not to licence third parties to produce within a given territory, the licence is a sole licence. Often exclusive or sole licensing is accompanied by sales restrictions that limit the parties in where they may sell products incorporating the licensed technology.

163. Reciprocal exclusive licensing between competitors falls under Article 4(1)(c), which identifies market sharing between competitors as a hardcore restriction. Reciprocal sole licensing between competitors is block exempted up to the market share threshold of 20%. Under such an agreement the parties mutually commit not to license their competing technologies to third parties. In cases where the parties have a significant degree of market power such agreements may facilitate collusion by ensuring that the parties are the only sources of output in the market based on the licensed technologies.

164. Non-reciprocal exclusive licensing between competitors is block exempted up to the market share threshold of 20%. Above the market share threshold it is necessary to analyse what are the likely anti-competitive effects of such exclusive licensing. Where the exclusive licence is world-wide it implies that the licensor leaves the market. In cases where exclusivity is limited to a particular territory such as a Member State the agreement implies that the licensor abstains from producing goods and services inside the territory in question. In the context of Article 81(1) it must in particular be assessed what is the competitive significance of the licensor. If the licensor has a limited market position on the product market or lacks the capacity to effectively exploit the technology in the licensee's territory, the agreement is unlikely to be caught by Article 81(1). A special case is where the licensor and the licensee only compete on the technology market and the licensor, for instance being a research institute or a small research based undertaking, lacks the production and distribution assets to effectively bring to market products incorporating the licensed technology. In such cases Article 81(1) is unlikely to be infringed.

165. Exclusive licensing between non-competitors – to the extent that it is caught by Article 81(1) (64) – is likely to fulfil the conditions of Article 81(3). The right to grant an exclusive licence is generally necessary in order to induce the licensee to invest in the licensed technology and to bring the products to market in a timely manner. This is in particular the case where the licensee must make large investments in further developing the licensed technology. To intervene against the exclusivity once the licensee has made a commercial success of the licensed technology would deprive the licensee of the fruits of his success and would be detrimental to competition, the dissemination of technology and innovation. The Commission will therefore only exceptionally intervene against exclusive licensing in agreements between non-competitors, irrespective of the territorial scope of the licence.

(64) See the judgment in Nungesser cited in note 13.

166. The main situation in which intervention may be warranted is where a dominant licensee obtains an exclusive licence to one or more competing technologies. Such agreements are likely to be caught by Article 81(1) and unlikely to fulfil the conditions of Article 81(3). It is a condition however that entry into the technology market is difficult and the licensed technology constitutes a real source of competition on the market. In such circumstances an exclusive licence may foreclose third party licensees and allow the licensee to preserve his market power.

167. Arrangements whereby two or more parties cross licence each other and undertake not to licence third parties give rise to particular concerns when the package of technologies resulting from the cross licences creates a de facto industry standard to which third parties must have access in order to compete effectively on the market. In such cases the agreement creates a closed standard reserved for the parties. The Commission will assess such arrangements according to the same principles as those applied to technology pools (see section 4 below). It will normally be required that the technologies which support such a standard be licensed to third parties on fair, reasonable and non-discriminatory terms (65). Where the parties to the arrangement compete with third parties on an existing product market and the arrangement relates to that product market a closed standard is likely to have substantial exclusionary effects. This negative impact on competition can only be avoided by licensing also to third parties.

(65) See in this respect the Commission's Notice in the Canon/Kodak Case (O.J. C 330, 1.11.1997, p. 10) and the IGR Stereo Television Case mentioned in the XI Report on Competition Policy, paragraph 94.

2.2.2. Sales restrictions

168. Also as regards sales restrictions there is an important distinction to be made between licensing between competitors and between non-competitors.

169. Restrictions on active and passive sales by one or both parties in a reciprocal agreement between competitors are hardcore restrictions of competition under Article 4(1)(c). Sales restrictions on either party in a reciprocal agreement between competitors are caught by Article 81(1) and are unlikely to fulfil the conditions of Article 81(3). Such restrictions are generally considered market sharing, since they prevent the affected party from selling actively and passively into territories and to customer groups which he actually served or could realistically have served in the absence of the agreement.

170. In the case of non-reciprocal agreements between competitors the block exemption applies to restrictions on active and passive sales by the licensee or the licensor into the exclusive territory or to the exclusive customer group reserved for the other party (cf. Article 4(1)(c)(iv). Above the market share threshold of 20% sales restrictions between licensor and licensee are caught by Article 81(1) when one or both of the parties have a significant degree of market power. Such restrictions, however, may be indispensable for the dissemination of valuable technologies and therefore fulfil the conditions of Article 81(3). This may be the case where the licensor has a relatively weak market position in the territory where he exploits himself the technology. In such circumstances restrictions on active sales in particular may be indispensable to induce the licensor to grant the licence. In the absence thereof the licensor would risk facing active competition in his main area of activity. Similarly, restrictions on active sales by the licensor may be indispensable, in particular, where the licensee has a relatively weak market position in the territory allocated to him and has to make significant investments in order to efficiently exploit the licensed technology.

171. The block exemption also covers restrictions on active sales into the territory or to the customer group allocated to another licensee, who was not a competitor of the licensor at the time when he concluded the licence agreement with the licensor. It is a condition, however, that the agreement between the parties in question is non-reciprocal. Above the market share threshold such active sales restrictions are likely to be caught by Article 81(1) when the parties have a significant degree of market power. However, the restraint is likely to be indispensable within the meaning of Article 81(3) for the period of time required for the protected licensee to penetrate a new market and establish a market presence in the allocated territory or vis-à-vis the allocated customer group. This protection against active sales allows the licensee to overcome the asymmetry, which he faces due to the fact that some of the licensees are competing undertakings of the licensor and thus already established on the market. Restrictions on passive sales by licensees into a territory or to a customer group allocated to another licensee are hardcore restrictions under Article 4(1)(c) of the TTBER.

172. In the case of agreements between non-competitors sales restrictions between the licensor and a licensee are block exempted up to the market share threshold of 30%. Above the market share threshold restrictions on active and passive sales by licensees to territories or customer groups reserved for the licensor may fall outside Article 81(1) where on the basis of objective factors it can be concluded that in the absence of the sales restrictions licensing would not occur. A technology owner cannot normally be expected to create direct competition with himself on the basis of his own technology. In other cases sales restrictions on the licensee may be caught by Article 81(1) both where the licensor individually has a significant degree of market power and in the case of a cumulative effect of similar agreements concluded by licensors which together hold a strong position on the market.

173. Sales restrictions on the licensor, when caught by Article 81(1), are likely to fulfil the conditions of Article 81(3) unless there are no real alternatives to the licensor's technology on the market or such alternatives are licensed by the licensee from third parties. Such restrictions and in particular restrictions on active sales are likely to be indispensable within the meaning of Article 81(3) in order to induce the licensee to invest in the production, marketing and sale of the products incorporating the licensed technology. It is likely that the licensee's incentive to invest would be significantly reduced if he would face direct competition from the licensor whose production costs are not burdened by royalty payments, possibly leading to sub-optimal levels of investment.

174. As regards restrictions on sales between licensees in agreements between non-competitors, the TTBER block exempts restrictions on active selling between territories or customer groups. Above the market share threshold restrictions on active sales between licensees' territories and customer groups limit intra-technology competition and are likely to be caught by Article 81(1) when the individual licensee has a significant degree of market power. Such restrictions, however, may fulfil the conditions of Article 81(3) where they are necessary to prevent free riding and to induce the licensee to make the investment necessary for efficient exploitation of the licensed technology inside his territory and to promote sales of the licensed product. Restrictions on passive sales are covered by the hardcore list of Article 4(2)(b), cf. paragraph 101 above, when they exceed two years from the date on which the licensee benefiting from the restrictions first put the product incorporating the licensed technology on the market inside his exclusive territory. Passive sales restrictions exceeding this two-year period are unlikely to fulfil the conditions of Article 81(3).

2.3. Output restrictions

175. Reciprocal output restrictions in licence agreements between competitors constitute a hardcore restriction covered by Article 4(1)(b) of the TTBER (cf. point 82 above). Article 4(1)(b) does not cover output restrictions imposed on the licensee in a non-reciprocal agreement or on one of the licensees in an reciprocal agreement. Such restrictions are block exempted up to the market share threshold of 20%. Above the market share threshold, output restrictions on the licensee may restrict competition where the parties have a significant degree of market power. However, Article 81(3) is likely to apply in cases where the licensor's technology is substantially better than the licensee's technology and the output limitation substantially exceeds the output of the licensee prior to the conclusion of the agreement. In that case the effect of the output limitation is limited even in markets where demand is growing. In the application of Article 81(3) it must also be taken into account that such restrictions may be necessary in order to induce the licensor to disseminate his technology as widely as possible. For instance, a licensor may be reluctant to license his competitors if he cannot limit the licence to a particular production site with a specific capacity (a site licence). Where the licence agreement leads to a real integration of complementary assets, output restrictions on the licensee may therefore fulfil the conditions of Article 81(3). However, this is unlikely to be the case where the parties have substantial market power.

176. Output restrictions in licence agreements between non-competitors are block exempted up to the market share threshold of 30%. The main anti-competitive risk flowing from output restrictions on licensees in agreements between non-competitors is reduced intratechnology competition between licensees. The significance of such anti-competitive effects depends on the market position of the licensor and the licensees and the extent to which the output limitation prevents the licensee from satisfying demand for the products incorporating the licensed technology.

177. When output restrictions are combined with exclusive territories or exclusive customer groups, the restrictive effects are increased. The combination of the two types of restraints makes it more likely that the agreement serves to partition markets.

178. Output limitations imposed on the licensee in agreements between non-competitors may also have pro-competitive effects by promoting the dissemination of technology. As a supplier of technology, the licensor should normally be free to determine the output produced with the licensed technology by the licensee. If the licensor were not free to determine the output of the licensee, a number of licence agreements might not come into existence in the first place, which would have a negative impact on the dissemination of new technology. This is particularly likely to be the case where the licensor is also a producer, since in that case the output of the licensees may find their way back into the licensor's main area of operation and thus have a direct impact on these activities. On the other hand, it is less likely that output restrictions are necessary in order to ensure dissemination of the licensor's technology when combined with sales restrictions on the licensee prohibiting him from selling into a territory or customer group reserved for the licensor.

2.4. Field of use restrictions

179. Under a field of use restriction the licence is either limited to one or more technical fields of application or one or more product markets. There are many cases in which the same technology can be used to make different products or can be incorporated into products belonging to different product markets. A new moulding technology may for instance be used to make plastic bottles and plastic glasses, each product belonging to separate product markets. However, a single product market may encompass several technical fields of use. For instance a new engine technology may be employed in four cylinder engines and six cylinder engines. Similarly, a technology to make chipsets may be used to produce chipsets with up to four CPUs and more than four CPUs. A licence limiting the use of the licensed technology to produce say four cylinder engines and chipsets with up to four CPUs constitutes a technical field of use restriction.

180. Given that field of use restrictions are block exempted and that certain customer restrictions are hardcore restrictions under Articles 4(1)(c) and 4(2)(b) of the TTBER, it is important to distinguish the two categories of restraints. A customer restriction presupposes that specific customer groups are identified and that the parties are restricted in selling to such identified groups. The fact that a technical field of use restriction may correspond to certain groups of customers within a product market does not imply that the restraint is to be classified as a customer restriction. For instance, the fact that certain customers buy predominantly or exclusively chipsets with more than four CPUs does not imply that a licence which is limited to chipsets with up to four CPUs constitutes a customer restriction. However, the field of use must be defined objectively by reference to identified and meaningful technical characteristics of the licensed product.

181. A field of use restriction limits the exploitation of the licensed technology by the licensee to one or more particular fields of use without limiting the licensor's ability to exploit the licensed technology. In addition, as with territories, these fields of use can be allocated to the licensee under an exclusive or sole licence. Field of use restrictions combined with an exclusive or sole licence also restrict the licensor's ability to exploit his own technology, by preventing him from exploiting it himself, including by way of licensing to others. In the case of a sole license only licensing to third parties is restricted. Field of use restrictions combined with exclusive and sole licences are treated in the same way as the exclusive and sole licenses dealt with in section 2.2.1 above. In particular, for licensing between competitors, this means that reciprocal exclusive licensing is hardcore under Article 4(1)(c).

182. Field of use restrictions may have pro-competitive effects by encouraging the licensor to license his technology for applications that fall outside his main area of focus. If the licensor could not prevent licensees from operating in fields where he exploits the technology himself or in fields where the value of the technology is not yet well established, it would be likely to create a disincentive for the licensor to license or would lead him to charge a higher royalty. It must also be taken into account that in certain sectors licensing often occurs to ensure design freedom by preventing infringement claims. Within the scope of the licence the licensee is able to develop his own technology without fearing infringement claims by the licensor.

183. Field of use restrictions on licensees in agreements between actual or potential competitors are block exempted up to the market share threshold of 20%. The main competitive concern in the case of such restrictions is the risk that the licensee ceases to be a competitive force outside the licensed field of use. This risk is greater in the case of cross licensing between competitors where the agreement provides for asymmetrical field of use restrictions. A field of use restriction is asymmetrical where one party is permitted to use the licensed technology within one product market or technical field of use and the other party is permitted to use the other licensed technology within another product market or technical field of use. Competition concerns may in particular arise where the licensee's production facility, which is tooled up to use the licensed technology, is also used to produce with his own technology products outside the licensed field of use. If the agreement is likely to lead the licensee to reduce output outside the licensed field of use, the agreement is likely to be caught by Article 81(1). Symmetrical field of use restrictions, i.e. agreements whereby the parties are licensed to use each other's technologies within the same field(s) of use, are unlikely to

be caught by Article 81(1). Such agreements are unlikely to restrict competition that existed in the absence of the agreement. Article 81(1) is also unlikely to apply in the case of agreements that merely enable the licensee to develop and exploit his own technology within the scope of the licence without fearing infringement claims by the licensor. In such circumstances field of use restrictions do not in themselves restrict competition that existed in the absence of the agreement. In the absence of the agreement the licensee also risked infringement claims outside the scope of the licensed field of use. However, if the licensee without business justification terminates or scales back his activities in the area outside the licensed field of use this may be an indication of an underlying market sharing arrangement amounting to a hardcore restriction under Article 4(1)(c) of the TTBER.

184. Field of use restrictions on licensee and licensor in agreements between non-competitors are block exempted up to the market share threshold of 30%. Field of use restrictions in agreements between non-competitors whereby the licensor reserves one or more product markets or technical fields of use for himself are generally either non-restrictive of competition or efficiency enhancing. They promote dissemination of new technology by giving the licensor an incentive to license for exploitation in fields in which he does not want to exploit the technology himself. If the licensor could not prevent licensees from operating in fields where the licensor exploits the technology himself, it would be likely to create a disincentive for the licensor to licence.

185. In agreements between non-competitors the licensor is normally also entitled to grant sole or exclusive licences to different licensees limited to one or more fields of use. Such restrictions limit intra-technology competition between licensees in the same way as exclusive licensing and are analysed in the same way (cf. section 2.2.1 above).

2.5. Captive use restrictions

186. A captive use restriction can be defined as an obligation on the licensee to limit his production of the licensed product to the quantities required for the production of his own products and for the maintenance and repair of his own products. In other words, this type of use restriction takes the form of an obligation on the licensee to use the products incorporating the licensed technology only as an input for incorporation into his own production; it does not cover the sale of the licensed product for incorporation into the products of other producers. Captive use restrictions are block exempted up to the respective market share thresholds of 20% and 30%. Outside the scope of the block exemption it is necessary to examine what are the pro-competitive and anti-competitive effects of the restraint. In this respect it is necessary to distinguish agreements between competitors from agreements between non-competitors.

187. In the case of licence agreements between competitors a restriction that imposes on the licensee to produce under the licence only for incorporation into his own products prevents him from being a supplier of components to third party producers. If prior to the conclusion of the agreement, the licensee was not an actual or likely potential supplier of components to other producers, the captive use restriction does not change anything compared to the pre-existing situation. In those circumstances the restriction is assessed in the same way as in the case of agreements between non-competitors. If, on the other hand, the licensee is an actual or likely component supplier, it is necessary to examine what is the impact of the agreement on this activity. If by tooling up to use the licensor's technology the licensee ceases to use his own technology on a stand alone basis and thus to be a component supplier, the agreement restricts competition that existed prior to the agreement. It may result in serious negative market effects when the licensor has a significant degree of market power on the component market.

188. In the case of licence agreements between non-competitors there are two main competitive risks stemming from captive use restrictions: (a) a restriction of intra-technology competition on the market for the supply of inputs and (b) an exclusion of arbitrage between licensees enhancing the possibility for the licensor to impose discriminatory royalties on licensees.

189. Captive use restrictions, however, may also promote pro-competitive licensing. If the licensor is a supplier of components, the restraint may be necessary in order for the dissemination of technology between non-competitors to occur. In the absence of the restraint the licensor may not grant the licence or may do so only against higher royalties, because otherwise he would create direct competition to himself on the component market. In such cases a captive use restriction is normally either not restrictive of competition or covered by Article 81(3). It is a condition, however, that the licensee is not restricted in selling the licensed product as replacement parts for his own products. The licensee must be able to serve the after market for his own products, including independent service organisations that service and repair the products produced by him.

190. Where the licensor is not a component supplier on the relevant market, the above reason for imposing captive use restrictions does not apply. In such cases a captive use restriction may in principle promote the dissemination of technology by ensuring that licensees do not sell to producers that compete with the licensor on other markets. However, a restriction on the licensee not to sell into certain customer groups reserved for the licensor normally constitutes a less restrictive alternative. Consequently, in such cases a captive use restriction is normally not necessary for the dissemination of technology to take place.

2.6. Tying and bundling

191. In the context of technology licensing tying occurs when the licensor makes the licensing of one technology (the tying product) conditional upon the licensee taking a licence for another technology or purchasing a product from the licensor or someone designated by him (the tied product). Bundling occurs where two technologies or a technology and a product are only sold together as a bundle. In both cases, however, it is a condition that the products and technologies involved are distinct in the sense that there is distinct demand for each of the products and technologies forming part of the tie or the bundle. This is normally not the case where the technologies or products are by necessity linked in such a way that the licensed technology cannot be exploited without the tied product or both parts of the bundle cannot be exploited without the other. In the following the term «tying» refers to both tying and bundling.

192. Article 3 of the TTBER, which limits the application of the block exemption by market share thresholds, ensures that tying and bundling are not block exempted above the market share thresholds of 20% in the case of agreements between competitors and 30% in the case of agreements between non-competitors. The market share thresholds apply to any relevant technology or product market affected by the licence agreement, including the market for the tied product. Above the market share thresholds it is necessary to balance the anti-competitive and pro-competitive effects of tying.

193. The main restrictive effect of tying is foreclosure of competing suppliers of the tied product. Tying may also allow the licensor to maintain market power in the market for the tying product by raising barriers to entry since it may force new entrants to enter several markets at the same time. Moreover, tying may allow the licensor to increase royalties, in particular when the tying product and the tied product are partly substitutable and the two products are not used in fixed proportion. Tying prevents the licensee from switching to substitute inputs in the face of increased royalties for the tying product. These competition concerns are independent of whether the parties to the agreement are competitors or not. For tying to produce likely anti-competitive effects the licensor must have a significant degree of market power in the tying product so as to restrict competition in the tied product. In the absence of market power in the tying product the licensor cannot use his technology for the anticompetitive purpose of foreclosing suppliers of the tied product. Furthermore, as in the case of non-compete obligations, the tie must cover a certain proportion of the market for the tied product for appreciable foreclosure effects to occur. In cases where the licensor has market power on the market for the tied product rather than on the market for the tying product, the restraint is analysed as non-compete or quantity forcing, reflecting the fact that any competition problem has its origin on the market for the «tied» product and not on the market for the «tying» product (66).

(66) For the applicable analytical framework see section 2.7 below and paragraphs 138 et seq. of the Guidelines on Vertical Restraints cited in note 36.

194. Tying can also give rise to efficiency gains. This is for instance the case where the tied product is necessary for a technically satisfactory exploitation of the licensed technology or for ensuring that production under the licence conforms to quality standards respected by the licensor and other licensees. In such cases tying is normally either not restrictive of competition or covered by Article 81(3). Where the licensees use the licensor's trademark or brand name or where it is otherwise obvious to consumers that there is a link between the product incorporating the licensed technology and the licensor, the licensor has a legitimate interest in ensuring that the quality of the products are such that it does not undermine the value of his technology or his reputation as an economic operator. Moreover, where it is known to consumers that the licensees (and the licensor) produce on the basis of the same technology it is unlikely that licensees would be willing to take a licence unless the technology is exploited by all in a technically satisfactory way.

195. Tying is also likely to be pro-competitive where the tied product allows the licensee to exploit the licensed technology significantly more efficiently. For instance, where the licensor licenses a particular process technology the parties can also agree that the licensee buys a catalyst from the licensor which is developed for use with the licensed technology and which allows the technology to be exploited more efficiently than in the case of other catalysts. Where in such cases the restriction is caught by Article 81(1), the conditions of Article 81(3) are likely to be fulfilled even above the market share thresholds.

2.7. Non-compete obligations

196. Non-compete obligations in the context of technology licensing take the form of an obligation on the licensee not to use third party technologies which compete with the licensed technology. To the extent that a non-compete obligation covers a product or additional technology supplied by the licensor the obligation is dealt with in the preceding section on tying.

197. The TTBER exempts non-compete obligations both in the case of agreements between competitors and in the case of agreements between non-competitors up to the market share thresholds of 20% and 30% respectively.

198. The main competitive risk presented by non-compete obligations is foreclosure of third party technologies. Non-compete obligations may also facilitate collusion between licensors in the case of cumulative use. Foreclosure of competing technologies reduces competitive pressure on royalties charged by the licensor and reduces competition between the incumbent technologies by limiting the possibilities for licensees to substitute between competing technologies. As in both cases the main problem is foreclosure, the analysis can in general be the same in the case of agreements between competitors and agreements between non-competitors. However, in the case of cross licensing between competitors where both agree not to use third party technologies the agreement may facilitate collusion between them on the product market, thereby justifying the lower market share threshold of 20%.

199. Foreclosure may arise where a substantial part of potential licensees are already tied to one or, in the case of cumulative effects, more sources of technology and are prevented from exploiting competing technologies. Foreclosure effects may result from agreements concluded by a single licensor with a significant degree of market power or by a cumulative effect of agreements concluded by several licensors, even where each individual agreement or network of agreements is covered by the TTBER. In the latter case, however, a serious cumulative effect is unlikely to arise as long as less than 50% of the market is tied. Above this threshold significant foreclosure is likely to occur when there are relatively high barriers to entry for new licensees. If barriers to entry are low, new licensees are able to enter the market and exploit commercially attractive technologies held by third parties and thus represent a real alternative to incumbent licensees. In order to determine the real possibility for entry and expansion by third parties it is also necessary to take account of the extent to which distributors are tied to licensees by non-compete obligations. Third party technologies only have a real possibility of entry if they have access to the necessary production and distribution assets. In other words, the ease of entry depends not only on the availability of licensees but also the extent to which they have access to distribution. In assessing foreclosure effects at the distribution level the Commission will apply the analytical framework set out in section IV.2.1 of the Guidelines on Vertical Restraints (67).

(67) See note 36.

200. When the licensor has a significant degree of market power, obligations on licensees to obtain the technology only from the licensor can lead to significant foreclosure effects. The stronger the market position of the licensor the higher the risk of foreclosing competing technologies. For appreciable foreclosure effects to occur the non-compete obligations do not necessarily have to cover a substantial part of the market. Even in the absence thereof, appreciable foreclosure effects may occur where non-compete obligations are targeted at undertakings that are the most likely to license competing technologies. The risk of foreclosure is particularly high where there is only a limited number of potential licensees and the licence agreement concerns a technology which is used by the licensees to make an input for their own use. In such cases the entry barriers for a new licensor are likely to be high. Foreclosure may be less likely in cases where the technology is used to make a product that is sold to third parties; although in this case the restriction also ties production capacity for the input in question, it does not tie demand for the product incorporating the input produced with the licensed technology. To enter the market in the latter case licensors only need access to one or more licensee(s) that have suitable production capacity and unless only few undertakings possess or are able to obtain the assets required to take a licence, it is unlikely that by imposing non-compete obligations on its licensees the licensor is able to deny competitors access to efficient licensees.

201. Non-compete obligations may also produce pro-competitive effects. First, such obligations may promote dissemination of technology by reducing the risk of misappropriation of the licensed technology, in particular know-how. If a licensee is entitled to license competing technologies from third parties, there is a risk that particularly licensed know-how would be used in the exploitation of competing technologies and thus benefit competitors. When a licensee also exploits competing technologies, it normally also makes monitoring of royalty payments more difficult, which may act as a disincentive to licensing.

202. Second, non-compete obligations possibly in combination with an exclusive territory may be necessary to ensure that the licensee has an incentive to invest in and exploit the licensed technology effectively. In cases where the agreement is caught by Article 81(1) because of an appreciable foreclosure effect, it may be necessary in order to benefit from Article 81(3) to choose a less restrictive alternative, for instance to impose minimum output or royalty obligations, which normally have less potential to foreclose competing technologies.

203. Third, in cases where the licensor undertakes to make significant client specific investments for instance in training and tailoring of the licensed technology to the licensee's needs, non-compete obligations or alternatively minimum output or minimum royalty obligations may be necessary to induce the licensor to make the investment and to avoid hold-up problems. However, normally the licensor will be able to charge directly for such investments by way of a lump sum payment, implying that less restrictive alternatives are available.

3. Settlement and non-assertion agreements

204. Licensing may serve as a means of settling disputes or avoiding that one party exercises his intellectual property rights to prevent the other party from exploiting his own technology. Licensing including cross licensing in the context of settlement agreements and non-assertion agreements is not as such restrictive of competition since it allows the parties to exploit their technologies post agreement. However, the individual terms and conditions of such agreements may be caught by Article 81(1). Licensing in the context of settlement agreements is treated like other licence agreements. In the case of technologies that from a technical point of view are substitutes, it is therefore necessary to assess to what extent it is likely that the technologies in question are in a one-way or two-way blocking position (*cf.* paragraph 32 above). If so, the parties are not deemed to be competitors.

205. The block exemption applies provided that the agreement does not contain any hardcore restrictions of competition as set out in Article 4 of the TTBER. The hardcore list of Article 4(1) may in particular apply where it was clear to the parties that no blocking position exists and that consequently they are competitors. In such cases the settlement is merely a means to restrict competition that existed in the absence of the agreement.

206. In cases where it is likely that in the absence of the licence the licensee could be excluded from the market, the agreement is generally pro-competitive. Restrictions that limit intra-technology competition between the licensor and the licensee are often compatible with Article 81, see section 2 above.

207. Agreements whereby the parties cross license each other and impose restrictions on the use of their technologies, including restrictions on the licensing to third parties, may be caught by Article 81(1). Where the parties have a significant degree of market power and the agreement imposes restrictions that clearly go beyond what is required in order to unblock, the agreement is likely to be caught by Article 81(1) even if it is likely that a mutual blocking position exists. Article 81(1) is particularly likely to apply where the parties share markets or fix reciprocal running royalties that have a significant impact on market prices.

208. Where under the agreement the parties are entitled to use each other's technology and the agreement extends to future developments, it is necessary to assess what is the impact of the agreement on the parties' incentive to innovate. In cases where the parties have a significant degree of market power the agreement is likely to be caught by Article 81(1) where the agreement prevents the parties from gaining a competitive lead over each other. Agreements that eliminate or substantially reduce the possibilities of one party to gain a competitive lead over the other reduce the incentive to innovate and thus adversely affect an essential part of the competitive process. Such agreements are also unlikely to satisfy the conditions of Article 81(3). It is particularly unlikely that the restriction can be considered indispensable within the meaning of the third condition of Article 81(3). The achievement of the objective of the agreement, namely to ensure that the parties can continue to exploit their own technology without being blocked by the other party, does not require that the parties agree to share future innovations. However, the parties are unlikely to be prevented from gaining a competitive lead over each other where the purpose of the licence is to allow the parties to develop their respective technologies and where the licence does not lead them to use the same technological solutions. Such agreements merely create design freedom by preventing future infringement claims by the other party.

209. In the context of a settlement and non-assertion agreement, non-challenge clauses are generally considered to fall outside Article 81(1). It is inherent in such agreements that the parties agree not to challenge ex post the intellectual property rights covered by the agreement. Indeed, the very purpose of the agreement is to settle existing disputes and/or to avoid future disputes.

4. Technology pools

210. Technology pools are defined as arrangements whereby two or more parties assemble a package of technology which is licensed not only to contributors to the pool but also to third parties. In terms of their structure technology pools can take the form of simple arrangements between a limited number of parties or elaborate organisational arrangements whereby the organisation of the licensing of the pooled technologies is entrusted to a separate entity. In both cases the pool may allow licensees to operate on the market on the basis of a single licence.

211. There is no inherent link between technology pools and standards, but in some cases the technologies in the pool support (wholly or partly) a de facto or de jure industry standard. When technology pools do support an industry standard they do not necessarily support a single standard. Different technology pools may support competing standards (68).

(68) See in this respect the Commission's press release IP/02/1651 concerning the licensing of patents for third generation (3G) mobile services. This case involved five technology pools creating five different technologies, each of which could be used to produce 3G equipment.

212. Agreements establishing technology pools and setting out the terms and conditions for their operation are not – irrespective of the number of parties – covered by the block exemption (cf. section III.2.2 above). Such agreements are addressed only by these guidelines. Pooling arrangements give rise to a number of particular issues regarding the selection of the included technologies and the operation of the pool, which do not arise in the context of other types of licensing. The individual licences granted by the pool to third party licensees, however, are treated like other licence agreements, which are block exempted when the conditions set out in the TTBER are fulfilled, including the requirements of Article 4 of the TTBER containing the list of hardcore restrictions.

213. Technology pools may be restrictive of competition. The creation of a technology pool necessarily implies joint selling of the pooled technologies, which in the case of pools composed solely or predominantly of substitute technologies amounts to a price fixing cartel. Moreover, in addition to reducing competition between the parties, technology pools may also, in particular when they support an industry standard or establish a de facto industry standard, result in a reduction of innovation by foreclosing alternative technologies. The existence of the standard and the related technology pool may make it more difficult for new and improved technologies to enter the market.

214. Technology pools can also produce pro-competitive effects, in particular by reducing transaction costs and by setting a limit on cumulative royalties to avoid double marginalisation. The creation of a pool allows for one-stop licensing of the technologies covered by the pool. This is particularly important in sectors where intellectual property rights are prevalent and where in order to operate on the market licences need to be obtained from a significant number of licensors. In cases where licensees receive on-going services concerning the application of the licensed technology, joint licensing and servicing can lead to further cost reductions.

4.1. The nature of the pooled technologies

215. The competitive risks and the efficiency enhancing potential of technology pools depend to a large extent on the relationship between the pooled technologies and their relationship with technologies outside the pool. Two basic distinctions must be made, namely (a) between technological complements and technological substitutes and (b) between essential and non-essential technologies.

216. Two technologies (69) are complements as opposed to substitutes when they are both required to produce the product or carry out the process to which the technologies relate. Conversely, two technologies are substitutes when either technology allows the holder to produce the product or carry out the process to which the technologies relate. A technology is essential as opposed to non-essential if there are no substitutes for that technology inside or outside the pool and the technology in question constitutes a necessary part of the package of technologies for the purposes of producing the product(s) or carrying out the process(es) to which the pool relates. A technology for which there are no substitutes, remains essential as long as the technology is covered by at least one valid intellectual property right. Technologies that are essential are by necessity also complements.

(69) The term «technology» is not limited to patents. It covers also patent applications and intellectual property rights other than patents.

217. When technologies in a pool are substitutes, royalties are likely to be higher than they would otherwise be, because licensees do not benefit from rivalry between the technologies in question. When the technologies in the pool are complements the arrangement reduces transaction costs and may lead to lower overall royalties because the parties are in a position to fix a common royalty for the package as opposed to each fixing a royalty which does not take account of the royalty fixed by others.

218. The distinction between complementary and substitute technologies is not clear-cut in all cases, since technologies may be substitutes in part and complements in part. When due to efficiencies stemming from the integration of two technologies licensees are likely to demand both technologies the technologies are treated as complements even if they are partly substitutable. In such cases it is likely that in the absence of the pool licensees would want to licence both technologies due to the additional economic benefit of employing both technologies as opposed to employing only one of them.

219. The inclusion in the pool of substitute technologies restricts inter-technology competition and amounts to collective bundling. Moreover, where the pool is substantially composed of substitute technologies, the arrangement amounts to price fixing between competitors. As a general rule the Commission considers that the inclusion of substitute technologies in the pool constitutes a violation of Article 81(1). The Commission also considers that it is unlikely that the conditions of Article 81(3) will be fulfilled in the case of pools comprising to a significant extent substitute technologies. Given that the technologies in question are alternatives, no transaction cost savings accrue from including both technologies in the pool. In the absence of the pool licensees would not have demanded both technologies. It is not sufficient that the parties remain free to license independently. In order not to undermine the pool, which allows them to jointly exercise market power, the parties are likely to have little incentive to do so.

220. When a pool is composed only of technologies that are essential and therefore by necessity also complements, the creation of the pool as such generally falls outside Article 81(1) irrespective of the market position of the parties. However, the conditions on which licences are granted may be caught by Article 81(1).

221. Where non-essential but complementary patents are included in the pool there is a risk of foreclosure of third party technologies. Once a technology is included in the pool and is licensed as part of the package, licensees are likely to have little incentive to license a competing technology when the royalty paid for the package already covers a substitute technology. Moreover, the inclusion of technologies which are not necessary for the purposes of producing the product(s) or carrying out the process(es) to which the technology pool relates also forces licensees to pay for technology that they may not need. The inclusion of complementary patents thus amounts to collective bundling. When a pool encompasses non-essential technologies, the agreement is likely to be caught by Article 81(1) where the pool has a significant position on any relevant market.

222. Given that substitute and complementary technologies may be developed after the creation of the pool, the assessment of essentiality is an on-going process. A technology may therefore become non-essential after the creation of the pool due to the emergence of new third party technologies. One way to ensure that such third party technologies are not foreclosed is to exclude from the pool technologies that have become non-essential. However, there may be other ways to ensure that third party technologies are not foreclosed. In the assessment of technology pools comprising non-essential technologies, i.e. technologies for which substitutes exist outside the pool or which are not necessary in order to produce one or more products to which the pool relates, the Commission will in its overall assessment, inter alia, take account of the following factors:

(a) whether there are any pro-competitive reasons for including the non-essential technologies in the pool;

(b) whether the licensors remain free to license their respective technologies independently. Where the pool is composed of a limited number of technologies and there are substitute technologies outside the pool, licensees may want to put together their own technological package composed partly of technology forming part of the pool and partly of technology owned by third parties;

(c) whether, in cases where the pooled technologies have different applications some of which do not require use of all of the pooled technologies, the pool offers the technologies only as a single package or whether it offers separate packages for distinct applications. In the latter case it is avoided that technologies which are not essential to a particular product or process are tied to essential technologies;

(d) whether the pooled technologies are available only as a single package or whether licensees have the possibility of obtaining a licence for only part of the package with a corresponding reduction of royalties. The possibility to obtain a licence for only part of the package may reduce the risk of foreclosure of third party technologies outside the pool, in particular where the licensee obtains a corresponding reduction in royalties. This requires that a share of the overall royalty has been assigned to each technology in the pool. Where the licence agreements concluded between the pool and individual licensees are of relatively long duration and the pooled technology supports a de facto industry standard, it must also be taken into account that the pool may foreclose access to the market of new substitute technologies. In assessing the risk of foreclosure in such cases it is relevant to take into account whether or not licensees can terminate at reasonable notice part of the licence and obtain a corresponding reduction of royalties.

4.2. Assessment of individual restraints

223. The purpose of this section is to address a certain number of restraints that in one form or another are commonly found in technology pools and which need to be assessed in the overall context of the pool. It is recalled, cf. paragraph 212 above, that the TTBER applies to licence agreements concluded between the pool and third party licensees. This section is therefore limited to addressing the creation of the pool and licensing issues that are particular to licensing in the context of technology pools.

224. In making its assessment the Commission will be guided by the following main principles:

1. The stronger the market position of the pool the greater the risk of anti-competitive effects.

2. Pools that hold a strong position on the market should be open and non-discriminatory.

3. Pools should not unduly foreclose third party technologies or limit the creation of alternative pools.

225. Undertakings setting up a technology pool that is compatible with Article 81, and any industry standard that it may support, are normally free to negotiate and fix royalties for the technology package and each technology's share of the royalties either before or after the standard is set. Such agreement is inherent in the establishment of the standard or pool and cannot in itself be considered restrictive of competition and may in certain circumstances lead to more efficient outcomes. In certain circumstances it may be more efficient if the royalties are agreed before the standard is chosen and not after the standard is decided upon, to avoid that the choice of the standard confers a significant degree of market power on one or more essential technologies. On the other hand, licensees must remain free to determine the price of products produced under the licence. Where the selection of technologies to be included in the pool is carried out by an independent expert this may further competition between available technological solutions.

226. Where the pool has a dominant position on the market, royalties and other licensing terms should be fair and non-discriminatory and licences should be non-exclusive. These requirements are necessary to ensure that the pool is open and does not lead to foreclosure and other anticompetitive effects on down stream markets. These requirements, however, do not preclude different royalties for different uses. It is in general not considered restrictive of competition to apply different royalty rates to different product markets, whereas there should be no discrimination within product markets. In particular, the treatment of licensees should not depend on whether they are licensors or not. The Commission will therefore take into account whether licensors are also subject to royalty obligations.

227. Licensors and licensees must be free to develop competing products and standards and must also be free to grant and obtain licences outside the pool. These requirements are necessary in order to limit the risk of foreclosure of third party technologies and ensure that the pool does not limit innovation and preclude the creation of competing technological solutions. Where a pool supports a (*de facto*) industry standard and where the parties are subject to non-compete obligations, the pool creates a particular risk of preventing the development of new and improved technologies and standards.

228. Grant back obligations should be non-exclusive and be limited to developments that are essential or important to the use of the pooled technology. This allows the pool to feed on and benefit from improvements to the pooled technology. It is legitimate for the parties to ensure that the exploitation of the pooled technology cannot be held up by licensees that hold or obtain essential patents.

229. One of the problems identified with regard to patent pools is the risk that they shield invalid patents. Pooling raises the costs/risks for a successful challenge, because the challenge fails if only one patent in the pool is valid. The shielding of invalid patents in the pool may oblige licensees to pay higher royalties and may also prevent innovation in the field covered by an invalid patent. In order to limit this risk any right to terminate a licence in the case of a challenge must be limited to the technologies owned by the licensor who is the addressee of the challenge and must not extend to the technologies owned by the other licensors in the pool.

4.3. The institutional framework governing the pool

230. The way in which a technology pool is created, organised and operated can reduce the risk of it having the object or effect of restricting competition and provide assurances to the effect that the arrangement is pro-competitive.

231. When participation in a standard and pool creation process is open to all interested parties representing different interests it is more likely that technologies for inclusion into the pool are selected on the basis of price/quality considerations than when the pool is set up by a limited group of technology owners. Similarly, when the relevant bodies of the pool are composed of persons representing different interests, it is more likely that licensing terms and conditions, including royalties, will be open and non-discriminatory and reflect the value of the licensed technology than when the pool is controlled by licensor representatives.

232. Another relevant factor is the extent to which independent experts are involved in the creation and operation of the pool. For instance, the assessment of whether or not a technology is essential to a standard supported by a pool is often a complex matter that requires special expertise. The involvement in the selection process of independent experts can go a long way in ensuring that a commitment to include only essential technologies is implemented in practice.

233. The Commission will take into account how experts are selected and what are the exact functions that they are to perform. Experts should be independent from the undertakings that have formed the pool. If experts are connected to the licensors or otherwise depend on them, the involvement of the expert will be given less weight. Experts must also have the necessary technical expertise to perform the various functions with which they have been entrusted. The functions of independent experts may include, in particular, an assessment of whether or not technologies put forward for inclusion into the pool are valid and whether or not they are essential.

234. It is also relevant to consider the arrangements for exchanging sensitive information among the parties. In oligopolistic markets exchanges of sensitive information such as pricing and output data may facilitate collusion (70). In such cases the Commission will take into account to what extent safeguards have been put in place, which ensure that sensitive information is not exchanged. An independent expert or licensing body may play an important role in this respect by ensuring that output and sales data, which may be necessary for the purposes of calculating and verifying royalties is not disclosed to undertakings that compete on affected markets.

(70) See in this respect the judgment in John Deere cited in note 11.

235. Finally, it is relevant to take account of the dispute resolution mechanism foreseen in the instruments setting up the pool. The more dispute resolution is entrusted to bodies or persons that are independent of the pool and the members thereof, the more likely it is that the dispute resolution will operate in a neutral way.

Index of the guidelines

TABLE OF CONTENTS

			Paragraphs
I.		Introduction	1-4
II.		General principles	5-33
	1.	Article 81 and intellectual property rights	5-9
	2.	The general framework for applying Article 81	10-18
	3.	Market definition	19-25
	4.	The distinction between competitors and non-competitors	26-33
III.		Application of the block exemption regulation	34-129

1.		The effects of the Block Exemption Regulation	34-37
2.		Scope and duration of the Block Exemption Regulation	38-64
	2.1.	Agreements between two parties	38-40
	2.2.	Agreements for the production of contract products	41-45
	2.3.	The concept of technology transfer agreements	46-53
	2.4.	Duration	54-55
	2.5.	Relationship with other block exemption regulations	56-64
		2.5.1. The Block Exemption Regulations on specialisation and R&D agreements	57-60
		2.5.2. The Block Exemption Regulation on vertical agreements	61-64
3.		The safe harbour established by the Block Exemption Regulation	65-73
4.		Hardcore restrictions of competition under the Block Exemption Regulation	74-106
	4.1.	General principles	74-76
	4.2.	Agreements between competitors	77-95
	4.3.	Agreements between non-competitors	96-106
5.		Excluded restrictions	107-116
6.		Withdrawal and disapplication of the Block Exemption Regulation	117-129
	6.1.	Withdrawal procedure	117-122
	6.2.	Disapplication of the Block Exemption Regulation	123-129
IV.		Application of Article 81(1) and 81(3) outside the scope of the Block Exemption Regulation	130-235
	1.	The general framework for analysis	130-152
	1.1.	The relevant factors	132-140
	1.2.	Negative effects of restrictive licence agreements	141-145
	1.3.	Positive effects of restrictive licence agreements and the framework for analysing such effects	146-152
	2.	The application of Article 81 to various types of licensing restraints	153-203
	2.1.	Royalty obligations	156-160
	2.2.	Exclusive licensing and sales restrictions	161-174
		2.2.1.Exclusive and sole licences	162-167
		2.2.2. Sales restrictions	168-174
	2.3.	Output restrictions	175-178
	2.4.	Field of use restrictions	179-185
	2.5.	Captive use restrictions	186-190
	2.6.	Tying and bundling	191-195
	2.7.	Non-compete obligations	196-203
	3.	Settlement and non-assertion agreements	204-209
	4.	Technology pools	210-235
	4.1.	The nature of the pooled technologies	215-222
	4.2.	Assessment of individual restraints	223-229
	4.3.	The institutional framework governing the pool	230-235

2.1.2.5. Insurance sector

Commission Regulation (EU) N° 267/2010, 24 March 2010 – Agreements, decisions and concerted practices in the insurance sector 205

Communication from the Commission on the application of Article 101(3) of the Treaty on the functioning of the European Union to certain categories of agreements, decisions and concerted practices in the insurance sector 209

Commission Regulation (EU) N° 267/2010, 24 March 2010 on the application of Article 101(3) of the Treaty on the functioning of the European Union to certain categories of agreements, decisions and concerted practices in the insurance sector

(OJ L 83, 30 March 2010, p. 1)

THE EUROPEAN COMMISSION,

Having regard to the Treaty on the Functioning of the European Union,

Having regard to Council Regulation (EEC) N° 1534/91 of 31 May 1991 on the application of Article 85(3) of the Treaty to certain categories of agreements, decisions and concerted practices in the insurance sector (1), and in particular Article 1(1)*(a)*, *(b)*, *(c)* and *(e)* thereof,

Having published a draft of this Regulation,

After consulting the Advisory Committee on Restrictive Practices and Dominant Positions,

Whereas:

(1) Regulation (EEC) N° 1534/91 empowers the Commission to apply Article 101(3) of the Treaty on the Functioning of the European Union (2) by regulation to certain categories of agreements, decisions and concerted practices in the insurance sector which have as their object cooperation with respect to:

– the establishment of common risk premium tariffs based on collectively ascertained statistics or the number of claims;

– the establishment of common standard policy conditions;

– the common coverage of certain types of risks;

– the settlement of claims;

– the testing and acceptance of security devices;

– registers of, and information on, aggravated risks.

(2) Pursuant to Regulation (EEC) N° 1534/91, the Commission adopted Regulation (EC) N° 358/2003 of 27 February 2003 on the application of Article 81(3) of the Treaty to certain categories of agreements, decisions and concerted practices in the insurance sector (3). Regulation (EC) N° 358/2003 expires on 31 March 2010.

(3) Regulation (EC) N° 358/2003 does not grant an exemption to agreements concerning the settlement of claims and registers of, and information on, aggravated risks. The Commission considered that it lacked sufficient experience in handling individual cases to make use of the power conferred by Regulation (EEC) N° 1534/91 in those fields. That situation has not changed. Furthermore, although Regulation (EC) N° 358/2003 granted an exemption for the establishment of standard policy conditions and the testing and acceptance of security devices, this Regulation should not do so since the Commission's review of the functioning of Regulation (EC) N° 358/2003 revealed that it was no longer necessary to include such agreements in a sector specific block exemption regulation. In the context where those two categories of agreements are not specific to the insurance sector and, as the review showed, can also give rise to certain competition concerns, it is more appropriate that they be subject to self-assessment.

(4) Following a public consultation launched on 17 April 2008, the Commission adopted a report to the European Parliament and the Council on the functioning of Regulation (EC) N° 358/2003 (the Report) (4) on 24 March 2009. In the Report and its accompanying Working Document (the Working Document) preliminary amendments of Regulation (EC) N° 358/2003 were proposed. On 2 June 2009, the Commission held a public meeting with interested parties, including representatives of the insurance sector, consumer organisations and national competition authorities, on the findings and proposals in the Report and Working Document.

(5) This Regulation should ensure effective protection of competition while providing benefits to consumers and adequate legal security for undertakings. The pursuit of those objectives should take account of the Commission's experience in this field, and the results of the consultations leading up to the adoption of this Regulation.

(6) Regulation (EEC) N° 1534/91 requires the exempting regulation of the Commission to define the categories of agreements, decisions and concerted practices to which it applies, to specify the restrictions or clauses which may, or may not, appear in the agreements, decisions and concerted practices, and to specify the clauses which must be contained in the agreements, decisions and concerted practices or the other conditions which must be satisfied.

(7) Nevertheless, it is appropriate to continue the approach taken in Regulation (EC) N° 358/2003 of placing the emphasis on defining categories of agreements which are exempted up to a certain level of market share and on specifying the restrictions or clauses which are not to be contained in such agreements.

(8) The benefit of the block exemption established by this Regulation should be limited to those agreements which can be assumed with sufficient certainty to satisfy the conditions of Article 101(3) of the Treaty. For the application of Article 101(3) of the Treaty by regulation, it is not necessary to define those agreements which are capable of falling within Article 101(1) of the Treaty. At the same time, there is no presumption that agreements which do not benefit from this Regulation are either caught by Article 101(1) of the Treaty or that they fail to satisfy the conditions of Article 101(3) of the Treaty. In the individual assessment of agreements under Article 101(1) of the Treaty, account must be taken of several factors, and in particular the market structure on the relevant market.

(9) Collaboration between insurance undertakings or within associations of undertakings in the compilation of information (which may also involve some statistical calcu-

lations) allowing the calculation of the average cost of covering a specified risk in the past or, for life insurance, tables of mortality rates or of the frequency of illness, accident and invalidity, makes it possible to improve the knowledge of risks and facilitates the rating of risks for individual companies. This can in turn facilitate market entry and thus benefit consumers. The same applies to joint studies on the probable impact of extraneous circumstances that may influence the frequency or scale of claims, or the yield of different types of investments. It is, however, necessary to ensure that such collaboration is only exempted to the extent to which it is necessary to attain these objectives. It is therefore appropriate to stipulate in particular that agreements on commercial premiums are not exempted. Indeed, commercial premiums may be lower than the amounts indicated by the compilations, tables or study results in question, since insurers can use the revenues from their investments in order to reduce their premiums. Moreover, the compilations, tables or studies in question should be non-binding and serve only for reference purposes. The exchange of information not necessary to attain the objectives set out in this recital should not be covered by this Regulation.

(10) Moreover, the narrower the categories into which statistics on the cost of covering a specified risk in the past are grouped, the more leeway insurance undertakings have to differentiate their commercial premiums when they calculate them. It is therefore appropriate to exempt joint compilations of the past cost of risks on condition that the available statistics are provided with as much detail and differentiation as is actuarially adequate.

(11) Furthermore, access to the joint compilations, tables and study results is necessary both for insurance undertakings active on the geographic or product market in question and for those considering entering that market. Similarly access to such compilations, tables and study results may be of value to consumer organisations or customer organisations. Insurance undertakings not yet active on the market in question and consumer or customer organisations must be granted access to such compilations, tables and study results on reasonable, affordable and non-discriminatory terms, as compared with insurance undertakings already present on that market. Such terms might for example include a commitment from an insurance undertaking not yet present on the market to provide statistical information on claims, should it ever enter the market and might also include membership of the association of insurers responsible for producing the compilations. An exception to the requirement to grant access to consumer organisations and customer organisations should be possible on the grounds of public security, for example where the information relates to the security systems of nuclear plants or the weakness of flood prevention systems.

(12) The reliability of joint compilations, tables and studies becomes greater as the amount of statistics on which they are based is increased. Insurers with high market shares may generate sufficient statistics internally to be able to make reliable compilations, but those with small market shares may not be able to do so, and new entrants are even less likely to be able to generate such statistics. The inclusion in such joint compilations, tables and studies of information from all insurers on a market, including large ones, in principle promotes competition by helping smaller insurers, and facilitates market entry. Given this specificity of the insurance sector, it is not appropriate to subject any exemption for such joint compilations, tables and studies to market share thresholds.

(13) Co-insurance or co-reinsurance pools can, in certain limited circumstances, be necessary to allow the participating undertakings of a pool to provide insurance or reinsurance for risks for which they might only offer insufficient cover in the absence of the pool. Those types of pools do not generally give rise to a restriction of competition under Article 101(1) of the Treaty and are thus not prohibited by it.

(14) Co-insurance or co-reinsurance pools can allow insurers and reinsurers to provide insurance or reinsurance for risks even if pooling goes beyond what is necessary to ensure that such a risk is covered. However, such pools can involve restrictions of competition, such as the standardisation of policy conditions and even of amounts of cover and premiums. It is therefore appropriate to lay down the circumstances in which such pools can benefit from exemption.

(15) For genuinely new risks it is not possible to know in advance what subscription capacity is necessary to cover the risk, nor whether two or more pools could co-exist for the purposes of providing the specific type of insurance concerned. A pooling arrangement offering the co-insurance or co-reinsurance of such new risks can therefore be exempted for a limited period of time without a market share threshold. Three years should constitute an adequate period for the constitution of sufficient historical information on claims to assess the necessity or otherwise of a pool.

(16) Risks which did not previously exist should be considered as new risks. However, in exceptional circumstances, a risk may be considered as a new risk where an objective analysis indicates that the nature of the risk has changed so materially that it is not possible to know in advance what subscription capacity is necessary in order to cover such a risk.

(17) For risks which are not new, co-insurance and co-reinsurance pools which involve a restriction of competition may, in certain limited circumstances, involve benefits so as to justify an exemption under Article 101(3) of the Treaty, even if they could be replaced by two or more competing insurance entities. They may, for example, allow their participating undertakings to gain the necessary experience of the sector of insurance involved, or they may allow cost savings, or reduction of commercial premiums through joint reinsurance on advantageous terms. However, any exemption should be limited to agreements which do not afford the undertakings involved the possibility of eliminating competition in respect of a substantial part of the products in question. Consumers can benefit effectively from pools only if there is sufficient competition in the relevant markets in which the pools operate. This condition should be regarded as being met when the market share of a pool remains below a given threshold and can therefore be presumed to be subject to actual or potential competition from undertakings which are not participating in that pool.

(18) This Regulation should therefore grant an exemption to any such co-insurance or co-reinsurance pool which has existed for more than three years, or which is not created in order to cover a new risk, on condition that the combined market share held by the participating undertakings does not exceed certain thresholds. The threshold for co-insurance pools should be lower because co-insurance pools may involve uniform policy conditions and commercial premiums. For the assessment of whether a pool fulfils the market share condition, the overall market share of the participating undertakings should be aggregated. The market share

of each participating undertaking is based on the overall gross premium income of that participating undertaking both within and outside that pool in the same relevant market. These exemptions however should only apply if the pool in question meets the further conditions laid down in this Regulation, which are intended to keep to a minimum the restrictions of competition between the participating undertakings of the pool. An individual analysis would be necessary in such cases, in order to determine whether or not the conditions set out in this Regulation are fulfilled.

(19) In order to facilitate the conclusion of agreements, some of which can involve significant investment decisions, the period of validity of this Regulation should be fixed at seven years.

(20) The Commission may withdraw the benefit of this Regulation, pursuant to Article 29(1) of Council Regulation (EC) N° 1/2003 of 16 December 2002 on the implementation of the rules on competition laid down in Articles 81 and 82 of the Treaty (5), where it finds in a particular case that an agreement to which the exemptions provided for in this Regulation apply nevertheless has effects which are incompatible with Article 101(3) of the Treaty.

(21) The competition authority of a Member State may withdraw the benefit of this Regulation pursuant to Article 29(2) of Regulation (EC) N° 1/2003 in respect of the territory of that Member State, or a part thereof where, in a particular case, an agreement to which the exemptions provided for in this Regulation apply nevertheless has effects which are incompatible with Article 101(3) of the Treaty in the territory of that Member State, or in a part thereof, and where such territory has all the characteristics of a distinct geographic market.

(22) In determining whether the benefit of this Regulation should be withdrawn pursuant to Article 29 of Regulation (EC) N° 1/2003, the anti-competitive effects that may derive from the existence of links between a co-insurance or co-reinsurance pool and/or its participating undertakings and other pools and/or their participating undertakings on the same relevant market are of particular importance,

HAS ADOPTED THIS REGULATION:

(1) *OJ* L 143, 7.6.1991, p. 1.

(2) With effect from 1 December 2009, Article 81 of the EC Treaty has become Article 101 of the Treaty on the Functioning of the European Union. The two articles are, in substance, identical. For the purposes of this Regulation, references to Article 101 of the Treaty on the Functioning of the European Union should be understood as references to Article 81 of the EC Treaty where appropriate.

(3) *OJ* L 53, 28.2.2003, p. 8.

(4) COM(2009) 138.

(5) *OJ* L 1, 4.1.2003, p. 1.

CHAPTER I
DEFINITIONS

Art. 1. *Definitions*

For the purposes of this Regulation, the following definitions shall apply:

1. «agreement» means an agreement, a decision of an association of undertakings or a concerted practice;

2. «participating undertakings» means undertakings party to the agreement and their respective connected undertakings;

3. «connected undertakings» means:

(a) undertakings in which a party to the agreement, directly or indirectly:

(i) has the power to exercise more than half the voting rights; or

(ii) has the power to appoint more than half the members of the supervisory board, board of management or bodies legally representing the undertaking; or

(iii) has the right to manage the undertaking's affairs;

(b) undertakings which directly or indirectly have, over a party to the agreement, the rights or powers listed in point *(a)*;

(c) undertakings in which an undertaking referred to in point *(b)* has, directly or indirectly, the rights or powers listed in point *(a)*;

(d) undertakings in which a party to the agreement together with one or more of the undertakings referred to in points *(a)*, *(b)* or *(c)*, or in which two or more of the latter undertakings, jointly have the rights or powers listed in point *(a)*;

(e) undertakings in which the rights or powers listed in point *(a)* are jointly held by:

(i) parties to the agreement or their respective connected undertakings referred to in points *(a)* to *(d)*; or

(ii) one or more of the parties to the agreement or one or more of their connected undertakings referred to in points *(a)* to *(d)* and one or more third parties;

4. «co-insurance pools» means groups set up by insurance undertakings either directly or through brokers or authorised agents, with the exception of ad-hoc co-insurance agreements on the subscription market, whereby a certain part of a given risk is covered by a lead insurer and the remaining part of the risk is covered by follow insurers who are invited to cover that remainder, which:

(a) agree to underwrite, in the name and for the account of all the participants, the insurance of a specified risk category; or

(b) entrust the underwriting and management of the insurance of a specified risk category, in their name and on their behalf, to one of the insurance undertakings, to a common broker or to a common body set up for this purpose;

5. «co-reinsurance pools» means groups set up by insurance undertakings either directly or through broker or authorised agents, possibly with the assistance of one or more reinsurance undertakings, with the exception of ad-hoc co-reinsurance agreements on the subscription market, whereby a certain part of a given risk is covered by a lead insurer and the remaining part of this risk is covered by follow insurers who are then invited to cover that remainder in order to:

(a) reinsure mutually all or part of their liabilities in respect of a specified risk category;

(b) incidentally accept, in the name and on behalf of all the participants, the reinsurance of the same category of risks;

6. «new risks» means:

(a) risks which did not previously exist, and for which insurance cover requires the development of an entirely new insurance product, not involving an extension, improvement or replacement of an existing insurance product; or

(b) in exceptional cases, risks the nature of which has, on the basis of an objective analysis, changed so materially that it is not possible to know in advance what subscription capacity is necessary in order to cover such a risk;

7. «commercial premium» means the price which is charged to the purchaser of an insurance policy.

CHAPTER II
JOINT COMPILATIONS, TABLES, AND STUDIES

Art. 2. *Exemption*

Pursuant to Article 101(3) of the Treaty and subject to the provisions of this Regulation, Article 101(1) of the Treaty shall not apply to agreements entered into between two or more undertakings in the insurance sector with respect to:

(a) the joint compilation and distribution of information necessary for the following purposes:

(i) calculation of the average cost of covering a specified risk in the past (hereinafter compilations);

(ii) construction of mortality tables, and tables showing the frequency of illness, accident and invalidity in connection with insurance involving an element of capitalisation (hereinafter tables);

(b) the joint carrying-out of studies on the probable impact of general circumstances external to the interested undertakings, either on the frequency or scale of future claims for a given risk or risk category or on the profitability of different types of investment (hereinafter studies), and the distribution of the results of such studies.

Art. 3. *Conditions for exemption*

1. The exemption provided for in Article 2*(a)* shall apply on condition that the compilations or tables:

(a) are based on the assembly of data, spread over a number of risk years chosen as an observation period, which relate to identical or comparable risks in sufficient numbers to constitute a base which can be handled statistically and which will yield figures on the following, amongst others:

(i) the number of claims during the said period;

(ii) the number of individual risks insured in each risk year of the chosen observation period;

(iii) the total amounts paid or payable in respect of claims that have arisen during the said period;

(iv) the total amount of capital insured for each risk year during the chosen observation period;

(b) include as detailed a breakdown of the available statistics as is actuarially adequate;

(c) do not include in any way elements for contingencies, income deriving from reserves, administrative or commercial costs or fiscal or parafiscal contributions, and take into account neither revenues from investments nor anticipated profits.

2. The exemptions provided for in Article 2 shall apply on condition that the compilations, tables or study results:

(a) do not identify the insurance undertakings concerned or any insured party;

(b) when compiled and distributed, include a statement that they are non-binding;

(c) do not contain any indication of the level of commercial premiums;

(d) are made available on reasonable, affordable and non-discriminatory terms, to any insurance undertaking which requests a copy of them, including insurance undertakings which are not active on the geographic or product market to which those compilations, tables or study results refer;

(e) except where non-disclosure is objectively justified on grounds of public security, are made available on reasonable, affordable and non-discriminatory terms, to consumer organisations or customer organisations which request access to them in specific and precise terms for a duly justified reason.

Art. 4. *Agreements not covered by the exemption*

The exemptions provided for in Article 2 shall not apply where participating undertakings enter into an undertaking or commitment among themselves, or oblige other undertakings, not to use compilations or tables that differ from those referred to in Article 2*(a)*, or not to depart from the results of the studies referred to in Article 2*(b)*.

CHAPTER III
COMMON COVERAGE OF CERTAIN TYPES OF RISKS

Art. 5. *Exemption*

Pursuant to Article 101(3) of the Treaty and subject to the provisions of this Regulation, Article 101(1) of the Treaty shall not apply to agreements entered into between two or more undertakings in the insurance sector with respect to the setting-up and operation of pools of insurance undertakings or of insurance undertakings and reinsurance undertakings for the common coverage of a specific category of risks in the form of co-insurance or co-reinsurance.

Art. 6. *Application of exemption and market share thresholds*

1. As concerns co-insurance or co-reinsurance pools which are created in order exclusively to cover new risks, the exemption provided for in Article 5 shall apply for a period of three years from the date of the first establishment of the pool, regardless of the market share of the pool.

2. As concerns co-insurance or co-reinsurance pools which do not fall within the scope of paragraph 1, the exemption provided for in Article 5 shall apply as long as this Regulation remains in force, on condition that the combined market share held by the participating undertakings does not exceed:

(a) in the case of co-insurance pools, 20 % of any relevant market;

(b) in the case of co-reinsurance pools, 25 % of any relevant market.

3. In calculating the market share of a participating undertaking on the relevant market, account shall be taken of:

(a) the market share of the participating undertaking within the pool in question;

(b) the market share of the participating undertaking within another pool on the same relevant market as the pool in question, to which the participating undertaking is a party; and

(c) the market share of the participating undertaking on the same relevant market as the pool in question, outside any pool.

4. For the purposes of applying the market share thresholds provided for in paragraph 2, the following rules shall apply:

(a) the market share shall be calculated on the basis of gross premium income; if gross premium income data are not available, estimates based on other reliable market information, including insurance cover provided or insured risk value, may be used to establish the market share of the undertaking concerned;

(b) the market share shall be calculated on the basis of data relating to the preceding calendar year.

5. Where the market share referred to in paragraph 2*(a)* is initially not more than 20 % but subsequently rises above that level without exceeding 25 %, the exemption provided for in Article 5 shall continue to apply for a pe-

riod of two consecutive calendar years following the year in which the 20 % threshold was first exceeded.

6. Where the market share referred to in paragraph 2*(a)* is initially not more than 20 % but subsequently rises above 25 %, the exemption provided for in Article 5 shall continue to apply for a period of one calendar year following the year in which the level of 25 % was first exceeded.

7. The benefit of paragraphs 5 and 6 may not be combined so as to exceed a period of two calendar years.

8. Where the market share referred to in paragraph 2*(b)* is initially not more than 25 % but subsequently rises above that level without exceeding 30 %, the exemption provided for in Article 5 shall continue to apply for a period of two consecutive calendar years following the year in which the 25 % threshold was first exceeded.

9. Where the market share referred to in paragraph 2*(b)* is initially not more than 25 % but subsequently rises above 30 %, the exemption provided for in Article 5 shall continue to apply for a period of one calendar year following the year in which the level of 30 % was first exceeded.

10. The benefit of paragraphs 8 and 9 may not be combined so as to exceed a period of two calendar years.

Art. 7. *Conditions for exemption*

The exemption provided for in Article 5 shall apply on condition that:

(a) each participating undertaking having given a reasonable period of notice has the right to withdraw from the pool, without incurring any sanctions;

(b) the rules of the pool do not oblige any participating undertaking of the pool to insure or reinsure through the pool and do not restrict any participating undertaking of the pool from insuring or reinsuring outside the pool, in whole or in part, any risk of the type covered by the pool;

(c) the rules of the pool do not restrict the activity of the pool or its participating undertakings to the insurance or reinsurance of risks located in any particular geographical part of the Union;

(d) the agreement does not limit output or sales;

(e) the agreement does not allocate markets or customers; and

(f) the participating undertakings of a co-reinsurance pool do not agree on the commercial premiums which they charge for direct insurance.

CHAPTER IV
FINAL PROVISIONS

Art. 8. *Transitional period*

The prohibition laid down in Article 101(1) of the Treaty shall not apply during the period from 1 April 2010 to 30 September 2010 in respect of agreements already in force on 31 March 2010 which do not satisfy the conditions for exemption provided for in this Regulation but which satisfy the conditions for exemption provided for in Regulation (EC) N° 358/2003.

Art. 9. *Period of validity*

This Regulation shall enter into force on 1 April 2010. It shall expire on 31 March 2017.

Communication from the Commission on the application of Article 101(3) of the Treaty on the functioning of the European Union to certain categories of agreements, decisions and concerted practices in the insurance sector

(OJ C 82, 30 March 2010, p. 20)

1. INTRODUCTION AND BACKGROUND

1. Commission Regulation (EC) N° 358/2003 (1), the previous Insurance Block Exemption Regulation (BER) which expired on 31 March 2010, applied Article 101 (3) of the Treaty on the Functioning of the European Union (2) (the Treaty) to certain categories of agreements, decisions and concerted practices in the insurance sector.

(1) *OJ* L 53, 28.2.2003, p. 8.

(2) With effect from 1 December 2009, Article 81 of the EC Treaty has become Article 101 of the Treaty on the Functioning of the European Union. The two Articles are, in substance, identical. For the purposes of this Communication, references to Article 101 of the Treaty on the Functioning of the European Union should be understood as references to Article 81 of the EC Treaty where appropriate.

2. Following a lengthy review (the Review) of the functioning of Regulation (EC) N° 358/2003, the Commission published its Report to the European Parliament and the Council on the functioning of that Regulation (3) (the Report) as well as an accompanying Working Document (4) (the Working Document) on 24 March 2009.

(3) http://eur-lex.europa.eu/LexUriServ/LexUriServ.do?uri=CELEX:52009DC0138:EN:NOT

(4) http://ec.europa.eu/competition/sectors/financial_services/insurance_ber_working_document.pdf

3. As a result of its findings following the Review, the Commission has now adopted a new insurance BER which renews the exemptions for two of the four categories of agreements exempted in the previous BER; namely: (i) joint compilations, tables and studies; and (ii) common coverage of certain types of risks (pools).

2. FIRST PRINCIPLES ANALYSIS

4. The Commission's original objective when it adopted Regulation (EC) N° 358/2003 of reducing the number of notifications it received is no longer relevant since under Regulation (EC) N° 1/2003 undertakings can no longer notify their agreements to the Commission, but now must conduct their own self-assessment. In this context, a specific legal instrument such as a BER should only be adopted if cooperation in the insurance sector is «special» and different to other sectors which do not benefit from a BER (i.e. most sectors currently). The Commission's analysis as to whether or not to renew the BER addressed three key questions in relation to each of the four categories of agreements exempted by the BER, namely:

(a) whether the business risks or other issues in the insurance sector make it «special» and different to other sec-

tors such that this leads to an enhanced need for cooperation amongst insurers;

(b) if so, whether this enhanced need for cooperation requires a legal instrument such as the BER to protect or facilitate it; and

(c) if so, what is the most appropriate legal instrument (i.e. whether it is the current BER or whether partial renewal, amended renewal, or guidance would be more appropriate).

3. RENEWED EXEMPTIONS

5. On the basis of its Review and consultation of stakeholders which was conducted over a 2-year period, the Commission adopted the new BER (Commission Regulation (EU) N° 267/2010 of 24 March) renewing (with amendments) the exemptions for two forms of cooperation, namely (i) joint compilations, tables and studies; and (ii) common coverage of certain types of risks (pools).

6. When agreements falling within these categories of agreements do not meet all the conditions to benefit from the block exemption, an individual analysis under Article 101 of the Treaty is required. The analytical framework set out in the Commission's Guidelines on the applicability of Article 81 of the EC Treaty to horizontal cooperation agreements (5) (the Horizontal Guidelines) will assist businesses in assessing the compatibility of agreements with Article 101 of the Treaty (6).

(5) See paragraph 7 of Commission Notice of 6 January 2001: Guidelines on the applicability of Article 81 of the EC Treaty to horizontal cooperation agreements, OJ C 3, 6.1.2001, p. 2.

(6) The current Horizontal Guidelines are under review.

3.1. Joint compilations, tables and studies

7. Subject to certain conditions, the previous BER exempted agreements which relate to the joint establishment and distribution of (i) calculations of the average cost of covering a specified risk in the past, and (ii) mortality tables and tables showing the frequency of illness, accident and invalidity, in connection with insurance involving an element of capitalisation. It also exempted (subject to certain conditions) the joint carrying out of studies on the probable impact of general circumstances external to the interested undertakings, either on the frequency or scale of future claims for a given risk or risk category or on the profitability of different types of investment and the distribution of the results of such studies.

8. As summarised in the Report, the costs of insurance products are unknown at the time the price is agreed and the risk covered. Calculation of risk is a key issue in pricing all insurance products which appears to be a differentiating factor from other sectors including the banking sector. This makes access to past statistical data in order to technically price risks crucial. Therefore, the Commission considers that cooperation in this area is both specific to the insurance industry and necessary in order to price risks.

9. The Commission also considers that there are good reasons to protect and facilitate cooperation in this area with a BER and that it is appropriate that the BER be renewed for this category of agreements in order to avoid any reduction in such pro-competitive cooperation.

10. However, in renewing the exemption the Commission made the following key changes: (i) the term «joint calculations» was changed to «joint compilations» (which may also include some calculations); (ii) clarification that exchange of information is only allowed where it is necessary; and (iii) access to data shared is now also allowed for consumer organisations and customer organisations (as distinguished from individuals), with a public security exception.

3.2. Common coverage of certain types of risks (pools)

11. The previous BER exempted (7) the setting up and operation of co-(re)insurance pools for the common coverage of new risks as well as co-(re)insurance pools covering risks which are not new, subject to certain conditions, in particular to market share thresholds.

(7) For three years from the date of first establishment of the group, regardless of the market share of the group.

12. As a result of its Review, the Commission considers that risk sharing for certain types of risks (such as nuclear, terrorism and environmental risks), for which individual insurance companies are reluctant or unable to insure the entire risk alone, is crucial in order to ensure that all such risks can be covered. This makes the insurance sector different to other sectors and triggers an enhanced need for cooperation (8). Therefore, the new BER also exempts pools under certain conditions.

(8) An alternative method of covering risks through co-(re)insurance is *ad hoc* co-(re)insurance agreements on the subscription market, which may be a less restrictive option depending on the analysis on a case-by-case basis.

13. In renewing the exemption, the Commission made the following key changes: (i) a change to the approach to market share calculation in order to bring it into line with other general and sector-specific competition rules so that not only gross premium income earned within the pool by the participating undertakings, but also outside the pool will be taken into account; and (ii) an amendment and expansion to the definition of «new risks».

14. In terms of self-assessment it is important to consider that there are three types of pools and determine into which category a particular pool falls: (i) pools which do not require a BER as a safe harbour because they do not give rise to a restriction of competition as long as the pooling is necessary to allow their members to provide a type of insurance that they could not provide alone; (ii) pools which fall under Article 101(1) of the Treaty and which do not comply with the conditions of the new BER but may benefit from an individual exception under Article 101(3) of the Treaty; (iii) pools which fall under Article 101(1) of the Treaty but which comply with the conditions of the BER.

15. For both types (ii) and (iii) it is necessary to carefully define the relevant product and geographic market, as market definition is a prerequisite in order to assess compliance with the market share thresholds (9). The Commission's Notice on the definition of the relevant market for the purposes of Community competition law (10), together with relevant Commission decisions and comfort letters in the insurance sector can be used as guidance in order for pools to determine the relevant market on which they operate.

(9) Concerns were also raised about the definition of «new risks».

(10) OJ C 372, 9.12.1997, p. 5.

16. However, the Review showed that many insurers were incorrectly using the pool exemption in the BER as a «blanket» exemption, without carrying out the required careful legal assessment of a pool's compliance with the conditions of the BER (11).

(11) In particular in relation to market share thresholds. Furthermore, it is crucial that any pools covering new risks and purporting to fall within the BER ensure that they are in fact covered by the precise definition of new risks in Article 1 of the new BER, as mentioned in the Report and Working Document.

17. Also, it should be remembered that *ad hoc* co-(re)insurance agreements on the subscription market (12) have never been covered by the BER and they remain outside the scope of the new BER. As mentioned in the Commission's Final Report on the Business Insurance Sector Inquiry of 25 September 2007 (13), practices involving an alignment of premium (between co-(re)insurers through *ad hoc* co-(re)insurance agreements) may fall within the scope of Article 101(1) of the Treaty, but may benefit from the exemption afforded by Article 101(3) of the Treaty.

(12) Whereby a certain part of a given risk is covered by a lead insurer and the remaining part of the risk is covered by follow insurers who are invited to cover the remainder.

(13) COM(2007) 556 final: Communication from the Commission to the European Parliament, the Council, the European Economic and Social Committee and the Committee of the Regions – Sector Inquiry under Article 17 of Regulation (EC) N° 1/2003 on business insurance (Final Report).

18. The Commission intends to closely monitor, in cooperation with national competition authorities within the framework of the European Competition Network, the operation of pools to ensure that blanket applications of the BER or Article 101(3) of the Treaty are not occurring. This closer monitoring will be undertaken in line with enforcement cases where pools are found to fall foul of Article 101(1) of the Treaty and/or the BER.

4. NON-RENEWED EXEMPTIONS

19. On the basis of the Commission's analysis set out in the Report and Working Document, as well as in its Impact Assessment of the new BER, two of the four exemptions in the previous BER, namely agreements on standard policy conditions (SPCs) and security devices have not been renewed by the new BER. This is primarily because they are not specific to the insurance sector and therefore their inclusion in such an exceptional legal instrument may result in unjustified discrimination against other sectors which do not benefit from a BER. In addition, although these two forms of cooperation may give rise to some benefits to consumers, the Review showed that they can also give rise to certain competition concerns. Therefore, it is more appropriate that they be subject to self-assessment.

20. Although non-renewal of the BER in relation to these two types of cooperation will inevitably result in slightly less legal certainty, it should be emphasised that the insurance sector will benefit in this regard from the same level of legal certainty as the other sectors which do not benefit from a BER. Furthermore, as outlined below the Commission plans to address both these forms of cooperation in its Horizontal Guidelines.

4.1. Standard Policy Conditions

21. The previous BER exempted the joint establishment and distribution of non-binding standard policy conditions (SPCs) for direct insurance (14).

(14) Article 6(1)(*a*) to (*k*) of Regulation (EC) N° 358/2003.

22. On the basis of the evidence found during its Review, the Commission no longer considers that a sector specific BER is necessary since cooperation on SPCs is not specific to the insurance sector, but common to many others, such as the banking sector, which do not benefit from a BER. As SPCs are not specific to the insurance sector it is appropriate that any guidance on SPCs is afforded to industry as a whole and in the form of a horizontal instrument.

23. The Commission considers that in many cases SPCs can give rise to positive effects for competition and consumers. For example, SPCs allow the comparison of insurance policies offered by different insurers, allowing customers to verify the content of guarantees more easily and facilitating switching between insurers and insurance products. However, whilst there is a need for comparability between insurance products for consumers, too much standardisation can be harmful for consumers and can lead to a lack of non-price competition. In addition, given that certain SPCs can be imbalanced, it is more appropriate that undertakings conduct their own assessment on the basis of Article 101(3) of the Treaty in the event that Article 101(1) of the Treaty is applicable in order to demonstrate that the cooperation they are part of gives rise to efficiency gains, a fair share of which benefit consumers (15).

(15) Certain of the clauses listed in Article 6(1) of the previous BER, Regulation (EC) N° 358/2003, would remain relevant for self-assessment of agreements under Article 101 of the Treaty, in particular those which have an impact on prices and product innovation. Of particular relevance are, for example, clauses which: (i) contain any indication of the level of commercial premiums; (ii) indicate the amount of cover or the part which the policyholder must pay himself; or (iii) impose comprehensive cover including risks to which a significant number of policyholders are not simultaneously exposed; (iv) require the policyholder to obtain cover from the same insurer for different risks.

24. Accordingly, the Commission is planning to expand its Horizontal Guidelines to also address SPCs for all sectors. These are currently under review and it is planned to publish a draft of the revised Horizontal Guidelines for stakeholder consultation in the first half of 2010.

4.2. Security devices

25. The previous BER exempted: (i) technical specifications, rules or codes of practice regarding security devices and procedures for assessing and approving their compliance with these standards as well as (ii) technical specifications, rules or codes of practice for the installation and maintenance of security devices and procedures for assessing and approving the compliance of undertakings which install or maintain security devices with such standards.

26. However, the Commission considers that the setting of technical standards falls into the general domain of standard setting, which is not unique to the insurance sector. As these kinds of agreements are not specific to the insurance sector, it is appropriate that any guidance is afforded to the industry as a whole and in the form of a horizontal instrument. This is already the case, as point 6 of the Horizontal Guidelines provides guidance on the compliance of technical standards with Article 101 of the Treaty. Moreover, the Horizontal Guidelines are currently under review and it is planned to publish a draft of the revised Horizontal Guidelines for stakeholder consultation during the first half of 2010.

27. In addition, these agreements were covered by the BER in so far as no harmonisation exists at Union level. The Commission's Review showed that there is reduced scope for the BER, since such harmonisation is now extensive. As regards the limited area where there is not yet Union harmonisation, detailed national rules result in fragmentation of the internal market, reduction of competition between producers of security devices across the Member States and less choice for consumers as consumers do not obtain insurance in the event that their security devices do not comply with standards commonly established by insurers.

28. The Commission has therefore not renewed the BER for these categories of agreements.

5. CONCLUSIONS

29. It will be necessary for undertakings to carefully assess their cooperation on joint compilations, tables and studies and pools under the conditions established by the BER, in order to avoid blanket application of the BER.

30. As regards self-assessment under Article 101(3) of the Treaty for cooperation on SPCs and security devices, undertakings benefit from two legal instruments, namely the Horizontal Guidelines (currently being revised) and the Guidelines on the application of Article 81(3) of the Treaty (16).

(16) *OJ* C 101, 27.4.2004, p. 97.

2.1.3. Procedural rules

Guidelines 6 January 2010 – Guidance on procedures of the Hearing Officers	213
Commission Regulation (EC) N° 773/2004, 7 April 2004 – Conduct of proceedings by the Commission, Art. 81 and 82 Treaty	220
Best practice – Submission of economic evidence, data collection	224
Commission Notice – Cooperation within the Network of Competition Authorities	232
Commission Notice – Co-operation between the Commission and the courts of the EU	239
Commission Notice – Handling of complaints	245
Commission Notice – Informal guidance relating to novel questions, guidance letters	253
Commission Notice – Access to the Commission file	255
Guidelines – Method of setting fines	261
Commission Notice – Immunity from fines and reduction of fines in cartel cases	263
Explanatory note – Inspections, authorization	268
Commission Notice – Settlement procedures	269
White paper 2 April 2008 – White Paper on Damages Actions for Breach of the EC antitrust rules	274
Commission staff working paper 2 April 2008 – Damages Actions for Breach of the EC antitrust rules	278
Commission staff working paper 2 April 2008 – Damages actions for breach of the EC antitrust rules - Impact Assessment Report	278
Draft Guidance paper quantifying harm	278
Commission Decision 13 October 2011 – The function and terms of reference of the Hearing Officer	309
Commission Notice 20 October 2011 – Best practices for the conduct of proceedings	315
Brochure – Compliance matters	332

Communication 6 January 2010 – Guidance on procedures of the Hearing Officers in proceedings relating to Articles 101 and 102 TFEU

1. See the site: http://ec.europa.eu/competition/consultations/2010_best_practices/hearing_officers.pdf

Table of contents

	Pages
1. Scope and purpose of the Guidance (1)	213
2. The Hearing Officers' tasks (3)	214
3. The investigative phase (10)	214
4. Procedures potentially leading to a prohibition decision (12)	215
4.1 Access to File or other information	
4.1.1 Addressees of a Statement of Objections (13)	215
4.1.2 Complainants and other admitted third parties (16)	215
4.2 Disclosure of confidential information (19)	215
4.3 Deadlines to Reply	
4.3.1 Addressees of a Statement of Objections (25)	216
4.3.2 Complainants and other admitted third parties (30)	216
5. Admission of third parties to the procedure (17) (32)	216
6. The oral hearing (38)	217
6.1 Admission to Oral Hearings (40)	217
6.2 Applications to attend the Oral Hearing (41)	217
6.3 Preparation of the Oral Hearing (45)	217
6.4 Publication of Dates of Oral Hearings (48)	218
6.5 Organisation of the Oral Hearing (49)	218
6.5.1 Presentations (52)	218
6.5.2 *In camera* sessions (53)	218
6.5.3 Questions and discussion (56)	218
6.5.4 Limits on the disclosure of information (58)	218
6.5.5 Admission of written comments and/or documents (59)	218
6.5.6 Recording of the Oral Hearing (60)	218
7. Post-Oral Hearing	
7.1 Interim Report (61)	218
7.2 Supplementary Statement of Objections and Letter of Facts (64)	219
8. Other procedures	
8.1 Rejection of complaints (65)	219
8.2 Commitment Decisions (67)	219
9. Decision-making procedure (21)	
9.1 Final Report (69)	219
9.2 Publication (74)	219
9.3 Future revision (76)	219

1. SCOPE AND PURPOSE OF THE GUIDANCE

1. The objective of this document («Guidance») is to provide guidance for interested parties on the contribution of the Hearing Officers to the Commission's main proceedings relating to Articles 101 and 102 TFEU (ex- articles 81 and 82 EC). (1) In this regard, the Guidance seeks to increase understanding of the role of the Hearing Officers as the independent guardians of the rights of defence, and thereby to ensure a high degree of transparency, fairness and predictability in our procedures.

(1) The Guidance does not deal with specific procedures, for example for imposing fines on undertakings having provided misleading information (see Article 23(1) of Regulation 1/2003). Nor does it cover decisions on finding of inapplicability pursuant to Article 10 of Regulation 1/2003 or decisions on interim measures pursuant to Article 8 of Regulation 1/2003.

2. This Guidance is intended to be of general application to issues that fall within the Hearing Officers' competence. Nevertheless, if the particular circumstances of a case so require, the Hearing Officers reserve the right to deviate and exercise their discretion in relation to any of the issues addressed by this Guidance. It is built upon the experience of the Hearing Officers in the application of relevant legislation, in particular their terms of reference («Mandate»), (2) and jurisprudence and does not create any additional rights or obligations.

(2) Cf. Commission Decision of 23 May 2001 on the terms and reference of hearing officers in certain competition proceedings, OJ L 162, 19.6.2001, p 21. See also Regulation 1/2003 on the implementation of the rules on competition laid down in Articles 81 and 82 of the Treaty OJ L 1, 4.1.2003, p. 1 Regulation 773/2004 relating to the conduct of proceedings by the Commission pursuant to Articles 81 and 82 of the EC Treaty (Implementing Regulation), OJ L 123, 27.4.2004, p. 18.

2. THE HEARING OFFICERS' TASKS

3. The Commission has to conduct its competition proceedings fairly and objectively while respecting the parties' procedural rights. The Hearing Officers are, first of all, guardians of fair proceedings before the Commission. They safeguard the rights of defence of undertakings subject to proceedings relating to Articles 101 and 102 (ex-articles 81 and 82) as well as the procedural rights of complainants and all other parties to the proceedings.

4. Rights of defence relate mainly to questions concerning the truth and relevance of the facts and matters alleged and the documents used by the Commission to support a claim that there has been an infringement of competition law (3). Examples of rights of defence are the right to be informed about one's procedural status and the right to be heard by the Commission. The procedural rights of all other parties to a Commission procedure are in essence participation rights, the most important right being the right to be heard by the Commission.

(3) Joined cases C-238/99 P, C-244/99 P, C-245/99 P, C-247/99 P, C-250/99 P, C-252/99 P and C-254/99 P, Limburgse Vinyl Maatschappij and others v Commission (2002) ECR I-8375, para. 91, case 85/76, Hoffmann-La Roche v Commission (1979) ECR 461, para. 11.

5. The observation of procedural rights falls in the first place within the responsibility of DG Competition. Should, however, a disagreement arise between DG Competition and a party to the procedure, it may be referred to the Hearing Officers for independent review. To this effect, specific decision-making powers relating to the extension of deadlines, access to file and protection of confidentiality are conferred to the Hearing Officers by the Mandate. Disputes can thus be resolved effectively and efficiently while the procedure is on-going, without parties having to wait for the adoption of a Commission decision before addressing any disputes, for the first time, in litigation before the European courts. Depending on the nature of the decisions taken by the Hearing Officers, they can be challenged separately before the European courts or in the context of an application for annulment lodged against a final decision.

6. In addition to their dispute resolution competencies, the Hearing Officers are directly involved in specific parts of the procedure in competition cases. In particular, the Hearing Officers decide on the admission of third parties to the procedure and to oral hearings. They are also responsible for all matters relating to the organisation and conduct of oral hearings and report directly on these hearings to the Commissioner responsible for competition on the conclusions they draw from them. In addition, at the end of the procedure the Hearing Officers report to the College of Commissioners and, ultimately to the addressee of the decision and the public on whether procedural safeguards and the right to be heard have been respected throughout the proceedings.

7. Whilst the Hearing Officers oversee procedural matters, have decision-making powers and adjudicate disputes in this respect, they may also make observations on substantive issues to the Commissioner. They usually submit such observations, if any, when reporting to the Commissioner on the oral hearing (see point 62 below). More generally, they may throughout the proceedings make observations to the Commissioner on any matter arising from the proceedings.

8. In fulfilling their functions, the Hearing Officers will apply the procedures as laid down in the Mandate. They carry out specific tasks primarily at the request of parties, but may also do so on an ex officio basis. The Hearing Officers do not, however, monitor the handling of competition cases by DG Competition, nor are they responsible for ensuring the respect of the principle of sound administration. (4) Conversely, when parties are concerned about an issue relating to the fairness of the procedure, such as the right to be heard, that has not been resolved by DG Competition, they are encouraged to make contact with the Hearing Officers at any stage of a competition proceeding. Failure to bring a dispute with DG Competition before the Hearing Officers, for which they are conferred decision-making powers, can be taken as an acceptance of the position expressed by DG Competition and may result in the Commission bringing attention to this fact if a party subsequently raises the procedural matter before the European courts. (5)

(4) Cf. Code of good administrative behaviour for staff of the European Commission in their relations with the public, Commission Decision of 17 October 2000 amending its rules of procedure, Code of Good Behaviour, OJ L 267, p. 63.

(5) See, in the context of access to file, Case T-44/00, Mannesmannröhren-Werke v Commission (2004) ECR II-2223, para. 51 et seq.

9. In order to perform their functions properly the Hearing Officers are entirely independent from DG Competition. They are appointed by the College of Commissioners. They are attached, for administrative purposes, to the Commissioner responsible for competition. Currently, two Hearing Officers are appointed. They carry out their functions on an individual basis.

3. THE INVESTIGATIVE PHASE

10. The Hearing Officers play a limited role during the investigation phase of proceedings relating to Articles 101 and 102 TFEU (ex-articles 81 and 82), i.e. the period between the first measure of investigation and notification of the Statement of Objections. This flows from the fact that an undertaking subject to investigatory measures can rely in full on its rights of defence only once a Statement of Objections has been notified to it (6), as it is not until then that an undertaking has been formally informed of any objections against them relating to an infringement of the competition rules.

(6) Case C-407/04 P Dalmine v Commission (2007) ECR I-829, para. 59.

11. Notwithstanding the above, some issues are occasionally brought before the Hearing Officers during the investigation stage of the proceedings. Examples of rights of de-

fence issues during the investigation phase that may arise include the undertaking's right:
  (i) to be informed of the purpose and subject-matter of the investigation (7);
  (ii) not to self-incriminate itself; and
  (iii) to be represented by a lawyer. In addition, confidentiality issues may sometimes require the intervention of the Hearing Officer prior to the notification of a Statement of Objections. The Hearing Officer will look into such issues at the request of an undertaking and will, in any event, address them if raised in the reply to the Statement of Objections.

(7) Case T-99/04 AC-Treuhand AG v Commission (2008) ECR I-1501, para. 56.

4. PROCEDURES POTENTIALLY LEADING TO A PROHIBITION DECISION

12. An undertaking has the right to rely in full on its rights of defence once a Statement of Objections has been notified to it. The addressee of the Statement of Objections will be informed by the Hearing Office of the Hearing Officer dealing with its case (8), after DG Competition has informed the Hearing Office of the notification of the Statement of Objections. The following issues are regularly brought before the Hearing Officers during this interpartes phase of the proceedings.

(8) This practice does not, however, apply to letters sent to complainants under Article 7 of Regulation N° 773/2004.

4.1 Access to File or other information

4.1.1 Addressees of a Statement of Objections

13. In order to ensure the equality of arms (9), the addressee acquires the right to request access the Commission file as soon as a Statement of Objections is notified to it.

(9) The principle of equality of arms presupposes «... that the knowledge which the undertaking concerned has of the file used in the proceeding is the same as that of the Commission ...». Case T-30/97, Solvay SA v Commission (1995) ECR II-1775, para. 83.

14. Granting access to the Commission file is the responsibility of DG Competition. The principles and practice in this regard are primarily laid down in the Notice on Access to File (10). Where an undertaking that is an addressee of a Statement of Objections is of the view that the access to file accorded to it is insufficient to allow it to properly exercise its rights of defence, it should therefore address its concerns to DG Competition in the first place. Thereafter, if the addressee is still not satisfied with the access that has been granted, it may submit a reasoned request in writing to the Hearing Officer. Failure to do so can be taken as an acceptance of the position expressed by DG Competition.(11)

(10) Commission Notice on the rules for access to the Commission file in cases pursuant to Articles 81 and 82 of the EC Treaty, 2005/C 325/07.

(11) Case T-44/00, Mannesmannröhren-Werke AG v Commission (2004) ECR II-2223, para. 51 et seq.

15. The Hearing Officer will decide either that full or partial access 12 be provided to certain documents, or give a reasoned decision why access should not be granted. All efforts should be made by addressees to raise access to file issues as soon as possible.

(12) «Partial» access should be understood as meaning that (i) access to only some parts of the information may be granted, or (ii) the means by which access is granted is somehow restricted (for example, by way of a data room procedure).

4.1.2 Complainants and other admitted third parties

16. Contrary to an addressee of a Statement of Objections complainants or other third parties admitted to the proceedings do not have a right to access the Commission's investigation file.

17. A complainant has the right to be provided with a non-confidential version of the Statement of Objections and be afforded an opportunity to make its views known in writing. If, however, the complainant considers that it has not been put in a position to submit any meaningful comments, it may address its concerns to the Hearing Officer.

18. An interested third party has the right to be informed of the nature and subject matter of the proceedings and, similarly to a complainant, be afforded the opportunity to make its views known in writing. In this respect it should be noted that it falls on DG Competition to determine the means by which a third party will be informed. Should however, a third party consider that the information is insufficient to allow it to effectively make known its views, it may address its concerns to the Hearing Officer.

4.2 Disclosure of confidential information

19. In the event that a dispute arises between an addressee of a Statement of Objections or information provider and DG Competition as to whether a piece of information is confidential or not, the dispute may be brought by the addressee or provider before the Hearing Officer for determination. Prior to disclosing information for which confidentiality has been claimed the Hearing Officer will activate the procedure commonly referred to as the «AKZO procedure», (13) in application of Article 9 of the Mandate.

(13) Case 53/85, AKZO Chemie and AKZO Chemie UK v Commission (1986) ECR 168.

20. Claims of confidentiality, as well as requests for disclosure of the information, presented to the Hearing Officer cannot be couched in general terms. (14) The provider of the information must detail what documents (or parts thereof) are non-accessible, together with reasons justifying such confidentiality. Similarly, the addressee of a Statement of Objections must specify the documents to which access is requested and explain why further disclosure is necessary for its defence.

(14) Case T-53/03 BPB v Commission (2008) ECR II-1333, para. 33; Joined Cases T-191/98, T-212-214/98, Atlantic Container Line and others v Commission (2003) ECR II-3275, paras. 353-354.

21. Any general requests that are not detailed in this way will be rejected by the Hearing Officer as unsubstantiated.

22. The Hearing Officer will carry out an independent review of the documents concerned, and consider the arguments of the parties and those of DG Competition to firstly, determine whether the information is confidential per se. If the Hearing Officer comes to the conclusion that the confidentially claim is merited, it will, secondly, carry out a balancing test whereby the legitimate interests of an undertaking to have its confidential information protected will be weighed against the addressee's interest to be effectively heard on the information in question. If, following the balancing test, the Hearing Officer reaches the preliminary conclusion that the information must be fully or partially disclosed, the information provider will be informed of the preliminary conclusion and the reasons for it (often referred to as a «pre-Article 9 letter»). The information provider will be granted a deadline within which it can make known its views on the Hearing Officer's preliminary position. On the other hand, should the Hearing Officer find that the confidentiality claim is justified and that the information cannot be disclosed, the requesting party will be informed thereof. In practice, many confidentiality disputes are resolved at this stage of the procedure (15).

(15) The Hearing Officer may also find that partial disclosure be granted in the form of a data room.

23. If, after receiving the pre-Article 9 letter, the information provider continues to object to disclosure, and should the Hearing Officer, having considered the arguments, maintain that the information should be disclosed, a reasoned decision under Article 9 of the Mandate will normally be issued (an «Article 9 decision»). An Article 9 decision will specify the date on which the information will be disclosed, which cannot occur less than one week from the date of notification of the decision.

24. An undertaking, which has provided the information in question, is entitled to challenge an Article 9 decision immediately to the General Court of the European Union («the General Court»). It will however be requested to inform the Hearing Officer by a specified date whether it intends to lodge an application for annulment before the General Court and whether or not interim measures will be requested. If the information provider makes known its intention to challenge the decision and to request interim measures, the disputed information will not be disclosed until the President of the General Court has issued an order ruling on the application for the interim measure.

4.3 Deadlines to Reply

4.3.1 Addressees of a Statement of Objections

25. Any request for an extension of the time-limit to reply to a Statement of Objections should be made as soon as possible, at the latest before the expiry of the deadline set by DG Competition. The request should detail both the reasons and time required to submit a reply.

26. The Hearing Officer will determine whether and to what extent additional time is needed to allow the addressee of the Statement of Objections to fully express its views and exercise its procedural rights effectively, after having received comments from DG Competition. In doing so, the Hearing Officer will also bear in mind the need for an efficient procedure. In assessing whether an extension should be granted, the Hearing Officer may consider, *inter alia*, the following elements, depending on the particular circumstances of the case:

a. any obstacles caused by the Commission faced by the addressee of the Statement of Objections in providing its observations within the deadline set by DG Competition, e.g. the impact of any access to file disputes on the time needed by the addressee to reply to the objections; and/or

b. any other objective obstacles faced by the requesting addressee in providing its observations within the deadline set by DG Competition.

27. It should be noted that deadlines will normally start running when access to the main documents in the file has been granted, which would allow the addressee to start analyzing the objections raised against it. The fact that access to the entire file has not, in the addressee's view, been granted does not have the automatic consequence that a deadline set by DG Competition has not started running (16).

(16) Case T-44/00 Mannesmannröhren-Werke AG v Commission (2004) ECR II-2223, para. 65.

28. In exceptional circumstances, the Hearing Officer may however decide to suspend the running of a deadline until an access dispute has been resolved, if it becomes evident that the addressee would not be in a position to reply within the deadline granted to it and an extension would not be an adequate solution at that point in time.

29. Where a supplementary Statement of Objections or a Letter of Facts has been notified to an addressee it falls, in the first place, on DG Competition to set the time period within the addressee may submit its comments. Any request for extension of that time period should be addressed to the Hearing Officer, who will examine it in light of the principles described above.

4.3.2 Complainants and other admitted third parties

30. The time periods for a complainant and other admitted third parties to submit comments will be set by DG Competition. A request for an extension of that time period should be addressed to the Hearing Officer and be made as soon as possible, at the latest before the expiry of the deadline set by DG Competition.

31. When assessing an extension request from a complainant and/or a third party the Hearing Officer will apply the general principles described above for an addressee of a Statement of Objections, where applicable.

5. ADMISSION OF THIRD PARTIES TO THE PROCEDURE (17)

(17) It should be observed that complainants are admitted to the proceedings by DG Competition on the basis of a formal complaint pursuant to Article 5 of Regulation N° 773/2004.

32. The Hearing Officer has the responsibility to admit natural or legal persons with a sufficient interest to proceedings before the Commission. Applications for admission must be reasoned, clearly explaining the applicant's interest in the outcome of the proceedings. An application may be submitted to the Hearing Officers throughout the administrative proceedings. Potential interested third parties are encouraged to submit formal applications around the time a Statement of Objections is issued in order to make the most effective use of their procedural rights.

33. In assessing a request for third party status, the Hearing Officer will take into consideration in particular the contribution the party has made or is likely to make to establish the truth and relevance of the facts and circumstances pertinent to the proceedings, as opposed to an exclusively private interest, which would normally not be considered as sufficient. If necessary, the Hearing Officer may request any further information from the party in order to assess the application to be admitted to the proceedings.

34. In assessing an application by an association to be admitted to the proceedings, the Hearing Officer may consider, *inter alia*, the following elements, depending on the particular circumstances of the case:

a. the object of the association (notably whether its object includes the protection of the interests of its members);

b. whether the case raises questions of principle that are likely to affect the common interest of the association's members (or the association itself);

c. whether the mission of the association is sufficiently closely connected to the subject matter of the case.

In general terms, the fact that the Hearing Officer has admitted an association cannot be relied upon in support of an application to intervene by its individual members. On the contrary, in cases where a particular association has been admitted, individual members seeking to be granted third party status independently of the association should explain and justify why their individual interest would not be sufficiently represented in the proceedings by the association in question and it would thus not serve the interest in efficient proceedings to only admit the association.

35. The Hearing Officer will decide on a request for third party status, after having requested comments from DG Competition.

36. If admitted, DG Competition will subsequently inform the interested third party of the nature and subject matter of the proceedings and provide a time-limit within which the party may submit written comments. Contrary to complainants, who are entitled to a non-confidential version of the Statement of Objections, it falls on DG Competition to determine the means by which a third party will be informed (see however points 17 and 18 above).

37. The addressee(s) of a Statement of Objections will be informed of the identities of admitted third parties at the latest before the Oral Hearing. Only in exceptional circumstances may the Hearing Officer agree not to divulge an admitted third party's identity.

6. THE ORAL HEARING

38. The Oral Hearing provides addressees of the Statement of Objections as well as all other parties to the proceeding with the opportunity to orally express and develop their view as to the preliminary findings of the Commission. The purpose of the hearing is best served if the addressees and third parties explain whether and to what extent they disagree with the findings or can defend or justify themselves. These explanations may be supported by facts and evidence, including witness and/or expert testimony. The hearing also allows the Commission services to explain further the contested findings supported by facts and evidence, as contained in the Statement of Objections.

39. An addressee has a right to request an Oral Hearing within the time-limit for submitting its written comments to the Statement of Objections. On receiving a request it is for the Hearing Officer to determine where and when the hearing will take place. The Hearing Officer is not obliged to grant a request for an Oral Hearing if the request is not made within the deadline for receiving the comments. It is a matter of discretion for the Hearing Officer.

6.1 Admission to Oral Hearings

40. The Hearing Officer decides who will be invited to attend the Oral Hearing. With the exception of the competition authorities of the Member States, invited parties are expected to orally contribute to the hearing. Accordingly, observers will, as a general rule, not be invited.

6.2 Applications to attend the Oral Hearing

41. Parties other than the addressee of the Statement of Objections may attend only if their request to do so has been accepted by the Hearing Officer in advance of the hearing. Complainants and interested third parties admitted to the proceedings do not automatically have the right to attend an Oral Hearing.

42. As a general principle, applicants should be capable of contributing to the establishment of the truth and relevance of the facts and circumstances likely to be the focus of the hearing. Parties admitted to an Oral Hearing contribute to its purpose notably by means of an oral presentation. For reasons of effectiveness and efficiency it may be necessary to limit the number of participants. In this case the Hearing Officer may have to restrict admission, while ensuring that all views of the matter are fairly and sufficiently represented.

43. Where necessary, the Hearing Officer may request further information from the applicant in order to assess its interest in the outcome of the proceedings or clarify issues and facts, in particular where the applicant has not, prima facie, satisfied the Hearing Officer of its contribution to the Oral Hearing. The Hearing Officer normally also asks for information on the applicant's intended presentation, such as an outline of the presentation, the length of time required, the proposed speakers and the evidence upon which the applicant intends to rely.

44. Those invited to attend the Oral Hearing shall either appear in person, or be represented by persons duly authorised. These persons may be assisted by a lawyer. Whenever possible, undertakings should also be represented by a person from among their permanent staff and/or by persons that possess expertise of the relevant markets and industry, including, as the case may be, persons with direct knowledge of the facts. (18) All representatives, agents and participants must be authorised to participate in advance by the Hearing Officer.

(18) Case 49/69, Badische Anilin & Soda Fabrik AG v Commission, (1972) ECR 713, para. 11.

6.3 Preparation of the Oral Hearing

45. The Hearing Officer will determine the date, the duration and the location of the Oral Hearing. The Oral Hearing will normally not take place before the written exchange of views has been concluded between all parties admitted to the Oral Hearing, and all parties have had sufficient time to review the written comments, where such exchange of views has been made available by DG Competition (19). New documents may not be submitted at the Oral Hearing without the prior authorization of the Hearing Officer.

(19) Cf. DG Competition Best Practices on the conduct of proceedings concerning Articles 101 and 102 TFEU (ex-articles 81 and 82 EC), para. 89 et seq.

46. The Hearing Officer will also take all necessary preparatory steps to ensure the effectiveness and efficiency of the Oral Hearing. Such preparatory steps may include inviting specific persons to attend who are directly involved in the case, possess expertise of the relevant markets and industry or are able to contribute in any other useful way to clarify the issues a case raises. They may also include asking parties and/or a party in advance to address particular issues during the Oral Hearing, or present their views at the hearing on questions prepared in advance by the Hearing Officer.

The Hearing Officer may invite parties and/or persons for a meeting to properly prepare the Oral Hearing. Parties are encouraged to discuss issues that the hearing should focus on by means of preparatory meetings where necessary.

47. Prior to the Oral Hearing, parties will receive an information memorandum from the Hearing Office detailing what documents and the number of copies of documents they need to bring with them to the Oral Hearing (20) and other more detailed information relating to the organisation of the hearing.

(20) http://ec.europa.eu/competition/hearing_officers/index_en.html)

6.4 Publication of Dates of Oral Hearings

48. For reasons of transparency the Hearing Office will publish the dates of future Oral Hearings on its web-site, when these have been finalised and the parties to the case have been duly informed thereof. Such publication will be purely for information purposes only. The Oral Hearing itself is, however, not public.

6.5 Organisation of the Oral Hearing

49. A provisional list of participants, together with the provisional agenda, will be distributed by the Hearing Office to all invited parties wherever possible at the latest three working days before the Oral Hearing. Only those persons admitted by the Hearing Officer will be allowed entry into the hearing room.

50. The agenda will be determined by the Hearing Officer, taking into account the number of attendees, the estimated amount of time required by the speakers and the complexity of the case. For reasons of procedural efficiency, the Hearing Officer will ensure that the timing of the agenda is adhered to as strictly as possible.

51. Participants may request to be heard in an EU official language other than the language of proceedings. In such a case, interpretation into the language of the proceedings from this language, if it is another official EU language, will be provided as long as sufficient advance notice of such a language requirement is given to the Hearing Officer.

6.5.1 Presentations

52. Presentations will be given at the Oral Hearing by:
(i) the Commission;
(ii) the addressees of the Statement of Objections; and
(iii) third parties. As mentioned above (para. 43), the Hearing Officer may request the Commission, addressees and the third parties to provide an outline of their presentations in advance of the hearing (point 43 above).

6.5.2 In camera sessions

53. In order to protect their business secrets and any other confidential information, addressees and third parties invited to the Oral Hearing may request to give any sensitive parts of their presentation in a closed *in camera* session. Such requests must be made to the Hearing Officer in advance of the Oral Hearing, and must be duly motivated so as to allow a proper assessment of the need for an *in camera* session.

54. In order to prevent the potential abuse by parties of *in camera* sessions, the Hearing Officer retains the right to reconsider the confidential nature of the information presented while the *in camera* session is in progress and determine at any time that the nature of the information is not as such to justify an *in camera* session and may duly terminate it, if considered necessary.

55. Where an *in camera* session is permitted, the participants excluded from the session may only be advised of the subject matter of the presentation given. The party should be ready to give a summary (non-confidential) presentation either before or after the *in camera* session.

6.5.3 Questions and discussion

56. So as to ensure the maximum effectiveness and efficiency, and where necessary to ensure that all relevant facts – whether favourable or unfavourable to the parties concerned, and including the factual elements relating to the gravity and duration of the alleged infringement – are clarified as much as possible, the Hearing Officer will foresee time for questions and discussion during the hearing.

57. The Hearing Officer may allow questions on any of the issues raised by a written or oral submission to be addressed to any participant by any participant. In principle, questions asked should be answered during the Oral Hearing. In the event that they cannot be answered in whole or in part, the Hearing Officer may allow a party to submit its reply in writing within a given deadline. Any such written response will, in principle, be distributed to all participants at the Oral Hearing.

6.5.4 Limits on the disclosure of information

58. The Oral Hearing is not public and any information, discussions, presentations and documents disclosed during it may only be used for the purposes of judicial and/or administrative proceedings for the application of Articles 101 and 102 TFEU. They must not be disclosed or used for any other purpose by any participant at the hearing, even after the case is closed by the Commission. This use restriction also applies to the recording of the Oral Hearing (section 6.5.6 below), as well as any visual presentations, where appropriate.

6.5.5 Admission of written comments and/or documents

59. In exceptional circumstances the Hearing Officer may permit a party to submit written comments or documents on the merits of the case, within a deadline set after the end of the Oral Hearing. This will usually only be permitted where an issue is raised during the Oral Hearing that requires further elaboration.

6.5.6 Recording of the Oral Hearing

60. The Oral Hearing will be recorded, and for reasons of confidentiality any *in camera* sessions will be recorded separately. If requested, the recording will be made available to the parties who participated as soon as possible after the hearing has finished.

7. POST-ORAL HEARING

7.1 Interim Report

61. After the Oral Hearing, the Hearing Officer reports on the written and oral procedure to date to the Commissioner responsible for competition (Interim Report). In particular, this Report addresses all procedural issues of significance relating to the fairness of the procedure, such as whether the addressees' rights of defence have been respected. It may also make observations on any other specific procedural issues brought to the attention of the Hearing Officer by any party during the procedure.

62. In addition to the report on the procedural aspects of the case, the Hearing Officer usually also makes observations on the substance of the case to the Commissioner. Such observations focus on the Commission's findings contested by the parties, which are liable to have decisive importance for the outcome of the proceedings and may relate to the withdrawal of certain objections, the formulation of further objections or, in any other way, make suggestions as to the further progress of the proceedings.

63. The Interim Report and any additional observations are internal to the Commission's decision-making process and are therefore not accessible to the parties to the proceedings.

7.2 Supplementary Statement of Objections and Letter of Facts

64. Any issue with regard to the rights of defence in the context of a Supplementary Statement of Objections or a Letter of Facts that is not resolved with DG Competition may be addressed to the Hearing Officer.

8. OTHER PROCEDURES

8.1 Rejection of complaints

65. Where the Commission considers that there are insufficient grounds for pursuing a complaint it will inform the complainant thereof in writing and set a time-limit within which the complainant may submit its comments in writing. If the complainant considers that the time-period granted is insufficient, a reasoned request for an extension of the deadline may be submitted to the Hearing Officer.

66. A complainant that has been informed of the Commission's provisional intention to reject the complaint is entitled, upon request, to access the documents in the Commission's investigation file on which the Commission has based its preliminary assessment. If the complainant considers that the documents to which access has been granted are insufficient to allow it to effectively exercise the right to be heard, and has reason to believe that the Commission has in its possession more documents that have not been disclosed, a reasoned request for additional access can be submitted to the Hearing Officer. Such a request may not be couched in general terms (see above p. 20).

8.2 Commitment Decisions

67. In proceedings where the Commission intends to issue a commitment decision in application of Article 9 of Regulation N° 1/2003, the Hearing Officer, as in proceedings leading to the adoption of a prohibition decision, will safeguard the respect of an undertaking's rights of defence. If a commitment decision is adopted on the basis of a Preliminary Assessment not taking the form of a Statement of Objections, the undertaking's rights of defence are normally exercised in a less extensive manner than when such a decision is adopted after a Statement of Objections. This reflects the more consensual nature of such commitment procedures.

68. In cases where the Commission adopts a commitment Decision, the Hearing officer will produce a Final Report (see Section 9.1 below) taking into account, in particular, that the undertaking concerned has been put in a position to propose adequate commitments, or to modify them following a market test, to meet the competition concerns expressed by the Commission.

9. DECISION-MAKING PROCEDURE (21)

(21) This section does not apply to a decision adopted rejecting a complaint.

9.1 Final Report

69. Following the Oral Hearing the Hearing Officer is kept informed on the further progress of the proceedings by DG Competition and, where appropriate, participates directly in the Commission's further deliberations up to the stage of the draft Decision to be submitted to the College of Commissioners for adoption.

70. A draft Decision will be scrutinized by the Hearing Officer with a view to determining whether the addressees' rights of defence and the procedural rights of all parties to the proceedings have been safeguarded. Any findings in this regard will be recorded by the Hearing Officer in a Final Report. The Hearing Officer will also consider the extent to which the draft decision deviates in any material respects from the Statement of Objections.

71. A draft of the Final Report is provided to the Advisory Committee, so as to allow it to take the Hearing Officer's views into account in its assessment of the case.

72. After the Advisory Committee the Hearing Officer's Report will be finalized and submitted, together with the draft Decision, to the College of Commissioners to ensure that, when it reaches a decision on the case, it has been fully appraised of all relevant information as regards the course of the procedure and the procedural rights of all parties to the proceedings. The Hearing Officer may amend the Final Report in the light of any amendments to the draft Decision up to the time the Decision is adopted by the Commission.

73. Subsequently, the Final Report is sent to the addressees together with the Commission's Decision.

9.2 Publication

74. The Hearing Officer's Final Report, together with a summary of the Commission's Decision, is published in the *Official Journal of the European Union*. The Final Report is also made available on the Hearing Officers' web-site and on DG Competition's web-site to accompany the summary of the Decision and subsequently the non-confidential version of the Decision.

75. The Hearing Officer will decide on any disputes between a natural or legal person referred to in a Decision and DG Competition which concern the protection of personal and/or confidential information that may arise during the publication process of the non-confidential version of the Decision. The procedure applying to these disputes is the same as in the inter-partes phase (cf. section 4.1.2 above).

9.3 Future revision

76. This Guidance may be revised as and when required to reflect changes to legislation and/or administrative practice and the interpretation of those by the European courts.

Commission Regulation (EC) N° 773/2004, 7 April 2004 relating to the conduct of proceedings by the Commission pursuant to Articles 81 and 82 of the EC Treaty

(OJ L 123, 27 April 2004, p. 18)

1. Article 81 EC is now Article 101 TFEU and Article 82 EC is now Article 102 TFEU.

Amended by:
Commission Regulation (EC) N° 1792/2006 of 23 October 2006, O.J. L 362 p. 1 20.12.2006.
Commission Regulation (EC) N° 622/2008 of 30 June 2008, O.J., L 171, p. 3, 1.7.2008.

THE COMMISSION OF THE EUROPEAN COMMUNITIES,
Having regard to the Treaty establishing the European Community,
Having regard to the Agreement on the European Economic Area,
Having regard to Council Regulation (EC) N° 1/2003 of 16 December 2002 on the implementation of the rules on competition laid down in Articles 81 and 82 of the Treaty (1), and in particular Article 33 thereof,
After consulting the Advisory Committee on Restrictive Practices and Dominant Positions,
Whereas:

(1) Regulation (EC) N° 1/2003 empowers the Commission to regulate certain aspects of proceedings for the application of Articles 81 and 82 of the Treaty. It is necessary to lay down rules concerning the initiation of proceedings by the Commission as well as the handling of complaints and the hearing of the parties concerned.

(2) According to Regulation (EC) N° 1/2003, national courts are under an obligation to avoid taking decisions which could run counter to decisions envisaged by the Commission in the same case. According to Article 11(6) of that Regulation, national competition authorities are relieved from their competence once the Commission has initiated proceedings for the adoption of a decision under Chapter III of Regulation (EC) N° 1/2003. In this context, it is important that courts and competition authorities of the Member States are aware of the initiation of proceedings by the Commission. The Commission should therefore be able to make public its decisions to initiate proceedings.

(3) Before taking oral statements from natural or legal persons who consent to be interviewed, the Commission should inform those persons of the legal basis of the interview and its voluntary nature. The persons interviewed should also be informed of the purpose of the interview and of any record which may be made. In order to enhance the accuracy of the statements, the persons interviewed should also be given an opportunity to correct the statements recorded. Where information gathered from oral statements is exchanged pursuant to Article 12 of Regulation (EC) N° 1/2003, that information should only be used in evidence to impose sanctions on natural persons where the conditions set out in that Article are fulfilled.

(4) Pursuant to Article 23(1)(d) of Regulation (EC) N° 1/2003 fines may be imposed on undertakings and associations of undertakings where they fail to rectify within the time limit fixed by the Commission an incorrect, incomplete or misleading answer given by a member of their staff to questions in the course of inspections. It is therefore necessary to provide the undertaking concerned with a record of any explanations given and to establish a procedure enabling it to add any rectification, amendment or supplement to the explanations given by the member of staff who is not or was not authorised to provide explanations on behalf of the undertaking. The explanations given by a member of staff should remain in the Commission file as recorded during the inspection.

(5) Complaints are an essential source of information for detecting infringements of competition rules. It is important to define clear and efficient procedures for handling complaints lodged with the Commission.

(6) In order to be admissible for the purposes of Article 7 of Regulation (EC) N° 1/2003, a complaint must contain certain specified information.

(7) In order to assist complainants in submitting the necessary facts to the Commission, a form should be drawn up. The submission of the information listed in that form should be a condition for a complaint to be treated as a complaint as referred to in Article 7 of Regulation (EC) N° 1/2003.

(8) Natural or legal persons having chosen to lodge a complaint should be given the possibility to be associated closely with the proceedings initiated by the Commission with a view to finding an infringement. However, they should not have access to business secrets or other confidential information belonging to other parties involved in the proceedings.

(9) Complainants should be granted the opportunity of expressing their views if the Commission considers that there are insufficient grounds for acting on the complaint. Where the Commission rejects a complaint on the grounds that a competition authority of a Member State is dealing with it or has already done so, it should inform the complainant of the identity of that authority.

(10) In order to respect the rights of defence of undertakings, the Commission should give the parties concerned the right to be heard before it takes a decision.

(11) Provision should also be made for the hearing of persons who have not submitted a complaint as referred to in Article 7 of Regulation (EC) N° 1/2003 and who are not parties to whom a statement of objections has been addressed but who can nevertheless show a sufficient interest. Consumer associations that apply to be heard should generally be regarded as having a sufficient interest, where the proceedings concern products or services used by the end-consumer or products or services that constitute a direct input into such products or services. Where it considers this to be useful for the proceedings, the Commission should also be able to invite other persons to express their views in writing and to attend the oral hearing of the parties to whom a statement of objections has been addressed. Where appropriate, it should also be able to invite such persons to express their views at that oral hearing.

(12) To improve the effectiveness of oral hearings, the Hearing Officer should have the power to allow the parties concerned, complainants, other persons invited to the hearing, the Commission services and the authorities of the Member States to ask questions during the hearing.

(13) When granting access to the file, the Commission should ensure the protection of business secrets and other confidential information. The category of «other confidential information» includes information other than business secrets, which may be considered as confidential, insofar as its disclosure would significantly harm an undertaking or person. The Commission should be able to request un-

dertakings or associations of undertakings that submit or have submitted documents or statements to identify confidential information.

(14) Where business secrets or other confidential information are necessary to prove an infringement, the Commission should assess for each individual document whether the need to disclose is greater than the harm which might result from disclosure.

(15) In the interest of legal certainty, a minimum time-limit for the various submissions provided for in this Regulation should be laid down.

(16) This Regulation replaces Commission Regulation (EC) N° 2842/98 of 22 December 1998 on the hearing of parties in certain proceedings under Articles 85 and 86 of the EC Treaty (2), which should therefore be repealed.

(17) This Regulation aligns the procedural rules in the transport sector with the general rules of procedure in all sectors. Commission Regulation (EC) N° 2843/98 of 22 December 1998 on the form, content and other details of applications and notifications provided for in Council Regulations (EEC) N° 1017/68, (EEC) N° 4056/86 and (EEC) N° 3975/87 applying the rules on competition to the transport sector (3) should therefore be repealed.

(18) Regulation (EC) N° 1/2003 abolishes the notification and authorisation system. Commission Regulation (EC) N° 3385/94 of 21 December 1994 on the form, content and other details of applications and notifications provided for in Council Regulation N° 17 (4) should therefore be repealed,
HAS ADOPTED THIS REGULATION:

(1) O.J. L 1, 4.1.2003, p. 1. Regulation as amended by Regulation (EC) N° 411/2004 (O.J. L 68, 6.3.2004, p. 1).

(2) O.J. L 354, 30.12.1998, p. 18.

(3) O.J. L 354, 30.12.1998, p. 22.

(4) O.J. L 377, 31.12.1994, p. 28.

CHAPTER I
SCOPE

Art. 1. *Subject-matter and scope*

This regulation applies to proceedings conducted by the Commission for the application of Articles 81 and 82 of the Treaty.

CHAPTER II
INITIATION OF PROCEEDINGS

Art. 2. *Initiation of proceedings*

1. The Commission may decide to initiate proceedings with a view to adopting a decision pursuant to Chapter III of Regulation (EC) N° 1/2003 at any point in time, but no later than the date on which it issues a preliminary assessment as referred to in Article 9(1) of that Regulation, a statement of objections or a request for the parties to express their interest in engaging in settlement discussions, or the date on which a notice pursuant to Article 27(4) of that Regulation is published, whichever is the earlier.

2. The Commission may make public the initiation of proceedings, in any appropriate way. Before doing so, it shall inform the parties concerned.

3. The Commission may exercise its powers of investigation pursuant to Chapter V of Regulation (EC) N° 1/2003 before initiating proceedings.

4. The Commission may reject a complaint pursuant to Article 7 of Regulation (EC) N° 1/2003 without initiating proceedings.

CHAPTER III
INVESTIGATIONS BY THE COMMISSION

Art. 3. *Power to take statements*

1. Where the Commission interviews a person with his consent in accordance with Article 19 of Regulation (EC) N° 1/2003, it shall, at the beginning of the interview, state the legal basis and the purpose of the interview, and recall its voluntary nature. It shall also inform the person interviewed of its intention to make a record of the interview.

2. The interview may be conducted by any means including by telephone or electronic means.

3. The Commission may record the statements made by the persons interviewed in any form. A copy of any recording shall be made available to the person interviewed for approval. Where necessary, the Commission shall set a time-limit within which the person interviewed may communicate to it any correction to be made to the statement.

Art. 4. *Oral questions during inspections*

1. When, pursuant to Article 20(2)(e) of Regulation (EC) N° 1/2003, officials or other accompanying persons authorised by the Commission ask representatives or members of staff of an undertaking or of an association of undertakings for explanations, the explanations given may be recorded in any form.

2. A copy of any recording made pursuant to paragraph 1 shall be made available to the undertaking or association of undertakings concerned after the inspection.

3. In cases where a member of staff of an undertaking or of an association of undertakings who is not or was not authorised by the undertaking or by the association of undertakings to provide explanations on behalf of the undertaking or association of undertakings has been asked for explanations, the Commission shall set a time-limit within which the undertaking or the association of undertakings may communicate to the Commission any rectification, amendment or supplement to the explanations given by such member of staff. The rectification, amendment or supplement shall be added to the explanations as recorded pursuant to paragraph 1.

CHAPTER IV
HANDLING OF COMPLAINTS

Art. 5. *Admissibility of complaints*

1. Natural and legal persons shall show a legitimate interest in order to be entitled to lodge a complaint for the purposes of Article 7 of Regulation (EC) N° 1/2003.

Such complaints shall contain the information required by Form C, as set out in the Annex. The Commission may dispense with this obligation as regards part of the information, including documents, required by Form C.

2. Three paper copies as well as, if possible, an electronic copy of the complaint shall be submitted to the Commission. The complainant shall also submit a non-confidential version of the complaint, if confidentiality is claimed for any part of the complaint.

3. Complaints shall be submitted in one of the official languages of the Community.

Art. 6. *Participation of complainants in proceedings*

1. Where the Commission issues a statement of objections relating to a matter in respect of which it has received a complaint, it shall provide the complainant with a copy of the non-confidential version of the statement of objections, except in cases where the settlement procedure applies, where it shall inform the complainant in writing of the nature and subject matter of the procedure. The Commission shall also set a time limit within which the complainant may make known its views in writing.

2. The Commission may, where appropriate, afford complainants the opportunity of expressing their views at the oral hearing of the parties to which a statement of objections has been issued, if complainants so request in their written comments.

Art. 7. *Rejection of complaints*

1. Where the Commission considers that on the basis of the information in its possession there are insufficient grounds for acting on a complaint, it shall inform the complainant of its reasons and set a time-limit within which the complainant may make known its views in writing. The Commission shall not be obliged to take into account any further written submission received after the expiry of that time-limit.

2. If the complainant makes known its views within the time-limit set by the Commission and the written submissions made by the complainant do not lead to a different assessment of the complaint, the Commission shall reject the complaint by decision.

3. If the complainant fails to make known its views within the time-limit set by the Commission, the complaint shall be deemed to have been withdrawn.

Art. 8. *Access to information*

1. Where the Commission has informed the complainant of its intention to reject a complaint pursuant to Article 7(1) the complainant may request access to the documents on which the Commission bases its provisional assessment. For this purpose, the complainant may however not have access to business secrets and other confidential information belonging to other parties involved in the proceedings.

2. The documents to which the complainant has had access in the context of proceedings conducted by the Commission under Articles 81 and 82 of the Treaty may only be used by the complainant for the purposes of judicial or administrative proceedings for the application of those Treaty provisions.

Art. 9. *Rejections of complaints pursuant to Article 13 of Regulation (EC) N° 1/2003*

Where the Commission rejects a complaint pursuant to Article 13 of Regulation (EC) N° 1/2003, it shall inform the complainant without delay of the national competition authority which is dealing or has already dealt with the case.

CHAPTER V
EXERCISE OF THE RIGHT TO BE HEARD

Art. 10. *Statement of objections and reply*

1. The Commission shall inform the parties concerned of the objections raised against them. The statement of objections shall be notified in writing to each of the parties against whom objections are raised.

2. The Commission shall, when notifying the statement of objections to the parties concerned, set a time-limit within which these parties may inform it in writing of their views. The Commission shall not be obliged to take into account written submissions received after the expiry of that time-limit.

3. The parties may, in their written submissions, set out all facts known to them which are relevant to their defence against the objections raised by the Commission. They shall attach any relevant documents as proof of the facts set out. They shall provide a paper original as well as an electronic copy or, where they do not provide an electronic copy, 30 paper copies of their submission and of the documents attached to it. They may propose that the Commission hear persons who may corroborate the facts set out in their submission.

Art. 10a. *Settlement procedure in cartel cases*

1. After the initiation of proceedings pursuant to Article 11(6) of Regulation (EC) N° 1/2003, the Commission may set a time limit within which the parties may indicate in writing that they are prepared to engage in settlement discussions with a view to possibly introducing settlement submissions. The Commission shall not be obliged to take into account replies received after the expiry of that time limit.

If two or more parties within the same undertaking indicate their willingness to engage in settlement discussions pursuant to the first subparagraph, they shall appoint a joint representation to engage in discussions with the Commission on their behalf. When setting the time limit referred to in the first subparagraph, the Commission shall indicate to the relevant parties that they are identified within the same undertaking, for the sole purpose of enabling them to comply with this provision.

2. Parties taking part in settlement discussions may be informed by the Commission of:

(a) the objections it envisages to raise against them;

(b) the evidence used to determine the envisaged objections;

(c) non-confidential versions of any specified accessible document listed in the case file at that point in time, in so far as a request by the party is justified for the purpose of enabling the party to ascertain its position regarding a time period or any other particular aspect of the cartel; and

(d) the range of potential fines.

This information shall be confidential vis-à-vis third parties, save where the Commission has given a prior explicit authorisation for disclosure.

Should settlement discussions progress, the Commission may set a time limit within which the parties may commit to follow the settlement procedure by introducing settlement submissions reflecting the results of the settlement discussions and acknowledging their participation in an infringement of Article 81 of the Treaty as well as their liability. Before the Commission sets a time limit to introduce their settlement submissions, the parties concerned shall be entitled to have the information specified in Article 10a(2), first subparagraph disclosed to them, upon request, in a timely manner. The Commission shall not be obliged to take into account settlement submissions received after the expiry of that time limit.

3. When the statement of objections notified to the parties reflects the contents of their settlement submissions, the written reply to the statement of objections by the par-

ties concerned shall, within a time limit set by the Commission, confirm that the statement of objections addressed to them reflects the contents of their settlement submissions. The Commission may then proceed to the adoption of a Decision pursuant to Article 7 and Article 23 of Regulation (EC) N° 1/2003 after consultation of the Advisory Committee on Restrictive Practices and Dominant Positions pursuant to Article 14 of Regulation (EC) N° 1/2003.

4. The Commission may decide at any time during the procedure to discontinue settlement discussions altogether in a specific case or with respect to one or more of the parties involved, if it considers that procedural efficiencies are not likely to be achieved.

Art. 11. *Right to be heard*

1. The Commission shall give the parties to whom it addresses a statement of objections the opportunity to be heard before consulting the Advisory Committee referred to in Article 14(1) of Regulation (EC) N° 1/2003.

2. The Commission shall, in its decisions, deal only with objections in respect of which the parties referred to in paragraph 1 have been able to comment.

Art. 12. 1. The Commission shall give the parties to whom it addresses a statement of objections the opportunity to develop their arguments at an oral hearing, if they so request in their written submissions.

2. However, when introducing their settlement submissions the parties shall confirm to the Commission that they would only require having the opportunity to develop their arguments at an oral hearing, if the statement of objections does not reflect the contents of their settlement submissions.

Art. 13. *Hearing of other persons*

1. If natural or legal persons other than those referred to in Articles 5 and 11 apply to be heard and show a sufficient interest, the Commission shall inform them in writing of the nature and subject matter of the procedure and shall set a time-limit within which they may make known their views in writing.

2. The Commission may, where appropriate, invite persons referred to in paragraph 1 to develop their arguments at the oral hearing of the parties to whom a statement of objections has been addressed, if the persons referred to in paragraph 1 so request in their written comments.

3. The Commission may invite any other person to express its views in writing and to attend the oral hearing of the parties to whom a statement of objections has been addressed. The Commission may also invite such persons to express their views at that oral hearing.

Art. 14. *Conduct of oral hearings*

1. Hearings shall be conducted by a Hearing Officer in full independence.

2. The Commission shall invite the persons to be heard to attend the oral hearing on such date as it shall determine.

3. The Commission shall invite the competition authorities of the Member States to take part in the oral hearing. It may likewise invite officials and civil servants of other authorities of the Member States.

4. Persons invited to attend shall either appear in person or be represented by legal representatives or by representatives authorised by their constitution as appropriate. Undertakings and associations of undertakings may also be represented by a duly authorised agent appointed from among their permanent staff.

5. Persons heard by the Commission may be assisted by their lawyers or other qualified persons admitted by the Hearing Officer.

6. Oral hearings shall not be public. Each person may be heard separately or in the presence of other persons invited to attend, having regard to the legitimate interest of the undertakings in the protection of their business secrets and other confidential information.

7. The Hearing Officer may allow the parties to whom a statement of objections has been addressed, the complainants, other persons invited to the hearing, the Commission services and the authorities of the Member States to ask questions during the hearing.

8. The statements made by each person heard shall be recorded. Upon request, the recording of the hearing shall be made available to the persons who attended the hearing. Regard shall be had to the legitimate interest of the parties in the protection of their business secrets and other confidential information.

CHAPTER VI
ACCESS TO THE FILE AND TREATMENT OF CONFIDENTIAL INFORMATION

Art. 15. *Access to the file and use of documents*

1. If so requested, the Commission shall grant access to the file to the parties to whom it has addressed a statement of objections. Access shall be granted after the notification of the statement of objections.

1a. After the initiation of proceedings pursuant to Article 11(6) of Regulation (EC) N° 1/2003 and in order to enable the parties willing to introduce settlement submissions to do so, the Commission shall disclose to them the evidence and documents described in Article 10a(2) upon request and subject to the conditions established in the relevant subparagraphs. In view thereof, when introducing their settlement submissions, the parties shall confirm to the Commission that they will only require access to the file after the receipt of the statement of objections, if the statement of objections does not reflect the contents of their settlement submissions.

2. The right of access to the file shall not extend to business secrets, other confidential information and internal documents of the Commission or of the competition authorities of the Member States. The right of access to the file shall also not extend to correspondence between the Commission and the competition authorities of the Member States or between the latter where such correspondence is contained in the file of the Commission.

3. Nothing in this Regulation prevents the Commission from disclosing and using information necessary to prove an infringement of Articles 81 or 82 of the Treaty.

4. Documents obtained through access to the file pursuant to this Article shall only be used for the purposes of judicial or administrative proceedings for the application of Articles 81 and 82 of the Treaty.

Art. 16. *Identification and protection of confidential information*

1. Information, including documents, shall not be communicated or made accessible by the Commission in so far as it contains business secrets or other confidential information of any person.

2. Any person which makes known its views pursuant to Article 6(1), Article 7(1), Article 10(2) and Article 13(1)

and (3) or subsequently submits further information to the Commission in the course of the same procedure, shall clearly identify any material which it considers to be confidential, giving reasons, and provide a separate non-confidential version by the date set by the Commission for making its views known.

3. Without prejudice to paragraph 2 of this Article, the Commission may require undertakings and associations of undertakings which produce documents or statements pursuant to Regulation (EC) N° 1/2003 to identify the documents or parts of documents which they consider to contain business secrets or other confidential information belonging to them and to identify the undertakings with regard to which such documents are to be considered confidential. The Commission may likewise require undertakings or associations of undertakings to identify any part of a statement of objections, a case summary drawn up pursuant to Article 27(4) of Regulation (EC) N° 1/2003 or a decision adopted by the Commission which in their view contains business secrets.

The Commission may set a time-limit within which the undertakings and associations of undertakings are to:

(a) substantiate their claim for confidentiality with regard to each individual document or part of document, statement or part of statement;

(b) provide the Commission with a non-confidential version of the documents or statements, in which the confidential passages are deleted;

(c) provide a concise description of each piece of deleted information.

4. If undertakings or associations of undertakings fail to comply with paragraphs 2 and 3, the Commission may assume that the documents or statements concerned do not contain confidential information.

CHAPTER VII
GENERAL AND FINAL PROVISIONS

Art. 17. *Time-limits*

1. In setting the time limits provided for in Article 3(3), Article 4(3), Article 6(1), Article 7(1), Article 10(2), Article 10a(1), Article 10a(2), Article 10a(3) and Article 16(3), the Commission shall have regard both to the time required for preparation of the submission and to the urgency of the case.

2. The time-limits referred to in Article 6(1), Article 7(1) and Article 10(2) shall be at least four weeks. However, for proceedings initiated with a view to adopting interim measures pursuant to Article 8 of Regulation (EC) N° 1/2003, the time-limit may be shortened to one week.

3. The time limits referred to in Article 4(3), Article 10a(1), Article 10a(2) and Article 16(3) shall be at least two weeks. The time limit referred to in Article 3(3) shall be at least two weeks, except for settlement submissions, for which corrections shall be made within one week. The time limit referred to in Article 10a(3) shall be at least two weeks.

4. Where appropriate and upon reasoned request made before the expiry of the original time-limit, time-limits may be extended.

Art. 18. *Repeals*

Regulations (EC) N° 2842/98, (EC) N° 2843/98 and (EC) N° 3385/94 are repealed.

References to the repealed regulations shall be construed as references to this regulation.

Art. 19. *Transitional provisions*

Procedural steps taken under Regulations (EC) N° 2842/98 and (EC) N° 2843/98 shall continue to have effect for the purpose of applying this Regulation.

Art. 20. *Entry into force*

This Regulation shall enter into force on 1 May 2004.

This Regulation shall be binding in its entirety and directly applicable in all Member States.

Annex
Form C
Complaint pursuant to article 7 of Regulation (EC) N° 1/2003

1. Not included, see section Forms

Best Practices for the submission of economic evidence and data collection in cases concerning the application of Articles 101 and 102 TFEU and in Merger cases, not published in the Official Journal

1. See: http://europa.eu/rapid/pressReleasesAction.do?reference=IP/10/2&format=HTML&aged=0&language=EN&guiLanguage=en

Table of contents

	Pages
1. Scope and purpose (1)	225
2. Best Practices regarding the content and presentation of economic and econometric submissions (9)	225
2.1. Formulating the relevant question (16)	226
2.2. Data relevance and reliability (20)	226
2.3. Choice of empirical methodology (24)	227
2.4. Reporting and interpreting the results (32)	227
2.5. Robustness (37)	228
2.6. Further recommendations (41)	228
3. Best Practices on responding to requests for quantitative data (46)	229
3.1. General motivation for Data Requests (51)	229
3.2. Common elements of a Data Request (55)	229
3.3. Main criteria to consider when responding to a Data Request (60)	230
3.3.1. Completeness (62)	230
3.3.2. Correctness (64)	230
3.3.3. Timely submission (66)	230

3.4. Other Recommendations (67) 230
3.4.1. Cooperation in good-faith (68). 230
3.4.2. Early consultation with DG Competition to inform about what type of data is available (70). 231
3.4.3. Consultation on a Draft Data Requests and data samples (74). 231
3.4.4. Transparency regarding data collection, formatting and submission (76). 231
3.4.5. Direct access (80). 231
ANNEX 1. – Structure and basic elements of a sound empirical submission. 232

1. SCOPE AND PURPOSE

1. Economic analysis plays a central role in competition enforcement. Economics as a discipline provides a framework to think about the way in which each particular market operates and how competitive interactions take place. This framework further allows formulating the possible consequences of the practices under review, whether a merger, an agreement between firms, or single firm conduct. It also provides tools to identify the direction and magnitude of these effects empirically, if appropriate and relevant. In a number of cases, economic analysis may involve the production, handling and assessment of voluminous sets of quantitative data, including, when appropriate, the development of econometric models (1).

(1) Infringements «by object» do not require any substantive economic analysis because empirical evidence has shown that they generally lead to serious anti-competitive effects. However, the investigation of potential infringements «by effect» often requires a complex economic assessment by the Commission

2. Economic analysis needs to be framed in such a way that the Commission can evaluate its relevance and significance. Furthermore, as an administrative authority the Commission is required to take a decision within an appropriate or sometimes a statutory time limit. It is therefore necessary to:

(i) ensure that economic analysis meets certain minimum standards at the outset;

(ii) facilitate the efficient gathering and exchange of facts and evidence, in particular any underlying quantitative data; and

(iii) use in an efficient way reliable and relevant evidence obtained during the administrative procedure, whether quantitative or qualitative.

3. In order to determine the relevance and significance of an economic analysis for a particular case, it is first necessary to assess its intrinsic quality from a technical perspective, i.e. whether it has been generated and presented to adequate standards. This involves, in particular, an evaluation of whether the hypothesis to be tested is formulated without ambiguity and clearly related to facts, whether the assumptions of the economic model are consistent with the institutional features and other relevant facts of the industry, whether economic models are well established in the relevant literature, whether the empirical methods and the data are appropriate, whether the results are properly interpreted and robust and whether counterarguments have been given adequate consideration.

4. Second, one must assess the congruence and consistency of the economic analysis with other pieces of quantitative and qualitative evidence (such as customer responses, or documentary evidence).

5. The present document formulates best practices concerning the generation as well as the presentation of relevant economic and empirical evidence that may be taken into account in the assessment of a competition case. These best practices are organised along two themes:

i) first of all, it provides recommendations regarding the content and presentation of economic or econometric analysis. This is meant to facilitate its assessment and the replication of any empirical results by DG Competition and/or other parties;

ii) second, the document provides guidance to respond to Commission requests for quantitative data (2) to ensure that timely and relevant input for the investigation can be provided.

(2) Quantitative data means, generally, observations or measurements, expressed as numbers. For the purposes of these Best Practices, this concept is used to refer to large sets of quantitative data submitted and/or obtained for the purposes of the conduct of an assessment of an economic (and often econometric) nature.

6. The desire to ensure transparency and accountability that guide these best practices apply to all parties involved in proceedings concerning the application of Articles 101 and 102 TFEU (3) and mergers (4), that is the parties to the case and interested third parties (including complainants), as well as DG Competition.

(3) Proceedings before the European Commission concerning Articles 101 and 102 TFEU, in accordance with Council Regulation (EC) N° 1/2003 of 16 December 2002 on the implementation of the rules on competition laid down in Articles 81 and 82 of the Treaty (OJ L 1, 4.1.2003, p. 1, as amended).

(4) Proceedings under the Council Regulation (EC) N° 139/2004 of 20 January 2004 on the control of concentrations between undertakings (OJ L 24, 29.1.2004, p. 1).

7. These Best Practices do not create or alter rights or obligations as set out in the Treaty on the Functioning of the European Union and in secondary law, as amended from time to time and as interpreted by the case-law of the Courts of the European Union. The Best Practices also do not alter the Commission's interpretative notices and established decisional practice.

8. The principles contained here may be further developed and refined by DG Competition in individual cases when appropriate in light of future developments. The specificity of an individual case or particular circumstances may require an adaptation of, or deviation from, these Best Practices.

2. BEST PRACTICES REGARDING THE CONTENT AND PRESENTATION OF ECONOMIC AND ECONOMETRIC SUBMISSIONS

9. Economic reasoning is employed in competition cases notably in order to develop in a consistent manner or, conversely, to rebut because of its inconsistency, the economic evidence and arguments in a given case.

10. Any economic model which explicitly or implicitly supports a theoretical claim must rely on assumptions that are consistent with the facts of the industry under consideration. These assumptions should be carefully laid out and the sensitivity of its predictions to changes to the assumptions should be made explicit. While it is not necessary for economic submissions to actually formalize verbal arguments in a model, this will sometimes be helpful to clearly spell out the assumptions underlying an argument, to check its logic consistency, to assess effects of a high degree of complexity, or to use the model as the theoretical basis for an empirical estimation (5).

(5) If an economic submission is well-reasoned, then the fact that a particular argument is «theoretical» or «general» is often a strength rather than a weakness of the submission. This is the case when one has deduced a general conclusion (which holds irrespective of the precise magnitudes of the parameters of the analysis) from a set of assumptions that are considered consistent with the facts of the case. For instance, an economic submission may try to substantiate that irrespective of the size or existence of efficiencies, a particular conduct cannot possibly harm consumers.

11. An economic analysis may support an assessment of the anticompetitive or pro-competitive effects of a merger. Such analysis usually involves a comparison of the actual or likely future situation in the relevant market with the absence of the proposed merger.

12. By their very nature, economic models and arguments are based on simplifications of reality. It is therefore normally not sufficient to disprove a particular argument or model, to point out that it is «based on seemingly unrealistic assumptions». It is also necessary to explicitly identify which aspects of reality should be better reflected in the model or argumentation, and to indicate why this would alter the conclusions.

13. In many cases, economic theory is used to develop a testable hypothesis that is later checked against the data. In that case, the economic analysis makes predictions about reality that can be tested by observations and potentially rejected or verified. Thus, whenever feasible, an economic model should be accompanied by an appropriate empirical model – i.e. a model which is capable of testing the relevant hypotheses given the data available.

14. Very often simple but well focused measurement of economic variables (prices, cost, margins, capacity constraints, R&D intensity) will provide important insights into the significance of particular factors. Occasionally, more advanced statistical and econometric techniques may provide more useful evidence (6). In any case, otherwise valid economic analysis may not always produce unambiguous results when applied to the facts of a competition case. Contradictions may result from differences in the data, differences in the approach to economic modelling or in the assumptions used to interpret the data or differences in the empirical techniques and methodologies.

(6) For instance, an econometric analysis of the extent to which prices of an undertaking have been affected by the observed entry of a competitor may provide evidence of the competitive constraint exercised by that entrant. In turn this could provide insights with respect to the likely degree of harm, that would result if an incumbent dominant undertaking were to engage in practices resulting in anticompetitive foreclosure in that or related markets.

15. The following sections provide practical advice on the generation and communication of economic and econometric analyses. The goal of these recommendations is to ensure that every economic or econometric analysis submitted for consideration in a case states fully the economic reasoning and the observations on which it relies as well as to explain the relevance of its findings for the case at hand and the robustness of the results. This should allow DG Competition and all interested parties to scrutinise the economic evidence submitted during the proceedings so as to avoid that empirical results that are not robust be disguised as such and key assumptions in theoretical reasoning be presented as innocuous.

2.1. Formulating the relevant question

16. The first step in any economic analysis, theoretical or empirical, should be the formulation of a question that is relevant to the case at hand.

17. The question of interest must be:

(a) precisely formulated so that its answer can be interpreted without ambiguity;

(b) properly motivated taking into account the nature of the competition case, the institutional features of the markets under consideration and the relevant economic theory (7).

(7) Occasionally the parties might submit a literature survey or review regarding an economic question of particular relevance for the case. A literature review may be useful when it is accompanied by an explanation on the merits and shortcomings, of the existing studies and explains how the party's own reasoning or analysis relates to past research, academic or otherwise.

18. An economic or econometric report should explicitly formulate not only the hypothesis to be tested (the «null hypothesis» (8)) but also the alternative hypothesis (or hypotheses) under consideration, so that rejection of the null hypothesis can be properly interpreted (9).

(8) The null hypothesis is generally that which is presumed to be true initially. A null hypothesis is a hypothesis set up to be nullified or refuted in order to support an alternative hypothesis.

(9) For example, consider an empirical project aimed at testing whether certain conduct would lead to higher prices. One could define as the null hypothesis that prices did not increase in which case a rejection of the null hypothesis would imply that the agreement had a positive price impact. Alternatively, one could have defined as the null hypothesis that prices did not change as a result of the agreement. A rejection of the null hypothesis in that case would be harder to interpret: did prices rise or fall as a result of the exclusive relationship between buyer and seller?

19. One should explicitly discuss the link between the hypothesis being tested and any economic theory regarding the competitive effects under assessment to which it relates. Often, the empirical exercise being carried out will shed only indirect evidence on the economic theory under assessment. This evidence is nonetheless useful but should be properly qualified (10).

(10) For example, the analysis of scanner data (retail prices and quantities) may provide valuable evidence in the context of a merger between producers of fast moving consumption goods, even when the direct impact of the transaction would be felt at the wholesale level and not at the consumer level.

2.2. Data relevance and reliability

20. The intrinsic quality of an economic theory depends on the extent to which the underlying assumptions match the corresponding economic facts. Likewise, empirical analysis depends on the relevance and the reliability of the underlying data.

21. First, it is necessary to identify the relevant facts to validate the theoretical assumptions and employ data which is appropriate to respond to the empirical question under investigation (11).

(11) For example when discounts are important, the analysis of the price impact of a merger, agreement or practice must focus on prices paid by consumers rather than on list prices.

22. Second, not all facts can be observed or measured with high accuracy and most datasets are incomplete or otherwise imperfect. Hence, parties and/or DG Competition should become familiar with the facts and data and acknowledge its limitations explicitly. As regards quantitative data, for example, this requires:

(i) a thorough inspection of the data, including summary statistics and graphs; and

(ii) a sufficient understanding of how the data were gathered, the sample selection process, the measurement of the variables and whether they bear a close relationship with their theoretical counterparts. Quantitative data may contain anomalies because of miscoding or other errors, which should be discussed with the data providers to decide how to best adjust the data to address these problems.

23. Failure to observe and validate all key assumptions or deficiencies in the data should not prevent an economic analysis to be given weight, though caution must be exercised before relying on its conclusions (12). Furthermore, statistical techniques have been developed to deal with measurement errors, missing observations and sample selection problems. While these techniques may not be able to improve the data, they may help to deal with some of its imperfections.

(12) For example, assumptions regarding firms' expectations regarding the identity of the market leader may be inferred indirectly through observation of which firm first announces its future prices.

2.3. Choice of empirical methodology

24. The choice of methodology to empirically test a hypothesis or to validate the predictions of an economic model should be properly motivated, and its pros and cons should be made explicit, including potential identification problems (13).

(13) Problems of inference can be separated into statistical and identification problems. Studies of identification seek to characterize the conclusions that could be drawn if one could use the sampling process to obtain an unlimited number of observations. Studies of statistical inference seek to characterize the generally weaker conclusions that can be drawn from a finite number of observations.

25. Identification can be understood as clarifying the basis upon which one theory can be preferred to another. Similarly, the term can be used to refer to any situation where an econometric model will invariably have more than one set of parameters which generate the same distribution of observations.

26. It is necessary to motivate how the chosen methodology exploits the variation in the data, to at least partially discriminate between the tested (or null) hypothesis and the alternative hypotheses. At the very least, an economic model or argument must generate predictions that are consistent with a significant number of relevant observed facts.

27. The choice of methodology should seek consistency with:

(a) the dataset and its potential limitations;

(b) the features of the market under investigation; and

(c) the economic issues under consideration – i.e., it should be designed to test the hypothesis of interest and formulated under the relevant question (see also section 2.1 above).

28. If statistical and/or econometric methods are used, a number of further methodological choices need to be made and justified, regarding, *inter-alia*:

i) specification (what is the range of sensible general forms for the relationship under evaluation, including the relevant variables, the way they could interact, and the nature of errors or uncertainty);

ii) observation (how well do the measurements approximate the variables they are intended to represent);

iii) estimation (what do the data in the sample suggest as to the range of plausible relationships among variables).

29. Statistical techniques and tests should be based, to the extent possible, on generally accepted methods. In many circumstances standard econometric models and statistical tools may have to be adapted to the peculiarities of the case. In those cases, one should motivate the changes, describe the modified technique or model, and document the likely biases, if any, that the new method is likely to introduce.

30. In general, it is recommended to follow a «bottom-up» approach. In the context of multiple regression analysis, this would mean estimating simple models first and then engage in more refined estimation exercises if necessary in order to avoid bias (14).

(14) For example, it is sound practice to estimate an Ordinary Least Squares (OLS) regression first and then, to the extent endogeneity is thought to be a problem, move on to an instrumental variable (IV) estimation.

31. Finally, alternative methodologies should also be discussed. If possible, given time and data constraints, conducting multiple empirical analyses relying on different methodologies would help determine whether the conclusions of the empirical investigation are robust to different tests or models (see also section 2.5 below).

2.4. Reporting and interpreting the results

32. Parties should explain the details of their models, and share any documentation needed to allow timely replication (e.g. the programming code used to run the analysis). It is critical to take the reader through the reasoning or where necessary the various mathematical steps that build the economic or econometric model (15). Reports which do not allow for replication and in particular those that do not include the code and data in electronic form will receive less consideration and are consequently unlikely to be given much weight.

(15) Any mathematical notation should either *(a)* follow the standard notation in the literature; or *(b)* be very self-explanatory.

33. Commonly, results from economic analysis and statistical information are presented in tables. Although it is not necessary to comment on or restate every piece of information that a table contains an interpretation of the data in it must be provided.

34. The results of the empirical analyses should be reported in the standard format found in academic papers. For example, when reporting multiple regression results, one should report on the statistical significance (16) of the parameter estimates by following the convention of reporting coefficients, p-values, standard errors and the size of the sample. In the description of the results the emphasis should be on statistically significant findings to the 5 % level (i.e. p-value < 0.05). However findings significant around the 10 % level should not be ignored, in particular where the coefficient of interest is economically significant and the sample size is small. Detailed information should also be provided on all other specification tests and statistical diagnoses (see also section 2.5 on robustness).

(16) A statistically significant result is one that is unlikely to have occurred by chance. In hypothesis testing, the significance level is the criterion used for rejecting the null hypothesis. The p-value is the probability of obtaining a test statistic at least as extreme as the one that was actually observed, assuming that the null hypothesis is true. If the obtained p-value is smaller than or equal to the significance level, then the null hypothesis is rejected and the outcome is said to be statistically significant.

35. An empirical submission should not only discuss the statistical significance of the results but also their practical relevance. In general, with very large samples coefficients may be statistically significant even if they are of trivial magnitude (17). This creates the potentially misleading impression that certain variables are important. Therefore, the magnitude of the coefficients must always be examined and discussed. This requires interpreting the results in connection with the hypothesis that is being tested, so as to draw implications for the case under investigation.

(17) Statistical significance is determined, in part, by the number of observations in the data set. The more observations used to calculate the regression coefficients, the smaller the standard error of each coefficient. A smaller standard error reflects less random variability in the estimated coefficient (or estimate). Other things being equal, the statistical significance of a regression coefficient increases as the sample size increases. If the data set is sufficiently large, results that are economically significant are often also statistically significant. However, when the sample size is small it is not uncommon to obtain results that are economically significant but statistically insignificant.

36. The results of any statistical or econometric analysis should also be assessed with respect to the relevant economic theory. (18) When discussing the results of a multiple regression analysis, this requirement includes assessing not only the coefficient(s) of direct interest, but also the coefficients of all other explanatory variables, as they often provide a signal on the reliability of the analysis. For example, a finding that the sign of a particular coefficient is counter to what would be expected by economic theory (19) may be an indication of an omitted-variable problem (20), a selection bias (21), or some other identification problem (22).

(18) For example, econometric estimates of the elasticity of demand for a given product implying an upward sloping demand curve should be discarded in almost all cases, unless the product in question (can be shown to be a Giffen good – i.e., a product for which a rise in price of this product makes people buy even more of the product.

(19) For example, a study showing that an increase in the marginal costs of production of a given good is associated with lower prices for that product should, ceteris paribus, be discarded automatically.

(20) That is, when a relevant explanatory variable, which is correlated with the dependent variable has been omitted from the analysis, so that the coefficients of some or all other explanatory variables suffer from a bias of a priori unknown sign or magnitude.

(21) The bias that arises when the selection process influences the availability of data in a way that is related to the dependent variable.

(22) See note 13 *supra*.

2.5. Robustness

37. Economic and econometric analysis should always be accompanied by a thorough robustness analysis, except where its absence is appropriately justified.

38. First, it is necessary to check whether empirical results are sensitive to changes in:
   (a) the data;
   (b) the choice of empirical method; and
   (c) the precise modelling assumptions (23).

Similarly an economic model should generally be accompanied by a sensitivity analysis with respect to the key variables, to the extent only the plausible but not the exact value of each variable can be determined. All results from the sensitivity analysis conducted should also be reported and not only those that support the argument.

(23) For example, in a multiple regression analysis, one should indicate whether the results are severely affected by how the variables were defined, by the set of explanatory variables incorporated to the analysis, or the functional form.

39. It is also necessary to assess and test to the extent possible whether the results of the analysis can be generalised (24).

(24) For example, if the elasticity of demand for a given product has been estimated for a given country, where data is available, but the case at hand would require estimates of the elasticity of demand for various countries, one should consider whether or not, and under which assumptions, her results for one country apply to the others. Similarly, if an economic model assumes that firms make take-it-or-leave-it offers when interacting with intermediate buyers with certain characteristics, it may be necessary to assess whether such assumption extends to all types of intermediate buyers.

40. Finally, an economic or econometric analysis should explicitly discuss whether the theory or technique has been generally accepted in the scientific community and discuss its known or potential rate of error when applied. Importantly, the model needs to be consistent and reasonably predict observed past outcomes and behaviour.

Moreover, it is expected to compare the predictions of the economic model or the results of the empirical work in question with previous analysis and results. Congruent and convergent results strongly suggest the validity of the analysis under submission, whereas discrepancies should be carefully explained.

2.6. Further recommendations

41. The credibility of an economic submission is enhanced when the limitations with regards to accuracy or explanatory power of the underlying data and methodology are explicitly acknowledged. In this regard it is often advisable to address rather than minimize uncertainty.

42. The parties rely sometimes on data that they do not have the means to audit and verify. Hence, they should be careful not to misleadingly present economic opinions as statements of fact. The sources of information should be carefully acknowledged, and the facts properly documented and described without ambiguity. This applies whether the economic or econometric analysis is a stand alone report or part of a broader submission.

43. It is advisable that the parties consult DG Competition regarding the types of empirical analyses that they consider useful in testing the anticompetitive and/or efficiencies theories. In particular, the parties can suggest potential analyses which may be easier for DG Competition to conduct, given its access to data from third parties. DG Competition, in turn, may propose analyses it believes might be useful for the parties to conduct.

44. Where economic submissions rely on quantitative data the parties should provide the data and codes timely, in an appropriate format and in accordance with the criteria laid down in section 3 of this document. In particular, the absence of all the necessary elements needed for replication and assessment of an economic submission can constitute grounds for not taking it further into consideration.

45. When granting access to the file, DG Competition shall provide upon request the data and codes underlying its final economic analysis or, to the extent that they have been made available to the Commission, that of third parties on which it intends to rely or take into account. Where necessary to protect the confidentiality of other parties' data, access to the data and codes will be granted only at DG Competition premises in a so-called data room procedure, (25) subject to strict confidentiality obligations and secure procedures (26). Third parties or complainants are equally expected to submit all the underlying data used in the analysis. They are also ex-

pected to authorise DG Competition, where appropriate, to offer data room access to the parties upon request.

(25) See DG Competition Best Practices on the conduct of proceedings concerning Articles 101 and 102, paragraph 85.

(26) Similarly, DG Competition will endeavour to organise access to a data room, normally to the parties' economic advisors and external counsel, if necessary to ensure their rights of defence are fully respected.

3. BEST PRACTICES ON RESPONDING TO REQUESTS FOR QUANTITATIVE DATA

46. Pursuant to Article 18 of Regulation 1/2003 and Article 11 of the Merger Regulation, the Commission is empowered, in order to carry out its duties, to require undertakings and associations of undertakings to provide it with all necessary information. It is the Commission that defines the scope and the format of requests for information.

47. Most competition investigations involve:
(1) collecting data;
(2) analyzing data; and
(3) drawing inferences from data. This document provides guidance to respond to a request for quantitative data (27). However, many of the principles here identified apply, more generally, to responses to any request for economic information, quantitative or qualitative.

(27) For statistical purposes, «quantitative data» means a series of observations or measurements, expressed as numbers. A statistic may refer to a particular numerical value, derived from the data. For example, an HHI measure and a correlation coefficient are statistics.

48. Quantitative data may help DG Competition to conduct statistical analysis to define markets, establish a counterfactual, assess the potential anti-competitive effects of a notified merger, validate efficiency claims or predict the impact of remedies. In order to do that DG Competition needs to get accurate data, with sufficient time to analyze it.

49. DG Competition is aware of the costs that its procedures may impose on undertakings. One of the objectives of this section is, therefore, to provide recommendations to reduce the burden on the involved parties and DG Competition posed by the production and processing of quantitative data, while at the same time ensuring and enhancing the effectiveness of DG Competition's substantive review.

50. These best practices are intended as general guidance and do not supersede any specific instructions in any data request issued by DG Competition in specific cases.

3.1. General motivation for Data Requests

51. The primary objective of a Data Request is to obtain accurate information concerning **quantitative variables** such as prices, turnover, capacity and entry or exit decisions within the possible relevant markets over a reasonable period. Quantitative data may be necessary to understand current market conditions and competitive dynamics. In some cases, reliable quantitative data may allow to conduct statistical or econometric analysis to be submitted as evidence in an antitrust or merger investigation.

52. DG Competition will endeavour to ask for the adequate amount of data required to carry out the required analyses. DG Competition is mindful of time constraints and must balance the usefulness of each request against the opportunity cost of the time the request will consume as a proportion of the time left before any legal or procedural deadline. In appropriate cases, DG Competition may discuss in advance with the addressees or other affected parties the scope and the format of the data request.

53. DG Competition will carefully consider what is the proper sample to characterize a population. Inferences from the part to the whole are justified only when the sample is representative (28).

(28) For example, in certain circumstances it may be appropriate to limit the data request to a certain representative subset of the involved firms' customers, or to a particular geographic market which stands out for a valid given reason.

54. A further issue that may influence the scope of the data request is whether third party data will be necessary and available to conduct any meaningful analysis

3.2. Common elements of a Data Request

55. Examples of data necessary for a competition investigation include data on costs, output, sales, prices, capacity, product characteristics, delivery flows, customer characteristics, tender details, entry barriers, business strategies, and market shares of the parties involved and of the other participants in the relevant market.

56. The source of the information can be the parties involved in the procedure, third parties, trade associations, trade press, independent consultants, survey information or government sources.

57. Data may be costly to collect or hardly accessible in the relevant time frame. Often, however, requests for quantitative data in merger proceedings seek data that is readily available to the involved parties. Readily available data refers to data that is routinely collected and maintained for a reasonable period as part of the firm's normal business operations, for example to inform business strategy or for internal reporting. Readily available data also includes data that is regularly purchased from third parties, such as scanner data or survey data (29). In any event, in its investigations, the Commission is not limited to request only data that is readily available to the parties (see point 74 below). Deadlines for submitting data which is difficult or costly to retrieve will be decided by the Commission on a case-by-case basis.

(29) Where econometric analyses are to be conducted, the sample needs to be of sufficient size for meaningful inference. For instance, in the absence of cross-section variability, requests would generally cover at least a three year period of monthly observations.

58. A Data Request often includes the following sections, but each request will be tailored to the specific information needs and circumstances of the case:

(i) a glossary of terms, in particular key variables;
(ii) a list of the variables;
(iii) for each variable: the units of measurement; the level of aggregation over time (e.g. monthly); the time range (e.g. the last three fiscal years) and the geographic scope (e.g. countries, regions or cities);
(iv) the preferred electronic format (stata file, excel file, etc);
(v) suggestions or specific requests on data formatting, variable classification and tests to detect data inconsistencies;
(vi) deadline for compliance with the request.

59. In some instances, particularly where data is requested from different parties, DG Competition may provide a template to ensure all submissions are compatible and can be efficiently combined with minimal risk of error.

3.3. Main criteria to consider when responding to a Data Request

60. Responses to a Data Request must be:
 (i) complete;
 (ii) correct; and
 (iii) timely.

61. The Commission may impose on undertakings and associations of undertakings fines where, intentionally or negligently, they supply incorrect or misleading information or when, in response to a request made by decision, they supply incomplete information or do not supply information within the required time-limit (30). Furthermore, in merger cases, the relevant time limits for initiating proceedings and for the adoption of decisions may exceptionally be suspended where, owing to circumstances for which one of the undertakings involved in the concentration is responsible, the Commission has had to request information by decision or to order an inspection (31).

(30) Article 23(1)(a) and (b) of Regulation 1/2003 and Article 14(1)(a), (b) and (c) of the Merger Regulation.

(31) Article 10(4) of the Merger Regulation, but see also Article 8(6) thereof.

3.3.1. Completeness

62. The parties should provide all data requested, in any of the stated formats and follow indications regarding presentation and consistency checks. Subsidiary data that is necessary to construct or to understand any variable requested should also be provided, except when adequately justified and with prior approval by DG Competition.

63. It is strongly encouraged that problems of missing data are flagged to DG Competition well in advance of the deadline for compliance with the data request to allow, if appropriate, for either a modification of the request or an extension of the deadline. Any data missing from the original data request must be adequately justified. In any event, a response to a data request may not be considered complete unless accompanied by a memo:

 (i) describing the data compilation process: from raw data through aggregation and merging operations to the final database submitted. How was the sample selected and was it necessary to eliminate certain kinds of observations;

 (ii) identifying all relevant sources;

 (iii) labelling and thoroughly describing all variables;

 (iv) reporting on the reasons for potential measurement error such as missing information or any changes in the collection process;

 (v) describing any assumptions and estimations used to fill incomplete data; and

 (vi) reporting on consistency checking and all data cleaning operations.

3.3.2. Correctness

64. It is up to interested parties to ensure the correctness of the data submitted. Tests for accuracy of all variables should always be undertaken and reported (32).

(32) For example, negative sales volumes or zero transaction prices are normally inaccurate and are often indicative of data extraction errors, systematic measurement errors or inadequate accounting of rebates or taxes.

65. In order to detect incorrectness in data it will be expected that consistency checks are performed and documented prior to submission. In particular:

 i) Responses to the data request should be consistent with responses provided to other requests for information (e.g. turnover, market shares, etc);

 ii) Individual values within a variable must be consistent with the economic reality (33);

 iii) when aggregation of raw data is necessary, one needs to ensure the aggregation algorithm is sensible and applied consistently;

 iv) coherence between different variables is necessary (34);

 v) over time consistency across and within variables must also be ensured.

(33) For example, transaction prices (net of discounts) should generally be positive, missing or unexpected values (i.e. sales not in line with historical levels) should be checked.

(34) For example, shipments of one product must be related to shipments of any by-products. Also, charged prices should generally remain above transportation costs (i.e. ex-works negative prices cast doubts on either the correctness of the charged price and/or the transportation cost).

3.3.3. Timely submission

66. Deadlines for responses to data requests must be strictly respected. Where parties plan to submit data in connection with an empirical analysis conducted at their own initiative, it is useful to warn in advance DG Competition of the planned timing and scope of such a submission. Results that the parties intend to rely upon or discuss in a meeting with DG Competition should be submitted, including data and code to facilitate replication, at least 2 working days before the said meeting.

3.4. Other Recommendations

67. This section sets down further recommended best practices concerning responses to a data request.

3.4.1. Cooperation in good-faith

68. Data production is an area where cooperation between the parties and DG Competition is especially important. The parties will need to explain clearly the complexities that can be associated with requests that DG Competition may regard as simple. (35) DG Competition endeavours to define its requests as specifically and quickly as possible so the parties can understand what is being sought and why. This dialogue may help both sides deal more efficiently with data issues. In any event, it is for DG Competition to decide the scope, format and timing of the data request.

(35) Why, for example, it may be difficult, impossible or useless to simply «turn over» a «database,» or the burdens and costs associated with providing data in the precise manner DG Competition seeks.

69. It is important to emphasise in that regard that the integrity and efficiency of the process are undermined if, inter alia, the parties make representations about what data exist without reasonably diligent efforts to confirm their accuracy, if they ignore a carefully drafted and limited data request and produce large amounts of data points disregarding the submission format, scope, or data processing requirements, if they use non-obvious «definitions» of common terms in construing requests, or if they make unilateral and undisclosed inferences about what DG Competition is effectively seeking.

3.4.2. Early consultation with DG Competition to inform about what type of data is available

70. In some cases, the burden of compliance with data requests may be significantly reduced if the parties inform DG Competition at the earliest opportunity on the availability of quantitative data. Early consultation allows to determine not only what data is available and its suitability, but also in what form it can be provided, thereby making it easier and faster for the parties to provide the data, in the event DG Competition makes a data request. However, the Commission is not limited to request only data that is readily available to the parties.

71. To make these early discussions fruitful, parties must be prepared to thoroughly explain their information management systems and should be prepared to discuss certain issues such as: every field of information captured, how the underlying data is collected and formatted, the frequency of collection, what software is used, the size of the data set, what reports are routinely generated from that database, etc. It is recommended that the involved firms provide any written documentation and/or training materials to DG Competition in advance of any discussion. It is also generally useful that parties create a diagram to show how the relevant data is distributed throughout the organization. In any event, as a general rule, parties should provide relevant documents to support their contentions concerning the availability, scope and production time of quantitative data.

72. Preliminary meetings or telephone conversations with those responsible for data collection or analysis in the firms are often quite useful. Parties should make such personnel available as early as possible. These discussions should involve descriptions of the type of electronic (or other) data that the parties maintain (both in the ordinary course of business and what is archived, and in what form).

73. In the case of mergers, pre-notification discussions should routinely deal with data issues. Although, DG Competition will endeavour to identify all issues that may require a data request as soon as possible, certain issues may not be identified until later in the proceedings.

3.4.3. Consultation on a Draft Data Requests and data samples

74. When appropriate and useful, DG Competition will send a «draft» data request for quantitative data in order to facilitate a better identification of the format, and to allow for basic consistency checks (see section 3.3.2). The purpose of the draft data request is to invite parties to propose any modifications that could alleviate the compliance burden while producing the necessary information. Any reduction on the scope of the data request can only be accepted if it does not risk harming the investigation and may trigger, particularly in merger cases, a reduction in the deadline for response initially anticipated.

75. In this connection, providing samples of the data is generally very helpful as it helps DG Competition to determine what data is available and would be useful. As a result, on the basis of the sample it may be possible to draft a more focused data request, limiting the eventual burden on the parties.

3.4.4. Transparency regarding data collection, formatting and submission

76. A transparent process allows for all parties involved to be aware of any incidences during the data collection process and thus react more rapidly and effectively.

77. The parties must take care that quantitative data is submitted in a format that minimises the time and manipulation required to process the data for analysis. Parties should always be able to answer all the following questions:

i) how applicable is the data to the analyses under consideration;

ii) how reliable or «clean» is the data;

iii) is it enough to conduct a meaningful analysis;

iv) what institutional factors specific to the industry setting and/or company may impact the proper interpretation of the data.

78. The involved parties must draw DG Competition's attention early on to any limitations in the data. They should make clear how raw data has been compiled and what steps have been taken to ensure its reliability (36).

(36) For example, if the raw data is based on a sample of individual customer accounts, an explanation of how these accounts have been chosen and why they are representative of all customers should also be provided.

79. The involved parties are also strongly encouraged to conduct their own descriptive analysis to detect data problems before submitting the data to DG Competition. Also DG Competition may sometimes welcome efforts by the involved parties to deal with any remaining data imperfections using statistical analysis. In some cases statistics allows in various ways to average out errors in measurement and yield statistically sound estimates. All such statistical analysis should be adequately reported. In any event, raw data should be provided wherever possible because the aggregation and cleaning of data may have a significant impact on the outcome of statistical or econometric analysis. Also parties should provide the program files that manipulate, clean and complete the raw data in preparation for the analysis.

3.4.5. Direct access

80. In some instances, DG Competition will accept that as part of its response to a Data Request the involved parties provide direct electronic access to the underlying data. This alternative can provide an inexpensive and fast way to provide access to large amounts of data. Limited direct access can also provide a means to assess the value of certain corporate information.

81. The terms and conditions for direct access can be discussed in advance, addressing issues such as the availability of technical assistance, the ability to print or otherwise retrieve the data, the number of log-ins the company should provide, assurances that the activities of the services of DG Competition will not be tracked, that underlying data will not be removed without agreement of DG Competition and, most importantly, continued access throughout the entire course of the investigation. In limited instances, when providing direct access to corporate resources is unworkable, DG Competition may submit a set of queries to the firm so that reports can be generated.

Annex 1
Structure and basic elements of a sound empirical submission

(...)
🔍 **1.** – Not included

Commission Notice on co-operation within the Network of Competition Authorities
(OJ C 101, 27 April 2004, p. 43)

1. Article 81 EC is now Article 101 TFEU and Article 82 EC is now Article 102 TFEU.

1. INTRODUCTION

1. Council Regulation (EC) N° 1/2003 of 16 December 2002 on the implementation of the rules on competition laid down in Articles 81 and 82 of the Treaty (1) (hereafter the «Council Regulation») creates a system of parallel competences in which the Commission and the Member States' competition authorities (hereafter the «NCAs») (2) can apply Article 81 and Article 82 of the EC Treaty (hereafter the «Treaty»). Together the NCAs and the Commission form a network of public authorities: they act in the public interest and co-operate closely in order to protect competition. The network is a forum for discussion and cooperation in the application and enforcement of EC competition policy. It provides a framework for the co-operation of European competition authorities in cases where Articles 81 and 82 of the Treaty are applied and is the basis for the creation and maintenance of a common competition culture in Europe. The network is called «European Competition Network» (ECN).

(1) *O.J.* L 1, 4.1.2003, p. 1.

(2) In this notice, the European Commission and the NCAs are collectively referred to as «the competition authorities».

2. The structure of the NCAs varies between Member States. In some Member States, one body investigates cases and takes all types of decisions. In other Member States, the functions are divided between two bodies, one which is in charge of the investigation of the case and another, often a college, which is responsible for deciding the case. Finally, in certain Member States, prohibition decisions and/or decisions imposing a fine can only be taken by a court: another competition authority acts as a prosecutor bringing the case before that court. Subject to the general principle of effectiveness, Article 35 of the Council Regulation allows Member States to choose the body or bodies which will be designated as national competition authorities and to allocate functions between them. Under general principles of Community law, Member States are under an obligation to set up a sanctioning system providing for sanctions which are effective, proportionate and dissuasive for infringements of EC law (3). The enforcement systems of the Member States differ but they have recognised the standards of each other's systems as a basis for co-operation (4).

(3) Cf. ECJ case 68/88 – Commission v. Greece [1989] ECR 2965 (recitals 23 to 25).

(4) See paragraph 8 of the Joint Statement of the Council and the Commission on the functioning of the network available from the Council register at http://register.consilium.eu.int (document N° 15435/02 ADD 1).

3. The network formed by the competition authorities should ensure both an efficient division of work and an effective and consistent application of EC competition rules. The Council Regulation together with the joint statement of the Council and the Commission on the functioning of the European Competition Network sets out the main principles of the functioning of the network. This notice presents the details of the system.

4. Consultations and exchanges within the network are matters between public enforcers and do not alter any rights or obligations arising from Community or national law for companies. Each competition authority remains fully responsible for ensuring due process in the cases it deals with.

2. DIVISION OF WORK

2.1. Principles of allocation

5. The Council Regulation is based on a system of parallel competences in which all competition authorities have the power to apply Articles 81 or 82 of the Treaty and are responsible for an efficient division of work with respect to those cases where an investigation is deemed to be necessary. At the same time each network member retains full discretion in deciding whether or not to investigate a case. Under this system of parallel competences, cases will be dealt with by:

– a single NCA, possibly with the assistance of NCAs of other Member States; or
– several NCAs acting in parallel; or
– the Commission.

6. In most instances the authority that receives a complaint or starts an *ex-officio* procedure (5) will remain in charge of the case. Re-allocation of a case would only be envisaged at the outset of a procedure (see paragraph 18 below) where either that authority considered that it was not well placed to act or where other authorities also considered themselves well placed to act (see paragraphs 8 to 15 below).

(5) In this Notice the term «procedure» is used for investigations and/or formal proceedings for the adoption of a decision pursuant to the Council Regulation conducted by an NCA or the Commission, as the case may be.

7. Where re-allocation is found to be necessary for an effective protection of competition and of the Community interest, network members will endeavour to re-allocate cases to a single well placed competition authority as often as possible (6). In any event, re-allocation should be a quick and efficient process and not hold up ongoing investigations.

(6) See Recital 18 of the Council Regulation.

8. An authority can be considered to be well placed to deal with a case if the following three cumulative conditions are met:

1. the agreement or practice has substantial direct actual or foreseeable effects on competition within its territory, is implemented within or originates from its territory;

2. the authority is able to effectively bring to an end the entire infringement, i.e. it can adopt a cease-and-desist order the effect of which will be sufficient to bring an end to the infringement and it can, where appropriate, sanction the infringement adequately;

3. it can gather, possibly with the assistance of other authorities, the evidence required to prove the infringement.

9. The above criteria indicate that a material link between the infringement and the territory of a Member State must exist in order for that Member State's competition authority to be considered well placed. It can be expected that in most cases the authorities of those Member States where competition is substantially affected by an infringement will be well placed provided they are capable of effectively bringing the infringement to an end through either single or parallel action unless the Commission is better placed to act (see below paragraphs 14 and 15).

10. It follows that a single NCA is usually well placed to deal with agreements or practices that substantially affect competition mainly within its territory.

Example 1: *Undertakings situated in Member State A are involved in a price fixing cartel on products that are mainly sold in Member State A.*

The NCA in A is well placed to deal with the case.

11. Furthermore single action of an NCA might also be appropriate where, although more than one NCA can be regarded as well placed, the action of a single NCA is sufficient to bring the entire infringement to an end.

Example 2: *Two undertakings have set up a joint venture in Member State A. The joint venture provides services in Member States A and B and gives rise to a competition problem. A cease-and-desist order is considered to be sufficient to deal with the case effectively because it can bring an end to the entire infringement. Evidence is located mainly at the offices of the joint venture in Member State A. The NCAs in A and B are both well placed to deal with the case but single action by the NCA in A would be sufficient and more efficient than single action by NCA in B or parallel action by both NCAs.*

12. Parallel action by two or three NCAs may be appropriate where an agreement or practice has substantial effects on competition mainly in their respective territories and the action of only one NCA would not be sufficient to bring the entire infringement to an end and/or to sanction it adequately.

Example 3: *Two undertakings agree on a market sharing agreement, restricting the activity of the company located in Member State A to Member State A and the activity of the company located in Member State B to Member State B. The NCAs in A and B are well placed to deal with the case in parallel, each one for its respective territory.*

13. The authorities dealing with a case in parallel action will endeavour to coordinate their action to the extent possible. To that effect, they may find it useful to designate one of them as a lead authority and to delegate tasks to the lead authority such as for example the coordination of investigative measures, while each authority remains responsible for conducting its own proceedings.

14. The Commission is particularly well placed if one or several agreement(s) or practice(s), including networks of similar agreements or practices, have effects on competition in more than three Member States (crossborder markets covering more than three Member States or several national markets).

Example 4: *Two undertakings agree to share markets or fix prices for the whole territory of the Community. The Commission is well placed to deal with the case.*

Example 5: *An undertaking, dominant in four different national markets, abuses its position by imposing fidelity rebates on its distributors in all these markets. The Commission is well placed to deal with the case. It could also deal with one national market so as to create a «leading» case and other national markets could be dealt with by NCAs, particularly if each national market requires a separate assessment.*

15. Moreover, the Commission is particularly well placed to deal with a case if it is closely linked to other Community provisions which may be exclusively or more effectively applied by the Commission, if the Community interest requires the adoption of a Commission decision to develop Community competition policy when a new competition issue arises or to ensure effective enforcement.

2.2. Mechanisms of co-operation for the purpose of case allocation and assistance

2.2.1. Information at the beginning of the procedure (Article 11 of the Council Regulation)

16. In order to detect multiple procedures and to ensure that cases are dealt with by a well placed competition authority, the members of the network have to be informed at an early stage of the cases pending before the various competition authorities (7). If a case is to be re-allocated, it is indeed in the best interest both of the network and of the undertakings concerned that the re-allocation takes place quickly.

(7) For cases initiated following a leniency application see paragraphs 37 et subseq.

17. The Council Regulation creates a mechanism for the competition authorities to inform each other in order to ensure an efficient and quick re-allocation of cases. Article 11(3) of the Council Regulation lays down an obligation for NCAs to inform the Commission when acting under Article 81 or 82 of the Treaty before or without delay after commencing the first formal investigative measure. It also states that the information may be made available to other NCAs (8). The rationale of Article 11(3) of the Council Regulation is to allow the network to detect multiple procedures and address possible case re-allocation issues as soon as an authority starts investigating a case. Information should therefore be provided to NCAs and the Commission before or just after any step similar to the measures of investigation that can be undertaken by the Commission under Articles 18 to 21 of the Council Regulation. The Commission has accepted an equivalent obligation to inform NCAs under Article 11(2) of the Council Regulation. Network members will inform each other of pending cases by means of a standard form containing limited details of the case, such as the authority dealing with the case, the product, territories and parties concerned, the alleged infringement, the suspected duration of the infringement and the origin of the case. They will also provide each other with updates when a relevant change occurs.

(8) The intention of making any information exchanged pursuant to Article 11 available and easily accessible to all network members is however expressed in the Joint Statement on the functioning of the network mentioned above in footnote 4.

18. Where case re-allocation issues arise, they should be resolved swiftly, normally within a period of two months, starting from the date of the first information sent to the network pursuant to Article 11 of the Council Regulation. During this period, competition authorities will endeavour to reach an agreement on a possible re-allocation and, where relevant, on the modalities for parallel action.

19. In general, the competition authority or authorities that is/are dealing with a case at the end of the re-allocation period should continue to deal with the case until the completion of the proceedings. Re-allocation of a case after the initial allocation period of two months should only occur where the facts known about the case change materially during the course of the proceedings.

2.2.2. Suspension or termination of proceedings (Article 13 of the Council Regulation)

20. If the same agreement or practice is brought before several competition authorities, be it because they have received a complaint or have opened a procedure on their own initiative, Article 13 of the Council Regulation provides a legal basis for suspending proceedings or rejecting a complaint on the grounds that another authority is dealing with the case or has dealt with the case. In Article 13 of the Council Regulation, «dealing with the case» does not merely mean that a complaint has been lodged with another authority. It means that the other authority is investigating or has investigated the case on its own behalf.

21. Article 13 of the Council Regulation applies when another authority has dealt or is dealing with the competition issue raised by the complainant, even if the authority in question has acted or acts on the basis of a complaint lodged by a different complainant or as a result of an *ex-officio* procedure. This implies that Article 13 of the Council Regulation can be invoked when the agreement or practice involves the same infringement(s) on the same relevant geographic and product markets.

22. An NCA may suspend or close its proceedings but it has no obligation to do so. Article 13 of the Council Regulation leaves scope for appreciation of the peculiarities of each individual case. This flexibility is important: if a complaint was rejected by an authority following an investigation of the substance of the case, another authority may not want to re-examine the case. On the other hand, if a complaint was rejected for other reasons (e.g. the authority was unable to collect the evidence necessary to prove the infringement), another authority may wish to carry out its own investigation and deal with the case. This flexibility is also reflected, for pending cases, in the choice open to each NCA as to whether it closes or suspends its proceedings. An authority may be unwilling to close a case before the outcome of another authority's proceedings is clear. The ability to suspend its proceedings allows the authority to retain its ability to decide at a later point whether or not to terminate its proceedings. Such flexibility also facilitates consistent application of the rules.

23. Where an authority closes or suspends proceedings because another authority is dealing with the case, it may transfer – in accordance with Article 12 of the Council Regulation – the information provided by the complainant to the authority which is to deal with the case.

24. Article 13 of the Council Regulation can also be applied to part of a complaint or to part of the proceedings in a case. It may be that only part of a complaint or of an *ex-officio* procedure overlaps with a case already dealt or being dealt with by another competition authority. In that case, the competition authority to which the complaint is brought is entitled to reject part of the complaint on the basis of Article 13 of the Council Regulation and to deal with the rest of the complaint in an appropriate manner. The same principle applies to the termination of proceedings.

25. Article 13 of the Council Regulation is not the only legal basis for suspending or closing *ex-officio* proceedings or rejecting complaints. NCAs may also be able to do so according to their national procedural law. The Commission may also reject a complaint for lack of Community interest or other reasons pertaining to the nature of the complaint (9).

(9) See Commission notice on complaints.

2.2.3. Exchange and use of confidential information (Article 12 of the Council Regulation)

26. A key element of the functioning of the network is the power of all the competition authorities to exchange and use information (including documents, statements and digital information) which has been collected by them for the purpose of applying Article 81 or Article 82 of the Treaty. This power is a precondition for efficient and effective allocation and handling of cases.

27. Article 12 of the Council Regulation states that for the purpose of applying Articles 81 and 82 of the Treaty, the Commission and the competition authorities of the Member States shall have the power to provide one another with and use in evidence any matter of fact or of law, including confidential information. This means that exchanges of information may not only take place between an NCA and the Commission but also between and amongst NCAs. Article 12 of the Council Regulation takes precedence over any contrary law of a Member State. The question whether information was gathered in a legal manner by the transmitting authority is governed on the basis of the law applicable to this authority. When transmitting information the transmitting authority may inform the receiving authority whether the gathering of the information was contested or could still be contested.

28. The exchange and use of information contains in particular the following safeguards for undertakings and individuals.

(a) First, Article 28 of the Council Regulation states that «the Commission and the competition authorities of the Member States, their officials, servants and other persons working under the supervision of these authorities (…) shall not disclose information acquired or exchanged by them pursuant to the» Council Regulation which is «of the kind covered by the obligation of professional secrecy». However, the legitimate interest of undertakings in the protection of their business secrets may not prejudice the disclosure of information necessary to prove an infringement of Articles 81 and 82 of the Treaty. The term «professional secrecy» used in Article 28 of the Council Regulation is a Community law concept and includes in particular business secrets and other confidential information. This will create a common minimum level of protection throughout the Community.

(b) The second safeguard given to undertakings relates to the use of information which has been exchanged

within the network. Under Article 12(2) of the Council Regulation, information so exchanged can only be used in evidence for the application of Articles 81 and 82 of the Treaty and for the subject matter for which it was collected (10). According to Article 12(2) of the Council Regulation, the information exchanged may also be used for the purpose of applying national competition law in parallel in the same case. This is, however, only possible if the application of national law does not lead to an outcome as regards the finding of an infringement different from that under Articles 81 and 82 of the Treaty.

(c) The third safeguard given by the Council Regulation relates to sanctions on individuals on the basis of information exchanged pursuant to Article 12(1). The Council Regulation only provides for sanctions on undertakings for violations of Articles 81 and 82 of the Treaty. Some national laws also provide for sanctions on individuals in connection with violations of Articles 81 and 82 of the Treaty. Individuals normally enjoy more extensive rights of defence (e.g. a right to remain silent compared to undertakings which may only refuse to answer questions which would lead them to admit that they have committed an infringement (11)). Article 12(3) of the Council Regulation ensures that information collected from undertakings cannot be used in a way which would circumvent the higher protection of individuals. This provision precludes sanctions being imposed on individuals on the basis of information exchanged pursuant to the Council Regulation if the laws of the transmitting and the receiving authorities do not provide for sanctions of a similar kind in respect of individuals, unless the rights of the individual concerned as regards the collection of evidence have been respected by the transmitting authority to the same standard as they are guaranteed by the receiving authority. The qualification of the sanctions by national law («administrative» or «criminal») is not relevant for the purpose of applying Article 12(3) of the Council Regulation. The Council Regulation intends to create a distinction between sanctions which result in custody and other types of sanctions such as fines on individuals and other personal sanctions. If both the legal system of the transmitting and that of the receiving authority provide for sanctions of a similar kind (e.g. in both Member States, fines can be imposed on a member of the staff of an undertaking who has been involved in the violation of Article 81 or 82 of the Treaty), information exchanged pursuant to Article 12 of the Council Regulation can be used by the receiving authority. In that case, procedural safeguards in both systems are considered to be equivalent. If on the other hand, both legal systems do not provide for sanctions of a similar kind, the information can only be used if the same level of protection of the rights of the individual has been respected in the case at hand (see Article 12(3) of the Council Regulation). In that latter case however, custodial sanctions can only be imposed where both the transmitting and the receiving authority have the power to impose such a sanction.

(10) See ECJ case 85/87 – Dow Benelux, [1989] ECR 3137 (recitals 17-20).

(11) See ECJ case 374/87 – Orkem [1989] ECR 3283 and CFI, case T-112/98 – Mannesmannröhren-Werke AG, [2001] ECR II-729.

2.2.4. Investigations (Article 22 of the Council Regulation)

29. The Council Regulation provides that an NCA may ask another NCA for assistance in order to collect information on its behalf. An NCA can ask another NCA to carry out fact-finding measures on its behalf. Article 12 of the Council Regulation empowers the assisting NCA to transmit the information it has collected to the requesting NCA. Any exchange between or amongst NCAs and use in evidence by the requesting NCA of such information shall be carried out in accordance with Article 12 of the Council Regulation. Where an NCA acts on behalf of another NCA, it acts pursuant to its own rules of procedure, and under its own powers of investigation.

30. Under Article 22(2) of the Council Regulation, the Commission can ask an NCA to carry out an inspection on its behalf. The Commission can either adopt a decision pursuant to Article 20(4) of the Council Regulation or simply issue a request to the NCA. The NCA officials will exercise their powers in accordance with their national law. The agents of the Commission may assist the NCA during the inspection.

2.3. Position of undertakings

2.3.1. General

31. All network members will endeavour to make the allocation of cases a quick and efficient process. Given the fact that the Council Regulation has created a system of parallel competences, the allocation of cases between members of the network constitutes a mere division of labour where some authorities abstain from acting. The allocation of cases therefore does not create individual rights for the companies involved in or affected by an infringement to have the case dealt with by a particular authority.

32. If a case is re-allocated to a given competition authority, it is because the application of the allocation criteria set out above led to the conclusion that this authority is well placed to deal with the case by single or parallel action. The competition authority to which the case is re-allocated would have been in a position, in any event, to commence an *ex-officio* procedure against the infringement.

33. Furthermore, all competition authorities apply Community competition law and the Council Regulation sets out mechanisms to ensure that the rules are applied in a consistent way.

34. If a case is re-allocated within the network, the undertakings concerned and the complainant(s) are informed as soon as possible by the competition authorities involved.

2.3.2. Position of complainants

35. If a complaint is lodged with the Commission pursuant to Article 7 of the Council Regulation and if the Commission does not investigate the complaint or prohibit the agreement or practice complained of, the complainant has a right to obtain a decision rejecting his complaint. This is without prejudice to Article 7(3) of the Commission implementing regulation (12). The rights of complainants who lodge a complaint with an NCA are governed by the applicable national law.

(12) Commission Regulation (EC) N° 773/2004, O.J. L 123, 27.4.2004.

36. In addition, Article 13 of the Council Regulation gives all NCAs the possibility of suspending or rejecting a complaint on the ground that another competition authority is dealing or has dealt with the same case. That provision also allows the Commission to reject a complaint on the ground that a competition authority of a Member State is dealing or has dealt with the case. Article 12 of the Council Regula-

2.3.3. Position of applicants claiming the benefit of a leniency programme

37. The Commission considers (13) that it is in the Community interest to grant favourable treatment to undertakings which co-operate with it in the investigation of cartel infringements. A number of Member States have also adopted leniency programmes (14) relating to cartel investigations. The aim of these leniency programmes is to facilitate the detection by competition authorities of cartel activity and also thereby to act as a deterrent to participation in unlawful cartels.

(13) O.J. C 45, 19.2.2002, p. 3 at paragraph 3.

(14) In this Notice, the term «leniency programme» is used to describe all programmes (including the Commission's programme) which offer either full immunity or a significant reduction in the penalties which would otherwise have been imposed on a participant in a cartel, in exchange for the freely volunteered disclosure of information on the cartel which satisfies specific criteria prior to or during the investigative stage of the case. The term does not cover reductions in the penalty granted for other reasons. The Commission will publish on its website a list of those authorities that operate a leniency programme.

38. In the absence of a European Union-wide system of fully harmonised leniency programmes, an application for leniency to a given authority is not to be considered as an application for leniency to any other authority. It is therefore in the interest of the applicant to apply for leniency to all competition authorities which have competence to apply Article 81 of the Treaty in the territory which is affected by the infringement and which may be considered well placed to act against the infringement in question (15). In view of the importance of timing in most existing leniency programmes, applicants will also need to consider whether it would be appropriate to file leniency applications with the relevant authorities simultaneously. It is for the applicant to take the steps which it considers appropriate to protect its position with respect to possible proceedings by these authorities.

(15) See paragraphs 8 to 15 above.

39. As for all cases where Articles 81 and 82 of the Treaty are applied, where an NCA deals with a case which has been initiated as a result of a leniency application, it must inform the Commission and may make the information available to other members of the network pursuant to Article 11(3) of the Council Regulation (cf. paragraphs 16 et subseq.). The Commission has accepted an equivalent obligation to inform NCAs under Article 11(2) of the Council Regulation. In such cases, however, information submitted to the network pursuant to Article 11 will not be used by other members of the network as the basis for starting an investigation on their own behalf whether under the competition rules of the Treaty or, in the case of NCAs, under their national competition law or other laws (16). This is without prejudice to any power of the authority to open an investigation on the basis of information received from other sources or, subject to paragraphs 40 and 41 below, to request, be provided with and use information pursuant to Article 12 from any member of the network, including the network member to whom the leniency application was submitted.

(16) Similarly, information transmitted with a view to obtaining assistance from the receiving authority under Articles 20 or 21 of the Council Regulation or of carrying out an investigation or other fact-finding measure under Article 22 of the Council Regulation may only be used for the purpose of the application of the said Articles.

40. Save as provided under paragraph 41, information voluntarily submitted by a leniency applicant will only be transmitted to another member of the network pursuant to Article 12 of the Council Regulation with the consent of the applicant. Similarly other information that has been obtained during or following an inspection or by means of or following any other fact-finding measures which, in each case, could not have been carried out except as a result of the leniency application will only be transmitted to another authority pursuant to Article 12 of the Council Regulation if the applicant has consented to the transmission to that authority of information it has voluntarily submitted in its application for leniency. The network members will encourage leniency applicants to give such consent, in particular as regards disclosure to authorities in respect of which it would be open to the applicant to obtain lenient treatment. Once the leniency applicant has given consent to the transmission of information to another authority, that consent may not be withdrawn. This paragraph is without prejudice, however, to the responsibility of each applicant to file leniency applications to whichever authorities it may consider appropriate.

41. Notwithstanding the above, the consent of the applicant for the transmission of information to another authority pursuant to Article 12 of the Council Regulation is not required in any of the following circumstances:

1. No consent is required where the receiving authority has also received a leniency application relating to the same infringement from the same applicant as the transmitting authority, provided that at the time the information is transmitted it is not open to the applicant to withdraw the information which it has submitted to that receiving authority.

2. No consent is required where the receiving authority has provided a written commitment that neither the information transmitted to it nor any other information it may obtain following the date and time of transmission as noted by the transmitting authority, will be used by it or by any other authority to which the information is subsequently transmitted to impose sanctions:

(a) on the leniency applicant;

(b) on any other legal or natural person covered by the favourable treatment offered by the transmitting authority as a result of the application made by the applicant under its leniency programme;

(c) on any employee or former employee of any of the persons covered by *(a)* or *(b)*.

A copy of the receiving authority's written commitment will be provided to the applicant.

3. In the case of information collected by a network member under Article 22(1) of the Council Regulation on behalf of and for the account of the network member to whom the leniency application was made, no consent is required for the transmission of such information to, and its use by, the network member to whom the application was made.

42. Information relating to cases initiated as a result of a leniency application and which has been submitted to the Commission under Article 11(3) of the Council Regulation (17) will only be made available to those NCAs that have committed themselves to respecting the principles set out above (see paragraph 72). The same principle applies where a case has been initiated by the Commission as a result of a leniency application made to the Commission. This does not affect the power of any authority to be provided with information under Article 12 of the Council

Regulation, provided however that the provisions of paragraphs 40 and 41 are respected.

(17) See paragraph 17.

3. CONSISTENT APPLICATION OF EC COMPETITION RULES (18)

(18) Article 15 of the Council Regulation empowers NCAs and the Commission to submit written and, with the permission of the Court, oral submissions in court proceedings for the application of Articles 81 and 82 of the Treaty. This is a very important tool for ensuring consistent application of Community rules. In exercising this power NCAs and the Commission will cooperate closely.

3.1. Mechanism of co-operation (Article 11(4) and 11(5) of the Council Regulation)

43. The Council Regulation pursues the objective that Articles 81 and 82 of the Treaty are applied in a consistent manner throughout the Community. In this respect NCAs will respect the convergence rule contained in Article 3(2) of the Council Regulation. In line with Article 16(2) they cannot – when ruling on agreements, decisions and practices under Article 81 or Article 82 of the Treaty which are already the subject of a Commission decision – take decisions, which would run counter to the decisions adopted by the Commission. Within the network of competition authorities the Commission, as the guardian of the Treaty, has the ultimate but not the sole responsibility for developing policy and safeguarding consistency when it comes to the application of EC competition law.

44. According to Article 11(4) of the Council Regulation, no later than 30 days before the adoption of a decision applying Articles 81 or 82 of the Treaty and requiring that an infringement be brought to an end, accepting commitments or withdrawing the benefit of a blockexemption regulation, NCAs shall inform the Commission. They have to send to the Commission, at the latest 30 days before the adoption of the decision, a summary of the case, the envisaged decision or, in the absence thereof, any other document indicating the proposed course of action.

45. As under Article 11(3) of the Council Regulation, the obligation is to inform the Commission, but the information may be shared by the NCA informing the Commission with the other members of the network.

46. Where an NCA has informed the Commission pursuant to Article 11(4) of the Council Regulation and the 30 days deadline has expired, the decision can be adopted as long as the Commission has not initiated proceedings. The Commission may make written observations on the case before the adoption of the decision by the NCA. The NCA and the Commission will make the appropriate efforts to ensure the consistent application of Community law (cf. paragraph 3 above).

47. If special circumstances require that a national decision is taken in less than 30 days following the transmission of information pursuant to Article 11(4) of the Council Regulation, the NCA concerned may ask the Commission for a swifter reaction. The Commission will endeavour to react as quickly as possible.

48. Other types of decisions, i.e. decisions rejecting complaints, decisions closing an *ex-officio* procedure or decisions ordering interim measures, can also be important from a competition policy point of view, and the network members may have an interest in informing each other about them and possibly discussing them. NCAs can therefore on the basis of Article 11(5) of the Council Regulation inform the Commission and thereby inform the network of any other case in which EC competition law is applied.

49. All members of the network should inform each other about the closure of their procedures which have been notified to the network pursuant to Article 11(2) and (3) of the Council Regulation (19).

(19) See paragraph 24 of the Joint Statement on the functioning of the network mentioned above in footnote 4.

3.2. The initiation of proceedings by the Commission under Article 11(6) of the Council Regulation

50. According to the case law of the Court of Justice, the Commission, entrusted by Article 85(1) of the Treaty with the task of ensuring the application of the principles laid down in Articles 81 and 82 of the Treaty, is responsible for defining and implementing the orientation of Community competition policy (20). It can adopt individual decisions under Articles 81 and 82 of the Treaty at any time.

(20) See ECJ case C-344/98 – Masterfoods Ltd, [2000] ECR I-11369.

51. Article 11(6) of the Council Regulation states that the initiation by the Commission of proceedings for the adoption of a decision under the Council Regulation shall relieve all NCAs of their competence to apply Articles 81 and 82 of the Treaty. This means that once the Commission has opened proceedings, NCAs cannot act under the same legal basis against the same agreement(s) or practice(s) by the same undertaking(s) on the same relevant geographic and product market.

52. The initiation of proceedings by the Commission is a formal act (21) by which the Commission indicates its intention to adopt a decision under Chapter III of the Council Regulation. It can occur at any stage of the investigation of the case by the Commission. The mere fact that the Commission has received a complaint is not in itself sufficient to relieve NCAs of their competence.

(21) The ECJ has defined that concept in the case 48/72 – SA Brasserie de Haecht, [1973] ECR 77: «the initiation of a procedure within the meaning of Article 9 of Regulation N° 17 implies an authoritative act of the Commission, evidencing its intention of taking a decision.»

53. Two situations can arise. First, where the Commission is the first competition authority to initiate proceedings in a case for the adoption of a decision under the Council Regulation, national competition authorities may no longer deal with the case. Article 11(6) of the Council Regulation provides that once the Commission has initiated proceedings, the NCAs can no longer start their own procedure with a view to applying Articles 81 and 82 of the Treaty to the same agreement(s) or practice(s) by the same undertaking(s) on the same relevant geographic and product market.

54. The second situation is where one or more NCAs have informed the network pursuant to Article 11(3) of the Council Regulation that they are acting on a given case. During the initial allocation period (indicative time period of two months, see paragraph 18 above), the Commission can initiate proceedings with the effects of Article 11(6) of the Council Regulation after having consulted the authorities concerned. After the allocation phase, the Commission will in principle only apply Article 11(6) of the Council Regulation if one of the following situations arises:

  (a) Network members envisage conflicting decisions in the same case.

  (b) Network members envisage a decision which is obviously in conflict with consolidated case law; the standards defined in the judgements of the Community courts and in previous decisions and regulations of the Commission should serve as a yardstick; concerning the assessment of the facts (e.g. market definition), only a significant divergence will trigger an intervention of the Commission;

  (c) Network member(s) is (are) unduly drawing out proceedings in the case;

  (d) There is a need to adopt a Commission decision to develop Community competition policy in particular when a similar competition issue arises in several Member States or to ensure effective enforcement;

  (e) The NCA(s) concerned do not object.

55. If an NCA is already acting on a case, the Commission will explain the reasons for the application of Article 11(6) of the Council Regulation in writing to the NCA concerned and to the other members of the Network (22).

(22) See paragraph 22 of the Joint Statement mentioned above in footnote 4.

56. The Commission will announce to the network its intention of applying Article 11(6) of the Council Regulation in due time, so that Network members will have the possibility of asking for a meeting of the Advisory Committee on the matter before the Commission initiates proceedings.

57. The Commission will normally not – and to the extent that Community interest is not at stake – adopt a decision which is in conflict with a decision of an NCA after proper information pursuant to both Article 11(3) and (4) of the Council Regulation has taken place and the Commission has not made use of Article 11(6) of the Council Regulation.

4. THE ROLE AND THE FUNCTIONING OF THE ADVISORY COMMITTEE IN THE NEW SYSTEM

58. The Advisory Committee is the forum where experts from the various competition authorities discuss individual cases and general issues of Community competition law (23).

(23) In accordance with Article 14(2) of the Council Regulation, where horizontal issues such as block-exemption regulations and guidelines are being discussed, Member States can appoint an additional representative competent in competition matters and who does not necessarily belong to the competition authority.

4.1. Scope of the consultation

4.1.1. Decisions of the Commission

59. The Advisory Committee is consulted prior to the Commission taking any decision pursuant to Articles 7, 8, 9, 10, 23, 24(2) or 29(1) of the Council Regulation. The Commission must take the utmost account of the opinion of the Advisory Committee and inform the Committee of the manner in which its opinion has been taken into account.

60. For decisions adopting interim measures, the Advisory Committee is consulted following a swifter and lighter procedure, on the basis of a short explanatory note and the operative part of the decision.

4.1.2. Decisions of NCAs

61. It is in the interest of the network that important cases dealt with by NCAs under Articles 81 and 82 of the Treaty can be discussed in the Advisory Committee. The Council Regulation enables the Commission to put a given case being dealt with by an NCA on the agenda of the Advisory Committee. Discussion can be requested by the Commission or by any Member State. In either case, the Commission will put the case on the agenda after having informed the NCA(s) concerned. This discussion in the Advisory Committee will not lead to a formal opinion.

62. In important cases, the Advisory Committee could also serve as a forum for the discussion of case allocation. In particular, where the Commission intends to apply Article 11(6) of the Council Regulation after the initial allocation period, the case can be discussed in the Advisory Committee before the Commission initiates proceedings. The Advisory Committee may issue an informal statement on the matter.

4.1.3. Implementing measures, block-exemption regulations, guidelines and other notices (Article 33 of the Council Regulation)

63. The Advisory Committee will be consulted on draft Commission regulations as provided for in the relevant Council Regulations.

64. Beside regulations, the Commission may also adopt notices and guidelines. These more flexible tools are very useful for explaining and announcing the Commission's policy, and for explaining its interpretation of the competition rules. The Advisory Committee will also be consulted on these notices and guidelines.

4.2. Procedure

4.2.1. Normal procedure

65. For consultation on Commission draft decisions, the meeting of the Advisory Committee takes place at the earliest 14 days after the invitation to the meeting is sent by the Commission. The Commission attaches to the invitation a summary of the case, a list of the most important documents, i.e. the documents needed to assess the case, and a draft decision. The Advisory Committee gives an opinion on the Commission draft decision. At the request of one or several members, the opinion shall be reasoned.

66. The Council Regulation allows for the possibility of the Member States agreeing upon a shorter period of time between the sending of the invitation and the meeting.

4.2.2. Written procedure

67. The Council Regulation provides for the possibility of a written consultation procedure. If no Member State objects, the Commission can consult the Member States by sending the documents to them and setting a deadline within which they can comment on the draft. This deadline would not normally be shorter than 14 days, except for decisions on interim measures pursuant to Article 8 of the Council Regulation. Where a Member State requests that a meeting takes place, the Commission will arrange for such a meeting.

4.3. Publication of the opinion of the Advisory Committee

68. The Advisory Committee can recommend the publication of its opinion. In that event, the Commission will carry out such publication simultaneously with the decision, taking into account the legitimate interest of undertakings in the protection of their business secrets.

5. FINAL REMARKS

69. This Notice is without prejudice to any interpretation of the applicable Treaty and regulatory provisions by the Court of First Instance and the Court of Justice.

70. This Notice will be the subject of periodic review carried out jointly by the NCAs and the Commission. On the basis of the experience acquired, it will be reviewed no later than at the end of the third year after its adoption.

71. This notice replaces the Commission notice on cooperation between national competition authorities and the Commission in handling cases falling within the scope of Articles 81 and 82 of the Treaty published in 1997 (24).

(24) *O.J.* C 313, 15.10.1997, p. 3.

6. STATEMENT BY OTHER NETWORK MEMBERS

72. The principles set out in this notice will also be abided by those Member States' competition authorities which have signed a statement in the form of the Annex to this Notice. In this statement they acknowledge the principles of this notice, including the principles relating to the protection of applicants claiming the benefit of a leniency programme (25) and declare that they will abide by them. A list of these authorities is published on the website of the European Commission. It will be updated if appropriate.

(25) See paragraphs 37 et subseq.

Annex

Statement regarding the Commission Notice on Co-operation within the Network of Competition Authorities

In order to cooperate closely with a view to protecting competition within the European Union in the interest of consumers, the undersigned competition authority:

1. Acknowledges the principles set out in the Commission Notice of Cooperation within the Network of Competition Authorities; and

2. Declares that it will abide by those principles, which include principles relating to the protection of applicants claiming the benefit of a leniency programme, in any case in which it is acting or may act and to which those principles apply.

.....
(place)

.....
(date)

Commission Notice on the co-operation between the Commission and the courts of the EU Member States in the application of Articles 81 and 82 EC

(OJ C 101, 27 April 2004, p. 54)

1. Article 81 EC is now Article 101 TFEU and Article 82 EC is now Article 102 TFEU.

I. THE SCOPE OF THE NOTICE

1. The present notice addresses the co-operation between the Commission and the courts of the EU Member States, when the latter apply Articles 81 and 82 EC. For the purpose of this notice, the «courts of the EU Member States» (hereinafter «national courts») are those courts and tribunals within an EU Member State that can apply Articles 81 and 82 EC and that are authorised to ask a preliminary question to the Court of Justice of the European Communities pursuant to Article 234 EC (1).

(1) For the criteria to determine which entities can be regarded as courts or tribunals within the meaning of Article 234 EC, see e.g. case C-516/99 Schmid [2002] ECR I-4573, 34: «The Court takes account of a number of factors, such as whether the body is established by law, whether it is permanent, whether its jurisdiction is compulsory, whether its procedure is inter partes, whether it applies rules of law and whether it is independent».

2. The national courts may be called upon to apply Articles 81 or 82 EC in lawsuits between private parties, such as actions relating to contracts or actions for damages. They may also act as public enforcer or as review court. A national court may indeed be designated as a competition authority of a Member State (hereinafter «the national competition authority») pursuant to Article 35(1) of Regulation (EC) N° 1/2003 (hereinafter «the regulation») (2). In that case, the co-operation between the national courts and the Commission is not only covered by the present notice, but also by the notice on the co-operation within the network of competition authorities (3).

(2) Council Regulation (EC) N° 1/2003 of 16 December 2002 on the implementation of the rules on competition laid down in Articles 81 and 82 of the Treaty (*O.J.* L 1, 4.1.2003, p. 1).

(3) Notice on the co-operation within the network of competition authorities (*O.J.* C 101, 27.4.2004, p. 43). For the purpose of this notice, a «national competition authority» is the authority designated by a Member State in accordance with Article 35(1) of the regulation.

II. THE APPLICATION OF EC COMPETITION RULES BY NATIONAL COURTS

A. The competence of national courts to apply EC competition rules

3. To the extent that national courts have jurisdiction to deal with a case (4), they have the power to apply Articles 81 and 82 EC (5). Moreover, it should be remembered that Articles 81 and 82 EC are a matter of public policy and are essential to the accomplishment of the tasks entrusted to the Community, and, in particular, for the functioning of the internal market (6). According to the Court of Justice, where, by virtue of domestic law, national courts must raise of their own motion points of law based on binding domestic rules which have not been raised by the parties, such an obligation also exists where binding Community rules, such as the EC competition rules, are concerned. The position is the same if domestic law confers on national courts a discretion to apply of their own motion binding rules of law: national courts must apply the EC competition rules, even when the party with an interest in application of those provisions has not relied on them, where domestic law allows such application by the national court. However, Community law does not require national courts to raise of their own motion an issue concerning the breach of provisions of Community law where examination of that issue would oblige them to abandon the passive role assigned to them by going beyond the ambit of the dispute defined by the parties themselves and relying on facts and circumstances other than those on which the party with an interest in application of those provisions bases his claim (7).

(4) The jurisdiction of a national court depends on national, European and international rules of jurisdiction. In this context, it may be recalled that Council Regulation (EC) N° 44/2001 of 22 December 2000 on jurisdiction and the recognition and enforcement of judgements in civil and commercial matters (O.J. L 12, 16.1.2001, p. 1) is applicable to all competition cases of a civil or commercial nature.

(5) See Article 6 of the regulation.

(6) See Articles 2 and 3 EC, case C-126/97 Eco Swiss [1999] ECR I-3055, 36; case T-34/92 Fiatagri UK and New Holland Ford [1994] ECR II-905, 39 and case T-128/98 Aéroports de Paris [2000] ECR II-3929, 241.

(7) Joined cases C-430/93 and C-431/93 van Schijndel [1995] ECR I-4705, 13 to 15 and 22.

4. Depending on the functions attributed to them under national law, national courts may be called upon to apply Articles 81 and 82 EC in administrative, civil or criminal proceedings (8). In particular, where a natural or legal person asks the national court to safeguard his individual rights, national courts play a specific role in the enforcement of Articles 81 and 82 EC, which is different from the enforcement in the public interest by the Commission or by national competition authorities (9). Indeed, national courts can give effect to Articles 81 and 82 EC by finding contracts to be void or by awards of damages.

(8) According to the last sentence of recital 8 of Regulation (EC) N° 1/2003, the regulation does not apply to national laws which impose criminal sanctions on natural persons except to the extent that such sanctions are the means whereby competition rules applying to undertakings are enforced.

(9) Case T-24/90 Automec [1992] ECR II-2223, 85.

5. National courts can apply Articles 81 and 82 EC, without it being necessary to apply national competition law in parallel. However, where a national court applies national competition law to agreements, decisions by associations of undertakings or concerted practices which may affect trade between Member States within the meaning of Article 81(1) EC (10) or to any abuse prohibited by Article 82 EC, they also have to apply EC competition rules to those agreements, decisions or practices (11).

(10) For further clarification of the effect on trade concept, see the notice on this issue (O.J. L 101, 27.4.2004, p. 81).

(11) Article 3(1) of the regulation.

6. The regulation does not only empower the national courts to apply EC competition law. The parallel application of national competition law to agreements, decisions of associations of undertakings and concerted practices which affect trade between Member States may not lead to a different outcome from that of EC competition law. Article 3(2) of the regulation provides that agreements, decisions or concerted practices which do not infringe Article 81(1) EC or which fulfil the conditions of Article 81(3) EC cannot be prohibited either under national competition law (12). On the other hand, the Court of Justice has ruled that agreements, decisions or concerted practices that violate Article 81(1) and do not fulfil the conditions of Article 81(3) EC cannot be upheld under national law (13). As to the parallel application of national competition law and Article 82 EC in the case of unilateral conduct, Article 3 of the regulation does not provide for a similar convergence obligation. However, in case of conflicting provisions, the general principle of primacy of Community law requires national courts to disapply any provision of national law which contravenes a Community rule, regardless of whether that national law provision was adopted before or after the Community rule (14).

(12) See also the notice on the application of Article 81(3) EC (O.J. L 101, 27.4.2004, p. 2).

(13) Case 14/68 Walt Wilhelm [1969] ECR 1 and joined cases 253/78 and 1 to 3/79 Giry and Guerlain [1980] ECR 2327, 15 to 17.

(14) Case 106/77 Simmenthal [1978] ECR 629, 21 and case C-198/01, Consorzio Industrie Fiammiferi (CIF) [2003] 49.

7. Apart from the application of Articles 81 and 82 EC, national courts are also competent to apply acts adopted by EU institutions in accordance with the EC Treaty or in accordance with the measures adopted to give the Treaty effect, to the extent that these acts have direct effect. National courts may thus have to enforce Commission decisions (15) or regulations applying Article 81(3) EC to certain categories of agreements, decisions or concerted practices. When applying these EC competition rules, national courts act within the framework of Community law and are consequently bound to observe the general principles of Community law (16).

(15) E.g. a national court may be asked to enforce a Commission decision taken pursuant to Articles 7 to 10, 23 and 24 of the regulation.

(16) See e.g. case 5/88 Wachauf [1989] ECR 2609, 19.

8. The application of Articles 81 and 82 EC by national courts often depends on complex economic and legal assessments (17). When applying EC competition rules, national courts are bound by the case law of the Community courts as well as by Commission regulations applying Article 81(3) EC to certain categories of agreements, decisions or concerted practices (18). Furthermore, the application of Articles 81 and 82 EC by the Commission in a specific case binds the national courts when they apply EC competition rules in the same case in parallel with or subsequent to the Commission (19). Finally, and without prejudice to the ultimate interpretation of the EC Treaty by the Court of Justice, national courts may find guidance in Commission regulations and decisions which present elements of analogy with the case they are dealing with, as well as in Commission notices and guidelines relating to the application of Articles 81 and 82 EC (20) and in the annual report on competition policy (21).

(17) Joined cases C-215/96 and C-216/96 Bagnasco [1999] ECR I-135, 50.

(18) Case 63/75 Fonderies Roubaix [1976] ECR 111, 9 to 11 and case C-234/89 Delimitis [1991] ECR I-935, 46.

(19) On the parallel or consecutive application of EC competition rules by national courts and the Commission, see also points 11 to 14.

(20) Case 66/86 Ahmed Saeed Flugreisen [1989] ECR 803, 27 and case C-234/89 Delimitis [1991] ECR I-935, 50. A list of Commission guidelines, notices and regulations in the field of competition policy, in particular the regulations applying Article 81(3) EC to certain categories of agreements, decisions or concerted practices, are annexed to this notice. For the decisions of the Commission applying Articles 81 and 82 EC (since 1964), see http://www.europa.eu.int/comm/competition/antitrust/cases/.

(21) Joined cases C-319/93, C-40/94 and C-224/94 Dijkstra [1995] ECR I-4471, 32.

B. Procedural aspects of the application of EC competition rules by national courts

9. The procedural conditions for the enforcement of EC competition rules by national courts and the sanctions they can impose in case of an infringement of those rules, are largely covered by national law. However, to some extent, Community law also determines the conditions in which EC competition rules are enforced. Those Community law provisions may provide for the faculty of national courts to avail themselves of certain instruments, e.g. to ask for the Commission's opinion on questions concerning the application of EC competition rules (22) or they may create rules that have an obligatory impact on proceedings before them, e.g. allowing the Commission and national competition authorities to submit written observations (23). These Community law provisions prevail over national rules. Therefore, national courts have to set aside national rules which, if applied, would conflict with these Community law provisions. Where such Community law provisions are directly applicable, they are a direct source of rights and duties for all those affected, and must be fully and uniformly applied in all the Member States from the date of their entry into force (24).

(22) On the possibility for national courts to ask the Commission for an opinion, see further in points 27 to 30.

(23) On the submission of observations, see further in points 31 to 35.

(24) Case 106/77 Simmenthal [1978] ECR 629, 14 and 15.

10. In the absence of Community law provisions on procedures and sanctions related to the enforcement of EC competition rules by national courts, the latter apply national procedural law and – to the extent that they are competent to do so – impose sanctions provided for under national law. However, the application of these national provisions must be compatible with the general principles of Community law. In this regard, it is useful to recall the case law of the Court of Justice, according to which:

(a) where there is an infringement of Community law, national law must provide for sanctions which are effective, proportionate and dissuasive (25);

(b) where the infringement of Community law causes harm to an individual, the latter should under certain conditions be able to ask the national court for damages (26);

(c) the rules on procedures and sanctions which national courts apply to enforce Community law

– must not make such enforcement excessively difficult or practically impossible (the principle of effectiveness) (27) and they

– must not be less favourable than the rules applicable to the enforcement of equivalent national law (the principle of equivalence) (28).

On the basis of the principle of primacy of Community law, a national court may not apply national rules that are incompatible with these principles.

(25) Case 68/88 Commission v Greece [1989] ECR 2965, 23 to 25.

(26) On damages in case of an infringement by an undertaking, see case C-453/99 Courage and Crehan [2001] ECR 6297, 26 and 27. On damages in case of an infringement by a Member State or by an authority which is an emanation of the State and on the conditions of such state liability, see e.g. joined cases C-6/90 and C-9/90 Francovich [1991] ECR I-5357, 33 to 36; case C-271/91 Marshall v Southampton and South West Hampshire Area Health Authority [1993] ECR I-4367, 30 and 34 to 35; joined cases C-46/93 and C-48/93 Brasserie du Pêcheur and Factortame [1996] ECR I-1029; case C-392/93 British Telecommunications [1996] ECR I-1631, 39 to 46 and joined cases C-178/94, C-179/94 and C-188/94 to 190/94 Dillenkofer [1996] ECR I-4845, 22 to 26 and 72.

(27) See e.g. case 33/76 Rewe [1976] ECR 1989, 5; case 45/76 Comet [1976] ECR 2043, 12 and case 79/83 Harz [1984] ECR 1921, 18 and 23.

(28) See e.g. case 33/76 Rewe [1976] ECR 1989, 5; case 158/80 Rewe [1981] ECR 1805, 44; case 199/82 San Giorgio [1983] ECR 3595, 12 and case C-231/96 Edis [1998] ECR I-4951, 36 and 37.

C. Parallel or consecutive application of EC competition rules by the Commission and by national courts

11. A national court may be applying EC competition law to an agreement, decision, concerted practice or unilateral behaviour affecting trade between Member States at the same time as the Commission or subsequent to the Commission (29). The following points outline some of the obligations national courts have to respect in those circumstances.

(29) Article 11(6), *juncto* Article 35(3) and (4) of the regulation prevents a parallel application of Articles 81 or 82 EC by the Commission and a national court only when the latter has been designated as a national competition authority.

12. Where a national court comes to a decision before the Commission does, it must avoid adopting a decision that would conflict with a decision contemplated by the Commission (30). To that effect, the national court may ask the Commission whether it has initiated proceedings regarding the same agreements, decisions or practices (31) and if so, about the progress of proceedings and the likelihood of a decision in that case (32). The national court may, for reasons of legal certainty, also consider staying its proceedings until the Commission has reached a decision (33). The Commission, for its part, will endeavour to give priority to cases for which it has decided to initiate proceedings within the meaning of Article 2(1) of Commission Regulation (EC) N° 773/2004 and that are the subject of national proceedings stayed in this way, in particular when the outcome of a civil dispute depends on them. However, where the national court cannot reasonably doubt the Commission's contemplated decision or where the Commission has already decided on a similar case, the national court may decide on the case pending before it in accordance with that contemplated or earlier decision without it being necessary to ask the Commission for the information mentioned above or to await the Commission's decision.

(30) Article 16(1) of the regulation.

(31) The Commission makes the initiation of its proceedings with a view to adopting a decision pursuant to Article 7 to 10 of the regulation public (see Article 2(2) of Commission Regulation (EC) N° 773/2004 of 7 April relating to proceedings pursuant to Articles 81 and 82 of the EC Treaty (O.J. C 101, 27.4.2004). According to the Court of Justice, the initiation of proceedings implies an authoritative act of the Commission, evidencing its intention of taking a decision (case 48/72 Brasserie de Haecht [1973] ECR 77, 16).

(32) Case C-234/89 Delimitis [1991] ECR I-935, 53, and joined cases C-319/93, C-40/94 and C-224/94 Dijkstra [1995] ECR I-4471, 34. See further on this issue point 21 of this notice.

(33) See Article 16(1) of the regulation and case C-234/89 Delimitis [1991] ECR I-935, 47 and case C-344/98 Masterfoods [2000] ECR I-11369, 51.

13. Where the Commission reaches a decision in a particular case before the national court, the latter cannot take a decision running counter to that of the Commission. The binding effect of the Commission's decision is of course without prejudice to the interpretation of Community law by the Court of Justice. Therefore, if the national court doubts the legality of the Commission's decision, it cannot avoid the binding effects of that decision without a ruling to the contrary by the Court of Justice (34). Consequently, if a national court intends to take a decision that runs counter to that of the Commission, it must refer a question to the Court of Justice for a preliminary ruling (Article 234 EC). The latter will then decide on the compatibility of the Commission's decision with Community law. However, if the Commission's decision is challenged before the Community courts pursuant to Article 230 EC and the outcome of the dispute before the national court depends on the validity of the Commission's decision, the national court should stay its proceedings pending final judgment in the action for annulment by the Community courts unless it considers that, in the circumstances of the case, a reference to the Court of Justice for a preliminary ruling on the validity of the Commission decision is warranted (35).

(34) Case 314/85 Foto-Frost [1987] ECR 4199, 12 to 20.

(35) See Article 16(1) of the regulation and case C-344/98 Masterfoods [2000] ECR I-11369, 52 to 59.

14. When a national court stays proceedings, e.g. awaiting the Commission's decision (situation described in point 12 of this notice) or pending final judgement by the Community courts in an action for annulment or in a preliminary ruling procedure (situation described in point 13), it is incumbent on it to examine whether it is necessary to order interim measures in order to safeguard the interests of the parties (36).

(36) Case C-344/98 Masterfoods [2000] ECR, I-11369, 58.

III. THE CO-OPERATION BETWEEN THE COMMISSION AND NATIONAL COURTS

15. Other than the co-operation mechanism between the national courts and the Court of Justice under Article 234 EC, the EC Treaty does not explicitly provide for co-operation between the national courts and the Commission. However, in its interpretation of Article 10 EC, which obliges the Member States to facilitate the achievement of the Community's tasks, the Community courts found that this Treaty provision imposes on the European institutions and the Member States mutual duties of loyal co-operation with a view to attaining the objectives of the EC Treaty. Article 10 EC thus implies that the Commission must assist national courts when they apply Community law (37). Equally, national courts may be obliged to assist the Commission in the fulfilment of its tasks (38).

(37) Case C-2/88 Imm Zwartveld [1990] ECR I-3365, 16 to 22 and case C-234/89 Delimitis [1991] I-935, 53.

(38) C-94/00 Roquette Frères [2002] ECR 9011, 31.

16. It is also appropriate to recall the co-operation between national courts and national authorities, in particular national competition authorities, for the application of Articles 81 and 82 EC. While the co-operation between these national authorities is primarily governed by national rules, Article 15(3) of the regulation provides for the possibility for national competition authorities to submit observations before the national courts of their Member State. Points 31 and 33 to 35 of this notice are mutatis mutandis applicable to those submissions.

A. The Commission as amicus curiae

17. In order to assist national courts in the application of EC competition rules, the Commission is committed to help national courts where the latter find such help necessary to be able to decide on a case. Article 15 of the regulation refers to the most frequent types of such assistance: the transmission of information (points 21 to 26) and the Commission's opinions (points 27 to 30), both at the request of a national court and the possibility for the Commission to submit observations (points 31 to 35). Since the regulation provides for these types of assistance, it cannot be limited by any Member States' rule. However, in the absence of Community procedural rules to this effect and to the extent that they are necessary to facilitate these forms of assistance, Member States must adopt the appropriate procedural rules to allow both the national courts and the Commission to make full use of the possibilities the regulation offers (39).

(39) On the compatibility of such national procedural rules with the general principles of Community law, see points 9 and 10 of this notice.

18. The national court may send its request for assistance in writing to: European Commission – Directorate General for Competition – B-1049 Brussels – Belgium or send it electronically to comp-amicus@cec.eu.int

19. It should be recalled that whatever form the co-operation with national courts takes, the Commission will respect the independence of national courts. As a consequence, the assistance offered by the Commission does not bind the national court. The Commission has also to make sure that it respects its duty of professional secrecy and that it safeguards its own functioning and independence (40). In fulfilling its duty under Article 10 EC, of assisting national courts in the application of EC competition rules, the Commission is committed to remaining neutral and objective in its assistance. Indeed, the Commission's assistance to national courts is part of its duty to defend the public interest. It has therefore no intention to serve the private interests of the parties involved in the case pending before the national court. As a consequence, the Commission will not hear any of the parties about its assistance to the national court. In case the Commission has been contacted by any of the parties in the case pending before the court on issues which are raised before the national court, it will inform the national court thereof, independent of whether these contacts took place before or after the national court's request for co-operation.

(40) On these duties, see e.g. points 23 to 26 of this notice.

20. The Commission will publish a summary concerning its co-operation with national courts pursuant to this notice in its annual Report on Competition Policy. It may also make its opinions and observations available on its website.

1. The Commission's duty to transmit information to national courts

21. The duty for the Commission to assist national courts in the application of EC competition law is mainly reflected in the obligation for the Commission to transmit information it holds to national courts. A national court may, e.g., ask the Commission for documents in its possession or for information of a procedural nature to enable it to discover whether a certain case is pending before the Commission, whether the Commission has initiated a procedure or whether it has already taken a position. A national court may also ask the Commission when a decision is likely to be taken, so as to be able to determine the conditions for any decision to stay proceedings or whether interim measures need to be adopted (41).

(41) Case C-234/89 Delimitis [1991] ECR I-935, 53, and joined cases C-319/93, C-40/94 and C-224/94 Dijkstra [1995] ECR I-4471, 34.

22. In order to ensure the efficiency of the co-operation with national courts, the Commission will endeavour to provide the national court with the requested information within one month from the date it receives the request. Where the Commission has to ask the national court for further clarification of its request or where the Commission has to consult those who are directly affected by the transmission of the information, that period starts to run from the moment that it receives the required information.

23. In transmitting information to national courts, the Commission has to uphold the guarantees given to natural and legal persons by Article 287 EC (42). Article 287 EC prevents members, officials and other servants of the Commission from disclosing information covered by the obligation of professional secrecy. The information covered by professional secrecy may be both confidential information and business secrets. Business secrets are information of which not only disclosure to the public but also mere transmission to a person other than the one that provided the information might seriously harm the latter's interests (43).

(42) Case C-234/89 Delimitis [1991] I-935, 53.

(43) Case T-353/94 Postbank [1996] ECR II-921, 86 and 87 and case 145/83 Adams [1985] ECR 3539, 34.

24. The combined reading of Articles 10 and 287 EC does not lead to an absolute prohibition for the Commission to transmit information which is covered by the obligation of professional secrecy to national courts. The case law of the Community courts confirms that the duty of loyal co-operation requires the Commission to provide the national court with whatever information the latter asks for, even information covered by professional secrecy. However, in offering its co-operation to the national courts, the Commission may not in any circumstances undermine the guarantees laid down in Article 287 EC.

25. Consequently, before transmitting information covered by professional secrecy to a national court, the Commission will remind the court of its obligation under Community law to uphold the rights which Article 287 EC confers on natural and legal persons and it will ask the court whether it can and will guarantee protection of confidential information and business secrets. If the national court cannot offer such guarantee, the Commission shall not transmit the information covered by professional secrecy to the national court (44). Only when the national court has offered a guarantee that it will protect the confidential information and business secrets, will the Commission transmit the information requested, indicating those parts which are covered by professional secrecy and which parts are not and can therefore be disclosed.

(44) Case C-2/88 Zwartveld [1990] ECR I-4405, 10 and 11 and case T-353/94 Postbank [1996] ECR II-921, 93.

26. There are further exceptions to the disclosure of information by the Commission to national courts. Particularly, the Commission may refuse to transmit information to national courts for overriding reasons relating to the need to safeguard the interests of the Community or to avoid any interference with its functioning and independence, in particular by jeopardising the accomplishment of the tasks entrusted to it (45). Therefore, the Commission will not transmit to national courts information voluntarily submitted by a leniency applicant without the consent of that applicant.

(45) Case C-2/88 Zwartveld [1990] ECR I-4405, 10 and 11; case C-275/00 First and Franex [2002] ECR I-10943, 49 and case T-353/94 Postbank [1996] ECR II-921, 93.

2. Request for an opinion on questions concerning the application of EC competition rules

27. When called upon to apply EC competition rules to a case pending before it, a national court may first seek guidance in the case law of the Community courts or in Commission regulations, decisions, notices and guidelines applying Articles 81 and 82 EC (46). Where these tools do not offer sufficient guidance, the national court may ask the Commission for its opinion on questions concerning the application of EC competition rules. The national court may ask the Commission for its opinion on economic, factual and legal matters (47). The latter is of course without prejudice to the possibility or the obligation for the national court to ask the Court of Justice for a preliminary ruling regarding the interpretation or the validity of Community law in accordance with Article 234 EC.

(46) See point 8 of this notice.

(47) Case C-234/89 Delimitis [1991] ECR I-935, 53, and joined cases C-319/93, C-40/94 and C-224/94 Dijkstra [1995] ECR I-4471, 34.

28. In order to enable the Commission to provide the national court with a useful opinion, it may request the national court for further information (48). In order to ensure the efficiency of the co-operation with national courts, the Commission will endeavour to provide the national court with the requested opinion within four months from the date it receives the request. Where the Commission has requested the national court for further information in order to enable it to formulate its opinion, that period starts to run from the moment that it receives the additional information.

(48) Compare with case 96/81 Commission v the Netherlands [1982] ECR 1791, 7 and case 272/86 Commission v Greece [1988] ECR 4875, 30.

29. When giving its opinion, the Commission will limit itself to providing the national court with the factual information or the economic or legal clarification asked for, without considering the merits of the case pending before the national court. Moreover, unlike the authoritative interpretation of Community law by the Community courts, the opinion of the Commission does not legally bind the national court.

30. In line with what has been said in point 19 of this notice, the Commission will not hear the parties before formulating its opinion to the national court. The latter will have to deal with the Commission's opinion in accordance with the relevant national procedural rules, which have to respect the general principles of Community law.

3. The Commission's submission of observations to the national court

31. According to Article 15(3) of the regulation, the national competition authorities and the Commission may submit observations on issues relating to the application of Articles 81 or 82 EC to a national court which is called upon to apply those provisions. The regulation distinguishes between written observations, which the national competition authorities and the Commission may submit on their own initiative, and oral observations, which can only be submitted with the permission of the national court (49).

(49) According to Article 15(4) of the regulation, this is without prejudice to wider powers to make observations before courts conferred on national competition authorities under national law.

32. The regulation specifies that the Commission will only submit observations when the coherent application of Articles 81 or 82 EC so requires. That being the objective of its submission, the Commission will limit its observations to an economic and legal analysis of the facts underlying the case pending before the national court.

33. In order to enable the Commission to submit useful observations, national courts may be asked to transmit or ensure the transmission to the Commission of a copy of all documents that are necessary for the assessment of the case. In line with Article 15(3), second subparagraph, of the regulation, the Commission will only use those documents for the preparation of its observations (50).

(50) See also Article 28(2) of the regulation, which prevents the Commission from disclosing the information it has acquired and which is covered by the obligation of professional secrecy.

34. Since the regulation does not provide for a procedural framework within which the observations are to be submitted, Member States' procedural rules and practices determine the relevant procedural framework. Where a Member State has not yet established the relevant procedural framework, the national court has to determine which procedural rules are appropriate for the submission of observations in the case pending before it.

35. The procedural framework should respect the principles set out in point 10 of this notice. That implies amongst others that the procedural framework for the submission of observations on issues relating to the application of Articles 81 or 82 EC

(a) has to be compatible with the general principles of Community law, in particular the fundamental rights of the parties involved in the case;

(b) cannot make the submission of such observations excessively difficult or practically impossible (the principle of effectiveness) (51); and

(c) cannot make the submission of such observations more difficult than the submission of observations in court proceedings where equivalent national law is applied (the principle of equivalence).

(51) Joined cases 46/87 and 227/88 Hoechst [1989] ECR, 2859, 33. See also Article 15(3) of the regulation.

B. The national courts facilitating the role of the Commission in the enforcement of EC competition rules

36. Since the duty of loyal co-operation also implies that Member States' authorities assist the European institutions with a view to attaining the objectives of the EC Treaty (52), the regulation provides for three examples of such assistance: (1) the transmission of documents necessary for the assessment of a case in which the Commission would like to submit observations (see point 33), (2) the transmission of judgements applying Articles 81 or 82 EC); and (3) the role of national courts in the context of a Commission inspection.

(52) Case C-69/90 Commission v Italy [1991] ECR 6011, 15.

1. The transmission of judgements of national courts applying Articles 81 or 82 EC

37. According to Article 15(2) of the regulation, Member States shall send to the Commission a copy of any written judgement of national courts applying Articles 81 or 82 EC without delay after the full written judgement is notified to the parties. The transmission of national judgements on the application of Articles 81 or 82 EC and the resulting information on proceedings before national courts primarily enable the Commission to become aware in a timely fashion of cases for which it might be appropriate to submit observations where one of the parties lodges an appeal against the judgement.

2. The role of national courts in the context of a Commission inspection

38. Finally, national courts may play a role in the context of a Commission inspection of undertakings and associations of undertakings. The role of the national courts depends on whether the inspections are conducted in business premises or in non-business premises.

39. With regard to the inspection of business premises, national legislation may require authorisation from a national court to allow a national enforcement authority to assist the Commission in case of opposition of the undertaking concerned. Such authorisation may also be sought as a precautionary measure. When dealing with the request, the national court has the power to control that the Commission's inspection decision is authentic and that the coercive measures envisaged are neither arbitrary nor excessive having regard to the subject matter of the inspection. In its control of the proportionality of the coercive measures, the national court may ask the Commission, directly or through the national competition authority, for detailed explanations in particular on the grounds the Commission has for suspecting infringement of Articles 81 and 82 EC, as well as on the seriousness of the suspected infringement and on the nature of the involvement of the undertaking concerned (53).

(53) Article 20(6) to (8) of the regulation and case C-94/00 Roquette Frères [2002] ECR 9011.

40. With regard to the inspection of non-business premises, the regulation requires the authorisation from a national court before a Commission decision ordering such an inspection can be executed. In that case, the national court may control that the Commission's inspection decision is authentic and that the coercive measures envisaged are neither arbitrary nor excessive having regard in particular to the seriousness of the suspected infringement, to the importance of the evidence sought, to the involvement of the undertaking concerned and to the reasonable likelihood that business books and records relating to the subject matter of the inspection are kept in the premises for which the authorisation is requested. The national court may ask the Commission, directly or through the national competition authority, for detailed explanations on those elements that are necessary to allow its control of the proportionality of the coercive measures envisaged (54).

(54) Article 21(3) of the regulation.

41. In both cases referred to in points 39 and 40, the national court may not call into question the lawfulness of the Commission's decision or the necessity for the inspection nor can it demand that it be provided with information in the Commission's file (55). Furthermore, the duty of loyal co-operation requires the national court to take its decision within an appropriate timeframe that allows the Commission to effectively conduct its inspection (56).

(55) Case C-94/00 Roquette Frères [2002] ECR 9011, 39 and 62 to 66.

(56) See also *ibidem*, 91 and 92.

IV. FINAL PROVISIONS

42. This notice is issued in order to assist national courts in the application of Articles 81 and 82 EC. It does not bind the national courts, nor does it affect the rights and obligations of the EU Member States and natural or legal persons under Community law.

43. This notice replaces the 1993 notice on co-operation between national courts and the Commission in applying Articles 85 and 86 of the EEC Treaty (57).

(57) O.J. C 39, 13.2.93, p. 6.

Annex
Commission block exemption regulations, notices and guidelines

1. Not included

This list is also available and updated on the website of the Directorate General for Competition of the European Commission: http://ec.europa.eu/competition/antitrust/legislation/

Commission Notice on the handling of complaints by the Commission under Articles 81 and 82 of the EC Treaty
(OJ C 101, 27 April 2004, p. 65)

1. Article 81 EC is now Article 101 TFEU and Article 82 EC is now Article 102 TFEU.

I. INTRODUCTION AND SUBJECT-MATTER OF THE NOTICE

1. Regulation 1/2003 (1) establishes a system of parallel competence for the application of Articles 81 and 82 of the EC Treaty by the Commission and the Member States' competition authorities and courts. The Regulation recognises in particular the complementary functions of the Commission and Member States' competition authorities acting as public enforcers and the Member States' courts that rule on private lawsuits in order to safeguard the rights of individuals deriving from Articles 81 and 82 (2).

(1) Council Regulation (EC) N° 1/2003 of 16 December 2002 on the implementation of the rules on competition laid down in Articles 81 and 82 of the Treaty (O.J. L 1, 4.1.2003, pages 1-25).

(2) Cf. in particular Recitals 3-7 and 35 of Regulation 1/2003.

2. Under Regulation 1/2003, the public enforcers may focus their action on the investigation of serious infringements of Articles 81 and 82 which are often difficult to detect. For their enforcement activity, they benefit from information supplied by undertakings and by consumers in the market.

3. The Commission therefore wishes to encourage citizens and undertakings to address themselves to the public enforcers to inform them about suspected infringements of the competition rules. At the level of the Commission, there are two ways to do this, one is by lodging a complaint pursuant to Article 7(2) of Regulation 1/2003. Under Articles 5 to 9 of Regulation 773/2004 (3), such complaints must fulfil certain requirements.

(3) Commission Regulation (EC) N° 773/2004 of 7 April 2004 relating to the conduct of proceedings by the Commission pursuant to Articles 81 and 82 of the EC Treaty (O.J. 123, 27.4.2004).

4. The other way is the provision of market information that does not have to comply with the requirements for complaints pursuant to Article 7(2) of Regulation 1/2003. For this purpose, the Commission has created a special website to collect information from citizens and undertakings and their associations who wish to inform the Commission about suspected infringements of Articles 81 and 82. Such information can be the starting point for an investigation by the Commission (4). Information about suspected infringements can be supplied to the following address: http://europa.eu.int/dgcomp/info-on-anti-competitivepractices or to: Commission européenne/Europese Commissie – Competition DG – B-1049 Bruxelles/Brussel

(4) The Commission handles correspondence from informants in accordance with its principles of good administrative practice.

5. Without prejudice to the interpretation of Regulation 1/2003 and of Commission Regulation 773/2004 by the Community Courts, the present Notice intends to provide guidance to citizens and undertakings that are seeking relief from suspected infringements of the competition rules. The Notice contains two main parts:

– Part II gives indications about the choice between complaining to the Commission or bringing a lawsuit before a national court. Moreover, it recalls the principles related to the work-sharing between the Commission and the national competition authorities in the enforcement system established by Regulation 1/2003 that are explained in the Notice on cooperation within the network of competition authorities (5).

– Part III explains the procedure for the treatment of complaints pursuant to Article 7(2) of Regulation 1/2003 by the Commission.

(5) Notice on cooperation within the Network of competition authorities (p. 43).

6. This Notice does not address the following situations:

– complaints lodged by Member States pursuant to Article 7(2) of Regulation 1/2003,

– complaints that ask the Commission to take action against a Member State pursuant to Article 86(3) in conjunction with Articles 81 or 82 of the Treaty,

– complaints relating to Article 87 of the Treaty on state aids,

– complaints relating to infringements by Member States that the Commission may pursue in the framework of Article 226 of the Treaty (6).

(6) For the handling of such complaints, cf. Commission communication of 10 October 2002, COM(2002) 141.

II. DIFFERENT POSSIBILITIES FOR LODGING COMPLAINTS ABOUT SUSPECTED INFRINGEMENTS OF ARTICLES 81 OR 82

A. Complaints in the new enforcement system established by regulation 1/2003

7. Depending on the nature of the complaint, a complainant may bring his complaint either to a national court or to a competition authority that acts as public enforcer. The present chapter of this Notice intends to help potential complainants to make an informed choice about whether to address themselves to the Commission, to one of the Member States' competition authorities or to a national court.

8. While national courts are called upon to safeguard the rights of individuals and are thus bound to rule on cases brought before them, public enforcers cannot investigate all complaints, but must set priorities in their treatment of cases. The Court of Justice has held that the Commission, entrusted by Article 85(1) of the EC Treaty with the task of ensuring application of the principles laid down in Articles 81 and 82 of the Treaty, is responsible for defining and implementing the orientation of Community competition policy and that, in order to perform that task effectively, it is entitled to give differing degrees of priority to the complaints brought before it (7).

(7) Case C-344/98, *Masterfoods v HB Ice Cream*, [2000] ECR I-11369, para 46; Case C-119/97 P, *Union française de l'express (Ufex) and Others v Commission of the European Communities*, [1999] ECR I-1341, para 88; Case T-24/90, *Automec v Commission of the European Communities*, [1992] ECR II-2223, paras 73-77.

9. Regulation 1/2003 empowers Member States' courts and Member States' competition authorities to apply Articles 81 and 82 in their entirety alongside the Commission. Regulation 1/2003 pursues as one principal objective that Member States' courts and competition authorities should participate effectively in the enforcement of Articles 81 and 82 (8).

(8) Cf. in particular Articles 5, 6, 11, 12, 15, 22, 29, 35 and Recitals 2 to 4 and 6 to 8 of Regulation 1/2003.

10. Moreover, Article 3 of Regulation 1/2003 provides that Member States' courts and competition authorities have to apply Articles 81 and 82 to all cases of agreements or conduct that are capable of affecting trade between Member States to which they apply their national competition laws. In addition, Articles 11 and 15 of the Regulation create a range of mechanisms by which Member States' courts and competition authorities cooperate with the Commission in the enforcement of Articles 81 and 82.

11. In this new legislative framework, the Commission intends to refocus its enforcement resources along the following lines:

– enforce the EC competition rules in cases for which it is well placed to act (9), concentrating its resources on the most serious infringements (10);

– handle cases in relation to which the Commission should act with a view to define Community competition policy and/or to ensure coherent application of Articles 81 or 82.

(9) Cf. Notice on cooperation within the network of competition authorities..., points 5 ss.

(10) Cf. Recital 3 of Regulation 1/2003.

B. The complementary roles of private and public enforcement

12. It has been consistently held by the Community Courts that national courts are called upon to safeguard the rights of individuals created by the direct effect of Articles 81(1) and 82 (11).

(11) Settled case law, cf. Case 127/73, *Belgische Radio en Televisie (BRT) v SABAM and Fonior*, [1974] ECR 51, para 16; Case C-282/95 P, *Guérin automobiles v Commission of the European Communities*, [1997] ECR I-1503, para 39; Case C-453/99, *Courage v Bernhard Crehan*, [2001] ECR I-6297, para 23.

13. National courts can decide upon the nullity or validity of contracts and only national courts can grant damages to an individual in case of an infringement of Articles 81 and 82. Under the case law of the Court of Justice, any individual can claim damages for loss caused to him by a contract or by conduct which restricts or distorts competition, in order to ensure the full effectiveness of the Community competition rules. Such actions for damages before the national courts can make a significant contribution to the maintenance of effective competition in the Community as they discourage undertakings from concluding or applying restrictive agreements or practices (12).

(12) Case C-453/99, *Courage v Bernhard Crehan*, [2001] ECR I-6297, paras 26 and 27; the power of national courts to grant damages is also underlined in Recital 7 of Regulation 1/2003.

14. Regulation 1/2003 takes express account of the fact that national courts have an essential part to play in applying the EC competition rules (13). By extending the power to apply Article 81(3) to national courts it removes the possibility for undertakings to delay national court proceedings by a notification to the Commission and thus eliminates an obstacle for private litigation that existed under Regulation N° 17 (14).

(13) Cf. Articles 1, 6 and 15 as well as Recital 7 of Regulation 1/2003.

(14) Regulation N° 17: First Regulation implementing Articles 85 and 86 of the Treaty; O.J. P 13 of 21 February 1962, p. 204-211; English special edition: Series I Chapter 1959-1962 p. 87. Regulation N° 17 is repealed by Article 43 of Regulation 1/2003 with effect from 1 May 2004.

15. Without prejudice to the right or obligation of national courts to address a preliminary question to the Court of Justice in accordance with Article 234 EC, Article 15(1) of Regulation 1/2003 provides expressly that national courts may ask for opinions or information from the Commission. This provision aims at facilitating the application of Articles 81 and 82 by national courts (15).

(15) For more detailed explanations of this mechanism, cf. Notice on the co-operation between the Commission and the courts of the EU Member States in the application of Articles 81 and 82 EC...

16. Action before national courts has the following advantages for complainants:

– National courts may award damages for loss suffered as a result of an infringement of Article 81 or 82.

– National courts may rule on claims for payment or contractual obligations based on an agreement that they examine under Article 81.

– It is for the national courts to apply the civil sanction of nullity of Article 81(2) in contractual relationships between individuals (16). They can in particular assess, in the light of the applicable national law, the scope and consequences of the nullity of certain contractual provisions under Article 81(2), with particular regard to all the other matters covered by the agreement (17).

– National courts are usually better placed than the Commission to adopt interim measures (18).

– Before national courts, it is possible to combine a claim under Community competition law with other claims under national law.

– Courts normally have the power to award legal costs to the successful applicant. This is never possible in an administrative procedure before the Commission.

(16) Case T-24/90, Automec v Commission of the European Communities, [1992] ECR II-2223, para 93.

(17) Case C-230/96, Cabour and Nord Distribution Automobile v Arnor «SOCO», [1998] ECR I-2055, para 51; Joined Cases T-185/96, T-189/96 and T-190/96, Dalmasso and Others v Commission of the European Communities, [1999] ECR II-93, para 50.

(18) Cf. Article 8 of Regulation 1/2003 and para 80 below. Depending on the case, Member States' competition authorities may equally be well placed to adopt interim measures.

17. The fact that a complainant can secure the protection of his rights by an action before a national court, is an important element that the Commission may take into account in its examination of the Community interest for investigating a complaint (19).

(19) Cf. points 41 ss. below.

18. The Commission holds the view that the new enforcement system established by Regulation 1/2003 strengthens the possibilities for complainants to seek and obtain effective relief before national courts.

C. Work-sharing between the public enforcers in the European community

19. Regulation 1/2003 creates a system of parallel competence for the application of Articles 81 and 82 by empowering Member States' competition authorities to apply Articles 81 and 82 in their entirety (Article 5). Decentralised enforcement by Member States' competition authorities is further encouraged by the possibility to exchange information (Article 12) and to provide each other assistance with investigations (Article 22).

20. The Regulation does not regulate the work-sharing between the Commission and the Member States' competition authorities but leaves the division of case work to the cooperation of the Commission and the Member States' competition authorities inside the European Competition Network (ECN). The Regulation pursues the objective of ensuring effective enforcement of Articles 81 and 82 through a flexible division of case work between the public enforcers in the Community.

21. Orientations for the work sharing between the Commission and the Member States' competition authorities are laid down in a separate Notice (20). The guidance contained in that Notice, which concerns the relations between the public enforcers, will be of interest to complainants as it permits them to address a complaint to the authority most likely to be well placed to deal with their case.

(20) Notice on cooperation within the Network of competition authorities (p. 43).

22. The Notice on cooperation within the Network of Competition Authorities states in particular (21):

«An authority can be considered to be well placed to deal with a case if the following three cumulative conditions are met:

– the agreement or practice has substantial direct actual or foreseeable effects on competition within its territory, is implemented within or originates from its territory;

– the authority is able effectively to bring to an end the entire infringement, i.e. it can adopt a cease-and desist order, the effect of which will be sufficient to bring an end to the infringement and it can, where appropriate, sanction the infringement adequately;

– it can gather, possibly with the assistance of other authorities, the evidence required to prove the infringement.

The above criteria indicate that a material link between the infringement and the territory of a Member State must exist in order for that Member State's competition authority to be considered well placed. It can be expected that in most cases the authorities of those Member States where competition is substantially affected by an infringement will be well placed provided they are capable of effectively bringing the infringement to an end through either single or parallel action unless the Commission is better placed to act (see below [...]).

It follows that a single NCA is usually well placed to deal with agreements or practices that substantially affect competition mainly within its territory [...].

Furthermore single action of an NCA might also be appropriate where, although more than one NCA can be regarded as well placed, the action of a single NCA is sufficient to bring the entire infringement to an end [...].

Parallel action by two or three NCAs may be appropriate where an agreement or practice has substantial effects on competition mainly in their respective territories and the action of only one NCA would not be sufficient to bring the entire infringement to an end and/or to sanction it adequately [...].

The authorities dealing with a case in parallel action will endeavour to coordinate their action to the extent possible. To that effect, they may find it useful to designate one of them as a lead authority and to delegate tasks to the lead authority such as for example the coordination of investigative measures, while each authority remains responsible for conducting its own proceedings.

The Commission is particularly well placed if one or several agreement(s) or practice(s), including networks of similar agreements or practices, have effects on competition in more than three Member States (crossborder markets covering more than three Member States or several national markets) [...].

Moreover, the Commission is particularly well placed to deal with a case if it is closely linked to other Community provisions which may be exclusively or more effectively applied by the Commission, if the Community interest requires the adoption of a Commission decision to develop Community competition policy when a new competition issue arises or to ensure effective enforcement.».

(21) Notice on cooperation within the Network of competition authorities ..., points 8-15.

23. Within the European Competition Network, information on cases that are being investigated following a complaint will be made available to the other members of the network before or without delay after commencing the first formal investigative measure (22). Where the same complaint has been lodged with several authorities or where a case has not been lodged with an authority that is well placed, the members of the network will endeavour to determine within an indicative time-limit of two months which authority or authorities should be in charge of the case.

(22) Article 11(2) and (3) of Regulation 1/2003; Notice on cooperation within the Network of Competition Authorities..., points 16/17.

24. Complainants themselves have an important role to play in further reducing the potential need for reallocation of a case originating from their complaint by referring to the orientations on work sharing in the network set out in the present chapter when deciding on where to lodge their complaint. If nonetheless a case is reallocated within the network, the undertakings concerned and the complainant(s) are informed as soon as possible by the competition authorities involved (23).

(23) Notice on cooperation within the Network of Competition Authorities,..., point 34.

25. The Commission may reject a complaint in accordance with Article 13 of Regulation 1/2003, on the grounds that a Member State competition authority is dealing or has dealt with the case. When doing so, the Commission must, in accordance with Article 9 of Regulation 773/2004, inform the complainant without delay of the national competition authority which is dealing or has already dealt with the case.

III. THE COMMISSION'S HANDLING OF COMPLAINTS PURSUANT TO ARTICLE 7(2) OF REGULATION 1/2003

A. General

26. According to Article 7(2) of Regulation 1/2003 natural or legal persons that can show a legitimate interest (24) are entitled to lodge a complaint to ask the Commission to find an infringement of Articles 81 and 82 EC and to require that the infringement be brought to an end in accordance with Article 7(1) of Regulation 1/2003. The present part of this Notice explains the requirements applicable to complaints based on Article 7(2) of Regulation 1/2003, their assessment and the procedure followed by the Commission.

(24) For more extensive explanations on this notion in particular, cf. points 33 ss. below.

27. The Commission, unlike civil courts, whose task is to safeguard the individual rights of private persons, is an administrative authority that must act in the public interest. It is an inherent feature of the Commission's task as public enforcer that it has a margin of discretion to set priorities in its enforcement activity (25).

(25) Case C-119/97 P, Union française de l'express (Ufex) and Others v Commission of the European Communities, [1999] ECR I-1341, para 88; Case T-24/90, Automec v Commission of the European Communities, [1992] ECR II-2223, paras 73-77 and 85.

28. The Commission is entitled to give different degrees of priority to complaints made to it and may refer to the Community interest presented by a case as a criterion of priority (26). The Commission may reject a complaint when it considers that the case does not display a sufficient Community interest to justify further investigation. Where the Commission rejects a complaint, the complainant is entitled to a decision of the Commission (27) without prejudice to Article 7(3) of Regulation 773/2004.

(26) Settled case law since Case T-24/90, Automec v Commission of the European Communities, [1992] ECR II-2223, para 85.

(27) Case C-282/95 P, Guérin automobiles v Commission of the European Communities, [1997] ECR I-1503, para 36.

B. Making complaint pursuant to Article 7(2) of Regulation 1/2003

(a) Complaint form

29. A complaint pursuant to Article 7(2) of Regulation 1/2003 can only be made about an alleged infringement of Articles 81 or 82 with a view to the Commission taking action under Article 7(1) of Regulation 1/2003. A complaint under Article 7(2) of Regulation 1/2003 has to comply with Form C mentioned in Article 5(1) of Regulation 773/2004 and annexed to that Regulation.

30. Form C is available at http://europa.eu.int/dgcomp/complaints-form and is also annexed to this Notice. The complaint must be submitted in three paper copies as well as, if possible, an electronic copy. In addition, the complainant must provide a non-confidential version of the complaint (Article 5(2) of Regulation 773/2004). Electronic transmission to the Commission is possible via the website indicated, the paper copies should be sent to the following address: Commission européenne/Europese Commissie – Competition DG – B-1049 Bruxelles/Brussel

31. Form C requires complainants to submit comprehensive information in relation to their complaint. They should also provide copies of relevant supporting documentation reasonably available to them and, to the extent possible, provide indications as to where relevant information and documents that are unavailable to them could be obtained by the Commission. In particular cases, the Commission may dispense with the obligation to provide information in relation to part of the information required by Form C (Article 5(1) of Regulation 773/2004). The Commission holds the view that this possibility can in particular play a role to facilitate complaints by consumer associations where they, in the context of an otherwise substantiated complaint, do not have access to specific pieces of information from the sphere of the undertakings complained of.

32. Correspondence to the Commission that does not comply with the requirements of Article 5 of Regulation 773/2004 and therefore does not constitute a complaint within the meaning of Article 7(2) of Regulation 1/2003 will be considered by the Commission as general information that, where it is useful, may lead to an own-initiative investigation (cf. point 4 above).

(b) Legitimate interest

33. The status of formal complainant under Article 7(2) of Regulation 1/2003 is reserved to legal and natural persons who can show a legitimate interest (28). Member States are deemed to have a legitimate interest for all complaints they choose to lodge.

(28) Cf. Article 5(1) of Regulation 773/2004.

34. In the past practice of the Commission, the condition of legitimate interest was not often a matter of doubt as most complainants were in a position of being directly and adversely affected by the alleged infringement. However, there are situations where the condition of a «legitimate interest» in Article 7(2) requires further analysis to conclude that it is fulfilled. Useful guidance can best be provided by a non-exhaustive set of examples.

35. The Court of First Instance has held that an association of undertakings may claim a legitimate interest in lodging a complaint regarding conduct concerning its members, even if it is not directly concerned, as an undertaking operating in the relevant market, by the conduct complained of, provided that, first, it is entitled to represent the interests of its members and secondly, the conduct complained of is liable to adversely affect the interests of its members (29). Conversely, the Commission has been found to be entitled not to pursue the complaint of an association of undertakings whose members were not involved in the type of business transactions complained of (30).

(29) Case T-114/92, Bureau Européen des Médias et de l'Industrie Musicale (BEMIM) v Commission of the European Communities, [1995] ECR II-147, para 28. Associations of undertakings were also the complainants in the cases underlying the judgments in Case 298/83, Comité des industries cinématographiques des Communautés européennes (CICCE) v Commission of the European Communities, [1985] ECR 1105 and Case T-319/99, Federacion Nacional de Empresas (FENIN) v Commission of the European Communities, not yet published in [2003] ECR.

(30) Joined Cases T-133/95 and T-204/95, International Express Carriers Conference (IECC) v Commission of the European Communities, [1998] ECR II-3645, paras 79-83.

36. From this case law, it can be inferred that undertakings (themselves or through associations that are entitled to represent their interests) can claim a legitimate interest where they are operating in the relevant market or where the conduct complained of is liable to directly and adversely affect their interests. This confirms the established practice of the Commission which has accepted that a legitimate interest can, for instance, be claimed by the parties to the agreement or practice which is the subject of the complaint, by competitors whose interests have allegedly been damaged by the behaviour complained of or by undertakings excluded from a distribution system.

37. Consumer associations can equally lodge complaints with the Commission (31). The Commission moreover holds the view that individual consumers whose economic interests are directly and adversely affected insofar as they are the buyers of goods or services that are the object of an infringement can be in a position to show a legitimate interest (32).

(31) Case T-37/92, Bureau Européen des Unions des Consommateurs (BEUC) v Commission of the European Communities, [1994] ECR II-285, para 36.

(32) This question is currently raised in a pending procedure before the Court of First Instance (Joined cases T-213 and 214/01). The Commission has also accepted as complainant an individual consumer in its Decision of 9 December 1998 in Case IV/D-2/34.466, Greek Ferries, O.J. L 109/24 of 27 April 1999, para 1.

38. However, the Commission does not consider as a legitimate interest within the meaning of Article 7(2) the interest of persons or organisations that wish to come forward on general interest considerations without showing that they or their members are liable to be directly and adversely affected by the infringement (*pro bono publico*).

39. Local or regional public authorities may be able to show a legitimate interest in their capacity as buyers or users of goods or services affected by the conduct complained of. Conversely, they cannot be considered as showing a legitimate interest within the meaning of Article 7(2) of Regulation 1/2003 to the extent that they bring to the attention of the Commission alleged infringements *pro bono publico*.

40. Complainants have to demonstrate their legitimate interest. Where a natural or legal person lodging a complaint is unable to demonstrate a legitimate interest, the Commission is entitled, without prejudice to its right to initiate proceedings of its own initiative, not to pursue the complaint. The Commission may ascertain whether this condition is met at any stage of the investigation (33).

(33) Joined Cases T-133/95 and T-204/95, International Express Carriers Conference (IECC) v Commission of the European Communities, [1998] ECR II-3645, para 79.

C. Assessment of complaints

(a) Community interest

41. Under the settled case law of the Community Courts, the Commission is not required to conduct an investigation in each case (34) or, *a fortiori*, to take a decision within the meaning of Article 249 EC on the existence or non-existence of an infringement of Articles 81 or 82 (35), but is entitled to give differing degrees of priority to the complaints brought before it and refer to the Community interest in order to determine the degree of priority to be applied to the various complaints it receives (36). The position is different only if the complaint falls within the exclusive competence of the Commission (37).

(34) Case T-24/90, Automec v Commission of the European Communities, [1992] ECR II-2223, para 76; Case C-91/95 P, Roger Tremblay and Others v Commission of the European Communities, [1996] ECR I-5547, para 30.

(35) Case 125/78, GEMA v Commission of the European Communities, [1979] ECR 3173, para 17; Case C-119/97/P, Union française de l'express (Ufex) and Others v Commission of the European Communities, [1999] ECR I-1341, para 87.

(36) Settled case law since the Case T-24/90, Automec v Commission of the European Communities, [1992] ECR II-2223, paras 77 and 85; Recital 18 of Regulation 1/2003 expressly confirms this possibility.

(37) Settled case law since Case T-24/90, Automec v Commission of the European Communities, [1992] ECR II-2223, para 75. Under Regulation 1/2003, this principle may only be relevant in the context of Article 29 of that Regulation.

42. The Commission must however examine carefully the factual and legal elements brought to its attention by the complainant in order to assess the Community interest in further investigation of a case (38).

(38) Case 210/81, Oswald Schmidt, trading as Demo-Studio Schmidt v Commission of the European Communities, [1983] ECR 3045, para 19; Case C-119/97 P, Union française de l'express (Ufex) and Others v Commission of the European Communities, [1999] ECR I-1341, para 86.

43. The assessment of the Community interest raised by a complaint depends on the circumstances of each individual case. Accordingly, the number of criteria of assessment to which the Commission may refer is not limited, nor is the Commission required to have recourse exclusively to certain criteria. As the factual and legal circumstances may differ considerably from case to case, it is permissible to apply new criteria which had not before been considered (39). Where appropriate, the Commission may give priority to a single criterion for assessing the Community interest (40).

(39) Case C-119/97 P, Union française de l'express (Ufex) and Others v Commission of the European Communities, [1999] ECR I-1341, paras 79-80.

(40) Case C-450/98 P, International Express Carriers Conference (IECC) v Commission of the European Communities, [2001] ECR I-3947, paras 57-59.

44. Among the criteria which have been held relevant in the case law for the assessment of the Community interest in the (further) investigation of a case are the following:

– The Commission can reject a complaint on the ground that the complainant can bring an action to assert its rights before national courts (41).

– The Commission may not regard certain situations as excluded in principle from its purview under the task entrusted to it by the Treaty but is required to assess in each case how serious the alleged infringements are and how persistent their consequences are. This means in particular that it must take into account the duration and the extent of the infringements complained of and their effect on the competition situation in the Community (42).

– The Commission may have to balance the significance of the alleged infringement as regards the functioning of the common market, the probability of establishing the existence of the infringement and the scope of the investigation required in order to fulfil its task of ensuring that Articles 81 and 82 of the Treaty are complied with (43).

– While the Commission's discretion does not depend on how advanced the investigation of a case is, the stage of the investigation forms part of the circumstances of the case which the Commission may have to take into consideration (44).

– The Commission may decide that it is not appropriate to investigate a complaint where the practices in question have ceased. However, for this purpose, the Commission will have to ascertain whether anticompetitive effects persist and if the seriousness of the infringements or the persistence of their effects does not give the complaint a Community interest (45).

– The Commission may also decide that it is not appropriate to investigate a complaint where the undertakings concerned agree to change their conduct in such a way that it can consider that there is no longer a sufficient Community interest to intervene (46).

(41) Case T-24/90, Automec v Commission of the European Communities, [1992] ECR II-2223, paras 88ss.; Case T-5/93, Roger Tremblay and Others v Commission of the European Communities, [1995] ECR II-185, paras 65ss.; Case T-575/93, Casper Koelman v Commission of the European Communities, [1996] ECR II-1, paras 75-80; see also part II above where more detailed explanations concerning this situation are given.

(42) Case C-119/97 P, Union française de l'express (Ufex) and Others v Commission of the European Communities, [1999] ECR I-1341, paras 92/93.

(43) Settled case law since Case T-24/90, Automec v Commission of the European Communities, [1992] ECR II-2223, para 86.

(44) Case C-449/98 P, International Express Carriers Conference (IECC) v Commission of the European Communities [2001] ECR I-3875, para 37.

(45) Case T-77/95, Syndicat français de l'Express International and Others v Commission of the European Communities [1997] ECR II-1, para 57; Case C-119/97 P, Union française de l'express (Ufex) and Others v Commission of the European Communities, [1999] ECR I-1341, para 95. Cf. also Case T-37/92, Bureau Européen des Unions des Consommateurs (BEUC) v Commission of the European Communities, [1994] ECR II-285, para 113, where an unwritten commitment between a Member State and a third county outside the common commercial policy was held not to suffice to establish that the conduct complained of had ceased.

(46) Case T-110/95, International Express Carriers (IECC) v Commission of the European Communities and Others, [1998] ECR II-3605, para 57, upheld by Case 449/98 P, International Express Carriers (IECC) v Commission of the European Communities and Others, [2001] ECR I-3875, paras 44-47.

45. Where it forms the view that a case does not display sufficient Community interest to justify (further) investigation, the Commission may reject the complaint on that ground. Such a decision can be taken either before commencing an investigation or after taking investigative measures (47). However, the Commission is not obliged to set aside a complaint for lack of Community interest (48).

(47) Case C-449/98 P, International Express Carriers (IECC) v Commission of the European Communities e.a. [2001] ECR I-3875, para 37.

(48) Cf. Case T-77/92, Parker Pen v Commission of the European Communities, [1994] ECR II-549, paras 64/65.

(b) Assessment under Articles 81 and 82

46. The examination of a complaint under Articles 81 and 82 involves two aspects, one relating to the facts to be established to prove an infringement of Articles 81 or 82 and the other relating to the legal assessment of the conduct complained of.

47. Where the complaint, while complying with the requirements of Article 5 of Regulation 773/2004 and Form C, does not sufficiently substantiate the allegations put forward, it may be rejected on that ground (49). In order to reject a complaint on the ground that the conduct complained of does not infringe the EC competition rules or does not fall within their scope of application, the Commission is not obliged to take into account circumstances that have not been brought to its attention by the complainant and that it could only have uncovered by the investigation of the case (50).

(49) Case 298/83, Comité des industries cinématographiques des Communautés européennes (CICCE) v Commission of the European Communities, [1985] ECR 1105, paras 21-24; Case T-198/98, Micro Leader Business v Commission of the European Communities, [1999] ECR II-3989, paras 32-39.

(50) Case T-319/99, Federación Nacional de Empresas (FENIN) v Commission of the European Communities, not yet published in [2003] ECR, para 43.

48. The criteria for the legal assessment of agreements or practices under Articles 81 and 82 cannot be dealt with exhaustively in the present Notice. However, potential complainants should refer to the extensive guidance available from the Commission (51), in addition to other sources and in particular the case law of the Community Courts and the case practice of the Commission. Four specific issues are mentioned in the following points with indications on where to find further guidance.

(51) Extensive guidance can be found on the Commission's website at http://europa.eu.int/comm/competition/index_en.html.

49. Agreements and practices fall within the scope of application of Articles 81 and 82 where they are capable of affecting trade between Member States. Where an agreement or practice does not fulfil this condition, national competition law may apply, but not EC competition law. Extensive guidance on this subject can be found in the Notice on the effect on trade concept (52).

(52) Notice on the effect on trade concept contained in Articles 81 and 82 of the Treaty (p. 81).

50. Agreements falling within the scope of Article 81 may be agreements of minor importance which are deemed not to restrict competition appreciably. Guidance on this issue can be found in the Commission's de minimis Notice (53).

(53) Commission Notice on agreements of minor importance which do not appreciably restrict competition under Article 81(1) of the Treaty establishing the European Community (de minimis), O.J. C 368 of 22 December 2002, p. 13.

51. Agreements that fulfil the conditions of a block exemption regulation are deemed to satisfy the conditions of Article 81(3) (54). For the Commission to withdraw the benefit of the block exemption pursuant to Article 29 of Regulation 1/2003, it must find that upon individual assessment an agreement to which the exemption regulation applies has certain effects which are incompatible with Article 81(3).

(54) The texts of all block exemption regulations are available on the Commission's website at http://europa.eu.int/comm/competition/index_en.html.

52. Agreements that restrict competition within the meaning of Article 81(1) EC may fulfil the conditions of Article 81(3) EC. Pursuant to Article 1(2) of Regulation 1/2003 and without a prior administrative decision being required, such agreements are not prohibited. Guidance on the conditions to be fulfilled by an agreement pursuant to Article 81(3) can be found in the Notice on Article 81(3) (55).

(55) Commission Notice – Guidelines on the application of Article 81(3) of the Treaty (p. 97).

D. The Commission's procedures when dealing with complaints

(a) Overview

53. As recalled above, the Commission is not obliged to carry out an investigation on the basis of every complaint submitted with a view to establishing whether an infringement has been committed. However, the Commission is under a duty to consider carefully the factual and legal issues brought to its attention by the complainant, in order to assess whether those issues indicate conduct which is liable to infringe Articles 81 and 82 (56).

(56) Case 210/81, Oswald Schmidt, trading as Demo-Studio Schmidt v Commission of the European Communities, [1983] ECR 3045, para 19; Case T-24/90, Automec v Commission of the European Communities, [1992] ECR II-2223, para 79.

54. In the Commission's procedure for dealing with complaints, different stages can be distinguished (57).

(57) Cf. Case T-64/89, Automec v Commission of the European Communities, [1990] ECR II-367, paras 45-47; Case T-37/92, Bureau Européen des Unions des Consommateurs (BEUC) v Commission of the European Communities, [1994] ECR II-285, para 29.

55. During the first stage, following the submission of the complaint, the Commission examines the complaint and may collect further information in order to decide what action it will take on the complaint. That stage may include an informal exchange of views between the Commission and the complainant with a view to clarifying the factual and legal issues with which the complaint is concerned. In this stage, the Commission may give an initial reaction to the complainant allowing the complainant an opportunity to expand on his allegations in the light of that initial reaction.

56. In the second stage, the Commission may investigate the case further with a view to initiating proceedings pursuant to Article 7(1) of Regulation 1/2003 against the undertakings complained of. Where the Commission considers that there are insufficient grounds for acting on the complaint, it will inform the complainant of its reasons and offer the complainant the opportunity to submit any further comments within a time-limit which it fixes (Article 7(1) of Regulation 773/2004).

57. If the complainant fails to make known its views within the time-limit set by the Commission, the complaint is deemed to have been withdrawn (Article 7(3) of Regulation 773/2004). In all other cases, in the third stage of the procedure, the Commission takes cognisance of the observations submitted by the complainant and either initiates a procedure against the subject of the complaint or adopts a decision rejecting the complaint (58).

(58) Case C-282/95 P, Guérin automobiles v Commission of the European Communities, [1997] ECR I-1503, para 36.

58. Where the Commission rejects a complaint pursuant to Article 13 of Regulation 1/2003 on the grounds that another authority is dealing or has dealt with the case, the Commission proceeds in accordance with Article 9 of Regulation 773/2004.

59. Throughout the procedure, complainants benefit from a range of rights as provided in particular in Articles 6 to 8 of Regulation 773/2004. However, proceedings of the Commission in competition cases do not constitute adversarial proceedings between the complainant on the one hand and the companies which are the subject of the investigation on the other hand. Accordingly, the procedural rights of complainants are less far-reaching than the right to a fair hearing of the companies which are the subject of an infringement procedure (59).

(59) Joined Cases 142 and 156/84, British American Tobacco Company and R. J. Reynolds Industries v Commission of the European Communities [1987] ECR 249, paras 19/20.

(b) Indicative time limit for informing the complainant of the Commission's proposed action

60. The Commission is under an obligation to decide on complaints within a reasonable time (60). What is a reasonable duration depends on the circumstances of each case and in particular, its context, the various procedural steps followed by the Commission, the conduct of the parties in the course of the procedure, the complexity of the case and its importance for the various parties involved (61).

(60) Case C-282/95 P, Guérin automobiles v Commission of the European Communities, [1997] ECR I-1503, para 37.

(61) Joined Cases T-213/95 and T-18/96, Stichting Certificatie Kraanverhuurbedrijf (SCK) and Federatie van Nederlandse Kraanbedrijven (FNK) v Commission of the European Communities, [1997] ECR 1739, para 57.

61. The Commission will in principle endeavour to inform complainants of the action that it proposes to take on a complaint within an indicative time frame of four months from the reception of the complaint. Thus, subject to the circumstances of the individual case and in particular the possible need to request complementary information from the complainant or third parties, the Commission will in principle inform the complainant within four months whether or not it intends to investigate its case further. This time-limit does not constitute a binding statutory term.

62. Accordingly, within this four month period, the Commission may communicate its proposed course of action to the complainant as an initial reaction within the first phase

of the procedure (see point 55 above). The Commission may also, where the examination of the complaint has progressed to the second stage (see point 56 above), directly proceed to informing the complainant about its provisional assessment by a letter pursuant to Article 7(1) of Regulation 773/2004.

63. To ensure the most expeditious treatment of their complaint, it is desirable that complainants cooperate diligently in the procedures (62), for example by informing the Commission of new developments.

(62) The notion of «diligence» on the part of the complainant is used by the Court of First Instance in Case T-77/94, Vereniging van Groothandelaren in Bloemkwekerijprodukten and Others v Commission of the European Communities, [1997] ECR II-759, para 75.

(c) Procedural rights of the complainant

64. Where the Commission addresses a statement of objections to the companies complained of pursuant to Article 10(1) of Regulation 773/2004, the complainant is entitled to receive a copy of this document from which business secrets and other confidential information of the companies concerned have been removed (non-confidential version of the statement of objections; cf. Article 6(1) of Regulation 773/2004). The complainant is invited to comment in writing on the statement of objections. A time-limit will be set for such written comments.

65. Furthermore, the Commission may, where appropriate, afford complainants the opportunity of expressing their views at the oral hearing of the parties to which a statement of objections has been addressed, if the complainants so request in their written comments (63).

(63) Article 6(2) of Commission Regulation 773/2004.

66. Complainants may submit, of their own initiative or following a request by the Commission, documents that contain business secrets or other confidential information. Confidential information will be protected by the Commission (64). Under Article 16 of Regulation 773/2004, complainants are obliged to identify confidential information, give reasons why the information is considered confidential and submit a separate non-confidential version when they make their views known pursuant to Article 6(1) and 7(1) of Regulation 773/2004, as well as when they subsequently submit further information in the course of the same procedure. Moreover, the Commission may, in all other cases, request complainants which produce documents or statements to identify the documents or parts of the documents or statements which they consider to be confidential. It may in particular set a deadline for the complainant to specify why it considers a piece of information to be confidential and to provide a non-confidential version, including a concise description or non-confidential version of each piece of information deleted.

(64) Article 287 EC, Article 28 of Regulation 1/2003 and Articles 15 and 16 of Regulation 773/2004.

67. The qualification of information as confidential does not prevent the Commission from disclosing and using information where that is necessary to prove an infringement of Articles 81 or 82 (65). Where business secrets and confidential information are necessary to prove an infringement, the Commission must assess for each individual document whether the need to disclose is greater than the harm which might result from disclosure.

(65) Article 27(2) of Regulation 1/2003.

68. Where the Commission takes the view that a complaint should not be further examined, because there is no sufficient Community interest in pursuing the case further or on other grounds, it will inform the complainant in the form of a letter which indicates its legal basis (Article 7(1) of Regulation 773/2004), sets out the reasons that have led the Commission to provisionally conclude in the sense indicated and provides the complainant with the opportunity to submit supplementary information or observations within a time-limit set by the Commission. The Commission will also indicate the consequences of not replying pursuant to Article 7(3) of Regulation 773/2004, as explained below.

69. Pursuant to Article 8(1) of Regulation 773/2004, the complainant has the right to access the information on which the Commission bases its preliminary view. Such access is normally provided by annexing to the letter a copy of the relevant documents.

70. The time-limit for observations by the complainant on the letter pursuant to Article 7(1) of Regulation 773/2004 will be set in accordance with the circumstances of the case. It will not be shorter than four weeks (Article 17(2) of Regulation 773/2004). If the complainant does not respond within the time-limit set, the complaint is deemed to have been withdrawn pursuant to Article 7(3) of Regulation 773/2004. Complainants are also entitled to withdraw their complaint at any time if they so wish.

71. The complainant may request an extension of the time-limit for the provision of comments. Depending on the circumstances of the case, the Commission may grant such an extension.

72. In that case, where the complainant submits supplementary observations, the Commission takes cognisance of those observations. Where they are of such a nature as to make the Commission change its previous course of action, it may initiate a procedure against the companies complained of. In this procedure, the complainant has the procedural rights explained above.

73. Where the observations of the complainant do not alter the Commission's proposed course of action, it rejects the complaint by decision (66).

(66) Article 7(2) of Regulation 773/2004; Case C-282/95 P, Guérin automobiles v Commission of the European Communities, [1997] ECR I-1503, para 36.

(d) The Commission decision rejecting a complaint

74. Where the Commission rejects a complaint by decision pursuant to Article 7(2) of Regulation 773/2004, it must state the reasons in accordance with Article 253 EC, i.e. in a way that is appropriate to the act at issue and takes into account the circumstances of each case.

75. The statement of reasons must disclose in a clear and unequivocal fashion the reasoning followed by the Commission in such a way as to enable the complainant to ascertain the reasons for the decision and to enable the competent Community Court to exercise its power of review. However, the Commission is not obliged to adopt a position on all the arguments relied on by the complainant in support of its complaint. It only needs to set out the facts and legal considerations which are of decisive importance in the context of the decision (67).

(67) Settled case law, cf. i.a. Case T-114/92, Bureau Européen des Médias et de l'Industrie Musicale (BEMIM) v Commission of the European Communities, [1995] ECR II-147, para 41.

76. Where the Commission rejects a complaint in a case that also gives rise to a decision pursuant to Article 10 of Regulation 1/2003 (Finding of inapplicability of Articles 81 or 82) or Article 9 of Regulation 1/2003 (Commitments), the decision rejecting a complaint may refer to that other decision adopted on the basis of the provisions mentioned.

77. A decision to reject a complaint is subject to appeal before the Community Courts (68).

(68) Settled case law since Case 210/81, Oswald Schmidt, trading as Demo-Studio Schmidt v Commission of the European Communities, [1983] ECR 3045.

78. A decision rejecting a complaint prevents complainants from requiring the reopening of the investigation unless they put forward significant new evidence. Accordingly, further correspondence on the same alleged infringement by former complainants cannot be regarded as a new complaint unless significant new evidence is brought to the attention of the Commission. However, the Commission may re-open a file under appropriate circumstances.

79. A decision to reject a complaint does not definitively rule on the question of whether or not there is an infringement of Articles 81 or 82, even where the Commission has assessed the facts on the basis of Articles 81 and 82. The assessments made by the Commission in a decision rejecting a complaint therefore do not prevent a Member State court or competition authority from applying Articles 81 and 82 to agreements and practices brought before it. The assessments made by the Commission in a decision rejecting a complaint constitute facts which Member States' courts or competition authorities may take into account in examining whether the agreements or conduct in question are in conformity with Articles 81 and 82 (69).

(69) Case T-575/93, Casper Koelman v Commission of the European Communities, [1996] ECR II-1, paras 41-43.

(e) Specific situations

80. According to Article 8 of Regulation 1/2003 the Commission may on its own initiative order interim measures where there is the risk of serious and irreparable damage to competition. Article 8 of Regulation 1/2003 makes it clear that interim measures cannot be applied for by complainants under Article 7(2) of Regulation 1/2003. Requests for interim measures by undertakings can be brought before Member States' courts which are well placed to decide on such measures (70).

(70) Depending on the case, Member States' competition authorities may equally be well placed to adopt interim measures.

81. Some persons may wish to inform the Commission about suspected infringements of Articles 81 or 82 without having their identity revealed to the undertakings concerned by the allegations. These persons are welcome to contact the Commission. The Commission is bound to respect an informant's request for anonymity (71), unless the request to remain anonymous is manifestly unjustified.

(71) Case 145/83, Stanley George Adams v Commission of the European Communities, [1985] ECR 3539.

Commission Notice on informal guidance relating to novel questions concerning Articles 81 and 82 of the EC Treaty that arise in individual cases

(OJ C 101, 27 April 2004, p. 78)

1. Article 81 EC is now Article 101 TFEU and Article 82 EC is now Article 102 TFEU.

I. REGULATION 1/2003

1. Regulation 1/2003 (1) sets up a new enforcement system for Articles 81 and 82 of the Treaty. While designed to restore the focus on the primary task of effective enforcement of the competition rules, the Regulation also creates legal certainty inasmuch as it provides that agreements (2) which fall under Article 81(1) but fulfil the conditions in Article 81(3) are valid and fully enforceable ab initio without a prior decision by a competition authority (Article 1 of Regulation 1/2003).

(1) Council Regulation (EC) N° 1/2003 of 16 December 2002 on the implementation of the rules on competition laid down in Articles 81 and 82 of the Treaty (O.J. L 1, 4.1.2003, pages 1-25).

(2) In this Notice, the term «agreement» is used for agreements, decisions by associations of undertakings and concerted practices. The term «practices» refers to the conduct of dominant undertakings. The term «undertakings» equally covers «associations of undertakings».

2. The framework of Regulation 1/2003, while introducing parallel competence of the Commission, Member States' competition authorities and Member States' courts to apply Article 81 and 82 in their entirety, limits risks of inconsistent application by a range of measures, thereby ensuring the primary aspect of legal certainty for companies as reflected in the case law of the Court of Justice, i.e. that the competition rules are applied in a consistent way throughout the Community.

3. Undertakings are generally well placed to assess the legality of their actions in such a way as to enable them to take an informed decision on whether to go ahead with an agreement or practice and in what form. They are close to the facts and have at their disposal the framework of block exemption regulations, case law and case practice as well as extensive guidance in Commission guidelines and notices (3).

(3) All texts mentioned are available at: http://europa.eu.int/comm/competition/index_en.html.

4. Alongside the reform of the rules implementing Articles 81 and 82 brought about by Regulation 1/2003, the Commission has conducted a review of block exemption regulations, Commission notices and guidelines, with a view to further assist self-assessment by economic operators. The Commission has also produced guidelines on the application of Article 81(3) (4). This allows undertakings in the vast majority of cases to reliably assess their agreements with regard to Article 81. Furthermore, it is the practice of the Commission to impose more than symbolic fines (5) only in cases where it is established, either in horizontal instruments or in the case law and practice that a certain behaviour constitutes an infringement.

(4) Commission Notice – Guidelines on the application of Article 81(3) of the Treaty (p. 97).

(5) Symbolic fines are normally set at 1 000 EUR, cf. Commission Guidelines on the method of setting fines imposed pursuant to Article 15(2) of Regulation N° 17 and Article 65(5) of the ECSC Treaty, (O.J. C 9, 14.1.1998).

5. Where cases, despite the above elements, give rise to genuine uncertainty because they present novel or unresolved questions for the application of Articles 81 and 82, individual undertakings may wish to seek informal guidance from the Commission (6). Where it considers it appropriate and subject to its enforcement priorities, the Commission may provide such guidance on novel questions concerning the interpretation of Articles 81 and/or 82 in a written statement (guidance letter). The present Notice sets out details of this instrument.

(6) Cf. Recital 38 of Regulation 1/2003.

II. FRAMEWORK FOR ASSESSING WHETHER TO ISSUE A GUIDANCE LETTER

6. Regulation 1/2003 confers powers on the Commission to effectively prosecute infringements of Articles 81 and 82 and to impose sanctions (7). One major objective of the Regulation is to ensure efficient enforcement of the EC competition rules by removing the former notification system and thus allowing the Commission to focus its enforcement policy on the most serious infringements (8).

(7) Cf. in particular Articles 7 to 9, 12, 17-24, 29 of Regulation 1/2003.

(8) Cf. in particular Recital 3 of Regulation 1/2003.

7. While Regulation 1/2003 is without prejudice to the ability of the Commission to issue informal guidance to individual undertakings (9), as set out in this Notice, this ability should not interfere with the primary objective of the Regulation, which is to ensure effective enforcement. The Commission may therefore only provide informal guidance to individual undertakings in so far as this is compatible with its enforcement priorities.

(9) Cf. Recital 38 of Regulation 1/2003.

8. Subject to point 7, the Commission, seized of a request for a guidance letter, will consider whether it is appropriate to process it. Issuing a guidance letter may only be considered if the following cumulative conditions are fulfilled:

(a) The substantive assessment of an agreement or practice with regard to Articles 81 and/or 82 of the Treaty, poses a question of application of the law for which there is no clarification in the existing EC legal framework including the case law of the Community Courts, nor publicly available general guidance or precedent in decision-making practice or previous guidance letters.

(b) A *prima facie* evaluation of the specificities and background of the case suggests that the clarification of the novel question through a guidance letter is useful, taking into account the following elements:

– the economic importance from the point of view of the consumer of the goods or services concerned by the agreement or practice, and/or

– the extent to which the agreement or practice corresponds or is liable to correspond to more widely spread economic usage in the marketplace and/or

– the extent of the investments linked to the transaction in relation to the size of the companies concerned and the extent to which the transaction relates to a structural operation such as the creation of a non-full function joint venture.

(c) It is possible to issue a guidance letter on the basis of the information provided, i.e. no further fact-finding is required.

9. Furthermore, the Commission will not consider a request for a guidance letter in either of the following circumstances:

– the questions raised in the request are identical or similar to issues raised in a case pending before the European Court of First Instance or the European Court of Justice;

– the agreement or practice to which the request refers is subject to proceedings pending with the Commission, a Member State court or Member State competition authority.

10. The Commission will not consider hypothetical questions and will not issue guidance letters on agreements or practices that are no longer being implemented by the parties. Undertakings may however present a request for a guidance letter to the Commission in relation to questions raised by an agreement or practice that they envisage, i.e. before the implementation of that agreement or practice. In this case the transaction must have reached a sufficiently advanced stage for a request to be considered.

11. A request for a guidance letter is without prejudice to the power of the Commission to open proceedings in accordance with Regulation 1/2003 with regard to the facts presented in the request.

III. INDICATIONS ON HOW TO REQUEST GUIDANCE

12. A request can be presented by an undertaking or undertakings which have entered into or intend to enter into an agreement or practice that could fall within the scope of Articles 81 and/or 82 of the Treaty with regard to questions of interpretation raised by such agreement or practice.

13. A request for a guidance letter should be addressed to the following address: Commission européenne/Europese Commissie – Competition DG – B-1049 Bruxelles/Brussel.

14. There is no form. A *memorandum* should be presented which clearly states:

– the identity of all undertakings concerned as well as a single address for contacts with the Commission;

– the specific questions on which guidance is sought;

– full and exhaustive information on all points relevant for an informed evaluation of the questions raised, including pertinent documentation;

– a detailed reasoning, having regard to point 8 *a)*, why the request presents *(a)* novel question(s);

– all other information that permits an evaluation of the request in the light of the aspects explained in points 8-10 of this Notice, including in particular a declaration that the agreement or practice to which the request refers is not subject to proceedings pending before a Member State court or competition authority;

– where the request contains elements that are considered business secrets, a clear identification of these elements;

– any other information or documentation relevant to the individual case.

IV. PROCESSING OF THE REQUEST

15. The Commission will in principle evaluate the request on the basis of the information provided. Notwithstanding point 8 *c)*, the Commission may use additional information at its disposal from public sources, former proceedings or any other source and may ask the applicant(s) to provide supplementary information. The normal rules on professional secrecy apply to the information supplied by the applicant(s).

16. The Commission may share the information submitted to it with the Member States' competition authorities and receive input from them. It may discuss the substance of the request with the Member States' competition authorities before issuing a guidance letter.

17. Where no guidance letter is issued, the Commission shall inform the applicant(s) accordingly.

18. An undertaking can withdraw its request at time. In any case, information supplied in the context of a request for guidance remains with the Commission and can be used in subsequent procedures under Regulation 1/2003 (cf. point 11 above).

V. GUIDANCE LETTERS

19. A guidance letter sets out:
 – a summary description of the facts on which it is based;
 – the principal legal reasoning underlying the understanding of the Commission on novel questions relating to Articles 81 and/or 82 raised by the request.

20. A guidance letter may be limited to part of the questions raised in the request. It may also include additional aspects to those set out in the request.

21. Guidance letters will be posted on the Commission's webb-site, having regard to the legitimate interest of undertakings in the protection of their business secrets. Before issuing a guidance letter, the Commission will agree with the applicants on a public version.

VI. THE EFFECTS OF GUIDANCE LETTERS

22. Guidance letters are in the first place intended to help undertakings carry out themselves an informed assessment of their agreements and practices.

23. A guidance letter cannot prejudge the assessment of the same question by the Community Courts.

24. Where an agreement or practice has formed the factual basis for a guidance letter, the Commission is not precluded from subsequently examining that same agreement or practice in a procedure under Regulation 1/2003, in particular following a complaint. In that case, the Commission will take the previous guidance letter into account, subject in particular to changes in the underlying facts, to any new aspects raised by a complaint, to developments in the case law of the European Courts or wider changes of the Commission's policy.

25. Guidance letters are not Commission decisions and do not bind Member States' competition authorities or courts that have the power to apply Articles 81 and 82. However, it is open to Member States' competition authorities and courts to take account of guidance letters issued by the Commission as they see fit in the context of a case.

Commission Notice on the rules for access to the Commission file in cases pursuant to Articles 81 and 82 of the EC Treaty, Articles 53, 54 and 57 of the EEA Agreement and Council Regulation (EC) N° 139/2004

(OJ C 325, 22 December 2005, p. 7)

1. Article 81 EC is now Article 101 TFEU and Article 82 EC is now Article 102 TFEU.

2. See above, section 2.1.3. Procedural rules

I. INTRODUCTION AND SUBJECT-MATTER OF THE NOTICE

1. Access to the Commission file is one of the procedural guarantees intended to apply the principle of equality of arms and to protect the rights of the defence. Access to the file is provided for in Article 27(1) and (2) of Council Regulation (EC) N° 1/2003 (1), Article 15(1) of Commission Regulation (EC) N° 773/2004 («the Implementing Regulation») (2), Article 18(1) and (3) of the Council Regulation (EC) N° 139/2004 («Merger Regulation») (3) and Article 17(1) of Commission Regulation (EC) N° 802/2004 («the Merger Implementing Regulation») (4). In accordance with these provisions, before taking decisions on the basis of Articles 7, 8, 23 and 24(2) of Regulation (EC) N° 1/2003 and Articles 6(3), 7(3), 8(2) to (6), 14 and 15 of the Merger Regulation, the Commission shall give the persons, undertakings or associations of undertakings, as the case may be, an opportunity of making known their views on the objections against them and they shall be entitled to have access to the Commission's file in order to fully respect their rights of defence in the proceedings. The present notice provides the framework for the exercise of the right set out in these provisions. It does not cover the possibility of the provision of documents in the context of other proceedings. This notice is without prejudice to the interpretation of such provisions by the Community Courts. The principles set out in this Notice apply also when the Commission enforces Articles 53, 54 and 57 of the EEA Agreement (5).

(1) Council Regulation (EC) N° 1/2003 of 16 December 2002 on the implementation of the rules on competition laid down in Articles 81 and 82 of the Treaty, O.J. L 1, 4.1.2003, p. 1-25.

(2) Commission Regulation (EC) N° 773/2004 of 7 April 2004 relating to the conduct of proceedings by the Commission pursuant to Articles 81 and 82 of the EC Treaty, O.J. L 123, 27.4.2004, p. 18-24.

(3) Council Regulation (EC) N° 139/2004 of 20 January 2004 on the control of concentrations between undertakings, O.J. L 24, 29.1.2004, p. 1-22.

(4) Commission Regulation (EC) N° 802/2004 of 21 April 2004 implementing Council Regulation (EC) N° 139/2004 on the control of concentrations between undertakings, O.J. L 133, 30.4.2004, p. 1-39. Corrected in the O.J. L 172, 6.5.2004, p. 9.

(5) References in this Notice to Articles 81 and 82 therefore apply also to Articles 53 and 54 of the EEA Agreement.

2. This specific right outlined above is distinct from the general right to access to documents under Regulation (EC) N° 1049/2001 (6), which is subject to different criteria and exceptions and pursues a different purpose.

(6) Regulation (EC) N° 1049/2001 of the European Parliament and of the Council of 30 May 2001 regarding public access to European Parliament, Council and Commission documents, O.J. L 145, 31.5.2001, p. 43. See for instance Case T-2/03, Verein für Konsumenteninformation v. Commission, judgment of 13 April 2005, not yet reported.

3. The term access to the file is used in this notice exclusively to mean the access granted to the persons, undertakings or association of undertakings to whom the Commission has addressed a statement of objections. This notice clarifies who has access to the file for this purpose.

4. The same term, or the term access to documents, is also used in the above-mentioned regulations in respect of complainants or other involved parties. These situations are, however, distinct from that of the addressees of a statement of objections and therefore do not fall under the definition of access to the file for the purposes of this notice. These related situations are dealt with in a separate section of the notice.

5. This notice also explains to which information access is granted, when access takes place and what are the procedures for implementing access to the file.

6. As from its publication, this notice replaces the 1997 Commission notice on access to the file (7). The new rules take account of the legislation applicable as of 1 May 2004, namely the above referred Regulation (EC) N° 1/2003, Merger Regulation, Implementing Regulation and Merger Implementing Regulation, as well as the Commission Decision of 23 May 2001 on the terms of reference of Hearing Officers in certain competition proceedings (8). It also takes into account the recent case law of the Court of Justice and the Court of First Instance of the European Communities (9) and the practice developed by the Commission since the adoption of the 1997 notice.

(7) Commission notice on the internal rules of procedure for processing requests for access to the file in cases under Articles 85 and 86 [now 81 and 82] of the EC Treaty, Articles 65 and 66 of the ECSC Treaty and Council Regulation (EEC) N° 4064/89, O.J. C 23, 23.1.1997, p. 3.

(8) O.J. L 162, 19.6.2001, p. 21.

(9) In particular Joint Cases T-25/95 et al., Cimenteries CBR SA et al. v Commission, [2000] ECR II-0491.

II. SCOPE OF ACCESS TO THE FILE

A. Who is entitled to access to the file?

7. Access to the file pursuant to the provisions mentioned in paragraph 1 is intended to enable the effective exercise of the rights of defence against the objections brought forward by the Commission. For this purpose, both in cases under Articles 81 and 82 EC and in cases under the Merger Regulation, access is granted, upon request, to the persons, undertakings or associations of undertakings (10), as the case may be, to which the Commission addresses its objections (11) (hereinafter, «the parties»).

(10) In the remainder of this Notice, the term «undertaking» includes both undertakings and associations of undertakings. The term «person» encompasses natural and legal persons. Many entities are legal persons and undertakings at the same time; in this case, they are covered by both terms. The same applies where a natural person is an undertaking within the meaning of Articles 81 and 82. In Merger proceedings, account must also be taken of persons referred to in Article 3(1)(b) of the Merger Regulation, even when they are natural persons. Where entities without legal personality which are also not undertakings become involved in Commission competition proceedings, the Commission applies, where appropriate, the principles set out in this Notice *mutatis mutandis*.

(11) Cf. Article 15(1) of the Implementing Regulation, Article 18(3) of the Merger Regulation and Article 17(1) of the Merger Implementing Regulation.

B. To which documents is access granted?

1. The content of the Commission file

8. The «Commission file» in a competition investigation (hereinafter also referred to as «the file») consists of all documents (12), which have been obtained, produced and/or assembled by the Commission Directorate General for Competition, during the investigation.

(12) In this notice the term «document» is used for all forms of information support, irrespective of the storage medium. This covers also any electronic data storage device as may be or become available.

9. In the course of investigation under Articles 20, 21 and 22(2) of Regulation (EC) N° 1/2003 and Articles 12 and 13 of the Merger Regulation, the Commission may collect a number of documents, some of which may, following a more detailed examination, prove to be unrelated to the subject matter of the case in question. Such documents may be returned to the undertaking from which those have been obtained. Upon return, these documents will no longer constitute part of the file.

2. Accessible documents

10. The parties must be able to acquaint themselves with the information in the Commission's file, so that, on the basis of this information, they can effectively express their views on the preliminary conclusions reached by the Commission in its objections. For this purpose they will be granted access to all documents making up the Commission file, as defined in paragraph 8, with the exception of internal documents, business secrets of other undertakings, or other confidential information (13).

(13) Cf. Article 27(2) of Regulation (EC) N° 1/2003, Articles 15(2) and 16(1) of the Implementing Regulation, and Article 17(3) of the Merger Implementing Regulation. Those exceptions are also mentioned in Case T-7/89, Hercules Chemicals v Commission, [1991] ECR II-1711, paragraph 54. The Court has ruled that it does not belong to the Commission alone to decide which documents in the file may be useful for the purposes of the defence (Cf. Case T-30/91 Solvay v. Commission, [1995] ECR II-1775, paragraphs 81-86, and Case T-36/91 ICI vs. Commission, [1995] ECR II-1847, paragraphs 91-96).

11. Results of a study commissioned in connection with proceedings are accessible together with the terms of reference and the methodology of the study. Precautions may however be necessary in order to protect intellectual property rights.

3. Non-accessible documents

3.1. Internal documents

3.1.1. General principles

12. Internal documents can be neither incriminating nor exculpatory (14). They do not constitute part of the evidence on which the Commission can rely in its assessment of a case. Thus, the parties will not be granted access to internal documents in the Commission file (15). Given their lack of evidential value, this restriction on access to internal documents does not prejudice the proper exercise of the parties' right of defence (16).

(14) Examples of internal documents are drafts, opinions, memos or notes from the Commission departments or other public authorities concerned.

(15) Cf. Article 27(2) of Regulation (EC) N° 1/2003, Article 15(2) of the Implementing Regulation, and Article 17(3) of the Merger Implementing Regulation.

(16) Cf. paragraph 1 above.

13. There is no obligation on the Commission departments to draft any minutes of meetings (17) with any person or undertaking. If the Commission chooses to make notes of such meetings, such documents constitute the Commission's own interpretation of what was said at the meetings, for which reason they are classified as internal documents. Where, however, the person or undertaking in question has agreed the minutes, such minutes will be made accessible after deletion of any business secrets or other confidential information. Such agreed minutes constitute part of the evidence on which the Commission can rely in its assessment of a case (18).

(17) Cf. judgement of 30.9.2003 in Joined Cases T-191/98 and T-212/98 to T-214/98 Atlantic Container Line and others v Commission (TACA), [2003] ECR II-3275, paragraphs 349-359.

(18) Statements recorded pursuant to Article 19 or Article 20(2)(e) of Regulation 1/2003 or Article 13(2)(e) of Merger Regulation will also normally belong to the accessible documents (see paragraph 10 above).

14. In the case of a study commissioned in connection with proceedings, correspondence between the Commission and its contractor containing evaluation of the contractor's work or relating to financial aspects of the study, are considered internal documents and will thus not be accessible.

3.1.2. Correspondence with other public authorities

15. A particular case of internal documents is the Commission's correspondence with other public authorities and the internal documents received from such authorities (whether from EC Member States («the Member States») or non-member countries). Examples of such non-accessible documents include:

– correspondence between the Commission and the competition authorities of the Member States, or between the latter (19);

– correspondence between the Commission and other public authorities of the Member States (20);

– correspondence between the Commission, the EFTA Surveillance Authority and public authorities of EFTA States (21);

– correspondence between the Commission and public authorities of non-member countries, including their competition authorities, in particular where the Community and a third country have concluded an agreement governing the confidentiality of the information exchanged (22).

(19) Cf. Article 27(2) of Regulation (EC) N° 1/2003, Article 15(2) of the Implementing Regulation, Article 17(3) of the Merger Implementing Regulation.

(20) Cf. Order of the Court of First Instance in Cases T-134/94 et al NMH Stahlwerke and Others v Commission [1997] ECR II-2293, paragraph 36, and Case T-65/89, BPB Industries and British Gypsum [1993] ECR II-389, paragraph 33.

(21) In this notice the term «EFTA States» includes the EFTA States that are parties to the EEA Agreement.

(22) For example, Article VIII.2 of the Agreement between the European Communities and the Government of the United States of America regarding the application of their competition laws (O.J. N° L 95, 27.4.1995, p. 47) stipulates that information provided to it in confidence under the Agreement must be protected «to the fullest extent possible». That Article creates an international-law obligation binding the Commission.

16. In certain exceptional circumstances, access is granted to documents originating from Member States, the EFTA Surveillance Authority or EFTA States, after deletion of any business secrets or other confidential information. The Commission will consult the entity submitting the document prior to granting access to identify business secrets or other confidential information.

This is the case where the documents originating from Member States contain allegations brought against the parties, which the Commission must examine, or form part of the evidence in the investigative process, in a way similar to documents obtained from private parties. These considerations apply, in particular, as regards:

– documents and information exchanged pursuant to Article 12 of Regulation (EC) N° 1/2003, and information provided to the Commission pursuant to Article 18(6) of Regulation (EC) N° 1/2003;

– complaints lodged by a Member State under Article 7(2) of Regulation (EC) N° 1/2003.

Access will also be granted to documents originating from Member States or the EFTA Surveillance Authority in so far as they are relevant to the parties' defence with regard to the exercise of competence by the Commission (23).

(23) In the merger control area, this may apply in particular to submissions by a Member State under Article 9 (2) of the Merger Regulation with regard to a case referral.

3.2. Confidential information

17. The Commission file may also include documents containing two categories of information, namely business secrets and other confidential information, to which access may be partially or totally restricted (24). Access will be granted, where possible, to non-confidential versions of the original information. Where confidentiality can only be assured by summarising the relevant information, access will be granted to a summary. All other documents are accessible in their original form.

(24) Cf. Article 16(1) of the Implementing Regulation and Article 17(3) of the Merger Implementing Regulation; Case T- 7/89 Hercules Chemicals NV v Commission, [1991] ECR II-1711, paragraph 54; Case T-23/99, LR AF 1998 A/S v Commission, [2002] ECR II-1705, paragraph 170.

3.2.1. Business secrets

18. In so far as disclosure of information about an undertaking's business activity could result in a serious harm to the same undertaking, such information constitutes business secrets (25). Examples of information that may qualify as business secrets include: technical and/or financial information relating to an undertaking's know-how, methods of assessing costs, production secrets and processes, supply sources, quantities produced and sold, market shares, customer and distributor lists, marketing plans, cost and price structure and sales strategy.

(25) Judgement of 18.9.1996 in Case T-353/94, Postbank NV v Commission, [1996] ECR II-921, paragraph 87.

3.2.2. Other confidential information

19. The category «other confidential information» includes information other than business secrets, which may be considered as confidential, insofar as its disclosure would significantly harm a person or undertaking. Depending on the specific circumstances of each case, this may apply to information provided by third parties about undertakings which are able to place very considerable economic or commercial pressure on their competitors or on their trading partners, customers or suppliers. The Court of First Instance and the Court of Justice have acknowledged that it is legitimate to refuse to reveal to such undertakings certain letters received from their customers, since their disclosure might easily expose the authors to the risk of retaliatory measures (26). Therefore the notion of other confidential information may include information that would enable the parties to identify complainants or other third parties where those have a justified wish to remain anonymous.

(26) The Community Courts have pronounced upon this question both in cases of alleged abuse of a dominant position (Article 82 of the EC Treaty) (Case T-65/89, BPB Industries and British Gypsum [1993] ECR II-389; and Case C-310/93P, BPB Industries and British Gypsum [1995] ECR I-865), and in merger cases (Case T-221/95 Endemol v Commission [1999] ECR II-1299, paragraph 69, and Case T-5/02 Laval v. Commission [2002] ECR II-4381, paragraph 98 et seq.).

20. The category of other confidential information also includes military secrets.

3.2.3. Criteria for the acceptance of requests for confidential treatment

21. Information will be classified as confidential where the person or undertaking in question has made a claim to this effect and such claim has been accepted by the Commission (27).

(27) See paragraph 40 below.

22. Claims for confidentiality must relate to information which is within the scope of the above descriptions of business secrets or other confidential information. The reasons for which information is claimed to be a business secret or other confidential information must be substantiated (28). Confidentiality claims can normally only pertain to information obtained by the Commission from the same person or undertaking and not to information from any other source.

(28) See paragraph 35 below.

23. Information relating to an undertaking but which is already known outside the undertaking (in case of a group, outside the group), or outside the association to which it has been communicated by that undertaking, will not normally be considered confidential (29). Information that has lost its commercial importance, for instance due to the passage of time, can no longer be regarded as confidential. As a general rule, the Commission presumes that information pertaining to the parties' turnover, sales, market-share data and similar information which is more than 5 years old is no longer confidential (30).

(29) However, business secrets or other confidential information which are given to a trade or professional association by its members do not lose their confidential nature with regard to third parties and may therefore not be passed on to complainants. Cf. Joined Cases 209 to 215 and 218/78, Fedetab, [1980] ECR 3125, paragraph 46.

(30) See paragraphs 35-38 below on asking undertakings to identify confidential information.

24. In proceedings under Articles 81 and 82 of the Treaty, the qualification of a piece of information as confidential is not a bar to its disclosure if such information is necessary to prove an alleged infringement («inculpatory document») or could be necessary to exonerate a party («exculpatory document»). In this case, the need to safeguard the rights of the defence of the parties through the provision of the widest possible access to the Commission file may outweigh the concern to protect confidential information of other parties (31). It is for the Commission to assess whether those circumstances apply to any specific situation. This calls for an assessment of all relevant elements, including:
– the relevance of the information in determining whether or not an infringement has been committed, and its probative value;
– whether the information is indispensable;
– the degree of sensitivity involved (to what extent would disclosure of the information harm the interests of the person or undertaking in question)
– the preliminary view of the seriousness of the alleged infringement.

Similar considerations apply to proceedings under the Merger Regulation when the disclosure of information is considered necessary by the Commission for the purpose of the procedure (32).

(31) Cf. Article 27(2) of Regulation (EC) N° 1/2003 and Article 15(3) of the Implementing Regulation.

(32) Article 18(1) of the Merger Implementing Regulation.

25. Where the Commission intends to disclose information, the person or undertaking in question shall be granted the possibility to provide a non-confidential version of the documents where that information is contained, with the same evidential value as the original documents (33).

(33) Cf. paragraph 42 below.

C. When is access to the file granted?

26. Prior to the notification of the Commission's statement of objections pursuant to the provisions mentioned in paragraph 1, the parties have no right of access to the file.

1. In antitrust proceedings under Articles 81 and 82 of the Treaty

27. Access to the file will be granted upon request and, normally, on a single occasion, following the notification of the Commission's objections to the parties, in order to ensure the principle of equality of arms and to protect their rights of defence. As a general rule, therefore, no access will be granted to other parties' replies to the Commission's objections.

A party will, however, be granted access to documents received after notification of the objections at later stages of the administrative procedure, where such documents may constitute new evidence – whether of an incriminating or of an exculpatory nature –, pertaining to the allegations concerning that party in the Commission's statement of objections. This is particularly the case where the Commission intends to rely on new evidence.

2. In proceedings under the Merger Regulation

28. In accordance with Article 18(1) and (3) of the Merger Regulation and Article 17(1) of the Merger Implementing Regulation, the notifying parties will be given access to the Commission's file upon request at every stage of the procedure following the notification of the Commission's objections up to the consultation of the Advisory Committee. In contrast, this notice does not address the possibility of the provision of documents before the Commission states its objections to undertakings under the Merger Regulation (34).

(34) This question is dealt with in the Directorate General Competition document «DG COMP Best Practices on the conduct of EC merger control proceedings», available on the web-site of the Directorate General for Competition: http://europa.eu.int/comm/competition/index_en.html.

III. PARTICULAR QUESTIONS REGARDING COMPLAINANTS AND OTHER INVOLVED PARTIES

29. The present section relates to situations where the Commission may or has to provide access to certain documents contained in its file to the complainants in antitrust proceedings and other involved parties in merger proceedings. Irrespective of the wording used in the antitrust and merger implementing regulations (35), these two situations are distinct – in terms of scope, timing, and rights – from access to the file, as defined in the preceding section of this notice.

(35) Cf. Article 8(1) of the Implementing Regulation, which speaks about «access to documents» to complainants and Article 17(2) of Merger Implementing Regulation which speaks about «access to file» to other involved parties «in so far as this is necessary for the purposes of preparing their comments».

A. Provision of documents to complainants in antitrust proceedings

30. The Court of First Instance has ruled (36) that complainants do not have the same rights and guarantees as the parties under investigation. Therefore complainants cannot claim a right of access to the file as established for parties.

(36) See Case T-17/93 Matra-Hachette SA v Commission, [1994] ECR II-595, paragraph 34. The Court ruled that the rights of third parties, as laid down by Article 19 of the Council Regulation N° 17 of 6.2.1962 (now replaced by Article 27 of Regulation (EC) N° 1/2003), were limited to the right to participate in the administrative procedure.

31. However, a complainant who, pursuant to Article 7(1) of the Implementing Regulation, has been informed of the Commission's intention to reject its complaint (37), may request access to the documents on which the Commission has based its provisional assessment (38). The complainant will be provided access to such documents on a single occasion, following the issuance of the letter informing the complainant of the Commission's intention to reject its complaint.

(37) By means of a letter issued in accordance with Article 7(1) of the Implementing Regulation.

(38) Cf. Article 8(1) of the Implementing Regulation.

32. Complainants do not have a right of access to business secrets or other confidential information which the Commission has obtained in the course of its investigation (39).

(39) Cf. Article 8(1) of the Implementing Regulation.

B. Provision of documents to other involved parties in merger proceedings

33. In accordance with Article 17(2) of the Merger Implementing Regulation, access to the file in merger proceedings shall also be given, upon request, to other involved parties who have been informed of the objections in so far as this is necessary for the purposes of preparing their comments.

34. Such other involved parties are parties to the proposed concentration other than the notifying parties, such as the seller and the undertaking which is the target of the concentration (40).

(40) Cf. Article 11(b) of the Merger Implementing Regulation.

IV. PROCEDURE FOR IMPLEMENTING ACCESS TO THE FILE

A. Preparatory procedure

35. Any person which submits information or comments in one of the situations listed hereunder, or subsequently submits further information to the Commission in the course of the same procedures, has an obligation to clearly identify any material which it considers to be confidential, giving reasons, and provide a separate non-confidential version by the date set by the Commission for making its views known (41):

a) In antitrust proceedings

– an addressee of a Commission's statement of objections making known its views on the objections (42);

– a complainant making known its views on a Commission statement of objections (43);

– any other natural or legal person, which applies to be heard and shows a sufficient interest, or which is invited by the Commission to express its views, making known its views in writing or at an oral hearing (44);

– a complainant making known his views on a Commission letter informing him on the Commission's intention to reject the complaint (45).

(41) Cf. Article 16(2) of the Implementing Regulation and Article 18(2) of the Merger Implementing Regulation.

(42) Pursuant to Article 10(2) of the Implementing Regulation.

(43) Pursuant to Article 6(1) of the Implementing Regulation.

(44) Pursuant to Article 13(1) and (3) of the Implementing Regulation.

(45) Pursuant to Article 7(1) of the Implementing Regulation.

b) In merger proceedings

– notifying parties or other involved parties making known their views on Commission objections adopted with a view to take a decision with regard to a request for a derogation from suspension of a concentration and which adversely affects one or more of those parties, or on a provisional decision adopted in the matter (46);

– notifying parties to whom the Commission has addressed a statement of objections, other involved parties who have been informed of those objections or parties to whom the Commission has addressed objections with a view to inflict a fine or a periodic penalty payment, submitting their comments on the objections (47);

– third persons who apply to be heard, or any other natural or legal person invited by the Commission to express their views, making known their views in writing or at an oral hearing (48);

– any person which supplies information pursuant to Article 11 of the Merger Regulation.

(46) Article 12 of the Merger Implementing Regulation.

(47) Article 13 of the Merger Implementing Regulation.

(48) Pursuant to Article 16 of the Merger Implementing Regulation.

36. Moreover, the Commission may require undertakings (49), in all cases where they produce or have produced documents, to identify the documents or parts of documents, which they consider to contain business secrets or other confidential information belonging to them, and to identify the undertakings with regard to which such documents are to be considered confidential (50).

(49) In merger proceedings the principles set out in the present and subsequent paragraphs also apply to the persons referred to in Article 3(1)(b) of Merger Regulation.

(50) Cf. Article 16(3) of the Implementing Regulation and Article 18(3) of the Merger Implementing Regulation. This also applies to documents gathered by the Commission in an inspection pursuant to Article 13 of the Merger Regulation and Articles 20 and 21 of Regulation (EC) N° 1/2003.

37. For the purposes of quickly dealing with confidentiality claims referred to in paragraph 36 above, the Commission may set a time-limit within which the undertakings shall:

(i) substantiate their claim for confidentiality with regard to each individual document or part of document;

(ii) provide the Commission with a non-confidential version of the documents, in which the confidential passages are deleted (51). In antitrust proceedings the undertakings in question shall also provide within the said time-limit a concise description of each piece of deleted information (52).

(51) Cf. Article 16(3) of the Implementing Regulation and Article 18(3) of the Merger Implementing Regulation.

(52) Cf. Article 16(3) of the Implementing Regulation.

38. The non-confidential versions and the descriptions of the deleted information must be established in a manner that enables any party with access to the file to determine whether the information deleted is likely to be relevant for its defence and therefore whether there are sufficient grounds to request the Commission to grant access to the information claimed to be confidential.

B. Treatment of confidential information

39. In antitrust proceedings, if undertakings fail to comply with the provisions set out in paragraphs 35 to 37 above, the Commission may assume that the documents or statements concerned do not contain confidential information (53). The Commission may consequently assume that the undertaking has no objections to the disclosure of the documents or statements concerned in their entirety.

(53) Cf. Article 16 of the Implementing Regulation.

40. In both antitrust proceedings and in proceedings under the Merger Regulation, should the person or undertaking in question meet the conditions set out in paragraphs 35 to 37 above, to the extent they are applicable, the Commission will either:

– provisionally accept the claims which seem justified; or

– inform the person or undertaking in question that it does not agree with the confidentiality claim in whole or in part, where it is apparent that the claim is unjustified.

41. The Commission may reverse its provisional acceptance of the confidentiality claim in whole or in part at a later stage.

42. Where the Directorate General for Competition does not agree with the confidentiality claim from the outset or where it takes the view that the provisional acceptance of the confidentiality claim should be reversed, and thus intends to disclose information, it will grant the person or undertaking in question an opportunity to express its views. In such cases, the Directorate General for Competition will inform the person or undertaking in writing of its intention to disclose information, give its reasons and set a time-limit within which such person or undertaking may inform it in writing of its views. If, following submission of those views, a disagreement on the confidentiality claim persists, the matter will be dealt with by the Hearing Officer according to the applicable Commission terms of reference of Hearing Officers (54).

(54) Cf. Article 9 of the Commission Decision of 23.5.2001 on the terms of reference of hearing officers in certain competition proceedings, O.J. L 162 19.6.2001, p. 21.

43. Where there is a risk that an undertaking which is able to place very considerable economic or commercial pressure on its competitors or on its trading partners, customers or suppliers will adopt retaliatory measures against those, as a consequence of their collaboration in the investigation carried out by the Commission (55), the Commission will protect the anonymity of the authors by providing access to a non-confidential version or summary of the responses in question (56). Requests for anonymity in such circumstances, as well as requests for anonymity according to point 81 of the Commission Notice on the handling of complaints (57) will be dealt with according to paragraphs 40 to 42 above.

(55) Cf. paragraph 19 above.

(56) Cf. Case T-5/02, Tetra Laval vs. Commission, [2002] ECR II-4381, paragraph 98, 104 and 105.

(57) Commission Notice on the handling of complaints by the Commission under Articles 81 and 82 of the EC Treaty, O.J. C 101, 27.4.2004, p. 65.

C. Provision of access to file

44. The Commission may determine that access to the file shall be granted in one of the following ways, taking due account of the technical capabilities of the parties:

– by means of a CD-ROM(s) or any other electronic data storage device as may become available in future;

– through copies of the accessible file in paper form sent to them by mail;

– by inviting them to examine the accessible file on the Commission's premises.

The Commission may choose any combination of these methods.

45. In order to facilitate access to the file, the parties will receive an enumerative list of documents setting out the content of the Commission file, as defined in paragraph 8 above.

46. Access is granted to evidence as contained in the Commission file, in its original form: the Commission is under no obligation to provide a translation of documents in the file (58).

(58) Cf. Case T-25/95 et al. Cimenteries, paragraph 635.

47. If a party considers that, after having obtained access to the file, it requires knowledge of specific nonaccessible information for its defence, it may submit a reasoned request to that end to the Commission. If the services of the Directorate General for Competition are not in a position to accept the request and if the party disagrees with that view, the matter will be resolved by the Hearing Officer, in accordance with the applicable terms of reference of Hearing Officers (59).

(59) Cf. Article 8 of the Commission Decision of 23.5.2001 on the terms of reference of hearing officers in certain competition proceedings, O.J. L 162, 19.6.2001, p. 21.

48. Access to the file in accordance with this notice is granted on the condition that the information thereby obtained may only be used for the purposes of judicial or administrative proceedings for the application of the Community competition rules at issue in the related administrative proceedings (60). Should the information be used for a different purpose, at any point in time, with the involvement of an outside counsel, the Commission may report the incident to the bar of that counsel, with a view to disciplinary action.

(60) Cf. Articles 15(4) and 8(2) of the Implementing Regulation, respectively, and Article 17(4) of the Merger Implementing Regulation.

49. With the exception of paragraphs 45 and 47, this section C applies equally to the grant of access to documents to complainants (in antitrust proceedings) and to other involved parties (in merger proceedings).

Guidelines on the method of setting fines imposed pursuant to Article 23(2)(a) of Regulation N° 1/2003

(OJ C 210, 1 September 2006, p. 2)

1. Article 81 EC is now Article 101 TFEU and Article 82 EC is now Article 102 TFEU.

INTRODUCTION

1. Pursuant to Article 23(2)(a) of Regulation N° 1/2003 (1), the Commission may, by decision, impose fines on undertakings or associations of undertakings where, either intentionally or negligently, they infringe Article 81 or 82 of the Treaty.

(1) Council Regulation (EC) N° 1 of 16 December 2002 on the implementation of the rules on competition laid down in Articles 81 and 82 of the Treaty (O.J. L 1, 4.1.2003, p. 1).

2. In exercising its power to impose such fines, the Commission enjoys a wide margin of discretion (2) within the limits set by Regulation N° 1/2003. First, the Commission must have regard both to the gravity and to the duration of the infringement. Second, the fine imposed may not exceed the limits specified in Article 23(2), second and third subparagraphs, of Regulation N° 1/2003.

(2) See, for example, Case C-189/02 P, C-202/02 P, C-205/02 P to C-208/02 P and C-213/02 P, Dansk Rørindustri A/S and others v Commission [2005] ECR I-5425, paragraph 172.

3. In order to ensure the transparency and impartiality of its decisions, the Commission published on 14 January 1998 guidelines on the method of setting fines (3). After more than eight years of implementation, the Commission has acquired sufficient experience to develop further and refine its policy on fines.

(3) Guidelines on the method of setting fines imposed pursuant to Article 15(2) of Regulation N° 17 and Article 65(5) of the ECSC Treaty (O.J. C 9, 14.1.1998, p. 3).

4. The Commission's power to impose fines on undertakings or associations of undertakings which, intentionally or negligently, infringe Article 81 or 82 of the Treaty is one of the means conferred on it in order for it to carry out the task of supervision entrusted to it by the Treaty. That task not only includes the duty to investigate and sanction individual infringements, but it also encompasses the duty to pursue a general policy designed to apply, in competition matters, the principles laid down by the Treaty and to steer the conduct of undertakings in the light of those principles (4). For this purpose, the Commission must ensure that its action has the necessary deterrent effect (5). Accordingly, when the Commission discovers that Article 81 or 82 of the Treaty has been infringed, it may be necessary to impose a fine on those who have acted in breach of the law. Fines should have a sufficiently deterrent effect, not only in order to sanction the undertakings concerned (specific deterrence) but also in order to deter other undertakings from engaging in, or continuing, behaviour that is contrary to Articles 81 and 82 of the EC Treaty (general deterrence).

(4) See, for example, Dansk Rørindustri A/S and others v Commission, cited above, paragraph 170.

(5) See Joined Cases 100/80 to 103/80 Musique Diffusion française and others v Commission [1983] ECR 1825, paragraph 106.

5. In order to achieve these objectives, it is appropriate for the Commission to refer to the value of the sales of goods or services to which the infringement relates as a basis for setting the fine. The duration of the infringement should also play a significant role in the setting of the appropriate amount of the fine. It necessarily has an impact on the potential consequences of the infringement on the market. It is therefore considered important that the fine should also reflect the number of years during which an undertaking participated in the infringement.

6. The combination of the value of sales to which the infringement relates and of the duration of the infringement is regarded as providing an appropriate proxy to reflect the economic importance of the infringement as well as the relative weight of each undertaking in the infringement. Reference to these factors provides a good indication of the order of magnitude of the fine and should not be regarded as the basis for an automatic and arithmetical calculation method.

7. It is also considered appropriate to include in the fine a specific amount irrespective of the duration of the infringement, in order to deter companies from even entering into illegal practices.

8. The sections below set out the principles which will guide the Commission when it sets fines imposed pursuant to Article 23(2)(a) of Regulation N° 1/2003.

METHOD FOR THE SETTING OF FINES

9. Without prejudice to point 37 below, the Commission will use the following two-step methodology when setting the fine to be imposed on undertakings or associations of undertakings.

10. First, the Commission will determine a basic amount for each undertaking or association of undertakings (see Section 1 below).

11. Second, it may adjust that basic amount upwards or downwards (see Section 2 below).

1. Basic amount of the fine

12. The basic amount will be set by reference to the value of sales and applying the following methodology.

A. Calculation of the value of sales

13. In determining the basic amount of the fine to be imposed, the Commission will take the value of the undertaking's sales of goods or services to which the infringement directly or indirectly (6) relates in the relevant geographic area within the EEA. It will normally take the sales made by the undertaking during the last full business year of its participation in the infringement (hereafter «value of sales»).

(6) Such will be the case for instance for horizontal price fixing arrangements on a given product, where the price of that product then serves as a basis for the price of lower or higher quality products.

14. Where the infringement by an association of undertakings relates to the activities of its members, the value of sales will generally correspond to the sum of the value of sales by its members.

15. In determining the value of sales by an undertaking, the Commission will take that undertaking's best available figures.

16. Where the figures made available by an undertaking are incomplete or not reliable, the Commission may determine the value of its sales on the basis of the partial figures it has obtained and/or any other information which it regards as relevant and appropriate.

17. The value of sales will be determined before VAT and other taxes directly related to the sales.

18. Where the geographic scope of an infringement extends beyond the EEA (e.g. worldwide cartels), the relevant sales of the undertakings within the EEA may not properly reflect the weight of each undertaking in the infringement. This may be the case in particular with worldwide market-sharing arrangements.

In such circumstances, in order to reflect both the aggregate size of the relevant sales within the EEA and the relative weight of each undertaking in the infringement, the Commission may assess the total value of the sales of goods or services to which the infringement relates in the relevant geographic area (wider than the EEA), may determine the share of the sales of each undertaking party to the infringement on that market and may apply this share to the aggregate sales within the EEA of the undertakings concerned. The result will be taken as the value of sales for the purpose of setting the basic amount of the fine.

B. Determination of the basic amount of the fine

19. The basic amount of the fine will be related to a proportion of the value of sales, depending on the degree of gravity of the infringement, multiplied by the number of years of infringement.

20. The assessment of gravity will be made on a case-by-case basis for all types of infringement, taking account of all the relevant circumstances of the case.

21. As a general rule, the proportion of the value of sales taken into account will be set at a level of up to 30% of the value of sales.

22. In order to decide whether the proportion of the value of sales to be considered in a given case should be at the lower end or at the higher end of that scale, the Commission will have regard to a number of factors, such as the nature of the infringement, the combined market share of all the undertakings concerned, the geographic scope of the infringement and whether or not the infringement has been implemented.

23. Horizontal price-fixing, market-sharing and output-limitation agreements (7), which are usually secret, are, by their very nature, among the most harmful restrictions of competition. As a matter of policy, they will be heavily fined. Therefore, the proportion of the value of sales taken into account for such infringements will generally be set at the higher end of the scale.

(7) This includes agreements, concerted practices and decisions by associations of undertakings within the meaning of Article 81 of the Treaty.

24. In order to take fully into account the duration of the participation of each undertaking in the infringement, the amount determined on the basis of the value of sales (see points 20 to 23 above) will be multiplied by the number of years of participation in the infringement. Periods of less than six months will be counted as half a year; periods longer than six months but shorter than one year will be counted as a full year.

25. In addition, irrespective of the duration of the undertaking's participation in the infringement, the Commission will include in the basic amount a sum of between 15% and 25% of the value of sales as defined in Section A above in order to deter undertakings from even entering into horizontal price-fixing, market-sharing and outputlimitation agreements. The Commission may also apply such an additional amount in the case of other infringements. For the purpose of deciding the proportion of the value of sales to be considered in a given case, the Commission will have regard to a number of factors, in particular those referred in point 22.

26. Where the value of sales by undertakings participating in the infringement is similar but not identical, the Commission may set for each of them an identical basic amount. Moreover, in determining the basic amount of the fine, the Commission will use rounded figures.

2. Adjustments to the basic amount

27. In setting the fine, the Commission may take into account circumstances that result in an increase or decrease in the basic amount as determined in Section 1 above. It will do so on the basis of an overall assessment which takes account of all the relevant circumstances.

A. Aggravating circumstances

28. The basic amount may be increased where the Commission finds that there are aggravating circumstances, such as:

– where an undertaking continues or repeats the same or a similar infringement after the Commission or a national competition authority has made a finding that the undertaking infringed Article 81 or 82: the basic amount will be increased by up to 100 % for each such infringement established;

– refusal to cooperate with or obstruction of the Commission in carrying out its investigations;

– role of leader in, or instigator of, the infringement; the Commission will also pay particular attention to any steps taken to coerce other undertakings to participate in the infringement and/or any retaliatory measures taken against other undertakings with a view to enforcing the practices constituting the infringement.

B. Mitigating circumstances

29. The basic amount may be reduced where the Commission finds that mitigating circumstances exist, such as:

– where the undertaking concerned provides evidence that it terminated the infringement as soon as the Commission intervened: this will not apply to secret agreements or practices (in particular, cartels);

– where the undertaking provides evidence that the infringement has been committed as a result of negligence;

– where the undertaking provides evidence that its involvement in the infringement is substantially limited and thus demonstrates that, during the period in which it was party to the offending agreement, it actually avoided applying it by adopting competitive conduct in the market: the mere fact that an undertaking participated in an infringement for a shorter duration than others will not be regarded as a mitigating circumstance since this will already be reflected in the basic amount;

– where the undertaking concerned has effectively co-operated with the Commission outside the scope of the Leniency Notice and beyond its legal obligation to do so;

– where the anti-competitive conduct of the undertaking has been authorized or encouraged by public authorities or by legislation. (8)

(8) This is without prejudice to any action that may be taken against the Member State concerned.

C. Specific increase for deterrence

30. The Commission will pay particular attention to the need to ensure that fines have a sufficiently deterrent effect; to that end, it may increase the fine to be imposed on undertakings which have a particularly large turnover beyond the sales of goods or services to which the infringement relates.

31. The Commission will also take into account the need to increase the fine in order to exceed the amount of gains improperly made as a result of the infringement where it is possible to estimate that amount.

D. Legal maximum

32. The final amount of the fine shall not, in any event, exceed 10% of the total turnover in the preceding business year of the undertaking or association of undertakings participating in the infringement, as laid down in Article 23(2) of Regulation N° 1/2003.

33. Where an infringement by an association of undertakings relates to the activities of its members, the fine shall not exceed 10% of the sum of the total turnover of each member active on the market affected by that infringement.

E. Leniency Notice

34. The Commission will apply the leniency rules in line with the conditions set out in the applicable notice.

F. Ability to pay

35. In exceptional cases, the Commission may, upon request, take account of the undertaking's inability to pay in a specific social and economic context. It will not base any reduction granted for this reason in the fine on the mere finding of an adverse or loss-making financial situation. A reduction could be granted solely on the basis of objective evidence that imposition of the fine as provided for in these Guidelines would irretrievably jeopardise the economic viability of the undertaking concerned and cause its assets to lose all their value.

FINAL CONSIDERATIONS

36. The Commission may, in certain cases, impose a symbolic fine. The justification for imposing such a fine should be given in its decision.

37. Although these Guidelines present the general methodology for the setting of fines, the particularities of a given case or the need to achieve deterrence in a particular case may justify departing from such methodology or from the limits specified in point 21.

38. These Guidelines will be applied in all cases where a statement of objections is notified after their date of publication in the *Official Journal*, regardless of whether the fine is imposed pursuant to Article 23(2) of Regulation N° 1/2003 or Article 15(2) of Regulation 17/62 (9).

(9) Article 15(2) of Regulation 17/62 of 6 February 1962: First Regulation implementing Articles 85 and 86 [now 81 and 82] of the Treaty (O.J. 13, 21.2.1962, p. 204).

Commission Notice on Immunity from fines and reduction of fines in cartel cases

(OJ C 298, 8 December 2006, p. 17)

1. Article 81 EC is now Article 101 TFEU.

I. INTRODUCTION

1. This notice sets out the framework for rewarding cooperation in the Commission investigation by undertakings which are or have been party to secret cartels affecting the Community. Cartels are agreements and/or concerted practices between two or more competitors aimed at coordinating their competitive behaviour on the market and/or influencing the relevant parameters of competition through practices such as the fixing of purchase or selling prices or other trading conditions, the allocation of production or sales quotas, the sharing of markets including bid-rigging, restrictions of imports or exports and/or anti-competitive actions against other competitors. Such practices are among the most serious violations of Article 81 EC (1).

2. By artificially limiting the competition that would normally prevail between them, undertakings avoid exactly those pressures that lead them to innovate, both in terms of product development and the introduction of more efficient production methods. Such practices also lead to more expensive raw materials and components for the Community companies that purchase from such producers. They ultimately result in artificial prices and reduced choice for the consumer. In the long term, they lead to a loss of competitiveness and reduced employment opportunities.

3. By their very nature, secret cartels are often difficult to detect and investigate without the cooperation of undertakings or individuals implicated in them. Therefore, the Commission considers that it is in the Community interest to reward undertakings involved in this type of illegal practices which are willing to put an end to their participation and co-operate in the Commission's investigation, independently of the rest of the undertakings involved in the cartel. The interests of consumers and citizens in ensuring that secret cartels are detected and punished outweigh the interest in fining those undertakings that enable the Commission to detect and prohibit such practices.

4. The Commission considers that the collaboration of an undertaking in the detection of the existence of a cartel has an intrinsic value. A decisive contribution to the opening of an investigation or to the finding of an infringement may justify the granting of immunity from any fine to the undertaking in question, on condition that certain additional requirements are fulfilled.

5. Moreover, co-operation by one or more undertakings may justify a reduction of a fine by the Commission. Any reduction of a fine must reflect an undertaking's actual contribution, in terms of quality and timing, to the Commission's establishment of the infringement. Reductions are to be limited to those undertakings that provide the Commission with evidence that adds significant value to that already in the Commission's possession.

6. In addition to submitting pre-existing documents, undertakings may provide the Commission with voluntary presentations of their knowledge of a cartel and their role therein prepared specially to be submitted under this leniency programme. These initiatives have proved to be useful for the effective investigation and termination of cartel infringements and they should not be discouraged by discovery orders issued in civil litigation. Potential leniency applicants might be dissuaded from cooperating with the Commission under this Notice if this could impair their position in civil proceedings, as compared to companies who do not cooperate. Such undesirable effect would significantly harm the public interest in ensuring effective public enforcement of Article 81 EC in cartel cases and thus its subsequent or parallel effective private enforcement.

7. The supervisory task conferred on the Commission by the Treaty in competition matters does not only include the duty to investigate and punish individual infringements, but also encompasses the duty to pursue a general policy. The protection of corporate statements in the public interest is not a bar to their disclosure to other addressees of the statement of objections in order to safeguard their rights of defence in the procedure before the Commission, to the extent that it is technically possible to combine both interests by rendering corporate statements accessible only at the Commission premises and normally on a single occasion following the formal notification of the objections. Moreover, the Commission will process personal data in the context of this notice in conformity with its obligations under Regulation (EC) N° 45/2001 (2).

II. IMMUNITY FROM FINES

A. Requirements to qualify for immunity from fines

8. The Commission will grant immunity from any fine which would otherwise have been imposed to an undertaking disclosing its participation in an alleged cartel affecting the Community if that undertaking is the first to submit information and evidence which in the Commission's view will enable it to:

(a) carry out a targeted inspection in connection with the alleged cartel (3); or

(b) find an infringement of Article 81 EC in connection with the alleged cartel.

9. For the Commission to be able to carry out a targeted inspection within the meaning of point (8)*(a)*, the undertaking must provide the Commission with the information and evidence listed below, to the extent that this, in the Commission's view, would not jeopardize the inspections:

(a) A corporate statement (4) which includes, in so far as it is known to the applicant at the time of the submission:

– A detailed description of the alleged cartel arrangement, including for instance its aims, activities and functioning; the product or service concerned, the geographic scope, the duration and the estimated market volumes affected by the alleged cartel; the specific dates, locations, content of and participants in alleged cartel contacts, and all relevant explanations in connection with the pieces of evidence provided in support of the application.

– The name and address of the legal entity submitting the immunity application as well as the names and addresses of all the other undertakings that participate(d) in the alleged cartel;

– The names, positions, office locations and, where necessary, home addresses of all individuals who, to the applicant's knowledge, are or have been involved in the alleged cartel, including those individuals which have been involved on the applicant's behalf;

– Information on which other competition authorities, inside or outside the EU, have been approached or are intended to be approached in relation to the alleged cartel; and

(b) Other evidence relating to the alleged cartel in possession of the applicant or available to it at the time of the submission, including in particular any evidence contemporaneous to the infringement.

10. Immunity pursuant to point (8)*(a)* will not be granted if, at the time of the submission, the Commission had already sufficient evidence to adopt a decision to carry out an inspection in connection with the alleged cartel or had already carried out such an inspection.

11. Immunity pursuant to point (8)*(b)* will only be granted on the cumulative conditions that the Commission did not have, at the time of the submission, sufficient evidence to find an infringement of Article 81 EC in connection with the alleged cartel and that no undertaking had been granted conditional immunity from fines under point (8)*(a)* in connection with the alleged cartel. In order to qualify, an undertaking must be the first to provide contemporaneous, incriminating evidence of the alleged cartel as well as a corporate statement containing the kind of information specified in point (9)*(a)*, which would enable the Commission to find an infringement of Article 81 EC.

12. In addition to the conditions set out in points (8)*(a)*, (9) and (10) or in points (8)*(b)* and 11, all the following conditions must be met in any case to qualify for any immunity from a fine:

(a) The undertaking cooperates genuinely (5), fully, on a continuous basis and expeditiously from the time it submits its application throughout the Commission's administrative procedure. This includes:

– providing the Commission promptly with all relevant information and evidence relating to the alleged cartel that comes into its possession or is available to it;

– remaining at the Commission's disposal to answer promptly to any request that may contribute to the establishment of the facts;

– making current (and, if possible, former) employees and directors available for interviews with the Commission;

– not destroying, falsifying or concealing relevant information or evidence relating to the alleged cartel; and

– not disclosing the fact or any of the content of its application before the Commission has issued a statement of objections in the case, unless otherwise agreed;

(b) The undertaking ended its involvement in the alleged cartel immediately following its application, except for what would, in the Commission's view, be reasonably necessary to preserve the integrity of the inspections;

(c) When contemplating making its application to the Commission, the undertaking must not have destroyed, falsified or concealed evidence of the alleged cartel nor disclosed the fact or any of the content of its contemplated application, except to other competition authorities.

13. An undertaking which took steps to coerce other undertakings to join the cartel or to remain in it is not eligible for immunity from fines. It may still qualify for a reduction of fines if it fulfils the relevant requirements and meets all the conditions therefor.

B. Procedure

14. An undertaking wishing to apply for immunity from fines should contact the Commission's Directorate General for Competition. The undertaking may either initially apply for a marker or immediately proceed to make a formal application to the Commission for immunity from fines in order to meet the conditions in points (8)*(a)* or (8)*(b)*, as appropriate. The Commission may disregard any application for immunity from fines on the ground that it has been submitted after the statement of objections has been issued.

15. The Commission services may grant a marker protecting an immunity applicant's place in the queue for a period to be specified on a case-by-case basis in order to allow for the gathering of the necessary information and evidence. To be eligible to secure a marker, the applicant must provide the Commission with information concerning its name and address, the parties to the alleged cartel, the affected product(s) and territory(-ies), the estimated duration of the alleged cartel and the nature of the alleged cartel conduct. The applicant should also inform the Commission on other past or possible future leniency applications to other authorities in relation to the alleged cartel and justify its request for a marker. Where a marker is granted, the Commission services determine the period within which the applicant has to perfect the marker by submitting the information and evidence required to meet the relevant threshold for immunity. Undertakings which have been granted a marker cannot perfect it by making a formal application in hypothetical terms. If the applicant perfects the marker within the period set by the Commission services, the information and evidence provided will be deemed to have been submitted on the date when the marker was granted.

16. An undertaking making a formal immunity application to the Commission must:

(a) provide the Commission with all information and evidence relating to the alleged cartel available to it, as specified in points (8) and (9), including corporate statements; or

(b) initially present this information and evidence in hypothetical terms, in which case the undertaking must present a detailed descriptive list of the evidence it proposes to disclose at a later agreed date. This list should accurately reflect the nature and content of the evidence, whilst safeguarding the hypothetical nature of its disclosure. Copies of documents, from which sensitive parts have been removed, may be used to illustrate the nature and content of the evidence. The name of the applying undertaking and of other undertakings involved in the alleged cartel need not be disclosed until the evidence described in its application is submitted. However, the product or service concerned by the alleged cartel, the geographic scope of the alleged cartel and the estimated duration must be clearly identified.

17. If requested, the Directorate General for Competition will provide an acknowledgement of receipt of the undertaking's application for immunity from fines, confirming the date and, where appropriate, time of the application.

18. Once the Commission has received the information and evidence submitted by the undertaking under point (16)*(a)* and has verified that it meets the conditions set out in points (8)*(a)* or (8)*(b)*, as appropriate, it will grant the undertaking conditional immunity from fines in writing.

19. If the undertaking has presented information and evidence in hypothetical terms, the Commission will verify that the nature and content of the evidence described in the detailed list referred to in point (16)*(b)* will meet the conditions set out in points (8)*(a)* or (8)*(b)*, as appropriate, and inform the undertaking accordingly. Following the disclosure of the evidence no later than on the date agreed and having verified that it corresponds to the description made in the list, the Commission will grant the undertaking conditional immunity from fines in writing.

20. If it becomes apparent that immunity is not available or that the undertaking failed to meet the conditions set out in points (8)*(a)* or (8)*(b)*, as appropriate, the Commission will inform the undertaking in writing. In such case, the undertaking may withdraw the evidence disclosed for the purposes of its immunity application or request the Commission to consider it under section III of this notice. This does not prevent the Commission from using its normal powers of investigation in order to obtain the information.

21. The Commission will not consider other applications for immunity from fines before it has taken a position on an existing application in relation to the same alleged infringement, irrespective of whether the immunity application is presented formally or by requesting a marker.

22. If at the end of the administrative procedure, the undertaking has met the conditions set out in point (12), the Commission will grant it immunity from fines in the relevant decision. If at the end of the administrative procedure, the undertaking has not met the conditions set out in point (12), the undertaking will not benefit from any favorable treatment under this Notice. If the Commission, after having granted conditional immunity ultimately finds that the immunity applicant has acted as a coercer, it will withhold immunity.

III. REDUCTION OF A FINE

A. Requirements to qualify for reduction of a fine

23. Undertakings disclosing their participation in an alleged cartel affecting the Community that do not meet the conditions under section II above may be eligible to benefit from a reduction of any fine that would otherwise have been imposed.

24. In order to qualify, an undertaking must provide the Commission with evidence of the alleged infringement which represents significant added value with respect to the evidence already in the Commission's possession and must meet the cumulative conditions set out in points (12)*(a)* to (12)*(c)* above.

25. The concept of «added value» refers to the extent to which the evidence provided strengthens, by its very nature and/ or its level of detail, the Commission's ability to prove the alleged cartel. In this assessment, the Commission will generally consider written evidence originating from the period of time to which the facts pertain to have a greater value than evidence subsequently established. Incriminating evidence directly relevant to the facts in question will generally be considered to have a greater value than that with only indirect relevance. Similarly, the degree of corroboration from other sources required for the evidence submitted to be relied upon against other undertakings involved in the case will have an impact on the value of that evidence, so that compelling evidence will be attributed a greater value than evidence such as statements which require corroboration if contested.

26. The Commission will determine in any final decision adopted at the end of the administrative procedure the level of reduction an undertaking will benefit from, relative to the fine which would otherwise be imposed. For the:

– first undertaking to provide significant added value: a reduction of 30-50%,

– second undertaking to provide significant added value: a reduction of 20-30%,

– subsequent undertakings that provide significant added value: a reduction of up to 20%.

In order to determine the level of reduction within each of these bands, the Commission will take into account the time at which the evidence fulfilling the condition in point (24) was submitted and the extent to which it represents added value.

If the applicant for a reduction of a fine is the first to submit compelling evidence in the sense of point (25) which the Commission uses to establish additional facts increasing the gravity or the duration of the infringement, the Commission will not take such additional facts into account when setting any fine to be imposed on the undertaking which provided this evidence.

B. Procedure

27. An undertaking wishing to benefit from a reduction of a fine must make a formal application to the Commission and it must present it with sufficient evidence of the alleged cartel to qualify for a reduction of a fine in accordance with point (24) of this Notice. Any voluntary submission of evidence to the Commission which the undertaking that submits it wishes to be considered for the beneficial treatment of section III of this Notice must be clearly identified at the time of its submission as being part of a formal application for a reduction of a fine.

28. If requested, the Directorate General for Competition will provide an acknowledgement of receipt of the undertaking's application for a reduction of a fine and of any subsequent submissions of evidence, confirming the date and, where appropriate, time of each submission. The Commission will not take any position on an application for a reduction of a fine before it has taken a position on any existing applications for conditional immunity from fines in relation to the same alleged cartel.

29. If the Commission comes to the preliminary conclusion that the evidence submitted by the undertaking constitutes significant added value within the meaning of points (24) and (25), and that the undertaking has met the conditions of points (12) and (27), it will inform the undertaking in writing, no later than the date on which a statement of objections is notified, of its intention to apply a reduction of a fine within a specified band as provided in point (26).

The Commission will also, within the same time frame, inform the undertaking in writing if it comes to the preliminary conclusion that the undertaking does not qualify for a reduction of a fine. The Commission may disregard any application for a reduction of fines on the grounds that it has been submitted after the statement of objections has been issued.

30. The Commission will evaluate the final position of each undertaking which filed an application for a reduction of a fine at the end of the administrative procedure in any decision adopted. The Commission will determine in any such final decision:

(a) whether the evidence provided by an undertaking represented significant added value with respect to the evidence in the Commission's possession at that same time;

(b) whether the conditions set out in points (12)*(a)* to (12)*(c)* above have been met;

(c) the exact level of reduction an undertaking will benefit from within the bands specified in point (26).

If the Commission finds that the undertaking has not met the conditions set out in point (12), the undertaking will not benefit from any favourable treatment under this Notice.

IV. CORPORATE STATEMENTS MADE TO QUALIFY UNDER THIS NOTICE

31. A corporate statement is a voluntary presentation by or on behalf of an undertaking to the Commission of the undertaking's knowledge of a cartel and its role therein prepared specially to be submitted under this Notice. Any statement made vis-à-vis the Commission in relation to this notice, forms part of the Commission's file and can thus be used in evidence.

32. Upon the applicant's request, the Commission may accept that corporate statements be provided orally unless the applicant has already disclosed the content of the corporate statement to third parties. Oral corporate statements will be recorded and transcribed at the Commission's premises. In accordance with Article 19 of Council Regulation (EC) N° 1/2003 (6) and Articles 3 and 17 of Commission Regulation (EC) N° 773/2004 (7), undertakings making oral corporate statements will be granted the opportunity to check the technical accuracy of the recording, which will be available at the Commission's premises and to correct the substance of their oral statements within a given time limit. Undertakings may waive these rights within the said time-limit, in which case the recording will from that moment on be deemed to have been approved. Following the explicit or implicit approval of the oral statement or the submission of any corrections to it, the undertaking shall listen to the recordings at the Commission's premises and check the accuracy of the transcript within a given time limit. Non-compliance with the last requirement may lead to the loss of any beneficial treatment under this Notice.

33. Access to corporate statements is only granted to the addressees of a statement of objections, provided that they commit, – together with the legal counsels getting access on their behalf –, not to make any copy by mechanical or electronic means of any information in the corporate statement to which access is being granted and to ensure that the information to be obtained from the corporate statement will solely be used for the purposes mentioned below. Other parties such as complainants will not be granted access to corporate statements. The Commission considers that this specific protection of a corporate statement is not justified as from the moment when the applicant discloses to third parties the content thereof.

34. In accordance with the Commission Notice on rules for access to the Commission file (8), access to the file is only granted to the addressees of a statement of objections on the condition that the information thereby obtained may only be used for the purposes of judicial or administrative proceedings for the application of the Community competition rules at issue in the related administrative proceedings. The use of such information for a different purpose during the proceeding may be regarded as lack of cooperation within the meaning of points (12) and (27) of this Notice. Moreover, if any such use is made after the Commission has already adopted a prohibition decision in the proceeding, the Commission may, in any legal proceedings before the Community Courts, ask the Court to increase the fine in respect of the responsible undertaking. Should the information be used for a different purpose, at any point in time, with the involvement of an outside counsel, the Commission may report the incident to the bar of that counsel, with a view to disciplinary action.

35. Corporate statements made under the present Notice will only be transmitted to the competition authorities of the Member States pursuant to Article 12 of Regulation N° 1/2003, provided that the conditions set out in the Network Notice (9) are met and provided that the level of protection against disclosure awarded by the receiving competition authority is equivalent to the one conferred by the Commission.

V. GENERAL CONSIDERATIONS

36. The Commission will not take a position on whether or not to grant conditional immunity, or otherwise on whether or not to reward any application, if it becomes apparent that the application concerns infringements covered by the five years limitation period for the imposition of penalties stipulated in Article 25(1)(b) of Regulation 1/2003, as such applications would be devoid of purpose.

37. From the date of its publication in the *Official Journal*, this notice replaces the 2002 Commission notice on immunity from fines and reduction of fines in cartel cases for all cases in which no undertaking has contacted the Commission in order to take advantage of the favourable treatment set out in that notice. However, points (31) to (35) of the current notice will be applied from the moment of its publication to all pending and new applications for immunity from fines or reduction of fines.

38. The Commission is aware that this notice will create legitimate expectations on which undertakings may rely when disclosing the existence of a cartel to the Commission.

39. In line with the Commission's practice, the fact that an undertaking cooperated with the Commission during its administrative procedure will be indicated in any decision, so as to explain the reason for the immunity or reduction of the fine. The fact that immunity or reduction in respect of fines is granted cannot protect an undertaking from the civil law consequences of its participation in an infringement of Article 81 EC.

40. The Commission considers that normally public disclosure of documents and written or recorded statements received in the context of this notice would undermine certain public or private interests, for example the protection of the purpose of inspections and investigations, within the meaning of Article 4 of Regulation (EC) N° 1049/2001 (10), even after the decision has been taken.

(1) Reference in this text to Article 81 EC also covers Article 53 EEA when applied by the Commission according to the rules laid down in Article 56 of the EEA Agreement.

(2) O.J. L 8, 12.1.2001, p. 1.

(3) The assessment of the threshold will have to be carried out ex ante, i.e. without taking into account whether a given inspection has or has not been successful or whether or not an inspection has or has not been carried out. The assessment will be made exclusively on the basis of the type and the quality of the information submitted by the applicant.

(4) Corporate statements may take the form of written documents signed by or on behalf of the undertaking or be made orally.

(5) This requires in particular that the applicant provides accurate, not misleading, and complete information. Cfr judgement of the European Court of Justice of 29 June 2006 in case C-301/04 P, Commission v SGL Carbon AG a.o., at paragraphs 68-70, and judgement of the European Court of Justice of 28 June 2005 in cases C-189/02 P, C-202/02 P, C-205/02 P, C-208/02 P and C-213/02 P, Dansk Rørindustri A/S a.o. v. Commission, at paragraphs 395-399.

(6) O.J. L 1, 4.1.2003, p. 1.

(7) O.J. L 123, 27.4.2004, p. 18.

(8) O.J. C 325, 22.12.2005, p. 7.

(9) Commission Notice on cooperation within the Network of Competition Authorities, O.J.C 101, 27.4.2004, p. 43.

(10) O.J. L 145, 31.5.2001, p. 43.

Inspections – Explanatory note to an authorization to conduct an inspection in execution of a Commission Decision under Article 20(4) of Council Regulation N° 1/2003, March 2008

1. See: http://ec.europa.eu/competition/antitrust/legislation/explanatory_note.pdf

This note is for information only and is without prejudice to any formal interpretation of the Commission's powers of investigation.

1. Undertakings (1) are legally obliged to submit to an inspection ordered by decision of the Commission under Article 20(4) of Council Regulation N° 1/2003. Written authorisations serve to name the officials and other accompanying persons authorised by the Commission to conduct the inspection. They prove their identity by means of their staff card.

2. Officials and other accompanying persons authorised by the Commission to conduct the inspection cannot be required to enlarge upon the subject matter as set out in the decision or to justify in any way the taking of the decision. They may however explain procedural matters, particularly confidentiality, and the possible consequences of a refusal to submit to the inspection.

3. A certified copy of the decision is to be handed to the undertaking. The minute of notification of service serves only to certify delivery and its signature by the recipient does not imply submission.

4. The officials and other accompanying persons are empowered, pursuant to Article 20(2) of Regulation N° 1/2003:

a) to enter any premises, land and means of transport of undertakings and associations of undertakings;

b) to examine the books and other records related to the business, irrespective of the medium on which they are stored;

c) to take or obtain in any form copies of or extracts from such books or records;

d) to seal any business premises and books or records for the period and to the extent necessary for the inspection;

e) to ask any representative or member of staff of the undertaking or association of undertakings for explanations on facts or documents relating to the subject-matter and purpose of the inspection and to record the answers.

5. Officials of and those authorised or appointed by the competition authority of the Member State in whose territory the inspection is conducted are entitled to actively assist the officials and other accompanying persons authorised by the Commission in carrying out their duties. To this end, they enjoy the same powers under Article 20(2) of Council Regulation N° 1/2003 as the officials and other accompanying persons authorised by the Commission (see paragraph 4 above). They shall prove their identity in accordance with the relevant national rules.

6. The undertaking may consult a legal adviser during the inspection. This consultation of the lawyer can be carried out by telephone. However, the presence of a lawyer is not a legal condition for the validity of the inspection. The officials or other accompanying persons authorised by the Commission can enter the premises, notify the decision ordering the inspection and occupy the offices of their choice without waiting for the undertaking to consult its lawyer. The officials and other accompanying persons authorised by the Commission will accept only a short delay pending consultation of the lawyer before starting examining the books and other records related to the business, taking copies or extracts of those documents, sealing business premises and books or records if needed or asking for oral explanations. Any such delay must be kept to the strict minimum.

7. Where any representative or member of staff of the undertaking gives pursuant to Article 4(1) of the Commission Regulation N° 773/2004 oral explanations on the spot on facts or documents relating to the subject-matter and purpose of the inspection at the request of the officials or other accompanying persons authorised by the Commission, the explanations may be recorded in any form. A copy of any such recording will be made available to the undertaking concerned after the inspection pursuant to Article 4(2) of the Commission Regulation N° 773/2004.

8. In cases where a member of staff of an undertaking who is not or was not authorised by the undertaking to provide explanations on behalf of the undertaking has been asked for explanations, the Commission shall set a time-limit within which the undertaking may communicate to the Commission any rectification, amendment or supplement to the explanations given by such member of staff. The rectification, amendment or supplement shall be added to the explanations as recorded during the inspection.

9. The officials and other accompanying persons authorised by the Commission are entitled to examine any books and records related to the business, irrespective of the medium on which they are stored, and to take or obtain in any form copies of or extracts from such books or records. This includes also the examination of electronic information and taking digital or paper copies of such information.

10. As part of its investigation, the Commission can search the IT environment, storage media and hardware of the undertaking. The officials and other accompanying persons authorised by the Commission may use the search tools built in the storage media investigated. The investigation may also include searches based on keywords and the use of dedicated software and/or hardware brought by the officials and other accompanying persons authorised by the Commission. The dedicated software allows the Commission to search and recover data whilst respecting the integrity of the undertakings' systems and data.

11. If the officials or other accompanying persons authorised by the Commission consider it appropriate, an integral copy of a digital storage medium, such as a forensic image, can be taken as well. This may occur, by way of example, where the Commission's selection of documents and data is not finished *in situ*, or when the officials or other accompanying persons authorised by the Commission find it necessary for the preservation of information that otherwise could be lost or when the access to the selected data or documents is not possible *in situ*. If the selection of the relevant documents for the investigation is not finished during the inspection the digital copy (DVD, Hard Disk, …) of the data still to be searched is put in an envelop which will be sealed *in situ* and carried off by the officials. A replicate of the digital copy is given to the undertaking.

The undertaking will then be invited by the Commission to attend the opening of the sealed envelop and the selection process in the Commission's premises.

12. The undertaking will receive a copy of all the documents and the data copied by the Commission services and may request a signed list of the copies and extracts taken by the Commission officials during the inspection.

Where the undertaking makes available photocopies of documents at the request of the Commission officials, the Commission shall, at the request of the undertaking, reimburse the cost of the photocopies.

13. The documents and the data copied during an inspection will be covered by the provisions of Article 28 of Council Regulation N° 1/2003 concerning professional secrecy. If, at a later stage of the procedure, it becomes necessary to grant other parties access to those documents and data, the undertakings will be asked to identify any business secrets or other confidential information contained in the documents or data, to justify those claims and to provide non-confidential copies for the purpose of granting access to the file.

14. In addition to the documents and the data requested and inspected by the officials, other accompanying persons authorised by the Commission and officials of and those authorised or appointed by the competition authority of the Member State, the undertaking is entitled to draw attention to other documents, data or information where it considers this necessary for the purpose of protecting its legitimate interest in a complete and objective clarification of the matters raised, provided that the inspection is not thereby unduly delayed.

15. Where the officials and other accompanying persons authorised by the Commission decide to seal business premises and books or records, a minute will be made. The undertaking has to ensure that seals that have been affixed as well as the immediate environment of the place where they have been affixed (e.g. door, doorframe, cupboard) remain untouched until the seals are removed by the Commission's representative. The officials and other accompanying persons authorised by the Commission will also record any changes in the seals following their affixation and, if such changes are found, the time when the seal is removed, in a separate minute.

16. Any personal data, as defined in Regulation N° 45/2001 in documents copied or obtained during the inspection will be processed in compliance with that Regulation.

(1) In this note the term «undertaking» includes both undertakings and associations of undertakings.

Commission Notice on the conduct of settlement procedures in view of the adoption of Decisions pursuant to Article 7 and Article 23 of Council Regulation (EC) n° 1/2003 in cartel cases

(OJ C 167, 2 July 2008, p. 1)

1. Article 81 EC is now Article 101 TFEU and Article 82 EC is now Article 102 TFEU.

1. INTRODUCTION

1. This Notice sets out the framework for rewarding cooperation in the conduct of proceedings commenced in view of the application of Article 81 of the EC Treaty (1) to cartel cases (2). The settlement procedure may allow the Commission to handle more cases with the same resources, thereby fostering the public interest in the Commission's delivery of effective and timely punishment, while increasing overall deterrence. The cooperation covered by this Notice is different from the voluntary production of evidence to trigger or advance the Commission's investigation, which is covered by the Commission Notice on Immunity from fines and reduction of fines in cartel cases (3) (the Leniency Notice). Provided that the cooperation offered by an undertaking qualifies under both Commission Notices, it can be cumulatively rewarded accordingly (4).

(1) References in this text to Article 81 also cover Article 53 EEA when applied by the Commission in accordance with the rules laid down in Article 56 of the EEA Agreement.

(2) Cartels are agreements and/or concerted practices between two or more competitors aimed at coordinating their competitive behaviour on the market and/or influencing the relevant parameters of competition through practices such as the fixing of purchase or selling prices or other trading conditions, the allocation of production or sales quotas, the sharing of markets including bid-rigging, restrictions of imports or exports and/or anti-competitive actions against other competitors. Such practices are among the most serious violations of Article 81 EC.

(3) O.J. C 298, 8.12.2006, p. 17.

(4) See point 33.

2. When parties to the proceedings are prepared to acknowledge their participation in a cartel violating Article 81 of the Treaty and their liability therefore, they may also contribute to expediting the proceedings leading to the adoption of the corresponding decision pursuant to Article 7 and Article 23 of Council Regulation (E.C.) n° 1/2003 of 16 December 2002 on the implementation of the rules on competition laid down in Articles 81 and 82 of the Treaty (5) in the way and with the safeguards specified in this Notice. Whilst the Commission, as the investigative authority and the guardian of the Treaty empowered to adopt enforcement decisions subject to judicial control by the Community Courts, does not negotiate the question of the existence of an infringement of Community law and the appropriate sanction, it can reward the cooperation described in this Notice.

(5) O.J. L 1, 4.1.2003, p. 1. Regulation as last amended by Regulation (E.C.) n° 1419/2006 (O.J. L 269, 28.9.2006, p. 1).

3. Commission Regulation (E.C.) n° 773/2004 of 7 April 2004 relating to the conduct of proceedings by the Commission pursuant to Articles 81 and 82 of the EC Treaty (6) lays down the core practical rules concerning the conduct of proceedings in antitrust cases including those applicable in the variant for settlement. In this regard, Regulation (E.C.) n° 773/2004 bestows on the Commission the discretion whether to explore the settlement procedure or not in cartel cases, while ensuring that the choice of the settlement procedure cannot be imposed on the parties.

(6) O.J. L 123, 27.4.2004, p. 18. Regulation as last amended by Regulation (E.C.) n° 622/2008 (O.J. L 171, 1.7.2008, p. 3).

4. Effective enforcement of Community competition law is compatible with full respect of the parties' rights of defence, which constitutes a fundamental principle of Community law to be respected in all circumstances, and in particular in antitrust procedures which may give rise to penalties. It follows that the rules established to conduct the Commission proceedings to enforce Article 81 of the Treaty should ensure that the undertakings and associations of undertakings concerned are afforded the opportunity effectively to make known their views on the truth and relevance of the facts, objections and circumstances put forward by the Commission (7), throughout the administrative procedure.

(7) Case 85/76, Hoffmann-La Roche v Commission (1979) E.C.R. 461, at paragraphs 9 and 11.

2. PROCEDURE

5. The Commission retains a broad margin of discretion to determine which cases may be suitable to explore the parties' interest in engaging in settlement discussions, as well as to decide to engage in them or discontinue them or to definitely settle. In this regard, account may be taken of the probability of reaching a common understanding regarding the scope of the potential objections with the parties involved within a reasonable timeframe, in view of factors such as number of parties involved, foreseeable conflicting positions on the attribution of liability, extent of contestation of the facts. The prospect of achieving procedural efficiencies in view of the progress made overall in the settlement procedure, including the scale of burden involved in providing access to non-confidential versions of documents from the file, will be considered. Other concerns such as the possibility of setting a precedent might apply. The Commission may also decide to discontinue settlement discussions if the parties to the proceedings coordinate to distort or destroy any evidence relevant to the establishment of the infringement or any part thereof or to the calculation of the applicable fine. Distortion or destruction of evidence relevant to the establishment of the infringement or any part thereof may also constitute an aggravating circumstance within the meaning of point 28 of the Commission Guidelines on the method of setting fines imposed pursuant to Article 23(2)(a) of Regulation (E.C.) n° 1/2003 (8) (the Guidelines on fines), and may be regarded as lack of cooperation within the meaning of points 12 and 27 of the Leniency Notice. The Commission may only engage in settlement discussions upon the written request of the parties concerned.

(8) *O.J.* C 210, 1.9.2006, p. 2.

6. While parties to the proceedings do not have a right to settle, should the Commission consider that a case may, in principle, be suitable for settlement, it will explore the interest in settlement of all parties to the same proceedings.

7. The parties to the proceedings may not disclose to any third party in any jurisdiction the contents of the discussions or of the documents which they have had access to in view of settlement, unless they have a prior explicit authorization by the Commission. Any breach in this regard may lead the Commission to disregard the undertaking's request to follow the settlement procedure. Such disclosure may also constitute an aggravating circumstance, within the meaning of point 28 of the Guidelines on fines and may be regarded as lack of cooperation within the meaning of points 12 and 27 of the Leniency Notice.

2.1. Initiation of proceedings and exploratory steps regarding settlement

8. Where the Commission contemplates the adoption of a decision pursuant to Article 7 and/or Article 23 of Regulation (E.C.) n° 1/2003, it is required in advance to identify and recognize as parties to the proceedings the legal persons on whom a penalty may be imposed for an infringement of Article 81 of the Treaty.

9. To this end, the initiation of proceedings pursuant to Article 11(6) of Regulation (E.C.) n° 1/2003 in view of adopting such a decision can take place at any point in time, but no later than the date on which the Commission issues a statement of objections against the parties concerned. Article 2(1) of Regulation (E.C.) n° 773/2004 further specifies that, should the Commission consider it suitable to explore the parties' interest in engaging in settlement discussions, it will initiate proceedings no later than the date on which it either issues a statement of objections or requests the parties to express in writing their interest to engage in settlement discussions, whichever is the earlier.

10. After the initiation of proceedings pursuant to Article 11(6) of Regulation (E.C.) n° 1/2003, the Commission becomes the only competition authority competent to apply Article 81 of the Treaty to the case in point.

11. Should the Commission consider it suitable to explore the parties' interest to engage in settlement discussions, it will set a time-limit of no less than two weeks pursuant to Articles 10a(1) and 17(3) of Regulation (E.C.) n° 773/2004 within which parties to the same proceedings should declare in writing whether they envisage engaging in settlement discussions in view of possibly introducing settlement submissions at a later stage. This written declaration does not imply an admission by the parties of having participated in an infringement or of being liable for it.

12. Whenever the Commission initiates proceedings against two or more parties within the same undertaking, the Commission will inform each of them of the other legal entities which it identifies within the same undertaking and which are also concerned by the proceedings. In such a case, should the concerned parties wish to engage in settlement discussions, they must appoint joint representatives duly empowered to act on their behalf by the end of the time-limit referred to in point 11. The appointment of joint representatives aims solely to facilitate the settlement discussions and it does not prejudge in any way the attribution of liability for the infringement amongst the different parties.

13. The Commission may disregard any application for immunity from fines or reduction of fines on the ground that it has been submitted after the expiry of the time-limit referred to in point 11.

2.2. Commencing the settlement procedure: settlement discussions

14. Should some of the parties to the proceedings request settlement discussions and comply with the requirements referred to in points 11 and 12, the Commission may decide to pursue the settlement procedure by means of bilateral contacts between the Commission Directorate-General for Competition and the settlement candidates.

15. The Commission retains discretion to determine the appropriateness and the pace of the bilateral settlement discussions with each undertaking. In line with Article 10a(2) of Regulation (E.C.) n° 773/2004, this includes determining, in view of the progress made overall in the settlement procedure, the order and sequence of the bilateral settlement discussions as well as the timing of the disclosure of information, including the evidence in the Commission file used to establish the envisaged objections and the potential fine (9). information will be disclosed in a timely manner as settlement discussions progress.

(9) Reference to the «potential fine» in Article 10a(2) of Regulation (E.C.) n° 773/2004 affords the Commission services the possibility to inform the parties concerned by settlement discussions of an estimate of their potential fine in view of the guidance contained in the Guidelines on fines, the provisions of this Notice and the Leniency Notice, where applicable.

16. Such an early disclosure in the context of settlement discussions pursuant to Article 10a(2) and Article 15(1a) of Regulation (E.C.) n° 773/2004 will allow the parties to be informed of the essential elements taken into consideration so far, such as the facts alleged, the classification of those facts, the gravity and duration of the alleged cartel, the attribution of liability, an estimation of the range of likely fines, as well as the evidence used to establish the potential objections. This will enable the parties effectively to assert their views on the potential objections against them and will allow them to make an informed decision on whether or not to settle. Upon request by a party, the Commission services will also grant it access to non-confidential versions of any specified accessible document listed in the case file at that point in time, in so far as this is justified for the purpose of enabling the party to ascertain its position regarding a time period or any other aspect of the cartel (10).

(10) For that purpose, the parties will be provided with a list of all accessible documents in the case file at that point in time.

17. When the progress made during the settlement discussions leads to a common understanding regarding the scope of the potential objections and the estimation of the range of likely fines to be imposed by the Commission, and the Commission takes the preliminary view that procedural efficiencies are likely to be achieved in view of the progress made overall, the Commission may grant a final time-limit of at least 15 working days for an undertaking to introduce a final settlement submission pursuant to Articles 10a(2) and 17(3) of Regulation (E.C.) n° 773/2004. The time-limit can be extended following a reasoned request. Before granting such time-limit, the parties will be entitled to have the information specified in point 16 disclosed to them upon request.

18. The parties may call upon the Hearing Officer at any time during the settlement procedure in relation to issues that might arise relating to due process. The Hearing Officer's duty is to ensure that the effective exercise of the rights of defence is respected.

19. Should the parties concerned fail to introduce a settlement submission, the procedure leading to the final decision in their regard will follow the general provisions, in particular Articles 10(2), 12(1) and 15(1) of Regulation (E.C.) n° 773/2004, instead of those regulating the settlement procedure.

2.3. Settlement submissions

20. Parties opting for a settlement procedure must introduce a formal request to settle in the form of a settlement submission. The settlement submission provided for in Article 10a(2) of Regulation (E.C.) n° 773/2004 should contain:

(a) an acknowledgement in clear and unequivocal terms of the parties' liability for the infringement summarily described as regards its object, its possible implementation, the main facts, their legal qualification, including the party's role and the duration of their participation in the infringement in accordance with the results of the settlement discussions;

(b) an indication (11) of the maximum amount of the fine the parties foresee to be imposed by the Commission and which the parties would accept in the framework of a settlement procedure;

(c) the parties' confirmation that, they have been sufficiently informed of the objections the Commission envisages raising against them and that they have been given sufficient opportunity to make their views known to the Commission;

(d) the parties' confirmation that, in view of the above, they do not envisage requesting access to the file or requesting to be heard again in an oral hearing, unless the Commission does not reflect their settlement submissions in the statement of objections and the decision;

(e) the parties' agreement to receive the statement of objections and the final decision pursuant to Articles 7 and 23 of Regulation (E.C.) n° 1/2003 in an agreed official language of the European Community.

(11) This would result from the discussions as set out in points 16 and 17.

21. The acknowledgments and confirmations provided by the parties in view of settlement constitute the expression of their commitment to cooperate in the expeditious handling of the case following the settlement procedure. However, those acknowledgments and confirmations are conditional upon the Commission meeting their settlement request, including the anticipated maximum amount of the fine.

22. Settlement requests cannot be revoked unilaterally by the parties which have provided them unless the Commission does not meet the settlement requests by reflecting the settlement submissions first in a statement of objections and ultimately, in a final decision (see in this regard points 27 and 29). The statement of objections would be deemed to have endorsed the settlement submissions if it reflects their contents on the issues mentioned in point 20(a). Additionally, for a final decision to be deemed to have reflected the settlement submissions, it should also impose a fine which does not exceed the maximum amount indicated therein.

2.4. Statement of objections and reply

23. Pursuant to Article 10(1) of Regulation (E.C.) n° 773/2004, the notification of a written statement of objections to each of the parties against whom objections are raised is a mandatory preparatory step before adopting any final decision. Therefore, the Commission will issue a statement of objections also in a settlement procedure (12).

(12) In the context of settlement procedures, statements of objections should contain the information necessary to enable the parties to corroborate that it reflects their settlement submissions.

24. For the parties' rights of defence to be exercised effectively, the Commission should hear their views on the objections against them and supporting evidence before adopting a final decision and take them into account by amending its preliminary analysis, where appropriate (13). The Commission must be able not only to accept or reject the parties' relevant arguments expressed during the administrative procedure, but also to make its own analysis of the matters put forward by them in order to either abandon such objections because they have been shown to be unfounded or to supplement and reassess its arguments both in fact and in law, in support of the objections which it maintains.

(13) In line with settled case-law, the Commission shall base its decisions only on objections on which the parties concerned have been able to comment and, to this end, they shall be entitled to have access to the Commission's file, subject to the legitimate interest of undertakings in the protection of their business secrets.

25. By introducing a formal settlement request in the form of a settlement submission prior to the notification of the statement of objections, the parties concerned enable the Commission to effectively take their views into account (14) already when drafting the statement of objections, rather than only before the consultation of the Advisory Committee on Restrictive Practices and Dominant Positions (hereinafter the «Advisory Committee») or before the adoption of the final decision (15).

(14) In this regard, recital 2 of Regulation (E.C.) n° 622/2008 states: «(...) Such early disclosure should enable the parties concerned to put forward their views on the objections which the Commission intends to raise against them as well as on their potential liability».

(15) As required by Article 11(1) of Regulation (E.C.) n° 773/2004 and Article 27(1) of Regulation (E.C.) n° 1/2003, respectively.

26. Should the statement of objections reflect the parties' settlement submissions, the parties concerned should within a time-limit of at least two weeks set by the Commission in accordance with Articles 10a(3) and 17(3) of Regulation (E.C.) n° 773/2004, reply to it by simply confirming (in unequivocal terms) that the statement of objections corresponds to the contents of their settlement submissions and that they therefore remain committed to follow the settlement procedure. In the absence of such a reply, the Commission will take note of the party's breach of its commitment and may also disregard the party's request to follow the settlement procedure.

27. The Commission retains the right to adopt a statement of objections which does not reflect the parties' settlement submission. If so, the general provisions in Articles 10(2), 12(1) and 15(1) of Regulation (E.C.) n° 773/2004 will apply. The acknowledgements provided by the parties in the settlement submission would be deemed to be withdrawn and could not be used in evidence against any of the parties to the proceedings. Hence, the parties concerned would no longer be bound by their settlement submissions and would be granted a time-limit allowing them, upon request, to present their defence anew, including the possibility to access the file and to request an oral hearing.

2.5. Commission decision and settlement reward

28. Upon the parties' replies to the statement of objections confirming their commitment to settle, Regulation (E.C.) n° 773/2004 allows the Commission to proceed, without any other procedural step, to the adoption of the subsequent final decision pursuant to Articles 7 and/or 23 of Regulation (E.C.) n° 1/2003, after consultation of the Advisory Committee pursuant to Article 14 of Regulation (E.C.) n° 1/2003. In particular, this implies that no oral hearing or access to the file may be requested by those parties once their settlement submissions have been reflected by the statement of objections, in line with Articles 12(2) and 15(1a) of Regulation (E.C.) n° 773/2004.

29. The Commission retains the right to adopt a final position which departs from its preliminary position expressed in a statement of objections endorsing the parties' settlement submissions, either in view of the opinion provided by the Advisory Committee or for other appropriate considerations in view of the ultimate decisional autonomy of the Commission to this effect. However, should the Commission opt to follow that course, it will inform the parties and notify to them a new statement of objections in order to allow for the exercise of their rights of defence in accordance with the applicable general rules of procedure. It follows that the parties would then be entitled to have access to the file, to request an oral hearing and to reply to the statement of objections. The acknowledgments provided by the parties in the settlement submissions would be deemed to have been withdrawn and could not be used in evidence against any of the parties to the proceedings.

30. The final amount of the fine in a particular case is determined in the decision finding an infringement pursuant to Article 7 and imposing a fine pursuant to Article 23 of Regulation (E.C.) n° 1/2003.

31. In line with the Commission's practice, the fact that an undertaking cooperated with the Commission under this Notice during the administrative procedure will be indicated in the final decision, so as to explain the reason for the level of the fine.

32. Should the Commission decide to reward a party for settlement in the framework of this Notice, it will reduce by 10% the amount of the fine to be imposed after the 10% cap has been applied having regard to the Guidelines on the method of setting fines imposed pursuant to Article 23(2)(a) of Regulation (E.C.) n° 1/2003 (16). Any specific increase for deterrence (17) used in their regard will not exceed a multiplication by two.

(16) O.J. C 210, 1.9.2006, p. 2.

(17) Point 30 of the Guidelines on fines.

33. When settled cases involve also leniency applicants, the reduction of the fine granted to them for settlement will be added to their leniency reward.

3. GENERAL CONSIDERATIONS

34. This Notice applies to any case pending before the Commission at the time of or after its publication in the Official Journal of the European Union.

35. Access to settlement submissions is only granted to those addressees of a statement of objections who have not requested settlement, provided that they commit – together with the legal counsels getting access on their behalf – not to make any copy by mechanical or electronic means of any information in the settlement submissions to which access is being granted and to ensure that the information to be obtained from the settlement submission will solely be used for the purposes of judicial or administrative proceedings for the application of the Community competition rules at issue in the related proceedings. Other parties such as complainants will not be granted access to settlement submissions.

36. The use of such information for a different purpose during the proceeding may be regarded as lack of cooperation within the meaning of points 12 and 27 of the Leniency Notice. Moreover, if any such use is made after the Commission has already adopted a prohibition decision in the proceedings, the Commission may, in any legal proceedings before the Community Courts, ask the Court to increase the fine in respect of the responsible undertaking. Should the information be used for a different purpose, at any point in time, with the involvement of an outside counsel, the Commission may report the incident to the bar of that counsel, with a view to disciplinary action.

37. Settlement submissions made under this Notice will only be transmitted to the competition authorities of the Member States pursuant to Article 12 of Regulation (E.C.) n° 1/2003, provided that the conditions set out in the Network Notice (18) are met and provided that the level of protection against disclosure awarded by the receiving competition authority is equivalent to the one conferred by the Commission.

(18) Commission Notice on cooperation within the Network of Competition Authorities (*O.J.* C 101, 27.4.2004, p. 43).

38. Upon the applicant's request, the Commission may accept that settlement submissions be provided orally. Oral settlement submissions will be recorded and transcribed at the Commission's premises. In accordance with Article 19 of Regulation (E.C.) n° 1/2003 and Articles 3(3) and 17(3) of Regulation (E.C.) n° 773/2004 undertakings making oral settlement submissions will be granted the opportunity to check the technical accuracy of the recording, which will be available at the Commission's premises and to correct the substance of their oral settlement submissions and the accuracy of the transcript without delay.

39. The Commission will not transmit settlement submissions to national courts without the consent of the relevant applicants, in line with the provisions in the Commission Notice on the co-operation between the Commission and the courts of the EU Member States in the application of Articles 81 and 82 EC (19).

(19) *O.J.* C 101, 27.4.2004, p. 54; point 26.

40. The Commission considers that normally public disclosure of documents and written or recorded statements (including settlement submissions) received in the context of this Notice would undermine certain public or private interests, for example the protection of the purpose of inspections and investigations, within the meaning of Article 4 of Regulation (E.C.) n° 1049/2001 of the European Parliament and of the Council of 30 May 2001 regarding public access to European Parliament, Council and Commission documents (20), even after the decision has been taken.

(20) *O.J.* L 145, 31.5.2001, p. 43.

41. Final decisions taken by the Commission under Regulation (E.C.) n° 1/2003 are subject to judicial review in accordance with Article 230 of the Treaty. Moreover, as provided in Article 229 of the Treaty and Article 31 of Regulation (E.C.) n° 1/2003, the Court of justice has unlimited jurisdiction to review decisions on fines adopted pursuant to Article 23 of Regulation (E.C.) n° 1/2003.

Overview of the procedure leading to the adoption of a (settlement) Decision pursuant to Articles 7 and 23 of Regulation n° (E.C.) 1/2003

I. INVESTIGATION AS USUAL

– parties may express their interest in a hypothetical settlement.

II. EXPLORATORY STEPS REGARDING SETTLEMENT

– Letter to all companies (and MS) informing of the decision to initiate proceedings in view of settlement (Article 11(6)) and requesting them to express their interest in settlement.

III. BILATERAL ROUNDS OF SETTLEMENT DISCUSSIONS

– Disclosure and exchange of arguments on potential objections, liability, fines range.

– Disclosure of evidence used to establish potential objections, liability, fines.

– Disclosure of other non-confidential versions of documents in the file, when justified.

IV. SETTLEMENT

– Conditional settlement submissions by the companies, jointly represented where applicable.

– DG COMP sends acknowledgement of receipt.

V. «SETTLED» STATEMENT OF OBJECTIONS

– Notification of streamlined SO endorsing company's settlement submissions, where appropriate.

– Company's reply to SO confirming clearly that it reflects its settlement submission.

VI. «SETTLEMENT» DECISION PURSUANT TO ARTICLES 7 AND 23 OF REGULATION N° (E.C.) 1/2003

– Advisory Committee on a draft streamlined final decision.

If College of commissioners agrees:

– Adoption of streamlined final decision.

White Paper 2 April 2008 on Damages Actions for Breach of the EC antitrust rules, COM(2008) 165

1. Article 81 EC is now Article 101 TFEU and Article 82 EC is now Article 102 TFEU.

1. PURPOSE AND SCOPE OF THE WHITE PAPER

1.1. Why a White Paper on damages actions for breaches of the EC antitrust rules?

Any citizen or business who suffers harm as a result of a breach of EC antitrust rules (Articles 81 and 82 of the EC Treaty) must be able to claim reparation from the party who caused the damage. This right of victims to compensation is guaranteed by Community law, as the European Court of Justice recalled in 2001 and 2006. (1)

(1) Case C-453/99, Courage and Crehan, (2001) ECR I-6297, and Joined Cases C-295 298/04, Manfredi, (2006) ECR I-6619.

Despite the requirement to establish an effective legal framework turning exercising the right to damages into a realistic possibility, and although there have recently been some signs of improvement in certain Member States, to date in practice victims of EC antitrust infringements only rarely obtain reparation of the harm suffered. The amount of compensation that these victims are forgoing is in the range of several billion euros a year. (2)

(2) See section 2.2 of the Impact Assessment Report (IAR).

In its 2005 Green Paper, the Commission concluded that this failure is largely due to various legal and procedural hurdles in the Member States' rules governing actions for antitrust damages before national courts. Indeed, such antitrust damages cases display a number of particular characteristics that are often insufficiently addressed by traditional rules on civil liability and procedure. This gives rise to a great deal of legal uncertainty. (3) These particularities include the very complex factual and economic analysis required, the frequent inaccessibility and concealment of crucial evidence in the hands of defendants and the often unfavourable risk/reward balance for claimants.

(3) See *ibid.*, section 2.3.

The current ineffectiveness of antitrust damages actions is best addressed by a combination of measures at both Community and national levels, in order to achieve effective minimum protection of the victims' right to damages under Articles 81 and 82 in every Member State and a more level playing field and greater legal certainty across the EU.

The European Parliament (4) concurred with the findings in the Green Paper, as did other stakeholders, and called upon the Commission to prepare a White Paper with detailed proposals to address the obstacles to effective antitrust damages actions.

(4) Resolution of 25 April 2007 (2006/2207(INI)).

1.2. Objectives, guiding principles and scope of the White Paper

This White Paper considers and puts forward proposals for policy choices and specific measures that would ensure, more than is the case today, that all victims of infringements of EC competition law have access to effective redress mechanisms so that they can be fully compensated for the harm they suffered.

This White Paper is to be read in conjunction with two Commission staff working documents:

(a) a Commission staff working paper on EC antitrust damages actions («the SWP») which explains in greater detail the considerations underlying the White Paper and also provides a concise overview of the already existing acquis communautaire; and

(b) an Impact Assessment Report (the «IAR») analysing the potential benefits and costs of various policy options, and an executive summary of this report.

The primary objective of this White Paper is to improve the legal conditions for victims to exercise their right under the Treaty to reparation of all damage suffered as a result of a breach of the EC antitrust rules. Full compensation is, therefore, the first and foremost guiding principle.

More effective compensation mechanisms mean that the costs of antitrust infringements would be borne by the infringers, and not by the victims and law-abiding businesses. Effective remedies for private parties also increase the likelihood that a greater number of illegal restrictions of competition will be detected and that the infringers will be held liable. (5) Improving compensatory justice would therefore inherently also produce beneficial effects in terms of deterrence of future infringements and greater compliance with EC antitrust rules. Safeguarding undistorted competition is an integral part of the internal market and important for implementing the Lisbon strategy. A competition culture contributes to better allocation of resources, greater economic efficiency, increased innovation and lower prices.

(5) See the IAR, section 2.1.

The Commission followed the further guiding principle that the legal framework for more effective antitrust damages actions should be based on a genuinely European approach. The policy choices proposed in this White Paper therefore consist of balanced measures that are rooted in European legal culture and traditions.

Another important guiding principle of the Commission's policy is to preserve strong public enforcement of Articles 81 and 82 by the Commission and the competition authorities of the Member States. Accordingly, the measures put forward in this White Paper are designed to create an effective system of private enforcement by means of damages actions that complements, but does not replace or jeopardise, public enforcement.

In view of the foregoing and in line with the requirement set out by the Court of Justice that any victim of antitrust infringements must be able to exercise his right to compensation effectively, the issues addressed in the White Paper concern, in principle, all categories of victim, all types of breach of Articles 81 and 82 and all sectors of the economy. The Commission also considers it appropriate that the policy should cover both actions for damages which do, and actions which do not, rely on a prior finding of an infringement by a competition authority.

2. THE PROPOSED MEASURES AND POLICY CHOICES

2.1. Standing: indirect purchasers and collective redress

In the context of legal standing to bring an action, the Commission welcomes the confirmation by the Court of Justice that «any individual» who has suffered harm caused by an antitrust infringement must be allowed to claim damages before national courts .(6) This principle also applies to indirect purchasers, i.e. purchasers who had no direct dealings with the infringer, but who nonetheless may have suffered considerable harm because an illegal overcharge was passed on to them along the distribution chain.

(6) Manfredi (see footnote 1), point 61.

With respect to collective redress, the Commission considers that there is a clear need for mechanisms allowing aggregation of the individual claims of victims of antitrust infringements. Individual consumers, but also small businesses, especially those who have suffered scattered and relatively low-value damage, are often deterred from bringing an individual action for damages by the costs, delays, uncertainties, risks and burdens involved. As a result, many of these victims currently remain uncompensated. At the rare occasions where a multitude of individual actions are brought in relation to the same infringement, procedural inefficiencies arise, for claimants, defendants and the judicial system alike.

The Commission therefore suggests (7) a combination of two complementary mechanisms of collective redress to address effectively those issues in the field of antitrust:

• representative actions, which are brought by qualified entities, such as consumer associations, state bodies or trade associations, on behalf of identified or, in rather restricted cases, identifiable victims. These entities are either:
 (i) officially designated in advance; or
 (ii) certified on an *ad hoc* basis by a Member State for a particular antitrust infringement to bring an action on behalf of some or all of their members; and

• opt-in collective actions, in which victims expressly decide to combine their individual claims for harm they suffered into one single action.

(7) For the underlying reasons see Chapter 2 of the SWP.

Considering that qualified entities will not be able or willing to pursue every claim, it is necessary that these two types of action complement each other to ensure effective collective redress for victims of antitrust infringements. In addition, it is important that victims are not deprived of their right to bring an individual action for damages if they so wish. However, safeguards should be put in place to avoid that the same harm is compensated more than once.

These suggestions on damages actions in the field of antitrust are part of the Commission's wider initiative to strengthen collective redress mechanisms in the EU and may develop further within this context.

2.2. Access to evidence: disclosure inter partes

Competition cases are particularly fact-intensive. Much of the key evidence necessary for proving a case for antitrust damages is often concealed and, being held by the defendant or by third parties, is usually not known in sufficient detail to the claimant.

Whilst it is essential to overcome this structural information asymmetry and to improve victims' access to relevant evidence, it is also important to avoid the negative effects of overly broad and burdensome disclosure obligations, including the risk of abuses.

The Commission therefore suggests that across the EU a minimum level of disclosure inter partes for EC antitrust damages cases should be ensured. Building on the approach in the Intellectual Property Directive (Directive 2004/48/EC), access to evidence should be based on fact-pleading and strict judicial control of the plausibility of the claim and the proportionality of the disclosure request. The Commission therefore suggests (8) that:

• national courts should, under specific conditions, have the power to order parties to proceedings or third parties to disclose precise categories of relevant evidence;

• conditions for a disclosure order should include that the claimant has:

 – presented all the facts and means of evidence that are reasonably available to him, provided that these show plausible grounds to suspect that he suffered harm as a result of an infringement of competition rules by the defendant;

 – shown to the satisfaction of the court that he is unable, applying all efforts that can reasonably be expected, otherwise to produce the requested evidence;

 – specified sufficiently precise categories of evidence to be disclosed; and

 – satisfied the court that the envisaged disclosure measure is both relevant to the case and necessary and proportionate;

• adequate protection should be given to corporate statements by leniency applicants and to the investigations of competition authorities;

• to prevent destruction of relevant evidence or refusal to comply with a disclosure order, courts should have the power to impose sufficiently deterrent sanctions, including the option to draw adverse inferences in the civil proceedings for damages.

(8) For the underlying reasons see Chapter 3 of the SWP.

2.3. Binding effect of NCA decisions

Whenever the European Commission finds a breach of Article 81 or 82 of the EC Treaty, victims of the infringement can, by virtue of established case law and Article 16(1) of Regulation 1/2003, rely on this decision as binding proof in civil proceedings for damages. For decisions by national competition authorities (NCAs) finding a breach of Article 81 or 82, similar rules currently exist in only some Member States.

The Commission sees no reason why a final decision (9) on Article 81 or 82 taken by an NCA in the European Competition Network (ECN), and a final judgment by a review court upholding the NCA decision or itself finding an infringement, should not be accepted in every Member State as irrebuttable proof of the infringement in subsequent civil antitrust damages cases.

(9) In all Member States, NCA decisions are subject to judicial review. NCA decisions are considered final when they can no longer be reviewed, i.e. decisions that were not appealed within the applicable time limits and thus accepted by their addressees, and those that were confirmed by the competent review courts.

A rule to this effect would ensure a more consistent application of Articles 81 and 82 by different national bodies and increase legal certainty. It would also significantly increase the effectiveness and procedural efficiency of actions for antitrust damages: if defendants can call into question their own breach of Article 81 or 82 established in a decision by an NCA and, possibly, confirmed by a review court, the courts seized with an action for damages are required to re-examine the facts and legal issues already investigated and assessed by a specialised public authority (and a review court). Such duplication of factual and legal analysis leads to considerable extra costs, duration and imponderability for the victim's action for damages.

The Commission therefore suggests (10) the following rule:

• national courts that have to rule in actions for damages on practices under Article 81 or 82 on which an NCA in the ECN has already given a final decision finding an infringement of those articles, or on which a review court has given a final judgment upholding the NCA decision or itself finding an infringement, cannot take decisions running counter to any such decision or ruling.

This obligation should apply without prejudice to the right, and possible obligation, of national courts to seek clarification on the interpretation of Article 81 or 82 under Article 234 of the EC Treaty.

The rule set out above confers binding effect only on decisions that are final, i.e. where the defendant has exhausted all appeal avenues, and relates only to the same practices and same undertaking(s) for which the NCA or the review court found an infringement.

(10) For the underlying reasons see Chapter 4 of the SWP.

2.4. Fault requirement

If the breach of Article 81 or 82 has been proven, Member States take diverse approaches concerning the requirement of fault to obtain damages.

Some Member States require no fault at all as a condition for an antitrust damages claim, or irrebuttably presume the existence of fault once an infringement has been proven. The Commission sees no policy grounds against such an approach.

As regards the other Member States, the Court's case law on the conditions of civil liability for breaches of directly applicable Treaty rules, such as Articles 81 and 82, and the principle of effectiveness suggest that any fault requirements under national law would have to be limited. The Commission sees no reasons to relieve infringers from liability on grounds of absence of fault other than in cases where the infringer made an excusable error.

The Commission therefore suggests (11) a measure to make it clear, for Member States that require fault to be proven, that:

• once the victim has shown a breach of Article 81 or 82, the infringer should be liable for damages caused unless he demonstrates that the infringement was the result of a genuinely excusable error;

• an error would be excusable if a reasonable person applying a high standard of care could not have been aware that the conduct restricted competition.

(11) For the underlying reasons see Chapter 5 of the SWP.

2.5. Damages

The Commission welcomes the confirmation by the Court of Justice of the types of harm for which victims of antitrust infringements should be able to obtain compensation. (12) The Court emphasised that victims must, as a minimum, receive full compensation of the real value of the loss suffered. The entitlement to full compensation therefore extends not only to the actual loss due to an anti-competitive price increase, but also to the loss of profit as a result of any reduction in sales and encompasses a right to interest.

(12) Manfredi (see footnote 1), points 95 and 97.

For reasons of legal certainty and to raise awareness amongst potential infringers and victims, the Commission suggests codifying in a Community legislative instrument the current acquis communautaire on the scope of damages that victims of antitrust infringements can recover.

Once the scope of damages is clear, the quantum of these damages must be calculated. This calculation, implying a comparison with the economic situation of the victim in the hypothetical scenario of a competitive market, is often a very cumbersome exercise. It can become excessively difficult or even practically impossible, if the idea that the exact amount of the harm suffered must always be precisely calculated is strictly applied. Moreover, far-reaching calculation requirements can be disproportionate to the amount of damage suffered.

To facilitate the calculation of damages, the Commission therefore intends: (13)

• to draw up a framework with pragmatic, non-binding guidance for quantification of damages in antitrust cases, e.g. by means of approximate methods of calculation or simplified rules on estimating the loss.

(13) For the underlying reasons see Chapter 6 of the SWP.

2.6. Passing-on overcharges

If the direct customer of the infringer fully or partially passed on the illegal overcharge to his own customers (the indirect purchasers), several legal issues can arise. At present, these create a great degree of legal uncertainty and difficulties in antitrust damages actions.

Problems arise, on the one hand, if the infringer invokes the passing-on of overcharges as a defence against a damages claimant, arguing that the claimant suffered no loss because he passed on the price increase to his customers.

The Commission recalls the Court's emphasis on the compensatory principle and its premise that damages should be available to any injured person who can show a sufficient causal link with the infringement. Against this background, infringers should be allowed to invoke the possibility that the overcharge might have been passed on. Indeed, to deny this defence could result in unjust enrichment of purchasers who passed on the overcharge and in undue multiple compensation for the illegal overcharge by the defendant. The Commission therefore suggests (14) that:

• defendants should be entitled to invoke the passing-on defence against a claim for compensation of the overcharge. The standard of proof for this defence should be not lower than the standard imposed on the claimant to prove the damage.

(14) For the underlying reasons see Chapter 7 of the SWP.

Difficulties also arise, on the other hand, if an indirect purchaser invokes the passing-on of overcharges as a basis to show the harm suffered. Purchasers at, or near the end of the distribution chain are often those most harmed by antitrust infringements, but given their distance from the infringement they find it particularly difficult to produce sufficient proof of the existence and extent of passing-on of the illegal overcharge along the distribution chain. If such claimants are unable to produce this proof, they will not be compensated and the infringer, who may have successfully used the passing-on defence against another claimant upstream, would retain an unjust enrichment.

To avoid such scenario, the Commission therefore proposes to lighten the victim's burden and suggests (15) that:

• indirect purchasers should be able to rely on the rebuttable presumption that the illegal overcharge was passed on to them in its entirety.

(15) For the underlying reasons see ibid.

In the case of joint, parallel or consecutive actions brought by purchasers at different points in the distribution chain, national courts are encouraged to make full use of all mechanisms at their disposal under national, Community and international law in order to avoid under- and over-compensation of the harm caused by an infringement of competition law.

2.7. Limitation periods

While limitation periods play an important role in providing legal certainty, they can also be a considerable obstacle to recovery of damages, both in stand-alone and follow-on cases.

As regards the commencement of limitation periods, victims can face practical difficulties in the event of a continuous or repeated infringement or when they cannot reasonably have been aware of the infringement. The latter occurs frequently in relation to the most serious and harmful competition law infringements, such as cartels, which often remain covert both during and after their lifespan. The Commission therefore suggests (16) that the limitation period should not start to run:

• in the case of a continuous or repeated infringement, before the day on which the infringement ceases;

• before the victim of the infringement can reasonably be expected to have knowledge of the infringement and of the harm it caused him.

(16) For the underlying reasons see Chapter 8 of the SWP.

To keep open the possibility of follow-on actions, measures should be taken to avoid limitation periods expiring while public enforcement of the competition rules by competition authorities (and review courts) is still ongoing. To this end, the Commission prefers the option of a new limitation period, which starts once a competition authority or a review court adopts an infringement decision, over the option of suspending the limitation period during the public proceedings.

In the latter case, claimants (and defendants) will sometimes find it difficult to calculate the remaining period precisely, given that the opening and closure of proceedings by competition authorities are not always publicly known. Moreover, if a suspension were to commence at a very late stage of the limitation period, there may not be enough time left to prepare a claim.

The Commission therefore suggests (17) that:

• a new limitation period of at least two years should start once the infringement decision on which a follow-on claimant relies has become final.

(17) For the underlying reasons see ibid.

2.8. Costs of damages actions

The costs associated with antitrust damages actions, and also the cost allocation rules, can be a decisive disincentive to bringing an antitrust damages claim, given that these actions may be particularly costly and are generally more complex and time-consuming than other kinds of civil action.

The Commission considers that it would be useful for Member States to reflect on their cost rules and to examine the practices existing across the EU, in order to allow meritorious actions where costs would otherwise prevent claims being brought, particularly by claimants whose financial situation is significantly weaker than that of the defendant.

Due consideration should be given to mechanisms fostering early resolution of cases, e.g. by settlements. This could significantly reduce or eliminate litigation costs for the parties and also the costs for the judicial system.

Member States could also consider introducing, where appropriate, limits on the level of court fees applicable to antitrust damages actions.

Finally, Member States are invited to reflect on their cost allocation rules in order to reduce the uncertainty for potential claimants about the costs for which they may be liable. The «loser pays» principle, which prevails in the EU Member States, plays an important function in filtering out unmeritorious cases. However, under certain circumstances, this principle could also discourage victims with meritorious claims. National courts may therefore have to be empowered to derogate from this principle, for example by guaranteeing that an unsuccessful claimant will not have to bear the defendants' costs that were unreasonably or vexatiously incurred or are otherwise excessive.

The Commission therefore encourages (18) Member States:

• to design procedural rules fostering settlements, as a way to reduce costs;

• to set court fees in an appropriate manner so that they do not become a disproportionate disincentive to antitrust damages claims;

• to give national courts the possibility of issuing cost orders derogating, in certain justified cases, from the normal cost rules, preferably upfront in the proceedings. Such cost orders would guarantee that the claimant, even if unsuccessful, would not have to bear all costs incurred by the other party.

(18) For the underlying reasons see Chapter 9 of the SWP.

2.9. Interaction between leniency programmes and actions for damages

It is important, for both public and private enforcement, to ensure that leniency programmes are attractive.

Adequate protection against disclosure in private actions for damages must be ensured for corporate statements submitted by a leniency applicant in order to avoid placing the applicant in a less favourable situation than the co-infringers. Otherwise, the threat of disclosure of the confession submitted by a leniency applicant could have a negative influence on the quality of his submissions, or even dissuade an infringer from applying for leniency altogether.

The Commission therefore suggests (19) that such protection should apply:

• to all corporate statements submitted by all applicants for leniency in relation to a breach of Article 81 of the EC Treaty (also where national antitrust law is applied in parallel);

- regardless of whether the application for leniency is accepted, is rejected or leads to n° decision by the competition authority.

(19) For the underlying reasons see Chapter 10, section B.1 of the SWP.

This protection applies where disclosure is ordered by a court, be it before or after adoption of a decision by the competition authority. Voluntary disclosure of corporate statements by applicants for immunity and reduction of fines should be precluded at least until a statement of objections has been issued.

A further measure to ensure that leniency programmes continue to be fully attractive could be to limit the civil liability of successful immunity applicants. The Commission therefore puts forward for further consideration (20) the possibility of limiting the civil liability of the immunity recipient to claims by his direct and indirect contractual partners. This would help to make the scope of damages to be paid by immunity recipients more predictable and more limited, without unduly sheltering them from civil liability for their participation in an infringement. The immunity recipient would have to bear the burden of proving the extent to which his liability would be limited. However, consideration should be given, in particular, to the need for such a measure and the impact it would have on the full compensation of victims of cartels and on the position of the co-infringers, especially other leniency applicants.

(20) For the underlying reasons see Chapter 10, section B.2 of the SWP.

The Commission invites comments on this White Paper. They may be sent, by 15 July 2008, either by e-mail to:
comp-damages-actions@ec.europa.eu
or by post to:
European Commission
Directorate-General for Competition, Unit A 5
Damages actions for breach of the EC antitrust rules
B-1049 Brussels.

It is standard practice within DG Competition to publish submissions received in response to a public consultation. However, it is possible to request that submissions, or parts thereof, remain confidential. Should this be the case, please indicate clearly on the front page of your submission that it should not be made public and also send a non-confidential version of your submission to DG Competition for publication.

Commission staff working paper 2 April 2008 accompanying the White paper on damages actions for breach of the EC antitrust rules

http://eur-lex.europa.eu/LexUriServ/LexUriServ.do?uri=SEC:2008:0404:FIN:EN:PDF

Commission Staff Working Paper 2 April 2008 – document accompanying document to the White paper on damages actions for breach of the EC antitrust rules – Impact assessment

http://eur-lex.europa.eu/LexUriServ/LexUriServ.do?uri=SEC:2008:405:FIN:EN:PDF

DG Competition, Draft Guidance paper: Quantifying harm in actions for damages on breaches of Article 101 or 102 of the Treaty on the Functioning of the European Union, June 2011, not published in the Official Journal

1. See: http://ec.europa.eu/competition/consultations/2011_actions_damages/draft_guidance_paper_en.pdf

PART 1
CONTEXT AND GENERAL APPROACH TO QUANTIFYING HARM IN COMPETITION CASES

I. LEGAL CONTEXT

A. The right to compensation

1. Everyone who has suffered harm because of an infringement of Article 101 or 102 of the Treaty on the Functioning of the European Union (TFEU) has a right to be compensated for that harm. The Court of Justice of the EU held that this right is guaranteed by primary EU law [3]. Compensation means placing the injured party in the position it would have been in had there been no infringement. Therefore, compensation includes reparation not only for actual loss suffered (*damnum emergens*), but also for loss of profit (*lucrum cessans*) and the payment of interest [4]. Actual loss means a reduction in a person's assets; loss of profit means that an increase in those assets, which would have occurred without the infringement, did not happen [5].

[3] See Case C-453/99 *Courage* (2001) ECR I-6297, paragraph 26; Joined Cases C-295/04 to C-298/04 *Manfredi* (2006) ECR I-6619, paragraph 60. These cases directly concern Article 101 TFEU (ex Article 81 EC Treaty); the same principles apply however also to Article 102 TFEU (ex Article 82 EC Treaty).

[4] See Joined Cases C-295/04 to C-298/04 *Manfredi* (2006) ECR I-6619, paragraph 95.

[5] See Opinion of Advocate General Capotorti in Case 238/78 *Ireks-Arkady GmbH v Council and Commission* (1979) ECR 2955, paragraph 9.

2. In so far as there are no EU rules governing the matter, it is for the domestic legal system of each Member State to lay down the detailed rules governing the exercise of this right to compensation guaranteed by EU law. Such rules, however, must not render excessively difficult or practically impossible the exercise of rights conferred on individuals by EU law (principle of effectiveness), and they must not be less favourable than those governing damages actions for breaches of similar rights conferred by domestic law (principle of equivalence) [6].

[6] See Case C-453/99 *Courage* (2001) ECR I-6297, paragraph 29; Joined Cases C-295/04 to C-298/04 *Manfredi* (2006) ECR I-6619, paragraph 62.

B. National rules on quantification and this Guidance Paper

3. In an action for compensation of harm suffered because of an infringement of Article 101 or 102 TFEU, national courts have to determine the amount to be awarded to the claimant in the event that the claim is well-founded [7]. Assessing and proving the quantum of damages in actions for damages is often difficult. This is particularly true in competition law cases [8].

[7] This Guidance Paper is only concerned with the assessment of harm in the context of claims for financial compensation. While the present paper does not specifically cover the determination of the award in other civil law remedies, its insights may also be used in making such determination, in particular with regard to actions (under applicable national law) for restitution.

[8] See, in more detail, paragraphs 10 *et seq.* in Section II below.

4. National law – which has to be laid down and applied in accordance with the rules and principles of EU law referred to in paragraphs 1 and 2 above – determines the legal framework in which courts fulfil their function of adjudicating disputes between parties. With regard to quantifying damages, this legal framework will, for instance, include rules on:

• the heads of damages to be compensated and general rules of liability governing claims for compensation;

• requirements such as causality or proximity that define a link between the illegal act and the harm which justifies that the infringer is held liable for reparation of that harm [9];

[9] The Court of Justice has clarified in this respect that whilst any individual must be able to claim compensation for the harm suffered where there is a causal relationship between that harm and an agreement or practice prohibited under EU competition law, it is for national law to prescribe the rules governing the exercise of that right, including those on the application of the concept of «causal relationship», provided that the principles of equivalence and effectiveness are observed; see Joined Cases C-295/04 to C-298/04 *Manfredi* (2006) ECR I-6619, paragraphs 61, 64; Case C-453/99 *Courage* (2001) ECR I- 6297, paragraph 29.

• the procedural framework in which claims for damages are adjudicated. National rules typically provide for an allocation of the burden of proof and of the respective responsibilities of the parties to make factual submissions to the court [10];

[10] See, for an example of such distribution of this burden in competition cases, *Kammergericht Berlin* (Higher Regional Court, Berlin), decision of 1 October 2009, case No 2 U 10/03 Kart (*Vitaminpreise*).

• the appropriate standard of proof, which may vary between different stages of the proceedings, and may also be different for questions of liability for damages and those of the quantum of damages;

• to what extent and how courts are empowered to quantify the harm suffered on the basis of approximate best estimates or equitable considerations; and

• the admissibility and the role of evidence in civil litigation and its evaluation (and in particular of expert evidence).

5. Within their respective legal frameworks, legislators and courts have often adopted pragmatic approaches in determining the amount of damages to be awarded. For instance, they have established presumptions and allowed for the burden of proof to shift, e.g. once a party has provided a certain amount of facts and evidence. Also, the law of the Member States may provide that the illicit profit made by the infringing undertaking(s) plays a role – either directly or indirectly – in estimating the harm suffered by injured parties [11].

[11] See paragraph 126 in Part 3 below.

6. The purpose of this Guidance Paper is to place at the disposal of courts and parties to damages actions economic and practical insights that may be of use when national rules and practices are applied. To this end, the Guidance Paper outlines insights into the harm caused through anticompetitive practices prohibited by the Treaty and information on the main methods and techniques available to quantify such harm [12]. Such guidance may also help parties in finding a consensual resolution of their disputes, be it within or outside the context of judicial proceedings or alternative dispute resolution mechanisms.

[12] The Commission has found useful assistance in preparing this Guidance Paper in various studies it commissioned as well as in the comments received from external experts; see http://ec.europa.eu/ competition/antitrust/actionsdamages/index.html.

7. This Guidance Paper is purely informative, does not bind national courts and does not alter the legal rules applicable in the Member States to damages actions based on infringements of Article 101 or 102 TFEU [13]. In particular, whether any and, if so, which of the methods and techniques described in this Guidance Paper are considered appropriate to use in a given case before the courts of the Member States depends on national law applied in accordance with the above-mentioned EU law principles of effectiveness and equivalence. Relevant considerations in this respect are likely to include whether a certain method or technique meets the standard required under national law, whether sufficient data are available to the party charged with the burden of proof to apply the method or technique and whether the burden and costs involved are proportionate to the value of the damages claim at stake. Excessive difficulties in exercising the right to damages guaranteed by EU law and therefore concerns in view of the principle of effectiveness could arise, for instance, through disproportionate costs or through overly demanding requirements regarding the degree of certainty and precision of a quantification of the harm suffered [14]. It may be that national courts, in a particular case, can use pieces of direct evidence relevant for the quantification of harm, such as documents produced by an infringing undertaking in the course of business regarding agreed price increases and their implementation or assessing the development of its market position. The availability of such evidence may play an important role when a court decides whether any, and if so which, of the methods and techniques set out below are necessary to be used by a party to meet the required standard of proof under applicable law [15].

[13] Neither does it affect the rights and obligations of Member States and natural or legal persons under EU law.

[14] See also paragraphs 13 and 14 below.

[15] Which substantive law is applicable in a given individual case will often be determined by EU Regulations, in particular Article 6 of Regulation 864/2007 on the law applicable to non-contractual obligations, O.J. 2007 L 199/40. The applicable procedural rules will usually be those in force in the country of the court hearing the action (*lex fori*).

8. Nothing in this Guidance Paper should be understood as arguing against the use of such direct evidence or against the use of more pragmatic approaches, or as raising or lowering the standard of proof or the level of detail of the factual submissions required from the parties in the legal systems of the Member States. Under applicable rules, and in accordance with the principles of effectiveness and equivalence, it may well be sufficient (including in cases where courts are called upon to make a finding based on approximate estimates or equitable considerations) for the parties to provide facts and evidence on the quantum of damages that are less detailed than the methods and techniques discussed in this Guidance Paper.

9. It should also be noted that the economic insights into the harm caused by antitrust infringements and methods and techniques to quantify such harm can evolve over time along with theoretical and empirical research and the judicial practice in this area.

II. GENERAL APPROACH TO QUANTIFYING HARM IN COMPETITION CASES

10. Compensation for harm suffered aims to place the injured party in the position in which it would have been had the infringement of Article 101 or 102 TFEU not occurred. Quantification of harm suffered therefore requires the actual position of the injured party to be compared with the position in which this party would have been but for the infringement. This assessment is sometimes called «but-for analysis».

11. The central question in antitrust damages quantification is hence to determine what is likely to have happened without the infringement. This hypothetical situation cannot, however, be observed and some form of estimation is therefore necessary to construct a reference scenario with which the actual situation can be compared. This reference scenario is referred to as the «non-infringement scenario» or the «counterfactual scenario».

12. The type of harm for which the claimant seeks compensation determines which kind of economic variables (such as, for instance, prices, sales volumes, profits, costs or market shares) need to be considered. For example, in a cartel leading to higher prices for customers of the cartelists, a non-infringement price will need to be estimated to have a reference point for comparing it with the price actually paid by these customers. In an abuse of dominance case leading to the market foreclosure of competitors, the profits lost by these competitors may be measured by comparing their actual turnover and profit margins with the turnover and profit margins they were likely to have generated without the infringement.

13. It is impossible to know with certainty how a market would have exactly evolved in the absence of the infringement of Article 101 or 102 TFEU. Prices, sales volumes, and profit margins depend on a range of factors and complex interactions between market participants that are not easily estimated. Estimation of the hypothetical non-infringement scenario will thus by definition rely on a number of assumptions [16]. In practice, the unavailability or inaccessibility of data will often add to this intrinsic limitation.

[16] The limits and implications of such assessment of a hypothetical situation have been recognised by the Court of Justice (in the context of quantifying loss of earnings in an action for damages against the European Community in the agricultural sector): «the loss of earnings is the result not of a simple mathematical calculation but of an evaluation and assessment of complex economic data. The Court is thus called upon to evaluate economic activities which are of a largely hypothetical nature. Like a national court, it therefore has a broad discretion as to both the figures and the statistical data to be chosen and also, above all, as to the way in which they are to be used to calculate and evaluate the damage», see Joined Cases C-104/89 and C-37/90 *Mulder and others v Council and Commission* (2000) ECR I-203, at paragraph 79.

14. For these reasons, quantification of harm in competition cases is, by its very nature, subject to considerable limits as to the degree of certainty and precision that can be expected. There cannot be a single «true» value of the harm suffered that could be determined, but only best estimates relying on assumptions and approximations. Applicable national legal rules and their interpretation should reflect these inherent limits in the quantification of harm in damages actions for breaches of Articles 101 and 102 TFEU in accordance with the EU law principle of effectiveness so that the exercise of the right to damages guaranteed by the Treaty is not made practically impossible or excessively difficult.

15. This Guidance Paper outlines a number of methods and techniques that have been developed in economics and legal practice to establish a suitable reference scenario and to estimate the value of the economic variable of interest (for example, in a price cartel the likely price that would have been charged for the product had the infringement not occurred) [17]. The methods and techniques are based on different approaches and vary in terms of the underlying assumptions and the variety and detail of data needed. They also differ in the extent to which they control for factors other than the infringement that may have affected the situation of the claimant. As a result, these methods and techniques may be more or less difficult, time-consuming and cost-intensive to apply.

[17] See Part 2 below.

16. Once a value for the relevant economic variable (such as, price or, for instance, profit margins, or sales volumes) in the hypothetical non-infringement scenario has been estimated, a comparison with the actual circumstances (e.g. the price actually paid by the injured party) is necessary to quantify the harm caused by the infringement of Article 101 or 102 TFEU.

17. Addition of interest will also need to be considered. The award of interest, pursuant to the applicable national rules, is an essential component of compensation for harm suffered through infringements of rights conferred by the Treaty. As the Court of Justice has emphasised, full compensation for the harm sustained must include the reparation of the adverse effects resulting from the lapse of time since the occurrence of the harm caused by the infringement [18]. These effects are monetary devaluation [19] and the lost opportunity for the injured party to have the capital at its disposal [20]. National law may account for these effects in the form of statutory interest or other forms of interest, as long as they are in accordance with the above-mentioned principles of effectiveness and equivalence.

[18] See Case C-271/91 *Marshall* (1993) ECR I-4367, paragraph 31; Joined Cases C-295/04 to C-298/04 *Manfredi* (2006) ECR I-6619, paragraph 97; see also European Commission, White Paper on damages actions for breach of

the EC antitrust rules (COM(2008) 165), section 2.5 and the accompanying Commission Staff Working Paper (SEC(2008) 404), paragraph 187.

[19] See Case C-308/87 *Grifoni II* (1994) ECR I-341, paragraph 40 and Opinion of Advocate General Tesauro in Case C-308/87 *Grifoni II* (1994) ECR I-341, paragraph 25; Joined Cases C-104/89 and C-37/90 *Mulder and others v Council and Commission* (2000) ECR I-203, paragraph 51. In the context of loss of purchasing power, see Joined Cases T-17/89, T-21/89 and T-25/89 *Brazzelli Lualdi* (1992) ECR II-293, paragraph 40.

[20] See opinion of Advocate General Saggio in Joined Cases C-104/89 and C-37/90 *Mulder and others v Council and Commission* (2000) ECR I-203, paragraph 105.

III. STRUCTURE OF THE GUIDANCE PAPER

18. The basis of a claim for damages is the submission that an infringement of Article 101 or 102 TFEU adversely affected the situation of the claimant. Broadly speaking, two principal categories of harmful effects of such infringements can be distinguished:

(a) infringers can exploit their market power by raising the prices their direct customers pay [21]. Among the infringements having such effect are exploitative abuses within the meaning of Article 102 TFEU. Undertakings can also raise prices to their customers by engaging in the kind of practices forbidden by Article 101 TFEU. Typical examples are price fixing, market sharing or output limitation cartels.

[21] Where the infringement affects the buying activity of the infringing undertakings, the corresponding effect will be the decrease in the purchase prices that these undertakings have to pay to their suppliers. See paragraph 115 in Part 3, Section 1 for more details.

Raised prices mean that the customers who purchase the affected product or service [22] pay an overcharge. Moreover, a rise in prices may also lead to less demand and may entail a loss of profits for customers who use the product for their own commercial activities [23];

[22] For ease of presentation, in the following reference will only be made to «products» affected by an infringement, which should however be understood as also referring to the «services» affected.

[23] See paragraphs 109 *et seq.* in Part 3, Section I for more details.

(b) undertakings can also infringe Articles 101 and 102 TFEU by excluding competitors from a market or reducing their market share. Typical examples are abuses of a dominant position through margin squeeze, predatory pricing or tying, or certain vertical exclusivity agreements between suppliers and distributors that infringe competition law [24]. Such practices have a significant effect on competitors, who suffer harm as they forego business opportunities and profit in this market. Where foreclosure of competitors is successful and competitive pressure in a market diminishes, customers will be harmed too, typically by a rise in prices.

[24] Vertical agreements are those concluded between undertakings from different levels of the supply chain.

19. Infringements of Articles 101 and 102 TFEU can also have further harmful effects, for example adverse impacts on product quality and innovation. The Guidance Paper focuses on the two principal categories of harm and the categories of injured parties [25] described in paragraph 18. The methods and techniques described in the Guidance Paper may, nonetheless, also be relevant in damages actions concerning other types of harm and other injured parties.

[25] The Guidance Paper does not specifically address the situation of persons other than those mentioned in points (a) and (b) of paragraph 18, although other persons (such as suppliers of the infringers or customers of law-abiding competitors of the infringers) may also be harmed by infringements leading to price overcharges or the exclusion of competitors; see also footnote 112.

20. Part 3 of the Guidance Paper addresses specifically the quantification of the kind of harm referred to in paragraph 18*(a)*. This part includes a description of the basic effects on the market of price increases resulting from an infringement and illustrates how these types of harm (in particular the harm resulting from the payment of an overcharge and the harm associated with a reduction in demand) can be quantified.

21. Part 4 of the Guidance Paper addresses specifically the quantification of the kind of harm referred to in paragraph 18*(b)*. This part includes a description of the possible effects of the exclusion of competitors from a market and illustrates through examples how these types of harm (namely the loss of profit of the excluded competitor and the harm to customers) can be quantified.

22. The main methods and techniques available to quantify the harm resulting from infringements of Article 101 or 102 TFEU are common to all kinds of harm caused by such infringements. Part 2 of the Guidance Paper therefore provides a general overview of these methods and techniques. In particular, it gives more information on the basic assumptions on which these methods rely and explains their application in practice.

PART 2
METHODS AND TECHNIQUES

I. OVERVIEW

23. Various methods are available to construct a non-infringement scenario for the purposes of quantifying the harm in damages actions in competition cases. The methods most widely used by parties and courts estimate what would have happened without the infringement by looking at the time periods before or after the infringement or at other markets that have not been affected by the infringement. Such comparator-based methods take the data (prices, sales volumes, profit margins or other economic variables) observed in the unaffected period or on the unaffected markets as an indication of the hypothetical scenario without the infringement. The implementation of these methods is sometimes refined by the use of econometric techniques [26]. Various comparator-based methods and techniques to implement these methods are described in Section II below.

[26] Econometrics combines economic theory with statistical or quantitative methods to identify and measure economic relationships between variables.

24. Methods other than comparator-based are addressed in Section III below. One of these methods uses economic models fitted to the actual market to simulate the likely market outcome that would have occurred without the infringement. These models draw on economic theory to explain the likely functioning of a market in view of its main features (e.g. the number of competitors, the way these compete with each other, the degree of product differentiation, entry barriers). Further methods include the cost-based method, which uses production costs for the affected product and a mark-up for a «reasonable» profit margin to estimate the hypothetical non-infringement scenario.

25. Each of these methods and techniques has particular features, strengths and weaknesses that may make them more or less suitable to estimate the harm suffered in a given set of circumstances. In particular, they differ in the degree to which they rely on data that are the outcome of actual market interactions or on assumptions based on economic theory and in the extent to which they control for factors other than the infringement that may have affected the claimant for damages. Moreover, the methods and techniques differ in the degree to which they are simple to use and in the amount of data required.

26. While these methods seek to construct how the market in question would have evolved absent the infringement, more direct evidence available to the parties and to the court (for instance, internal documents of the infringing undertakings on agreed price increases) may also provide, under applicable national legal rules, useful information for assessing quantum of damages in a given case [27].

[27] See for an example of such an approach *Oberlandesgericht Karlsruhe* (Higher Regional Court, Karlsruhe), decision of 11 June 2010, case No 6 U 118/05 (appeal pending), where specifically agreed price increases of the infringing undertakings of a cartel were used, under applicable legal rules on the distribution of fact pleading and the establishment of *prima facie* evidence, to determine the damages award.

27. Section IV below sets out considerations on the choice of method, which will usually depend on the specific features of that case and on the requirements under applicable law [28].

[28] See, in this context, paragraph 7 above.

II. COMPARATOR-BASED METHODS

28. To appreciate how comparator-based methods work in practice, it is useful to consider a (entirely fictitious) example of a hypothetical damages action based on a cartel infringing Article 101 TFEU [29].

[29] This example is further developed at paragraph 127.

The flour cartel

Assume that all of the milling companies in a particular Member State have been found, by the national competition authority, to have fixed among themselves the prices for the grinding of cereals and the production of flour.

A bakery that regularly purchased flour in recent years brings a damages claim against one of the milling companies. The bakery submits that the infringement has led to an illegal rise in prices for the flour it purchased from that milling company. The bakery asks for compensation for this price overcharge it paid over the past years.

29. The key question regarding the quantification of harm in the aforementioned example is to find out what price the claimant bakery would have paid for flour had there been no infringement. If a comparator-based method is used to do so, these methods compare the price in the infringement scenario with a non-infringement scenario that is established on the basis of price data observed either:

• on the same market at a time before and/or after the infringement (1); or

• on a different but similar geographic market (2); or

• on a different but similar product market (3).

It is also possible to combine a comparison over time with a comparison across different geographic or product markets (4).

30. In the example of the flour cartel, the application of the methods focuses on price. It is, however, likewise possible to use these methods to estimate other economic variables such as market shares, profit margins, rate of return on capital, value of assets, or the level of costs of an undertaking. Which economic variable can be usefully considered for the purposes of damages quantification depends on the circumstances of the case at hand.

31. The data used in such a comparison across markets or over time can be data that relate to the entire market (i.e. the average of the price for flour charged to all bakeries operating in a neighbouring geographic market) or data that relate to certain specific market participants only (i.e. the price charged for flour to certain customer groups such as wholesale purchasers operating in a neighbouring market). It could also be appropriate, in particular in cases concerning exclusionary practices, to compare data relating to only one market participant. An example for such a comparison between individual companies, i.e. the injured party and a sufficiently similar comparator firm, may be the comparison between the profits achieved by a company trying to enter a new market where it faced exclusionary practices in breach of the EU competition rules and the profits that a comparable new entrant achieved on a different but similar geographic market without being affected by anticompetitive practices. Sections A.1 to 4 below cover the comparison with aggregated market data and firm-level data alike [30].

[30] The comparison with firm-level data of another company could, theoretically, be made not only for companies that operate in *another* geographic or product market as discussed in Sections 2-4 below, but also for data of companies operating in the *same* product and geographic market as the injured party. In practice, such intra-market comparisons do not play a significant role, possibly because within the same market it can be difficult to find a sufficiently comparable other company that was not affected by the infringement. The following sections therefore do not further discuss such comparisons within a market.

32. The strength of all comparator-based methods lies in the fact that they use real-life data that are observed on the same or a similar market [31]. The comparator-based methods rely on the premise that the comparator scenario can be considered representative of the likely non-infringement scenario and that the difference between the infringement data and the data chosen as a comparator is due to the infringement. Whether the level of similarity between infringement and comparator markets or time periods is considered sufficient in order to perform a comparison depends on national legal systems. Where significant differences exist between the time periods or markets considered, various techniques are available to account for such differences [32].

[31] This aspect is emphasised, for instance, by the *Bundesgerichtshof* (Federal Court of Justice, Germany), decision of 19 June 2007, case No KRB 12/07 (*Paper Wholesale Cartel*).

[32] See for more detail paragraphs 53-84 in Section B below.

A. Methods for establishing a non-infringement scenario

(1) Comparison over time on the same market

33. One frequently used method consists in comparing the actual situation during the period when the infringement produced effects with the situation on the same market before the infringement produced effects or after they ceased [33]. For instance, where an undertaking abused its dominant position by foreclosing a competitor from the market during 2004 and 2005, the method could look at e.g. the competitor's profits during the infringement period and its profits in 2002 and 2003 when there was not yet an infringement [34]. Another example would be a price fixing cartel (such as the flour cartel example mentioned above) that lasted from 2005 to 2007 where the method could compare the price paid by the cartel customers during the infringement period with the price paid by customers in a period after the infringement, e.g. in 2008 and 2009 [35].

[33] See, for example, *Corte d'Appello di Milano* (Court of Appeal, Milan), decision of 11 July 2003, (*Bluvacanze*) and *Corte d'Appello di Milano* (Court of Appeal, Milan), decision of 3 February 2000, case No I, 308 (*Inaz Paghe v Associazione Nazionale Consulenti del Lavoro*) (in both cases, comparison before, during and after); *Landgericht Dortmund* (Regional Court, Dortmund), decision of 1 April 2004, case No 13 O 55/02 Kart (*Vitaminpreise*) (during and after comparison); *Landesgericht für Zivilrechtssachen Graz* (Regional Civil Court of Graz), decision of 17 August 2007, case No 17 R 91/07 p (*Driving school*) (accepting a comparison during and after).

[34] For more detailed examples of the method's application in cases of exclusionary practices, see Part 4 below.

[35] For more detailed examples of the method's application in cases of infringements that lead to a price overcharge, see Part 3 below.

34. There are, in principle, three different points of reference that can be used for the comparison over time: [36]

[36] The comparison over time method is also referred to as the «before-after method» or «benchmark method».

• an unaffected *pre*-infringement period (comparison «before and during» – in the flour cartel example: comparison of the prices paid for flour in the same market *before* the infringement had effects with those affected by the infringement);

• an unaffected *post*-infringement period (comparison «during and after» – in the flour cartel example: comparison of the prices affected by the infringement with prices paid in the same market *after* the infringement ended); and

• both an unaffected *pre*- and *post*-infringement period (comparison «before, during and after»).

35. An advantage of all methods comparing, over time, data from the *same* geographic and product market is that market characteristics such as the degree of competition, market structure, costs and demand characteristics may be more comparable than in a comparison with different product or geographic markets. However, also in comparisons over time it happens that some differences between the two data sets are not only due to the infringement. In such cases, it may be appropriate to make adjustments to the data observed in the comparator period to account for differences with the infringement period [37] or to choose a different comparator period or market. For instance, in the case of a long-lasting infringement, the assumption that e.g. prices of 10 years ago would have remained unchanged over time absent the infringement is probably overly strong and may lead to opting e.g. for a comparison with the pre-infringement period *and* the post-infringement period [38].

[37] On such adjustments and, in particular, the possibility to use regression analysis, see paragraphs 53-84 in Section B below.

[38] In cases of long infringement periods, it may also be appropriate to address practical issues of comparability of data that result from changes in the way that data have been recorded by companies (e.g. changes in accounting practices or changes in the data organisation software).

36. In a comparison over time, choosing among the reference periods described in paragraph 34 above will depend on the specifics of the case, including market characteristics and availability of data. For example, in the case of long-lasting infringements, data from the pre-infringement period may simply no longer be available.

37. Where data are available, the choice between a comparison «before and during», «during and after» or «before, during and after» can be determined by a range of factors. It is highly unlikely to find any reference period where market circumstances exactly represent what would have happened in the infringement period had the infringement not occurred. It is only possible to identify a sufficiently similar time period that allows a likely non-infringement scenario to be reasonably approximated. Factors to be considered in this context may include uncertainties as to which time periods were actually not affected by the infringement. Some infringements start, or cease, gradually; and often doubts exist regarding the exact beginning of an infringement and, in particular, the effects it produces. Indeed, decisions of competition authorities regularly mention evidence suggesting that the infringement may have started earlier than the period established as the infringement period for the purposes of the decision [39]. Econometric analysis of observed data can be a way to identify when the infringement's effects started or ceased.

[39] It is possible that a competition authority limits the finding of an infringement to a certain period, while in fact the infringement may have had a longer duration.

38. The ending of an infringement and its effects may be more easily established than its beginning, but here too uncertainties could arise as to whether the period immediately after the infringement's end is unaffected by the anticompetitive behaviour [40]. For example, when there is some delay until market conditions return to a non-infringement level, using data from the period immediately after the infringement could lead to an underestimation of the effect of the infringement [41]. The pre-infringement period may be a more suitable reference point where central market characteristics changed radically towards the end of the infringement period due to exogenous factors (e.g. a steep increase in raw material costs or an increase in demand for the product) [42].

[40] See the decision of the *Oberlandesgericht Karlsruhe* (Higher Regional Court, Karlsruhe) of 11 June 2010 in case No 6 U 118/05 (appeal pending), for an example where a national court ruled that the prices charged in the five months after the infringement ended were still influenced by the cartel.

[41] It may also occur that prices are, for a short period after the end of a cartel, particularly low as companies might temporarily engage in aggressive pricing strategies until the «normal», i. e. non-infringement, equilibrium on the market is reached.
Specifically in oligopolistic markets another issue may arise, namely that the participants in a cartel can use the knowledge gained through the cartel to coordinate their behaviour afterwards without infringing Article 101. In such a situation, post-infringement prices are likely to be higher than without the infringement and can only serve to make a lower-bound estimate of the harm suffered; see also paragraphs 134 *et seq.* in Part 3, Section II below.

[42] For the short period of the infringement after such a change, post-infringement data can be the more appropriate comparator as they may better reflect the market characteristics after the change. However, where the change in market characteristics was caused by the infringement itself (e.g. where due to anticompetitive foreclosure several competitors exited the market), the post-infringement period is obviously not a suitable comparator to estimate the situation that would have existed without the infringement.

39. Nonetheless, even when there are doubts as to whether or not a certain period before or after the infringement was affected by the infringement, this period could, in principle, still serve as a reference period in order to obtain a safe estimate of the harm that will at least have been suffered («lower-bound» estimate or «minimum damage») [43].

[43] If during the infringement exogenous factors lead to a decrease in prices (e.g. a sharp fall in input costs of the infringer), the inference of a lower bound could be rebutted.

40. In certain circumstances, the non-infringement scenario may be appropriately estimated on the basis of two reference periods (before and after the infringement), for example, by using the average from these periods or by using other techniques to reflect a trend in the development of market circumstances during the infringement [44].

[44] For example interpolation or regression analysis. For these different techniques to implement comparator-based methods, see paragraphs 53-84 in Section B below.

Pre-infringement data could also be used as the reference period up to a certain point during the infringement when a significant change in market circumstances occurred, and post-infringement data as the reference period for the time thereafter.

41. Also the choice of data can contribute to building a sufficiently similar basis for the comparison: there can be situations where aggregated data such as industry price averages (or averages for certain groups of firms) are sufficiently representative, [45] whilst in other situations it would be more appropriate to use only data from pre- or post-infringement transactions by the injured company or average data that relate to similar companies. For example, where the injured party or the infringer belongs to a specific group of market players such as wholesale customers (as opposed to end customers), pre- or post-infringement prices charged to wholesale customers may be an appropriate reference point.

[45] For further detail on the use of averages in implementing comparator-based approaches, see paragraph 64 in Part 2, Section II below.

42. Making an informed choice of reference period and type of data will usually require good knowledge of the industry in question. The choice will also be influenced by the availability of data and the requirements of applicable rules regarding the standard and burden of proof.

(2) Comparison with data from other geographic markets

43. Another comparator-based method consists in looking at data observed in a different geographic market [46] for the purpose of estimating a non-infringement scenario [47]. These may be data observed across the entire geographic comparator market or data observed in relation to certain market participants only. For instance, in the example of a flour cartel mentioned above at paragraph 28, the prices paid by the claimant bakery during the infringement period could be compared with the prices paid on average by similar bakeries, in a different geographic market untouched by the infringement. The same type of comparison can, in principle, be undertaken with regard to any other economic variable, e.g. the market shares, profit margins, rate of return on capital, value of assets, or level of costs of an undertaking. A comparison with the commercial performance of firms active on another geographic market that is unaffected by the infringement [48] will be particularly relevant in cases of exclusionary behaviour.

[46] For the concepts of relevant (geographic and product) market, see Commission Notice on the definition of the relevant market for the purposes of Community competition law, O.J. C 372, 9.12.1997, p. 5.

[47] This method is also referred to as «yardstick method» or «cross-sectional method». These terms are also used to refer to the comparator-based method that looks at data observed in different but similar product markets, see paragraphs 48-49 in Section 3 below.
For examples of the use of the comparator-based method looking at different geographic markets see, for instance, Cour d'Appel de Paris (Court of Appeal, Paris), decision of 23 June 2003 (Lescarcelle-De Memoris v OGF); Juzgado Mercantil numero 5 de Madrid (Commercial Court, Madrid), decision of 11 November 2005, case No 85/2005 (Conduit-Europe, S.A. v Telefónica de España S.A.), confirmed by Audiencia Provincial de Madrid (Court of Appeal, Madrid), decision of 25 May 2006, case No 73/2006; Bundesgerichtshof (Federal Court of Justice, Germany), decision of 19 June 2007, case No KBR 12/07 (Paper Wholesale Cartel) (in the context of assessing the illicit gain by cartelists for the purpose of calculating a fine).

[48] The comparator firm might, in principle, also be a firm active on the infringement market provided that its performance was not significantly influenced by the exclusionary behaviour. Even if the comparator firm was not directly affected by the infringement, it may still have been indirectly affected, e.g. by gaining market shares from a foreclosed competitor. The risk of being directly or indirectly influenced by the infringement is lower if the comparison is carried out in relation to a similar firm active on another geographic market. Characteristics that could be relevant when considering the sufficient similarity of firms include their size, cost structure, customers and features of the product they sell.

44. The more a geographic market is similar (except for the infringement effects) to the market affected by the infringement, the more it is likely to be suitable as a comparator market. This means that the products traded in the two geographic markets compared should be the same or, at least, sufficiently similar. Also the competitive characteristics of the geographic comparator market should be similar to the characteristics of the affected market except for the infringement. This may well be a market that is not perfectly competitive.

45. The method of using geographic comparator markets for deriving a non-infringement scenario is, in practice, mainly used when the infringement concerns geographic markets that are local, regional or national in scope [49]. Where the infringement market and the geographic comparator market are neighbouring areas, possibly within one country, there may be an increased likelihood that they are sufficiently similar for the purpose of a comparison [50].

[49] It might, however, also be used when the relevant market is wider than national provided that a sufficiently similar comparator market can be identified.

[50] See, however, paragraph 47 below.

46. The comparator market does not always need to be sufficiently similar in its entirety. Where, for instance, the prices paid by one customer group (e.g. wholesalers) or the profits earned by one competitor company (e.g. a new entrant) in the comparator market are used as a reference, it is important that the market position of this customer group or this competitor is sufficiently similar to that of the injured party on the infringement market [51].

[51] This may, however, not easily be the case if the overall characteristics on the comparator market are all too different from the infringement market.

47. The choice of a geographic comparator market may also be influenced by uncertainties about the geographic scope of an infringement. Geographic markets on which the same or a similar infringement occurred are, in principle, not good candidates for being used as comparator markets. Also neighbouring markets on which no similar infringement occurred may still have been influenced by the anticompetitive practices on the infringement market (e.g. because prices on the neighbouring market were raised in view of the increased prices on the infringement market and lesser competitive pressure emanating from this market). A comparison with such markets will not show the full extent of the harm suffered, but they may, nonetheless, constitute a useful basis to establish a lower-bound estimate of the harm caused on the infringement market. This means that a party to an action for damages could, in principle, safely choose to rely on the comparison with a geographic market that was

influenced by the same or a similar infringement, in particular where such influence is likely to have been rather small.

(3) Comparison with data from other product markets

48. Similar to the comparison across geographic markets is the approach to look at a different product market [52] with similar market characteristics [53]. For example, in a case of exclusionary behaviour partially foreclosing a company selling one product, the profit margin earned by that company in the infringement market could be compared with the profit margin for another product that is traded (by a similar or the same company) in a distinct but similar product market.

[52] For the concepts of the relevant (geographic and product) market, see Commission Notice on the definition of the relevant market for the purposes of Community competition law, *O.J.* C 372, 9.12.1997, p. 5.

[53] This method is sometimes also referred to as «yardstick method» or «cross-sectional method» (as is the the comparator-based method looking at different geographic markets).

49. The considerations discussed in the context of geographic comparator markets are, *mutatis mutandis*, also likely to be relevant for the choice of a suitable comparator product market. They will often relate to the degree of similarity between the two product markets. In particular, the comparator product should be carefully chosen with a view to the nature of the products compared, the way they are traded and the characteristics of the market e.g. in terms of number of competitors, their cost structure and the buying power of customers [54]. Uncertainties as to whether a potential comparator product market was affected by the infringement or a similar infringement of Article 101 or 102 TFEU can also play a role.

[54] Similarity of market characteristics may be more likely if the two products compared are traded in the same geographic market. Although the circumstances may also be sufficiently similar where the same or similar products from different geographic markets are compared.

(4) Combining comparisons over time and across markets

50. Where sufficient data are available, it may be possible to combine comparisons over time and comparisons across markets. This approach is sometimes called the «difference in differences» method because it looks at the development of the relevant economic variable (e.g. the price for flour) in the infringement market during a certain period (difference over time on the infringement market) and compares it to the development of the same variable during the same time period on an unaffected comparator market (difference over time on the non-infringement market) [55]. The comparison shows the difference between these two differences over time. This gives an estimate of the change in the variable produced by the infringement and excludes all those factors that affected both the infringement and the comparator market in the same way. The method is thus a way to isolate the effects of the infringement from other influences on the relevant variable.

[55] This can be a geographic or a product comparator market.

51. A simple example derived from the flour cartel mentioned above may illustrate the method: assume that a before, during and after comparison reveals an increase in price of € 40 per 100 kg bag of flour in the Member State where the cartel occurred between 2005 and 2008. Looking at an unaffected geographic market over the same period may show that prices for flour rose by € 10 per 100 kg bag due to increased costs for an input product (cereals). Assuming that the increased input costs also concerned the infringement market, a comparison of the different development of prices on the infringement and the comparator market would indicate the price difference caused by the flour cartel. In the example, this would be € 30 per unit.

52. The strength of the «difference in differences» method is therefore that it can subtract out changes unrelated to the infringement that occurred during the same time period as the infringement [56]. It rests, however, to a large extent on the assumption that these other changes affected both markets similarly [57]. The considerations regarding the application of the comparison over time and across market methods, in particular the need for sufficient similarity, are also relevant for the difference in differences method. From a practical point of view, this method usually requires a range of data from different markets and periods of time that may not always be easy to obtain; lesser amounts of data may, however, still allow lower-bound or approximate estimates to be derived [58].

[56] Compared to a simple comparison across markets, the difference in differences method also has the advantage of filtering out fixed differences between markets (such as differences due to constantly lower input costs in one of the markets).

[57] If, for example, price increases unrelated to the infringement were higher in the affected market than in the comparator market during the infringement period, application of the difference in differences method using simple averages would overestimate the amount of damages. An econometric implementation of the difference in differences technique may help control for such factors.

[58] See, for an example of a national court establishing a lower bound in the course of estimating the quantum of damages (although not using the difference-in-differences method, but the comparison over time method), *Kammergericht Berlin* (Higher Regional Court, Berlin), decision of 1 October 2009, case No 2 U 10/03 Kart.

B. Implementing the method in practice: techniques for estimating the price or other economic variable in the non-infringement scenario

53. Once a suitable comparator-based method for establishing a non-infringement scenario has been chosen, various techniques are available to implement this method in practice. These techniques differ mainly in the degree to which they rely on individual or average data (e.g. price observations), and in the degree to which the data observed in the comparator market [59] or period are subject to further adjustment. As a consequence, these techniques differ in the amount of data they require in order to be carried out.

[59] As mentioned in paragraph 31 above, the data used in such comparison across markets or over time can be data that relate to the entire market or data that relate to certain specific market participants only.

54. One possibility in implementing comparator-based methods is to use comparator data directly in the form they are observed and to estimate on this basis a value for the economic variable under consideration in the non-infringement scenario (e.g., in the above example, the price of flour). Where more than one data observation is available (e.g. the price of flour in a range of transactions on a geographic comparator market), they can be combined through a calculation of averages into one or more values for the non-infringement scenario. Such average value(s) for the non-infringement scenarios could then be compared to the average value(s) actually observed during the infringement, e.g. the prices really paid for flour (see in more detail in Section (1) below).

55. Where certain factors (such as an increase in raw material prices) have influenced only the comparator or only the infringement market or period, it should be considered, depending on the standard of proof required and depending on applicable rules regarding causality, whether adjustments need to be made to the observed data in order to account for such influences. These could be simple adjustments to the data in cases where the influencing factor and the magnitude of its effects can be relatively easily ascertained and accounted for (see Section (1) below). More sophisticated adjustments of observed comparator data can be obtained on the basis of econometric techniques, in particular through the use of regression analysis, which is described in Section (2) below. Whether it is for the defendant or the claimant to plead, substantiate and prove such adjustments is a matter of applicable law [60].

[60] See, for instance, *Kammergericht Berlin* (Higher Regional Court, Berlin), decision of 1 October 2009, case No 2 U 10/03 Kart., as an example of the distribution of fact pleading obligations in the quantification of harm.

56. In a given case, the choice between these different techniques depends on the specific circumstances of the case and applicable legal rules, taking account of the different advantages and disadvantages of these techniques, for instance with regard to their accuracy and precision and the data requirements they entail (see Section (3) below).

(1) Simple techniques: individual data observations, averages, interpolation and simple adjustments

57. Depending on the requirements under applicable national law and on the circumstances of the case, especially the degree of similarity between the infringement market and the comparator market or period, the data observed may be compared directly, i.e. without further adjustments, with the data observed in the infringement market [61].

[61] For instance, time-based comparison could be based on the simple observation of prices before and during the infringement. For an example of the legal implications of such method see *Corte Suprema di Cassazione* (Supreme Court of Cassation, Italy), decision of 2 February 2007, case No 2305 (*Fondiaria SAI SpA* v *Nigriello*).

58. The amount of data observed for the variable of interest (e.g., in the flour cartel example, the price for flour) in the comparator markets or comparator time periods may range from only one or very few data observations (i.e. the price observed in a small number of transactions) to a large number of data observations. In bidding markets, for example, auctions may occur very infrequently and at the time of the damages estimation only the price observed in the one tender after the infringement may be available. A similar situation could occur in industries where long-term contracts are common. It may be appropriate to use damages estimations based on single data observations where these are sufficiently representative for the period of interest.

59. Where looking at comparator markets or time periods produces a greater number of data observations, e.g. the prices paid by the injured party in a series of post-infringement transactions, or the prices paid by a number of customers in another geographic market, these data observations can be used either individually or in the form of averages [62].

[62] For the purposes of this Guidance Paper, the term «average» is used as referring to the mean, i.e. the average calculated by dividing the sum of observations by the number of observations. There may, however, be situations where it may be more appropriate to use other descriptive statistics (i.e. the median or the mode). For example, where in a market of 25 companies, 21 charge a price of € 50 and four a price of € 75, the modal price of € 50 (the price most observed in the sample) may be the more meaningful representation of the market price than the mean of € 54 (in this example, the modal price equals the median price, which is the price charged by the middle-ranked company).

60. The use of various forms of averages or other forms of data aggregation can be appropriate, provided that like with like is compared. For example, where a wholesaler claims damages for having purchased a product in January, May, July and October 2009 from the participants in a price cartel and where the chosen method is comparison with another geographic market, the monthly average prices paid in that market by the same type of customer (wholesaler) during the same months may be the appropriate reference point (i.e. comparing January data with January data, May data with May data, and so forth). Comparing data from the same months will, for instance, account for seasonal differences over a year and thus make the comparison more reliable. If, however, little monthly price variation exists, the average price on the comparator market for the entire year of 2009 may be considered an appropriate indicator. It may also be the case that yearly data or other average data (e.g. aggregated industry data) are simply the only information available. Legal systems in the Member States may generally allow parties to rely on average data whilst granting the defendant the opportunity to show that significant differences exist, and they may require the use of more disaggregated data where available.

61. Another simple technique for deriving a comparator value from a range of data observations is linear interpolation. Where a comparison over time has produced price series from before and after the infringement, the «non-infringement» or «counterfactual» price during the infringement period can be estimated by drawing a line between the pre-infringement price and the post-infringement price, as shown in the illustration below. From this line, a comparator value can be read for each relevant point in time during the infringement period. Compared with the calculation of a single average value for price during the entire infringement period, interpolation therefore allows to some degree to account for trends in price developments over time that are not due to the infringement. Reading comparator data from the interpolated line will, therefore, produce more accurate results than using an average value for the period, e.g. in cases where damages are claimed that result from transactions (or other events) which occurred only towards the beginning or the end of the infringement period [63]. The following illustration gives a simple example of linear interpolation (the dotted line shows the interpolated non-infringement price, the full line the actually observed prices):

[63] Interpolation likewise has advantages over using averages where the number of transactions (or other events) is unevenly distributed during the infringement period.

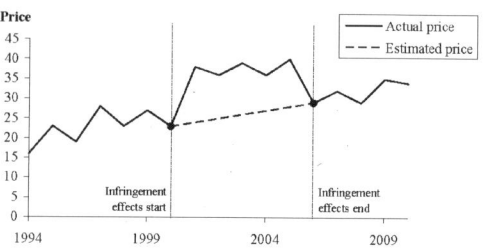

Linear extrapolation works similarly to interpolation except that the line is continued from either only pre- or only post-infringement data[64].

[64] Extrapolation thus extends a trend existing in a time series either before or after the infringement. For example, if in the three years before a cartel prices were € 12, € 13.20, and € 14.52 respectively (reflecting a 10 % increase each year), a simple technique would be to estimate that prices during the two-year duration of a cartel were € 15.97 and € 17.57 respectively; a more accurate estimation of the underlying trend could be obtained through using regression analysis.

62. There may be situations where it is quite straightforward to identify a differentiating factor between an infringement market (or period) and a comparator market (or period) and to make the corresponding adjustment to the value of the observed comparator data. For example, certain seasonal effects occurring on a market may have a pattern and a magnitude that can in some cases be rather easily understood from internal business records of a party or from other sources, such as expert statements. In these cases, for example, the straight line obtained in a simple linear interpolation should be adjusted to reflect such patterns [65].

[65] Such adjustment, could, data permitting, be done in a more sophisticated way by using regression analysis as explained in the following section.

(2) Regression analysis

a. Concept and purpose of regression analysis

63. Regression analysis uses statistical techniques to investigate patterns in the relationship between economic variables and to measure to what extent a certain variable of interest [66] (e.g., in the flour cartel example, the price for flour [67]) is influenced by other variables that are not affected by the infringement [68] (e.g. raw material costs, variations in customer demand, product characteristics, the level of market concentration [69]). Regression analysis therefore makes it possible to assess whether, and by how much, factors other than the infringement have contributed to the difference between the value of the variable of interest observed on the infringement market during the infringement period and the value observed in a comparator market or during a comparator time period. Regression analysis is thus a way to account for alternative causes for the difference between the compared data sets. All comparator-based methods are, in principle, capable of being implemented through regression analysis provided that sufficient data observations are available [70].

[66] Also referred to as an «explained variable» or «dependent variable».

[67] Possible other variables of interest for which regression analysis may be applied include, for instance, sales volumes, market shares or profit margins (e.g. those of an excluded competitor who claims damages for loss of profits through a reduction of sales or a decrease in its margins), costs of production (which may also be relevant in the context of a loss of profits estimation).

[68] Also referred to as «explanatory variable(s)» or «influencing variable(s)».

[69] Other factors influencing the variable of interest may, for example, include customer and order sizes, the technology used for production, the size and cost structure of the firms offering the product, or advertising expenditure.

[70] A sufficient number of data observations is, however, required to apply statistical methods in a meaningful manner. Such sets of data observations could be obtained (in comparisons over time) from time series of observations, or (in comparisons at one point in time) from a range of comparator markets or from a range of firms or a range of transactions, or a combination of both (observations over time from a range of markets, firms or transactions).

64. In a regression analysis, a number of data observations for the variable of interest and the likely influencing variables are examined by means of statistical techniques.

The relationship identified is usually described in the form of an equation (referred to as a «regression equation» or «regression model»). This equation makes it possible to estimate the effects of influencing variables on the variable of interest and to isolate them from the effects of the infringement. Regression analysis estimates how closely the relevant variables are correlated [71] with each other, which may in some instances be suggestive of a causal influence of one variable on the other [72].

[71] In multivariate regression analysis (see in more detail below), the correlation established is a conditional correlation, i.e. one where the effect of other variables is controlled for.

[72] Provided this is consistent with a coherent economic framework and with other pieces of qualitative and quantitative evidence.

65. There are two main approaches to carrying out a regression analysis for damages estimation, depending on whether only data from non-infringement periods (markets) are used to build the regression equation or whether, in addition to non-infringement data, also data from within the infringement period (market) are used. If only data from non-infringement periods are used to estimate the regression, the regression equation would be used to «forecast» the effect on the variable of interest during the infringement period on the basis of the pattern identified outside this period («forecasting approach») [73]. Where, in addition, also data from the infringement period (market) are used to estimate the regression, the effect of the infringement would be accounted for in the regression equation through a separate indicator variable (called «dummy variable») [74]. Whether it is more appropriate to apply the forecasting or the dummy variable approach will depend on the circumstances of the case [75].

[73] This «forecasting approach» is sometimes also referred to as a «residual model approach». This approach is illustrated in the graph in paragraph 72 below.

[74] Such a «dummy variable» measures whether there has been an upward shift in the variable of interest during the infringement period.

[75] In particular, while the forecasting method has the advantage of allowing the choice of a regression model that is only based on data observations from the non-infringement period (and hence, untainted by the effects of the infringement), using data from both periods/markets may allow a more precise and accurate estimation of the parameters of interest, in particular if the available non-infringement data are limited or do not allow the dynamics of the industry at hand to be fully captured. In practice, both methods can often be combined, e.g. by selecting the model on the basis of the pre-infringement period and estimating a dummy-variable regression using data from both periods (and allowing, if appropriate, the effects of the other influencing variables to vary in the infringement and non-infringement periods).

b. Examples and illustrations

66. A simple example that, for illustrative purposes, looks only at one potential influencing variable may show the basic steps in regression analysis. Assume that, in the above-mentioned example of a flour cartel, the prices paid by bakeries during the cartel period to the milling companies are compared with the prices paid by bakeries to the milling companies in the pre-infringement period, and that this comparison shows a price increase during the infringement period of 20 %. Assume further that there are indications that this increase is not exclusively due to the cartel but that during the infringement period costs for an important input material (e.g. cereals) also increased significantly. It is therefore not clear how much of the increase in price for flour is due to the infringement and how much is due to the increased input costs (the rise in cereals prices).

67. One option to address this uncertainty could be to use data from another period or market where input costs (price for cereals) were more similar and no infringement existed, but there may be situations where this is not possible [76]. Regression analysis can offer a tool to account for the variation in input costs, by showing the statistical relationship between input costs and price for flour. To this end, a range of data observations on input costs (cereal prices) and on prices for flour during the period not affected by the infringement could be examined [77]. Through applying statistical techniques to these data observations, it is possible to establish a pattern of how the prices for cereals influenced the price for flour in a period where the flour prices were not influenced by the infringement. It is then possible to deduce a statistical relationship between the price for flour and the price for cereals from this period. By applying the insight on this relationship to the prices for flour from the infringement period, it is possible to eliminate the part of the increase of prices for flour not imputable to the infringement, but to the change in input costs. This allows to «forecast» prices for flour without the cartel overcharge but including the price increase caused by higher input costs.

[76] For instance, because reliable data from other periods (or markets) are not available or because in such other periods (or markets) market characteristics differed significantly.

[77] On the possibility of whether or not to also consider data from the infringement period (market), see paragraph 75 below.

68. The following graph gives a simple illustration of how such a statistical relationship is deduced. The chart shows several data observations of the input costs (cereals prices) and the corresponding price for flour at the same point in time during a non-infringement period. For instance, when at one particular moment the price for cereals was 60, the price for flour was 128. It is possible to calculate the coordinates of the line that best fits all data observations in order to represent the statistical relationship (correlation) between the price for cereals and the price for flour. This relationship is expressed in the graph below as a line and can be, and usually is, also expressed as an equation [78]. The steepness of this line shows what increase in the price for flour is associated with a certain increase in the price for cereals. In the example shown in the graph, the identified relationship indicates that e.g. a rise in the price for cereals from 50 to 60 relates to a rise in price for flour from 120 to 130. As an increase in input costs (cereals) by € 10 is associated with a flour price increase of € 10, the statistical relationship thus shows that an increase in this input cost is fully passed on.

[78] Estimating a regression of price (as the variable of interest) over input costs (as the influencing variable) provides the coordinates of this line. In this example, the ordinary least squares (OLS) technique is used to calculate the coordinates of a straight line that is located at a minimal distance («least squares») from the set of data points on the graph. The OLS technique is a common statistical method to estimate the parameters of a linear regression model. Which statistical technique is used and how it is adjusted to the case at hand will depend on what is known about the general functioning of the industry in question.

69. Knowing the pattern of how the input cost (cereals prices) influenced prices for flour outside the infringement period makes it possible to estimate («forecast») how much the observed higher values of these costs (cereals prices) during the infringement period influenced prices for flour. Excluding these effects from the price comparison allows the price overcharge caused by the infringement to be estimated on a more reliable basis than without the regression analysis. In the above example, if during the infringement period the price for flour was 140 instead of 120 during the non-infringement period, but the input cost (cereals prices) increased from 50 to 60, the likely price for flour without the cartel would not be 120 but 130.

70. Whilst the example described so far concerned only the influence of a *single* other variable (cereals price as input cost) on the variable of interest (flour price), regression analysis in competition practice usually has to account for several other factors influencing the variable of interest (*multiple* regression analysis [79]). In this situation, data need to be observed for all additional relevant influencing variables and a regression equation needs to be deduced from these data that reflects their relationship to the variable of interest. For instance, in the above-mentioned flour cartel example, it may be the case that during the infringement period the milling companies not only had to pay higher prices for cereals, but were also subject to an increase in energy and labour costs and introduced a more efficient milling and packaging technology, all of which may have had an impact on the price of the flour they sold to bakeries during the cartel period. To identify the statistical pattern of how these factors influenced the flour price, series of data observations for each of these influencing variables need to be analysed.

[79] Also referred to as «multivariate regression analysis» as opposed to «single variable («univariate») regression analysis' as used in the above example.

71. When undertaking a regression analysis, it is important to consider all variables that are relevant in the specific case. Suppose that either the defendant or the claimant uses, in a comparison of the flour prices charged by a mill before and during an infringement, a multiple regression analysis to control for the potential influence on the flour price of the above-mentioned factors (i.e. the cereal prices, energy and labour costs and milling and packaging technology). If, however, a significant demand change took place during the cartel (e.g. higher demand by bakeries for flour due to an increased demand by end customers for bread and cake) and if the influence of this event on the price for flour is not accounted for in the regression equation, the estimate of the infringement effect is likely to be biased, despite the otherwise comprehensive regression analysis[80]. It is for the applicable national law to determine, in accordance with the principle of effectiveness, the party on which the burden falls to invoke and prove facts, such as the above-mentioned change in demand or the completeness of the variables considered in a regression analysis.

[80] It is, however, important not only to include all relevant factors in the regression model, but also to refrain from including variables that appear clearly irrelevant (on the basis of industry knowledge). In fact, damages estimates could be wrongly lowered (even down to zero) if irrelevant variables are included in order to explain the price variation in the model.

72. The basis of each damages quantification using regression analysis is thus the statistical relationship between the variable of interest (e.g. price) and the relevant explanatory variable(s) expressed in a regression equation. When the forecasting approach is used,[81] the estimation of a regression equation using data from the non-infringement period constitutes the first step. In a second step, using this regression equation and the observed values of these relevant variables during the infringement period, the price injured parties are likely to have paid without the infringement can then be estimated. In a third step, the difference between this likely non-infringement price and the price actually paid by the injured parties gives an estimate of the overcharge resulting from the infringement. The graph below illustrates the second and the third step. When the dummy variable approach is used, the regression analysis combines the three steps described above [82].

[81] The alternative approach is the dummy variable approach; see paragraph 65 above. Unlike the forecasting approach, the dummy variable approach estimates the effect of the infringement in a single step, by carrying out a regression analysis using data from both the infringement and non-infringement periods. In the case of the example above, this approach would estimate the effect of the cartel as the upward shift in price that is observed during the cartel period (i.e. the coefficient of the dummy variable in the regression equation) and is not explained by changes in other influencing variables, such as raw material costs.

[82] In this case, the regression equation is estimated using data from both the infringement and non-infringement periods and directly indicates how much the variable of interest changed during the infringement period after accounting for the effect of other explanatory variables.

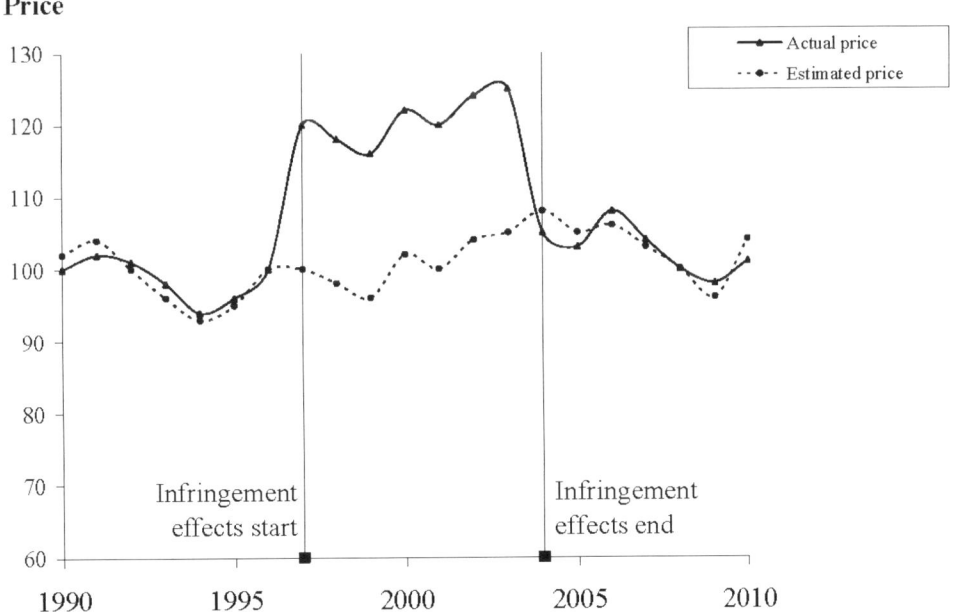

73. The regression analysis illustrated in this graph is based on the forecasting approach, in which a regression is carried out on pre- and post-infringement data to establish in an equation the statistical relationship between price and various relevant explanatory variables (input costs and other relevant factors). Using this equation and the observed values of the relevant explanatory variables, an estimated price can be derived that is likely to have prevailed absent the infringement (dotted line). The continuous line is the actually observed price. The difference between the continuous and the dotted line during the infringement period is the estimated overcharge. The dotted line outside the infringement period is also derived from the regression equation and can serve, through comparison with the actually observed non-infringement prices (continuous line), to assess the predictive power of the regression model.

c. Requirements for applying regression analysis

74. Carrying out a regression analysis requires knowledge of various statistical techniques to measure the relationship between variables, to construct an appropriate regression equation and to calculate the precision of the parameters in this equation. In addition, it is necessary to have a good understanding of the industry concerned, in the first place, to formulate the right hypotheses when constructing the regression equation and to make the right choices as to the factors that are likely to have significantly influenced the variable of interest (and which should therefore be included in the analysis). Industry understanding is furthermore necessary to make informed choices about which statistical techniques to use in a given situation, for instance, to account for unusual observations (outliers) or other specific features in data sets. In particular, where the influencing variables were themselves affected by the infringement, biased results may occur if this aspect is not taken into account, e.g. through applying specific statistical techniques [83] or through using data observations that lie outside the infringement period or market [84].

[83] For example, the use of instrumental variables, an econometric technique that may be applied to correct such bias.

[84] In particular, by using the forecasting approach described above, where the value of the influencing variables included in the model to predict the counterfactual are corrected for the infringement effect on these variables.

75. Without a sufficient number of data observations, statistical analysis cannot identify relationships between economic variables. To identify the effect of influencing variables on the variable of interest therefore requires that a sufficient range of data observations is available for all variables considered. Regression analysis therefore typically requires extensive data. However, statistical techniques may help to overcome some gaps in data or biases in their interpretation [85] and there can be situations where also the analysis of a smaller number of data observations is meaningful.

[85] E.g. where a sample of data observations is not fully representative.

76. Data observations can, in principle, be gathered at different levels of aggregation. For example, where the relationship between price and input cost is to be analysed, data series either for the prices charged in individual transactions, for annual industry average prices or –in between – monthly data at firm level could be examined next to data series either for individual input costs per unit or for industry cost averages respectively. Using disaggregated data makes it possible to analyse a greater number of observations and therefore to obtain more precise estimates. Where such disaggregated data do not exist or are not accessible to the party carrying out the regression analysis, the analysis of aggregated data may still produce informative results, in particular if the aggregated data have a high frequency.

77. Where used appropriately and on the basis of sufficient data observations, regression analysis can considerably refine the damages estimation through comparator-based methods. It should be stressed, however, that even very sophisticated regression equations rely on a range of assumptions and will (like any technique to predict a hypothetical situation) only be able to deliver estimates. It is good practice to consider the assumptions underlying a regression equation, because some assumptions may be more appropriate than others in a given situation and may lead to significantly different results.

78. Whether, by which party and at which stage of the proceedings a regression analysis is carried out in a court case will *inter alia* depend on the existence or accessibility of data and the rules under applicable law regarding fact pleading requirements, disclosure of evidence, the standard of proof and the allocation of the burden of proof between the claimant and the defendant.

79. The different forms of regression analysis mentioned above (paragraphs 65 *et seq.*) are sometimes referred to as «reduced form» approaches, as they directly estimate parameters of an equation that are themselves derived from other economic relationships (e.g. the interaction of supply and demand), without modelling these explicitly. Alternatively, econometric models can be built to estimate these underlying economic relationships. Although such econometric models, which are usually referred to as «structural», often rely on particularly strong assumptions, they may bring a deeper understanding of the market concerned and form an integral part of simulation exercises to estimate damages (as further detailed in section III.A).

(3) Choice of techniques

80. Sections 1 and 2 above have described different techniques whereby comparator-based methods can be implemented in practice. In a given case, the choice of technique will usually depend on a range of aspects, in particular the legal requirements and the factual circumstances of the case. Considerations relating to the standard and burden of proof are likely to be very relevant in practice.

81. Econometric techniques can increase the degree of accuracy of a damages estimate and may thus help in meeting a higher standard of proof if required under applicable rules. Whether regression analysis is required (possibly in addition to other evidence available) to meet such a standard, and on which party the burden of proof falls in this respect are questions of applicable law, including the EU law principle of effectiveness. It should be considered that carrying out an econometric analysis usually requires a significant number of data observations, which may not always be accessible. Moreover, it may also be that in a given procedural situation the applicable standard of proof does not require the party charged with the burden of proof to go further than the techniques mentioned in Section 1 above. This could be because the national legal system concerned considers the markets or periods compared as sufficiently similar and the estimate of damages resulting from the simple comparison as sufficiently accurate for what the party has to show in the given procedural situation. It may also be that the legal system, in view of the damages estimation presented by a claimant and the data that are reasonably accessible to him, provides for a shift of the burden of proof from the claimant to the defendant. In such a situation, the defendant may consider carrying out a regression analysis to rebut the submission of the claimant.

82. Considerations of proportionality may also play an important role, as the gathering of data and their econometric analysis can entail considerable costs (including those of third parties) that may be disproportionate to or even exceed the value of the damages claim at hand. Such considerations may also become relevant with a view to the principle of effectiveness [86].

[86] See above paragraph 2 in Part 1, Section 1.

83. Courts in the EU have mainly used straightforward implementations of comparator-based methods without regression analysis, often on the basis of averages [87]. They have also accepted simple adjustments to the value of observed data when it is quite straightforward to identify a differentiating factor between an infringement market (or period) and a comparator market (or period). To date, little experience exists with econometric analysis in actions for antitrust damages before courts in the EU, [88] although such techniques can, as described above, provide valuable help in quantifying the harm suffered through infringements of Article 101 or 102 TFEU.

[87] The use of averages was accepted in e.g. *Landgericht Dortmund* (Regional Court, Dortmund), decision of 1 April 2004, Case No 13 O 55/02 Kart (*Vitaminpreise*); WuW/DE-R 1352.

[88] For a recent example concerning lost profits in an exclusionary case see *Juzgado Mercantil numero 2 de Barcelona* (Commercial Court, Barcelona), decision of 20 January 2011, case No 45/2010 (Céntrica Energia S.L.U./ Endesa Distribuciòn Eléctrica S.A.)

84. Courts in the EU sometimes also apply a «safety discount», i.e. they deduct from the observed data values an amount sufficient, under the standards of applicable law, to take account of uncertainties in a damages estimate [89]. Regression analysis can also be considered to account for these other possible influencing factors, and to obtain a «lower bound estimate» of the damages incurred [90].

[89] For instance, to exclude the effects on the variable of interest of possible other factors. See e.g. *Kammergericht Berlin* (Higher Regional Court, Berlin), decision of 1 October 2009, case No 2 U 10/03 Kart.; *Oberlandesgericht Karlsruhe* (Higher Regional Court, Karlsruhe) of 11 June 2010 in case No 6 U 118/05 (appeal pending).

[90] Indeed, in addition to providing damages estimates that already control for the influence of other factors, regression analysis also measures the precision of these estimates (in the form of *standard errors*), from which lower (and upper) bounds on the estimated damages can be obtained.

III. SIMULATION MODELS, COST-BASED ANALYSIS AND OTHER METHODS

85. Alongside comparator-based methods, other methods exist to establish an estimate for the hypothetical non-infringement situation. Such other methods include, in particular, the simulation of market outcomes on the basis of economic models (A), and the approach to estimate a likely non-infringement scenario on the basis of costs of production and a reasonable profit margin (B).

A. Simulation models

86. Simulation methods draw on economic models of market behaviour. Economic studies on how markets function and how firms compete with each other have shown that markets with certain characteristics may allow the likely outcomes of market interaction to be predicted, for instance the likely price or production levels or profit margins. The branch of economics known as industrial organisation has developed models of competition for various types of markets that can simulate such outcomes. These models range from monopoly models to, at the other end of the spectrum, perfect competition models. Intermediate models designed to reflect firm behaviour in oligopolistic markets are, in particular, those designed originally in the 19th century by the economists Augustin Cournot and Joseph Bertrand and numerous extensions and variations of the Cournot and Bertrand models. These include, in particular, also dynamic oligopoly models based on game theory [91] that take into account the repeated interaction between firms in the market [92].

[91] Game theory is the study of how people and firms behave in strategic situations in which they must consider how others respond to their action.

[92] Taking into account the repeated interaction between firms in the market can be useful to explain, for instance, coordinated behaviour between firms or market entry of a new competitor. Dynamic models can be particularly useful for explaining exclusionary behaviour and to build a counterfactual to estimate the resulting damage.

87. Prices are likely to be highest (and sales volumes lowest) in a monopoly and prices are likely to be lowest (and sales volumes highest) in a situation of perfect competition. The particular oligopolies described by Bertrand («Bertrand oligopoly») [93] in markets with differentiated goods [94] and by Cournot («Cournot oligopoly») [95] will normally lead to prices and volumes somewhere between perfect competition and monopoly levels; the exact outcome depends on the number of firms in the market and barriers to entry, on the degree of differentiation between them and their products and on other characteristics of the market at hand, such as demand characteristics (especially, how sensitive customers are to changes in price), and the capacities and cost structure of producers.

[93] The Bertrand oligopoly model of competition describes a market with a relatively small number of firms (and high barriers to entry) that compete on price, not output quantity. Firms set their price based on their beliefs about the prices their competitors will charge. In this model, prices increase with the degree of product differentiation.

[94] In a market with homogeneous goods with no capacity constraints, Bertrand price competition will, in contrast, lead to very competitive outcomes. Homogeneous goods are goods that have little differences in terms of quality or features.

[95] The Cournot oligopoly model of competition describes a market with a relatively small number of firms (and high barriers to entry) that compete on the amount of output they will produce. Before they choose prices, they set their quantity (or capacity) simultaneously on the basis of how much they each believe the other firms will produce.

88. Based on such theoretical insights that link the market outcome e.g. in terms of prices to a given set of market characteristics, simulation models can be built to estimate the prices (or other variables) that are likely to have prevailed in the market had an infringement of Article 101 or 102 TFEU not occurred. The simulation model should be constructed in such a way that it replicates *(a)* the most significant factors influencing supply (in particular, the way competition takes place between firms («competitive interactions») [96] and the cost structure of firms; and *(b)* demand conditions (in particular, the extent to which customers respond to price changes). These factors would be expressed as a set of equations in which a number of parameter values need to be included. These values may be known, estimated econometrically or assumed so that the output of the model matches some observed variables. When using simulation models to generate a non-infringement scenario, the relevant market structure and other characteristics must be those that would have existed without the infringement; these may correspond to the structure and other characteristics of the market observed in the infringement scenario, but they may also differ to some extent [97].

[96] The term «competitive interactions» is used to indicate how competition between firms takes place, e.g. (but not limited to) Bertrand or Cournot competition, or how firms refrain from competing between each other (in the case of collusive behaviour infringing competition rules). Markets on which price formation occurs through auctions or other bidding processes may also be conducive to modelling as interaction between competitors often follows fixed rules (prices or output quantities likely to result from an auction or other bidding process not affected by the infringement could, in particular, be estimated by oligopoly models that incorporate game theory to simulate the likely bidding behaviour of competitors in a non-infringement scenario).

[97] As the infringement may have led to a change in the market structure or may have prevented changes in the market that would otherwise have occurred (e.g. the exit of an inefficient competitor), the (hypothetical) market characteristics in the non-infringement scenario are not necessarily the same as those that could be observed in the infringement scenario. In addition, market shares observed during an infringement may significantly differ from those that would have prevailed in the absence of the infringement as cartel members may allocate markets between themselves.

89. An example may illustrate the use of simulation modelling to estimate damages. In the example of a cartel on a differentiated product market (e.g. confectionary chocolates), non-infringement prices could be estimated as follows, using data from the non-infringement period. First, one would estimate how the demand for each chocolate product varies with its own price (own-price elasticity) and with the price of competing products (cross-price elasticity) [98]. Second, one would decide which model appropriately reflects the competitive interaction between firms in the non-infringement period (e.g. the Bertrand model of competition in the confectionary chocolates example). On this basis, it can be calculated at which prices the profits of the firms are maximised in view of the cost parameters (e.g. marginal costs) and demand parameters (e.g. the level of demand) [99]. The value of some of these parameters can then be adapted to reflect the relevant conditions during the infringement period (e.g. supposing the cost of cocoa increases by 10 %). With all this information expressed in equations, it can be simulated (under the assumption that firms strive for maximised profits) what prices these firms are likely to have charged during the infringement period. The cartel overcharge can then be estimated by taking the difference between the observed prices and the simulated non-infringement prices.

[98] Technically, this would involve estimating a demand system, which is an example of the structural econometric analysis mentioned in paragraph 79.

[99] The value of these parameters (e.g. the value for marginal costs used in the calculation) in the non-infringement period can be determined so that the derived prices and volumes match the observed data.

90. This example is particularly demanding in terms of data requirements and assumptions. Simpler simulation models may be envisaged to estimate damages but they rely even more heavily on crucial assumptions that are difficult to verify. For example, damages following a cartel infringement could be calculated by comparing monopoly prices (aimed at reflecting prices during the cartel) with prices expected under a Cournot model (aimed at reflecting prices in the non-infringement scenario), using data such as market shares, costs, and market price elasticity. However, such a method crucially depends on the assumed competitive interactions in the infringement and non-infringement scenarios and entails the risk that these do not mirror sufficiently closely the way in which the cartel operates during the infringement period and the way in which competition on the market would have operated absent the infringement.

91. Simulation models can be used to estimate market outcomes not only in cartel cases (or other price raising infringements), but also in cases of exclusionary behaviour. For example, an oligopoly model could be used to simulate the sales volume and the market share a foreclosed competitor would have attained had the infringement not taken place.

92. Each model simulating market outcomes is an approximation of reality and relies on theoretical and often also factual assumptions regarding market characteristics and the likely behaviour of producers and customers. Although, by their very nature, models rely on simplification of reality, even simple models may in certain cases provide useful insights regarding the likely damages [100]. Building a comprehensive model that replicates a range of specific features of the market in question, if it can be properly solved and evaluated, can increase the likelihood that the result of the simulation is a reasonable estimate for the hypothetical non-infringement scenario. Even very comprehensive models, though, still depend very much on the right assumptions being made, in particular regarding the central questions of what is the likely mode of competition and the likely customer demand in the non-infringement scenario. Moreover, the development of complex simulation models can be technically demanding and may require significant amounts of data that may not always be accessible to the party concerned or possible to be estimated with sufficient reliability.

[100] Therefore, pointing out that a model relies on seemingly simplifying assumptions should therefore on its own not be sufficient to dismiss it; rather, one should consider how some of the simplifying assumptions are likely to affect its results.

93. Nonetheless, both simple and more complex simulation models could provide useful insights when estimating the outcomes that a market would have produced absent an infringement of Article 101 or 102 TFEU. Whether and in which procedural situation legal systems will consider that the use of an economic simulation is appropriate and its results are sufficiently reliable will depend on the specific circumstances of the case in point and the requirements under applicable legal rules.

B. Cost-based method

94. Another approach to estimating the likely prices that would have emerged absent the infringement is provided by the cost-based method [101]. This method consists in using some measure of production costs per unit, and adding a mark-up for a profit that would have been «reasonable» in the non-infringement scenario. The resulting estimate for a per unit non-infringement price can be compared to the per unit price actually charged by the infringing undertaking(s) to obtain an estimate of the overcharge [102].

[101] This method is also referred to as the «cost plus method» or «bottom-up costing method». It is mentioned, as a subsidiary approach in cases where comparator-based methods are not appropriate, by the *Bundesgerichtshof* (Federal Court of Justice, Germany), decision of 19 June 2007, case No KBR 12/07 (*Paper Wholesale Cartel*).

[102] Usually, the cost-based method is considered for quantifying price overcharges. The method, or elements of it, may, however, also be used for quantifying other forms of harm such as the profits lost by foreclosed competitors. For instance, the *Oberlandesgericht Düsseldorf* (Higher Regional Court, Düsseldorf), decision of 16 April 2008, case No VI-2 U (kart) 8/06, 2 U 8/06 (*Stadtwerke Düsseldorf*), estimated the lost profits of a foreclosed competitor by considering the costs of the competitor and the likely profit margin expressed as a proportion of these costs.

95. Different types of production costs may be suitable for implementing the cost-based method, depending on the characteristics of the industry concerned. It is, however, essential to ensure that the treatment of costs and margins is consistent. For example, if variable costs (i.e. costs that vary with the level of production) are considered as the basis of this exercise, a gross margin (i.e. the margin earned once variable costs have been deducted) should be added to calculate the price. It should also be noted that the relevant cost for determining prices may be not only the cost of the infringer, but also the cost of one of its competitors (e.g. if the price in the market is determined by the least efficient producer).

96. The first step of the cost-based method is to determine the production cost per unit. Per unit costs can be estimated by dividing the actual relevant production costs incurred by the infringer(s) for the relevant business activity by the total number of products produced. This approach can be rather straightforward where companies or separate business divisions of companies produce only one main product. Such companies or business divisions sometimes publish their major cost data or file this information as part of their audited accounts with public registries. In other situations, the access to data and the allocation of costs to the product affected by the infringement is more difficult. Where accounting data are available, adjustments may be necessary given that the notions of costs in accounting terms can differ from the notions of costs in economic terms.

97. It may occur that the observed production costs during the infringement are not representative of the production costs that would have been likely without the infringement. This could mainly be for two reasons: first, in the event of infringements of Article 101, companies which due to their collusive behaviour are not subject to the competitive pressure that would exist in the non-infringement scenario may operate less efficiently and therefore generate higher production costs than under competitive pressure. Second, infringers may restrict output and may therefore, during the infringement, forego economies of scale that would have led to lower production costs. Where indications for such situations exist, adjustments to the observed costs data of the infringer(s) may be appropriate. Where such adjustments are not made, the observed costs may still contribute, under the cost-based method, to a lower-bound estimate of the possible price overcharge.

98. The second step of the cost-based method requires a «reasonable» profit margin to be estimated and added to the per unit production costs. Various approaches exist to estimate a «reasonable» profit margin. They are based either on a comparison over time or across markets, or on economic models, and thus have commonalities with the methods described in the preceding Sections. For instance, an estimate for the profit margin that could reasonably be expected in a non-infringement scenario may be derived from the profit margins made by similar undertakings in a comparable geographic market not affected by the infringement or in comparable product markets [103]. Similarly, the profit margins of the infringing (or a similar) undertaking during the pre- or post infringement periods could be used as a basis for the estimate. Both these comparator-based methods rest on the assumption that the reference period, market or firm are sufficiently similar, [104] in particular with respect to market characteristics that are relevant for profit margins such as the level of competition in the market, [105] the cost structure of producers (including costs of innovation), capacity utilisation and capacity constraints. These assumptions are not always easily verified, as a large number of factors and strategic decisions are likely to determine a firm's price and margin setting.

[103] See *Bundesgerichtshof* (Federal Court of Justice, Germany), decision of 19 June 2007, case No KBR 12/07 (*Paper Wholesale Cartel*), referring to the profit margins generated in «comparable industries».

[104] For relevant considerations regarding sufficient similarity see above paragraphs 33-52 in Part 2, Section II.

[105] E.g. whether competition would have been so strong as to drive the price downwards towards marginal costs (as assumed in the model of perfect competition) or whether profit margins, due to an oligopolistic structure, would have been higher even without the infringement.

99. Another approach to estimating a «reasonable» profit margin is to consider the nature of competition and the characteristics of the market absent the infringement and to derive a likely profit margin from the insights from industrial organisation models [106]. For instance, absent the infringement, prices may be likely to tend towards costs due to relative homogeneity of goods and overcapacities in the market; in such cases, the likely profit margin of producers would be relatively low [107].

[106] See above paragraphs 86 *et seq.* in Part 2, Section III.

[107] The cost of capital (i.e. the cost at which a firm can obtain capital on the market) is sometimes considered as an approximation of a «reasonable» profit margin in such cases. However, margins in the absence of an infringement may significantly differ from the cost of capital, for example in the absence of perfect competition or in the presence of firm-specific cost advantages for certain firms, or demand and supply shocks.

100. It is clear from the above that both the estimation of likely non-infringement costs and the estimation of a «reasonable» profit margin can, in practice, require a range of difficult issues to be considered. In addition, the cost-based method supposes access to data that may be in the possession of the opposing party or a third party. Nonetheless, depending on the circumstances of the particular case and on the requirements under applicable legal rules, it may provide useful insights to support an estimation of the harm suffered through an antitrust infringement.

C. Other methods

101. The methods described in this Guidance Paper are those that have received most consideration so far in legal practice and academic scholarship. They should, however, not be seen as an exhaustive list, firstly, as the methods described could further evolve or others could be developed in practice.

102. Secondly, there are methods *not* discussed in this Guidance Paper could nonetheless prove useful, in particular, in order to establish an upper- or lower-bound [108] or approximate estimate [109] for the harm suffered. Especially where the legal systems provide for the possibility of an approximate estimation, national courts have opted for pragmatic techniques rather than a sophisticated implementation of the methods set out in Sections A and B above to establish the amount of damages to be awarded to injured parties. For instance, in cases where a new entrant has been foreclosed in breach of Article 101 or 102 TFEU, business plans have sometimes been used [110] as a source of information on the likely profits of a business, albeit in some instances adjusted depending on the market circumstances or through the use of data from a comparator market or undertaking.

[108] For example, an upper-bound estimation could be obtained through critical loss analysis. This technique assesses for a price increase what loss in quantities would make that price increase unprofitable.

[109] For instance, counterfactual profits could be *prima facie* identified by taking as a benchmark the cost of capital, on the assumption that, absent the infringement, the undertaking would have earned the cost of capital, which represents the minimum return required by providers of capital to an undertaking. On the limitations of this approach, see footnote 107.

[110] See for instance *Højesteret* (Danish Supreme Court), judgment of 20 April 2005, case UFR 2005.2 17H (*GT Linien A/S v De Danske Statsbaner DSB and Scandlines A/S*).

103. It is for national courts to establish whether, under the applicable rules, a method can be accepted for the quantification of harm in a given case, provided that the principles of effectiveness and equivalence of EU law are observed.

IV. CHOICE OF METHODS

104. Each of the methods described in Sections II and III above can, in principle, provide useful insights in relation to all infringements of Article 101 or 102 TFEU and the different types of harm such infringements tend to produce. In particular, they make it possible to estimate not only the amount of illegal price overcharge in a price fixing cartel but also, for example, the sales volume or the profit lost by a company suffering harm through an exclusionary abuse by a dominant competitor.

105. It should be stressed that it is only possible to estimate, not to measure with certainty and precision, what the hypothetical non-infringement scenario is likely to have looked like. There is no method that could be singled out as the one that would in all cases be more appropriate than others. Each of the methods described above has particular features, strengths and weaknesses that may make it more or less suitable to estimate the harm suffered in a given set of circumstances. In particular, the methods differ in the degree to which they are simple to apply, in the degree to which they rely on data that are the outcome of actual market interactions or on assumptions based on economic theory and in the extent to which they take into account factors other than the infringement that may have affected the situation of the parties.

106. In the specific circumstances of any given case, the appropriate approach to quantification must be determined under the applicable rules of law. Relevant considerations may include, alongside the standard and burden of proof under applicable legal rules, the availability of data, the costs and time involved and their proportionality in relation to the value of the damages claim at stake. The costs to be considered in this context may not only be those incurred when the party bearing the burden of proof applies the method, but also include the costs for the other party to rebut its submissions and the costs to the judicial system when the court assesses the results produced by the method, possibly with the help of a court-appointed expert. The costs and burden for an injured party and their proportionality may become particularly relevant with a view to the principle of effectiveness [111]. Moreover, the decision under applicable law as to whether and, if so, which of the methods and techniques described in this Guidance Paper should be used may also depend on the availability of other evidence, for instance documentary evidence produced by the undertakings on the course of business showing that an illegally agreed price increase was actually implemented at a certain amount.

[111] See above paragraph 2 in Part 1, Section 1.

107. It may be that in a given case the application of *several* methods (e.g. comparison over time and comparison across geographic markets) is envisaged, either alternatively or cumulatively. Where two different methods yield results that are similar, such findings may lead a legal system to attribute stronger evidentiary value to the damages estimate, possibly a lower bound, based on these methods. Where, however, the application of two methods produces apparently contradictory results (especially when two opposing parties each rely on a different method), it is normally not appropriate either to simply take the average of the two results nor would it be appropriate to consider that the contradictory results cancel each other out in the sense that *both* methods should be disregarded. In such a scenario it would rather be appropriate to examine the reasons for the diverging results and to carefully consider the strengths and weaknesses of each method and its implementation in the case at hand.

PART 3

QUANTIFYING HARM CAUSED BY A RISE IN PRICES

I. EFFECTS OF INFRINGEMENTS LEADING TO A RISE IN PRICES

108. Anticompetitive practices can have the effect of raising the prices that direct and often also indirect customers [112] of the infringing undertakings pay for the product concerned. Typical examples of infringements leading to such increases are price cartels, or excessive pricing by a dominant undertaking. Customers can also be affected by practices that limit output or allocate customers or markets – distortions of competition which in turn normally lead to a rise in prices. A different type of harm is caused where infringements adversely affect the market position of competitors; the quantification of such harm and its consequences for customers is discussed in Part 4 below.

[112] The direct customers of the infringing undertakings are those who purchase a product directly from one of the infringing undertakings; indirect customers are those who purchase a product affected by the infringement from such direct customers or from other indirect customers. In some instances, undertakings that do not infringe the competition rules themselves can raise their prices, as market prices are higher because of the infringement. Customers who purchase from these undertakings are sometimes referred to as «umbrella customers». To what extent such customers can claim compensation for the harm from the infringing undertakings depends on the applicable legal rules.

109. In so far as infringements lead to a rise in prices for the products concerned, two main kinds [113] of harm caused by such infringement can be distinguished:

(*a*) the harm resulting from the fact that direct and indirect customers of the infringing undertakings have to pay more for each product they purchase than without the infringement (the «overcharge»). This type of harm is further discussed in Section II; and

[113] For other kinds of harm, see above paragraph 19 in Part 1, Section III.

(*b*) the harm resulting from the so-called «volume effect», which is caused by the fact that fewer of the products in question are bought due to the rise in prices. This type of harm is further discussed in Section III.

The following figure represents in a stylised way these two main effects:

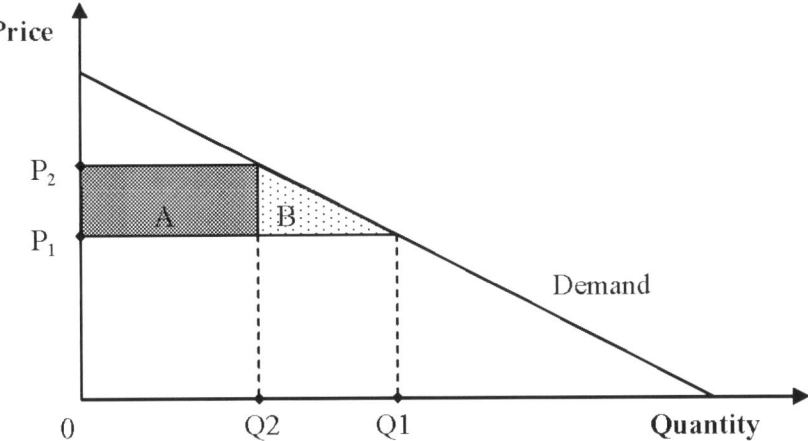

110. P1 is the price charged if no infringement of Article 101 or 102 TFEU affects the market. In a perfectly competitive market, this price will equal the supplier's marginal cost [114] of providing that product. Many markets are in fact not perfectly competitive and non-infringement prices on these markets will be above the level of marginal costs. At price P1, Q1 is the quantity of the product bought by customers.

[114] These are the costs for suppliers to produce one more unit.

111. P2 is the higher price resulting from an infringement having an effect on price. This in turn leads to lower demand (Q2) because some customers will consider that the higher price they have to pay exceeds the value of owning the product or of benefiting from the service. This effect is referred to as the «volume effect» or the «quantity effect». The degree to which a rise in prices affects demand depends on demand elasticity [115].

[115] Demand elasticity measures by what percentage the quantity sold of a product in a given market varies in response to a one percent price change for a particular demand level, and provides a useful indication of the magnitude of the volume effect for small price changes.

112. Rectangle A represents the value transferred from the customers to the infringers due to the infringement: the customers who buy at the higher price P2 have to transfer more money to the infringing undertaking(s) in order to obtain the product. They can demand compensation for having had to pay more and Section II below will explain how to quantify this harm.

113. Triangle B represents the volume effect and thus the value foregone by those who would have bought the product for price P1, but refrain from doing so when the price rises to P2 [116].

[116] For the economy as a whole, this triangle therefore represents the loss in value for customers due to a reduction in output: while the overcharge affects the distribution of assets within the economy, triangle B means welfare not created because of the infringement. This is referred to in economics as «deadweight loss».

114. Some customers use the product in question for their own commercial activities – for example to sell it on or to manufacture other goods. When they do not buy at price P2 (or buy less), they forego the profit they would have made had they been able to purchase at price P1. They can claim reparation for this loss of profit and Section III below will illustrate how to quantify this harm. Other customers are end-consumers. If these do not purchase at price P2 this means that they fail to enjoy the utility of these products or services, for which they would have been prepared to pay price P1 [117]. Applicable legal rules may provide that some or all of such harm should be compensated for such failure to enjoy the usefulness of the product. At a minimum, end-consumers who have to bear higher costs (for example for the purchase of a substitute good) and who therefore have suffered an actual loss [118] must be able to obtain compensation.

[117] It is also possible that customers would have been prepared to pay a price higher than P1, but lower than P2.

[118] See, for this legal term, Joined Cases C-295/04 to C-298/04 Manfredi (2006) ECR I-6619, paragraph 95.

115. The foregoing summarises the basic effects on the market of infringements that lead to a *higher* selling price. Infringements of Article 101 or 102 TFEU can also affect the demand side and lead to lower purchasing prices paid by infringers in their own supply with products, for example in the case of a buyers' cartel or in the abuse of market power exercised by a dominant buyer vis-à-vis its suppliers. In such a case, the price effects would consist in an «undercharge» for the supplier of the infringer, and often also an overcharge on the downstream markets, i.e. for the direct and indirect customers of the infringer [119]. The same methods used to quantify an overcharge can, in principle, also be used to quantify the undercharge, e.g. the lower prices paid by the members of a buyers' cartel vis-à-vis their suppliers.

[119] In order to drive down input prices, the cartel members/dominant buyers with downstream market power are likely to restrict their input purchases, hence also reducing output sales and increasing downstream prices.

116. The same methods can, in principle, also be used [120] where at first sight no overcharge is visible, because the infringement served to artificially stabilise prices over a certain period of time in which prices would under normal market circumstances (i.e. without infringement) have declined. In the following, the term «overcharge» designates also these situations.

[120] Only the method based on comparison between time periods in the variant of «before and during» comparison (i.e. comparing the infringement prices with pre-infringement prices) would obviously be unsuitable, unless regression analysis or simple adjustments are applied to account for the factors that would lead to a price decrease under normal market circumstances (e.g. decreased raw material costs).

II. QUANTIFYING THE OVERCHARGE

117. Different types of infringements lead directly or indirectly to overcharges. Antitrust damages actions often deal with overcharges caused by cartels, which will be addressed in Section A below. The quantification of overcharges caused by other types of infringements will be addressed in Section B below.

A. Quantifying overcharges caused by cartels

118. In an action for compensation, it will be necessary – within the framework of applicable legal rules – to quantify the overcharge paid by the claimant(s). Economic and legal studies have analysed the effects of cartels; some insights from these studies are set out below in Section 1. In actions for damages, it is useful to distinguish between the initial overcharge paid by the direct customer of the infringing undertaking (see below Section 2) and the possible harm that such overcharge causes to indirect customers at different levels of the supply chain (Section 3).

(1) Effects of cartels

119. Cartels are agreements and concerted practices between two or more undertakings aimed at influencing the parameters of competition through practices such as fixing the purchase or selling price or other trading conditions, allocating production or sales quotas or sharing markets (including bid-rigging). For the purpose of finding whether such practices infringe Article 101 TFEU there is no need to quantify the concrete effects of such a practice, because the object of the cartel agreement is the prevention, restriction or distortion of competition [121].

[121] See judgments of the General Court in Joined Cases T-25/95 etc. *Cimenteries CBR SA* v *Commission* (2000) ECR II-491, paragraphs 837, 1531, 2589; Case T-202/98 *Tate & Lyle* v *Commission* (2001) ECR II-2035, paragraphs 72–74; see also Communication from the Commission: Guidelines on the application of Article 81(3) of the Treaty, *O.J.* C 101, 27.4.2004, p. 97, paragraphs 20–23.

120. Infringing the competition rules exposes the cartel members to the risk of being discovered and thus subject to a decision finding an infringement and imposing fines. The fact alone that undertakings nonetheless engage in such illegal activity suggests that they expect to reap substantial benefits from their actions, i.e. that they expect the cartel to have effects on the market and, hence, on their customers [122].

[122] See also the decision of the *Kammergericht Berlin* (Higher Regional Court, Berlin) of 1 October 2009 in case No 2 U 10/03, where the court referred to a similar argument.

121. A study undertaken for the Commission examined the empirical evidence on the existence of overcharge effects and on their magnitude [123]. This study draws on a range of existing empirical studies on the effects of cartels. In particular, it refines the sample of cartels examined in the most comprehensive existing study by considering only cartels: *(a)* that started after 1960 (thus taking into account only more recent cartels); *(b)* for which an estimate of the average overcharge was available (rather than only an estimate of the highest or lowest overcharge); *(c)* for which the relevant background study explicitly explained the method for calculating the average overcharge estimate; and *(d)* which were discussed in peer-reviewed academic articles or chapters in books [124]. While some care is required in interpreting the results of this exercise, [125] the study undertaken for the Commission contains some useful information as to the effects of cartels.

[123] See the external study prepared for the Commission «Quantifying antitrust damages» (2009), pages 88 et seq., available at http://ec.europa.eu/competition/antitrust/actionsdamages/index.html.

[124] In all, the study considers 114 cartels based on different types of collusion, including bid-rigging. The sample includes international and national cartels that affected a wide range of different industries. The geographic spread of the sample extends to the US and Canada as well as cartels from Europe and other regions.

[125] In particular, it seems possible that cartels that do have an effect on the market receive more attention in empirical studies than those that have no effects, which may lead to a certain bias in the findings; see the study «Quantifying antitrust damages», page 89 (ref. in footnote 123), for further details about the interpretation of the data used in the study.

122. On the basis of the data observed, this study found that in 93 % of all cartel cases considered, cartels do lead to an overcharge. As to the magnitude of the cartel overcharge, this study made the following findings [126]:

[126] Study «Quantifying antitrust damages», page 91 (ref. in footnote 123). That magnitude is expressed as a percentage of the actual price. This means that if the actual price (meaning the price paid as influenced by the infringement) is € 100 and the overcharge is said to be 10 %, the price absent the infringement is deemed to be € 90.

123. According to this study, there is thus a considerable spread of the overcharges observed (with some cartels even having an overcharge of more than 50 %). About 70 % of all cartels considered in this study have an overcharge of between 10 % and 40 %. The average overcharge observed in these cartels is around 20 %.

124. The insights of this study concord with those of other available empirical studies, namely that: *(a)* the vast majority of cartels do in fact lead to an overcharge; and *(b)* there is considerable variance in the overcharges observed. Also, all of these other empirical studies come largely to a similar estimate of the magnitude of the average overcharges as described above [127].

[127] For details and further references see the study «Quantifying antitrust damages», pages 89 et seq. (ref. in footnote 123).

125. These insights into the effects of cartels do not replace the quantification of the specific harm suffered by claimants in a particular case. However, national courts have, on the basis of such empirical knowledge, asserted that it is likely that cartels normally do lead to an overcharge and that the longer and more sustainable a cartel was, the more difficult it would be for a defendant to argue that no adverse impact on price did take place in a concrete case [128]. Such inferences, however, are a matter for national legal systems.

[128] See for example *Bundesgerichtshof* (Federal Court of Justice, Germany), decision of 28 June 2005, case No KRB 2/05 (*Transportable concrete*) (in the context of assessing the illicit gain by cartelists for the purpose of calculating a fine).

(2) The initial overcharge paid by the direct customer

126. All of the methods and techniques described above in Part 2 can, in principle, be used to quantify the initial overcharge paid by the direct customers of the infringing undertakings [129]. Also, other types of evidence (such as, for instance, a specific agreement on the rise in prices as shown by internal documents) may also provide valuable insights into the scope of the overcharge. As the initial overcharge is a transfer of money from the direct customer to the infringing undertaking(s), any information that may exist on the illicit profits made by infringers can also serve to quantify this overcharge [130].

[129] These methods and techniques can also be used to quantify the overcharge paid by the umbrella customers (see footnote 112 above), provided that applicable legal rules provide that they are entitled to receive compensation.

[130] See also Section 33(3)(3) of the German Act against restraints on competition (*Gesetz gegen Wettbewerbsbeschränkungen*), which states that the proportion of the profit which the infringing undertaking made from the infringement may be taken into account when estimating damages.

127. In order to illustrate how methods and techniques can be used to estimate prices in a non-infringement scenario and, based on this estimate, to determine the overcharge paid by the customers of infringing undertakings, it is useful to consider the stylised example of a flour cartel already mentioned in Part 2 [131].

[131] Any resemblance of this fictitious example to real events would be purely coincidental; the example cannot be seen as reflecting the Commission's views regarding any specific undertaking or sector or the market definition in such a sector.

The flour cartel

In this example, all the flour in a certain Member State is produced by four milling companies (Mill A, Mill B, Mill C and Mill D). These mills purchase cereals from various farmers, grind the cereals and apply the appropriate treatments, package the flour and sell it on to bakers. These bakers use the flour to bake bread, which they sell on to consumers as well as to supermarkets.

The national competition authority investigates the market on suspicion of price-fixing and in January 2008 carries out unannounced inspections on the premises of the milling companies. In July 2010 the competition authority adopts a decision in which it establishes that all four milling companies infringed Article 101 TFEU by participating, during the period from 1 January 2005 till 31 December 2007, in a single and continuous infringement regarding the production of flour, covering the whole Member State, which consisted of fixing prices.

A bakery company having purchased flour from one of the milling companies (Mill A) sues this company for compensation of the harm suffered because of the infringement of Article 101 TFEU [132]. The bakery claims that the infringement has led to a rise in prices for the flour and demands compensation for the payment of this overcharge for all purchases made in 2005, 2006 and 2007.

---

[132] National law might well provide that all members of a cartel are jointly and severally liable for the entire harm caused by the cartel. The present example has no implications for these rules.

128. The bakery is a direct customer of one of the infringing undertakings. If the infringement caused higher prices, the bakery paid an overcharge for each of the units of flour purchased while price was affected. Application of the methods and techniques described will yield an estimate of the price which the bakery would have paid for the flour had there been no infringement. By subtracting that non-infringement price from the price actually paid by the bakery, the cartel overcharge per unit purchased can be determined. That figure has to be multiplied by the number of units bought by the bakery in order to determine the actual direct overcharge loss (assuming that there were no significant changes in the overcharge during the infringement period).

129. As discussed above in Part 2, several methods and techniques are generally suitable to quantify the non-infringement price. It should be stressed that this non-infringement price is necessarily hypothetical and can therefore only be an estimate [133]. The choice of a method and technique in a given litigation scenario will depend on a wide range of factors, in particular the standard of proof under applicable legal rules and the availability of data [134]. For the estimation of the overcharge paid by the bakery in the present example, the use of comparator-based methods will be illustrated as these are most often used in practice and will often yield helpful results in quantifying the initial overcharge.

[133] See above paragraphs 10-15 in Part 1, Section II.

[134] See above paragraphs 101-103 in Part 2, Section III.

a. Comparison over time

130. In the present example, the claimant bakery company bought flour from Mill A before, during and after the time for which the national competition authority found an infringement. As described above, using the prices actually paid before or after the infringement to reconstruct the prices as they would have been without the infringement makes it necessary, first, to determine which prices were affected by the infringement and which were not. This means finding out at which point the cartel infringement began to have an effect on the flour market and at which point that effect ended.

131. In the present case, the national competition authority has determined the duration of the infringement. In fact, the decision details the evidence the authority had, which indicates that the milling companies met in January 2005 to discuss prices and thereafter continued to meet on a monthly basis, adjusting their pricing arrangements. The last meeting was held in December 2007. The authority found no evidence of meetings after it inspected the companies in January 2008. In a first step, therefore, the prices before January 2005 and after December 2007 appear to be suitable material for a time-based comparison. However, as described in Part 2, further consideration should be given to the extent to which these figures are useful to serve as comparators.

132. As mentioned above, the decision by a competition authority might limit the finding of an infringement to a certain period for which solid evidence is available to the authority, while indicating that the infringement might have had a longer duration [135]. It may then be appropriate not to use the relevant price data for the period that might have been affected by the infringement (and thus include an overcharge), although such data may nonetheless be used to determine a lower bound for the damages estimation, i.e. a safe estimate of what the harm suffered has been at least.

[135] See paragraph 37 in Part 2, Section II.

133. Also, the timing of the cartel infringement may be different from the timing of the effects of the infringement: the milling companies infringed Article 101 TFEU by entering into an anticompetitive agreement. For the purpose of determining which prices observed could be regarded as unaffected by the infringement, it is necessary to look at the timing of the effects of that agreement, not its conclusion. If it can be shown that the companies met in January 2005 for the first time, but that their agreement was implemented from March 2005 onwards, prices before March 2005 would not be tainted by the infringement.

134. As regards the suitability of using post-infringement price observations, it is possible that the cartel produced effects on the market even after the cartel members had ceased to engage in the kind of cooperation forbidden by Article 101 TFEU [136]. This may, in particular, be the case in oligopoly markets, where the information gathered because of the cartel might allow cartel members to adopt on a sustainable basis – after the cartel infringement has ended – a course of action aimed at selling at a price higher than the price likely associated with absence of the cartel infringement, without engaging in the sort of practices forbidden by Article 101 TFEU [137]. It is also possible that, after the end of the cartel, former cartel members resort to another type of infringement of the competition rules that raises prices for their customers. In these cases any time comparison based on the prices observed after the infringement ceased might lead to an underestimation of the overcharge paid by the customers of the infringers, as the post-infringement prices might still be influenced by an infringement. Where in the present example, the claimant bakery has reasons to believe that this might be the case for the prices paid in 2008 and thereafter, it could only use these prices in its submission to the court to estimate a lower bound of the overcharge harm suffered.

[136] See also paragraph 38 in Part 2, Section II.

[137] For further insights into the workings of such «coordinated effects», see Commission, Guidelines on the assessment of horizontal mergers under the Council Regulation on the control of concentrations between undertakings, O.J. C 31, 5.2.2004, p. 5, paragraph 39.

135. In the present example, the claimant bakery finds that the prices paid before the infringement are well suited to estimate the likely hypothetical price. If the bakery compares infringement and non-infringement prices as they are observed, it implicitly assumes that the entire difference between the prices paid in the non-infringement years 2003 and 2004 and the prices paid in the infringement years 2005, 2006 and 2007 is due to the infringement. It is possible, however, that causes other than the infringement had a significant influence on the development of prices during the infringement period. Changes in grain prices, for instance, might be an alternative cause that influenced price developments, and they may be accounted for by using the techniques set out in Part 2, Section II B above. In so far as significant other influences can be identified and the price data are adjusted for their effects, the submission that the remaining difference between the prices in the non-infringement and the infringement periods is due to the infringement gains additional strength [138].

The circumstances in which such adjustments would be required from claimants or defendants will depend on the rules of applicable law.

[138] This is without implications for the application of national rules allowing the claimant to use the basic, unadjusted comparisons between prices charged in infringement and non-infringement periods to make an initial pleading, or to fulfil the duties incumbent upon him under national legal rules with regard to fact-pleading (in particular where national law allows a court to determine the damages award by way of approximate estimation or determination on an *ex-aequo-et-bono* basis). Also, rules on the standard and the burden of proof remain unaffected.

b. Other comparator-based methods

136. Besides comparisons over time, other comparator-based methods as described above in Part 2 may also be useful in quantifying the amount of the initial overcharge paid by the direct customer. In the example of the flour cartel, the claimant bakery could alternatively use a comparison with prices from another geographic market or another product market to show what the prices in its own market are likely to have been without the infringement.

137. One possibility would be the comparison with price data observed on a different geographic market for flour. On the assumption that the flour cartel as described above covered a national market, price data from another Member State could be used to construct the non-infringement price. In the case of markets with a sub-national regional scope, sales prices for flour from a different regional market could be a suitable reference point.

138. In order to be a suitable indicator for the prices as they would have been absent the infringement, the comparator prices should themselves not be influenced by the same or a similar infringement of the competition rules. If in the example of the flour cartel price data from a neighbouring geographic market are used and there is evidence that the anti-competitive agreement also covered that neighbouring market, prices from that market would lead to an underestimation of the overcharge. Also, in the case of neighbouring markets, the infringement in one market may have had an influence on that neighbouring market (for example through a rise in demand in the market without infringement), which might therefore not reflect non-infringement prices either.

139. Where the comparator market has different market characteristics, price data from that market might likewise not be sufficiently indicative of the prices as they would have been had there been no infringement. In the present example, the market concerned by the infringement is supplied by four milling companies. For instance, if it can be shown that prior to entering into the infringing practices, vigorous competition existed, price data from a neighbouring market characterised by the presence of a dominant milling company might not adequately reflect the prices as they would have been had there been no cartel and may only serve as a basis for a lower-bound estimate.

140. If the claimant bakery uses price data from a different geographic market in the form in which they are observed, it makes the implicit assumption that the remaining differences actually paid to the infringers and the prices prevailing on that comparator market are due to the infringement. Depending on the circumstances of the case and requirements under applicable law, the techniques described in Part 2 Section II B above may be used to identify and account for possible alternative influences on prices. It is a matter of applicable law to determine which party bears the burden of proof for such alternative influences or other counterarguments against the claimant's estimation of a quantum of damages.

141. A further possibility to estimate the non-infringement price is comparison with price data observed on other product markets. In the case of flour, it may, however, be difficult to find a sufficiently similar product market not affected by the same or a similar infringement.

(3) The pass-on of overcharges

142. Direct customers of the infringing undertakings who pay an overcharge caused by the cartel may themselves sell on the affected products (or use them as input for their own production of other goods or services). In the example of the flour cartel discussed above, the bakeries are the direct customers of the infringing undertakings and they use the purchased flour to bake bread, which they then sell on either directly to final customers or to supermarkets. These direct customers (bakeries), in reaction to the price increase they face, may raise the prices for their own goods or services (the bread they sell on), thereby passing on some or the entire initial overcharge to their own customers (the consumers or supermarkets). The same effect exists where it is *indirect* customers (such as, for instance, the supermarkets in the present example) who themselves raise their own selling prices in their business deals with their customers, thereby passing on an overcharge which was first passed on to them.

143. Such pass-on of overcharges normally entails a volume effect: as described above in paragraphs 109 *et seq.*, a rise in prices normally leads to a decrease in demand. In the example of the flour cartel, in so far as the bakery passes on the overcharge by raising the prices it charges for the bread to the supermarkets and end customers, it may reduce the adverse financial impact of the overcharge on itself, but it will suffer decreased demand [139]. This decrease in demand means, for the bakery, less sales and a loss of profit – harm that is also caused by the infringement and should be compensated (see Section III below).

[139] This connection between a company passing on an overcharge and its own sales volume has, in a different context, also been emphasised by the Court of Justice in Case C-147/01 *Weber's Wine World* (2003) ECR I-11365, at paragraphs 98-99: «even where it is established that the ... charge ... has been passed on in whole or in part to third parties ... the person may suffer as a result of a fall in the volume of his sales».

144. The price increase through pass-on and the reduction in sales are thus intrinsically connected. In fact, both pass-on and volume effects are determined by the same factors, in particular, the elasticity of demand from downstream customers. This is because the market conditions regarding downstream demand affect both the sales price and the corresponding sales volumes at which the bakery would maximise its profits.

145. In the context of a claim for compensation of overcharges in an antitrust damages action, the pass-on of overcharges can become relevant in two different types of situations:

(a) In an action brought by the direct customer claiming reparation for the initial overcharge paid by him (in the present example: the claim by the bakery against Mill A), the defendant cartel infringer might argue that the direct customer should not, in fact, be compensated for the overcharge harm to the extent that he raised his own prices and thus passed on the overcharge. This is commonly referred to as the «passing-on defence». Pass-on by the purchaser may, as mentioned above, lead to a loss of sales and therefore a loss of profit for him;

(b) an action brought by an indirect customer against the infringer (for example, a supermarket or a consumer who purchased bread from the bakery and who brings a claim against the milling companies) will also depend on a pass-on argument. Indeed, the indirect purchaser can claim compensation for an overcharge only where the initial overcharge paid by the direct customer has been passed on partially or entirely to him. This can be of relevance for claimants situated at different levels of the supply chain, including end customers.

146. Different legal rules exist concerning the availability of the passing-on defence and the burden of proof in this context [140]. The economic insights into the quantification of pass-on set out in paragraphs 148 *et seq.* below can be of use no matter how these rules are designed.

[140] See Commission White Paper on damages actions for breach of the EC antitrust rules (COM(2008) 165 final, 2.4.2008) for policy proposals concerning the treatment of pass-on in antitrust damages actions.

147. In both situations considered above, claimants and defendants could rely on two different approaches to substantiate their claim that the overcharge was passed on to the indirect customer: they could either: *(a)* quantify the initial overcharge and determine the pass-on rate to the indirect customer, possibly at several levels of the supply chain and using the econometric techniques outlined above; or *(b)* use the methods and techniques outlined above to determine whether the indirect customer concerned paid an overcharge. For instance, where an indirect customer brings a claim for compensation of an overcharge caused by a cartel, that indirect customer can either show that there was an initial overcharge and that this overcharge was passed on to him [141] or he may quantify the overcharge passed on to his level in the same manner as a direct customer would quantify an initial overcharge, namely by comparing the actual price he paid with the likely price in a non-infringement scenario: comparator-based methods can provide useful insights into the amount of overcharge paid by indirect customers, without it being necessary to identify the degree of pass-on. By using a time comparison, for instance, for the prices paid by the indirect customer before and during the infringement, it can be possible to ascertain how much those prices rose because of the infringement, without having to make a finding concerning the pass-on rate.

[141] Where the indirect customer substantiates his claim with reference to a pass-on rate and the infringement concerns a cost factor which is small compared to the entire cost of the product, the pass-on rates of other, more important cost factors that may be more easily estimated might serve as a useful indicator.

148. It is not possible to establish a typical pass-on rate that would apply in most situations. Rather, careful examination of all the characteristics of the market in question will be necessary to assess pass-on rates. In a specific case, the existence and degree of pass-on is determined by a range of different criteria and can therefore only be assessed having regard to the conditions of the market in question.

149. Where the direct customer of the infringing undertakings uses the cartelised goods to compete in a downstream market, it is likely that the direct customer will normally not be able to pass on this increase in cost (or only to a very limited degree) if his own competitors in that downstream market are not subject to the same or a similar overcharge (for example, where they receive their input from a market that is not subject to the cartel). In the example of the flour cartel, the claimant bakery is in competition with other bakeries for the production and supply of bread. In so far as these other bakeries do not obtain their flour from the cartel members, but are able to buy it at a lower price elsewhere, the bakery having to buy from the cartel is placed at a competitive disadvantage vis-à-vis its own competitors that prevents it from passing on the extra cost of the overcharge.

150. Where all the undertakings in that downstream market are hit by the cartel and are thus similarly exposed to the payment of the direct overcharge, it is likely that the direct customer will be able to pass on at least part of that overcharge. The degree of such pass-on is influenced by the intensity of competition in the downstream market: if the downstream market is perfectly competitive, the pass-on rate in this case will be virtually 100 %. This reflects the fact that in perfectly competitive markets, price equals marginal costs and a rise in prices for the input will therefore directly lead to an equal rise in cost/output price. For less than perfectly competitive markets, it is likely that affected firms will pass on at least part of the overcharge, though not necessarily 100 %. For example, if the direct customer is a monopolist on the downstream market, he will choose a pass-on rate that reflects – for him – a profit-maximising price in view of the decrease in demand that the pass-on of the overcharge is likely to generate [142].

[142] The exact extent of this pass-on will depend on the demand the direct customer faces and his cost structure. For example, in the simple case of a monopolist facing linear demand (meaning that the relationship between the quantity and price can be represented by a straight line) and constant marginal costs, the pass-on will be 50 % of the direct overcharge.

151. The other characteristics that may also have an influence on the degree of pass-on in such situations (everything else being constant) include:

- the price elasticity of demand and the question whether customers become more or less sensitive to price as prices rise. In particular, pass-on is generally more likely if customers do not easily switch to other products following a price increase (inelastic demand) and if customers become less sensitive to price increases when prices are higher;
- the variation of marginal cost with output changes. For instance, a substantial pass-on is less likely if marginal cost significantly decreases following a reduction in output, because the lower output would become less costly to produce (e.g. in the presence of capacity constraints). Conversely, a substantial pass-on is more likely if marginal cost does not significantly decrease following a reduction in output (e.g. due to the absence of capacity constraints);
- the impact of the infringement on different types of costs. Where the infringement impacts on variable costs, this renders pass-on more likely than if the impact is on fixed costs;
- the duration of the infringement and the frequency of business exchanges. Where infringements last for a long time, it is more likely that some level of pass-on occurs; the same applies to sectors where business exchanges and price adjustments are frequent.

B. Quantifying overcharges caused by other types of infringements leading to overcharge harm

152. Cartels are but one of the infringements leading to a rise in prices for customers of the infringing undertakings and thus to overcharge harm (or, in the case of infringements pertaining to the supply to the infringing undertakings, to an «undercharge»). Other examples of behaviour that can lead to overcharge harm include infringements of Article 101 TFEU by way of certain anti-competitive joint ventures and the abusive charging of excessive prices by a dominant undertaking within the meaning of Article 102 TFEU.

153. A common feature of these infringements is the fact that they may directly or indirectly allow the infringing undertaking(s) to raise the prices for their customers [143]. The payment of such overcharge in turn leads to a decrease in demand and thus to a volume effect as described above.

[143] Or, if the infringement relates to the supply to the infringing undertakings, to lower the price these suppliers obtain from their customers.

154. The methods and techniques whose application to the case of cartel overcharge has been described above [144] can be used to quantify the overcharge harm caused by other infringements.

[144] See paragraphs 130 and following, and 136 and following.

III. QUANTIFYING THE HARM CAUSED BY THE VOLUME EFFECT

155. A rise in prices for a particular product leads to less demand. The degrees to which both prices rise and quantities decrease following an infringement depends on the same cost and demand parameters, and are determined jointly. Hence, the overcharge and volume effects are intrinsically linked.

156. For an overcharge to an intermediate customer (as discussed above in paragraphs 142 *et seq.*), the volume effect is also closely linked to the pass-on of overcharges along the supply chain to the final customer: where a customer of the infringing undertakings does not pass on the overcharge and thus absorbs it entirely, his own sales will not decrease because of the infringement as his customers will not experience a rise in prices due to the infringement. Where, however, the overcharge is passed on partly or entirely to the final customer, that customer will be subject to the rise in prices described in paragraph 109 and will reduce his demand. This in turn will reduce demand upstream in the supply chain.

157. As explained above, for those direct or indirect customers of the infringing undertakings who use the product in question for their own commercial activities, this decrease in demand («volume effect») means that they sell less because of the infringement and therefore forego the profit they would have made on the units they failed to sell because of this effect. This loss of profit is harm for which compensation may be awarded [145] and, in principle, the methods and techniques described above in Part 2 could be used to quantify it [146].

[145] Joined Cases C-295/04 to C-298/04 Manfredi (2006) ECR I-6619, paragraph 95.

[146] Except for the cost-based method.

158. In particular, the comparator-based methods and techniques, whose application to the quantification of the initial overcharge paid by the direct customer is discussed above, can provide the claimant with useful insights in determining the decrease in his turnover and profits. For instance, a comparison over time or across markets can be used to reconstruct the sales volume in the non-infringement scenario, i.e. how many units the claimant would have been able to sell had there been no infringement. Likewise, the application of these methods and techniques can be used to arrive at the hypothetical profit margin in a non-infringement scenario. In some instances, a court may also agree to these methods being used in a simplified fashion, for instance by determining an average profit margin per transaction and then multiplying it by the units that were not sold because of the infringement [147].

[147] See also below, paragraph 171.

159. Loss of profit is a form of harm often associated with infringements that have the effect of excluding competitors from the market. Part 4 of the Guidance Paper discusses the quantification of such harm in more detail. The insights presented in that part can also be relevant when it comes to quantifying the loss of profit caused by a rise in prices.

PART 4
QUANTIFYING HARM FROM EXCLUSIONARY PRACTICES

I. EFFECTS OF EXCLUSIONARY PRACTICES

160. Infringements of Article 101 or 102 TFEU can have the effect of completely excluding competitors from a market or of reducing their market shares. Such effects of infringements on competitors are commonly referred to as «foreclosure». Examples of these practices are abuses of a dominant position prohibited by Article 102 TFEU through, for instance, predation, exclusive dealing, refusal to supply, tying, bundling, or margin squeeze [148]. Such abuses are called «exclusionary abuses». Foreclosure of a competitor can also be the object or effect of a practice prohibited by Article 101 TFEU. It is therefore possible to refer to «exclusionary pratices», covering both infringements of Article 101 and of Article 102 TFEU.

[148] For a description of these practices see also Communication from the Commission – Guidance on the Commission's enforcement priorities in applying Article 82 of the EC Treaty to abusive exclusionary conduct by dominant undertakings, O.J. C 45, 24.2.2009, p. 7.

161. Through exclusionary practices prohibited by the Treaty's competition rules, infringers distort competition in order to improve or artificially maintain their position on the market. This immediately affects their competitors by deteriorating their position in a market, driving them out of a market or preventing them from entering a market. Exclusionary practices can affect the costs borne by a competitor, the price it is able to charge for its products, or the quantities it is capable of producing and selling. They typically lead to a loss of profit for the competitors concerned.

162. Moreover, by illegally affecting the market position of competitors and thereby the level of competition in the market, such practices lead to harm to customers in the form of higher prices or reduced choice, quality or innovation. However, the detrimental effects of exclusionary practices on customers may not always manifest themselves immediately, as these practices target competitors in the first place, thereby reducing the competitive constraints exerted by them on the infringer(s). Whereas infringements of the kind described in Part 3 normally produce an immediate illegal profit for the infringers and immediate harm for their customers, exclusionary practices could result in an initial disadvantage for the infringers and in better prices for customers in the short run, as typically occurs in predatory pricing. The following sections will separately approach the issues of quantifying harm suffered by competitors (Section II) and harm suffered by customers (Section III).

163. The Treaty guarantees consumers and undertakings that have suffered harm caused by an exclusionary practice a right to compensation regardless of whether they are customers or competitors of the infringers. As already stated, the Court of Justice has specified that such compensation encompasses the actual loss suffered (*damnum emergens*), compensation for the profit they have lost due to the infringement (*lucrum cessans*), and the payment of interest [149]. For the purposes of quantifying harm from exclusionary practices, the following Sections will primarily refer to the concept of «loss of profit», in line with the case-law of the Court of Justice. The concept of «loss of profit» will be used in a broad sense, as meaning any difference between the actual profits generated by an undertaking and the profits it would have generated in the absence of the infringement. The approaches to quantifying such loss of profit described in the following are without prejudice to the possibility of injured parties to claim compensation under other heads of damage under national law. Indeed, some elements of lost profits in a broad sense may be classified under different legal concepts under the law of Member States (such as loss of chance [150] or loss of reputation) and there may also be heads of damage caused by exclusionary behaviour that go beyond the notion of lost profits.

[149] Joined Cases C-295/04 to 298/04 *Manfredi* (2006) ECR I-6619, paragraph 95.

[150] Loss of a chance identifies the business opportunities forgone by an undertaking due to the illegal exclusionary practice.

II. QUANTIFYING HARM TO COMPETITORS

164. Loss of profit to competitors can be caused by reduced revenues (e.g. through the reduction in the quantity that such competitors can sell) or increased costs (e.g. when the infringement affects the price of an input). The overall situation can be reflected in a decrease in the competitor's market share. In the following Sections, after a short description of how exclusionary practices affect competitors over time (A), and an outline of the general approach to the quantification of lost profits (B), some typical situations in the quantification of exclusionary practices will be addressed, namely in cases where they affect existing competitors (C) and new entrants (D) and when the harm they produce extends also to the future (E).

A. The time dimension of exclusionary practices

165. Depending on the period considered, exclusionary practices can affect competitors in different ways. When an exclusionary practice starts, competitors typically face difficulties in selling their products or (where the practice concerns the upstream market) obtaining supplies. This translates into a deterioration of their profit through higher costs or reduced revenues. Competitors may typically suffer a drop in their market shares, or a lower market share than they could have expected absent the infringement (for instance where their expansion is prevented). This phase may coincide with an increase in profits for infringers. This is, however, not necessarily so, since infringers may have to bear costs due to the implementation of the exclusionary practice (e.g. by lowering their price, by not supplying a competitor and thus reducing their own sales, or by offering rebates or other advantages to customers that could lower profits in the short term). Competitors may eventually be forced out of the market.

166. Once competitors have been successfully prevented from entering a market, or once their market presence has been reduced or eliminated, infringers usually recoup and benefit from increased profits to the detriment of customers and foreclosed competitors. When this occurs (either very soon after the infringement started or after a certain period of time), customers may have to pay a higher price and suffer a loss of quality or choice. The full exclusion of a competitor from a market is not a prerequisite for these effects on customers. Such effects may occur also from the very beginning of the exclusionary practice, and even if competitors are still on the market, provided the competitive pressure they exercise is weakened.

167. When the exclusionary practice is detected by public enforcers or brought to an end as a result of private actions, competitive conditions could be progressively restored. It is important to stress that the restoration of market conditions as if the infringement had not occurred is factually impossible in many cases. This depends mainly on structural effects of the infringement that may be difficult and lengthy to undo (existing contractual obligations, network effects, or other barriers to the re-entry of a foreclosed competitor). Therefore, in some instances full convergence between the non-infringement scenario and the actual market development cannot take place.

B. General approach to the quantification of lost profits

168. In order to determine whether and to what extent competitors have suffered a loss of profits, it is necessary to compare the profit obtained by competitors during the infringement in the market affected by it with the profit they would have obtained from those products in a non-infringement scenario (i.e. the counterfactual scenario) [151]. Whenever it can be shown that the foreclosed competitor would have earned higher profits in a non-infringement scenario, and that the difference is caused by the infringement, the competitor has suffered harm, even if its market share is unchanged or profits increased due to other factors [152].

[151] This does not concern claims aimed at recovering only part of that loss, e.g. only the additional costs incurred. Such claims arise in practice also because of the availability of more straightforward approaches to quantifying the harm suffered. See below, paragraph 172.

[152] For instance, a new entrant with high potential for growth may maintain its profit levels but would have increased them absent the infringement.

169. The actual profits earned by the undertaking in question are normally determined by deducting the actual costs incurred from the actual revenues earned. Similarly, profits that would have been obtained in a non-infringement scenario (counterfactual profits) can be determined by deducting the estimated costs in a non-infringement scenario (counterfactual costs) [153] from the revenues expected in the absence of the infringement (counterfactual revenues) [154]. The amount of profits lost is the difference between counterfactual and actual profits. In the case of prevented entry, the actual profits are normally zero, or can even be a negative number if the foreclosed competitor incurred costs (e.g. investment to enter the market) that did not return any revenue.

[153] When estimating the profit lost by the undertaking in question, it is necessary to take into account the additional costs it would have naturally faced to increase production. In this respect, the cost per unit incurred by the undertaking does not necessarily correspond to its cost per unit in the counterfactual scenario. For instance, in the case of increasing returns to scale, the cost per unit in the counterfactual scenario would be lower than the observed cost as the undertaking's production would be higher in the counterfactual scenario (i.e. had it not been affected by the infringement).

[154] E.g. *Stockholms tingsrätt* (Stockholm District Court), judgment of 20 November 2008, joined cases T 32799-05 and T 34227-05 (*Europe Investor Direct AB and others v VPC Aktiebolag*), appeal pending.

170. This basic approach to calculating lost profits can be put into practice in different ways. For instance, it is possible to compare the revenues of the foreclosed competitor in the non-infringement scenario with actual revenues from the market as affected by the infringement. Once the lost revenues have been established, it is possible to deduct the costs that the undertaking has avoided due to the lower volumes produced, in order to obtain a value of lost profits. This approach to assessing lost profits does not make it necessary to quantify the entire costs that would have been incurred by the company, but only an estimate of those costs that have not been incurred because of the infringement.

171. There are also some further pragmatic approaches to assessing lost profits that may be suitable in certain specific cases. For instance, an average profit margin per unit of the product traded in the non-infringement scenario could be estimated and then multiplied by the number of units that have not been sold due to the infringement [155]. Such an estimate of the average per unit profit may be based on one or more transactions that can be considered as sufficiently representative of the claimant's business for the product concerned. It is worth noting that in this calculation the avoided costs would implicitly be included [156].

[155] For an example of a pragmatic approach based on real data on costs and revenues implemented through regression techniques, see *Juzgado Mercantil numero 2 de Barcelona* (Commercial Court, Barcelona), decision of 20 January 2011, case No 45/2010 (*Céntrica Energìa S.L.U./Endesa Distribuciòn Eléctrica S.A.*)

[156] In order to estimate the average profit margin, it could be still appropriate to consider how costs and revenues in the counterfactual scenario would have evolved without the infringement. For example, profit margins observed in a pre-infringement period could have been reduced during the infringement period for reasons unrelated to the infringement, due to a reduction in demand or an increase in input costs that are caused by other factors. In addition, the reduction in the output of the excluded competitor could affect its unit cost, hence also affecting the margin on the units it continues to sell.

172. Practice of antitrust damages actions shows that foreclosed competitors sometimes choose to claim damages only for part of the harm, for instance the costs incurred in order to respond to an exclusionary practice, [157] the non recoverable costs ('sunk costs') incurred with a view to entering a market from which they have been foreclosed [158] or the amount judged excessive in cases of margin squeeze or of discriminatory pricing [159] that infringe EU competition law. The quantification methods and techniques illustrated in the present Guidance Paper do not prejudice the possibility to bring claims only for part of the harm suffered. This choice is sometimes prompted by the consideration that quantifying such heads of damage is more straightforward or may require less data, and that evidence is more easily available. Also when claimants seek compensation for loss of profits, quantification of harm on the basis of additional costs incurred (sunk and non-sunk) will generally constitute a lower bound when estimating the full loss of profit.

[157] E.g. additional marketing expenses necessary to retain the market position.

[158] E.g. the costs of building a new factory on that market.

[159] See e.g. *Lietuvos apeliacinis teismas* (Lithuanian Court of Appeal), decision of 26 May 2006, case No 2A-41/2006 (*Stumbras*); *Højesteret* (Supreme Court, Denmark), decision of 20 April 2005, case No 387/2002 (*GT Linien A/S v DSB*).

173. Whichever the method or technique chosen, quantifying lost profits may entail evaluating complex data referring to a hypothetical non-infringement situation against which the actual position of the foreclosed competitor needs to be assessed, often with a view at likely future developments. Assessing the profits that a company would have made, including future profits, may depend on such a number of factors that it could be appropriate to provide for less demanding requirements when it comes to quantification. Therefore, legal systems may allow courts to exercise some

discretion as to the figures and statistical method to be chosen, and the way in which they are to be used to evaluate the damage [160].

[160] See for instance Joined Cases C-104/89 and C-37/90 *Mulder and others* v *Council and Commission* (2000) ECR I-203, paragraph 79.

C. Existing competitors

174. In order to quantify the harm they suffered because of an exclusionary practice, competitors may choose to rely on the methods or techniques described in Part 2. The non-infringement scenario could be reconstructed by comparison with the performance of the same undertaking in a time period that was not affected by an infringement, a similar undertaking on the same market, aggregated industry profits [161] or the performance of the same or a similar undertaking in a market other than the one in which the exclusionary practice occurred. Alternatively, methods based on simulations may provide an estimate of the non-infringement scenario, i.e. simulating on the basis of a number of assumptions (regarding e.g. the type of competitive interactions among firms) what the likely situation would have been if the excluded competitor could have been active on the market and unaffected by the exclusionary practice. The use of other methods is also possible, e.g. financial data from the undertakings involved could provide useful insights on the likely returns of companies had they not been affected by an infringement.

[161] See above at paragraphs 31, 41 and 60.

Refusal to supply an essential input for commercial solvents
Worldco is a leading international producer of raw materials that are an essential input in the manufacturing of commercial solvents. Eusolv is a company that has been active on the market for commercial solvents since 1995, and most of its turnover is made from sales of Betanol. In order to produce Betanol, Eusolv purchases Rawbeta from Worldco. Worldco is dominant in the production of Rawbeta, which is the only raw material suitable for producing Betanol on an industrial scale and at prices that enable Betanol to be marketed. Worldco also supplies Rawbeta to its subsidiary Subco, which since 2004 has been producing Betanol and competes with Eusolv.
In 2006, Worldco decides to stop supplying Rawbeta to companies selling Betanol in the European Union, with the exception of its own subsidiary Subco. Eusolv initially tries to acquire sufficient Rawbeta from alternative suppliers or to replace its Rawbeta input with other raw materials produced through experimental processes, which are significantly more costly and produce sharp rises in the sales price of Betanol, together with a decrease in its quality and suitability for commercial purposes. As a consequence, Eusolv suffers a progressive decline in its sales and finally discontinues the production of Betanol in 2010. In the same year, Eusolv brings a damages action against Worldco and its subsidiary Subco in order to recover the profits it lost due to the refusal to supply. The court holds that Worldco's practice amounted to an abuse of a dominant position prohibited by Article 102 TFEU.

(1) Comparison over time

175. When an exclusionary practice affects existing competitors, it is likely that data from the same undertaking in an unaffected period are available. In such cases, the profits lost by the harmed competitor could be estimated by means of a comparison over time. The non-infringement scenario could, for example, be constructed by reference to data on revenues and costs of the harmed undertaking before the exclusionary infringement produced effects [162]. In many exclusionary practices cases, data from after the infringement may not be available or would not be equally suitable, particularly if the infringement produced effects that may alter the structure of a market and are unlikely to disappear in the short term, for instance when the competitor is excluded from the market and there are barriers to re-entry in the short term, or when the competitor has lost market shares that could be difficult to regain because of network effects [163].

In the Betanol example, reliable data from after the infringement are not available, since Eusolv, the harmed undertaking, is no longer active on the market, and its effective re-entry into the market may not occur promptly after the termination of the infringement. Eusolv thus decides to construct a likely non-infringement scenario by using data from before 2006, when the exclusionary practice was initiated.

[162] For an example of the application of a before and during comparison to estimate the harm from an exclusionary practice prohibited by Article 101 TFEU see *Corte d'Appello di Milano* (Court of Appeal, Milan), decision of 3 February 2000, case No I, 308 (*Inaz Paghe* v *Associazione Nazionale Consulenti del Lavoro*).

[163] A product is subject to network effects if its value for each user increases as the number of users increases.

176. Under some circumstances, the pre-infringement revenue and cost data used for the comparison could be refined. For instance, and depending on applicable national rules on evidence and on the burden of proof, a defendant may challenge the amount estimated by the claimant by indicating other elements that may have adversely influenced the performance of an undertaking and are not related to the infringement, such as a drop in marketing investment, a loss of competitiveness of the product, or an increase in the cost of inputs that is specific to the competitor claiming damages. Conversely, it could be shown that the harmed competitor's situation in the non-infringement scenario would have been better than it was before the infringement, for instance because it had a potential for growth. Generally, the reference to an earlier unaffected time period on the same market is likely to be more reliable the longer the competitor has been on that market and the more stable its market position has been. In other words, the reference to a pre-infringement scenario could benefit more from adjustments [164] if the harmed competitor was a recent entrant on the market, since its market share could have been more likely subject to fluctuations.

[164] Such adjustments could be performed through the techniques described above at paragraphs 53 *et seq*.

In the example, Eusolv provides data on its overall actual revenues and costs from the production and sale of Betanol, as set out in the following chart:

In order to establish a reliable non-infringement scenario, data from before 2004 are not taken into account because Subco, the most significant competitor of Eusolv, was not yet active on the market, whereas after 2004 and until 2006 Eusolv held a stable share of the market.

Eusolv, in accordance with national rules on the burden and the standard of proof, provides figures on the «counterfactual» quantities, revenues and costs that would have occurred in the absence of the infringement.

Due to increasing industrial applications of Betanol, it is observed that the total demand for this product (thus, the size of the market) has grown steadily. The stability of Eusolv's market share after Subco's entry into the Betanol market is used by Eusolv to rely on the assumption that, absent the infringement, it would have maintained a similar market share. On this assumption Eusolv provides figures on its «counterfactual» revenues for the years 2006-2010, calculated on the basis of the total value of the market and Eusolv's share of it. From its internal accounts, Eusolv provides figures on its unit costs for the years 2004 to 2006 [165]. It is shown that costs closely followed the prices of the inputs for the production of Betanol, i.e. that, for instance, a rise in the input prices directly leads to a corresponding increase in costs. Using available industry data on input prices, Eusolv's experts estimate «counterfactual» unit costs and, e.g. through regression analysis, account for the evolution in input prices and efficiencies related to the production of higher volumes. The figure for overall «counterfactual» costs in the years 2006-2010 is then obtained by multiplying the estimated «counterfactual» unit cost by the number of units it would have sold in the absence of the infringement.

[165] These include sunk costs, distributed over time.

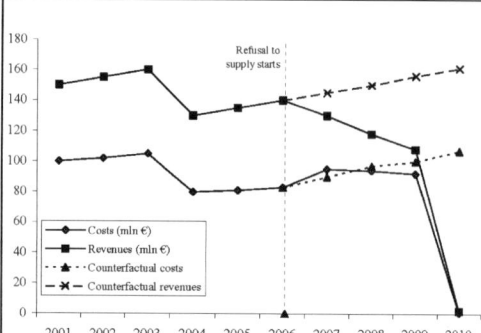

The figures obtained are compared with the actual revenues and costs faced by Eusolv as follows: the actual profits (actual revenues minus actual costs) are deducted from counterfactual profits (counterfactual revenues minus counterfactual costs). This constitutes the final estimate of the damages claimed by Eusolv.

However, Worldco and Subco argue that in order to be able to supply the expected increasing number of units in 2006-2010, Eusolv would have needed to expand its capacity, facing extra sunk costs that have not been included in the calculation. The defence is accepted by the court, and the compensation for lost profits is reduced accordingly (by deducting the expected extra sunk costs for the years in question, on a pro-rata basis, from the figure submitted by Eusolv).

177. In exclusionary practices cases, market shares can play an important role as an indicator in the calculation of lost profits through comparator-based methods such as time comparisons. For instance, a comparator-based method could be used to obtain the likely market share of the foreclosed competitor absent the infringement. Lost profits could then be quantified by multiplying the observed data on actual per-unit costs and revenues (or the actual average profit margin) by the extra quantities corresponding to the higher «counterfactual» market share expected in the absence of the infringement. This relies on the assumption that costs and revenues per unit would not have significantly changed in the non-infringement scenario, and could be accepted by a legal system as an estimate of the harm suffered, possibly as *prima facie* evidence or as sufficient to shift the burden of proof [166]. A more refined estimate would assess the evolution of costs and revenues in the non-infringement scenario, provided that sufficient data are available.

[166] For an example of a court estimation based on multiplying the total number of contracts concluded by the infringer by the market share held by claimants before the exclusionary practice started, see *Corte d'Appello di Roma* (Court of Appeal, Rome), decision of 20 January 2003, case No I, 2474 (*Albacom S.p.A. v Telecom Italia S.p.A.*).

178. When the market share is taken as an indicator in the estimation of lost profits, consideration should be given to the fact that it may be subject to fluctuations due to factors other than the infringement, such as the 2004 fall in Eusolv's market share in the Betanol example due to the entry of Subco as a competitor [167]. It may also be the case that if the infringement shrank the total size of the market, revenues for the excluded competitor estimated on the basis of actual market shares would result in an underestimate.

[167] For this reason, in the example the market share considered for the quantification is the stable market share held by Eusolv after 2004.

(2) Other comparator-based methods

179. Other geographic or product markets may also be used as a comparator in order to construct the non-infringement scenario [168]. Thus, costs and revenues of the same or a similar undertaking on a different market could be taken as a reference to estimate the costs and revenues that would have been yielded by the harmed competitor had the infringement not occurred. These methods can also be used as a means to assess the reliability of an estimation obtained by a comparison over time or other methods. For instance, if the pre-infringement performance of the sole competitor of a historically monopolistic undertaking indicates that it would have held a certain market share absent the infringement, the estimation could be comforted by the finding that the same or a similar undertaking which competes with the formerly monopolistic incumbent on a comparable geographic market actually holds a similar market share, taking into account possible differences between the undertakings or the markets concerned.

[168] See *Juzgado Mercantil numero 5 de Madrid* (Commercial Court, Madrid), decision of 11 November 2005, case No 85/2005 (*Conduit-Europe, S. A. v Telefónica de España S.A.*), confirmed by *Audiencia Provincial de Madrid* (Court of Appeal, Madrid), decision of 25 May 2006, case No 73/2006.

D. Prevented entry of competitors

180. Exclusionary practices can not only lead to the deterioration of the market position of an existing competitor, but also prevent the entry of a potential competitor that was not already active on the market. The foreclosure of new entrants can cause them a very significant harm for which they are entitled to compensation. Legal systems should take account of the inherent difficulties of quantifying such harm and should ensure that damages actions by prevented market entrants are not made practically impossible or excessively difficult [169].

[169] In some cases it is possible under applicable legal rules to quantify this harm through pragmatic approaches, such as calculation of the total value of the lost market in terms of profits, multiplied by a percentage expressing the share of the market that the foreclosed undertaking would have been likely to acquire. For instance if the total profits generated by undertakings active on the relevant market after the infringement amount to 200 million euros, and it is estimated that, in the absence of the infringement, the foreclosed competitor would have held a market share of 30 per cent, the lost profit could be estimated, under this approach, at 60 million euros.

181. The situation of prevented entry presents some peculiar circumstances that can be taken into account when quantifying the harm. In particular, if the harmed undertaking was willing to enter a market where it was not active before, there is an inherent lack of observable data on its performance on that market.

182. The general approach to quantifying the profits lost by competitors in such situations is not essentially different from the situation of foreclosure of competitors that see their existing market position deteriorate, as it also involves an assessment of the profits that could have been yielded by the excluded competitor absent the infringement. These can then be compared with the actual situation. In cases of prevented entry, it is likely that the excluded competitor made no profits or even sustained losses (for instance where the competitor had to bear costs it did not recover through not being able to enter the market).

183. As mentioned above, foreclosed competitors may decide to seek damages only in relation to the costs borne in order to enter the market rather than the whole of the profits foregone. This approach can be more straightforward than claiming compensation for loss of profits as it only involves quantifying the sunk costs incurred by the claimant.

The medical equipment case

Newco is an undertaking that was committed to entering the market for a particular type of medical device in a Member State where Medco has a dominant position. In order to be profitable, Newco would have needed to achieve a minimum size on the market to take advantage of economies of scale.

Fearing to lose substantial sales to Newco, Medco concluded exclusive purchasing agreements with a number of customers in order to prevent Newco from achieving this minimum scale. As a result, Newco could not compete with Medco for these customers and was unable to profitably enter the market, which led to higher average prices for consumers than if Newco had entered the market. As Medco's conduct was considered to infringe Article 102 TFEU, Newco would be entitled to claim compensation for the profits it lost as a result of the infringement. However, in order to avoid carrying out a full loss of profit analysis, Newco only claimed compensation for the sunk costs it had already incurred to set up a new plant and enter the market (including e.g. financial costs and non-recoverable losses on purchased input material).

---

184. In cases where entry of competitors is prevented, there are no pre-infringement revenue and cost data for the market concerned, while post-infringement data could equally not lend themselves to be a reference for a time comparison because of the effects of the infringement. In such instances, reference to a comparable geographic or product market where the same or a comparable undertaking is active could prove a better means to construct a non-infringement scenario. Product or geographic markets concerned should offer a sufficient degree of similarity, although it may be possible to adjust for some differences between the markets [170].

[170] This could be done, for instance, through regression analysis, provided that sufficient data are available. See above, paragraph 63 *et seq*. For an example of an exclusionary practice where the use of a different geographic market was, in principle, accepted as a comparator see *Juzgado Mercantil numero 5 de Madrid* (Commercial Court, Madrid), decision of 11 November 2005, case No 85/2005 (*Conduit-Europe, S.A. v Telefónica de España S.A.*), confirmed by *Audiencia Provincial de Madrid* (Court of Appeal, Madrid), decision of 25 May 2006, case No 73/2006.

185. In some cases, assessment of the competitor's financial performance may suffice to find data in order to estimate the profits in the non-infringement scenario [171].

[171] For an illustration of the quantification of harm to a foreclosed new entrant in a bidding market see *Oberlandesgericht Düsseldorf* (Higher Regional Court, Düsseldorf), decision of 16 April 2008, case No VI-2 U (kart) 8/06, 2 U 8/06 (*Stadtwerke Düsseldorf*).

In the situation referred in the example above, assume that Newco is willing to supply the three biggest private health centres in a Member State with an innovative type of films for X-ray machines. Assume that normally the market for this type of medical equipment for private health centres is a bidding market. Thanks to a technological improvement, Newco is capable of offering its products at a lower price than Medco. However, Medco, which holds a dominant position in the market for X-ray machines, ties the products by applying a higher price for X-ray machines to centres that do not purchase films from it. As a result, Newco does not obtain any contract. In such circumstances, Newco showed that it was actually capable of supplying the quantities demanded by the centres for the price offered, and provided detailed data on its own costs. On the basis of these data, and on the assumption that Newco would have been chosen as a contractor in those instances where it offered the lowest price, expected profit margins could be estimated without resorting to a comparison in time or with other geographic or product markets.

E. Compensation for future loss

186. When foreclosed competitors claim compensation, they may seek compensation not only for the profits lost during the infringement period, but also for the profits foregone after its termination [172]. This is relevant, in particular, where they could not re-enter the market or fully recover their market share because of lasting effects of the terminated infringement. Compensation would then be asked for future profits, i.e. profits that are likely to be lost after the claim for compensation is brought and adjudicated.

[172] For an example of a damages award also for the period subsequent to the end of an infringement see *Østre landsrets* (Eastern High Court, Denmark), decision of 20 May 2009, case No B-3355-06. (*Forbruger-Kontakt a-s v Post Danmark A/S*).

187. The challenges for quantifying such loss not only lie in the techniques to be deployed, but also have to do with the time frame during which a lost profit can still be identified and compensated. National law plays an important role in this context, for instance by determining under which circumstances a future loss can be recovered, or by establishing pragmatic rules to address this issue on a case-by-case basis [173].

[173] When future profits are estimated, it is normally appropriate to discount their value in order to reflect the loss in the value of money over time.

188. Factors likely to affect the choice of the relevant limit in time for claiming loss of future profit may encompass, for instance, the likely time needed to re-enter the market in question. In other cases, this assessment could be easier because of the circumstances of the case. For instance, in the X-ray machine example above, the duration of the contracts Newco was bidding for could constitute a reasonable lapse of time over which loss of future profits should be compensated under applicable national rules. In other cases, the time over which the undertaking could reasonably have continued producing goods or providing services in the absence of new investments could also be considered.

In the Betanol example, Eusolv may claim compensation also for the profits it could have obtained after 2010, when it was driven out of the market and brought an action for damages. In such a case, it would be possible to use the same techniques employed to reconstruct the non-infringement scenario in the years 2006–2010 and project it further into the future. Of course, lost profits for the future cannot be claimed for an indefinite duration. Eusolv decided to take as a benchmark the likely lapse of time that would be needed for Eusolv to re-enter the market once the infringement was brought to an end.

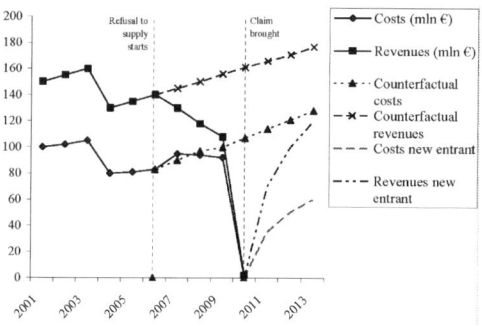

III. QUANTIFYING HARM TO CUSTOMERS

189. Undertakings that collude or abuse their dominant position in order to foreclose a competitor might face costs or a temporary reduction in their profits in order to implement the infringement. This sacrifice is borne in order to achieve a distortion of the competitive process that will eventually place the infringers in a position where they gain higher profits thanks to the distorted market conditions achieved, thus allowing them to recoup, at the expense of their customers, the temporary loss or reduction in profits borne in order to attain that position. The following sections will address two typical situations of harm to customers caused by exclusionary practices. For the purposes of quantification, the harm caused to customers by exclusionary practices can be analogous to that caused by infringements leading to a rise in prices, which is discussed in more detail in Part 3 of the Guidance Paper.

A. Recoupment

190. The most straightforward example of the harm caused to customers in the recoupment phase of exclusionary practices is price predation, where an undertaking abuses its dominant position by setting its prices at an artificially low level that cannot be matched by its competitors, who will eventually leave the market or suffer a reduction in their market share. Once the competitors have been excluded from the market, or once a higher market share has been achieved, infringers can enjoy higher profits due to the weaker competitive constraints.

191. Recoupment can be seen as a complementary phase of the infringement that can result in overcharge effects for the customers of the infringers. These overcharge effects constitute harm caused by the exclusionary practice, and compensation for them can be sought by customers.

Recoupment in a predatory pricing case

Consider, for example, the market for flights on a particular route between two cities. Operating on this market in a dominant position is Titan Airlines, an established undertaking which offers high quality in-flight service for a standard fare of 1.000 euros. Another player on this specific market is the smaller Bluesky Airlines, which recently started operating on the same route with prices of 800 euros. Titan Airlines engages in predatory pricing by strategically lowering its fares to a standard price of 500 euros. Bluesky Airlines experiences difficulties in meeting these predatory fares, as a result of which it fails to remain profitable, and is eventually driven out of the market. The dominant Titan Airlines will in that case take advantage of the reduction of competition and increase its profits by raising fares to a level beyond pre-predation fares, i.e. exceeding its initial standard price of 1.000 euros. If Titan Airlines, until re-entry of a competitor, were to charge a price of 1.100 euros, its customers would, due to the infringement, pay an overcharge of 100 euros.

---

192. When overcharges resulting from recoupment are to be quantified, the conceptual framework that applies is in principle not different from that discussed in Part 3, namely regarding infringements leading more directly to a rise in prices. Since the harm caused by an exclusionary practice is not confined to competitors of the infringer but extends to all customers in a specific market, the issues discussed in the framework of overcharge harm are thus relevant also in this scenario.

193. The position achieved by an undertaking on the market due to an exclusionary infringement does not lead in all cases to a rise in price for customers of the infringing undertaking. However, also in such cases customers may still be harmed by the infringement, for instance if it results in reduced quality. In the example, it could happen that the dominant undertaking Titan Airlines reinstates the same standard price of 1.000 euros, not exceeding the fares it charged prior to the exclusion of Bluesky Airlines. Passengers travelling on this particular route are nevertheless adversely affected, for instance, if Titan Airlines seizes the opportunity of less competitive constraints to lower the standard of its in-flight service.

194. Customers of the foreclosed competitor could be in a different situation than customers of the infringers, because they may have to switch to the products sold by the infringing undertaking as the competitor is driven out of the market. Apart from the possibility of reduced quality, they may also have to pay to the infringing undertaking prices that are higher than the prices paid for the products sold by the foreclosed undertaking. Depending on applicable legal rules, they could be allowed to show that, in the absence of the infringement, they would have purchased from the foreclosed competitor at a lower price. In such case, the effect to be considered is, in principle, similar to an overcharge. The overcharge can be calculated by comparing the price of the product sold by the infringing undertaking in the actual scenario with that charged by the foreclosed undertaking in the non-infringement scenario.

For instance, passengers travelling with Bluesky Airlines prior to its foreclosure may face an overcharge when, due to Bluesky Airlines' exclusion from the market, they are forced to fly at more expensive fares with Titan Airlines. The overcharge could be estimated as the difference between the actual price of 1.000 euros paid to Titan Airlines and the price of 800 euros which Bluesky Airlines would have charged, had it not been driven out of the market. In such case, the overcharge suffered by passengers constrained to switch from Bluesky Airlines to Titan Airline could be estimated at 200 euros.

B. Harm to competitors as customers of the infringers

195. In cases where a competitor is also a customer of the infringer, the exclusionary practice could damage the competitor in so far as it purchases from the infringer. In these situations, the foreclosed competitor can not only claim compensation for the increase in costs produced by the infringement, but also choose to claim compensation for the profits lost because the resulting volumes produced or sold are lower than if the infringement had not occurred [174].

[174] For an example of the estimation of damages in a discriminatory pricing affecting a competitor as a customer of the infringer, see *Højesteret* (Supreme Court, Denmark), decision of 20 April 2005, case No 387/2002 (*GT Linien A/S v DSB*).

196. It can be observed that for the purposes of quantification, competitors that suffer an overcharge are in a position analogous to that of customers of the members of a cartel or another infringement leading to an overcharge. In order to explain this, it is possible to take the example of Betanol, and assume that rather than refusing to supply Rawbeta to Eusolv, the dominant firm Worldco decides to increase the price of Rawbeta charged to Eusolv so as to squeeze its profit margins. In such a situation, similar considerations arise as in the case of an increase in price generated by other types of infringements. In the example Eusolv would claim compensation for the overcharge represented by the difference between the price it paid as a result of the exclusionary practice and the price it would have paid in the absence of the infringement. If the overcharge has been passed on, claims for damages could be also brought by Eusolv's own customers, and Eusolv itself could claim compensation for the volumes lost because of the price increase.

TABLE OF CASES CITED

Court of Justice of the EU

Case 238/78 *Ireks-Arkady GmbH v Council and Commission* (1979) ECR 2955.

Case C-271/91 *marshall* (1993) ECR I-4367.

Case C-308/87 *Grifoni II* (1994) ECR I-341.

Joined Cases C-104/89 and C-37/90 *Mulder and others v Council and Commission* (2000) ECR I-203. Case C-453/99 *Courage* (2001) ECR I-6297.

Case C-147/01 *Weber's Wine World* (2003) ECR I-11365.

Joined Cases C-295/04 to 298/04 *Manfredi* (2006) ECR I-6619.

General Court

Case T-202/98 *Tate & Lyle* v *Commission* (2001) ECR II-2035

Joined Cases T-25/95 etc. *Cimenteries CBR SA* v *Commission* (2000) ECR II-491.

Courts of the Member States

Corte d'Appello di Milano (Court of Appeal, Milan), decision of 3 February 2000, case No I, 308 (*Inaz Paghe* v *Associazione Nazionale Consulenti del Lavoro*).

Corte d'Appello di Roma (Court of Appeal, Rome), decision of 20 January 2003, case No I, 2474 (*Albacom S.p.A.* v *Telecom Italia S.p.A.*).

Corte d'Appello di Milano (Court of Appeal, Milan), decision of 11 July 2003, (*Bluvacanze*)

Cour d'Appel de Paris (Court of Appeal, Paris), decision of 23 June 2003 (*Lescarcelle-De Memoris* v *OGF*)

Landgericht Dortmund (Regional Court, Dortmund), decision of 1 April 2004, Case No 13 O 55/02 Kart (*Vitaminpreise*).

Højesteret (Supreme Court, Denmark), decision of 20 April 2005, case No 387/2002 (*GT Linien A/S* v *DSB*).

Bundesgerichtshof (Federal Court of Justice, Germany), decision of 28 June 2005, case No KRB 2/05. (*Transportable concrete*)

Juzgado Mercantil numero 5 de Madrid (Commercial Court, Madrid), decision of 11 November 2005, case No 85/2005 (*Conduit-Europe, S.A.* v *Telefónica de España S.A.*),

Audiencia Provincial de Madrid (Court of Appeal, Madrid), decision of 25 May 2006, case No 73/2006.

Lietuvos apeliacinis teismas (Lithuanian Court of Appeal), decision of 26 May 2006, case No 2A-41/2006. (*Stumbras*)

Corte Suprema di Cassazione (Supreme Court of Cassation, Italy), decision of 2 February 2007, case No 2305 (*Fondiaria SAI SpA* v *Nigriello*).

Bundesgerichtshof (Federal Court of Justice, Germany), decision of 19 June 2007, case No KBR 12/07 (*Paper Wholesale Cartel*)

Landesgericht für Zivilrechtssachen Graz (Regional Civil Court of Graz), decision of 17 August 2007, case No 17 R91/07 p (*Driving school*).

Oberlandesgericht Düsseldorf (Higher Regional Court, Düsseldorf), decision of 16 April 2008, case No VI-2 U (kart) 8/06, 2 U 8/06 (*Stadtwerke Düsseldorf*).

Stockholms tingsrätt (Stockholm District Court), judgment of 20 November 2008, joined cases T 32799-05 and T 34227-05 (*Europe Investor Direct AB and others* v *VPC Aktiebolag*), appeal pending.

Østre landsrets (Eastern High Court, Denmark), decision of 20 May 2009, case No B-3355-06 (*Forbruger-Kontakt a-s* v *Post Danmark A/S*).

Kammergericht Berlin (Higher Regional Court, Berlin), decision of 1 October 2009, case No 2 U 10/03 Kart.

Oberlandesgericht Karlsruhe (Higher Regional Court, Karlsruhe) of 11 June 2010 in case No 6 U 118/05 (appeal pending)

Juzgado Mercantil numero 2 de Barcelona (Commercial Court, Barcelona), decision of 20 January 2011, case No 45/2010 (Céntrica Energìa S.L.U./Endesa Distribuciòn Eléctrica S.A.).

PRIVACY STATEMENT

Public consultation «Quantification of harm in actions for damages based on breaches of Articles 101 or 102 of the Treaty»

(referred as «consultation» in the text)

1. *Objective*

The objective of this consultation is to receive the views of stakeholders or people concerned by the topic of the consultation and potentially to publish them on the Internet, under the responsibility of the Head of the Unit «*COMP.A1*», Directorate-General *Competition*, acting as the Controller.

As this consultation collects and further processes personal data, Regulation (EC) 45/2001, of the European Parliament and of the Council of 18 December 2000 on the protection of individuals with regard to the processing of personal data by the Community institutions and bodies and on the free movement of such data, is applicable.

2. *What personal information do we collect and through which technical means?*

Identification Data

The personal data collected and further processed are data necessary for the participation in the consultation, such as name/surname/profession/ postal & e-mail addresses/phone number/fax number ..., of the contributors, including their views on the topics concerned. The processing operations on personal data linked to the organisation and management of this consultation are necessary for the management and functioning of the Commission, as mandated by the Treaties, and more specifically articles 5, 7 and 211 - 219 of the EC Treaty.

Technical information

Your reply and personal data will be collected through post or e-mail. The e-mail system of the European Commission abides by the Commission's security decisions and provisions established by the Directorate of Security.

3. *Who has access to your information and to whom is it disclosed?*

Received contributions, together with the identity of the contributor, will be published on the Internet, unless the contributor objects to publication of the personal data on the grounds that such publication would harm his or her legitimate interests. In this case the contribution may be published in anonymous form. Otherwise the contribution will not be published nor will, in principle, its content be taken into account. Any objections concerning publication of personal data should be sent to the service responsible for the consultation (see Contact information below).

4. *How do we protect and safeguard your information?*

Your replies, together with your chosen language used for drafting the reply, are recorded in a secured and protected database hosted by the Data Centre of the European Commission, the operations of which abide by the Commission's security decisions and provisions established by the Directorate of Security for this kind of servers and services. The database is not accessible from outside the Commission. Inside the Commission the database can be accessed using a UserId/Password.

5. *How can you verify, modify or delete your information?*

In case you want to verify which personal data is stored on your behalf by the responsible controller, have it modified, corrected or deleted, please contact the Controller by using the Contact Information below and by explicitly specifying your request.

6. *How long do we keep your data?*

All replies to the consultation will remain in the database until the results have been completely analysed, and they will be archived for reference purposes thereafter. Your personal data will be part of a list of contact details shared internally amongst the staff under the responsibility of the Controller for the purpose of contacting you in the future in the context of further activities related to the consultation. If you do not agree with this, please indicate this in your reply. If you have already sent your reply, please contact the Controller by using the Contact Information below specifying your request.

7. *Contact Information*

In case you wish to verify which personal data is stored on your behalf by the responsible controller, have it modified, corrected, or deleted, or if you have questions regarding the consultation, or concerning any information processed in the context of the consultation, or on your rights, feel free to contact the support team, operating under the responsibility of the Controller, using the following contact information:

European Commission

Directorate-General for Competition

Unit A1 – Private Enforcement

Reference: HT 2290. comp-damages-actions@ec.europa.eu

8. *Recourse*

Complaints, in case of conflict, can be addressed to the European Data Protection Supervisor.

Decision of the President of the European Commission 13 October 2011 on the function and terms of reference of the hearing officer in certain competition proceedings (Text with EEA relevance)

(PB. L 275, 20 October 2011, p. 29)

1. See above, section 2.1.3. Procedural rules

THE PRESIDENT OF THE EUROPEAN COMMISSION,

Having regard to the Treaty on European Union,

Having regard to the Treaty on the Functioning of the European Union,

Having regard to the Agreement on the European Economic Area,

Having regard to the Rules of Procedure of the Commission (1), and in particular Article 22 thereof,

Whereas:

(1) Under the system for competition law enforcement established under the Treaty on the Functioning of the European Union (hereinafter «the Treaty»), the Commission investigates and decides on cases by administrative decision, subject to judicial review by the Court of Justice of the European Union (hereinafter «the Court of Justice»).

(2) The Commission has to conduct its competition proceedings fairly, impartially and objectively and must ensure respect of the procedural rights of the parties concerned as set out in Council Regulation (EC) No 1/2003 of 16 December 2002 on the implementation of the rules on competition laid down in Articles 81 and 82 of the Treaty (2), Council Regulation (EC) No 139/2004 of 20 January 2004 on the control of concentrations between undertakings (the EC Merger Regulation) (3), Commission Regulation (EC) No 773/2004 of 7 April 2004 relating to the conduct of proceedings by the Commission pursuant to Articles 81 and 82 of the EC Treaty (4), and Commission Regulation (EC) No 802/2004 of 7 April 2004 implementing Council Regulation (EC) No 139/2004 on the control of concentrations between undertakings (5), as well as in the relevant case-law of the Court of Justice. In particular, the right of the parties concerned to be heard before the adoption of any individual decision adversely affecting them is a fundamental right of European Union law recognised by the Charter of Fundamental Rights, and in particular Article 41 thereof (6).

(3) In order to ensure the effective exercise of the procedural rights of the parties concerned, other involved parties within the meaning of Article 11(b) of Regulation (EC) No 802/2004 (hereinafter «other involved parties»), complainants within the meaning of Article 7(2) of Regulation (EC) No 1/2003 (hereinafter «complainants») and persons other than those referred to in Articles 5 and 11 of Regulation (EC) No 773/2004 and third persons within the meaning of Article 11 of Regulation (EC) No 802/2004 (hereinafter «third persons») involved in competition proceedings, responsibility for safeguarding the observance of such rights should be entrusted to an independent person experienced in competition matters who has the integrity necessary to contribute to the objectivity, transparency and efficiency of those proceedings.

(4) The Commission created the function of hearing officer for these purposes in 1982, revised it in Commission Decision 94/810/ECSC, EC of 12 December 1994 on the terms of reference of hearing officers in competition procedures before the Commission (7) and in Commission Decision 2001/462/EC, ECSC of 23 May 2001 on the terms of reference of hearing officers in certain competition proceedings (8). It is now necessary to clarify and further strengthen the role of the hearing officer and to adapt the terms of reference of the hearing officer in the light of developments in Union competition law.

(5) The function of the hearing officer has been generally perceived as an important contribution to the competition proceedings before the Commission due to the independence and expertise that hearing officers have brought to these proceedings. In order to ensure the continued independence of the hearing officer from the Directorate-General for Competition, he or she should be attached, for administrative purposes, to the member of the Commission with special responsibility for competition.

(6) The hearing officer should be appointed in accordance with the rules laid down in the Staff Regulations of Officials and the Conditions of Employment of Other Servants of the European Union. In accordance with those rules, consideration may also be given to candidates who are not officials of the Commission. Transparency as regards the appointment, termination of appointment and transfer of hearing officers should be ensured.

(7) The Commission may appoint one or more hearing officers and should provide for their supporting staff. Where

the hearing officer perceives a conflict of interests in the performance of his or her functions, the hearing officer should cease from acting on a case. If the hearing officer is unable to act, his or her role should be carried out by another hearing officer.

(8) The hearing officer should operate as an independent arbiter who seeks to resolve issues affecting the effective exercise of the procedural rights of the parties concerned, other involved parties, complainants or interested third persons where such issues could not be resolved through prior contacts with the Commission services responsible for the conduct of competition proceedings, which must respect these procedural rights.

(9) The terms of reference of the hearing officer in competition proceedings should be framed in such a way as to safeguard the effective exercise of procedural rights throughout proceedings before the Commission pursuant to Articles 101 and 102 of the Treaty and Regulation (EC) No 139/2004, in particular the right to be heard.

(10) In order to strengthen this role, the hearing officer should be attributed with the function of safeguarding the effective exercise of procedural rights of undertakings and associations of undertakings in the context of the Commission's powers of investigation under Chapter V of Regulation (EC) No 1/2003, as well as pursuant to Article 14 of Regulation (EC) No 139/2004 which empowers the Commission to impose fines on undertakings and associations of undertakings. The hearing officer should also be attributed with specific functions during this investigative phase in relation to claims for legal professional privilege, the privilege against self-incrimination, deadlines for replying to decisions requesting information pursuant to Article 18(3) of Regulation (EC) No 1/2003, as well as with regard to the right of undertakings and associations of undertakings subject to an investigative measure by the Commission under Chapter V of Regulation (EC) No 1/2003 to be informed of their procedural status, namely whether they are subject to an investigation and, if so, the subject matter and purpose of that investigation. In assessing claims made in relation to privilege against self-incrimination, the hearing officer may consider whether undertakings make clearly unfounded claims for protection merely as a delaying tactic.

(11) The hearing officer should be able to facilitate the resolution of claims that a document is covered by legal professional privilege. To this end, if the undertaking or association of undertakings making the claim agrees, the hearing officer will be allowed to examine the document concerned and make an appropriate recommendation, referring to the applicable case-law of the Court of Justice.

(12) The hearing officer should be responsible for deciding whether a third person shows a sufficient interest to be heard. Consumer associations that apply to be heard should be generally regarded as having a sufficient interest, where the proceedings concern products or services used by end-consumers or products or services that constitute a direct input into such products or services.

(13) The hearing officer should decide whether to admit complainants and interested third persons to the oral hearing, taking into account the contribution they can make to the clarification of the relevant facts of the case.

(14) The right of the parties concerned to be heard before a final decision adversely affecting their interests is taken is guaranteed through their right to reply in writing to the preliminary position of the Commission, as set out in the statement of objections and their right to develop their arguments, if they so request, at the oral hearing. In order to exercise these rights effectively, parties to whom a statement of objections has been addressed have the right of access to the Commission's investigation file.

(15) In order to safeguard the effective exercise of the rights of defence of parties to whom a statement of objections has been addressed, the hearing officer should be responsible for ensuring that disputes about access to the file or about the protection of business secrets and other confidential information between those parties and the Commission's Directorate-General for Competition are resolved. In exceptional circumstances, the hearing officer may suspend the running of the time period in which an addressee of a statement of objections should reply to that statement until a dispute about access to file has been resolved, if the addressee would not be in a position to reply within the deadline granted and an extension would not be an adequate solution at that point in time.

(16) In order to safeguard the effective exercise of procedural rights while respecting the legitimate interests of confidentiality, the hearing officer should, where appropriate, be able to order specific measures for access to the Commission's file. In particular, the hearing officer should have the power to decide that parts of the file are made accessible to the party requesting access in a restricted manner, for example by limiting the number or category of persons having access, and the use of the information being accessed.

(17) The hearing officer should be responsible for deciding on requests for the extension of time limits set for the reply to a statement of objections, a supplementary statement of objections or a letter of facts or time limits within which other involved parties, complainants or interested third persons may make comments, in case of disagreement between any such person and the Directorate-General for Competition.

(18) The hearing officer should promote the effectiveness of the oral hearing, by, inter alia, taking all appropriate preparatory measures, including the circulation, in due time before the hearing, of a provisional list of participants and a provisional agenda.

(19) The oral hearing allows the parties to whom the Commission has addressed a statement of objections and other involved parties to further exercise their right to be heard by developing their arguments orally before the Commission, which should be represented by the Directorate-General for Competition as well as other services that contribute to the further preparation of a decision to be taken by the Commission. It should provide an additional opportunity to ensure that all relevant facts – whether favourable or unfavourable to the parties concerned, including the factual elements relating to the gravity and duration of the alleged infringement – are clarified as much as possible. The oral hearing should also allow the parties to present their arguments as to the matters that may be of importance for the possible imposition of fines.

(20) To ensure the effectiveness of oral hearings, the hearing officer may allow the parties to whom a statement of objections has been addressed, other involved parties, complainants, other persons invited to the hearing, the Commission services and the authorities of the Member States to ask questions during the hearing. The oral hearing should not be public so as to guarantee that all participants can express themselves freely. Therefore, informa-

tion disclosed during the oral hearing should not be used for a purpose other than judicial and/or administrative proceedings for the application of Articles 101 and 102 of the Treaty. Where justified to protect business secrets and other confidential information, the hearing officer should be able to hear persons in a closed session.

(21) Parties to the proceedings which offer commitments pursuant to Article 9 of Regulation (EC) No 1/2003, as well as parties which engage in settlement procedures in cartel cases pursuant to Article 10a of Regulation (EC) No 773/2004, should be able to call upon the hearing officer in relation to the effective exercise of their procedural rights.

(22) The hearing officer should report on the respect for the effective exercise of procedural rights throughout competition proceedings. Moreover, and separately from his or her reporting function, the hearing officer should also be able to make observations on the further progress and objectivity of the proceedings and thereby contribute to ensuring that competition proceedings are concluded on the basis of a sound assessment of all relevant facts.

(23) When disclosing information about natural persons, the hearing officer should have regard, in particular, to Regulation (EC) No 45/2001 of the European Parliament and of the Council of 18 December 2000 on the protection of individuals with regard to the processing of personal data by the Community institutions and bodies and on the free movement of such data (9).

(24) Decision 2001/462/EC, ECSC should be repealed, HAS DECIDED AS FOLLOWS:

(1) O.J. L 308, 8.12.2000, p. 26.
(2) O.J. L 1, 4.1.2003, p. 1.
(3) O.J. L 24, 29.1.2004, p. 1.
(4) O.J. L 123, 27.4.2004, p. 18.
(5) O.J. L 133, 30.4.2004, p. 1.
(6) O.J. C 303, 14.12.2007, p. 1.
(7) O.J. L 330, 21.12.1994, p. 67.
(8) O.J. L 162, 19.6.2001, p. 21.
(9) O.J. L 8, 12.1.2001, p. 1.

CHAPTER 1
ROLE, APPOINTMENT AND DUTIES OF THE HEARING OFFICER

Art. 1. *The Hearing Officer*

1. There shall be one or more hearing officers for competition proceedings, whose powers and functions are laid down in the present decision.

2. The hearing officer shall safeguard the effective exercise of procedural rights throughout competition proceedings before the Commission for the implementation of Articles 101 and 102 of the Treaty, and under Regulation (EC) No 139/2004 (hereinafter «competition proceedings»).

Art. 2. *Appointment, Termination of Appointment and Deputising*

1. The Commission shall appoint the hearing officer. The appointment shall be published in the *Official Journal of the European Union*. Any interruption, termination or transfer of the hearing officer shall be the subject of a reasoned decision of the Commission. That decision shall be published in the *Official Journal of the European Union*.

2. The hearing officer shall be attached, for administrative purposes, to the member of the Commission with special responsibility for competition (hereinafter «the competent member of the Commission»).

3. Where the hearing officer is unable to act, his or her role shall be carried out by another hearing officer. If no hearing officer is able to act, the competent member of the Commission, where appropriate after consultation of the hearing officer, shall designate another competent Commission official, who is not involved in the case in question, to carry out the hearing officer's duties.

4. In case of an actual or potential conflict of interests, the hearing officer shall refrain from acting on a case. Paragraph 3 shall apply.

Art. 3. *Method of Operation*

1. In exercising his or her functions, the hearing officer shall act independently.

2. In exercising his or her functions, the hearing officer shall take account of the need for effective application of the competition rules in accordance with Union legislation in force and the principles laid down by the Court of Justice.

3. In exercising his or her functions, the hearing officer shall have access to any files relating to competition proceedings.

4. The hearing officer shall be kept informed by the director responsible for investigating the case in the Directorate-General for Competition (hereinafter «the director responsible») about the development of the procedure.

5. The hearing officer may present observations on any matter arising out of any Commission competition proceeding to the competent member of the Commission.

6. If the hearing officer makes reasoned recommendations to the competent member of the Commission or takes decisions as foreseen in this decision, the hearing officer shall provide a copy of these documents to the director responsible and the Legal Service of the Commission.

7. Any issue regarding the effective exercise of the procedural rights of the parties concerned, other involved parties within the meaning of Article 11(b) of Regulation (EC) No 802/2004 (hereinafter «the other involved parties»), complainants within the meaning of Article 7(2) of Regulation (EC) No 1/2003 (hereinafter «complainants») and interested third persons within the meaning of Article 5 of this Decision involved in such proceedings shall first be raised by those persons with the Directorate-General for Competition. If the issue is not resolved, it may be referred to the hearing officer for independent review. Requests related to a measure for which a time limit applies must be made in due time, within the original time limit.

CHAPTER 2
INVESTIGATION

Art. 4. *Procedural rights in the investigation phase*

1. The hearing officer shall safeguard the effective exercise of procedural rights which arise in the context of the exercise of the Commission's powers of investigation under Chapter V of Regulation (EC) No 1/2003 and in proceedings that can result in the imposition of fines pursuant to Article 14 of Regulation (EC) No 139/2004.

2. In particular, the hearing officer shall have the following functions, subject to Article 3(7):

(a) the hearing officer may be asked by undertakings or associations of undertakings to examine claims that a document required by the Commission in the exercise of powers conferred on it pursuant to Article 18, 20 or 21 of Regulation (EC) No 1/2003, in inspections pursuant to Article 13 of Regulation (EC) No 139/2004 or in the context of investigatory measures in proceedings that can result in the imposition of fines pursuant to Article 14 of Regulation (EC) No 139/2004 and which was withheld from the Commission is covered by legal professional privilege, within the meaning of the case-law of the Court of Justice. The hearing officer may only review the matter if the undertaking or association of undertakings making the claim consent to the hearing officer viewing the information claimed to be covered by legal professional privilege as well as related documents that the hearing officer considers necessary for his or her review. Without revealing the potentially privileged content of the information, the hearing officer shall communicate to the director responsible and the undertaking or association of undertakings concerned his or her preliminary view, and may take appropriate steps to promote a mutually acceptable resolution. Where no resolution is reached, the hearing officer may formulate a reasoned recommendation to the competent member of the Commission, without revealing the potentially privileged content of the document. The party making the claim shall receive a copy of this recommendation;

(b) where the addressee of a request for information pursuant to Article 18(2) of Regulation (EC) No 1/2003 refuses to reply to a question in such a request invoking the privilege against self-incrimination, as determined by the case-law of the Court of Justice, it may refer the matter, in due time following the receipt of the request, to the hearing officer. In appropriate cases, and having regard to the need to avoid undue delay in proceedings, the hearing officer may make a reasoned recommendation as to whether the privilege against self-incrimination applies and inform the director responsible of the conclusions drawn, to be taken into account in case of any decision taken subsequently pursuant to Article 18(3) of Regulation (EC) No 1/2003. The addressee of the request shall receive a copy of the reasoned recommendation;

(c) where the addressee of a decision requesting information pursuant to Article 18(3) of Regulation (EC) No 1/2003 considers that the time limit imposed for its reply is too short, it may refer the matter to the hearing officer, in due time before the expiry of the original time limit set. The hearing officer shall decide on whether an extension of the time limit should be granted, taking account of the length and complexity of the request for information and the requirements of the investigation;

(d) undertakings or associations of undertakings subject to an investigative measure by the Commission under Chapter V of Regulation (EC) No 1/2003 shall have the right to be informed of their procedural status, namely whether they are subject to an investigation and, if so, the subject matter and purpose of that investigation. If such an undertaking or association of undertakings considers that it has not been properly informed by the Directorate-General for Competition of its procedural status, it may refer the matter to the hearing officer for resolution. The hearing officer shall take a decision that the Directorate-General for Competition will inform the undertaking or association of undertakings that made the request of their procedural status. This decision shall be communicated to the undertaking or association of undertakings that made the request.

CHAPTER 3

APPLICATIONS TO BE HEARD

Art. 5. *Interested third persons*

1. Applications to be heard from persons other than those referred to in Articles 5 and 11 of Regulation (EC) No 773/2004 and third persons within the meaning of Article 11 of Regulation (EC) No 802/2004 (hereinafter «third persons») shall be made in accordance with Article 13(1) of Regulation (EC) No 773/2004 and Article 16 of Regulation (EC) No 802/2004. Applications shall be submitted in writing and explain the applicant's interest in the outcome of the procedure.

2. The hearing officer shall decide as to whether third persons are to be heard after consulting the director responsible. In assessing whether a third person shows a sufficient interest, the hearing officer shall take into account whether and to what extent the applicant is sufficiently affected by the conduct which is the subject of the competition proceedings or whether the applicant fulfils the requirements of Article 18(4) of Regulation (EC) No 139/2004.

3. Where the hearing officer considers that an applicant has not shown a sufficient interest to be heard, he or she shall inform the applicant in writing of the reasons thereof. A time limit shall be fixed within which the applicant may make known its views in writing. If the applicant makes known its views in writing within the time limit set by the hearing officer and the written submission does not lead to a different assessment, that finding shall be stated in a reasoned decision which shall be notified to the applicant.

4. The hearing officer shall inform parties to competition proceedings as from the initiation of proceedings pursuant to Article 11(6) of Regulation (EC) No 1/2003 or Article 6(1)*(c)* of Regulation (EC) No 139/2004 of the identities of interested third persons to be heard, unless such disclosure would significantly harm a person or undertaking.

Art. 6. *Right to an oral hearing; participation of complainants and third persons in the oral hearing*

1. At the request of parties to whom the Commission has addressed a statement of objections or other involved parties, the hearing officer shall conduct an oral hearing so that such parties can further develop their written submissions.

2. The hearing officer may, where appropriate and after consulting the director responsible, decide to afford complainants and interested third persons within the meaning of Article 5 the opportunity to express their views at the oral hearing of the parties to which a statement of objections has been issued, provided they so request in their written comments. The hearing officer may also invite representatives from competition authorities from third countries to attend the oral hearing as observers in accordance with agreements concluded between the Union and third countries.

CHAPTER 4
ACCESS TO FILE, CONFIDENTIALITY AND BUSINESS SECRETS

Art. 7. *Access to File and Access to Documents and Information*

1. Where a party which has exercised its right of access to the file has reason to believe that the Commission has in its possession documents which have not been disclosed to it and that those documents are necessary for the proper exercise of the right to be heard, it may make a reasoned request for access to these documents to the hearing officer, subject to Article 3(7).

2. Subject to Article 3(7), other involved parties, complainants and interested third persons within the meaning of Article 5 may make a reasoned request to the hearing officer in the circumstances listed hereafter:

(a) other involved parties who have reason to believe that they have not been informed of the objections addressed to the notifying parties in accordance with Article 13(2) of Regulation (EC) No 802/2004;

(b) a complainant who has been informed by the Commission of its intention to reject a complaint pursuant to Article 7(1) of Regulation (EC) No 773/2004 and has reason to believe that the Commission has in its possession documents which have not been disclosed to it and that those documents are necessary for the proper exercise of its rights in accordance with Article 8(1) of Regulation (EC) No 773/2004;

(c) a complainant who considers that it has not received a copy of the non-confidential version of the statement of objections in accordance with Article 6(1) of Regulation (EC) No 773/2004 or that the non-confidential version of the statement of objections has not been established in a manner which enables it to exercise its rights effectively, with the exception of cases where the settlement procedure applies;

(d) an interested third person within the meaning of Article 5 of this Decision who has reason to believe that it has not been informed of the nature and subject matter of a procedure in accordance with Article 13(1) of Regulation (EC) No 773/2004 and Article 16(1) of Regulation (EC) No 802/2004. The same applies to a complainant in a case to which the settlement procedure applies who has reason to believe that it has not been informed of the nature and subject matter of the procedure in accordance with Article 6(1) of Regulation (EC) No 773/2004.

3. The hearing officer shall take a reasoned decision on a request addressed to him or her under paragraph 1 or 2 and communicate such decision to the person that made the request and to any other person concerned by the procedure.

Art. 8. *Business secrets and other confidential information*

1. Where the Commission intends to disclose information which may constitute a business secret or other confidential information of any undertaking or person, the latter shall be informed in writing of this intention and the reasons thereof by the Directorate-General for Competition. A time limit shall be fixed within which the undertaking or person concerned may submit any written comments.

2. Where the undertaking or person concerned objects to the disclosure of the information it may refer the matter to the hearing officer. If the hearing officer finds that the information may be disclosed because it does not constitute a business secret or other confidential information or because there is an overriding interest in its disclosure that finding shall be stated in a reasoned decision which shall be notified to the undertaking or person concerned. The decision shall specify the date after which the information will be disclosed. This date shall not be less than 1 week from the date of notification.

3. Paragraphs 1 and 2 shall apply *mutatis mutandis* to the disclosure of information by publication in the *Official Journal of the European Union*.

4. Where appropriate in order to balance the effective exercise of a party's rights of defence with legitimate interests of confidentiality, the hearing officer may decide that parts of the file which are indispensable for the exercise of the party's rights of defence will be made accessible to the party requesting access in a restricted manner, the details of which shall be determined by the hearing officer.

CHAPTER 5
EXTENSION OF TIME LIMITS

Art. 9. *Requests for extension of time limits*

1. If an addressee of a statement of objections considers that the time limit imposed for its reply to the statement of objections is too short, it may seek an extension of that time limit by means of a reasoned request addressed to the director responsible. Such a request must be made in due time before the expiry of the original time limit in proceedings pursuant to Articles 101 and 102 of the Treaty and at least 5 working days before the expiry of the original time limit in proceedings under Regulation (EC) No 139/2004. If such a request is not granted or the addressee of the statement of objections making the request disagrees with the length of the extension granted, it may refer the matter to the hearing officer for review before the expiry of the original time limit. After hearing the director responsible, the hearing officer shall decide on whether an extension of the time limit is necessary to allow the addressee of a statement of objections to exercise its right to be heard effectively, while also having regard to the need to avoid undue delay in proceedings. In proceedings pursuant to Articles 101 and 102 of the Treaty, the hearing officer shall take into account, among others, the following elements:

(a) the size and complexity of the file;

(b) whether the addressee of the statement of objections making the request has had prior access to information;

(c) any other objective obstacles which may be faced by the addressee of the statement of objections making the request in providing its observations.

For the purposes of assessing point *(a)* of the first subparagraph, the number of infringements, the alleged duration of the infringement(s), the size and number of documents and the size and complexity of expert studies may be taken into consideration.

2. If other involved parties, a complainant or an interested third person within the meaning of Article 5 considers that the time limit to make its views known is too short, it may seek an extension of that time limit by means of a reasoned request addressed to the director responsible in due time before the expiry of the original time limit. If such a request is not granted or the other involved party, complainant or interested third person disagrees with this decision, it may refer the matter to the hearing officer for review. After hearing the director responsible, the hearing officer shall decide on whether an extension of the time limit should be granted.

CHAPTER 6
THE ORAL HEARING

Art. 10. *Organisation and function*

1. The hearing officer shall organise and conduct the hearings provided for in the provisions implementing Articles 101 and 102 of the Treaty and Regulation (EC) No 139/2004.

2. The oral hearing shall be conducted by the hearing officer in full independence.

3. The hearing officer shall ensure that the hearing is properly conducted and shall contribute to the objectivity of the hearing itself and of any decision taken subsequently.

4. The hearing officer shall ensure that the oral hearing provides addressees of the statement of objections, other involved parties, as well as complainants and interested third persons within the meaning of Article 5 which have been admitted to the oral hearing, with sufficient opportunity to develop their views as to the preliminary findings of the Commission.

Art. 11. *Preparation of the oral hearing*

1. The hearing officer shall be responsible for the preparation of the oral hearing and shall take all appropriate measures in that regard. In order to ensure the proper preparation of the oral hearing, the hearing officer may, after consulting the director responsible, supply in advance to the persons invited to the hearing a list of questions on which they are invited to make known their views. The hearing officer may also indicate to the persons invited to the hearing the focal areas for debate, having regard, in particular, to the facts and issues that the addressees of a statement of objections who have requested an oral hearing want to raise.

2. For this purpose, after consulting the director responsible, the hearing officer may hold a meeting with the persons invited to the hearing and, where appropriate, the Commission services, in order to prepare for the hearing itself.

3. The hearing officer may also ask for prior written notification of the essential contents of the intended statements of persons invited to the hearing.

4. The hearing officer may set a time limit for all persons invited to the oral hearing to provide a list of participants who will attend on their behalf. The hearing officer shall make this list available to all persons invited to the oral hearing in due time before the date of the hearing.

Art. 12. *Timing and conduct*

1. After consulting the director responsible, the hearing officer shall determine the date, the duration and the place of the hearing. Where a postponement is requested, the hearing officer shall decide whether or not to allow it.

2. The hearing officer shall decide whether new documents should be admitted during the hearing and which persons should be heard on behalf of a party.

3. The hearing officer may allow the parties to whom a statement of objections has been addressed, other involved parties, complainants, other persons invited to the hearing, the Commission services and the authorities of the Member States to ask questions during the hearing. To the extent that, exceptionally, a question cannot be answered in whole or in part at the oral hearing, the hearing officer may allow the reply to be given in writing within a set time limit. Such written reply shall be distributed to all participants in the oral hearing, unless the hearing officer decides otherwise in order to protect the rights of defence of an addressee of a statement of objections or the business secrets or other confidential information of any person.

4. Where required by the need to ensure the right to be heard, the hearing officer may, after consulting the director responsible, afford the parties concerned, other involved parties, complainants or interested third persons within the meaning of Article 5 the opportunity to submit further written comments after the oral hearing. The hearing officer shall fix a date by which such submissions may be made. The Commission shall not be obliged to take into account written comments received after that date.

Art. 13. *Protection of business secrets and confidentiality at the oral hearing*

Each person shall normally be heard in the presence of all other persons invited to attend the oral hearing. The hearing officer may also decide to hear persons separately in a closed session, having regard to their legitimate interest in the protection of their business secrets and other confidential information.

CHAPTER 7
INTERIM REPORT AND RIGHT TO MAKE OBSERVATIONS

Art. 14. *Interim report and observations*

1. The hearing officer shall submit an interim report to the competent member of the Commission on the hearing and the conclusions he or she draws with regard to the respect for the effective exercise of procedural rights. The observations in this report shall concern procedural issues including the following:

(a) disclosure of documents and access to the file;

(b) time limits for replying to the statement of objections;

(c) the observance of the right to be heard;

(d) the proper conduct of the oral hearing.

A copy of the report shall be given to the Director-General for Competition, to the director responsible and to the other competent services of the Commission.

2. In addition to, and separately from, the report referred to in paragraph 1, the hearing officer may make observations on the further progress and impartiality of the proceedings. In so doing, the hearing officer shall seek to ensure in particular that, in the preparation of draft Commission decisions, due account is taken of all the relevant facts, whether favourable or unfavourable to the parties concerned, including the factual elements relevant to the gravity and duration of any infringement. Such observations may relate to, inter alia, the need for further information, the withdrawal of certain objections, the formulation of further objections or suggestions for further investigative measures pursuant to Chapter V of Regulation (EC) No 1/2003.

The Director-General for Competition, the director responsible and the Legal Service shall be informed of such observations.

CHAPTER 8
COMMITMENTS AND SETTLEMENTS

Art. 15. *Commitments and settlements*

1. Parties to the proceedings which offer commitments to meet the concerns expressed to them by the Commission in its preliminary assessment pursuant to Article 9 of Regulation (EC) No 1/2003 may call upon the hearing officer at

any stage in the procedure pursuant to Article 9, in order to ensure the effective exercise of their procedural rights.

2. Parties to proceedings in cartel cases which engage in settlement discussions pursuant to Article 10a of Regulation (EC) No 773/2004 may call upon the hearing officer at any stage during the settlement procedure in order to ensure the effective exercise of their procedural rights.

CHAPTER 9
FINAL REPORT

Art. 16. *Content and transmission prior to the adoption of a decision*

1. The hearing officer shall, on the basis of the draft decision to be submitted to the Advisory Committee in the case in question, prepare a final report in writing on the respect for the effective exercise of procedural rights, as referred to in Article 14(1), at any stage of the proceedings. That report will also consider whether the draft decision deals only with objections in respect of which the parties have been afforded the opportunity of making known their views.

2. The final report shall be submitted to the competent member of the Commission, the Director-General for Competition, the director responsible and the other competent services of the Commission. It shall be communicated to the competent authorities of the Member States and, in accordance with the provisions on cooperation laid down in Protocols 23 and 24 of the EEA Agreement, to the EFTA Surveillance Authority.

Art. 17. *Submission to the Commission and publication*

1. The hearing officer's final report shall be presented to the Commission together with the draft decision submitted to it, in order to ensure that, when it reaches a decision on an individual case, the Commission is fully apprised of all relevant information as to the course of the procedure and that the effective exercise of procedural rights has been respected throughout the proceedings.

2. The final report may be modified by the hearing officer in the light of any amendments to the draft decision prior to its adoption by the Commission.

3. The Commission shall communicate the hearing officer's final report, together with the decision, to the addressees of the decision. It shall publish the hearing officer's final report in the *Official Journal of the European Union*, together with the decision, having regard to the legitimate interest of undertakings in the protection of their business secrets.

CHAPTER 10
FINAL PROVISIONS

Art. 18. *Repeal and transitional provision*

1. Decision 2001/462/EC, ECSC is repealed.

2. Procedural steps already taken under Decision 2001/462/EC, ECSC shall continue to have effect. In relation to investigatory measures that were taken before the entry into force of this Decision, the hearing officer may decline to exercise his or her powers pursuant to Article 4.

In cases where the initiation of proceedings pursuant to Article 11(6) of Regulation (EC) No 1/2003 or the initiation of proceedings pursuant to Article 6(1)(c) of Regulation (EC) No 139/2004 took place before the entry into force of the present Decision, the interim report pursuant to Article 14 of the present Decision and the final report pursuant to Article 16 shall not cover the investigation phase, unless the hearing officer decides otherwise.

Art. 19. *Entry into force*

This Decision shall enter into force on the day following its publication in the *Official Journal of the European Union*.

Commission notice 20 October 2011 Best practices for the conduct of proceedings concerning Articles 101 and 102 TFEU

(O.J. C 308, 20 October 2011, p. 6)

1. SCOPE AND PURPOSE OF THE NOTICE

1. The principal purpose of this notice is to provide practical guidance on the conduct of proceedings before the European Commission (Commission) concerning Articles 101 and 102 of the Treaty on the Functioning of the European Union (TFEU) (1) in accordance with Regulation (EC) No 1/2003 (2), its Implementing Regulation (3) and the case law of the Court of Justice of the European Union. In this regard, the notice seeks to increase understanding of the Commission's investigation process (4) and thereby enhance the efficiency of investigations and ensure a high degree of transparency and predictability in the process. The notice covers the main proceedings (5) concerning alleged infringements of Articles 101 and 102 TFEU.

(1) With effect from 1 December 2009, Articles 81 and 82 of the EC Treaty have become Articles 101 and 102 respectively of the TFEU. The two sets of provisions are in substance identical. For the purposes of this document, references to Articles 101 and 102 TFEU should be understood as references to Articles 81 and 82 of the EC Treaty when appropriate.

(2) Council Regulation (EC) No 1/2003 of 16 December 2002 on the implementation of the rules on competition laid down in Articles 81 and 82 of the Treaty (O.J. L 1, 4.1.2003, p. 1), as amended by Council Regulation (EC) No 411/2004 of 26 February 2004 repealing Regulation (EEC) No 3975/87 and amending Regulations (EEC) No 3976/87 and (EC) No 1/2003, in connection with air transport between the Community and third countries (O.J. L 68, 6.3.2004, p. 1) and Council Regulation (EC) No 1419/2006 of 25 September 2006 repealing Regulation (EEC) No 4056/86 laying down detailed rules for the application of Articles 85 and 86 of the Treaty to maritime transport, and amending Regulation (EC) No 1/2003 as regards the extension of its scope to include cabotage and international tramp services (O.J. L 269, 28.9.2006, p. 1).

(3) Commission Regulation (EC) No 773/2004 of 7 April 2004 relating to the conduct of proceedings by the Commission pursuant to Articles 81 and 82 of the EC Treaty (O.J. L 123, 27.4.2004, p. 18), as amended by Commission Regulation (EC) No 622/2008 of 30 June 2008 amending Regulation (EC) No 773/2004, as regards the conduct of settlement procedures in cartel cases (O.J. L 171, 1.7.2008, p. 3).

(4) This notice applies exclusively to the Commission's procedures for the enforcement of Articles 101 and 102 TFEU and does not concern the national competition authorities when they apply these provisions.

(5) This notice does not deal with specific procedures, for example for imposing fines on undertakings having provided misleading information, refused to submit to inspections or breached seals affixed by officials (see Article 23(1) of Regulation (EC) No 1/2003). It covers neither decisions on interim measures pursuant to Article 8 of Regulation (EC) No 1/2003 nor decisions on finding of inapplicability pursuant to Article 10 of Regulation (EC) No 1/2003.

2. Infringement proceedings against Member States based notably on Article 106 TFEU in conjunction with Articles 101 and 102 TFEU fall outside the scope of this notice. Nor does it apply to proceedings under the Merger Regulation (6) or to State aid proceedings (7).

(6) See Council Regulation (EC) No 139/2004 of 20 January 2004 on the control of concentrations between undertakings (O.J. L 24, 29.1.2004, p. 1). See in this respect the Directorate-General for Competition's Best Practices on the conduct of EC Merger Proceedings of 20 January 2004, published on the Directorate-General for Competition's website (http://ec.europa.eu/competition/mergers/legislation/proceedings.pdf).

(7) See Council Regulation (EC) No 659/1999 of 22 March 1999 laying down detailed rules for the application of Article 93 (now Article 108 TFEU) of the EC Treaty (O.J. L 83, 27.3.1999, p. 1). See in this respect the Commission notice on a Code of Best Practice for the conduct of State aid control procedures (O.J. C 136, 16.6.2009, p. 13).

3. Proceedings concerning the application of Articles 101 and 102 TFEU (hereafter generally referred to as «proceedings») are in particular regulated by Regulation (EC) No 1/2003 and the Implementing Regulation. The Commission's notices on access to file (8) and handling of complaints (9), as well as the terms of reference of the hearing officer (10) are also relevant for the conduct of proceedings. As regards submissions of reports of economic experts and submission of quantitative data, reference is made to the Best Practices on the submission of economic evidence (11). This notice should therefore not be taken as an exhaustive account of all measures governing proceedings before the Commission. The notice should be read in conjunction with other such instruments and any relevant jurisprudence.

(8) Commission notice on the rules for access to the Commission file in cases pursuant to Articles 81 and 82 of the EC Treaty, Articles 53, 54 and 57 of the EEA Agreement and Council Regulation (EC) No 139/2004 (O.J. C 325, 22.12.2005, p. 7).

(9) Commission notice on the handling of complaints by the Commission under Articles 81 and 82 of the EC Treaty (O.J. C 101, 27.4.2004, p. 65).

(10) Decision C(2011) 5742 of the President of the European Commission of 13 October 2011 on the function and terms of reference of the hearing officer in certain competition proceedings.

(11) Staff working paper on Best Practices for the submission of economic evidence and data collection in cases concerning the application of Articles 101 and 102 TFEU and merger cases, http://ec.europa.eu/competition/index_en.html

4. The investigation of cartels, as defined in the Leniency Notice (12), may also be subject to the specific procedures on applications for leniency and on settlements (13). These specific procedures are not covered by this notice. Moreover, the particular nature of cartel proceedings in some circumstances requires special provisions, in order not to interfere with possible leniency applications (14) or settlement discussions (15). These special provisions are indicated where applicable.

(12) Commission notice on immunity from fines and reduction of fines in cartel cases (O.J. C 298, 8.12.2006, p. 17) (Leniency Notice), i.e. secret «agreements and/or concerted practices between two or more competitors aimed at coordinating their competitive behaviour on the market and/or influencing the relevant parameters of competition through practices such as the fixing of purchase or selling prices or other trading conditions, the allocation of production or sales quotas, the sharing of markets including bid-rigging, restrictions of imports or exports and/or anti-competitive actions against other competitors. Such practices are among the most serious violations of (Article 101 TFEU)».

(13) Commission Regulation (EC) No 622/2008 of 30 June 2008 amending Regulation (EC) No 773/2004, as regards the conduct of settlement procedures in cartel cases (O.J. L 171, 1.7.2008, p. 3); Commission notice on the conduct of settlement procedures in view of the adoption of Decisions pursuant to Article 7 and Article 23 of Council Regulation (EC) No 1/2003 in cartel cases O.J. C 167, 2.7.2008, p. 1.

(14) It should be noted that the Commission may disregard any application for immunity from fines on the ground that it has been submitted after the statement of objections has been issued (see paragraphs 14 and 29 of the Leniency Notice).

(15) The Commission may disregard any application for immunity from fines or reductions of fines under the Leniency Notice on the ground that it has been submitted after the expiry of the time limit set for parties to declare in writing whether they envisage engaging in settlement discussions (see paragraph 13 of the Settlement Notice).

5. This notice is structured in the following way. Section 2 sets out the procedure followed during the investigative phase. This part is relevant for any investigation regardless of whether it leads to a prohibition decision (Article 7 of Regulation (EC) No 1/2003), a commitment decision (Article 9 of Regulation (EC) No 1/2003) or a rejection of complaint decision (Article 7 of the Implementing Regulation). Section 3 describes the main procedural steps and rights of defence in the context of procedures leading to prohibition decisions. Section 4 describes the specific features of the commitment procedure. Section 5 covers rejection of complaints. The remaining sections are of general application: Section 6 describes the limits to use of information, Section 7 deals with the adoption, notification and publication of decisions and Section 8 with future revisions.

6. This notice is notably built upon the experience to date in the application of Regulation (EC) No 1/2003 and the Implementing Regulation. It reflects the views of the Commission at the time of publication and will be applied as from the date of publication for pending (16) and future cases. The specific features of an individual case may however require an adaptation of, or deviation from this notice, depending on the case at issue.

(16) With regard to cases which are pending at the time of the publication of this document, the latter will apply to any procedural steps that remain to be taken after publication.

7. This notice does not create any new rights or obligations, nor alter, the rights or obligations which arise from the Treaty on the Functioning of the European Union (TFEU), Regulation (EC) No 1/2003, the Implementing Regulation and the case law of the Court of Justice of the European Union.

8. The Commission encourages the use of electronic information (e-mails or digital devices) for any case-related correspondence.

2. THE INVESTIGATIVE PHASE

2.1. Origin of cases

9. A case concerning an alleged infringement of Article 101 or 102 TFEU may be based on a complaint by undertakings, other natural and legal persons and even Member States.

10. Information from citizens and undertakings is important in triggering investigations by the Commission. The Commission therefore encourages citizens and undertakings to inform it about suspected infringements of the competition rules (17). This can be done either by lodging a formal complaint (18) or by simply providing market information to the Commission. Anyone who is able to show a legitimate interest as a complainant, and who submits a complaint in compliance with form C (19), enjoys certain procedural rights. The details of the procedure to be followed are set out in the Implementing Regulation and in the notice on the handling of complaints. Natural and legal persons, other than complainants, which show a sufficient interest to be heard and which are admitted to the proceedings by the hearing officer also enjoy certain procedural rights in accordance with Article 13 of the Implementing Regulation.

(17) Or, when appropriate, the relevant national competition authority.

(18) Pursuant to Article 7(2) of Regulation (EC) No 1/2003. Under Articles 5 to 9 of the Implementing Regulation, formal complaints have to fulfil certain requirements. Information contained in submissions that do not respect these requirements may nevertheless be taken into account as market information.

(19) See Article 5(1) of the Implementing Regulation.

11. The Commission may also open a case on its own initiative (*ex officio*). It may do so when certain facts have been brought to its attention, or further to information gathered in the context of sector enquiries, informal meetings with industry, monitoring of markets or on the basis of information exchanged within the European Competition Network (ECN) or with competition authorities of third countries. Cartel cases can also be initiated on the basis of an application for leniency by one of the cartel members.

2.2. Initial assessment and case allocation

12. All cases, irrespective of their origin, are subject to an initial assessment phase. During this phase the Commission examines whether the case merits further investigation (20) and, if so, provisionally defines its focus, in particular with regard to the parties, the markets and the conduct to be investigated. During this phase, the Commission may make use of investigative measures such as requests for information in accordance with Article 18(2) of Regulation (EC) No 1/2003.

(20) The Court of Justice of the European Union has recognised that the Commission is entitled to give differing degrees of priority to the complaints that it receives. This is settled case law since Case T-24/90, Automec v Commission (hereinafter «Automec II») (1992) ECR II-2223, para 85.

13. In practice, the system of initial assessment means that some cases will be discarded at a very early stage because they are not deemed to merit further investigation. In this regard, the Commission focuses its enforcement resources on cases where it appears likely that an infringement may be found, in particular on cases with the most significant impact on the functioning of competition in the internal market and risk of consumer harm, as well as on cases which are likely to contribute to defining EU competition policy and/or to ensuring the coherent application of Articles 101 and/or 102 TFEU (21).

(21) The Commission has made public a non-exhaustive list of criteria which it intends to use when examining whether or not complaints show a sufficient «European Union interest». The criteria were published in the Annual Report on Competition Policy 2005, adopted in June 2006. See as well paragraph 44 of the notice on handling of complaints.

14. This initial assessment phase also attempts to address, at an early stage, the allocation of cases within the ECN. Regulation (EC) No 1/2003 introduced the possibility of reallocating cases to other network members if they are well placed to deal with them. Accordingly, the Commission may reallocate a case to a national competition authority and vice versa (22).

(22) See paragraphs 5 to 15 of the Commission notice on cooperation within the Network of Competition Authorities (O.J. C 101, 27.4.2004, p. 43).

15. When the first investigative measure is addressed to them (normally a request for information (23) or an inspection), addressees are informed of the fact that they are subject to a preliminary investigation and about the subject matter and purpose of such investigation. In the context of requests for information, they will further be reminded that if the behaviour under investigation is confirmed to have taken place this might constitute an infringement of Articles 101 and/or 102 TFEU. After having received a request for information or being subject to an inspection, parties (24) may at any time inquire with the Directorate-General for Competition about the status of the investigation, including before the opening of proceedings. If such an undertaking considers that it has not been properly informed by the Directorate-General for Competition of its procedural status, it may refer the matter to the hearing officer for resolution, after having raised the matter with the Directorate-General for Competition (25). The hearing officer shall take a decision that the Directorate-General for Competition will inform the undertaking or association of undertakings that made the request of their procedural status. This decision shall be communicated to the undertaking or association of undertakings that made the request. If at any stage during the initial assessment phase, the Commission decides not to investigate the case further (and thus not to open proceedings), the Commission will, at its own initiative, inform the party subject to the preliminary investigation thereof.

(23) See Case T-99/04 AC Treuhand v Commission (2008) ECR II-1501, para. 56.

(24) In this notice, «parties» are defined as the parties subject to the investigation. If not explicitly mentioned, «parties» does not include complainants and admitted third persons (also referred to as «third parties» in this notice).

(25) Article 4(2)(d) of the terms of reference of the hearing officer.

16. In cases based on a complaint, the Commission will endeavour to inform complainants within four months from the receipt of the complaint of the action that it proposes to take with regard to the complaint (26). This time frame is indicative and will depend on the circumstances of the individual case and whether the Directorate-General for Competition has received sufficient information from the complainant or third parties, notably in response to its requests for information, in order for it to decide whether or not to investigate the case further.

(26) Notice on the handling of complaints, paragraph 61.

2.3. Opening of proceedings

17. The Commission will open proceedings (27) under Article 11(6) of Regulation (EC) No 1/2003 when the initial assessment leads to the conclusion that the case merits further investigation and where the scope of the investigation has been sufficiently defined.

(27) According to Article 2 of the Implementing Regulation, the Commission may decide to initiate proceedings with a view to adopting a decision (e.g. a decision finding an infringement or a commitment decision) at any point in time, but no later than the date on which it issues a statement of objections, a preliminary assessment (as referred to in Article 9(1) of Regulation (EC) No 1/2003) or a notice pursuant to Article 27(4) of Regulation (EC) No 1/2003, whichever is the earlier.

18. The opening of proceedings determines the allocation of the case within the ECN (28) and in relation to the parties and the complainant, if applicable. It also signals a commitment on the part of the Commission to further investigate the case. The Commission will thus allocate resources to the case and will endeavour to deal with the case in a timely manner.

(28) The opening of proceedings relieves the national competition authorities of their competence to apply Articles 101 and 102 TFEU, see Article 11(6) of Regulation (EC) No 1/2003.

19. The decision to open proceedings identifies the parties subject to the proceedings and briefly describes the scope of the investigation. In particular, it sets out the behaviour constituting the alleged infringement of Articles 101 and/or 102 TFEU to be covered by the investigation and normally identifies the territory and sector(s) where that behaviour takes place.

20. Pursuant to Article 2 of the Implementing Regulation, the Commission may make the opening of proceedings public. The Commission's policy is to publish the opening of proceedings on the website of the Directorate-General for Competition and issue a press release, unless such publication may harm the investigation.

21. The parties subject to the investigation are informed orally or in writing of the opening of proceedings sufficiently in advance before the opening of proceedings is made public so as to enable them to prepare their own communication (in particular in relation to shareholders, the financial institutions and the press).

22. It should be emphasised that the opening of proceedings does not prejudge in any way the existence of an infringement. It merely indicates that the Commission will further pursue the case. This important clarification will be mentioned in the decision opening the proceedings (notified to the parties), as well as in all public communications concerning the opening of the case.

23. The opening of proceedings does not limit the right of the Commission to extend the scope and/or the addressees of the investigation at a later point in time. In case of such an extension of the scope of the investigation, the measures in paragraphs (20) to (21) apply.

24. In cartel cases, the opening of proceedings normally takes place simultaneously with the adoption of the Statement of Objections (see paragraph (4) above), though it may take place earlier.

2.4. Languages

25. Pursuant to Article 3 of Regulation No 1 (29), documents which the Commission sends to an undertaking based in the European Union will be drafted in the language of the Member State in which the undertaking is based.

(29) EEC Council: Regulation No 1 determining the languages to be used by the European Economic Community (O.J. 17, 6.10.1958, p. 385; Consolidated version of 1.1.2007).

26. Pursuant to Article 2 of that same Regulation, documents which an undertaking sends to the Commission may be drafted in any one of the official languages of the European Union selected by the sender. The reply and subsequent correspondence will be drafted in the same language.

27. In order to avoid delays due to translation, the addressees may waive their right to receive the text in the language resulting from the above rule and opt for another language. Duly authorised language waivers can be given for some specific documents and/or for the whole procedure.

28. As regards simple requests for information it is standard practice to send the cover letter in the language of the addressee's location or in English (including a reference to Article 3 of Regulation No 1) and to attach the questionnaire in English. The addressee is also clearly informed – in the language of the addressee's location – of its right to obtain a translation of the cover letter and/or questionnaire into the language of the addressee's location, as well as the right to reply in that language. This practice allows for more expeditious treatment of information requests, while preserving the rights of addressees.

29. The Statement of Objections, Preliminary Assessment and decisions pursuant to Articles 7, 9 and 23(2) of Regulation (EC) No 1/2003 are notified in the authentic language of the addressee unless it has signed the above mentioned language waiver.

30. Pursuant to Article 2 of Regulation No 1, the reply and the subsequent correspondence addressed to the complainant will be in the language of their complaint.

31. Participants in the oral hearing may request to be heard in an EU official language other than the language of proceedings. In that case, interpretation will be provided during the oral hearing, as long as sufficient advance notice of this requirement is given to the hearing officer.

2.5. Information requests

32. Pursuant to Article 18 of Regulation (EC) No 1/2003, the Commission is empowered to require undertakings and associations of undertakings to provide it with all necessary information. Information can be requested by letter («simple request» (Article 18(2)) or by decision (Article 18(3)) (30). It should be underlined that requests for information are regularly sent not only to the undertakings under investigation, but also to other undertakings or associations of undertakings which may have information relevant for the case.

(30) Non-respect of an Article 18(3) decision requesting information (supplying incomplete information or not respecting the time limit set out) can lead to fines and periodic penalties, see Articles 23 and 24 of Regulation (EC) No 1/2003. Submitting incorrect or misleading information may lead to fines being imposed both in case of an Article 18(2) letter and an Article 18(3) decision (see Article 23 of Regulation (EC) No 1/2003).

2.5.1. Scope of request for information

33. Pursuant to Article 18 of Regulation (EC) No 1/2003, the Commission may require undertakings and associations of undertakings to provide all necessary information. Information is necessary, in particular, if it may enable the Commission to verify the existence of the alleged infringement referred to in the request. The Commission enjoys a margin of appreciation in this respect (31).

(31) As regards the Commission's discretion in shaping the enquiry, see Case T-141/94 Thyssen Stahl v Commission (1999) ECR II-347, paragraph 110; Case T-9/99 HFB and Others v Commission (2002) ECR II-1487, paragraph 384; Case T-48/00 Corus UK v Commission (2004) ECR II-2325, paragraph 212. In exercising its discretion, the Commission is bound by the principle of proportionality and, in relation to Article 18(3) decisions, must respect the privilege against self-incrimination.

34. It is for the Commission to define the scope and the format of the request for information. Where appropriate, the Directorate-General for Competition might however discuss with the addressees the scope and the format of the request for information. This may be particularly useful in cases of requests concerning quantitative data (32).

(32) See the Best Practices on the submission of economic evidence.

35. When, in a reply to a request for information, undertakings submit manifestly irrelevant information (in particular documents which are clearly not related to the subject matter of the investigation), the Directorate-General for Competition may, in order not to unnecessarily burden the often voluminous administrative file, return such information to the addressee of the request as early as possible after having received the reply. A short notice reporting this fact will be put in the file.

2.5.2. Self-incrimination

36. Where the addressee of a request for information pursuant to Article 18(2) of Regulation (EC) No 1/2003 refuses to reply to a question in such a request invoking the privilege against self-incrimination, as defined by the case law of the Court of Justice of the European Union (33), it may refer the matter in due time following the receipt of the request to the hearing officer, after having raised the matter with the Directorate-General for Competition before the expiry of the original time limit set (34). In appropriate cases, and having regard to the need to avoid undue delay in proceedings, the hearing officer may make a reasoned recommendation as to whether the privilege against self-incrimination applies and inform the director responsible for the conclusions drawn, to be taken into account in case of any decision taken subsequently pursuant to Article 18(3) of Regulation (EC) No 1/2003. The addressee of the request shall receive a copy of the reasoned recommendation. The addressee of an Article 18(3) decision will be reminded of the privilege against self-incrimination as defined by case law of the Court of Justice of the European Union (35).

(33) See for example Case C-301/04 P Commission v SGL, (2006) ECR I-5915, which specifies that addressees of an Article 18(3) decision may be required to provide pre-existing documents, such as minutes of cartel meetings, even if those documents may incriminate the party providing them.

(34) Article 4(2)(b) of the terms of reference of the hearing officer.

(35) See footnote 33.

2.5.3. Time limits

37. The request for information specifies which information is required and fixes the time limit within which the information is to be provided.

38. Addressees are given a reasonable time limit to reply to the request, according to the length and complexity of the request taking into account the requirements of the investigation. In general, this time limit will be at least two weeks from the receipt of the request. If from the outset, it is considered that a longer period is required, the time limit to reply to the request will be set accordingly. When the scope of the request is limited, for example if it only covers a short clarification of information previously provided or information readily available to the addressee of the request, the time limit will normally be shorter (one week or less).

39. If they have difficulties responding within the time limit set, addressees may ask for it to be extended. A reasoned request should be made or confirmed in writing (letter or e-mail), sufficiently in advance of the expiry of the time limit. If the Commission considers the request to be justified, additional time (depending on the complexity of the information asked and other factors) will be granted. The Commission may also agree with the addressee of the request that certain parts of the requested information that are of particular importance or easily available for the addressee will be supplied within a shorter time limit, whereas additional time will be granted for supplying the remaining information.

40. Where the addressee of a decision requesting information pursuant to Article 18(3) Regulation (EC) No 1/2003 is unable to resolve its concerns about the time limit through the procedure outlined above, it may refer the matter to the hearing officer. Such a request should be made in due time before the expiry of the original time limit set (36). The hearing officer shall decide on whether an extension of the time limit should be granted, taking account of the length and complexity of the request for information and the requirements of the investigation.

(36) Article 4(2)(c) of the terms of reference of the hearing officer.

2.5.4. Confidentiality

41. The cover letter of the request for information also requires the addressee to indicate whether it considers that information provided in the reply is confidential. In that case, in accordance with Article 16(3) of the Implementing Regulation, the addressee must substantiate its claims individually with regard to each item of information and provide a non-confidential version of the information. Such a non-confidential version shall be provided in the same format as the confidential information, replacing deleted passages by summaries thereof. Unless otherwise agreed, a non-confidential version should be provided at the same time as the original submission. If undertakings fail to comply with these requirements, the Commission may assume that the documents or statements concerned do not contain confidential information pursuant to Article 16(4) of the Implementing Regulation.

2.5.5. Meetings and other contacts with the parties and third parties

42. During the investigative phase, the Directorate-General for Competition may hold meetings (or conduct phone calls) with the parties subject to the proceedings, complainants, or third parties. In particular, it will hold State of Play meetings or may hold triangular meetings as outlined in Sections 2.9 or 2.10 below.

43. When a meeting takes place at the request of the parties, complainants or third parties, they should as a general rule submit in advance a proposed agenda of topics to be discussed at the meeting, as well as a memorandum or a presentation which covers these issues in more detail. After meetings or phone calls on substantive issues, the parties, complainants or third parties may substantiate their statements or presentations in writing.

44. Any written documentation prepared by the undertakings which attended a meeting that is communicated to the Directorate-General for Competition will be put on the file. A non-confidential version of such documentation, together with a brief note prepared by the Directorate-General for Competition, will be made accessible to the parties subject to the investigation during their access to the file, if the case is further pursued. Subject to any anonymity requests (37) this note will mention the undertaking(s) attending the meeting (or participating in the phone call relating to substantive issues) and the timing and topic(s) covered by the meeting (or phone call) (38). Such a brief note will also be prepared when the meeting takes place on the Commission's initiative (e.g. State of Play meetings).

(37) See paragraph 143 below.

(38) The provisions of this section also apply to State of Play meetings and triangular meetings (see Section 2.10 below).

45. The Commission may, after a meeting or other informal contact with the parties, complainants or third parties, request that they provide information in writing pursuant to Article 18 of Regulation (EC) No 1/2003 or invite them to make a statement pursuant to Article 19 of that Regulation.

2.5.6. Power to take statements (interviews)

46. Regulation (EC) No 1/2003 and the Implementing Regulation establish a specific procedure for taking statements from natural or legal persons who may be in possession of useful information concerning an alleged infringement of Articles 101 and 102 TFEU (see Article 19 of Regulation (EC) No 1/2003 and Article 3 of the Implementing Regulation) (39).

(39) This power to take statements pursuant to Article 19 of Regulation (EC) No 1/2003 should be distinguished from the power of the Commission, during an inspection, to ask any representative or member of staff of the undertaking or association of undertakings for explanations on facts or documents relating to the subject matter and purpose of the inspection and to record the answers, pursuant to Article 20(2)(e) of Regulation (EC) No 1/2003.

47. The Commission may, under this procedure, interview by any means, such as by telephone or video conference, any natural or legal person who consents to be interviewed for the purpose of collecting information relating to the subject matter of an investigation.

48. Before taking such statements, the Directorate-General for Competition will inform the interviewee of the legal basis of the interview, its voluntary nature and the right of the interviewee to consult a lawyer. The Directorate-General for Competition will further inform the interviewee of the purpose of the interview and of its intention to make a record of the interview. In practice this will be done by providing a document explaining the procedure to be signed by the interviewee. In order to enhance the accuracy of the statements, a copy of any recording will be made available shortly thereafter to the person interviewed for approval.

49. The procedure for taking statements pursuant to Article 19 of Regulation (EC) No 1/2003 and Article 3 of the Implementing Regulation applies only when it is expressly agreed between the interviewee and the Directorate-General for Competition that the conversation will be recorded as a formal interview under Article 19. It is within the discretion of the Commission to decide when to propose interviews. A party may however also make a request to the Directorate-General for Competition to have its statement recorded as an interview. Such a request will in principle be accepted, subject to the needs and requirements of the proper conduct of the investigation.

2.6. Inspections

50. In the context of an investigation the Commission has the power to conduct inspections at the premises of an undertaking and in certain circumstances at other premises, including private premises. The Commission's practice in relation to inspections at the premises of an undertaking is currently described in an explanatory note available on the website of the Directorate-General for Competition (40).

(40) See: http://ec.europa.eu/competition/antitrust/legislation/legislation.html

2.7. Legal professional privilege

51. According to the case law of the Court of Justice of the European Union (41), the main features of which are summarised below, certain communications between lawyer and client may, subject to strict conditions, be protected by legal professional privilege (also referred to as «LPP») and thus be confidential as regards the Commission, as an exception to the latter's powers of investigation and examination of documents (42). Communications between lawyer and client are protected by legal professional privilege provided that they are made for the purpose and interest of the exercise of the client's rights of defence in competition proceedings and that they emanate from independent lawyers (43).

(41) The exclusion of certain communications between lawyers and clients from the Commission's powers of enquiry derives from the general principles of law common to the laws of the Member States as clarified by the Court of Justice of the European Union: Case 155/79 AM&S Europe Limited v Commission (hereinafter «AM&S») (1982) ECR 1575; Order in Case T-30/89 Hilti v Commission (hereinafter «Hilti») (1990) ECR II-163; Joined Cases T-125/03 and T-253/03 Akzo Nobel Chemicals and Akcros Chemicals v Commission (hereinafter «Akzo») (2007) ECR II-3523, as confirmed by Case C-550/07 P, Akzo Nobel Chemicals and Akcros Chemicals v Commission, judgment of 14 September 2010.

(42) The Court of Justice of the European Union has considered that the protection of the confidentiality of communications between lawyer and client is an essential corollary to the full exercise of the rights of defence (AM&S, paragraphs 18 and 23). In any event, the principle of legal professional privilege does not prevent a lawyer's client from disclosing the written communications between them if the client considers that it is in his interest to do so (AM&S, paragraph 28).

(43) AM&S, paragraphs 21, 22 and 27. According to the case law, the substantive scope of the protection of legal professional privilege covers also, further to written communications with an independent lawyer made for the purposes of the exercise of the client's rights of defence, (i) internal notes circulated within an undertaking which are confined to reporting the text or the content of communications with independent lawyers containing legal advice (Hilti, paragraphs 13, 16 to 18) and (ii) preparatory documents prepared by the client, even if not exchanged with a lawyer or not created for the purpose of being sent physically to a lawyer, provided that they were drawn up exclusively for the purpose of seeking legal advice from a lawyer in exercise of the rights of the defence (Akzo, paragraphs 120 to 123). As for the personal scope of the protection of legal professional privilege, it only applies to the extent that the lawyer is independent (i.e. not bound to his client by a relationship of employment); in-house lawyers are explicitly excluded from legal professional privilege, irrespective of their membership of a Bar or Law Society or their subjection to professional discipline and ethics or protection under national law: AM&S, paragraphs 21, 22, 24 and 27; Akzo, paragraphs 166 to 168; confirmed by ECJ in its judgment of 14 September 2010, Case C-550/07 P, paragraphs 44 to 51. Moreover, according to the case law, protection under legal professional privilege applies only to lawyers entitled to practise their profession in one of the EU Member States, regardless of the country in which the client lives (AM&S, paragraphs 25 and 26), and does not extend to other professional advisers such as patent attorneys, accountants, etc. Finally, it shall be observed that the protection of legal professional privilege covers, in principle, written communications exchanged after the initiation of the administrative procedure that may lead to a decision on the application of Articles 101 and/or 102 TFEU or to a decision imposing a pecuniary sanction on the undertaking; this protection can also extend to earlier written communications made for the purpose of exercising rights of the defence and which have a relationship to the subject matter of that procedure (AM&S, paragraph 23).

52. It is for the undertaking claiming the protection of legal professional privilege with regard to a given document to provide the Commission with appropriate justification and relevant material to substantiate its claim, while not being bound to disclose the contents of such document (44). Redacted versions removing the parts covered by legal professional privilege should be submitted. Where the Commission considers that such evidence has not been provided, it may order production of the document in question and, if necessary, impose on the undertaking fines or periodic penalty payments for its refusal either to supply such additional necessary evidence or to produce the contested document (45).

(44) Hence, the mere fact that an undertaking claims that a document is protected by legal professional privilege is not sufficient to prevent the Commission from reading that document if the undertaking produces no relevant material of such a kind (*Akzo*, paragraph 80; see below). In order to substantiate its claim, the undertaking concerned may, in particular, inform the Directorate-General for Competition of the author of the document and for whom it was intended, explain the respective duties and responsibilities of each, and refer to the objective and the context in which the document was drawn up. Similarly, it may also mention the context in which the document was found, the way in which it was filed and any related documents (*Akzo*, paragraph 80).

(45) AM&S, paragraphs 29 to 31. The undertaking may subsequently bring an action for the annulment of such a decision, where appropriate, coupled with a request for interim relief (AM&S, paragraphs 32; see below).

53. In many cases, a mere cursory look by Commission officials, normally during an inspection, at the general layout, heading, title or other superficial features of a document will enable them to confirm or not the accuracy of the reasons invoked by the undertaking. However, an undertaking is entitled to refuse to allow the Commission officials to take even a cursory look, provided that it gives appropriate reasons to justify why such a cursory look would be impossible without revealing the content of the document (46).

(46) *Akzo*, paragraphs 81 and 82.

54. Where, in the course of an inspection, the Commission officials consider that the undertaking has: (i) not substantiated its claim that the document concerned is covered by legal professional privilege; (ii) has only invoked reasons that, according to the case law, cannot justify such protection; or (iii) bases itself on factual assertions that are manifestly wrong, the Commission officials may immediately read the contents of the document and take a copy of it (without using the sealed envelope procedure).

However, where, in the course of an inspection, the Commission officials consider that the material presented by the undertaking is not of such a nature as to prove that the document in question is protected by legal professional privilege as defined by the case law of the Court of Justice of the European Union, in particular where that undertaking refuses to give the Commission officials a cursory look at a document, but where it cannot be excluded that the document may be protected, the officials may place a copy of the contested document in a sealed envelope and bring it to the Commission's premises, with a view to a subsequent resolution of the dispute.

55. The hearing officer may be asked by undertakings or associations of undertakings to examine claims that a document required by the Commission in the exercise of Articles 18, 20 or 21 of Regulation (EC) No 1/2003 and which was withheld from the Commission is covered by legal professional privilege, within the meaning of the case law, if the undertaking has been unable to resolve the matter with the Directorate-General for Competition (47). The undertaking making the claim may refer the matter to the hearing officer if they consent to the hearing officer viewing the information claimed to be covered by legal professional privilege and any other material necessary for the hearing officer's assessment. Without revealing the potentially privileged content of the information, the hearing officer shall communicate to the director responsible and the undertaking or association of undertakings concerned his or her preliminary view, and may take appropriate steps to promote a mutually acceptable resolution.

(47) Article 4(2)(*a*) of the terms of reference of the hearing officer.

56. Where no resolution is reached, the hearing officer may formulate a reasoned recommendation to the competent member of the Commission, without revealing the potentially privileged content of the document. The party making the claim shall receive a copy of this recommendation. If the matter is not resolved on this basis, the Commission will examine the matter further. Where appropriate, it may adopt a decision rejecting the claim.

57. In cases where the undertaking has claimed the protection of legal professional privilege and has provided reasons substantiating its claims, the Commission (with the exception of the hearing officer if a claim has been referred to him or her on the basis of Article 4(2)(*a*) of the terms of reference of the hearing officer) will not read the contents of the document before it has adopted a decision rejecting this claim and allowed the undertaking concerned to refer the matter to the Court of Justice of the European Union. Thus, if the company brings an action for annulment and applies for interim relief within the specified time limit, the Commission will not open the sealed envelope and will not read the documents until the Court of Justice of the European Union has decided on this application for interim measures (48).

(48) Thus, the Commission will wait until the time limit for bringing an action against the rejection decision has expired before reading the contents of the contested document. However, since such an action does not have suspensory effect, it is for the undertaking concerned to make a prompt application for interim relief seeking suspension of operation of the decision rejecting the request for legal professional privilege.

58. Undertakings making clearly unfounded claims for protection under legal professional privilege merely as delaying tactics or opposing, without objective justification, any cursory look at the documents during an investigation may be subject to fines pursuant to Article 23(1) of Regulation (EC) No 1/2003, if the other conditions of this provision are met. Similarly, such actions may be taken into account as aggravating circumstances in any decision imposing a fine for infringement of Articles 101 and/or 102 TFEU (49).

(49) *Akzo*, paragraph 89.

2.8. Information exchange between competition authorities

59. In the context of an investigation the Commission may also exchange information with national competition authorities pursuant to Article 12 of Regulation (EC) No 1/2003. The Commission's practice in relation to these exchanges is currently described in the Commission notice on cooperation within the Network of Competition Authorities (50).

(50) *O.J.* C 101, 27.4.2004, p. 43.

2.9. State of Play meetings

60. Throughout the procedure the Directorate-General for Competition endeavours to give, on its own initiative or upon request, parties subject to the proceedings ample opportunity for open and frank discussions – taking into account the stage of the investigation – and to make their points of view known.

61. In this respect the Commission will offer State of Play meetings at certain stages of the procedure. State of Play meetings, which are completely voluntary in nature for the parties, can contribute to the quality and efficiency of the decision making process and to ensure transparency and communication between the Directorate-General for Competition and the parties, notably to inform them of the status of the proceedings at key points in the procedure. State of Play meetings will only be offered to the parties being investigated and not to the complainant (except where the Commission has opened proceedings pursuant to Article 11(6) of Regulation (EC) No 1/2003 and intends to inform the complainant that it will reject its complaint by formal letter under Article 7(1) of the Implementing Regulation) nor to third parties. Where several parties are investigated, State of Play meetings will be offered to each party separately. In cartel proceedings, a State of Play meeting will be offered as provided for in paragraph (65).

2.9.1. Format of the State of Play meetings

62. State of Play meetings are normally conducted at the Commission's premises, but if appropriate, they may also be held by telephone or videoconference. Senior management of the Directorate-General for Competition (Director or Deputy Director-General) will normally chair the meeting. However, in cases involving multiple parties, the meeting may be chaired by the responsible head of unit.

2.9.2. Timing of the State of Play meetings

63. The Directorate-General for Competition will offer State of Play meetings at several key stages of the case. These correspond, in principle (although not normally in the context of cartel proceedings), to the following events:

1) shortly after the opening of proceedings: the Directorate-General for Competition will inform the parties subject to the proceedings of the issues identified at this stage and of the anticipated scope of the investigation. This meeting provides the parties with an opportunity to react initially to the issues identified and may also serve to assist the Directorate-General for Competition in deciding on the appropriate framework for its further investigation. This meeting may also be used to discuss with the parties any relevant language waivers that may be appropriate for the conduct of the investigation. The Directorate-General for Competition will normally at this stage indicate a tentative timetable for the case. Such tentative timetable will, if appropriate, be updated at following State of Play meetings;

2) at a sufficiently advanced stage in the investigation: this meeting gives the parties subject to the proceedings an opportunity to understand the Commission's preliminary views on the status of the case following its investigation and on the competition concerns identified. The meeting may also be used by the Directorate-General for Competition and by the parties to clarify certain issues and facts relevant for the outcome of the case.

64. Where a Statement of Objections is issued, the parties will also be offered a State of Play meeting after their reply to the Statement of Objections or after the Oral Hearing, should one be held: the parties will at this meeting normally be informed of the Commission's preliminary view on how it intends to pursue the case further.

65. In the context of cartel proceedings one State of Play meeting will be offered after the oral hearing. Furthermore, two specific State of Play Meetings will be offered in the context of procedures leading to commitment decisions (see Section 4 below) and to complainants where the Commission has opened proceedings under Article 11(6) of Regulation (EC) No 1/2003 and intends to inform the complainant that it will reject its complaint by formal letter under Article 7(1) of the Implementing Regulation (see Section 5 below).

66. State of Play meetings do not in any way preclude discussions between the parties, complainants or third parties and the Directorate-General for Competition on substance or on timing issues on other occasions throughout the procedure as appropriate.

2.10. Triangular meetings

67. In addition to bilateral meetings between the Directorate-General for Competition and each individual party such as the State of Play meetings, the Commission may exceptionally decide to invite the parties subject to the proceedings, and possibly also the complainant and/or third parties, to a so-called «triangular» meeting. Such a meeting will be organised if the Directorate-General for Competition believes it to be in the interests of the investigation to hear the views on, or to verify the accuracy of, factual issues of all the parties in a single meeting. Such a meeting could be useful to the investigation, for example, where two or more opposing views or information have been put forward as to key data or evidence.

68. Any triangular meeting would normally take place at the initiative of the Commission and on a voluntary basis. Triangular meetings are normally chaired by senior management of the Directorate- General for Competition (Director or Deputy Director-General). A triangular meeting does not replace the formal Oral Hearing.

69. Where triangular meetings are held, this should be done as early as possible during the investigatory phase (after the opening of proceedings and before any issuing of Statement of Objections) in order to help the Commission reach a conclusion on substantive issues before the Commission decides whether to issue a Statement of Objections, although the holding of such meetings after the issue of the Statement of Objections in appropriate cases is not excluded. Triangular meetings should be prepared on the basis of an agenda established by the Directorate-General for Competition after consulting all parties that agree to attend the meeting. The preparation of the meeting may include a mutual exchange of non-confidential submissions between the attending parties sufficiently in advance of the meeting.

2.11. Meetings with the Commissioner or the Director-General

70. If the parties so request, it is normal practice to offer senior officers of the parties subject to the proceedings and the complainant an opportunity to discuss the case either with the Director-General for competition, the Deputy Director-General for antitrust, or if appropriate, with the Commissioner responsible for Competition. The senior officers may be accompanied by their legal and/or economic advisors.

2.12. Review of key submissions

71. In the spirit of encouraging an open exchange of views the Commission will, in cases based on formal complaints, provide the parties subject to the proceedings, at an early stage (unless such is considered to likely prejudice the investigation) and at the latest shortly after the opening of proceedings, with the opportunity of commenting on a non-confidential version of the complaint (51). However, this may not be the case where the complaint is rejected at an early stage without further in-depth investigation (e.g. based on «insufficient grounds for acting», also known as «lack of European Union interest»).

(51) A non-confidential version of the reply of the party subject to the investigation to the complaint may thereafter be provided to the complainant.

72. Early access to the complaint may allow the parties to provide useful information at an early stage of the procedure and facilitate the assessment of the case.

73. In the same spirit, the Commission's objective will be to provide the parties subject to the proceedings shortly after the opening of proceedings with the opportunity to review non-confidential versions of other «key submissions» already submitted to the Commission. This would include significant submissions of the complainant or interested third parties, but not, for example, replies to requests for information. After this early stage, other such submissions will only be shared with the parties if this is in the interest of the investigation and would not risk unduly slowing down the investigative phase. The Commission will respect justified requests by the complainant or interested third parties for non-disclosure of their submissions prior to the issuing of a Statement of Objections where they have genuine concerns regarding confidentiality, including fears of retaliation and the protection of business secrets.

74. The review of key submissions will not be offered in the context of cartel proceedings (see paragraph (4) above).

2.13. Possible outcomes of the investigation phase

75. Once the Commission has reached a preliminary view of the main issues raised by a case, different procedural paths may be envisaged.

– The Commission may decide to proceed towards the adoption of a Statement of Objections with a view to adopting a prohibition decision relating to all or some of the issues identified at the opening of proceedings (see Section 3 below).

– The parties subject to the investigation may consider offering commitments which address the competition concerns arising from the investigation, or at least show their willingness to discuss such a possibility; in that case, the Commission may decide to engage in discussion with a view to a commitment decision (see Section 4 below).

– The Commission may decide that there are no grounds to continue the proceedings with regard to all or some of the parties and close the proceedings accordingly. If the case originated via a complaint, the Commission shall, before closing the case, give the complainant the possibility to express its views (see Section 5 on rejection of complaints).

76. When closing a case in relation to one or several parties in multi-party proceedings at an early stage after proceedings have been formally opened, the Commission will normally not only notify the decision to those parties but also in those cases where the opening of proceedings has been made public, note the closure on its website and/or issue a press release. The same applies in cases where proceedings have not been formally opened but the Commission has already made public its investigation (e.g. by having confirmed that inspections have taken place).

3. PROCEDURES LEADING TO A PROHIBITION DECISION

77. An important procedural step in procedures which may lead to a prohibition decision is the adoption of a Statement of Objections. However, the adoption of a Statement of Objections does not prejudge the final outcome of the investigation. It may well lead to the closing of the case without the adoption of a prohibition decision or a commitment decision.

3.1. Right to be heard

78. The right of the parties to the proceedings to be heard before a final decision adversely affecting their interests is taken is a fundamental principle of EU law. The Commission is committed to ensuring that the effective exercise of the right to be heard is respected in its proceedings (52).

(52) Article 27 of Regulation (EC) No 1/2003, mentioned above.

79. The hearing officers have the function of safeguarding the effective exercise of procedural rights, in particular the right to be heard, in competition proceedings (53). The hearing officers carry out their tasks in full independence from the Directorate-General for Competition, and disputes arising between the latter and any party subject to the proceedings can be brought before the relevant hearing officer for resolution.

(53) Article 1 of terms of reference of the hearing officer.

80. The hearing officer is directly involved throughout antitrust proceedings, including in particular the organisation and conduct of the oral hearing, if one is held. After the oral hearing, and taking into account the parties' written replies to the Statement of Objections, the hearing officer reports to the Commissioner responsible for Competition on the hearing and the conclusions to be drawn from it. Moreover, prior to a final decision being taken by the College of Commissioners, the hearing officer informs it whether the right to exercise procedural rights effectively has been respected throughout the administrative proceedings. The final report is sent to the parties subject to the proceedings, together with the Commission's final decision, and is published in the *Official Journal of the European Union*.

3.1.1. Statement of Objections

81. Before adopting a decision adversely affecting the interests of an addressee, in particular, a decision finding an infringement of Article 101 and 102 TFEU and ordering its termination (Article 7 of Regulation (EC) No 1/2003) and/or imposing fines (Article 23 of Regulation (EC) No 1/2003), the Commission will give the parties subject to the proceedings the opportunity to be heard on the matters to which the Commission has objected (54). The Commission will do this by adopting a Statement of Objections, which is notified to each of the parties subject to the proceedings.

(54) Article 27 of Regulation (EC) No 1/2003.

3.1.1.1. Purpose and content of the Statement of Objections

82. The Statement of Objections sets out the preliminary position of the Commission on the alleged infringement of Articles 101 and/or 102 TFEU, after an in-depth investigation. Its purpose is to inform the parties concerned of the objections raised against them with a view to enabling them to exercise their rights of defence in writing and orally (at the hearing). It thus constitutes an essential procedural safeguard which ensures that the right to be heard is observed. The parties concerned will be provided with all the information they need to defend themselves effectively and to comment on the allegations made against them.

3.1.1.2. Possible imposition of remedies and arguments of the parties

83. If the Commission intends to impose remedies on the parties, in accordance with Article 7(1) of Regulation (EC) No 1/2003, the Statement of Objections will indicate the remedies envisaged that may be necessary to bring the suspected infringement to an end. The information given should be sufficiently detailed to allow the parties to defend themselves as to the necessity and proportionality of the remedies envisaged. If structural remedies are envisaged, in accordance with Article 7(1) of Regulation (EC) No 1/2003, the Statement of Objections will spell out why there is no equally effective behavioural remedy or why the Commission considers any equally effective behavioural remedy would be more burdensome for the undertaking concerned than the structural remedy.

3.1.1.3. Possible imposition off in es and arguments of the parties

84. The Statement of Objections will clearly indicate whether the Commission intends to impose fines on the undertakings, should the objections be upheld (Article 23 of Regulation (EC) No 1/2003). In such cases, the Statement of Objections will refer to the relevant principles laid down in the Guidelines on setting fines (55). In the Statement of Objections the Commission will indicate the essential facts and matters of law which may result in the imposition of a fine, such as the duration and gravity of the infringement and that the infringement was committed intentionally or by negligence. The Statement of Objections will also mention in a sufficiently precise manner that certain facts may give rise to aggravating circumstances and, to the extent possible, to attenuating circumstances.

(55) Guidelines on the method of setting fines imposed pursuant to Article 23(2)(a) of Regulation (EC) No 1/2003 (O.J. C 210, 1.9.2006, p. 2).

85. Although under no legal obligation in this respect, in order to increase transparency, the Commission will endeavour to include in the Statement of Objections (using information available) further matters relevant to any subsequent calculation of fines, including the relevant sales figures to be taken into account and the year(s) that will be considered for the value of such sales. Such information may also be provided to the parties after the Statement of Objections. In both cases, the parties will be provided with an opportunity to comment.

86. Should the Commission intend to depart in its final decision from the elements of fact or of law set out in the Statement of Objections to the disadvantage of one or more parties or should the Commission intend to take account of additional inculpatory evidence, the party or parties concerned will always be given the opportunity to make their views known thereon in an appropriate manner.

87. In the Statement of Objections the Commission will also inform parties that in exceptional cases, it may, upon request, take account of the undertaking's inability to pay and reduce or cancel the fine that might otherwise be imposed if that fine would irretrievably jeopardise the economic viability of the undertaking, according to point 35 of the Guidelines on setting fines (56).

(56) See footnote 55.

88. The undertakings making such a request should be prepared to provide, detailed and up-to-date financial information to support their request. Usually, the Directorate-General for Competition will be in contact with the parties in order to collect additional information and/or clarify the information obtained, which will allow the parties to bring further relevant information to the attention of the Commission. When assessing an undertaking's claim that it is unable to pay, the Commission looks in particular at the financial statements for recent years and forecasts for the current and coming years; at ratios measuring the financial strength, profitability, solvency and liquidity; and the undertaking's relations with outside financial partners and with shareholders. The Commission also examines the specific social and economic context of each undertaking and assesses whether the fine would likely cause its assets to lose significantly their value (57).

(57) See Note SEC(2010) 737/2 of 12 June 2010.

89. The assessment of the financial situation is carried out for all undertakings that have made an inability to pay request close to the adoption of the decision and on the basis of up-to-date information, irrespective of when the request was submitted.

90. The parties may also present their arguments as to the matters that may be of importance for the possible imposition of fines at the oral hearing (58).

(58) See paragraph 107 below.

3.1.1.4. Transparency

91. In order to enhance the transparency of the proceedings, the Commission will, as a general rule, publish a press release setting out the key issues in the Statement of Objections shortly after it is received by its addressees. This press release will explicitly state that the Statement of Objections does not predetermine the final outcome of the proceedings, once the parties have been heard.

3.1.2. Access to file

92. The addressees of the Statement of Objections are granted access to the Commission's file, in accordance with Article 27(2) of Regulation (EC) No 1/2003 and Articles 15 and 16 of the Implementing Regulation, so as to allow them to effectively express their views on the preliminary conclusions reached by the Commission in its Statement of Objections.

93. The practicalities of access to the file, as well as detailed indications on the type of documents that will be accessible and confidentiality issues, are covered by a separate notice on access to file (59). Granting access to the

Commission file is primarily the responsibility of the Directorate-General for Competition. The hearing officers will decide disputes between the parties, the information providers and the Directorate-General for Competition over access to information contained in the Commission's file in accordance with the notice on access to file, the applicable regulations and the principles laid down in the relevant case law. Lastly, special rules govern access to corporate statements in cartel cases and settlement procedures (60).

(59) Notice on the rules for access to the Commission file, mentioned above.

(60) Commission Notice on Immunity from fines and reduction of fines in cartel cases (mentioned above), paragraphs 31 to 35 and Commission Notice on the conduct of settlement procedures (mentioned above), paragraphs 35 to 40.

94. Efficient access to file depends to a large extent on the cooperation of the parties and other undertakings having provided information included in the file. As noted in paragraph (41) above, information providers must, in accordance with Article 16(3) of the Implementing Regulation, substantiate their confidentiality claims and provide a non-confidential version of the information. Such a non-confidential version must be provided in the same format as the confidential information, replacing deleted passages with summaries thereof. Unless otherwise agreed, a non-confidential version should be provided at the same time as the original submission. In the case of a failure to provide a non-confidential version, it may be assumed that the documents do not contain confidential information (61).

(61) See Article 16(4) of the Implementing Regulation.

3.1.3. Procedures for facilitating the exchange of confidential information between parties to the proceedings

95. Further to the possibilities contemplated in the notice on access to the file, two additional procedures may be used for the purpose of alleviating the burden of drawing up non-confidential versions of submissions: the negotiated disclosure to a restricted circle of persons and the data room procedure.

96. First, the Directorate-General for Competition may accept in certain cases, especially those with a very voluminous file that the parties agree voluntarily to use a negotiated disclosure procedure. Under this procedure, the party entitled to access to file agrees bilaterally with the information providers claiming confidentiality to receive all or some of the information which the latter have provided to the Commission, including confidential information. The party being granted access to file limits access to the information to a restricted circle of persons (to be decided by the parties on a case-by-case basis, if requested, under the supervision of the Directorate-General for Competition). To the extent that such negotiated access to the file would amount to restricting a party's right to have access to the investigation file, that party must waive its right to access to the file vis-à-vis the Commission. Normally, the party would receive the information subject to the negotiated disclosure procedure directly from the information provider. However, if the information that is subject to such an agreement would, exceptionally, be provided to the restricted circle of persons by the Commission, the information providers must waive their rights to confidentiality vis-à-vis the Commission.

97. Second, the Directorate-General for Competition may organise the so-called data room procedure. This procedure is typically used for the disclosure of quantitative data relevant for econometric analysis. Under this procedure, part of the file, including confidential information, is gathered in a room, at the Commission's premises (the data room). Access to the data room is granted to a restricted group of persons, i.e. the external legal counsel and/or the economic advisers of the party (collectively known as the «advisers»), under the supervision of a Commission official. The advisers may make use of the information contained in the data room for the purpose of defending their client but may not disclose any confidential information to their client. The data room is equipped with several PC workstations and the necessary software (and if relevant the necessary data sets and a log of the regressions used to support the Commission's case). There is no network connection and no external communication is allowed. The advisers are permitted to remain in the data room during normal working hours and, if justified, access may be provided for several days. The advisers are strictly prohibited from taking copies, notes or summaries of the documents and may only remove a final report from the data room, which is to be verified by the case team in order to ensure that it does not contain any confidential information. Each adviser will sign a confidentiality agreement and will be presented with the conditions of special access to the data room before entering. To the extent that the use of such a data room procedure would restrict a party's right to have full access to the investigation file, the procedural guarantees provided for in Article 8 of the terms of reference of the hearing officer apply.

98. The hearing officer may decide pursuant to Article 8(4) of the terms of reference of the hearing officer that the data room procedure shall be used in those limited cases where access to certain confidential information is indispensible for a party's rights of defence and where the hearing officer considers that, on balance, the conflict between respect for confidentiality and the rights of defence is best solved in this way. The hearing officer will not take such decisions if he or she considers that the data room is not appropriate and that access to the information should be given in a different form (e.g. a non- confidential version).

3.1.4. Written reply to the Statement of Objections

99. Pursuant to Article 27(1) of Regulation (EC) No 1/2003, the Commission shall give the addressees of a Statement of Objections the opportunity of being heard on matters to which the Commission has taken objection. The written reply gives the parties subject to the proceedings the opportunity to set out their views on the objections raised by the Commission.

100. The time limit for the reply to the Statement of Objections will take into account both the time required for the preparation of the submission and the urgency of the case (62). The addressees of the Statement of Objections have the right to a minimum period of four weeks to reply in writing (63). A longer period (normally, a period of two months, although this may be longer or shorter depending on the circumstances of the case) will be granted by the Directorate-General for Competition taking into account, inter alia, the following elements:

(62) See Case T-44/00 Mannesmannröhren-Werke AG v Commission (2004) ECR II-2223, para. 65.

(63) See Article 17(2) of the Implementing Regulation. For the rule applicable to settlement procedures, see Article 10(a) of the Implementing Regulation.

– the size and complexity of the file (e.g. the number of infringements, the alleged duration of the infringement(s), the size and number of documents and/or the size and complexity of expert studies); and/or

– whether the addressee of the statement of objection making the request has had prior access to information (e.g. key submissions, leniency applications); and/or

– any other objective obstacles which may be faced by the addressee of the Statement of Objections making the request in providing its observations.

101. An addressee of a Statement of Objections may, within the original time limit, seek an extension of the time limit to reply by means of a reasoned request to the Directorate-General for Competition at least 10 working days before the expiry of the original time limit. If such a request is not granted or the addressee of the Statement of Objections disagrees with the length of the extension granted, it may refer the matter to the hearing officer for review before the expiry of the original time limit.

102. The time limit will start to run from the date when access to the main documents of the file has been granted (64). In particular, time limits will normally not start running before the addressee of the Statement of Objections has been offered access to documents which are only accessible on Commission premises, e.g. corporate statements. The fact that access to the entire file has not been granted does not have the automatic consequence that a time limit has not started running (65).

(64) In most cases, parties will be given access to the complete file by means of a CD-Rom containing all documents in the file.

(65) See Case T-44/00, Mannesmannröhren-Werke AG v Commission, (2004) ECR II-2223, para 65. See also recital 15 of the terms of reference of the hearing officer which states «In exceptional circumstances, the hearing officer may suspend the running of the time period in which an addressee of a statement of objections should reply to that statement until a dispute about access to file has been resolved, if the addressee would not be in a position to reply within the deadline granted and an extension would not be an adequate solution at that point in time.»

103. Where required by the rights of defence (66), or where it may in the Commission's view help to further clarify factual and legal issues relevant for the case, the Commission may give parties a copy of the non-confidential version (or specific parts thereof) of other parties' written replies to the Statement of Objections. This would normally be done prior to the oral hearing, so as to allow parties to comment on them at the oral hearing. The Commission may also decide to do so in appropriate cases with respect to complainants and admitted third parties. If access to other parties' replies is granted because it is required for the rights of the defence parties are also entitled to have sufficient additional time to comment on these replies.

(66) See Joined Cases T-191/98 and T-212/98 to T-214/98 Atlantic Container Line and Others v Commission (2003) ECR II- 3275; Case T-54/03 Lafarge v Commission (2008) ECR II-120, paras 69-73; Case T-52/03 Knauf v Commission (2008) ECR II-115, paras 41-47, 67-79; Case C-407/08P Knauf v Commission, judgment of 1 July 2010 (not yet reported), paras 23-28.

3.1.5. Rights of complainants and interested third persons

104. Complainants are closely associated with the proceedings. Pursuant to Article 6(1) of the Implementing Regulation, they are entitled to receive a non-confidential version of the Statement of Objections, and the Commission shall set a time limit in which the complainant may make its views known in writing. A request for an extension of this time limit may be made by way of a reasoned request to the Commission in due time before the expiry of the original time limit. If such a request is not granted or the Directorate-General for Competition and the complainant disagree about a requested extension, the complainant may refer the matter to the hearing officer, by means of a reasoned request (67).

(67) Article 9(2) of the terms of reference of the hearing officer.

105. Upon application, the Commission shall also hear other natural or legal persons which can demonstrate a sufficient interest in the outcome of the procedure in accordance with Article 13 of the Implementing Regulation. The hearing officer takes the decision on whether such third persons are admitted to the proceedings. Persons who have been admitted shall be informed in writing of the nature and subject matter of the procedure and a time limit shall be set by the Commission in which they may make their views known in writing. A request for an extension of this time limit may be made by way of a reasoned request to the Directorate-General for Competition in due time before the expiry of the original time limit. If such a request is not granted or the Directorate-General for Competition and the third person admitted to the proceedings disagree about a requested extension the third person may refer the matter to the hearing officer, by means of a reasoned request (68).

(68) See footnote 67.

3.1.6. Oral hearing

106. Every party to which a Statement of Objections has been addressed has the right to an oral hearing. An oral hearing may be requested within the time limit set for their written reply to the Statement of Objections.

107. The oral hearing allows the parties to develop orally the arguments that they submitted in writing and to supplement, where appropriate, the written evidence, or to inform the Commission of other matters that may be relevant. The oral hearing also allows the parties to present their arguments as to the matters that may be of importance for the possible imposition of fines. The fact that the hearing is not public guarantees that all attendees can express themselves freely. Any information disclosed during the hearing shall only be used for the purposes of judicial and/or administrative proceedings for the application of Articles 101 and 102 TFEU and shall not be disclosed or used for any other purpose by any participant in a hearing. This restriction also applies to the recording of the oral hearing, as well as any visual presentations. Should information disclosed during the oral hearing be used for a purpose other than judicial and/or administrative proceedings for the application of Articles 101 and 102 TFEU at any point in time with the involvement of outside counsel, the Commission may report the incident to the bar of that counsel, with a view to disciplinary action.

108. In view of the importance of the oral hearing, it is the practice of the Directorate-General for Competition to ensure the continuous presence of senior management of the Directorate-General for Competition (Director or Deputy Director-General), together with the case team of Commission officials responsible for the investigation. The competition authorities of the Member States, the Chief Economist's team, and associated Commission services (69), including the Legal Service, are also invited to attend by the hearing officer.

(69) See further the document «Key actors and checks and balances», available on the Directorate-General for Competition's website.

3.1.7. Supplementary Statement of Objections and letter of facts

109. If, after the Statement of Objections has been issued, new evidence is identified which the Commission intends to rely upon or if the Commission intends to change its legal assessment to the disadvantage of the undertakings concerned, the undertakings in question shall be given an opportunity to present their observations on these new aspects.

110. If additional objections are issued or the intrinsic nature of the infringement with which an undertaking is charged is modified (70), the Commission shall notify this to the parties in a Supplementary Statement of Objections. Before doing so, a State of Play meeting will normally be offered to the parties. The rules on setting the time limit for the reply to a Statement of Objections apply (see above), although a shorter time limit will typically be set in this context.

(70) For example a supplementary Statement of Objections would be issued if the new evidence allows the Commission to extend the duration of the infringement, the geographic scope or the nature or scope of the infringement.

111. If, however, the objections already raised against the undertakings in the Statement of Objections are only corroborated by new evidence that the Commission intends to rely on, it will bring this to the attention of the parties concerned by a simple letter (letter of facts) (71). The letter of facts gives undertakings the opportunity to provide written comments on the new evidence within a fixed time limit. A request for an extension of this time limit may be made by way of a reasoned request to the Commission. If the Directorate-General for Competition and the addressee disagree about a requested extension, the addressee may refer the matter to the hearing officer, by means of a reasoned request.

(71) When the Commission merely communicates to a party a non-confidential version (or specific excerpts thereof) of the other parties' written replies to the Statement of Objections and gives it the opportunity to submit its comments (see paragraph 103 above), this does not constitute a letter of facts.

112. The procedural rights which are triggered by the sending of the Statement of Objections apply *mutatis mutandis* where a Supplementary Statement of Objections is issued, including the right of the parties to request an oral hearing. Access to all evidence gathered between the initial Statement of Objections and the Supplementary Statement of Objections will also be provided. If a letter of facts is issued, access will in general be granted to evidence gathered after the Statement of Objections up to the date of the said letter of facts. However, in cases where the Commission only intends to rely upon specific evidence that concerns one or a limited number of parties and/or isolated issues (in particular those regarding the determination of the amount of the fine or issues of parental liability), access will be provided only to the parties directly concerned and to the evidence relating to the issue(s) in question.

3.2. Possible outcomes of this phase

113. If, having regard to the parties' replies given in writing and/or at the oral hearing and on the basis of a thorough assessment of all information obtained up to this stage the objections are substantiated, the Commission will proceed towards adopting a decision finding an infringement of the relevant competition rules. The Commission can also decide to withdraw certain objections and to continue towards a decision finding an infringement for the remaining part.

114. If, however, the objections at this stage are not substantiated, the Commission will close the case. In this case, the information measures described above in paragraph (76) would also apply.

4. COMMITMENT PROCEDURES

115. Article 9 of Regulation (EC) No 1/2003 provides the possibility for undertakings to offer commitments that are intended to address the competition concerns identified by the Commission. If the Commission accepts these commitments, it may adopt a decision which makes them binding on the parties subject to the proceedings. It is at the discretion of the Commission whether or not to accept commitments. In light of the principle of proportionality, the Commission must verify that the commitments address the identified competition concerns and that the commitments offered do not manifestly go beyond what is necessary to address these concerns. When carrying out that assessment, the Commission will take into consideration the interests of third parties. However, it is not obliged to compare such voluntary commitments with measures it could impose under Article 7 of Regulation (EC) No 1/2003 and to regard as disproportionate any commitments which go beyond such measures (72).

(72) Case C-441/07 P Commission v Alrosa, judgment of 29 June 2010, paragraph 120.

116. Commitment decisions are not appropriate in cases where the Commission considers that the nature of the infringement calls for the imposition of a fine (73). Consequently, the Commission does not apply the Article 9 procedure to secret cartels that fall under the Notice on immunity from fines and reduction of fines in cartel cases.

(73) See recital 13 of Regulation (EC) No 1/2003.

117. The main difference between a prohibition decision pursuant to Article 7 and a commitment decision pursuant to Article 9 of Regulation (EC) No 1/2003 is that the former contains a finding of an infringement while the latter makes the commitments binding without concluding whether there was or still is an infringement. A commitment decision concludes that there are no longer grounds for action by the Commission. Moreover, commitments are offered by undertakings on a voluntary basis. Conversely, by an Article 7 decision, the Commission can impose remedies which are necessary to bring the infringement to an end (and/or fines) on undertakings.

4.1. Initiation of commitment discussions

118. Undertakings may contact the Directorate-General for Competition at any time to explore the Commission's readiness to pursue the case with the aim of reaching a commitment decision. The Commission encourages undertakings to signal at the earliest possible stage their interest in discussing commitments.

119. A State of Play meeting will be offered to the parties at that point. The Directorate-General for Competition will indicate to the undertaking the timeframe within which the discussions on potential commitments should be concluded and will present to them the preliminary competition concerns arising from the investigation.

120. In order to avoid delays due to translation, that meeting and the following steps of the procedure may be conducted in an agreed language on the basis of a duly provided «language waiver» by which the parties accept to receive and submit documents in a language other than the language of the Member State in which they are located (see above Section 2.4).

4.2. Preliminary Assessment

121. Once the Commission is convinced of the undertakings' genuine willingness to propose commitments which will effectively address the competition concerns, a Preliminary Assessment will be issued. Pursuant to Article 9 of Regulation (EC) No 1/2003 the Preliminary Assessment summarises the main facts of the case and identifies the competition concerns that would warrant a decision requiring that the infringement is brought to an end. Prior to issuing the Preliminary Assessment, the parties will also be offered a State of Play meeting.

122. The Preliminary Assessment will serve as a basis for the parties to formulate appropriate commitments addressing the competition concerns expressed by the Commission, or to better define previously discussed commitments.

123. If a Statement of Objections has already been sent to the parties, commitments may nevertheless still be accepted, in appropriate cases. In these circumstances, a Statement of Objections fulfils the requirements of a Preliminary Assessment, as it contains a summary of the main facts as well as an assessment of the competition concerns identified.

124. Parties to the proceedings which offer commitments to meet the concerns expressed to them by the Commission in its Preliminary Assessment may call upon the hearing officer at any time during which the procedure under Article 9 is followed in relation to the effective exercise of their procedural rights (74).

(74) Article 15(1) of the terms of reference of the hearing officer.

125. The Commission or the undertaking(s) concerned may decide at any moment during the commitment procedure to discontinue their discussions. The Commission can then normally continue formal proceedings pursuant to Article 7 of Regulation (EC) No 1/2003 (75).

(75) See Section 3 of this notice.

4.3. Submission of the commitments

126. After receiving the Preliminary Assessment, the parties will normally have one month to formally submit their commitments. If the parties have received a Statement of Objections and subsequently decide to submit commitments, the time limit to reply to the Statement of Objections will generally not be extended. The submission of commitments does not necessarily imply that the parties agree with the Commission's Preliminary Assessment.

127. The parties can offer commitments of a behavioural or structural nature that address adequately the competition concerns identified. Commitments which do not adequately remedy these concerns will not be accepted by the Commission.

128. Commitments must be unambiguous and self-executing (76). If need be, a trustee can be appointed to assist the Commission in their implementation (monitoring and/or divestiture trustee). Furthermore, when commitments cannot be implemented without the agreement of third parties (e.g. where a third party that would not be a suitable buyer under the commitments holds a pre-emption right), the undertaking should submit evidence of the third party's agreement.

(76) That is, their implementation must not be dependant on the will of a third party which is not bound by the commitments.

4.4. The «market test» and subsequent discussions with the parties

129. In accordance with Article 27(4) of Regulation (EC) No 1/2003 the Commission must conduct a market test of the commitments before making them binding by decision. The Commission will only conduct a market test if it considers that the commitments offered prima facie address the competition concerns identified. The Commission must publish in the *Official Journal of the European Union* a notice (market test notice) containing a concise summary of the case and the main content of the commitments, whilst respecting the obligations of professional secrecy (77). It will also publish on the Directorate-General for Competition's website the full text of the commitments (78) in the authentic language (79). In order to enhance the transparency of the process, the Commission will also publish a press release setting out the key issues of the case and the proposed commitments. If the case is based on a complaint, the Commission will at this stage also inform the complainant about the market test and invite the complainant to submit comments. Similarly, third parties admitted to the procedure will be informed and invited to submit comments. At the Commission's discretion, triangular meetings with the parties and the complainant and/or admitted third parties may be held.

(77) Article 28 of Regulation (EC) No 1/2003.
(78) Non-confidential version.
(79) Without translation.

130. Interested third parties are invited to submit their observations within a fixed time limit of not less than one month in accordance with Article 27(4) of Regulation (EC) No 1/2003.

131. The Commission may send the market test document to other parties that may be potentially concerned by the outcome of the case (e.g. consumer associations).

132. After receipt of the replies to the market test, a State of Play meeting will be organised with the parties. The Commission will inform the parties orally or in writing of the substance of the replies.

133. Where the Commission is of the view, on the basis of the results of the market test (and any other information available) that the competition concerns identified have not been addressed or that changes in the text of the commitments are necessary to make them effective, this will be brought to the attention of the undertakings offering the commitments. If the latter are willing to address the problems identified by the Commission, they should submit an amended version of the commitments. If the amended version of the commitments alters the very nature or scope of the commitments, a new market test will be conducted. If the undertakings are unwilling to submit an amended version of the commitments, where this is required by the Commission's assessment of the result of the market test, the Commission can revert to the Article 7 procedure.

5. PROCEDURE FOR REJECTION OF COMPLAINTS

134. Formal complaints are an important tool in the implementation of the competition rules and are therefore carefully examined by the Commission. However, after appropriate assessment of the factual and legal circumstances of the individual case, the Commission may reject a complaint pursuant to the grounds and procedure set out below (80).

(80) See also Commission notice on the handling of complaints (mentioned above).

5.1. Grounds for rejection

135. The rejection of complaints can be based on «insufficient grounds for acting» (also known as «lack of European Union interest»), lack of competence or lack of evidence to establish the existence of an infringement.

136. Rejections based on «insufficient grounds for acting» (81) concern in particular complaints where, given the limited likelihood of establishing the proof of the alleged infringements and the substantial investigatory resources which the Commission would have to invest in order to verify their existence, allocating the resources necessary to further investigate the case would be disproportionate, in light of its expected limited impact on the functioning of the internal market and/or the possibility of the complainant to have recourse to other means (82).

(81) Cf. in particular Case T-24/90, Automec II, (1992) ECR II-2223 and Case C-119/97 P, Ufex, (1999) ECR I-1341.

(82) The Commission notice on the handling of complaints lists in paragraph 44 certain criteria that can be used in isolation or combination for rejections on the grounds of lack of «European Union interest». Moreover, the Commission identified in its Report on Competition Policy 2005 some criteria that it could use to decide whether or not there is «European Union interest». See also Case T-427/08, Confédération européenne des associations d'horlogeurs-réparateurs (CEAHR) v Commission, not yet reported.

137. The Commission may also reject complaints for lack of substantiation (when the complainant fails to submit even a minimum of prima facie evidence necessary to substantiate an infringement of Articles 101 and/or 102 TFEU) or on substantive grounds (absence of an infringement).

138. If a national competition authority is dealing or has already dealt with the same case (83), the Commission shall inform the complainant accordingly. In such a situation, the complainant may withdraw the complaint. If the complainant maintains the complaint, the Commission may reject it by decision pursuant to Article 13 of Regulation (EC) No 1/2003 and in accordance with Article 9 of the Implementing Regulation (84). If a national court is dealing or has already dealt with the same case, the Commission may reject the complaint based on «insufficient grounds for acting» (85).

(83) The notion of same case essentially implies: infringement of the same nature, same product market, same geographic market, at least one of the same undertakings, same period of time.

(84) Paragraph 25 of the Commission's notice on the handling of complaints.

(85) See Annual Report on Competition Policy 2005, adopted in June 2006, p. 25 ff.

5.2. Procedure

139. If the Commission, after careful examination of the case, comes to the preliminary conclusion that it should not pursue the case for any of the reasons mentioned above, it will first inform the complainant in a meeting or by phone that it has come to the preliminary view that the case may be rejected. Once informed, the complainant may decide to withdraw the complaint. Otherwise, the Commission will inform the complainant by a formal letter pursuant to Article 7(1) of the Implementing Regulation of its preliminary conclusion that there are insufficient grounds for acting and set a time limit for its written observations (86). In this context, the complainant has the right to request access to the documents on which the Commission bases its provisional assessment (87). If in the course of its examination of the complaint, the Commission has opened proceedings pursuant to Article 11(6) of Regulation (EC) No 1/2003 a State of Play meeting will be offered to the complainant prior to sending such a formal letter. The time limit set in the formal letter shall be at least four weeks (88). The time limit will start to run from the date when access to the main documents on which the assessment was made has been granted. Where appropriate and upon reasoned request to the Directorate-General for Competition made before the expiry of the original time limit, the time limit may be extended (89). If such a request is not granted or the Directorate-General for Competition and the complainant disagree about the extension requested, the addressee may refer the matter to the hearing officer, by means of a reasoned request (90).

(86) Article 7(1) of the Implementing Regulation; paragraph 68 of the Commission's notice on the handling of complaints.

(87) Article 8 of Regulation of the Implementing Regulation; paragraph 69 of the Commission's notice on the handling of complaints.

(88) Article 17(2) of the Implementing Regulation.

(89) Article 17(4) of the Implementing Regulation.

(90) See footnote 67.

140. If the complainant does not react to the above mentioned letter of the Commission within the time limit, the complaint shall be deemed to have been withdrawn pursuant to Article 7(3) of the Implementing Regulation. The complainant will be informed accordingly about the administrative closure of the case.

141. If the submissions of the complainant in response to the above mentioned letter of the Commission, does not lead the Commission to a different assessment of the complaint, it will reject the complaint by formal decision pursuant to Article 7(2) of the Implementing Regulation. If the submissions of the complainant lead to a different assessment of the complaint, the Commission will continue its investigation.

6. LIMITS ON THE USE OF INFORMATION

142. Information exchanged in the course of these procedures, in particular in the context of access to file and review of key submissions, shall only be used for the purposes of judicial or administrative proceedings for the application of Articles 101 and 102 TFEU (91).

(91) Cf. Article 15(4) of the Implementing Regulation.

143. At all stages of the proceedings, the Commission will respect genuine and justified requests from complainants or from information providers regarding the confidential nature of their submissions or contacts with the Commission, including, where appropriate, their identity, in order to protect their legitimate interests (in particular in case of possible retaliation) and to avoid discouraging them from coming forward to the Commission (92).

(92) See Article 16(1) of Regulation (EC) No 1/2003.

144. Commission officials and the members of the Advisory Committee are bound by the obligation of professional secrecy set out in Article 28 of Regulation (EC) No 1/2003. They are therefore prohibited from disclosing any information of the kind covered by this obligation which they have acquired or exchanged in the context of the investigation and the preparation of, and the deliberations in, the Advisory Committee. As regards the Advisory Committee, its members also must not reveal the opinion of the Advisory Committee prior to its publication, if any, or any information concerning the deliberations which led to the formulation of the opinion.

7. ADOPTION, NOTIFICATION AND PUBLICATION OF DECISIONS

145. All decisions pursuant to Articles 7, 9, 23 and 24 of Regulation (EC) No 1/2003 are adopted by the Commission, on a proposal of the Commissioner responsible for competition policy.

146. Immediately after the decision has been adopted, the addressees will be informed of the decision. The Directorate-General for Competition endeavours to send a courtesy copy to the parties. A certified copy of the full text of the decision as well as a copy of the final report of the hearing officer will then be notified to the addressees by express courier service.

147. A press release will be published after the adoption of the decision by the Commission. The press release describes the scope of the case and the nature of the infringement. It also indicates (where appropriate) the amount of fines for each undertaking concerned and/or the remedies imposed or, in decisions pursuant to Article 9 of Regulation (EC) No 1/2003, the commitments rendered binding.

148. The summary of the decision, the hearing officer's final report as well as the Opinion of the Advisory Committee will be published shortly after the adoption of the decision in the *Official Journal of the European Union* in all official languages (93).

(93) With the exception of Irish (see Article 2 of Council Regulation (EC) No 920/2005 of 13 June 2005).

149. In addition to the requirements set out in Article 30(1) of Regulation (EC) No 1/2003, the Directorate-General for Competition will endeavour to publish as soon as possible on its website a non-confidential version of the decision in the authentic languages as well as in additional languages, if such versions are available. A non-confidential version of the decision will also be sent to the complainant. The addressees of the decision will normally be asked to provide the Commission within two weeks with a non-confidential version of the decision and to approve the summary. Should disputes arise regarding the deletion of business secrets, a provisional version of the decision excluding all information for which confidentiality has been requested will be made available on the website of the Directorate-General for Competition in any of the official languages in anticipation of a final version after resolution of the disputed parts.

150. In the interest of transparency, the Commission intends to make public on its website its decisions rejecting complaints (pursuant to Article 7 of the Implementing Regulation) or a summary thereof. If required for the protection of legitimate interests of the complainant, the published version of the decision will not identify the complainant. Decisions adopted pursuant to Article 7 of Regulation (EC) No 1/2003 or modifying commitments that have been made binding under Article 9 of that Regulation will also be made public on the website. Other types of decisions may also be published in appropriate cases.

8. FUTURE REVISION

151. This notice may be revised to reflect changes in the applicable legislation, significant developments in the case law of the Court of Justice of the European Union, or further experience gained in applying the competition rules. The Commission intends to engage in regular dialogue with the business and legal community and other interested parties on the experience gained through the application of this notice, of Regulation (EC) No 1/2003, the Implementing Regulation and its various notices and guidelines.

Annex 1

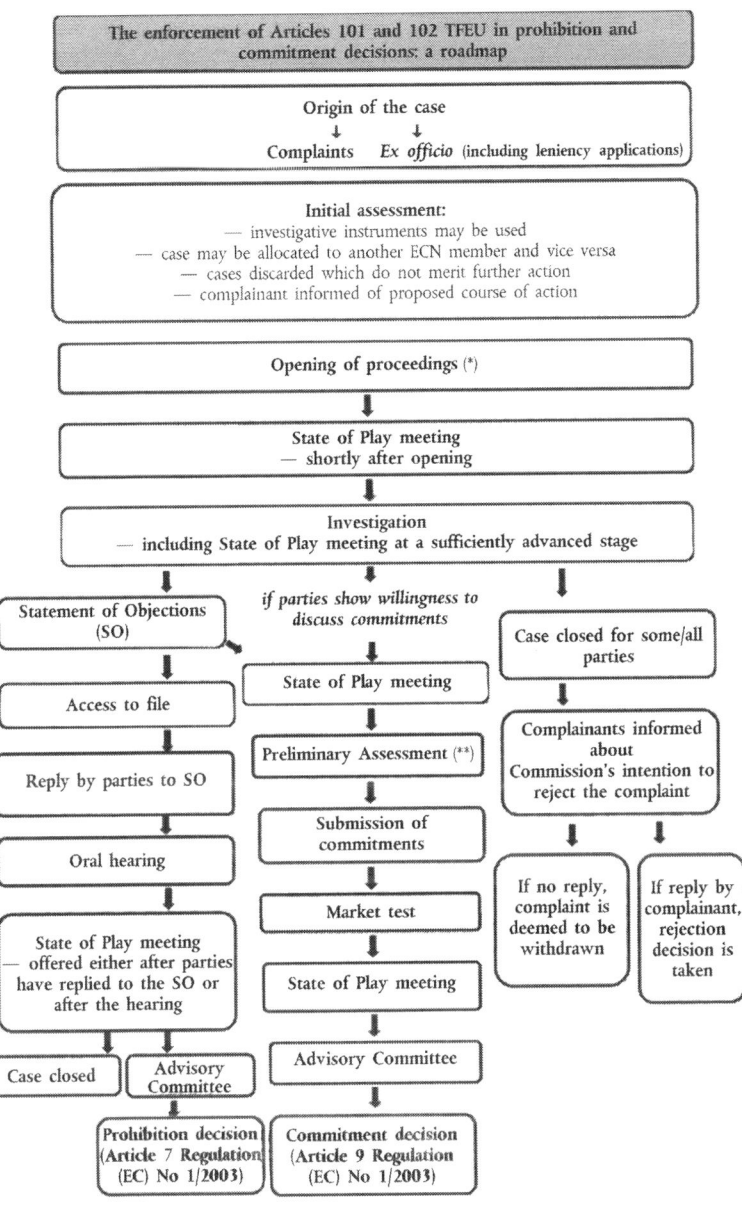

(*) With the exception of cartel proceedings, where the opening of proceedings normally takes place simultaneously with the adoption of the Statement of Objections.
(**) If an SO has already been issued, a Preliminary Assessment is not required.

Brochure DG Competition – Compliance matters, November 2011, – What companies can do better to respect EU competition rules, not published in the Official Journal

1. See: http://ec.europa.eu/competition/antitrust/compliance/compliance_matters_en.pdf

1. COMPLYING WITH COMPETITION RULES IN EUROPE: A COMPANY'S RESPONSIBILITY

EU competition rules concern everyone who does business in the EU, as they apply directly to all undertakings which are active within the EU. This means not only managers, who have choices to make in the interest of their companies, but also employees, who require guidance on how to implement these choices. Companies whose market behaviour fails to comply with EU competition rules run the risk of incurring high fines and facing other negative consequences.

Although under EU competition rules individuals are not penalised, their careers and jobs can be negatively affected by the wrong choices and even a company's existence may be threatened. In some Member States anti-competitive conduct may result in the individuals involved being penalised (including possible imprisonment), possibly in parallel to fines being imposed on companies.

1.1. General obligation to comply

The prime responsibility for complying with the law, as in any other field, lies with those who are subject to it. EU competition rules applying to undertakings are a fact of daily business life that has to be reckoned with, because ignorance of the law will not shield undertakings from the consequences of breaking it.

While it is clear that companies are under an obligation to comply with the rules, they are largely free to decide how to go about it. This is only natural, given that the size of companies, their resources for seeking advice, their field of activity and their exposure to the risk of becoming involved in infringements of EU competition rules vary considerably. It goes without saying that awareness of the rules is always a precondition for effective adherence to them.

1.2. Benefits of compliance

One important reason why a company should comply with competition rules, apart from being seen as doing business ethically, is the potentially high cost of non-compliance. But compliance can also – and indeed should – be approached positively.

An active and supportive strategy of compliance with the law and business ethics can certainly enhance a company's reputation and attractiveness for promotional and recruitment purposes, in much the same way as an explicit environmental or family-friendly agenda would do. It can help to raise job satisfaction of staff and contribute to a constructive sense of belonging, even pride, within the company. Staff who are aware of what constitutes illegal behaviour will also be more alert to wrongdoing by competitors or other commercial partners.

Your company can do more to help ensure that a level playing field is maintained by bringing potential malpractice to the attention of the competition authorities. First, it may inform the Commission 1 or a national competition authority 2 of any suspected infringement which comes to its attention. Second, it may apply for immunity from and/ or reduction of fines if it has been involved in an infringement. Finally, it may lodge a complaint if it is the victim of an infringement by other companies 3.

1 Concerns can by reported to the Commission by email to compmarket-information@ec.europa.eu. Please indicate your name and address, identify the companies and products concerned and describe the practice you have observed. This will help the European Commission to detect problems in the market and can be the starting point for an investigation.

2 The link to contact details of the national competition authorities of the EU Member States, members of the European Competition Network, is provided at the end of this brochure.

3 Citizens and/or companies may want to lodge a formal complaint if they are directly affected by a practice which they suspect restricts competition and are able to provide specific information. Certain requirements which must be fulfilled are explained in detail in the Commission Notice on the handling of complaints (O.J. C 101/65 of 27.04.2004), a summary of which can be found at http://europa.eu/legislation_summaries/competition/companies/l26111_en.htm. You can also send an email to comp-market-information@ec.europa.eu if you want more information on how to lodge a formal complaint.

1.3. Effectiveness: the sole benchmark of success

Any effort by a company to ensure compliance with EU competition rules is laudable. But what matters ultimately is that the rules are actually complied with. When it comes to taking practical steps to ensure compliance, companies should keep in mind that their efforts will be assessed on the basis of results, in other words they will be judged by their success in avoiding infringements. Merely paying lip-service to an abstract or formalistic commitment to comply will get them nowhere. Any credible compliance programme must be built on a firm foundation of management commitment and supported by a «topdown» compliance culture.

2. THE COSTS OF NON-COMPLIANCE FOR A COMPANY

2.1. Fines on companies

The fines which the European Commission imposes on companies that infringe EU competition rules can be very substantial, even as high as 10 % of a company's annual worldwide turnover. It should be noted that fines may be imposed even where the illegal purpose of an infringement was not actually achieved.

For example, members of a cartel that are found to have fixed prices will face high fines irrespective of whether or not the price levels rose as intended.

Several years ago the Commission set out its fining policy in writing 4, so as to make companies fully aware of the financial risk which they run if they do not comply with EU competition rules.

4 Guidelines on the method of setting fines imposed pursuant to Article 23(2) (a) of Regulation No 1/2003, published in the Offcial Journal of the EU under number O.J. C 210 of 1.9.2006, p. 2.

The risk of engaging in anti-competitive behaviour is thus considerable for a company, as evidenced particularly by the number of anti-cartel decisions in recent years, causing substantial fines to be imposed.

Cartels

Despite the Commission's and national competition authorities' determined fight against them, cartels still appear in many sectors, from basic industries to service markets, and companies of all sizes are involved in these infringements, from big multinational groups to small businesses.

In most of the cases investigated, unlawful behaviour had been encouraged and often directly perpetrated at the highest levels of responsibility. This shows that in certain circles, infringing the most essential rules of a market economy is still considered a rational way of doing business and maximising revenue.

In recent years, and in particular since 2001, the Commission has increased the frequency of its decisions prohibiting and fining cartels, imposing several billions of euros *in fine*s overall. Most of these decisions have been upheld on appeal.

The international removals cartel

In 2008, the Commission fined international removal companies a total of more than € 31 million for having participated in a cartel in Belgium.

Between 1984 and 2003 the companies fixed prices, shared the market and manipulated the procedures for submission of tenders, in particular by issuing false quotes («cover quotes») to customers and through a compensation system for rejected offers.

The Commission started the investigation on its own initiative with surprise inspections which proved particularly successful and abundant evidence of cartel activities was obtained.

One company received a reduction of 50 % of its fine under the Commission's Leniency Notice for providing the Commission with evidence of significant added value.

The industrial sewing thread cartel

In 2005, the Commission fined thread producers from Germany, Belgium, the Netherlands, France, Switzerland and the United Kingdom over € 43 million for their participation in different cartels.

Industrial thread is used in a variety of industries to sew or embroider various products such as clothes, home furnishings, motor vehicle seats and seatbelts, leather products, mattresses, footwear and ropes.

Between 1990 and 2001, these companies took part in regular meetings and had bilateral contacts to agree on price increases and/or target prices, to exchange sensitive information on price lists or prices charged to various consumers, to avoid undercutting the incumbent supplier's prices, and to arrange customer allocation.

National competition authorities have also targeted similar types of cartel behaviour in such sectors as coffee roasters, bath and personal care products, contact lenses, and flour.

Abusive behaviour by dominant companies is also of great – and indeed growing – concern for the Commission. This has led to a number of decisions imposing fines in the last few years relating to the ICT sector and to recently liberalised or partially liberalised markets, such as the energy, telecommunication and postal sectors. However, other sectors are not devoid of abusive practices by dominant companies.

2.2. Sanctions on individuals

In addition to imposing fines on undertakings, a number of Member States provide for sanctions on individuals (e.g. fines, director disqualification). The laws of some countries even allow custodial sanctions for individuals involved in general competition law infringements and/or in certain pre-defined types of infringements (e.g. bid-rigging). Such sanctions can be separate or cumulatively applied on top of pecuniary sanctions. Company managers who behave in an unlawful way therefore run the risk of jail in certain Member States.

2.3. Illegal agreements are void and may attract damages

Restrictive agreements which are incompatible with EU competition rules are automatically void and therefore cannot be enforced in court by the parties involved.

This means that a party cannot be obliged to honour an agreement which is illegal. Negative consequences for business can be considerable.

If an infringement of EU competition rules causes or has caused harm to a third party, the victim may bring a claim for damages before a national court against the perpetrator. For example, in the airfreight cartel case 5, damages claims were filed even before the Commission had fined 11 air cargo carriers for fixing prices.

5 See also Commission Press Release IP/10/1487 of 9.11.2010.

2.4. Bad press for lawbreakers and other collateral consequences

The Commission issues a press release whenever it has made a finding of illegal conduct and has fined the companies involved.

The resulting media coverage, both general and specialised, could have a detrimental impact on the reputation of those companies. Moreover, they may face hostility from clients and consumers who feel cheated.

Investigations by competition authorities can be time-consuming and costly for companies. Managers may become embroiled in lengthy legal discussions, thereby distracting attention from the core business activity.

3. COMPLIANCE WITH EU COMPETITION RULES – ARE YOU CERTAIN YOU HAVE COVERED THE RISK?

Two main provisions of the Treaty on the Functioning of the European Union (TFEU) deal with the market behaviour of companies. **Article 101** prohibits agreements between companies which restrict competition, unless they produce substantial benefits to customers and consumers, while **Article 102** outlaws abuses by dominant companies.

These fundamental rules and prohibitions are further clarified by legal texts adopted by the Council or the European Commission, as the case may be, spelling out how the basic principles are applied to particular sectors or to particular types of agreements or behaviour by companies. Note that at national level behaviour purely affecting competition within a Member State is similarly prohibited.

3.1. EU competition rules are directly applicable to your company

EU rules are about the competitive behaviour of companies and they apply directly in all EU Member States. No transposition into national law is required. This makes it all the more important for companies to be aware of them, as they are directly enforceable by both the European Commission and national competition authorities and courts.

It is worth noting that EU competition rules apply to «undertakings», a term which encompasses any entity engaged in an economic activity. Groupings of undertakings, such as trade associations and other industry groupings, while generally pursuing legitimate purposes and operating as a useful business forum, also have an obligation to comply with EU competition rules.

As indicated above, there are two basic types of behaviour in which companies may feel tempted to engage in the marketplace, but which are prohibited by EU competition law:

Illegal contacts and agreements between companies

Anti-competitive contacts between companies which, irrespective of their form, may distort the normal play of competitive forces are prohibited. Such contacts can take many forms and do not require the formal acceptance by the companies involved through an agreement. Even informal arrangements among business representatives can be considered illegal.

The most striking examples of anticompetitive contacts between companies include price fixing, sharing markets or customer allocation, production or output limitation, whether through bid rigging or otherwise. Such practices are often kept secret and generally referred to as «cartels». They are qualified as «hardcore» restrictions of competition in legal jargon as they are by their very nature most likely to restrict competition. These hardcore infringements are vigorously pursued by the Commission and can result in companies being heavily fined.

Private exchanges between competing companies of individualised information concerning their intended future prices or quantities can also amount to a hardcore infringement. More generally all exchanges of confidential, strategic information between competitors can give rise to competition concerns.

This concerns all types of information that reduces strategic uncertainty in the market, for example relating to production costs, customer lists, turnover, sales, capacities, qualities, marketing plans, etc.

Furthermore, even the unilateral disclosure of strategic information by one company via mail, email, phone calls or meetings to its competitor(s) can be considered problematic.

Agreements between companies at different levels of the supply chain, typically distribution agreements between suppliers and re-sellers, which aim at fixing prices or artificially partitioning the internal market, are also illegal.

For instance, a supplier may not oblige its distributors to refuse to sell goods to customers residing outside of a given territory. In addition, it may not impose on its distributors a resale price for a given product.

In short, the following basic «DON'Ts» should always be kept in mind by managers and employees of companies when they deal with competitors:

DON'T fix purchase or selling prices or other trading conditions;

DON'T limit production, markets, technical development or investment;

DON'T share markets or sources of supply;

DON'T exchange individualised information on intended future prices or quantities or other strategic information.

It is important to keep in mind that agreements between competitors and companies at different levels of the supply chain can also have anticompetitive effects even if they do not contain any of the above-mentioned hardcore restrictions.

For example, the agreement might have a negative impact on one of the parameters of competition, namely price, output, innovation, or the quality or variety of goods and services.

Such restrictive effects also need to be assessed by companies. A detailed framework for analysing the competitive impact of such agreements is provided by the Commission in specific guidelines.

Abuse of a dominant position

If companies have a large proportion of the business in a particular market, they are likely to hold a dominant position in that market. Such companies have a special responsibility not to engage in behaviour which is considered abusive. They should not act in a way that prevents competitors from competing effectively or drives them out of the market.

Examples of abusive conduct on the part of dominant companies are: charging unreasonably high prices which may exploit customers; charging unrealistically low prices which may be used to drive competitors out of the market; unjustified discrimination between customers; and forcing unjustified trading conditions on trading partners.

What about Small & Medium Enterprises?

All companies are subject to competition rules, with no differentiation according to their size. Being small is n° excuse for not complying with the applicable EU or national competition rules.

3.2. Activities by public authorities

It falls to both European and national competition authorities and courts to ensure that EU competition rules are complied with.

Enforcement against illegal practices

The European Commission ensures effective application of these rules throughout the EU. It investigates suspected infringements and addresses binding decisions to companies in order to bring established infringements to an end. The Commission also has the power to impose fines on companies which have been found to infringe EU competition law.

The enforcement activity by national competition authorities, which are equally empowered to apply EU competition rules, needs to be added to that of the Commission.

National courts also play an important role. They may declare an agreement void if it is in breach of EU competition rules. They may also hear claims for damages resulting from a company's infringement of EU competition rules and award compensation to plaintiffs.

Further explaining the rules

The Commission endeavours to make it easier for companies to acquaint themselves with and know the rules which they must respect.

Certain types of agreements are exempted from general prohibition if their restrictive nature can be justified by benefits for consumers and the economy as a whole. The hardcore practices mentioned above are very unlikely to bring such benefits.

Companies have to assess for themselves whether their behaviour complies with competition rules and in doing so they might consider seeking legal advice.

General guidance as to whether an agreement is deemed exempted or not is provided by the Commission in particular by way of so-called Block Exemption Regulations. Mostly, such Regulations exempt restrictions in certain categories of agreements (e.g. Research & Development, Specialisation or Distribution agreements) up to a certain level of market power, defined in terms of market share, providing there are no «hardcore» restrictions and certain conditions are met.

Outside the «safe harbour» of the block exemption, guidelines such as those on horizontal cooperation agreements 6 or on vertical restraints 7 also set out the Commission's policy and decision-making practice on a variety of competition issues.

6 Commission Guidelines on the applicability of Article 101 of the Treaty on the Functioning of the European Union to horizontal cooperation agreements, O.J. C 11 of 14.1.2011, p. 1.

7 Commission Guidelines on vertical restraints, O.J. C 130 of 19.5.2010, p. 1.

As regards abusive behaviour, the Commission has published guidance on its enforcement priorities in applying Article 102 TFEU 8.

8 Communication from the Commission, O.J. C 45 of 24.2.2009, p. 7.

Furthermore, formal Commission decisions 9 and Court judgments are publicly available, and the Commission publishes the formal opening and closing of proceedings on its website and/or by issuing a press release 10.

9 Article 30 of Council Regulation 1/2003.

10 The same applies in cases where proceedings have not been formally opened but DG Competition has already made public the fact that it is investigating a case (e.g. by having publicly confirmed certain inspections). See Commission Notice on Best Practices for the conduct of proceedings concerning Articles 101 and 102 TFEU, O.J. C 308 of 20.10.2011, p. 6.

Finally, the Commission also publishes an annual report on competition policy and a number of informative brochures 11.

11 See last section of this brochure «Where to find further relevant information».

4. HOW CAN YOUR COMPANY ENSURE COMPLIANCE?

4.1. A clear strategy

In order to ensure effective compliance with EU competition rules, companies should think ahead, develop an approach tailor-made for their particular situation and set it out in writing, rather than react to problems only when they occur.

The ultimate goal of such a strategy is to raise awareness of potential conflicts with EU competition law and disseminate adequate knowledge of how to avoid them at all levels of the company, from employees to middle and top management.

Identifying the overall risk and individual exposure

A successful company's compliance strategy would be based on a comprehensive analysis of the areas in which it is most likely to run a risk of infringing EU competition rules.

These areas will depend on factors such as:

• the sector of activity; for example a history of previous infringements in the sector indicates a need for particular attention.

• (frequency/level of) the company's interaction with competitors; for example in the course of industry meetings or within trade associations, but also in day-to-day commercial dealings.

• the characteristics of the market: position of the company and its competitors, barriers to entry ... If a company holds a dominant position in a market, the preventive measures to be taken will differ from those where the risk factor is more in the nature of «cartelisation».

But the exposure to that risk may vary greatly according to the position held by each member of staff. Employees whose specific areas of responsibility cause them to be particularly exposed (for example, employees who frequently interact with competitors as part of their job or through trade associations) would be made aware of what is at stake and of the basic principles to keep in mind.

Making the strategy explicit

In the interest of genuine compliance it is also important to disseminate the company's compliance strategy throughout its entire organisational structure. For the sake of internal clarity the strategy would preferably be laid down in writing, plainly worded and in all the working languages of the company, so that it is understood by everyone. It could for example take the form of a manual.

Such internal guidance would ideally contain a general description of EU competition law and its purpose, explain the way it is enforced and highlight the potential costs of non-compliance for the company. In this way, employees will better understand the reason behind the compliance strategy and its importance.

In addition, guidance in particular risk areas would be provided. For instance, a company which mainly deals in homogeneous products or has management or employee level contacts with competitors on a regular basis could stress the ban on cartels.

A practical set of «DON'Ts» and «RED FLAGS» can be a useful tool:

• a list of «DON'Ts» could include clearly illegal conduct such as price-fixing agreements, the exchange of future pricing intentions, allocation of production quotas and the fixing of market shares;

• «RED FLAGs» are warning signs which serve to identify situations in which infringements of competition rules can be suspected. They would encourage managers and employees to exercise particular caution in seeking to avoid any infringement on the part of their own company.

Visible and lasting commitment to the compliance strategy by senior management

Apart from choosing the right strategy and making it accessible to all staff, unequivocal senior management support is vital. The message that compliance with the law is a fundamental policy of a company needs to be clearly endorsed. This is an essential element of creating a culture of respect for the law within the company.

Designating an individual member of the senior management to take overall responsibility for compliance is considered advisable to ensure lasting commitment to and visibility for this objective.

Small and medium-sized companies have the advantage that the «tone from the top» can more easily be disseminated to the employees, who are fewer in number.

Whilst the Commission does not wish to be prescriptive, a company should devote sufficient resources appropriate to its size and the risks it faces – to ensure it has a credible programme.

4.2. Formal acts of acknowledgement by staff and consideration of compliance efforts in staff evaluation

Backup measures taken by companies as regards adherence of their staff to the adopted compliance strategy might include:
• asking staff for written acknowledgement of receipt of relevant information on compliance with EU competition law, for example when providing them with a manual or after dedicated training sessions. This form of explicit recognition helps to make individual staff members more aware that compliance concerns each and every one of them;
• putting in place positive incentives for employees to consider this objective with utmost seriousness. Compliance duties could for instance be part of job descriptions. A particularly vigilant attitude in that respect may also form part of the staff evaluation criteria;
• penalties for breach of the internal compliance rules. Such penalties would however have to be consistent with national employment law and doublechecked with legal advisers first.

Proper internal reporting mechanisms

A further essential feature of a successful compliance strategy is the inclusion of clear reporting mechanisms. Staff must not only be aware of potential conflicts with EU competition law, but also need to know whom to contact and in what form when concrete situations of conflict arise.

A company may for example consider appointing a compliance officer who directly reports to the company's management. The communication channels should in any event allow management to take swift action. Time is usually of the essence, irrespective of whether or not competition authorities are already aware of the particular problem.

If an employee or manager discovers or even suspects an infringement, the compliance strategy should provide her/him with concrete guidance on how to proceed.

An environment that encourages employees to speak up when they are confronted with questionable situations can be decisive for the effectiveness of the compliance strategy.

4.3. Constant update, contact points for advice and training

Obviously it is not enough just to put down a strategy on paper. Where a manual is made available to staff, it should be reviewed regularly. There should also be a clearly identified contact point where advice can be sought by staff in case of doubts about the compatibility of certain types of behaviour or agreements with EU competition law.

Training on applicable EU competition rules also plays an important role. Many companies already offer their staff, in particular newcomers, an ambitious training programme. In such cases the development of a module on competitive behaviour would be advisable. Where a company's analysis has indicated particular risk areas, training should be provided to those staff members who are most likely to be confronted with situations that could lead to the company becoming involved in infringements, for example sales personnel and sales managers as regards price agreements between competitors and anyone attending trade associations or industry events.

The specific details will vary from one business to another, depending on available resources and expertise. In any case, a compliance strategy will be more effective if it incorporates a clear mechanism for ensuring that updates of the written policy can be obtained by staff at any time and that all employees and managers are kept informed about new developments.

4.4. Monitoring/Auditing

Monitoring and auditing can serve as effective tools to prevent and detect anti-competitive behaviour inside the company. Monitoring, for instance by verifying the company's own behaviour in the competitive process in bidding markets, would mean a more preventive approach.

Auditing would tend to discover anticompetitive behaviour only after it had already occurred.

Both mechanisms can also be combined. The appropriate procedure depends on the specific needs of the undertaking, but some form of control is surely important to underpin the internal credibility of a compliance strategy.

4.5. The strategy has failed to ensure full compliance? It may still serve to limit exposure!

An effective compliance strategy will be expected to simply prevent any infringement from happening. Yet it may prove insufficient to ensure compliance, and there may nevertheless be instances of wrongdoing.

Stopping the infringement at the earliest possible stage

In such a case, the existence of a compliance strategy – on condition that it incorporates appropriate reporting mechanisms – will allow mishaps to be nipped in the bud.

It will enable the company to take appropriate measures without delay, so that any potential infringement is swiftly brought to an end. This will contribute to limiting damage to competition and minimising the company's exposure.

Cooperating under the leniency programme and the settlement procedure: limiting the damage of cartel behaviour

The detection mechanisms provided by an effective compliance strategy can also help to get the best out of the Commission's leniency programme. Aimed at enabling the detection of secret agreements between competitors – some of the most egregious infringements of competition law – it offers a unique opportunity, for companies willing to cooperate with the Commission (or with the national competition authorities), to receive immunity from fines or to get a fine reduced.

Full immunity can be granted to the company that is the first to denounce a secret cartel to the Commission or to provide the Commission with sufficient corroborative evidence. Companies which, despite their willingness to cooperate, file their leniency application after another competitor has qualified for immunity, can only hope to obtain a reduction of up to 50 % of any fine imposed on them.

However, remember that competition authorities are also on constant lookout for markets showing signs of distorted competition. When such signs appear, they may launch investigations themselves.

The exact conditions under which immunity from or reduction of fines in cartel cases is granted are explained in the corresponding Commission Notice 12.

12 O.J. C 45 of 19.2.2002.

Therefore, if you believe your company is or has been involved in a cartel, you might consider filing an application under the Commission's leniency programme and seeking legal advice in that respect.

Initial contact with the Commission should be made through the following dedicated fax number:

+ 32 2 299 45 85

Or through the following dedicated telephone numbers:

+ 32 2 298 41 90

+32 2 298 41 91

Further information on the Commission's leniency programme is available on the Internet at

http://ec.europa.eu/ competition/cartels/ leniency/leniency.html 13

13 See also Commission Press Release IP/06/1705 and Memo MEMO/06/469 of 7.12.2006.

Finally, if companies are prepared to acknowledge their participation in a cartel, the Commission may invite them to participate in a swifter conclusion of the procedure. The companies' cooperation in this «settlement» procedure is rewarded with a 10 % reduction of the fine in addition to any reductions for leniency.

4.6. The Commission welcomes compliance efforts by companies

The Commission welcomes and supports all compliance efforts by companies as they contribute to the firm rooting of a truly competitive culture in all sectors of the European economy.

Companies, supported by the legal profession, have already contemplated and indeed implemented schemes to ensure compliance with EU competition law. These schemes are usually referred to as «business compliance programmes» or just «compliance programmes».

In practice, they are often developed in reaction to past infringements or even after fines have been imposed. Increasingly such programmes are seen as an essential element of good corporate governance.

The Commission would advocate a more proactive approach that avoids infringements of EU competition rules from the outset. It cannot be overemphasised that a compliance programme worthy of the name must ensure that companies do not infringe competition law.

As has already been pointed out, it is not so much the effort made, but the result achieved, which counts once competition authorities become involved and launch an investigation. The quality of a compliance programme stands or falls by its effectiveness.

The Commission's attitude towards compliance programmes can, therefore, be summarised as follows:

• **Compliance programmes need to be tailor-made to the company concerned**. The range of situations that a compliance programme may need to address is wide. Equally the type, size and resources of companies which may find it useful to adopt a compliance programme vary considerably.

Consequently, there is **no «one size fits all» model**: an exhaustive allencompassing model would not be adequate. It is for each company to reflect on its needs to ensure compliance and develop its own strategy. Further legal advice can be sought if considered appropriate.

• **Access to useful information can be provided by the Commission but there will be no endorsement of any individual compliance programme**. While the Commission constantly seeks to improve the accessibility of relevant legislation and information on EU competition rules, it considers it not to be the task of competition authorities to formally advise on or approve individual compliance programmes.

Indeed, companies know best what is required for their own compliance strategy. This brochure provides companies with food for thought about the nature of their own compliance strategy. This includes for example creating the necessary positive and negative incentives to ensure compliance.

• Although all compliance efforts are welcomed, **the mere existence of a compliance programme is not enough to counter the finding of an infringement of competition rules** 14 – companies and their employees must, in fact, comply. If a company which has put a compliance programme in place is nevertheless found to have committed an infringement of EU competition rules, the question of whether there is any positive impact on the level of fines frequently arises. The answer is: No Compliance programmes should not be perceived by companies as an abstract and formalistic tool for supporting the argument that any fine to be imposed should be reduced if the company is «caught». The purpose of a compliance programme should be to avoid an infringement in the first place.

14 See, for example, Case C-189/02 P Dansk Rørindustri, paragraph 373.

For the purpose of setting the level of fines, the specific situation of a company is duly taken into account. But **the mere existence of a compliance programme will not be considered as an attenuating circumstance** 15. Nor will the setting-up of a compliance programme be considered as a valid argument justifying a reduction of the fine in the wake of investigation of an infringement. It would nevertheless be encouraged by competition authorities as a preventive means to avoid the occurrence and possible repetition of illegal behaviour in the first place.

15 See, for example, Joined Cases T-101/05 and T-111/05, BASF and UCB, paragraph 52, and Case T-138/07, Schindler Holding, paragraph 282.

It goes without saying that **the existence of a compliance programme will not be considered an aggravating circumstance** if an infringement is found by the enforcement authorities: if the programme has failed to deliver results, the sanction will come in the form of the fine imposed. In other words: a credible competition compliance programme can only deliver benefits to a company.

5. WHERE TO FIND FURTHER RELEVANT INFORMATION

Competition website on «Europa», the Internet site of the European Commission:

http://ec.europa.eu/competition

On this site, easy access to relevant legislative texts, Commission decisions, Press Releases, Annual Reports, sector-specific and other background information is provided. Links to other important sources of information, like the website of the Court of Justice of the European Union and the General Court, are equally available.

Publications on competition matters published by the European Commission:

http://ec.europa.eu/competition/publications/

Contact details of European Competition Authorities/members of the European Competition Network, available via:

http://ec.europa.eu/competition/ecn/competition_authorities.html

2.2. Concentration control

TABLE OF CONTENTS

2.2.1. Core legislation	338
2.2.2. Substantive rules	363
2.2.3. Procedural rules	436

2.2.1. Core legislation

Council Regulation (EC) N° 139/2004, 20 January 2004 – EC Merger Regulation	338
Communication from the Commission 18 June 2009 – Report on the functioning of Regulation No 139/2004	354
Commission Regulation (EC) N° 802/2004, 21 April 2004 – Implementing Regulation	356

Council Regulation (EC) N° 139/2004, 20 January 2004 on the control of concentrations between undertakings (the EC Merger Regulation)

(OJ L 24, 29 January 2004, p. 1)

1. The EC is now the EU. Articles 83 and 308 TEC are now articles 103 and 352 TFEU.

THE COUNCIL OF THE EUROPEAN UNION,

Having regard to the Treaty establishing the European Community, and in particular Articles 83 and 308 thereof,

Having regard to the proposal from the Commission (1),

Having regard to the opinion of the European Parliament (2),

Having regard to the opinion of the European Economic and Social Committee (3),

Whereas:

(1) Council Regulation (EEC) N° 4064/89 of 21 December 1989 on the control of concentrations between undertakings (4) has been substantially amended. Since further amendments are to be made, it should be recast in the interest of clarity.

(2) For the achievement of the aims of the Treaty, Article 3(1)(g) gives the Community the objective of instituting a system ensuring that competition in the internal market is not distorted. Article 4(1) of the Treaty provides that the activities of the Member States and the Community are to be conducted in accordance with the principle of an open market economy with free competition. These principles are essential for the further development of the internal market.

(3) The completion of the internal market and of economic and monetary union, the enlargement of the European Union and the lowering of international barriers to trade and investment will continue to result in major corporate reorganisations, particularly in the form of concentrations.

(4) Such reorganisations are to be welcomed to the extent that they are in line with the requirements of dynamic competition and capable of increasing the competitiveness of European industry, improving the conditions of growth and raising the standard of living in the Community.

(5) However, it should be ensured that the process of reorganisation does not result in lasting damage to competition; Community law must therefore include provisions governing those concentrations which may significantly impede effective competition in the common market or in a substantial part of it.

(6) A specific legal instrument is therefore necessary to permit effective control of all concentrations in terms of their effect on the structure of competition in the Community and to be the only instrument applicable to such concentrations. Regulation (EEC) N° 4064/89 has allowed a Community policy to develop in this field. In the light of experience, however, that Regulation should now be recast into legislation designed to meet the challenges of a more integrated market and the future enlargement of the European Union. In accordance with the principles of subsidiarity and of proportionality as set out in Article 5 of the Treaty, this Regulation does not go beyond what is necessary in order to achieve the objective of ensuring that competition in the common market is not distorted, in accordance with the principle of an open market economy with free competition.

(7) Articles 81 and 82, while applicable, according to the case-law of the Court of Justice, to certain concentrations, are not sufficient to control all operations which may prove to be incompatible with the system of undistorted competition envisaged in the Treaty. This Regulation should therefore be based not only on Article 83 but, principally, on Article 308 of the Treaty, under which the Community may give itself the additional powers of action necessary for the attainment of its objectives, and also powers of action with regard to concentrations on the markets for agricultural products listed in Annex I to the Treaty.

(8) The provisions to be adopted in this Regulation should apply to significant structural changes, the impact of which on the market goes beyond the national borders of any one Member State. Such concentrations should, as a general rule, be reviewed exclusively at Community level, in application of a «one-stop shop» system and in compliance with the principle of subsidiarity. Concentrations not covered by this Regulation come, in principle, within the jurisdiction of the Member States.

(9) The scope of application of this Regulation should be defined according to the geographical area of activity of the undertakings concerned and be limited by quantitative

thresholds in order to cover those concentrations which have a Community dimension. The Commission should report to the Council on the implementation of the applicable thresholds and criteria so that the Council, acting in accordance with Article 202 of the Treaty, is in a position to review them regularly, as well as the rules regarding pre-notification referral, in the light of the experience gained; this requires statistical data to be provided by the Member States to the Commission to enable it to prepare such reports and possible proposals for amendments. The Commission's reports and proposals should be based on relevant information regularly provided by the Member States.

(10) A concentration with a Community dimension should be deemed to exist where the aggregate turnover of the undertakings concerned exceeds given thresholds; that is the case irrespective of whether or not the undertakings effecting the concentration have their seat or their principal fields of activity in the Community, provided they have substantial operations there.

(11) The rules governing the referral of concentrations from the Commission to Member States and from Member States to the Commission should operate as an effective corrective mechanism in the light of the principle of subsidiarity; these rules protect the competition interests of the Member States in an adequate manner and take due account of legal certainty and the «one-stop shop» principle.

(12) Concentrations may qualify for examination under a number of national merger control systems if they fall below the turnover thresholds referred to in this Regulation. Multiple notification of the same transaction increases legal uncertainty, effort and cost for undertakings and may lead to conflicting assessments. The system whereby concentrations may be referred to the Commission by the Member States concerned should therefore be further developed.

(13) The Commission should act in close and constant liaison with the competent authorities of the Member States from which it obtains comments and information.

(14) The Commission and the competent authorities of the Member States should together form a network of public authorities, applying their respective competences in close cooperation, using efficient arrangements for information-sharing and consultation, with a view to ensuring that a case is dealt with by the most appropriate authority, in the light of the principle of subsidiarity and with a view to ensuring that multiple notifications of a given concentration are avoided to the greatest extent possible. Referrals of concentrations from the Commission to Member States and from Member States to the Commission should be made in an efficient manner avoiding, to the greatest extent possible, situations where a concentration is subject to a referral both before and after its notification.

(15) The Commission should be able to refer to a Member State notified concentrations with a Community dimension which threaten significantly to affect competition in a market within that Member State presenting all the characteristics of a distinct market. Where the concentration affects competition on such a market, which does not constitute a substantial part of the common market, the Commission should be obliged, upon request, to refer the whole or part of the case to the Member State concerned. A Member State should be able to refer to the Commission a concentration which does not have a Community dimension but which affects trade between Member States and threatens to significantly affect competition within its territory.

Other Member States which are also competent to review the concentration should be able to join the request. In such a situation, in order to ensure the efficiency and predictability of the system, national time limits should be suspended until a decision has been reached as to the referral of the case. The Commission should have the power to examine and deal with a concentration on behalf of a requesting Member State or requesting Member States.

(16) The undertakings concerned should be granted the possibility of requesting referrals to or from the Commission before a concentration is notified so as to further improve the efficiency of the system for the control of concentrations within the Community. In such situations, the Commission and national competition authorities should decide within short, clearly defined time limits whether a referral to or from the Commission ought to be made, thereby ensuring the efficiency of the system. Upon request by the undertakings concerned, the Commission should be able to refer to a Member State a concentration with a Community dimension which may significantly affect competition in a market within that Member State presenting all the characteristics of a distinct market; the undertakings concerned should not, however, be required to demonstrate that the effects of the concentration would be detrimental to competition. A concentration should not be referred from the Commission to a Member State which has expressed its disagreement to such a referral. Before notification to national authorities, the undertakings concerned should also be able to request that a concentration without a Community dimension which is capable of being reviewed under the national competition laws of at least three Member States be referred to the Commission. Such requests for pre-notification referrals to the Commission would be particularly pertinent in situations where the concentration would affect competition beyond the territory of one Member State. Where a concentration capable of being reviewed under the competition laws of three or more Member States is referred to the Commission prior to any national notification, and no Member State competent to review the case expresses its disagreement, the Commission should acquire exclusive competence to review the concentration and such a concentration should be deemed to have a Community dimension. Such pre-notification referrals from Member States to the Commission should not, however, be made where at least one Member State competent to review the case has expressed its disagreement with such a referral.

(17) The Commission should be given exclusive competence to apply this Regulation, subject to review by the Court of Justice.

(18) The Member States should not be permitted to apply their national legislation on competition to concentrations with a Community dimension, unless this Regulation makes provision therefor. The relevant powers of national authorities should be limited to cases where, failing intervention by the Commission, effective competition is likely to be significantly impeded within the territory of a Member State and where the competition interests of that Member State cannot be sufficiently protected otherwise by this Regulation. The Member States concerned must act promptly in such cases; this Regulation cannot, because of the diversity of national law, fix a single time limit for the adoption of final decisions under national law.

(19) Furthermore, the exclusive application of this Regulation to concentrations with a Community dimension is

without prejudice to Article 296 of the Treaty, and does not prevent the Member States from taking appropriate measures to protect legitimate interests other than those pursued by this Regulation, provided that such measures are compatible with the general principles and other provisions of Community law.

(20) It is expedient to define the concept of concentration in such a manner as to cover operations bringing about a lasting change in the control of the undertakings concerned and therefore in the structure of the market. It is therefore appropriate to include, within the scope of this Regulation, all joint ventures performing on a lasting basis all the functions of an autonomous economic entity. It is moreover appropriate to treat as a single concentration transactions that are closely connected in that they are linked by condition or take the form of a series of transactions in securities taking place within a reasonably short period of time.

(21) This Regulation should also apply where the undertakings concerned accept restrictions directly related to, and necessary for, the implementation of the concentration. Commission decisions declaring concentrations compatible with the common market in application of this Regulation should automatically cover such restrictions, without the Commission having to assess such restrictions in individual cases. At the request of the undertakings concerned, however, the Commission should, in cases presenting novel or unresolved questions giving rise to genuine uncertainty, expressly assess whether or not any restriction is directly related to, and necessary for, the implementation of the concentration. A case presents a novel or unresolved question giving rise to genuine uncertainty if the question is not covered by the relevant Commission notice in force or a published Commission decision.

(22) The arrangements to be introduced for the control of concentrations should, without prejudice to Article 86(2) of the Treaty, respect the principle of non-discrimination between the public and the private sectors. In the public sector, calculation of the turnover of an undertaking concerned in a concentration needs, therefore, to take account of undertakings making up an economic unit with an independent power of decision, irrespective of the way in which their capital is held or of the rules of administrative supervision applicable to them.

(23) It is necessary to establish whether or not concentrations with a Community dimension are compatible with the common market in terms of the need to maintain and develop effective competition in the common market. In so doing, the Commission must place its appraisal within the general framework of the achievement of the fundamental objectives referred to in Article 2 of the Treaty establishing the European Community and Article 2 of the Treaty on European Union.

(24) In order to ensure a system of undistorted competition in the common market, in furtherance of a policy conducted in accordance with the principle of an open market economy with free competition, this Regulation must permit effective control of all concentrations from the point of view of their effect on competition in the Community. Accordingly, Regulation (EEC) N° 4064/89 established the principle that a concentration with a Community dimension which creates or strengthens a dominant position as a result of which effective competition in the common market or in a substantial part of it would be significantly impeded should be declared incompatible with the common market.

(25) In view of the consequences that concentrations in oligopolistic market structures may have, it is all the more necessary to maintain effective competition in such markets. Many oligopolistic markets exhibit a healthy degree of competition. However, under certain circumstances, concentrations involving the elimination of important competitive constraints that the merging parties had exerted upon each other, as well as a reduction of competitive pressure on the remaining competitors, may, even in the absence of a likelihood of coordination between the members of the oligopoly, result in a significant impediment to effective competition. The Community courts have, however, not to date expressly interpreted Regulation (EEC) N° 4064/89 as requiring concentrations giving rise to such non-coordinated effects to be declared incompatible with the common market. Therefore, in the interests of legal certainty, it should be made clear that this Regulation permits effective control of all such concentrations by providing that any concentration which would significantly impede effective competition, in the common market or in a substantial part of it, should be declared incompatible with the common market. The notion of «significant impediment to effective competition» in Article 2(2) and (3) should be interpreted as extending, beyond the concept of dominance, only to the anti-competitive effects of a concentration resulting from the non-coordinated behaviour of undertakings which would not have a dominant position on the market concerned.

(26) A significant impediment to effective competition generally results from the creation or strengthening of a dominant position. With a view to preserving the guidance that may be drawn from past judgments of the European courts and Commission decisions pursuant to Regulation (EEC) N° 4064/89, while at the same time maintaining consistency with the standards of competitive harm which have been applied by the Commission and the Community courts regarding the compatibility of a concentration with the common market, this Regulation should accordingly establish the principle that a concentration with a Community dimension which would significantly impede effective competition, in the common market or in a substantial part thereof, in particular as a result of the creation or strengthening of a dominant position, is to be declared incompatible with the common market.

(27) In addition, the criteria of Article 81(1) and (3) of the Treaty should be applied to joint ventures performing, on a lasting basis, all the functions of autonomous economic entities, to the extent that their creation has as its consequence an appreciable restriction of competition between undertakings that remain independent.

(28) In order to clarify and explain the Commission's appraisal of concentrations under this Regulation, it is appropriate for the Commission to publish guidance which should provide a sound economic framework for the assessment of concentrations with a view to determining whether or not they may be declared compatible with the common market.

(29) In order to determine the impact of a concentration on competition in the common market, it is appropriate to take account of any substantiated and likely efficiencies put forward by the undertakings concerned. It is possible that the efficiencies brought about by the concentration counteract the effects on competition, and in particular the potential harm to consumers, that it might otherwise have and that, as a consequence, the concentration would not significantly impede effective competition, in the com-

mon market or in a substantial part of it, in particular as a result of the creation or strengthening of a dominant position. The Commission should publish guidance on the conditions under which it may take efficiencies into account in the assessment of a concentration.

(30) Where the undertakings concerned modify a notified concentration, in particular by offering commitments with a view to rendering the concentration compatible with the common market, the Commission should be able to declare the concentration, as modified, compatible with the common market. Such commitments should be proportionate to the competition problem and entirely eliminate it. It is also appropriate to accept commitments before the initiation of proceedings where the competition problem is readily identifiable and can easily be remedied. It should be expressly provided that the Commission may attach to its decision conditions and obligations in order to ensure that the undertakings concerned comply with their commitments in a timely and effective manner so as to render the concentration compatible with the common market. Transparency and effective consultation of Member States as well as of interested third parties should be ensured throughout the procedure.

(31) The Commission should have at its disposal appropriate instruments to ensure the enforcement of commitments and to deal with situations where they are not fulfilled. In cases of failure to fulfil a condition attached to the decision declaring a concentration compatible with the common market, the situation rendering the concentration compatible with the common market does not materialise and the concentration, as implemented, is therefore not authorised by the Commission. As a consequence, if the concentration is implemented, it should be treated in the same way as a non-notified concentration implemented without authorisation. Furthermore, where the Commission has already found that, in the absence of the condition, the concentration would be incompatible with the common market, it should have the power to directly order the dissolution of the concentration, so as to restore the situation prevailing prior to the implementation of the concentration. Where an obligation attached to a decision declaring the concentration compatible with the common market is not fulfilled, the Commission should be able to revoke its decision. Moreover, the Commission should be able to impose appropriate financial sanctions where conditions or obligations are not fulfilled.

(32) Concentrations which, by reason of the limited market share of the undertakings concerned, are not liable to impede effective competition may be presumed to be compatible with the common market. Without prejudice to Articles 81 and 82 of the Treaty, an indication to this effect exists, in particular, where the market share of the undertakings concerned does not exceed 25 % either in the common market or in a substantial part of it.

(33) The Commission should have the task of taking all the decisions necessary to establish whether or not concentrations with a Community dimension are compatible with the common market, as well as decisions designed to restore the situation prevailing prior to the implementation of a concentration which has been declared incompatible with the common market.

(34) To ensure effective control, undertakings should be obliged to give prior notification of concentrations with a Community dimension following the conclusion of the agreement, the announcement of the public bid or the acquisition of a controlling interest. Notification should also be possible where the undertakings concerned satisfy the Commission of their intention to enter into an agreement for a proposed concentration and demonstrate to the Commission that their plan for that proposed concentration is sufficiently concrete, for example on the basis of an agreement in principle, a memorandum of understanding, or a letter of intent signed by all undertakings concerned, or, in the case of a public bid, where they have publicly announced an intention to make such a bid, provided that the intended agreement or bid would result in a concentration with a Community dimension. The implementation of concentrations should be suspended until a final decision of the Commission has been taken. However, it should be possible to derogate from this suspension at the request of the undertakings concerned, where appropriate. In deciding whether or not to grant a derogation, the Commission should take account of all pertinent factors, such as the nature and gravity of damage to the undertakings concerned or to third parties, and the threat to competition posed by the concentration. In the interest of legal certainty, the validity of transactions must nevertheless be protected as much as necessary.

(35) A period within which the Commission must initiate proceedings in respect of a notified concentration and a period within which it must take a final decision on the compatibility or incompatibility with the common market of that concentration should be laid down. These periods should be extended whenever the undertakings concerned offer commitments with a view to rendering the concentration compatible with the common market, in order to allow for sufficient time for the analysis and market testing of such commitment offers and for the consultation of Member States as well as interested third parties. A limited extension of the period within which the Commission must take a final decision should also be possible in order to allow sufficient time for the investigation of the case and the verification of the facts and arguments submitted to the Commission.

(36) The Community respects the fundamental rights and observes the principles recognised in particular by the Charter of Fundamental Rights of the European Union (5). Accordingly, this Regulation should be interpreted and applied with respect to those rights and principles.

(37) The undertakings concerned must be afforded the right to be heard by the Commission when proceedings have been initiated; the members of the management and supervisory bodies and the recognised representatives of the employees of the undertakings concerned, and interested third parties, must also be given the opportunity to be heard.

(38) In order properly to appraise concentrations, the Commission should have the right to request all necessary information and to conduct all necessary inspections throughout the Community. To that end, and with a view to protecting competition effectively, the Commission's powers of investigation need to be expanded. The Commission should, in particular, have the right to interview any persons who may be in possession of useful information and to record the statements made.

(39) In the course of an inspection, officials authorised by the Commission should have the right to ask for any information relevant to the subject matter and purpose of the inspection; they should also have the right to affix seals during inspections, particularly in circumstances where there are reasonable grounds to suspect that a concentration has been implemented without being notified; that incorrect, incomplete or misleading information has been

supplied to the Commission; or that the undertakings or persons concerned have failed to comply with a condition or obligation imposed by decision of the Commission. In any event, seals should only be used in exceptional circumstances, for the period of time strictly necessary for the inspection, normally not for more than 48 hours.

(40) Without prejudice to the case-law of the Court of Justice, it is also useful to set out the scope of the control that the national judicial authority may exercise when it authorises, as provided by national law and as a precautionary measure, assistance from law enforcement authorities in order to overcome possible opposition on the part of the undertaking against an inspection, including the affixing of seals, ordered by Commission decision. It results from the case-law that the national judicial authority may in particular ask of the Commission further information which it needs to carry out its control and in the absence of which it could refuse the authorisation. The case-law also confirms the competence of the national courts to control the application of national rules governing the implementation of coercive measures. The competent authorities of the Member States should cooperate actively in the exercise of the Commission's investigative powers.

(41) When complying with decisions of the Commission, the undertakings and persons concerned cannot be forced to admit that they have committed infringements, but they are in any event obliged to answer factual questions and to provide documents, even if this information may be used to establish against themselves or against others the existence of such infringements.

(42) For the sake of transparency, all decisions of the Commission which are not of a merely procedural nature should be widely publicised. While ensuring preservation of the rights of defence of the undertakings concerned, in particular the right of access to the file, it is essential that business secrets be protected. The confidentiality of information exchanged in the network and with the competent authorities of third countries should likewise be safeguarded.

(43) Compliance with this Regulation should be enforceable, as appropriate, by means of fines and periodic penalty payments. The Court of Justice should be given unlimited jurisdiction in that regard pursuant to Article 229 of the Treaty.

(44) The conditions in which concentrations, involving undertakings having their seat or their principal fields of activity in the Community, are carried out in third countries should be observed, and provision should be made for the possibility of the Council giving the Commission an appropriate mandate for negotiation with a view to obtaining non-discriminatory treatment for such undertakings.

(45) This Regulation in no way detracts from the collective rights of employees, as recognised in the undertakings concerned, notably with regard to any obligation to inform or consult their recognised representatives under Community and national law.

(46) The Commission should be able to lay down detailed rules concerning the implementation of this Regulation in accordance with the procedures for the exercise of implementing powers conferred on the Commission. For the adoption of such implementing provisions, the Commission should be assisted by an Advisory Committee composed of the representatives of the Member States as specified in Article 23,

HAS ADOPTED THIS REGULATION:

(1) OJ C 20, 28.1.2003, p. 4.

(2) Opinion delivered on 9.10.2003 (not yet published in the *Official Journal*).

(3) Opinion delivered on 24.10.2003 (not yet published in the *Official Journal*).

(4) OJ L 395, 30.12.1989, p. 1. Corrected version in OJ L 257, 21.9.1990, p. 13. Regulation as last amended by Regulation (EC) N° 1310/97 (OJ L 180, 9.7.1997, p. 1). Corrigendum in OJ L 40, 13.2.1998, p. 17.

(5) OJ C 364, 18.12.2000, p. 1.

Art. 1. *Scope*

1. Without prejudice to Article 4(5) and Article 22, this Regulation shall apply to all concentrations with a Community dimension as defined in this Article.

2. A concentration has a Community dimension where:

(a) the combined aggregate worldwide turnover of all the undertakings concerned is more than EUR 5.000 million; and

(b) the aggregate Community-wide turnover of each of at least two of the undertakings concerned is more than EUR 250 million,

unless each of the undertakings concerned achieves more than two-thirds of its aggregate Community-wide turnover within one and the same Member State.

3. A concentration that does not meet the thresholds laid down in paragraph 2 has a Community dimension where:

(a) the combined aggregate worldwide turnover of all the undertakings concerned is more than EUR 2.500 million;

(b) in each of at least three Member States, the combined aggregate turnover of all the undertakings concerned is more than EUR 100 million;

(c) in each of at least three Member States included for the purpose of point *(b)*, the aggregate turnover of each of at least two of the undertakings concerned is more than EUR 25 million; and

(d) the aggregate Community-wide turnover of each of at least two of the undertakings concerned is more than EUR 100 million,

unless each of the undertakings concerned achieves more than two-thirds of its aggregate Community-wide turnover within one and the same Member State.

4. On the basis of statistical data that may be regularly provided by the Member States, the Commission shall report to the Council on the operation of the thresholds and criteria set out in paragraphs 2 and 3 by 1 July 2009 and may present proposals pursuant to paragraph 5.

5. Following the report referred to in paragraph 4 and on a proposal from the Commission, the Council, acting by a qualified majority, may revise the thresholds and criteria mentioned in paragraph 3.

Art. 2. *Appraisal of concentrations*

1. Concentrations within the scope of this Regulation shall be appraised in accordance with the objectives of this Regulation and the following provisions with a view to establishing whether or not they are compatible with the common market.

In making this appraisal, the Commission shall take into account:

(a) the need to maintain and develop effective competition within the common market in view of, among other things, the structure of all the markets concerned and the

actual or potential competition from undertakings located either within or outwith the Community;

(b) the market position of the undertakings concerned and their economic and financial power, the alternatives available to suppliers and users, their access to supplies or markets, any legal or other barriers to entry, supply and demand trends for the relevant goods and services, the interests of the intermediate and ultimate consumers, and the development of technical and economic progress provided that it is to consumers' advantage and does not form an obstacle to competition.

2. A concentration which would not significantly impede effective competition in the common market or in a substantial part of it, in particular as a result of the creation or strengthening of a dominant position, shall be declared compatible with the common market.

3. A concentration which would significantly impede effective competition, in the common market or in a substantial part of it, in particular as a result of the creation or strengthening of a dominant position, shall be declared incompatible with the common market.

4. To the extent that the creation of a joint venture constituting a concentration pursuant to Article 3 has as its object or effect the coordination of the competitive behaviour of undertakings that remain independent, such coordination shall be appraised in accordance with the criteria of Article 81(1) and (3) of the Treaty, with a view to establishing whether or not the operation is compatible with the common market.

5. In making this appraisal, the Commission shall take into account in particular:

– whether two or more parent companies retain, to a significant extent, activities in the same market as the joint venture or in a market which is downstream or upstream from that of the joint venture or in a neighbouring market closely related to this market;

– whether the coordination which is the direct consequence of the creation of the joint venture affords the undertakings concerned the possibility of eliminating competition in respect of a substantial part of the products or services in question.

Art. 3. *Definition of concentration*

1. A concentration shall be deemed to arise where a change of control on a lasting basis results from:

(a) the merger of two or more previously independent undertakings or parts of undertakings; or

(b) the acquisition, by one or more persons already controlling at least one undertaking, or by one or more undertakings, whether by purchase of securities or assets, by contract or by any other means, of direct or indirect control of the whole or parts of one or more other undertakings.

2. Control shall be constituted by rights, contracts or any other means which, either separately or in combination and having regard to the considerations of fact or law involved, confer the possibility of exercising decisive influence on an undertaking, in particular by:

(a) ownership or the right to use all or part of the assets of an undertaking;

(b) rights or contracts which confer decisive influence on the composition, voting or decisions of the organs of an undertaking.

3. Control is acquired by persons or undertakings which:

(a) are holders of the rights or entitled to rights under the contracts concerned; or

(b) while not being holders of such rights or entitled to rights under such contracts, have the power to exercise the rights deriving therefrom.

4. The creation of a joint venture performing on a lasting basis all the functions of an autonomous economic entity shall constitute a concentration within the meaning of paragraph 1*(b)*.

5. A concentration shall not be deemed to arise where:

(a) credit institutions or other financial institutions or insurance companies, the normal activities of which include transactions and dealing in securities for their own account or for the account of others, hold on a temporary basis securities which they have acquired in an undertaking with a view to reselling them, provided that they do not exercise voting rights in respect of those securities with a view to determining the competitive behaviour of that undertaking or provided that they exercise such voting rights only with a view to preparing the disposal of all or part of that undertaking or of its assets or the disposal of those securities and that any such disposal takes place within one year of the date of acquisition; that period may be extended by the Commission on request where such institutions or companies can show that the disposal was not reasonably possible within the period set;

(b) control is acquired by an office-holder according to the law of a Member State relating to liquidation, winding up, insolvency, cessation of payments, compositions or analogous proceedings;

(c) the operations referred to in paragraph 1*(b)* are carried out by the financial holding companies referred to in Article 5(3) of Fourth Council Directive 78/660/EEC of 25 July 1978 based on Article 54(3)*(g)* of the Treaty on the annual accounts of certain types of companies (6) provided however that the voting rights in respect of the holding are exercised, in particular in relation to the appointment of members of the management and supervisory bodies of the undertakings in which they have holdings, only to maintain the full value of those investments and not to determine directly or indirectly the competitive conduct of those undertakings.

Art. 4. *Prior notification of concentrations and pre-notification referral at the request of the notifying parties*

1. Concentrations with a Community dimension defined in this Regulation shall be notified to the Commission prior to their implementation and following the conclusion of the agreement, the announcement of the public bid, or the acquisition of a controlling interest.

Notification may also be made where the undertakings concerned demonstrate to the Commission a good faith intention to conclude an agreement or, in the case of a public bid, where they have publicly announced an intention to make such a bid, provided that the intended agreement or bid would result in a concentration with a Community dimension.

For the purposes of this Regulation, the term «notified concentration» shall also cover intended concentrations notified pursuant to the second subparagraph. For the purposes of paragraphs 4 and 5 of this Article, the term «concentration» includes intended concentrations within the meaning of the second subparagraph.

2. A concentration which consists of a merger within the meaning of Article 3(1)*(a)* or in the acquisition of joint control within the meaning of Article 3(1)*(b)* shall be notified

jointly by the parties to the merger or by those acquiring joint control as the case may be. In all other cases, the notification shall be effected by the person or undertaking acquiring control of the whole or parts of one or more undertakings.

3. Where the Commission finds that a notified concentration falls within the scope of this Regulation, it shall publish the fact of the notification, at the same time indicating the names of the undertakings concerned, their country of origin, the nature of the concentration and the economic sectors involved. The Commission shall take account of the legitimate interest of undertakings in the protection of their business secrets.

4. Prior to the notification of a concentration within the meaning of paragraph 1, the persons or undertakings referred to in paragraph 2 may inform the Commission, by means of a reasoned submission, that the concentration may significantly affect competition in a market within a Member State which presents all the characteristics of a distinct market and should therefore be examined, in whole or in part, by that Member State.

The Commission shall transmit this submission to all Member States without delay. The Member State referred to in the reasoned submission shall, within 15 working days of receiving the submission, express its agreement or disagreement as regards the request to refer the case. Where that Member State takes no such decision within this period, it shall be deemed to have agreed.

Unless that Member State disagrees, the Commission, where it considers that such a distinct market exists, and that competition in that market may be significantly affected by the concentration, may decide to refer the whole or part of the case to the competent authorities of that Member State with a view to the application of that State's national competition law.

The decision whether or not to refer the case in accordance with the third subparagraph shall be taken within 25 working days starting from the receipt of the reasoned submission by the Commission. The Commission shall inform the other Member States and the persons or undertakings concerned of its decision. If the Commission does not take a decision within this period, it shall be deemed to have adopted a decision to refer the case in accordance with the submission made by the persons or undertakings concerned.

If the Commission decides, or is deemed to have decided, pursuant to the third and fourth subparagraphs, to refer the whole of the case, no notification shall be made pursuant to paragraph 1 and national competition law shall apply. Article 9(6) to (9) shall apply *mutatis mutandis*.

5. With regard to a concentration as defined in Article 3 which does not have a Community dimension within the meaning of Article 1 and which is capable of being reviewed under the national competition laws of at least three Member States, the persons or undertakings referred to in paragraph 2 may, before any notification to the competent authorities, inform the Commission by means of a reasoned submission that the concentration should be examined by the Commission.

The Commission shall transmit this submission to all Member States without delay.

Any Member State competent to examine the concentration under its national competition law may, within 15 working days of receiving the reasoned submission, express its disagreement as regards the request to refer the case.

Where at least one such Member State has expressed its disagreement in accordance with the third subparagraph within the period of 15 working days, the case shall not be referred. The Commission shall, without delay, inform all Member States and the persons or undertakings concerned of any such expression of disagreement.

Where no Member State has expressed its disagreement in accordance with the third subparagraph within the period of 15 working days, the concentration shall be deemed to have a Community dimension and shall be notified to the Commission in accordance with paragraphs 1 and 2. In such situations, no Member State shall apply its national competition law to the concentration.

6. The Commission shall report to the Council on the operation of paragraphs 4 and 5 by 1 July 2009. Following this report and on a proposal from the Commission, the Council, acting by a qualified majority, may revise paragraphs 4 and 5.

Art. 5. *Calculation of turnover*

1. Aggregate turnover within the meaning of this Regulation shall comprise the amounts derived by the undertakings concerned in the preceding financial year from the sale of products and the provision of services falling within the undertakings' ordinary activities after deduction of sales rebates and of value added tax and other taxes directly related to turnover. The aggregate turnover of an undertaking concerned shall not include the sale of products or the provision of services between any of the undertakings referred to in paragraph 4.

Turnover, in the Community or in a Member State, shall comprise products sold and services provided to undertakings or consumers, in the Community or in that Member State as the case may be.

2. By way of derogation from paragraph 1, where the concentration consists of the acquisition of parts, whether or not constituted as legal entities, of one or more undertakings, only the turnover relating to the parts which are the subject of the concentration shall be taken into account with regard to the seller or sellers.

However, two or more transactions within the meaning of the first subparagraph which take place within a two-year period between the same persons or undertakings shall be treated as one and the same concentration arising on the date of the last transaction.

3. In place of turnover the following shall be used:

(a) for credit institutions and other financial institutions, the sum of the following income items as defined in Council Directive 86/635/EEC (7), after deduction of value added tax and other taxes directly related to those items, where appropriate:

(i) interest income and similar income;
(ii) income from securities:
– income from shares and other variable yield securities;
– income from participating interests;
– income from shares in affiliated undertakings;
(iii) commissions receivable;
(iv) net profit on financial operations;
(v) other operating income.

The turnover of a credit or financial institution in the Community or in a Member State shall comprise the income items, as defined above, which are received by the branch or division of that institution established in the Community or in the Member State in question, as the case may be;

(b) for insurance undertakings, the value of gross premiums written which shall comprise all amounts received and receivable in respect of insurance contracts issued by or on behalf of the insurance undertakings, including also outgoing reinsurance premiums, and after deduction of taxes and parafiscal contributions or levies charged by reference to the amounts of individual premiums or the total volume of premiums; as regards Article 1(2)(b) and (3)(b), (c) and (d) and the final part of Article 1(2) and (3), gross premiums received from Community residents and from residents of one Member State respectively shall be taken into account.

4. Without prejudice to paragraph 2, the aggregate turnover of an undertaking concerned within the meaning of this Regulation shall be calculated by adding together the respective turnovers of the following:

(a) the undertaking concerned;

(b) those undertakings in which the undertaking concerned, directly or indirectly:

(i) owns more than half the capital or business assets; or

(ii) has the power to exercise more than half the voting rights; or

(iii) has the power to appoint more than half the members of the supervisory board, the administrative board or bodies legally representing the undertakings; or

(iv) has the right to manage the undertakings' affairs;

(c) those undertakings which have in the undertaking concerned the rights or powers listed in (b);

(d) those undertakings in which an undertaking as referred to in (c) has the rights or powers listed in (b);

(e) those undertakings in which two or more undertakings as referred to in (a) to (d) jointly have the rights or powers listed in (b).

5. Where undertakings concerned by the concentration jointly have the rights or powers listed in paragraph 4(b), in calculating the aggregate turnover of the undertakings concerned for the purposes of this Regulation:

(a) no account shall be taken of the turnover resulting from the sale of products or the provision of services between the joint undertaking and each of the undertakings concerned or any other undertaking connected with any one of them, as set out in paragraph 4(b) to (e);

(b) account shall be taken of the turnover resulting from the sale of products and the provision of services between the joint undertaking and any third undertakings. This turnover shall be apportioned equally amongst the undertakings concerned.

Art. 6. *Examination of the notification and initiation of proceedings*

1. The Commission shall examine the notification as soon as it is received:

(a) where it concludes that the concentration notified does not fall within the scope of this Regulation, it shall record that finding by means of a decision;

(b) where it finds that the concentration notified, although falling within the scope of this Regulation, does not raise serious doubts as to its compatibility with the common market, it shall decide not to oppose it and shall declare that it is compatible with the common market.

A decision declaring a concentration compatible shall be deemed to cover restrictions directly related and necessary to the implementation of the concentration;

(c) without prejudice to paragraph 2, where the Commission finds that the concentration notified falls within the scope of this Regulation and raises serious doubts as to its compatibility with the common market, it shall decide to initiate proceedings. Without prejudice to Article 9, such proceedings shall be closed by means of a decision as provided for in Article 8(1) to (4), unless the undertakings concerned have demonstrated to the satisfaction of the Commission that they have abandoned the concentration.

2. Where the Commission finds that, following modification by the undertakings concerned, a notified concentration no longer raises serious doubts within the meaning of paragraph 1(c), it shall declare the concentration compatible with the common market pursuant to paragraph 1(b).

The Commission may attach to its decision under paragraph 1(b) conditions and obligations intended to ensure that the undertakings concerned comply with the commitments they have entered into vis-à-vis the Commission with a view to rendering the concentration compatible with the common market.

3. The Commission may revoke the decision it took pursuant to paragraph 1(a) or (b) where:

(a) the decision is based on incorrect information for which one of the undertakings is responsible or where it has been obtained by deceit; or

(b) the undertakings concerned commit a breach of an obligation attached to the decision.

4. In the cases referred to in paragraph 3, the Commission may take a decision under paragraph 1, without being bound by the time limits referred to in Article 10(1).

5. The Commission shall notify its decision to the undertakings concerned and the competent authorities of the Member States without delay.

Art. 7. *Suspension of concentrations*

1. A concentration with a Community dimension as defined in Article 1, or which is to be examined by the Commission pursuant to Article 4(5), shall not be implemented either before its notification or until it has been declared compatible with the common market pursuant to a decision under Articles 6(1)(b), 8(1) or 8(2), or on the basis of a presumption according to Article 10(6).

2. Paragraph 1 shall not prevent the implementation of a public bid or of a series of transactions in securities including those convertible into other securities admitted to trading on a market such as a stock exchange, by which control within the meaning of Article 3 is acquired from various sellers, provided that:

(a) the concentration is notified to the Commission pursuant to Article 4 without delay; and

(b) the acquirer does not exercise the voting rights attached to the securities in question or does so only to maintain the full value of its investments based on a derogation granted by the Commission under paragraph 3.

3. The Commission may, on request, grant a derogation from the obligations imposed in paragraphs 1 or 2. The request to grant a derogation must be reasoned. In deciding on the request, the Commission shall take into account inter alia the effects of the suspension on one or more undertakings concerned by the concentration or on a third party and the threat to competition posed by the concentration. Such a derogation may be made subject to conditions and obligations in order to ensure conditions of effective competition. A derogation may be applied for and granted at any time, be it before notification or after the transaction.

4. The validity of any transaction carried out in contravention of paragraph 1 shall be dependent on a decision pursuant to Article 6(1)(b) or Article 8(1), (2) or (3) or on a presumption pursuant to Article 10(6).

This Article shall, however, have no effect on the validity of transactions in securities including those convertible into other securities admitted to trading on a market such as a stock exchange, unless the buyer and seller knew or ought to have known that the transaction was carried out in contravention of paragraph 1.

Art. 8. *Powers of decision of the Commission*

1. Where the Commission finds that a notified concentration fulfils the criterion laid down in Article 2(2) and, in the cases referred to in Article 2(4), the criteria laid down in Article 81(3) of the Treaty, it shall issue a decision declaring the concentration compatible with the common market.

A decision declaring a concentration compatible shall be deemed to cover restrictions directly related and necessary to the implementation of the concentration.

2. Where the Commission finds that, following modification by the undertakings concerned, a notified concentration fulfils the criterion laid down in Article 2(2) and, in the cases referred to in Article 2(4), the criteria laid down in Article 81(3) of the Treaty, it shall issue a decision declaring the concentration compatible with the common market.

The Commission may attach to its decision conditions and obligations intended to ensure that the undertakings concerned comply with the commitments they have entered into vis-à-vis the Commission with a view to rendering the concentration compatible with the common market.

A decision declaring a concentration compatible shall be deemed to cover restrictions directly related and necessary to the implementation of the concentration.

3. Where the Commission finds that a concentration fulfils the criterion defined in Article 2(3) or, in the cases referred to in Article 2(4), does not fulfil the criteria laid down in Article 81(3) of the Treaty, it shall issue a decision declaring that the concentration is incompatible with the common market.

4. Where the Commission finds that a concentration:

(a) has already been implemented and that concentration has been declared incompatible with the common market; or

(b) has been implemented in contravention of a condition attached to a decision taken under paragraph 2, which has found that, in the absence of the condition, the concentration would fulfil the criterion laid down in Article 2(3) or, in the cases referred to in Article 2(4), would not fulfil the criteria laid down in Article 81(3) of the Treaty,

the Commission may:

– require the undertakings concerned to dissolve the concentration, in particular through the dissolution of the merger or the disposal of all the shares or assets acquired, so as to restore the situation prevailing prior to the implementation of the concentration; in circumstances where restoration of the situation prevailing before the implementation of the concentration is not possible through dissolution of the concentration, the Commission may take any other measure appropriate to achieve such restoration as far as possible;

– order any other appropriate measure to ensure that the undertakings concerned dissolve the concentration or take other restorative measures as required in its decision.

In cases falling within point *(a)* of the first subparagraph, the measures referred to in that subparagraph may be imposed either in a decision pursuant to paragraph 3 or by separate decision.

5. The Commission may take interim measures appropriate to restore or maintain conditions of effective competition where a concentration:

(a) has been implemented in contravention of Article 7, and a decision as to the compatibility of the concentration with the common market has not yet been taken;

(b) has been implemented in contravention of a condition attached to a decision under Article 6(1)(b) or paragraph 2 of this Article;

(c) has already been implemented and is declared incompatible with the common market.

6. The Commission may revoke the decision it has taken pursuant to paragraphs 1 or 2 where:

(a) the declaration of compatibility is based on incorrect information for which one of the undertakings is responsible or where it has been obtained by deceit; or

(b) the undertakings concerned commit a breach of an obligation attached to the decision.

7. The Commission may take a decision pursuant to paragraphs 1 to 3 without being bound by the time limits referred to in Article 10(3), in cases where:

(a) it finds that a concentration has been implemented

(i) in contravention of a condition attached to a decision under Article 6(1)(b); or

(ii) in contravention of a condition attached to a decision taken under paragraph 2 and in accordance with Article 10(2), which has found that, in the absence of the condition, the concentration would raise serious doubts as to its compatibility with the common market; or

(b) a decision has been revoked pursuant to paragraph 6.

8. The Commission shall notify its decision to the undertakings concerned and the competent authorities of the Member States without delay.

Art. 9. *Referral to the competent authorities of the Member States*

1. The Commission may, by means of a decision notified without delay to the undertakings concerned and the competent authorities of the other Member States, refer a notified concentration to the competent authorities of the Member State concerned in the following circumstances.

2. Within 15 working days of the date of receipt of the copy of the notification, a Member State, on its own initiative or upon the invitation of the Commission, may inform the Commission, which shall inform the undertakings concerned, that:

(a) a concentration threatens to affect significantly competition in a market within that Member State, which presents all the characteristics of a distinct market; or

(b) a concentration affects competition in a market within that Member State, which presents all the characteristics of a distinct market and which does not constitute a substantial part of the common market.

3. If the Commission considers that, having regard to the market for the products or services in question and the geographical reference market within the meaning of paragraph 7, there is such a distinct market and that such a threat exists, either:

(a) it shall itself deal with the case in accordance with this Regulation; or

(b) it shall refer the whole or part of the case to the competent authorities of the Member State concerned with a view to the application of that State's national competition law.

If, however, the Commission considers that such a distinct market or threat does not exist, it shall adopt a decision to that effect which it shall address to the Member State concerned, and shall itself deal with the case in accordance with this Regulation.

In cases where a Member State informs the Commission pursuant to paragraph 2*(b)* that a concentration affects competition in a distinct market within its territory that does not form a substantial part of the common market, the Commission shall refer the whole or part of the case relating to the distinct market concerned, if it considers that such a distinct market is affected.

4. A decision to refer or not to refer pursuant to paragraph 3 shall be taken:

(a) as a general rule within the period provided for in Article 10(1), second subparagraph, where the Commission, pursuant to Article 6(1)*(b)*, has not initiated proceedings; or

(b) within 65 working days at most of the notification of the concentration concerned where the Commission has initiated proceedings under Article 6(1)*(c)*, without taking the preparatory steps in order to adopt the necessary measures under Article 8(2), (3) or (4) to maintain or restore effective competition on the market concerned.

5. If within the 65 working days referred to in paragraph 4*(b)* the Commission, despite a reminder from the Member State concerned, has not taken a decision on referral in accordance with paragraph 3 nor has taken the preparatory steps referred to in paragraph 4*(b)*, it shall be deemed to have taken a decision to refer the case to the Member State concerned in accordance with paragraph 3*(b)*.

6. The competent authority of the Member State concerned shall decide upon the case without undue delay.

Within 45 working days after the Commission's referral, the competent authority of the Member State concerned shall inform the undertakings concerned of the result of the preliminary competition assessment and what further action, if any, it proposes to take. The Member State concerned may exceptionally suspend this time limit where necessary information has not been provided to it by the undertakings concerned as provided for by its national competition law.

Where a notification is requested under national law, the period of 45 working days shall begin on the working day following that of the receipt of a complete notification by the competent authority of that Member State.

7. The geographical reference market shall consist of the area in which the undertakings concerned are involved in the supply and demand of products or services, in which the conditions of competition are sufficiently homogeneous and which can be distinguished from neighbouring areas because, in particular, conditions of competition are appreciably different in those areas. This assessment should take account in particular of the nature and characteristics of the products or services concerned, of the existence of entry barriers or of consumer preferences, of appreciable differences of the undertakings' market shares between the area concerned and neighbouring areas or of substantial price differences.

8. In applying the provisions of this Article, the Member State concerned may take only the measures strictly necessary to safeguard or restore effective competition on the market concerned.

9. In accordance with the relevant provisions of the Treaty, any Member State may appeal to the Court of Justice, and in particular request the application of Article 243 of the Treaty, for the purpose of applying its national competition law.

Art. 10. *Time limits for initiating proceedings and for decisions*

1. Without prejudice to Article 6(4), the decisions referred to in Article 6(1) shall be taken within 25 working days at most. That period shall begin on the working day following that of the receipt of a notification or, if the information to be supplied with the notification is incomplete, on the working day following that of the receipt of the complete information.

That period shall be increased to 35 working days where the Commission receives a request from a Member State in accordance with Article 9(2) or where, the undertakings concerned offer commitments pursuant to Article 6(2) with a view to rendering the concentration compatible with the common market.

2. Decisions pursuant to Article 8(1) or (2) concerning notified concentrations shall be taken as soon as it appears that the serious doubts referred to in Article 6(1)*(c)* have been removed, particularly as a result of modifications made by the undertakings concerned, and at the latest by the time limit laid down in paragraph 3.

3. Without prejudice to Article 8(7), decisions pursuant to Article 8(1) to (3) concerning notified concentrations shall be taken within not more than 90 working days of the date on which the proceedings are initiated. That period shall be increased to 105 working days where the undertakings concerned offer commitments pursuant to Article 8(2), second subparagraph, with a view to rendering the concentration compatible with the common market, unless these commitments have been offered less than 55 working days after the initiation of proceedings.

The periods set by the first subparagraph shall likewise be extended if the notifying parties make a request to that effect not later than 15 working days after the initiation of proceedings pursuant to Article 6(1)*(c)*. The notifying parties may make only one such request. Likewise, at any time following the initiation of proceedings, the periods set by the first subparagraph may be extended by the Commission with the agreement of the notifying parties. The total duration of any extension or extensions effected pursuant to this subparagraph shall not exceed 20 working days.

4. The periods set by paragraphs 1 and 3 shall exceptionally be suspended where, owing to circumstances for which one of the undertakings involved in the concentration is responsible, the Commission has had to request information by decision pursuant to Article 11 or to order an inspection by decision pursuant to Article 13.

The first subparagraph shall also apply to the period referred to in Article 9(4)*(b)*.

5. Where the Court of Justice gives a judgment which annuls the whole or part of a Commission decision which is subject to a time limit set by this Article, the concentration shall be re-examined by the Commission with a view to adopting a decision pursuant to Article 6(1).

The concentration shall be re-examined in the light of current market conditions.

The notifying parties shall submit a new notification or supplement the original notification, without delay, where the original notification becomes incomplete by reason of intervening changes in market conditions or in the information provided. Where there are no such changes, the parties shall certify this fact without delay.

The periods laid down in paragraph 1 shall start on the working day following that of the receipt of complete information in a new notification, a supplemented notification, or a certification within the meaning of the third subparagraph.

The second and third subparagraphs shall also apply in the cases referred to in Article 6(4) and Article 8(7).

6. Where the Commission has not taken a decision in accordance with Article 6(1)(b), (c), 8(1), (2) or (3) within the time limits set in paragraphs 1 and 3 respectively, the concentration shall be deemed to have been declared compatible with the common market, without prejudice to Article 9.

Art. 11. *Requests for information*

1. In order to carry out the duties assigned to it by this Regulation, the Commission may, by simple request or by decision, require the persons referred to in Article 3(1)(b), as well as undertakings and associations of undertakings, to provide all necessary information.

2. When sending a simple request for information to a person, an undertaking or an association of undertakings, the Commission shall state the legal basis and the purpose of the request, specify what information is required and fix the time limit within which the information is to be provided, as well as the penalties provided for in Article 14 for supplying incorrect or misleading information.

3. Where the Commission requires a person, an undertaking or an association of undertakings by decision, to supply information by decision, it shall state the legal basis and the purpose of the request, specify what information is required and fix the time limit within which it is to be provided. It shall also indicate the penalties provided for in Article 14 and indicate or impose the penalties provided for in Article 15. It shall further indicate the right to have the decision reviewed by the Court of Justice.

4. The owners of the undertakings or their representatives and, in the case of legal persons, companies or firms, or associations having no legal personality, the persons authorised to represent them by law or by their constitution, shall supply the information requested on behalf of the undertaking concerned. Persons duly authorised to act may supply the information on behalf of their clients. The latter shall remain fully responsible if the information supplied is incomplete, incorrect or misleading.

5. The Commission shall without delay forward a copy of any decision taken pursuant to paragraph 3 to the competent authorities of the Member State in whose territory the residence of the person or the seat of the undertaking or association of undertakings is situated, and to the competent authority of the Member State whose territory is affected. At the specific request of the competent authority of a Member State, the Commission shall also forward to that authority copies of simple requests for information relating to a notified concentration.

6. At the request of the Commission, the governments and competent authorities of the Member States shall provide the Commission with all necessary information to carry out the duties assigned to it by this Regulation.

7. In order to carry out the duties assigned to it by this Regulation, the Commission may interview any natural or legal person who consents to be interviewed for the purpose of collecting information relating to the subject matter of an investigation. At the beginning of the interview, which may be conducted by telephone or other electronic means, the Commission shall state the legal basis and the purpose of the interview.

Where an interview is not conducted on the premises of the Commission or by telephone or other electronic means, the Commission shall inform in advance the competent authority of the Member State in whose territory the interview takes place. If the competent authority of that Member State so requests, officials of that authority may assist the officials and other persons authorised by the Commission to conduct the interview.

Art. 12. *Inspections by the authorities of the Member States*

1. At the request of the Commission, the competent authorities of the Member States shall undertake the inspections which the Commission considers to be necessary under Article 13(1), or which it has ordered by decision pursuant to Article 13(4). The officials of the competent authorities of the Member States who are responsible for conducting these inspections as well as those authorised or appointed by them shall exercise their powers in accordance with their national law.

2. If so requested by the Commission or by the competent authority of the Member State within whose territory the inspection is to be conducted, officials and other accompanying persons authorised by the Commission may assist the officials of the authority concerned.

Art. 13. *The Commission's powers of inspection*

1. In order to carry out the duties assigned to it by this Regulation, the Commission may conduct all necessary inspections of undertakings and associations of undertakings.

2. The officials and other accompanying persons authorised by the Commission to conduct an inspection shall have the power:

(a) to enter any premises, land and means of transport of undertakings and associations of undertakings;

(b) to examine the books and other records related to the business, irrespective of the medium on which they are stored;

(c) to take or obtain in any form copies of or extracts from such books or records;

(d) to seal any business premises and books or records for the period and to the extent necessary for the inspection;

(e) to ask any representative or member of staff of the undertaking or association of undertakings for explanations on facts or documents relating to the subject matter and purpose of the inspection and to record the answers.

3. Officials and other accompanying persons authorised by the Commission to conduct an inspection shall exercise their powers upon production of a written authorisation specifying the subject matter and purpose of the inspection and the penalties provided for in Article 14, in the production of the required books or other records related to the business which is incomplete or where answers to questions asked under paragraph 2 of this Article are incorrect or misleading. In good time before the inspection, the Commission shall give notice of the inspection to the competent authority of the Member State in whose territory the inspection is to be conducted.

4. Undertakings and associations of undertakings are required to submit to inspections ordered by decision of the Commission. The decision shall specify the subject matter

and purpose of the inspection, appoint the date on which it is to begin and indicate the penalties provided for in Articles 14 and 15 and the right to have the decision reviewed by the Court of Justice. The Commission shall take such decisions after consulting the competent authority of the Member State in whose territory the inspection is to be conducted.

5. Officials of, and those authorised or appointed by, the competent authority of the Member State in whose territory the inspection is to be conducted shall, at the request of that authority or of the Commission, actively assist the officials and other accompanying persons authorised by the Commission. To this end, they shall enjoy the powers specified in paragraph 2.

6. Where the officials and other accompanying persons authorised by the Commission find that an undertaking opposes an inspection, including the sealing of business premises, books or records, ordered pursuant to this Article, the Member State concerned shall afford them the necessary assistance, requesting where appropriate the assistance of the police or of an equivalent enforcement authority, so as to enable them to conduct their inspection.

7. If the assistance provided for in paragraph 6 requires authorisation from a judicial authority according to national rules, such authorisation shall be applied for. Such authorisation may also be applied for as a precautionary measure.

8. Where authorisation as referred to in paragraph 7 is applied for, the national judicial authority shall ensure that the Commission decision is authentic and that the coercive measures envisaged are neither arbitrary nor excessive having regard to the subject matter of the inspection. In its control of proportionality of the coercive measures, the national judicial authority may ask the Commission, directly or through the competent authority of that Member State, for detailed explanations relating to the subject matter of the inspection. However, the national judicial authority may not call into question the necessity for the inspection nor demand that it be provided with the information in the Commission's file. The lawfulness of the Commission's decision shall be subject to review only by the Court of Justice.

Art. 14. *Fines*

1. The Commission may by decision impose on the persons referred to in Article 3(1)*b*, undertakings or associations of undertakings, fines not exceeding 1 % of the aggregate turnover of the undertaking or association of undertakings concerned within the meaning of Article 5 where, intentionally or negligently:

(a) they supply incorrect or misleading information in a submission, certification, notification or supplement thereto, pursuant to Article 4, Article 10(5) or Article 22(3);

(b) they supply incorrect or misleading information in response to a request made pursuant to Article 11(2);

(c) in response to a request made by decision adopted pursuant to Article 11(3), they supply incorrect, incomplete or misleading information or do not supply information within the required time limit;

(d) they produce the required books or other records related to the business in incomplete form during inspections under Article 13, or refuse to submit to an inspection ordered by decision taken pursuant to Article 13(4);

(e) in response to a question asked in accordance with Article 13(2)*(e)*,

– they give an incorrect or misleading answer;

– they fail to rectify within a time limit set by the Commission an incorrect, incomplete or misleading answer given by a member of staff; or

– they fail or refuse to provide a complete answer on facts relating to the subject matter and purpose of an inspection ordered by a decision adopted pursuant to Article 13(4);

(f) seals affixed by officials or other accompanying persons authorised by the Commission in accordance with Article 13(2)*(d)* have been broken.

2. The Commission may by decision impose fines not exceeding 10 % of the aggregate turnover of the undertaking concerned within the meaning of Article 5 on the persons referred to in Article 3(1)*b* or the undertakings concerned where, either intentionally or negligently, they:

(a) fail to notify a concentration in accordance with Articles 4 or 22(3) prior to its implementation, unless they are expressly authorised to do so by Article 7(2) or by a decision taken pursuant to Article 7(3);

(b) implement a concentration in breach of Article 7;

(c) implement a concentration declared incompatible with the common market by decision pursuant to Article 8(3) or do not comply with any measure ordered by decision pursuant to Article 8(4) or (5);

(d) fail to comply with a condition or an obligation imposed by decision pursuant to Articles 6(1)*(b)*, Article 7(3) or Article 8(2), second subparagraph.

3. In fixing the amount of the fine, regard shall be had to the nature, gravity and duration of the infringement.

4. Decisions taken pursuant to paragraphs 1, 2 and 3 shall not be of a criminal law nature.

Art. 15. *Periodic penalty payments*

1. The Commission may by decision impose on the persons referred to in Article 3(1)*b*, undertakings or associations of undertakings, periodic penalty payments not exceeding 5 % of the average daily aggregate turnover of the undertaking or association of undertakings concerned within the meaning of Article 5 for each working day of delay, calculated from the date set in the decision, in order to compel them:

(a) to supply complete and correct information which it has requested by decision taken pursuant to Article 11(3);

(b) to submit to an inspection which it has ordered by decision taken pursuant to Article 13(4);

(c) to comply with an obligation imposed by decision pursuant to Article 6(1)*(b)*, Article 7(3) or Article 8(2), second subparagraph; or

(d) to comply with any measures ordered by decision pursuant to Article 8(4) or (5).

2. Where the persons referred to in Article 3(1)*(b)*, undertakings or associations of undertakings have satisfied the obligation which the periodic penalty payment was intended to enforce, the Commission may fix the definitive amount of the periodic penalty payments at a figure lower than that which would arise under the original decision.

Art. 16. *Review by the Court of Justice*

The Court of Justice shall have unlimited jurisdiction within the meaning of Article 229 of the Treaty to review decisions whereby the Commission has fixed a fine or periodic penalty payments; it may cancel, reduce or increase the fine or periodic penalty payment imposed.

Art. 17. *Professional secrecy*

1. Information acquired as a result of the application of this Regulation shall be used only for the purposes of the relevant request, investigation or hearing.

2. Without prejudice to Article 4(3), Articles 18 and 20, the Commission and the competent authorities of the Member States, their officials and other servants and other persons working under the supervision of these authorities as well as officials and civil servants of other authorities of the Member States shall not disclose information they have acquired through the application of this Regulation of the kind covered by the obligation of professional secrecy.

3. Paragraphs 1 and 2 shall not prevent publication of general information or of surveys which do not contain information relating to particular undertakings or associations of undertakings.

Art. 18. *Hearing of the parties and of third persons*

1. Before taking any decision provided for in Article 6(3), Article 7(3), Article 8(2) to (6), and Articles 14 and 15, the Commission shall give the persons, undertakings and associations of undertakings concerned the opportunity, at every stage of the procedure up to the consultation of the Advisory Committee, of making known their views on the objections against them.

2. By way of derogation from paragraph 1, a decision pursuant to Articles 7(3) and 8(5) may be taken provisionally, without the persons, undertakings or associations of undertakings concerned being given the opportunity to make known their views beforehand, provided that the Commission gives them that opportunity as soon as possible after having taken its decision.

3. The Commission shall base its decision only on objections on which the parties have been able to submit their observations. The rights of the defence shall be fully respected in the proceedings. Access to the file shall be open at least to the parties directly involved, subject to the legitimate interest of undertakings in the protection of their business secrets.

4. In so far as the Commission or the competent authorities of the Member States deem it necessary, they may also hear other natural or legal persons. Natural or legal persons showing a sufficient interest and especially members of the administrative or management bodies of the undertakings concerned or the recognised representatives of their employees shall be entitled, upon application, to be heard.

Art. 19. *Liaison with the authorities of the Member States*

1. The Commission shall transmit to the competent authorities of the Member States copies of notifications within three working days and, as soon as possible, copies of the most important documents lodged with or issued by the Commission pursuant to this Regulation. Such documents shall include commitments offered by the undertakings concerned vis-à-vis the Commission with a view to rendering the concentration compatible with the common market pursuant to Article 6(2) or Article 8(2), second subparagraph.

2. The Commission shall carry out the procedures set out in this Regulation in close and constant liaison with the competent authorities of the Member States, which may express their views upon those procedures. For the purposes of Article 9 it shall obtain information from the competent authority of the Member State as referred to in paragraph 2 of that Article and give it the opportunity to make known its views at every stage of the procedure up to the adoption of a decision pursuant to paragraph 3 of that Article; to that end it shall give it access to the file.

3. An Advisory Committee on concentrations shall be consulted before any decision is taken pursuant to Article 8(1) to (6), Articles 14 or 15 with the exception of provisional decisions taken in accordance with Article 18(2).

4. The Advisory Committee shall consist of representatives of the competent authorities of the Member States. Each Member State shall appoint one or two representatives; if unable to attend, they may be replaced by other representatives. At least one of the representatives of a Member State shall be competent in matters of restrictive practices and dominant positions.

5. Consultation shall take place at a joint meeting convened at the invitation of and chaired by the Commission. A summary of the case, together with an indication of the most important documents and a preliminary draft of the decision to be taken for each case considered, shall be sent with the invitation. The meeting shall take place not less than 10 working days after the invitation has been sent. The Commission may in exceptional cases shorten that period as appropriate in order to avoid serious harm to one or more of the undertakings concerned by a concentration.

6. The Advisory Committee shall deliver an opinion on the Commission's draft decision, if necessary by taking a vote. The Advisory Committee may deliver an opinion even if some members are absent and unrepresented. The opinion shall be delivered in writing and appended to the draft decision. The Commission shall take the utmost account of the opinion delivered by the Committee. It shall inform the Committee of the manner in which its opinion has been taken into account.

7. The Commission shall communicate the opinion of the Advisory Committee, together with the decision, to the addressees of the decision. It shall make the opinion public together with the decision, having regard to the legitimate interest of undertakings in the protection of their business secrets.

Art. 20. *Publication of decisions*

1. The Commission shall publish the decisions which it takes pursuant to Article 8(1) to (6), Articles 14 and 15 with the exception of provisional decisions taken in accordance with Article 18(2) together with the opinion of the Advisory Committee in the Official Journal of the European Union.

2. The publication shall state the names of the parties and the main content of the decision; it shall have regard to the legitimate interest of undertakings in the protection of their business secrets.

Art. 21. *Application of the Regulation and jurisdiction*

1. This Regulation alone shall apply to concentrations as defined in Article 3, and Council Regulations (EC) N° 1/2003 (8), (EEC) N° 1017/68 (9), (EEC) N° 4056/86 (10) and (EEC) N° 3975/87 (11) shall not apply, except in relation to joint ventures that do not have a Community dimension and which have as their object or effect the coordination of the competitive behaviour of undertakings that remain independent.

2. Subject to review by the Court of Justice, the Commission shall have sole jurisdiction to take the decisions provided for in this Regulation.

3. No Member State shall apply its national legislation on competition to any concentration that has a Community dimension.

The first subparagraph shall be without prejudice to any Member State's power to carry out any enquiries necessary for the application of Articles 4(4), 9(2) or after referral, pursuant to Article 9(3), first subparagraph, indent (b), or Article 9(5), to take the measures strictly necessary for the application of Article 9(8).

4. Notwithstanding paragraphs 2 and 3, Member States may take appropriate measures to protect legitimate interests other than those taken into consideration by this Regulation and compatible with the general principles and other provisions of Community law.

Public security, plurality of the media and prudential rules shall be regarded as legitimate interests within the meaning of the first subparagraph.

Any other public interest must be communicated to the Commission by the Member State concerned and shall be recognised by the Commission after an assessment of its compatibility with the general principles and other provisions of Community law before the measures referred to above may be taken. The Commission shall inform the Member State concerned of its decision within 25 working days of that communication.

Art. 22. *Referral to the Commission*

1. One or more Member States may request the Commission to examine any concentration as defined in Article 3 that does not have a Community dimension within the meaning of Article 1 but affects trade between Member States and threatens to significantly affect competition within the territory of the Member State or States making the request.

Such a request shall be made at most within 15 working days of the date on which the concentration was notified, or if no notification is required, otherwise made known to the Member State concerned.

2. The Commission shall inform the competent authorities of the Member States and the undertakings concerned of any request received pursuant to paragraph 1 without delay.

Any other Member State shall have the right to join the initial request within a period of 15 working days of being informed by the Commission of the initial request.

All national time limits relating to the concentration shall be suspended until, in accordance with the procedure set out in this Article, it has been decided where the concentration shall be examined. As soon as a Member State has informed the Commission and the undertakings concerned that it does not wish to join the request, the suspension of its national time limits shall end.

3. The Commission may, at the latest 10 working days after the expiry of the period set in paragraph 2, decide to examine, the concentration where it considers that it affects trade between Member States and threatens to significantly affect competition within the territory of the Member State or States making the request. If the Commission does not take a decision within this period, it shall be deemed to have adopted a decision to examine the concentration in accordance with the request.

The Commission shall inform all Member States and the undertakings concerned of its decision. It may request the submission of a notification pursuant to Article 4.

The Member State or States having made the request shall no longer apply their national legislation on competition to the concentration.

4. Article 2, Article 4(2) to (3), Articles 5, 6, and 8 to 21 shall apply where the Commission examines a concentration pursuant to paragraph 3. Article 7 shall apply to the extent that the concentration has not been implemented on the date on which the Commission informs the undertakings concerned that a request has been made.

Where a notification pursuant to Article 4 is not required, the period set in Article 10(1) within which proceedings may be initiated shall begin on the working day following that on which the Commission informs the undertakings concerned that it has decided to examine the concentration pursuant to paragraph 3.

5. The Commission may inform one or several Member States that it considers a concentration fulfils the criteria in paragraph 1. In such cases, the Commission may invite that Member State or those Member States to make a request pursuant to paragraph 1.

Art. 23. *Implementing provisions*

1. The Commission shall have the power to lay down in accordance with the procedure referred to in paragraph 2:

(a) implementing provisions concerning the form, content and other details of notifications and submissions pursuant to Article 4;

(b) implementing provisions concerning time limits pursuant to Article 4(4), (5) Articles 7, 9, 10 and 22;

(c) the procedure and time limits for the submission and implementation of commitments pursuant to Article 6(2) and Article 8(2);

(d) implementing provisions concerning hearings pursuant to Article 18.

2. The Commission shall be assisted by an Advisory Committee, composed of representatives of the Member States:

(a) before publishing draft implementing provisions and before adopting such provisions, the Commission shall consult the Advisory Committee;

(b) consultation shall take place at a meeting convened at the invitation of and chaired by the Commission. A draft of the implementing provisions to be taken shall be sent with the invitation. The meeting shall take place not less than 10 working days after the invitation has been sent;

(c) the Advisory Committee shall deliver an opinion on the draft implementing provisions, if necessary by taking a vote. The Commission shall take the utmost account of the opinion delivered by the Committee.

Art. 24. *Relations with third countries*

1. The Member States shall inform the Commission of any general difficulties encountered by their undertakings with concentrations as defined in Article 3 in a third country.

2. Initially not more than one year after the entry into force of this Regulation and, thereafter periodically, the Commission shall draw up a report examining the treatment accorded to undertakings having their seat or their principal fields of activity in the Community, in the terms referred to in paragraphs 3 and 4, as regards concentrations in third countries. The Commission shall submit those reports to the Council, together with any recommendations.

3. Whenever it appears to the Commission, either on the basis of the reports referred to in paragraph 2 or on the basis of other information, that a third country does not grant undertakings having their seat or their principal fields of activity in the Community, treatment comparable to that granted by the Community to undertakings from that country, the Commission may submit proposals to the Council for an appropriate mandate for negotiation with a view to obtaining

comparable treatment for undertakings having their seat or their principal fields of activity in the Community.

4. Measures taken under this Article shall comply with the obligations of the Community or of the Member States, without prejudice to Article 307 of the Treaty, under international agreements, whether bilateral or multilateral.

Art. 25. *Repeal*

1. Without prejudice to Article 26(2), Regulations (EEC) N° 4064/89 and (EC) N° 1310/97 shall be repealed with effect from 1 May 2004.

2. References to the repealed Regulations shall be construed as references to this Regulation and shall be read in accordance with the correlation table in the Annex.

Art. 26. *Entry into force and transitional provisions*

1. This Regulation shall enter into force on the 20th day following that of its publication in the *Official Journal of the European Union*.

It shall apply from 1 May 2004.

2. Regulation (EEC) N° 4064/89 shall continue to apply to any concentration which was the subject of an agreement or announcement or where control was acquired within the meaning of Article 4(1) of that Regulation before the date of application of this Regulation, subject, in particular, to the provisions governing applicability set out in Article 25(2) and (3) of Regulation (EEC) N° 4064/89 and Article 2 of Regulation (EEC) N° 1310/97.

3. As regards concentrations to which this Regulation applies by virtue of accession, the date of accession shall be substituted for the date of application of this Regulation.

(6) OJ L 222, 14. 8. 1978, p. 11. Directive as last amended by Directive 2003/51/EC of the European Parliament and of the Council (OJ L 178, 17.7.2003, p. 16).

(7) OJ L 372, 31. 12. 1986, p. 1. Directive as last amended by Directive 2003/51/EC of the European Parliament and of the Council.

(8) OJ L 1, 4.1.2003, p. 1.

(9) OJ L 175, 23. 7. 1968, p. 1. Regulation as last amended by Regulation (EC) N° 1/2003 (OJ L 1, 4.1.2003, p. 1).

(10) OJ L 378, 31. 12. 1986, p. 4. Regulation as last amended by Regulation (EC) N° 1/2003.

(11) OJ L 374. 31. 12. 1987, p. 1. Regulation as last amended by Regulation (EC) N° 1/2003.

Annex
Correlation table

Regulation (EEC) N° 4064/89	This Regulation
Article 1(1), (2) and (3)	Article 1(1), (2) and (3)
Article 1(4)	Article 1(4)
Article 1(5)	Article 1(5)
Article 2(1)	Article 2(1)
–	Article 2(2)
Article 2(2)	Article 2(3)
Article 2(3)	Article 2(4)
Article 2(4)	Article 2(5)
Article 3(1)	Article 3(1)
Article 3(2)	Article 3(4)
Article 3(3)	Article 3(2)
Article 3(4)	Article 3(3)
–	Article 3(4)
Article 3(5)	Article 3(5)
Article 4(1) first sentence	Article 4(1) first subparagraph
Article 4(1) second sentence	–
–	Article 4(1) second and third subparagraphs
Article 4(2) and (3)	Article 4(2) and (3)
–	Article 4(4) to (6)
Article 5(1) to (3)	Article 5(1) to (3)
Article 5(4), introductory words	Article 5(4), introductory words
Article 5(4) point *(a)*	Article 5(4) point *(a)*
Article 5(4) point *(b)*, introductory words	Article 5(4) point *(b)*, introductory words
Article 5(4) point *(b)*, first indent	Article 5(4) point *(b)*(i)
Article 5(4) point *(b)*, second indent	Article 5(4) point *(b)*(ii)
Article 5(4) point *(b)*, third indent	Article 5(4) point *(b)*(iii)
Article 5(4) point *(b)*, fourth indent	Article 5(4) point *(b)*(iv)
Article 5(4) points *(c)*, *(d)* and *(e)*	Article 5(4) points *(c)*, *(d)* and *(e)*
Article 5(5)	Article 5(5)
Article 6(1), introductory words	Article 6(1), introductory words
Article 6(1) points *(a)* and *(b)*	Article 6(1) points *(a)* and *(b)*
Article 6(1) point *(c)*	Article 6(1) point *(c)*, first sentence
Article 6(2) to (5)	Article 6(2) to (5)
Article 7(1)	Article 7(1)
Article 7(3)	Article 7(2)
Article 7(4)	Article 7(3)
Article 7(5)	Article 7(4)
Article 8(1)	Article 6(1) point *(c)*, second sentence
Article 8(2)	Article 8(1) and (2)
Article 8(3)	Article 8(3)
Article 8(4)	Article 8(4)
–	Article 8(5)
Article 8(5)	Article 8(6)
Article 8(6)	Article 8(7)
–	Article 8(8)
Article 9(1) to (9)	Article 9(1) to (9)
Article 9(10)	–
Article 10(1) and (2)	Article 10(1) and (2)
Article 10(3)	Article 10(3) first subparagraph, first sentence
–	Article 10(3) first subparagraph, second sentence
–	Article 10(3) second subparagraph
Article 10(4)	Article 10(4) first subparagraph
–	Article 10(4), second subparagraph
Article 10(5)	Article 10(5), first and fourth subparagraphs
–	Article 10(5), second, third and fifth subparagraphs
Article 10(6)	Article 10(6)
Article 11(1)	Article 11(1)
Article 11(2)	–

Regulation (EEC) N° 4064/89	This Regulation
Article 11(3)	Article 11(2)
Article 11(4)	Article 11(4) first sentence
–	Article 11(4) second and third sentences
Article 11(5) first sentence	–
Article 11(5) second sentence	Article 11(3)
Article 11(6)	Article 11(5)
–	Article 11(6) and (7)
Article 12	Article 12
Article 13(1) first subparagraph	Article 13(1)
Article 13(1) second subparagraph, introductory words	Article 13(2) introductory words
Article 13(1) second subparagraph, point *(a)*	Article 13(2) point *(b)*
Article 13(1) second subparagraph, point *(b)*	Article 13(2) point *(c)*
Article 13(1) second subparagraph, point *(c)*	Article 13(2) point *(e)*
Article 13(1) second subparagraph, point *(d)*	Article 13(2) point *(a)*
–	Article 13(2) point *(d)*
Article 13(2)	Article 13(3)
Article 13(3)	Article 13(4) first and second sentences
Article 13(4)	Article 13(4) third sentence
Article 13(5)	Article 13(5), first sentence
–	Article 13(5), second sentence
Article 13(6) first sentence	Article 13(6)
Article 13(6) second sentence	–
–	Article 13(7) and (8)
Article 14(1) introductory words	Article 14(1) introductory words
Article 14(1) point *(a)*	Article 14(2) point *(a)*
Article 14(1) point *(b)*	Article 14(1) point *(a)*
Article 14(1) point *(c)*	Article 14(1) points *(b)* and *(c)*
Article 14(1) point *(d)*	Article 14(1) point *(d)*
–	Article 14(1) points *(e)* and *(f)*
Article 14(2) introductory words	Article 14(2) introductory words
Article 14(2) point *(a)*	Article 14(2) point *(d)*
Article 14(2) points *(b)* and *(c)*	Article 14(2) points *(b)* and *(c)*
Article 14(3)	Article 14(3)
Article 14(4)	Article 14(4)
Article 15(1) introductory words	Article 15(1) introductory words
Article 15(1) points *(a)* and *(b)*	Article 15(1) points *(a)* and *(b)*
Article 15(2) introductory words	Article 15(1) introductory words
Article 15(2) point *(a)*	Article 15(1) point *(c)*
Article 15(2) point *(b)*	Article 15(1) point *(d)*
Article 15(3)	Article 15(2)
Articles 16 to 20	Articles 16 to 20
Article 21(1)	Article 21(2)
Article 21(2)	Article 21(3)
Article 21(3)	Article 21(4)
Article 22(1)	Article 21(1)
Article 22(3)	–
–	Article 22(1) to (3)
Article 22(4)	Article 22(4)
Article 22(5)	–
–	Article 22(5)

Regulation (EEC) N° 4064/89	This Regulation
Article 23	Article 23(1)
–	Article 23(2)
Article 24	Article 24
–	Article 25
Article 25(1)	Article 26(1), first subparagraph
–	Article 26(1), second subparagraph
Article 25(2)	Article 26(2)
Article 25(3)	Article 26(3)
–	Annex

Communication 18 June 2009 from the Commission to the Council – Report on the functioning of Regulation N° 139/2004, COM (2009) 281 final

1. BACKGROUND

1. Council Regulation (EEC) N° 4064/89, the «EC Merger Regulation», entered into force on 21 September 1990. The EC Merger Regulation applies to concentrations which are deemed to have a Community dimension, i.e. where the turnover of the parties concerned satisfy the thresholds set out in Article 1 of the EC Merger Regulation.

2. One of the main principles of the EC Merger Regulation is the exclusive jurisdiction of the Commission with respect to concentrations having a Community dimension. The concept that the Commission should have sole competence to deal with mergers with a Community dimension follows from the principle of subsidiarity. From the viewpoint of the European business community, the Commission's exclusive jurisdiction also provides a «one-stop-shop» advantage, which is widely regarded as an essential part of keeping the regulatory costs associated with cross-border transactions at a reasonable level. In addition, the Commission's exclusive jurisdiction to vet such mergers is an important element in providing a «level playing field» for the concentrations that were bound to result from the completion of the internal market. This principle is widely accepted as the most efficient way of ensuring that all mergers with a significant cross-border impact are subject to a uniform set of rules.

3. In 1998, after a careful review of the experience gained, the EC Merger Regulation was amended, through Council Regulation N° 1310/97. In relation to Article 1, a new sub-paragraph – Article 1(3) – providing for an alternative turnover threshold was introduced. The objective of this provision was to address the problem that a significant number of cases failed to meet the turnover requirements of Article 1(2) and had to be notified in several Member States. Many such concentrations had a significant cross-border impact but did not benefit from the one-stop-shop principle. The EC Merger Regulation had therefore not fully succeeded in creating a level playing field and a set of coherent rules for this category of cases.

4. The adoption of the recast EC Merger Regulation on 20 January 2004 (1) (also referred to as the «EC Merger Regulation») was the next step to further improve the merger case allocation between the Commission and the Member States. It was the result of a far reaching review and a broad debate with all concerned parties which was launched in 2001 with the Commission Green Paper (2).

(1) Council Regulation (EC) N° 139/2004 of 20 January 2004 on the control of concentrations between undertakings (O.J. L 24, 29.1.2004, p. 1).

(2) COM(2001) 745, 11.12.2001.

5. The recast EC Merger Regulation introduced a number of substantive and procedural changes. The review had found that, notwithstanding the introduction of the threshold under Article 1(3), there was still further scope for improved case allocation between the Commission and the national competition authorities («NCAs»). Therefore, while the turnover thresholds set out in Articles 1(2) and 1(3) were left unchanged, a set of voluntary pre-notification referral mechanisms was introduced in order to «further improve the efficiency of the system for the control of concentrations within the Community» (3). The principles guiding the system were those that decisions taken with regard to the referral of cases should take due account «in particular which is the authority more appropriate for carrying out the investigation, the benefits inherent in a «one-stop-shop» system, and the importance of legal certainty with regard to jurisdiction» (4).

(3) Recital 16 of the EC Merger Regulation. Other instruments that should also be mentioned are: the Commission Notice on Case Referral in respect of concentrations (Commission Notice on Case Referral in respect of concentrations – O.J. C 56, 5.3.2005, p. 2), which sets out the guiding principles of the referral system. On 10 July 2007, the Commission adopted the Consolidated Jurisdictional Notice under Council Regulation (EC) N° 139/2004 on the control of concentrations between undertakings (Corrected French and German versions of the Commission Consolidated Jurisdictional Notice and the remaining languages versions of the Notice were adopted by the Commission on 17 March 2008). The Consolidated Jurisdictional Notice replaces the previous four jurisdictional Notices, all adopted by the Commission in 1998 under the previous EC Merger Regulation. The Consolidated Jurisdictional Notice covers all issues of jurisdiction relevant for establishing the Commission's competence under the EC Merger Regulation, including in particular, the concept of a concentration, the notion of control, the concept of full-function joint ventures and the calculation of turnover.

(4) Commission Notice on Case Referral in respect of concentrations (O.J. C 56, 5.3.2005, p. 2-23, paragraph 8).

2. SCOPE AND PURPOSE OF THE REPORT

6. This Report is a stock-taking exercise, the aim of which is to understand and assess how the jurisdictional thresholds and their corrective mechanisms have operated since the entry into force of the recast EC Merger Regulation on 1 May 2004, as provided by its Articles 1(4) and 4(6). It is to be read in conjunction with the accompanying Commission Staff Working Paper which contains a more detailed review.

7. In a number of areas, this Report highlights aspects which merit further discussion, but leaves open the question as to whether any amendment to the existing rules or practice is appropriate. It will serve as a basis for the Commission to assess, at a further stage, whether it is appropriate to take further policy initiatives.

3. A SYSTEM OF JURISDICTIONAL THRESHOLDS AND CORRECTIVE MECHANISMS

8. The division of competence between the Commission and the NCAs is based on the application of the turnover thresholds set out in Article 1 (5) and includes three corrective mechanisms. The first corrective mechanism is the so-called «two-thirds rule». The objective of this rule is to exclude from the Commission's jurisdiction certain cases which contain a clear national nexus to one Member State (6).

(5) Article 1(2) of the EC Merger Regulation stipulates that: «A concentration has a Community dimension where: *(a)* the combined aggregate worldwide turnover of all the undertakings concerned is more than EUR 5.000 million; and *(b)* the aggregate Community-wide turnover of each of at least two of the undertakings concerned is more than ECU 250 million, unless each of the undertakings concerned achieves more than two-thirds of its aggregate Community-wide turnover within one and the same Member State.» Article 1(3) stipulates that: «A concentration that does not meet the thresholds laid down in paragraph 2 has a Community dimension where: *(a)* the combined aggregate worldwide turnover of all the undertakings concerned is more than EUR 2.500 million; *(b)* in each of at least three Member States, the combined aggregate turnover of all the undertakings concerned is more than EUR 100 million; *(c)* in each of at least three Member States included for the purpose of point *(b)*, the aggregate turnover of

each of at least two of the undertakings concerned is more than EUR 25 million; and (d) the aggregate Community-wide turnover of each of at least two of the undertakings concerned is more than EUR 100 million; unless each of the undertakings concerned achieves more than two-thirds of its aggregate Community-wide turnover within one and the same Member State.»

(6) The threshold is construed in a way that even if the general thresholds under Articles 1(2) and 1(3) are met, notification under the EC Merger Regulation is not required if each of the parties concerned realises more than two thirds of its EU-wide turnover in one and the same Member State, see footnote above.

9. The second corrective mechanism is the pre-notification referral system introduced in 2004. This mechanism allows for the re-allocation of jurisdiction to the Member States under Article 4(4) or the Commission under Article 4(5) if certain conditions are fulfilled (7). The initiative is in the hands of the parties prior to notification. However, referral is subject to approval by the Member States and the Commission under Article 4(4) and by the Member States under Article 4(5).

(7) Under Article 4(4), unless the Member State expresses its disagreement, the Commission, when it considers that the concentration may significantly affect competition in a market within a Member State which presents all the characteristics of a distinct market, may decide to refer the whole or part of the case to the competent authorities of that Member State with a view to the application of that State's national competition law. Under Article 4(5) concentrations which do not have a Community dimension and which are capable of being reviewed under the national competition laws of at least three Member States can be referred to the Commission unless any Member State competent to examine the concentration under its national competition law expresses its disagreement.

10. The third corrective mechanism is the post-notification referral system whereby one or more Member States can request that the Commission assess mergers that fall below the thresholds of the EC Merger Regulation under certain conditions (Article 22) (8). Conversely, a Member State may, in cases that have been notified under the EC Merger Regulation, request the transfer of competence to the NCA under certain conditions (Article 9) (9).

(8) For a referral to the Commission to be available under Article 22 the concentration must: (i) affect trade between Member States; and (ii) it must threaten to significantly affect competition within the territory of the Member State(s) making the request.

(9) Under Article 9, a Member State may request that a case be referred to it in either of the following circumstances: (i) the concentration must «threaten to affect significantly competition in a market» and the market in question must be within the requesting Member State and present all the characteristics of a distinct market, or (ii) the concentration must affect competition in a market and the market in question must be within the requesting Member State and present all the characteristics of a distinct market and does not constitute a substantial part of the common market.

4. JURISDICTIONAL THRESHOLDS

11. It appears that the threshold criteria in Article 1(2) and 1(3), considered in conjunction with the available corrective mechanisms, operate in a satisfactory way in allocating jurisdiction.

12. Nevertheless, the Commission's analysis of cases reported by the NCAs indicates that there are still a significant number of transactions which need to be notified in more than one Member State. In this regard, available data for 2007 indicate that there were at least 100 transactions which were notifiable in three or more Member States (10). These concentrations together required more than 360 parallel investigations by the NCAs.

(10) At least 240 cases were reviewable in two or more Member States in 2007.

13. A large majority of the cases with filing requirements in three or more member States involve markets which are wider than national or relate to several national or narrower markets. Consequently, there are a number of transactions with significant cross-border effects which would appear to remain outside the scope of the EC Merger Regulation. Against this background, one can conclude that there is further scope for «one-stop-shop» review.

14. Available data also suggest that around 6% of the cases notified in at least three Member State gave rise to competition concerns. This is an indication that a number of additional concentrations may be appropriate candidates for review by the Commission also when considering the principle of the «more appropriate authority». In fact, the negative consequences of parallel proceedings and the potential for a contradictory outcome are particularly important for those cases which raise substantive competition issues.

15. Looking beyond the application of the existing jurisdictional thresholds and their corrective mechanisms, in order to fully achieve the objective of a level playing field in the Common Market, the public consultation has suggested that efforts towards further convergence of the various national rules governing merger control and their relation to Community rules should be envisaged to alleviate difficulties encountered in the context of multiple filings.

5. THE TWO-THIRDS RULE

16. There were at least 126 cases that fell under the two-thirds rule over the reference period (11). There were thus few cases that met this threshold compared to the overall case load at the Member State level (12). Furthermore, it has mostly been applied in relation to concentrations within large Member States. The two-thirds rule has, in most cases appropriately distinguished between concentrations that in terms of their cross-border effects, have a Community relevance and those that do not. However, there are a small number of cases with potential cross-border effects in the Community which nevertheless fall under the competence of the NCAs as a result of this rule. In a substantive respect, public interest considerations other than competition policy have been applied in a number of cases falling under this threshold to authorise mergers which could have given rise to competition concerns. More generally, it is desirable that, independently of which authority is the reviewing agency, merger control across the EU ensures the protection of undistorted competition. Against this background, the present form of the two-thirds rule merits further consideration.

(11) Reference period between 2001 and 2008.

(12) In the same reference period, more than 26,000 cases where reported at a Member State level.

6. PRE-NOTIFICATION REFERAL MECHANISMS

17. The Commission's own experience as well as the comments received from the NCAs and stakeholders clearly support the view that the pre-notification referral mechanisms introduced in 2004 have considerably enhanced the efficiency and jurisdictional flexibility of merger control in the EU. They have substantially improved the allocation of cases between the Commission and the Member States taking into account the principles of «one-stop-shop» and «more appropriate authority».

18. In fact, available information clearly supports the view that these mechanisms have allowed the appropriate authority to handle cases while also avoiding unnecessary parallel proceedings and inconsistent enforcement efforts. In fact, it is estimated that these mechanisms have allowed for the reduction of the number of proceedings to around 150 from almost a thousand potential parallel proceedings in the period between 2004 and 2008. Furthermore, they have allowed for the re-allocation of 40 cases from the Commission to the Member States over the same period. Referrals were refused only in four cases under Article 4(5) and in one case under Article 4(4).

19. Nevertheless, there are some problems that have been highlighted, in particular in a procedural respect. Stakeholders have expressed concerns notably with regard to the overall timing and cumbersomeness of the referral process. These factors have been identified as the main cause of parties' decisions not to request referral in a large number of cases.

20. In this respect, based on available data with regard to the number of multiple filings and having regard to stakeholder comments, there appears to be further scope to use the referral mechanism under Article 4(5) in more cases and thus to achieve increased «one-stop-shop» (13). Conversely, there may be scope for more referrals in the direction of the Member States in application of Article 4(4).

(13) Furthermore, it must be recalled that the Member States' refusal powers under Article 4(5) have been rarely used. Many stakeholders therefore consider, having regard to the experience they acquired over the past years, that one should re-examine the possibilities of shifting to a system of automatic notification under the EC Merger Regulation when the three Member State criterion is met (or other intermediary solutions) as was initially proposed in the process leading up to the current system. This would in their view significantly increase transparency while lowering the cost and time for the review.

7. POST-NOTIFICATION REFERRAL MECHANISMS

21. The post-notification mechanisms provided by Articles 9 and 22 of the EC Merger Regulation have proven to continue to be useful corrective instruments also after the introduction of the pre-notification referral mechanisms. This is a reflection of the different function of the post-notification mechanisms, allowing for a flexible reallocation of cases at the initiative of the Member States or the Commission when appropriate. Nevertheless, the business community's concern regarding the timing and cumbersomeness of the referral procedures described above extends also to these mechanisms.

8. CONCLUSION

22. This report gives account to the Council of the operation of the notification thresholds under Article 1 of the EC Merger Regulation in allocating merger cases between the Community level and the national level and of the referral mechanisms provided for by its Articles 4, 9 and 22. The conclusions of this report are limited to taking stock of the situation to date without proposing any measures. Following this report and considering in particular the reactions of the Council, the Commission may, pursuant to Articles 1(5) and 4(6) of the EC Merger Regulation, present proposals to revise the notification thresholds or the referral mechanisms.

23. The Commission concludes that overall, the jurisdictional thresholds and the set of corrective mechanisms provided for by the EC Merger Regulation have provided an appropriate legal framework for allocating cases between the Community level and the Member States. This framework has in most cases been effective in distinguishing cases that have a Community relevance from those with a primarily national nexus, in pursuit of the objectives of «one-stop-shop» and the principle of the «more appropriate authority». Notwithstanding this success, there is scope for further improvements of the current system of case allocation in a number of respects as set out in this Report.

24. The Commission invites the Council to take note of the information set out in this report. The Commission also submits this report for information to the European Parliament and the European Economic and Social Committee.

Commission Regulation (EC) N° 802/2004, 21 April 2004 implementing Council Regulation N° 139/2004 on the control of concentrations between undertakings

(OJ L 133, 30 April 2004, p. 1)

Amended by:
Commission Regulation (EC) N° 1792/2006 of 23 October 2006, O.J., L 362, p. 1, 20.12.2006.
Commission Regulation (EC) N° 1033/2008 of 20 October 2008, O.J., L 279, p. 3, 22.10.2008.
Corrected by:
Corrigendum, O.J., L 172, 6.5.2004, p. 9 (802/2004)

THE COMMISSION OF THE EUROPEAN COMMUNITIES,

Having regard to the Treaty establishing the European Community,

Having regard to the Agreement on the European Economic Area,

Having regard to Council Regulation (EC) N° 139/2004 of 20 January 2004 on the control of concentrations between undertakings (EC Merger Regulation) (1), and in particular Article 23(1) thereof,

Having regard to Council Regulation (EEC) N° 4064/89 of 21 December 1989 on the control of concentrations between undertakings (2), as last amended by Regulation (EC) N° 1310/97 (3), and in particular Article 23 thereof,

Having consulted the Advisory Committee,

Whereas:

(1) Council Regulation (EEC) N° 4064/89 of 21 December 1989 on the control of concentrations between undertakings has been recast, with substantial amendments to various provisions of that Regulation.

(2) Commission Regulation (EC) N° 447/98 (4) of 1 March 1998 on the notifications, time-limits and hearings provided for in Council Regulation (EEC) N° 4064/89 must be modified in order to take account of those amendments. For the sake of clarity it should therefore be repealed and replaced by a new regulation.

(3) The Commission has adopted measures concerning the terms of reference of hearing officers in certain competition proceedings.

(4) Regulation (EC) N° 139/2004 is based on the principle of compulsory notification of concentrations before they are put into effect. On the one hand, a notification has important legal consequences which are favourable to the parties to the proposed concentration, while, on the other hand, failure to comply with the obligation to notify renders the parties liable to fines and may also entail civil law disadvantages for them. It is therefore necessary in the interests of legal certainty to define precisely the subject matter and content of the information to be provided in the notification.

(5) It is for the notifying parties to make a full and honest disclosure to the Commission of the facts and circumstances which are relevant for taking a decision on the notified concentration.

(6) Regulation (EC) N° 139/2004 also allows the undertakings concerned to request, in a reasoned submission, prior to notification, that a concentration fulfilling the requirements of that Regulation be referred to the Commission by one or more Member States, or referred by the Commission to one or more Member States, as the case may be. It is important to provide the Commission and the competent authorities of the Member States concerned with sufficient information, in order to enable them to assess, within a short period of time, whether or not a referral ought to be made. To that end, the reasoned submission requesting the referral should contain certain specific information.

(7) In order to simplify and expedite examination of notifications and of reasoned submissions, it is desirable to prescribe that forms be used.

(8) Since notification sets in motion legal time-limits pursuant to Regulation (EC) N° 139/2004, the conditions governing such time-limits and the time when they become effective should also be determined.

(9) Rules must be laid down in the interests of legal certainty for calculating the time-limits provided for in Regulation (EC) N° 139/2004. In particular, the beginning and end of time periods and the circumstances suspending the running of such periods must be determined, with due regard to the requirements resulting from the exceptionally tight legal timeframe available for the proceedings.

(10) The provisions relating to the Commission's procedure must be framed in such a way as to safeguard fully the right to be heard and the rights of defence. For these purposes, the Commission should distinguish between the parties who notify the concentration, other parties involved in the proposed concentration, third parties and parties regarding whom the Commission intends to take a decision imposing a fine or periodic penalty payments.

(11) The Commission should give the notifying parties and other parties involved in the proposed concentration, if they so request, an opportunity before notification to discuss the intended concentration informally and in strict confidence. In addition, the Commission should, after notification, maintain close contact with those parties, to the extent necessary to discuss with them any practical or legal problems which it discovers on a first examination of the case, with a view, if possible, to resolving such problems by mutual agreement.

(12) In accordance with the principle of respect for the rights of defence, the notifying parties must be given the opportunity to submit their comments on all the objections which the Commission proposes to take into account in its decisions. The other parties involved in the proposed concentration should also be informed of the Commission's objections and should be granted the opportunity to express their views.

(13) Third parties demonstrating a sufficient interest must also be given the opportunity of expressing their views, if they make a written application to that effect.

(14) The various persons entitled to submit comments should do so in writing, both in their own interests and in the interests of sound administration, without prejudice to their right to request a formal oral hearing, where appropriate, to supplement the written procedure. In urgent cases, however, the Commission must be enabled to proceed immediately to formal oral hearings of the notifying parties, of other parties involved or of third parties.

(15) It is necessary to define the rights of persons who are to be heard, to what extent they should be granted access to the Commission's file and on what conditions they may be represented or assisted.

(16) When granting access to the file, the Commission should ensure the protection of business secrets and other confidential information. The Commission should be able to ask undertakings that have submitted documents or statements to identify confidential information.

(17) In order to enable the Commission to carry out a proper assessment of commitments offered by the notifying parties with a view to rendering the concentration compatible with the common market, and to ensure due consultation with other parties involved, with third parties and with the authorities of the Member States as provided for in Regulation (EC) N° 139/2004, in particular Article 18(1), 18(4), Article 19(1), 19(2), 19(3) and 19(5) thereof, the procedure and time-limits for submitting the commitments referred to in Article 6(2) and Article 8(2) of that Regulation should be laid down.

(18) It is also necessary to define the rules applicable to certain time limits set by the Commission.

(19) The Advisory Committee on Concentrations must deliver its opinion on the basis of a preliminary draft decision. It must therefore be consulted on a case after the inquiry in to that case has been completed. Such consultation does not, however, prevent the Commission from reopening an inquiry if need be.

HAS ADOPTED THIS REGULATION:

(1) O.J. L 24, 29.1.2004, p. 1.

(2) O.J. L 395, 30.12.1989, p. 1.

(3) O.J. L 180, 9.7.1997, p. 1.

(4) O.J. L 61, 2.3.1998, p. 1. Regulation as amended by the 2003 Act of Accession.

CHAPTER I
SCOPE

Art. 1. *Scope*

This Regulation shall apply to the control of concentrations conducted pursuant to Regulation (EC) N° 139/2004.

CHAPTER II

NOTIFICATIONS AND OTHER SUBMISSIONS

Art. 2. *Persons entitled to submit notifications*

1. Notifications shall be submitted by the persons or undertakings referred to in Article 4(2) of Regulation (EC) N° 139/2004.

2. Where notifications are signed by representatives of persons or of undertakings, such representatives shall produce written proof that they are authorised to act.

3. Joint notifications shall be submitted by a joint representative who is authorised to transmit and to receive documents on behalf of all notifying parties.

Art. 3. *Submission of notifications*

1. Notifications shall be submitted in the manner prescribed by Form CO as set out in Annex I. Under the conditions set out in Annex II, notifications may be submitted in Short Form as defined therein. Joint notifications shall be submitted on a single form.

2. One original and 37 copies of the Form CO and the supporting documents shall be submitted to the Commission. The notification shall be delivered to the address referred to in Article 23(1) and in the format specified by the Commission.

3. The supporting documents shall be either originals or copies of the originals; in the latter case the notifying parties shall confirm that they are true and complete.

4. Notifications shall be in one of the official languages of the Community. For the notifying parties, this language shall also be the language of the proceeding, as well as that of any subsequent proceedings relating to the same concentration. Supporting documents shall be submitted in their original language. Where the original language is not one of the official languages of the Community, a translation into the language of the proceeding shall be attached.

5. Where notifications are made pursuant to Article 57 of the Agreement on the European Economic Area, they may also be submitted in one of the official languages of the EFTA States or the working language of the EFTA Surveillance Authority. If the language chosen for the notifications is not an official language of the Community, the notifying parties shall simultaneously supplement all documentation with a translation into an official language of the Community. The language which is chosen for the translation shall determine the language used by the Commission as the language of the proceeding for the notifying parties.

Art. 4. *Information and documents to be provided*

1. Notifications shall contain the information, including documents, requested in the applicable forms set out in the Annexes. The information shall be correct and complete.

2. The Commission may dispense with the obligation to provide any particular information in the notification, including documents, or with any other requirement specified in Annexes I and II where the Commission considers that compliance with those obligations or requirements is not necessary for the examination of the case.

3. The Commission shall without delay acknowledge in writing to the notifying parties or their representatives receipt of the notification and of any reply to a letter sent by the Commission pursuant to Article 5(2) and 5(3).

Art. 5. *Effective date of notification*

1. Subject to paragraphs 2, 3 and 4, notifications shall become effective on the date on which they are received by the Commission.

2. Where the information, including documents, contained in the notification is incomplete in any material respect, the Commission shall inform the notifying parties or their representatives in writing without delay. In such cases, the notification shall become effective on the date on which the complete information is received by the Commission.

3. Material changes in the facts contained in the notification coming to light subsequent to the notification which the notifying parties know or ought to know, or any new information coming to light subsequent to the notification which the parties know or ought to know and which would have had to be notified if known at the time of notification, shall be communicated to the Commission without delay. In such cases, when these material changes or new information could have a significant effect on the appraisal of the concentration, the notification may be considered by the Commission as becoming effective on the date on which the relevant information is received by the Commission; the Commission shall inform the notifying parties or their representatives of this in writing and without delay.

4. Incorrect or misleading information shall be considered to be incomplete information.

5. When the Commission publishes the fact of the notification pursuant to Article 4(3) of Regulation (EC) N° 139/2004, it shall specify the date upon which the notification has been received. Where, further to the application of paragraphs 2, 3 and 4 of this Article, the effective date of notification is later than the date specified in that publication, the Commission shall issue a further publication in which it shall state the later date.

Art. 6. *Specific provisions relating to reasoned submissions, supplements and certifications*

1. Reasoned submissions within the meaning of Article 4(4) and 4(5) of Regulation (EC) N° 139/2004 shall contain the information, including documents, requested in accordance with Annex III to this Regulation.

2. Article 2, Article 3(1), third sentence, 3(2) to (5), Article 4, Article 5(1), 5 (2) first sentence, 5 (3), 5 (4), Article 21 and Article 23 of this Regulation shall apply *mutatis mutandis* to reasoned submissions within the meaning of Article 4(4) and 4(5) of Regulation (EC) N° 139/2004.

Article 2, Article 3(1), third sentence, 3(2) to (5), Article 4, Article 5(1) to (4), Article 21 and Article 23 of this Regulation shall apply *mutatis mutandis* to supplements to notifications and certifications within the meaning of Article 10(5) of Regulation (EC) N° 139/2004.

CHAPTER III

TIME-LIMITS

Art. 7. *Beginning of time periods*

Time periods shall begin on the working day, as defined in Article 24 of this Regulation, following the event to which the relevant provision of Regulation (EC) N° 139/2004 refers.

Art. 8. *Expiry of time periods*

A time period calculated in working days shall expire at the end of its last working day.

A time period set by the Commission in terms of a calendar date shall expire at the end of that day.

Art. 9. *Suspension of time limit*

1. The time limits referred to in Articles 9(4), Article 10(1) and 10(3) of Regulation (EC) N° 139/2004 shall be suspended where the Commission has to take a decision pursuant to Article 11(3) or Article 13(4) of that Regulation, on any of the following grounds:

(a) information which the Commission has requested pursuant to Article 11(2) of Regulation (EC) N° 139/2004 from one of the notifying parties or another involved party, as defined in Article 11 of this Regulation, is not provided or not provided in full within the time limit fixed by the Commission;

(b) information which the Commission has requested pursuant to Article 11(2) of Regulation (EC) N° 139/2004 from a third party, as defined in Article 11 of this Regulation, is not provided or not provided in full within the time limit fixed by the Commission owing to circumstances for which one of the notifying parties or another involved party, as defined in Article 11 of this Regulation, is responsible;

(c) one of the notifying parties or another involved party, as defined in Article 11 of this Regulation, has refused to submit to an inspection deemed necessary by the Commission on the basis of Article 13(1) of Regulation (EC) N° 139/2004 or to cooperate in the carrying out of such an inspection in accordance with Article 13(2) of that Regulation;

(d) the notifying parties have failed to inform the Commission of material changes in the facts contained in the notification, or of any new information of the kind referred to in Article 5(3) of this Regulation.

2. The time limits referred to in Articles 9(4), Article 10(1) and 10(3) of Regulation (EC) N° 139/2004 shall be suspended where the Commission has to take a decision pursuant to Article 11(3) of that Regulation, without proceeding first by way of simple request for information, owing to circumstances for which one of the undertakings involved in the concentration is responsible.

3. The time limits referred to in Articles 9(4), Article 10(1) and (3) of Regulation (EC) N° 139/2004 shall be suspended:

(a) in the cases referred to in points *(a)* and *(b)* of paragraph 1, for the period between the expiry of the time limit set in the simple request for information, and the receipt of the complete and correct information required by decision;

(b) in the cases referred to in point *(c)* of paragraph 1, for the period between the unsuccessful attempt to carry out the inspection and the completion of the inspection ordered by decision;

(c) in the cases referred to in point *(d)* of paragraph 1, for the period between the occurrence of the change in the facts referred to therein and the receipt of the complete and correct information;

(d) in the cases referred to in paragraph 2 for the period between the expiry of the time limit set in the decision and the receipt of the complete and correct information required by decision.

4. The suspension of the time limit shall begin on the working day following the date on which the event causing the suspension occurred. It shall expire with the end of the day on which the reason for suspension is removed. Where such a day is not a working day, the suspension of the time-limit shall expire with the end of the following working day.

Art. 10. *Compliance with the time-limits*

1. The time limits referred to in Article 4(4), fourth subparagraph, Article 9(4), Article 10(1) and (3), and Article 22(3) of Regulation (EC) N° 139/2004 shall be met where the Commission has taken the relevant decision before the end of the period.

2. The time limits referred to in Article 4(4), second subparagraph, Article 4(5), third subparagraph, Article 9(2), Article 22(1), second subparagraph, and 22(2), second subparagraph, of Regulation (EC) N° 139/2004 shall be met by a Member State concerned where that Member State, before the end of the period, informs the Commission in writing or makes or joins the request in writing, as the case may be.

3. The time limit referred to in Article 9(6) of Regulation (EC) N° 139/2004 shall be met where the competent authority of a Member State concerned informs the undertakings concerned in the manner set out in that provision before the end of the period.

CHAPTER IV
EXERCISE OF THE RIGHT TO BE HEARD; HEARINGS

Art. 11. *Parties to be heard*

For the purposes of the rights to be heard pursuant to Article 18 of Regulation (EC) N° 139/2004, the following parties are distinguished:

(a) notifying parties, that is, persons or undertakings submitting a notification pursuant to Article 4(2) of Regulation (EC) N° 139/2004;

(b) other involved parties, that is, parties to the proposed concentration other than the notifying parties, such as the seller and the undertaking which is the target of the concentration;

(c) third persons, that is natural or legal persons, including customers, suppliers and competitors, provided they demonstrate a sufficient interest within the meaning of Article 18(4), second sentence, of Regulation (EC) N° 139/2004, which is the case in particular:

– for members of the administrative or management bodies of the undertakings concerned or the recognised representatives of their employees;

– for consumer associations, where the proposed concentration concerns products or services used by final consumers;

(d) parties regarding whom the Commission intends to take a decision pursuant to Article 14 or Article 15 of Regulation (EC) N° 139/2004.

Art. 12. *Decisions on the suspension of concentrations*

1. Where the Commission intends to take a decision pursuant to Article 7(3) of Regulation (EC) N° 139/2004 which adversely affects one or more of the parties, it shall, pursuant to Article 18(1) of that Regulation, inform the notifying parties and other involved parties in writing of its objections and shall set a time limit within which they may make known their views in writing.

2. Where the Commission, pursuant to Article 18(2) of Regulation (EC) N° 139/2004, has taken a decision referred to in paragraph 1 of this Article provisionally without having given the notifying parties and other involved parties the opportunity to make known their views, it shall without delay send them the text of the provisional decision and shall set a time limit within which they may make known their views in writing.

Once the notifying parties and other involved parties have made known their views, the Commission shall take a final decision annulling, amending or confirming the provisional decision. Where they have not made known their views in writing within the time limit set, the Commission's provisional decision shall become final with the expiry of that period.

Art. 13. *Decisions on the substance of the case*

1. Where the Commission intends to take a decision pursuant to Article 6(3) or Article 8(2) to (6) of Regulation (EC) N° 139/2004, it shall, before consulting the Advisory Committee on Concentrations, hear the parties pursuant to Article 18(1) and (3) of that Regulation.

Article 12(2) of this Regulation shall apply *mutatis mutandis* where, in application of Article 18(2) of Regulation (EC) N° 139/2004, the Commission has taken a decision pursuant to Article 8(5) of that Regulation provisionally.

2. The Commission shall address its objections in writing to the notifying parties.

The Commission shall, when giving notice of objections, set a time limit within which the notifying parties may inform the Commission of their comments in writing.

The Commission shall inform other involved parties in writing of these objections.

The Commission shall also set a time limit within which those other involved parties may inform the Commission of their comments in writing.

The Commission shall not be obliged to take into account comments received after the expiry of a time limit which it has set.

3. The parties to whom the Commission's objections have been addressed or who have been informed of those objections shall, within the time limit set, submit in writing their comments on the objections. In their written comments, they may set out all facts and matters known to them which are relevant to their defence, and shall attach any relevant documents as proof of the facts set out. They may also propose that the Commission hear persons who may corroborate those facts. They shall submit one original and 10 copies of their comments to the Commission to the address of the Commission's Directorate General for Competition. An electronic copy shall also be submitted at the same address and in the format specified by the Commission. The Commission shall forward copies of such written comments without delay to the competent authorities of the Member States.

4. Where the Commission intends to take a decision pursuant to Article 14 or Article 15 of Regulation (EC) N° 139/2004, it shall, before consulting the Advisory Committee on Concentrations, hear the parties pursuant to Article 18(1) and (3) of that Regulation the parties regarding whom the Commission intends to take such a decision.

The procedure provided for in paragraph 2, first and second subparagraphs, and paragraph 3 shall apply, *mutatis mutandis*.

Art. 14. *Oral hearings*

1. Where the Commission intends to take a decision pursuant to Article 6(3) or Article 8(2) to (6) of Regulation (EC) N° 139/2004, it shall afford the notifying parties who have so requested in their written comments the opportunity to develop their arguments in a formal oral hearing. It may also, at other stages in the proceedings, afford the notifying parties the opportunity of expressing their views orally.

2. Where the Commission intends to take a decision pursuant to Article 6(3) or Article 8(2) to (6) of Regulation (EC) N° 139/2004, it shall also afford other involved parties who have so requested in their written comments the opportunity to develop their arguments in a formal oral hearing. It may also, at other stages in the proceedings, afford other involved parties the opportunity of expressing their views orally.

3. Where the Commission intends to take a decision pursuant to Article 14 or Article 15 of Regulation (EC) N° 139/2004, it shall afford parties on whom it proposes to impose a fine or periodic penalty payment the opportunity to develop their arguments in a formal oral hearing, if so requested in their written comments. It may also, at other stages in the proceedings, afford such parties the opportunity of expressing their views orally.

Art. 15. *Conduct of formal oral hearings*

1. Formal oral hearings shall be conducted by the Hearing Officer in full independence.

2. The Commission shall invite the persons to be heard to attend the formal oral hearing on such date as it shall determine.

3. The Commission shall invite the competent authorities of the Member States to take part in any formal oral hearing.

4. Persons invited to attend shall either appear in person or be represented by legal representatives or by representatives authorised by their constitution as appropriate. Undertakings and associations of undertakings may also be represented by a duly authorised agent appointed from among their permanent staff.

5. Persons heard by the Commission may be assisted by their lawyers or other qualified and duly authorised persons admitted by the Hearing Officer.

6. Formal oral hearings shall not be public. Each person may be heard separately or in the presence of other persons invited to attend, having regard to the legitimate interest of the undertakings in the protection of their business secrets and other confidential information.

7. The Hearing Officer may allow all parties within the meaning of Article 11, the Commission services and the competent authorities of the Member States to ask questions during the formal oral hearing.

The Hearing Officer may hold a preparatory meeting with the parties and the Commission services, so as to facilitate the efficient organisation of the formal oral hearing.

8. The statements made by each person heard shall be recorded. Upon request, the recording of the formal oral hearing shall be made available to the persons who attended that hearing. Regard shall be had to the legitimate interest of the undertakings in the protection of their business secrets and other confidential information.

Art. 16. *Hearing of third persons*

1. If third persons apply in writing to be heard pursuant to Article 18(4), second sentence, of Regulation (EC) N° 139/2004, the Commission shall inform them in writing of the nature and subject matter of the procedure and shall set a time limit within which they may make known their views.

2. The third persons referred to in paragraph 1 shall make known their views in writing within the time limit set. The Commission may, where appropriate, afford such third parties who have so requested in their written comments the opportunity to participate in a formal hearing. It may also in other cases afford such third parties the opportunity of expressing their views orally.

3. The Commission may likewise invite any other natural or legal person to express its views, in writing as well as orally, including at a formal oral hearing.

CHAPTER V
ACCESS TO THE FILE AND TREATMENT OF CONFIDENTIAL INFORMATION

Art. 17. *Access to the file and use of documents*

1. If so requested, the Commission shall grant access to the file to the parties to whom it has addressed a statement of objections, for the purpose of enabling them to exercise their rights of defence. Access shall be granted after the notification of the statement of objections.

2. The Commission shall, upon request, also give the other involved parties who have been informed of the objections access to the file in so far as this is necessary for the purposes of preparing their comments.

3. The right of access to the file shall not extend to confidential information, or to internal documents of the Commission or of the competent authorities of the Member States. The right of access to the file shall equally not extend to correspondence between the Commission and the competent authorities of the Member States or between the latter.

4. Documents obtained through access to the file pursuant to this Article may only be used for the purposes of the relevant proceeding pursuant to Regulation (EC) N° 139/2004.

Art. 18. *Confidential information*

1. Information, including documents, shall not be communicated or made accessible by the Commission in so far as it contains business secrets or other confidential information the disclosure of which is not considered necessary by the Commission for the purpose of the procedure.

2. Any person which makes known its views or comments pursuant to Articles 12, Article 13 and Article 16 of this Regulation, or supplies information pursuant to Article 11 of Regulation (EC) N° 139/2004, or subsequently submits further information to the Commission in the course of the same procedure, shall clearly identify any material which it considers to be confidential, giving reasons, and provide a separate non-confidential version by the date set by the Commission.

3. Without prejudice to paragraph 2, the Commission may require persons referred to in Article 3 of Regulation (EC) N° 139/2004, undertakings and associations of undertakings in all cases where they produce or have produced documents or statements pursuant to Regulation (EC) N° 139/2004 to identify the documents or parts of documents which they consider to contain business secrets or other confidential information belonging to them and to identify the undertakings with regard to which such documents are to be considered confidential.

The Commission may also require persons referred to in Article 3 of Regulation (EC) N° 139/2004, undertakings or associations of undertakings to identify any part of a statement of objections, case summary or a decision adopted by the Commission which in their view contains business secrets.

Where business secrets or other confidential information are identified, the persons, undertakings and associations of undertakings shall give reasons and provide a separate non-confidential version by the date set by the Commission.

4. If persons, undertakings or associations of undertakings fail to comply with paragraphs 2 or 3, the Commission may assume that the documents or statements concerned do not contain confidential information.

CHAPTER VI
COMMITMENTS OFFERED BY THE UNDERTAKINGS CONCERNED

Art. 19. *Time limits for submission of commitments*

1. Commitments offered by the undertakings concerned pursuant to Article 6(2) of Regulation (EC) N° 139/2004 shall be submitted to the Commission within not more than 20 working days from the date of receipt of the notification.

2. Commitments offered by the undertakings concerned pursuant to Article 8(2) of Regulation (EC) N° 139/2004 shall be submitted to the Commission within not more than 65 working days from the date on which proceedings were initiated.

Where pursuant to Article 10(3), second subparagraph, of Regulation (EC) N° 139/2004 the period for the adoption of a decision pursuant to Article 8(1), (2) and (3) is extended, the period of 65 working days for the submission of commitments shall automatically be extended by the same number of working days.

In exceptional circumstances, the Commission may accept commitments offered after the expiry of the time limit for their submission within the meaning of this paragraph provided that the procedure provided for in Article 19(5) of Regulation (EC) N° 139/2004 is complied with.

3. Articles 7, 8 and 9 shall apply *mutatis mutandis*.

Art. 20. *Procedure for the submission of commitments*

1. One original and 10 copies of commitments offered by the undertakings concerned pursuant to Article 6(2) or Article 8(2) of Regulation (EC) N° 139/2004 shall be submitted to the Commission at the address of the Commission's Directorate General for Competition. An electronic copy shall also be submitted at the same address and in the format specified by the Commission. The Commission shall forward copies of such commitments without delay to the competent authorities of the Member States.

1*a*. In addition to the requirements set out in paragraph 1, the undertakings concerned shall, at the same time as offering commitments pursuant to Article 6(2) or Article 8(2) of Regulation (EC) N° 139/2004, submit one original and 10 copies of the information and documents prescribed by the Form RM relating to remedies (Form RM) as set out in Annex IV to this Regulation. The information submitted shall be correct and complete.

2. When offering commitments pursuant to Articles 6(2) or Article 8(2) of Regulation (EC) N° 139/2004, the undertakings concerned shall at the same time clearly identify any information which they consider to be confidential, giving reasons, and shall provide a separate non-confidential version.

Art. 20.*a***.** *Trustees*

1. The commitments offered by the undertakings concerned pursuant to Article 6(2) or Article 8(2) of Regulation (EC) N° 139/2004 may include, at the own expense of the undertakings concerned, the appointment of an independent trustee (or trustees) assisting the Commission in overseeing the parties' compliance with the commitments or having a mandate to implement the commitments. The trustee may be appointed by the parties, after the Commission has approved its identity, or by the Commission. The trustee shall carry out its tasks under the supervision of the Commission.

2. The Commission may attach such trustee-related provisions of the commitments as conditions and obligations pursuant to Article 6(2) or Article 8(2) of Regulation (EC) N° 139/2004.

CHAPTER VII
MISCELLANEOUS PROVISIONS

Art. 21. *Transmission of documents*

1. Transmission of documents and invitations from the Commission to the addressees may be effected in any of the following ways:

(a) delivery by hand against receipt;
(b) registered letter with acknowledgement of receipt;
(c) fax with a request for acknowledgement of receipt;
(d) telex;
(e) electronic mail with a request for acknowledgement of receipt.

2. Unless otherwise provided in this Regulation, paragraph 1 also applies to the transmission of documents from the notifying parties, from other involved parties or from third parties to the Commission.

3. Where a document is sent by telex, by fax or by electronic mail, it shall be presumed that it has been received by the addressee on the day on which it was sent.

Art. 22. *Setting of time limits*

In setting the time limits provided for pursuant to Article 12(1) and (2), Article 13(2) and Article 16(1), the Commission shall have regard to the time required for the preparation of statements and to the urgency of the case. It shall also take account of working days as well as public holidays in the country of receipt of the Commission's communication.

Time limits shall be set in terms of a precise calendar date.

Art. 23. *Receipt of documents by the Commission*

1. In accordance with the provisions of Article 5(1) of this Regulation, notifications shall be delivered to the Commission at the address of the Commission's Directorate General for Competition as published by the Commission in the *Official Journal of the European Union*.

2. Additional information requested to complete notifications must reach the Commission at the address referred to in paragraph 1.

3. Written comments on Commission communications pursuant to Article 12(1) and (2), Article 13(2) and Article 16(1) of this Regulation must have reached the Commission at the address referred to in paragraph 1 before the expiry of the time limit set in each case.

Art. 24. *Definition of working days*

The expression working days in Regulation (EC) N° 139/2004 and in this Regulation means all days other than Saturdays, Sundays, and Commission holidays as published in the *Official Journal of the European Union* before the beginning of each year.

Art. 25. *Repeal and transitional provision*

1. Without prejudice to paragraphs 2 and 3, Regulation (EC) N° 447/98 is repealed with effect from 1 May 2004.

References to the repealed Regulation shall be construed as references to this Regulation.

2. Regulation (EC) N° 447/98 shall continue to apply to any concentration falling within the scope of Regulation (EEC) N° 4064/89.

3. For the purposes of paragraph 2, Sections 1 to 12 of the Annex to Regulation (EC) N° 447/98 shall be replaced by Sections 1 to 11 of Annex I to this Regulation. In such cases references in those sections to the «EC Merger Regulation» and to the «Implementing Regulation» shall be read as referring to the corresponding provisions of Regulation (EEC) N° 4064/89 and Regulation (EC) N° 447/98, respectively.

Art. 26. *Entry into force*

This Regulation shall enter into force on 1 May 2004.

This Regulation shall be binding in its entirety and directly applicable in all Member States.

ANNEX I

Form CO Relating to the notification of a concentration pursuant to Regulation (EC) N° 139/2004

1. Not included; see section Forms

Annex II

Short Form for the notification of a concentration pursuant to Regulation (EC) N° 139/2004

1. Not included; see section Forms

Annex III

FORM RS
(Form for reasoned submission pursuant to Article 4(4) and (5) of Council Regulation (EC) N° 139/2004)

1. Not included; see section Forms

Annex IV

Form RM relating to the information concerning commitments submitted pursuant to Article 6(2) and Article 8(2) of Regulation (EC) N° 139/2004

1. Not included; see section Forms

2.2.2. Substantive rules

Commission Notice – Relevant market...	363
Commission Notice – Remedies acceptable under Council Regulation (EC) No 139/2004 and under Commission Regulation (EC) No 802/2004.....................	363
Merger Remedies Study..	381
Guidelines – Assessment of horizontal mergers...............................	381
Guidelines – Assessment of non-horizontal mergers.........................	392
Commission Notice – Restrictions directly related and necessary to concentrations....	404
Commission Notice – Commission Consolidated Jurisdictional Notice under the Merger Regulation	408
Commission Notice – Average rate used to calculate the turnover, simplified method.	435

Commission Notice on the definition of relevant market for the purposes of Community competition law

(OJ C 372, 9 December 1997, p. 5)

1. See above, section 2.1.2.1. General rules

2. In 1999, Articles 85 and 86 became Articles 81 and 82 EC, and are now Articles 101 and 102 TFEU.

Commission Notice on remedies acceptable under Council Regulation (EC) N° 139/2004 and under Commission Regulation (EC) N° 802/2004

(OJ C 267, 22 October 2008, p. 1)

I. INTRODUCTION

1. Council Regulation (E.C.) N° 139/2004 of 20 January 2004 on the control of concentrations between undertakings (1) (hereinafter referred to as «the Merger Regulation») in Articles 6(2) and 8(2) expressly provides that the Commission may decide to declare a concentration compatible with the common market following modification by the parties (2), both before and after the initiation of proceedings. To that end, the Commission may attach to its decision conditions and obligations intended to ensure that the undertakings concerned comply with the commitments they have entered into vis-à-vis the Commission with a view to rendering the concentration compatible with the common market (3).

(1) O.J. L 24, 29.1.2004, p. 1-22.

(2) The references to «parties» and «merging parties» also cover situations with one notifying party.

(3) Articles 6(2) and 8(2), second subparagraphs respectively. See also Recital 30 of the Merger Regulation which states that «where the undertakings concerned modify a notified concentration, in particular by offering commitments with a view to rendering the concentration compatible with the common market, the Commission should be able to declare the concentration, as modified, compatible with the common market. Such commitments should be proportionate to the competition problem and entirely eliminate it». Recital 30 further explains that «it is also appropriate to accept commitments before the initiation of proceedings where the competition problem is readily identifiable and can easily be remedied».

2. The purpose of this Notice is to provide guidance on modifications to concentrations, in particular commitments by the undertakings concerned to modify a concentration. Such modifications are more commonly described as «remedies» since their object is to eliminate the competition concerns (4) identified by the Commission. The guidance set out in this Notice reflects the Commission's evolving experience with the assessment, acceptance and implementation of remedies under the Merger Regulation since its entry into force on 21 September 1990. The revision of the Commission's 2001 Notice on remedies (5) is entailed by the entry into force of the recast Merger Regulation (E.C.) N° 139/2004 (6) and of Commission Regulation (E.C.) N° 802/2004 (the «Implementing Regulation») (7) on 1 May 2004, case-law of the Court of justice and the Court of First Instance, the conclusions drawn from the systematic ex post review of the Commission of past remedies case (8), and decisional practice of the Commission in cases involving remedies in recent years. The principles contained herein will be applied and further developed and refined by the Commission in individual cases. The guidance provided in this Notice is without prejudice to the interpretation which may be given by the Court of justice or by the Court of First Instance of the European Communities.

(4) Save where the contrary is indicated, in the following, the term «competition concerns» corresponds, according to the stage of the procedure, to serious doubts or preliminary findings that the concentration is likely to significantly impede effective competition in the common market or in a substantial part of it, in particular as a result of the creation or strengthening of a dominant position.

(5) Commission Notice on remedies acceptable under Council Regulation (E.E.C.) N° 4064/89 and under Commission Regulation (EC) N° 447/98 (O.J. C 68, 2.3.2001, p. 3).

(6) Regulation replacing Council Regulation (E.E.C.) N° 4064/89 (O.J. L 395, 30.12.1989, corrected version in O.J. L 257, 21.9.1990, p. 13.

(7) Commission Regulation (E.C.) N° 802/2004 of 7 April 2004 implementing Council Regulation (E.C.) N° 139/2004 on the control of concentrations between undertakings (O.J. L 133, 30.4.2004, p. 1). This Regulation replaces Commission Regulation (E.C.) N° 447/98 implementing Council Regulation (E.E.C.) N° 4064/89 on the control of concentrations between undertakings (O.J. L 61, 2.3.1998, p. 1).

(8) DG COMP, Merger Remedies Study, October 2005.

3. This Notice sets out the general principles applicable to remedies acceptable to the Commission, the main types of commitments that may be accepted by the Commission in cases under the Merger Regulation, the specific requirements which proposals of commitments need to fulfil in both phases of the procedure, and the main requirements for the implementation of commitments. In any case, the Commission will take due account of the particular circumstances of the individual case.

II. GENERAL PRINCIPLES

4. Under the Merger Regulation, the Commission assesses the compatibility of a notified concentration with the common market on the basis of its effect on the structure of competition in the Community (9). The test for compatibility under Article 2(2) and (3) of the Merger Regulation is whether or not a concentration would significantly impede effective competition in the common market or a substantial part of it, in particular as a result of the creation or strengthening of a dominant position. A concentration that significantly impedes effective competition as described above is incompatible with the common market and the Commission is required to prohibit it. For the creation of a joint venture, the Commission will also examine the concentration under Article 2(4) of the Merger Regulation. The principles set out in this Notice will generally also apply to remedies submitted to eliminate competition concerns identified under Article 2(4).

(9) Recital 6 of the Merger Regulation.

5. Where a concentration raises competition concerns in that it could significantly impede effective competition, in particular as a result of the creation or strengthening of a dominant position, the parties may seek to modify the concentration in order to resolve the competition concerns and thereby gain clearance of their merger. Such modifications may be fully implemented in advance of a clearance decision. However, it is more common that the parties submit commitments with a view to rendering the concentration compatible with the common market and that those commitments are implemented following clearance.

6. Under the structure of the Merger Regulation, it is the responsibility of the Commission to show that a concentration would significantly impede competition (10). The Commission communicates its competition concerns to the parties to allow them to formulate appropriate and corresponding remedies proposals (11). It is then for the parties to the concentration to put forward commitments; the Commission is not in a position to impose unilaterally any conditions to an authorisation decision, but only on the basis of the parties' commitments (12). The Commission will inform the parties about its preliminary assessment of remedies proposals. If, however, the parties do not validly propose remedies adequate to eliminate the competition concerns, the only option for the Commission will be to adopt a prohibition decision (13).

(10) In phase I and before the issuance of a Statement of Objections, this corresponds to serious doubts as to the significant impediment to effective competition.

(11) The Merger Regulation provides for formal steps where the parties are informed of the competition concerns identified by the Commission (Article 6(1)(c) decision, Statement of Objections). In addition, the DG COMPETITION Best Practices on the conduct of EC merger control proceedings foresee that «state of play» meetings will normally be offered at key stages of the procedure where the Commission will explain its concerns to the parties in order to allow them to respond with remedies proposals.

(12) Judgment of the CFI in Case T-210/01 *General Electric v Commission* (2005) ECR II-5575, paragraph 52; see judgment of the CFI in Case T-87/05 *EDP v Commission* (2005) ECR II-3745, paragraph 105.

(13) See Case COMP/M.2220 – *GE/Honeywell* of 3 July 2001, confirmed by judgment of the CFI in Case T-210/01 *General Electric v Commission* (2005) ECR II-5575, paragraph 555 et seq., 612 et seq.; Case COMP/M.3440 – EDP/ENI/GDP of 9 December 2004, confirmed by judgment of the CFI in Case T-87/05 *EDP v Commission* (2005) ECR II-3745, paragraphs 63 et seq., 75 et seq.; Case IV/M.469 – *MSG Media service* of 9 November 1994; Case IV/M.490 – *Nordic Satellite Distribution* of 19 July 1995; Case IV/M.553 – *RTL/Veronica/Endemol* of 20 September 1995; Case IV/M.993 – *Bertelsmann/Kirch/Prèmiere* of 27 May 1998; Case IV/M.1027 – *Deutsche Telekom BetaResearch* of 27 May 1998; Case IV/M.774 – *St Gobain/Wacker Chemie* of 4 December 1996; Case IV/M.53 – *Aerospatiale/Alenia/De Havilland* of 2 October 1991; Case IV/M.619 – *Gencor/Lonrho* of 24 April 1996, confirmed by judgment of the CFI in Case T-102/96 *Gencor v Commission* (1999) ECR II-753.

7. The Commission has to assess whether the proposed remedies, once implemented, would eliminate the competition concerns identified. Only the parties have all the relevant information necessary for such an assessment, in particular as to the feasibility of the commitments proposed and the viability and competitiveness of the assets proposed for divestiture. It is therefore the responsibility of the parties to provide all such information available that is necessary for the Commission's assessment of the remedies proposal. To this end, the Implementing Regulation obliges the notifying parties to provide, with the commitments, detailed information on the content of the commitments offered, the conditions for their implementation and showing their suitability to remove any significant impediment of effective competition, as set out in the annex to the Implementing Regulation («Form RM»). For commitments consisting in the divestiture of a business, parties have to describe in detail in particular how the business to be divested is currently operated. This information will enable the Commission to assess the viability, competitiveness and marketability of the business by comparing its current operation to its proposed scope under the commitments. The Commission can adapt the precise requirements to the information necessary in the individual case at hand and will be available to discuss the scope of the information required with the parties in advance of submission of Form R.M.

8. Whereas the parties have to propose commitments sufficient to remove the competition concerns and submit the necessary information to assess them, it is for the Commission to establish whether or not a concentration, as modified by commitments validly submitted, must be declared incompatible with the common market because it leads, despite the commitments, to a significant impediment of effective competition. The burden of proof for a prohibition or authorisation of a concentration modified by commitments is therefore subject to the same criteria as an unmodified concentration (14).

(14) See judgment of the CFI in Case T-87/05 *EDP v Commission* (2005) ECR II-3745, paragraphs 62 ff.

Basic conditions for acceptable commitments

9. Under the Merger Regulation, the Commission only has power to accept commitments that are deemed capable of rendering the concentration compatible with the common market so that they will prevent a significant impediment of effective competition. The commitments have to eliminate the competition concerns entirely (15) and have to be

comprehensive and effective from all points of view (16). Furthermore, commitments must be capable of being implemented effectively within a short period of time as the conditions of competition on the market will not be maintained until the commitments have been fulfilled.

(15) See recital 30 of the Merger Regulation and judgment of the CFI in Case T-282/02 *Cementbouw v Commission* (2006) ECR II-319, paragraph 307.

(16) CFI, Case T-210/01 *General Electrics v Commission* (2005) ECR II-5575, paragraph 52; Case T-87/05 *EDP v Commission* (2005) ECR II-3745, paragraph 105.

10. Structural commitments, in particular divestitures, proposed by the parties will meet these conditions only in so far as the Commission is able to conclude with the requisite degree of certainty that it will be possible to implement them and that it will be likely that the new commercial structures resulting from them will be sufficiently workable and lasting to ensure that the significant impediment to effective competition will not materialise (17).

(17) CFI, Case T-210/01 *General Electric v Commission* (2005) ECR II-5575, paragraphs 555, 612.

11. The requisite degree of certainty concerning the implementation of the proposed commitments may in particular be affected by risks in relation to the transfer of a business to be divested, such as conditions attached by the parties to the divestiture, third party rights in relation to the business or the risks of finding a suitable purchaser, as well as risks in relation to the degradation of the assets until the divestiture has taken place. It is incumbent on the parties to remove such uncertainties as to the implementation of the remedy when submitting it to the Commission (18).

(18) Depending on the nature of the risks, specific safeguards may aim at compensating for them. For example, the risk arising from third party rights in relation to the assets to be divested may be compensated by the proposal of an alternative divestiture. Such safeguards will be discussed in more detail below.

12. In assessing the second condition, whether the proposed commitment will likely eliminate the competition concerns identified, the Commission will consider all relevant factors relating to the proposed remedy itself, including, inter alia, the type, scale and scope of the remedy proposed, judged by reference to the structure and particular characteristics of the market in which the competition concerns arise, including the position of the parties and other players on the market.

13. In order for the commitments to comply with these principles, there has to be an effective implementation and ability to monitor the commitments (19). Whereas divestitures, once implemented, do not require any further monitoring measures, other types of commitments require effective monitoring mechanisms in order to ensure that their effect is not reduced or even eliminated by the parties. Otherwise, such commitments would have to be considered as mere declarations of intention by the parties and would not amount to binding obligations, as, due to the lack of effective monitoring mechanisms, any breach of them could not result in the revocation of the decision according to the provisions of the Merger Regulation (20).

(19) CFI, Case T-177/04 *easyJet v Commission* (2006) ECR II-1931, paragraph 188.

(20) CFI, Case T-177/04 *easyJet v Commission* (2006) ECR II-1931, paragraph 186 et seq.; CFI, judgment in Case T-87/05 *EDP v Commission* (2005) ECR II-3745, paragraph 72.

14. Where, however, the parties submit remedies proposals that are so extensive and complex that it is not possible for the Commission to determine with the requisite degree of certainty, at the time of its decision, that they will be fully implemented and that they are likely to maintain effective competition in the market, an authorisation decision cannot be granted (21). The Commission may reject such remedies in particular on the grounds that the implementation of the remedies cannot be effectively monitored and that the lack of effective monitoring diminishes, or even eliminates, the effect of the commitments proposed.

(21) See, as an example for such a complex and inappropriate remedy, Case COMP/M.3440 – *ENI/EDP/GDP* of 9 December 2004; confirmed by CFI, judgment in Case T-87/05 *EDP v Commission* (2005) ECR II-3745, paragraph 102; Case COMP/M.1672 – *Volvo/Scania* of 15 March 2000.

Appropriateness of different types of remedies

15. According to the case law of the Court, the basic aim of commitments is to ensure competitive market structures (22). accordingly, commitments which are structural in nature, such as the commitment to sell a business unit, are, as a rule, preferable from the point of view of the Merger Regulation's objective, inasmuch as such commitments prevent, durably, the competition concerns which would be raised by the merger as notified, and do not, moreover, require medium or long-term monitoring measures. Nevertheless, the possibility cannot automatically be ruled out that other types of commitments may also be capable of preventing the significant impediment of effective competition (23).

(22) See recital 8 of the Merger Regulation; judgment of CFI in Case T-102/96 *Gencor v Commission* (1999) ECR II-753, at paragraph 316; ECJ in Case C-12/03 P *Commission v Tetra Laval* (2005) ECR I-987, paragraph 86; judgment of CFI in Case T-158/00 *ARD v Commission* (2003) ECR II-3825, at paragraphs 192 et seq.

(23) ECJ, judgment in Case C-12/03 P *Commission v Tetra Laval* (2005) ECR I-987, paragraph 86; CFI, judgment of 25 March 1999 in Case T-102/96 *Gencor v Commission* (1999) ECR II-753, paragraphs 319 et seq.; CFI, judgment of 30 September 2003 in Case T-158/00 *ARD v Commission* (2003) ECR II-3825, paragraph 193; CFI in Case T-177/04 *easyJet v Commission* (2006) ECR II-1931, paragraph 182; CFI, judgment in Case T-87/05 *EDP v Commission* (2005) ECR II-3745, paragraph 101.

16. The Commission stresses that the question of whether a remedy and, more specifically, which type of remedy is suitable to eliminate the competition concerns identified, has to be examined on a case-by-case basis.

17. Nevertheless, a general distinction can be made between divestitures, other structural remedies, such as granting access to key infrastructure or inputs on non-discriminatory terms, and commitments relating to the future behaviour of the merged entity. Divestiture commitments are the best way to eliminate competition concerns resulting from horizontal overlaps, and may also be the best means of resolving problems resulting from vertical or conglomerate concerns (24). Other structural commitments may be suitable to resolve all types of concerns if those remedies are equivalent to divestitures in their effects, as explained in more detail below in paragraphs 61 et seq. Commitments relating to the future behaviour of the merged entity may be acceptable only exceptionally in very specific circumstances (25). In particular, commitments in the form of undertakings not to raise prices, to reduce product ranges or to remove brands, etc., will generally not eliminate competition concerns resulting from horizontal overlaps. In any case, those types of remedies can only exceptionally be accepted if their workability is fully ensured by effective implementation and monitoring in line with the considerations set out in paragraphs 13-14, 66, 69, and if they do not risk leading to distorting effects on competition (26).

(24) See divestiture of storage facilities in Case COMP/M.3868 – *DONG/Elsam/Energi E2* of 14 March 2006, paragraphs 170 et seq.; Case COMP/M.3696 – *E.ON/MOL* of 21 December 2005, paragraphs 735 et seq., for an example of «ownership unbundling» to eliminate structural links between the parties in the gas storage sector; further Case COMP/M.4314 – *Johnson&Johnson/Pfizer* of 11 December 2006, Case COMP/M.4494 – *Evraz/Highveld* of 20 February 2007.

(25) See, in relation to conglomerate effects of a concentration, ECJ, judgment of 15 February 2005 in Case C-12/03 P *Commission v Tetra Laval* (2005) ECR I-987, paragraphs 85, 89.

(26) For example, commitments regarding a certain pricing behaviour such as price caps which contain the risk to lead to an anticompetitive alignment of prices among competitors.

Procedure

18. The Commission may accept commitments in either phase of the procedure (27). However, given the fact that an in-depth market investigation is only carried out in phase II, commitments submitted to the Commission in phase I must be sufficient to clearly rule out «serious doubts» within the meaning of Article 6(1)(c) of the Merger Regulation (28). Pursuant to Article 10(2) of the Merger Regulation, the Commission has to take a clearance decision as soon as the serious doubts referred to in Article 6(1)(c) of the Merger Regulation are removed as a result of commitments submitted by the parties. This rule applies to commitments proposed in phase II-proceedings before the Commission issues a Statement of Objections (29). If the Commission reaches the preliminary view that the merger leads to a significant impediment to effective competition and issues a Statement of Objections, the commitments must be sufficient to eliminate such a significant impediment to effective competition.

(27) As foreseen in recital 30 of the Merger Regulation, the Commission will ensure transparency and effective consultation of Member States in both phases of the procedure.

(28) Commitments in phase I can only be accepted in certain types of situations; see below in paragraph 81.

(29) See, inter alia, Case COMP/M.2972 – *DSM/Roche Vitamins* of 23 July 2003; Case COMP/M.2861 – *Siemens/Drägerwerk/JV* of 30 April 2003; Case IV/JV.15 – *BT/AT & T* of 30 March 1999; Case IV/M.1532 – *BP Amoco/Arco* of 29 September 1999.

19. Whilst commitments have to be offered by the parties, the Commission will ensure the enforceability of commitments by making the authorisation of the merger subject to compliance with the commitments. A distinction must be made between conditions and obligations. The requirement for achievement of the structural change of the market is a condition – for example, that a business is to be divested. The implementing steps which are necessary to achieve this result are generally obligations on the parties, e.g. such as the appointment of a trustee with an irrevocable mandate to sell the business.

20. Where the undertakings concerned commit a breach of an obligation, the Commission may revoke clearance decisions issued either under Article 6(2) or Article 8(2) of the Merger Regulation, acting pursuant to Article 6(3) or Article 8(6), respectively. In case of a breach of an obligation, the parties may also be subject to fines and periodic penalty payments as provided in Article 14(2)(d) and 15(1)(c) respectively of the Merger Regulation. Where, however, a condition is breached, e.g. a business is not divested in the time-frame foreseen in the commitments or afterwards re-acquired, the compatibility decision is no longer applicable. In such circumstances, the Commission may, first, take interim measures appropriate to maintain conditions of effective competition pursuant to Article 8(5)(b) of the Merger Regulation. Second, it may, if the conditions of Article 8(4)(b) are met, order any appropriate measure to ensure that the undertakings concerned dissolve the concentration or take other restorative measures or, according to Article 8(7), take a decision pursuant to Article 8(1)-(3). In addition, the parties may also be subject to fines as provided in Article 14(2)(d).

Model Texts for divestiture commitments

21. The Commission services have issued Best Practice Guidelines for divestiture commitments, consisting of a Model Text for Divestiture Commitments and a Model Text for Trustee Mandates (30). These model texts are neither intended to provide an exhaustive coverage of all issues that may become relevant in all cases, nor are they legally binding upon parties in a merger procedure. They complement the present Notice as they outline the typical arrangements for divestiture commitments in a format which can be used by the parties. At the same time, the model texts leave the flexibility to adapt them to the requirements of the specific case.

(30) See website of DG COMP, released in May 2003, available at:http:&ec.europa.eu/comm/competition/mergers/legislation/legislation.html. The model texts may be continuously up-dated and, if there should be a need, further best practice guidelines in the field of remedies may be issued.

III. DIFFERENT TYPES OF REMEDIES

1. Divestiture of a business to a suitable purchaser

22. Where a proposed concentration threatens to significantly impede effective competition the most effective way to maintain effective competition, apart from prohibition, is to create the conditions for the emergence of a new competitive entity or for the strengthening of existing competitors via divestiture by the merging parties.

1.1. Divestiture of a viable and competitive business

23. The divested activities must consist of a viable business that, if operated by a suitable purchaser, can compete effectively with the merged entity on a lasting basis and that is divested as a going concern (31). For the business to be viable, it may also be necessary to include activities which are related to markets where the Commission did not identify competition concerns if this is required to create an effective competitor in the affected markets (32).

(31) This includes, under certain conditions, businesses that have to be carved out from a party's business or individual assets; see below paragraphs 35 ff.

(32) Case IV/M.913 – *Siemens/Elektrowatt* of 18 November 1997; Case IV/M.1578 – *Sanitec/Sphinx* of 1 December 1999, at paragraph 255; Case COMP/M.1802 – *Unilever/Amora-Maille* of 8 March 2000; Case COMP/M.1990 – *Unilever/Bestfoods* of 28 September 2000.

24. In proposing a viable business for divestiture, it is necessary to take into account the uncertainties and risks related to the transfer of a business to a new owner. These risks may limit the competitive impact of the divested business, and, therefore, may lead to a market situation where the competition concerns at stake will not necessarily be eliminated.

Scope of the business to be divested

25. The business has to include all the assets which contribute to its current operation or which are necessary to ensure its viability and competitiveness and all personnel which is currently employed or which is necessary to ensure the business' viability and competitiveness (33).

(33) Notifying parties will have to undertake in the commitments that the business to be divested includes all those assets and personnel. Where the detailed description of the business, to be provided by the parties as set out in paragraph 27, will at a later point in time appear to be incomplete in that respect and the parties do not complement the business with the necessary additional assets or personnel, the Commission may consider revoking the conditional clearance decision.

26. Personnel and assets which are currently shared between the business to be divested and other businesses of the parties, but which contribute to the operation of the business or which are necessary to ensure its viability and competitiveness, also have to be included. Otherwise, the viability and competitiveness of the business to be divested would be endangered. Therefore, the divested business has to contain the personnel providing essential functions for the business such as, for instance, group R / D and information technology staff even where such personnel is currently employed by another business unit of the parties – at least in a sufficient proportion to meet the on-going needs of the divested business. In the same way shared assets have to be included even if those assets are owned by or allocated to another business unit.

27. In order for the Commission to be able to identify the scope of the business to be divested, the parties have to include a precise definition of the scope of the divested business in the commitments (the «description of the business»). The description of the business has to be adapted to the individual case at hand and should contain all the elements that are part of the business to be divested: tangible (e.g. R / D, production, distribution, sales and marketing activities) and intangible assets (such as intellectual property rights, know-how and goodwill); licences, permits and authorisations by governmental organisations granted to the business; contracts, leases and commitments (e.g. arrangements with suppliers and customers) for the benefit of the business to be divested; and customer, credit and other records. In the description of the business, the parties have to include the personnel to be transferred in general terms, including staff seconded and temporary employees, and to insert a list of the key personnel, i.e. the personnel essential for the viability and competitiveness of the business. The transfer of those employees is without prejudice to the application of the Council directives on collective redundancies (34); on safeguarding employees' rights in the event of transfers of undertakings (35); and on informing and consulting employees (36) as well as national provisions implementing those directives and other national laws. The remedy has to include a non-solicitation commitment by the parties with regard to the key personnel.

(34) Council directive 98/59/EC of 20 July 1998 on the approximation of the laws of the Member States relating to collective redundancies (O.J. L 225, 12.8.1998, p. 16).

(35) Council directive 2001/23/EC of 12 March 2001 on the approximation of the laws of the Member States relating to the safeguarding of employees' rights in the event of transfers of undertakings, businesses or parts of undertakings or businesses (O.J. L 82, 22.3.2001, p. 16).

(36) Council directive 94/45/EC of 22 September 1994 on the establishment of a European Works Council or a procedure in Community-scale undertakings and Community-scale groups of undertakings for the purposes of informing and consulting employees (O.J. L 254, 30.9.1994, p. 64); directive 2002/14/EC of the European Parliament and of the Council of 11 March 2002 establishing a general framework for informing and consulting employees in the European Community (O.J. L 80, 23.3.2002, p. 29).

28. In the description of the business, the parties also have to set out the arrangements for the supply of products and services by them to the divested business or by the divested business to them. Such on-going relationships of the divested business may be necessary to maintain the full economic viability and competitiveness of the divested business for a transitional basis. The Commission will only accept such arrangements if they do not affect the independence of the divested business from the parties.

29. In order to avoid any misunderstanding about the business to be divested, assets or personnel that are used within or employed by the business but that should not, according to the parties, be transferred with the divestiture, have to be expressly excluded by the parties in the commitments text. The Commission will only be able to accept such exclusion of assets or personnel if the parties can clearly show that this does not affect the viability and competitiveness of the business.

30. The business to be divested has to be viable as such. Therefore, the resources of a possible or even presumed future purchaser are not taken into account by the Commission at the stage of assessing the remedy. The situation is different if already during the procedure a sale and purchase agreement with a specific purchaser is concluded whose resources can be taken into account at the time of the assessment of the commitment. This situation will be dealt with in more detail below in paragraphs 56 ff.

31. Once a purchaser is identified after adoption of an authorisation decision, some of the assets or personnel included in the divested business may not be needed by the proposed purchaser. In the purchaser approval process, the Commission may, upon request by the parties, approve the divestiture of the business to the proposed purchaser without one or more assets or parts of the personnel if this does not affect the viability and competitiveness of the business to be divested after the sale, taking account of the resources of the proposed purchaser.

1.2. Stand-alone business and conditions for acceptability of alternatives

32. Normally, a viable business is a business that can operate on a stand-alone-basis, which means independently of the merging parties as regards the supply of input materials or other forms of cooperation other than during a transitory period.

33. The Commission has a clear preference for an existing stand-alone business. This may take the form of a pre-existing company or group of companies, or of a business division which was not previously legally incorporated as such.

34. Where the competition concern results from a horizontal overlap, the parties may be able to choose between two businesses. In cases involving a hostile bid, a commitment to divest activities of the target company may, in such circumstances of limited information available to the notifying parties about the business to be divested, increase the risk that this business might not, after a divestiture, result in a viable competitor which could effectively compete in the market on a lasting basis. It may therefore be more appropriate for the parties to propose to divest activities of the acquiring company in such scenarios.

Carve-outs

35. Even though normally the divestiture of an existing viable stand-alone business is required, the Commission, taking into account the principle of proportionality, may also consider the divestiture of businesses which have existing strong links or are partially integrated with businesses retained by the parties and therefore need to be «carved out» in those respects. In order to reduce the risks for the viability and competitiveness to a minimum in such circumstances, an option for the parties is to submit commitments proposing to carve out those parts of an existing business which do not necessarily have to be divested. In effect, an existing, stand-alone business is being divested in those circumstances although, by way of a «reverse carve-out», the parties may carve-out the limited parts which they may keep.

36. In any case, the Commission will only be able to accept commitments which require the carve-out of a business if it can be certain that, at least at the time when the business is transferred to the purchaser, a viable business on a stand-alone basis will be divested and the risks for the viability and competitiveness caused by the carve-out will thereby be reduced to a minimum. The parties therefore have to ensure, as set out in detail below in paragraph 113, that the carve-out is started in the interim period, i.e. the period between the adoption of the Commission decision up to the completion of the divestiture (meaning the legal and factual transfer of the business to the purchaser). Consequently, at the end of this period, a viable business on a stand-alone basis will be divested. If this should not be possible or if the carve-out should be particularly difficult, parties may provide the requisite degree of certainty for the Commission by proposing an up-front buyer solution, as further detailed below in paragraph 55.

Divestiture of assets, in particular of brands and licences

37. A divestiture consisting of a combination of certain assets which did not form a uniform and viable business in the past creates risks as to the viability and competitiveness of the resulting business. This is in particular the case if assets from more than one party are involved. Such an approach may be accepted by the Commission only if the viability of the business is ensured notwithstanding the fact that the assets did not form a uniform business in the past. This may be the case if the individual assets can already be considered a viable and competitive business (37). Similarly, only in exceptional cases a divestiture package including only brands and supporting production and/or distribution assets may be sufficient to create the conditions for effective competition (38). In such circumstances, the package consisting of brands and assets must be sufficient to allow the Commission to conclude that the resulting business will be immediately viable in the hands of a suitable purchaser.

(37) Case COMP/M.1806 – *AstraZeneca/Novartis* of 26 July 2000; COMP/M.1628 – *TotalFina/Elf* of 9 February 2000; Case IV/M.603 – *Crown Cork & Seal/CarnaudMetalbox* of 14 November 1995.

(38) Case COMP/M.2544 – *Masterfoods/Royal Canin* of 15 February 2002; Case COMP/M.2337 – *Nestlé/Ralston Purina* of 27 July 2001; Case IV/M.623 – *Kimberly-Clark/Scott Paper* of 16 January 1996; Case COMP/M.3779 – *Pernod Ricard/Allied Domecq* of 24 June 2005.

38. Divestitures of a business generally appear preferable to the granting of licenses to IP rights, as the granting of a license involve more uncertainties, will not enable the licensee to compete immediately in the market, requires an ongoing relationship with the parties which may allow the licensor to influence the licensee in its competitive behaviour and may give rise to disputes between the licensor and the licensee over the scope and the terms and conditions of the license. The granting of a license will therefore generally not be considered appropriate where a divestiture of a business seems feasible. Where the competition concerns arise from the market position held for such a technology or such IP rights, a divestiture of the technology or the IP rights is the preferable remedy as it eliminates a lasting relationship between the merged entity and its competitors (39). However, the Commission may accept licensing arrangements as an alternative to divestiture where, for instance, a divestiture would impede efficient, on-going research or where a divestiture would be impossible due to the nature of the business (40). Such licences will have to enable the licensee to compete effectively with the parties in a similar way as if a divestiture had taken place. They will normally be exclusive licences and have to be without any field-of-use and any geographical restrictions on the licensee. Where there might be any uncertainty as regards the scope of the licence or its terms and conditions, the parties will have to divest the underlying IP right, but may obtain a licence back. If there is uncertainty that the license will actually be granted to a suitable licensee, the parties may consider to propose an up-front licensee or a fix-it-first solution according to the considerations set out below in paragraphs 56, in order to enable the Commission to conclude with the requisite degree of certainty that the remedy will be implemented (41).

(39) See Case COMP/M.2972 – *DSM/Roche Vitamins* of 23 July 2003; Case IV/M.1378 – *Hoechst/Rhône-Poulenc* of 9 August 1999; Case COMP/M.1601 – *Allied Signal/Honeywell* of 1 December 1999; Case COMP/M.1671 – *Dow/UCC* of 3 May 2000.

(40) Case COMP/M.2949 – *Finmeccanica/Alenia Telespazio* of 30 October 2002; Case COMP/M.3593 – *Apollo/Bakelite* of 11 April 2005, commitment on carbon bond refractory licence; for cases from the pharmaceutical industry see Case COMP/M.2972 – *DSM/Roche Vitamins* of 23 July 2003; Case IV/M.555 – *Glaxo/Wellcome* of 28 February 1995.

(41) Case COMP/M.2972 – *DSM/Roche Vitamins* of 23 July 2003.

Re-branding

39. In exceptional cases, the Commission has accepted commitments to grant an exclusive, time-limited licence for a brand with the purpose of allowing the licensee to re-brand the product in the period foreseen. After the first licence phase of these so-called re-branding commitments, the parties commit in a second phase to abstain from any use of the brand (blackout phase). The goal of such commitments is to allow the licensee to transfer the customers from the licensed brand to its own brand in order to create a viable competitor, without the licensed brand being permanently divested.

40. A re-branding remedy carries substantially higher risks for restoring effective competition than a divestiture, including the divestiture of a brand as there is considerable uncertainty whether the licensee will succeed in establishing itself as an active competitor in the market on the basis of the re-branded product. A re-branding remedy may be acceptable in circumstances where the brand at stake is widely used and a high proportion of its turnover is generated in markets outside those in which competition concerns have been identified (42). In those circumstances, a re-branding remedy has to be defined in such a way as to ensure that the granting of the licence will effectively maintain competition in the market on a lasting basis and that the licensee will be an effective competitor after re-branding the products.

(42) However, even in these conditions a divestiture of the brand may be more appropriate, especially if the resulting split in the ownership of the brand corresponds to common practice in the industry, see for the pharmaceutical industry Case COMP/M.3544 – *Bayer Healthcare/Roche* (O.T.C.) of 19 November 2004, paragraph 59 concerning the divestiture of the Desenex brand.

41. As the success of re-branding commitments is substantially linked to the viability of the licensed brand a number of preconditions have to be met for the design of such commitments. Firstly, the brand to be transferred must be well-known and one of considerable strength to guarantee both immediate viability of the licensed brand and its economic survival in the re-branding period. Secondly, part of the assets related to the production or the distribution of the products marketed under the licensed brand or the transfer of know-how may be necessary to ensure the viability of the remedy (43). Thirdly, the licence has to be exclusive and normally comprehensive, i.e. not limited to a certain range of products within a specific market, and has to include the intellectual property rights to ensure that customers will acknowledge the familiarity of the re-branded product. The parties will not be allowed to use similar words or signs as this could undermine the effect of the re-branding exercise (44). Fourthly, both the licence and the black-out period have to be sufficiently long, account being taken of the particularities of the case, so that the re-branding remedy is in its effects similar to a divestiture (45).

(43) COMP/M.3149 – *Procter&Gamble/Wella* paragraph 60; IV/M.623 – *Kimberly-Clark/Scott Paper* of 16 January 1996, paragraph 236(*i*). This is particularly important during the licence phase in which the licensee has to prepare for the launch of a new competitive brand. Such a launch of a new brand appears to not be feasible if the purchaser had to spend considerable resources on the production process, marketing and distribution of the licensed brand; COMP/M.2337 – *Nestlé/Ralston Purina* of 27 July 2001, paragraphs 67 et seq.; COMP/M.2621 – *SEB/Moulinex* of 8 January 2002, paragraph 140.

(44) COMP/M.3149 – *Procter&Gamble/Wella* of 30 July 2003, paragraph 61; COMP/M.2337 – *Nestlé/Ralstone Purina* of 27 July 2001, paragraph 68; COMP/M.2621 – *SEB/Moulinex* of 8 January 2002, paragraph 141; IV/M.623 – *Kimberly-Clark/Scott Paper* of 16 January 1996, paragraph 236(*ii*).

(45) For example taking into account the life cycle of products, c.f. COMP/M.2621 – *SEB/Moulinex* of 8 January 2002, paragraph 141, where effectively the duration of the commitments covered a period equal to about three product life cycles; confirmed by judgment of CFI in Case T-119/02 *Royal Philips Electronics NV v Commission* (2003) ECR II-1433, paragraphs 112 et seq.

42. The identity of the potential licensee will be a key factor for the success of the commitment. If there is uncertainty that a number of suitable licensees are available, being able and having strong incentives to carry out the re-branding exercise, the parties may consider proposing an up-front or fix-it-first solution, in line with the considerations set out in paragraph 53 below.

1.3. Non-reacquisition clause

43. In order to maintain the structural effect of a remedy, the commitments have to foresee that the merged entity cannot subsequently acquire influence (46) over the whole or parts of the divested business. The commitments will normally have to foresee that no re-acquisition of material influence is possible for a significant period, generally of 10 years. However, the commitments can also provide for a waiver allowing the Commission to relieve the parties from this obligation if it subsequently finds that the structure of the market has changed to such an extent that the absence of influence over the divested business is no longer necessary to render the concentration compatible with the common market. Even in the absence of an explicit clause, a re-acquisition of the business would violate an implicit obligation on the parties under the commitments as this would affect the effectiveness of the remedies.

(46) An influence by the previous owner of the business in the competitive behaviour of the divested business risking to frustrate the objective of the remedy.

1.4. Alternative divestiture commitments: Crown Jewels

44. In certain cases, the implementation of the parties' preferred divestiture option (of a viable business solving the competition concerns) might be uncertain in view, for example, of third parties' pre-emption rights or uncertainty as to the transferability of key contracts, intellectual property rights, or the uncertainty of finding a suitable purchaser. Nevertheless, the parties may consider that they would be able to divest this business to a suitable purchaser within a very short time period.

45. In such circumstances, the Commission cannot take the risk that, in the end, effective competition will not be maintained. accordingly, the Commission will only accept such divestiture commitments under the following conditions: *(a)* absent the uncertainty, the first divestiture proposed in the commitments would consist of a viable business, and *(b)* the parties will have to propose a second alternative divestiture which the parties will be obliged to implement if they are not able to implement the first commitment within the given time frame for the first divestiture (47). Such an alternative commitment normally has to be a «crown jewel» (48), i.e. it should be as least as good as the first proposed divestiture in terms of creating a viable competitor once implemented, it should not involve any uncertainties as to its implementation and it should be capable of being implemented quickly in order to avoid that the overall implementation period exceeds what would normally be regarded as acceptable in the conditions of the market in question. In order to limit the risks in the interim period, it is indispensable that interim preservation and holding separate measures apply to all assets included in both divestiture alternatives. Furthermore, the commitment has to establish clear criteria and a strict timetable as to how and when the alternative divestiture obligation will become effective and the Commission will require shorter periods for its implementation.

(47) See judgment of the CFI in Case T-210/01 *General Electric v Commission* (2005) ECR II-5575, paragraph 617; COMP/M.1453 – *AXA/GRE* of 8 April 1999.

(48) The alternative may consist of an entirely different business or, in case of uncertainty as to finding a suitable buyer, of additional businesses and assets that are added to the initial package.

46. If there is uncertainty as to the implementation of the divestiture due to third party rights or as to finding a suitable purchaser crown jewel commitments and up-front buyers as discussed below in paragraphs 54 address the same concerns, and the parties may therefore choose between both structures.

1.5. Transfer to a suitable purchaser

47. The intended effect of the divestiture will only be achieved if and once the business is transferred to a suitable purchaser in whose hands it will become an active competitive force in the market. The potential of a business to attract a suitable purchaser is an important element already of the Commission's assessment of the appropriateness of the proposed commitment (49). In order to ensure that the business is divested to a suitable purchaser, the commitments have to include criteria to define its suitability which will allow the Commission to conclude that the divestiture of the business to such a purchaser will likely remove the competition concerns identified.

(49) Case IV/M.913 – *Siemens/Elektrowatt* of 18 November 1997.

(a) Suitability of a purchaser

48. The standard purchaser requirements are the following:
– the purchaser is required to be independent of and unconnected to the parties,
– the purchaser must possess the financial resources, proven relevant expertise and have the incentive and ability to maintain and develop the divested business as a viable and active competitive force in competition with the parties and other competitors, and
– the acquisition of the business by a proposed purchaser must neither be likely to create new competition problems nor give rise to a risk that the implementation of the commitments will be delayed. Therefore, the proposed purchaser must reasonably be expected to obtain all necessary approvals from the relevant regulatory authorities for the acquisition of the business to be divested.

49. The standard purchaser requirements may have to be supplemented on a case-by-case basis. An example is the requirement, where appropriate, that the purchaser should be an industrial, rather than a financial purchaser (50). The commitments will normally contain such a clause where, due to the specific circumstances of the case, a financial buyer might not be able or might not have the incentives to develop the business as a viable and competitive force in the market even considering that it could obtain the necessary management expertise (*e.g.* by recruiting managers experienced in the sector at stake) and therefore the acquisition by a financial buyer would not remove the competition concerns with sufficient certainty.

(50) See commitments in Case COMP/M.2621 – *SEB/Moulinex* of 8 January 2002, which foresee that the licensee needs to have its own trademark used in the sector concerned. Certain markets may require a sufficient degree of recognition by customers for a purchaser to be able to translate the business to be divested into a competitive force on the market.

(b) Identification of a suitable purchaser

50. In general, there are three ways to ensure that the business is transferred to a suitable purchaser. First, the business is transferred within a fixed time-limit after adoption of the decision to a purchaser which is approved by the Commission on the basis of the purchaser requirements. Second, in addition to the conditions set out for the first category, the commitments foresee that the parties may not complete the notified operation before having entered into a binding agreement with a purchaser for the business, approved by the Commission (so-called «up-front-buyer»). Third, the parties identify a purchaser for the business and enter into a binding agreement already during the Commission's procedure (51) (so-called «fix-it-first» (52) remedy). The main difference between the two latter options is that in the case of an up-front buyer, the identity of the purchaser is not known to the Commission prior to the authorisation decision.

(51) The transfer of the business may be implemented after the Commission decision.

(52) This terminology might be used differently in other jurisdictions.

51. The choice of the category depends on the risks involved in the case and therefore on the measures which enable the Commission to conclude with the requisite degree of certainty that the commitment will be implemented. This will depend on the nature and the scope of the business to be divested, the risks of degradation of the business in the interim period up to divestiture and any uncertainties inherent in the transfer and implementation, in particular the risks of finding a suitable purchaser.

1) Sale of the divested business within a fixed time-limit after the decision

52. In the first category, the parties may proceed with the sale of the divested business on the basis of the purchaser requirements within a fixed time-limit after the adoption of the decision. This procedure is likely to be appropriate in the majority of cases, provided that a number of purchasers can be envisaged for a viable business and that no specific issues complicate or stand in the way of the divestiture. Where the purchaser needs to have special qualifications, this procedure may be appropriate if there are sufficient interested potential purchasers available which fulfil the specific purchaser requirements to be included in the commitments in such cases. In these circumstances the Commission may be able to conclude that the divestiture will be implemented and that there are no reasons for the implementation of the notified concentration to be suspended after the Commission decision.

2) Up-front buyer

53. There are cases where only the proposal of an up-front buyer will allow the Commission to conclude with the requisite degree of certainty that the business will be effectively divested to a suitable purchaser. The parties therefore have to undertake in the commitments that they are not going to complete the notified operation before having entered into a binding agreement with a purchaser for the divested business, approved by the Commission (53).

(53) Case COMP/M.3796 – *Omya/Huber PCC* of 19 July 2006; Case COMP/M.2972 – *DSM/Roche Vitamins* of 23 July 2003; Case COMP/M.2060 – *Bosch/Rexroth* of 13 December 2000; Case COMP/M.2337 – *Nestlé/Ralston Purina* of 27 July 2001; Case COMP/M.2544 – *Masterfoods/Royal Canin* of 15 February 2002; Case COMP/M.2947 – *Verbund/Energie Allianz* of 11 June 2003.

54. First, this concerns cases where there are considerable obstacles for a divestiture, such as third party rights, or uncertainties as to finding a suitable purchaser (54). In such cases, an up-front buyer will allow the Commission to conclude with the requisite degree of certainty that the commitments will be implemented, as such a commitment creates greater incentives for the parties to close the divestiture in order to be able to complete their own concentration. In these circumstances, parties may choose between proposing an up-front buyer and an alternative divestiture commitment, as set out above in paragraph 46.

(54) See Case COMP/M.2060 – *Bosch/Rexroth* of 13 December 2000, paragraph 92.

55. Second, an up-front buyer may be necessary in cases which cause considerable risks of preserving the competitiveness and saleability of the divestment business in the interim period until divestiture. This category comprises cases where the risks of a degradation of the divestment business appear to be high, in particular due to a risk of losing employees being key for the business, or where the interim risks are increased as the parties are not able to undertake the carve-out process in the interim period, but the carve-out process can only take place once a sales and purchase agreement with a purchaser is entered into. The up-front buyer provision may accelerate the transfer of the business to be divested – given the increased incentives for the parties to close the divestiture in order to be able to complete their own concentration – to such an extent that the commitments may allow the Commission to conclude with the requisite degree of certainty that those risks are limited and the divestiture will be effectively implemented (55).

(55) See Case COMP/M.2060 – *Bosch/Rexroth* of 13 December 2000, paragraph 95.

3) Fix-it-first remedies

56. The third category involves cases where the parties identify and enter into a legally binding agreement with a buyer outlining the essentials of the purchase during the Commission procedure (56). The Commission will be able to decide in the final decision whether the transfer of the divested business to the identified purchaser will remove the competition concerns. If the Commission authorises the notified concentration, no additional Commission decision for the purchaser approval will be needed and the closing of the sale of the divested business may take place shortly afterwards.

(56) Such agreements are normally conditional to the final Commission decision accepting the remedy in question.

57. The Commission welcomes fix-it-first remedies in particular in cases where the identity of the purchaser is crucial for the effectiveness of the proposed remedy. This concerns cases where, given the circumstances, only very few potential purchasers can be considered suitable, in particular as the divested business is not a viable business in itself, but its viability will only be ensured by specific assets of the purchaser, or where the purchaser needs to have specific characteristics in order for the remedy to solve the competition concerns (57). If the parties choose to enter into a binding agreement with a suitable purchaser during the procedure by way of a fix-it-first solution, the Commission can in those circumstances conclude with the requisite degree of certainty that the commitments will be implemented with a sale to a suitable purchaser. In these situations, an «upfront buyer» solution containing specific requirements as to the suitability of a buyer will generally be considered equivalent and acceptable.

(57) See Case COMP/M.3916 – *T-Mobile Austria/tele.ring* of April 2006, the divestiture of certain mobile telephony sites and frequencies, not constituting a viable business, could only take place to a competitor which was likely to play a similar role in the market as tele.ring; Case COMP/M.4000 – *Inco/Falconbridge* of 4 July 2006, the divestiture of a nickel processing business could only take place to a competitor vertically integrated into the supply of nickel; Case COMP/M.4187 – *Metso/Aker Kvaerner* of 12 December 2006, only one purchaser was suitable for acquiring the businesses to be divested as it was the only one with the necessary know-how and the necessary presence in neighbouring markets; Case COMP/M.3436 – *Continental/Phoenix* of 26 October 2004, only the partner in the distribution joint venture was able to render the divested business viable; Case COMP/M.3136 – *GE/Agfa* of 5 December 2003.

2. Removal of links with competitors

58. Divestiture commitments may also be used for removing links between the parties and competitors in cases where these links contribute to the competition concerns raised by the merger. The divestiture of a minority shareholding in a joint venture may be necessary in order to sever a structural link with a major competitor (58), or, similarly, the divestiture of a minority shareholding in a competitor (59).

(58) Case IV/M.942 – *VEBA/Degussa* of 3 December 1997.

(59) Case COMP/M.3653 – *Siemens/VA Tech* of 13 July 2005, paragraphs 491, 493 ff.

59. Although the divestiture of such stakes is the preferable solution, the Commission may exceptionally accept the waiving of rights linked to minority stakes in a competitor where it can be excluded, given the specific circumstances of the case, that the financial gains derived from a minority shareholding in a competitor would in themselves raise competition concerns (60). In such circumstances, the parties have to waive all the rights linked to such a shareholding which were relevant for behaviour in terms of competition, such as representations on the board, veto rights and also information rights (61). The Commission may only be able to accept such a severing of the link with a competitor if those rights are waived comprehensively and in a permanent way (62).

(60) See Case COMP/M.3653 – *Siemens/VA Tech* of 13 July 2005, paragraphs 327 ff., where effects from the minority stake in financial respect could be excluded as a put option for the sale of this stake had already been exercised.

(61) Case COMP/M.4153 – *Toshiba/Westinghouse* of 19 September 2006.

(62) See Case COMP/M.3440 – *ENI/EDP/GDP* of 9 December 2004, paragraphs 648 f., 672.

60. Where competition concerns result from agreements with companies supplying the same products or providing the same services, a suitable remedy may be the termination of the respective agreement, such as distribution agreements with competitors (63) or agreements resulting in the coordination of certain commercial behaviour (64). However, the termination of a distribution agreement alone will only remove the competition concerns if it is ensured that the product of a competitor will also be distributed in the future and exercise effective competitive pressure on the parties.

(63) See for the termination of distribution agreements Case COMP/M.3779 – *Pernod Ricard/Allied Domecq* of 24 June 2005; Case COMP/M.3658 – *Orkla/Chips* of 3 March 2005.

(64) See particularly the sea transport sector, Case COMP/M.3829 – *Maersk/PONL* of 29 July 2005 and Case COMP/M.3863 – *TUI/CP Ships* of 12 October 2005. In those cases, the parties committed to withdraw from certain liner conferences and consortia.

3. Other remedies

61. Whilst being the preferred remedy, divestitures or the removal of links with competitors are not the only remedy possible to eliminate certain competition concerns. However, divestitures are the benchmark for other remedies in terms of effectiveness and efficiency. The Commission therefore may accept other types of commitments, but only in circumstances where the other remedy proposed is at least equivalent in its effects to a divestiture (65).

(65) Case COMP/M.3680 – *Alcatel/Finmeccanica/Alcatel Alenia Space & Telespazio* of 28 April 2005, where a divestiture was impossible.

Access remedies

62. In a number of cases, the Commission has accepted remedies foreseeing the granting of access to key infrastructure, networks, key technology, including patents, know-how or other intellectual property rights, and essential inputs. Normally, the parties grant such access to third parties on a non-discriminatory and transparent basis.

63. Commitments granting access to infrastructure and networks may be submitted in order to facilitate market entry by competitors. They may be acceptable to the Commission in circumstances where it is sufficiently clear that there will be actual entry of new competitors that would eliminate any significant impediment to effective competition (66). Other examples of access commitments are commitments granting access to pay-TV platforms (67) and to energy via gas release programs (68). Often, a sufficient reduction of entry barriers is not achieved by individual measures, but by a package comprising a combination of divestiture remedies and access commitments or a commitments package aimed at overall facilitating entry of competitors by a whole range of different measures. If those commitments actually make the entry of sufficient new competitors timely and likely, they can be considered to have a similar effect on competition in the market as a divestiture. If it cannot be concluded that the lowering of the entry barriers by the proposed commitments will likely lead to the entry of new competitors in the market, the Commission will reject such a remedies package (69).

(66) See judgment of the CFI in Case T-177/04 *easyJet v Commission* (2006) ECR II-1931, at paragraphs 197 et seq.

(67) See Case COMP/M.2876 – *Newscorp/Telepiù* of 2 April 2003, paragraphs 225 et seq., where the commitments package included access of competitors to all essential elements of a pay-TV network, such as 1. access to the necessary content; 2. access to the technical platform as well as 3. access to the necessary technical services. Similarly, in Case COMP/JV.37 – *BskyB/Kirch Pay TV* of 21 March 2000, confirmed by judgment of CFI in Case T-158/00 *ARD v Commission* (2003) ECR II-3825, the Commission accepted a commitments package which allowed other operators comprehensive access to the pay-TV market.

(68) See Case COMP/M.3696 – *E.ON/MOL* of 21 December 2005; Case COMP/M.3868 – *DONG/Elsam/Energi E2* of 14 March 2006.

(69) In air transport mergers, a mere reduction of barriers to entry by a commitment of the parties to offer slots on specific airports may not always be sufficient to ensure the entry of new competitors on those routes where competition problems arise and to render the remedy equivalent in its effects to a divestiture.

64. Commitments granting non-discriminatory access to infrastructure or networks of the merging parties may also be submitted in order to ensure that competition is not significantly impeded as a result of foreclosure. In past Commission decisions, commitments have foreseen the granting of access to pipelines (70) and to telecom or similar networks (71). The Commission will only accept such commitments if it can be concluded that these commitments will be effective and competitors will likely use them so that foreclosure concerns will be eliminated. In specific cases, it may be appropriate to link such a commitment with an up-front or fix-it-first provision in order to allow the Commission to conclude with the requisite degree of certainty that the commitment will be implemented (72).

(70) Case COMP/M.2533 – *BP/E.ON* of 20 December 2001, access to pipelines in addition to divestiture of shares in a pipeline company; Case COMP/M.2389 – *Shell/DEA* of 20 December 2001, access to an ethylene import terminal.

(71) For access to telecom networks, see Case COMP/M.2803 – *Telia/Sonera* of 10 July 2002; Case IV/M.1439 – *Telia/Telenor* of 13 October 1999; Case COMP/M.1795 – *Vodafone/Mannesmann* of 12 April 2000. See also Case COMP/M.2903 – *DaimlerChrysler/Deutsche Telekom/JV* of 30 April 2003, where the Commission accepted a commitments package to grant third parties access to a telematics network and to reduce the entry barriers by allowing them to use parts of a telematics device, designed for toll collection, provided by the parties.

(72) See the «qualitative moratorium» in Case COMP/M.2903 – *DaimlerChrysler/Deutsche Telekom/JV* of 30 April 2003, paragraph 76.

65. Similarly, the control of key technology or IP rights may lead to concerns of foreclosure of competitors which depend on the technology or IP rights as essential input for the activities in a downstream market. This, for example, concerns cases where competition problems arise as the parties may withhold information necessary for the interoperability of different equipment. In such circumstances, commitments to grant competitors access to the necessary information may eliminate the competition concerns (73). Similarly, in sectors where players commonly have to cooperate by licensing patents to each other, concerns that the merged entity would no longer have the incentive to provide licences to the same extent and under the same conditions as before may be eliminated by commitments to grant licenses on the same basis also in the future (74). In those cases, commitments should foresee non-exclusive licences or the disclosure of information on a non-exclusive basis to all third parties which depend on the IP rights or information for their activities. It has to be further ensured that the terms and conditions under which the licenses are granted do not impede the effective implementation of such a license remedy. If no clearly determined terms and conditions for the granting of licenses exist in the market at stake, the terms and conditions, including the pricing, should be clearly apparent from the commitments (*e.g.* by way of pricing formulas). An alternative solution may be to rely on royalty-free licences. Furthermore, depending on the case, the granting of licenses may also transmit sensitive information to the licensor on the competitive behaviour of the licensees which are active as competitors in the downstream market, *e.g.* by transmitting the number of licenses used in the downstream market. In such cases, in order for the remedy to be suitable, the commitments will have to exclude such confidentiality problems. Generally, as set out in the preceding paragraph, the Commission will only accept such commitments if it can be concluded that they will be effective and competitors will likely use them.

(73) Case COMP/M.3083 – *GE/Instrumentarium* of 2 September 2003; Case COMP/M.2861 – *Siemens/Draegerwerk* of 30 April 2003.

(74) See Case COMP/M.3998 – *Axalto/Gemplus* of 19 May 2006.

66. Access commitments are often complex in nature and necessarily include general terms for determining the terms and conditions under which access is granted. In order to render them effective, those commitments have to contain the procedural requirements necessary for monitoring them, such as the requirement of separate accounts for the infrastructure in order to allow a review of the costs involved (75), and suitable monitoring devices. Normally, such monitoring has to be done by the market participants themselves, *e.g.* by those undertakings wishing to benefit from the commitments. Measures allowing third parties themselves to enforce the commitments are in particular access to a fast dispute resolution mechanism via arbitration proceedings (together with trustees) (76) or via arbitration proceedings involving national regulatory authorities if existing for the markets concerned (77). If the Commission can conclude that the mechanisms foreseen in the commitments will allow the market participants themselves to effectively enforce them in a timely manner, no permanent monitoring of the commitments by the Commission is required. In those cases, an intervention by the Commission would only be necessary in cases where the parties do not comply with the solutions found by those dispute resolution mechanisms (78). However, the Commission will only be able to accept such commitments where the complexity does not lead to a risk of their effectiveness from the outset and where the monitoring devices proposed ensure that those commitments will be effectively implemented and the enforcement mechanism will lead to timely results (79).

(75) See e.g. Case COMP/M.2803 – *Telia/Sonera* of 10 July 2002; Case COMP/M.2903 – *DaimlerChrysler/Deutsche Telekom/JV* of 30 April 2003.

(76) As to the effects of arbitration clauses, see judgment of CFI in Case T-158/00 *ARD v Commission* (2003) ECR II-3825, paragraphs 212, 295, 352; CFI judgment in Case T-177/04 *easyJet v Commission* (2006) ECR II-1931, paragraph 186.

(77) See Case COMP/M.2876 – *Newscorp/Telepiù*; Case COMP/M.3916 – *T-Mobile Austria/tele.ring*.

(78) CFI, judgment in Case T-158/00 *ARD v Commission* (2003) ECR II-3825, paragraphs 212, 295, 352.

(79) See judgments of the CFI in Case T-87/05 *EDP v Commission* (2005) ECR II-3745, at paragraphs 102 et seq.; and Case T-177/04 *easyJet v Commission* (2006) ECR II-1931, at paragraph 188.

Change of long-term exclusive contracts

67. The change in the market structure resulting from a proposed concentration can cause existing contractual arrangements to be inimical to effective competition. This is in particular true for exclusive long-term supply agreements if such agreements foreclose either, up-stream, the input for competitors or, down-stream, their access to customers. Where the merged entity will have the ability and the incentives to foreclose competitors in this way, the foreclosure effects resulting from existing exclusive agreements may contribute to significantly impeding effective competition (80).

(80) See Commission Notice on non-horizontal mergers (...); Case IV/M.986 – *AGFA Gevaert/DuPont* of 11 February 1998.

68. In such circumstances, the termination or change of existing exclusive agreements may be considered appropriate to eliminate the competition concerns (81). However, the available evidence must allow the Commission to clearly determine that no de facto exclusivity will be maintained. Furthermore, such change of long-term agreements will normally only be sufficient as part of a remedies package to remove the competition concerns identified.

(81) Case COMP/M.2876 – *Newscorp/Telepiù* of 2 April 2003, paragraphs 225 et seq., granting unilateral termination rights to suppliers of TV content, limiting the scope of the exclusivity clauses and limiting the duration of future exclusive agreements relating to supply of content; Case COMP/M.2822 – *ENI/EnBW/GVS* of 17 December 2002, granting of early termination rights to all local gas distributors concerning long-term gas supply agreements; Case IV/M.1571 – *New Holland* of 28 October 1999; Case IV/M.1467 – *Rohm and Haas/Morton* of 19 April 1999.

Other non-divestiture remedies

69. As indicated above in paragraph 17, non-structural types of remedies, such as promises by the parties to abstain from certain commercial behaviour (e.g. bundling products), will generally not eliminate the competition concerns resulting from horizontal overlaps. In any case, it may be difficult to achieve the required degree of effectiveness of such a remedy due to the absence of effective monitoring of its implementation, as already set out above in paragraph 13(f) (82). Indeed, it may be impossible for the Commission to verify whether or not the commitment is complied with and even other market participants, such as competitors, may not be able to establish at all or with the requisite degree of certainty whether the parties meet the conditions of the commitment in practice. In addition, competitors may also not have an incentive to alert the Commission as they do not directly benefit from the commitments. Therefore, the Commission may examine other types of non-divestiture remedies, such as behavioural promises, only exceptionally in specific circumstances, such as in respect of competition concerns arising in conglomerate structures (83).

(82) See, as an example for such remedies, Case COMP/M.3440 – *ENI/EDP/GDP* of 9 December 2004, paragraphs 663, 719.

(83) See, in relation to conglomerate effects of a concentration, ECJ, judgment of 15 February 2005 in Case C-12/03 P *Commission v Tetra Laval* (2005) ECR I-987, paragraphs 85, 89.

Time limit for non-divestiture remedies

70. The Commission may accept that non-divestiture remedies are limited in their duration. The acceptability of a time limit and the duration will depend on the individual circumstances of the case and cannot be pre-defined in a general manner in the present Notice.

4. Review Clause

71. Irrespective of the type of remedy, commitments will usually include a review clause (84). This may allow the Commission, upon request by the parties showing good cause, to grant an extension of deadlines or, in exceptional circumstances, to waive, modify or substitute the commitments.

(84) However, the review clause is of particular relevance for access remedies, which systematically should include such a clause; see below paragraph 74.

72. Modifying commitments by extending the deadlines is in particular relevant for divestiture commitments. parties have to submit a request for an extension within the deadline. Where parties apply for an extension for the first divestiture period, the Commission will only accept that they have shown good cause if the parties were not able to meet the deadline for reasons outside their responsibility and if it can be expected that the parties subsequently will succeed in divesting the business within a short time-frame. Otherwise, the divestiture trustee may be better placed to undertake the divestiture and to fulfil the commitments for the parties.

73. The Commission may grant waivers or accept modifications or substitutions of the commitments only in exceptional circumstances. This will very rarely be relevant for divestiture commitments. As divestiture commitments have to be implemented within a short time-frame after the decision, it is very unlikely that changes of market circumstances will have occurred in such a short time-frame and the Commission will normally not accept any modifications under the general review clause. For specific situations the commitments normally foresee more targeted review clauses (85).

(85) As mentioned in paragraph 30, the Commission may approve a purchaser without some of the assets or personnel foreseen if this does not affect the competitiveness and viability of the divested business. Similarly, the non-requisition clause, as explained in paragraph 43, prohibits the reacquisition of control over the assets divested only if the Commission has not previously found that that the market structure has changed to such an extent that the divestiture is no longer necessary.

74. A waiver, modification or substitution of commitments may be more relevant for non-divestiture commitments, such as access commitments, which may be on-going for a number of years and for which not all contingencies can be predicted at the time of the adoption of the Commission decision. Exceptional circumstances justifying a waiver, modification or substitution may, first, be accepted for such commitments if parties show that market circumstances have changed significantly and on a permanent basis. For showing this, a sufficient long time-span, normally at least several years, between the Commission decision and a request by the parties is required. Second, exceptional circumstances may also be present if the parties can show that the experience gained in the application of the remedy demonstrates that the objective pursued with the remedy will be better achieved if modalities of the commitment are changed. For any waiver, modification or substitution of commitments, the Commission will also take into account the view of third parties and the impact a modification may have on the position of third parties and thereby on the overall effectiveness of the remedy. In this regard, the Commission will also consider whether modifications affect the right already acquired by third parties after implementation of the remedy (86).

(86) See examples in judgment of CFI in Case T-119/02 *Royal Philips Electronics NV v Commission* (2003) ECR II-1433, paragraph 184.

75. If at the time of the adoption of the decision the Commission for particular reasons cannot anticipate all contingencies in relation to the implementation of such commitments, it may also be appropriate for the parties to include a clause in the commitments, allowing the Commission to trigger a limited modification to the commitments. Such modifications may be necessary if the original commitments do not achieve the envisaged results set out in those commitments, and therefore do not effectively remove the competition concerns. Procedurally, the parties may be obliged in such cases to propose a change to the commitments in order to achieve the result defined in those commitments, or the Commission may itself, after hearing the parties, modify the conditions and obligations to this end. This type of clause will typically be limited to cases where specific modalities risk to jeopardise effective implementation of the commitments. Such clauses have been used, for example, in relation to the modalities of gas release programs (87).

(87) See Case COMP/M.3868 – *DONG/Elsam/Energi E2* of 14 March 2006, paragraph 24 of the Annex.

76. The Commission may, upon request, adopt a formal decision for any waiver, modification or substitution of commitments or simply take note of satisfactory amendments of the remedy by the parties, where such amendments improve the effectiveness of the remedy and result in legally binding obligations of the parties, e.g. by contractual arrangements. A change of the commitments will normally only be effective ex nunc. Consequently, a modification of the commitments will not heal retroactively any breach of the commitments which has been committed before the time of the modification. The Commission may therefore, where appropriate, further pursue a breach under Articles 14, 15 of the Merger Regulation.

IV. ASPECTS OF PROCEDURE FOR SUBMISSION OF COMMITMENTS

1. Phase I

77. Pursuant to Article 6(2) of the Merger Regulation the Commission may declare a concentration compatible with the common market also before the initiation of proceedings, where it is confident that following modification a notified concentration no longer raises serious doubts within the meaning of paragraph 1(c).

78. Parties can submit proposals for commitments to the Commission on an informal basis, even before notification. parties have to submit commitments within not more than 20 working days from the date of the receipt of the notification (88). The Commission informs the parties about its serious doubts in due time before that deadline (89). Where the parties submit commitments, the deadline for the Commission's decision pursuant to Article 6(1) of the Merger Regulation is extended from 25 to 35 working days (90).

(88) Article 19(1) of the Implementing Regulation.

(89) The notifying parties will normally be offered the opportunity of attending a state of play meeting in such circumstances, see point 33 of the DG COMPETITION Best Practices on the conduct of EC merger control proceedings.

(90) Article 10(1), subparagraph 2 of the Merger Regulation.

79. In order to form the basis of a decision pursuant to Article 6(2), proposals for commitments must meet the following requirements:

(a) they shall fully specify the substantive and implementing commitments entered into by the parties;

(b) they shall be signed by a person duly authorised to do so;

(c) they shall be accompanied by the information on the commitments offered as provided for in the Implementing Regulation (as explained above in paragraph 7); and

(d) they shall be accompanied by a non-confidential version of the commitments (91) for the purposes of market testing them with third parties. The non-confidential version of the commitments must allow third parties to fully assess the workability and the effectiveness of the proposed remedies to remove the competition concerns.

(91) Article 20(2) of the Implementing Regulation.

80. Proposals submitted by the parties in accordance with these requirements will be assessed by the Commission. The Commission will consult the authorities of the Member States on the proposed commitments and, when considered appropriate, also third parties in the form of a market test, including in particular those third parties and the recognised representatives (92) of those employees whose positions are directly affected by the proposed remedies. In markets with national regulatory authorities the Commission may also, if appropriate, consult the competent national regulatory authorities (93). In addition, in cases involving a geographic market that is wider than the European Economic Area («E.E.A.») or where, for reasons related to the viability of the business, the scope of the business to be divested is wider than the E.E.A. territory, the non-confidential version of the proposed remedies may also be discussed with non-EEA competition authorities in the framework of the Community's bilateral cooperation agreements with these countries.

(92) Cf. Article 2(1)(c) of Council directive 2001/23/EC of 12 March 2001 on the approximation of the laws of the Member States relating to the safeguard-

ing of employees' rights in the event of transfers of undertakings, businesses or parts of undertakings or businesses (*O.J.* L 82, 22.3.2001, p. 16). See also Article 2(1)(g) of Council directive 94/45/EC of 22 September 1994 on the establishment of a European Works Council or a procedure in Community-scale undertakings and Community-scale groups of undertakings for the purposes of informing and consulting employees (*O.J.* L 254, 30.9.1994, p. 64).

(93) For the role of national regulatory authorities in a dispute resolution mechanism, see paragraph 66.

81. Commitments in phase I can only be accepted where the competition problem is readily identifiable and can easily be remedied (94). The competition problem therefore needs to be so straightforward and the remedies so clear-cut that it is not necessary to enter into an in-depth investigation and that the commitments are sufficient to clearly rule out «serious doubts» within the meaning of Article 6(1)(c) of the Merger Regulation (95). Where the assessment confirms that the proposed commitments remove the grounds for serious doubts on this basis, the Commission clears the merger in phase I.

(94) See recital 30 of the Merger Regulation.

(95) See judgment of CFI in Case T-119/02 *Royal Philips Electronics NV v Commission* (2003) ECR II-1433, paragraphs 79 et seq.

82. Due to the time-constraints in phase I, it is particularly important for the parties to submit in a timely manner to the Commission the information required in the Implementing Regulation to properly assess the content and workability of the commitments and their suitability to maintain conditions of effective competition in the common market on a permanent basis. If the parties do not comply with the obligation in the Implementing Regulation, the Commission may not be able to conclude that the proposed commitments will remove the grounds for serious doubts.

83. Where the assessment shows that the commitments offered are not sufficient to remove the competition concerns raised by the concentration, the parties will be informed accordingly. Given that phase I remedies are designed to provide a clear-cut answer to a readily identifiable competition concern, only limited modifications can be accepted to the proposed commitments. Such modifications, presented as an immediate response to the result of the consultations, may include clarifications, refinements and/or other improvements designed to ensure that the commitments are workable and effective. However, such modifications may only be accepted in circumstances where it is ensured that the Commission can carry out a proper assessment of those commitments (96).

(96) See recital 17 of the Implementing Regulation and judgment of the CFI, Case T-119/02 *Royal Philips Electronics NV v Commission* (2003) ECR II-1433, paragraphs 237 et seq.

84. If the Commission's final assessment of a case shows that there are no competition concerns in one or more markets, the parties will be informed accordingly and may withdraw the unnecessary commitments for such markets. If the parties do not withdraw them, the Commission will normally ignore them in the decision. In any event, such commitment proposals do not constitute a condition for clearance.

85. Where the parties are informed that the Commission intends to maintain in its final decision that the transaction raises competition concerns for a specific market, it is for the parties to propose commitments. The Commission is not in a position to impose unilaterally any conditions to an authorisation decision, but only on the basis of the parties' commitments (97). However, the Commission will review whether the commitments submitted by the parties are proportionate to the competition problem when assessing whether to attach them as conditions or obligations to its final decision (98). Nevertheless, it has to be stressed that, in a commitments proposal, all those elements which are required to fulfil the basic conditions for acceptable commitments as set out above in paragraphs 9 et seq. will be considered necessary. This paragraph as well as the previous one also applies to commitments in phase II.

(97) See above paragraph 6.

(98) See judgment of ECJ of 18 December 2007 in Case C-202/06 P *Cementbouw v Commission* (2007), paragraph 54.

86. If the Commission concludes that the commitments offered by the parties do not remove the serious doubts, it will issue an Article 6(1)(c) decision and open proceedings.

2. Phase II

87. Pursuant to Article 8(2) of the Merger Regulation, the Commission must declare a concentration compatible with the common market, where following modification a notified concentration does no longer significantly impede effective competition within the meaning of Article 2(3) of the Merger Regulation.

88. Commitments proposed to the Commission pursuant to Article 8(2) must be submitted to the Commission within not more than 65 working days from the day on which proceedings were initiated. Where the deadlines for the final decision have been extended according to Article 10(3) of the Merger Regulation, also the deadline for remedies is automatically extended by the same number of days (99). Only in exceptional circumstances, the Commission may accept that commitments are submitted for the first time after the expiry of this period. The request by the parties for an extension of the deadline must be received within the period and has to set forth the exceptional circumstances which, according to the parties, justify it. In addition to the existence of exceptional circumstances, an extension is only possible where there is sufficient time to make a proper assessment of the proposal by the Commission and to allow adequate consultation with Member States and third parties (100).

(99) Article 19(2), subparagraph 2 of the Implementing Regulation.

(100) Article 19(2), subparagraph 3 of the Implementing Regulation. See Case COMP/M.1439 – *Telia/Telenor* of 13 October 1999; Case IV/M.754 – *Anglo American Corporation/Lonrho* of 23 April 1997.

89. The question whether or not submitting remedies will extend the deadline for the Commission to take a final decision depends on the time in the procedure when the commitments are submitted. Where the parties submit commitments within less than 55 working days after the initiation of proceedings, the Commission has to take a final decision within not more than 90 working days of the date of initiation of proceedings (101). Where the parties submit commitments on working day 55 or afterwards (even after working day 65, if those commitments should be acceptable due to exceptional circumstances as described above in paragraph 88), the period for the Commission to take a final decision is increased to 105 working days according to Article 10(3), subparagraph 2. Where the parties submit commitments within less than 55 working days, but submit a modified version on day 55 or thereafter, the period to take a final decision will also be extended to 105 working days.

(101) Where the deadlines for the final decision have been extended according to Article 10(3) subparagraph 2 of the Merger Regulation before working day 55, this period is also extended.

90. The Commission is available to discuss suitable commitments well in advance of the end of the 65 working day period. The parties are encouraged to submit draft proposals dealing with both substantive and implementation aspects which are necessary to ensure that the commitments are fully workable. If the parties are of the opinion that more time is needed for the investigation of the competition concerns and for the corresponding design of appropriate commitments, they may also suggest to the Commission to extend the final deadline under Article 10(3), subparagraph 1. Such a request will have to be made before the end of the 65 working day period. Indeed, the Commission will normally not extend the period for adopting a final decision according to Article 10(3), subparagraph 1 where the request for extension is presented after the deadline for submitting remedies foreseen in the Implementing Regulation, i.e. after working day 65 (102).

(102) The Court of First Instance confirmed that the Merger Regulation and the Implementing Regulation do not impose any obligations on the Commission to accept commitments which are submitted after the legal deadline, as set out below in paragraph 94, see Case T-87/05 *EDP v Commission* (2005) ECR II-3745, at paragraph 161. Therefore, the Commission is not bound to consider any remedies which are submitted by the parties after the deadline for remedies, even if the parties were to agree to extend the final deadline. Moreover, this would not correspond to the purpose, as explained in recital 35 of the Merger Regulation, of the extensions foreseen in Article 10(3). The extension foreseen in Article 10(3), subparagraph 1 is to allow for sufficient time for the investigation of the competitive concerns, whereas it is the purpose of the extension laid down in Article 10(3), subparagraph 2 to allow for sufficient time for the analysis and market testing of commitments.

91. In order to meet the requirements for a decision pursuant to Article 8(2), commitments must meet the following requirements:

(a) they shall address all competition concerns raised by the concentration and shall fully specify the substantive and implementing commitments entered into by the parties;

(b) they shall be signed by a person duly authorised to do so;

(c) they shall by accompanied by the information on the commitments offered as provided for in the Implementing Regulation (as explained above in paragraph 7); and

(d) they shall be accompanied by a non-confidential version of the commitments (103) for the purposes of market testing them with third parties, fulfilling the requirements set out above in paragraph 79.

(103) Article 20(2) of the Implementing Regulation.

92. Proposals submitted by the parties in accordance with these requirements will be assessed by the Commission. If the assessment confirms that the proposed commitments remove the serious doubts (if no Statement of Objection has been issued yet by the Commission) or the competition concerns raised in the Statement of Objections, following the consultations as set out in paragraph 80 above, the Commission will adopt a conditional clearance decision.

93. Conversely, where the assessment leads to the conclusion that the proposed commitments appear not to be sufficient to resolve the competition concerns raised by the concentration, the parties will be informed accordingly (104).

(104) See paragraphs 30 ff. of the DG Competition Best Practices on the conduct of EC merger proceedings which provide for several state of play meetings between the Commission and the parties throughout the procedure.

94. The Merger Regulation does not impose any obligation on the Commission to accept commitments after the legal deadline for remedies, unless the Commission voluntarily undertakes to assess commitments in specific circumstances (105). In view of this, where parties subsequently modify the proposed commitments after the deadline of 65 working days, the Commission will only accept these modified commitments where it can clearly determine – on the basis of its assessment of information already received in the course of the investigation, including the results of prior market testing, and without the need for any other market test – that such commitments, once implemented, fully and unambiguously resolve the competition concerns identified and where there is sufficient time to allow for an adequate assessment by the Commission and for proper consultation with Member States (106) (107). The Commission will normally reject modified commitments which do not fulfil those conditions (108).

(105) See judgment of CFI in Case T-87/05 *EDP v Commission* (2005) ECR II-3745, at paragraphs 161 et seq. See also judgement of CFI in case T-290/94 *Kaysersberg SA v Commission* (1997) ECR II-2137.

(106) Case COMP/M.3440 – *ENI/EDP/GDP* of 9 December 2004, paragraphs 855 et seq.; confirmed by Judgment of CFI in Case T-87/05 *EDP v Commission* (2005) ECR II-3745, at paragraphs 162 et seq.; Case COMP/M.1628 – *TotalFina/Elf* of 9 March 2000, at paragraph 345.

(107) This consultation normally requires that the Commission has to be able to send a draft of the final decision, including an assessment of the modified commitments, to the Member States not less than 10 working days before the Advisory Committee with Member States. This period may only be shortened in exceptional circumstances (Article 19(5) of the Merger Regulation).

(108) See Case COMP/M.3440 – *ENI/EDP/GDP* of 9 December 2004, paragraph 913.

V. REQUIREMENTS FOR IMPLEMENTATION OF COMMITMENTS

95. Commitments are offered as a means of securing a clearance, with the implementation normally taking place after the decision. Commitments therefore require safeguards to ensure their effective and timely implementation. These implementing provisions will normally form part of the commitments entered into by the parties vis-à-vis the Commission.

96. In the following, detailed guidance is given on the implementation of divestiture commitments, as the most typical commitment. Afterwards, some aspects of the implementation of other types of commitments are discussed.

1. Divestiture process

97. The divestiture has to be completed within a fixed time period agreed between the parties and the Commission. In the Commission's practice, the total time period is divided into a period for entering into a final agreement and a further period for the closing, the transfer of legal title, of the transaction. The period for entering into a binding agreement is further normally divided into a first period in which the parties can look for a suitable purchaser (the «first divestiture period») and, if the parties do not succeed to divest the business, a second period in which a divestiture trustee obtains the mandate to divest the business at no minimum price (the «trustee divestiture period»).

98. The Commission's experience has shown that short divestiture periods contribute largely to the success of the divestiture as, otherwise, the business to be divested will be exposed to an extended period of uncertainty. The time periods should therefore be as short as feasible. The Commission will normally consider a period of around six months for the first divestiture period and an additional period of three months for the trustee divestiture period as appropriate. A period of further three months is normally foreseen for closing the transaction. These periods may be modified on a case-by-case basis. In particular, they may have to be shortened if there is a high risk of degradation of the business' viability in the interim period.

99. The deadline for the divestiture shall normally start on the day of the adoption of the Commission decision. An exception might be justified for a transaction via public bid where the parties commit to divest a business belonging to the target. Where in such circumstances the parties cannot prepare for the divestiture of the target's business before closing of the notified concentration, the Commission might accept that the periods for such a divestiture only start with the date of closing the notified transaction. Similarly, such a solution may be considered if the date of closing of the concentration is not under the control of the parties as it, e.g. requires state approval (109). In return, it may be appropriate to shorten the deadlines in order to reduce the time of uncertainty for the business to be divested.

(109) However, also in those circumstances, other provisions in the commitments, in particular the provisions establishing the safeguards in the interim period, should start running on the date of the adoption of the decision.

100. Whereas for up-front buyer solutions the above-described procedure applies, the procedure will be different for fix-it-first solutions. In general, a binding agreement with a purchaser will already be entered into during the procedure so that after the decision only a further period for the closing of the transaction has to be foreseen. If before the decision only a framework agreement has been concluded with the purchaser, the periods to be foreseen for entering into a full agreement and the closing afterwards will have to be decided on a case-by-case basis (110).

(110) See Case COMP/M.3916 – *T-Mobile Austria/tele.ring* of 20 April 2006.

2. Approval of the purchaser and of the sale and purchase agreement

101. In order to ensure the effectiveness of the commitment, the sale to a proposed purchaser is subject to prior approval by the Commission. When the parties (or the divestiture trustee) have reached a final agreement with a purchaser, they have to submit a reasoned and documented proposal to the Commission. The parties or the divestiture trustee, as the case may be, will be required to demonstrate to the satisfaction of the Commission that the proposed purchaser meets the purchaser requirements, and that the business is divested in a manner consistent with the Commission's decision and the commitments. Where the commitments allow that different purchasers are being proposed for different parts of the package, the Commission will assess whether each individual proposed purchaser is acceptable and that the total package solves the competition concern.

102. In assessing any proposed purchaser, the Commission will interpret the purchaser requirements in the light of the purpose of the commitments, to immediately maintain effective competition in the market where competition concerns had been found, and of the market circumstances as set out in the decision (111). Generally, the basis for the Commission's assessment of the purchaser requirements will be the submission of the parties, the assessment of the monitoring trustee and, in particular, discussions with the proposed purchaser and its business plan. The Commission will further analyse whether the underlying assumptions of the purchaser appear plausible according to the market circumstances.

(111) See judgment of the CFI in Case T-342/00 *Petrolessence v Commission* (2003) ECR II-1161.

103. The requirement that the purchaser has to have the necessary financial resources extends in particular to the way the acquisition is financed by the proposed purchaser. The Commission will normally not accept any financing of the divestiture by the seller, and, in particular, any seller financing if this were to give the seller a share in the profits of the divested business in the future.

104. In assessing whether the proposed purchaser threatens to create competition problems, the Commission will undertake a prima facie assessment in the light of the information available to the Commission in the purchaser approval process. Where the purchase results in a concentration that has a Community dimension, this new operation will have to be notified under the Merger Regulation and cleared under normal procedures (112). Where this is not the case, the Commission's approval of a proposed purchaser is without prejudice to the merger control jurisdiction of national authorities. In addition, the proposed purchaser must be expected to obtain all other necessary approvals from the relevant regulatory authorities. Where it can be foreseen, in the light of the information available to the Commission, that difficulties in obtaining merger control clearance or other approvals may unduly delay the timely implementation of the commitment, it will be considered that the proposed purchaser does not meet the purchaser requirements. Otherwise, the competition concerns identified by the Commission would not be removed in the appropriate time-frame.

(112) Case IV/M.1383 – *Exxon/Mobil* of 29 September 1999 and the follow-up Cases COMP/M.1820 – *BP/JV Dissolution* of 2 February 2000 and COMP/M.1822 – *Mobil/JV Dissolution* of 2 February 2000.

105. The requirement for an approval by the Commission does usually not only extend to the identity of the purchaser, but also to the sale and purchase agreement and any other agreement entered into between the parties and the proposed purchaser, including transitory agreements. The Commission will verify whether the divestiture according to the agreements is in line with the commitments (113).

(113) As discussed above, the parties may apply to the Commission to approve the divestiture of the business to the proposed purchaser without one or more assets or parts of the personnel if this does not affect the viability and competitiveness of the Divestment Business after the sale, taking account of the resources of the proposed purchaser.

106. The Commission will communicate its view as to the suitability of the proposed purchaser to the parties. If the Commission concludes that the proposed purchaser does not meet the purchaser requirements, it will adopt a decision that the proposed purchaser is not a purchaser under the commitments (114). If the Commission concludes that the sale and purchase agreement (or any ancillary agreements) does not foresee a divestiture in line with the commitments, the Commission will communicate this to the parties without necessarily rejecting the purchaser as such. If the Commission concludes that the purchaser is suitable under the commitments and that the contracts agree a divestiture in line with the commitments, the Commission will approve the divestiture to the proposed purchaser

(115). The Commission will issue the necessary approvals as expeditiously as possible.

(114) COMP/M.1628 – *TotalFina/Elf* of 9 February 2000, motorway service stations; confirmed by judgment of the CFI in Case T-342/00 *Petrolessence v Commission* (2003) ECR II-1161.

(115) Depending on the circumstances of the divestiture, the parties may also have to ensure, for example through appropriate provisions in the purchase agreement, that the purchaser will maintain the divested business as a competitive force in the market and will not sell on the business within a short time-span.

3. Obligations of the parties in the interim period

107. Parties have to fulfil certain obligations in the interim period (as defined above in paragraph 36). The following should normally be included in the commitments in this respect: *(i)* safeguards for the interim preservation of the viability to the business; *(ii)* the necessary steps for a carve-out process, if relevant; and *(iii)* the necessary steps to prepare the divestiture of the business.

Interim preservation of the divested business

108. It is the parties' responsibility to reduce to the minimum any possible risk of loss of competitive potential of the business to be divested resulting from the uncertainties inherent in the transfer of a business. Up to the transfer of the business to the purchaser, the Commission will require the parties to offer commitments to maintain the independence, economic viability, marketability and competitiveness of the business. Only such commitments will allow the Commission to conclude with the requisite degree of certainty that the divestiture of the business will be implemented in the way as proposed by the parties in the commitments.

109. Generally, these commitments should be designed to keep the business separate from the business retained by the parties, and to ensure that it is managed as a distinct and saleable business in its best interest, with a view to ensuring its continued economic viability, marketability and competitiveness and its independence from the businesses retained by the parties.

110. The parties will be required to ensure that all assets of the business are maintained, pursuant to good business practice and in the ordinary course of business, and that no acts which might have a significant adverse impact on the business are carried out. This relates in particular to the maintenance of fixed assets, know-how or commercial information of a confidential or proprietary nature, the customer base and the technical and commercial competence of the employees. Furthermore, the parties must maintain the business in the same conditions as before the concentration, in particular provide sufficient resources, such as capital or a line of credit, on the basis and continuation of existing business plans, the same administrative and management functions, or other factors relevant for maintaining competition in the specific sector. The commitments also have to foresee that the parties should take all reasonable steps, including appropriate incentive schemes, to encourage all key personnel to remain with the business, and that the parties may not solicit or move any personnel to their remaining businesses.

111. The parties should further hold the business separate from its retained business and ensure that the key personnel of the business to be divested do not have any involvement into the retained businesses and vice versa. If the business to be divested is in corporate form and a strict separation of the corporate structure appears necessary, the parties' rights as shareholders, in particular the voting rights, should be exercised by the monitoring trustee which should also have the power to replace the board members appointed on behalf of the parties. In relation to information, the parties must ring-fence the business to be divested and take all necessary measures to ensure that the parties do not obtain any business secrets or other confidential information. Any documents or information confidential to the business obtained by the parties before adoption of the decision have to be returned to the business or destroyed.

112. The parties are further generally required to appoint a hold-separate manager with the necessary expertise, who will be responsible for the management of the business and the implementation of the hold-separate and ring-fencing obligations. The hold-separate manager should act under the supervision of the monitoring trustee who may issue instructions to the hold-separate manager. The commitments have to provide that the appointment should take place immediately after the adoption of the decision and even before the parties may close the notified concentration. Whereas the parties can appoint the hold-separate manager on their own, the commitments have to foresee that the monitoring trustee is able to remove the hold-separate manager if s/he does not act in line with the commitments or endangers their timely and proper implementation. A new appointment of a hold-separate manager afterwards will be subject to the approval of the monitoring trustee.

Steps for a carve-out

113. As outlined above in paragraph 35, the Commission may accept in appropriate circumstances that the divestiture of a business which needs to be carved out from the remaining businesses of the parties can be considered a suitable remedy. Nevertheless, also in such circumstances only the transfer of a viable business to a purchaser which can maintain and develop this business as an active competitive force in the market will remove the Commission's competition concerns. Therefore, the parties have to commit to a result-oriented obligation to carry out, in the interim period, a carve-out of the assets that contribute to the divested business. The result has to be that a viable and competitive business, which is stand-alone and separate from the other businesses of the parties, can be transferred to a suitable purchaser at the end of the interim period. The parties will have to bear the costs and risks of such a carve-out in the interim period.

114. The carve-out will need to be carried out by the parties under the supervision of the trustee and in cooperation with the hold-separate manager. First, those assets and parts of the personnel which are shared between the business to be divested and remaining businesses of the parties have to be allocated to the business to the extent that this is not excluded in the commitments (116). The allocation of the assets and the personnel will be monitored and has to be approved by the monitoring trustee. Second, the carve-out process may also require a replication for the business of assets held or functions performed by other parts of the parties' businesses if this is necessary to ensure the viability and competitiveness of the business to be divested. An example is the termination of the business' participation in a central information technology network and an installation of a separate IT system for the business. In general, the major steps of such a carve-out process and the functions to be replicated should be decided on a case-by-case basis and described in the commitments.

(116) See paragraph 26 above for the question how shared assets have to be dealt with in commitments.

115. At the same time, it has to be ensured that the viability of the business to be divested is not affected by such measures. In the interim period, the parties therefore have to maintain the use of shared assets by and to continue to provide services to the business to the same extent as in the past as long as the business is not yet viable on a stand-alone basis.

Specific obligations of the parties concerning the divestiture process

116. For the divestiture process, the commitments should foresee that potential purchasers can carry out a due diligence exercise and obtain, dependent on the stage of the procedure, sufficient information concerning the divested business to allow the purchaser to fully asses the value, scope and commercial potential of the business, and have direct access to its personnel. The parties further have to submit periodic reports on potential purchasers and developments in the negotiations. The divestiture will only be implemented once the transaction is closed, that is the legal title has passed to the approved purchaser, and the assets have been actually transferred. At the end of the process, the parties will have to send a final report, confirming the closing and the transfer of the assets.

4. The monitoring and the divestiture trustee

Role of the monitoring trustee

117. As the Commission cannot, on a daily basis, be directly involved in overseeing the implementation of the commitments, the parties have to propose the appointment of a trustee to oversee the parties' compliance with the commitments, in particular with their obligations in the interim period and the divestiture process (the so-called «monitoring trustee»). Thereby, the parties guarantee the effectiveness of the commitments submitted by them and allow the Commission to ensure that the modification of the notified concentration, as proposed by the parties, will be carried out with the requisite degree of certainty.

118. The monitoring trustee will carry out its tasks under the supervision of the Commission and is to be considered the Commission's «eyes and ears». It shall be the guardian that the business is managed and kept properly on a stand-alone basis in the interim period. The Commission may therefore give any orders and instructions to the monitoring trustee in order to ensure compliance with the commitments, and the trustee may propose to the parties any measures it considers necessary for carrying out its tasks. The parties, however, may not issue any instructions to the trustee without approval by the Commission.

119. The Commitments will generally set out the tasks of the monitoring trustee. Its duties and obligations will be specified in detail in the trustee mandate, to be concluded between the parties and the trustee, and its tasks shall be further detailed in a work-plan. The tasks of the monitoring trustee will normally start immediately after the adoption of the Commission decision and last until the legal and actual transfer of the business to the approved purchaser. Five main, non-exhaustive tasks can be distinguished which the monitoring trustee should carry out under the supervision of the Commission:

– first, the monitoring trustee will be called upon to oversee the safeguards for the business to be divested in the interim period,

– second, in carve-out cases, the monitoring trustee has to monitor the splitting of assets and the allocation of the personnel between the divested business and retained businesses by the parties as well as the replication of assets and functions in the business previously provided by the parties,

– third, the monitoring trustee shall be responsible for overseeing the parties' efforts to find a potential purchaser and to transfer the business. In general, it shall review the progress of the divestiture process and the potential purchasers included in the process. It shall verify that potential purchasers receive sufficient information relating to the business – in particular by reviewing the information memorandum (if available), the data room or the due diligence process. Once a purchaser is proposed, the monitoring trustee shall submit to the Commission a reasoned opinion as to whether the proposed purchaser fulfils the purchaser requirements in the commitments and whether the business is sold in a manner consistent with the commitments. At the end of the process, the monitoring trustee has to oversee the legal and actual transfer of the business to the purchaser and make a final report, confirming the transfer,

– fourth, the monitoring trustee shall act as a contact point for any requests by third parties, in particular potential purchasers, in relation to the commitments. The parties shall inform interested third parties of the identity and the tasks of the monitoring trustee, including any potential purchasers. In case of disagreement between the parties and third parties in relation to matters dealt with by the commitments, the monitoring trustee shall discuss those matters with both sides and report to the Commission. In order to be able to carry out its role, the monitoring trustee will keep confidential any business secrets of the parties and third parties,

– fifth, the monitoring trustee shall report on these issues to the Commission in periodic compliance reports and shall also submit additional reports upon request by the Commission.

120. The commitments will also comprehensively set out the monitoring trustee's needs for support by and cooperation with the parties; the Commission will supervise the relationship between the parties and the trustee also in this respect. In order to fulfil its tasks, the trustee shall have access to books and records of the parties and of the divested business, insofar and as long as this is relevant for the implementation of the commitments, may ask for managerial and administrative support by the parties, shall be informed of potential purchasers and all developments in the divestiture process, and shall be provided with the information submitted to potential purchasers. In addition, the parties shall indemnify the trustee and allow the trustee to appoint advisors, if appropriate for the fulfilment of its tasks under the commitments. The commitments will also enable the Commission to share the parties' information with the monitoring trustee in order to allow the monitoring trustee to fulfil its tasks. The monitoring trustee will be bound to keep this information confidential.

Role of the divestiture trustee

121. As for the monitoring trustee, the parties have to propose to appoint a divestiture trustee in order to make the commitments submitted by them effective and allow the Commission to ensure that the modification of the notified concentration, as proposed by them, will be carried out. If the parties do not succeed in finding a suitable purchaser within the first divestiture period, then in the trustee divestiture period, the divestiture trustee will be given an irrevocable and exclusive mandate to dispose of the business, under the supervision of the Commission, within a specific deadline at no minimum price to a suitable purchaser. The commitments shall allow the divestiture trustee to include in the sale and purchase agreement such terms and conditions as it considers appropriate for an expedient sale, in particular customary representations, warranties and indemnities. The sale of the business by the divestiture trustee is in the same way subject to the prior approval of the Commission as the sale by the parties.

122. The commitments will set out that the parties shall support and inform the divestiture trustee and cooperate with the trustee in the same way as this is foreseen for the monitoring trustee. For the divestiture, the parties have to grant to the divestiture trustee comprehensive powers of attorney, covering all stages of the divestiture.

Approval of the trustee and the trustee mandate

123. Depending on the commitment, the monitoring trustee may or may not be the same person or Institution as the divestiture trustee. The parties shall propose one or several potential trustees to the Commission, including the full terms of the mandate and an outline of a work-plan. It is of the essence that the monitoring trustee is in place immediately after the Commission decision. Therefore, the parties should propose a suitable trustee immediately after the Commission decision (117) and the commitments normally have to foresee that the notified concentration can only be implemented once the monitoring trustee is appointed, after being approved by the Commission (118). The situation is different for the divestiture trustee who should be appointed well ahead of the end of the first divestiture period (119) so that its mandate can take effect with the beginning of the trustee divestiture period.

(117) Normally, the commitments should foresee that a monitoring trustee is proposed within two weeks of the date of the decision.

(118) See Case COMP/M.4180 – *GdF/Suez* of 14 November 2006; Case COMP/M.4187 – *Metso/Aker Kvaerner* of 12 December 2006; Case COMP/M.3916 – *T-Mobile/tele.ring* of 20 April 2006.

(119) The Commission will normally require an appointment at least one month ahead of the end of the first divestiture period.

124. Both types of trustees will be appointed by the parties on the basis of a trustee mandate, entered into by the parties and the trustee. The appointment and the mandate will be subject to the approval by the Commission which will have discretion in the selection of the trustee and will assess whether the proposed candidate is suitable for the tasks in the specific case. The trustee shall be independent of the parties, possess the necessary qualifications to carry out its mandate and shall not be, or become, exposed to a conflict of interests.

125. The Commission will assess the necessary qualifications in the light of the requirements of the specific case, including the geographic area and the sector concerned. according to the Commission's experience, auditing firms and other consulting firms may be particularly well placed to fulfil the tasks of a monitoring trustee. Individuals who have worked in the specific industry may also be suitable candidates for performing such a role if they have the necessary resources available to deal with the tasks at stake. Investment banks seem to be particularly suitable for the role of a divestiture trustee. The independence of the trustee is crucial in order to enable the trustee to properly fulfil its role of monitoring the parties' compliance for the Commission and to ensure its credibility vis-à-vis third parties. In particular, the Commission will not accept persons or Institutions as trustees which are at the same time the parties' auditors or their investment advisors in the divestiture. However, no conflicts of interests will arise by relations of the trustee with the parties if those relations will not impair the Trustee's objectivity and independence in discharging its tasks. It is the parties' responsibility to supply the Commission with adequate information for it to verify that the trustee fulfils the requirements. The appointment of the trustee after approval by the parties is irrevocable unless the trustee is replaced with the approval of or upon request by the Commission.

126. The trustee mandate shall define the tasks as specified in the commitments further and shall include all provisions necessary to enable the trustee to fulfil its tasks under the commitments accepted by the Commission. The parties are responsible for remuneration of the trustee under the mandate, and the remuneration structure must be such as to not impede the trustee's independence and effectiveness in fulfilling the mandate. The Commission will approve a trustee only together with a suitable mandate. In appropriate cases, it may publish the identity of the trustee and a summary of its tasks.

127. When the specific commitments with which the trustee has been entrusted have been implemented – that is to say, when legal title for the business to be divested has passed, the assets have been actually transferred to the purchaser and specific arrangements which may continue post-divestiture have been fulfilled – the mandate will provide for the trustee to request the Commission for a discharge from further responsibilities. Even after the discharge has been given, it may be necessary for the Commission to require the reappointment of the trustee on the basis of the commitments, if it appears subsequently to the Commission that the relevant commitments might not have been fully and properly implemented.

5. Obligations of the parties following implementation of the divestiture

128. The Commitments also have to foresee that for a period of 10 years after the adoption of the decision accepting the commitments the Commission may request information from the parties. This will allow the Commission to monitor the effective implementation of the remedy.

6. Implementation of other commitments

129. Many of the principles discussed above for the implementation of divestiture commitments can equally be applied to other types of commitments if those commitments need to be implemented subsequent to the Commission decision. For example, if it is foreseen that the beneficiary of a licence needs to be approved by the Commission, the considerations regarding the purchaser approval can be applied. Given the wide range of non-divestiture commitments, no general and comprehensive requirements for the implementation of non-divestiture commitments can be set out.

130. However, given the long duration of non-divestiture commitments and their frequent complexity, they often require a very high monitoring effort and specific monitoring tools in order to allow the Commission to conclude that they will effectively be implemented. Therefore, the Commission will often require the involvement of a trustee to oversee the implementation of such commitments and the establishment of a fast-track arbitration procedure in order to provide for a dispute resolution mechanism and to render the commitments enforceable by the market participants themselves. In past cases, the Commission has often required both the appointment of a trustee and an arbitration clause (120). In those circumstances, the trustee will oversee the implementation of the commitments, but will also be able to assist in arbitral proceedings to the effect that they may be finalised in a short period of time.

(120) Such an approach of combined monitoring by arbitration and a monitoring trustee was, e.g. used in Case COMP/M.2803 – *Telia/Sonera* of 10 July 2002; Case COMP/M.3083 – *GE/Instrumentarium* of 2 September 2003; and Case COMP/M.3225 – *Alcan/Pechiney II* of 29 September 2003.

Merger Remedies Study, October 2005

See the site: http://ec.europa.eu/competition/mergers/legislation/remedies_study.pdf for the ex post analysis of 96 remedies included in merger decisions adopted in 1996-2000

Guidelines on the assessment of horizontal mergers under the Council Regulation on the control of concentrations between undertakings

(OJ C 31, 5 February 2004, p. 5)

I. INTRODUCTION

1. Article 2 of Council Regulation (EC) N° 139/2004 of 20 January 2004 on the control of concentrations between undertakings (1) (hereinafter: the «Merger Regulation'» provides that the Commission has to appraise concentrations within the scope of the Merger Regulation with a view to establishing whether or not they are compatible with the common market. For that purpose, the Commission must assess, pursuant to Article 2(2) and (3), whether or not a concentration would significantly impede effective competition, in particular as a result of the creation or strengthening of a dominant position, in the common market or a substantial part of it.

(1) Council Regulation (EC) N° 139/2004 of 20 January 2004 (*O.J.* L 24, 29.1.2004, p. 1).

2. Accordingly, the Commission must take into account any significant impediment to effective competition likely to be caused by a concentration. The creation or the strengthening of a dominant position is a primary form of such competitive harm. The concept of dominance was defined in the context of Council Regulation (EEC) N° 4064/89 of 21 December 1989 on the control of concentrations between undertakings (hereinafter «Regulation N° 4064/89») as:

«a situation where one or more undertakings wield economic power which would enable them to prevent effective competition from being maintained in the relevant market by giving them the opportunity to act to a considerable extent independently of their competitors, their customers and, ultimately, of consumers» (2).

(2) Case T-102/96, Gencor v Commission, [1999] ECR II-753, paragraph 200. See Joined Cases C-68/94 and C-30/95, France and others v Commission (hereinafter «Kali and Salz»), [1998] ECR I-1375, paragraph 221. In exceptional circumstances, a merger may give rise to the creation or the strengthening of a dominant position on the part of an undertaking which is not a party to the notified transaction (see Case IV/M.1383 – Exxon/Mobil, points 225-229; Case COMP/M.2434 – Grupo Villar MIR/EnBW/Hidroelectrica del Cantabrico, points 67-71).

3. For the purpose of interpreting the concept of dominance in the context of Regulation N° 4064/89, the Court of Justice referred to the fact that it «is intended to apply to all concentrations with a Community dimension insofar as they are likely, because of their effect on the structure of competition within the Community, to prove incompatible with the system of undistorted competition envisaged by the Treaty» (3).

(3) See also Joined Cases C-68/94 and C-30/95, Kali and Salz, paragraph 170.

4. The creation or strengthening of a dominant position held by a single firm as a result of a merger has been the most common basis for finding that a concentration would result in a significant impediment to effective competition. Furthermore, the concept of dominance has also been applied in an oligopolistic setting to cases of collective dominance. As a consequence, it is expected that most cases of incompatibility of a concentration with the common market will continue to be based upon a finding of dominance. That concept therefore provides an important indication as to the standard of competitive harm that is applicable when determining whether a concentration is likely to impede effective competition to a significant degree, and hence, as to the likelihood of intervention (4). To that effect, the present notice is intended to preserve the guidance that can be drawn from past decisional practice and to take full account of past case-law of the Community Courts.

(4) See Recitals 25 and 26 of the Merger Regulation.

5. The purpose of this notice is to provide guidance as to how the Commission assesses concentrations (5) when the undertakings concerned are actual or potential competitors on the same relevant market (6). In this notice such mergers will be denoted «horizontal mergers». While the notice presents the analytical approach used by the Commission in its appraisal of horizontal mergers it cannot provide details of all possible applications of this approach. The Commission applies the approach described in the notice to the particular facts and circumstances of each case.

(5) The term «concentration» used in the Merger Regulation covers various types of transactions such as mergers, acquisitions, takeovers, and certain types of joint ventures. In the remainder of this notice, unless otherwise specified, the term 'merger' will be used as a synonym for concentration and therefore cover all the above types of transactions.

(6) The notice does not cover the assessment of the effects of competition that a merger has in other markets, including vertical and conglomerate effects. Nor does it cover the assessment of the effects of a joint venture as referred to in Article 2(4) of the Merger Regulation.

6. The guidance set out in this notice draws and elaborates on the Commission's evolving experience with the appraisal of horizontal mergers under Regulation N° 4064/89 since its entry into force on 21 September 1990 as well as on the case-law of the Court of Justice and the Court of First Instance of the European Communities. The principles contained here will be applied and further developed and refined by the Commission in individual cases. The Commission may revise this notice from time to time in the light of future developments.

7. The Commission's interpretation of the Merger Regulation as regards the appraisal of horizontal mergers is without prejudice to the interpretation which may be given by the Court of Justice or the Court of First Instance of the European Communities.

II. OVERVIEW

8. Effective competition brings benefits to consumers, such as low prices, high quality products, a wide selection of goods and services, and innovation. Through its control of mergers, the Commission prevents mergers that would be likely to deprive customers of these benefits by significantly increasing the market power of firms. By «increased market power» is meant the ability of one or more firms to profitably increase prices, reduce output, choice or quality of goods and services, diminish innovation, or otherwise influence parameters of competition. In this notice, the expression «increased prices» is often used as shorthand for these various ways in which a merger may result in competitive harm (7). Both suppliers and buyers can have market power. However, for clarity, market power will usually refer here to a supplier's market power. Where a buyer's market power is the issue, the term «buyer power» is employed.

(7) The expression should be understood to also cover situations where, for instance, prices are decreased less, or are less likely to decrease, than they otherwise would have without the merger and where prices are increased more, or are more likely to increase, than they otherwise would have without the merger.

9. In assessing the competitive effects of a merger, the Commission compares the competitive conditions that would result from the notified merger with the conditions that would have prevailed without the merger (8). In most cases the competitive conditions existing at the time of the merger constitute the relevant comparison for evaluating the effects of a merger. However, in some circumstances, the Commission may take into account future changes to the market that can reasonably be predicted (9). It may, in particular, take account of the likely entry or exit of firms if the merger did not take place when considering what constitutes the relevant comparison (10).

(8) By analogy, in the case of a merger that has been implemented without having been notified, the Commission would assess the merger in the light of the competitive conditions that would have prevailed without the implemented merger.

(9) See, e.g. Commission Decision 98/526/EC in Case IV/M.950 – Hoffmann La Roche/Boehringer Mannheim, O.J. L 234, 21.8.1998, p. 14, point 13; Case IV/M.1846 – Glaxo Wellcome/SmithKline Beecham, points 70-72; Case COMP/M.2547 – Bayer/Aventis Crop Science, points 324 et seq.

(10) See, e.g. Case T-102/96, Gencor v Commission, [1999] ECR II-753, paragraphs 247-263.

10. The Commission's assessment of mergers normally entails:

(a) definition of the relevant product and geographic markets;

(b) competitive assessment of the merger.

The main purpose of market definition is to identify in a systematic way the immediate competitive constraints facing the merged entity. Guidance on this issue can be found in the Commission's Notice on the definition of the relevant market for the purposes of Community competition law (11). Various considerations leading to the delineation of the relevant markets may also be of importance for the competitive assessment of the merger.

(11) O.J. C 372, 9.12.1997, p. 5.

11. This notice is structured around the following elements:

(a) The approach of the Commission to market shares and concentration thresholds (Section III).

(b) The likelihood that a merger would have anticompetitive effects in the relevant markets, in the absence of countervailing factors (Section IV).

(c) The likelihood that buyer power would act as a countervailing factor to an increase in market power resulting from the merger (Section V).

(d) The likelihood that entry would maintain effective competition in the relevant markets (Section VI).

(e) The likelihood that efficiencies would act as a factor counteracting the harmful effects on competition which might otherwise result from the merger (Section VII).

(f) The conditions for a failing firm defence (Section VIII).

12. In order to assess the foreseeable impact (12) of a merger on the relevant markets, the Commission analyses its possible anti-competitive effects and the relevant countervailing factors such as buyer power, the extent of entry barriers and possible efficiencies put forward by the parties. In exceptional circumstances, the Commission considers whether the conditions for a failing firm defence are met.

(12) See Case T-102/96, Gencor v Commission, [1999] ECR II-753, paragraph 262, and Case T-342/99, Airtours v Commission, [2002] ECR II-2585, paragraph 280.

13. In the light of these elements, the Commission determines, pursuant to Article 2 of the Merger Regulation, whether the merger would significantly impede effective competition, in particular through the creation or the strengthening of a dominant position, and should therefore be declared incompatible with the common market. It should be stressed that these factors are not a 'checklist' to be mechanically applied in each and every case. Rather, the competitive analysis in a particular case will be based on an overall assessment of the foreseeable impact of the merger in the light of the relevant factors and conditions. Not all the elements will always be relevant to each and every horizontal merger, and it may not be necessary to analyse all the elements of a case in the same detail.

III. MARKET SHARE AND CONCENTRATION LEVELS

14. Market shares and concentration levels provide useful first indications of the market structure and of the competitive importance of both the merging parties and their competitors.

15. Normally, the Commission uses current market shares in its competitive analysis (13). However, current market shares may be adjusted to reflect reasonably certain future changes, for instance in the light of exit, entry or expansion (14). Post-merger market shares are calculated on the assumption that the post-merger combined market share of the merging parties is the sum of their pre-merger market shares (15). Historic data may be used if market shares have been volatile, for instance when the market is characterised by large, lumpy orders. Changes in historic market shares may provide useful information about the competitive process and the likely future importance of the various competitors, for instance, by indicating whether firms have been gaining or losing market shares. In any event, the Commission interprets market shares in the light of likely market conditions, for instance, if the market is highly dynamic in character and if the market structure is unstable due to innovation or growth (16).

(13 As to the calculation of market shares, see also Commission Notice on the definition of the relevant market for the purposes of Community competition law, O.J. C 372, 9.12.1997, p. 3, paragraphs 54-55.

(14) See, e.g. Case COMP/M.1806 – Astra Zeneca/Novartis, points 150 and 415.

(15) When relevant, market shares may be adjusted, in particular, to account for controlling interests in other firms (See, e.g. Case IV/M.1383 – Exxon/Mobil, points 446-458; Case COMP/M.1879 – Boeing/Hughes, points 60-79; Case COMP/JV 55 – Hutchison/RCPM/ECT, points 66-75), or for other arrangements with third parties (See, for instance, as regards subcontractors, Commission Decision 2001/769/EC in Case COMP/M.1940 – Framatome/Siemens/Cogema, O.J. L 289, 6.11.2001, p. 8, point 142).

(16) See, e.g. Case COMP/M.2256 – Philips/Agilent Health Care Technologies, points 31-32, and Case COMP/M.2609 – HP/Compaq, point 39.

16. The overall concentration level in a market may also provide useful information about the competitive situation. In order to measure concentration levels, the Commission often applies the Herfindahl-Hirschman Index (HHI) (17). The HHI is calculated by summing the squares of the individual market shares of all the firms in the market (18). The HHI gives proportionately greater weight to the market shares of the larger firms. Although it is best to include all firms in the calculation, lack of information about very small firms may not be important because such firms do not affect the HHI significantly. While the absolute level of the HHI can give an initial indication of the competitive pressure in the market post-merger, the change in the HHI (known as the «delta») is a useful proxy for the change in concentration directly brought about by the merger (19).

(17) See, e.g. Case IV/M.1365 – FCC/Vivendi, point 40; Case COMP/JV 55 – Hutchison/RCPM/ECT, point 50. If appropriate, the Commission may also use other concentration measures such as, for instance, concentration ratios, which measure the aggregate market share of a small number (usually three or four) of the leading firms in a market.

(18) For example, a market containing five firms with market shares of 40%, 20%, 15%, 15%, and 10%, respectively, has an HHI of 2.550 (40^2 + 20^2 + 15^2 + 15^2 + 10^2 = 2.550). The HHI ranges from close to zero (in an atomistic market) to 10 000 (in the case of a pure monopoly).

(19) The increase in concentration as measured by the HHI can be calculated independently of the overall market concentration by doubling the product of the market shares of the merging firms. For example, a merger of two firms with market shares of 30% and 15% respectively would increase the HHI by 900 (30 × 15 × 2 = 900). The explanation for this technique is as follows: Before the merger, the market shares of the merging firms contribute to the HHI by their squares individually: $(a)^2 + (b)^2$. After the merger, the contribution is the square of their sum: $(a + b)^2$, which equals $(a)^2 + (b)^2 + 2ab$. The increase in the HHI is therefore represented by $2ab$.

Market share levels

17. According to well-established case law, very large market shares – 50% or more – may in themselves be evidence of the existence of a dominant market position (20). However, smaller competitors may act as a sufficient constraining influence if, for example, they have the ability and incentive to increase their supplies. A merger involving a firm whose market share will remain below 50% after the merger may also raise competition concerns in view of other factors such as the strength and number of competitors, the presence of capacity constraints or the extent to which the products of the merging parties are close substitutes. The Commission has thus in several cases considered mergers resulting in firms holding market shares between 40% and 50% (21), and in some cases below 40% (22), to lead to the creation or the strengthening of a dominant position.

(20) Case T-221/95, Endemol v Commission, [1999] ECR II-1299, paragraph 134, and Case T-102/96, Gencor v Commission, [1999] ECR II-753, paragraph 205. It is a distinct question whether a dominant position is created or strengthened as a result of the merger.

(21) See, e.g. Case COMP/M.2337 – Nestlé/Ralston Purina, points 48-50.

(22) See, e.g. Commission Decision 1999/674/EC in Case IV/M.1221 – Rewe/Meinl, O.J. L 274, 23.10.1999, p. 1, points 98-114; Case COMP/M.2337 – Nestlé/Ralston Purina, points 44-47.

18. Concentrations which, by reason of the limited market share of the undertakings concerned, are not liable to impede effective competition may be presumed to be compatible with the common market. Without prejudice to Articles 81 and 82 of the Treaty, an indication to this effect exists, in particular, where the market share of the undertakings concerned does not exceed 25% (23) either in the common market or in a substantial part of it (24).

(23) The calculation of market shares depends critically on market definition. It must be emphasised that the Commission does not necessarily accept the parties' proposed market definition.

(24) Recital 32 of the Merger Regulation. However, such an indication does not apply to cases where the proposed merger creates or strengthens a collective dominant position involving the «undertakings concerned» and other third parties (see Joined Cases C-68/94 and C-30/95, Kali and Salz, [1998] ECR I-1375, paragraphs 171 et seq.; and Case T-102/96, Gencor v Commission, [1999] ECR II-753, paragraphs 134 et seq.).

HHI levels

19. The Commission is unlikely to identify horizontal competition concerns in a market with a post-merger HHI below 1.000. Such markets normally do not require extensive analysis.

20. The Commission is also unlikely to identify horizontal competition concerns in a merger with a post-merger HHI between 1.000 and 2.000 and a delta below 250, or a merger with a post-merger HHI above 2.000 and a delta below 150, except where special circumstances such as, for instance, one or more of the following factors are present:

(a) a merger involves a potential entrant or a recent entrant with a small market share;

(b) one or more merging parties are important innovators in ways not reflected in market shares;

(c) there are significant cross-shareholdings among the market participants (25);

(d) one of the merging firms is a maverick firm with a high likelihood of disrupting coordinated conduct;

(e) indications of past or ongoing coordination, or facilitating practices, are present;

(f) one of the merging parties has a pre-merger market share of 50% of more (26).

(25) In markets with cross-shareholdings or joint ventures the Commission may use a modified HHI, which takes into account such share-holdings (see, e.g. Case IV/M.1383 – Exxon/Mobil, point 256).

(26) See paragraph 17.

21. Each of these HHI levels, in combination with the relevant deltas, may be used as an initial indicator of the absence of competition concerns. However, they do not give rise to a presumption of either the existence or the absence of such concerns.

IV. POSSIBLE ANTI-COMPETITIVE EFFECTS OF HORIZONTAL MERGERS

22. There are two main ways in which horizontal mergers may significantly impede effective competition, in particular by creating or strengthening a dominant position:

(a) by eliminating important competitive constraints on one or more firms, which consequently would have increased market power, without resorting to coordinated behaviour (non-coordinated effects);

(b) by changing the nature of competition in such a way that firms that previously were not coordinating their behaviour, are now significantly more likely to coordinate and raise prices or otherwise harm effective competition. A merger may also make coordination easier, more stable or more effective for firms which were coordinating prior to the merger (coordinated effects).

23. The Commission assesses whether the changes brought about by the merger would result in any of these effects. Both instances mentioned above may be relevant when assessing a particular transaction.

Non-coordinated effects (27)

(27) Also often called «unilateral» effects.

24. A merger may significantly impede effective competition in a market by removing important competitive constraints on one or more sellers, who consequently have increased market power. The most direct effect of the merger will be the loss of competition between the merging firms. For example, if prior to the merger one of the merging firms had raised its price, it would have lost some sales to the other merging firm. The merger removes this particular constraint. Non-merging firms in the same market can also benefit from the reduction of competitive pressure that results from the merger, since the merging firms' price increase may switch some demand to the rival firms, which, in turn, may find it profitable to increase their prices (28). The reduction in these competitive constraints could lead to significant price increases in the relevant market.

25. (28) Such expected reactions by competitors may be a relevant factor influencing the merged entity's incentives to increase prices.

Generally, a merger giving rise to such non-coordinated effects would significantly impede effective competition by creating or strengthening the dominant position of a single firm, one which, typically, would have an appreciably larger market share than the next competitor post-merger. Furthermore, mergers in oligopolistic markets (29) involving the elimination of important competitive constraints that the merging parties previously exerted upon each other together with a reduction of competitive pressure on the remaining competitors may, even where there is little likelihood of coordination between the members of the oligopoly, also result in a significant impediment to competition. The Merger Regulation clarifies that all mergers giving rise to such non-coordinated effects shall also be declared incompatible with the common market (30).

(29) An oligopolistic market refers to a market structure with a limited number of sizeable firms. Because the behaviour of one firm has an appreciable impact on the overall market conditions, and thus indirectly on the situation of each of the other firms, oligopolistic firms are interdependent.

(30) Recital 25 of the Merger Regulation.

26. A number of factors, which taken separately are not necessarily decisive, may influence whether significant non-coordinated effects are likely to result from a merger. Not all of these factors need to be present for such effects to be likely. Nor should this be considered an exhaustive list.

Merging firms have large market shares

27. The larger the market share, the more likely a firm is to possess market power. And the larger the addition of market share, the more likely it is that a merger will lead to a significant increase in market power. The larger the increase in the sales base on which to enjoy higher margins after a price increase, the more likely it is that the merging firms will find such a price increase profitable despite the accompanying reduction in output. Although market shares and additions of market shares only provide first indications of market power and increases in market power, they are normally important factors in the assessment (31).

(31) See, in particular, paragraphs 17 and 18.

Merging firms are close competitors

28. Products may be differentiated (32) within a relevant market such that some products are closer substitutes than others (33). The higher the degree of substitutability between the merging firms' products, the more likely it is that the merging firms will raise prices significantly (34). For example, a merger between two producers offering products which a substantial number of customers regard as their first and second choices could generate a significant price increase. Thus, the fact that rivalry between the parties has been an important source of competition on the market may be a central factor in the analysis (35). High pre-merger margins (36) may also make significant price increases more likely. The merging firms' incentive to raise prices is more likely to be constrained when rival firms produce close substitutes to the products of the merging firms than when they offer less close substitutes (37). It is therefore less likely that a merger will significantly impede effective competition, in particular through the creation or strengthening of a dominant position, when there is a high degree of substitutability between the products of the merging firms and those supplied by rival producers.

(32) Products may be differentiated in various ways. There may, for example, be differentiation in terms of geographic location, based on branch or stores location; location matters for retail distribution, banks, travel agencies, or petrol stations. Likewise, differentiation may be based on brand image, technical specifications, quality or level of service. The level of advertising in a market may be an indicator of the firms' effort to differentiate their products. For other products, buyers may have to incur switching costs to use a competitor's product.

(33) For the definition of the relevant market, see the Commission's Notice on the definition of the relevant market for the purposes of Community competition law, cited above.

(34) See for example Case COMP/M.2817 – Barilla/BPS/Kamps, point 34; Commission Decision 2001/403/EC in Case COMP/M.1672 – Volvo/Scania, O.J. L 143, 29.5.2001, p. 74, points 107-148.

(35) See, e.g. Commission Decision 94/893/EC in Case IV/M.430 – Procter & Gamble/VP Schickedanz (II), O.J. L 354, 21.6.1994, p. 32, Case T-290/94, Kaysersberg v Commission, [1997] II-2137, paragraph 153; Commission Decision 97/610/EC in Case IV/M.774 – Saint-Gobain/ Wacker-Chemie/NOM, O.J. L 247, 10.9.1997, p. 1, point 179; Commission Decision 2002/156/EC in Case COMP/M.2097 – SCA/Metsä Tissue, O.J. L 57, 27.2.2002, p. 1, points 94-108; Case T-310/01, Schneider v Commission, [2002] II-4071, paragraph 418.

(36) Typically, the relevant margin (m) is the difference between price (p) and the incremental cost (c) of supplying one more unit of output expressed as a percentage of price ($m = (p - c)/p$).

(37) See, e.g. Case IV/M.1980 – Volvo/Renault VI, point 34; Case COMP/M.2256 – Philips Agilent/Health Care Solutions, points 33-35; Case COMP/M.2537 – Philips/Marconi Medical Systems, points 31-34.

29. When data are available, the degree of substitutability may be evaluated through customer preference surveys, analysis of purchasing patterns, estimation of the cross-price elasticities of the products involved (38), or diversion ratios (39). In bidding markets it may be possible to measure whether historically the submitted bids by one of the merging parties have been constrained by the presence of the other merging party (40).

(38) The cross-price elasticity of demand measures the extent to which the quantity of a product demanded changes in response to a change in the price of some other product, all other things remaining equal. The own-price elasticity measures the extent to which demand for a product changes in response to the change in the price of the product itself.

(39) The diversion ratio from product A to product B measures the proportion of the sales of product A lost due to a price increase of A that are captured by product B.

(40) Commission Decision 97/816/EC in Case IV/M.877 – Boeing/McDonnell Douglas, O.J. L 336, 8.12.1997, p. 16, points 58 et seq.; Case COMP/M.3083 – GE/Instrumentarium, points 125 et seq.

30. In some markets it may be relatively easy and not too costly for the active firms to reposition their products or extend their product portfolio. In particular, the Commission examines whether the possibility of repositioning or product line extension by competitors or the merging parties may influence the incentive of the merged entity to raise prices. However, product repositioning or product line extension often entails risks and large sunk costs (41) and may be less profitable than the current line.

(41) Sunk costs are costs which are unrecoverable upon exit from the market.

Customers have limited possibilities of switching supplier

31. Customers of the merging parties may have difficulties switching to other suppliers because there are few alternative suppliers (42) or because they face substantial switching costs (43). Such customers are particularly vulnerable to price increases. The merger may affect these customers' ability to protect themselves against price increases. In particular, this may be the case for customers that have used dual sourcing from the two merging firms as a means of obtaining competitive prices. Evidence of past customer switching patterns and reactions to price changes may provide important information in this respect.

(42) See e.g. Commission Decision 2002/156/EC in Case IV/M.877 – Boeing/McDonnell Douglas, O.J. L 336, 8.12.1997, p. 16, point 70.

(43) See, e.g. Case IV/M. 986 – Agfa Gevaert/DuPont, O.J. L 211, 29.7.1998, p. 22, points 63-71.

Competitors are unlikely to increase supply if prices increase

32. When market conditions are such that the competitors of the merging parties are unlikely to increase their supply substantially if prices increase, the merging firms may have an incentive to reduce output below the combined pre-merger levels, thereby raising market prices (44). The merger increases the incentive to reduce output by giving the merged firm a larger base of sales on which to enjoy the higher margins resulting from an increase in prices induced by the output reduction.

(44) See, e.g. Case COMP/M.2187 – CVC/Lenzing, points 162-170.

33. Conversely, when market conditions are such that rival firms have enough capacity and find it profitable to expand output sufficiently, the Commission is unlikely to find that the merger will create or strengthen a dominant position or otherwise significantly impede effective competition.

34. Such output expansion is, in particular, unlikely when competitors face binding capacity constraints and the expansion of capacity is costly (45) or if existing excess capacity is significantly more costly to operate than capacity currently in use.

(45) When analysing the possible expansion of capacity by rivals, the Commission considers factors similar to those described in Section VI on entry. See, e.g. Case COMP/M.2187 – CVC/Lenzing, points 162-173.

35. Although capacity constraints are more likely to be important when goods are relatively homogeneous, they may also be important where firms offer differentiated products.

Merged entity able to hinder expansion by competitors

36. Some proposed mergers would, if allowed to proceed, significantly impede effective competition by leaving the merged firm in a position where it would have the ability and incentive to make the expansion of smaller firms and potential competitors more difficult or otherwise restrict the ability of rival firms to compete. In such a case, competitors may not, either individually or in the aggregate, be in a position to constrain the merged entity to such a degree that it would not increase prices or take other actions detrimental to competition. For instance, the merged entity may have such a degree of control, or influence over, the supply of inputs (46) or distribution possibilities (47) that expansion or entry by rival firms may be more costly. Similarly, the merged entity's control over patents (48) or other types of intellectual property (e.g. brands (49)) may make expansion or entry by rivals more difficult. In markets where interoperability between different infrastructures or platforms is important (50), a merger may give the merged entity the ability and incentive to raise the costs or decrease the quality of service of its rivals (51). In making this assessment the

Commission may take into account, inter alia, the financial strength of the merged entity relative to its rivals (52).

(46) See, e.g. Case T-221/95, Endemol v Commission, [1999] ECR II-1299, paragraph 167.

(47) See, e.g. Case T-22/97, Kesko v Commission, [1999], ECR II-3775, paragraphs 141 et seq.

(48) See, e.g. Commission Decision 2001/684/EC in Case M.1671 – Dow Chemical/Union Carbide O.J. L 245, 14.9.2001, p. 1, points 107-114.

(49) See, e.g. Commission Decision 96/435/EC in Case IV/M.623 – Kimberly-Clark/Scott, O.J. L 183, 23.7.1996, p. 1; Case T-114/02, Babyliss SA v Commission («Seb/Moulinex»), [2003] ECR II-000, paragraphs 343 et seq.

(50) This is, for example, the case in network industries such as energy, telecommunications and other communication industries.

(51) Commission Decision 99/287/EC in Case IV/M.1069 – Worldcom/MCI, O.J. L 116, 4.5.1999, p. 1, points 117 et seq.; Case IV/M.1741 – MCI Worldcom/Sprint, points 145 et seq.; Case IV/M.1795 – Vodafone Airtouch/Mannesmann, points 44 et seq.

(52) Case T-156/98 RJB Mining v Commission [2001] ECR II-337.

Merger eliminates an important competitive force

37. Some firms have more of an influence on the competitive process than their market shares or similar measures would suggest. A merger involving such a firm may change the competitive dynamics in a significant, anti-competitive way, in particular when the market is already concentrated (53). For instance, a firm may be a recent entrant that is expected to exert significant competitive pressure in the future on the other firms in the market.

(53) Commission Decision 2002/156/EC in Case IV/M.877 – Boeing/McDonnell Douglas, O.J. L 336, 8.12.1997, p. 16, point 58; Case COMP/M.2568 – Haniel/Ytong, point 126.

38. In markets where innovation is an important competitive force, a merger may increase the firms' ability and incentive to bring new innovations to the market and, thereby, the competitive pressure on rivals to innovate in that market. Alternatively, effective competition may be significantly impeded by a merger between two important innovators, for instance between two companies with 'pipeline' products related to a specific product market. Similarly, a firm with a relatively small market share may nevertheless be an important competitive force if it has promising pipeline products (54).

(54) For an example of pipeline products of one merging party likely to compete with the other party's pipeline or existing products, see, e.g. Case IV/M.1846 – Glaxo Wellcome/SmithKline Beecham, point 188.

Coordinated effects

39. In some markets the structure may be such that firms would consider it possible, economically rational, and hence preferable, to adopt on a sustainable basis a course of action on the market aimed at selling at increased prices. A merger in a concentrated market may significantly impede effective competition, through the creation or the strengthening of a collective dominant position, because it increases the likelihood that firms are able to coordinate their behaviour in this way and raise prices, even without entering into an agreement or resorting to a concerted practice within the meaning of Article 81 of the Treaty (55). A merger may also make coordination easier, more stable or more effective for firms, that were already coordinating before the merger, either by making the coordination more robust or by permitting firms to coordinate on even higher prices.

(55) Case T-102/96, Gencor v Commission, [1999] ECR II-753, paragraph 277; Case T-342/99, Airtours v Commission, [2002] ECR II-2585, paragraph 61.

40. Coordination may take various forms. In some markets, the most likely coordination may involve keeping prices above the competitive level. In other markets, coordination may aim at limiting production or the amount of new capacity brought to the market. Firms may also coordinate by dividing the market, for instance by geographic area (56) or other customer characteristics, or by allocating contracts in bidding markets.

(56) This may be the case if the oligopolists have tended to concentrate their sales in different areas for historic reasons.

41. Coordination is more likely to emerge in markets where it is relatively simple to reach a common understanding on the terms of coordination. In addition, three conditions are necessary for coordination to be sustainable. First, the coordinating firms must be able to monitor to a sufficient degree whether the terms of coordination are being adhered to. Second, discipline requires that there is some form of credible deterrent mechanism that can be activated if deviation is detected. Third, the reactions of outsiders, such as current and future competitors not participating in the coordination, as well as customers, should not be able to jeopardise the results expected from the coordination (57).

(57) Case T-342/99, Airtours v Commission, [2002] ECR II-2585, paragraph 62.

42. The Commission examines whether it would be possible to reach terms of coordination and whether the coordination is likely to be sustainable. In this respect, the Commission considers the changes that the merger brings about. The reduction in the number of firms in a market may, in itself, be a factor that facilitates coordination. However, a merger may also increase the likelihood or significance of coordinated effects in other ways. For instance, a merger may involve a 'maverick' firm that has a history of preventing or disrupting coordination, for example by failing to follow price increases by its competitors, or has characteristics that gives it an incentive to favour different strategic choices than its coordinating competitors would prefer. If the merged firm were to adopt strategies similar to those of other competitors, the remaining firms would find it easier to coordinate, and the merger would increase the likelihood, stability or effectiveness of coordination.

43. In assessing the likelihood of coordinated effects, the Commission takes into account all available relevant information on the characteristics of the markets concerned, including both structural features and the past behaviour of firms (58). Evidence of past coordination is important if the relevant market characteristics have not changed appreciably or are not likely to do so in the near future (59). Likewise, evidence of coordination in similar markets may be useful information.

(58) See Commission Decision 92/553/EC in Case IV/M.190 – Nestlé/Perrier, O.J. L 356, 5.12.1992, p. 1, points 117-118.

(59) See, e.g. Case IV/M.580 – ABB/Daimler-Benz, point 95.

Reaching terms of coordination

44. Coordination is more likely to emerge if competitors can easily arrive at a common perception as to how the coordination should work. Coordinating firms should have similar views regarding which actions would be considered to be in accordance with the aligned behaviour and which actions would not.

45. Generally, the less complex and the more stable the economic environment, the easier it is for the firms to reach a common understanding on the terms of coordination. For instance, it is easier to coordinate among a few players than among many. It is also easier to coordinate on a price for a single, homogeneous product, than on hundreds of prices in a market with many differentiated products. Similarly, it is easier to coordinate on a price when demand and supply conditions are relatively stable than when they are continuously changing (60). In this context volatile demand, substantial internal growth by some firms in the market or frequent entry by new firms may indicate that the current situation is not sufficiently stable to make coordination likely (61). In markets where innovation is important, coordination may be more difficult since innovations, particularly significant ones, may allow one firm to gain a major advantage over its rivals.

(60) See, e.g. Commission Decision 2002/156/EC in Case COMP/M.2097 – SCA/Metsä Tissue, O.J. L 57, 27.2.2002, p. 1, point 148.

(61) See, e.g. Case IV/M.1298 – Kodak/Imation, point 60.

46. Coordination by way of market division will be easier if customers have simple characteristics that allow the coordinating firms to readily allocate them. Such characteristics may be based on geography; on customer type or simply on the existence of customers who typically buy from one specific firm. Coordination by way of market division may be relatively straightforward if it is easy to identify each customer's supplier and the coordination device is the allocation of existing customers to their incumbent supplier.

47. Coordinating firms may, however, find other ways to overcome problems stemming from complex economic environments short of market division. They may, for instance, establish simple pricing rules that reduce the complexity of coordinating on a large number of prices. One example of such a rule is establishing a small number of pricing points, thus reducing the coordination problem. Another example is having a fixed relationship between certain base prices and a number of other prices, such that prices basically move in parallel. Publicly available key information, exchange of information through trade associations, or information received through cross-shareholdings or participation in joint ventures may also help firms reach terms of coordination. The more complex the market situation is, the more transparency or communication is likely to be needed to reach a common understanding on the terms of coordination.

48. Firms may find it easier to reach a common understanding on the terms of coordination if they are relatively symmetric (62), especially in terms of cost structures, market shares, capacity levels and levels of vertical integration (63). Structural links such as cross-shareholding or participation in joint ventures may also help in aligning incentives among the coordinating firms (64).

(62) Case T-102/96, Gencor v Commission, [1999] ECR II-753, paragraph 222; Commission Decision 92/553/EC in Case IV/M.190 – Nestlé/Perrier, O.J. L 356, 5.12.1992, p. 1, points 63-123.

(63) In assessing whether or not a merger may increase the symmetry of the various firms present on the market, efficiency gains may provide important indications (see also paragraph 82 of the notice).

(64) See, e.g. Commission Decision 2001/519/EC in Case COMP/M.1673 – VEBA/VIAG, O.J. L 188, 10.7.2001, p. 1, point 226; Case COMP/M.2567 – Nordbanken/Postgirot, point 54.

Monitoring deviations

49. Coordinating firms are often tempted to increase their share of the market by deviating from the terms of coordination, for instance by lowering prices, offering secret discounts, increasing product quality or capacity or trying to win new customers. Only the credible threat of timely and sufficient retaliation keeps firms from deviating. Markets therefore need to be sufficiently transparent to allow the coordinating firms to monitor to a sufficient degree whether other firms are deviating, and thus know when to retaliate (65).

(65) See, e.g. Case COMP/M.2389 – Shell/DEA, points 112 et seq.; and Case COMP/M.2533 – BP/E.ON, points 102 et seq.

50. Transparency in the market is often higher, the lower the number of active participants in the market. Further, the degree of transparency often depends on how market transactions take place in a particular market. For example, transparency is likely to be high in a market where transactions take place on a public exchange or in an open outcry auction (66). Conversely, transparency may be low in a market where transactions are confidentially negotiated between buyers and sellers on a bilateral basis (67). When evaluating the level of transparency in the market, the key element is to identify what firms can infer about the actions of other firms from the available information (68). Coordinating firms should be able to interpret with some certainty whether unexpected behaviour is the result of deviation from the terms of coordination. For instance, in unstable environments it may be difficult for a firm to know whether its lost sales are due to an overall low level of demand or due to a competitor offering particularly low prices. Similarly, when overall demand or cost conditions fluctuate, it may be difficult to interpret whether a competitor is lowering its price because it expects the coordinated prices to fall or because it is deviating.

(66) See also Commission Decision 2000/42/EC in Case IV/M.1313 – Danish Crown/Vestjyske Slagterier, O.J. L 20, 25.1.2000, p. 1, points 176-179.

(67) See, e.g. Case COMP/M.2640 – Nestlé/Schöller, point 37; Commission Decision 1999/641/EC in Case COMP/M.1225 – Enso/Stora, O.J. L 254, 29.9.1999, p. 9, points 67-68.

(68) See, e.g. Case IV/M.1939 – Rexam (PLM)/American National Can, point 24.

51. In some markets where the general conditions may seem to make monitoring of deviations difficult, firms may nevertheless engage in practices which have the effect of easing the monitoring task, even when these practices are not necessarily entered into for such purposes. These practices, such as meeting-competition or most-favouredcustomer clauses, voluntary publication of information, announcements, or exchange of information through trade associations, may increase transparency or help competitors interpret the choices made. Cross-directorships, participation in joint ventures and similar arrangements may also make monitoring easier.

Deterrent mechanisms

52. Coordination is not sustainable unless the consequences of deviation are sufficiently severe to convince coordinating firms that it is in their best interest to adhere to the terms of coordination. It is thus the threat of future retaliation that keeps the coordination sustainable (69). However the threat is only credible if, where deviation by one of the firms is detected, there is sufficient certainty that some deterrent mechanism will be activated (70).

(69) See Case COMP/M.2389 – Shell/DEA, point 121, and Case COMP/M.2533 – BP/E.ON, point 111.

(70) Although deterrent mechanisms are sometimes called 'punishment' mechanisms, this should not be understood in the strict sense that such a mechanism necessarily punishes individually a firm that has deviated. The expectation that coordination may break down for a certain period of time, if a deviation is identified as such, may in itself constitute a sufficient deterrent mechanism.

53. Retaliation that manifests itself after some significant time lag, or is not certain to be activated, is less likely to be sufficient to offset the benefits from deviating. For example, if a market is characterised by infrequent, largevolume orders, it may be difficult to establish a sufficiently severe deterrent mechanism, since the gain from deviating at the right time may be large, certain and immediate, whereas the losses from being punished may be small and uncertain and only materialise after some time. The speed with which deterrent mechanisms can be implemented is related to the issue of transparency. If firms are only able to observe their competitors' actions after a substantial delay, then retaliation will be similarly delayed and this may influence whether it is sufficient to deter deviation.

54. The credibility of the deterrence mechanism depends on whether the other coordinating firms have an incentive to retaliate. Some deterrent mechanisms, such as punishing the deviator by temporarily engaging in a price war or increasing output significantly, may entail a short-term economic loss for the firms carrying out the retaliation. This does not necessarily remove the incentive to retaliate since the short-term loss may be smaller than the long-term benefit of retaliating resulting from the return to the regime of coordination.

55. Retaliation need not necessarily take place in the same market as the deviation (71). If the coordinating firms have commercial interaction in other markets, these may offer various methods of retaliation (72). The retaliation could take many forms, including cancellation of joint ventures or other forms of cooperation or selling of shares in jointly owned companies.

(71) See, e.g. Commission Decision 2000/42/EC in Case IV/M.1313 – Danish Crown/Vestjyske Slagterier, O.J. L 20, 25.1.2000, p. 1, point 177.

(72) See Case T-102/96, Gencor v Commission, [1999] ECR II-753, paragraph 281.

Reactions of outsiders

56. For coordination to be successful, the actions of non-coordinating firms and potential competitors, as well as customers, should not be able to jeopardise the outcome expected from coordination. For example, if coordination aims at reducing overall capacity in the market, this will only hurt consumers if non-coordinating firms are unable or have no incentive to respond to this decrease by increasing their own capacity sufficiently to prevent a net decrease in capacity, or at least to render the coordinated capacity decrease unprofitable (73).

(73) These elements are analysed in a similar way to non-coordinated effects.

57. The effects of entry and countervailing buyer power of customers are analysed in later sections. However, special consideration is given to the possible impact of these elements on the stability of coordination. For instance, by concentrating a large amount of its requirements with one supplier or by offering long-term contracts, a large buyer may make coordination unstable by successfully tempting one of the coordinating firms to deviate in order to gain substantial new business.

Merger with a potential competitor

58. Concentrations where an undertaking already active on a relevant market merges with a potential competitor in this market can have similar anti-competitive effects to mergers between two undertakings already active on the same relevant market and, thus, significantly impede effective competition, in particular through the creation or the strengthening of a dominant position.

59. A merger with a potential competitor can generate horizontal anti-competitive effects, whether coordinated or non-coordinated, if the potential competitor significantly constrains the behaviour of the firms active in the market. This is the case if the potential competitor possesses assets that could easily be used to enter the market without incurring significant sunk costs. Anticompetitive effects may also occur where the merging partner is very likely to incur the necessary sunk costs to enter the market in a relatively short period of time after which this company would constrain the behaviour of the firms currently active in the market (74).

(74) See, e.g. Case IV/M.1630 – Air Liquide/BOC, points 201 et seq. For an example of a case where entry by the other merging firm was not sufficiently likely in the short to medium term (Case T-158/00, ARD v Commission, [2003] ECR II-000, paragraphs 115-127).

60. For a merger with a potential competitor to have significant anti-competitive effects, two basic conditions must be fulfilled. First, the potential competitor must already exert a significant constraining influence or there must be a significant likelihood that it would grow into an effective competitive force. Evidence that a potential competitor has plans to enter a market in a significant way could help the Commission to reach such a conclusion (75). Second, there must not be a sufficient number of other potential competitors, which could maintain sufficient competitive pressure after the merger (76).

(75) Commission Decision 2001/98/EC in Case IV/M.1439 – Telia/Telenor, O.J. L 40, 9.2.2001, p. 1, points 330-331, and Case IV/M.1681 – Akzo Nobel/Hoechst Roussel Vet, point 64.

(76) Case IV/M.1630 – Air Liquide/BOC, point 219; Commission Decision 2002/164/EC in Case COMP/M.1853 – EDF/EnBW, O.J. L 59, 28.2.2002, p. 1, points 54-64.

Mergers creating or strengthening buyer power in upstream markets

61. The Commission may also analyse to what extent a merged entity will increase its buyer power in upstream markets. On the one hand, a merger that creates or strengthens the market power of a buyer may significantly impede effective competition, in particular by creating or strengthening a dominant position. The merged firm may be in a position to obtain lower prices by reducing its purchase of inputs. This may, in turn, lead it also to lower its level of output in the final product market, and thus harm consumer welfare (77). Such effects may in particular arise when upstream sellers are relatively fragmented. Competition in the downstream markets could also be adversely affected if, in particular, the merged entity were likely to use its buyer power vis-à-vis its suppliers to foreclose its rivals (78).

(77) See Commission Decision 1999/674/EC in Case M.1221 – Rewe/Meinl, O.J. L 274, 23.10.1999, p. 1, points 71-74.

(78) Case T-22/97, Kesko v Commission, [1999] ECR II-3775, paragraph 157; Commission Decision 2002/156/EC in Case M.877 – Boeing/ McDonnell Douglas, O.J. L 336, 8.12.1997, p. 16, points 105-108.

62. On the other hand, increased buyer power may be beneficial for competition. If increased buyer power lowers input costs without restricting downstream competition or total output, then a proportion of these cost reductions are likely to be passed onto consumers in the form of lower prices.

63. In order to assess whether a merger would significantly impede effective competition by creating or strengthening buyer power, an analysis of the competitive conditions in upstream markets and an evaluation of the possible positive and negative effects described above are therefore required.

V. COUNTERVAILIG BUYER POWER

64. The competitive pressure on a supplier is not only exercised by competitors but can also come from its customers. Even firms with very high market shares may not be in a position, post-merger, to significantly impede effective competition, in particular by acting to an appreciable extent independently of their customers, if the latter possess countervailing buyer power (79). Countervailing buyer power in this context should be understood as the bargaining strength that the buyer has vis-à-vis the seller in commercial negotiations due to its size, its commercial significance to the seller and its ability to switch to alternative suppliers.

(79) See, e.g. Case IV/M.1882 – Pirelli/BICC, points 73-80.

65. The Commission considers, when relevant, to what extent customers will be in a position to counter the increase in market power that a merger would otherwise be likely to create. One source of countervailing buyer power would be if a customer could credibly threaten to resort, within a reasonable timeframe, to alternative sources of supply should the supplier decide to increase prices (80) or to otherwise deteriorate quality or the conditions of delivery. This would be the case if the buyer could immediately switch to other suppliers (81), credibly threaten to vertically integrate into the upstream market or to sponsor upstream expansion or entry (82) for instance by persuading a potential entrant to enter by committing to placing large orders with this company. It is more likely that large and sophisticated customers will possess this kind of countervailing buyer power than smaller firms in a fragmented industry (83). A buyer may also exercise countervailing buying power by refusing to buy other products produced by the supplier or, particularly in the case of durable goods, delaying purchases.

(80) See, e.g. Case IV/M.1245 – Valeo/ITT Industries, point 26.

(81) Even a small number of customers may not have sufficient buyer power if they are to a large extent «locked in» because of high switching costs (see Case COMP/M.2187 – CVC/Lenzing, point 223).

(82) Commission Decision 1999/641/EC in Case COMP/M.1225 – Enso/Stora, O.J. L 254, 29.9.1999, p. 9, points 89-91.

(83) It may also be appropriate to compare the concentration existing on the customer side with the concentration on the supply side (Case COMP/JV 55 – Hutchison/RCPM/ECT, point 119, and Commission Decision 1999/641/EC in Case COMP/M.1225 – Enso/Stora, O.J. L 254, 29.9.1999, p. 9, point 97).

66. In some cases, it may be important to pay particular attention to the incentives of buyers to utilise their buyer power (84). For example, a downstream firm may not wish to make an investment in sponsoring new entry if the benefits of such entry in terms of lower input costs could also be reaped by its competitors.

(84) Case COMP/JV 55 – Hutchison/RCPM/ECT, points 129-130.

67. Countervailing buyer power cannot be found to sufficiently off-set potential adverse effects of a merger if it only ensures that a particular segment of customers (85), with particular bargaining strength, is shielded from significantly higher prices or deteriorated conditions after the merger (86). Furthermore, it is not sufficient that buyer power exists prior to the merger, it must also exist and remain effective following the merger. This is because a merger of two suppliers may reduce buyer power if it thereby removes a credible alternative.

(85) Commission Decision 2002/156/EC in Case COMP/M.2097 – SCA/ Metsä Tissue, O.J. L 57, 27.2.2002, point 88. Price discrimination between different categories of customers may be relevant in some cases in the context of market definition (See the Commission's notice on the definition of the relevant market, cited above, at paragraph 43).

(86) Accordingly, the Commission may assess whether the various purchasers will hold countervailing buyer power, see, e.g. Commission Decision 1999/641/EC in Case COMP/M.1225 – Enso/Stora, O.J. L 254, 29.9.1999, p. 9, points 84-97.

VI. ENTRY

68. When entering a market is sufficiently easy, a merger is unlikely to pose any significant anti-competitive risk. Therefore, entry analysis constitutes an important element of the overall competitive assessment. For entry to be considered a sufficient competitive constraint on the merging parties, it must be shown to be likely, timely and sufficient to deter or defeat any potential anti-competitive effects of the merger.

Likelihood of entry

69. The Commission examines whether entry is likely or whether potential entry is likely to constrain the behaviour of incumbents post-merger. For entry to be likely, it must be sufficiently profitable taking into account the price effects of injecting additional output into the market and the potential responses of the incumbents. Entry is thus less likely if it would only be economically viable on a large scale, thereby resulting in significantly depressed price levels. And entry is likely to be more difficult if the incumbents are able to protect their market shares by offering long-term contracts or giving targeted pre-emptive price reductions to those customers that the entrant is trying to acquire. Furthermore, high risk and costs of failed entry may make entry less likely. The costs of failed entry will be higher, the higher is the level of sunk cost associated with entry (87).

(87) Commission Decision 97/610/EC in Case IV/M.774 – Saint-Gobain/Wacker-Chemie/NOM, O.J. L 247, 10.9.1997, p. 1, point 184.

70. Potential entrants may encounter barriers to entry which determine entry risks and costs and thus have an impact on the profitability of entry. Barriers to entry are specific features of the market, which give incumbent firms advantages over potential competitors. When entry barriers are low, the merging parties are more likely to be constrained by entry. Conversely, when entry barriers are high, price increases by the merging firms would not be significantly constrained by entry. Historical examples of entry and exit in the industry may provide useful information about the size of entry barriers.

71. Barriers to entry can take various forms:

(a) Legal advantages encompass situations where regulatory barriers limit the number of market participants by, for example, restricting the number of licences (88). They also cover tariff and non-tariff trade barriers (89).

(b) The incumbents may also enjoy technical advantages, such as preferential access to essential facilities, natural resources (90), innovation and R & D (91), or intellectual property rights (92), which make it difficult for any firm to compete successfully. For instance, in certain industries, it might be difficult to obtain essential input materials, or patents might protect products or processes. Other factors such as economies of scale and scope, distribution and sales networks (93), access to important technologies, may also constitute barriers to entry.

(c) Furthermore, barriers to entry may also exist because of the established position of the incumbent firms on the market. In particular, it may be difficult to enter a particular industry because experience or reputation is necessary to compete effectively, both of which may be difficult to obtain as an entrant. Factors such as consumer loyalty to a particular brand (94), the closeness of relationships between suppliers and customers, the importance of promotion or advertising, or other advantages relating to reputation (95) will be taken into account in this context. Barriers to entry also encompass situations where the incumbents have already committed to building large excess capacity (96), or where the costs faced by customers in switching to a new supplier may inhibit entry.

(88) Case IV/M.1430 – Vodafone/Airtouch, point 27; Case IV/M.2016 – France Télécom/Orange, point 33.

(89) Commission Decision 2002/174/EC in Case COMP/M.1693 – Alcoa/Reynolds, O.J. L 58, 28.2.2002, point 87.

(90) Commission Decision 95/335/EC in Case IV/M.754 – Anglo American Corp./Lonrho, O.J. L 149, 20.5.1998, p. 21, points 118-119.

(91) Commission Decision 97/610/EC in Case IV/M.774 – Saint-Gobain/Wacker-Chemie/NOM, O.J. L 247, 10.9.1997, p. 1, points 184-187.

(92) Commission Decision 94/811/EC in Case IV/M.269 – Shell/Montecatini, O.J. L 332, 22.12.1994, p. 48, point 32.

(93) Commission Decision 98/327/EC in Case IV/M.833 – The Coca-Cola Company/Carlsberg A/S, O.J. L 145, 15.5.1998, p. 41, point 74.

(94) Commission Decision 98/327/EC in Case IV/M.833 – The Coca-Cola Company/Carlsberg A/S, O.J. L 145, 15.5.1998, p. 41, points 72-73.

(95) Commission Decision 2002/156/EC in Case COMP/M.2097 – SCA/Metsä Tissue, O.J. L 57, 27.2.2002, p. 1, points 83-84.

(96) Commission Decision 2001/432/EC in Case IV/M.1813 – Industri Kapital Nordkem/Dyno, O.J. L 154, 9.6.2001, p. 41, point 100.

72. The expected evolution of the market should be taken into account when assessing whether or not entry would be profitable. Entry is more likely to be profitable in a market that is expected to experience high growth in the future (97) than in a market that is mature or expected to decline (98). Scale economies or network effects may make entry unprofitable unless the entrant can obtain a sufficiently large market share (99).

(97) See, e.g. Commission Decision 98/475/EC in Case IV/M.986 – Agfa-Gevaert/Dupont, O.J. L 211, 29.7.1998, p. 22, points 84-85.

(98) Case T-102/96, Gencor v Commission, [1999] ECR II-753, paragraph 237.

(99) See, e.g. Commission Decision 2000/718/EC in Case IV/M.1578 – Sanitec/Sphinx, O.J. L 294, 22.11.2000, p. 1, point 114.

73. Entry is particularly likely if suppliers in other markets already possess production facilities that could be used to enter the market in question, thus reducing the sunk costs of entry. The smaller the difference in profitability between entry and non-entry prior to the merger, the more likely such a reallocation of production facilities.

Timeliness

74. The Commission examines whether entry would be sufficiently swift and sustained to deter or defeat the exercise of market power. What constitutes an appropriate time period depends on the characteristics and dynamics of the market, as well as on the specific capabilities of potential entrants (100). However, entry is normally only considered timely if it occurs within two years.

(100) See, e.g. Commission Decision 2002/174/EC in Case COMP/M.1693 – Alcoa/Reynolds, L 58, 28.2.2002, points 31-32, 38.

Sufficiency

75. Entry must be of sufficient scope and magnitude to deter or defeat the anti-competitive effects of the merger (101). Small-scale entry, for instance into some market 'niche', may not be considered sufficient.

(101) Commission Decision 91/535/EEC in Case IV/M.68 – Tetra Pak/Alfa Laval, O.J. L 290, 22.10.1991, p. 35, point 3.4.

VII. EFFICIENCIES

76. Corporate reorganisations in the form of mergers may be in line with the requirements of dynamic competition and are capable of increasing the competitiveness of industry, thereby improving the conditions of growth and raising the standard of living in the Community (102). It is possible that efficiencies brought about by a merger counteract the effects on competition and in particular the potential harm to consumers that it might otherwise have (103). In order to assess whether a merger would significantly impede effective competition, in particular through the creation or the strengthening of a dominant position, within the meaning of Article 2(2) and (3) of the Merger Regulation, the Commission performs an overall competitive appraisal of the merger. In making this appraisal, the Commission takes into account the factors mentioned in Article 2(1), including the development of technical and economic progress provided that it is to the consumers' advantage and does not form an obstacle to competition (104).

(102) See Recital 4 of the Merger Regulation.

(103) See Recital 29 of the Merger Regulation.

(104) *Cf.* Article 2(1)*(b)* of the Merger Regulation.

77. The Commission considers any substantiated efficiency claim in the overall assessment of the merger. It may decide that, as a consequence of the efficiencies that the merger brings about, there are no grounds for declaring the merger incompatible with the common market pursuant to Article 2(3) of the Merger Regulation. This will be the case when the Commission is in a position to conclude on the basis of sufficient evidence that the efficiencies generated by the merger are likely to enhance the ability and incentive of the merged entity to act pro-competitively for the benefit of consumers, thereby counteracting the adverse effects on competition which the merger might otherwise have.

78. For the Commission to take account of efficiency claims in its assessment of the merger and be in a position to reach the conclusion that as a consequence of efficiencies, there are no grounds for declaring the merger to be incompatible with the common market, the efficiencies have to benefit consumers, be merger-specific and be verifiable. These conditions are cumulative.

Benefit to consumers

79. The relevant benchmark in assessing efficiency claims is that consumers (105) will not be worse off as a result of the merger. For that purpose, efficiencies should be substantial and timely, and should, in principle, benefit consumers in those relevant markets where it is otherwise likely that competition concerns would occur.

(105) Pursuant to Article 2(1)(b), the concept of 'consumers' encompasses intermediate and ultimate consumers, i.e. users of the products covered by the merger. In other words, consumers within the meaning of this provision include the customers, potential and/or actual, of the parties to the merger.

80. Mergers may bring about various types of efficiency gains that can lead to lower prices or other benefits to consumers. For example, cost savings in production or distribution may give the merged entity the ability and incentive to charge lower prices following the merger. In line with the need to ascertain whether efficiencies will lead to a net benefit to consumers, cost efficiencies that lead to reductions in variable or marginal costs (106) are more likely to be relevant to the assessment of efficiencies than reductions in fixed costs; the former are, in principle, more likely to result in lower prices for consumers (107). Cost reductions, which merely result from anti-competitive reductions in output, cannot be considered as efficiencies benefiting consumers.

(106) Variable costs should be viewed as those costs that vary with the level of production or sales over the relevant time period. Marginal costs are those costs associated with expanding production or sales at the margin.

(107) Generally, fixed cost savings are not given such weight as the relationship between fixed costs and consumer prices is normally less direct, at least in the short run.

81. Consumers may also benefit from new or improved products or services, for instance resulting from efficiency gains in the sphere of R & D and innovation. A joint venture company set up in order to develop a new product may bring about the type of efficiencies that the Commission can take into account.

82. In the context of coordinated effects, efficiencies may increase the merged entity's incentive to increase production and reduce prices, and thereby reduce its incentive to coordinate its market behaviour with other firms in the market. Efficiencies may therefore lead to a lower risk of coordinated effects in the relevant market.

83. In general, the later the efficiencies are expected to materialise in the future, the less weight the Commission can assign to them. This implies that, in order to be considered as a counteracting factor, the efficiencies must be timely.

84. The incentive on the part of the merged entity to pass efficiency gains on to consumers is often related to the existence of competitive pressure from the remaining firms in the market and from potential entry. The greater the possible negative effects on competition, the more the Commission has to be sure that the claimed efficiencies are substantial, likely to be realised, and to be passed on, to a sufficient degree, to the consumer. It is highly unlikely that a merger leading to a market position approaching that of a monopoly, or leading to a similar level of market power, can be declared compatible with the common market on the ground that efficiency gains would be sufficient to counteract its potential anti-competitive effects.

Merger specificity

85. Efficiencies are relevant to the competitive assessment when they are a direct consequence of the notified merger and cannot be achieved to a similar extent by less anticompetitive alternatives. In these circumstances, the efficiencies are deemed to be caused by the merger and thus, merger-specific (108). It is for the merging parties to provide in due time all the relevant information necessary to demonstrate that there are no less anticompetitive, realistic and attainable alternatives of a non-concentrative nature (e.g. a licensing agreement, or a cooperative joint venture) or of a concentrative nature (e.g. a concentrative joint venture, or a differently structured merger) than the notified merger which preserve the claimed efficiencies. The Commission only considers alternatives that are reasonably practical in the business situation faced by the merging parties having regard to established business practices in the industry concerned.

(108) In line with the general principle set out in paragraph 9 of this notice.

Verifiability

86. Efficiencies have to be verifiable such that the Commission can be reasonably certain that the efficiencies are likely to materialise, and be substantial enough to counteract a merger's potential harm to consumers. The more precise and convincing the efficiency claims are, the better the Commission can evaluate the claims. Where reasonably possible, efficiencies and the resulting benefit to consumers should therefore be quantified. When the necessary data are not available to allow for a precise quantitative analysis, it must be possible to foresee a clearly identifiable positive impact on consumers, not a marginal one. In general, the longer the start of the efficiencies is projected into the future, the less probability the Commission may be able to assign to the efficiencies actually being brought about.

87. Most of the information, allowing the Commission to assess whether the merger will bring about the sort of efficiencies that would enable it to clear a merger, is solely in the possession of the merging parties. It is, therefore, incumbent upon the notifying parties to provide in due time all the relevant information necessary to demonstrate that the claimed efficiencies are merger-specific and likely to be realised. Similarly, it is for the notifying parties to show to what extent the efficiencies are likely to counteract any adverse effects on competition that might otherwise result from the merger, and therefore benefit consumers.

88. Evidence relevant to the assessment of efficiency claims includes, in particular, internal documents that were used by the management to decide on the merger, statements from the management to the owners and financial markets about the expected efficiencies, historical examples of efficiencies and consumer benefit, and pre-merger external experts' studies on the type and size of efficiency gains, and on the extent to which consumers are likely to benefit.

VIII. FAILING FIRM

89. The Commission may decide that an otherwise problematic merger is nevertheless compatible with the common market if one of the merging parties is a failing firm. The basic requirement is that the deterioration of the competitive structure that follows the merger cannot be said to be caused by the merger (109). This will arise where the competitive structure of the market would deteriorate to at least the same extent in the absence of the merger (110).

(109) Joined Cases C-68/94 and C-30/95, Kali and Salz, paragraph 110.

(110) Joined Cases C-68/94 and C-30/95, Kali and Salz, paragraph 114. See also Commission Decision 2002/365/EC in Case COMP/M.2314 – BASF/Pantochim/Eurodiol, O.J. L 132, 17.5.2002, p. 45, points 157-160. This requirement is linked to the general principle set out in paragraph 9 of this notice.

90. The Commission considers the following three criteria to be especially relevant for the application of a «failing firm defence». First, the allegedly failing firm would in the near future be forced out of the market because of financial difficulties if not taken over by another undertaking. Second, there is no less anti-competitive alternative purchase than the notified merger. Third, in the absence of a merger, the assets of the failing firm would inevitably exit the market (111).

(111) The inevitability of the assets of the failing firm leaving the market in question may, in particular in a case of merger to monopoly, underlie a finding that the market share of the failing firm would in any event accrue to the other merging party. See Joined Cases C-68/94 and C-30/95, Kali and Salz, paragraphs 115-116.

91. It is for the notifying parties to provide in due time all the relevant information necessary to demonstrate that the deterioration of the competitive structure that follows the merger is not caused by the merger.

Guidelines on the assessment of non-horizontal mergers under the Council Regulation on the control of concentrations between undertakings

(OJ C 265, 18 October 2008, p. 6)

I. INTRODUCTION

1. Article 2 of Council Regulation (EC) N° 139/2004 of 20 January 2004 on the control of concentrations between undertakings (1) (hereinafter: the «Merger Regulation») provides that the Commission has to appraise concentrations within the scope of the Merger Regulation with a view to establishing whether or not they are compatible with the common market. For that purpose, the Commission must assess, pursuant to Article 2(2) and (3), whether or not a concentration would significantly impede effective competition, in particular as a result of the creation or strengthening of a dominant position in the common market or a substantial part of it.

(1) Council Regulation (EC) N° 139/2004 of 20 January 2004 (O.J. L 24, 29.1.2004, p. 1).

2. This document develops guidance as to how the Commission assesses concentrations (2) where the undertakings concerned are active on different relevant markets (3). In this document, these concentrations will be called «non-horizontal mergers».

(2) The term concentration used in the Merger Regulation covers various types of transactions such as mergers, acquisitions, takeovers, and certain types of joint ventures. In the remainder of this Document, unless otherwise specified, the term «merger» will be used as a synonym for concentration and therefore cover all the above types of transactions.

(3) Guidance on the assessment of mergers involving undertakings which are actual or potential competitors on the same relevant market («horizontal mergers») is given in the Commission Notice: Guidelines on the assessment of horizontal mergers under the Council Regulation on the control of concentrations between undertakings (O.J. C 31, 5.2.2004, p. 5) («Notice on Horizontal Mergers»).

3. Two broad types of non-horizontal mergers can be distinguished: vertical mergers and conglomerate mergers.

4. Vertical mergers involve companies operating at different levels of the supply chain. For example, when a manufacturer of a certain product (the «upstream firm») merges with one of its distributors (the «downstream firm»), this is called a vertical merger (4).

(4) In the present document, the terms «downstream» and «upstream» are used to describe the (potential) commercial relationship that the merging entities have with each other. Generally the commercial relationship is one where the «downstream» firm purchases the output from the «upstream» firm and uses it as an input in its own production, which it then sells on to its customers. The market where the former transactions take place is referred to as the intermediate market (upstream market). The latter market is referred to as the downstream market.

5. Conglomerate mergers are mergers between firms that are in a relationship which is neither horizontal (as competitors in the same relevant market) nor vertical (as suppliers or customers) (5). In practice, the focus of the present guidelines is on mergers between companies that are active in closely related markets (e.g. mergers involving suppliers of complementary products or products that belong to the same product range).

(5) The distinction between conglomerate mergers and horizontal mergers may be subtle, e.g. when a conglomerate merger involves products that are weak substitutes for each other. The same holds true for the distinction between conglomerate mergers and vertical mergers. For instance, products may be supplied by some companies with the inputs already integrated (vertical relationship), whereas other producers leave it to the customers to select and assemble the inputs themselves (conglomerate relationship).

6. The general guidance already given in the Notice on horizontal mergers is also relevant in the context of non-horizontal mergers. The purpose of the present document is to concentrate on the competition aspects that are relevant to the specific context of non-horizontal mergers. In addition, it will set out the Commission's approach to market shares and concentration thresholds in this context.

7. In practice, mergers may entail both horizontal and non-horizontal effects. This may for instance be the case where the merging firms are not only in a vertical or conglomerate relationship, but are also actual or potential competitors of each other in one or more of the relevant markets concerned (6). In such a case, the Commission will appraise horizontal, vertical and/or conglomerate effects in accordance with the guidance set out in the relevant notices (7).

(6) For instance, in certain markets upstream or downstream firms are often well-placed potential entrants. See e.g. in the electricity and gas sector, Case COMP/M.3440 – EDP/ENI/GDP (2004). The same may hold for producers of complementary products. See e.g. in the liquid packaging sector, Case COMP/M.2416 – TetraLaval/Sidel (2001).

(7) Guidance on the assessment of mergers with a potential competitor is given in the Notice on horizontal mergers, in particular at paragraphs 58 to 60 thereof.

8. The guidance set out in this document draws and elaborates on the Commission's evolving experience with the appraisal of non-horizontal mergers under Regulation (EEC) N° 4064/89 since its entry into force on 21 September 1990, the Merger Regulation presently in force as well as on the case-law of the Court of Justice and the Court of First Instance of the European Communities. The principles contained here will be applied and further developed and refined by the Commission in individual cases. The Commission may revise the notice on non-horizontal mergers from time to time in the light of future developments and of evolving insight.

9. The Commission's interpretation of the Merger Regulation as regards the appraisal of non-horizontal mergers is without prejudice to the interpretation which may be given by the Court of Justice or the Court of First Instance of the European Communities.

II. OVERVIEW

10. Effective competition brings benefits to consumers, such as low prices, high quality products, a wide selection of goods and services, and innovation. Through its control of mergers, the Commission prevents mergers that would be likely to deprive customers of these benefits by significantly increasing the market power of firms. An «increase in market power» in this context refers to the ability of one or more firms to profitably increase prices, reduce output, choice or quality of goods and services, diminish innovation, or otherwise negatively influence parameters of competition (8).

(8) In this document, the expression «increased prices» is often used as shorthand for these various ways in which a merger may result in competitive harm. The expression should also be understood to cover situations where, for instance, prices are decreased less, or are less likely to decrease, than they otherwise would have without the merger and where prices are increased more, or are more likely to increase, than they otherwise would have without the merger.

11. Non-horizontal mergers are generally less likely to significantly impede effective competition than horizontal mergers.

12. First, unlike horizontal mergers, vertical or conglomerate mergers do not entail the loss of direct competition between the merging firms in the same relevant market (9). As a result, the main source of anti-competitive effect in horizontal mergers is absent from vertical and conglomerate mergers.

(9) Such a loss of direct competition can, nevertheless, arise where one of the merging firms is a potential competitor in the relevant market where the other merging firm operates. See paragraph 7 above.

13. Second, vertical and conglomerate mergers provide substantial scope for efficiencies. A characteristic of vertical mergers and certain conglomerate mergers is that the activities and/or the products of the companies involved are complementary to each other (10). The integration of complementary activities or products within a single firm may produce significant efficiencies and be pro-competitive. In vertical relationships for instance, as a result of the complementarity, a decrease in mark-ups downstream will lead to higher demand also upstream. A part of the benefit of this increase in demand will accrue to the upstream suppliers. An integrated firm will take this benefit into account. Vertical integration may thus provide an increased incentive to seek to decrease prices and increase output because the integrated firm can capture a larger fraction of the benefits. This is often referred to as the «internalisation of double mark-ups». Similarly, other efforts to increase sales at one level (e.g. improve service or stepping up innovation) may provide a greater reward for an integrated firm that will take into account the benefits accruing at other levels.

(10) In this document, products or services are called «complementary» (or «economic complements») when they are worth more to a customer when used or consumed together than when used or consumed separately. Also a merger between upstream and downstream activities can be seen as a combination of complements which go into the final product. For instance, both production and distribution fulfil a complementary role in getting a product to the market.

14. Integration may also decrease transaction costs and allow for a better co-ordination in terms of product design, the organisation of the production process, and the way in which the products are sold. Similarly, mergers which involve products belonging to a range or portfolio of products that are generally sold to the same set of customers (be they complementary products or not) may give rise to customer benefits such as one-stop-shopping.

15. However, there are circumstances in which non-horizontal mergers may significantly impede effective competition, in particular as a result of the creation or strengthening of a dominant position. This is essentially because a non-horizontal merger may change the ability and incentive to compete on the part of the merging companies and their competitors in ways that cause harm to consumers.

16. In the context of competition law, the concept of «consumers» encompasses intermediate and ultimate consumers (11). When intermediate customers are actual or potential competitors of the parties to the merger, the Commission focuses on the effects of the merger on the customers to which the merged entity and those competitors are selling. Consequently, the fact that a merger affects competitors is not in itself a problem. It is the impact on effective competition that matters, not the mere impact on competitors at some level of the supply chain (12). In particular, the fact that rivals may be harmed because a merger creates efficiencies cannot in itself give rise to competition concerns.

(11) See Article 2(1)(b) of the Merger Regulation and paragraph 84 of the Communication from the Commission – Notice – Guidelines on the application of Article 81(3) of the Treaty (O.J. C 101, 27.4.2004, p. 97).

(12) One example of this approach can be found in the case COMP/M.3653 – Siemens/VA Tech (2005), in which the Commission assessed the effect of the transaction on the two complementary markets for electrical rail vehicles and electrical traction systems for rail vehicles, which combine into a full rail vehicle. While the merger allegedly reduced the independent supply of electrical traction systems, there would still be several integrated suppliers which could deliver the rail vehicle. The Commission thus concluded that even if the merger had negative consequences for independent suppliers of electrical rail vehicles «sufficient competition would remain in the relevant downstream market for rail vehicles».

17. There are two main ways in which non-horizontal mergers may significantly impede effective competition: non-coordinated effects and coordinated effects (13).

(13) See section II of the Notice on Horizontal Mergers.

18. Non-coordinated effects may principally arise when non-horizontal mergers give rise to foreclosure. In this document, the term «foreclosure» will be used to describe any instance where actual or potential rivals' access to supplies or markets is hampered or eliminated as a result of the merger, thereby reducing these companies' ability and/or incentive to compete. As a result of such foreclosure, the merging companies – and, possibly, some of its competitors as well – may be able to profitably increase the price (14) charged to consumers. These instances give rise to a significant impediment to effective competition and are therefore referred to hereafter as «anticompetitive foreclosure».

(14) For the meaning of the expression «increased prices» see footnote 8.

19. Coordinated effects arise where the merger changes the nature of competition in such a way that firms that previously were not coordinating their behaviour, are now significantly more likely to coordinate to raise prices or otherwise harm effective competition. A merger may also make coordination easier, more stable or more effective for firms which were coordinating prior to the merger.

20. In assessing the competitive effects of a merger, the Commission compares the competitive conditions that would result from the notified merger with the conditions that would have prevailed without the merger (15). In most cases the competitive conditions existing at the time of the merger constitute the relevant comparison for evaluating the effects of a merger. However, in some circumstances, the Commission will take into account future changes to the market that can reasonably be predicted. It may, in particular, take account of the likely entry or exit of firms if the merger did not take place when considering what constitutes the relevant comparison. The Commission may take into account future market developments that result from impending regulatory changes (16).

(15) By analogy, in the case of a merger that has been implemented without having been notified, the Commission would assess the merger in the light of the competitive conditions that would have prevailed without the implemented merger.

(16) This may be particularly relevant in cases where effective competition is expected to arise in the future as a result of market opening. See e.g. Case COMP/M.3696 – *E.ON/MOL* (2005), at points 457 to 463.

21. In its assessment, the Commission will consider both the possible anti-competitive effects arising from the merger and the possible pro-competitive effects stemming from substantiated efficiencies benefiting consumers (17). The Commission examines the various chains of cause and effect with a view to ascertaining which of them is the most likely. The more immediate and direct the perceived anti-competitive effects of a merger, the more likely the Commission is to raise competition concerns. Likewise, the more immediate and direct the pro-competitive effects of a merger, the more likely the Commission is to find that they counteract any anti-competitive effects.

(17) See section VII on efficiencies in the Notice on Horizontal Mergers.

22. This document describes the main scenarios of competitive harm and sources of efficiencies in the context of vertical mergers and, subsequently, in the context of conglomerate mergers.

III. MARKET SHARE AND CONCENTRATION LEVELS

23. Non-horizontal mergers pose no threat to effective competition unless the merged entity has a significant degree of market power (which does not necessarily amount to dominance) in at least one of the markets concerned. The Commission will examine this issue before proceeding to assess the impact of the merger on competition.

24. Market shares and concentration levels provide useful first indications of the market power and the competitive importance of both the merging parties and their competitors (18).

(18) See also section III of the Notice on Horizontal Mergers. The calculation of market shares depends critically on market definition (see Commission notice on the definition of the relevant market for the purposes of Community competition law (O.J. C 372, 9.12.1997)). Special care must be taken in contexts where vertically integrated companies supply products internally.

25. The Commission is unlikely to find concern in non-horizontal mergers, be it of a coordinated or of a non-coordinated nature, where the market share post-merger of the new entity in each of the markets concerned is below 30% (19) and the post-merger H.H.I. is below 2000.

(19) In analogy to the indications given in Commission Regulation (EC) N° 2790/1999 of 22 December 1999 on the application of Article 81(3) of the Treaty to categories of vertical agreements and concerted practices (O.J. L 336, 29.12.1999, p. 21). Where a merged entity would have a market share just above the 30% threshold on one market but substantially below on other, related, markets competition concerns will be less likely.

26. In practice, the Commission will not extensively investigate such mergers, except where special circumstances such as, for instance, one or more of the following factors are present:

(a) a merger involves a company that is likely to expand significantly in the near future, e.g. because of a recent innovation;

(b) there are significant cross-shareholdings or cross-directorships among the market participants;

(c) one of the merging firms is a firm with a high likelihood of disrupting coordinated conduct;

(d) indications of past or ongoing coordination, or facilitating practices, are present.

27. The Commission will use the above market share and H.H.I. thresholds as an initial indicator of the absence of competition concerns. However, these thresholds do not give rise to a legal presumption. The Commission is of the opinion that it is less appropriate in this context to present market share and concentration levels above which competition concerns would be deemed to be likely, as the existence of a significant degree of market power in at least one of the markets concerned is a necessary condition for competitive harm, but is not a sufficient condition (20).

(20) See sections IV and V.

IV. VERTICAL MERGERS

28. This section sets out the Commission's framework of analysis in the context of vertical mergers. In its assessment, the Commission will consider both the possible anti-competitive effects arising from vertical mergers and the possible pro-competitive effects stemming from efficiencies substantiated by the parties.

A. Non-coordinated effects: foreclosure

29. A merger is said to result in foreclosure where actual or potential rivals' access to supplies or markets is hampered or eliminated as a result of the merger, thereby reducing these companies' ability and/or incentive to compete. Such foreclosure may discourage entry or expansion of rivals or encourage their exit. Foreclosure thus can be found even if the foreclosed rivals are not forced to exit the market: It is sufficient that the rivals are disadvantaged and consequently led to compete less effectively. Such foreclosure is regarded as anti-competitive where the merging companies – and, possibly, some of its competitors as well – are as a result able to profitably increase the price charged to consumers (21).

(21) For the meaning of the expression «increased prices» see footnote 8. For the meaning of «consumers», see footnote 16.

30. Two forms of foreclosure can be distinguished. The first is where the merger is likely to raise the costs of downstream rivals by restricting their access to an important input (input foreclosure). The second is where the merger is likely to foreclose upstream rivals by restricting their access to a sufficient customer base (customer foreclosure) (22).

(22) See Merger Regulation, Article 2(1)(b), referring to «access to supplies» and «access to (...) markets», respectively.

1. Input foreclosure

31. Input foreclosure arises where, post-merger, the new entity would be likely to restrict access to the products or services that it would have otherwise supplied absent the merger, thereby raising its downstream rivals' costs by making it harder for them to obtain supplies of the input under similar prices and conditions as absent the merger. This may lead the merged entity to profitably increase the price charged to consumers, resulting in a significant impediment to effective competition. As indicated above, for input foreclosure to lead to consumer harm, it is not necessary that the merged firm's rivals are forced to exit the market. The relevant benchmark is whether the increased input costs would lead to higher prices for consumers. Any efficiencies resulting from the merger may, however, lead the merged entity to reduce price, so that the overall likely impact on consumers is neutral or positive. A graphical presentation of this mechanism is provided in Figure 1.

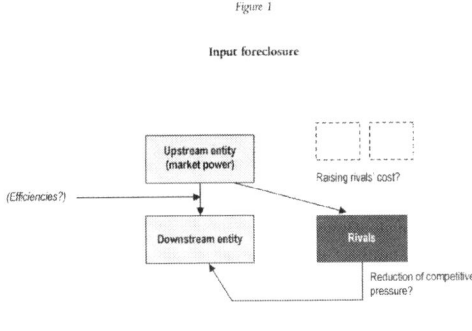

Figure 1

Input foreclosure

32. In assessing the likelihood of an anticompetitive input foreclosure scenario, the Commission examines, first, whether the merged entity would have, post-merger, the ability to substantially foreclose access to inputs, second, whether it would have the incentive to do so, and third, whether a foreclosure strategy would have a significant detrimental effect on competition downstream (23). In practice, these factors are often examined together since they are closely intertwined.

(23) See e.g. Case COMP/M.4300 – Philips/Intermagnetics, COMP/M.4314 – Johnson & Johnson/Pfizer Consumer Healthcare, COMP/M.4389 – WLR/BST, COMP/M.4403 – Thales/Finmeccanica/Alcatel Alenia Space and Telespazio, COMP/M.4494 – Evraz/Highveld, and COMP/M.4561 – GE/Smiths Aerospace.

A. Ability to foreclose access to inputs (24)

(24) The term «inputs» is used here as a generic term and may also cover services, access to infrastructure and access to intellectual property rights.

33. Input foreclosure may occur in various forms. The merged entity may decide not to deal with its actual or potential competitors in the vertically related market. Alternatively, the merged firm may decide to restrict supplies and/or to raise the price it charges when supplying competitors and/or to otherwise make the conditions of supply less favourable than they would have been absent the merger (25). Further, the merged entity may opt for a specific choice of technology within the new firm which is not compatible with the technologies chosen by rival firms (26). Foreclosure may also take more subtle forms, such as the degradation of the quality of input supplied (27). In its assessment, the Commission may consider a series of alternative or complementary possible strategies.

(25) See e.g. Case COMP/M.1693 – Alcoa/Reynolds (2000), Case COMP/M.4403 – Thales/Finmeccanica/Alcatel Alenia Space/Telespazio, points 257-260.

(26) See e.g. Case COMP/M.2861 – Siemens/Drägerwerk/JV (2003), Case COMP/M.3998 – Axalto, point 75.

(27) See e.g. Case COMP/M.4314 – Johnson & Johnson/Pfizer Consumer Healthcare, points 127-130.

34. Input foreclosure may raise competition problems only if it concerns an important input for the downstream product (28). This is the case, for example, when the input concerned represents a significant cost factor relative to the price of the downstream product. Irrespective of its cost, an input may also be sufficiently important for other reasons. For instance, the input may be a critical component without which the downstream product could not be manufactured or effectively sold on the market (29), or it may represent a significant source of product differentiation for the downstream product (30). It may also be that the cost of switching to alternative inputs is relatively high.

(28) See e.g. Case COMP/M.3868 – Dong/Elsam/Energi E2, Case COMP/M.4094 – Ineos/BP Dormagen, points 183-184, Case COMP/M.4561 – GE/Smiths Aerospace, points 48-50.

(29) For instance, an engine starter can be considered a critical component to an engine (Case T-210/01, General Electric v Commission (2005) ECR II-000); see also, e.g. Case COMP/M.3410 – Total/GDF, points 53-54 and 60-61.

(30) For instance, personal computers are often sold with specific reference to the type of microprocessor they contain.

35. For input foreclosure to be a concern, the vertically integrated firm resulting from the merger must have a significant degree of market power in the upstream market. It is only in these circumstances that the merged firm can be expected to have a significant influence on the conditions of competition in the upstream market and thus, possibly, on prices and supply conditions in the downstream market.

36. The merged entity would only have the ability to foreclose downstream competitors if, by reducing access to its own upstream products or services, it could negatively affect the overall availability of inputs for the downstream market in terms of price or quality. This may be the case where the remaining upstream suppliers are less efficient, offer less preferred alternatives, or lack the ability to expand output in response to the supply restriction, for example because they face capacity constraints or, more generally, face decreasing returns to scale (31). Also, the presence of exclusive contracts between the merged entity and independent input providers may limit the ability of downstream rivals to have adequate access to inputs.

(31) See e.g. Case COMP/M.4494 – *Evraz/Highveld*, point 92 and points 97-112.

37. When determining the extent to which input foreclosure may occur, it must be taken into account that the decision of the merged entity to rely on its upstream division's supply of inputs may also free up capacity on the part of the remaining input suppliers from which the downstream division used to purchase before. In fact, the merger may merely realign purchase patterns among competing firms.

38. When competition in the input market is oligopolistic, a decision of the merged entity to restrict access to its inputs reduces the competitive pressure exercised on remaining input suppliers, which may allow them to raise the input price they charge to non-integrated downstream competitors. In essence, input foreclosure by the merged entity may expose its downstream rivals to non-vertically integrated suppliers with increased market power (32). This increase in third-party market power will be greater the lower the degree of product differentiation between the merged entity and other upstream suppliers and the higher the degree of upstream concentration. However, the attempt to raise the input price may fail when independent input suppliers, faced with a reduction in the demand for their products (from the downstream division of the merged entity or from independent downstream firms), respond by pricing more aggressively (33).

(32) The analysis of the likely effect of the removal of a competitive constraint is similar to the analysis of non-coordinated effects with horizontal mergers (see section IV of the Notice on Horizontal Mergers).

(33) Also the nature of the supply contracts between upstream suppliers and the downstream independent firms may be important in this respect. For instance, when these contracts use a price system combining a fixed fee and a per-unit supply price, the effect on downstream competitors' marginal costs may be affected less than when these contracts involve only per-unit supply prices.

39. In its assessment, the Commission will consider, on the basis of the information available, whether there are effective and timely counter-strategies that the rival firms would be likely to deploy. Such counterstrategies include the possibility of changing their production process so as to be less reliant on the input concerned or sponsoring the entry of new suppliers upstream.

B. Incentive to foreclose access to inputs

40. The incentive to foreclose depends on the degree to which foreclosure would be profitable. The vertically integrated firm will take into account how its supplies of inputs to competitors downstream will affect not only the profits of its upstream division, but also of its downstream division. Essentially, the merged entity faces a trade-off between the profit lost in the upstream market due to a reduction of input sales to (actual or potential) rivals and the profit gain, in the short or longer term, from expanding sales downstream or, as the case may be, being able to raise prices to consumers.

41. The trade-off is likely to depend on the level of profits the merged entity obtains upstream and downstream (34). Other things constant, the lower the margins upstream, the lower the loss from restricting input sales. Similarly, the higher the downstream margins, the higher the profit gain from increasing market share downstream at the expense of foreclosed rivals (35).

(34) See e.g. Case COMP/M.4300 – *Philips/Intermagnetics*, points 56-62, Case COMP/M.4576 – *AVR/Van Gansewinkel*, points 33-38.

(35) It has to be considered that upstream and downstream margins may change as a result of the merger. This may impact upon the merged entity's incentive to engage in foreclosure.

42. The incentive for the integrated firm to raise rivals' costs further depends on the extent to which downstream demand is likely to be diverted away from foreclosed rivals and the share of that diverted demand that the downstream division of the integrated firm can capture (36). This share will normally be higher the less capacity constrained the merged entity will be relative to non-foreclosed downstream rivals and the more the products of the merged entity and foreclosed competitors are close substitutes. The effect on downstream demand will also be higher if the affected input represents a significant proportion of downstream rivals' costs or if the affected input represents a critical component of the downstream product (37).

(36) See e.g. Case COMP/M.3943 – *Saint-Gobain/BPB* (2005), point 78. The Commission noted that it would be very unlikely that BPB, the main supplier of plaster board in the UK, would cut back on supplies to rival distributors of Saint-Gobain, in part because expansion of Saint-Gobain's distribution capacity was difficult.

(37) Conversely, if the input accounts only for a small share of the downstream product and is not a critical component, even a high market share upstream may not give the merged entity the incentive to foreclose downstream rivals because few, if any, sales would be diverted to the integrated firm's downstream unit. See e.g. Case COMP/M.2738 – *GEES/Unison*; Case COMP M.4561 – *GE/Smiths Aerospace*, points 60-62.

43. The incentive to foreclose actual or potential rivals may also depend on the extent to which the downstream division of the integrated firm can be expected to benefit from higher price levels downstream as a result of a strategy to raise rivals' costs (38). The greater the market shares of the merged entity downstream, the greater the base of sales on which to enjoy increased margins (39).

(38) See e.g. Case COMP/M.4314 – *Johnson & Johnson/Pfizer Consumer Healthcare*, points 131-132.

(39) It must be noted that the less the merged firm can target a specific downstream market, the less it is likely to raise its prices for the input it supplies, as it would have to incur opportunity costs in other downstream markets. In this respect, the extent to which the merged entity can price discriminate when the merged entity supplies several downstream markets and/or ancillary markets may be taken into account (e.g. for spare parts).

44. An upstream monopolist that is already able to fully extract all available profits in vertically related markets may not have any incentive to foreclose rivals following a vertical merger. The ability to extract available profits from the consumers does not follow immediately from a very high market share (40). Such a finding would require a more thorough analysis of the actual and future constraints under which the monopolist operates. When all available profits cannot be extracted, a vertical merger – even if it involves an upstream monopolist – may give the merged entity the incentive to raise the costs of downstream rivals, thereby reducing the competitive constraint they exert on the merged entity in the downstream market.

(40) One situation in which this may not be the case would be when the monopolist has a so-called commitment problem which it is unable to solve. For example, a downstream buyer may be willing to pay a high price to an upstream monopolist if the latter does not subsequently sell additional quantities to a competitor. But once the terms of supply are fixed with one downstream firm, the upstream supplier may have an incentive to increase its supplies to other downstream firms, thereby making the

first purchase unprofitable. Since downstream firms will anticipate this kind of opportunistic behavior, the upstream supplier will be unable to fully exploit its market power. Vertical integration may restore the upstream supplier's ability to commit not to expand input sales as this would harm its own downstream division. Another case in which the monopolist cannot obtain all available monopoly profits may arise when the company cannot differentiate its prices among customers.

45. In its assessment of the likely incentives of the merged firm, the Commission may take into account various considerations such as the ownership structure of the merged entity (41), the type of strategies adopted on the market in the past (42) or the content of internal strategic documents such as business plans.

(41) For instance, in cases where two companies have joint control over a firm active in the upstream market, and only one of them is active downstream, the company without downstream activities may have little interest in foregoing input sales. In such cases, the incentive to foreclose is smaller than when the upstream company is fully controlled by a company with downstream activities. See e.g. Case COMP/M.3440 – EDP/ENI/GDP (2004), Case COMP/M.4403 – Thales/Finmeccanica/Alcatel Alenia Space/Telespazio, points 121 and 268.

(42) The fact that, in the past, a competitor with a similar market position as the merged entity has stopped supplying inputs may demonstrate that it is commercially rational to adopt such a strategy (see e.g. COMP/M.3225 – Alcan/Pechiney (2004), at point 40).

46. In addition, when the adoption of a specific course of conduct by the merged entity is an essential step in foreclosure, the Commission examines both the incentives to adopt such conduct and the factors liable to reduce, or even eliminate, those incentives, including the possibility that the conduct is unlawful. Conduct may be unlawful inter alia because of competition rules or sector-specific rules at the EU or national levels. This appraisal, however, does not require an exhaustive and detailed examination of the rules of the various legal orders which might be applicable and of the enforcement policy practised within them (43). Moreover, the illegality of a conduct may be likely to provide significant disincentives for the merged entity to engage in such conduct only in certain circumstances. In particular, the Commission will consider, on the basis of a summary analysis: *(i)* the likelihood that this conduct would be clearly, or highly probably, unlawful under Community law (44), *(ii)* the likelihood that this illegal conduct could be detected (45), and *(iii)* the penalties which could be imposed.

(43) Case C-12/03 P, *Commission v Tetra Laval BV* (2003) ECR I-000, paragraphs 74-76. Case T-210/01, *General Electric v Commission* (2005) ECR II-000, at paragraph 73.

(44) Case T-210/01, *General Electric v Commission* (2005) ECR II-000, specifically at points 74-75 and 311-312.

(45) For instance, in Case COMP/M.3696 – *E.ON/MOL* (2005), points 433 and 443-446, the Commission attached importance to the fact that the national Hungarian regulator for the gas sector indicated that in a number of settings, although it has the right to control and to force market players to act without discrimination, it would not be able to obtain adequate information on the commercial behaviour of the operators. See also Case COMP/M.3440 – *EDP/ENI/GDP* (2004), point 424.

C. Overall likely impact on effective competition

47. In general, a merger will raise competition concerns because of input foreclosure when it would lead to increased prices in the downstream market thereby significantly impeding effective competition.

48. First, anticompetitive foreclosure may occur when a vertical merger allows the merging parties to increase the costs of downstream rivals in the market thereby leading to an upward pressure on their sales prices. Significant harm to effective competition normally requires that the foreclosed firms play a sufficiently important role in the competitive process on the downstream market. The higher the proportion of rivals which would be foreclosed on the downstream market, the more likely the merger can be expected to result in a significant price increase in the downstream market and, therefore, to significantly impede effective competition therein (46). Despite a relatively small market share compared to other players, a specific firm may play a significant competitive role compared to other players (47), for instance because it is a close competitor of the vertically integrated firm or because it is a particularly aggressive competitor.

(46) See e.g. Case COMP/M.4494 – *Evraz/Highveld*, points 97-112.

(47) See e.g. Case COMP/M.3440 – *EDP/ENI/GDP* (2004).

49. Second, effective competition may be significantly impeded by raising barriers to entry to potential competitors (48). A vertical merger may foreclose potential competition on the downstream market when the merged entity would be likely not to supply potential downstream entrants, or only on less favourable terms than absent the merger. The mere likelihood that the merged entity would carry out a foreclosure strategy post-merger may already create a strong deterrent effect on potential entrants (49). Effective competition on the downstream market may be significantly impeded by raising barriers to entry, in particular if input foreclosure would entail for such potential competitors the need to enter at both the downstream and the upstream level in order to compete effectively on either market. The concern of raising entry barriers is particularly relevant in those industries that are opening up to competition or are expected to do so in the foreseeable future (50).

(48) See e.g. Case COMP/M.4180 – *Gaz de France/Suez*, points 876-931, Case COMP/M.4576 – *AVR/Van Gansewinkel*, points 33-38.

(49) See Case COMP/M.3696 – *E.ON/MOL* (2005), at point 662 et seq.

(50) See paragraph 20. It is important that regulatory measures aimed at opening a market are not rendered ineffective through vertically-related incumbent companies merging and thereby closing off the market, or eliminating each other as potential entrants.

50. If there remain sufficient credible downstream competitors whose costs are not likely to be raised, for example because they are themselves vertically integrated (51) or they are capable of switching to adequate alternative inputs, competition from those firms may constitute a sufficient constraint on the merged entity and therefore prevent output prices from rising above pre-merger levels.

(51) See e.g. Case COMP/M.3653 – *Siemens/VA Tech* (2005), at point 164.

51. The effect on competition on the downstream market must also be assessed in light of countervailing factors such as the presence of buyer power (52) or the likelihood that entry upstream would maintain effective competition (53).

(52) See section V on countervailing buyer power in the Notice on Horizontal Mergers.

(53) See section VI on entry in the Notice on Horizontal Mergers.

52. Further, the effect on competition needs to be assessed in light of efficiencies substantiated by the merging parties (54) The Commission may decide that, as a consequence of the efficiencies that the merger brings about, there are no grounds for declaring the merger incompatible with the common market pursuant to Article 2(3) of the Merger Regulation. This will be the case when the Commission is in a position to conclude on the basis of sufficient evidence that the efficiencies generated by the merger are likely to enhance the ability and incentive of the merged entity to act pro-competitively for the benefit of consumers, thereby counteracting the adverse effects on competition which the merger might otherwise have.

(54) See section VII on efficiencies in the Notice on Horizontal Mergers.

53. When assessing efficiencies in the context of non-horizontal mergers, the Commission applies the principles already set out in section VII of the Notice on Horizontal Mergers In particular, for the Commission to take account of efficiency claims in its assessment of the merger, the efficiencies have to benefit consumers, be merger-specific and be verifiable. These conditions are cumulative (55).

(55) See, more specifically, paragraphs 79 to 88 of the Notice on Horizontal Mergers.

54. Vertical mergers may entail some specific sources of efficiencies, the list of which is not exhaustive.

55. In particular, a vertical merger allows the merged entity to internalise any pre-existing double mark-ups resulting from both parties setting their prices independently pre-merger (56). Depending on the market conditions, reducing the combined mark-up (relative to a situation where pricing decisions at both levels are not aligned) may allow the vertically integrated firm to profitably expand output on the downstream market (57).

(56) See also paragraph 13 above.

(57) It is important to recognise, however, that the problem of double mark-ups is not always present or significant pre-merger, for instance because the merging parties had already concluded a supply agreement with a price mechanism providing for volume discounts eliminating the mark-up. The efficiencies associated with the elimination of double mark-ups may thus not always be merger specific because vertical cooperation or vertical agreements may, short of a merger, achieve similar benefits with less anti-competitive effects. In addition, a merger may not fully eliminate the double mark-up when the supply of the input is limited by capacity constraints and there is an equally profitable alternative use for the input. In such circumstances, the internal use of the input entails an opportunity cost for the vertically integrated company: using more of the input internally to increase output downstream means selling less in the alternative market. As a result, the incentive to use the input internally and increase output downstream is less than when there is no opportunity cost.

56. A vertical merger may further allow the parties to better coordinate the production and distribution process, and therefore to save on inventories costs.

57. More generally, a vertical merger may align the incentives of the parties with regard to investments in new products, new production processes and in the marketing of products. For instance, whereas before the merger, a downstream distributor entity might have been reluctant to invest in advertising and informing customers about the qualities of products of the upstream entity when such investment would also have benefited the sale of other downstream firms, the merged entity may reduce such incentive problems.

2. Customer foreclosure

58. Customer foreclosure may occur when a supplier integrates with an important customer in the downstream market (58). Because of this downstream presence, the merged entity may foreclose access to a sufficient customer base to its actual or potential rivals in the upstream market (the input market) and reduce their ability or incentive to compete. In turn, this may raise downstream rivals' costs by making it harder for them to obtain supplies of the input under similar prices and conditions as absent the merger. This may allow the merged entity profitably to establish higher prices on the downstream market. Any efficiencies resulting from the merger, however, may lead the merged entity to reduce price, so that there is overall not a negative impact on consumers. For customer foreclosure to lead to consumer harm, it is thus not necessary that the merged firm's rivals are forced to exit the market. The relevant benchmark is whether the increased input costs would lead to higher prices for consumers. A graphical presentation of this mechanism is provided in Figure 2.

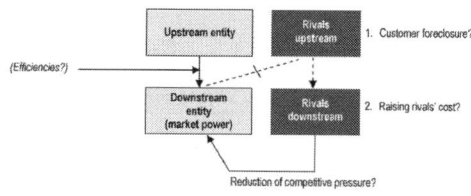

(58) See footnote 4 for the definition of «downstream» and «upstream».

59. In assessing the likelihood of an anticompetitive customer foreclosure scenario, the Commission examines, first, whether the merged entity would have the ability to foreclose access to downstream markets by reducing its purchases from its upstream rivals, second, whether it would have the incentive to reduce its purchases upstream, and third, whether a foreclosure strategy would have a significant detrimental effect on consumers in the downstream market (59).

(59) See e.g. Case COMP/M.4389 – WLR/BST.

A. Ability to foreclose access to downstream markets

60. A vertical merger may affect upstream competitors by increasing their cost to access downstream customers or by restricting access to a significant customer base. Customer foreclosure may take various forms. For instance, the merged entity may decide to source all of its required goods or services from its upstream division and, as a result, may stop purchasing from its upstream competitors. It may also reduce its purchases from upstream rivals, or purchase from those rivals on less favourable terms than it would have done absent the merger (60).

(60) For instance, in cases involving distribution, the merged entity may be less likely to grant access to its outlets under the same conditions as absent the merger.

61. When considering whether the merged entity would have the ability to foreclose access to downstream markets, the Commission examines whether there are sufficient economic alternatives in the downstream market for the upstream rivals (actual or potential) to sell their output (61). For customer foreclosure to be a concern, it must be the case that the vertical merger involves a company which is an important customer with a significant degree of market power in the downstream market (62). If, on the contrary, there is a sufficiently large customer base, at present or in the future, that is likely to turn to independent suppliers, the Commission is unlikely to raise competition concerns on that ground (63).

(61) The loss of the integrated firm as a customer is normally less significant if that firm's pre-merger purchases from non-integrated firms are a small share of the available sales base for those firms. In that case, sufficient alternative customers are more likely to be available. The presence of exclusive contracts between the merged entity and other downstream firms may limit the ability of upstream rivals to reach a sufficient sales volume.

(62) See e.g. Case COMP/M.2822 – *ENBW/ENI/GVS* (2002) at points 54-57.

(63) See e.g. Case COMP/M.81 – *VIAG/Continental Can* (1991), point 51, see e.g. Case COMP/M.4389 – *WLR/BST*, points 33-35.

62. Customer foreclosure can lead to higher input prices in particular if there are significant economies of scale or scope in the input market or when demand is characterised by network effects (64). It is mainly in such circumstances that the ability to compete of upstream rivals, be they actual or potential, can be impaired.

(64) Economies of scale or scope exist when an increase in scale or scope of production leads to a reduction in average unit cost. Network effects occur when the value of a product for a customer increases when the number of other customers also using it increases. Examples include communication devices, specific software programmes, products requiring standardisation, and platforms bringing together buyers and sellers.

63. For instance, customer foreclosure can lead to higher input prices when existing upstream rivals operate at or close to their minimum efficient scale. To the extent that customer foreclosure and the corresponding loss of output for the upstream rivals increases their variable costs of production, this may result in an upward pressure on the prices they charge to their customers operating in the downstream market.

64. In the presence of economies of scale or scope, customer foreclosure may also render entry upstream by potential entrants unattractive by significantly reducing the revenue prospects of potential entrants. When customer foreclosure effectively results in entry deterrence, input prices may remain at a higher level than otherwise would have been the case, thereby raising the cost of input supply to downstream competitors of the merged firm.

65. Further, when customer foreclosure primarily impacts upon the revenue streams of upstream rivals, it may significantly reduce their ability and incentive to invest in cost reduction, R & D and product quality (65). This may reduce their ability to compete in the long run and possibly even cause their exit from the market.

(65) An input supplier foreclosed from an important customer may prefer to stay out of the market if it fails to reach some minimum viable scale following the investment. Such minimum viable scale may be achieved, however, if a potential entrant has access to a broader customer base including customers in other relevant markets. See Case COMP/M.1879 – *Boeing/Hughes* (2000); Case COMP/M.2978 – *Lagardère/Natexis/VUP* (2003).

66. In its assessment, the Commission may take into account the existence of different markets corresponding to different uses for the input. If a substantial part of the downstream market is foreclosed, an upstream supplier may fail to reach efficient scale and may also operate at higher costs in the other market(s). Conversely, an upstream supplier may continue to operate efficiently if it finds other uses or secondary markets for its input without incurring significantly higher costs.

67. In its assessment, the Commission will consider, on the basis of the information available, whether there are effective and timely counter-strategies, sustainable over time, that the rival firms would be likely to deploy. Such counterstrategies include the possibility that upstream rivals decide to price more aggressively to maintain sales levels in the downstream market, so as to mitigate the effect of foreclosure (66).

(66) For instance, in Case COMP/M.1879 – *Boeing/Hughes* (2000), point 100, it was considered, among several other factors, that in view of the high fixed costs involved, if competing satellite launch vehicle providers were to become less cost-competitive relative to the merged entity, they would try to cut prices in order to salvage volume and recoup at least part of their fixed costs rather than accept losing a contract and incur a higher loss. The most likely impact would therefore be greater price competition rather than market monopolisation.

B. Incentive to foreclose access to downstream markets

68. The incentive to foreclose depends on the degree to which it is profitable. The merged entity faces a trade-off between the possible costs associated with not procuring products from upstream rivals and the possible gains from doing so, for instance, because it allows the merged entity to raise price in the upstream or downstream markets.

69. The costs associated with reducing purchases from rival upstream suppliers are higher, when the upstream division of the integrated firm is less efficient than the foreclosed suppliers. Such costs are also higher if the upstream division of the merged firm is capacity constrained or rivals' products are more attractive due to product differentiation.

70. The incentive to engage in customer foreclosure further depends on the extent to which the upstream division of the merged entity can benefit from possibly higher price levels in the upstream market arising as a result of upstream rivals being foreclosed. The incentive to engage in customer foreclosure also becomes higher, the more the downstream division of the integrated firm can be expected to enjoy the benefits of higher price levels downstream resulting from the foreclosure strategy. In this context, the greater the market shares of the merged entity's downstream operations, the greater the base of sales on which to enjoy increased margins (67).

(67) If the vertically integrated firm partially supplies inputs to downstream competitors it may benefit from the ability to expand sales, or as the case may be, to increase input prices.

71. When the adoption of a specific conduct by the merged entity is an essential step in foreclosure, the Commission examines both the incentives to adopt such conduct and the factors liable to reduce, or even eliminate, those incentives, including the possibility that the conduct is unlawful (68).

(68) The analysis of these incentives will be conducted as set out in paragraph 46 above.

C. Overall likely impact on effective competition

72. Foreclosing rivals in the upstream market may have an adverse impact in the downstream market and harm consumers. By denying competitive access to a significant customer base for the foreclosed rivals' (upstream) products, the merger may reduce their ability to compete in the foreseeable future. As a result, rivals downstream are likely to be put at a competitive disadvantage, for example in the form of raised input costs. In turn, this may allow the merged entity to profitably raise prices or reduce the overall output on the downstream market.

73. The negative impact on consumers may take some time to materialise when the primary impact of customer foreclosure is on the revenue streams of upstream rivals, reducing their incentives to make investments in cost reduction, product quality or in other competitive dimensions so as to remain competitive.

74. It is only when a sufficiently large fraction of upstream output is affected by the revenue decreases resulting from the vertical merger that the merger may significantly impede effective competition on the upstream market. If there remain a number of upstream competitors that are not affected, competition from those firms may be sufficient to prevent prices from rising in the upstream market and, consequently, in the downstream market. Sufficient competition from these non-foreclosed upstream firms requires that they do not face barriers to expansion *e.g.* through capacity constraints or product differentiation (69). When the reduction of competition upstream affects a significant fraction of output downstream, the merger is likely, as with input foreclosure, to result in a significant increase of the price level in the downstream market and, therefore, to significantly impede effective competition (70).

(69) The analysis of such non-coordinated effects bears similarities with the analysis of non-coordinated effects in horizontal mergers (see section IV of the Notice on Horizontal Mergers).

(70) See paragraph 47-50 of the present Notice.

75. Effective competition on the upstream market may also be significantly impeded by raising barriers to entry to potential competitors. This may be so in particular if customer foreclosure would entail for such potential competitors the need to enter at both the downstream and the upstream level in order to compete effectively on either market. In such a context, customer foreclosure and input foreclosure may thus be part of the same strategy. The concern of raising entry barriers is particularly relevant in those industries that are opening up to competition or are expected to do so in the foreseeable future (71).

(71) It is important that regulatory measures aimed at opening a market are not rendered ineffective through vertically-related incumbent companies merging and thereby closing off the market, or eliminating each other as potential entrants.

76. The effect on competition must be assessed in light of countervailing factors such as the presence of countervailing buyer power (72) or the likelihood that entry would maintain effective competition in the upstream or downstream markets (73).

(72) See section V on countervailing buyer power in the Notice on Horizontal Mergers.

(73) See section VI on entry in the Notice on Horizontal Mergers.

77. Further, the effect on competition needs to be assessed in light of efficiencies substantiated by the merging parties (74).

(74) For the assessment of efficiencies in a vertical context, see section V.A.1 above.

B. Other non-coordinated effects

78. The merged entity may, by vertically integrating, gain access to commercially sensitive information regarding the upstream or downstream activities of rivals (75). For instance, by becoming the supplier of a downstream competitor, a company may obtain critical information, which allows it to price less aggressively in the downstream market to the detriment of consumers (76). It may also put competitors at a competitive disadvantage, thereby dissuading them to enter or expand in the market.

(75) See Case COMP/M.1879 – *Boeing/Hughes* (2000); Case COMP/M.2510 – *Cendant/Galileo*, point 37; Case COMP/M.2738 – *Gees/Unison*, point 21; Case COMP/M.2925 – *Charterhouse/CDC/Telediffusion de France*, point 37-38; Case COMP/M.3440 – *EDP/ENI/GDP* (2004).

(76) See *e.g.* Case COMP/M.2822 – *ENBW/ENI/GVS* (2002), at point 56; Case COMP/M.3440 – *EDP/ENI/GDP* (2004), points 368-379; Case COMP/M.3653 – *Siemens/VA Tech* (2005) points 159-164.

C. Coordinated effects

79. As set out in section IV of the Notice on Horizontal Mergers, a merger may change the nature of competition in such a way that firms that previously were not coordinating their behaviour, are now significantly more likely to coordinate and raise prices or otherwise harm effective competition. A merger may also make coordination easier, more stable or more effective for firms which were coordinating prior to the merger (77).

(77) See Case COMP/M.3101 – *Accor/Hilton/Six Continents*, points 23-28.

80. Market coordination may arise where competitors are able, without entering into an agreement or resorting to a concerted practice within the meaning of Article 81 of the Treaty, to identify and pursue common objectives, avoiding the normal mutual competitive pressure by a coherent system of implicit threats. In a normal competitive setting, each firm constantly has an incentive to compete. This incentive is ultimately what keeps prices low, and what prevents firms from jointly maximising their profits. Coordination involves a departure from normal competitive conditions in that firms are able to sustain prices in excess of what independent short term profit maximisation would yield. Firms will refrain from undercutting the high prices charged by their competitors in a coordinated way because they anticipate that such behaviour would jeopardise coordination in the future. For coordinated effects to arise, the profit that firms could make by competing aggressively in the short term («deviating») has to be less than the expected reduction in revenues that this behaviour would entail in the longer term, as it would be expected to trigger an aggressive response by competitors («a punishment»).

81. Coordination is more likely to emerge in markets where it is relatively simple to reach a common understanding on the terms of coordination. In addition, three conditions are necessary for coordination to be sustainable. First, the coordinating firms must be able to monitor to a sufficient degree whether the terms of coordination are being adhered to. Second, discipline requires that there is some form of deterrent mechanism that can be activated if deviation is detected. Third, the reactions of outsiders, such as current and future competitors not participating in the coordination, as well as customers, should not be able to jeopardise the results expected from the coordination (78).

(78) See Case T-342/99, *Airtours v Commission* (2002) ECR II-2585, paragraph 62.

Reaching terms of coordination

82. A vertical merger may make it easier for the firms in the upstream or downstream market to reach a common understanding on the terms of coordination (79).

(79) See *e.g.* Case COMP/M.3314 – *Air Liquide/Messer Targets*, points 91-100.

83. For instance, when a vertical merger leads to foreclosure (80), it results in a reduction in the number of effective competitors in the market. Generally speaking, a reduction in the number of players makes it easier to coordinate among the remaining market players.

(80) Foreclosure would have to be shown by the Commission along the lines of Part A of this section.

84. Vertical mergers may also increase the degree of symmetry between firms active in the market (81). This may increase the likelihood of coordination by making it easier to reach a common understanding on the terms of coordination. Likewise, vertical integration may increase the level of market transparency, making it easier to coordinate among the remaining market players.

(81) See Case COMP/M.2389 – *Shell/DEA*; Case COMP/M.2533 – *BP/EON*. Alternatively, vertical integration may also decrease the degree of symmetry between firms active in the market, rendering coordination more difficult.

85. Further, a merger may involve the elimination of a maverick in a market. A maverick is a supplier that for its own reasons is unwilling to accept the co-ordinated outcome and thus maintains aggressive competition. The vertical integration of the maverick may alter its incentives to such an extent that co-ordination will no longer be prevented.

Monitoring deviations

86. Vertical integration may facilitate coordination by increasing the level of market transparency between firms through access to sensitive information on rivals or by making it easier to monitor pricing. Such concerns may arise, for example, if the level of price transparency is higher downstream than upstream. This could be the case when prices to final consumers are public, while transactions at the intermediate market are confidential. Vertical integration may give upstream producers control over final prices and thus monitor deviations more effectively.

87. When it leads to foreclosure, a vertical merger may also induce a reduction in the number of effective competitors in a market. A reduction in the number of players may make it easier to monitor each other's actions in the market.

Deterrent mechanisms

88. Vertical mergers may affect coordinating firms' incentives to adhere to the terms of coordination. For instance, a vertically integrated company may be in a position to more effectively punish rival companies when they choose to deviate from the terms of coordination, because it is either a crucial customer or supplier to them (82).

(82) For instance, in a case that was subsequently withdrawn (Case COMP/M.2322 – *CRH/Addtek* (2001)) the merger involved an upstream dominant supplier of cement and a downstream producer or pre-cast concrete products, both active in Finland. The Commission provisionally took the view in the administrative procedure that the new entity would be able to discipline the downstream rivals by using the fact that they would be highly dependent on cement supplies of the merged entity. As a result, the downstream entity would be able to increase the price of its pre-cast concrete products while making sure that the competitors would follow these price increases and avoiding that they turn to cement imports from the Baltic States and Russia.

Reactions of outsiders

89. Vertical mergers may reduce the scope for outsiders to destabilise the coordination by increasing barriers to enter the market or otherwise limiting the ability to compete on the part of outsiders to the coordination.

90. A vertical merger may also involve the elimination of a disruptive buyer in a market. If upstream firms view sales to a particular buyer as sufficiently important, they may be tempted to deviate from the terms of co-ordination in an effort to secure their business. Similarly, a large buyer may be able to tempt the co-ordinating firms to deviate from these terms by concentrating a large amount of its requirements on one supplier or by offering long term contracts. The acquisition of such a buyer may increase the risk of co-ordination in a market.

V. CONGLOMERATE MERGERS

91. Conglomerate mergers are mergers between firms that are in a relationship which is neither purely horizontal (as competitors in the same relevant market) nor vertical (as supplier and customer). In practice, the focus is on mergers between companies that are active in closely related markets (83) (*e.g.* mergers involving suppliers of complementary products or of products which belong to a range of products that is generally purchased by the same set of customers for the same end use).

(83) See also Form CO, section IV, 6.3(c).

92. Whereas it is acknowledged that conglomerate mergers in the majority of circumstances will not lead to any competition problems, in certain specific cases there may be harm to competition. In its assessment, the Commission will consider both the possible anti-competitive effects arising from conglomerate mergers and the possible pro-competitive effects stemming from efficiencies substantiated by the parties.

A. Non-coordinated effects: foreclosure

93. The main concern in the context of conglomerate mergers is that of foreclosure. The combination of products in related markets may confer on the merged entity the ability and incentive to leverage (84) a strong market position from one market to another by means of tying or bundling or other exclusionary practices (85). Tying and bundling as such are common practices that often have no anticompetitive consequences. Companies engage in tying and bundling in order to provide their customers with better products or offerings in cost-effective ways. Nevertheless, in certain circumstances, these practices may lead to a reduction in actual or potential rivals' ability or incentive to compete. This may reduce the competitive pressure on the merged entity allowing it to increase prices.

(84) There is no received definition of «leveraging» but, in a neutral sense, it implies being able to increase sales of a product in one market (the «tied market» or «bundled market»), by virtue of the strong market position of the product to which it is tied or bundled (the «tying market» or «leveraging market»).

(85) These concepts are defined further below.

94. In assessing the likelihood of such a scenario, the Commission examines, first, whether the merged firm would have the ability to foreclose its rivals, second, whether it would have the economic incentive to do so and, third, whether a foreclosure strategy would have a significant detrimental effect on competition, thus causing harm to consumers (86). In practice, these factors are often examined together as they are closely intertwined.

(86) See Case T-210/01, *General Electric v Commission* (2005) ECR II-000, paragraphs 327, 362-363, 405; Case COMP/M.3304 – *GE/Amersham* (2004), point 37, and Case COMP/M.4561 – *GE/Smiths Aerospace*, points 116-126.

A. Ability to foreclose

95. The most immediate way in which the merged entity may be able to use its market power in one market to foreclose competitors in another is by conditioning sales in a way that links the products in the separate markets together. This is done most directly either by tying or bundling.

96. «Bundling» usually refers to the way products are offered and priced by the merged entity. One can distinguish in this respect between pure bundling and mixed bundling. In the case of pure bundling the products are only sold jointly in fixed proportions. With mixed bundling the products are also available separately, but the sum of the stand-alone prices is higher than the bundled price (87). Rebates, when made dependent on the purchase of other goods, may be considered a form of mixed bundling.

(87) The distinction between mixed bundling and pure bundling is not necessarily clear-cut. Mixed bundling may come close to pure bundling when the prices charged for the individual offerings are high.

97. «Tying» usually refers to situations where customers that purchase one good (the tying good) are required to also purchase another good from the producer (the tied good). Tying can take place on a technical or contractual basis. For instance, technical tying occurs when the tying product is designed in such a way that it only works with the tied product (and not with the alternatives offered by competitors). Contractual tying entails that the customer when purchasing the tying good undertakes only to purchase the tied product (and not the alternatives offered by competitors).

98. The specific characteristics of the products may be relevant for determining whether any of these means of linking sales between separate markets are available to the merged entity. For instance, pure bundling is very unlikely to be possible if products are not bought simultaneously or by the same customers (88). Similarly, technical tying is only an option in certain industries.

(88) See e.g. Case COMP/M.3304 – GE/Amersham (2004), point 35.

99. In order to be able to foreclose competitors, the new entity must have a significant degree of market power, which does not necessarily amount to dominance, in one of the markets concerned. The effects of bundling or tying can only be expected to be substantial when at least one of the merging parties' products is viewed by many customers as particularly important and there are few relevant alternatives for that product, e.g. because of product differentiation (89) or capacity constraints on the part of rivals.

(89) For instance, in the context of branded products, particularly important products are sometimes referred to as «must stock» products. See e.g. Case COMP/M.3732 – Procter&Gamble/Gillette (2005), point 110.

100. Further, for foreclosure to be a potential concern it must be the case that there is a large common pool of customers for the individual products concerned. The more customers tend to buy both products (instead of only one of the products), the more demand for the individual products may be affected through bundling or tying. Such a correspondence in purchasing behaviour is more likely to be significant when the products in question are complementary.

101. Generally speaking, the foreclosure effects of bundling and tying are likely to be more pronounced in industries where there are economies of scale and the demand pattern at any given point in time has dynamic implications for the conditions of supply in the market in the future. Notably, where a supplier of complementary goods has market power in one of the products (product A), the decision to bundle or tie may result in reduced sales by the non-integrated suppliers of the complementary good (product B). If further there are network externalities at play (90) this will significantly reduce these rivals' scope for expanding sales of product B in the future. Alternatively, where entry into the market for the complementary product is contemplated by potential entrants, the decision to bundle by the merged entity may have the effect of deterring such entry. The limited availability of complementary products with which to combine may, in turn, discourage potential entrants to enter market A.

(90) When a product features network externalities, this means that customers or producers derive benefit from the fact that other customers or producers are using the same products as well. Examples include communication devices, specific software programmes, products requiring standardisation, and platforms bringing together buyers and sellers.

102. It can also be noted that the scope for foreclosure tends to be smaller where the merging parties cannot commit to making their tying or bundling strategy a lasting one, for example through technical tying or bundling which is costly to reverse.

103. In its assessment, the Commission considers, on the basis of the information available, whether there are effective and timely counter-strategies that the rival firms may deploy. One such example is when a strategy of bundling would be defeated by single-product companies combining their offers so as to make them more attractive to customers (91). Bundling is further less likely to lead to foreclosure if a company in the market would purchase the bundled products and profitably resell them unbundled. In addition, rivals may decide to price more aggressively to maintain market share, mitigating the effect of foreclosure (92).

(91) See e.g. Case COMP/M.3304 – GE/Amersham (2004), point 39.

(92) See e.g. Case COMP/M.1879 – Boeing/Hughes (2000), point 100; Case COMP/M.3304 – GE/Amersham (2004), point 39. The resulting loss of revenues may, however, in certain circumstances, have an impact on the ability of rivals to compete. See section C.

104. Customers may have a strong incentive to buy the range of products concerned from a single source (one-stop-shopping) rather than from many suppliers, e.g. because it saves on transaction costs. The fact that the merged entity will have a broad range or portfolio of products does not, as such, raise competition concerns (93).

(93) See e.g. Case COMP/M.2608 – INA/FAG, point 34.

B. Incentive to foreclose

105. The incentive to foreclose rivals through bundling or tying depends on the degree to which this strategy is profitable. The merged entity faces a trade-off between the possible costs associated with bundling or tying its products and the possible gains from expanding market shares in the market(s) concerned or, as the case may be, being able to raise price in those market(s) due to its market power.

106. Pure bundling and tying may entail losses for the merged company itself. For instance, if a significant number of customers are not interested in buying the bundle, but instead prefers to buy only one product (e.g. the product used to leverage), sales of that product (as contained in the bundle) may significantly fall. Furthermore, losses on the leveraging product may arise where customers who, before the merger, used to «mix and match» the leveraging product of a merging party with the product of another company, decide to purchase the bundle offered by rivals or no longer to purchase at all (94).

(94) See e.g. Case COMP/M.3304 – *GE/Amersham* (2004), point 59.

107. In this context it may thus be relevant to assess the relative value of the different products. By way of example, it is unlikely that the merged entity would be willing to forego sales on one highly profitable market in order to gain market shares on another market where turnover is relatively small and profits are modest.

108. However, the decision to bundle and tie may also increase profits by gaining market power in the tied goods market, protecting market power in the tying goods market, or a combination of the two (see section C below).

109. In its assessment of the likely incentives of the merged firm, the Commission may take into account other factors such as the ownership structure of the merged entity (95), the type of strategies adopted on the market in the past or the content of internal strategic documents such as business plans.

(95) For instance, in cases where two companies have joint control over a firm active in one market, and only one of them is active on the neighbouring market, the company without activities on the latter market may have little interest in foregoing sales in the former market. See e.g. Case T-210/01, *General Electric v Commission* (2005) ECR II-000, paragraph 385 and Case COMP/M.4561 – *GE/Smiths Aerospace*, point 119.

110. When the adoption of a specific conduct by the merged entity is an essential step in foreclosure, the Commission examines both the incentives to adopt such conduct and the factors liable to reduce, or even eliminate, those incentives, including the possibility that the conduct is unlawful (96).

(96) The analysis of these incentives will be conducted as set out in paragraph 46 above.

C. Overall likely impact on prices and choice

111. Bundling or tying may result in a significant reduction of sales prospects faced by single-component rivals in the market. The reduction in sales by competitors is not in and of itself a problem. Yet, in particular industries, if this reduction is significant enough, it may lead to a reduction in rivals' ability or incentive to compete. This may allow the merged entity to subsequently acquire market power (in the market for the tied or bundled good) and/or to maintain market power (in the market for the tying or leveraging good).

112. In particular, foreclosure practices may deter entry by potential competitors. They may do so for a specific market by reducing sales prospects for potential rivals in that market to a level below minimum viable scale. In the case of complementary products, deterring entry in one market through bundling or tying may also allow the merged entity to deter entry in another market if the bundling or tying forces potential competitors to enter both product markets at the same time rather than entering only one of them or entering them sequentially. The latter may have a significant impact in particular in those industries where the demand pattern at any given point in time has dynamic implications for the conditions of supply in the market in the future.

113. It is only when a sufficiently large fraction of market output is affected by foreclosure resulting from the merger that the merger may significantly impede effective competition. If there remain effective single-product players in either market, competition is unlikely to deteriorate following a conglomerate merger. The same holds when few single-product rivals remain, but these have the ability and incentive to expand output.

114. The effect on competition needs to be assessed in light of countervailing factors such as the presence of countervailing buyer power (97) or the likelihood that entry would maintain effective competition in the upstream or downstream markets (98).

(97) See section V on countervailing buyer power in the Notice on Horizontal Mergers.

(98) See e.g. Case COMP/M.3732 – *Procter&Gamble/Gillette* (2005), point 131. See also section VI on entry in the Notice on Horizontal Mergers.

115. Further, the effect on competition needs to be assessed in light of the efficiencies substantiated by the merging parties (99).

(99) See section VII on efficiencies in the Notice on Horizontal Mergers.

116. Many of the efficiencies identified in the context of vertical mergers may, *mutatis mutandis*, also apply to conglomerate mergers involving complementary products.

117. Notably, when producers of complementary goods are pricing independently, they will not take into account the positive effect of a drop in the price of their product on the sales of the other product. Depending on the market conditions, a merged firm may internalise this effect and may have a certain incentive to lower margins if this leads to higher overall profits (this incentive is often referred to as the «Cournot effect»). In most cases, the merged firm will make the most out of this effect by means of mixed bundling, i.e. by making the price drop conditional upon whether or not the customer buys both products from the merged entity (100).

(100) It is important to recognise however that the problem of double mark-ups is not always present or significant pre-merger. In the context of mixed bundling, it must further be noted that while the merged entity may have an incentive to reduce the price for the bundle, the effect on the prices of the individual products is less clear cut. The incentive for the merged entity to raise its single product prices may come from the fact that it counts on selling more bundled products instead. The merged entity's bundle price and prices of the individually sold products (if any) will further depend on the price reactions of rivals in the market.

118. Specific to conglomerate mergers is that they may produce cost savings in the form of economies of scope (either on the production or the consumption side), yielding an inherent advantage to supplying the goods together rather than apart (101). For instance, it may be more efficient that certain components are marketed together as a bundle rather than separately. Value enhancements for the customer can result from better compatibility and quality assurance of complementary components. Such economies of scope however are necessary but not sufficient to provide an efficiency justification for bundling or tying. Indeed, benefits from economies of scope frequently can be realised without any need for technical or contractual bundling.

(101) See e.g. Case COMP/M.3732 – *Procter&Gamble/Gillette* (2005), point 131.

B. Co-ordinated effects

119. Conglomerate mergers may in certain circumstances facilitate anticompetitive co-ordination in markets, even in the absence of an agreement or a concerted practice within the meaning of Article 81 of the Treaty. The framework set out in section IV of the Notice on Horizontal Mergers also applies in this context. In particular, co-ordination is more likely to emerge in markets where it is fairly easy to identify the terms of co-ordination and where such co-ordination is sustainable.

120. One way in which a conglomerate merger may influence the likelihood of a coordinated outcome in a given market is by reducing the number of effective competitors to such an extent that tacit coordination becomes a real possibility. Also when rivals are not excluded from the market, they may find themselves in a more vulnerable situation. As a result, foreclosed rivals may choose not to contest the situation of co-ordination, but may prefer instead to live under the shelter of the increased price level.

121. Further, a conglomerate merger may increase the extent and importance of multi-market competition. Competitive interaction on several markets may increase the scope and effectiveness of disciplining mechanisms in ensuring that the terms of co-ordination are being adhered to.

Commission Notice on restrictions directly related and necessary to concentrations
(OJ C 56, 5 March 2005, p. 24)

I. INTRODUCTION

1. Council Regulation (EC) N° 139/2004 of 20 January 2004 on the control of concentrations between undertakings (the EC Merger Regulation) (1) provides in Article 6(1)(b), second subparagraph, in Article 8(1), second subparagraph and in Article 8(2), third subparagraph that a decision declaring a concentration compatible with the common market «shall be deemed to cover restrictions directly related and necessary to the implementation of the concentration».

(1) O.J. L 24, 29.1.2004, p. 1.

2. The amendment of the rules governing the assessment of restrictions directly related and necessary to the implementation of the concentration (hereinafter also referred to as «ancillary restraints») introduces a principle of self-assessment of such restrictions. This reflects the intention of the legislature not to oblige the Commission to assess and individually address ancillary restraints. The treatment of ancillary restraints under the EC Merger Regulation is further explained in recital 21 in the preamble to the EC Merger Regulation, which states that «Commission decisions declaring concentrations compatible with the common market in application of this Regulation should automatically cover such restrictions, without the Commission having to assess such restrictions in individual cases». While the Recital envisages that the Commission will exercise a residual function with regard to specific novel or unresolved issues giving rise to genuine uncertainty, it is in all other scenarios the task of the undertakings concerned to assess for themselves whether and to what extent their agreements can be regarded as ancillary to a transaction. Disputes as to whether restrictions are directly related and necessary to the implementation of the concentration, and thus automatically covered by the Commission's clearance decision, may be resolved before national courts.

3. The Commission's residual function is addressed in recital 21 of the Merger Regulation, where it is stated that the Commission should, at the request of the undertakings concerned, expressly assess the ancillary character of restrictions if a case presents «novel and unresolved questions giving rise to genuine uncertainty». The Recital subsequently defines a «novel or unresolved question giving rise to genuine uncertainty» as a question that is «not covered by the relevant Commission notice in force or a published Commission decision».

4. In order to provide legal certainty to the undertakings concerned, this Notice provides guidance on the interpretation of the notion of ancillary restraints. The guidance given in the following sections reflects the essence of the Commission's practice, and sets out principles for assessing whether and to what extent the most common types of agreements are deemed to be ancillary restraints.

5. However, cases involving exceptional circumstances that are not covered by this Notice may justify departing from these principles. Parties may find further guidance in published Commission decisions (2) as to whether their agreements can be regarded as ancillary restraints or not. To the extent that cases involving exceptional circumstances have been previously addressed by the Commission in its published decisions (3), they do not constitute «novel or unresolved questions» within the meaning of recital 21) of the Merger Regulation.

(2) For the purpose of this Notice, a decision is considered to be published when it is published in the *Official Journal of the European Union* or when it is made available to the public on the Commission's web site.

(3) See for example Commission Decision of 1 September 2000 (COMP/M.1980 – Volvo/Renault V.I., paragraph 56) – high degree of customer loyalty; Commission Decision of 23 October 1998 (IV/M.1298 – Kodak/Imation, paragraph 73) – long product life cycle; Commission Decision of 13 March 1995 (IV/M.550 – Union Carbide/Enichem, paragraph 99) – limited number of alternative producers; Commission Decision of 30 April 1992 (IV/M.197 – Solvay-Laporte/Interox, paragraph 50) – longer protection of know-how required.

6. Accordingly, a case presents a «novel and unresolved question giving rise to genuine uncertainty» if those restrictions are not covered by this Notice and have not been previously addressed by the Commission in its published decisions. As envisaged in recital 21 of the Merger Regulation, the Commission will, at the request of the parties, expressly assess such restrictions in these cases. Subject to confidentiality requirements, the Commission will provide adequate publicity as regards such assessments that further develop the principles set out in this Notice.

7. To the extent that restrictions are directly related and necessary to the implementation of the concentration, Article 21(1) of the Merger Regulation provides that this Regulation alone applies, to the exclusion of Council Regulations (EC) N° 1/2003 (4), (EEC) N° 1017/68 (5) and (EEC) N° 4056/86 (6). By contrast, for restrictions that cannot be regarded as directly related and necessary to the implementation of the concentration, Articles 81 and 82 of the EC Treaty remain potentially applicable. However, the mere fact that an agreement or arrangement is not deemed to be ancillary to a concentration is not, as such, prejudicial to the legal status thereof. Such agreements or arrangements are to be assessed in accordance with Article 81 and 82 of the EC Treaty and the related regulatory texts and notices (7). They may also be subject to any applicable national competition rules. Hence, agreements which contain a restriction on competition, but are not considered directly related and necessary to the implementation of the concentration pursuant to this notice, may nevertheless be covered by those provisions.

(4) Council Regulation (EC) N° 1/2003 of 16 December 2002 on the implementation of the rules on competition laid down in Articles 81 and 82 of the Treaty, O.J. L 1, 4.1.2003, p. 1; Regulation as last amended by Regulation (EC) N° 411/2004 (O.J. L 68, 6.3.2004, p. 1).

(5) Council Regulation (EEC) 1017/68 of 19 July 1968 applying rules of competition to transport by rail, road and inland waterway, O.J. L 175, 23.7.1968, p. 1; Regulation as last amended by Regulation (EC) N° 1/2003.

(6) Council Regulation (EEC) N° 4056/86 of 22 December 1986 laying down detailed rules for the application of Articles 81 and 82 of the Treaty to maritime transport, O.J. L 378, 31.12.1986, p. 4; Regulation as last amended by Regulation (EC) N° 1/2003.

(7) See, for example, for licence agreements Regulation (EC) N° 772/2004 of 27 April 2004 on the application of Article 81(3) of the Treaty to categories of technology transfer agreements, O.J. L 123, 27.4.2004, p. 11; see for supply and purchase agreements e.g. Commission Regulation (EC) N° 2790/1999 of 22 December 1999 on the application of Article 81(3) of the Treaty to categories of vertical agreements and concerted practices, O.J. L 336, 29.12.1999, p. 21.

8. The Commission's interpretation of Article 6(1)(*b*), second subparagraph, and Article 8(1), second subparagraph, and (2), third subparagraph, of the Merger Regulation is without prejudice to the interpretation which may be given by the Court of Justice or the Court of First Instance of the European Communities.

9. This Notice replaces the Commission's previous Notice regarding restrictions directly related and necessary to concentrations (8).

(8) O.J. C 188, 4.7.2001, p. 5.

II. GENERAL PRINCIPLES

10. A concentration consists of contractual arrangements and agreements establishing control within the meaning of Article 3(2) of the Merger Regulation. All agreements which carry out the main object of the concentration (9), such as those relating to the sale of shares or assets of an undertaking, are integral parts of the concentration. In addition to these arrangements and agreements, the parties to the concentration may enter into other agreements which do not form an integral part of the concentration but can restrict the parties' freedom of action in the market. If such agreements contain ancillary restraints, these are automatically covered by the decision declaring the concentration compatible with the Common Market.

(9) See e.g. Commission Decision of 10 August 1992 (IV/M.206 – Rhône-Poulenc/SNIA, paragraph 8.3); Commission Decision of 19 December 1991 (IV/M.113 – Courtaulds/SNIA, paragraph 35); Commission Decision of 2 December 1991 (IV/M.102 – TNT/Canada Post/DBP Postdienst/La Poste/PTT Poste & Sweden Post, paragraph 46).

11. The criteria of direct relation and necessity are objective in nature. Restrictions are not directly related and necessary to the implementation of a concentration simply because the parties regard them as such.

12. For restrictions to be considered «directly related to the implementation of the concentration», they must be closely linked to the concentration itself. It is not sufficient that an agreement has been entered into in the same context or at the same time as the concentration (10). Restrictions which are directly related to the concentration are economically related to the main transaction and intended to allow a smooth transition to the changed company structure after the concentration.

(10) Likewise, a restriction could, if all other requirements are fulfilled, be «directly related» even if it has not been entered into at the same time as the agreement carrying out the main object of the concentration.

13. Agreements must be «necessary to the implementation of the concentration» (11), which means that, in the absence of those agreements, the concentration could not be implemented or could only be implemented under considerably more uncertain conditions, at substantially higher cost, over an appreciably longer period or with considerably greater difficulty (12). Agreements necessary to the implementation of a concentration are typically aimed at protecting the value transferred (13), maintaining the continuity of supply after the break-up of a former economic entity (14), or enabling the start-up of a new entity (15). In determining whether a restriction is necessary, it is appropriate not only to take account of its nature, but also to ensure that its duration, subject matter and geographical field of application does not exceed what the implementation of the concentration reasonably requires. If equally effective alternatives are available for attaining the legitimate aim pursued, the undertakings must choose the one which is objectively the least restrictive of competition.

(11) See European Court of Justice, Case 42/84 (Remia), [1985] ECR 2545, paragraph 20; Court of First Instance, Case T-112/99 (Métropole Télévision – M6), [2001] ECR II-2459, paragraph 106.

(12) Commission Decision of 18 December 2000 (COMP/M.1863 – Vodafone/BT/Airtel JV, paragraph 20).

(13) Commission Decision of 30 July 1998 (IV/M.1245 – VALEO/ITT Industries, paragraph 59); Commission Decision of 3 March 1999 (IV/M.1442 – MMP/AFP, paragraph 17); Commission Decision of 9 March 2001 (COMP/M.2330 – Cargill/Banks, paragraph 30); Commission Decision of 20 March 2001 (COMP/M.2227 – Goldman Sachs/Messer Griesheim, paragraph 11).

(14) Commission Decision of 25 February 2000 (COMP/M.1841 – Celestica/IBM, paragraph 21).

(15) Commission Decision of 30 March 1999 (IV/JV.15 – BT/AT&T, paragraphs 207-214); Commission Decision of 22 December 2000 (COMP/M.2243 – Stora Enso/Assidoman/JV, paragraphs 49, 56 and 57).

14. For concentrations which are carried out in stages, the contractual arrangements relating to the stages before the establishment of control within the meaning of Article 3(1) and (2) of the Merger Regulation cannot normally be considered directly related and necessary to the implementation of the concentration. However, an agreement to abstain from material changes in the target's business until completion is considered directly related and necessary to the implementation of the joint bid (16). The same applies, in the context of a joint bid, to an agreement by the joint purchasers of an undertaking to abstain from making separate competing offers for the same undertaking, or otherwise acquiring control.

(16) Commission Decision of 27 July 1998 (IV/M.1226 – GEC/GPTH, paragraph 22); Commission Decision of 2 October 1997 (IV/M.984 – Dupont/ICI, paragraph 55); Commission Decision of 19 December 1997 (IV/M.1057 – Terra Industries/ ICI, paragraph 16); Commission Decision of 18 December 1996 (IV/M.861 – Textron/Kautex, paragraphs 19 and 22); Commission Decision of 7 August 1996 (IV/M.727 – BP/Mobil, paragraph 50).

15. Agreements which serve to facilitate the joint acquisition of control are to be considered directly related and necessary to the implementation of the concentration. This will apply to arrangements between the parties for the joint acquisition of control aimed at implementing the division of assets in order to divide the production facilities or distribution networks among themselves, together with the existing trademarks of the undertaking acquired jointly.

16. To the extent that such a division involves the break-up of a pre-existing economic entity, arrangements that make the break-up possible under reasonable conditions are to be considered directly related and necessary to the implementation of the concentration, under the principles set out below.

III. PRINCIPLES APPLICABLE TO COMMONLY ENCOUNTERED RESTRICTIONS IN CASES OF ACQUISITION OF AN UNDERTAKING

17. Restrictions agreed between the parties in the context of a transfer of an undertaking may be to the benefit of the purchaser or of the vendor. In general terms, the need for the purchaser to benefit from certain protection is more compelling than the corresponding need for the vendor. It is the purchaser who needs to be assured that she/he will be able to acquire the full value of the acquired business. Thus, as a general rule, restrictions which benefit the vendor are either not directly related and necessary to the implementation of the concentration at all (17), or their scope and/or duration need to be more limited than that of clauses which benefit the purchaser (18).

(17) Commission Decision of 27 July 1998 (IV/M.1226 – GEC/GPTH, paragraph 24).

(18) See, for example, for a clause aiming at the protection of a part of the business remaining with the vendor: Commission Decision of 30 August 1993 (IV/M.319 – BHF/CCF/Charterhouse, paragraph 16).

A. Non-competition clauses

18. Non-competition obligations which are imposed on the vendor in the context of the transfer of an undertaking or of part of it can be directly related and necessary to the implementation of the concentration. In order to obtain the full value of the assets transferred, the purchaser must be able to benefit from some protection against competition from the vendor in order to gain the loyalty of customers and to assimilate and exploit the know-how. Such non-competition clauses guarantee the transfer to the purchaser of the full value of the assets transferred, which in general include both physical assets and intangible assets, such as the goodwill accumulated or the know-how (19) developed by the vendor. These are not only directly related to the concentration but are also necessary to its implementation because, without them, there would be reasonable grounds to expect that the sale of the undertaking or of part of it could not be accomplished.

(19) As defined in Article 1(1)(i) of Regulation (EC) N° 772/2004.

19. However, such non-competition clauses are only justified by the legitimate objective of implementing the concentration when their duration, their geographical field of application, their subject matter and the persons subject to them do not exceed what is reasonably necessary to achieve that end (20).

(20) See European Court of Justice, Case 42/84 (Remia), [1985] ECR 2545, paragraph 20; Court of First Instance, Case T-112/99 (Métropole Télévision – M6), [2001] ECR II-2459, paragraph 106.

20. Non-competition clauses are justified for periods of up to three years (21), when the transfer of the undertaking includes the transfer of customer loyalty in the form of both goodwill and know-how (22). When only goodwill is included, they are justified for periods of up to two years (23).

(21) See for exceptional cases in which longer periods may be justified e.g. Commission Decision of 1 September 2000 (COMP/M.1980 – Volvo/Renault V.I., paragraph 56); Commission Decision of 27 July 1995 (IV/M.612 – RWE-DEA/ Enichem Augusta, paragraph 37); Commission decision of 23 October 1998 (IV/M.1298 – Kodak/Imation, paragraph 74).

(22) Commission Decision of 2 April 1998 (IV/M.1127 – Nestlé/Dalgety, paragraph 33); Commission Decision of 1 September 2000 (COMP/M.2077 – Clayton Dubilier & Rice/Iteltel, paragraph 15); Commission Decision of 2 March 2001 (COMP/M.2305 – Vodafone Group PLC/EIRCELL, paragraphs 21 and 22).

(23) Commission Decision of 12 April 1999 (IV/M.1482 – KingFisher/Grosslabor, paragraph 26); Commission Decision of 14 December 1997 (IV/M.884 – KNP BT/Bunzl/Wilhelm Seiler, paragraph 17).

21. By contrast, non-competition clauses cannot be considered necessary when the transfer is in fact limited to physical assets (such as land, buildings or machinery) or to exclusive industrial and commercial property rights (the holders of which could immediately take action against infringements by the transferor of such rights).

22. The geographical scope of a non-competition clause must be limited to the area in which the vendor has offered the relevant products or services before the transfer, since the purchaser does not need to be protected against competition from the vendor in territories not previously penetrated by the vendor (24). That geographical scope can be extended to territories which the vendor was planning to enter at the time of the transaction, provided that he had already invested in preparing this move.

(24) Commission Decision of 14 December 1997 (IV/M.884 – KNP BT/Bunzl/Wilhelm Seiler, paragraph 17); Commission Decision of 12 April 1999 (IV/M.1482 – KingFisher/Grosslabor, paragraph 27); Commission Decision of 6 April 2001 (COMP/M.2355 – Dow/Enichem Polyurethane, paragraph 28); Commission Decision of 4 August 2000 (COMP/M.1979 – CDC/Banco Urquijo/JV, paragraph 18).

23. Similarly, non-competition clauses must remain limited to products (including improved versions or updates of products as well as successor models) and services forming the economic activity of the undertaking transferred. This can include products and services at an advanced stage of development at the time of the transaction, or products which are fully developed but not yet marketed. Protection against competition from the vendor in product or service markets in which the transferred undertaking was not active before the transfer is not considered necessary (25).

(25) Commission Decision of 14 December 1997 (IV/M.884 – KNP BT/Bunzl/Wilhelm Seiler, paragraph 17); Commission Decision of 2 March 2001 (COMP/M.2305 – Vodafone Group PLC/EIRCELL, paragraph 22); Commission Decision of 6 April 2001 (COMP/M.2355 – Dow/Enichem Polyurethane, paragraph 28); Commission Decision of 4 August 2000 (COMP/M.1979 – CDC/Banco Urquijo/JV, paragraph 18).

24. The vendor may bind herself/himself, her/his subsidiaries and commercial agents. However, an obligation to impose similar restrictions on others would not be regarded as directly related and necessary to the implementation of the concentration. This applies, in particular, to clauses which would restrict the freedom of resellers or users to import or export.

25. Clauses which limit the vendor's right to purchase or hold shares in a company competing with the business transferred shall be considered directly related and necessary to the implementation of the concentration under the same conditions as outlined above for non-competition clauses, unless they prevent the vendor from purchasing or holding shares purely for financial investment purposes, without granting him/her, directly or indirectly, management functions or any material influence in the competing company (26).

(26) Commission Decision of 4 February 1993 (IV/M.301 – Tesco/Catteau, paragraph 14); Commission Decision of 14 December 1997 (IV/

M.884 – KNP BT/Bunzl/Wilhelm Seiler, paragraph 19); Commission Decision of 12 April 1999 (IV/M.1482 – Kingfisher/Grosslabor, paragraph 27); Commission Decision of 6 April 2000 (COMP/M.1832 – Ahold/ ICA Förbundet/Canica, paragraph 26).

26. Non-solicitation and confidentiality clauses have a comparable effect and are therefore evaluated in a similar way to non-competition clauses (27).

(27) Accordingly, confidentiality clauses on customer details, prices and quantities cannot be extended. By contrast, confidentiality clauses concerning technical know-how may exceptionally be justified for longer periods, see Commission Decision of 29 April 1998 (IV/M.1167 – ICI/Williams, paragraph 22); Commission Decision of 30 April 1992 (IV/ M.197 – Solvay-Laporte/Interox, paragraph 50).

B. Licence agreements

27. The transfer of an undertaking or of part of it can include the transfer to the purchaser, with a view to the full exploitation of the assets transferred, of intellectual property rights or know-how. However, the vendor may remain the owner of the rights in order to exploit them for activities other than those transferred. In these cases, the usual means for ensuring that the purchaser will have the full use of the assets transferred is to conclude licensing agreements in his/her favour. Likewise, where the vendor has transferred intellectual property rights with the business, she/he may still want to continue using some or all of these rights for activities other than those transferred; in such a case the purchaser will grant a licence to the vendor.

28. Licences of patents (28), of similar rights, or of know-how (29), can be considered necessary to the implementation of the concentration. They may equally be considered an integral part of the concentration and, in any event, need not be limited in time. These licences can be simple or exclusive and may be limited to certain fields of use, to the extent that they correspond to the activities of the undertaking transferred.

(28) Including patent applications, utility models, applications for registration of utility models, designs, topographies of semiconductor products, supplementary protection certificates for medicinal products or other products for which such supplementary protection certificates may be obtained and plant breeder's certificates (as referred to in Article 1(1)(h) of Regulation (EC) N° 772/2004.

(29) As defined in Article 1(1)(i) of Regulation (EC) N° 772/2004.

29. However, territorial limitations on manufacture reflecting the territory of the transferred activity are not necessary to the implementation of the operation. As regards licences granted by the seller of a business to the buyer, the seller can be made subject to territorial restrictions in the licence agreement under the same conditions as laid down for non-competition clauses in the context of the sale of a business.

30. Restrictions in licence agreements going beyond the above provisions, such as those which protect the licensor rather than the licensee, are not necessary to the implementation of the concentration (30).

(30) To the extent that they fall within Article 81(1) of the EC Treaty, such agreements may nevertheless fall under Regulation (EC) N° 772/2004, or other Community legislation.

31. Similarly, in the case of licences of trademarks, business names, design rights, copyrights or similar rights, there may be situations in which the vendor wishes to remain the owner of such rights in relation to activities retained, but the purchaser needs those rights in order to market the goods or services produced by the undertaking or part of the undertaking transferred. Here, the same considerations as above apply (31).

(31) Commission Decision of 1 September 2000 (COMP/M.1980 – Volvo/ Renault V.I., paragraph 54).

C. Purchase and supply obligations

32. In many cases, the transfer of an undertaking or of part of it can entail the disruption of traditional lines of purchase and supply which have existed as a result of the previous integration of activities within the economic unity of the vendor. In order to enable the break-up of the economic unity of the vendor and the partial transfer of the assets to the purchaser under reasonable conditions, it is often necessary to maintain, for a transitional period, the existing or similar links between the vendor and the purchaser. This objective is normally attained by purchase and supply obligations for the vendor and/or the purchaser of the undertaking or of part of it. Taking into account the particular situation resulting from the break-up of the economic unity of the vendor, such obligations can be recognised as directly related and necessary to the implementation of the concentration. They may be in favour of the vendor as well as the purchaser, depending on the particular circumstances of the case.

33. The aim of such obligations may be to ensure the continuity of supply to either of the parties of products necessary for carrying out the activities retained by the vendor or taken over by the purchaser. However, the duration of purchase and supply obligations must be limited to a period necessary for the replacement of the relationship of dependency by autonomy in the market. Thus, purchase or supply obligations aimed at guaranteeing the quantities previously supplied can be justified for a transitional period of up to five years (32).

(32) Commission Decision of 5 February 1996 (IV/M.651 – AT&T/Philips, VII.); Commission Decision of 30 March 1999 (IV/JV.15 – BT/AT&T, paragraph 209; see for exceptional cases Commission Decision of 13 March 1995 (IV/M.550 – Union Carbide/Enichem, paragraph 99); Commission Decision of 27 July 1995 (IV/M.612 – RWE-DEA/Enichem Augusta, paragraph 45).

34. Both supply and purchase obligations providing for fixed quantities, possibly with a variation clause, are recognised as directly related and necessary to the implementation of the concentration. However, obligations providing for unlimited quantities (33), exclusivity or conferring preferred-supplier or preferred-purchaser status (34), are not necessary to the implementation of the concentration.

(33) In line with the principle of proportionality, obligations providing for fixed quantities with a variation clause are, in these cases, less restrictive on competition, see e.g. Commission Decision of 18 September 1998 (IV/M.1292 – Continental/ ITT, paragraph 19).

(34) Commission Decision of 30 July 1998 (IV/M.1245 – VALEO/ITT Industries, paragraph 64); see for exceptional cases (e.g. absence of a market) Commission Decision of 13 March 1995 (IV/M.550 – Union Carbide/ Enichem, paragraphs 92 to 96); Commission Decision of 2 July 1995 (IV/M.612 – RWE-DEA/Enichem Augusta, paragraphs 38 et seq.).

35. Service and distribution agreements are equivalent in their effect to supply arrangements; consequently the same considerations as above shall apply.

IV. PRINCIPLES APPLICABLE TO COMMONLY ENCOUNTERED RESTRICTIONS IN CASES OF JOINT VENTURES WITHIN THE MEANING OF ARTICLE 3(4° OF THE MERGER REGULATION

A. Non-competition obligations

36. A non-competition obligation between the parent undertakings and a joint venture may be considered directly related and necessary to the implementation of the concentration where such obligations correspond to the products, services and territories covered by the joint venture agreement or its bylaws. Such non-competition clauses reflect, inter alia, the need to ensure good faith during negotiations; they may also reflect the need to fully utilise the joint venture's assets or to enable the joint venture to assimilate know-how and goodwill provided by its parents; or the need to protect the parents' interests in the joint venture against competitive acts facilitated, inter alia, by the parents' privileged access to the know-how and goodwill transferred to or developed by the joint venture. Such non-competition obligations between the parent undertakings and a joint venture can be regarded as directly related and necessary to the implementation of the concentration for the lifetime of the joint venture (35).

(35) Commission Decision of 15 January 1998 (IV/M.1042 – Eastman Kodak/Sun Chemical, paragraph 40); Commission Decision of 7 August 1996 (IV/M.727 - BP/Mobil, paragraph 51); Commission Decision of 3 July 1996 (IV/M.751 – Bayer/Hüls, paragraph 31); Commission Decision of 6 April 2000 (COMP/M.1832 – Ahold/ICA Förbundet/Canica, paragraph 26).

37. The geographical scope of a non-competition clause must be limited to the area in which the parents offered the relevant products or services before establishing the joint venture (36). That geographical scope can be extended to territories which the parent companies were planning to enter at the time of the transaction, provided that they had already invested in preparing this move.

(36) Commission Decision of 29 August 2000 (COMP/M.1913 – Lufthansa/Menzies/LGS/JV; paragraph 18); Commission Decision of 22 December 2000 (COMP/M.2243 – Stora Enso/Assidoman/JV, paragraph 49, last sentence).

38. Similarly, non-competition clauses must be limited to products and services constituting the economic activity of the joint venture. This may include products and services at an advanced stage of development at the time of the transaction, as well as products and services which are fully developed but not yet marketed.

39. If the joint venture is set up to enter a new market, reference will be made to the products, services and territories in which it is to operate under the joint venture agreement or by-laws. However, the presumption is that one parent's interest in the joint venture does not need to be protected against competition from the other parent in markets other than those in which the joint venture will be active from the outset.

40. Additionally, non-competition obligations between non-controlling parents and a joint venture are not directly related and necessary to the implementation of the concentration.

41. The same principles as for non-competition clauses apply to non-solicitation and confidentiality clauses.

B. Licence agreements

42. A licence granted by the parent undertakings to the joint venture may be considered directly related and necessary to the implementation of the concentration. This applies regardless of whether or not the licence is an exclusive one and whether or not it is limited in time. The licence may be restricted to a particular field of use which corresponds to the activities of the joint venture.

43. Licences granted by the joint venture to one of its parents, or cross-licence agreements, can be regarded as directly related and necessary to the implementation of the concentration under the same conditions as in the case of the acquisition of an undertaking. Licence agreements between the parents are not considered directly related and necessary to the implementation of a joint venture.

C. Purchase and supply obligations

44. If the parent undertakings remain present in a market upstream or downstream of that of the joint venture, any purchase and supply agreements, including service and distribution agreements are subject to the principles applicable in the case of the transfer of an undertaking.

Commission Consolidated Jurisdictional Notice under Council Regulation (EC) N° 139/2004 on the control of concentrations between undertakings

(OJ C 95, 16 April 2008, p. 1)

A. INTRODUCTION

1. The purpose of this Notice is to provide guidance as to jurisdictional issues under Council Regulation (E.C.) N° 139/2004, *O.J.* L 24, 29.1.2003, page 1 (the Merger Regulation) (1). This formal guidance should enable firms to establish more quickly, in advance of any contact with the Commission, whether and to what extent their operations may be covered by Community control of concentrations.

(1) Where it is necessary in this Notice to distinguish between Regulation 139/2004 and Council Regulation (E.E.C.) N° 4064/89 (*O.J.* L 395, 30.12.1989, corrected version in *O.J.* L 257, 21.9.1990, p. 13, Regulation last amended by Regulation (E.C.) N° 1310/97, *O.J.* L 180, 9.7.1997, p. 1, corrigendum in *O.J.* L 40, 13.2.1998, p. 17), the former will be referred to as the «recast Merger Regulation» whereas the latter will be referred to as the «former Merger Regulation». Articles without reference refer to the recast Merger Regulation.

2. This Notice replaces the Notice on the concept of concentration (2), the Notice on the concept of full-function joint ventures (3), the Notice on the concept of undertakings concerned (4) and the Notice on calculation of turnover (5).

(2) *O.J.* C 66, 2.3.1998, p. 5.
(3) *O.J.* C 66, 2.3.1998, p. 1.
(4) *O.J.* C 66, 2.3.1998, p. 14.
(5) *O.J.* C 66, 2.3.1998, p. 25.

3. This Notice deals with the concepts of a concentration and of a full-function joint venture, undertakings concerned and the calculation of turnover as set out in Articles 1, 3 and 5 of the Merger Regulation. Issues concerning referrals are dealt with in the Notice on referrals (6). The Commission's interpretation of Articles 1, 3 and 5 in the present Notice is without prejudice to the interpretation which may be given by the Court of Justice or by the Court of First Instance of the European Communities.

(6) O.J. C 56, 5.3.2005, p. 2.

4. The guidance set out in this Notice reflects the Commission's experience in applying the recast Merger Regulation and the former Merger Regulation since the latter entered into force on 21 September 1990. The general principles governing the issues dealt with in this Notice have not been changed by the entry into force of Regulation (E.C.) N° 139/2004, but where changes have occurred, the Notice deals with them explicitly. The principles contained in the Notice will be applied and further developed by the Commission in individual cases.

5. According to Article 1, the Merger Regulation only applies to operations that satisfy two conditions. First, there must be a concentration of two or more undertakings within the meaning of Article 3 of the Merger Regulation. Secondly, the turnover of the undertakings concerned, calculated in accordance with Article 5, must satisfy the thresholds set out in Article 1 of the Regulation. The notion of a concentration (including the particular requirements for joint ventures), as the first condition, is dealt with under Part B; the identification of undertakings concerned and the calculation of their turnover as relevant for the second condition are dealt with under Part C.

6. The Commission addresses the question of its jurisdiction over a concentration in decisions according to Article 6 of the Merger Regulation (7).

(7) See also opinion of AG Kokott in Case C-202/06 Cementbouw v Commission of 26 April 2007, paragraph 56 (not yet reported).

B. THE CONCEPT OF CONCENTRATION

7. According to Article 3(1) of the Merger Regulation, a concentration only covers operations where a change of control in the undertakings concerned occurs on a lasting basis. Recital 20 in the preamble to the Merger Regulation further explains that the concept of concentration is intended to relate to operations which bring about a lasting change in the structure of the market. Because the test in Article 3 is centred on the concept of control, the existence of a concentration is to a great extent determined by qualitative rather than quantitative criteria.

8. Article 3(1) of the Merger Regulation defines two categories of concentrations:
– those arising from a merger between previously independent undertakings (point *(a)*);
– those arising from an acquisition of control (point *(b)*).
These are treated respectively in Sections I and II below.

I. MERGERS BETWEEN PREVIOUSLY INDEPENDENT UNDERTAKINGS

9. A merger within the meaning of Article 3(1)*(a)* of the Merger Regulation occurs when two or more independent undertakings amalgamate into a new undertaking and cease to exist as separate legal entities. A merger may also occur when an undertaking is absorbed by another, the latter retaining its legal identity while the former ceases to exist as a legal entity (8).

(8) See, for example, Case COMP/M. 1673 – Veba/VIAG of 13 June 2000; Case COMP/M.1806 – AstraZeneca/Novartis of 26 July 2000; Case COMP/M.2208 – Chevron/Texaco of 26 January 2001; and Case IV/M.1383 – Exxon/Mobil of 29 September 1999. A merger in the meaning of Article 3(1)*(a)* is not deemed to occur if a target company is merged with a subsidiary of the acquiring company to the effect that the parent company acquires control of the target undertaking under Article 3(1)(b), see Case COMP/M.2510 – Cendant/Galileo of 24 September 2001.

10. A merger within the meaning of Article 3(1)*(a)* may also occur where, in the absence of a legal merger, the combining of the activities of previously independent undertakings results in the creation of a single economic unit (9). This may arise in particular where two or more undertakings, while retaining their individual legal personalities, establish contractually a common economic management (10) or the structure of a dual listed company (11). If this leads to a *de facto* amalgamation of the undertakings concerned into a single economic unit, the operation is considered to be a merger. A prerequisite for the determination of such a *de facto* merger is the existence of a permanent, single economic management. Other relevant factors may include internal profit and loss compensation or a revenue distribution as between the various entities within the group, and their joint liability or external risk sharing. The *de facto* amalgamation may be solely based on contractual arrangements (12), but it can also be reinforced by cross-shareholdings between the undertakings forming the economic unit.

(9) In determining the previous independence of undertakings, the issue of control may be relevant as the merger might otherwise only be an internal restructuring within the group. In this specific context, the assessment of control also follows the general concept set out below and includes de jure as well as *de facto* control.

(10) This could apply for example in the case of a «Gleichordnungskonzern» in German law, certain «Groupements d'Intérêt Economique» in French law, and the amalgamation of partnerships, as in Case IV/M.1016 – Price Waterhouse/Coopers&Lybrand of 20 May 1998.

(11) Case IV/M.660 – RTZ/CRA of 7 December 1995; Case COMP/M.3071 – Carnival Corporation/P&O Princess II of 24 July 2002.

(12) See Case IV/M.1016 – Price Waterhouse/Coopers&Lybrand of 20 May 1998; Case COMP/M.2824 – Ernst & Young/Andersen Germany of 27 August 2002.

II. ACQUISITION OF CONTROL

1. Concept of control

1.1. Person or undertaking acquiring control

11. Article 3(1)*(b)* provides that a concentration occurs in the case of an acquisition of control. Such control may be acquired by one undertaking acting alone or by several undertakings acting jointly.

Person controlling another undertaking

12. Control may also be acquired by a person in circumstances where that person already controls (whether solely or jointly) at least one other undertaking or, alternatively, by a combination of persons (which control another undertaking) and undertakings. The term «person» in this context extends to public bodies (13) and private entities, as well as natural persons. Acquisitions of control by natural persons are only considered to bring about a lasting change in the structure of the undertakings concerned if those natural persons carry out further economic activities on their own account or if they control at least one other undertaking (14).

(13) Including the State itself, e.g. Case IV/M.157 – Air France/Sabena, of 5 October 1992 in relation to the Belgian State, or other public bodies such as the Treuhandanstalt in Case IV/M.308 – Kali und Salz/MDK/Treuhand, of 14 December 1993. See, however, recital 22 of the Merger Regulation.

(14) Case IV/M.82 – Asko/Jakobs/Adia of 16 May 1991 including a private individual as undertaking concerned.; Case COMP/M.3762 – Apax/Travelex of 16 June 2005 in which a private individual acquiring joint control was not considered an undertaking concerned.

Acquirer of control

13. Control is normally acquired by persons or undertakings which are the holders of the rights or are entitled to rights conferring control under the contracts concerned (Article 3(3)(a)). However, there are also situations where the formal holder of a controlling interest differs from the person or undertaking having in fact the real power to exercise the rights resulting from this interest. This may be the case, for example, where an undertaking uses another person or undertaking for the acquisition of a controlling interest and has the power to exercise the rights conferring control through this person or undertaking, i.e. the latter is formally the holder of the rights, but acts only as a vehicle. In such a situation, control is acquired by the undertaking which in reality is behind the operation and in fact enjoys the power to control the target undertaking (Article 3(3)(b)). The Court of First Instance concluded from this provision that control held by commercial companies can be attributed to their exclusive shareholder, their majority shareholders or to those jointly controlling the companies since these companies comply in any event with the decisions of those shareholders (15). A controlling shareholding which is held by different entities in a group is normally attributed to the undertaking exercising control over the different formal holders of the rights. In other cases, the evidence needed to establish this type of indirect control may include, either separately or in combination and to be assessed on a case-by-case basis, factors such as shareholdings, contractual relations, source of financing or family links (16).

(15) Judgment in Case T-282/02 Cementbouw v Commission, paragraph 72, (2006) ECR II-319.

(16) See Case M.754 – Anglo American Corporation/Lonrho of 23 April 1997.

Acquisition of control by investment funds

14. Specific issues may arise in the case of acquisitions of control by investment funds. The Commission will analyse structures involving investment funds on a case-by-case basis, but some general features of such structures can be set out on the basis of the Commission's past experience.

15. Investment funds are often set up in the legal form of limited partnerships, in which the investors participate as limited partners and normally do not exercise control, either individually or collectively. The investment funds usually acquire the shares and voting rights which confer control over the portfolio companies. Depending on the circumstances, control is normally exercised by the investment company which has set up the fund as the fund itself is typically a mere investment vehicle; in more exceptional circumstances, control may be exercised by the fund itself. The investment company usually exercises control by means of the organisational structure, e.g. by controlling the general partner of fund partnerships, or by contractual arrangements, such as advisory agreements, or by a combination of both. This may be the case even if the investment company itself does not own the company acting as a general partner, but their shares are held by natural persons (who may be linked to the investment company) or by a trust. Contractual arrangements with the investment company, in particular advisory agreements, will become even more important if the general partner does not have any own resources and personnel for the management of the portfolio companies, but only constitutes a company structure whose acts are performed by persons linked to the investment company. In these circumstances, the investment company normally acquires indirect control within the meaning of Article 3(1)(b) and 3(3)(b) of the Merger Regulation, and has the power to exercise the rights which are directly held by the investment fund (17).

(17) This structure also has an effect on how the turnover is calculated in situations involving investment funds, see paragraphs 189ff.

1.2. Means of control

16. Control is defined by Article 3(2) of the Merger Regulation as the possibility of exercising decisive influence on an undertaking. It is therefore not necessary to show that the decisive influence is or will be actually exercised. However, the possibility of exercising that influence must be effective (18). Article 3(2) further provides that the possibility of exercising decisive influence on an undertaking can exist on the basis of rights, contracts or any other means, either separately or in combination, and having regard to the considerations of fact and law involved. A concentration therefore may occur on a legal or a *de facto* basis, may take the form of sole or joint control, and extend to the whole or parts of one or more undertakings (*cf.* Article 3(1)(b)).

(18) Judgment in Case T-282/02 Cementbouw v Commission, paragraph 58, (2006) ECR II-319

Control by the acquisition of shares or assets

17. Whether an operation gives rise to an acquisition of control therefore depends on a number of legal and/or factual elements. The most common means for the acquisition of control is the acquisition of shares, possibly combined with a shareholders' agreement in cases of joint control, or the acquisition of assets.

Control on a contractual basis

18. Control can also be acquired on a contractual basis. In order to confer control, the contract must lead to a similar control of the management and the resources of the other undertaking as in the case of acquisition of shares or assets. In addition to transferring control over the management and the resources, such contracts must be characterised by a very long duration (ordinarily without a possibility of early termination for the party granting the contractual rights). Only such contracts can result in a structural change in the market (19). Examples of such contracts are organisational contracts under national company law (20) or other types of contracts, e.g. in the form of agreements for the lease of the business, giving the acquirer control over the management and the resources despite the fact that property rights or shares are not transferred. In this respect, Article 3(2)(a) specifies that control may also be constituted by a right to use the assets of an undertaking (21). Such contracts may also lead to a situation of joint control if both the owner of the assets as well as the undertaking controlling the management enjoy *veto* rights over strategic business decisions (22).

(19) In Case COMP/M.3858 – Lehman Brothers/SCG/Starwood/Le Meridien of 20 July 2005 the management agreements had a duration of 10-15 years; in Case COMP/M.2632 – Deutsche Bahn/ECT International/United Depots/JV of 11 February 2002 the contract had a duration of 8 years.

(20) Examples of such specific contracts under national company law are the «Beherrschungsvertrag» in German law or the «Contrato de subordinação» in Portuguese law; such contracts do not exist in all Member States.

(21) See Case COMP/M.2060 – Bosch/Rexroth of 12 January 2001 concerning a control contract (Beherrschungsvertrag) in combination with a business lease; Case COMP/M.3136 – GE/Agfa NDT of 5 December 2003 concerning a specific contract to transfer control over entrepreneurial resources, management and risks; Case COMP/M.2632 – Deutsche Bahn/ECT International/United Depots/JV of 11 February 2002 concerning a business lease.

(22) Case COMP/M.3858 – Lehman Brothers/SCG/Starwood/Le Meridien of 20 July 2005; see also case IV/M.126 – Accor/Wagon-Lits of 28 April 1992 in the context of Article 5(4)(b) of the Merger Regulation.

Control by other means

19. In line with these considerations, franchising agreements as such do not normally confer control over the franchisee's business on the franchisor. The franchisee usually exploits the entrepreneurial resources on its own account even if essential parts of the assets may belong to the franchisor (23). Furthermore, purely financial agreements, such as sale-and-lease-back transactions with arrangements for a buyback of the assets at the end of the term, do not normally constitute a concentration as they do not change control over the management and the resources.

(23) Case M.940 – UBS/Mister Minit, in the context of Article 5(4)(b) of the Merger Regulation. For the treatment of franchising relationships in the competitive assessment, see Case COMP/M.4220 – Food Service Project/Tele Pizza of 6 June 2006. The situation in Case IV/M.126 – Accor/Wagon-Lits of 28 April 1992 has to be distinguished from franchising agreements. In this case, again in the context of Article 5(4)(b), the hotel company had a right to manage also hotels in which it only owned a minority stake as it had entered into long-term hotel management agreements giving it decisive influence over the day-to-day operations of these hotels, including decisions on budgetary matters.

20. Furthermore, control can also be established by any other means. Purely economic relationships may play a decisive role for the acquisition of control. In exceptional circumstances, a situation of economic dependence may lead to control on a *de facto* basis where, for example, very important long-term supply agreements or credits provided by suppliers or customers, coupled with structural links, confer decisive influence (24). In such a situation, the Commission will carefully analyse whether such economic links, combined with other links, are sufficient to lead to a change of control on a lasting basis (25).

(24) See Case IV/M.794 – Coca-Cola/Amalgamated Beverages GB of 22 January 1997; Case IV/ECSC.1031 – US/Sollac/Bamesa of 28 July 1993; Case IV/M.625 – Nordic Capital/Transpool of 23 August 1995; for the criteria see also Case IV/M.697 – Lockheed Martin Corporation/Loral Corporation, of 27 March 1996.

(25) See Case IV/M.258 – CCIE/GTE, of 25 September 1992 where the Commission did not find control due to the temporary nature of the commercial agreements involved.

21. There may be an acquisition of control even if it is not the declared intention of the parties or if the acquirer is only passive and the acquisition of control is triggered by action of third parties. Examples are situations where the change of control results from the inheritance of a shareholder or where the exit of a shareholder triggers a change of control, in particular a change from joint to sole control (26). Article 3(1)(b) covers such scenarios in specifying that control may also be acquired «by any other means».

(26) See Case COMP/M.3330 – RTL/M6 of 12 March 2004; Case COMP/M.452 – Avesta (II) of 9 June 1994.

Control and national company law

22. National legislation within a Member State may provide specific rules on the structure of bodies representing the organization of decision-making within an undertaking. While such legislation may confer some power of control upon persons other than the shareholders, in particular on representatives of employees, the concept of control under the Merger Regulation is not related to such a means of influence as the Merger Regulation focuses on decisive influence enjoyed on the basis of rights, assets or contracts or equivalent *de facto* means. Restrictions in the articles of association or in general law concerning the persons eligible to sit on the board, such as a provisions requiring the appointment of independent members or excluding persons holding office or employment in the parent companies, do not exclude the existence of control as long as the shareholders decide the composition of the decision-making bodies (27). Similarly, despite provisions of national law foreseeing that decisions of a company must be taken by its company organs in its interests, those persons holding the voting rights have the power to adopt those decisions and therefore have the possibility to exercise decisive influence on the company (28).

(27) Judgment in Case T-282/02 Cementbouw v Commission, paragraphs 70, 73, 74 (2006) ECR II-319.

(28) Judgment in Case T-282/02 Cementbouw v Commission, paragraphs 79 (2006) ECR II-319.

Control in other areas of legislation

23. The concept of control under the Merger Regulation may be different from that applied in specific areas of Community and national legislation concerning, for example, prudential rules, taxation, air transport or the media. The interpretation of «control» in other areas is therefore not necessarily decisive for the concept of control under the Merger Regulation

1.3. Object of control

24. The Merger Regulation provides in Article 3(1)(b), (2) that the object of control can be one or more, or also parts of, undertakings which constitute legal entities, or the assets of such entities, or only some of these assets. The acquisition of control over assets can only be considered a concentration if those assets constitute the whole or a part of an undertaking, i.e. a business with a market presence, to which a market turnover can be clearly attributed (29). The transfer of the client base of a business can fulfil these criteria if this is sufficient to transfer a business with a market turnover (30). A transaction confined to intangible assets such as brands, patents or copyrights may also be considered to be a concentration if those assets constitute a business with a market turnover. In any case, the transfer of licences for brands, patents or copyrights, without additional assets, can only fulfil these criteria if the licences are exclusive at least in a certain territory and the transfer of such licences will transfer the turnover-generating activity (31). For non-exclusive licences it can be excluded that they may constitute on their own a business to which a market turnover is attached.

(29) See, e.g., Case COMP/M. 3867 – Vattenfall/Elsam and E2 Assets of 22 December 2005.

(30) Case COMP/M.2857 – ECS/IEH of 23 December 2002.

(31) In addition, the granting of licences and the transfer of patent licences will only constitute a concentration if this is done on a lasting basis. In this respect, similar considerations as set out above in paragraph 18 for the acquisition of control by (long-term) agreements apply.

25. Specific issues arise in cases where an undertaking outsources in-house activities, such as the provision of services or the manufacturing of products, to a service provider. Typical cases are the outsourcing of IT services to specialised IT companies. Outsourcing contracts can take several forms; their common characteristic is that the outsourcing service supplier shall provide those services to the customer which the latter has performed in-house before. Cases of simple outsourcing do not involve any transfer of assets or employees to the outsourcing service suppliers, but it is usually the case that any assets or employees are retained by the customer. Such an outsourcing contract is akin to a normal service contract and even if the outsourcing service supplier acquires a right to direct those assets and employees of the customer, no concentration arises if the assets and employees will be used exclusively to service the customer.

26. The situation may be different if the outsourcing service supplier, in addition to taking over a certain activity which was previously provided internally, is transferred the associated assets and/or personnel. A concentration only arises in these circumstances if the assets constitute the whole or part of an undertaking, i.e. a business with access to the market. This requires that the assets previously dedicated to in-house activities of the seller will enable the outsourcing service supplier to provide services not only to the outsourcing customer but also to third parties, either immediately or within a short period after the transfer. This will be the case if the transfer relates to an internal business unit or a subsidiary already engaged in the provision of services to third parties. If third parties are not yet supplied, the assets transferred in the case of manufacturing should contain production facilities, the product know-how (it is sufficient if the assets transferred allow the build-up of such capabilities in the near future) and, if there is no existing market access, the means for the purchaser to develop a market access within a short period of time (e.g. including existing contracts or brands) (32). As regards the provision of services, the assets transferred should include the required know-how (e.g. the relevant personnel and intellectual property) and those facilities which allow market access (such as, e.g., marketing facilities) (33). The assets transferred therefore have to include at least those core elements that would allow an acquirer to build up a market presence in a time-frame similar to the start-up period for joint ventures as set out below under paragraphs 97, 100. As in the case of joint ventures, the Commission will take account of substantiated business plans and general market features for assessing this.

(32) See Case COMP/M.1841 – Celestica/IBM of 25 February 2000; Case COMP/M.1849 – Solectron/Ericsson of 29 February 2000; Case COMP/M.2479 – Flextronics/Alcatel – of 29 June 2001; Case COMP/M.2629 – Flextronics/Xerox of 12 November 2001.

(33) See, in the context of joint ventures, Case IV/M.560 – EDS/Lufthansa of 11 May 1995; Case COMP/M.2478 – IBM Italia/Business Solutions/JV of 29 June 2001.

27. If the assets transferred do not allow the purchaser to at least develop a market presence, it is likely that they will be used only for providing services to the outsourcing customer. In such circumstances, the transaction will not result in a lasting change in the market structure and the outsourcing contract is again similar to a service contract. The transaction will not constitute a concentration. The specific requirements under which a joint venture for the provision of outsourcing services is qualified as a concentration are assessed in the present Notice in the section on full-function joint ventures.

1.4. Change of control on a lasting basis

28. Article 3(1) of the Merger Regulation defines the concept of a concentration in such a manner as to cover operations only if they bring about a lasting change in the control of the undertakings concerned and, as recital 20 adds, in the structure of the market. The Merger Regulation therefore does not deal with transactions resulting only in a temporary change of control. However, a change of control on a lasting basis is not excluded by the fact that the underlying agreements are entered into for a definite period of time, provided those agreements are renewable. A concentration may arise even in cases in which agreements envisage a definite end-date, if the period envisaged is sufficiently long to lead to a lasting change in the control of the undertakings concerned (34).

(34) See, in cases of joint ventures, Case COMP/M.2903 – DaimlerChrysler/Deutsche Telekom/JV of 30 April 2003 where a period of 12 years was considered sufficient; Case COMP/M.2632 – Deutsche Bahn/ECT International/United Depots/JV of 11 February 2002 with a contract duration of 8 years. In Case COMP/M.3858 Lehman Brothers/Starwood/Le Meridien of 20 July 2005, the Commission considered a minimum period of 10-15 years sufficient, but not a period of three years. The acquisition of control by the acquisition of shares or assets is not normally confined to a definite period of time and is therefore assumed to lead to a change of control on a lasting basis. Only in the scenarios set out in paragraphs 29 ff., will an acquisition of control by shares or assets be exceptionally considered to be transitory in nature and thus not to lead to a lasting change in the control of the undertakings concerned.

29. The question whether an operation results in a lasting change in the market structure is also relevant for the assessment of several operations occurring in succession, where the first transaction is only transitory in nature. Several scenarios can be distinguished in this respect.

30. In one scenario, several undertakings come together solely for the purpose of acquiring another company on the basis of an agreement to divide up the acquired assets according to a pre-existing plan immediately upon completion of the transaction. In such circumstances, in a first step, the acquisition of the entire target company is carried out by one or several undertakings. In a second step, the acquired assets are divided among several undertakings. The question is then whether the first transaction is to be considered as a separate concentration, involving an acquisition of sole control (in the case of a single purchaser) or of joint control (in the case of a joint purchase) of the entire target undertaking, or whether only the acquisitions in the second step constitute concentrations, whereby each of the acquiring undertakings acquires its relevant part of the target undertaking.

31. The Commission considers that the first transaction does not constitute a concentration, and examines the acquisitions of control by the ultimate acquirers, provided a number of conditions are met: First, the subsequent break-up must be agreed between the different purchasers in a legally binding way. Second, there must not be any uncertainty that the second step, the division of the acquired assets, will take place within a short time period after the first acquisition. The Commission considers that normally the maximum timeframe for the division of the assets should be one year (35).

(35) See, e.g., Cases COMP/M. Case N° COMP/M.3779 – Pernod Ricard/Allied Domecq of 24 June 2005 and COMP/M.3813 – Fortune Brands/Allied Domecq of 10 June 2005, where the split-up of the assets was foreseen to become effective within 6 months after the acquisition.

32. If both conditions are met, the first acquisition does not result in a structural change on a lasting basis. There is no effective concentration of economic power between the acquirer(s) and the target company as a whole since the acquired assets are not held in an undivided way on a lasting basis, but only for the time necessary to carry out the immediate split-up of the acquired assets. In those circumstances, only the acquisitions of the different parts of the undertaking in the second step will constitute concentrations, whereby each of these acquisitions by different purchasers will constitute a separate concentration. This is irrespective of whether the first acquisition is carried out by only one undertaking (36) or jointly by the undertakings which are also involved in the second step (37). In any case, it must be noted that the scope of a clearance decision will only allow for a takeover of the entire target if the break-up can proceed within a short time-frame afterwards and the different parts of the target undertaking are directly sold on to the respective ultimate buyer.

(36) For a first acquisition by only one undertaking see Case COMP/M.3779 – Pernod Ricard/Allied Domecq of 24 June 2005 and Case COMP/M.3813 – Fortune Brands/Allied Domecq/Pernod Ricard of 10 June 2005; Case COMP/M.2060 – Bosch/Rexroth of 12 January 2001.

(37) For a joint acquisition see Case COMP/M.1630 – Air Liquide/BOC of 18 January 2000; Case COMP/M.1922 – Siemens/Bosch/Atecs of 11 August 2000; Case COMP/M.2059 – Siemens/Dematic/VDO Sachs of 29 August 2000.

33. However, if these conditions are not fulfilled, in particular if it is not certain that the second step will proceed within a short time-frame after the first acquisition, the Commission will consider the first transaction as a separate concentration, involving the entire target undertaking. This, e.g., is the case if the first transaction may also proceed independently of the second transaction (38) or if a longer transitory period is needed to divide up the target undertaking (39).

(38) See Case COMP/M.2498 – UPM-Kymmene/Haindl of 21 November 2001 and Case COMP/M.2499 – Norske Skog/Parenco/Walsum of 21 November 2001.

(39) Case COMP/M.3372 – Carlsberg/Holsten of 16 March 2004.

34. A second scenario is an operation leading to joint control for a starting-up period but, according to legally binding agreements, this joint control will be converted to sole control by one of the shareholders. As the joint control situation may not constitute a lasting change of control, the whole operation may be considered to be an acquisition of sole control. In the past, the Commission accepted that such a start-up period could last up to three years (40). Such a period seems to be too long to exclude that the joint control scenario has an impact on the structure of the market. The period therefore should, in general, not exceed one year and the joint control period should be only transitory in nature (41). Only such a relatively short period will make it unlikely that the joint control period will have a distinct impact on the market structure and can therefore be considered as not leading to a change in control on a lasting basis.

(40) Case IV/M.425 – British Telecom/Santander of 28 March 1994.

(41) See Case M.2389 – Shell/DEA of 20 December 2001 where the ultimate acquirer of sole control had a strong influence in the operational management during the joint control period; Case M.2854 – RAG/Degussa of 18 November 2002 where the transitional period was designed to facilitate internal post-merger restructuring.

35. In a third scenario, an undertaking is «parked» with an interim buyer, often a bank, on the basis of an agreement on the future onward sale of the business to an ultimate acquirer. The interim buyer generally acquires shares «on behalf» of the ultimate acquirer, which often bears the major part of the economic risks and may also be granted specific rights. In such circumstances, the first transaction is only undertaken to facilitate the second transaction and the first buyer is directly linked to the ultimate acquirer. Contrary to the situation described in the first scenario in paragraphs 30-33, no other ultimate acquirer is involved, the target business remains unchanged, and the sequence of transactions is initiated alone by the sole ultimate acquirer. From the date of the adoption of this Notice, the Commission will examine the acquisition of control by the ultimate acquirer, as provided for in the agreements entered into by the parties. The Commission will consider the transaction by which the interim buyer acquires control in such circumstances as the first step of a single concentration comprising the lasting acquisition of control by the ultimate buyer.

1.5. Interrelated transactions

1.5.1. Relation between Article 3 and Article 5(2) second subparagraph

36. Several transactions can be treated as a single concentration under the Merger Regulation either according to the general rule of Article 3 – as the transactions are interdependent – or according to the specific provision of Article 5(2) second subparagraph.

37. Article 5(2) second subparagraph governs a different question from that referred to by Article 3 of the Merger Regulation. Article 3 defines the existence of a «concentration» in general and material terms, but does not directly determine the question of the Commission's competence in respect of concentrations. Article 5 intends to specify the scope of the Merger Regulation, in particular by defining the turnover to be taken into account for the purpose of determining whether a concentration has Community dimension, and Article 5(2) second subparagraph allows the Commission in this respect to consider two or more concentrative transactions to constitute a single concentration for the purposes of calculating the turnover of the undertakings concerned. The assessment whether, in application of Article 3, a number of transactions give rise to a single concentration or whether those transactions must be regarded as giving rise to a number of concentrations, is thereby logically precedent to the question addressed in Article 5(2) second subparagraph (42).

(42) Judgment in Case T-282/02 Cementbouw v Commission, paragraphs 113-119 (2006) ECR II-319.

1.5.2. Interdependent transactions under Article 3

38. The general and teleological definition of a concentration set out in Article 3(1) – the result being control of one or more undertakings – implies that it makes no difference whether control was acquired by one or several legal transactions, provided that the end result constitutes a single concentration. Two or more transactions constitute a single concentration for the purposes of Article 3 if they are unitary in nature. It should therefore be determined whether the result leads to conferring one or more undertakings direct or indirect economic control over the activities of one or more other undertakings. For the assessment, the economic reality underlying the transactions is to be identified and thus the economic aim pursued by the parties. In other words, in order to determine the unitary nature of the transactions in question, it is necessary, in each individual case, to ascertain whether those transactions are interdependent, in such a way that one transaction would not have been carried out without the other (43).

(43) Judgment in Case T-282/02 Cementbouw v Commission, paragraphs 104-109 (2006) ECR II-319.

39. Recital 20 to the Merger Regulation explains in this respect that it is appropriate to treat as a single concentration transactions that are closely connected in that they are linked by condition. The requirement that the transactions are interdependent as set out by the Court of First Instance in the Cementbouw judgment (44) thereby corresponds to the explanation set out in recital 20 that the transactions are linked by condition.

(44) Judgment in Case T-282/02 Cementbouw v Commission, paragraphs 106-109 (2006) ECR II-319.

40. This general approach reflects, on the one hand, that under the Merger Regulation transactions which stand or fall together according to the economic objectives pursued by the parties should also be analysed in one procedure. In these circumstances, the change of the market structure is brought about by these transactions together. On the other hand, if different transactions are not interdependent and if the parties would proceed with one of the transactions if the other ones would not succeed, it seems appropriate to assess these transactions individually under the Merger Regulation.

41. However, several transactions, even if linked by condition upon each other, can only be treated as a single concentration, if control is acquired ultimately by the same undertaking(s). Only in these circumstances two or more transactions can be considered to be unitary in nature and therefore to constitute a single concentration for the purposes of Article 3 (45). This excludes de-mergers of joint ventures by which different parts of an undertaking are split between its former parent companies. The Commission will consider those transactions as separate concentrations (46). The same applies to transactions where two (or more) companies exchange assets in transactions involving de-mergers of joint ventures or assets swaps. Although the parties will normally consider those transactions as interdependent, the purpose of the Merger Regulation requires a separate assessment of the results of each of the transactions: Several undertakings acquire control of different assets; a separate combination of resources takes place for each of the acquiring undertakings; and the impact on the market of each of those acquisitions of control needs to be analysed separately under the Merger Regulation.

(45) This also covers situations where an undertaking sells a business to a purchaser and then acquirers the seller including the business sold, see Case COMP/M.4521 – LGI/Telenet of 26 February 2007.

(46) See parallel cases COMP/M.3293 – Shell/BEB and COMP/M.3294 – ExxonMobil/BEB of 20 November 2003; case IV/M.197 – Solvay/Laporte of 30 April 1992.

42. The acquisition of different degrees of control (for example joint control of one business and sole control of another business) raises specific questions. An operation involving the acquisition of joint control of one part of an undertaking and sole control of another part is in principle regarded as two separate concentrations under the Merger Regulation (47). Those transactions constitute only one concentration if they are interdependent and if the undertaking acquiring sole control is also acquiring joint control. In any case, such a scenario is considered to constitute one concentration where a corporate entity is acquired to which both the solely controlled and the jointly controlled undertaking belong. On the basis of the interpretation in recital 20, the situation where the same undertaking acquires sole and joint control of other undertakings based on interdependent agreements is not to be treated differently. These transactions, if they are interdependent, therefore constitute a single concentration.

(47) See Case IV/M.409 ABB/Renault Automation of 9 March 1994.

Requirement of conditionality of transactions

43. The required conditionality implies that none of the transactions would take place without the others and they therefore constitute a single operation (48). Such conditionality is normally demonstrated if the transactions are linked de jure, i.e. the agreements themselves are linked by mutual conditionality. If *de facto* conditionality can be satisfactorily demonstrated, it may also suffice for treating the transactions as a single concentration. This requires an economic assessment of whether each of the transactions necessarily depends on the conclusion of the others (49). Further indications of the interdependence of several transactions may be the statements of the parties themselves or the simultaneous conclusion of the relevant agreements. A conclusion of *de facto* interconditionality of several transactions will be difficult to reach in the absence of their simultaneity. A pronounced lack of simultaneity of legally inter-conditional transactions may likewise put into doubt their true interdependence.

(48) Judgment in Case T-282/02 Cementbouw v Commission, paragraphs 127 et seq. (2006) ECR II-319.

(49) Judgment in Case T-282/02 Cementbouw v Commission, paragraphs 131 et seq. (2006) ECR II-319. See Case COMP/M.4521 – LGI/Telenet of 26 February 2007, where the interdependence was based on the fact that two transactions were decided and carried out simultaneously and that, according to the economic aims of the parties, each of the transactions would not have been carried out without the other.

44. The principle that several transactions can be treated as a single concentration under the mentioned conditions only applies if the result is that control of one or more undertakings is acquired by the same person(s) or undertaking(s). First, this may be the case if a single business or undertaking is acquired via several legal transactions. Second, also the acquisition of control of several undertakings – which could constitute concentrations in themselves – can be linked in such a way that it constitutes a single concentration. However, it is not possible under the Merger Regulation to link different legal transactions which only partly concern the acquisition of control of undertakings, but partly also the acquisition of other assets, such as non-controlling minority stakes in other companies. It would not be in line with the general framework and the purpose of the Merger Regulation if different transactions, linked by conditionality, were assessed as a whole under the Merger Regulations if only some of these transactions lead to a change in control of a given target.

Acquisition of a single business

45. A single concentration may therefore exist if the same purchaser(s) acquire control of a single business, i.e. a single economic entity, via several legal transactions if those are inter-conditional. This is the case irrespective of whether the business is acquired in a corporate structure, consisting of one or several companies, or whether various assets are acquired which form a single business, i.e. a single economic entity managed for a common commercial purpose to which all the assets contribute. Such a business may comprise majority and minority stakes in companies as well as tangible and intangible assets. If several legal transactions which are interdependent are required to transfer such a business, these transactions constitute one concentration (50).

(50) See Case IV/M.470 – Gencor/Shell of 29 August 1994; COMP/M.3410 – Total/Gaz de France of 8 October 2004; Case IV/M.957 – L'Oreal/Procasa/Cosmetique Iberica/Albesa of 19 September 1997; Case IV/M.861 – Textron/Kautex of 18 December 1996 where all the assets were also used in the same product market. The same considerations apply if a joint venture is created by several companies, forming a single business, see Case M.4048 – Sonae Industria/Tarkett of 12 June 2006 where the interdependence of transactions establishing, respectively, a production and a distribution joint venture was necessary in order to demonstrate that there was a single concentration that would create a full-function joint venture.

Parallel and serial acquisitions of control

46. For the treatment of several acquisitions of control as a single concentration, several scenarios have arisen in the Commission's past decisional practice. One such scenario is a parallel acquisition of control, i.e. undertaking A acquires control of undertaking B and C in parallel from separate sellers on condition that A is not obliged to buy either and neither seller is obliged to sell, unless both transactions proceed (51). Another scenario is a serial acquisition of control, i.e. undertaking A acquires control of undertaking B conditional on B's prior or simultaneous acquisition of undertaking C, as illustrated by the Kingfisher case (52).

(51) Case COMP/M.2926 – EQT/H&R/Dragoco – of 16 September 2002; the same considerations apply to the question when several mergers constitute one concentration in the meaning of Article 3(1)(a), Case COMP/M. 2824 – Ernst & Young/Andersen Germany of 27 August 2002.

(52) Case IV/M.1188 – Kingfisher/Wegert/ProMarkt of 18 June 1998; case COMP/M.2650 – Haniel/Cementbouw/JV (CVK) of 26 June 2002.

Serial acquisition of sole/joint control

47. In the same way as the Kingfisher scenario, the Commission approaches cases where, in a serial transaction, an undertaking agrees to acquire first sole control of a target undertaking, with a view to directly selling on parts of the acquired stake in the target to another undertaking, finally resulting in joint control of both acquirers over the target company. If both acquisitions are inter-conditional, the two transactions constitute a single concentration and only the acquisition of joint control, as the final result of the transactions, will be considered by the Commission (53).

(53) Case COMP/M.2420 – Mitsui/CVRD/Caemi of 30 October 2001.

1.5.3. Series of transactions in securities

48. Recital 20 of the Merger Regulation further explains that a single concentration will also arise in cases where control over one undertaking is acquired by a series of transactions in securities from one or several sellers taking place within a reasonably short period of time. The concentration in these scenarios is not limited to the acquisition of the «one and decisive» share, but will cover all the acquisitions of securities which take place in the reasonably short period of time.

1.5.4. Article 5(2) subparagraph 2

49. Article 5(2) subparagraph 2 provides a specific rule which allows the Commission to consider successive transactions occurring in a fixed period of time a single concentration for the purposes of calculating the turnover of the undertakings concerned. The purpose of this provision is to ensure that the same persons do not break a transaction down into series of sales of assets over a period of time, with the aim of avoiding the competence conferred on the Commission by the Merger Regulation (54).

(54) Judgment in Case T-282/02 Cementbouw v Commission, paragraph 118 (2006) ECR II-319.

50. If two or more transactions (each of them bringing about an acquisition of control) take place within a two-year period between the same persons or undertakings, they shall be qualified as a single concentration (55), irrespective of whether or not those transactions relate to parts of the same business or concern the same sector. This does not apply where the same persons or undertakings are joined by other persons or undertakings for only some of the transactions involved. It is sufficient if the transactions, although not carried out between the same companies, are carried out between companies belonging to the same respective groups. The provision also applies to two or more transactions between the same persons or undertakings if they are carried out simultaneously. Whenever they lead to acquisitions of control by the same undertaking, such simultaneous transactions between the same parties form a single concentration even if they are not conditional upon each other (56). However, Article 5(2) subparagraph 2 would not appear to apply to different transactions at least one of which involves an undertaking concerned which is distinct from the common seller(s) and buyer(s). In situations involving two transactions where one transaction results in sole control and the other in joint control, Article 5(2) subparagraph 2 therefore does not apply unless the other jointly controlling parent(s) in the latter transaction are the seller(s) of the solely controlling stake in the former transaction.

(55) See Case COMP/M.3173 – E.ON/Fortum Burghausen/Smaland/Endenderry of 13 June 2003. This also applies to situations where sole control is acquired whereby only parts of the undertaking were previously jointly controlled by the acquiring undertaking, case COMP/M. 2679 – EdF/TXU/Europe/24 Seven of 20 December 2001.

(56) Case IV/M.1283 – Volkswagen/RollsRoyce/Cosworth of 24 August 1998.

1.6. Internal restructuring

51. A concentration within the meaning of the Merger Regulation is limited to changes in control. An internal restructuring within a group of companies does not constitute a concentration. This applies, e.g., to increases in shareholdings not accompanied by changes of control or to restructuring operations such as a merger of a dual listed company into a single legal entity or a merger of subsidiaries. A concentration could only arise if the operation leads to a change in the quality of control of one undertaking and therefore is no longer purely internal.

1.7. Concentrations involving State-owned undertakings

52. An exceptional situation exists where both the acquiring and acquired undertakings are companies owned by the same State (or by the same public body or municipality). In this case, whether the operation is to be regarded as an internal restructuring depends in turn on the question whether both undertakings were formerly part of the same economic unit. Where the undertakings were formerly part of different economic units having an independent power of decision, the operation will be deemed to constitute a concentration and not an internal restructuring (57). However, where the different economic units will continue to have an independent power of decision also after the operation, the operation is only to be regarded as an internal restructuring, even if the shares of the undertakings, constituting different economic units, should be held by a single entity, such as a pure holding company (58).

(57) Case IV/M.097 – Péchiney/Usinor, of 24 June 1991; Case IV/M.216 – CEA Industrie/France Telecom/SGS-Thomson, of 22 February 1993; Case IV/M.931 – Neste/IVO of 2 June 1998. See also recital 22 of the Merger Regulation.

(58) Specific issues concerning the calculation of turnover for state-owned companies are dealt with in paragraphs 192-194.

53. However, the prerogatives exercised by a State acting as a public authority rather than as a shareholder, in so far as they are limited to the protection of the public interest, do not constitute control within the meaning of the Merger Regulation to the extent that they have neither the aim nor the effect of enabling the State to exercise a decisive influence over the activity of the undertaking (59).

(59) Case IV/M.493 – Tractebel/Distrigaz II, of 1 September 1994.

2. Sole control

54. Sole control is acquired if one undertaking alone can exercise decisive influence on an undertaking. Two general situations in which an undertaking has sole control can be distinguished. First, the solely controlling undertaking enjoys the power to determine the strategic commercial decisions of the other undertaking. This power is typically achieved by the acquisition of a majority of voting rights in a company. Second, a situation also conferring sole control exists where only one shareholder is able to *veto* strategic decisions in an undertaking, but this shareholder does not have the power, on his own, to impose such decisions (the so-called negative sole control). In these circumstances, a single shareholder possesses the same level of influence as that usually enjoyed by an individual shareholder which jointly-controls a company, i.e. the power to block the adoption of strategic decisions. In contrast to the situation in a jointly controlled company, there are no other shareholders enjoying the same level of influence and the shareholder enjoying negative sole control does not necessarily have to cooperate with specific other shareholders in determining the strategic behaviour of the controlled undertaking. Since this shareholder can produce a deadlock situation, the shareholder acquires decisive influence within the meaning of Article 3(2) and therefore control within the meaning of the Merger Regulation (60).

(60) Since this shareholder is the only undertaking acquiring a controlling influence, only this shareholder is obliged to submit a notification under the Merger Regulation.

55. Sole control can be acquired on a de jure and/or *de facto* basis.

De jure sole control

56. Sole control is normally acquired on a legal basis where an undertaking acquires a majority of the voting rights of a company. In the absence of other elements, an acquisition which does not include a majority of the voting rights does not normally confer control even if it involves the acquisition of a majority of the share capital. Where the company statutes require a supermajority for strategic decisions, the acquisition of a simple majority of the voting rights may not confer the power to determine strategic decisions, but may be sufficient to confer a blocking right on the acquirer and therefore negative control.

57. Even in the case of a minority shareholding, sole control may occur on a legal basis in situations where specific rights are attached to this shareholding. These may be preferential shares to which special rights are attached enabling the minority shareholder to determine the strategic commercial behaviour of the target company, such as the power to appoint more than half of the members of the supervisory board or the administrative board. Sole control can also be exercised by a minority shareholder who has the right to manage the activities of the company and to determine its business policy on the basis of the organisational structure (e.g. as a general partner in a limited partnership which often does not even have a shareholding).

58. A typical situation of negative sole control occurs where one shareholder holds 50% in an undertaking whilst the remaining 50% is held by several other shareholders (assuming this does not lead to positive sole control on a *de facto* basis), or where there is a supermajority required for strategic decisions which in fact confers a *veto* right upon only one shareholder, irrespective of whether it is a majority or a minority shareholder (61).

(61) See consecutive Cases COMP/M.3537 – BBVA/BNL of 20 August 2004 and M.3768 – BBVA/BNL of 27 April 2005; Case M.3198 – VW-Audi/VW-Audi Vertriebszentren of 29 July 2003; Case COMP/M.2777 – Cinven Limited/Angel Street Holdings of 8 May 2002; Case IV/M.258 – CCIE/GTE, of 25 September 1992. In Case COMP/M.3876 – Diester Industrie/Bunge/JV of 30 September 2005, there was the specific situation that a joint venture held a stake in a company by which it had negative sole control over this company.

De facto sole control

59. A minority shareholder may also be deemed to have sole control on a *de facto* basis. This is in particular the case where the shareholder is highly likely to achieve a majority at the shareholders' meetings, given the level of its shareholding and the evidence resulting from the presence of shareholders in the shareholders' meetings in previous years (62). Based on the past voting pattern, the Commission will carry out a prospective analysis and take into account foreseeable changes of the shareholders' presence which might arise in future following the operation (63). The Commission will further analyse the position of other shareholders and assess their role. Criteria for such an assessment are in particular whether the remaining shares are widely dispersed, whether other important shareholders have structural, economic or family links with the large minority shareholder or whether other shareholders have a strategic or a purely financial interest in the target company; these criteria will be assessed on a case-by-case basis (64). Where, on the basis of its shareholding, the historic voting pattern at the shareholders' meeting and the position of other shareholders, a minority shareholder is likely to have a stable majority of the votes at the shareholders' meeting, then that large minority shareholder is taken to have sole control (65).

(62) Case IV/M.343 – Société Générale de Belgique/Générale de Banque, of 3 August 1993; Case COMP/M.3330 – RTL/M6 of 12 March 2004; Case IV/M.159 – Mediobanca/Generali of 19 December 1991.

(63) See Case COMP/M.4336 – MAN/Scania of 20 December 2006 as regards the question whether Volkswagen had acquired control of MAN.

(64) Case IV/M.754 – Anglo American/Lonrho of 23 April 1997; Case IV/M.025 – Arjomari/Wiggins Teape, of 10 February 1990.

(65) See also Case COMP/M.2574 – Pirelli/Edizione/Olivetti/Telecom Italia of 20 September 2001; Case IV/M.1519 – Renault/Nissan of 12 May 1999.

60. An option to purchase or convert shares cannot in itself confer sole control unless the option will be exercised in the near future according to legally binding agreements (66). However, in exceptional circumstances an option, together with other elements, may lead to the conclusion that there is *de facto* sole control (67).

(66) Judgment in Case T 2/93, Air France v Commission (1994) ECR II-323. Even though an option does normally not in itself lead to a concentration, it can be taken into account for the substantive assessment in a related concentration, see Case COMP/M.3696 – E.ON/MOL of 21 December 2005, at paragraphs 12-14, 480, 762 et subseq.

(67) Case IV/M.397 – Ford/Hertz of 7 March 1994.

Sole control acquired by other means than voting rights

61. Apart from the acquisition of sole control on the basis of voting rights, the considerations outlined in section 1.2 concerning the acquisition of sole control by purchase of assets, by contract, or by any other means also apply.

3. Joint control

62. Joint control exists where two or more undertakings or persons have the possibility of exercising decisive influence over another undertaking. Decisive influence in this sense normally means the power to block actions which determine the strategic commercial behaviour of an undertaking. Unlike sole control, which confers upon a specific shareholder the power to determine the strategic decisions in an undertaking, joint control is characterized by the possibility of a deadlock situation resulting from the power of two or more parent companies to reject proposed strategic decisions. It follows, therefore, that these shareholders must reach a common understanding in determining the commercial policy of the joint venture and that they are required to cooperate (68).

(68) See also Judgment in Case T-282/02 Cementbouw v Commission, paragraphs 42, 52, 67 (2006) ECR II-319.

63. As in the case of sole control, the acquisition of joint control can also be established on a de jure or *de facto* basis. There is joint control if the shareholders (the parent companies) must reach agreement on major decisions concerning the controlled undertaking (the joint venture).

3.1. Equality in voting rights or appointment to decision-making bodies

64. The clearest form of joint control exists where there are only two parent companies which share equally the voting rights in the joint venture. In this case, it is not necessary for a formal agreement to exist between them. However, where there is a formal agreement, it must be consistent with the principle of equality between the parent companies, by laying down, for example, that each is entitled to the same number of representatives in the management bodies and that none of the members has a casting vote (69). Equality may also be achieved where both parent companies have the right to appoint an equal number of members to the decision-making bodies of the joint venture.

(69) Case COMP/M.3097 – Maersk Data/Eurogate IT; Global Transport Solutions JV of 12 March 2003; Case IV/M.272 – Matra/CAP Gemini Sogeti, of 17 March 1993.

3.2. Veto rights

65. Joint control may exist even where there is no equality between the two parent companies in votes or in representation in decision-making bodies or where there are more than two parent companies. This is the case where minority shareholders have additional rights which allow them to *veto* decisions which are essential for the strategic commercial behaviour of the joint venture (70). These *veto* rights may be set out in the statute of the joint venture or conferred by agreement between its parent companies. The *veto* rights themselves may operate by means of a specific quorum required for decisions taken at the shareholders' meeting or by the board of directors to the extent that the parent companies are represented on this board. It is also possible that strategic decisions are subject to approval by a body, e.g. supervisory board, where the minority shareholders are represented and form part of the quorum needed for such decisions.

(70) Case T 2/93, Air France v Commission (1994) ECR II-323; Case IV/M.010 – Conagra/Idea, of 3 May 1991.

66. These *veto* rights must be related to strategic decisions on the business policy of the joint venture. They must go beyond the *veto* rights normally accorded to minority shareholders in order to protect their financial interests as investors in the joint venture. This normal protection of the rights of minority shareholders is related to decisions on the essence of the joint venture, such as changes in the statute, an increase or decrease in the capital or liquidation. A *veto* right, for example, which prevents the sale or winding-up of the joint venture does not confer joint control on the minority shareholder concerned (71).

(71) Case IV/M.062 – Eridania/ISI, of 30 July 1991.

67. In contrast, *veto* rights which confer joint control typically include decisions on issues such as the budget, the business plan, major investments or the appointment of senior management. The acquisition of joint control, however, does not require that the acquirer has the power to exercise decisive influence on the day-to-day running of an undertaking. The crucial element is that the *veto* rights are sufficient to enable the parent companies to exercise such influence in relation to the strategic business behaviour of the joint venture. Moreover, it is not necessary to establish that an acquirer of joint control of the joint venture will actually make use of its decisive influence. The possibility of exercising such influence and, hence, the mere existence of the *veto* rights, is sufficient.

68. In order to acquire joint control, it is not necessary for a minority shareholder to have all the *veto* rights mentioned above. It may be sufficient that only some, or even one such right, exists. Whether or not this is the case depends upon the precise content of the *veto* right itself and also the importance of this right in the context of the specific business of the joint venture.

Appointment of senior management and determination of budget

69. Very important are the *veto* rights concerning decisions on the appointment and dismissal of the senior management and the approval of the budget. The power to co-determine the structure of the senior management, such as the members of the board, usually confers upon the holder the power to exercise decisive influence on the commercial policy of an undertaking. The same is true with respect to decisions on the budget since the budget determines the precise framework of the activities of the joint venture and, in particular, the investments it may make.

Business plan

70. The business plan normally provides details of the aims of a company together with the measures to be taken in order to achieve those aims. A *veto* right over this type of business plan may be sufficient to confer joint control even in the absence of any other *veto* right. In contrast, where the business plan contains merely general declarations concerning the business aims of the joint venture, the existence of a *veto* right will be only one element in the general assessment of joint control but will not, on its own, be sufficient to confer joint control.

Investments

71. In the case of a *veto* right on investments, the importance of this right depends, first, on the level of investments which are subject to the approval of the parent companies and, secondly, on the extent to which investments constitute an essential feature of the market in which the joint venture is active. In relation to the first criterion, where the level of investments necessitating approval of the parent companies is extremely high, this *veto* right may be closer to the normal protection of the interests of a minority shareholder than to a right conferring a power of co-determination over the commercial policy of the joint venture. With regard to the second, the investment policy of an undertaking is normally an important element in assessing whether or not there is joint control. However, there may be some markets where investment does not play a significant role in the market behaviour of an undertaking.

Market-specific rights

72. Apart from the typical *veto* rights mentioned above, there exist a number of other possible *veto* rights related to specific decisions which are important in the context of the particular market of the joint venture. One example is the decision on the technology to be used by the joint venture where technology is a key feature of the joint venture's activities. Another example relates to markets characterized by product differentiation and a significant degree of innovation. In such markets, a *veto* right over decisions relating to new product lines to be developed by the joint venture may also be an important element in establishing the existence of joint control.

Overall context

73. In assessing the relative importance of *veto* rights, where there are a number of them, these rights should not be evaluated in isolation. On the contrary, the determination of whether or not joint control exists is based upon an assessment of these rights as a whole. However, a *veto* right which does not relate either to strategic commercial policy, to the appointment of senior management or to the budget or business plan cannot be regarded as giving joint control to its owner (72).

(72) Case IV/M.295 – SITA-RPC/SCORI, of 19 March 1993.

3.3. Joint exercise of voting rights

74. Even in the absence of specific *veto* rights, two or more undertakings acquiring minority shareholdings in another undertaking may obtain joint control. This may be the case where the minority shareholdings together provide the means for controlling the target undertaking. This means that the minority shareholders, together, will have a majority of the voting rights; and they will act together in exercising these voting rights. This can result from a legally binding agreement to this effect, or it may be established on a *de facto* basis.

75. The legal means to ensure the joint exercise of voting rights can be in the form of a (jointly controlled) holding company to which the minority shareholders transfer their rights, or an agreement by which they undertake to act in the same way (pooling agreement).

76. Very exceptionally, collective action can occur on a *de facto* basis where strong common interests exist between the minority shareholders to the effect that they would not act against each other in exercising their rights in relation to the joint venture. The greater the number of parent companies involved in such a joint venture, however, the more remote is the likelihood of this situation occurring.

77. Indicative for such a commonality of interests is a high degree of mutual dependency as between the parent companies to reach the strategic objectives of the joint venture. This is in particular the case when each parent company provides a contribution to the joint venture which is vital for its operation (e.g. specific technologies, local know-how or supply agreements) (73). In these circumstances, the parent companies may be able to block the strategic decisions of the joint venture and, thus, they can operate the joint venture successfully only with each other's agreement on the strategic decisions even if there is no express provision for any *veto* rights. The parent companies will therefore be required to cooperate (74). Further factors are decision making procedures which are tailored in such a way as to allow the parent companies to exercise joint control even in the absence of explicit agreements granting *veto* rights or other links between the minority shareholders related to the joint venture (75).

(73) Case COMP/JV.55 Hutchison/RCPM/ECT of 3 July 2001; see also Case IV/M.553 – RTL/Veronica/Endemol of 20 September 1995.

(74) Judgment in Case T-282/02 Cementbouw v Commission, paragraphs 42, 52, 67 (2006) ECR II-319.

(75) Case COMP/JV.55 Hutchison/RCPM/ECT of 3 July 2001. See also Case IV/M.553 – RTL/Veronica/Endemol of 20 September 1995.

78. Such a scenario may not only occur in a situation where two or more minority shareholders jointly control an undertaking on a *de facto* basis, but also where there is high degree of dependency of a majority shareholder on a minority shareholder. This may be the case where the joint venture economically and financially depends on the minority shareholder or where only the minority shareholder has the required know-how for, and will play a major role in, the operation of the joint undertaking whereas the majority shareholder is a mere financial investor (76). In such circumstances, the majority shareholder will not be able to enforce its position, but the joint venture partner may be able to block strategic decisions so that both parent undertakings will be required to cooperate permanently. This leads to a situation of *de facto* joint control which prevails over a pure de jure assessment according to which the majority shareholder could have been considered to have sole control.

(76) Case IV/M. 967 – KLM/Air UK of 22 September 1997; Case COMP/M.4085 – Arcelor/Oyak/Erdemir of 13 February 2006.

79. These criteria apply to the formation of a new joint venture as well as to acquisitions of minority shareholdings, together conferring joint control. In case of acquisitions of shareholdings, there is a higher probability of a commonality of interests if the shareholdings are acquired by means of concerted action. However, an acquisition by way of a concerted action is not alone sufficient for the purposes of establishing *de facto* joint control. In general, a common interest as financial investors (or creditors) of a company in a return on investment does not constitute a commonality of interests leading to the exercise of *de facto* joint control.

80. In the absence of strong common interests such as those outlined above, the possibility of changing coalitions between minority shareholders will normally exclude the assumption of joint control. Where there is no stable majority in the decision-making procedure and the majority can on each occasion be any of the various combinations possible amongst the minority shareholders, it cannot be assumed that the minority shareholders (or a certain group thereof) will jointly control the undertaking (77). In this context, it is not sufficient that there are agreements between two or more parties having an equal shareholding in the capital of an undertaking which establish identical rights and powers between the parties, where these fall short of strategic *veto* rights. For example, in the case of an undertaking where three shareholders each own one-third of the share capital and each elect one-third of the members of the Board of Directors, the shareholders do not have joint control since decisions are required to be taken on the basis of a simple majority.

(77) Case IV/JV.12 – Ericsson/Nokia/Psion/Motorola of 22 December 1998.

3.4. Other considerations related to joint control

Unequal role of the parent companies

81. Joint control is not incompatible with the fact that one of the parent companies enjoys specific knowledge of and experience in the business of the joint venture. In such a case, the other parent company can play a modest or even non-existent role in the daily management of the joint venture where its presence is motivated by considerations of a financial, long-term-strategy, brand image or general policy nature. Nevertheless, it must always retain the real possibility of contesting the decisions taken by the other parent company on the basis of equality in voting rights or rights of appointment to decision making bodies or of *veto* rights related to strategic issues. Without this, there would be sole control.

Casting vote

82. For joint control to exist, there should not be a casting vote for one parent company only as this would lead to sole control of the company enjoying the casting vote. However, there can be joint control when this casting vote is in practice of limited relevance and effectiveness. This may be the case when the casting vote can be exercised only after a series of stages of arbitration and attempts at reconciliation or in a very limited field or if the exercise of the casting vote triggers a put option implying a serious financial burden or if the mutual interdependence of the parent companies would make the exercise of the casting vote unlikely (78).

(78) Case COMP/M.2574 – Pirelli/Edizione/Olivetti/Telecom Italia of 20 September 2001; Case IV/M.553 – RTL/Veronica/Endemol of 20 September 1995; Case IV/M.425 – British Telecom/Banco Santander, of 28 March 1994.

III. CHANGES IN THE QUALITY OF CONTROL

83. The Merger Regulation covers operations resulting in the acquisition of sole or joint control, including operations leading to changes in the quality of control. First, such a change in the quality of control, resulting in a concentration, occurs if there is a change between sole and joint control. Second, a change in the quality of control occurs between joint control scenarios before and after the transaction if there is an increase in the number or a change in the identity of controlling shareholders. However, there is no change in the quality of control if a change from negative to positive sole control occurs. Such a change affects neither the incentives of the negatively controlling shareholder nor the nature of the control structure, as the controlling shareholder did not necessarily have to cooperate with specific shareholders at the time when it enjoyed negative control. In any case, mere changes in the level of shareholdings of the same controlling shareholders, without changes of the powers they hold in a company and of the composition of the control structure of the company, do not constitute a change in the quality of control and therefore are not a notifiable concentration.

84. These changes in the quality of control will be discussed in two categories: first, an entrance of one or more new controlling shareholders irrespective of whether or not they replace existing controlling shareholders and, second, a reduction of the number of controlling shareholders.

1. Entry of controlling shareholders

85. An entry of new controlling shareholders leading to a joint control scenario can either result from a change from sole to joint control, or from the entry of an additional shareholder or a replacement of an existing shareholder in an already jointly controlled undertaking.

86. A move from sole control to joint control is considered a notifiable operation as this changes the quality of control of the joint venture. First, there is a new acquisition of control for the shareholder entering the controlled undertaking. Second, only the new acquisition of control makes the controlled undertaking to a joint venture which changes decisively also the situation for the remaining controlling undertaking under the Merger Regulation: In the future, it has to take into account the interests of one or more other controlling shareholder(s) and it is required to cooperate permanently with the new shareholder(s). Before, it could either determine the strategic behaviour of the controlled undertaking alone (in the case of sole control) or was not forced to take into account the interests of specific other shareholders and was not forced to cooperate with those shareholders permanently.

87. The entry of a new shareholder in a jointly controlled undertaking – either in addition to the already controlling shareholders or in replacement of one of them – also constitutes a notifiable concentration, although the undertaking is jointly controlled before and after the operation (79). First, also in this scenario there is a shareholder newly acquiring control of the joint venture. Second, the quality of control of the joint venture is determined by the identity of all controlling shareholders. It lies in the nature of joint control that, since each shareholder alone has a blocking right concerning strategic decisions, the jointly controlling shareholders have to take into account each others interests and are required to cooperate for the determination of the strategic behaviour of the joint venture (80). The nature of joint control therefore does not exhaust itself in a pure mathematical addition of the blocking rights exercised by several shareholders, but is determined by the composition of the jointly controlling shareholders. One of the most obvious scenarios leading to a decisive change in the nature of the control structure of a jointly controlled undertaking is a situation where in a joint venture, jointly controlled by a competitor of the joint venture and a financial investor, the financial investor is replaced by another competitor. In these circumstances, the control structure and the incentives of the joint venture may entirely change, not only because of the entry of the new controlling shareholder, but also due to the change in the behaviour of the remaining shareholder. The replacement of a controlling shareholder or the entry of a new shareholder in a jointly controlled undertaking therefore constitutes a change in the quality of control (81).

(79) See, e.g., Case COMP/M.3440 – ENI/EDP/GdP of 9 December 2004.

(80) Judgment in Case T-282/02 Cementbouw v Commission, paragraph 67 (2006) ECR II-319.

(81) Generally, it should be noted that the Commission will not assess as a separate concentration the indirect replacement of a controlling shareholder in a joint control scenario which takes place via an acquisition of control of one of its parent undertakings. The Commission will assess any changes occurring in the competitive situation of the joint venture in the framework of the overall acquisition of control of its parent undertaking. In those circumstances, the other controlling shareholders in the joint venture will therefore not be undertakings concerned by the concentration which relates to its parent undertaking.

88. However, the entry of new shareholders only results in a notifiable concentration if one or several shareholders acquire sole or joint control by virtue of the operation. The entry of new shareholders may lead to a situation where joint control can neither be established on a de jure basis nor on a *de facto* basis as the entry of the new shareholder leads to the consequence that changing coalitions between minority shareholders are possible (82).

(82) Case IV/JV.12 – Ericsson/Nokia/Psion/Motorola of 22 December 1998.

2. Reduction in the number of shareholders

89. A reduction in the number of controlling shareholders constitutes a change in the quality of control and is thus to be considered as a concentration if the exit of one or more controlling shareholders results in a change from joint to sole control. Decisive influence exercised alone is substantially different from decisive influence exercised jointly, since in the latter case the jointly controlling shareholders have to take into account the potentially different interests of the other party or parties involved (83).

(83) See Case IV/M023 – ICI/Tioxide, of 28 November 1990; see also paragraph 5 (d) of the Commission Notice on a simplified procedure for treatment of certain concentrations under Council Regulation (E.C.) N° 139/2004.

90. Where the operation involves a reduction in the number of jointly controlling shareholders, without leading to a change from joint to sole control, the transaction will normally not lead to a notifiable concentration.

IV. JOINT VENTURES – THE CONCEPT OF FULL-FUNCTIONALITY

91. Article 3(1)(b) provides that a concentration shall be deemed to arise where control is acquired by one or more undertakings of the whole or parts of another undertaking. The new acquisition of another undertaking by several jointly controlling undertakings therefore constitutes a concentration under the Merger Regulation. As in the case of the acquisition of sole control of an undertaking, such an acquisition of joint control will lead to a structural change in the market even if, according to the plans of the acquiring undertakings, the acquired undertaking would no longer be considered full-function after the transaction (e.g. because it will sell exclusively to the parent undertakings in future). Thus, a transaction involving several undertakings acquiring joint control of another undertaking or parts of another undertaking, fulfilling the criteria set out in paragraph 24, from third parties will constitute a concentration according to Article 3(1) without it being necessary to consider the full-functionality criterion (84).

(84) These considerations do not apply to Article 2(4) in the same way. Whereas the interpretation of Article 3, paragraphs (1) and (4) relates to the applicability of the Merger Regulation to joint ventures, Article 2(4) relates to the substantive analysis of joint ventures. The «creation of a joint venture constituting a concentration pursuant to Article 3», as provided for in Article 2(4), comprises the acquisition of joint control according to Article 3, paragraphs (1) and (4).

92. Article 3(4) provides in addition that the creation of a joint venture performing on a lasting basis all the functions of an autonomous economic entity (so called full-function joint ventures) shall constitute a concentration within the meaning of the Merger Regulation. The full-functionality criterion therefore delineates the application of the Merger Regulation for the creation of joint ventures by the parties, irrespective of whether such a joint venture is created as a «greenfield operation» or whether the parties contribute assets to the joint venture which they previously owned individually. In these circumstances, the joint venture must fulfil the full-functionality criterion in order to constitute a concentration.

93. The fact that a joint venture may be a full-function undertaking and therefore economically autonomous from an operational viewpoint does not mean that it enjoys autonomy as regards the adoption of its strategic decisions. Otherwise, a jointly controlled undertaking could never be considered a full-function joint venture and therefore the condition laid down in Article 3(4) would never be complied with (85). It is therefore sufficient for the criterion of full-functionality if the joint venture is autonomous in operational respect.

(85) Judgment in Case T-282/02 Cementbouw v Commission, paragraph 62 (2006) ECR II-319.

1. Sufficient resources to operate independently on a market

94. Full function character essentially means that a joint venture must operate on a market, performing the functions normally carried out by undertakings operating on the same market. In order to do so the joint venture must have a management dedicated to its day-to-day operations and access to sufficient resources including finance, staff, and assets (tangible and intangible) in order to conduct on a lasting basis its business activities within the area provided for in the joint-venture agreement (86). The personnel do not necessarily need to be employed by the joint venture itself. If it is standard practice in the industry where the joint venture is operating, it may be sufficient if third parties envisage the staffing under an operational agreement or if staff is assigned by an interim employment agency. The secondment of personnel by the parent companies may also be sufficient if this is done either only for a start-up period or if the joint venture deals with the parent companies in the same way as with third parties. The latter case requires that the joint venture deals with the parents at arm's length on the basis of normal commercial conditions and that the joint venture is also free to recruit its own employees or to obtain staff via third parties.

(86) Case IV/M.527 – Thomson CSF/Deutsche Aerospace, of 2 December 1994 – intellectual rights, Case IV/M.560 EDS/Lufthansa of 11 May 1995 – outsourcing, Case IV/M.585 – Voest Alpine Industrieanlagenbau GmbH/Davy International Ltd, of 7 September 1995 – joint venture's right to demand additional expertise and staff from its parent companies, Case IV/M.686 – Nokia/Autoliv, of 5 February 1996, joint venture able to terminate «service agreements» with parent company and to move from site retained by parent company, Case IV/M.791 – British Gas Trading Ltd/Group 4 Utility Services Ltd, of 7 October 1996, joint venture's intended assets will be transferred to leasing company and leased by joint venture.

2. Activities beyond one specific function for the parents

95. A joint venture is not full-function if it only takes over one specific function within the parent companies' business activities without its own access to or presence on the market. This is the case, for example, for joint ventures limited to R&D or production. Such joint ventures are auxiliary to their parent companies' business activities. This is also the case where a joint venture is essentially limited to the distribution or sales of its parent companies' products and, therefore, acts principally as a sales agency. However, the fact that a joint venture makes use of the distribution network or outlet of one or more of its parent companies normally will not disqualify it as «full-function» as long as the parent companies are acting only as agents of the joint venture (87).

(87) Case IV/M.102 – TNT/Canada Post etc. of 2 December 1991.

96. A frequent example where this question arises are joint ventures involved in the holding of real estate property, which are typically set up for tax and other financial reasons. As long as the purpose of the joint venture is limited to the acquisition and/or holding of certain real estate for the parents and based on financial resources provided by the parents, it will not usually be considered to be full-function, as it lacks an autonomous, long term business activity on the market and will typically also lack the necessary resources to operate independently. This has to be distinguished from joint ventures that are actively managing a real estate portfolio and who act on their own behalf on the market, which typically indicates full-functionality (88).

(88) See Case IV/M.929 – DIA/Veba Immobilien/Deutschbau of 23 June 1997; Case COMP/M. 3325 – Morgan Stanley/Glick/Canary Wharf of 23 January 2004.

3. Sale/purchase relations with the parents

97. The strong presence of the parent companies in upstream or downstream markets is a factor to be taken into consideration in assessing the full-function character of a joint venture where this presence results in substantial sales or purchases between the parent companies and the joint venture. The fact that, for an initial start-up period only, the joint venture relies almost entirely on sales to or purchases from its parent companies does not normally affect its full-function character. Such a start-up period may be necessary in order to establish the joint venture on a market. But the period will normally not exceed a period of three years, depending on the specific conditions of the market in question (89).

(89) Case IV/M.560 – EDS/Lufthansa of 11 May 1995; Case IV/M.686 Nokia/Autoliv of 5 February 1996; to be contrasted with Case IV/M.904 – RSB/Tenex/Fuel Logistics of 2 April 1997 and Case IV/M.979 – Preussag/Voest-Alpine of 1 October 1997. A special case exists where sales by the joint venture to its parent are caused by a legal monopoly downstream of the joint venture, see Case IV/M.468 – Siemens/Italtel of 17 February 1995, or where the sales to a parent company consist of by-products, which are of minor importance to the joint venture, see Case IV/M.550 – Union Carbide/Enichem of 13 March 1995.

Sales to the parents

98. Where sales from the joint venture to the parent companies are intended to be made on a lasting basis, the essential question is whether, regardless of these sales, the joint venture is geared to play an active role on the market and can be considered economically autonomous from an operational viewpoint. In this respect the relative proportion of sales made to its parents compared with the total production of the joint venture is an important factor. Due to the particularities of each individual case, it is impossible to define a specific turnover ratio which distinguishes full-function from other joint ventures. If the joint venture achieves more than 50% of its turnover with third parties, this will typically be an indication of full-functionality. Below this indicative threshold, a case-by-case analysis is required, whereby, for the finding of operational autonomy, the relationship between the joint venture and its parents must be truly commercial in character. For this purpose, it is to be demonstrated that the joint venture will supply its goods or services to the purchaser who values them most and will pay most and that the joint venture will also deal with its parents' companies at arm's length on the basis of normal commercial conditions (90). Under these circumstances, i.e. if the joint venture will treat its parent companies in the same commercial way as third parties, it may be sufficient that at least 20% of the joint venture's predicted sales will go to third parties. However, the greater the proportion of sales likely to be made to the parents, the greater will be the need for clear evidence of the commercial character of the relationship.

(90) Case IV/M.556 – Zeneca/Vanderhave of 9 April 1996; Case IV/M.751 – Bayer/Hüls of 3 July 1996.

99. For the determination of the proportion between sales to the parents and to third parties, the Commission will take past accounts and substantiated business plans into account. However, especially where substantial third-party sales cannot be readily foreseen, the Commission will base its finding also on the general market structure. This may be a relevant factor as well for the assessment whether the joint venture will deal with its parents on an arm's length basis.

100. These issues frequently arise with regard to outsourcing agreements, where an undertaking creates a joint venture with a service provider (91) which will carry out functions that were previously dealt with by the undertaking in-house. The JV typically cannot be considered to be full-function in these scenarios: it provides its services exclusively to the client undertaking, and it is dependent for its services on input from the service provider. The fact that the joint venture's business plan often at least does not exclude that the joint venture can provide its services to third parties does not alter this assessment, as in the typical outsourcing setup any third party revenues are likely to remain ancillary to the joint venture's main activities for the client undertaking. However, this general rule does not exclude that there are outsourcing situations where the joint venture partners, for example for reasons of economies of scale, set up a joint venture with the perspective of significant market access. This could qualify the joint venture as full function if significant third-party sales are foreseen and if the relationship between the joint venture and its parent will be truly commercial in character and if the joint venture deals with its parents on the basis of normal commercial conditions.

(91) The question under which circumstances an outsourcing arrangement qualifies as a concentration is dealt with in paragraphs 25ff. of this Notice.

Purchases from the parents

101. In relation to purchases made by the joint venture from its parent companies, the full-function character of the joint venture is questionable in particular where little value is added to the products or services concerned at the level of the joint venture itself. In such a situation, the joint venture may be closer to a joint sales agency.

Trade markets

102. However, in contrast to this situation where a joint venture is active in a trade market and performs the normal functions of a trading company in such a market, it normally will not be an auxiliary sales agency but a full-function joint venture. A trade market is characterised by the existence of companies which specialise in the selling and distribution of products without being vertically integrated in addition to those which are integrated, and where different sources of supply are available for the products in question. In addition, many trade markets may require operators to invest in specific facilities such as outlets, stockholding, warehouses, depots, transport fleets and sales and service personnel. In order to constitute a full-function joint venture in a trade market, an undertaking must have the necessary facilities and be likely to obtain a substantial proportion of its supplies not only from its parent companies but also from other competing sources (92).

(92) Case IV/M.788 – AgrEVO/Marubeni of 3 September 1996.

4. Operation on a lasting basis

103. Furthermore, the joint venture must be intended to operate on a lasting basis. The fact that the parent companies commit to the joint venture the resources described above normally demonstrates that this is the case. In addition, agreements setting up a joint venture often provide for certain contingencies, for example, the failure of the joint venture or fundamental disagreement as between the parent companies (93). This may be achieved by the incorporation of provisions for the eventual dissolution of the joint venture itself or the possibility for one or more parent companies to withdraw from the joint venture. This kind of provision does not prevent the joint venture from being considered as operating on a lasting basis. The same is normally true where the agreement specifies a period for the duration of the joint venture where this period is sufficiently long in order to bring about a lasting change in the structure of the undertakings concerned (94), or where the agreement provides for the possible continuation of the joint venture beyond this period.

(93) Case IV/M.891 – Deutsche Bank/Commerzbank/J.M. Voith of 23 April 1997.

(94) See Case COMP/M.2903 – DaimlerChrysler/Deutsche Telekom/JV of 30 April 2003 where a period of 12 years was considered sufficient; Case COMP/M.2632 – Deutsche Bahn/ECT International/United Depots/JV of 11 February 2002 with a contract duration of 8 years. In Case COMP/M.3858 Lehman Brothers/Starwood/Le Meridien of 20 July 2005, the Commission considered a minimum period of 10-15 years sufficient, but not a period of three years.

104. By contrast, the joint venture will not be considered to operate on a lasting basis where it is established for a short finite duration. This would be the case, for example, where a joint venture is established in order to construct a specific project such as a power plant, but it will not be involved in the operation of the plant once its construction has been completed.

105. A joint venture also lacks the sufficient operations on a lasting basis at a stage where there are decisions of third parties outstanding that are of an essential core importance for starting the joint venture's business activity. Only decisions that go beyond mere formalities and the award of which is typically uncertain qualify for these scenarios. Examples are the award of a contract (e.g., in public tenders), licences (e.g., in the telecoms sector) or access rights to property (e.g., exploration rights for oil and gas). Pending the decision on such factors, it is unclear whether the joint venture will become operational at all. Thus, at that stage the joint venture cannot be considered to perform economic functions on a lasting basis and consequently does not qualify as full function. However, once a decision has been taken in favour of the joint venture in question, this criterion is fulfilled and a concentration arises (95).

(95) Subject to the other criteria mentioned in this chapter of the Notice.

5. Changes in the activities of the joint venture

106. The parents may decide to enlarge the scope of the activities of the joint venture in the course of its lifetime. This will be considered as a new concentration that may trigger a notification requirement if this enlargement entails the acquisition of the whole or part of another undertaking from the parents that would, considered in isolation, qualify as a concentration as explained in paragraph 24 of this Notice (96).

(96) See Case COMP/M.3039 – Soprol/Céréol/Lesieur of 30 January 2003.

107. A concentration may also arise if the parent companies transfer significant additional assets, contracts, know-how or other rights to the joint venture and these assets and rights constitute the basis or nucleus of an extension of the activities of the joint venture into other product or geographic markets which were not the object of the original joint venture, and if the joint venture performs such activities on a full-function basis. As the transfer of the assets or rights shows that the parents are the real players behind the extension of the joint venture's scope, the enlargement of the activities of the joint venture can be considered in the same way as the creation of a new joint venture within the meaning of Article 3(4) (97).

(97) The triggering event for the notification in such a case will be the agreement or other legal act underlying the transfer of the assets, contracts, know-how or other rights.

108. If the scope of a joint venture is enlarged without additional assets, contracts, know-how or rights being transferred, no concentration will be deemed to arise.

109. A concentration arises if a change in the activity of an existing non-full-function joint venture occurs so that a full-function joint venture within the meaning of Article 3(4) is created. The following examples may be given: a change of the organisational structure of a joint venture so that it fulfils the full functionality criterion (98); a joint venture that used to supply only the parent companies, which subsequently starts a significant activity on the market; or scenarios, as described in paragraph 105 above, where a joint venture can only start its activity on the market once it has essential input (such as a licence for a joint venture in the telecoms sector). Such a change in the activity of the joint venture will frequently require a decision by its shareholders or its management. Once the decision is taken that leads to the joint venture meeting the full functionality criterion, a concentration arises.

(98) Case COMP/M.2276 – The Coca-Cola Company/Nestlé/JV of 27 September 2001.

V. EXCEPTIONS

110. Article 3(5) sets out three exceptional situations where the acquisition of a controlling interest does not constitute a concentration under the Merger Regulation.

111. First, the acquisition of securities by companies whose normal activities include transactions and dealing in securities for their own account or for the account of others is not deemed to constitute a concentration if such an acquisition is made in the framework of these businesses and if the securities are held on only a temporary basis (Article 3(5)(a)). In order to fall within this exception, the following requirements must be fulfilled:
– the acquiring undertaking must be a credit or other financial institution or insurance company the normal activities of which are described above;
– the securities must be acquired with a view to their resale;
– the acquiring undertaking must not exercise the voting rights with a view to determining the strategic commercial behaviour of the target company or must exercise these rights only with a view to preparing the total or partial disposal of the undertaking, its assets or the securities;
– the acquiring undertaking must dispose of its controlling interest within one year of the date of the acquisition, that is, it must reduce its shareholding within this one-year period at least to a level which no longer confers control. This period, however, may be extended by the Commission where the acquiring undertaking can show that the disposal was not reasonably possible within the one-year period.

112. Second, there is no change of control, and hence no concentration within the meaning of the Merger Regulation, where control is acquired by an office-holder according to the law of a Member State relating to liquidation, winding-up, insolvency, cessation of payments, compositions or analogous proceedings (Article 3(5)(b));

113. Third, a concentration does not arise where a financial holding company within the meaning of Article 5(3) of the Council Directive 78/660/EEC (99) acquires control. The notion of «financial holding company» is thus limited to companies whose sole purpose it is to acquire holdings in other undertakings without involving themselves directly or indirectly in the management of those undertakings, the foregoing without prejudice to their rights as shareholders. Such investment companies must be further structured in a way that compliance with these limitations can be supervised by an administrative or judicial authority. The Merger Regulation provides for an additional condition for this exception to apply: such companies may exercise the voting rights in the other undertakings only to maintain the full value of those investments and not to determine directly or indirectly the strategic commercial conduct of the controlled undertaking.

(99) Fourth Council Directive 78/660/EEC of 25 July 1978 based on Article 54 (3) (g) of the Treaty on the annual accounts of certain types of companies, O.J. L 222, 14.8.1978, p. 11, as last amended by Directive 2003/51/EC of 18 June 2003, O.J. L 178, 17.7.2003, p. 16. Article 5(3) of this Directive defines financial holding companies as «those companies the sole objective of which is to acquire holdings in other undertakings, and to manage such holdings and turn them to profit, without involving themselves directly or indirectly in the management of those undertakings, the foregoing without prejudice to their rights as shareholders. The limitations imposed on the activities of these companies must be such that compliance with them can be supervised by an administrative or judicial authority».

114. The exceptions under Article 3(5) of the Merger Regulation only apply to a very limited field. First, these exceptions only apply if the operation would otherwise be a concentration in its own right, but not if the transaction is part of a broader, single concentration, in circumstances in which the ultimate acquirer of control would not fall within the terms of Article 3(5) (see e.g. paragraph 35 above). Second, the exceptions under Article 3(5)(a) and (c) only apply to acquisitions of control by way of purchase of securities, not to acquisitions of assets.

115. The exceptions do not apply to typical investment fund structures. According to their objectives, these funds usually do not limit themselves in the exercise of the voting rights, but adopt decisions to appoint the members of the management and the supervisory bodies of the undertakings or to even restructure those undertakings. This would not be compatible with the requirement under both Article 3(5)(a) and (c) that the acquiring companies do not exercise the voting rights with a view to determine the competitive conduct of the other undertaking (100).

(100) Case IV/M.669 – Charterhouse/Porterbrook, of 11 December 1995.

116. The question may arise whether an operation to rescue an undertaking before or from insolvency proceedings constitutes a concentration under the Merger Regulation. Such a rescue operation typically involves the conversion of existing debt into a new company, through which a syndicate of banks may acquire joint control of the company concerned. Where such an operation meets the criteria for joint control, as outlined above, it will normally be considered to be a concentration (101). Although the primary intention of the banks is to restructure the financing of the undertaking concerned for its subsequent resale, the exception set out in Article 3(5)(a) is normally not applicable to such an operation. In a similar way as set out for investment funds, the restructuring programme normally requires the controlling

banks to determine the strategic commercial behaviour of the rescued undertaking. Furthermore, it is not normally a realistic proposition to transform a rescued company into a commercially viable entity and to resell it within the permitted one-year period. Moreover, the length of time needed to achieve this aim may be so uncertain that it would be difficult to grant an extension of the disposal period.

(101) Case IV/M.116 – Kelt/American Express, of 28 August 1991.

VI. ABANDONMENT OF CONCENTRATIONS

117. A concentration ceases to exist and the Merger Regulation ceases to be applicable if the undertakings concerned abandon the concentration.

118. In this respect, the revised Merger Regulation 139/2004 introduced a new provision related to the closure of procedures concerning the control of concentrations without a final decision after the Commission has initiated proceedings under Article 6(1)(c), first sentence. That sentence reads as follows: «Without prejudice to Article 9, such proceedings shall be closed by means of a decision as provided for in Article 8(1) to (4), unless the undertakings concerned have demonstrated to the satisfaction of the Commission that they have abandoned the concentration». Prior to the initiation of proceedings, such requirements do not apply.

119. As a general principle, the requirements for the proof of the abandonment must correspond in terms of legal form, intensity etc. to the initial act that was considered sufficient to make the concentration notifiable. In case the parties proceed from that initial act to a strengthening of their contractual links during the procedure, for example by concluding a binding agreement after the transaction was notified on the basis of a good faith intention, the requirements for the proof of the abandonment must correspond also to the nature of the latest act.

120. In line with this principle, in case of implementation of the concentration prior to a Commission decision, the re-establishment of the status quo ante has to be shown. The mere withdrawal of the notification is not considered as sufficient proof that the concentration has been abandoned in the sense of Article 6(1)(c). Likewise, minor modifications of a concentration which do not affect the change in control or the quality of that change, cannot be considered as an abandonment of the original concentration (102).

– Binding agreement: proof of the legally binding cancellation of the agreement in the form envisaged by the initial agreement (i.e. usually a document signed by all the parties) will be required. Expressions of intention to cancel the agreement or not to implement the notified concentration, as well as unilateral declarations by (one of) the parties will not be considered sufficient (103).

– Good faith intention to conclude an agreement: In case of a letter of intent or memorandum of understanding reflecting such good faith intention, documents proving that this basis for the good faith intention has been cancelled will be required. As for possible other forms that indicated the good faith intention, the abandonment must reverse this good faith intention and correspond in terms of form and intensity to the initial expression of intent.

– Public announcement of a public bid or of the intention to make a public bid: a public announcement terminating the bidding procedure or renouncing to the intention to make a public bid will be required. The format and public reach of this announcement must be comparable to the initial announcement.

– Implemented concentrations: In case the concentration has been implemented prior to a Commission decision, the parties will be required to show that the situation prevailing before the implementation of the concentration has been re-established.

(102) This paragraph does not prejudge the assessment whether the modification requires submitting additional information to the Commission under Article 5(3) of Regulation (E.C.) N° 802/2004.

(103) See Case COMP/M.4381 – JCI/VB/FIAMM of 10 May 2007, paragraph 15, where only one party did no longer wished to implement an agreement, whereas the other party still considered the agreement to be binding and enforceable.

121. It is for the parties to submit the necessary documentation to meet these requirements in due time.

VII. CHANGES OF TRANSACTIONS AFTER A COMMISSION AUTHORISATION DECISION

122. In some cases, parties may wish not to implement the concentration in the form foreseen after authorisation of the concentration by the Commission. The question arises whether the Commission's authorisation decision still covers the changed structure of the transaction.

123. Broadly speaking, if, before implementation of the authorised concentration, the transactional structure is changed from an acquisition of control, falling under Article 3(1)(b), to a merger according to Article 3(1)(a), or vice versa, then the change in the transactional structure is considered a different concentration under the Merger Regulation and a new notification is required (104). However, less significant modifications of the transaction, for example minor changes in the shareholding percentages which do not affect the change in control or the quality of that change, changes in the offer price in the case of public bids or changes in the corporate structure by which the transaction is implemented without effects on the relevant control situation under the Merger Regulation, are considered as being covered by the Commission's authorisation decision.

(104) See cases COMP/M.2706 – Carnival Corporation/P&O Princess of 11 April 2002 and COMP/M.3071 – Carnival Corporation/P&O Princess of 10 February 2003. In such circumstances, the identity of the notifying parties changes, as both parties to a merger must notify, whereas only the party acquiring control must do so. However, if the parties implement an acquisition of control over a target company and only subsequently decide to merge with the newly acquired subsidiary, this would be regarded as an internal restructuring that does not give rise to a change in control and would thus not fall within the terms of Article 3 of the Merger Regulation.

C. COMMUNITY DIMENSION

I. THRESHOLDS

124. A two fold test defines the operations to which the Merger Regulation applies. The first test is that the operation must be a concentration within the meaning of Article 3. The second comprises the turnover thresholds contained in Article 1, designed to identify those operations which have an impact upon the Community and can be deemed to be of «Community dimension». Turnover is used as a proxy for the economic resources being combined in a concentration, and is allocated geographically in order to reflect the geographic distribution of those resources.

125. Two sets of thresholds are set out in Article 1 to establish whether the operation has a Community dimension. Article 1(2) establishes three different criteria: The worldwide turnover threshold is intended to measure the overall dimension of the undertakings concerned; the Community turnover threshold seek to determine whether the concentration involves a minimum level of activities in the Community; and the two-thirds rule aims to exclude purely domestic transactions from Community jurisdiction.

126. This second set of thresholds, contained in Article 1(3), is designed to tackle those concentrations which fall short of achieving Community dimension under Article 1(2), but would have a substantial impact in at least three Member States leading to multiple notifications under national competition rules of those Member States. For this purpose, Article 1(3) provides for lower turnover thresholds, both worldwide and Community-wide, and for a minimum level of activities of the undertakings concerned, jointly and individually, in at least three Member States. Similarly to Article 1(2), Article 1(3) also contains a two-thirds rule excluding predominantly domestic concentrations (105).

(105) A concentration is further deemed to have a Community dimension if it is referred to the Commission under Article 4(5) of the Merger Regulation. These cases are dealt with in the Commission Notice on Case Referral in respect of concentrations, O.J. C 56, 5.3.2005, p. 2.

127. The thresholds as such are designed to govern jurisdiction and not to assess the market position of the parties to the concentration nor the impact of the operation. In so doing they include turnover derived from, and thus the resources devoted to, all areas of activity of the parties, and not just those directly involved in the concentration. The thresholds are purely quantitative, since they are only based on turnover calculation instead of market share or other criteria. They pursue the objective to provide a simple and objective mechanism that can be easily handled by the companies involved in a merger in order to determine if their transaction has a Community dimension and is therefore notifiable.

128. Whereas Article 1 sets out the numerical thresholds to establish jurisdiction, the purpose of Article 5 is to explain how turnover should be calculated to ensure that the resulting figures are a true representation of economic reality.

II. NOTION OF UNDERTAKING CONCERNED

1. General

129. From the point of view of determining jurisdiction, the undertakings concerned are those participating in a concentration, i.e. a merger or an acquisition of control as foreseen in Article 3(1). The individual and aggregate turnover of those undertakings will be decisive in determining whether the thresholds are met.

130. Once the undertakings concerned have been identified in a given transaction, their turnover for the purposes of determining jurisdiction is to be calculated according to the rules set out in Article 5. Article 5(4) sets out detailed criteria to identify undertakings whose turnover may be attributed to the undertaking concerned because of certain direct or indirect links with the latter. The legislator's intention was to lay down concrete rules which, seen together, can be taken to establish the notion of a «group» for the purposes of the turnover thresholds in the Merger Regulation. The term «group» will be used in the following sections exclusively to refer to the collection of undertakings whose relations with an undertaking concerned come within the terms of one or more of the sub-paragraphs of Article 5(4) of the Merger Regulation.

131. It is important, when referring to the various undertakings which may be involved in a procedure, not to confuse the concept of «undertakings concerned» under Articles 1 and 5 with the terminology used elsewhere in the Merger Regulation and in Commission Regulation (E.C.) N° 802/2004 of 7 April 2004 implementing Council Regulation (E.C.) N° 139/2004 on the control of concentrations between undertakings (hereinafter referred to as the «Implementing Regulation») (106) referring to the various undertakings which may be involved in a procedure. This terminology refers to the notifying parties, other involved parties, third parties and parties who may be subject to fines or periodic penalty payments, and they are defined in Chapter IV of the Implementing Regulation, along with their respective rights and duties.

(106) O.J. L 133, 30.4.2004, p. 1.

2. Mergers

132. In a merger the undertakings concerned are each of the merging entities.

3. Acquisition of control

133. In the remaining cases, it is the concept of «acquiring control» that will determine which are the undertakings concerned. On the acquiring side, there can be one or more undertakings acquiring sole or joint control. On the acquired side, there can be one or more undertakings as a whole or parts thereof. As a general rule, each of these undertakings will be an undertaking concerned within the meaning of the Merger Regulation.

Acquisition of sole control

134. Acquisition of sole control of the whole undertaking is the most straightforward case of acquisition of control. The undertakings concerned will be the acquiring undertaking and the target undertaking.

135. Where the target undertaking is acquired by a group through one of its subsidiaries, the undertakings concerned are the target undertaking and the acquiring subsidiary if this is not a mere acquisition vehicle. However, even though the subsidiary is normally the undertaking concerned for the purpose of calculating turnover, the turnover of all undertakings with which the undertaking concerned has the links as specified in Article 5(4) shall be included in the threshold calculations. In this respect, the group is considered to be a single economic unit and the different companies belonging to the same group cannot be considered as different undertakings concerned for jurisdictional purposes under the Merger Regulation. The actual notification can be made by the subsidiary concerned or by its parent company.

Acquisition of parts of an undertaking and staggered operations – Article 5(2)

136. The first subparagraph of Article 5(2) of the Merger Regulation provides that when the operation concerns the acquisition of parts of one or more undertakings, only those parts which are the subject of the transaction shall be taken into account with regard to the seller. The possible impact of the transaction on the market will depend only on the combination of the economic and financial resources that are the subject of the transaction with those of the acquirer and not on the remaining business of the seller. In this case, the undertakings concerned will be the acquirer(s) and the acquired part(s) of the target undertaking, but the remaining businesses of the seller will be ignored.

137. The second subparagraph of Article 5(2) includes a special provision on staggered operations or follow-up deals. The previous concentrations (within two years) involving the same parties become (re)notifiable with the most recent transaction, provided this constitutes a concentration, if the thresholds are met whether for one or more of the transactions taken in isolation or cumulatively. In this case, the undertakings concerned are the acquirer(s) and the different acquired part(s) of the target company taken as a whole.

Change from joint to sole control

138. If the acquisition of control occurs by way of a change from joint control to sole control, one shareholder normally acquires the stake previously held by the other shareholder(s). In this situation, the undertakings concerned are the acquiring shareholder and the joint venture. As is the case for any other seller, the «exiting» shareholder is not an undertaking concerned (107).

(107) Case IV/M.023 – ICI/Tioxide, of 28 November 1990.

Acquisition of joint control

139. In the case of acquisition of joint control of a newly-created undertaking, the undertakings concerned are each of the companies acquiring control of the newly set-up joint venture (which, as it does not yet exist, cannot be considered to be an undertaking concerned and moreover, as yet, has no turnover of its own). The same rule applies where one undertaking contributes a pre-existing subsidiary or a business (over which it previously exercised sole control) to a newly created joint venture. In these circumstances, each of the jointly-controlling undertakings is considered an undertaking concerned whereas any company or business contributed to the joint venture is not an undertaking concerned, and its turnover is part of the turnover of the initial parent company.

140. The situation is different if undertakings newly acquire joint control of a pre-existing undertaking or business. The undertakings concerned are each of the undertakings acquiring joint control on the one hand, and the pre-existing acquired undertaking or business on the other.

141. The acquisition of a company with a view to immediately split up the assets is, as explained above in paragraph 32, mostly not considered as an acquisition of joint control of the entire target company, but as the acquisition of sole control by each of the ultimate acquirers of the respective parts of the target company. In line with the considerations for the acquisition of sole control, undertakings concerned are the acquiring undertakings and the acquired parts in each of the transactions.

Changes of controlling shareholders in cases of joint control of an existing joint venture

142. A notifiable concentration may arise, as explained above, where a change in the quality of control occurs in a joint control structure due to the entrance of new controlling shareholders, irrespective of whether or not they replace existing controlling shareholders.

143. In the case where one or more shareholders acquire control, either by entry or by substitution of one or more shareholders, in a situation of joint control both before and after the operation, the undertakings concerned are the shareholders (both existing and new) who exercise joint control and the joint venture itself (108). On the one hand, similar to the acquisition of joint control of an existing company, the joint venture itself can be considered as an undertaking concerned as it is an already pre-existing undertaking. On the other hand, as set out above, the entry of a new shareholder is not only in itself a new acquisition of control, but also leads to a change in the quality of control for the remaining controlling shareholders as the quality of control of the joint venture is determined by the identity and composition of the controlling shareholders and therefore also by the relationship between them. Furthermore, the Merger Regulation considers a joint venture as a combination of the economic resources of the parent companies, together with the joint venture if it already generates turnover on the market. For these reasons, the newly entering controlling shareholders are undertakings concerned alongside with the remaining controlling shareholders. Due to the change of the quality in control, all of them are considered to undertake an acquisition of control.

(108) See Case IV/M.376 – Synthomer/Yule Catto, of 22 October 1993.

144. As Article 4(2) first sentence of the Merger Regulation foresees that all acquisitions of joint control shall be notified jointly by the undertakings acquiring joint control, existing and new shareholders in principle have to notify concentrations arising from such changes in joint control scenarios jointly.

Acquisition of control by a joint venture

145. In transactions where a joint venture acquires control of another company, the question arises whether or not the joint venture should be regarded as the undertaking concerned (the turnover of which would include the turnover of its parent companies), or whether each of its parent companies should individually be regarded as undertakings concerned. This question may be decisive for jurisdictional purposes (109). Whereas, in principle, the undertaking concerned is the joint venture as the direct participant in the acquisition of control, there may be circumstances where companies set up «shell» companies and the parent companies will individually be considered as undertakings concerned. In this type of situation, the Commission will look at the economic reality of the operation to determine which are the undertakings concerned.

(109) Assume the following scenario: The target company has an aggregate Community turnover of less than EUR 250 million, and the acquiring parties are two (or more) undertakings, each with a Community turnover exceeding EUR 250 million. If the target is acquired by a «shell» company set up between the acquiring undertakings, there would only be one undertaking (the «shell» company) with a Community turnover exceeding EUR 250 million, and thus one of the cumulative threshold conditions for Community jurisdiction, namely, the existence of at least two undertak-

ings with a Community turnover exceeding EUR 250 million, would not be fulfilled. Conversely, if instead of acting through a «shell» company, the acquiring undertakings acquire the target undertaking themselves, then the turnover threshold would be met and the Merger Regulation would apply to this transaction. The same considerations apply to the national turnover thresholds referred to in Article 1(3).

146. Where the acquisition is carried out by a full-function joint venture, with the features set out above, and already operates on the same market, the Commission will normally consider the joint venture itself and the target undertaking to be the undertakings concerned (and not the joint venture's parent companies).

147. Conversely, where the joint venture can be regarded as a mere vehicle for an acquisition by the parent companies, the Commission will consider each of the parent companies themselves to be the undertakings concerned, rather than the joint venture, together with the target company. This is the case in particular where the joint venture is set up especially for the purpose of acquiring the target company or has not yet started to operate, where an existing joint venture has no full-function character as referred to above or where the joint venture is an association of undertakings. The same applies where there are elements which demonstrate that the parent companies are in fact the real players behind the operation. These elements may include a significant involvement by the parent companies themselves in the initiation, organisation and financing of the operation. In those cases, the parent companies are regarded as undertakings concerned.

Break-up of joint ventures and exchange of assets

148. When two (or more) undertakings break up a joint venture and split the assets (constituting businesses) between them, this will normally be considered as more than one acquisition of control, as explained above in paragraph 41. For example, undertakings A and B form a joint venture and subsequently split it up, in particular with a new asset configuration. The break-up of the joint venture involves a change from joint control over the joint venture's entire assets to sole control over the divided assets by each of the acquiring undertakings (110).

(110) See parallel cases COMP/M.3293 – Shell/BEB and COMP/M.3294 – ExxonMobil/BEB of 20 November 2003; Case IV/M.197 – Solvay/Laporte of 30 April 1992.

149. For each break-up operation, and in line with the consideration to the acquisition of sole control, the undertakings concerned will be, on the one hand, the acquiring party and, on the other, the assets that this undertaking will acquire.

150. Similar to the break-up scenario is the situation where two (or more) companies exchange assets constituting a business on each side. In this case, each acquisition of control is considered an independent acquisition of sole control. The undertakings concerned will be, for each transaction, the acquiring companies and the acquired undertaking or assets.

Acquisitions of control by natural persons

151. Control may also be acquired by natural persons, within the meaning of Article 3 of the Merger Regulation, if those persons themselves carry out further economic activities (and are therefore classified as economic undertakings in their own right) or if they control one or more other economic undertakings. In such a situation, the undertakings concerned are the target undertaking and the individual acquirer (with the turnover of the undertaking(s) controlled by that natural person being included in the calculation of the natural person's turnover to the extent that the terms of Article 5(4) are satisfied) (111).

152. An acquisition of control of an undertaking by its managers is also an acquisition by natural persons, and paragraph 151 above is also relevant. However, the managers may pool their interests through a «vehicle company», so that it acts with a single voice and also to facilitate decision-making. Such a vehicle company may be, but is not necessarily, an undertaking concerned. The general guidance given above in paragraphs 145-147 on acquisitions of control by a joint venture also applies here.

(111) See Case IV/M.082 – Asko/Jacobs/Adia, of 16 May 1991 where a private individual with other economic activities acquired joint control of an undertaking and was considered an undertaking concerned.

Acquisition of control by a State-owned undertaking

153. As described above, a merger or an acquisition of control arising between two undertakings owned by the same State (or the same public body) may constitute a concentration if the undertakings were formerly part of different economic units having an independent power of decision. If this is the case, both of them will qualify as undertakings concerned although both are owned by the same State (112).

(112) See recital 22 of the Merger Regulation, directly related to the calculation of turnover of a state-owned undertaking concerned in the context of Article 5(4).

III. RELEVANT DATE FOR ESTABLISHING JURISDICTION

154. The legal situation for establishing the Commission's jurisdiction has been changed under the recast Merger Regulation. Under the former Merger Regulation, the relevant date was the triggering event for a notification according to Article 4(1) of this Regulation – the conclusion of a final agreement or the announcement of a public bid or the acquisition of a controlling interest – or, at the latest, the time when the parties were obliged to notify (i.e. one week after a triggering event for a notification) (113).

(113) See Case COMP/M.1741 – MCI Worldcom/Sprint of 28 June 2000.

155. Under the recast Merger Regulation, there is no longer an obligation for the parties to notify within a certain time-frame (provided the parties do not implement the planned concentration before notification). Moreover, according to Article 4(1) second subparagraph, the undertakings concerned can already notify the transaction on the basis of a good faith intention to conclude an agreement or, in the case of a public bid, where they have publicly announced an intention to make such a bid. At the time of the notification at the latest, the Commission – as well as national competition authorities – must be able to determine their jurisdiction. Article 4(1) subparagraph 1 of the Merger Regulation provides, generally, that concentrations shall be notified following the conclusion of the agreement, the announcement of the public bid, or the acquisition of a controlling interest. The dates of these events are therefore still decisive under the recast Merger Regulation in order to determine the relevant date for establishing jurisdiction, if a notification does not occur before such events on the basis of a good faith intention or an announced intention (114).

(114) The alternative possibility that turnover should be defined on the latest date when the relevant parties are obliged to notify (seven days after the «triggering event» under the former Merger Regulation) cannot be retained under the recast merger Regulation, because there is no deadline for notification.

156. The relevant date for establishing Community jurisdiction over a concentration is therefore the date of the conclusion of the binding legal agreement, the announcement of a public bid or the acquisition of a controlling interest or the date of the first notification, whichever date is earlier (115). Regarding the date of notification, a notification to either the Commission or to a Member State authority is relevant. The relevant date needs in particular to be considered for the question whether acquisitions or divestitures which occur after the period covered by the relevant account, but before the relevant date, require adaptations to those accounts according to the principles set out in paragraphs 172 and 173.

(115) See also opinion of AG Kokott in Case C-202/06 Cementbouw v Commission of 26 April 2007, paragraph 46 (not yet reported). Only the recast merger Regulation has provided for the possibility to take into account the first notification if this is earlier than the date of the conclusion of the binding legal agreement, the announcement of a public bid or the acquisition of a controlling interest, see fn. 35 of the opinion.

IV. TURNOVER

1. The concept of turnover

157. The concept of turnover as used in Article 5 of the Merger Regulation comprises «the amounts derived (...) from the sale of products and the provision of services». Those amounts generally appear in company accounts under the heading «sales». In the case of products, turnover can be determined without difficulty, namely by identifying each commercial act involving a transfer of ownership.

158. In the case of services, the method of calculating turnover in general does not differ from that used in the case of products: the Commission takes into consideration the total amount of sales. However, the calculation of the amounts derived from the provision of services may be more complex as this depends on the exact service provided and the underlying legal and economic arrangements in the sector in question. Where one undertaking provides the entire service directly to the customer, the turnover of the undertaking concerned consists of the total amount of sales for the provision of services in the last financial year.

159. In other areas, this general principle may have to be adapted to the specific conditions of the service provided. In certain sectors of activity (such as package holidays and advertising), the service may be sold through intermediaries (116). Even if the intermediary invoices the entire amount to the final customer, the turnover of the undertaking acting as an intermediary consists solely of the amount of its commission. For package holidays, the entire amount paid by the final customer is then allocated to the tour operator which uses the travel agency as distribution network. In the case of advertising, only the amounts received (without the commission) are considered to constitute the turnover of the TV channel or the magazine since media agencies, as intermediaries, do not constitute the distribution channel for the sellers of advertising space, but are chosen by the customers, i.e. those undertakings wishing to place advertising.

(116) An undertaking will normally not act as an intermediary if it sells products via a commercial act which involves a transfer of ownership, Judgment in Case T-417/05, Endesa v Commission, paragraph 213, (2006) ECR II-2533.

160. The examples mentioned show that, due to the diversity of services, many different situations may arise and the underlying legal and economic relations have to be carefully analysed. Similarly, specific situations for the calculation of turnover may arise in the areas of credit, financial services and insurance. These issues will be dealt with in Section VI.

2. Ordinary activities

161. Article 5(1) provides that the amounts to be included in the calculation of turnover should correspond to the «ordinary activities» of the undertakings concerned. This is the turnover achieved from the sale of products or the provision of services in the normal course of its business. It generally excludes those items which are listed under the headers «financial income» or «extraordinary income» in the company's accounts. Such extraordinary income may be derived from the sale of businesses or of fixed assets. However, company accounts do not necessarily delineate the revenues derived from ordinary activities in the way required for the purposes of turnover calculation under the Merger Regulation. In some cases, the qualification of the items in the accounts may have to be adapted to the requirements of the Merger Regulation (117).

(117) In Case IV/M.126 – Accor/Wagons-Lits, of 28 April 1992, the Commission decided to consider certain income from car-hire activities as revenues from ordinary activities although they were included as «other operating proceeds» in Wagons-Lits' profit and loss account.

162. The revenues do not necessarily have to be derived from the customer of the products or services. With regard to aid granted to undertakings by public bodies, any aid has to be included in the calculation of turnover if the undertaking is itself the recipient of the aid and if the aid is directly linked to the sale of products and the provision of services by the undertaking. The aid is therefore an income of the undertaking from the sale of products or provision of services in addition to the price paid by the consumer (118).

(118) See Case IV/M.156 – Cereol/Continentale Italiana of 27 November 1991. In this case, the Commission excluded Community aid from the calculation of turnover because the aid was not intended to support the sale of products manufactured by one of the undertakings involved in the merger, but the producers of the raw materials (grain) used by the undertaking, which specialised in the crushing of grain.

163. Specific issues have arisen for the calculation of turnover of a business unit which only had internal revenues in the past. This may in particular apply for transactions involving the outsourcing of services by transfer of a business unit. If such a transaction constitutes a concentration on the basis of the considerations outlined in paragraphs 25 ff. of this Notice, the Commission's practice is that the turnover should normally be calculated on the basis of the previously internal turnover or of publicly quoted prices where such prices exist (e.g. in the oil industry). Where the previously internal turnover does not appear to correspond to a market valuation of the activities in question (and, thus, to the expected future turnover on the market), the forecast revenues to be received on the basis of an agreement with the former parent may be a suitable proxy.

3. «Net» turnover

164. The turnover to be taken into account is «net» turnover, after deduction of a number of components specified in the Regulation. The aim is to adjust turnover in such a way as to enable it to reflect the real economic strength of the undertaking.

3.1. Deduction of rebates and taxes

165. Article 5(1) provides for the «deduction of sales rebates and of value added tax and other taxes directly related to turnover». «Sales rebates» mean all rebates or discounts which are granted by the undertakings to their customers and which have a direct influence on the amounts of sales.

166. As regards the deduction of taxes, the Merger Regulation refers to VAT and «other taxes directly related to turnover». The concept of «taxes directly related to turnover» refers to indirect taxation linked to turnover, such as, for example, taxes on alcoholic beverages or cigarettes.

3.2. The treatment of «internal» turnover

167. The first subparagraph of Article 5(1) states that «the aggregate turnover of an undertaking concerned shall not include the sale of products or the provision of services between any of the undertakings referred to in paragraph 4», i.e. the group to which the undertaking concerned belongs. The aim is to exclude the proceeds of business dealings within a group so as to take account of the real economic weight of each entity in the form of market turnover. Thus, the «amounts» taken into account by the Merger Regulation reflect only the transactions which take place between the group of undertakings on the one hand and third parties on the other.

168. Article 5(5)(a) of the Merger Regulation applies the principle that double counting is to be avoided specifically to the situation where two or more undertakings concerned in a concentration jointly have the rights or powers listed in Article 5(4)(b) in another company. According to this provision, the turnover resulting from the sale of products or the provision of services between the joint venture and each of the undertakings concerned (or any other undertaking connected with any one of them in the sense of Article 5(4)) should be excluded. As regards joint ventures between undertakings concerned and third parties, insofar as their turnover is taken into account according to Article 5(4)(b) as set out in paragraph 181 below, the turnover generated by sales between the joint venture and the undertaking concerned (as well as undertakings linked to the undertaking concerned in accordance with the criteria set out in Article 5(4)) is not taken into account according to Article 5(1).

4. Turnover calculation and financial accounts

4.1. The general rule

169. The Commission seeks to base itself upon the most accurate and reliable figures available. Generally, the Commission will refer to accounts which relate to the closest financial year to the date of the transaction and which are audited under the standard applicable to the undertaking in question and compulsory for the relevant financial year (119). An adjustment of the audited figures should only take place if this is required by the provisions of the Merger Regulation, including the cases explained in more detail in paragraph 172.

(119) See Case COMP/M.3986 – Gas Natural/Endesa of 15 November 2005; confirmed by Judgment in Case T-417/05, Endesa v Commission, paragraphs 128, 131, (2006) ECR II-2533.

170. The Commission is reluctant to rely on management or any other form of provisional accounts in any but exceptional circumstances (120). Where a concentration takes place within the first months of the year and audited accounts are not yet available for the most recent financial year, the figures to be taken into account are those relating to the previous year. Where there is a major divergence between the two sets of accounts, due to significant and permanent changes in the undertaking concerned, and, in particular, when the final draft figures for the most recent year have been approved by the board of management, the Commission may decide to take those figures into account.

(120) See Case COMP/M.3986 – Gas Natural/Endesa of 15 November 2005; confirmed by Judgment in Case T-417/05, Endesa v Commission, paragraphs 176, 179, (2006) ECR II-2533.

171. Despite the general rule, in cases where major differences between the Community's accounting standards and those of a non-member country are observed, the Commission may consider it necessary to restate these accounts in accordance with Community standards in respect of turnover.

4.2. Adjustments after the date of the last audited accounts

172. Notwithstanding the foregoing paragraphs, an adjustment must always be made to account for permanent changes in the economic reality of the undertakings concerned, such as acquisitions or divestments which are not or not fully reflected in the audited accounts. Such changes have to be taken into account in order to identify the true resources being concentrated and to better reflect the economic situation of the undertakings concerned. Those adjustments are only selective in nature and do not endanger the principle that there should be a simple and objective mechanism to determine the Commission's jurisdiction as they do not require a complete revision of the audited accounts (121). First, this applies to acquisitions, divestments or closure of part of its business subsequent to the date of the audited accounts. This is relevant if a company closes a transaction concerning the divestment and closure of part of its business at any time before the relevant date for establishing jurisdiction (see paragraph 154) or where such a divestment or closure of a business is a pre-condition for the operation (122). In this case, the turnover to be attributed to that part of the business must be subtracted from the turnover of the notifying party as shown in its last audited accounts. If an agreement for the sale of part of its business is signed, but the closing of the sale (in other words, its legal implementation and the transfer of the legal title to the shares or assets acquired) has not yet occurred, such a change is not taken into account (123), unless the sale is a pre-condition for the notified operation. Conversely, the turnover of those businesses whose acquisition has been closed subsequent to the preparation of the most recent audited accounts, but before the relevant date for establishing jurisdiction, must be added to a company's turnover for notification purposes.

(121) Judgment in Case T-417/05, Endesa v Commission, paragraph 209, (2006) ECR II-2533.

(122) See Judgment in Case T-3/93, Air France v Commission, (1994) ECR II-121 paragraphs 100 et seq. in relation to Case IV/M.278 – British Airways/Dan Air; Case IV/M.588 – Ingersoll-Rand/Clark Equipment.

(123) Case IV/M.632 – Rhône Poulenc Rorer/Fisons of 21 September 1995; Case COMP/M.1741 – MCI Worldcom/Sprint of 28 June 2000.

173. Second, an adjustment may also be necessary for acquisitions, divestments or closure of part of the business which have taken place during the financial year for which the audited accounts are drawn up. If acquisitions, divestments or closure of part of the business within this period are made, the changes in the economic resources may only partly be reflected in the audited accounts of the undertaking concerned. As the turnover of the businesses acquired may be included in the accounts only from the time of their acquisition, this may not reflect the full annual turnover of the acquired business. Conversely, the turnover of the businesses divested or closed may still be included in the audited accounts up to the point in time of their actual divestment or closure. In these cases, adjustments have to be made to remove the turnover generated by the divested or closed businesses from the audited accounts until the time of de-consolidation and to add the turnover which the acquired businesses have generated in the year until the time they have been consolidated in the accounts. As a result, the turnover of the businesses divested or closed must be excluded in full and the full annual turnover of the businesses acquired must be included.

174. Other factors that may affect turnover on a temporary basis such as a decrease in orders for the product or a slow-down in the production process within the period prior to the transaction will be ignored for the purposes of calculating turnover. No adjustment to the definitive accounts will be made to incorporate them.

5. Attribution of turnover under Article 5(4)

5.1. Identification of undertakings whose turnover is taken into account

175. When an undertaking concerned by a concentration belongs to a group, not only the turnover of the undertaking concerned is considered, but the Merger Regulation requires to also take into account the turnover of those undertakings with which the undertaking concerned has links consisting in the rights or powers listed in Article 5(4) in order to determine whether the thresholds contained in Article 1 of the Merger Regulation are met. The aim is again to capture the total volume of the economic resources that are being combined through the operation irrespective of whether the economic activities are carried out directly by the undertaking concerned or whether they are undertaken indirectly via undertakings with which the undertaking concerned possesses the links described in Article 5(4).

176. The Merger Regulation does not delineate the concept of a group in a single abstract definition, but sets out in Article 5(4)(b) certain rights or powers. If an undertaking concerned directly or indirectly has such links with other companies, those are to be regarded as part of its group for purposes of turnover calculation under the Merger Regulation.

177. Article 5(4) of the Merger Regulation provides the following:

«Without prejudice to paragraph 2 (acquisitions of parts), the aggregate turnover of an undertaking concerned within the meaning of Article 1(2) and (3) shall be calculated by adding together the respective turnovers of the following:

(a) the undertaking concerned;

(b) those undertakings in which the undertaking concerned directly or indirectly:

(i) owns more than half the capital or business assets, or

(ii) has the power to exercise more than half the voting rights, or

(iii) has the power to appoint more than half the members of the supervisory board, the administrative board or bodies legally representing the undertakings, or

(iv) has the right to manage the undertaking's affairs;

(c) those undertakings which have in an undertaking concerned the rights or powers listed in *(b)*;

(d) those undertakings in which an undertaking as referred to in *(c)* has the rights or powers listed in *(b)*;

(e) those undertakings in which two or more undertakings as referred to in *(a)* to *(d)* jointly have the rights or powers listed in *(b)*.»

An undertaking which has in another undertaking the rights and powers mentioned in Article 5(4)(b) will be referred to as the «parent» of the latter in the present section of this Notice dealing with the calculation of turnover, whereas the latter is referred to as «subsidiary» of the former. In short, Article 5(4) therefore provides that the turnover of the undertaking concerned by the concentration (point *(a)*) should include its subsidiaries (point *(b)*), its parent companies (point *(c)*), the other subsidiaries of its parent undertakings (point *(d)*) and any other subsidiary jointly held by two or more of the undertakings identified under *(a)*-*(d)* (point *(e)*).

178. A graphic example is as follows:
The undertaking concerned and its group:

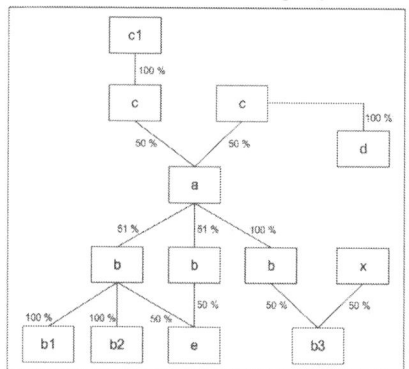

a : The undertaking concerned (124)

(124) For the graph it is assumed that the joint venture itself is the undertaking concerned according to the criteria set out in paragraph 146 (acquisition by a full-function JV operating on the same market).

b : Its subsidiaries, jointly held companies together with third parties (b3) and their own subsidiaries (b1 and b2)

c : Its parent companies and their own parent companies (c1)

d : Other subsidiaries of the parent companies of the undertaking concerned

e : Companies jointly held by two (or more) companies of the group

x : Third party

Note: the letters a – e correspond to the relevant points of Article 5(4). Percentages set out in the graph relate to the percentage of voting rights held by the respective parent company.

179. The rights or powers listed in Article 5(4)(b)(i)-(iii) can be identified in a rather straightforward way as they refer to quantitative thresholds. These thresholds are fulfilled if the undertaking concerned owns more than half of the capital or business assets of other undertakings, has more than half of the voting rights or has legally the power to appoint more than half of the board members in other undertakings. However, the thresholds are also met if the undertaking concerned *de facto* has the power to exercise more than half of the voting rights in the shareholders' assembly or the power to appoint more than half of the board members in other undertakings (125).

(125) Case IV/M.187 – Ifint/Exor of 2 March 1992; Case IV/M.062 – Eridania/ISI of 30 July 1991.

180. The provision contained in Article 5(4)*(b)(iv)* refers to the right to manage the undertaking's affairs. Such a right to manage exists under company law in particular on the basis of organisational contracts such as a «Beherrschungsvertrag» under German law, on the basis of business lease agreements or on the basis of the organisation structure for the general partner in a limited partnership (126). However, the «right to manage» may also result from the holding of voting rights (alone or in combination with contractual arrangements, such as a shareholders' agreement) which enable, on a stable, de jure basis, to determine the strategic behaviour of an undertaking.

(126) Case IV/M.126 – Accor/WagonLits of 28 April 1992.

181. The right to manage also covers situations in which the undertaking concerned jointly has the right to manage an undertaking's affairs together with third parties (127). The underlying consideration is that the undertakings exercising joint control have jointly the right to manage the controlled undertakings' affairs even if each of them individually may have those rights only in a negative sense, i.e. in the form of *veto* rights. In the example, the undertaking (b3) which is jointly controlled by the undertaking concerned *(a)* and a third party *(x)* is taken into account as both *(a)* and *(x)* have *veto* rights in (b3) on the basis of their equal shareholding in (b3) (128). Under Article 5(4)*(b)(iv)* the Commission only takes into account those joint ventures in which the undertaking concerned and third parties have de jure rights that give rise to a clear-cut right to manage. The inclusion of joint ventures is therefore limited to situations where the undertaking concerned and third parties have a joint right to manage on the basis of an agreement, e.g. a shareholders' agreement, or where the undertaking concerned and a third party have an equality of voting rights to the effect that they have the right to appoint an equal number of members to the decision-making bodies of the joint venture.

(127) Case COMP/M.1741 – MCI Worldcom/Sprint; Case IV/M. 187 – Ifint/Exor; Case IV/M.1046 – Ameritech/Tele Danmark.
(128) However, only half of the turnover generated by b3 is taken into account, see paragraph 187.

182. In the same way, where two or more companies jointly control the undertaking concerned in the sense that the agreement of each and all of them is needed in order to manage the undertaking affairs, the turnover of all of them is included. In the example, the two parent companies *(c)* of the undertaking concerned *(a)* would be taken into account as well as their own parent companies (c1 in the example). This interpretation results from the referral from Article 5(4)*(c)*, dealing with this case, to Article 5(4)*(b)*, which is applicable to jointly controlled companies as set out in the preceding paragraph.

183. When any of the companies identified on the basis of Article 5(4) also has links as defined in Article 5(4) with other undertakings, these should also be brought into the calculation. In the example, one of the subsidiaries of the undertaking concerned a (called b) has in turn its own subsidiaries b1 and b2 and one of the parent companies (called c) has its own subsidiary *(d)*.

184. Article 5(4) sets out specific criteria for identifying undertakings whose turnover can be attributed to the undertaking concerned. These criteria, including the «right to manage the undertaking's affairs», are not coextensive with the notion of «control» under Article 3(2). There are significant differences between Articles 3 and 5, as those provisions fulfil different roles. The differences are most apparent in the field of *de facto* control. Whereas under Article 3(2) even a situation of economic dependence may lead to control on a *de facto* basis (see in detail above), a solely controlled subsidiary is only taken into account on a *de facto* basis under Article 5(4)*(b)* if it is clearly demonstrated that the undertaking concerned has the power to exercise more than half of the voting rights or to appoint more than half of the board members. Concerning joint control scenarios, Article 5(4)*(b)(iv)* covers those scenarios where the controlling undertakings jointly have a right to manage on the basis of individual *veto* rights. However, Article 5(4) would not cover situations where joint control occurs on a *de facto* basis due to strong common interests between different minority shareholders of the joint venture company on the basis of shareholders' attendance. The difference is reflected in the fact that Article 5(4)*(b)(iv)* refers to the right to manage, and not a power (as in subparagraph *(b)(ii)* and *(iii)*) and is explained by the need for precision and certainty in the criteria used for calculating turnover so that jurisdiction can be readily verified. Under Article 3(3), however, the question whether a concentration arises can be much more comprehensively investigated. In addition, situations of negative sole control are only exceptionally covered (if the conditions of Article 5(4)*(b)(i)-(iii)* are met in the specific case); the «right to manage» under Article 5(4)*(b)(iv)* does not cover negative control scenarios. Finally, Article 5(4)*(b)(i)*, for example, covers situations where «control» under Article 3(2) may not exist.

5.2. Allocation of turnover of the undertakings identified

185. In general, as long as the test under Article 5(4)*(b)* is fulfilled, the whole turnover of the subsidiary in question will be taken into account regardless of the actual shareholding which the undertaking concerned holds in the subsidiary. In the chart, the whole turnover of the subsidiaries called b of the undertaking concerned a will be taken into account.

186. However, the Merger Regulation includes specific rules for joint ventures. Article 5(5)*(b)* provides that for joint ventures between two or more undertakings concerned, the turnover of the joint venture (as far as the turnover is generated from activities with third parties as set out above in paragraph 168) should be apportioned equally amongst the undertakings concerned, irrespective of their share of the capital or the voting rights.

187. The principle contained in Article 5(5)*(b)* is followed by analogy for the allocation of turnover for joint ventures between undertakings concerned and third parties if their turnover is taken into account according to Article 5(4)*(b)* as set out above in paragraph 181. The Commission's practice has been to allocate to the undertaking concerned the turnover of the joint venture on a per capita basis according to the number of undertakings exercising joint control. In the example, half of the turnover of b3 is taken into account.

188. The rules of Article 5(4) also have to be adapted in situations involving a change from joint to sole control in order to avoid double counting of the turnover of the joint venture. Even if the acquiring undertaking has rights or powers in the joint venture which satisfy the requirements of Article 5(4), the turnover of the acquiring shareholder has to be calculated without the turnover of the joint venture, and the turnover of the joint venture has to be taken without the turnover of the acquiring shareholder.

5.3. Allocation of turnover in case of investment funds

189. The investment company, as set out above in paragraph 15, normally acquires indirect control over portfolio companies held by an investment fund. In the same way, the investment company may be considered to indirectly have the powers and rights which are set out in Article 5(4)(b), in particular to indirectly have the power to exercise the voting rights held by the investment fund in the portfolio companies.

190. The same considerations, as set out above in the framework of Article 3 (paragraph 15), may also apply if an investment company sets up several investment funds with possibly different investors. Typically, on the basis of the organisational structure, in particular links between the investment company and the general partner(s) of the different funds organised as limited partnerships, or contractual arrangements, especially advisory agreements between the general partner or the investment fund and the investment company, the investment company will indirectly have the power to exercise the voting rights held by the investment fund in the portfolio companies or indirectly have one of the other powers or rights set out in Article 5(4)(b). In these circumstances, the investment company may exercise a common control structure over the different funds which it has set up and the common operation of the different funds by the investment company is often indicated by a common brand for the funds.

191. Consequently, such an organisation of the different funds by the investment company may lead to the result that the turnover of all portfolio companies held by different funds is taken into account for the purpose of assessing whether the turnover thresholds in Article 1 are met if the investment company acquires indirect control of a portfolio company via one of the funds.

5.4. Allocation of turnover for State-owned undertakings

192. As regards the calculation of turnover of State-owned undertakings, Article 5(4) should be read in conjunction with recital 22 of the Merger Regulation. This recital declares that, in order to avoid discrimination between the public and private sectors, «in the public sector, calculation of the turnover of an undertaking concerned in a concentration needs, therefore, to take account of undertakings making up an economic unit with an independent power of decision, irrespective of the way in which their capital is held or of the rules of administrative supervision applicable to them» (129).

(129) See also Case IV/M.216 – CEA Industrie/France Telecom/Finmeccanica/SGS-Thomson, of 22 February 1993.

193. This recital clarifies that Member States (or other public bodies) are not considered as «undertakings» under Article 5(4) simply because they have interests in other undertakings which satisfy the conditions of Article 5(4). Therefore, for the purposes of calculating turnover of State-owned undertakings, account is only taken of those undertakings which belong to the same economic unit, having the same independent power of decision.

194. Thus, where a State-owned company is not subject to any coordination with other State-controlled holdings, it should be treated as independent for the purposes of Article 5, and the turnover of other companies owned by that State should not be taken into account. Where, however, several State-owned companies are under the same independent centre of commercial decision-making, then the turnover of those businesses should be considered part of the group of the undertaking concerned for the purposes of Article 5.

V. GEOGRAPHIC ALLOCATION OF TURNOVER

195. The thresholds concerning Community-wide and Member State turnover in Article 1(2) and (3) aim to identify cases which have sufficient turnover within the Community in order to be of Community interest and which are primarily cross-border in nature. They require turnover to be allocated geographically to the Community and to individual Member States. Since audited accounts often do not provide a geographical breakdown as required by the Merger Regulation, the Commission will rely on the best figures available provided by the undertakings. The second subparagraph of Article 5(1) provides that the location of turnover is determined by the location of the customer at the time of the transaction:

«Turnover, in the Community or in a Member State, shall comprise products sold and services provided to undertakings or consumers, in the Community or in that Member State as the case may be.»

General rule

196. The Merger Regulation does not discriminate between «products sold» and «services provided» for the geographic allocation of turnover. In both cases, the general rule is that turnover should be attributed to the place where the customer is located. The underlying principle is that turnover should be allocated to the location where competition with alternative suppliers takes place. This location is normally also the place where the characteristic action under the contract in question is to be performed, i.e. where the service is actually provided and the product is actually delivered. In the case of Internet transactions, it may be difficult for the undertakings to determine the location of the customer at the time when the contract is concluded via the Internet. If the product or the service itself is not supplied via the Internet, focusing on the place where the characteristic action under the contract is performed may avoid those difficulties. In the following, the sale of goods and the provision of services are dealt with separately as they exhibit certain different features in terms of allocation of turnover.

Sale of goods

197. For the sale of goods, particular situations may arise in situations in which the place where the customer was located at the time of concluding the purchase agreement is different from the billing address and/or the place of delivery. In these situations, the place where the purchase agreement was entered into and the place of delivery are more important than the billing address. As the delivery is in general the characteristic action for the sale of goods, the place of delivery may even be prevailing over the place where the customer was located at the time when the purchase agreement was concluded. This will depend on whether the place of delivery is to be considered the place where competition takes place for the sale of goods or whether competition rather takes place at the residence of the customer. In the case of a sale of mobile goods, such as a motor car, to a final consumer, the place where the car is delivered to the customer is decisive even if the agreement was concluded via the phone or the Internet before.

198. A specific situation arises in cases where a multinational corporation has a Community buying strategy and sources all its requirements for a good from one location. As a central purchasing organisation can take different forms, it is necessary to consider its concrete form since this may determine how to allocate the turnover. Where goods are purchased by and delivered to the central purchasing organisation and are subsequently re-distributed internally to different plants in a variety of Member States, turnover is allocated only to the Member State where the central purchasing organisation is located. In this case, competition takes place at the location of the central purchasing organisation and this is also the place where the characteristic action under the sales contract is performed. The situation is different in case of direct links between the seller and the different subsidiaries. This comprises the case where the central purchasing organisation concludes a mere framework agreement, but the individual orders are placed by and the products are directly delivered to the subsidiaries in different Member States as well as the case where the individual orders are placed via the central purchasing organisation, but the products are directly delivered to the subsidiaries. In both cases, turnover is to be allocated to the different Member States in which the subsidiaries are located, irrespective of whether the central purchasing organisation or the subsidiaries receive the bills and effect the payment. The reason is that in both cases competition with alternative suppliers takes place for the delivery of products to the different subsidiaries even though the contract is concluded centrally. In the first case, in addition, the subsidiaries actually decide upon the quantities to be delivered and on an element essential for competition on their own.

Provision of services

199. For services, the Merger Regulation foresees that the place of their provision to the customer is relevant. Services containing cross-border elements can be considered to fall into three general categories. The first category comprises cases where the service provider travels, the second category cases where the customer travels. The third category comprises those cases where a service is provided without either the service provider or the customer having to travel. In the first two categories, the turnover generated is to be allocated to the place of destination of the traveller, i.e. the place where the service is actually provided to the customer. In the third category, the turnover is generally to be allocated to the location of the customer. For the central sourcing of services the above outlined principles for the central purchasing of goods apply in an analogous way.

200. An example of the first category would be a situation where a non-European company provides special airplane maintenance services to a carrier in a Member State. In this case, the service provider travels to the Community where the service is actually provided and where also competition for this service takes place. If a European tourist hires a car or books a hotel directly in the United States, this falls into the second category as the service is provided outside the Community and also competition takes place between hotels and rental car companies at the location chosen. However, the case is different for package holidays. For this kind of holiday, the service starts with the sale of the package through a travel agent at the customer's location and competition for the sale of holidays through travel agents takes place locally, as with retail shopping, even though parts of the service may be provided in a number of distant locations. The case therefore falls into the third category and the turnover generated is to be allocated to the customer's location. The third category also comprises cases like the supply of software or the distribution of films which are made outside the Community, but are supplied to a customer in a Member State so that the service is actually provided to the customer within the Community.

201. Cases concerning the transport of goods are different as the customer, to whom those services are provided, does not travel, but the transport service is provided to the customer at its location. Those cases fall into the third category and the location of the customer is the relevant criterion for the allocation of the turnover.

202. In telecom cases, the qualification of call termination services may raise problems. Although call termination would appear to fall into the third category, there are reasons to treat it differently. Call termination services are provided, e.g., in situations where a call, originating from a European operator, is being terminated in the United States. Although neither the European nor the US operator travels, the signal travels and the service is provided by the US network to the European operator in the United States. This is also the place where competition takes place (if any). The turnover is therefore to be considered as non-Community turnover (130).

(130) This does not affect the turnover which the European telephony operator generates vis-à-vis its own customer with this call.

Specific sectors

203. Certain sectors do, however, pose very particular problems with regard to the geographical allocation of turnover. These will be dealt with in Section VI below.

VI. CONVERSION OF TURNOVER INTO EURO

204. When converting turnover figures into euro great care should be taken with the exchange rate used. The annual turnover of a company should be converted at the average rate for the twelve months concerned. This average can be obtained via DG Competition's website (131). The audited annual turnover figures should be converted as such and not be broken down into quarterly or monthly figures which would then be converted individually.

(131) See http://europa.eu.int/comm/competition/mergers/others/exchange_rates.html#footnote_1. The website makes reference to the European Central Bank's Monthly Bulletin.

205. When a company has sales in a range of currencies, the procedure is no different. The total turnover given in the consolidated audited accounts and in that company's reporting currency is converted into euros at the yearly average rate. Local currency sales should not be converted directly into euros since these figures are not from the consolidated audited accounts of the company.

VII. PROVISIONS FOR CREDIT AND OTHER FINANCIAL INSTITUTIONS AND INSURANCE UNDERTAKINGS

1. Scope of application

206. Due to the specific nature of the sector, Article 5(3) contains specific rules for the calculation of turnover of credit and other financial institutions as well as insurance undertakings.

207. In order to define the terms «credit institutions and other financial institutions» under the Merger Regulation, the Commission in its practice has consistently adopted the definitions provided in the applicable European regulation in the banking sector. The Directive on the taking up and pursuit of the business of credit institutions foresees that (132):

– «Credit institution shall mean an undertaking whose business is to receive deposits or other repayable funds from the public and to grant credits for its own account.»

– «Financial institution shall mean an undertaking other than a credit institution, the principal activity of which is to acquire holdings or to carry on one or more of the activities listed in points 2 to 12 of Annex 1.»

(132) The definitions are to be found in Article 1 (1) and (5) of Directive 2000/12/EC of the European Parliament and of the Council of 20 March 2000 relating to the taking up and pursuit of the business of credit institutions (O.J. L 126, 26.5.2000, p. 1).

208. Financial institutions within the meaning of Article 5(3) of the Merger Regulation are, accordingly, on the one hand holding companies and, on the other hand, undertakings which perform on a regular basis as a principal activity one or more activities expressly mentioned in points 2 to 12 of the Annex of the banking Directive. These activities include:

– lending (comprising activities such as consumer credit, mortgage credit, factoring);

– financial leasing;

– money transmission services;

– issuing and administering means of payment (e.g. credit cards, travellers' cheques and bankers' drafts);

– guarantees and commitments;

– trading for own account or for account of customers in money market instruments, (cheques, bills, certificates of deposit, etc.), foreign exchange, financial futures and options, exchange and interest-rate instruments, transferable securities;

– participation in securities issues and the provision of services related to such issues;

– money broking;

– portfolio management and advice; and

– safekeeping and administration of securities.

2. Calculation of turnover

209. Article 5(3) of the Merger Regulation sets out the methods of calculation of turnover for credit and other financial institutions and for insurance undertakings. In the following Section, some supplementary questions related to turnover calculation for the abovementioned types of undertakings are addressed.

2.1. Calculation of turnover of credit and financial institutions (other than financial holding companies)

2.1.1. General

210. There are normally no particular difficulties in applying the banking income criterion for the definition of the worldwide turnover to credit institutions and other kinds of financial institutions.

For the geographic allocation of turnover to the Community and to individual Member States, the specific provision of Article 5(3)(a) second subparagraph applies. It specifies that the turnover is to be allocated to the branch or division established in the Community or in the Member State which receives this income.

2.1.2. Turnover of leasing companies

211. There is a fundamental distinction to be made between financial leases and operating leases. Basically, financial leases are made for longer periods than operating leases and ownership is generally transferred to the lessee at the end of the lease term by means of a purchase option included in the lease contract. Under an operating lease, on the contrary, ownership is not transferred to the lessee at the end of the lease term and the costs of maintenance, repair and insurance of the leased equipment are included in the lease payments. A financial lease therefore functions as a loan by the lessor to enable the lessee to purchase a given asset.

212. As already mentioned above, a company performing as its principal activity financial leasing is a financial institution within the meaning of Article 5(3)(a) and its turnover is to be calculated according to the specific rules set out in this provision. All payments on financial leasing contracts, except for the redemption part, are to be taken into account; a sale of future leasing payments at the beginning of the contract for re-financing purposes is not relevant.

213. Operational leasing activities are, however, not considered to be carried out by financial institutions, and therefore the general turnover calculation rules of Article 5(1) apply (133).

(133) See Case IV/M.234 – GECC/Avis Lease, 15 July 1992.

2.2. Insurance undertakings

214. In order to measure the turnover of insurance undertakings, Article 5(3)(b) of the Merger Regulation provides that gross premiums written are taken into account. The gross premiums written are the sum of received premiums, including any received reinsurance premiums if the undertaking concerned has activities in the field of reinsurance. Outgoing or outward reinsurance premiums, i.e. all amounts paid and payable by the undertaking concerned to get reinsurance cover, are only costs related to the provision of insurance coverage and are not to be deducted from the gross premiums written.

215. The premiums to be taken into account are not only related to new insurance contracts made during the accounting year being considered but also to all premiums related to contracts made in previous years which remain in force during the period taken into consideration.

216. In order to constitute appropriate reserves allowing for the payment of claims, insurance undertakings, usually hold a portfolio of investments in shares, interest-bearing securities, land and property and other assets providing annual revenues. The annual revenues coming from those sources are not considered as turnover for insurance undertakings under Article 5(3)(b). However, a distinction has to be made between pure financial investments, which do not confer the rights and powers specified in Article 5(4) to the insurance undertaking in the undertakings in which the investment has been made, and those investments leading to the acquisition of an interest which meets the criteria specified in Article 5(4)(b). In the latter case, Article 5(4) of the Merger Regulation applies, and the turnover of this undertaking has to be added to the turnover of the insurance undertaking, as calculated according to Article 5(3)(b), for the determination of the thresholds laid down in the Merger Regulation (134).

(134) See Case IV/M.018 – AG/AMEV, of 21 November 1990.

2.3. Financial holding companies

217. As an «other financial institution» within the meaning of Article 5(3)(a) of the Merger Regulation, the turnover of a financial holding company has to be calculated according to the specific rules set out in this provision. However, in the same way as mentioned above for insurance undertakings, Article 5(4) applies to those participations which meet the criteria specified in Article 5(4)(b). Thus, the turnover of a financial holding is to be basically calculated according to Article 5(3), but it may be necessary to add turnover of undertakings falling within the categories set out in Article 5(4) («Art. 5(4) companies») (135).

(135) The principles for financial holding companies may to a certain extent be applied to fund management companies.

218. In practice, the turnover of the financial holding company (non-consolidated) must first be taken into account. Then the turnover of the Art. 5(4) companies must be added, whilst taking care to deduct dividends and other income distributed by those companies to the financial holdings. The following provides an example for this kind of calculation:

	(EUR million)
1. Turnover related to financial activities (from non-consolidated P&L)	3000
2. Turnover related to insurance Art. 5(4) companies (gross premiums written)	300
3. Turnover of industrial Article 5(4) companies	2000
4. Deduct dividends and other income derived from Art. 5(4) companies 2 and 3	200
Total turnover financial holding and its group	5100

219. In such calculations different accounting rules may need to be taken into consideration. Whilst this consideration applies to any type of undertaking concerned by the Merger Regulation, it is particularly important in the case of financial holding companies (136) where the number and the diversity of enterprises controlled and the degree of control the holding holds on its subsidiaries, affiliated companies and other companies in which it has shareholding requires careful examination.

(136) See for example Case IV/M.166 – Torras/Sarrió, of 24 February 1992.

220. Turnover calculation for financial holding companies as described above may in practice prove onerous. Therefore a strict and detailed application of this method will be necessary only in cases where it seems that the turnover of a financial holding company is likely to be close to the Merger Regulation thresholds; in other cases it may well be obvious that the turnover is far from the thresholds of the Merger Regulation, and therefore the published accounts are adequate for the establishment of jurisdiction.

Simplified method to obtain the average rate used to calculate the turnover

This is the methodology to calculate the annual average rate, when the financial year does not correspond with the calendar year.

Example: from 01 april 1993 to 31 March 1994

Average rate (April – March) =

((average 1993/04) + (average 1993/05) + (average 1993/06)

+ (average 1993/07) + (average 1993/08) + (average 1993/09)

+ (average 1993/10) + (average 1993/11) + (average 1993/12)

+ (average 1994/01) + (average 1994/02) + (average 1994/03)) / 12

2.2.3. Procedural rules

Best practice on divestiture commitments	436
Model texts for divestiture commitments	440
Model texts for trustee mandates	440
Best practices on merger control proceedings	440
Competition Information note on Art. 6 (1) c 2nd sentence of Regulation 139/2004 (abandonment of concentration)	445
Communication from the Commission – Address for delivery, Implementing Regulation	446
Commission Notice – Case referral in respect of concentrations	446
Commission Notice – Simplified procedure for treatment of certain concentrations	461
Communication from the Commission – Format of notifications and reasoned submissions, Implementing Regulation	463
Commission Notice – Access to the Commission file	464
Merger notification and procedures template	464
Market share ranges in non confidential versions of merger decisions	474
Best Practices submission of economic evidence and data collection	475
Decision 13 October 2011 – The function and terms of reference of the Hearing Officer	475
Best Practices on Co-operation in Merger Review	475

Best Practice Guidelines – The Commission's Model Texts for Divestiture Commitments and the Trustee Mandate under the EC Merger Regulation, not published in the Official Journal

1. See the site: http://ec.europa.eu/competition/mergers/legislation/note.pdf

1. The European Commission's model texts for divestiture commitments and trustee mandates are designed to serve as best practice guidelines for notifying parties submitting commitments under the EC Merger Regulation (1). These texts are (1) the model to be used for divestiture commitments (the «Standard Model for Divestiture Commitments» or the «Standard Commitments»); and (2) the model for the mandate of the two types of trustees referred to in the Standard Commitments, that is, the mandate appointing monitoring and divestiture trustees (the «Standard Trustee Mandate»).

(1) Council Regulation (EEC) N° 4064/89 of 21 December 1989 on the control of concentrations between undertakings, as amended, O.J. L 395, 30.12.1989, p. 1; corrigendum O.J. L 257, 21.9.1990, p. 13.

2. The model texts (the «Standard Models») are based upon the experience the Commission has gained to date in fashioning remedies from previous merger cases and are drafted in line with the remedies policy set out in the Commission's Notice on Remedies (2) (the «Remedies Notice»). The Standard Models are neither intended to provide an exhaustive coverage of all issues that may become relevant in all cases, nor are they legally binding upon parties in a merger procedure. Rather, they contain the elements for all standard provisions that should be included in commitments and trustee mandates relating to divestitures. In providing a framework for commitments and trustee mandates to be submitted in concrete cases, the Standard Models leave the flexibility to adapt the texts to the specific requirements of the case in question.

(2) See Commission Notice on remedies acceptable under Council Regulation (EEC) N° 4064/89 and Regulation (EC) N° 447/98 at Official Journal C 68, 02.03.2001, pages 3-11; published on http://europa.eu.int/eur-lex/pri/en/O.J./dat/2001/c_068/c_06820010302en00030011.pdf

3. The Standard Models are designed to apply to all remedy proceedings in both Phase I and Phase II, therefore to all Commission decisions according to Articles 6(2) and 8(2) of the Merger Regulation. The Standard Models deal specifically with divestiture commitments inasmuch as the Commission's Remedies Notice stipulates that divestiture commitments are normally the preferred form of merger remedies; they are also the most common. However, it should be underlined that the Commission will consider the acceptability of other types of commitments in appropriate circumstances, as set out in the Remedies Notice. Individual provisions contained in the Standard Models can be used in cases involving such other types of commitments.

4. Finally, it is expected that the text of these models will evolve, based on ongoing practice, and will be regularly up-dated by the Commission, taking into consideration both the developments of the Commission's remedies policy and the experience gained from working with the merging parties and trustees in future matters.

THE PURPOSE OF THE STANDARD MODELS

5. The Commission recognises that timing is crucial when merging parties reach the remedies stage in merger review procedures, where they offer commitments in order to resolve the Commission's competition concerns in a given case. Through the use of standardised models, the merging parties and the Commission will be relieved of the heavy demands – both in terms of time and resources – that would otherwise be required to negotiate the standard terms and provisions for commitments and trustee mandates under tight time constraints. The use of standardised models will expedite the proceedings and allow the merging parties to concentrate more on the actual substance and implementation of the commitments.

6. The use of the standard models will ensure consistency across cases and will thereby contribute to increasing the level of transparency and legal certainty for the merging parties offering commitments to the Commission.

OVERVIEW OF THE CONTENTS OF THE STANDARD MODELS

7. The Standard Model for Divestiture Commitments sets out all requirements for achieving full and effective compliance with divestiture commitments offered by the merging parties (the «Parties») to obtain a clearance decision. More specifically, this Model is designed (i) to describe clearly the business to be divested («Divestment Business»), the divestiture procedure and the obligations of the parties in relation to the Divestment Business for the interim period until divestiture has been completed, (ii) to set out the various responsibilities that the merging parties will thereby have, respectively, to the Commission, the Trustee, and the Divestment Business; and (iii) to enshrine the importance which the Commission places upon requiring an acceptable purchaser for the Divestment Business in order to ensure the viability and competitiveness of the new entity in the market where the divestiture takes place.

8. The Standard Model for Trustee Mandates sets out the role and functions of the Trustee, as provided in the Standard Commitments, in a contractual relationship between the Parties responsible for the divestiture and the Trustee. As the Commitments set out the basis for the responsibilities of the Trustee, the Standard Trustee Mandate has been prepared in conformity with the requirements laid down for the Trustee in the Standard Model for Divestiture Commitments.

9. Although the Standard Trustee Mandate is a bilateral contract between the Parties responsible for the divestiture and the Trustee, this document forms the basis for a tri-partite relationship among the Commission, the Trustee, and the Parties. The relationship between the Parties and the Trustee is not a traditional trusteeship. The Trustee rather benefits from a status which makes it independent from the Parties and which is characterised by the role of the Trustee to monitor (Monitoring Trustee) or even to effectuate (Divestiture Trustee) the Parties' compliance with the commitments. Accordingly, the Parties are not entitled to give instructions to the Trustee, whereas the Commission is allowed to do so. This specific relationship is also confirmed by the fact that the Trustee Mandate requires the Commission's approval.

10. The Standard Trustee Mandate is designed (i) to facilitate the smooth and timely appointment of the Trustee and the approval of the Trustee Mandate; (ii) to clarify the relationship among the Commission, the Trustee, and the Parties; and (iii) to set out the tasks of the Trustee in the process in order to enable the Trustee to expedite compliance with the commitments. Whereas the Standard Trustee Mandate defines the role of a Monitoring and a Divestiture Trustee in one text, they can be assigned to different Trustees in practice.

11. In providing guidance for the interpretation of the Standard Texts, a certain hierarchy is established. The Standard Trustee Mandate should be interpreted in the light of the Standard Commitments, as they lay the foundation for the application of the Trustee Mandate. To the extent that they are attached as conditions and obligations, the commitments are to be interpreted in the light of the respective Commission decision. Moreover, both Standard Texts should be interpreted in the general framework of Community law, in particular in the light of the EC Merger Regulation, and by reference to the Commission's Remedies Notice setting out the Commission's remedies policy.

DESCRIPTION OF THE PROVISIONS OF THE STANDARD MODELS

12. The most important provisions contained in both Standard Models are briefly set out below.

STANDARD MODEL FOR DIVESTITURE COMMITMENTS

13. The Standard Model for Commitments consists of the following main elements:

14. Section A contains a definitions section.

15. Section B contains the commitment to divest and the definition of the Divestment Business. After spelling out the general obligation to divest the Divestment Business as a going concern, paragraph 1 describes the divestiture procedure, which may take two phases. The Commitments provide that in the first phase (that is, the Divestiture Period), the Parties have the sole responsibility for finding a suitable purchaser for the Divestment Business. If the Parties do not succeed in divesting the business on their own in the Divestiture Period, then a Divestiture Trustee will be appointed with an exclusive mandate to dispose of the Divestment Business at no minimum price, in the Extended Divestiture Period. The individual deadlines are determined in the definitions section. The experience of the Commission has shown that short divestiture periods contribute largely to the success of the divestiture as, otherwise, the Divestment Business will be exposed to an extended period of uncertainty. The Commission will normally consider a period of around 6 months for the Divestiture Period and an additional period of 3 to 6 months for the Extended Divestiture Period as appropriate. These periods may be modified according to the particular requirements of the case in question.

16. The divestiture commitment will take a special form in those cases where the Parties propose an up-front buyer. The Parties commit not to implement the proposed concentration unless and until they have entered into a binding agreement with a purchaser for the Divestment Business, approved by the Commission. The qualification of the buyer are the same as in other divestiture commitments. The up-front buyer concept has been applied in several cases (3) and will be used in the specific circumstances as described in the Notice (4). The structure of the divestiture commitment also needs to be adapted in cases of alternative divestitures, in particular «Crown Jewels» structures, i.e. structures in which the Parties commit to divest a very attractive business if they have not divested the originally proposed business until the end of a period fixed in the commitments. The circumstances in which the Commission will accept alternative divestiture commitments are also set out in the Remedies Notice (5).

(3) Cases COMP/M.2060 – Bosch/Rexroth; COMP/M.1915 – The Post Office/TPG/SPPL; COMP/M.2544 – Masterfood/Royal Canin.

(4) Paragraph 18 of the Remedies Notice.

(5) Paragraphs 22, 23 of the Remedies Notice.

17. The divestiture commitment includes the commitment not to re-acquire direct or indirect influence over the Divestment Business (paragraph 3). This re-acquisition prohibition is limited to ten years after the date of the decision and serves to maintain the structural effects of the Commitments. The Commission may grant a waiver if the structure of the market has changed to such an extent that the absence of influence over the Divestment Business is no longer necessary to render the concentration compatible with the common market.

18. Section B, together with the Schedule to the Commitments, defines what is included in the Divestment Business. The clear identification of the Divestment Business is of great importance as thereby the scope of the divestiture and of the hold-separate obligations are defined. As set out in the Notice, the Divestment Business is considered to be an existing entity that can operate on a stand-alone-basis (6). The Divestment Business is the minimum which is to be divested by the Parties in order to comply with the Commitments. In order to make the package more attractive to buyers, the Parties may add, on their own initiative, other assets (7). The Divestment Business must include all the assets and personnel necessary to ensure the viability of the divested activities. Whereas this principle is set out as an undertaking of the Parties in paragraph 3 of the Standard Commitments, the Parties have to give a detailed factual description of the Divestment Business in the Schedule to the Standard Commitments.

(6) Cf. paragraph 14 of the Remedies Notice. The importance of the divestiture of an on-going business for the success of the remedy has also been underlined by the FTC in a published study entitled A Study of the Commission's Divestiture Process, prepared by the Staff of the Bureau of Competition of the Federal Trade Commission, p. 10 ff.

(7) Cf. paragraph 21 of the Remedies Notice.

19. The Divestment Business must comprise the Personnel and the Key Personnel retained by the Divestment Business as well as the personnel providing essential functions for the Divestment Business, such as the central R&D staff. The personnel (according to groups and functions performed) is to be listed in the Schedule to the Commitments, the Key Personnel is to be listed separately. The principle, indicated in paragraph 4 (d), is that the personnel should be transferred with the Divestment Business. If the Divestment Business takes the form of a company or if the transfer of undertakings legislation applies, the personnel will normally be transferred by operation of law. In other cases, the acquirer of the business can retain and select the personnel and can make offers of employment. The transfer – whichever form it takes – is without prejudice to the application of Council Directives, where applicable, on collective redundancies (8); on safeguarding employees rights in the event of transfers of undertakings (9); and on informing and consulting employees (10), as well as relevant national law on these matters.

(8) Council Directive 98/59/EC of 20 July 1998 on the approximation of the laws of the Member States relating to collective redundancies (O.J. L 225, 12.8.1998, p. 16).

(9) Council Directive 77/187/EEC on the approximation of the laws of the Member States relating to the safeguarding of employees rights in the event of transfers of undertakings, businesses or parts of a business (O.J. L 61, 5.3.1977, p. 26) as amended by Council Directive 98/50/EC (O.J. L 201, 17.7.1998, p. 88).

(10) Council Directive 94/45/EC of 22 September 1994 on the establishment of a European Works Council or a procedure in Community-scale undertakings and Community-scale groups of undertakings for the purposes of informing and consulting employees (O.J. L 254, 30.9.1994, p. 64) as amended by Directive 97/74/EC (O.J. L 10, 16.1.1998, p. 22).

20. Furthermore, the Standard Commitments foresee that the Divestment Business shall be entitled to benefit from products or services provided by the Parties for a transitional period, determined on a case-by-case basis, if this is necessary to maintain the full economic viability and competitiveness of the Divestment Business (paragraph 4 (e) of the Standard Commitments referring to the products or services listed in the Schedule).

21. Section C contains a number of related commitments, which are designed to maintain, pending divestiture, the viability, marketability and competitiveness of the Divestment Business. These provisions deal with the preservation of the divested entity's viability and independence, as well as the hold-separate and ring-fencing obligations. The Hold Separate Manager, to be appointed by the Parties and normally the manager of the Divestment Business, is responsible for the management of the Divestment Business as a distinct entity separate from the businesses retained by the Parties, and is supervised by the Monitoring Trustee.

22. In certain cases it may also be necessary for the hold-separate obligation to apply to the corporate structure itself. That is, in cases where the Divestment Business takes the form of a company and a strict separation of the corporate structure is necessary, the Monitoring Trustee must be given the authority to (i) exercise the Parties' rights as shareholders in the Divestment Business and (ii) to replace members of the supervisory board or non-executive directors on the board of directors who have been appointed on behalf of the Parties (cf. paragraph 8 of the Standard Commitments and paragraph 6 (d) of the Standard Trustee Mandate).

23. Of particular importance is the ring-fencing of competitively sensitive information of the Divestment Business. The parties are obliged to implement all necessary measures to ensure that they do not obtain such information of the Divestment Business and, in particular, to sever its participation in a central information technology network. The Monitoring Trustee may allow the disclosure of information to the divesting party if this is reasonably necessary for the divestiture of the Divestment Business or required by law (e.g. information necessary for group accounts).

24. The related commitments further contain a non-solicitation clause for Key Personnel of the Divestment Business. According to the experience of the Commission, the non-solicitation period, dependent on the circumstances of the case, should normally be two years. In addition, the Commission may request the inclusion of a non-compete clause in the commitments protecting the customers of the Divestment Business for a start-up period. This may be required to enable the Divestment Business to be active as a viable competitor in the market. The period for such customer protection clause will depend on the market in question.

25. During the Divestiture Phase, the divestiture lies in the hands of the divesting party. The Commission does not have a preference as to the method the parties use to select an acceptable purchaser as long as they meet the objective of the divestiture, to maintain or restore competition. However, as part of the due diligence procedure, it is foreseen that the divesting party shall provide to potential purchasers sufficient information as regards the Divestment Business and allow them access to its personnel (paragraph 11 of the Standard Commitments) in order to enable them to determine whether it will be possible to maintain and to develop the Divestment Business as active and viable competitive force in the market after the divestiture.

26. The divesting party shall further submit regular reports on potential purchasers and developments in the divestiture process to the Commission and the Monitoring Trustee (paragraph 12 of the Standard Commitments). This reporting mechanism gives the Monitoring Trustee the basis on which to assess the progress of the divestiture process as well as potential purchasers (for the Trustee's report, see paragraph 23 (vi) of the Standard Commitments) and keeps the Commission informed.

27. Section D sets out the requirements to be met by the Purchaser. The aim of this section is to ensure that the Divestment Business will be sold to a suitable purchaser who is independent of and unconnected to the Parties, and who possesses the financial resources, proven expertise and incentive to maintain and develop the Divestment Business as a viable and active competitive force in the marketplace. These Purchaser Requirements can generally be met by either industrial or financial investors. The latter must demonstrate the necessary management capabilities and «proven expertise» which can in particular be met by financing a management buy-out.

28. Section D also deals with the approval process. After finalising the agreement(s), the divesting party shall submit a fully documented and reasoned proposal to the Commission. The Commission will verify that the purchaser will fulfil the requirements and that the Divestment Business is being sold in a manner consistent with the Commitments. One element for its assessment will be the report of the Monitoring Trustee according to paragraph 23 (vii). The Commission may approve the sale of the Divestment Business without parts of the assets or personnel of the Divestment Business if this does not affect the viability and competitiveness of the Divestment Business, in particular if the Purchaser provides for such assets or personnel itself.

29. Section E deals with both the Monitoring and Divestiture Trustees. It identifies the terms for their appointment, as well as the content of the Trustee Mandates, and conditions for replacement of the Trustee during the divestiture periods if that becomes necessary. A Monitoring Trustee must be proposed by the Parties within one week after the adoption of the decision, whereas a Divestiture Trustee must be proposed no later than one month before the end of the Divestiture Period, (paragraph 16 of the Standard Commitments). The Commission wishes to emphasise the importance it attaches to compliance with these deadlines in practise, as otherwise the Parties are in breach of the commitments and the divestiture procedure is endangered.

30. Section E also sets out the duties and obligations of both types of Trustees. The Monitoring Trustee's responsibilities (mainly set out in paragraph 23 Standard Commitments) relate to both the management of the Divestment Business during the hold-separate period and the monitoring of the divestiture process itself. The supervision of the management shall in particular ensure the viability, marketability and competitiveness of the Divestment Business and the compliance with the hold-separate and ring-fencing obligations. The Standard Commitments further assign certain monitoring tasks concerning the divestiture process to the Monitoring Trustee in the Divestiture Period. Once the Parties have proposed a purchaser for the Divestment Business, the Monitoring Trustee assesses the independence and suitability of the proposed purchaser and the viability of the Divestment Business after the sale to the purchaser, in order to assist the Commission in assessing the suitability of the proposed purchaser.

31. In the Extended Divestiture Period, the Divestiture Trustee will have an exclusive mandate to sell the Divestment Business at no minimum price and is empowered to include in the sale and purchase agreement such terms and conditions as it considers appropriate for an expedient sale. However, it is foreseen that the Trustee has to protect the legitimate financial interests of the divesting parties, subject to its unconditional obligation to divest at no minimum price. The Divestiture Trustee must report regularly on the progress of the divestiture process.

32. Also in Section E (paragraphs 26-30), the duties and obligations of the Parties vis-à-vis the Trustee are defined. Beside the provision of information, the Parties are in particular obliged to provide the Monitoring Trustee with all managerial and administrative support necessary for the Divestment Business and to grant to the Divestiture Trustee comprehensive powers of attorney covering all steps of the sale of the Divestment Business. An indemnification clause is included in order to reinforce the independent status of the Trustee from the Parties. Such a clause is already common practice in the trustee mandates submitted to the Commission for approval. The Trustee may further, at the expense of the Parties, retain advisors with specialised skills, in particular for corporate finance or legal advice.

33. Section E further foresees that trustees may only be removed in exceptional circumstances and with the approval of the Commission before the complete implementation of the Commitments.

34. Section F contains a review clause, which allows the Commission to extend the periods specified in the Commitments and to waive or modify the undertakings in the Commitments. The Parties must show good cause in order to be able to benefit from the exercise of the review clause. Requests for the extension of time periods shall, normally, be submitted no later than one month before the expiry of the time period in question.

STANDARD MODEL FOR TRUSTEE MANDATES

35. The Standard Model for Trustee Mandates sets out the duties and responsibilities of both Monitoring and Divestiture Trustee in a single text. However, the language makes clear that the Commission does not have a preference for the appointment of a single person to serve in the dual role of both Monitoring and Divestiture Trustee. Rather, the decision as to whether one or more trustees are appointed should be determined on a case-by-case basis by the Parties. If more than one trustee shall serve in these roles, only the provisions relevant for the Monitoring or Divestiture Trustee, respectively, have to be included in the individual mandate.

36. The Standard Trustee Mandate consists of the following main elements:

37. Section A contains some definitions and references the definitions included in the Standard Commitments.

38. Sections B to G contain provisions regarding the appointment of the Trustee (Section B), its general duties (Section C), the specific duties and obligations of the Monitoring and Divestiture Trustees (Sections D and E), reporting obligations identifying certain important subjects that should be discussed in each report (Section G), and duties and obligations of the Parties vis-à-vis the Trustee (Section F). These arrangements are based on the provisions established in the Standard Commitments in relation to the Trustee and described above.

39. Sections H to J cover additional trustee-related provisions, including provisions regarding the remuneration of the Trustee(s), procedures concerning the termination of the Mandate, and certain additional provisions, such as determination of applicable national law.

40. In particular, the independence of the trustee and the absence of conflicts of interests of the trustee are of great importance for the Commission in deciding on the approval of the Trustee and the respective mandate. The provisions in the Standard Trustee Mandate (paragraphs 20 to 23) ensuring the independence of the trustee from the parties and the absence of conflicts of interest foresee the following procedure: (1) The Trustee must disclose all current relationships with the Parties (paragraph 20) at the time at which the Trustee Mandate is entered into. (2) During the term of the mandate, the Trustee undertakes not to create a conflict of interest by having or accepting employment or appointment as a Member of the Board of the Parties or by having or accepting any assignments or other business relationships with, or financial interests in, the Parties. (3) As legal consequences it is foreseen that, if the Trustee becomes aware of a conflict of interest during the Mandate, the Trustee must notify the Commission and resolve the problem immediately and, if the conflict of interest cannot subsequently be resolved, the Commission may require the termination of the trustee mandate. These rules concerning conflicts of interests apply to the Trustee itself, members of the Trustee Team and the Trustee Partner Firms as members of the same organisation. (4) For a period of one year following termination of the Mandate, the members of the Trustee Team shall not provide services to the Parties without the Commission's prior approval and must establish measures to ensure the integrity of the members of the Trustee Team.

41. In addition to the rules laid down in the Standard Trustee Mandate, it is up to the Parties and the Trustee to include provisions dealing with other potential conflicts of interests, such as conflicts of interests of the Trustee with potential purchasers.

Model texts for divestiture commitments – Commitments to the European Commission, 2 May 2003, not published in the Official Journal

1. See the site: http://ec.europa.eu/competition/mergers/legislation/commitments.pdf
2. See below, section Forms

Model texts for trustee mandates, 2 May 2003, not published in the Official Journal

1. See the site: http://ec.europa.eu/competition/mergers/legislation/trustee_mandate.pdf
2. See below, section Forms

DG Competition 20 January 2004 – Best Practices on the conduct of EC merger control proceedings, not published in the Official Journal

1. See the site: http://ec.europa.eu/competition/mergers/legislation/proceedings.pdf

1. SCOPE AND PURPOSE OF THE BEST PRACTICES

1. The principal aim of these Best Practices is to provide guidance for interested parties on the day-to-day conduct of EC merger control proceedings. They are intended to foster and build upon a spirit of co-operation and better understanding between DG Competition and the legal and business community. In this regard, the Best Practices seek to increase understanding of the investigation process and thereby to further enhance the efficiency of investigations and to ensure a high degree of transparency and predictability of the review process. In particular, they aim at making the short time available in EC merger procedures as productive and efficient as possible for all parties concerned.

2. The Best Practices are built on the experience to date of DG Competition in the application of Council Regulation (EEC) N° 4064/89 (1) (the Merger Regulation) and replace the current Best Practices of 1999. They reflect the views and practice of DG Competition at the time of publication (2).

The specificity of an individual case may require an adaptation of, or deviation from these Best Practices depending on the case at hand.

(1) Council Regulation N° 4064/89, *OJ* L 395, 30.12.1989 p. 1; *corrigendum OJ* L 257 of 21.9.1990, p. 13; Regulation as last amended by Regulation (EC) N° 1310/97 (*OJ* L 180, 9.7.1997, p. 1, *corrigendum OJ* L 40, 13.2.1998, p. 17).

(2) It is to be noted that a recast Merger Regulation replacing Regulation 4064/89 will apply from 1 May 2004. The Best Practices are equally applicable under Regulation 4064/89 and will continue to be applicable, possibly with further amendments, under the recast Merger Regulation. Appropriate references to the recast Merger Regulation are made throughout the Best Practices by means of footnotes. Those references will only become applicable from 1st of May 2004.

2. RELATIONSHIP TO COMMUNITY LAW

3. These Best Practices should not be taken as a full or comprehensive account of the relevant legislative, interpretative and administrative measures which govern Community merger control. They should be read in conjunction with such measures.

4. The Best Practices do not create or alter any rights or obligations as set out in the Treaty establishing the European Community, the Merger Regulation, its Implementing Regulation (3) as amended from time to time and as interpreted by the case-law of the Community Courts. Nor do they alter the Commission's interpretative notices. The Best Practices do not apply to proceedings under Council Regulation N° 17 (4), to be replaced by Council Regulation N° 1/2003 (5) as of 1 May 2004, implementing Articles 81 and 82 of the Treaty.

(3) Commission Regulation (EC) N° 447/98 of 1 March 1998 on the notifications, time limits and hearings provided for in the Merger Regulation, OJ L 61, 2.3.1998, p. 1.

(4) OJ P 013, 21/02/1962, p. 204-211.

(5) Council Regulation (EC) N° 1/2003 of 16 December 2002 on the implementation of the rules on competition laid down in Articles 81 and 82 of the Treaty, OJ L 1, 04.01.2003, p. 1-25.

3. PRE-NOTIFICATION

Purpose of pre-notification contacts

5. In DG Competition's experience the pre-notification phase of the procedure is an important part of the whole review process. As a general rule, DG Competition finds it useful to have pre-notification contacts with notifying parties even in seemingly non-problematic cases. DG Competition will therefore always give notifying parties and other involved parties the opportunity, if they so request, to discuss an intended concentration informally and in confidence prior to notification (cf. also Recital 10 Implementing Regulation).

6. Pre-notification contacts provide DG Competition and the notifying parties with the possibility, prior to notification, to discuss jurisdictional and other legal issues. They also serve to discuss issues such as the scope of the information to be submitted and to prepare for the upcoming investigation by identifying key issues and possible competition concerns (theories of harm) at an early stage.

7. Further, it is in the interests of DG Competition and the business and legal community to ensure that notification forms are complete from the outset so that declarations of incompleteness are avoided as far as possible. It is DG Competition's experience that in cases in which notifications have been declared incomplete, usually there were no or very limited pre-notification contacts. Accordingly, for this reason it is recommended that notifying parties contact DG Competition prior to notification.

8. Pre-notification discussions are held in strict confidence. The discussions are a voluntary part of the process and remain without prejudice to the handling and investigation of the case following formal notification. However, the mutual benefits for DG Competition and the parties of a fruitful pre-notification phase can only materialise if discussions are held in an open and co-operative atmosphere, where all potential issues are addressed in a constructive way.

9. In DG Competition's experience it is generally preferable that both legal advisers and business representatives, who have a good understanding of the relevant markets, are available for pre-notification discussions with the case-team. This normally results in more informed discussions on the business rationale for the transaction and the functioning of the markets in question.

Timing and extent of pre-notification contacts

10. Pre-notification contacts should preferably be initiated at least two weeks before the expected date of notification. The extent and format of the pre-notification contacts required is, however, linked to the complexity of the individual case in question. In more complex cases a more extended pre-notification period may be appropriate and in the interest of the notifying parties. In all cases it is advisable to make contact with DG Competition as soon as possible as this will facilitate planning of the case.

11. Pre-notification contacts should be launched with a submission that allows the selection of an appropriate DG Competition case-team (6). This memorandum should provide a brief background to the transaction, a brief description of the relevant sector(s) and market(s) involved and the likely impact of the transaction on competition in general terms. It should also indicate the case language. In straightforward cases, the parties may chose to submit a draft Form CO as a basis for further discussions with DG Competition.

(6) Case teams for new cases are normally set up in weekly DG Competition's Merger Management Meetings.

12. After initial contacts have been made between the case-team and the notifying parties, it will be decided, whether it will suffice for DG Competition to make comments orally or in writing on the submissions made. This would typically be considered in straightforward cases. In more complex cases and cases that raise jurisdictional or other procedural issues, one or more pre-notification meetings are normally considered appropriate.

13. The first pre-notification meeting is normally held on the basis of a more substantial submission or a first draft Form CO. This allows for a more fruitful discussion about the proposed transaction in question or potential issue in point. Subsequent meetings may cover additional information submitted or outstanding issues.

14. Any submission sent to DG Competition should be provided sufficiently ahead of meetings or other contacts in order to allow for well prepared and fruitful discussions. In this regard, preparatory briefing memoranda/ draft Form COs sent in preparation of meetings should be filed in good time before the meeting (at least three working days) unless agreed otherwise with the case team. In case of voluminous submissions and in less straightforward cases, this time may need to be extended to allow DG Competition to properly prepare for the meeting.

15. Irrespective of whether pre-notification meetings have taken place or not, it is advisable that the notifying parties systematically provide a substantially complete draft Form CO before filing a formal notification. DG Competition would thereafter normally require five working days to review the draft before being asked to comment, at a meeting or on the telephone, on the adequacy of the draft. In case of voluminous submissions, this time will normally be extended.

Information to be provided / preparation of the Form CO

16. The format and the timing of all prenotification submissions should be decided together with the case-team. Notifying parties are advised to fully and frankly disclose information relating to all potentially affected markets and possible competition concerns, even if they may ultimately consider

that they are not affected and notwithstanding that they may take a particular view in relation to, for example, the issue of market definition. This will allow for an early market testing of alternative market definitions and/or the notifying parties' position on the market/s in question. In DG Competition's experience this approach minimises surprise submissions from third parties, and may avoid requests for additional information from the notifying parties at a late stage in the procedure and possible declarations of incompleteness under Article 4(2) of the Implementing Regulation or a decision under Article 11(5) of the Merger Regulation.

17. In addition, DG Competition recommends that notifying parties should, as early as possible in pre-notification, submit internal documents such as board presentations, surveys, analyses, reports and studies discussing the proposed concentration, the economic rationale for the concentration and competitive significance or the market context in which it takes place. Such documents provide DG Competition with an early and informed view of the transaction and its potential competitive impact and can thus allow for a productive discussion and finalisation of the Form CO.

18. Where appropriate, it is also recommended that notifying parties put forward, already at the pre-notification stage, any elements demonstrating that the merger leads to efficiency gains that they would like the Commission to take into account for the purposes of its competitive assessment of the proposed transaction. Such claims are likely to require extensive analysis. It is thus in the interests of the notifying parties to present these claims as early as possible to allow sufficient time for DG Competition to appropriately consider these elements in its assessment of a proposed transaction.

19. Pre-notification discussions provide the opportunity for the Commission and the notifying parties to discuss the amount of information to be provided in a notification. The notifying parties may in pre-notification request the Commission to waive the obligation to provide certain information that is not necessary for the examination of the case. All requests to omit any part of the information specified should be discussed in detail and any waiver has to be agreed with DG Competition prior to notification (7).

(7) See Article 3(2) Implementing Regulation. See also Commission Notice on a simplified procedure for treatment of certain concentrations under Council Regulation (EEC) N° 4064/89, *OJ* C 217, 29.07.2000, p. 32.

Completeness of the notification

20. Given that a notification is not considered effective until the information to be submitted in Form CO is complete in all material respects, the notifying parties and their advisers should ensure that the information contained in Form CO has been carefully prepared and verified: incorrect and misleading information is considered incomplete information (8). In this regard, the notifying parties should take special care that the appropriate contact details are provided for customers, suppliers and competitors. If such information is not correct or provided in full it will significantly delay the investigation and therefore may lead to a declaration of incompleteness.

(8) In addition, the Commission may impose fines on the notifying parties where they supply incorrect or misleading information in a notification under Article 14 (1)*(b)* Merger Regulation.

21. Further, to facilitate the effective and expeditious handling of their notification, notifying parties should also endeavour to provide the contact details required in Form CO electronically, at the latest on the day of notification, using the appropriate electronic form which can be provided by the case team.

22. Provided that the notifying parties follow the above described guidance, DG Competition will in principle, be prepared to confirm informally the adequacy of a draft notification at the pre-notification stage or, if appropriate, to identify in what material respects the draft Form CO is incomplete. However it has to be recognised that it will not be possible for DG Competition to exclude the fact that it may have to declare a notification incomplete in appropriate cases after notification.

23. In the event that DG Competition discovers omissions in the Form CO after formal notification, the notifying parties may be given an opportunity to urgently put right such omissions before a declaration of incompleteness is adopted. Due to the time constraints in merger procedures, the time allowed for such rectification is normally limited to 1 or 2 days. This opportunity will not be granted, however, in cases where DG Competition finds that the omissions immediately hinder the proper investigation of the proposed transaction.

Procedural questions and inter-agency co-operation

24. In addition to substantive issues, the notifying parties may in the pre-notification phase seek DG Competition's opinion on procedural matters such as jurisdictional questions.

25. Informal guidance may be provided if they are directly related to an actual, planned transaction and if sufficiently detailed background information is submitted by the notifying parties to properly assess the issue in question (9). Further matters for pre-notification discussions include the possibility of referrals to or from national EU jurisdictions (10), parallel proceedings in other non-EU jurisdictions and the issue of waivers on information sharing with other jurisdictions. As regards transactions likely to be reviewed in more than one jurisdiction, DG Competition invites the notifying parties to discuss the timing of the case with a view to enhance efficiency of the respective investigations, to reduce burdens on the merging parties and third parties, and to increase overall transparency of the merger review process. In this regard, notifying parties should also have regard to the EU-US Best Practices on co-operation in merger investigations (11).

(9) Such informal guidance cannot be regarded as creating legitimate expectations regarding the proper interpretation of applicable jurisdictional or other rules.

(10) Such jurisdictional discussions will become particularly pertinent under the recast Merger Regulation, which becomes applicable from 1 May 2004. Pursuant to Articles 4(4) and 4(5) of the recast Merger Regulation, notifying parties may, before notification, request on the basis of a reasoned submission, referral of a case to or from the Commission. DG Competition will be ready to discuss with notifying parties informally the possibility of such pre-notification referrals and to guide them through the pre-notification referral process.

(11) http://europa.eu.int/comm/competition/mergers/others/eu_us.pdf

4. FACT FINDING/REQUESTS FOR INFORMATION

26. In carrying out its duties the Commission may obtain all necessary information from relevant persons, undertakings, associations of undertakings and competent authorities of Member States (see Article 11(1) Merger Regulation). That investigation normally starts after the notification of a proposed concentration. However, DG Competition may exceptionally decide that, in the interest of its investigation, market contacts could be initiated informally prior to notification. Such pre-notification contacts/enquiries would only take place if the existence of the transaction is in the public domain and once the notifying parties have had the opportunity to express their views on such measures.

27. The Commission's investigation is mainly conducted in the form of written Requests for Information (requests pursuant to Article 11 of the Merger Regulation) to customers, suppliers, competitors and other relevant parties. Such requests may also be addressed to the notifying parties. In addition to such Article 11 requests, the views of the notifying parties, other involved parties and third parties are also sought orally.

28. In the interest of an efficient investigation, DG Competition may consult the notifying parties, other involved parties or third parties on methodological issues regarding data and information gathering in the relevant economic sector. It may also seek external economic and/or industrial expertise and launch its own economic studies.

5. COMMUNICATION AND MEETINGS WITH THE NOTIFYING PARTIES, OTHER INVOLVED PARTIES AND 3RD PARTIES

29. One of the aims of these Best Practices is to enhance transparency in the day to day handling of merger cases and in particular, to ensure good communication between DG Competition, the merging parties and third parties. In this regard, DG Competition endeavours to give all parties involved in the proceeding ample opportunity for open and frank discussions and to make their points of view known throughout the procedure.

5.1. State of Play meetings with notifying parties

Aim and format of the State of Play meetings

30. The objective of the State of Play meetings is to contribute to the quality and efficiency of the decision-making process and to ensure transparency and communication between DG Competition and the notifying parties. As such these meetings should provide a forum for the mutual exchange of information between DG Competition and the notifying parties at key points in the procedure. They are entirely voluntary in nature.

31. State of Play meetings may be conducted in the form of meetings at the Commission's premises, or alternatively, if appropriate, by telephone or videoconference. In order for the meetings to operate properly they should be carefully prepared on the basis of an agenda agreed in advance. Further, senior DG Competition management will normally chair the meetings.

32. The State of Play meetings will not exclude discussions and exchanges of information between the notifying parties and DG Competition at other occasions throughout the procedure as appropriate. In this regard, notifying parties are advised to inform DG Competition, as soon as possible, about any important procedural or substantive developments that may be of relevance for the assessment of the proposed transaction. Such developments may include any remedy proposals the notifying parties are offering or are considering to offer in other jurisdictions, so as to facilitate co-ordination of the timing and substance of such remedy proposals. This also concerns matters already discussed at a State of Play meeting, in respect of which the parties consider it necessary to provide additional comments.

Timing of the State of Play meetings

33. Notifying parties will normally be offered the opportunity of attending a State of Play meeting at the following five different points in the Phase I and Phase II procedure:

a) where it appears that «serious doubts» within the meaning of Article 6(1)(c) of the Merger Regulation are likely to be present a meeting will be offered before the expiry of 3 weeks (12) into Phase I. In addition to informing the notifying parties of the preliminary result of the initial investigation, this meeting provides an opportunity for the notifying parties to prepare the formulation of a possible remedy proposal in Phase I before expiry of the deadline provided in Article 18 of the Implementing Regulation.

(12) Fifteen working days under the recast Merger Regulation.

b) normally within 2 weeks following the adoption of the Article 6(1)(c) decision. In order to prepare for this meeting, the notifying parties should provide DG Competition with their comments on the Article 6(1)(c) decision and on any documents in the Commission's file, which they may have had the opportunity to review (see below section 7.2) by way of a written memorandum in advance of the meeting. The notifying parties should contact the case team to discuss an appropriate schedule for the filing of this memorandum.

The main purpose of the post Article 6(1)(c) meeting is to facilitate the notifying parties' understanding of the Commission's concerns at an early stage of the Phase II proceedings. The meeting also serves to assist DG Competition in deciding the appropriate framework for its further investigation by discussing with the notifying parties matters such as the market definition and competition concerns outlined in the Article 6(1)(c) decision. The meeting is also intended to serve as a forum for mutually informing each other of any planned economic or other studies. The approximate timetable of the Phase II procedure may also be discussed (13).

(13) Once the recast Merger Regulation becomes applicable, this post Article 6(1)(c) State of Play meeting will also serve to discuss the possibility of any extensions to the Phase II deadline pursuant to Article 10(3) of the recast Merger Regulation.

c) before the issuing of a Statement of Objections (SO). This pre-SO meeting gives the notifying parties an opportunity to understand DG Competition's preliminary view on the outcome of the Phase II investigation and to be informed of the type of objections DG Competition may set out in the SO. The meeting may also be used by DG Competition to clarify certain issues and facts before it finalises its proposal on the issuing of a SO.

d) following the reply to the SO and the Oral Hearing. This post-SO State of Play meeting provides the notifying parties with an opportunity to understand DG Competition's position after it has considered their reply and heard them at an Oral Hearing. If DG Competition indicates that it is minded to maintain some or all of its objections, the meeting may also serve as an opportunity to discuss the scope and timing of possible remedy proposals (14).

(14) It is to be noted that, under the recast Merger Regulation (Article 10(3)), the submission of remedies could lead to an automatic extension of the Phase II deadline.

e) before the Advisory Committee meets. The primary purpose of this meeting is to enable the notifying parties to discuss with DG Competition its views on any proposed remedies and where relevant, the results of the market testing of such remedies. It also provides the notifying parties where necessary, with the opportunity to formulate improvements to their remedies proposal (15).

(15) Modifications to remedies are only possible under those conditions set out in Article 18 of the Implementing Regulation and point 43 of the Commission's Notice on Remedies.

5.2. Involvement of third parties

34. According to Community merger control law, third parties considered as having a «sufficient interest» in the Commission's procedure include customers, suppliers, competitors, members of the administration or management organs of the undertakings concerned or recognised workers' representatives of those undertakings (16). Their important role in the Commission's procedure is stressed in particular in Article 18(4) of the Merger Regulation and Articles 16(1) and (2) of the Implementing Regulation. In addition, the Commission also welcomes the views of any other interested third parties including consumer organisations (17).

(16) See Article 11 of the Implementing Regulation.

(17) Article 16(3) Implementing Regulation. To this effect, DG Competition has appointed a Consumer Liaison Officer responsible for contacts with consumer organisations.

35. The primary way for third parties to contribute to the Commission's investigation is by means of replies to requests for information (Article 11 Merger Regulation) (18). However, DG Competition also welcomes any individual submission apart from direct replies to questionnaires, where third parties provide information and comments they consider relevant for the assessment of a given transaction. DG Competition may also invite third parties for meetings to discuss and clarify specific issues raised.

(18) Article 11(7) of the recast Merger Regulation expressly provides for the Commission's competence to interview any natural or legal person who consents to be interviewed for the purpose of collecting information relating to the subject-matter of an investigation.

36. In addition, DG Competition may in the interest of the investigation in appropriate cases provide third parties that have shown a sufficient interest in the procedure with an edited version of the SO from which business secrets have been removed, in order to allow them to make their views known on the Commission's preliminary assessment. In such cases, the SO is provided under strict confidentiality obligations and restrictions of use, which the third parties have to accept prior to receipt.

37. If third parties wish to express competition concerns as regards the transaction in question or to put forward views on key market data or characteristics that deviate from the notifying parties' position, it is essential that they are communicated as early as possible to DG Competition, so that they can be considered, verified and taken into account properly. Any point raised should be substantiated and supported by examples, documents and other factual evidence. Furthermore, in accordance with Article 17(2) of the Implementing Regulation, third parties should always provide the DG Competition with a non-confidential version of their submissions at the time of filing or shortly thereafter to facilitate access to the file and other measures intended to ensure transparency for the benefit of the decision making process (see further below section 7).

5.3. «Triangular» and other meetings

38. In addition to bilateral meetings between DG Competition and the notifying parties, other involved parties or third parties, DG Competition may decide to invite third parties and the notifying parties to a «triangular» meeting where DG Competition believes it is desirable, in the interests of the fact-finding investigation, to hear the views of the notifying parties and such third parties in a single forum. Such triangular meetings, which will be on a voluntary basis and which are not intended to replace the formal oral hearing, would take place in situations where two or more opposing views have been put forward as to key market data and characteristics and the effects of the concentration on competition in the markets concerned.

39. Triangular meetings should ideally be held as early in the investigation as possible in order to enable DG Competition to reach a more informed conclusion as to the relevant market characteristics and to clarify issues of substance before deciding on the issuing of an SO. Triangular meetings are normally chaired by senior DG Competition management. They are prepared in advance on the basis of an agenda established by DG Competition after consultation of all parties that agreed to attend the meeting. The preparation will normally include a mutual exchange of non-confidential submissions between the notifying parties and the third party in question sufficiently in advance of the meeting. The meeting will not require the disclosure of confidential information or business secrets, unless otherwise agreed by the parties.

6. REMEDIES DISCUSSIONS

40. As stated above, the State of Play meetings in both Phase I and Phase II, in addition to providing a forum for discussing issues related to the investigation, also serve to discuss possible remedy proposals. Detailed guidance on the requirements for such proposals is set out in the Commission Notice on remedies acceptable under Council Regulation (EEC) N° 4064/89 and under Commission Regulation (EC) N° 447/98 (19) (the Remedies Notice). In particular, the Remedies Notice sets out the general principles applicable to remedies, the main types of commitments that have previously been accepted by the Commission, the specific requirements which proposals of remedies need to fulfil in both phases of the procedure, and guidance on the implementation of remedies. As regards the design of divestiture commitment proposals, the notifying parties are advised to take due account of the Commission's «Best Practice Guidelines on Divestiture Commitments» (20).

(19) *OJ* C 68, 02.03.2001, p. 3-11.

(20) Available under http://europa.eu.int/comm/competition/mergers/legislation/divestiture_commitments/

41. Although it is for the notifying parties to formulate suitable remedies proposals, DG Competition will provide guidance to the parties as to the general appropriateness of their draft proposal in advance of submission. In order to allow for such discussions, a notifying party should contact DG Competition in good time before the relevant deadline in Phase I or Phase II, in order to be able to address comments DG Competition may have on the draft proposal (21).

(21) It is to be noted that under the recast Merger Regulation (Articles 10(1) and (3)), the submission of remedies could lead to an automatic extension of the Phase I and II deadlines.

7. PROVISION OF DOCUMENTS IN THE COMMISSION'S FILE/CONFIDENTIALITY

7.1. Access to the file

42. According to Community law, the notifying parties have upon request a right to access the Commission's file after the Commission has issued an SO (see Article 18(3) of the Merger Regulation and Article 13(3) of the Implementing Regulation).

43. Further, the notifying parties will be given the opportunity to have access to documents received after the issuing of the SO up until the consultation of the Advisory Committee.

44. Access to the file will be provided subject to the legitimate interest of the protection of third parties' business secrets and other confidential information.

7.2. Review of key documents

45. DG Competition believes in the merits of an open exchange of views with ample opportunities for the notifying parties and third parties to make their points of view known throughout the procedure. This enables DG Competition to assess the main issues arising during the investigation with as much information at its disposal as possible. In this spirit, DG Competition's objective will be to provide the notifying parties with the opportunity of reviewing and commenting on «key documents» obtained by the Commission. Such documents would comprise substantiated submissions of third parties running counter to the notifying parties' own contentions received during Phase I and thereafter (22), including key submissions to which specific reference is made in the Article 6(1)(c) decision and market studies.

(22) This would in particular include substantiated «complaints» contending that the notified transaction may give rise to competition concerns. The word «complaint» is to be understood in the non-technical sense of the term as no formal complaints procedure exists in merger cases.

46. DG Competition will use its best endeavours to provide notifying parties in a timely fashion, with the opportunity to review such documents following the initiation of proceedings and thereafter on an *ad hoc* basis. DG Competition will respect justified requests by third parties for non-disclosure of their submissions prior to the issuing of the SO relating to genuine concerns regarding confidentiality, including fears of retaliation and the protection of business secrets.

7.3. Confidentiality Rules

47. In accordance with Article 287 of the EC Treaty and Article 17(1) of the Implementing Regulation, the Commission will, throughout its investigation, protect confidential information and business secrets contained in submissions provided by all parties involved in EC merger proceedings. Given the short legal deadlines of EC merger procedures, parties are encouraged to clarify as soon as possible any queries related to confidentiality claims with members of the case team. Guidance on what is considered to be business secrets or other confidential information is provided in the Commission's Notice on Access to file (23).

(23) OJ C 23, 23/01/97, p. 3.

8. RIGHT TO BE HEARD AND OTHER PROCEDURAL RIGHTS

48. The right of the parties concerned to be heard before a final decision affecting their interests is taken is a fundamental principle of Community law. That right is also set out in the Merger Regulation (Article 18) and the Implementing Regulation (Articles 14-16). These Best Practices do not alter any such rights under Community law.

49. Any issues related to the right to be heard and other procedural issues, including access to the file, time limits for replying to the SO and the objectivity of any enquiry conducted in order to assess the competition impact of commitments proposed in EC merger proceedings can be raised with the Hearing Officer, in accordance with Commission Decision of 23 May 2001 on the terms of reference of hearing officers in certain competition proceedings (24).

(24) OJ L 162, 19/06/2001 p. 21–24. The text can also be found at: http://europa.eu.int/comm/competition/hearings/officers/

9. FUTURE REVIEW

50. These Best Practices may be revised to reflect changes to legislative, interpretative and administrative measures or due to case law of the European Courts, which govern EC merger control or any experience gained in applying such framework. DG Competition further intends to engage, on a regular basis, in a dialogue with the business and legal community on the experience gained through the application of the Merger Regulation in general, and these Best Practices in particular.

DG Competition Information note on Art. 6, (1), c), 2nd sentence, of Regulation 139/2004 (abandonment of concentrations), 20 January 2004, not published in the Official Journal

1. See the site: http://ec.europa.eu/competition/mergers/legislation/abandonment.pdf

The revised EC Merger Regulation introduced a new provision related to the closure of merger control procedures without a final decision after the Commission has initiated proceedings under Art. 6, (1), c), 1st sentence. That sentence reads as follows: «Without prejudice to Article 9, such proceedings shall be closed by means of a decision as provided for in Article 8, (1) to (4), unless the undertakings concerned have demonstrated to the satisfaction of the Commission that they have abandoned the concentration». Prior to the initiation of proceedings, such requirements do not apply.

This note sets out the requirements for this satisfaction to be achieved.

As a general principle, the requirements for the proof of the abandonment must correspond in terms of legal form, format, intensity *etc.* to the initial act that was considered sufficient to make the concentration notifiable. In case the parties proceed from that initial act to a strengthening of their contractual links during the procedure, for example by concluding a binding agreement after the transaction was notified on the basis of a good faith intention, the requirements for the proof of the abandonment must correspond also to the latest act.

In line with this principle, in case of implementation of the concentration prior to a Commission decision, the re-establishment of the status quo ante has to be shown.

In other cases, the mere withdrawal of the notification is not considered as sufficient proof that the concentration has been abandoned in the sense of Article 6, (1), c). Likewise, minor modifications of a concentration, for example as regards the agreed time of implementation or minor changes in the shareholding percentages which do not affect the change in control or the quality of that change, cannot be considered as an abandonment of the original concentration.

❑ Binding agreement: proof of the legally binding cancellation of the agreement in the form envisaged by the initial agreement (i.e. usually a document signed by all the parties) will be required. Expressions of intention to cancel the agreement or not to implement the notified concentration, as well as unilateral declarations by the parties will not be considered sufficient.

❑ Good faith intention to conclude an agreement: In case of a letter of intent or memorandum of understanding reflecting such good faith intention, documents proving that this basis for the good faith intention has been cancelled will be required. As for possible other forms that indicated the good faith intention, the abandonment must reverse this good faith intention and correspond in terms of form and intensity to the initial expression of intent.

❑ Public announcement of a public bid or of the intention to make a public bid: a public announcement terminating the bidding procedure will be required. The format and public reach of this announcement must be comparable to the initial announcement.

❑ Implemented concentrations: In case the concentration has been implemented prior to a Commission decision, the parties will be required to show that the situation prevailing before the implementation of the concentration has been re-established.

It is for the parties to submit the necessary documentation to meet these requirements.

This information is without prejudice to the interpretation of Community law which may be given by the Court of Justice or the Court of First Instance of the European Communities.

Communication from the Commission pursuant to Article 23(1) of Commission Regulation (EC) N° 802/2004 implementing Council Regulation (EC) N° 139/2004 on the control of concentrations between undertakings

(OJ C 139, 19 May 2004, p. 2)

(2004/C 139/02)
(Text with EEA relevance)
Address of the Commission's Directorate General for Competition
European Commission

Directorate General for Competition
Merger Registry
Rue Joseph II / Jozef II Straat, 70
B-1000 Bruxelles / Brussel

Commission Notice on case referral in respect of concentrations

(OJ C 56, 5 March 2005, p. 2)

1. The purpose of this Notice is to describe in a general way the rationale underlying the case referral system in Article 4(4) and (5), Article 9 and Article 22 of Council Regulation (EC) N° 139/2004 of 20 January 2004 on the control of concentrations between undertakings (the EC Merger Regulation) (1) (hereinafter «the Merger Regulation»), including the recent changes made to the system, to catalogue the legal criteria that must be fulfilled in order for referrals to be possible, and to set out the factors which may be taken into consideration when referrals are decided upon. The Notice also provides practical guidance regarding the mechanics of the referral system, in particular regarding the pre-notification referral mechanism provided for in Article 4(4) and (5) of the Merger Regulation. The guidance provided in this notice applies, mutatis mutandis, to the referral rules contained in the EEA Agreement (2).

(1) O.J. L 24, 29.1.2004, p. 1. This Regulation has recast Council Regulation (EEC) N° 4064/89 of 21 December 1989 on the control of concentrations between undertakings (O.J. L 395, 30.12.1989, p. 1. Corrected version in O.J. L 257, 21.9.1990, p. 13).

(2) See EEA Joint Committee Decision N° 78/2004 of 8 June 2004 (O.J. L 219, 8.6.2004, p. 13).

I. INTRODUCTION

2. Community jurisdiction in the field of merger control is defined by the application of the turnoverrelated criteria contained in Articles 1(2) and 1(3) of the Merger Regulation. When dealing with concentrations, the Commission and Member States do not have concurrent jurisdiction.

Rather, the Merger Regulation establishes a clear division of competence. Concentrations with a «Community dimension», i.e. those above the turnover thresholds in Article 1 of the Merger Regulation, fall within the exclusive jurisdiction of the Commission; Member States are precluded from applying national competition law to such concentrations by virtue of Article 21 of the Merger Regulation. Concentrations falling below the thresholds remain within the competence of the Member States; the Commission has no jurisdiction to deal with them under the Merger Regulation.

3. Determining jurisdiction exclusively by reference to fixed turnover-related criteria provides legal certainty for merging companies. While the financial criteria generally serve as effective proxies for the category of transactions for which the Commission is the more appropriate authority, Regulation (EEC) N° 4064/89 complemented this «bright-line» jurisdictional scheme with a possibility for cases to be re-attributed by the Commission to Member States and *vice versa*, upon request and provided certain criteria were fulfilled.

4. When Regulation (EEC) N° 4064/89 was first introduced, it was envisaged by the Council and Commission that case referrals would only be resorted to in «exceptional circumstances» and where «the interests in respect of competition of the Member State concerned could not be adequately protected in any other way» (3). There have, however, been a number of developments since the adoption of Regulation (EEC) N° 4064/89. First, merger control laws have been introduced in almost all Member States. Second, the Commission has exercised its discretion to refer a number of cases to Member States pursuant to Article 9 in circumstances where it was felt that the Member State in question was in a better position to carry out the investigation than the Commission (4). Likewise, in a number of cases (5), several Member States decided to make a joint referral of a case pursuant to Article 22 in circumstances where it was felt that the Commission was the authority in a better position to carry out the investigation (6). Third, there has been an increase in the number of transactions not meeting the thresholds in Article 1 of the Merger Regulation which must be filed in multiple Member State jurisdictions, a trend which is likely to continue in line with the Community's growing membership. Many of these transactions affect competition beyond the territories of individual Member States (7).

(3) See the Notes on Council Regulation (EEC) N° 4064/89 [«Merger Control in the European union», European Commission, Brussels-Luxembourg, 1998, at p. 54]. See also Case T-119/02 Philips v Commission [2003] ECR II-1433 (Case M.2621 SEB/Moulinex) at paragraph 354.

(4) It is a fact that some concentrations of Community dimension affect competition in national or sub-national markets within one or more Member States.

(5) M.2698 Promatech/Sulzer; M.2738 GE/Unison; M.3136 GE/AGFA.

(6) In the same vein, Member States' competition authorities, in the context of the European Competition Authorities' association, have issued a recommendation designed to provide guidance as to the principles upon which national competition authorities should deal with cases eligible for joint referrals under Article 22 of the EC Merger Regulation – Principles on the application, by National Competition Authorities within the ECA network, of Article 22 of the EC Merger Regulation.

(7) While the introduction of Article 1(3) in 1997 has brought some such cases under the jurisdiction of the Merger Regulation, many are unaffected. See paragraph 21 et seq of the Commission's Green Paper of 11 December 2001 (COM(2001) 745 final).

5. The revisions made to the referral system in the Merger Regulation are designed to facilitate the reattribution of cases between the Commission and Member States, consistent with the principle of subsidiarity, so that the more appropriate authority or authorities for carrying out a particular merger investigation should in principle deal with the case. At the same time, the revisions are intended to preserve the basic features of the Community merger control system introduced in 1989, in particular the provision of a «one-stop-shop» for the competition scrutiny of mergers with a cross-border impact and an alternative to multiple merger control notifications within the Community (8). Such multiple filings often entail considerable cost for competition authorities and businesses alike.

(8) See Recitals 11, 12 and 14 to the Merger Regulation.

6. The case re-attribution system now provides that a referral may also be triggered before a formal filing has been made in any Member State jurisdiction, thereby affording merging companies the possibility of ascertaining, at as early as possible a stage, where jurisdiction for scrutiny of their transaction will ultimately lie. Such pre-notification referrals have the advantage of alleviating the additional cost, notably in terms of time delay, associated with post-filing referral.

7. The revisions made to the referral system in Regulation (EC) N° 139/2004 were motivated by a desire that it should operate as a jurisdictional mechanism which is flexible (9) but which at the same time ensures effective protection of competition and limits the scope for «forum shopping» to the greatest extent possible. However, having regard in particular to the importance of legal certainty, it should be stressed that referrals remain a derogation from the general rules which determine jurisdiction based upon objectively determinable turnover thresholds. Moreover, the Commission and Member States retain a considerable margin of discretion in deciding whether to refer cases falling within their «original jurisdiction», or whether to accept to deal with cases not falling within their «original jurisdiction», pursuant to Article 4(4) and (5), Article 9(2)(a) and Article 22 (10). To that extent, the current Notice is intended to provide no more than general guidance regarding the appropriateness of particular cases or categories of cases for referral.

(9) See Recital 11 to the Merger Regulation.

(10) See, however, *infra*, footnote 14. It should moreover be noted that, pursuant to Article 4(5), the Commission has no discretion as to whether or not to accept a case not falling within its original jurisdiction.

II. REFERRAL OF CASES

Guiding principles

8. The system of merger control established by the Merger Regulation, including the mechanism for reattributing cases between the Commission and Member States contained therein, is consistent with the principle of subsidiarity enshrined in the EC Treaty (11). Decisions taken with regard to the referral of cases should accordingly take due account of all aspects of the application of the principle of subsidiarity in this context, in particular which is the authority more appropriate for carrying out the investigation, the benefits inherent in a «one-stop-shop» system, and the importance of legal certainty with regard to jurisdiction (12). These factors are inter-linked and the respective weight placed upon each of them will depend upon the specificities of a particular case. Above all, in considering whether or not to exercise their discretion to make or accede to a referral, the Commission and Member States should bear in mind the need to ensure effective protection of competition in all markets affected by the transaction (13).

(11) See Article 5 of the EC Treaty.

(12) See Recitals 11 and 14 to the Merger Regulation.

(13) See Article 9(8) of the Merger Regulation; see also Philips v Commission (paragraph 343) where the Court of First Instance of the European Communities states that «... although the first subparagraph of Article 9(3) of Regulation (EEC) N° 4064/89 confers on the Commission broad discretion as to whether or not to refer a concentration, it cannot decide to make such a referral if, when the Member State's request for referral is examined, it is clear, on the basis of a body of precise and coherent evidence, that such a referral cannot safeguard effective competition on the relevant market»; see also T-346/02 and T-347/02 Cableuropa SA v Commission of 30 September 2003, case not yet reported (paragraph 215). Circumstances relevant for the purpose of the Commission assessment include, inter alia, the fact that a Member State: *(i)* has specific laws for the control of concentrations on competition grounds and specialised bodies to ensure that these laws are implemented under the supervision of the national courts; *(ii)* has accurately identified the competition concerns raised by the concentration on the relevant markets in that Member State (see paragraphs 346-347 of Philips v Commission, cited above).

More appropriate authority

9. In principle, jurisdiction should only be re-attributed to another competition authority in circumstances where the latter is the more appropriate for dealing with a merger, having regard to the specific characteristics of the case as well as the tools and expertise available to the authority. Particular regard should be had to the likely locus of any impact on competition resulting from the merger. Regard may also be had to the implications, in terms of administrative effort, of any contemplated referral (14).

(14) This may involve consideration of the relative cost, time delay, legal uncertainty and the risk of conflicting assessment which may be associated with the investigation, or a part of the investigation, being carried out by multiple authorities.

10. The case for re-attributing jurisdiction is likely to be more compelling where it appears that a particular transaction may have a significant impact on competition and thus may deserve careful scrutiny.

One-stop-shop

11. Decisions on the referral of cases should also have regard to the benefits inherent in a «one-stopshop», which is at the core of the Merger Regulation (15). The provision of a one-stop-shop is beneficial to competition authorities and businesses alike. The handling of a merger by a single competition authority normally increases administrative efficiency, avoiding duplication and fragmentation of enforcement effort as well as potentially incoherent treatment (regarding investigation, assessment and possible remedies) by multiple authorities. It normally also brings advantages to businesses, in particular to merging firms, by reducing the costs and burdens arising from multiple filing obligations and by eliminating the risk of conflicting decisions resulting from the concurrent assessment of the same transaction by a number of competition authorities under diverse legal regimes.

(15) See Recital 11 of the Merger Regulation.

12. Fragmentation of cases through referral should therefore be avoided where possible (16), unless it appears that multiple authorities would be in a better position to ensure that competition in all markets affected by the transaction is effectively protected. Accordingly, while partial referrals are possible under Article 4(4) and Article 9, it would normally be appropriate for the whole of a case (or at least all connected parts thereof) to be dealt with by a single authority (17).

(16) The Court of First Instance in Philips v Commission took the view, obiter dictum, that «fragmentation» of cases, while possible as a result of the application of Article 9, is «undesirable in view of the «one-stop-shop» principle on which Regulation (EEC) N° 4064/89 is based». Moreover, the Court, while recognising that the risk of «inconsistent, or even irreconcilable» decisions by the Commission and Member States» is inherent in the referral system established by Article 9», made it clear that this is not, in its view, desirable. (See paragraphs 350 and 380).

(17) This is consistent with the Commission's decision in cases M.2389 Shell/DEA and M.2533 BP/E.ON to refer to Germany all of the markets for downstream oil products. The Commission retained the parts of the cases involving upstream markets. Likewise, in M.2706 P&O Princess/Carnival, the Commission exercised its discretion not to refer a part of the case to the United Kingdom, because it wished to avoid a fragmentation of the case (See Commission press release of 11.4.2002, IP/02/552).

Legal certainty

13. Due account should also be taken of the importance of legal certainty regarding jurisdiction over a particular concentration, from the perspective of all concerned (18). Accordingly, referral should normally only be made when there is a compelling reason for departing from «original jurisdiction» over the case in question, particularly at the post-notification stage. Similarly, if a referral has been made prior to notification, a post-notification referral in the same case should be avoided to the greatest extent possible (19).

(18) See Recital 11 of the Merger Regulation.

(19) See Recital 14 to the Merger Regulation. This is of course subject to the parties having made a full and honest disclosure of all relevant facts in their request for a pre-filing referral.

14. The importance of legal certainty should also be borne in mind with regard to the legal criteria for referral, and particularly – given the tight deadlines – at the pre-notification stage. Accordingly, pre-filing referrals should in principle be confined to those cases where it is relatively straightforward to establish, from the outset, the scope of the geographic market and/or the existence of a possible competitive impact, so as to be able to promptly decide upon such requests

Case referrals: legal requirements and other factors to be considered

Pre-notification referrals

15. The system of pre-notification referrals is triggered by a reasoned submission lodged by the parties to the concentration. When contemplating such a request, the parties to the concentration are required, first, to verify whether the relevant legal requirements set out in the Merger Regulation are fulfilled, and second, whether a pre-notification referral would be consistent with the guiding principles outlined above.

Referral of cases by the Commission to Member States under Article 4(4)

Legal requirements

16. In order for a referral to be made by the Commission to one or more Member States pursuant to Articles 4(4), two legal requirements must be fulfilled:

(i) there must be indications that the concentration may significantly affect competition in a market or markets;

(ii) the market(s) in question must be within a Member State and present all the characteristics of a distinct market.

17. As regards the first criterion, the requesting parties are in essence required to demonstrate that the transaction is liable to have a potential impact on competition on a distinct market in a Member State, which may prove to be significant, thus deserving close scrutiny. Such indications may be no more than preliminary in nature, and would be without prejudice to the outcome of the investigation. While the parties are not required to demonstrate that the effect on competition is likely to be an adverse one (20), they should point to indicators which are generally suggestive of the existence of some competitive effects stemming from the transaction (21).

(20) See Recital 16, which states that «the undertakings concerned should not ... be required to demonstrate that the effects of the concentration would be detrimental to competition».

(21) The existence of «affected markets» within the meaning of Form RS would generally be considered sufficient to meet the requirements of Article 4(4). However, the parties can point to any factors which may be relevant for the competitive analysis of the case (market overlap, vertical integration, etc.).

18. As regards the second criterion, the requesting parties are required to show that a geographic market in which competition is affected by the transaction in the manner just described (paragraph 17) is national, or narrower than national in scope (22).

(22) To this end, the requesting parties should consider those factors which are typically suggestive of national or narrower than national markets, such as, primarily, the product characteristics (e.g. low value of the product as opposed to significant costs of transport), specific characteristics of demand (e.g. end consumers sourcing in proximity to their centre of activity) and supply, significant variation of prices and market shares across countries, national consumer habits, different regulatory frameworks, taxation or other legislation. Further guidance can be found in the Commission Notice on the definition of the relevant market for the purposes of Community competition law (O.J. C 372, 9.12.1997, p. 5).

Other factors to be considered

19. Other than verification of the legal requirements, in order to anticipate to the greatest extent possible the likely outcome of a referral request, merging parties contemplating a request should also consider whether referral of the case is likely to be considered appropriate. This will involve an examination of the application of the guiding principles referred to above (paragraphs 8 to 14), and in particular whether the competition authority or authorities to which they are contemplating requesting the referral of the case is the most appropriate authority for dealing with the case. To this end, consideration should be given in turn both to the likely locus of the competitive effects of the transaction and to how appropriate the national competition authority (NCA) would be for scrutinising the operation.

20. Concentrations with a Community dimension which are likely to affect competition in markets that have a national or narrower than national scope, and the effects of which are likely to be confined to, or have their main economic impact in, a single Member State (23), are the most appropriate candidate cases for referral to that Member State. This applies in particular to cases where the impact would occur on a distinct market which does not constitute a substantial part of the common market. To the extent that referral is made to one Member State only, the benefit of a «one-stop-shop» is also preserved.

(23) See, for example, the Commission's referral of certain distinct oil storage markets for assessment by the French authorities in Cases M.1021 Compagnie Nationale de Navigation-SOGELF, M.1464 Total/Petrofina, and Case M.1628 Totalfina/Elf Aquitaine, Case M.1030 Lafarge/Redland, Case M.1220 Alliance Unichem/Unifarma, Case M.2760 Nehlsen/ Rethmann/ SWB/Bremerhavener Energiewirtschaft, and Case M.2154 C3D/Rhone/Go-ahead; Case M.2845 Sogecable/Canal Satelite Digital/Vias Digital.

21. The extent to which a concentration with a Community dimension which, despite having a potentially significant impact on competition in a nation-wide market, nonetheless potentially engenders substantial cross-border effects (e.g. because the effects of the concentration in one geographic market may have significant repercussions in geographic markets in other Member States, or because it may involve potential foreclosure effects and consequent fragmentation of the common market (24)), may be an appropriate candidate for referral will depend on the specific circumstances of the case. As both the Commission and Member States may be equally well equipped or be in an equally good position to deal with such cases, a considerable margin of discretion should be retained in deciding whether or not to refer such cases.

(24) See Case M.580 ABB/Daimler Benz, where the Commission did not accede to Germany's request for referral of a case under Article 9 in circumstances where, while the competition concerns were confined to German markets, the operation (which would create the largest supplier of railway equipment in the world) would have significant repercussions throughout Europe. See also Case M.2434 Hidroelectrica del Cantabrico/EnBW/Grupo Vilar Mir, where, despite a request by Spain to have the case referred under Article 9, the Commission pursued the investigation and adopted a decision pursuant to Article 8(2).

22. The extent to which concentrations with a Community dimension, and potentially affecting competition in a series of national or narrower than national markets in more than one Member State, may be appropriate candidates for referral to Member States will depend on factors specific to each individual case, such as the number of national markets likely to be significantly affected, the prospect of addressing any possible concerns by way of proportionate, non-conflicting remedies, and the investigative efforts that the case may require. To the extent that a case may engender competition concerns in a number of Member States, and require coordinated investigations and remedial action, this may militate in favour of the Commission retaining jurisdiction over the entirety of the case in question (25). On the other hand, to the extent that the case gives rise to competition concerns which, despite involving national markets in more than one Member State, do not appear to require coordinated investigation and/or remedial action, a referral may be appropriate. In a limited number of cases (26), the Commission has even found it appropriate to refer a concentration to more than one Member State, in view of the significant differences in competitive conditions that characterised the affected markets in the Member States concerned. While fragmentation of the treatment of a case deprives the merging parties of the benefit of a one-stop-shop in such cases, this consideration is less pertinent at the pre-notification stage, given that the referral is triggered by a voluntary request from the merging parties.

(25) For some examples, see M.1383 Exxon/Mobil, where the Commission, despite the United Kingdom request to have the part of the concentration relating to the market for motor fuel retailing in North west of Scotland referred to it, pursued the investigation as the case required a single and coherent remedy package designed to address all the problematic is-

sues in the sector concerned; see also M.2706 P&O Princess/Carnival, where, despite the fact that the UK authorities were assessing a rival bid by Royal Caribbean, the Commission did not accede to a request for a partial referral, so as to avoid a fragmentation of the case and secure a single investigation of the various national markets affected by the operation.

(26) See M. 2898, Le Roy Merlin/Brico, M.1030, Redland/Lafarge, M. 1684, Carrefour/Promodes.

23. Consideration should also, to the extent possible, be given to whether the NCA(s) to which referral of the case is contemplated may possess specific expertise concerning local markets (27), or be examining, or about to examine, another transaction in the sector concerned (28).

(27) In Case M.330 MacCormick/CPC/Rabobank/Ostmann, the Commission referred a case to Germany, because it was better placed to investigate local conditions in 85,000 sales points in Germany; a referral to the Netherlands was made in Case M.1060 Vendex/KBB, because it was better placed to assess local consumer tastes and habits; See also Case M.1555 Heineken/Cruzcampo, Case M.2621 SEB/Moulinex (where consumer preferences and commercial and marketing practice swere specific to the French market); Case M.2639 Compass/Restorama/Rail Gourmet/Gourmet, and Case M.2662 Danish-Crown/Steff-Houlberg.

(28) In Case M.716 Gehe/Lloyds Chemists, for example, the Commission referred a case because Lloyds was also subject to another bid not falling under ECMR thresholds but being scrutinised by the UK authorities: the referral allowed both bids to be scrutinised by the same authority; in M.1001/M.1019 Preussag/Hapag-Lloyd/TUI, a referral was made to Germany of two transactions, which together with a third one notified in Germany, would present competition concerns: the referral ensured that all three operations were dealt with in like manner; in case M.2044 Interbrew/Bass, the Commission referred the case to the UK authorities, because they were at the same time assessing Interbrew's acquisition of another brewer, Whitbread, and because of their experience in recent investigations in the same markets; similarly, see also Cases M.2760 Nehlsen/Rethmann/SWB/Bremerhavener Energiewirtschaft, M.2234 Metsalilitto Osuuskunta/Vapo Oy/JV, M.2495 Haniel/Fels, M.2881 Koninklijke BAM NBM/HBG, and M.2857/M.3075-3080 ECS/IEH and six other acquisitions by Electrabel of local distributors. In M.2706 P&O Princess/Carnival, however, despite the fact that the UK authorities were already assessing a rival bid by Royal Caribbean, the Commission did not accede to a request for a partial referral. The Commission had identified preliminary competition concerns in other national markets affected by the merger and thus wished to avoid a fragmentation of the case (See Commission press release of 11.4.2002, IP/02/552).

Referral of cases from Member States to the Commission under Article 4(5)

Legal requirements

24. Under Article 4(5), only two legal requirements must be met in order for the parties to the transaction to request the referral of the case to the Commission: the transaction must be a concentration within the meaning of Article 3 of the Merger Regulation, and the concentration must be capable of being reviewed under the national competition laws for the control of mergers of at least three Member States (see also paragraphs 65 et seq and 70 et seq).

Other factors to be considered

25. Other than verification of the legal requirements, in order to anticipate to the greatest extent possible the likely outcome of a referral request, merging parties contemplating a request should also consider whether referral of the case is likely to be considered appropriate. This will involve an examination of the application of the guiding principles referred to above, and in particular whether the Commission is the more appropriate authority for dealing with the case.

26. In this regard, Recital 16 to the Merger Regulation states that «requests for pre-notification referrals to the Commission would be particularly pertinent in situations where the concentration would affect competition beyond the territory of one Member State.» Particular consideration should therefore be given to the likely locus of any competitive effects resulting from the transaction, and to how appropriate it would be for the Commission to scrutinise the operation.

27. It should in particular be assessed whether the case is genuinely cross-border in nature, having regard to elements such as its likely effects on competition and the investigative and enforcement powers likely to be required to address any such effects. In this regard, particular consideration should be given to whether the case is liable to have a potential impact on competition in one or more markets affected by the concentration. In any case, indications of possible competitive impact may be no more than preliminary in nature (29), and would be without prejudice to the outcome of the investigation. Nor would it be necessary for the parties to demonstrate that the effect on competition is likely to be an adverse one.

(29) The existence of «affected markets» within the meaning of Form RS would generally be considered sufficient. However, the parties can point to any factors which may be relevant for the competitive analysis of the case (market overlap, vertical integration, etc).

28. Cases where the market(s) in which there may be a potential impact on competition is/are wider than national in geographic scope (30), or where some of the potentially affected markets are wider than national and the main economic impact of the concentration is connected to such markets, are the most appropriate candidate cases for referral to the Commission. In such cases, as the competitive dynamics extend over territories reaching beyond national boundaries, and may consequently require investigative efforts in several countries as well as appropriate enforcement powers, the Commission is likely to be in the best position to carry out the investigation.

(30) See the joint referral by seven Member States to the Commission of a transaction affecting worldwide markets in M.2738 GE/Unison, and the joint referral by seven Member States to the Commission of a transaction affecting a Western European market in M.2698 Promatech/Sulzer; See also Principles on the application, by National Competition Authorities within the ECA network, of Article 22 of the EC Merger Regulation, a paper published by the European Competition Authorities (ECA), at paragraph 11.

29. The Commission may be more appropriately placed to treat cases (including investigation, assessment and possible remedial action) that give rise to potential competition concerns in a series of national or narrower than national markets located in a number of different Member States (31). The Commission is likely to be in the best position to carry out the investigation in such cases, given the desirability of ensuring consistent and efficient scrutiny across the different countries, of employing appropriate investigative powers, and of addressing any competition concerns by way of coherent remedies.

(31) This may, for example, be the case in relation to operations where the affected markets, while national (or even narrower than national in scope for the purposes of a competition assessment), are nonetheless characterised by common Europe-wide or world-wide brands, by common Europe-wide or world-wide intellectual property rights, or by centralised manufacture or distribution — at least to the extent that such centralised manufacture or distribution would be likely to impact upon any remedial measures.

30. Similarly to what has been said above in relation to Article 4(4), the appropriateness of referring concentrations which, despite having a potentially significant impact on competition in a nation-wide market, nonetheless potentially engender substantial cross-border effects, will depend on the specific circumstances of the case. As both the Commission and Member States may be in an equally good position to deal with such cases, a considerable margin of discretion should be retained in deciding whether or not to refer such cases.

31. Consideration should also, to the extent possible, be given to whether the Commission is particularly well equipped to properly scrutinise the case, in particular having regard to factors such as specific expertise, or past experience in the sector concerned. The greater a merger's potential to affect competition beyond the territory of one Member State, the more likely it is that the Commission will be better equipped to conduct the investigation, particularly in terms of fact finding and enforcement powers.

32. Finally, the parties to the concentration might submit that, despite the apparent absence of an effect on competition, there is a compelling case for having the operation treated by the Commission, having regard in particular to factors such as the cost and time delay involved in submitting multiple Member State filings (32).

(32) See Recitals 12 and 16 of the Merger Regulation.

Post-notification referrals

Referrals from the Commission to Member States pursuant to Article 9

33. Under Article 9 there are two options for a Member State wishing to request referral of a case following its notification to the Commission: Articles 9(2)(a) and 9(2)(b) respectively.

Article 9(2)(a)

Legal requirements

34. In order for a referral to be made to a Member State or States pursuant to Article 9(2)(a), the following legal requirements must be fulfilled:

(i) the concentration must threaten to affect significantly competition in a market; and

(ii) the market in question must be within the requesting Member State, and present all the characteristics of a distinct market.

35. As regards the first criterion, in essence a requesting Member State is required to demonstrate that, based on a preliminary analysis, there is a real risk that the transaction may have a significant adverse impact on competition, and thus that it deserves close scrutiny. Such preliminary indications may be in the nature of prima facie evidence of such a possible significant adverse impact, but would be without prejudice to the outcome of a full investigation.

36. As regards the second criterion, the Member State is required to show that a geographic market(s) in which competition is affected by the transaction in the manner just described (paragraph 35) is/are national, or narrower than national in scope (33). Other factors to be considered

(33) See Commission notice on the definition of relevant market for the purposes of Community competition law (O.J. C 372, 9.12.1997, p. 5).

37. Other than verification of the legal requirements, other factors should also be considered in assessing whether referral of a case is likely to be considered appropriate. This will involve an examination of the application of the guiding principles referred to above, and in particular whether the competition authority or authorities requesting the referral of the case is/are in the best position to deal with the case. To this end, consideration should be given in turn both to the likely locus of the competitive effects of the transaction and to how well equipped the NCA would be to scrutinise the operation (see above at paragraphs 19-23)

Article 9(2)(b)

Legal requirements

38. In order for a referral to be made to a Member State or States pursuant to Article 9(2)(b), the following legal requirements must be fulfilled:

(i) the concentration must affect competition in a market; and

(ii) the market in question must be within the requesting Member State, present all the characteristics of a distinct market, and must not constitute a substantial part of the common market.

39. As regards the first criterion, a requesting Member State is required to show, based on a preliminary analysis, that the concentration is liable to have an impact on competition in a market. Such preliminary indications may be in the nature of prima facie evidence of a possible adverse impact, but would be without prejudice to the outcome of a full investigation.

40. As to the second criterion, a requesting Member State is required to show not only that the market in which competition is affected by the operation in the manner just described (paragraph 38) constitutes a distinct market within a Member State, but also that the market in question does not constitute a substantial part of the common market. In this respect, based on the past practice and caselaw (34), it appears that such situations are generally limited to markets with a narrow geographic scope, within a Member State.

(34) See Commission referrals granted under Article 9(2)(b) in: M.2446, Govia/Connex South Central, where the operation affected competition on specific railway routes in the London/Gatwick-Brighton area in the United Kingdom; in M.2730, Connex/DNVBVG, where the transaction affected competition in local public transport services in the Riesa area (Saxony, Germany); and in M. 3130, Arla Foods/Express Diaries, where the transaction affected competition in the market for the supply of bottled milk to doorstep deliverers in the London, Yorkshire and Lancashire regions of the United Kingdom. For the purpose of defining the notion of a non-substantial part of the common market, some guidance can also be found in the case-law relating to the application of Article 82 of EC Treaty. In that context, the Court of Justice has articulated quite a broad notion of what may constitute a substantial part of the common market, resorting inter alia to empirical evidence. In the case-law there can be found, for instance, indications essentially based on practical criteria such as «the pattern and volume of the production and consumption of the said product as well as the habits and economic opportunities of vendors and purchasers», see Case 40/73, Suiker Unie v Commission, [1975] ECR 1663. See also Case C-179/90, Porto di Genova [1991] ECR 5889, where the Port of Genova was considered as constituting a substantial part of the common market. In its case-law the Court has also stated that a series of separate markets may be regarded as together constituting a substantial part of the common market. See, for example, Case C-323/93, Centre d'insémination de la Crespelle [1994] ECR I-5077, paragraph. 17, where the Court stated «In this case, by making the operation of the insemination centres subject to authorization and providing that each centre should have the exclusive right to serve a defined area, the national legislation granted those centres exclusive rights. By thus establishing, in favour of those undertakings, a contiguous series of monopolies territorially limited but together covering the entire territory of a Member State, those national provisions create a dominant position, within the meaning of Article 86 of the Treaty, in a substantial part of the common market».

41. If these conditions are met, the Commission has an obligation to refer the case.

Referrals from Member States to the Commission pursuant to Article 22

Legal requirements

42. In order for a referral to be made by one or more Member States to the Commission pursuant to Article 22, two legal requirements must be fulfilled:

(i) the concentration must affect trade between Member States; and

(ii) it must threaten to significantly affect competition within the territory of the Member State or States making the request.

43. As to the first criterion, a concentration fulfils this requirement to the extent that it is liable to have some discernible influence on the pattern of trade between Member States (35).

(35) See also, by analogy, the Commission Notice – Guidelines on the effect on trade concept contained in Articles 81 and 82 of the Treaty (O.J. C 101, 27.4.2004, p. 81).

44. As to the second criterion, as under Article 9(2)*(a)*, a referring Member State or States is/are required in essence to demonstrate that, based on a preliminary analysis, there is a real risk that the transaction may have a significant adverse impact on competition, and thus that it deserves close scrutiny. Such preliminary indications may be in the nature of prima facie evidence of such a possible significant adverse impact, but would be without prejudice to the outcome of a full investigation.

Other factors to be considered

45. As post-notification referrals to the Commission may entail additional cost and time delay for the merging parties, they should normally be limited to those cases which appear to present a real risk of negative effects on competition and trade between Member States, and where it appears that these would be best addressed at the Community level (36). The categories of cases normally most appropriate for referral to the Commission pursuant to Article 22 are accordingly the following:

– cases which give rise to serious competition concerns in one or more markets which are wider than national in geographic scope, or where some of the potentially affected markets are wider than national, and where the main economic impact of the concentration is connected to such markets,

– cases which give rise to serious competition concerns in a series of national or narrower than national markets located in a number of Member States, in circumstances where coherent treatment of the case (regarding possible remedies, but also, in appropriate cases, the investigative efforts as such) is considered desirable, and where the main economic impact of the concentration is connected to such markets.

(36) See the joint referral by seven Member States to the Commission of a transaction affecting worldwide markets in M.2738 GE/Unison, and the joint referral by seven Member States to the Commission of a transaction affecting a Western European market in M.2698 Promatech/Sulzer; See also Principles on the application, by National Competition Authorities within the ECA network, of Article 22 of the EC Merger Regulation, a paper published by the European Competition Authorities (ECA), at paragraph 11.

III. MECHANICS OF THE REFERRAL SYSTEM

A. Overview of the referral system

46. The Merger Regulation sets out the relevant legal rules for the functioning of the referral system. The rules contained in Article 4(4) and (5), Article 9 and Article 22 set out in detail the various steps required for a case to be referred from the Commission to Member States and *vice versa*.

47. Each of the four relevant referral provisions establishes a self-contained mechanism for the referral of a given category of concentration. The provisions can be categorised in the following way:

(a) Pre-notification referrals:
(i) From the Commission to Member States (Article 4(4))
(ii) From Member States to the Commission (Article 4(5))
(b) Post-notification referrals:
(i) From the Commission to Member States (Article 9)
(ii) From Member States to the Commission (Article 22).

48. The flowcharts in Annex I to this Notice describe in graphical form the various procedural steps to be followed in the referral mechanisms set out in Articles 4(4) and (5), Article 9 and Article 22.

Pre-notification referrals

49. Pre-notification referrals can only be requested by the undertakings concerned (37). It is for the undertakings concerned to verify whether the concentration meets the criteria specified in Article 4(4) (that the concentration has a Community dimension but may significantly affect competition in a distinct market within a Member State) or Article 4(5) (that the concentration does not have a Community dimension but is capable of being reviewed under the national competition laws of at least three Member States). The undertakings concerned may then decide to request a referral to or from the Commission by submitting a reasoned request on Form RS. The request is transmitted without delay by the Commission to all Member States. The remainder of the process differs under Article 4(4) and Article 4(5).

(37) The term «undertakings concerned» includes «persons» within the meaning of Article 3(1)*(b)*.

– Under Article 4(4), the Member State or States concerned (38) have 15 working days from the date they receive the submission to express agreement or disagreement with the request. Silence on the part of a Member State is deemed to constitute agreement (39). If the Member State or States concerned agree to the referral, the Commission has an additional period of approximately 10 working days (25 working days from the date the Commission received Form RS) in which it may decide to refer the case. Silence on the part of the Commission is deemed to constitute assent. If the Commission assents, the case (or one or more parts thereof) is referred to the Member States or States as requested by the undertakings concerned. If the referral is made, the Member State or States concerned apply their national law to the referred part of the case (40). Articles 9(6) to 9(9) apply.

(38) The Member State or States concerned are the ones identified in Form RS to which the case will be referred if the request is granted.

(39) This mechanism is an essential feature of all referral procedures set out in the Merger Regulation. The mechanism may be termed «positive silence» or non-opposition: that is to say that failure to take a decision on the part of the Commission or a Member State will be deemed to constitute the taking of a positive decision. This mechanism was already a feature of Regulation

(EEC) N° 4064/89, in Article 9(5). It is now included in Article 4(4) (second and fourth sub-paragraphs), Article 4(5) (fourth sub-paragraph), Article 9(5) and Article 22(3) (first sub-paragraph, last sentence) of the Merger Regulation. The positive silence mechanism is, however, not applicable with regard to decisions by Member States to join a request under Article 22(2).

(40) Article 4(4) allows merging parties to request partial or full referrals. The Commission and Member States must either accede to or refuse the request, and may not vary its scope by, for example, referring only a part of case when a referral of the whole of the case had been requested. In the case of a partial referral, the Member State concerned will apply its national competition law to the referred part of the case. For the remainder of the case, the Merger Regulation will continue to apply in the normal way, that is the undertakings concerned will be obliged to make a notification of the non-referred part of the concentration on Form CO pursuant to Article 4(1) of the Merger Regulation. By contrast, if the whole of the case is referred to a Member State, Article 4(4) final subparagraph specifies that there will be no obligation to notify the case also to the Commission. The case will thus not be examined by the Commission. The Member State concerned will apply its national law to the whole of the case; no other Member State can apply national competition law to the concentration in question.

– Under Article 4(5), the Member States concerned (41) have 15 working days from the date they receive the submission to express agreement or disagreement with the request. At the end of that period, the Commission checks whether any Member State competent to examine the concentration under its national competition law has expressed disagreement. If there is no expression of disagreement by any such competent Member State, the case is deemed to acquire a Community dimension and is thus referred to the Commission which has exclusive jurisdiction over it. It is then for the parties to notify the case to the Commission, using Form CO. On the other hand, if one or more competent Member States have expressed their disagreement, the Commission informs all Member States and the undertakings concerned without delay of any such expression of disagreement and the referral process ends. It is then for the parties to comply with any applicable national notification rules.

(41) That is, those that would be competent to review the case under their national competition law in the absence of a referral. For the concept of «competent to review the case», see section B5 below.

Post-notification referrals

50. Pursuant to Article 9(2) and Article 22(1), post-notification referrals are triggered by Member States either on their own initiative or following an invitation by the Commission pursuant to Article 9(2) and Article 22(5) respectively. The procedures differ according to whether the referral is from or to the Commission.

– Under Article 9, a Member State may request that the Commission refer to it a concentration with Community dimension, or a part thereof, which has been notified to the Commission and which threatens to significantly affect competition within a distinct market within that Member State (Article 9(2)(a)), or which affects such a distinct market not constituting a substantial part of the common market (Article 9(2)(b)). The request must be made within 15 working days from the date the Member State received a copy of Form CO. The Commission must first verify whether those legal criteria are met. It may then decide to refer the case, or a part thereof, exercising its administrative discretion. In the case of a referral request made pursuant to Article 9(2)(b), the Commission must (i.e. has no discretion) make the referral if the legal criteria are met. The decision must be taken within 35 working days from notification or, where the Commission has initiated proceedings, within 65 working days (42). If the referral is made, the Member State concerned applies its own national competition law, subject only to Article 9(6) and (8).

(42) As regards cases where the Commission takes preparatory steps within 65 working days, see Article 9(4)(b) and (5).

– Under Article 22, a Member State may request that the Commission examine a concentration which has no Community dimension but which affects trade between Member States and threatens to significantly affect competition within its territory. The request must be made within 15 working days from the date of national notification or, where no notification is required, the date when the concentration was «made known» (43) to the Member State concerned. The Commission transmits the request to all Member States. Any other Member States can decide to join the request (44) within a period of 15 working days from the date they receive a copy of the initial request. All national time limits relating to the concentration are suspended a decision has been taken as to where it will be examined; a Member State can restart the national time limits before the expiry of the 15 working day period by informing the Commission and the merging parties that it does not wish to join the request. At the latest 10 working days following the expiry of the 15 working day period, the Commission must decide whether to accept the case from the requesting Member State(s). If the Commission accepts jurisdiction, national proceedings in the referring Member State(s) are terminated and the Commission examines the case pursuant to Article 22(4) of the Merger Regulation on behalf of the requesting State(s) (45). Non-requesting States can continue to apply national law.

(43) The notion of «made known», derived from the wording of Article 22, should in this context be interpreted as implying sufficient information to make a preliminary assessment as to the existence of the criteria for the making of a referral request pursuant to Article 22.

(44) It should be noted that Article 22 enables a Member State to join the initial request even if the concentration has not yet been notified to it. However, Member States may be unable to do so if they have not yet received the necessary information from the merging parties at the time of being informed by the Commission that a referral request has been lodged by another Member State. Notwithstanding the Member State's ability to contact the merging parties in order to verify whether they are competent to review any particular transaction, the notifying parties are therefore strongly encouraged to file, where feasible, their notification to all competent Member States simultaneously.

(45) Where the Commission examines a concentration on behalf of one or more Member States pursuant to Article 22, it can adopt all the substantive decisions provided for in Articles 6 and 8 of the Merger Regulation. This is established in Article 22(4) of that Regulation. It is to be noted that the Commission examines the concentration upon the request of and on behalf of the requesting Member States. This provision should therefore be interpreted as requiring the Commission to examine the impact of the concentration within the territory of those Member States. The Commission will not examine the effects of the concentration in the territory of Member States which have not joined the request unless this examination is necessary for the assessment of the effects of the concentration within the territory of the requesting Member States (for example, where the geographic market extends beyond the territory/ or territories of the requesting Member State(s).

51. The following section of the Notice focuses on a number of detailed elements of the system with the aim in particular of providing further guidance to undertakings contemplating making requests at the pre-notification stage, or who may be party to transactions subject to the possibility of post-notification referral.

B. Details of the referral mechanism

52. This section of this Notice provides guidance regarding certain aspects of the functioning of the referral system set out in Article 4(4) and(5), Article 9 and Article 22 of the Merger Regulation.

1. The network of competition authorities

53. Article 19(2) of the Merger Regulation provides that the Commission is to carry out the procedures set out in that Regulation in close and constant liaison with the competent authorities of the Member States (the NCAs). Cooperation and dialogue between the Commission and the NCAs, and between the NCAs themselves, is particularly important in the case of concentrations which are subject to the referral system set out in the Merger Regulation.

54. According to Recital 14 to the Merger Regulation, «the Commission and the NCAs should form together a network of public authorities, applying their respective competences in close cooperation using efficient arrangements for information sharing and consultation with a view to ensuring that a case is dealt with by the most appropriate authority, in the light of the principle of subsidiarity, and with a view to ensuring that multiple notifications of a given concentration are avoided to the greatest extent possible».

55. The network should ensure the efficient re-attribution of concentrations according to the principles described in section II above. This involves facilitating the smooth operation of the pre-notification referral mechanism, as well as providing, to the extent foreseeable, a system whereby potential postnotification referral requests are identified as soon as possible (46).

(46) Advance knowledge of the possibility of a referral request might, for example, be taken into account by the Commission in deciding not to accede to a request for derogation from the suspensive effect pursuant to Article 7(3) of the Merger Regulation.

56. Pursuant to Article 4(4) and (5), the Commission must transmit reasoned requests made by the undertakings concerned «without delay» (47). The Commission will endeavour to transmit such documents on the working day following that on which they are received or issued. Information within the network will be exchanged by various means, depending on the circumstances: e-mail, surface mail, courier, fax, telephone. It should be noted that for sensitive information or confidential information exchanges will be carried out by secure e-mail or by any other protected means of communication between these contact points.

(47) It should be noted that, as provided for in Article 19(1) of the Merger Regulation, the Commission is also under an obligation to transmit to the NCAs copies of notifications and of the most important documents lodged with or issued by the Commission.

57. All members of the network, including the Commission and all NCAs, their officials and other servants, and other persons working under the supervision of those authorities as well as officials and civil servants of other authorities of the Member States, will be bound by the professional secrecy obligations set out in Article 17 of the Merger Regulation. They must not disclose non-public information they have acquired through the application of the Merger Regulation, unless the natural or legal person who provided that information has consented to its disclosure.

58. Consultations and exchanges within the network is a matter between public enforcement agencies and do not alter any rights or obligations arising from Community or national law for companies. Each competition authority remains fully responsible for ensuring that due process is observed in the cases it deals with.

2. Triggering the pre-notification referral system; information to be provided by the requesting parties

59. For the referral system to work swiftly and smoothly, it is crucial that the requesting parties, provide complete and accurate information, whenever required, in a timely fashion and in the most efficient way possible. Legal requirements concerning the information to be provided and the consequences of providing incorrect, incomplete or misleading information are set out in the Merger Regulation, Regulation (EC) N° 802/2004 (hereinafter «the Merger Implementing Regulation») and Form RS (48).

(48) Form RS is annexed to Commission Regulation (EC) N° 802/2004 of 7 April 2004 implementing Council Regulation (EC) N° 139/2004 on the control of concentrations between undertakings (O.J. L 133, 30.4.2004, p. 1).

60. Form RS states that all information submitted in a reasoned submission must be correct and complete. If parties submit incorrect or incomplete information, the Commission has the power to either adopt a decision pursuant to Article 6(1)(a) of the Merger Regulation (where failure to fulfil the conditions of Article 4(5) comes to its attention during the course of the investigation), or to revoke any decision it adopts pursuant to Article 6 or Article 8, following an Article 4(5) referral, pursuant to Article 6(3)(a) or 8(6)(a) of the Merger Regulation. Following the adoption of a decision pursuant to Article 6(1)(a) or following revocation, national competition laws would once again be applicable to the transaction. In the case of referrals under Article 4(4) made on the basis of incorrect or incomplete information, the Commission may require a notification pursuant to Article 4(1). In addition, the Commission has the power to impose fines under Article 14(1)(a) of the Merger Regulation. Finally, parties should also be aware that, if a referral is made on the basis of incorrect or incomplete information included in Form RS, the Commission and/or the Member States may consider making a post-notification referral reversing a pre-notification referral based on such incorrect or incomplete information (49).

(49) This would be the appropriate «remedy» where the requesting parties have submitted incorrect or incomplete information not affecting fulfilment of the conditions of Article 4(5), which comes to the Commission's attention during the course of the investigation.

61. When providing information on Form RS or generally in making a request for a pre-notification referral, it is not envisaged or necessary for the undertakings concerned to show that their concentration will lead to detrimental effects on competition (50). They should, however, provide as much information as possible showing clearly in what way the concentration meets the relevant legal criteria set out in Article 4(4) and (5) and why the concentration would be most appropriately dealt with by the competition authority or authorities specified in the request. The Merger Regulation does not require publication of the fact that a Form RS has been lodged, and it is not intended to do so. A non-public transaction can consequently be the subject of a pre-notification referral request.

(50) See Recital 16 to the Merger Regulation.

62. Even though, according to the Merger Implementing Regulation, the Commission will accept Form RS in any official Community language, undertakings concerned providing information which is to be distributed to the network are strongly encouraged to use a language which will be understood by all addressees of the information. This will facilitate Member State treatment of such requests.

Moreover, as regards requests for referral to a Member State or States, the requesting parties are strongly encouraged to include a copy of the request in the language(s) of the Member State(s) to which the referral is being requested.

63. Beyond the legal requirements specified in Form RS, the undertakings concerned should be prepared to provide additional information, if required, and to discuss the matter with the Commission and the NCAs in a frank and open manner in order to enable the Commission and the NCAs to assess whether the concentration in question should be the subject of referral.

64. Informal contacts between merging parties contemplating lodging a pre-filing referral request, on the one hand, and the Commission and/or Member State authorities, on the other, are actively encouraged, even following the submission of Form RS. The Commission is committed to providing informal, early guidance to firms wishing to use the pre-notification referrals system set out in Article 4(4) and (5) of the Merger Regulation (51).

(51) A request for derogation from the suspensive effect pursuant to Article 7(3) of the Merger Regulation would normally be inconsistent with an intention to make a pre-notification referral request pursuant to Article 4(4).

3. Concentrations eligible for referral

65. Only concentrations within the meaning of Article 3 of the Merger Regulation are eligible for referral pursuant to Article 4(5) and Article 22. Only concentrations falling within the ambit of the relevant national competition laws for the control of mergers are eligible for referral pursuant to Article 4(4) and Article 9 (52).

(52) By contrast, the reference to «national legislation on competition» in Article 21(3) and Article 22(3) should be understood as referring to all aspects of national competition law.

66. Pre-filing referral requests pursuant to Article 4(4) and (5) of the Merger Regulation must concern concentrations the plans for which are sufficiently concrete. In that regard, there must at least exist a good faith intention to merge on the part of the undertakings concerned, or, in the case of a public bid, at least a public announcement of an intention to make such a bid (53).

(53) See Recital 34 to, and Article 4(1) of, the Merger Regulation.

4. The concept of «prior to notification» under Article 4(4) and (5)

67. Article 4(4) and (5) only apply at the pre-notification stage.

68. Article 4(4) specifies that the undertakings concerned may make a referral request by means of reasoned submission (Form RS), «prior to the notification of a concentration within the meaning of paragraph 1». This means that the request can only be made where no Form CO has been submitted pursuant to Article 4(1).

69. Likewise, Article 4(5) specifies that the request may be made «before any notification to the competent [national] authorities». This means that the concentration in question must not have been formally notified in any Member State jurisdiction for that provision to apply. Even one notification anywhere in the Community will preclude the undertakings concerned from triggering the mechanism of Article 4(5). In the Commission's view, no penalty should be imposed for non-notification of a transaction at the national level while a request pursuant to Article 4(5) is pending.

5. The concept of a «concentration capable of being reviewed under national competition law» and the concept of «competent Member State» in Article 4(5)

70. Article 4(5) enables the undertakings concerned to request a pre-notification referral of a concentration which does not have a Community dimension and which is «capable of being reviewed under the national competition laws of at least three Member States».

71. «Capable of being reviewed» or reviewable should be interpreted as meaning a concentration which falls within the jurisdiction of a Member State under its national competition law for the control of mergers. There is no need for a mandatory notification requirement, i.e. it is not necessary for the concentration to be required to be notified under national law (54).

(54) Even in circumstances where a notification is voluntary de jure, the parties may in practice wish or be expected to file a notification.

72. Pursuant to the third and fourth subparagraphs of Article 4(5), where at least one Member State «competent to examine the concentration under its national competition law» has expressed its disagreement with the referral, the case must not be referred. A «competent» Member State is one where the concentration is reviewable and which therefore has the power to examine the concentration under its national competition law.

73. All Member States, and not only those «competent» to review the case, receive a copy of the Form RS. However, only Member States «competent» to review the case are counted for the purposes of the third and fourth subparagraphs of Article 4(5). Pursuant to the third subparagraph of Article 4(5), «competent» Member States have 15 working days from the date they receive the Form RS to express their agreement or disagreement with the referral. If they all agree, the case will be deemed to acquire a Community dimension pursuant to the fifth subparagraph of Article 4(5). According to the fourth subparagraph of Article 4(5), by contrast, if even only one «competent» Member State disagrees, no referral will take place from any Member State.

74. Given the above mechanism, it is crucial to the smooth operation of Article 4(5) that all Member States where the case is reviewable under national competition law, and which are hence «competent» to examine the case under national competition law, are identified correctly. Form RS therefore requires the undertakings concerned to provide sufficient information to enable each and every Member State to identify whether or not it is competent to review the concentration pursuant to its own national competition law.

75. In situations where Form RS has been filled in correctly, no complications should arise. The undertakings concerned will have identified correctly all Member States which are competent to review the case. In situations, however, where the undertakings concerned have not filled in Form RS correctly, or where there is a genuine disagreement as to which Member States are «competent» to review the case, complications may arise.

– Within the period of 15 working days provided for in the third subparagraph of Article 4(5), a Member State which is not identified in Form RS as being competent may inform the Commission that it is competent and may, like any other competent Member State, express its agreement or disagreement with the referral.

– Likewise, within the period of 15 working days provided for in the third subparagraph of Article 4(5), a Member State which has been identified as competent in Form RS may inform the Commission that it is not «competent». That Member State would then be disregarded for the purposes of Article 4(5).

76. Once the period of 15 working days has expired without any disagreement having been expressed, the referral, will be considered valid. This ensures the validity of Commission decisions taken under Articles 6 or 8 of the Merger Regulation following an Article 4(5) referral.

77. This is not to say, however, that undertakings concerned can abuse the system by negligently or intentionally providing incorrect information, including as regards the reviewability of the concentration in the Member States, on Form RS. As noted at paragraph 60 above, the Commission may take measures to rectify the situation and to deter such violations. The undertakings concerned should also be aware that, in such circumstances, where a referral has been made on the basis of incorrect or incomplete information, a Member State which believes it was competent to deal with the case but did not have the opportunity to veto the referral due to incorrect information being supplied, may request a post-notification referral.

6. Notification and Publication of Decisions

78. According to the fourth subparagraph of Article 4(4), the fourth subparagraph of Article 4(5), Article 9(1) and the second subparagraph of Article 22(3), the Commission is obliged to inform the undertakings or persons concerned and all Member States of any decision taken pursuant to those provisions as to the referral of a concentration.

79. The information will be provided by means of a letter addressed to the undertakings concerned (or for decisions adopted pursuant to Article 9(1) or Article 22(3), a letter addressed to the Member State concerned). All Member States will receive a copy thereof.

80. There is no requirement that such decisions be published in the *Official Journal of the European Union* (55). The Commission will, however, give adequate publicity to such decisions on DG Competition's website, subject to confidentiality requirements.

(55) Pursuant to Article 20 of the Merger Regulation this is only required for decisions taken under Article 8(1)-(6) and Articles 14 and 15.

7. Article 9(6)

81. Article 9(6) provides that, when the Commission refers a notified concentration to a Member State in accordance with Article 4(4) or Article 9(3), the NCA concerned must deal with the case «without undue delay». Accordingly, the competent authority concerned should deal as expeditiously as possible with the case under national law.

82. In addition, Article 9(6) provides that the competent national authority must, within 45 working days after the Commission's referral or following receipt of a notification at the national level if requested inform the undertakings concerned of the result of the «preliminary competition assessment» and what «further action», if any, it proposes to take. Accordingly, within 45 working days after the referral or notification, as appropriate, the merging parties should be provided with sufficient information to enable them to understand the nature of any preliminary competition concerns the authority may have and be informed of the likely extent and duration of the investigation. The Member State concerned may only exceptionally suspend this time limit, where necessary information has not been provided to it by the undertakings concerned as required under its national competition law.

IV. FINAL REMARKS

83. This Notice will be the subject of periodic review, in particular following any revision of the referral provisions in the Merger Regulation. In that regard, it should be noted that, according to Article 4(6) of the Merger Regulation, the Commission must report to the Council on the operation of the prenotification referral provisions in Article 4(4) and (5), by 1 July 2009.

84. This Notice is without prejudice to any interpretation of the applicable Treaty and regulatory provisions by the Court of First Instance and the Court of Justice of the European Communities.

Annex

Referal charts

Article 4(4)

Legislation • 2. Rules adressed to undertakings • 2.2. Concentration control
Commission Notice - Case referral

Concentration with Community Dimenstion

Article 4(5)

Concentration without Community Dimension reviewable in at least three MS under national law

Article 9

Legislation • 2. Rules adressed to undertakings • 2.2. Concentration control
Commission Notice - Case referral

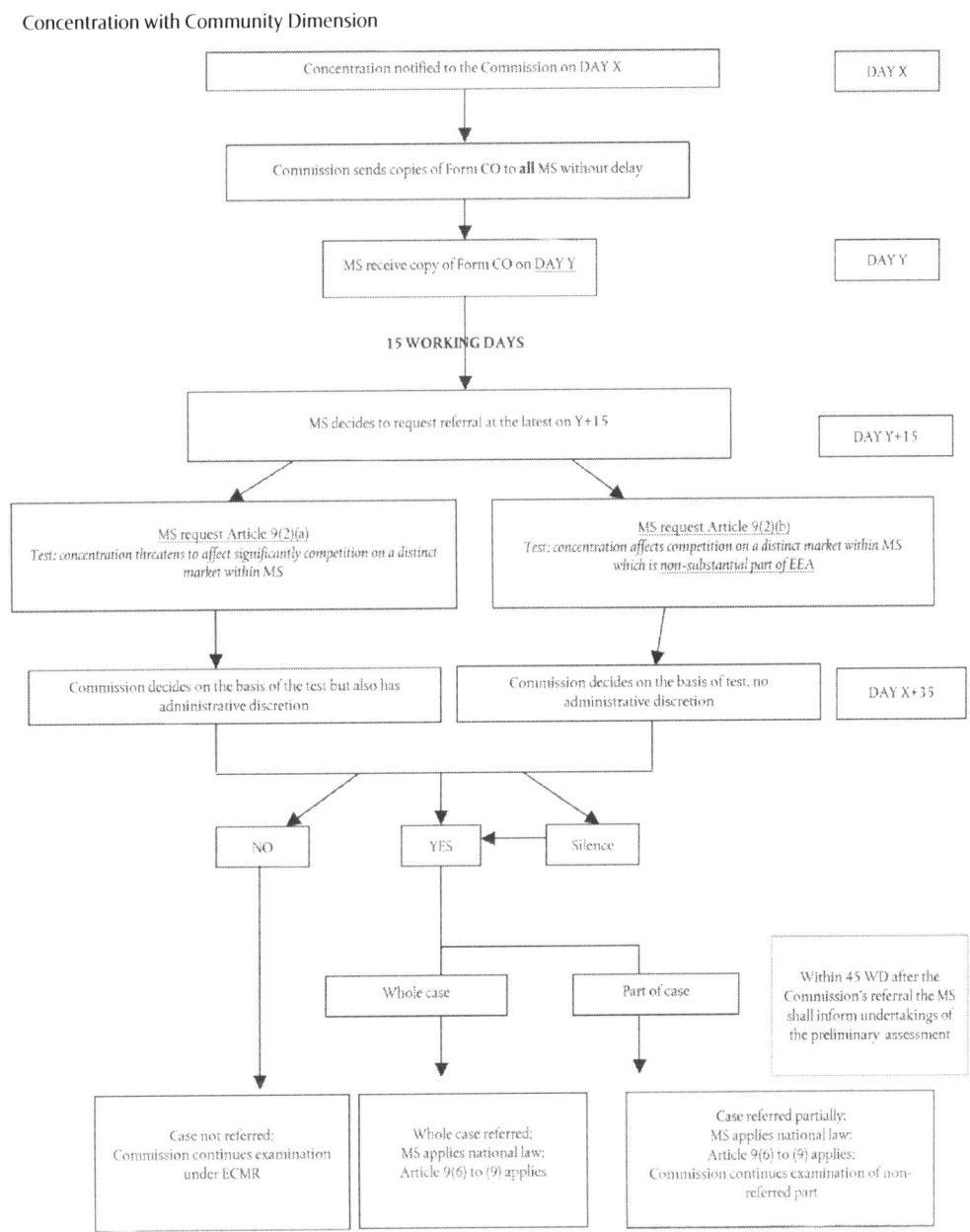

Legislation · 2. Rules adressed to undertakings · 2.2. Concentration control
Commission Notice - Case referral

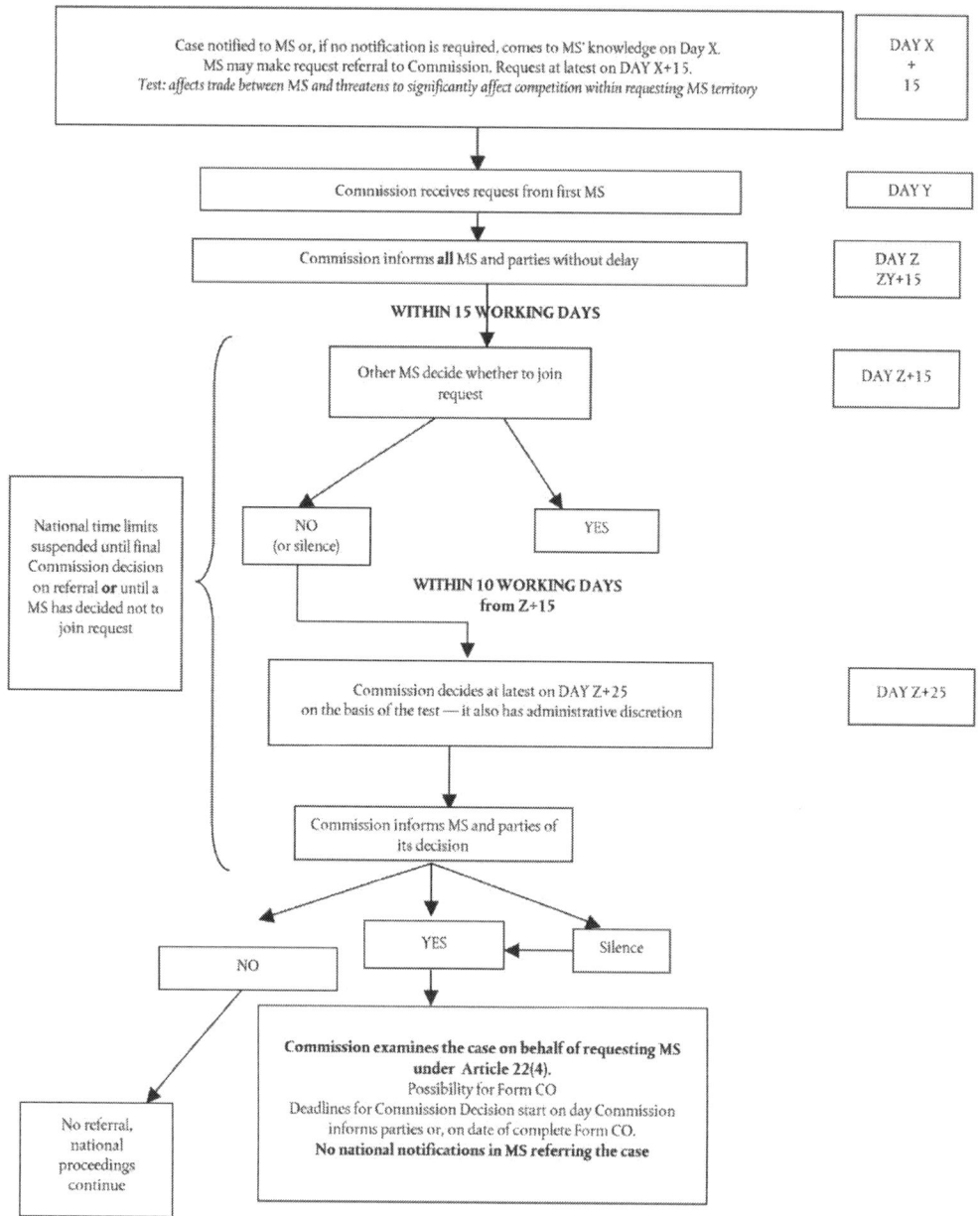

Commission Notice on a simplified procedure for treatment of certain concentrations under Council Regulation (EC) N° 139/2004

(OJ C 56, 5 March 2005, p. 32)

I. INTRODUCTION

1. This Notice sets out a simplified procedure under which the Commission intends to treat certain concentrations pursuant to Council Regulation (EC) N° 139/2004 of 20 January 2004, on the control of concentrations between undertakings (the EC Merger Regulation) (1) on the basis that they do not raise competition concerns.

(1) O.J. L 24, 29.1.2004, p. 1.

This Notice replaces the Notice on a simplified procedure for treatment of certain concentrations under Council Regulation (EEC) N° 4064/89 (2). The Commission's experience gained in applying Council Regulation (EEC) N° 4064/89 of 21 December 1989 on the control of concentrations between undertakings (3) has shown that certain categories of notified concentrations are normally cleared without having raised any substantive doubts, provided that there were no special circumstances.

(2) O.J. C 217, 29.7.2000, p. 32.

(3) O.J. L 395, 30.12.1989, p. 1; corrected version O.J. L 257, 21.9.1990, p. 13.

2. The purpose of this Notice is to set out the conditions under which the Commission usually adopts a short-form decision declaring a concentration compatible with the common market pursuant to the simplified procedure and to provide guidance in respect of the procedure itself.

When all necessary conditions set forth at point 5 of this Notice are met and provided there are no special circumstances, the Commission adopts a short-form clearance decision within 25 working days from the date of notification, pursuant to Article 6(1)*(b)* of the EC Merger Regulation (4).

(4) The notification requirements are set out in Annexes I and II to Commission Regulation (EC) N° 802/2004 implementing Council Regulation (EC) N° 139/2004 on the control of concentrations between undertakings.

3. However, if the safeguards or exclusions set forth at points 6 to 11 of this Notice are applicable, the Commission may launch an investigation and/or adopt a full decision under the EC Merger Regulation.

4. By following the procedure outlined in the following sections, the Commission aims to make Community merger control more focused and effective.

II. CATEGORIES OF CONCENTRATIONS SUITABLE FOR TREATMENT UNDER THE SIMPLIFIED PROCEDURE

Eligible concentrations

5. The Commission will apply the simplified procedure to the following categories of concentrations:

(a) two or more undertakings acquire joint control of a joint venture, provided that the joint venture has no, or negligible, actual or foreseen activities within the territory of the European Economic Area (EEA). Such cases occur where:

(i) the turnover (5) of the joint venture and/or the turnover of the contributed activities (6) is less than EUR 100 million in the EEA territory; and

(ii) the total value of assets (7) transferred to the joint venture is less than EUR 100 million in the EEA territory (8);

(b) two or more undertakings merge, or one or more undertakings acquire sole or joint control of another undertaking, provided that none of the parties to the concentration are engaged in business activities in the same product and geographical market, or in a product market which is upstream or downstream of a product market in which any other party to the concentration is engaged (9);

(c) two or more undertakings merge, or one or more undertakings acquire sole or joint control of another undertaking and:

(i) two or more of the parties to the concentration are engaged in business activities in the same product and geographical market (horizontal relationships) provided that their combined market share is less than 15%; or

(ii) one or more of the parties to the concentration are engaged in business activities in a product market which is upstream or downstream of a product market in which any other party to the concentration is engaged (vertical relationships) (10), provided that none of their individual or combined market shares is at either level 25% or more (11);

(d) a party is to acquire sole control of an undertaking over which it already has joint control.

(5) The turnover of the joint venture should be determined according to the most recent audited accounts of the parent companies, or the joint venture itself, depending upon the availability of separate accounts for the resources combined in the joint venture.

(6) The expression «and/or» refers to the variety of situations covered; for example:
– in the case of a joint acquisition of a target company, the turnover to be taken into account is the turnover of this target (the joint venture),
– in the case of the creation of a joint venture to which the parent companies contribute their activities, the turnover to be taken into account is that of the contributed activities,
– in the case of entry of a new controlling party into an existing joint venture, the turnover of the joint venture and the turnover of the activities contributed by the new parent company (if any) must be taken into account.

(7) The total value of assets of the joint venture should be determined according to the last prepared and approved balance sheet of each parent company. The term «assets» includes: (1) all tangible and intangible assets that will be transferred to the joint venture (examples of tangible assets include production plants, wholesale or retail outlets, and inventory of goods; examples of intangible assets include intellectual property, goodwill, etc.), and (2) any amount of credit or any obligations of the joint venture which any parent company of the joint venture has agreed to extend or guarantee.

(8) Where the assets transferred generate turnover, then neither the value of the assets nor that of the turnover may exceed EUR 100 million.

(9) See Commission Notice on the definition of relevant market for the purposes of Community competition law (O.J. C 372, 9.12.1997, p. 5).

(10) See footnote 6.

(11) This means that only concentrations, which do not lead to affected markets, as defined in Section 6 III of Form CO, fall into this category. The thresholds for horizontal and vertical relationships apply to market shares both at national and at EEA levels and to any plausible alternative product market definition that may have to be considered in a given case. It is important that the underlying market definitions set out in the notification are precise enough to justify the assessment that these thresholds are not met, and that all plausible alternative market definitions are mentioned (including geographic markets narrower than national).

Safeguards and exclusions

6. In assessing whether a concentration falls into one of the categories referred to in point 5, the Commission will ensure that all relevant circumstances are established with sufficient clarity. Given that market definitions are likely to be a key element in this assessment, the parties should provide information on all plausible alternative market definitions during the pre-notification phase (see point 15). Notifying parties are responsible for describing all alternative relevant product and geographic markets on which the notified concentration could have an impact and for providing data and information relating to the definition of such markets (12). The Commission retains the discretion to take the ultimate decision on market definition, basing its decision on an analysis of the facts of the case. Where it is difficult to define the relevant markets or to determine the parties' market shares, the Commission will not apply the simplified procedure. In addition, to the extent that concentrations involve novel legal issues of a general interest, the Commission would normally abstain from adopting short-form decisions, and would normally revert to a normal first phase merger procedure.

(12) As with all other notifications, the Commission may revoke the short-form decision if it is based on incorrect information for which one of the undertakings concerned is responsible (Article 6(3)(a), of the EC Merger Regulation).

7. While it can normally be assumed that concentrations falling into the categories referred to in point 5 will not raise serious doubts as to their compatibility with the common market, there may nonetheless be certain situations, which exceptionally require a closer investigation and/or a full decision. In such cases, the Commission may revert to a normal first phase merger procedure.

8. The following are indicative examples of types of cases which may be excluded from the simplified procedure. Certain types of concentrations may increase the parties' market power, for instance by combining technological, financial or other resources, even if the parties to the concentration do not operate in the same market. Concentrations where at least two parties to the concentration are present in closely related neighbouring markets (13) may also be unsuitable for the simplified procedure, in particular, where one or more of the parties to the concentration holds individually a market share of 25% or more in any product market in which there is no horizontal or vertical relationship between the parties but which is a neighbouring market to a market where another party is active. In other cases, it may not be possible to determine the parties' precise market shares. This is often the case when the parties operate in new or little developed markets. Concentrations in markets with high entry barriers, with a high degree of concentration (14) or other known competition problems may also be unsuitable.

(13) Product markets are closely related neighbouring markets when the products are complementary to each other or when they belong to a range of products that is generally purchased by the same set of customers for the same end use.

(14) See Guidelines on the assessment of horizontal mergers under the Council Regulation on the control of concentrations between undertakings O.J. C 31, 5.2.2004, p. 5, points 14-21.

9. The Commission's experience to date has shown that a change from joint to sole control may exceptionally require closer investigation and/or a full decision. A particular competition concern could arise in circumstances where the former joint venture is integrated into the group or network of its remaining single controlling shareholder, whereby the disciplining constraints exercised by the potentially diverging incentives of the different controlling shareholders are removed and its strategic market position could be strengthened. For example, in a scenario in which undertaking A and undertaking B jointly control a joint venture C, a concentration pursuant to which A acquires sole control of C may give rise to competition concerns in circumstances in which C is a direct competitor of A and where C and A will hold a substantial combined market position and where this removes a degree of independence previously held by C (15). In cases where such scenarios require a closer analysis, the Commission may revert to a normal first phase merger procedure (16).

(15) Case N° IV/M.1328 KLM/Martinair, XXIXth Report on Competition Policy 1999 – SEC(2000) 720 final, points 165-166.

(16) Case N° COMP/M.2908 Deutsche Post/DHL (II), Decision of 18.9.2002.

10. The Commission may also revert to a normal first phase merger procedure where neither the Commission nor the competent authorities of Member States have reviewed the prior acquisition of joint control of the joint venture in question.

11. Furthermore, the Commission may revert to a normal first phase merger procedure where an issue of coordination as referred to in Article 2(4) of the EC Merger Regulation arises.

12. If a Member State expresses substantiated concerns about the notified concentration within 15 working days of receipt of the copy of the notification, or if a third party expresses substantiated concerns within the time-limit laid down for such comments, the Commission will adopt a full decision. The time-limits set out in Article 10(1) of the EC Merger Regulation apply.

Referral requests

13. The simplified procedure will not be applied if a Member State requests the referral of a notified concentration pursuant to Article 9 of the EC Merger Regulation or if the Commission accepts a request from one or more Member States for referral of a notified concentration pursuant to Article 22 of the EC Merger Regulation.

Pre-notification referrals at the request of the notifying parties

14. Subject to the safeguards and exclusions set out in this Notice, the Commission may apply the simplified procedure to concentrations where:

(i) following a reasoned submission pursuant to Article 4(4) of the EC Merger Regulation, the Commission decides not to refer the case to a Member State; or

(ii) following a reasoned submission pursuant to Article 4(5) of the EC Merger Regulation the case is referred to the Commission.

III. PROCEDURAL PROVISIONS

Pre-notification contacts

15. The Commission has found pre-notification contacts between notifying parties and the Commission beneficial even in seemingly unproblematic cases (17). The Commission's experience of the simplified procedure has shown that candidate cases for the simplified procedure may raise complex issues for instance, of market definition (see point 6) which should preferably be resolved prior to notification. Such contacts allow the Commission and the notifying parties to determine the precise amount of information to be provided in a notification. Pre-notification contacts should be initiated at least two weeks prior to the expected date of notification. Notifying parties are therefore advised to engage in pre-notification contacts, particularly where they request the Commission to waive full-form notification in accordance with Article 3(1) of Commission Regulation (EC) N° 802/2004 of 7 April 2004 implementing Council Regulation (EC) N° 139/ 2004 on the control of concentrations between undertakings (18) on the grounds that the operation to be notified will not raise competition concerns.

(17) See DG Competition Best Practices on the conduct of EC merger control proceedings available at: http://europa.eu.int/comm/competition/mergers/legislation/regulation/ best_practices.pdf.

(18) O.J. L 133, 30.4.2004, p. 1.

Publication of the fact of notification

16. The information to be published in the *Official Journal of the European Union* upon receipt of a notification (19) will include the names of the parties to the concentration, their country of origin, the nature of the concentration and the economic sectors involved, as well as an indication that, on the basis of the information provided by the notifying party, the concentration may qualify for a simplified procedure. Interested parties will then have the opportunity to submit observations, in particular on circumstances which might require an investigation.

(19) Article 4(3) of the EC Merger Regulation.

Short-form decision

17. If the Commission is satisfied that the concentration fulfils the criteria for the simplified procedure (see point 5), it will normally issue a short-form decision. This includes appropriate cases not giving rise to any competition concerns where it receives a full form notification. The concentration will thus be declared compatible with the common market, within 25 working days from the date of notification, pursuant to Article 10(1) and (6) of the EC Merger Regulation. The Commission will endeavour to issue a short-form decision as soon as practicable following expiry of the 15 working day period during which Member States may request referral of a notified concentration pursuant to Article 9 of the EC Merger Regulation. However, in the period leading up to the 25 working day deadline, the option of reverting to a normal first phase merger procedure and thus launching investigations and/or adopting a full decision remains open to the Commission, should it judge such action appropriate in the case in question.

Publication of the short-form decision

18. The Commission will publish a notice of the fact of the decision in the *Official Journal of the European Union* as it does for full clearance decisions. The public version of the decision will be made available on DG Competition's Internet website for a limited period. The short-form decision will contain the information about the notified concentration published in the *Official Journal* at the time of notification (names of the parties, their country of origin, nature of the concentration and economic sectors concerned) and a statement that the concentration is declared compatible with the common market because it falls within one or more of the categories described in this Notice, with the applicable category(ies) being explicitly identified.

IV. ANCILLARY RESTRICTIONS

19. The simplified procedure is not suited to cases in which the undertakings concerned request an express assessment of restrictions which are directly related to, and necessary for, the implementation of the concentration.

Communication pursuant to Article 3(2) of Commission Regulation (EC) N° 802/2004 implementing Council Regulation (EC) N° 139/2004 on the control of concentrations between undertakings

(OJ C 251, 17 October 2006, p. 2)

INTRODUCTION

The Commission hereby lays down, pursuant to Article 3(2) of Commission Regulation (EC) N° 802/2004 (1), the format in which notifications and reasoned submissions should be delivered. Article 3(2) of Regulation 802/2004 requires notifications and reasoned submissions to be delivered in one original and 35 copies.

NOTIFICATIONS: FORM CO AND SHORT FORM CO (ANNEXES I AND II TO COMMISSION REGULATION (EC) N° 802/2004)

1) One signed original on paper.

2) Five paper copies of the entire Form CO or Short Form CO and its annexes («notification»).

3) Thirty copies of the notification in CD- or DVD-ROM format (the «medium»). The following specifications shall be adhered to:

a) The files comprising the notification in this medium shall be in Portable Document Format (*.pdf) and should preferably not exceed 5 MB (mega-bytes) each in size. The copy of the notification may be contained on several CD- or DVD-ROMs. Documents which were originally produced in *.doc, *.xls and *.ppt format shall also be saved in this format in the same medium.

b) Files should be named in a way which allows easy identification of the section in the Form CO or Short Form CO they refer to.

c) A list of all files in the medium shall be delivered as a separate file in the medium.

d) Each file shall bear the number and name of the proceeding for which the notification is submitted.

REASONED SUBMISSIONS (2): – FORM RS (ANNEX III TO COMMISSION REGULATION (EC) N° 802/2004)

1) One signed original on paper.

2) Five paper copies of the entire Form RS and its annexes («Reasoned submission»)

3) One CD- or DVD-ROM (the «medium») which contains the complete reasoned submission. The following specifications shall be adhered to:

a) The files comprising the reasoned submission in this medium shall be in Portable Document Format (*.pdf) and may not exceed 1 MB (mega-byte) each in size. Documents which were originally produced in *.doc, *.xls and *.ppt format shall also be saved in this format in the same medium.

b) Files should be named in a way which allows easy identification of the section in the Form RS they refer to.

c) A list of files in the medium shall be delivered as a separate file in the medium itself.

d) Each file shall bear the number and name of the proceeding for which the Reasoned submission is made.

4) If the files on the CD- or DVD-ROM cannot be kept under 1MB (mega-byte) each in size and/or if the total size of the files on the CD- or DVD-ROM exceeds 5MB, the instructions for submitting Form CO should be followed instead, i.e. 30 copies in CD- or DVD-ROM format should be submitted.

DATE OF APPLICABILITY OF THIS COMMUNICATION

The instructions contained in this communication shall be applicable 20 days following the date of publication of this communication in the *Official Journal of the European Union*.

(1) Article 3(2) should be read together with Article 6(2) of Commission Regulation (EC) N° 802/2004.

(2) Reasoned submissions within the meaning of Article 4(4) and 4(5) of Council Regulation (EC) N° 139/2004.

Commission Notice on the rules for access to the Commission file in cases pursuant to Articles 81 and 82 of the EC Treaty, Articles 53, 54 and 57 of the EEA Agreement and Council Regulation (EC) N° 139/2004

(OJ C 325, 22 December 2005, p. 7)

1. Article 81 EC is now Article 101 TFEU and Article 82 EC is now Article 102 TFEU.
2. See above, section 2.1.3. Procedural rules

Merger notification and procedures template, March 2008, not published in the Official Journal

1. See the site: http://ec.europa.eu/competition/contacts/2008_03_template.pdf

IMPORTANT NOTE:
This template is intended to provide introductory material. Reading the template is not a substitute for consulting the referenced statutes and regulations. If you are analyzing a particular transaction, this template should be a starting point only.

The following explanations are made available for information purposes only and do not constitute an official publication of the European Commission with legally binding effects. The official versions of the applicable texts are published in the Official Journal of the European Communities.

1. Merger notification and review materials (please provide title(s), popular name(s) and citation(s))	
A. Notification provisions	Article 4 of the Merger Regulation; Articles 1-5 of the Implementing Regulation
	Please note that the materials referred to here and below, as well as non-confidential versions of the Commission's decisions in merger cases and other kinds of merger-related information are available at:
	http://europa.eu.int/comm/competition/index_en.html
B. Notification forms or information requirements	Form CO relating to the notification of a concentration pursuant to Regulation (EC) N° 139/2004 (Annex of the Implementing Regulation (EC) 802/2004)
C. Substantive merger control provisions	Council Regulation (EC) N° 139/2004 of 20 January 2004 on the control of concentrations between undertakings, «the Merger Regulation», (OJ L 24/1, 29.1.2004)
D. Implementing regulations	Commission Regulation (EC) N° 802/04 of of 7 April 2004 implementing Council Regulation (EC) N° 139/04 on the control of concentrations between undertakings (OJ L 133/1, 30.4.2004) (hereinafter referred to as «the Implementing Regulation»)
E. Interpretive guidelines and notices	Commission Notices:
	– Commission Consolidated Jurisdictional Notice under Council Regulation (EC) N° 139/2004

	– Commission Notice on the definition of the relevant market for the purposes of Community competition law (*OJ* C 372, 9.12.1997, p. 5)
	– Commission Notice on a simplified procedure for treatment of certain concentrations under Council Regulation (EC) N° 139/2004 (*OJ* C 56, 05.03.2005, p. 32).
	– Commission Notice on Case Referral in respect of concentrations *Official Journal* C 56, 05.03.2005, p. 2-23
	– Commission Notice on remedies acceptable under Council Regulation (EEC) N° 4064/89 and under Commission Regulation (EC) N° 447/98 (*OJ* C 68, 02.03.2001, p. 3)
	– Commission Notice on restrictions directly related and necessary to concentrations (*OJ* C 56, 05.03.2005, p. 24)
	– Commission Guidelines on the assessment of horizontal mergers under the Council Regulation on the control of concentrations between undertakings (*OJ* C 31/5, 5.2.2004)
	– Commision Notice on the assessment of non-horizontal mergers under the council regulation on the control of concentrations between undertakings http://ec.europa.eu/comm/competition/mergers/legislation/nonhorizontalguidelines.pdf
	– DG Competition Best Practices on the conduct of EC merger control proceedings
	At any given time the relevant materials are available at: http://ec.europa.eu/comm/competition/mergers/legislation/legislation.html
F. Annual report	Annual Report on Competition Policy – available on the internet : http://europa.eu.int/comm/competition/annual_reports/
2. Authority or authorities responsible for merger enforcement.	
A. Name of authority. If there is more than one authority, please describe allocation of responsibilities.	European Commission, Directorate General for Competition
	The European Commission has exclusive merger control jurisdiction for concentrations with a Community dimension as defined in Article 1 of the Merger Regulation (see Article 21 of the Merger Regulation). In addition, cases may be referred to the Commission by one or several Member States pursuant to Article 22(3) of the Merger Regulation. In turn, the Commission can refer or partially refer cases to the competent authorities of Member States upon their request (see Article 9 of the Merger Regulation).
	In addition pursuant to Art. 4(4) and 4(5) of the Merger Regulation notifying parties may request a transfer of jurisdiction either from or to the Commission prior to notification. In the case of requests for referral from the Commission to a particular Member State, Article 4(4) provides that where the concentration may significantly affect competition in a market within a Member State which presents all the characteristics of a distinct market the notifying parties may make a reasoned submission requesting that the transaction should therefore be examined, in whole or in part, by that Member State. Requests should be made on the basis of a reasoned submission from the parties using the Form RS which is an annex to the Implementing Regulation. Article 4 (5) provides that where a concentration does not have a Community dimension within the meaning of Art. 1 and where it is capable of being reviewed under the national competition laws of at least three Member States the notifying parties may, prior to notification to the competent authorities, request that the concentration is examined by the Commission, using the above mentioned Form.
	The Commission is preparing a guidance Notice on the functioning of the referral provisions, a draft of which is
	Commission Notice on Case Referral in respect of concentrations*Official Journal* C 56, 05.03.2005, p. 2-23
B. Address, telephone and fax (including country code), e-mail, website address and languages available.	European Commission
	DG COMP
	postal address: B-1049 Brussels
	Belgium
	office address: 70, Rue Joseph II,
	B-1000 Brussels,
	Belgium
	Tel: +32.2.299.11.11 / Fax: +32.2.296.43.01)
	E-Mail: comp-mergers@ec.europa.eu (caution: this e-mail address is a contact point for external queries only; it may not be used for any specific messages relating to individual merger cases, in particular not for merger notifications)
	Website: http://ec.europa.eu/comm/competition/index_en.html

C. Is agency staff available for prenotification consultation? If yes, please provide contact points for questions on merger filing requirements and/or consultations.	Yes. The European Commission even encourages notifying parties to enter into pre-notification contacts with the relevant service. See our best practice guidelines: http://ec.europa.eu/comm/competition/mergers/legislation/proceedings.pdf
	Please send a fax with your query to the European Commission, addressed to the deputy Director General formergers (Fax N° +32.2.296.43.01). You may also send an e-mail to the following address: compmergers@ ec.europa.eu
3. Notification requirements	
A. Is notification mandatory pre-merger?	Notification is mandatory pre-merger.
B. Is notification mandatory post-merger?	Please see section 3.A: Notification is mandatory pre-merger. This obligation to notify remains unchanged should the parties illegally implement the merger without prior notification to the Commission.
C. Can parties make a voluntary pre- or postmerger filing even if filing is not mandatory?	Not applicable. The Merger Regulation provides for a system of mandatory *ex-ante* merger control. Concentrations which fall within the scope of the Merger Regulation must be notified to the Commission. Concentrations which do not fall within the scope of the Merger Regulation cannot be notified to the Commission; they may, however, be notifiable in one or several EU Member States pursuant to their respective national competition laws.
4. Covered transactions	
A. Definitions of potentially covered transactions	Pursuant to Article 3(1) and 3(4) of the Merger Regulation:
	(1) A concentration shall be deemed to arise where:
	(a) two ore more previously independent undertakings merge; or
	(b) one ore more persons already controlling at least one undertaking, or – one or more undertakings acquire, whether by purchase of securities or assets, by contract or by any other means, direct or indirect control of the whole or parts of one or more other undertakings.
	(4) The creation of a joint venture performing on a lasting basis all the functions of an autonomous economic entity, shall constitute a concentration within the meaning of paragraph 1*(b)*.
	Article 3 of the Merger Regulation contains provisions concerning control and the acquisition of control.
	See also the Commission Consolidated Jurisdictional Notice under Council Regulation (EC) N° 139/2004 http://ec.europa.eu/comm/competition/mergers/legislation/jn_en.pdf
B. If change of control is a determining factor, how is control defined?	Pursuant to Article 3(3) of the Merger Regulation:
	For the purpose of the Merger Regulation, control shall be constituted by rights, contracts or any other means which, either separately or in combination and having regard to the considerations of fact or law involved, confer the possibility of exercising decisive influence on an undertaking, in particular by: *(a)* ownership or the right to use all or part of the assets of an undertaking;*(b)* rights or contracts which confer decisive influence on the composition, voting or decisions of the organs of an undertaking.
	Article 3(5) of the Merger Regulation contains specific provisions concerning the circumstances under which a concentration shall not be deemed to arise.
	See also the Commission Consolidated Jurisdictional Notice under Council Regulation (EC) N° 139/2004 http://ec.europa.eu/comm/competition/mergers/legislation/jn_en.pdf
C. Are partial (less than 100 %) stock acquisitions/minority shareholdings covered? At what levels?	Yes, as long as the transaction is a concentration and has a Community dimension within the meaning of Articles 1 and 3 of the Merger Regulation.
D. Do the notification requirements cover production joint ventures or any other type of joint venture?	Yes. Article 3(4) of the Merger Regulation provides that the creation of a joint venture performing on a lasting basis all the functions of an autonomous economic entity shall constitute a concentration within the meaning of the Merger Regulation.
	See also the Commission Consolidated Jurisdictional Notice under Council Regulation (EC) N° 139/2004 http://ec.europa.eu/comm/competition/mergers/legislation/jn_en.pdf
E. Are any sectors excluded from notification requirements? If so, which sectors?	No.

F. Are transactions that do not meet merger notification thresholds subject to substantive merger control?	The Merger Regulation only applies to concentrations with a Community dimension as defined in Articles 1 and 3 thereof. The European Commission has exclusive merger control jurisdiction for concentrations with a Community dimension (see Article 21 of the Merger Regulation).
	Note that concentrations that do not fall within the Merger Regulation's scope may be notifiable in individual member states.
	In addition, Article 22(3) of the Merger Regulation provides that the Commission may, at the request of a Member State or at the joint request of two or more Member States, investigate a concentration as defined in Article 3 of the Merger Regulation that has no Community dimension within the meaning of Article 1 of the Merger Regulation, insofar as that concentration affects trade between Member States.
5. Thresholds for notification	
A. What are the general thresholds? Are the thresholds subject to adjustment: (e.g. annually for inflation)? If adjusted, state on what basis and how frequently.	(1) Pursuant to Article 1 of the Merger Regulation, the Merger Regulation shall apply to all concentrations with a Community dimension defined as follows:
	(a) the combined aggregate worldwide turnover of all the undertakings concerned is more than EUR 5 billion; and
	(b) the aggregate Community-wide turnover of each of at least two of the undertakings concerned is more than EUR 250 million, unless each of the undertakings concerned achieves more than two-thirds of its aggregate Community-wide turnover within one and the same Member State.
	(2) A concentration that does not meet these thresholds has a Community dimension where:
	(a) the combined aggregate worldwide turnover of all the undertakings concerned is more than EUR 2.5 billion;
	(b) in each of at least three Member States, the combined aggregate turnover of all the undertakings concerned is more than EUR 100 million;
	(c) in each of at least three Member States included for the purpose of point (b), the aggregate turnover of each of at least two of the undertakings concerned is more than EUR 25 million; and
	(d) the aggregate Community-wide turnover of each of at least two of the undertakings concerned is more than EUR 100 million;
	unless each of the undertakings concerned achieves more than two-thirds of its aggregate Community-wide turnover within one and the same Member State.
B. To what period(s) of time do the thresholds relate (e.g., most recent calendar year, fiscal year; for assets-based tests, calendar year-end, fiscal year-end, other)?	Pursuant to Article 5(1), first subparagraph, of the Merger Regulation, aggregate turnover within the meaning of the Merger Regulation shall comprise the amounts derived by the undertakings concerned in the preceding financial year from the sale of products and the provision of services falling within the undertakings' ordinary activities after deduction of sales rebates and of value added tax and other taxes directly related to turnover.
C. Describe methodology for identifying and calculating any values necessary to determine if notification is required, including:	
i. The methodology for identifying and calculating the value of the transaction, if applicable.	According to point 3.2 of the Form CO, the notifying parties must state the value of the transaction (the purchase price or the value of all the assets involved, as the case may be.
ii. The methodology for identifying and calculating relevant sales or turnover, if applicable.	Pursuant to Article 5(1), second subparagraph, of the Merger Regulation, turnover, in the Community or in a Member State, shall comprise products sold and services provided to undertakings or consumers, in the Community or in that Member State as the case may be.
	See also the Commission Consolidated Jurisdictional Notice under Council Regulation (EC) N° 139/2004 http://ec.europa.eu/comm/competition/mergers/legislation/jn_en.pdf
iii. The methodology for identifying and calculating the value of relevant assets, if applicable.	Pursuant to Article 5(2) of the Merger Regulation, where the concentration consists of the acquisition of parts, whether or not constituted as legal entities, of one or more undertakings, only the turnover relating to the parts which are the subject of the transaction shall be taken into account with regard to the seller or sellers.
	However, two or more such transactions which take place within a two-year period between the same persons or undertakings shall be treated as one and the same concentration arising on the date of the last transaction.
	See also the Commission Consolidated Jurisdictional Notice under Council Regulation (EC) N° 139/2004 http://ec.europa.eu/comm/competition/mergers/legislation/jn_en.pdf

iv. Methodology for calculating exchange rates.	The European Commission suggests relying on the exchange rates published by the European Central bank, to the extent applicable.
D. Do thresholds apply to worldwide sales/assets, to sales/assets within the jurisdiction, or both?	The stated tests apply to worldwide figures, Community-wide figures and figures relating to Member States.
E. How is the nexus to the jurisdiction determined? If based on an «effects doctrine», please describe how this is applied.	The thresholds laid down in Article 1 of the Merger Regulation determine jurisdictional nexus as far as the obligation to notify is concerned (for details regarding these thresholds, please refer to section 5.A). See also Judgment of the Court of First Instance of the European Communities of 25 March 1999 in case T-102/96 – Gencor Ltd. / Commission, (1999) ECR II-879, at paragraphs 76-111. The judgment can be found at the following webpage: http://curia.eu.int/en/jurisp/index.htm
F. If national sales are relevant, how are they allocated geographically (e.g., location of customer, location of seller)?	Pursuant to Article 5(1), second subparagraph, of the Merger Regulation, turnover, in the Community or in a Member State, shall comprise products sold and services provided to undertakings or consumers, in the Community or in that Member State as the case may be. The Commission Notice on calculation of turnover under Council Regulation (EEC) N° 4064/89 on the control of concentrations between undertakings (*OJ* C 66, 2.3.1998, p. 25) clarifies «that the location of the turnover is determined by the location of the customer at the time of the transaction.».
G. If there are market share tests, are there guidelines for calculating market shares?	The jurisdiction of the European Commission does not depend on a market share test.
H. If there are market share tests, do they apply even if there is no horizontal overlap in the parties' activities, either in the jurisdiction or worldwide?	The jurisdiction of the European Commission does not depend on a market share test.
I. Describe the methodology for determining relevant undertakings/firms for threshold purposes (e.g., group-wide? only the acquired entity? If based on control, how is control determined?).	Pursuant to Article 5(4) of the Merger Regulation, and without prejudice to Article 5(2), the aggregate turnover of an undertaking concerned within the meaning of Article 1 (2) and 3 shall be calculated by adding together the respective turnovers of the following:
	(a) the undertaking concerned;
	(b) those undertakings in which the undertaking concerned, directly or indirectly;
	– owns more than half the capital or business assets; or
	– has the power to exercise more than half the voting rights; or
	– has the power to appoint more than half the members of the supervisory board, the administrative board or bodies legally representing the undertakings; or
	– has the right to manage the undertakings' affairs;
	(c) those undertakings which have in an undertaking concerned the rights or powers listed in *(b)*;
	(d) those undertakings in which an undertaking as referred to in *(c)* has the rights or powers listed in *(b)*;
	(e) those undertakings in which two or more undertakings as referred to in *(a)* to *(d)* jointly have the rights or powers listed in *(b)*.
	Pursuant to Article 5(1), first subparagraph, second sentence, of the Merger Regulation, the aggregate turnover of an undertaking concerned shall not include the sale of products or the provision of services between any of the undertakings referred to in Article 5(4).
	See also the Commission Consolidated Jurisdictional Notice under Council Regulation (EC) N° 139/2004 http://ec.europa.eu/comm/competition/mergers/legislation/jn_en.pdf
J. Are there special threshold calculations for joint ventures?	Pursuant to Article 5(5) of the Merger Regulation, where undertakings concerned by the concentration jointly have the rights or powers listed in Article 5(4)*(b)*, in calculating the aggregate turnover of the undertakings concerned for the purposes of Article 1 (2) and (3):
	(a) no account shall be taken of the turnover resulting from the sale of products or the provision of services between the joint undertaking and each of the undertakings concerned or any other undertaking connected with any one of them, as set out in Article 5(4)*(b)* to *(e)*;
	(b) account shall be taken of the turnover resulting from the sale of products and the provision of services between the joint undertaking and any third undertakings. This turnover shall be apportioned equally amongst the undertakings concerned.
	See also the Commission Consolidated Jurisdictional Notice under Council Regulation (EC) N° 139/2004 http://ec.europa.eu/comm/competition/mergers/legislation/jn_en.pdf

K. Are there special threshold calculations for particular sectors (e.g., banking, airlines) or particular types of transactions (e.g. partnerships, financial investments)?	Pursuant to Article 5(3) of the Merger Regulation, in place of turnover the following shall be used:
	(*a*) for credit institutions and other financial institutions, as regards Article 1 (2) and (3) of the Merger Regulation, the sum of the following income items as defined in Council Directive 86/635/EEC of 8 December 1986 on the annual accounts and consolidated accounts of banks and other financial institutions, after deduction of value added tax and other taxes directly related to those items, where appropriate:
	(i) interest income and similar income;
	(ii) income from securities:
	– income from shares and other variable yield securities;
	– income from participating interests;
	– income from shares in affiliated undertakings;
	(iii) commissions receivable;
	(iv) net profit on financial operations;
	(v) other operating income.
	The turnover of a credit or financial institution in the Community or in a Member State shall comprise the income items, as defined above, which are received by the branch or division of that institution established in the Community or in the Member State in question, as the case may be;
	(*b*) for insurance undertakings, the value of gross premiums written which shall comprise all amounts received and receivable in respect of insurance contracts issued by or on behalf of the insurance undertakings, including also outgoing reinsurance premiums, and after deduction of taxes and parafiscal contributions or levies charged by reference to the amounts of individual premiums or the total volume of premiums; as regards Version 2 – March, 2008 Page 10 of 3 Article 1(2)(*b*) and (3)(*b*), (*c*) and (*d*) and the final part of Article 1(2) and (3) of the Merger Regulation, gross premiums received from Community residents and from residents of one Member State respectively shall be taken into account.
	See also the Commission Consolidated Jurisdictional Notice under Council Regulation (EC) N° 139/2004 http://ec.europa.eu/comm/competition/mergers/legislation/jn_en.pdf
6. Transactions in which the acquiring and acquired parties are foreign Are there special rules or exemptions	
A. With respect to application of jurisdictional thresholds?	No
B. With respect to information required (e.g. information submitted or document legalization)?	No
C. With respect to waiting periods?	No
7. Simplified procedures	

Describe any special procedures for notifying transactions that do not raise competition concerns (e.g., short form, simplified procedures, advanced ruling certificates, waivers, etc.).	Pursuant to the Form CO and the Commission Notice on a simplified procedure for treatment of certain concentrations, the Commission may allow a short form notification and dispense with a full-form notification on the grounds that the operation to be notified will not raise competition concerns.
	If the Commission is satisfied that the concentration qualifies for the simplified procedure, it will normally issue a short form clearance decision within one month from the date of notification, pursuant to Article 10(1) and 6(1)(b) of the Merger Regulation.
	The categories of concentrations eligible for simplified procedure treatment, which are laid down in Form CO and the aforementioned Commission Notice, are the following:
	(a) in the case of a joint venture, the joint venture has no, or negligible, actual or foreseen activities within the territory of the Version 2 – March, 2008 Page 11 of 3 European Economic Area (EEA). Such cases occur where:
	the turnover of the joint venture and/or the turnover of the contributed activities is less than EUR 100 million in the EEA territory; and
	the total value of the assets transferred to the joint venture is less than EUR 100 million in the EEA territory;
	(b) none of the parties to the concentration are engaged in business activities in the same relevant product and geographic market (no horizontal overlap), or in a market which is upstream or downstream of a market in which another party to the concentration is engaged (no vertical relationship);
	(c) two or more of the parties to the concentration are engaged in business activities in the same relevant product and geographic market (horizontal relationships), provided that their combined market share is less than 15 %; and/or one or more of the parties to the concentration are engaged in business activities in a market which is upstream or downstream of a market in which any other party to the concentration is engaged (vertical relationships), and provided that none of their individual or combined market shares at either level is 25 % or more; or
	(d) a party is to acquire sole control of an undertaking over which it has joint control.
	In order to assess in detail the applicability of the simplified procedure and of the short form notification, the Commission is available for pre-notification contacts (for details, please refer to section 2.F). It is also advisable to refer to the Commission Notice on a simplified procedure for treatment of certain concentrations.
8. Timing of notification	
A. What is the earliest that a transaction can be notified (e.g., is a definitive agreement required; if so, when is an agreement considered definitive?)?	Pursuant to Article 4(1) of the Merger Regulation, concentrations with a Community dimension defined in the Merger Regulation shall be notified to the Commission prior to implementation and following the conclusion of the agreement, or the announcement of the public bid, or the acquisition of a controlling interest.
	Notification is also possible where the undertakings concerned satisfy the Commission of their intention to enter into an agreement for a proposed concentration and demonstrate to the Commission that their plan for that proposed concentration is sufficiently concrete, for example on the basis of an agreement in principle, a memorandum of understanding, or a letter of intent Version 2 – March, 2008 Page 12 of 3 signed by all undertakings concerned, or, in the case of a public bid, where they have publicly announced an intention to make such a bid, provided that the intended agreement or bid would result in a concentration with a Community dimension.
B. Must notification be made within a specified period following a triggering event? If so, describe the triggering event (e.g., definitive agreement) and the deadline following the event.	No
9. Documents to be submitted	
A. Describe the types of documents that parties must submit with the notification (e.g., agreement, annual reports, market studies, transaction documents).	Section 5 of the notification Forms (Annexes I and II to the Implementing Regulation) specify the information and the documents that must be provided by an undertaking or undertakings when notifying a proposed concentration to the Commission.
	At a pre-notification stage, the parties can approach the Commission in order to discuss the exact type of information and documentation which should be provided in a given case.
B. Are there any document legalization requirements (e.g., notarization or apostille)?	Pursuant to Article 2(3) of the Implementing Regulation, the supporting documents shall be either originals or copies of the originals; in the latter case, the notifying parties shall confirm that they are true and complete.

Describe any requirements to submit translations of documents with the initial notification, or later in response to requests for information, including the categories or types of documents for which translation is required, requirements for certification, language(s) accepted, and whether selected excerpts are accepted in lieu of complete documents.	Article 21(3) of the Treaty establishing the European Community (the EC Treaty) provides that every citizen of the Union may write to any of the institutions or bodies, referred to in this Article or in Article 7 (the European Parliament, the Council, the Commission, the Court of Justice, and the Court of Auditors) in one of the languages mentioned in Article 314 of the EC Treaty and have an answer in the same language.
	Pursuant to Article 3(4) of the Implementing Regulation, notifications shall be in one of the official languages of the Community. This language, which notifying parties are free to choose when submitting their notification, shall also be the language of the proceeding for the notifying parties. Where the original language is not one of the official languages of the Community, a translation into the language of the proceeding shall be attached.
	Article 4(2) of the Implementing Regulation provides that the Commission may dispense with the obligation to provide any particular information, including documents, requested by Form CO where the Commission considers that such information is not necessary for the examination of the case.
11. Review and waiting periods / Suspensive effects	
A. Describe any applicable review and/or waiting periods following notification, including whether closing is suspended during any initial review or waiting period and/or further review periods (i.e., second-phase proceedings).	Initial waiting period during the preliminary investigation («Phase I»):
	Pursuant to Article 10(1) of the Merger Regulation, the decision referred to in Article 6(1) (the «Phase I decision») must be taken within 25 working days at most. That period shall begin on the working day following that of the receipt of a notification or, if the information to be supplied with the notification is incomplete, on the working day following that of the receipt of the complete information.
	That period shall be increased to 35 days if the Commission receives a request from a Member State in accordance with Article 9(2) of the Merger Regulation (request for referral of the case to that Member State), or where, after notification of a concentration, the undertakings concerned submit commitments pursuant to Article 6(2) of the Merger Regulation, which are intended by the parties to form the basis for a decision pursuant to Article 6(1)(b) («Phase I» clearance decision).
	Extended waiting period after the initiation of proceedings («Phase II»):
	Article 10(2) of the Merger Regulation provides that decisions taken pursuant to Article 8 («Phase II» decisions) concerning notified concentrations must be taken as soon as it appears that the serious doubts referred to in Article 6(1)(c) have been removed, particularly as a result of modifications made by the undertakings concerned.
	Pursuant to Article 10(3) of the Merger Regulation, without prejudice to Article 8(7), decisions taken pursuant to Article 8(3) (prohibition decisions) concerning notified concentrations must be taken within not more than 90 working days of the date on which proceedings are initiated (date of the «Phase I» decision based on Article 6(1)(c) of the Merger Regulation).
	Pursuant to Article 10 (3) that period shall be increased to 105 working days where the undertakings concerned offer commitments pursuant to Article 8(2) second sub-paragraph, with a view to rendering the concentration compatible with the common market, unless these commitments have been offered Version 2 – March, 2008 Page 14 of 3 less than 55 working days after the initiation of proceedings. These periods may also be extended by up to 20 working days wat the notifying parties' request or with their agreement.
	Obligation to suspend closing:
	Article 7(1) of the Merger Regulation provides that a concentration as defined in Article 1 shall not be implemented either before its notification or until it has been declared compatible wirth the common market pursuant to a decision under Article 6(1)(b), 8(1) or 8(2) or on the basis of a presumption according to Article 10(6) of the Merger Regulation. As regards exceptions to this rule, please refer to sections 11.B, 11.C, and 11.F.
B. Are there different rules for public tenders (e.g. open market stock purchases or hostile bids)?	Pursuant to Article 7(2) of the Merger Regulation, the obligation to suspend the concentration laid down in Article 7(1) shall not prevent the implementation of a public bid or a series of transactions on the stock exchange, provided the concentration is notified without delay to the Commission in accordance with Article 4(1), and provided that the acquirer does not exercise the voting rights attached to the securities in question or does so only to maintain the full value of those investments and on the basis of a derogation granted by the Commission under paragraph 3.

C. Are the applicable waiting periods limited to aspects of the transaction that occur within the jurisdiction (e.g., acquisition or merger of local undertakings/business units)? If not, to what extent do they apply to the parties' ability to proceed with the transaction outside the jurisdiction? Describe any procedures available to permit consummation outside the jurisdiction prior to the expiration of the local waiting period and/or clearance. (e.g. request for a derogation from the bar on closing, commitment to hold separate the local business operations.)	Territorial scope of application of the waiting periods
	The applicable waiting periods are not limited to aspects of the transaction that occur within the Commission's jurisdiction. They apply to the proposed concentration as a whole.
	Derogations from the suspensive effect
	Pursuant to Article 7(3) of the Merger Regulation, the Commission may, on request, grant a derogation from the obligations (to suspend the concentration) imposed in paragraph 1 or 3. The request to grant a derogation must be reasoned. In deciding on the request, the Commission shall take into account inter alia the effects of the suspension on one or more undertakings concerned by a concentration or on a third party and the threat to competition posed by the concentration. That derogation may be made subject to conditions and obligations in order to ensure conditions of effective competition. A derogation may be applied for and granted at any time, even before notification or after the transaction.
D. Describe any provisions or procedures available to the enforcement authority, the parties and/or third parties to extend the waiting period. Is there a statutory maximum for extensions of the review period by the authority.	The «Phase-I» period of 25 working days shall be increased to 35 working days if the Commission receives a request for referral from a Member State pursuant to Article 9 of the Merger Regulation, or where, after notification of a concentration, the undertakings concerned submit commitments pursuant to Article 6(2) of the Merger Regulation, which are intended by the parties to form the basis for a «Phase I» clearance decision (Art. 10(1), second subparagraph, of the Merger Regulation)
	Pursuant to Article 10(4) of the Merger Regulation, the periods set by paragraphs 1 and 3 shall exceptionally be suspended where, owing to circumstances for which one of the undertakings involved in the concentration is responsible, the Commission has had to request information by decision pursuant to Article 11 or to order an investigation by decision pursuant to Article 13
E. Describe any procedures for obtaining early termination of the applicable waiting period, and the criteria and timetable for deciding whether to grant early termination.	Article 10(2) of the Merger Regulation provides that decisions taken pursuant to Article 8(2) («Phase II» clearance decisions) concerning notified concentrations must be taken as soon as it appears that the serious doubts referred to in Article 6(1)(c) have been removed, particularly as a result of modifications made by the undertakings concerned..
F. Describe any provisions or procedures allowing the parties to close at their own risk before waiting periods expire or clearance is granted (e.g., allowing the transaction to close if no «irreversible measures» are taken).	The possible means of derogation from the obligation to suspend implementation are described in section 11B and C above.
12. Responsibility for notification / representation	
A. Who is responsible for notifying – the acquiring person(s), acquired person(s), or both?	Article 4(2) of the Merger Regulation provides that a concentration which consists of a merger within the meaning of Article 3(1)(a) or in the acquisition of joint control within the meaning of Article 3(1)(b) shall be notified jointly by the parties to the merger or by those acquiring joint control, as the case may be. In all other cases, the notification shall be effected by the person or undertaking acquiring control of the whole or parts of one or more undertakings.
B. Do different rules apply to public tenders (e.g. open market stock purchases or hostile bids)?	No.
	Nonetheless, at a pre-notification stage, the parties can approach the Commission in order to discuss any issues of unavailability of information on the target company, for example in hostile bids.
C. Are the parties required to appoint a joint representative?	Article 2(3) of the Implementing Regulation provides that joint notifications shall be submitted by a joint representative who is authorised to transmit and to receive documents on behalf of all notifying parties.
D. Are there any rules as to who can represent the notifying parties (e.g., must a lawyer representing the parties be a member of a local bar)?	No
E. How does the validity of the representation need to be attested (e.g., power of attorney)? Are there special rules for foreign representatives or firms? Must a power of attorney be notarized, legalized or apostilled?	Article 2(2) of the Implementing Regulation provides that where notifications are signed by representatives of persons or of undertakings, such representatives shall produce written proof that they are authorised to act.
	There are no special rules for foreign representatives or firms
13. Filing fees	
A. Are any filing fees assessed for notification? If so, in what amount and how is the amount determined?	There are no filing fees for notifications to the European Commission.
B. Who is responsible for payment?	Not applicable
C. When is payment required?	Not applicable

D. What are the procedures for making payments (e.g., accepted forms of payment, proof of payment required, wire transfer instructions)?	Not applicable
14. Confidentiality	
A. To what extent, if any, does your agency make public the fact that a premerger notification filing was made or the contents of the notification?	Article 4(3) of the Merger Regulation provides that where the Commission finds that a notified concentration falls within the scope of this Regulation, it shall publish the fact of the notification, at the same time indicating the names of the parties, the nature of the concentration and the economic sectors involved. The Commission takes account of the legitimate interest of undertakings in the protection of their business secrets.
B. Do notifying parties have access to the authority's file? If so, under what circumstances can the right of access be exercised?	Art. 17 of the Implementing Regulation provides that the Commission shall, upon request, give notifying parties access to the file. Access is granted when the Commission has addressed to the notifying parties a Statement of Objections, for the purpose of enabling them to exercise their rights of defence. Insofar as this is necessary for the purposes of preparing their observations, the Commission shall, upon request, also give access to the file to the «other involved parties» (such as the seller and the company which is the target of the concentration) who have been informed of the Commission's objections.
C. Can third parties or other government agencies obtain access to notification materials? If so, under what circumstances?	Pursuant to Article 19(1) of the Merger Regulation, the Commission shall transmit to the competent authorities of the Member State copies of notifications within three working days and, as soon as possible, copies of the most important documents lodged with or issued by the Commission pursuant to the Merger Regulation. Such documents shall include commitments which are intended by the parties to form the basis for a decision pursuant to Articles 6(2) or 8(2) of the Merger Regulation (conditional «Phase I» or «Phase II» clearance decisions).
	Article 17(1) of the Merger Regulation provides that information acquired as a result of the investigation of a merger case shall be used only for the purposes of that case. Pursuant to Article 17(2) of the Merger Regulation, without prejudice to Articles 4(3), 18 and 20, the Commission and the competent authorities of the Member States, their officials and other servants are under an obligation of professional secrecy; they shall not disclose information they have acquired through the application of the Merger Regulation of the kind covered by the obligation of professional secrecy.
	As a general rule, third parties do not have access to notification materials.
D. Are procedures available to request confidential treatment of the fact of notification and/or notification materials? If so, please describe.	No confidential treatment can be granted with regard to the fact of the notification. As regards notification materials, please see section B. above.
E. Is the agency or government a party to any agreements that permit the exchange of information with foreign competition authorities? If so, with which foreign authorities? Are the agreements publicly available?	The Agreements to which the European Community is party do not permit the exchange of case related information provided by the parties or third parties without their prior consent.
	For further information, please refer to the following internet website:
	http://ec.europa.eu/comm/competition/international/overview/index_en.html
15. Sanctions / penalties	
A. What are the sanctions/penalties for failure to file a notification and/or failure to observe any mandatory waiting periods?	Sanctions:
	Pursuant to Article 14(1) of the Merger Regulation, the Commission may by decision impose fines not exceeding 1 % of the aggregate turnover of the undertaking or association of undertakings concerned where intentionally or negligently parties:
	– supply incorrect or misleading information in a submission, certification, notification or supplement thereto pursuant to Article 4, Article 10(5) or Article 22(3)
	– supply incorrect or misleading information in repsonse to a request made pursuant to Art. 11 (2);
	– in response to a request made by decision pursuant to Article 11 (3), supply incorrect, incomplete or misleading information ro do not supply informaiton within the required time limit;
	– they produce books or records related to the business in incomplete form suring an inspection or refuse to submit to an inspection ordered by decision pursuant to Art. 13 (4);
	– in response to a question put during an oral inteview they provide an incorrect or misleading answer, fail to rectify an incoreect answer or fail or refuse to provide a complete answer in relation to information requested pursuant to Art. 13 (4).
	Article 14(2) of the Merger Regulation provides that the Commission may by decision impose fines not exceeding 10 % of the aggregate turnover of the undertakings concerned within the meaning of Article 5 on the persons referred to in Article 3(1)b or undertakings concerned where, intentionnally or negligently, they:
	– fail to notify a notify a concentation in accordance with Articles 4 and 22 (3) prior to its implementation;

	— implement a concentration in breach of Article 7 of the Merger Regulation;
	— implement a concentration declared incompatible with the common market by decision pursuant to Article 8(3) or do nt comply with any measure ordered by decision pursuant to Article 8(4) or (5);
	– fail to comply with a condition or an obligation imposed by decision pursuant to Articles 6(1)(b), 7(3) or 8(2) of the Merger Regulation;
	Other consequences:
	Pursuant to Articles 6(3) and 8(6) of the Merger Regulation, the Commission may revoke a clearance decision it has taken where this decision is based on incorrect information for which one of the undertakings is responsible or where this decision has been obtained by deceit, or where the undertakings concerned commit a breach of an obligation attached to the decision.
B. Which party/ies are potentially liable?	The persons referred to in Article 3(1)(b) of the Merger Regulation, undertakings or associations of undertakings.
16. Judicial review	
Describe the provisions and timetable for judicial review or other rights of appeal/review of agency decisions on merger notification and review.	The legality of decisions adopted by the Commission can be reviewed by the Court of First Instance and the Court of Justice of the European Communities under the conditions and within the time-limits laid down in the Treaty establishing the European Community, in particular Article 230 thereof, as well as the Statute of the Court of Justice and the Rules of Procedure of the Community courts. The Rules of Procedure of the Community courts provide, for instance, the possibility of applying an expedited procedure.
	(Internet links:
	http://ec.europa.eu/comm/competition/court/index.html http://www.curia.eu.int/)
	Pursuant to Article 10(5) of the Merger Regulation, where the Court of Justice annuls a Commission decision taken under the Merger Regulation in whole or in part, the periods laid down in the Merger Regulation shall start again from the date of the receipt of a new complete notification, a supplement to the original notification or a certification that there have been no changes to the facts contained in the original notification.
17. Additional filings	
Are any additional filings/clearances required for some types of transactions, e.g., foreign investment or regulated sectors?	Article 21(3) of the Merger Regulation provides that Member States may take appropriate measures to protect legitimate interests other than those taken into consideration by the Merger Regulation and compatible with the general principles and other provisions of the Community law.
	Public security, plurality of the media and prudential rules shall be regarded as such legitimate interests.
	Any other public interest must be communicated to the Commission by the Member State concerned and shall be recognized by the Commission after an assessment of its compatibility with the general principles and other provisions of Community law before the measures referred to above may be taken. The Commission shall inform the Member State concerned of its decision within one month of that communication.
18. Closing deadlines	
When a transaction is cleared or approved, is there a time period within which the parties must close for it to remain authorized?	No

Market share ranges in non confidential versions of merger decisions (11 December 2008)

In order to prepare non-confidential versions of final decisions in merger cases the notifying party(ies) has/have to provide the Commission within seven days with a proposal for a non-confidential version of the decision by replacing all business secrets by (...) and replacing market shares by ranges.

Save exceptional circumstances, DG Competition considers that the following market share ranges are suitable for protecting business secrets contained in a decision:

Ranges to be used in non-confidential version:

Between 0 and 4.99%	[0-5]%
Between 5.0 and 9.99%	[5-10]%
Between 10.0 and 19.99%	[10-20]%
Between 20.0 and 29.99%	[20-30]%
Between 30.0 and 39.99%	[30-40]%
Between 40.0 and 49.99%	[40-50]%
Between 50.0 and 59.99%	[50-60]%
Between 60.0 and 69.99%	[60-70]%
Between 70.0 and 79.99%	[70-80]%
Between 80.0 and 89.99%	[80-90]%
Between 90.0 and 100%	[90-100]%.

Best practices for the submission of economic evidence and data collection in cases concerning the application of Articles 101 and 102 TFEU and in Merger cases, not published in the Official Journal

1. See the site: http://ec.europa.eu/rapid/pressReleasesAction.do?reference=IP/10/2&format=HTML&aged=0&language=EN&guilanguage=en
2. See above, section 2.1.3. Procedural rules

Decision of the President of the European Commission 13 October 2011 on the function and terms of reference of the hearing officer in certain competition proceedings (Text with EEA relevance)

(PB. L 275, 20 October 2011, p. 29)

1. See above, section 2.1.3. Procedural rules

EU Merger Working Group 8 November 2011 Best Practices on Cooperation between EU National Competition Authorities in Merger Review, not published in the Official Journal

1. See: http://ec.europa.eu/competition/ecn/nca_best_practices_merger_review_en.pdf

1. INTRODUCTION

1.1. The national competition authorities of the EU who have responsibility for merger review («NCAs») operate in compliance with different national legal systems. They believe, however, that it is desirable to cooperate in the review of some mergers which meet the requirements for notification or investigation in more than one Member State («multi-jurisdictional mergers»), and have therefore decided jointly to publish an agreed set of Best Practices on Co-operation in Merger Review.

1.2. This document, which has been drawn up by the EU Merger Working Group [1], sets out the Best Practices which the NCAs, to the extent consistent with their respective laws and enforcement priorities, aim to follow when they review the same merger transaction. It also sets out the steps that merging parties and third parties are encouraged to take in order to facilitate cooperation between NCAs. Cooperation extending beyond the existing ECA Notice system [2] is limited to NCAs who are reviewing the same merger transaction («the NCAs concerned»). It is not intended that cooperation should provide a forum whereby NCAs not concerned will be involved in the review of a specific case [3].

[1] The EU Merger Working Group («the Working Group») was established in Brussels in January 2010. It consists of representatives of the European Commission and the national competition authorities («NCAs») of the European Union («EU») together with observers from the NCAs of the European Economic Area («EEA»). The objective of the Working Group is to foster increased convergence and cooperation between the EU merger jurisdictions in order to ensure effective administration and enforcement of merger control laws.

[2] The European Competition Authorities («ECA») Notice system is an information system among the NCAs of the EU and EEA EFTA States («ECAs»). An ECA Notice is a notice which is distributed to all other ECAs by the first NCA to be notified of a multi-jurisdictional merger. It sets out the names of the merging parties, the sector/industry concerned and/or products concerned, the date of the notification, the name of the case handler, and the other member states concerned. See ECA procedures guide on the exchange of information between members on multi-jurisdictional mergers (2001); Available for example on http://ec.europa.eu/competition/ecn/eca_information_exchange_procedures_en.pdf.

[3] Some cooperation may, however, be necessary in order to determine the NCAs concerned. NCAs may also wish to consult non-involved NCAs about past experiences with similar mergers both as regards the substantive assessment and remedies, and these Best Practices do not preclude such discussions. For example, it may be helpful to exchange non-confidential information when assessing the effectiveness of a remedy, e.g. if the remedy concerns facilities or assets located in another Member State that is not reviewing the merger.

1.3. This document is intended to provide a non-binding reference for cooperation between NCAs. NCAs reserve their full discretion in the implementation of these Best Practices and nothing in this document is intended to create new rights or obligations which may fetter that discretion.

2. OBJECTIVES OF COOPERATION

2.1. Cooperation is beneficial for the NCAs concerned, for the merging parties themselves and for third parties. The Best Practices are intended to provide clarity on how cooperation among NCAs will operate in multi-jurisdictional merger cases. Where the merging parties provide full and consistent information to NCAs concerned, cooperation can reduce burdens on merging parties and third parties by facilitating, where possible, the alignment of timing and the overall efficiency, transparency, effectiveness and timeliness of the merger review processes.

2.2. In cases where serious concerns or difficult analytical issues arise, cooperation can be invaluable in helping to reach informed and consistent or at least non-conflicting outcomes. In such cases, cooperation will ensure that NCAs are in a better position to exchange views on, for example, possible conceptual frameworks for the assessment of the transaction and theories of competitive harm, types of empirical evidence and so on.

2.3. Cooperation is also beneficial both for the NCAs concerned and for the merging parties in relation to any remedial action which may be necessary. Remedies in a merger that is reviewable in more than one jurisdiction may differ across jurisdictions depending on the competition concern identified in each one; indeed, remedies may not be necessary in every jurisdiction. Nevertheless, where the merger affects a market or markets in more than one jurisdiction, a remedy accepted in one jurisdiction may have an impact in another jurisdiction (see section 3.2(iii)). Cooperation can therefore contribute to avoiding inconsistent remedies and obtaining those that are more coherent.

2.4. These Best Practices are intended to promote the achievement of all these ends.

3. SCOPE OF APPLICATION OF BEST PRACTICES

3.1. These Best Practices address cooperation in multi-jurisdictional merger cases. While it is always useful for NCAs to provide basic case information [4] to each other in merger cases which are notifiable in more than one Member State, further cooperation will not be necessary, or even efficient, in the case of every multi-jurisdictional merger. This is particularly the case where it is clear during the early stages of an investigation that the merger does not raise any significant competition or procedural issues in any Member State or that it does so only in one Member State, or where such issues are not decisive for the outcome of any of the different merger reviews. Close cooperation is not an end in itself: its benefits depend on the specific circumstances of each case.

[4] See model ECA notice (cf. Fn 2 above) as agreed in the ECA procedures guide on the exchange of information between members on multijurisdictional mergers (2001); available for example on http://ec.europa.eu/competition/ecn/eca_information_exchange_procedures_en.pdf.

3.2. Where multi-jurisdictional mergers raise similar or comparable issues in relation to jurisdictional or substantive questions, the NCAs concerned will decide on a case-by-case basis whether cooperation may be necessary or appropriate [5]. For example:

[5] Although the NCAs concerned will keep under review throughout the merger control process the need for cooperation, it will sometimes be possible for them to form a view in this regard at an early stage of the process, i.e. during pre-notification contacts (where such contacts take place) or following notification.

(i) Cooperation may assist the NCAs in forming a view as to whether a transaction qualifies for notification or investigation under merger control laws in their respective jurisdictions. It is noted that although jurisdictional rules and practices may differ across jurisdictions, cooperation may assist the NCAs in reaching an informed view.

(ii) Cooperation may assist the NCAs in relation to mergers which may have an impact on competition in more than one Member State, when markets affected by the transaction cover more than one Member State or when a merger affects national or sub-national markets in more than one Member State, if such national or subnational markets are the same or similar from the product standpoint.

(iii) Cooperation may also be of value in relation to mergers where remedies need to be designed or examined in more than one Member State, such as in situations where the same remedy is designed to address competition issues in different Member States or where one remedy affects the effectiveness of a different remedy in another Member State.

3.3. These Best Practices are without prejudice to the existing guidance on the system of reattribution of cases between the Member States and the Commission (see the Commission's referral notice and ECA's Principles on the application of Art. 4(5) and 22 of Regulation 139/2004) [6]. Nevertheless, the enhanced cooperation recommended in these Best Practices may also facilitate the smooth functioning of the reattribution mechanisms set out in Regulation (EC) 139/2004. In particular, where NCAs are contemplating an Article 22 referral request, contacts between them can facilitate the referral, and, if done before notification, can also assist merging parties in forming a view whether it is appropriate for them to speed up the referral process by themselves making an Art. 4(5) referral request (see further the description of pre-notification contacts in section 5.5).

[6] Article 4(5) provides for referral of cases from the Member States to the Commission prior to notification with the purpose of providing a "one-stop-shop" review. Article 22 provides for referral from the Member States to the Commission after notification where it is considered that the Commission is better positioned to investigate a merger. See also Commission Notice on Case Referral in respect of concentrations (OJ C 56, 05.03.2005, p. 2-23). See ECA principles on the application, by National Competition Authorities within the ECA, of Articles 4 (5) and 22 of the Merger Regulation (2005). Available for example on http://ec.europa.eu/competition/ecn/eca_referral_principles_en.pdf.

4. ROLE OF NATIONAL COMPETITION AUTHORITIES

4.1. In all cases that relate to a merger transaction that is reviewable in more than one EU Member State, the NCAs concerned will inform the other NCAs by means of the existing ECA Notice system, which involves the exchange of basic non-confidential case information after received [7].

[7] See model ECA notice as agreed in the ECA procedures guide on the exchange of information between members on multijurisdictional mergers (2001); Available for example on http://ec.europa.eu/competition/ecn/eca_information_exchange_procedures_en.pdf.

4.2. To facilitate cooperation, the NCAs concerned will aim to update the information contained in the ECA notice by informing the other NCAs about any decision to commence second phase proceedings/in-depth investigations, and any final decision, including a decision with remedies.

4.3. In cases where closer cooperation is necessary or appropriate (see paragraph 3.2 above), the NCAs, having due regard to confidentiality issues (see section 6 below), will aim to cooperate in particular in the following ways:

(i) The NCAs concerned will liaise with one another and keep one another appraised of their progress at key stages of their respective investigations. The key stages will vary depending on the procedural framework of each NCA concerned. The NCAs concerned will keep each other informed of the outcome of the first phase investigation, including, where relevant, the intention to open an in-depth investigation, and the outcome of the in-depth investigation. The NCAs concerned will also keep each other appraised of the launch and progress of any remedies discussions, if not conducted jointly.

(ii) Where it is helpful to do so, the NCAs concerned may discuss their respective jurisdictional and/or substantive analyses. Where necessary, having regard to the possible effects of the transaction on the national territories of the NCAs concerned, such discussions may relate to issues such as market definition, assessment of competitive effects, efficiencies, theories of competitive harm, and the empirical evidence needed to test those theories. NCAs concerned will also, where it is helpful to do so, exchange views on necessary remedial measures or submitted remedies.

5. ROLE OF MERGING PARTIES

5.1. Effective cooperation between NCAs requires the active assistance of the merging parties at all stages of the review process, both as regards the jurisdictional and/or substantive review and, where required, the assessment of remedies.

5.2. Parties to merger investigations play an important role with regard to cooperation between the NCAs concerned. They can contribute significantly to the alignment of the review proceedings in different Member States, taking into account, among other things, procedural requirements and review periods. Such alignment will be of benefit both to merging parties and to NCAs.

5.3. Therefore, where a transaction is expected to fulfil the requirements for notification or investigation in more than one jurisdiction, the merging parties are encouraged, unless it is clear and obvious from the outset that paragraph 3.2 above does not apply, to contact each of the NCAs concerned as soon as practicable and provide them with the following basic information:

 i. the name of each jurisdiction in which they intend to make a filing;
 ii. the date of the proposed filing in each jurisdiction;
 iii. the names and activities of the merging parties;
 iv. the geographic areas in which they carry on business (8);

(8) The phrase «carry on business» does not include a situation where an undertaking is merely registered in a particular place.

 v. the sector or sectors involved (short description and/or NACE code).

5.4. It is important to note that the provision of this information by the parties will not of itself be a trigger for cooperation among the NCAs concerned. That will depend rather upon whether the case is one where cooperation is necessary or appropriate, as set out in paragraph 3.2 of these Best Practices. However, it will assist the NCAs concerned to decide at an early stage whether there might be a need for cooperation in the particular case.

5.5. Depending on the circumstances of the case it may be possible to provide much of this information at the pre-notification stage. For this purpose, and where it is permitted by law, it may be helpful for merging parties and the NCAs concerned to organize pre-notification contacts as early as possible. Such contacts can assist the parties and the NCAs concerned to align as far as possible the timing of parallel proceedings and can, ultimately, contribute to the reduction of the overall burden that falls on merging parties in the course of a multijurisdictional merger. It may at times, where circumstances permit, be useful for the merging parties and the NCAs concerned to engage in joint pre-notification contacts.

5.6. Merging parties have a crucial role in helping NCAs to ensure that remedies in different Member States do not lead to inconsistent or untenable results. As already stated above, remedies in a merger that is reviewable in more than one Member State may differ across Member States depending on the competition concern identified in each one; indeed, remedies may not be necessary in every Member State. Nevertheless, a remedy accepted in one Member State may have an impact on the effectiveness of remedies targeted at competition problems in another Member State. It is therefore clearly in the interest of the merging parties to coordinate the timing and substance of remedy proposals to the NCAs concerned, so as to ensure coherent remedies and to avoid inconsistent remedies. In certain cases, where circumstances permit, it might be appropriate for merging parties and the reviewing NCAs to engage in joint discussions on proposed remedies.

6. CONFIDENTIAL INFORMATION

6.1. It will often be helpful for the NCAs concerned to be able to exchange and discuss confidential information when reviewing the same merger. Therefore, while a certain degree of cooperation is feasible through the exchange of non-confidential information, waivers of confidentiality executed by merging parties can enable more effective communication between the NCAs concerned regarding evidence that is relevant to the investigation.

APPENDIX A
ICN Model Waiver Form

(DATE)

(CONTACT NAME AT AGENCY A)
(ADDRESS)

Re: (CASE REFERENCE)

Dear -----:

On behalf of COMPANY A, I confirm that COMPANY A, subject to the conditions and limitations set forth herein, agrees to waive the confidentiality restrictions under (RELEVANT STATUTORY OR REGULATORY AUTHORITY) and other applicable laws and rules (collectively the «Confidentiality Obligations») that prevent AGENCY X from disclosing to FOREIGN AGENCY Y confidential information obtained from COMPANY A in connection with its proposed transaction with COMPANY B. Specifically, COMPANY A agrees that AGENCY X staff may share with FOREIGN AGENCY Y (any of COMPANY A's documents, statements, data and information, as well as AGENCY A's own internal analyses that contain or refer to COMPANY A's materials that would otherwise be foreclosed by the confidentiality Obligations) (1).

(1) NOTE: This model language is intended for those situations where a waiver with respect to any and all documents and information provided to Agency X is contemplated. There may be instances where such a broad waiver is not desired. In those cases, the parties may opt for a waiver limited in scope, such as to allow the agencies to discuss potential remedies that each is considering and the reasons for such remedies, or to discuss specific limited issues such as product market definition or barriers to entry. Parties and agency staff should consider the scope of the waiver that is desired to assist them in their investigation so as to not unnecessarily burden parties or other competition agencies.

This waiver is granted only with respect to disclosures to FOREIGN AGENCY Y and only on the condition that FOREIGN AGENCY Y will treat as confidential information it obtains from AGENCY X in accordance with the terms of the attached letter from (CONTACT NAME) of FOREIGN AGENCY Y (2). This agreement does not constitute a waiver by COMPANY A of its rights under the Confidentiality Obligations with respect to the protection afforded to COMPANY A against the direct or indirect disclosures of information to any third-party other than FOREIGN AGENCY Y.

(2) NOTE: «Foreign Agency Y» should provide a letter describing the confidentiality protections provided by that country. (In some cases, the parties and Agency X staff may be satisfied if that letter is directed to that contact person by representatives of the parties, with a written confirmation that Foreign Agency Y agrees to the terms of that letter.) Attached to this model form at Appendix (D) are sample confidentiality letters.

COMPANY A submits this waiver under the condition and understanding that, with respect to information that AGENCY X obtains from COMPANY A and provides to the FOREIGN AGENCY Y pursuant to this waiver, AGENCY X should continue to protect the confidentiality of such information with respect to other outside parties in accordance with the Confidentiality Obligations.

A copy of this letter is being sent to (CONTACT PERSON AT FOREIGN AGENCY Y).

Sincerely,

(ATTORNEY FOR COMPANY A)

cc: (CONTACT FOR FOREIGN AGENCY Y)